Securing Enterprise Networks with Cisco Meraki

Ryan Chaney, CCIE No. 16666
Simerjit Singh, CCIE No. 38710

Cisco Press

Securing Enterprise Networks with Cisco Meraki

Ryan Chaney, Simerjit Singh

Published by:
Cisco Press
Hoboken, New Jersey

1 2024

Library of Congress Control Number: 2024943927

ISBN-13: 978-0-13-829818-0

ISBN-10: 0-13-829818-1

Warning and Disclaimer

This book is designed to provide information about securing an enterprise network with Cisco Meraki. Every effort has been made to make this book as complete and as accurate as possible, but no warranty or fitness is implied.

The information is provided on an "as is" basis. The authors, Cisco Press, and Cisco Systems, Inc., shall have neither liability nor responsibility to any person or entity with respect to any loss or damages arising from the information contained in this book or from the use of the discs or programs that may accompany it.

The opinions expressed in this book belong to the authors and are not necessarily those of Cisco Systems, Inc.

Trademark Acknowledgments

All terms mentioned in this book that are known to be trademarks or service marks have been appropriately capitalized. Cisco Press or Cisco Systems, Inc., cannot attest to the accuracy of this information. Use of a term in this book should not be regarded as affecting the validity of any trademark or service mark.

Special Sales

For information about buying this title in bulk quantities, or for special sales opportunities (which may include electronic versions; custom cover designs; and content particular to your business, training goals, marketing focus, or branding interests), please contact our corporate sales department at corpsales@pearsoned.com or (800) 382-3419.

For government sales inquiries, please contact governmentsales@pearsoned.com.

For questions about sales outside the U.S., please contact intlcs@pearson.com.

Feedback Information

At Cisco Press, our goal is to create in-depth technical books of the highest quality and value. Each book is crafted with care and precision, undergoing rigorous development that involves the unique expertise of members from the professional technical community.

Readers' feedback is a natural continuation of this process. If you have any comments regarding how we could improve the quality of this book, or otherwise alter it to better suit your needs, you can contact us through email at feedback@ciscopress.com. Please make sure to include the book title and ISBN in your message.

We greatly appreciate your assistance.

GM K12, Early Career and Professional Learning: Soo Kang

Alliances Manager, Cisco Press: Caroline Antonio

Director, ITP Product Management: Brett Bartow

Managing Editor: Sandra Schroeder

Development Editor: Christopher Cleveland

Senior Project Editor: Tonya Simpson

Copy Editor: Chuck Hutchinson

Technical Editors: Akhil Behl, Jeffry Handal

Editorial Assistant: Cindy Teeters

Cover Designer: Chuti Prasertsith

Composition: codeMantra

Indexer: Timothy Wright

Proofreader: Jennifer Hinchliffe

cisco.

Americas Headquarters
Cisco Systems, Inc.
San Jose, CA

Asia Pacific Headquarters
Cisco Systems (USA) Pte. Ltd.
Singapore

Europe Headquarters
Cisco Systems International BV Amsterdam,
The Netherlands

Cisco has more than 200 offices worldwide. Addresses, phone numbers, and fax numbers are listed on the Cisco Website at **www.cisco.com/go/offices.**

About the Authors

Ryan Chaney, the lead author on this book, started his Cisco journey in his early 20s, completing his first CCIE (R+S) at the age of 25, before completing his second CCIE (Security) just 2 years later. Before joining Cisco, he worked in a variety of networking roles across the world, including time as a network architect for Visa in London. Ryan spent the first 10 years of his 15 years at Cisco as a systems engineer, educating customers, designing, and building IT solutions. His first experience with Meraki came while volunteering at the Royal Far West Centre for Country Kids, where he designed and built the network for their new headquarters in Manly, Sydney. At the time, no books had been published on Meraki. This experience and wanting to share his learnings with fellow network engineers, like you, became the inspiration for this book. Ryan lives in Bondi Beach, Australia.

Simerjit Singh, the contributing author on this book, is a seasoned Meraki solutions engineer with more than 17 years' tenure at Cisco. From his wealth of experience working with customers in the Enterprise and SMB segments, Simerjit contributes his vast experience of the diverse needs of these customers and relevant Meraki solutions. Simerjit holds highly regarded qualifications in networking and security, including a bachelor of technology in computer science, as well as both CCIE and ISC2 Certified Cloud Security Professional (CCSP) certifications. Committed to continuous learning and professional growth, Simerjit is currently pursuing a master's degree in cybersecurity from the Royal Melbourne Institute (RMIT). Simerjit lives in Melbourne with his mother, wife, and two sons.

About the Technical Reviewers

Akhil Behl is a passionate technologist and business development practitioner. He has more than 19 years of experience in the IT industry working across several leadership, advisory, consultancy, and business development profiles across OEMs, Telcos, and SI organizations. Akhil believes in cultivating an entrepreneurial culture, working across high-performance teams, identifying emerging technology trends, and ongoing innovation. For the last 7+ years he has been working extensively with hyperscalers across industry verticals—FSI, RCPG, transport, public sector, and mining. He is employed at Red Hat and leads the Global System Integrator (GSI) partner alliances for ANZ region across modernization, automation, cloud first Go-To-Market (GTM) motions.

Akhil is a published author. Over the span of past few years, he has authored multiple titles on security and business communication technologies. He has contributed as technical editor for more than a dozen books on security, networking, and information technology. He has published four books with Pearson Education's Cisco Press. He has published several research papers in national and international journals, including IEEE Xplore, and presented at various IEEE conferences, as well as other prominent ICT, security, and telecom events. Writing and mentoring is his passion and a part of his life. This is his fifth book.

Akhil holds CCIE No. 19564 Emeritus (Collaboration and Security), CompTIA Data+, Azure Solutions Architect Expert, Google Professional Cloud Architect, Azure AI Certified Associate, Azure Data Fundamentals, CCSK, CHFI, PMP, ITIL, VCP, TOGAF, CEH, ISM, CCDP, and other industry certifications. He has bachelors in Technology and masters in Business Administration degrees.

Akhil lives in Melbourne, Australia with his better half, Kanika, and two sons, Shivansh (11 years) and Shaurya (9 years). Both of them are passionate gamers and are excellent musicians, sporting guitar and keyboard, respectively.

In his spare time, Akhil likes to play cricket and console games with his sons, watch movies with family, and write articles or blogs.

Jeffry Handal is a principal solutions engineer at Cisco. He completed his bachelors and masters degrees in electrical engineering at Louisiana State University (LSU) and has more than 18 years of experience in the area of information communication technology, with special interest in IPv6, cybersecurity, big data, and experimental networks. Before joining Cisco, Jeffry was a very active customer, always pushing the envelope designing and maintaining networks with new technologies, testing new protocols, and providing Cisco and others a large-scale testbed for new products, features, and functionality. Currently, he plays an active role in several Cisco groups (TACops, IPv6 Ambassadors, Security Technical Advisory Group, Meraki).

Outside of work, Jeffry is an active volunteer in organizations ranging from search and rescue operations with the Air Force to humanitarian technology groups such as NetHope. He sits on several boards within IEEE, actively promotes IPv6 adoption via different task forces, volunteers to teach networking classes in third-world countries, and promotes STEM for women and minorities. In addition, Jeffry serves the public through his participation in conferences and standards bodies (IETF, IEEE); speaks at local and international events (Internet2, CANS, IPv6 Summits, AI/ML Symposiums, IEEE events, WALC, Cisco Live); contributes to and reviews publications; and appears as a guest in podcasts like *IPv6 Buzz* and *Meraki Unboxed*. He is a big promoter of technological change for the betterment of humanity.

Dedications

First and foremost, I'd like to dedicate this book to my proud parents, Steve and Susanne, who encouraged me to fly high, enjoy life, and dream big. I could never have imagined such a project without their interest and enthusiasm for both reading and technology.

—*Ryan Chaney*

This book goes out to my family. My wife, your faith in my dreams has been my driving force. My sons, who carried on without me when I was working on this book. They always provided me with incredible support, and I simply couldn't achieve my goals without them. And to my brothers, who have given me encouragement, love, and wisdom to shape me into the person I am today. My mother, her unwavering love, patience, and encouragement have carried me through every storm and celebrated every success.

—*Simerjit Singh*

Acknowledgments

We'd like to heartfully acknowledge all those wonderful people, including many new names and faces, who selflessly supported us in our efforts to create this fantastic book.

First, we'd like to start by thanking Rob Soderbery, former SVP at Cisco and current CEO of Western Digital, for taking the time to share his memories of Cisco's acquisition of Meraki.

I (Ryan) would like to thank my contributing author, Simerjit Singh, for his time, knowledge, and professional network, which made this book possible.

We'd like to personally thank Fady Sharobeem, solutions engineer with Meraki and fellow CCIE, for his technical support and enthusiasm for this project. Likewise, Kabeer Noorudeen, CCIE, rock star and solutions engineer at Cisco, for his support.

I (Simerjit) would like to acknowledge Dimitri Polydorou for being an exceptional mentor. Dimitri, you have not only imparted guidance and support but also instilled confidence and inspired me to strive for excellence.

Thanks also to Sheela Kishan, security solutions engineer with Cisco, Duo guru, and fellow CCIE, for her help and support on all things Duo.

Similarly, a big thank you to Shweta Palande, technical marketing engineer at Meraki, for her technical support on ServiceNow.

A shout out and thanks go to Harry Lewins from AlgoSec. We could not have included AlgoSec without your support.

A big thank you to Tim Mallyon, Jacqueline Emery, Pip Crooks, and the whole Royal Far West team. It was working together that provided the inspirational spark for this book.

This book in its final form would not be what it is without the insights and enormous experience of our technical reviewers, Akhil Behl and Jeffry Handal.

Last, but most important, this book would not have been possible without the support of many people in the Cisco Press team. We'd like to thank Brett Bartow, director, IT Professional Product Management at Pearson Education, who was instrumental in sponsoring this book. A big thank you to Chris Cleveland, development editor, for your expertise and keeping us on track. Thanks also to Tonya Simpson, senior project editor, for getting us across the finish line. Finally, many thanks to the many other Pearson folks behind the scenes who made this project possible.

Contents at a Glance

Reader Services

Register your copy at www.ciscopress.com/title/9780138298180 for convenient access to downloads, updates, and corrections as they become available. To start the registration process, go to www.ciscopress.com/register and log in or create an account*. Enter the product ISBN 9780138298180 and click Submit. When the process is complete, you will find any available bonus content under Registered Products.

*Be sure to check the box that you would like to hear from us to receive exclusive discounts on future editions of this product.

Contents

Introduction

Despite Meraki's huge success and wide adoption, at the time we started this project, no one had written a book about Cisco's Meraki product lines. After helping organizations to deploy Meraki, we realized that it was time for this to change. As a result, we sought to create a book that enables more organizations to adopt cloud-managed infrastructure and build better, more modern, and more secure networks.

Our goal is to show you that Meraki can be used, not just to build secure networks, but as the foundation for a more secure enterprise as a whole. By researching as many of the common IT security standards and frameworks as we could find, we gathered together over a hundred common security requirements that we believe you can solve with a Meraki solution. With this goal in mind, we show how Cisco Meraki, either on its own or when easily integrated with complementary products, can be deployed to meet the requirements of the most common IT security standards.

Guided by the requirements of industry best practices, the topics in this book stretch beyond what might be considered traditional networking roles, perhaps with a view to secure networking roles of the future. As such, the target audience includes roles covering IT security, networking, and systems, such as:

- All new Meraki customers
- Experienced networking engineers looking to upskill on cloud-managed networking
- The next generation of networking and IT professionals who may be just starting their careers and have basic CCNA-level networking knowledge
- Multidisciplined, lean IT teams
- IT managers looking to streamline and modernize operations

The book is organized as follows:

- **Chapter 1, Meraki's History:** This chapter recounts the history of Meraki from its beginnings as a research project at the Massachusetts Institute of Technology (MIT). It charts the intersection of the explosive growth in Wi-Fi devices and broadband Internet, with the launch of Meraki as a start-up. The chapter concludes with the story of Meraki's acquisition by Cisco, including an interview with Rob Soderbery, then SVP of Cisco's Enterprise Networking Group.
- **Chapter 2, Security Frameworks and Industry Best Practices:** This chapter opens by highlighting the consequences of IT security failures. Common IT standards and frameworks are introduced as the conversation shifts to how to minimize IT risk and industry best practices. Finally, this chapter identifies the nine key themes that you must consider when designing and implementing Meraki solutions.

- **Chapter 3, Meraki Dashboard and Trust:** This chapter introduces the Meraki management portal, Meraki Dashboard, before addressing the common considerations when adopting cloud-managed infrastructure. This includes discussions around privacy, data security, resiliency, compliance, hardware, and software trust. With a full understanding of these topics and the steps Cisco has taken to address them, organizations should feel confident in adopting Cisco Meraki solutions.
- **Chapter 4, Role-Based Access Control (RBAC):** RBAC is one of the nine key themes identified from industry best practices. Being central to the principle of least privilege, RBAC receives its own dedicated chapter. This chapter introduces and demonstrates the RBAC capabilities available in Meraki Dashboard.
- **Chapter 5, Securing Administrator Access to Meraki Dashboard:** This chapter discusses the need for strong authentication and multifactor authentication (MFA) in relation to administrator access to Meraki Dashboard. Here, we guide you through the configuration of Meraki Dashboard's native controls. This chapter also demonstrates the enhanced capabilities available when using SAML single sign-on (SSO). This includes a full step-by-step guide, showing how to implement SAML SSO with MFA using Meraki, Cisco Duo, and Microsoft Entra.
- **Chapter 6, Security Operations:** This chapter covers the native Meraki toolset to support a security operations center. Also covered is the implementation of external solutions providing compliance reporting, centralized logging including Cisco Splunk, polling, the Meraki Dashboard API, alerting, and incident response.
- **Chapter 7, User Authentication:** User access authentication is an essential part of an enterprise's zero trust architecture. This chapter covers the configuration of the authentication infrastructure in support of authenticating user access via wired, wireless, and VPN. This includes implementing Meraki Cloud Authentication, SAML, and RADIUS (with and without MFA). This chapter covers RADIUS extensively, including the full configuration steps for Cisco Identity Services Engine (ISE) and Cisco Duo. This chapter is a prerequisite for Chapter 8.
- **Chapter 8, Wired and Wireless LAN Security:** This chapter covers two main topics—first, how to implement authentication for wired and wireless users. This includes step-by-step guided configuration of 802.1X, Sentry-based access, and MAC Authentication Bypass (MAB). The second major topic discusses those network-based security features available on Meraki MS and MR devices. This includes the implementation of firewalling, Layer 2 switching features such as port isolation, as well as group policies and adaptive policies.
- **Chapter 9, Meraki MX and WAN Security:** Encryption is vital for protecting the confidentiality and integrity of data over public networks. This chapter shows how various VPN types—client VPN, Sentry VPN, AnyConnect VPN, and site-to-site VPN (Auto VPN)—can be implemented using Meraki MX. This chapter also introduces Meraki virtual MX (vMX), stepping through how to extend your secure Meraki SD-WAN into public cloud. This includes a step-by-step guide to setting up Meraki vMX in Amazon Web Services (AWS).

- **Chapter 10, Securing User Traffic:** This chapter discusses the various ways administrators can secure Internet traffic both natively and using the recently released Secure Connect. This includes such features as URL filtering, IDS/IPS, content filtering, Advanced Malware Protection (AMP), and much more. Secure Connect is a must-have solution bringing advanced functionality that will be new for a lot of readers. Of particular interest are the Cloud Access Security Broker (CASB) and Data Loss Prevention (DLP) capabilities. This chapter shows how, using these capabilities, administrators can reduce the risk of sensitive data leaving their organization via webmail, email attachments, file uploads, and via generative AI platforms like ChatGPT.
- **Chapter 11, Securing End-User Devices:** Meraki Systems Manager, Meraki's own mobile device management (MDM) solution, helps organizations manage corporate devices in line with industry best practices. This chapter shows how Systems Manager provides an important role through enabling organizations to take advantage of Sentry-based policies for 802.1X on wired and wireless. You also learn how to apply your own profiles to managed devices, simplifying the deployment of wireless and VPN access.
- **Chapter 12, Physical Security:** This chapter focuses on the capabilities of Meraki's MV smart camera solution, covering all the topics relevant for monitoring the physical environment, such as a data center. This chapter addresses important topics like privacy, before delving into video walls, motion alerts, motion search, and other capabilities required by today's security operation centers.
- **Appendix A, Comparison of Common Security Standards and Framework Requirements:** This book has been created to help you understand today's IT security requirements and how to meet them using Cisco Meraki. This appendix shows the mapping between IT security requirements, security standards, and where each topic is addressed in this book. This helpful resource enables you to visualize the breadth, commonality, and key themes across industry best practices.

Figure Credits

Cover Page: PeopleImages.com - Yuri A/Shutterstock.

Figures 1-1, 1-2: Sanjit Biswas

Figure 1-3: Rob Soderbery

Figures 2-1, 10-115, 10-117, 10-126d, 10-140, 10-142, 10-143: Google

Figures 5-73–5-92, 5-95–5-97, 5-105–5-113, 5-116–5-145, 5-161–5-163, 5-174, 5-175, 5-180, 5-183–5-185, 7-15–7-20, 7-27–7-38, 7-112, 7-133, 7-135, 7-136, 10-126c: Microsoft

Figure 6-35: Solarwinds

Figures 6-40–6-56: AlgoSec

Figures 6-62–6-71,6-78: PagerDuty

Figures 6-86, 7-89, 7-90, 8-6, 8-24, 8-48–8-50, 8-77, 8-78, 8-80, 8-81, 8-85, 8-127, 8-179, 8-180, 9-21, 9-22, 9-27–9-30, 9-42, 9-43, 10-3, 10-7, 10-13, 10-14, 10-17, 10-23, 10-28, 10-72, 10-73, 10-80, 10-126a, 11-3, 11-4, 11-25, 11-26, 11-34, 11-41–11-43: Apple Inc.

Figures 6-87–6-93: JetBrains

Figures 6-103–6-111: ServiceNow

Figures 7-134, 8-181, 8-182: Wireshark

Figures 9-47–9-73, 10-126b: Amazon Web Services, Inc.

Figure 10-27: EICAR

Figures 10-145, 10-146: Open AI

Chapter 1

Meraki's History

In this chapter, you learn the following:

- The history of Meraki from research project to start-up to Cisco's acquisition

In 2001, less than 12 percent of Americans had Internet access in the home, and of those who did, more than 40 percent were using dial-up. Even though the global home Internet access market was small, Internet subscribers were growing very quickly, making it a boom time for Internet service providers (ISPs). Furthermore, there was already a major shift to adopt premium broadband services, with the number of broadband customers in the US doubling between 2001 and 2003.[1] At that time, the cost to ISPs to provide wired broadband connectivity to homes, commonly referred to as the "last mile," was prohibitively expensive, at between US$75,000 and US$125,000 per square mile.[2]

Roofnet

Around this time, a research project named *Roofnet* was taking shape at the Massachusetts Institute of Technology (MIT) Computer Science and Artificial Intelligence Laboratory (CSAIL). The aim of this project was to build an ad hoc network infrastructure capable of providing pervasive high-speed network access. Recognizing the emergence of community wireless mesh networks, researchers sought to prove that wireless mesh technologies could be used as a lower-cost alternative to wired access in the last mile. To be successful, wireless mesh technologies would need to be both functional (reliable, fast, and cover a large geographic area) and inexpensive.

To keep the cost of the hardware as low as possible, the team built their own wireless access points using a small PC with a wireless card and running the Click Modular Router software. An omnidirectional antenna and mounting hardware completed kits, which included all the required antennas, cabling, and mounts needed (as shown in Figure 1-1).

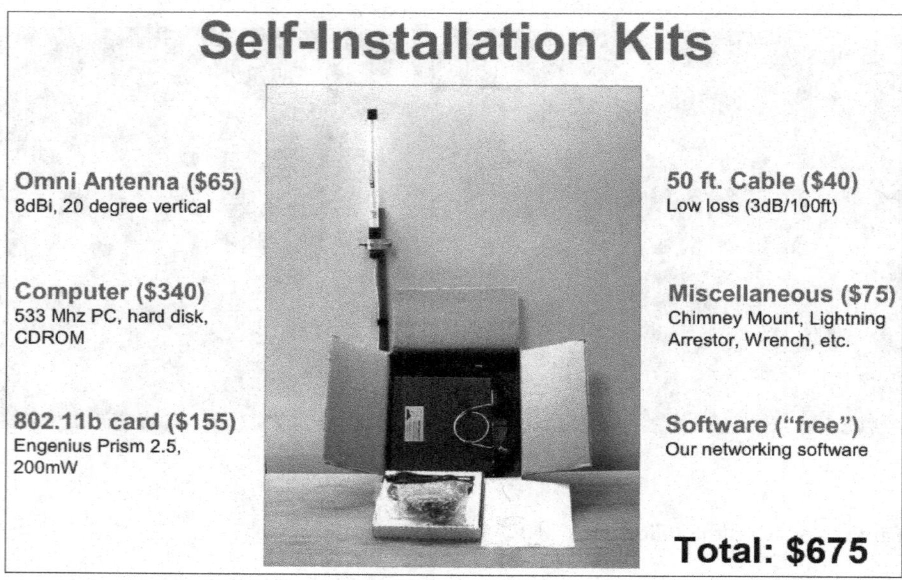

Figure 1-1 *The Original Roofnet Self-Installation Kit*

While cost could be kept low through careful selection of the hardware components, by far the largest proportion of cost in existing wireless deployments was the ongoing need for skilled engineering resources. These wireless networks had no capability to grow organically and relied on carefully planned point-to-point links for backhauling traffic to central sites. This meant that expensive engineering resources were required throughout the product's lifecycle to ensure optimal coverage and performance. In the case of Roofnet, researchers designed their kits to be simple enough that nontechnical users could install them themselves. Volunteers installed these nodes across MIT's Cambridge campus and used them to obtain free Internet access. Roofnet was an ad hoc network, so once nodes were installed, they became available for nearby users to connect to and for other users to route through. Because nodes could attach to the network automatically, the wireless network itself needed no configuration or planning, making it easy to both deploy and expand. To further reduce cost, Roofnet nodes were managed in-band, allowing for software upgrades to be done remotely without administrators needing to visit sites. You can already see the makings of plug-and-play provisioning and automatic software updates, which are key features of Meraki's solution today.

The Roofnet network enabled the researchers to study how real-life traffic performed over lossy, marginal links and how the network adapted to link failure and new paths in a multihop network. Network links in a switched wired network were comparatively more reliable than a wireless network (little or no packet loss). All other things being equal, finding the best path in a wired network simply required finding the shortest path between the source and destination. However, finding the best path in a wireless network meant dealing with asymmetric link loss rates, frequent changes in link loss rates, and the frequent loss of routing protocol packets. This meant that the problem the researchers had to solve was how to determine the best path in real-world wireless networks. To help solve this problem, the researchers developed a new routing protocol called SrcRR that could take the performance of links into consideration. If SrcRR was intended as an acronym, its meaning was never published.

The journal articles of this research are still available online. If you're interested, search "Roofnet" or read the following articles:

- Benjamin A. Chambers, *The Grid Roofnet: A Rooftop Ad Hoc Wireless Network*, MIT master's thesis, June 2002.
- Douglas S. J. De Couto, Daniel Aguayo, John Bicket, and Robert Morris, *A High-Throughput Path Metric for Multi-Hop Wireless Routing*, Proceedings of the 9th ACM International Conference on Mobile Computing and Networking (MobiCom '03), San Diego, California, September 2003.
- Daniel Aguayo, John Bicket, Sanjit Biswas, Glenn Judd, and Robert Morris, *Link-Level Measurements from an 802.11b Mesh Network*, SIGCOMM 2004, August 2004.
- John Bicket, *Bit-Rate Selection in Wireless Networks*, MIT master's thesis, February 2005.
- Sanjit Biswas, *Opportunistic Routing in Multi-Hop Wireless Networks*, MIT master's thesis, March 2005.
- John Bicket, Daniel Aguayo, Sanjit Biswas, and Robert Morris, *Architecture and Evaluation of an Unplanned 802.11b Mesh Network*, MobiCom 2005, August 2005.

Start-up

In 2006, Sanjit Biswas was invited to present the team's research findings to Google, which had been testing its first municipal Wi-Fi network in its hometown of Mountain View, California. After Mr. Biswas's talk, a Google engineer shared that people using Google's network had told them that they could get online at home only by holding their laptops against a window. Mr. Biswas was not surprised—using municipal Wi-Fi (radio transmitters on existing streetlamp posts) for residential coverage, he said, was "the equivalent of expecting streetlamps to light everyone's homes."[3] It was this discussion that made Sanjit Biswas and fellow PhD student John Bicket realize that their low-cost Roofnet node, which was installed closer to the users and designed for residential use, could solve this problem. With seed capital from Google and Sequoia Capital and an order for 1,000 nodes, Biswas, Bicket, and another MIT graduate, Hans Robertson, formed their own Silicon Valley start-up, Meraki Networks (see Figure 1-2).

Note In case you were wondering where the name came from, *Meraki* is a Greek word that means doing something with soul, creativity, or love.

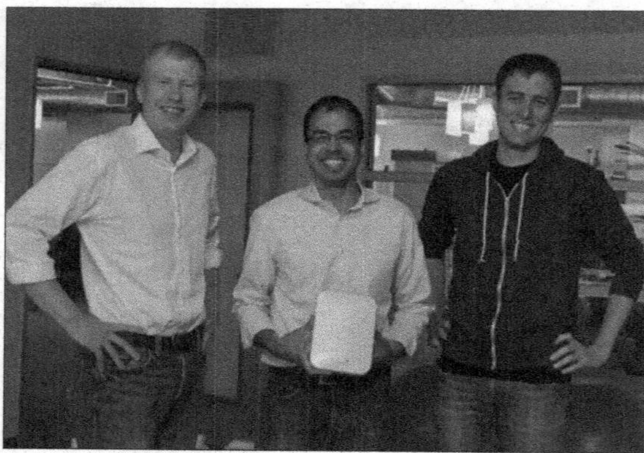

Figure 1-2 *Meraki's Original Founders: Hans Robertson, Sanjit Biswas, and John Bicket*

In 2009, now a private company, Meraki released its first cloud-based management platform, which it called the Meraki Cloud Controller; this is what we know today as the Meraki Dashboard. This platform was closely followed by the world's first line of enterprise-grade cloud-managed WLAN access points, which included the MR58, a rugged outdoor access point. Cloud network management made it drastically easier to roll out and manage networks. Consequently, this made Meraki's solution well suited to organizations with large numbers of sites and small IT teams (so-called Lean IT) such as retailers and schools. With the launch of the iPhone, the number of wireless clients was skyrocketing. This proliferation made the release of an easy-to-deploy and -manage wireless access solution especially timely. Being able to administer a network from anywhere made after-hours support much easier, and often avoided needing to travel to site.

By the end of 2010, customers, including household names such as Starbucks, Applebee's, and Burger King, had deployed over 17,000 Meraki networks worldwide. Now, with the further release of the iPad, these networks connected over 35 million client devices.

In 2011, Meraki introduced the industry's first cloud-managed security appliances, the Meraki MX50 and MX70. In 2012, Meraki introduced its MS range of cloud-managed switches. The world was now a vastly different place from the days of Roofnet. The worldwide annual production of wireless chipsets had grown from 200 million in 2007 to 1 billion in 2012.[4] The iPhone, iPod touch, and iPad had all been released and had seen phenomenal adoption. Meraki had grown to 330 employees, it had launched its Cloud Controller and three major product lines (MX, MS, and MR), grown its annual revenues to US$120 million, and was eyeing a share market listing (an initial public offering, or IPO for short).

Acquisition by Cisco

On November 28, 2012, Cisco announced its intention to acquire Meraki. In a statement to staff at the time, Meraki CEO Sanjit Biswas spoke about how "Cisco had been hearing from customers, partners and analysts that Meraki had built something truly different, and they wanted to see if Cisco could distribute the technology on a worldwide scale through their vast sales channels."[5] Rob Soderbery was senior vice president of Cisco's Enterprise Networking Group at the time. In an interview for this book, Rob stated that the number one driver for this acquisition was existing customers telling Cisco, "This is a wonderful product, and this is a wonderful company."

When a company embarks on a new product strategy, there is typically a consideration of whether to build it in-house or acquire another company that is already doing it. There was no doubt in this case that Cisco was not going to try to replicate what Meraki had built. Hilton Romanski, vice president of business development for Cisco, said in a blog post that "Meraki had built a unique cloud-based business from the ground up that addresses the broader networking shift towards cloud, not just within wireless." Meraki had created a massively scalable architecture that made networks easy to deploy, secure, and manage. Meraki "didn't obsess about the number of features, but instead focused on those that could be simplified or removed entirely." Rob Soderbery stated at the time that "the acquisition of Meraki enables Cisco to make simple, secure, cloud-managed networks available to our global customer base of mid-sized businesses and enterprises."[6] Furthermore, that "these companies have the same IT needs as larger organizations, but without the resources to integrate complex IT solutions."[7] After a relatively quick couple of months of negotiations, Cisco closed its 158th acquisition on December 20, 2012, with Meraki joining Cisco as a newly formed business unit known as the Cloud Networking Group. Figure 1-3 shows a memento given to staff to commemorate the closing of the Meraki acquisition. Note the original Meraki logo.

Figure 1-3 *A Totem Given to Staff as a Memento to Commemorate the Closing of the Meraki Acquisition*

Independence was highly important to the original founders, who realized that Meraki really had built something unique. To this day, Meraki still uses its own technology in its offices globally, including their headquarters in San Francisco, providing a great, real-world demo environment for staff. Meraki's focus on simplicity and the "Meraki Way" resonates with everyone you meet. Meraki has a distinct start-up culture, part of which is the near ban on business shirts and suits. So strong was this element of Meraki's culture that when driving between Cisco's campus in San Jose and Meraki's HQ in San Francisco, Rob Soderbery admitted he would change out of his business shirt before going up to meet with Meraki.

Since the acquisition, Cisco has seen Meraki sales increase by more than 10 times, making it one of its most successful acquisitions (see Figure 1-4). Today, there are well over 4 million+ active networks (and growing) as well as additional product lines for sensors, smart security cameras, and more. Meraki devices can be seen deployed all across the world in a wide range of sectors. As you're reading this book now, even if you haven't deployed your first Meraki network yet, you've no doubt already seen evidence of Meraki's huge success.

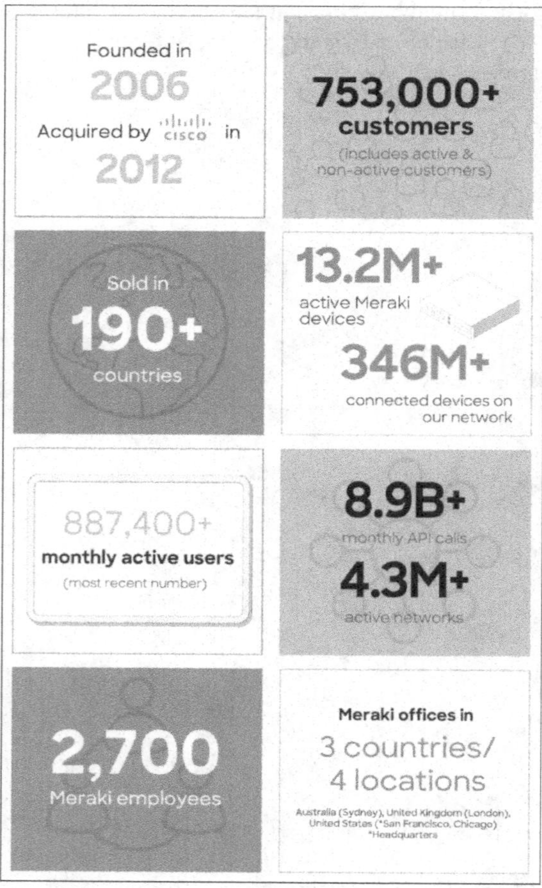

Figure 1-4 *Cisco Meraki Infographic Showing Global Size and Scale*

The Meraki Museum

If you're a passionate Meraki customer or partner, you might be interested in visiting the Meraki Museum (see Figure 1-5). Located upstairs in Meraki's San Francisco headquarters, the museum has a range of former products on display. The exhibits range from the very early days of Meraki (pre-acquisition, "free-the-net" era) to today. The museum is usually off limits to the public, so speak to your Meraki, Cisco, or partner account team to see if they can arrange a tour for you.

Figure 1-5 *A Display Case That Is Part of the Meraki Museum*

Summary

Meraki was founded at a time when the Internet was booming. Networks were growing in both size and clients, and Wi-Fi was exploding due to the popularity of new mobile devices. Meraki responded to the challenges of organizations with small IT teams with an extreme focus on simplicity and ease of management. The acquisition by Cisco further accelerated Meraki's success. Today, enterprises of all sizes and industries use cloud-managed IT in at least some part of their business. As a result, network engineers everywhere need to learn these new skills in order to future-proof their careers.

Notes

[1] National Telecommunications and Information Administration (NTIA). (2004). *A Nation Online: Entering the Broadband Age*. https://ntia.gov/report/2004/nation-online-entering-broadband-age

[2] Stross, R. (2007, February 4). Wireless Internet for All, Without the Towers, *New York Times*. https://www.nytimes.com/2007/02/04/business/yourmoney/04digi.html

[3] Ibid.

[4] Ibid.

[5] Cisco Meraki. (n.d.). *Cisco Acquisition: CEO's Letter to Employees*. https://meraki.cisco.com/company/cisco-acquisition-faq#sanjit-letter-to-employees

[6] Cisco. (2012, November 18). *Cisco Announces Intent to Acquire Meraki* [Blog]. https://blogs.cisco.com/news/cisco-announces-intent-to-acquire-meraki

[7] Cisco. (2012, November 18). *Cisco Announces Intent to Acquire Meraki* [Press Release]. https://newsroom.cisco.com/c/r/newsroom/en/us/a/y2012/m11/cisco-announces-intent-to-acquire-meraki.html

Further Reading

Aguayo, D., Bicket, J., Biswas, S., & De Couto, D. (2003). MIT Roofnet: Construction of a Production Quality Ad-Hoc Network. *Mobicom*. https://www.sigmobile.org/mobicom/2003/posters/13-Biswas.pdf

Aguayo, D., Bicket, J., Biswas, S., De Couto, D., & Morris, R. (2003). MIT Roofnet Implementation: August 2003. *Roofnet*. https://web.archive.org/web/20060831060307/http:/pdos.csail.mit.edu/roofnet/doku.php?id=design

Cisco. (2012, December 20). *Cisco Completes Acquisition of Meraki* [Press Release]. https://newsroom.cisco.com/c/r/newsroom/en/us/a/y2012/m12/cisco-completes-acquisition-of-meraki.html

Meraki. (2003, February 3). *Meraki Featured in The New York Times*. Meraki Blog. https://meraki.cisco.com/blog/2007/02/meraki-featured-in-the-new-york-times/

Meraki. (2011, November 16). *Meraki: Level 1 PCI DSS Certified*. Meraki Blog. https://meraki.cisco.com/blog/2011/11/meraki-level-1-pci-dss-certified/)

Meraki. (2012, January 18). *Introducing 100% Cloud Managed Switching & Security*. Meraki Blog. https://meraki.cisco.com/blog/2011/11/meraki-level-1-pci-dss-certified/)

Meraki. (2023, May 10). *Video: The Meraki Product Mission*. Meraki Community. https://community.meraki.com/t5/Learning-Spotlight/Video-The-Meraki-Product-Mission/ba-p/194080

Morris, R., Aguayo, D., Bicket, J., Biswas, S., & De Couto, D. (n.d.). *MIT Roofnet*. https://pdos.csail.mit.edu/archive/rtm/slides/intel03-roofnet.pdf

Rao, L. (2011, February 8). *Sequoia Leads $15 Million Round In Wireless Networking Company Meraki*. TechCrunch. https://techcrunch.com/2011/02/07/sequoia-leads-15-million-round-in-wireless-networking-company-meraki/

Sequoia Capital. (n.d.). Cisco Acquires Meraki: How 3 Guys from MIT Transformed the Networking Industry. Tumblr. https://sequoiacapital.tumblr.com/post/36033519237/cisco-acquires-meraki-how-3-guys-from-mit).

Shaw, S. (2008, December 13). *Wi-Fi: Mobile Feature or Fundamental RAN?* https://www.eetimes.com/wi-fi-mobile-feature-or-fundamental-ran/

Stross, R. (2007, February 4). Wireless Internet for All, Without the Towers. *New York Times*. https://www.nytimes.com/2007/02/04/business/yourmoney/04digi.html

Chapter 2

Security Frameworks and Industry Best Practices

In this chapter, you learn the following:

- How cybercrime affects enterprises
- Common industry security frameworks and standards
- The role network engineers play in mitigating cybercrime
- The key focus areas common across multiple security standards

The Cybersecurity Imperative

The threat of cybercrime is real and pervasive, and no one is too big or too small to avoid being a target. Every day there are headlines of cybersecurity incidents, hacks, scams, ransomware, data breaches, denial-of-service attacks, and malware. Figure 2-1 illustrates some search results using the keywords "cyber security breach hack leak ransom" on Google. Try it yourself and see what results you get. Read some of the articles; they are shocking.

The consequences in each of these incidents are huge:

- Massive loss of reputation and trust
- Loss of customers
- Loss of revenue
- Share price collapse
- Business failure
- Loss of employment

- Executives being called to appear in front of government inquiries
- Negative media coverage
- Abuse and ridicule (e.g., memes) on social networks

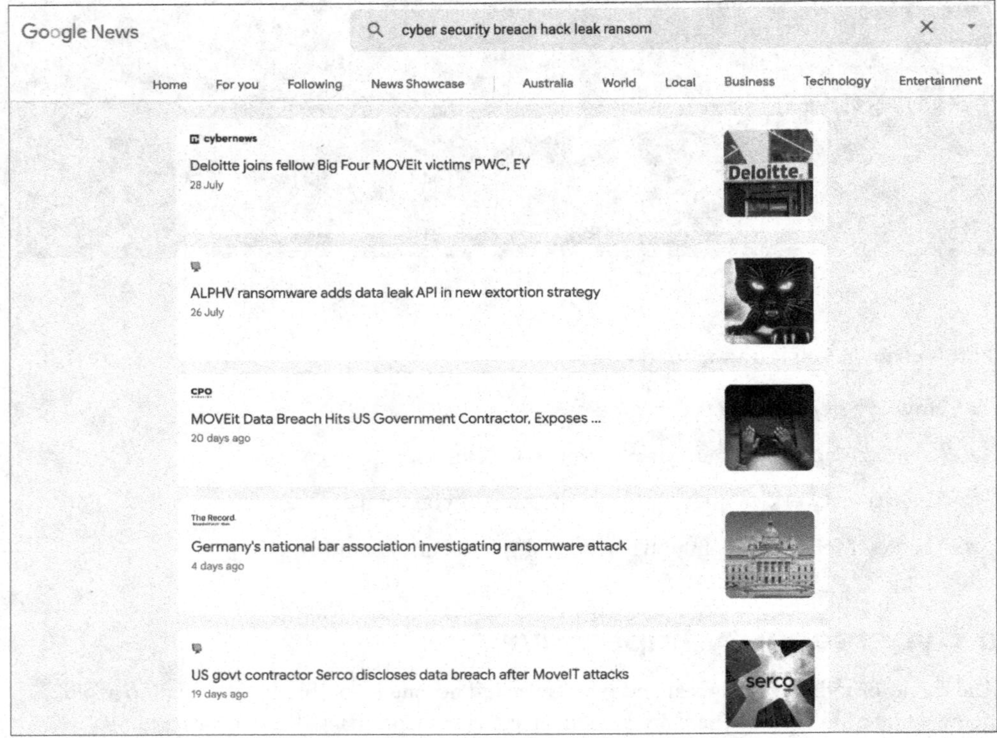

Figure 2-1 *Search Results for News Articles Related to Cybercrime*

Cybersecurity incidents lead to new security solutions being developed, improved IT security standards, and additional regulation. Cyber insurance does exist to protect organizations from some of these direct costs, such as lost revenue and the costs of notifying customers or recovering data. However, it's important to remember what cyber insurance doesn't cover. Cyber insurance won't bring back those customers who no longer trust you with their data. Nor will it restore the subsequent loss in business value. As insurance companies are looking to reduce their own risk, such policies typically stipulate minimum IT security requirements. Rather than being a substitute, cyber insurance reinforces the need for good IT security practices. As a network engineer, you have a vital role to play in protecting your organization from such consequences. This includes having preventative measures in place, while also adapting to changing best practice.

Adopting Industry Best Practice

IT security has come a long way in the past 25 years. In my early years as a network engineer, if a colleague had asked me, "Are we secure?" I would likely have replied, "Yes, we have a firewall." During the 2000s, if someone had asked me the same question, I would likely have replied, "Yes, we have two firewalls, and they are each from different vendors." While this is a true and somewhat amusing anecdote, what it really highlights is the change in the way that organizations have sought to reduce risk. Today's threats come with increased volume, sophistication, and an ever-increasing range of possible attack vectors. No one feature, product, or platform can provide an enterprise's entire cybersecurity needs. It's time to shift your thinking to minimizing risk, and the best way to reduce risk is to adopt industry best practice.

Industry Standards

Industry and government security experts are constantly developing and updating what is regarded as industry best practice. This practice is contained in numerous cybersecurity standards and frameworks. The best of these encompass continuous improvement, meaning that you should expect them to be updated every few years. Behind the scenes are cybersecurity professionals who live and breathe this stuff. They attend industry conferences, follow emerging technology, and research new exploits. These learnings are then incorporated into new and revised frameworks and standards. In this book, we refer to standards and frameworks jointly as industry best practice.

What is the difference between a framework and a standard? The simplest explanation is this: a framework tells you what to do, and standards tell you how to do it. Frameworks provide guidance and are helpful for determining the required scope of an organization's cybersecurity architecture, processes, and policies. Examples include the following:

- The National Institute of Standards and Technology (NIST) at the US Department of Commerce publishes its own cybersecurity framework (NIST CSF 2.0), which is mandatory for US federal agencies. That said, this framework has been designed so that it can be used by any organization, in any industry. The NIST CSF is designed to be used in conjunction with NIST's *Special Publication 800-53, Revision 5, Security and Privacy Controls*. NIST 800-53 is a security standard that maps applicable controls to the categories in the cybersecurity framework, so in practice they are used together. Even though NIST 800-53 was created in the US, it is common to see it used as a reference in many other nations.
- Australia has the Essential Eight framework, which is published by the Australian Cyber Security Centre (ACSC). All government agencies and departments of the Australian government must comply with the Essential Eight framework. You likely have an equivalent in your country as well.

In contrast, standards provide details in relation to the security capabilities required and their required features or specifications. Wherever there is sensitive data, you should expect to find an IT security standard mandating how best to protect it. Following are some of the more common examples:

- **Payments:** The Payment Card Industry Data Security Standard v4.0 (PCI DSS v4.0). Commonly referred to as PCI, this standard applies globally to organizations taking credit card payments and handling credit card data. PCI was once introduced to me as "IT Security for Dummies," because, to its credit, it is clearly written and the requirements are common sense, making it easy to apply. PCI shares many of its requirements with other standards and would apply to most businesses that sell to consumers as opposed to other businesses. If no standards seem to apply to your organization, we recommend you use PCI as your baseline.
- **Healthcare:** The Health Insurance Portability and Accountability Act (also referred to as HIPAA) sets standards to protect the confidentiality, integrity, and availability of electronic, protected health information. This standard applies in the US; however, there is likely an equivalent standard in your respective country.
- **Customer data:** In addition to the preceding standards, there are other popular standards related to protecting customer data (SOC 2) and best practice information systems management (ISO 27001). Being accredited as complying with these standards demonstrates that a firm can be trusted to safeguard customer information, which is important for outsourcing and cloud services.

Note A trend is emerging with newer standards where they could apply to your organization simply because of who you do business with. For example, the European Union's General Data Protection Regulation (GDPR), which protects the personal data of EU citizens, applies to any organization offering goods or services to the EU (yes, even if your enterprise is not based in the EU). Similarly, the NIST cybersecurity framework mandates that the cybersecurity requirements be reflected in contracts with third parties, including the same requirements for routine assessments and so on. This mandate prevents agencies simply contracting out their obligations. This trend is not likely to change, so you may also need to make those in your value chain aware of standards that apply to you, which by extension apply to them.

By having an awareness of industry best practice, organizations can design their IT and processes to be secure from the outset—the benefit being lower risk and faster detection and resolution of incidents. Now, imagine someone comes to you and asks, "Are we secure?" In this case, you're able to confidently reply, "Yes, we adhere to the latest [pick your applicable standard(s)], which is best practice for our industry. We were audited within the last year and certified to meet all applicable requirements." Rather than simply hoping that your organization has been diligent, now you can demonstrate that you are. This will be a significant change for many of today's organizations.

Security as a Team Sport

If you were to read the text of any of the industry best practices mentioned previously, you would quickly realize that they were not written just for network engineers. They can contain a lot of legalese, and you'll no doubt see a lot of requirements, thinking, "What does this have to do with me?" This is where this idea of security as a team sport comes in. Adhering to industry best practices really requires everyone in the organization to play their part. In fact, industry best practices mandate that one of the first things your organization should do is to clearly map out roles and responsibilities.

Understanding roles and responsibilities will help you to sort cybersecurity requirements into one of three buckets:

- Those that you're accountable for
- Those that you can support others to meet
- Those that others will be wholly accountable for

One of the obvious ways you can support other teams is by providing a second line of defense—for example, encrypting a WAN link even if only certain applications or data carried over that link need to be encrypted. This effort may be as simple as turning on capabilities in the platforms that you already have, in some cases without any additional cost.

Key Themes Across Security Standards

When setting out to write this book, we wanted to understand two things:

1. How similar were the network security requirements across different security standards?
2. Were there any common themes to these requirements?

We researched the standards mentioned previously and identified around 100 requirements relevant to IT teams (hopefully, we saved you a bunch of time). You can find a normalized view of these requirements in Appendix A, "A Comparison of Common Security Standards and Framework Requirements."

We have categorized these IT security requirements into the following key themes:

- The principle of least privilege, including role-based access control (RBAC).
- Strong authentication including multifactor authentication (MFA).
- The principle of zero trust. In networking, this is typically applied through requiring authentication before providing access to network resources.
- Controls, such as firewalls, intrusion prevention systems (IPS), and anti-malware.
- Encryption.
- Segmentation, including physical and logical isolation.

- Physical security.
- Logging.
- Monitoring (incident response).

In the following chapters, we cover each of these topics in depth and guide you through how to configure the Meraki platform to meet these requirements.

Continuous Improvement

Once you understand your obligations and implement the required controls, then what? Well, first you should definitely take the rest of the day off and do something you really enjoy. However, you're not done yet; it's important to keep in mind the principle of continuous improvement and make sure that you're aware of any changes in the standards. For example, when PCI DSS version 4.0 was released in 2022, one of the changes it introduced was to increase minimum password lengths from 7 to 12 characters. Before PSS DSS 3.2.1 was phased out in March 2024, all entities involved in payment processing were required to update their systems and processes to comply with the new rules. Because your annual audits will be based on the current standard of the day, it is important to stay up to date.

Note A key design consideration is ensuring that you have the ability to update policy centrally. In the example of the minimum password length, you can easily update this in Meraki Dashboard, as shown in Chapter 5, "Securing Administrator Access to Meraki Dashboard." However, if you're the one responsible for a large network and you're managing the configuration of each box manually, then you're about to have a very bad day!

Lastly, it is also highly recommended (and often mandated) that you audit the effectiveness of security controls. One way to test the effectiveness of controls is by hiring the services of a penetration tester. If you're doing this, ensure that you hire an organization that is both reputable and ethical. In regards to auditing your standards compliance, it is suggested that you perform this review at least annually and that you hire an external auditor for the most objective assessment. NIST CSF calls for "continuous evaluation," including reviews, audits, and assessments, and for the "routine" assessment of third parties. Be aware of the audit and review requirements of your applicable standard(s), because the frequency may be far more regular than you expect.

Comparison of Common Security Standards and Framework Requirements

Refer to Appendix A for a table showing six common standards and frameworks. We've selected the subset of requirements that would typically apply to or could be solved by the networking team. Not all standards use the same language, time periods, number of instances, and so on, so we've done our best to normalize them for easier comparison.

Summary

Although network engineers are only responsible for solving part of the overall IT security challenge, by having industry best practices as that wider lens, you can now connect your efforts to the aims of the overall organization. For effective IT security, you need this "north star" to guide you, adopt a relevant security standard, and ensure the key themes are addressed. Equally important is to implement an audit and compliance function to ensure adequate controls are in place and remain effective. Often the biggest challenge is one layer above the OSI model, the people. Therefore, don't underestimate the importance of continuous education for administrators, leaders, and users alike. Lastly, consider getting actively involved in the standards bodies and contribute to calls for comments when changes to frameworks are proposed.

Further Reading

American Institute of Certified Public Accountants (AICPA). (2022). 2017 Trust Services Criteria for Security, Availability, Processing Integrity, Confidentiality, and Privacy (with Revised Points of Focus – 2022). https://us.aicpa.org/content/dam/aicpa/interestareas/frc/assuranceadvisoryservices/downloadabledocuments/trust-services-criteria-2020.pdf

Australian Cyber Security Centre (ACSC). (2022, November 24). *Essential Eight Maturity Model*. https://www.cyber.gov.au/resources-business-and-government/essential-cyber-security/essential-eight/essential-eight-maturity-model

European Union. (2016). *General Data Protection Regulation (GDPR): Article 28*. https://gdpr-info.eu/art-28-gdpr/

International Standards Organization (ISO). (2022). *ISO/IEC 27001 Information Security Management Systems: Requirements*. https://www.iso.org/standard/27001

National Institute of Standards and Technology (NIST). (2020, September). *NIST 800-53 Rev. 5: Security and Privacy Controls for Information Systems and Organizations*. https://nvlpubs.nist.gov/nistpubs/SpecialPublications/NIST.SP.800-53r5.pdf

National Institute of Standards and Technology (NIST). (2023). *Public Draft: The NIST Cybersecurity Framework 2.0*. https://csrc.nist.gov/pubs/cswp/29/the-nist-cybersecurity-framework-20/ipd

PCI Security Standards Council. (2022, May). *Summary of Changes from PCI DSS Version 3.2.1 to 4.0 Revision 1*. https://listings.pcisecuritystandards.org/documents/PCI-DSS-v3-2-1-to-v4-0-Summary-of-Changes-r1.pdf

PCI Security Standards Council. (2022, December). PCI DSS: v4.0. https://www.pcisecuritystandards.org/document_library/

Tunggal, A. T. (2023, June 14). What Is SOC 2? *Upguard*. https://www.upguard.com/blog/soc-2

US Department of Health and Human Services. (2013, March 26). *HIPAA Administrative Simplification: Regulation Text*. https://www.hhs.gov/sites/default/files/ocr/privacy/hipaa/administrative/combined/hipaa-simplification-201303.pdf

Chapter 3

Meraki Dashboard and Trust

In this chapter, you learn the following:

- What Meraki Dashboard is
- The steps that Cisco takes to ensure the confidentiality, security, and availability of your data when using the Meraki platform
- How the Meraki platform can help your organization meet its IT compliance obligations
- How Meraki's hardware and software trust models work together to provide trustworthy infrastructure

Meraki Dashboard

Meraki Dashboard, or simply Dashboard, is the first step on your cloud-managed infrastructure journey. Meraki Dashboard is a centralized platform that enables you to manage your entire infrastructure stack in one place, with real-time monitoring, assurance, and analytics. Meraki has a full range of security appliances, Wi-Fi, mobile device management (MDM), switching, cameras, sensors, and more. Customers can choose as many products as they like and administer them all from one easy-to-use interface.

There are some inherent benefits to Meraki's cloud-hosted, Platform-as-a-Service (PaaS) based approach:

- It eliminates the need for setting up and maintaining multiple management platforms, thus reducing cost and management overhead.
- Configurations and templates can be created before hardware arrives on site, enabling zero-touch provisioning. Configuration changes are kept in sync with deployed devices.

- It enables automatic, scheduled software updates and patching, essential to maintaining a strong security posture.
- The native API interface enables simple integration with other cloud solutions. This integration enables enterprises to build end-to-end IT solutions and business capabilities quickly and easily.

Figure 3-1 shows the prevalence of Meraki networks around the globe, each reflected by the dark green dots.

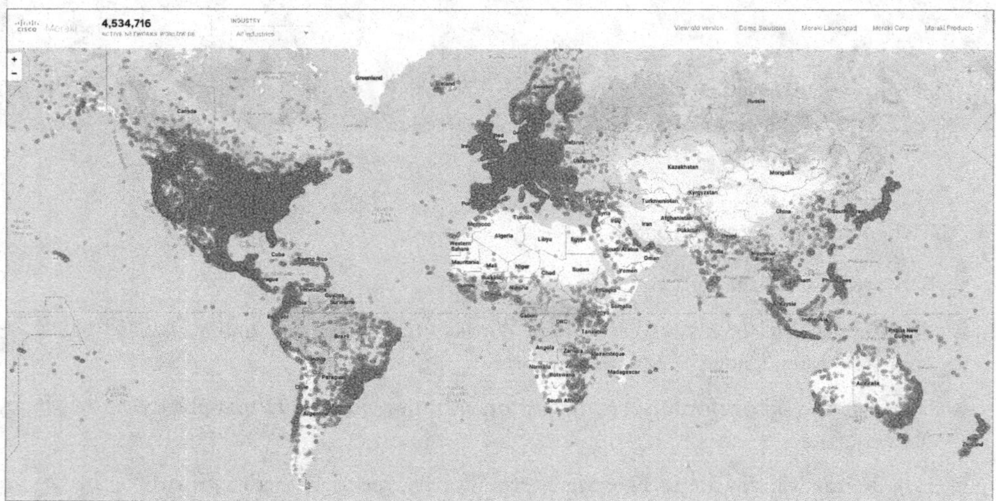

Figure 3-1 *Map with Dots Indicating the Meraki Networks Deployed Globally*

Out-of-Band Management

Meraki devices use an out-of-band encrypted tunnel to send management traffic to the Meraki Cloud. The Meraki Cloud is designed to be highly resilient. In the unlikely event that the Meraki Cloud is unavailable, customer networks continue to function because they rely on Dashboard only for management and not control plane or data plane functions. Figure 3-2 depicts this separation of user and management traffic.

Meraki Dashboard Hierarchy

Meraki Dashboard has a two-level policy hierarchy, as illustrated in Figure 3-3:

1. **Organization level:** An organization is a collection of networks that are all part of a single organizational entity, such as a company or government agency. Each organization is treated independently, meaning that all licensing, inventory, users, and configurations are kept within that organization.

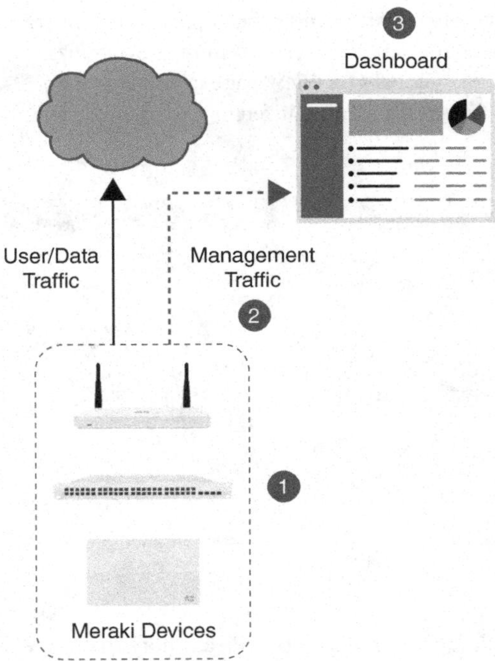

Figure 3-2 *Graphical Representation of Meraki's Separation of User and Management Traffic*

2. **Network level:** A network contains Cisco Meraki devices (such as switches, access points, and sensors), their configurations, statistics, and any client device information. A network can be dedicated to only network devices, only sensors (Environmental), only cameras (Camera), only Systems Manager devices, or a mix (Combined). For more information on network types, plus creating and deleting networks, refer to https://documentation.meraki.com/General_Administration/Organizations_and_Networks/Creating_and_Deleting_Dashboard_Networks.

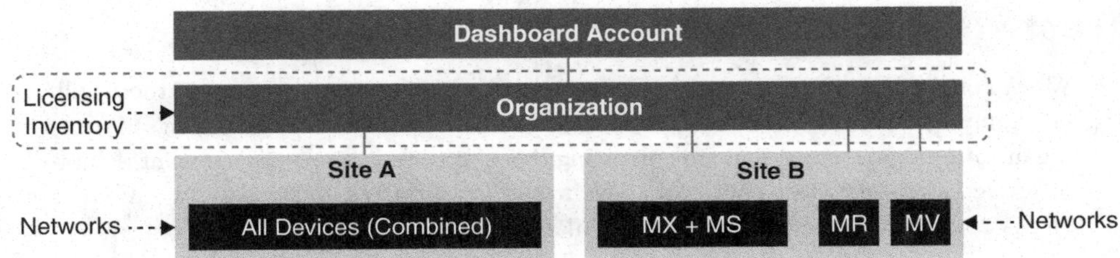

Figure 3-3 *The Meraki Dashboard Organizational Structure*

Each organization will have at least one administrator. A Dashboard account can have access to more than one organization if required. Managed service providers (MSPs) will typically manage each customer as a separate organization and have common administrators across all customers. When an admin account that has access to multiple organizations logs in, the admin's home page will be the Global Overview page (see Figure 3-4). This page allows an admin to quickly assess the health of the different environments, as well as switch between them easily.

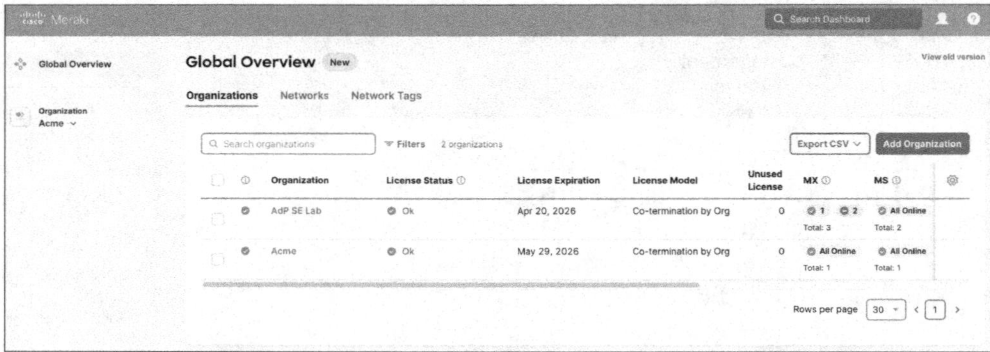

Figure 3-4 *The Global Overview Page*

To access Meraki Dashboard, go to https://dashboard.meraki.com. Please note that there are also other instances of Meraki Dashboard:

- China: https://dashboard.meraki.cn
- Canada: https://dashboard.meraki.ca
- Cisco Meraki for Government: https://dashboard.gov-meraki.com. Created for the US public sector, this dedicated instance of Meraki Dashboard is hosted in the US, FedRAMP approved, and FIPS 140-2 compliant.

In this book we reference https://dashboard.meraki.com whenever we instruct you to log in to Dashboard. If you require a different instance of Dashboard, substitute that instead.

Trust

When considering whether to locate assets or data outside of your premises, there will inevitably be a conversation about trust. Whether it's your pet, your firstborn, or your organization's data, when you are entrusting these to others, it's natural to want them to be looked after—typically, better than we would do ourselves. In the case of data, that means continuing to comply with the regulations that govern it.

Customer concerns typically fall into the following domains:

- Privacy
- Data security

- Data center resiliency
- Compliance with information standards, regulations, and industry best practices

We address each of these domains in the sections that follow.

Privacy

Meraki is built with privacy in mind and is designed so that it can be used in a manner consistent with global privacy requirements. Meraki takes privacy seriously and complies with industry best practices, including

- **ISO 9001:2008:** Quality Management
- **ISO 27001:2008:** Information Security Management
- **PCI DSS:** Protection of cardholder data[1]

Meraki and the EU Cloud are compliant with the following applicable European data protection regulatory frameworks and local laws:

- **EU Directive 95/46/EC:** Processing of personal data
- **German Federal Data Protection Act:** Protection of personal data
- **Article 29 Working Party Opinion of July 1, 2012:** Relevant issues for cloud computing service providers

Meraki Dashboard utilizes an out-of-band control plane that isolates network management data from user data. Outside of a few limited exceptions, no user traffic passes through Cisco Meraki's data centers. This makes the solution suitable for organizations requiring compliance with standards such as HIPAA and PCI.

In addition, Meraki complies with the General Data Protection Regulation (GDPR) in the EU. As a result, additional privacy-related tools have been introduced into Dashboard:

- **Data access and portability:** To honor customers' requests to export their information, Meraki has built functionality to enable accessibility and the export of Dashboard data.
- **The "right to be forgotten":** Customers can delete Dashboard data, either for themselves or in response to requests from users of their networks.
- **Restriction of processing:** In Meraki Dashboard, data can be identified, hidden, and removed upon a verified request to restrict processing.[2]

In summary, users whose personal data is processed by Meraki have the right to request access, rectification, suspension of processing, or deletion of their personal data.

Data Retention Policy

Dashboard stores customer data within the region where it is hosted. The period for which the data is retained varies from region to region:

- **EU:** 14 months (12 months + 2 months' worth of backups). This shorter period is intended to allow for annual reporting, while also ensuring that data is not kept for longer than necessary. This is done to align with the GDPR's storage limitation principles.
- **Rest of the world:** 26 months (24 months + 2 months' worth of backups).

Some data is stored for shorter periods, depending on the feature that it is used for. You can find this detail at https://documentation.meraki.com/General_Administration/Privacy_and_Security/Cloud_Data_Retention_Policies.

Data Security

Three major types of data are stored by Cisco Meraki:

- **Network configuration data:** This data includes device settings configured by customers in Meraki Dashboard.
- **Network analytics data:** Client traffic and location analytics data are used to provide visualizations and network insights of traffic and foot patterns.
- **Customer-uploaded assets:** This data includes any uploaded assets, such as custom floorplans and splash page logos.[3]

Meraki meets common data security requirements in the following ways:

- **All data transmission must be encrypted while in-transit and at-rest:**
  - Data in transit: Meraki devices communicating with the Meraki Cloud leverage a proprietary lightweight encrypted tunnel with AES256 encryption.[4]
  - Data at rest: All stored data is encrypted.[5]
  - Data in use is also encrypted.[6]
  - The Meraki platform supports FIPS 140-2, a US and Canadian government standard that specifies security requirements for cryptographic modules.
- **Supplier access to customer data must be restricted based on a "need-to-know" basis:** Access to customer data is restricted to personnel based on appropriate business need and limited by functional role.[7]
- **Data must be stored only in locations that are protected from unauthorized access:** Meraki's Cloud is protected as follows:
  - Access to Meraki's data centers is monitored 24×7 and restricted to only authorized personnel. All entries, exits, and cabinets are monitored by video surveillance.

- A high-security keycard system and biometric readers are utilized to control facility access.
- Security guards monitor all access in and out of the data centers 24×7, ensuring that entry processes are followed.
- Automated intrusion detection and firewalling are available 24×7.
- Remote access is restricted by an IP whitelist, PKI-based authentication, and is encrypted.
- All administrative activity is logged.[8]

- **The supplier must disclose all third parties/contractors who will have access to customer data:**
  - Meraki's third-party service providers are contracted to provide the same level of data protection and information security as Meraki.[9]
  - These third parties are disclosed on the Meraki Trust Center website at https://meraki.cisco.com/trust/#subprocessors.

Another common requirement is to understand exactly where your data will be located. The location will be one of the countries in Table 3-1, depending on the Dashboard region chosen at the time the organization was created.

Table 3-1 *Meraki Data Center Locations*

Dashboard Region	Location of Dashboard Data
North America	US
South America	US
Europe	Germany
Asia	Australia, Singapore
China	China
Canada	Canada

The Dashboard region cannot be changed later without creating a new organization. The Dashboard region can be verified at any time by simply viewing the bottom-middle of any page in Dashboard. There you will see "Data for <*Organization*> (organization ID: <XXXXXXXXXXXXXXXXXX>) is hosted in <Dashboard region>," as shown in Figure 3-5.

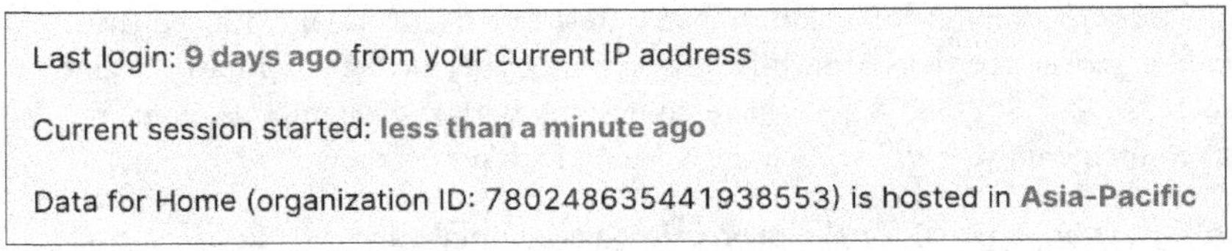

Last login: **9 days ago** from your current IP address

Current session started: **less than a minute ago**

Data for Home (organization ID: 780248635441938553) is hosted in **Asia-Pacific**

Figure 3-5 *The Organization ID as Shown in Meraki Dashboard*

Meraki publishes the latest list of its data center locations at https://documentation.meraki.com/General_Administration/Privacy_and_Security/Dashboard_Data_Storage_Privacy_and_Security.

Data Center Resiliency

Meraki has engineered its data centers to meet the highest standards of resiliency and availability. This includes the following:

- Data centers are globally distributed. In the event of a catastrophic data center failure, services fail over to another geographically separate site.
- Meraki's data centers are certified by industry-recognized standards, including ISO 9001:2008, ISO 27001, Payment Card Industry Data Security Standard (PCI DSS), SSAE16, and ISAE 3402 (SAS70) including Type II.
- There is a 99.99 percent uptime service-level agreement (that's under one hour per year) with failover procedures drilled weekly.
- Each data center has redundant WAN connectivity from at least two top-tier carriers.
- Automated failure detection is available 24×7. All servers are tested every five minutes from multiple locations.
- Diesel generators provide backup power in the event of power loss.
- Uninterruptible power supply (UPS) systems condition power and ensure an orderly shutdown in the event of a full power outage.
- Seismic bracing is provided for the raised floor, cabinets, and support systems.
- Overprovisioned heating, ventilation, and air conditioning (HVAC) systems provide cooling and humidity control via underfloor air distribution.
- Real-time replication of data occurs between data centers (within 60 seconds). Customer network configuration data and statistical data are replicated across independent data centers, with no common point of failure.
- Archival backups are made nightly for customer network configuration data and statistical data.[10]

Compliance with Information Standards, Regulations, and Industry Best Practices

In Chapter 2, "Security Frameworks and Industry Best Practices," we introduced the notion of industry best practices, drawn from common cybersecurity frameworks and standards such as NIST 800-53. When you're complying with such standards, here are some other requirements you will see and how Meraki addresses them:

- **Controls must be in place for the protection against malware:** Meraki operates 24×7 automated intrusion detection to protect against malware.[11]

- **Regular vulnerability assessments must be conducted by a third party:**
  - All Cisco Meraki data centers undergo daily vulnerability scanning by an independent third party (Qualys).
  - External vulnerability scans are performed at least once every three months by a PCI SSC Approved Scanning Vendor (ASV) (PCI DSS 4.0 requirement 11.3.2). Vulnerabilities are resolved and rescans are performed as needed to confirm that vulnerabilities are resolved.
  - In addition, Meraki runs a vulnerability rewards program for both hardware and software, encouraging external researchers to report vulnerabilities.
- **Regular penetration testing must be conducted by a third party:**
  - All Cisco Meraki data centers undergo thorough daily penetration testing.[12]
  - Cisco Meraki is verified to be free of vulnerabilities such as injection flaws, cross-site scripting, misconfiguration, and insecure session management.
- **The supplier must implement an information security policy and information security framework within its organization:** Meraki has implemented an information security policy including the following:
  - Designated information security responsibilities for employees, including industry standard confidentiality agreements
  - Comprehensive security training
  - A policy of no contract developers
  - Criminal background reviews of all Meraki personnel[13]
  - Documentation and business justification for use of all services, protocols, and ports allowed
  - Data control and access control policies and procedures
  - A Secure Development Lifecycle (SDL) approach
  - Vulnerability disclosure and management programs
  - Audit trails policy and procedures as well as a log retention policy and procedures

If you require more details or answers to other compliance questions, please refer to the following three Meraki resources:

- **Cisco Meraki Privacy Data Sheet:** https://trustportal.cisco.com/c/r/ctp/trust-portal.html#/1620320457399887
- **The Meraki Security Brief:** https://trustportal.cisco.com/c/r/ctp/trust-portal.html#/1599853130766928
- **The Meraki Trust Center:** https://meraki.cisco.com/trust/

Hardware Trust Model

The foundation of any secure networking solution lies in the trustworthiness of its hardware components. Cisco Meraki employs a hardware trust model that encompasses multiple layers of security measures to safeguard against hardware-level attack vectors. Following are some of the key elements to Meraki's platform integrity:

- Supply or value chain security
- Secure boot (including image signing and OS validation)
- Secure device onboarding

Supply Chain Security

Cisco maintains a highly controlled and audited supply chain process to prevent tainted and counterfeit products. From the initial manufacturing stage to the final deployment, every step is carefully monitored to ensure the integrity of hardware components. This includes rigorous quality checks, tamper-evident packaging, and strict adherence to industry standards and government regulations.

Cisco's layered security approach applies to the entire ecosystem, including parts manufacturers, completed product (warehouses), distribution centers, and channel partners. Cisco's value chain security practices ensure that solutions are retained in securely controlled development, manufacturing, logistics, and channel environments. This includes the following components:

- **Physical security:** Camera monitoring, security checkpoints, alarms, and electronic or biometric access control.
- **Logical security:** Systematic, repeatable, and auditable operational security processes, including encryption, materials and failure analysis segregation, and scrap weight validation.
- **Security technology:** Technical innovation to enhance counterfeit detection, identify nonauthorized components, and terminate functionality. This includes smart chips and proprietary holographic or intaglio security labels.
- **Information security:** Data and information systems protection, including
  - Limited remote access
  - Configuration management
  - Network segmentation
  - Multifactor authentication
  - Data classification[14]

Cisco solutions are developed using only Cisco-approved processes and tools, together with approved software modules and hardware components. These processes prevent the introduction of malware that could compromise functionality. In addition, Cisco maintains a TPAT Tier III accreditation, which encompasses all aspects of logistics security including physical access controls, personnel screening, container integrity, procedural security, and training. The net effect of all these measures is the peace of mind that your Meraki products are genuine, high quality, and trustworthy.

Secure Boot

Meraki devices employ secure boot mechanisms, where only trusted and digitally signed firmware images can be loaded during the boot process. This ensures that the device starts with a known, trusted state and guards against the execution of malicious or unauthorized firmware.

Secure boot is made possible by a hardware trust anchor module (TAM), which is a tamper-resistant module that features nonvolatile secure storage and crypto functions. The trust anchor module provides a secure place to store the Secure Unique Device Identifier (SUDI), which is an X.509 certificate that is installed by Cisco during manufacturing. The SUDI provides a cryptographic way to verify that the device is an authentic Cisco Meraki device, a process also known as remote attestation.

Through the use of signed images and trusted elements, a chain of trust can be created that boots the system securely and validates the integrity of Cisco software. The high-level process is as follows:

- On start-up, an initial micro loader stored on the trust anchor module performs an integrity check on itself. Once the check is successfully completed, this establishes the first step in the chain of trust and acts as the "root of trust."
- Next, the bootloader's (equivalent to BIOS on your PC or ROMMON on traditional Cisco devices) integrity is verified using its digital signature before being loaded.
- Lastly, the operating system software image is verified using its digital signature to ensure that it hasn't been tampered with either. If this check is successful, it too is loaded.

The boot process stops if any of the secure boot checks fail. Once the OS is loaded, the same verification process is used to validate that the device hardware and any expansion modules (all of which contain their own SUDIs) are genuine and unmodified. This protects against counterfeit hardware. While the instances of counterfeit hardware are extremely rare, these measures are important to dissuade attempts. Successful completion of the secure boot process guarantees the immutable authenticity of all software and hardware components.

Secure Device Onboarding

Following the secure boot process, before a device is permitted to join an organization in Meraki Dashboard, it must be added to the organization's inventory. The recommended way to add devices is by using the order number (an eight- or nine-digit number, typically starting with 5S, 5C, 4S, or 4C). This then acts as a form of whitelist, ensuring that only devices that were knowingly purchased from Cisco become part of your organization's Dashboard inventory.

Software Trust Model

In addition to its robust hardware trust model, Meraki follows a stringent Secure Development Lifecycle (SDL) process, integrating security at every stage. This includes secure coding practices, third-party software compliance, regular code reviews, and thorough vulnerability assessments to identify and address any potential security flaws or weaknesses. You can find more details on Cisco's Secure Development Lifecycle approach at https://www.cisco.com/c/dam/en_us/about/doing_business/trust-center/docs/cisco-secure-development-lifecycle.pdf.

Being connected to the cloud means that Meraki devices receive regular software updates and patches to address any newly discovered vulnerabilities. These updates are thoroughly tested before deployment and can be applied seamlessly. This ensures that the network remains protected against emerging threats.

To ensure robust and reliable firmware development, Meraki follows a consistent software release process to validate and deploy consistent and reliable firmware[15] (see Figure 3-6). Meraki's firmware development process has four stages: alpha, beta, stable release candidate (RC), and stable. If a particular build fails to pass Meraki's key metrics at any stage of the development process, a new build is created, and the process begins again.

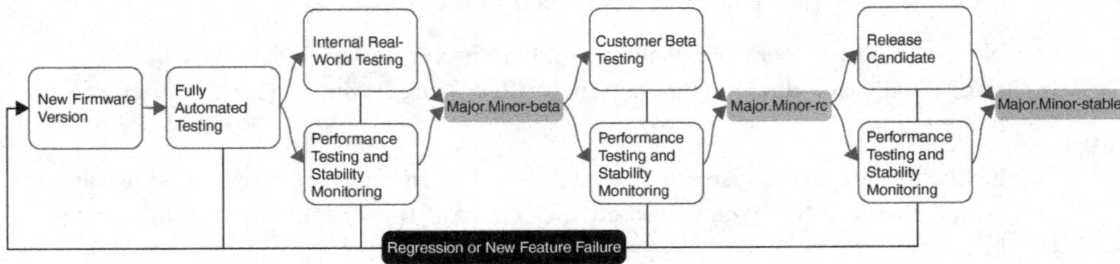

Figure 3-6 *Meraki's Firmware Quality Assurance Regime*

Meraki validates every release by running it through an ever-expanding number of testing suites (see Figure 3-7). The aim of this testing is to find regressions or new features that are not performing as expected. Key performance indicators (KPIs) for quantifying stable release candidate firmware quality include open support cases and engineering issues, firmware adoption, and stability metrics. A stable release candidate matures into a stable version over time as it is slowly rolled out to devices globally. When the Meraki install base hits a specified threshold for a major version (roughly 10–20 percent of nodes), that firmware revision will be promoted to stable, pending a final formal review.[16]

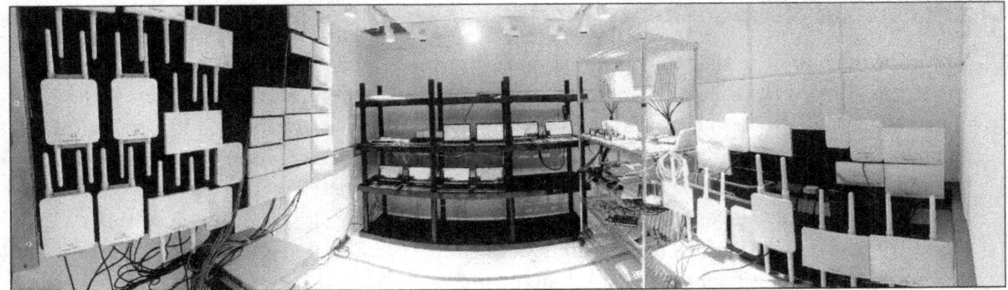

Figure 3-7 *Meraki's Wireless Test Facilities*

As previously discussed, Meraki does extensive testing before a release candidate progresses to a stable release. It would be a waste of time and effort to produce high-quality, secure software if it was never deployed. Industry best practice requires that software be patched and kept up to date. Therefore, there is an obligation on administrators to keep their software current. Meraki makes this easy through the ability to schedule automatic software upgrades, the firmware upgrade tool (**Organization > Firmware Upgrades**), and the ability to do staged software upgrades.

It is recommended that network administrators do the following:

- Ensure software is maintained at a "Good" level. You can view the firmware status on the Overview tab of the Firmware Upgrades page.
- Run the latest stable version for each respective product to ensure the best performance, stability, and protection from security vulnerabilities. To check the current firmware versions in your network, navigate to **Organization > Firmware Upgrades** (under Monitor) > **Schedule Upgrades.** The table located here lists your device types and their current firmware versions.
- View the firmware release notes. You can find these by navigating to **Organization > Firmware Upgrades** (under Monitor). Scroll down to Latest Firmware Versions and click the **Release Notes** button underneath the corresponding firmware version. The pop-up window lists the important information related to this release.
- Test firmware images in a noncritical area of the network before doing a widescale rollout.
- Specify the appropriate access point firmware upgrade strategy preference—either **Minimize Total Upgrade Time** or **Minimize Client Downtime.** You configure this in Dashboard under **Network-wide > General.** You can find additional details on how the two options work in practice on Meraki's website at https://documentation.meraki.com/MR/Other_Topics/Access_Point_Firmware_Upgrade_Strategy.

By combining a robust hardware trust model with robust integrity mechanisms and a comprehensive software trust model, Meraki establishes a solid foundation for a secure and reliable IT platform. Together, these measures ensure that the network infrastructure remains trustworthy and protected against potential threats.

Cloud Shared Responsibility Model

It's important to note that a shared responsibility model exists in relation to the Meraki platform. Shared responsibility models have existed for as long as the public cloud has been available. They are not new, but they might be new to enterprises shifting to cloud-managed networks. Under Cisco's shared responsibility model, responsibilities are either retained by the customer, shared with the customer, or transferred to Cisco. In the past, all components in the IT stack were located on a customer's site, and therefore their security was the customer's responsibility. With the Meraki platform, some of these components have shifted to the cloud, making them Cisco's responsibility. One of the aspects that customers really like about Meraki's solution is that they don't have to set up their own management servers. Meraki Dashboard, which is hosted in the Meraki Cloud, resides on infrastructure including hardware, software, and networking. The security of this infrastructure and the facilities in which it resides are Cisco's responsibility. These are referred to as inherited controls.

Some controls are shared, such as configuration. Customers are responsible for the configuration within Meraki Dashboard. This includes the configuration of access control to their Dashboard organization and the configuration of security features, like firewall rules. Likewise, Cisco is responsible for the configuration of access control and security features in relation to the infrastructure providing Meraki Dashboard, but not inside a customer's organization.

Lastly, some elements remain solely the responsibility of customers, such as the proper treatment of logging, alerts, and flow data that is exported out of Dashboard. This could also include integrations that provide additional functionality such as identity management or multifactor authentication.

The major benefit of a shared responsibility model is the reduction in the scope of what an organization is responsible for securing. The upside is that organizations free up existing resources, enabling more focus on better securing the remaining infrastructure. Organizations should take the time to understand shared responsibility models when determining IT security roles and responsibilities.

Summary

Meraki's Dashboard is a wildly popular, full-stack management interface. It does away with traditional management headaches such as setting up and maintaining management platforms, while bringing new benefits such as plug-and-play provisioning, access from anywhere, and automatic software updates. Operating out of the cloud brings with it new conversations about trust, resilience, data privacy, and security. Meraki has taken exhaustive steps to comply with common industry standards and government regulations. Lastly, Meraki's industry-leading hardware and software trust models ensure that customers know, with confidence, that their infrastructure is genuine and tamper free.

Notes

[1] Cisco Systems. (n.d.) *The Cisco Meraki EU Cloud*. https://meraki.cisco.com/lib/pdf/meraki_datasheet_eu_cloud.pdf

[2] Cisco Systems. (2022). Meraki and GDPR. https://meraki.cisco.com/gdpr

[3] Cisco Systems. (2023). Meraki Storage Architecture. https://meraki.cisco.com/trust/#storage-architecture

[4] Cisco Systems. (2023, October 10). Meraki Cloud Architecture. (https://documentation.meraki.com/Architectures_and_Best_Practices/Cisco_Meraki_Best_Practice_Design/Meraki_Cloud_Architecture)

[5] Cisco Systems. (2023, June 21). Cisco Meraki Privacy Data Sheet. https://trustportal.cisco.com/c/r/ctp/trust-portal.html#/1620320457399887

[6] Ibid.

[7] Cisco Meraki. (2024). Technical and Organizational Measures. https://meraki.cisco.com/trust/#tom

[8] Ibid.

[9] Cisco Systems. Cisco Meraki Privacy Data Sheet.

[10] Cisco Meraki. Technical and Organizational Measures.

[11] Cisco Systems. (n.d.) Cisco Value Chain Security Program. https://www.cisco.com/c/dam/en_us/about/doing_business/trust-center/docs/value-chain-security.pdf

[12] Cisco Meraki. Technical and Organizational Measures.

[13] Ibid.

[14] Cisco Systems. (n.d.) Cisco Value Chain Security Program.

[15] Cisco Systems. (n.d.). Best Practices for Meraki Firmware. https://documentation.meraki.com/Architectures_and_Best_Practices/Cisco_Meraki_Best_Practice_Design/Best_Practices_for_Meraki_Firmware

[16] Cisco Meraki. (2023, November 26). Meraki Firmware Release Process. https://documentation.meraki.com/General_Administration/Firmware_Upgrades/Meraki_Firmware_Release_Process

Further Reading

Amazon Cloud Services. (n.d.). Shared Responsibility Model. https://aws.amazon.com/compliance/shared-responsibility-model/

Carling, M. (2020). *Foundational Trust for Foundational Infrastructure*. Cisco Live. https://www.ciscolive.com/c/dam/r/ciscolive/apjc/docs/2020/pdf/BRKSEC-2634.pdf

Cisco Meraki. (2021, December 8). Information for Users in China. https://documentation.meraki.com/General_Administration/Support/Information_for_Users_in_China

Cisco Meraki. (2023, November 8). Managed Service Providers (MSPs). https://documentation.meraki.com/General_Administration/Managed_Service_Providers_(MSPs)

Cisco Meraki. (2024, April 3). Meraki Device-to-Cloud Connectivity – FIPS. https://documentation.meraki.com/General_Administration/Cross-Platform_Content/Meraki_Device_to_Cloud_Connectivity_-_FIPS

Cisco Meraki. (2024, May 3). Cisco Meraki Canada Region. https://documentation.meraki.com/General_Administration/Cross-Platform_Content/Cisco_Meraki_Canada_Region

Cisco Meraki. (2024, May 3). Information for Cisco Meraki for Government Users. https://documentation.meraki.com/General_Administration/Support/Information_for_Cisco_Meraki_for_Government_users

Cisco Systems. (2019, April 8). Cisco Trusted Platforms. Cisco Blogs. https://blogs.cisco.com/sp/cisco-trusted-platforms

Cisco Systems. (2021) *Cisco Value Chain Security Key Questions/Answers*. https://www.cisco.com/c/dam/en_us/about/doing_business/trust-center/docs/cisco-value-chain-security-faqs.pdf

Cisco Systems. (2021). *Cisco Trustworthy Technologies Data Sheet*. https://www.cisco.com/c/dam/en_us/about/doing_business/trust-center/docs/trustworthy-technologies-datasheet.pdf

Cisco Systems. (2021). *Cisco Secure Development Lifecycle.* https://www.cisco.com/c/dam/en_us/about/doing_business/trust-center/docs/cisco-secure-development-lifecycle.pdf

Cisco Systems. (2022). *Meraki Product Guidebook, Security Made Simple*. https://merakiresources.cisco.com/rs/010-KNZ-501/images/SecurityMadeSimple-Product-Guidebook-English.pdf

Cisco Systems. (2022, November 10). The Meraki Data Privacy and Protection Features. https://documentation.meraki.com/General_Administration/Privacy_and_Security/Meraki_Data_Privacy_and_Protection_Features

Cisco Systems. (2023). Login Attempts. https://documentation.meraki.com/General_Administration/Organizations_and_Networks/Organization_Menu/Login_Attempts

Cisco Systems. (2023, March 16). Dashboard Data Storage Privacy and Security. https://documentation.meraki.com/General_Administration/Privacy_and_Security/Dashboard_Data_Storage_Privacy_and_Security

Cisco Systems. (2023, June 21). Cisco Meraki Privacy Data Sheet. https://trustportal.cisco.com/c/r/ctp/trust-portal.html#/1620320457399887

Cisco Systems. (2023, August 8). Cloud Data Retention Policies. https://documentation.meraki.com/General_Administration/Privacy_and_Security/Cloud_Data_Retention_Policies

Cisco Systems. (2023, August 22). Managing Firmware Upgrades. https://documentation.meraki.com/General_Administration/Firmware_Upgrades/Managing_Firmware_Upgrades

Cisco Systems. (2023, October 10). Meraki Cloud Architecture. (https://documentation.meraki.com/Architectures_and_Best_Practices/Cisco_Meraki_Best_Practice_Design/Meraki_Cloud_Architecture)

Cisco Systems (2024), Meraki Security Brief. https://trustportal.cisco.com/c/r/ctp/trust-portal.html#/1599853130766928

European Union. (2016, April 27). Regulation (EU) 2016/679 of the European Parliament and of the Council. https://eur-lex.europa.eu/legal-content/EN/TXT/HTML/?uri=CELEX:32016R0679&from=EN#d1e1807-1-1

Microsoft. (2023, September 9). Shared Responsibility in the Cloud. https://learn.microsoft.com/en-us/azure/security/fundamentals/shared-responsibility

Patil, J. (2020, June 2). *Security Made Simple with Cisco Meraki*. Cisco Live. https://www.ciscolive.com/c/dam/r/ciscolive/us/docs/2020/pdf/DGTL-PSOMER-2000.pdf

Rodriguez, S. (2023). *Meraki Wireless: Ready for Enterprise – BRKEWN-2035*. Cisco Live. https://www.ciscolive.com/on-demand/on-demand-library.html?search=Meraki%20Wireless%3A%20Ready%20for%20Enterprise%20#/

Chapter 4

Role-Based Access Control (RBAC)

In this chapter, you learn the following:

- The organizational hierarchy and the built-in access levels available in Meraki Dashboard
- The various roles available in Meraki Dashboard
- How to configure role-based access control (RBAC) within Meraki Dashboard to adhere to the principle of least privilege

The principle of least privilege and role-based access control (RBAC) are key themes across industry best practices. RBAC is an essential feature that enables you to assign appropriate access rights to users based on their roles and responsibilities. Practical use cases for differentiated administrative roles include the following:

- Providing help-desk staff with limited access to Dashboard to be able to collect vital troubleshooting information, thereby enabling incidents to be resolved faster.
- Providing CCTV operators with the access they need to view and edit footage, while limiting access to network settings.
- Assigning limited read-write access for junior administrators. Having fewer admins with full access at the organizational level reduces the likelihood of mistakes that can have a wide-ranging impact.

Meraki Dashboard incorporates RBAC, providing a built-in way to precisely control administrative access to specific parts of the Meraki organization. In addition to the built-in roles, you can create distinct and granular roles if required.

Meraki Dashboard's Administration Hierarchy

Meraki Dashboard administrator privileges are controlled at the organization and network levels:

- Organization administrators have visibility of the organization and all its networks. Organizational admins do not necessarily have the highest permissions. Access can be restricted; for example, it is possible to have an organizational administrator with only read-only access.
- Network administrators have visibility of individual networks. Network administrators can have complete or limited control over these networks but do not have access to organization-level information (licensing, device inventory, and so on) unless granted such access at the organization level.

The privileges grant control over what a user can see and do in Meraki Dashboard. Permissions granted at the organization level cannot be reduced at the network level. If required, a user can have access to multiple networks and multiple organizations. We cover how to assign access to multiple networks later in the section titled "Assigning Permissions Using Network Tags."

For more information on the Meraki Dashboard's hierarchical structure, see https://documentation.meraki.com/General_Administration/Organizations_and_Networks/Meraki_Dashboard_Organizational_Structure.

Administrator Access Levels for Dashboard Organizations and Networks

Three levels of administrative access are available at the organization level:

- **None:** Users will have no access to the organization, meaning they cannot perform any actions or view any configurations at the organization level. They may, however, still have privileges assigned at the network level.
- **Read-Only:** Users with read-only access can view the Dashboard configurations for the organization but cannot make any changes. This includes the ability to view video footage if the organization has cameras. Be aware that administrators may still have privileges assigned at the network level.
- **Full:** Users with full access have access to all parts of Dashboard (including cameras), can make configuration changes, and can even delete the organization. This access level should be limited to suitably qualified and trusted personnel.

Four additional levels of access are available when configuring privileges at the network level:

- **Full:** This level grants full access to the target network, including the ability to view all of the Dashboard and change any configuration settings (see Figure 4-1).

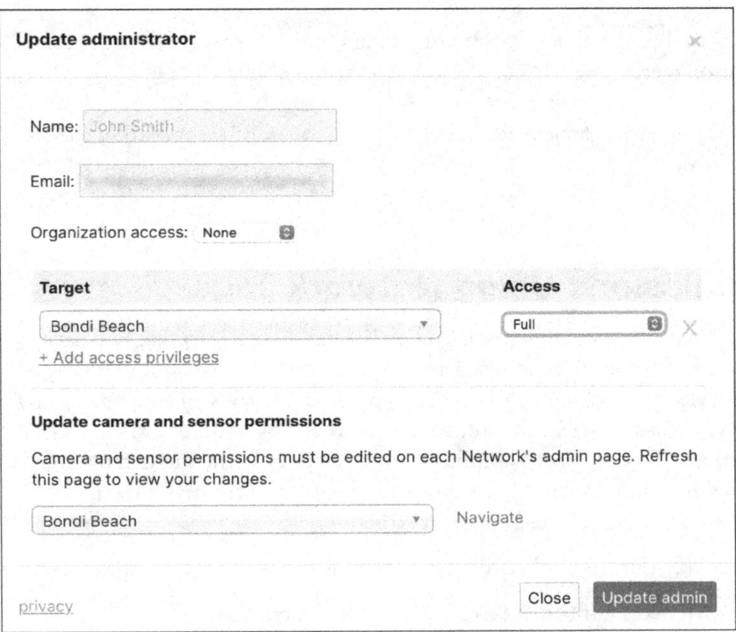

Figure 4-1 *An Example of an Administrator Configured as a Network-Only Admin*

- **Read-Only:** With this level, users can view all configurations in the target network but are restricted from making any modifications.
- **Monitor-Only:** Administrators with this access level can view a dedicated monitor page in the Dashboard but cannot make any changes. Users with this access level can monitor and analyze network performance metrics, troubleshoot issues, and gain insights into the network's health and performance.
- **Guest Ambassador:** This level of access is intended for managing user access to Wi-Fi or client VPN access. The most common use case for this role is a hotel receptionist or lobby ambassador needing to provide temporary (time-bound) Wi-Fi access for guests and visitors. Staff with this access level can manage guest users, granting or revoking access as needed. When logging in, the Guest Ambassador user is presented with a purpose-built user management portal. It allows them to efficiently manage guest user accounts without having access to other parts of the Dashboard.

Note You cannot assign full access to a user at the organization level and then assign only read-only permissions at the network level. Dashboard will give you a warning if you try to do this. If you want to create some network-focused admin users, you can grant read-only or no access (none) at the organization level and then the desired access at the network level.

> **Tip** For more information on managing Dashboard administrators and permissions, check out https://documentation.meraki.com/General_Administration/Managing_Dashboard_Access/Managing_Dashboard_Administrators_and_Permissions. Alternatively, search for "Managing Dashboard Administrators and Permissions" using Search Dashboard in the top right of Meraki Dashboard.

Assigning Permissions Using Network Tags

If you're not using configuration templates, then here's a handy little tip that will save you a ton of time when it comes to administering admin users. Because you will have a network for every location, grouping them together in a logical way will make assigning administrative rights far easier. In Dashboard, group networks by assigning them a common tag. Then, when granting access to administrators, select only the tag name rather than all the individual network names. Tagged networks appear with the prefix *Tag:* in the **Target** list on the **Organization Administrators** page.

Follow these steps to tag your networks and assign administrator access using them:

Step 1. Log in to Meraki Dashboard (https://dashboard.meraki.com).

Step 2. Navigate to **Organization** > **Overview** (under Monitor), as demonstrated in Figure 4-2.

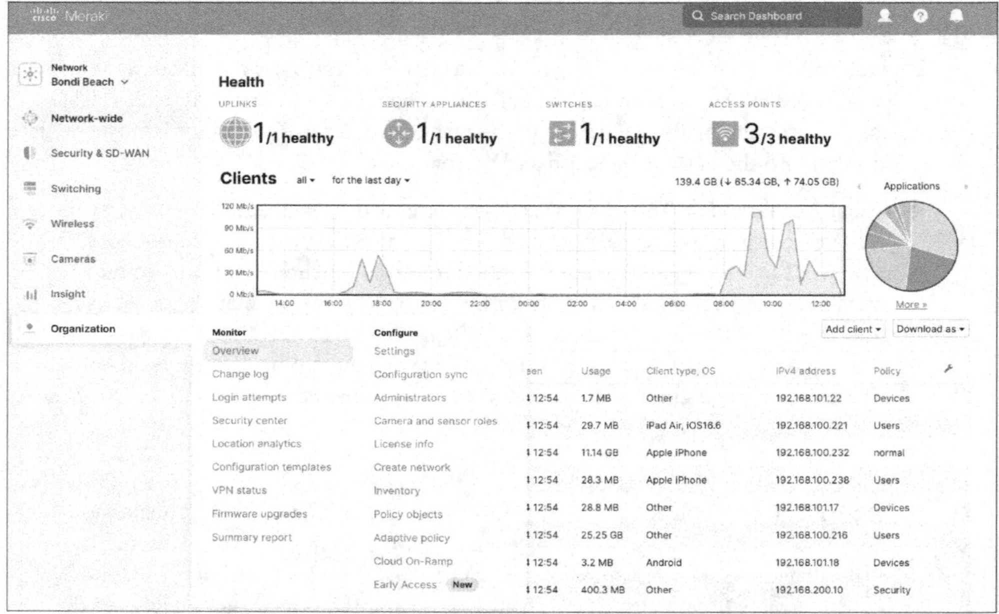

Figure 4-2 *Navigating to the Organization Overview Page*

Step 3. Select the check box or boxes next to the network(s) you want to tag, as demonstrated in Figure 4-3.

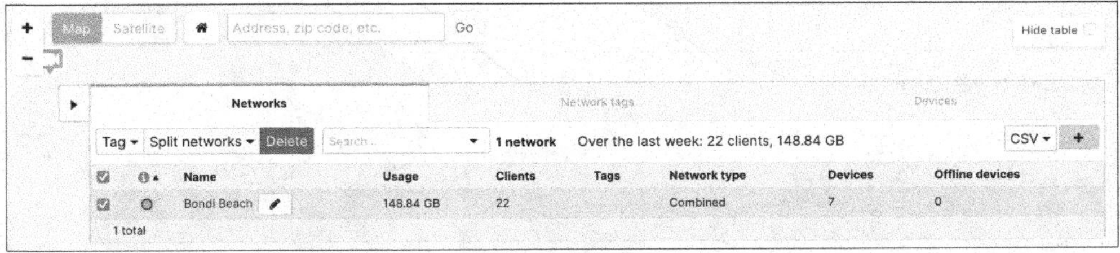

Figure 4-3 *The Organization Overview Page*

Step 4. Click **Tag** and then enter the tag name you would like to create. In the case illustrated in Figure 4-4, we used the tag **Stores.** Click **Add.** The Add button will change to Updating, then quickly turn green, then change to Updated, before changing back to Add.

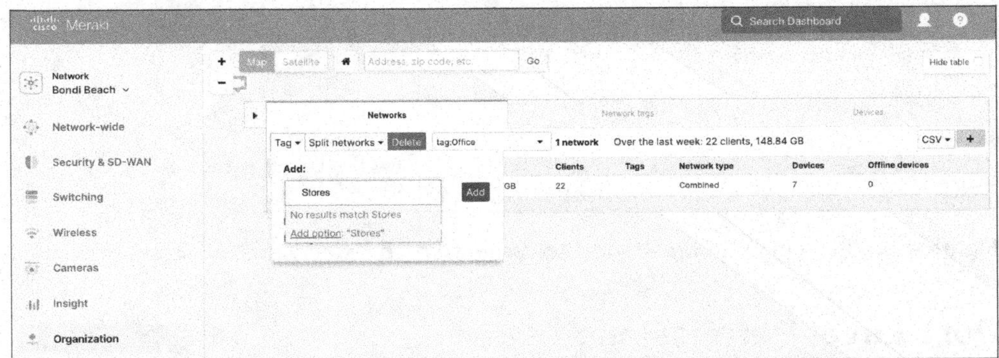

Figure 4-4 *Creating New Network Tags*

You can now see the tag next to the network name selected previously, confirming that the changes have been applied, as demonstrated in Figure 4-5.

Figure 4-5 *Confirming Networks Are Now Tagged*

Step 5. When updating organization administrator privileges (**Organization > Administrators**), you can now see the Stores group created with the prefix

Tag: in the **Target** list, as demonstrated in Figure 4-6. From here, just assign access the same way you would to a regular network, by choosing the access level from the **Access** drop-down menu and clicking **Update Admin.**

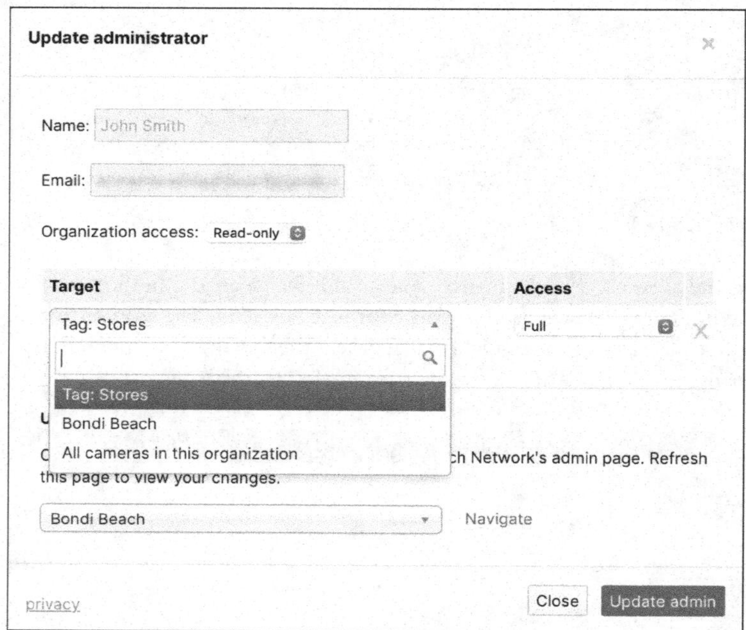

Figure 4-6 *Assigning Administrator Access to a Group Using Tags*

Port-Level Permissions

In Meraki Dashboard it is possible to provision read-only administrator accounts with read-write access to selected switchports. In traditional networks, doing this wasn't easy, so we avoided it. However, now that the capability exists, some immediate use cases come to mind:

- Labs, teaching environments, dormitories, and the like. If you have any such environments in your network, you can now provide limited admin access to staff or students without having to provide them with admin access to the rest of the network. With the access locked down, if required, you could continue to serve regular users off the remaining ports.
- Multitenanted environments like airports or shopping centers. In a multitenanted environment where you're responsible for providing network connectivity to businesses inside your premises, you could provide tenants with admin access to the ports serving just their premises. Because the control is down to the port level, potentially you could now share switches between tenants where you previously had provided a switch per tenant, reducing costs.

Follow these steps to tag your ports and configure roles with port-level permissions:

Step 1. Log in to Meraki Dashboard (https://dashboard.meraki.com).

Step 2. Navigate to **Switching > Switch Ports** (under Monitor), as demonstrated in Figure 4-7.

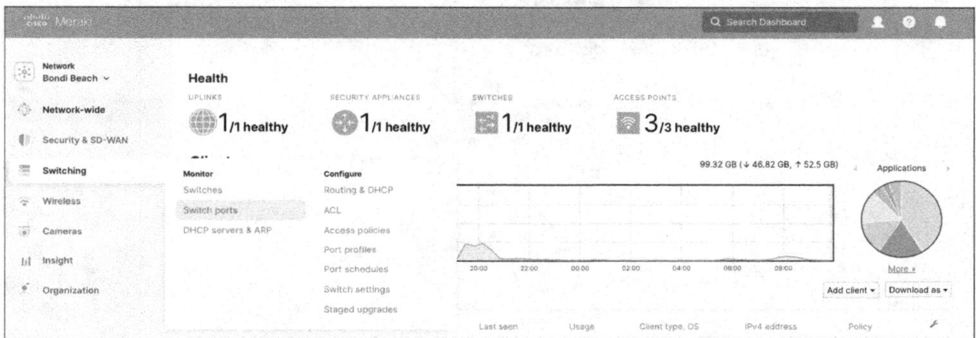

Figure 4-7 *Navigating to the Switch Ports Page*

Step 3. Select the ports that you want to tag using the check box next to their name, as demonstrated in Figure 4-8.

Switch Ports for the last day

Edit | Aggregate | Split | Mirror | Unmirror | Tags | not:enabled | help 3 of 10 switch ports, 2 selected (deselect all) | Download As

☐	Switch / Port ▲	Enabled	Type	VLAN	Allowed VLANs	Received bytes	Sent bytes	Status	CDP/LLDP
☐	Bondi-G-MS120-1 / 4 details	disabled	access	200	-	-	-		
☑	Bondi-G-MS120-1 / 9 details	disabled	access	100	-	-	-		
☑	Bondi-G-MS120-1 / 10 details	disabled	access	100	-	-	-		

Figure 4-8 *Selecting Ports to Tag*

Step 4. Click the **Tags** drop-down menu and enter the name for a new tag or select an existing tag. In the example in Figure 4-9, we added the tag **Lab.** Click **Add** to confirm the changes.

If you have the Tags column enabled (click the spanner symbol on the far-right column name to customize the columns displayed), you see the new tag associated with these ports, as demonstrated in Figure 4-10.

Step 5. Navigate to **Network-wide > Administration** to open the Network administration page, as demonstrated in Figure 4-11.

Step 6. Scroll down to the **Port Management Privileges** section and click **Add a Port Management Privilege.**

The privilege name is displayed in the **Access** drop-down menu when this role is assigned to administrators, as demonstrated in Figure 4-12. Enter a privilege name that makes sense for your use case; then select the port tags that apply.

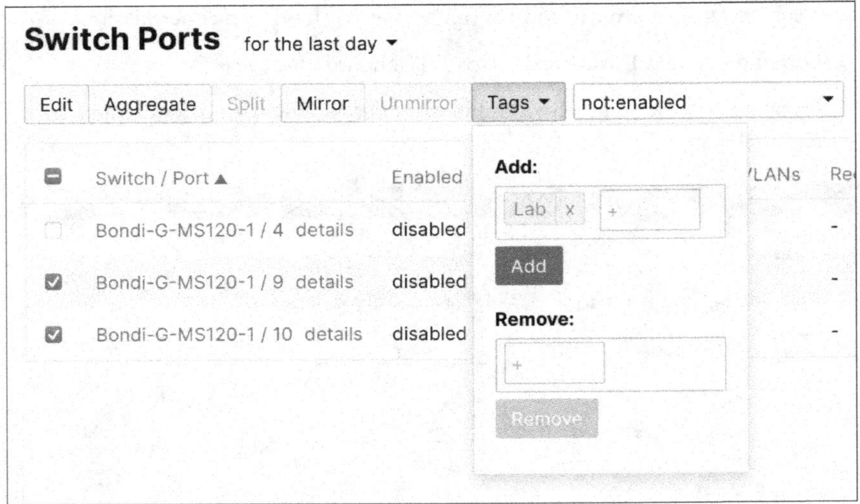

Figure 4-9 *Creating Port Tags*

Figure 4-10 *Showing Port Tags on the Switch Port Page*

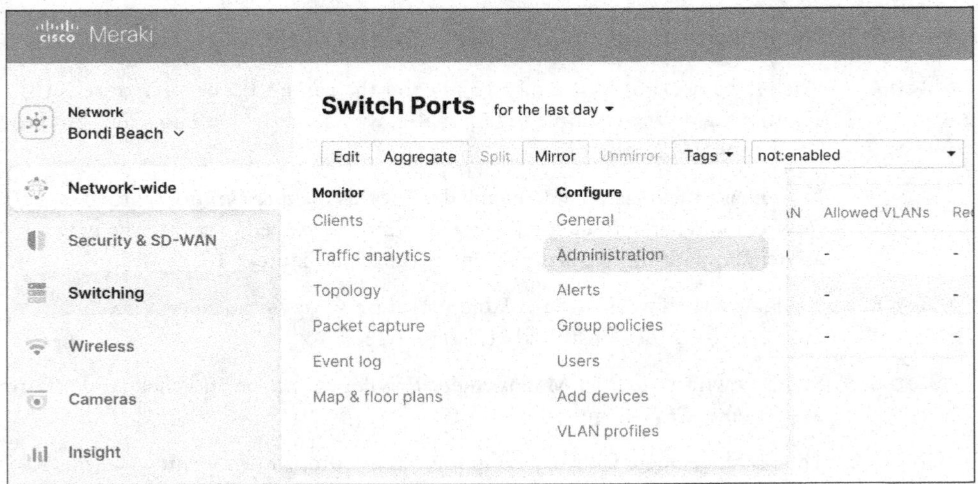

Figure 4-11 *Navigating to the Network Administration Page*

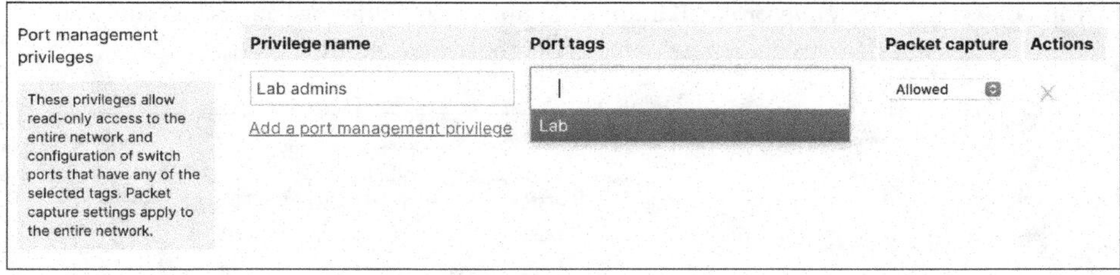

Figure 4-12 *Creating a Port Management Role*

Step 7. Decide whether this role should be able to do packet captures on these ports (the default is Allowed), as demonstrated in Figure 4-13, and then click **Save** in the bottom-right corner. A message at the top of the screen confirms that the changes have been saved.

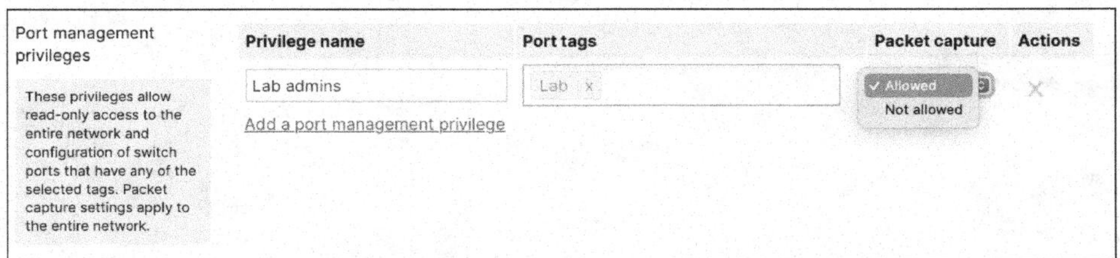

Figure 4-13 *Selecting Packet Capture Permissions*

Step 8. Navigate to **Organization > Administrators** to open the Organization administrators page, as demonstrated in Figure 4-14.

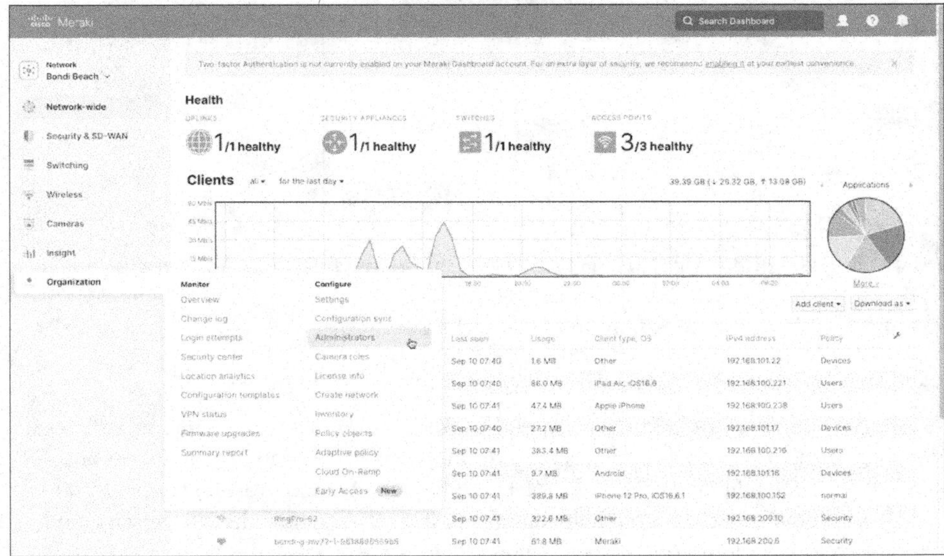

Figure 4-14 *Navigating to the Organization Administrators Page*

Step 9. Click the name or email address of an existing administrator that you want to modify (or create a new one), as demonstrated in Figure 4-15.

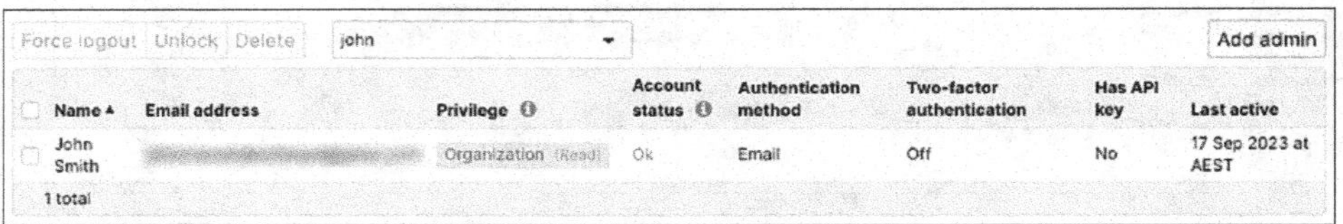

Figure 4-15 *The Organization Administrators Page (Port-Based Permissions)*

Step 10. Set the Organization access to **Read-only** or **None** and then select the target network. At the time of writing, the target network cannot be a tagged group of networks—that is, one starting with *Tag:*. In Figure 4-16, you can now select the Lab admins role created in the Access drop-down menu.

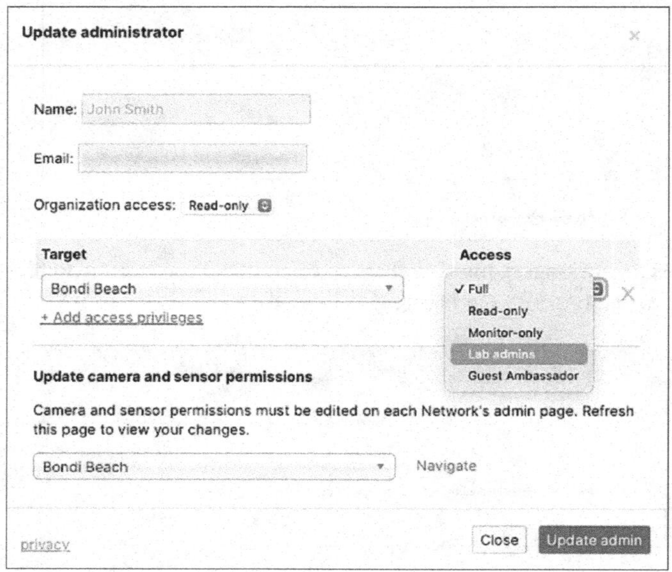

Figure 4-16 *Assigning Port-Level Permissions on the Organization Administrators Page*

Step 11. Click **Update Admin** to save the changes.

Perform the following steps to verify that these changes are now in effect:

Step 1. Log in to Meraki Dashboard as the user that was just configured. In the example in Figure 4-17, this is the user John Smith. You can see on the network-wide administrators page (**Network-wide > Administrators**) that this user is configured with the Lab admins privileges. Note how the X is missing under the Actions column, confirming the user has read-only access.

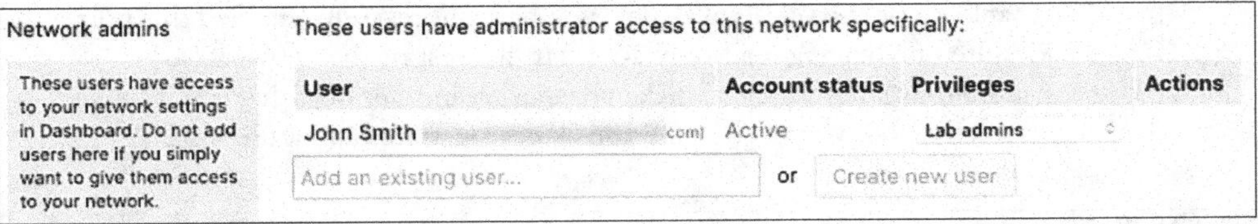

Figure 4-17 *A Network Admin with Lab Admin Privileges*

Step 2. Navigate to the switch ports page (**Switching > Switch Ports**). Here, the Tags column is enabled to make it clear which ports you have access to. Select those port(s) with the tag to which this user has read-write permissions; then click **Edit**. In this example, the lab admin has selected port 1/9, as shown in Figure 4-18.

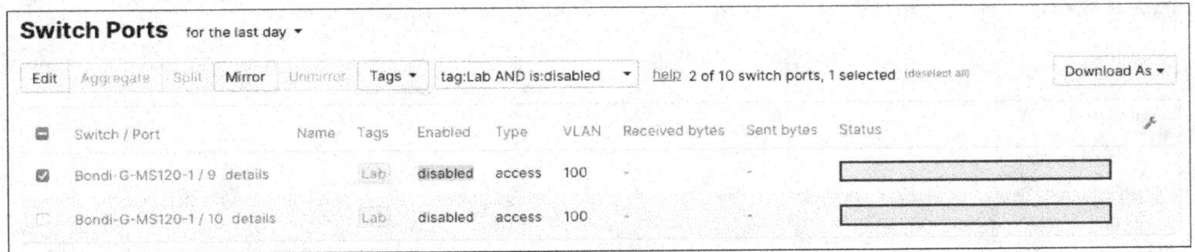

Figure 4-18 *A Lab Admin Selecting Switch Ports to Modify*

Step 3. On the update port page, as shown in Figure 4-19, change the port status to **Enabled** and click **Update**.

Update 1 port
Switch / Port Bondi-G-MS120-1 / 9
Name
Port status Enabled Disabled
Link negotiation Auto negotiate
Port schedule Unscheduled
Tags Lab
Port profile Enabled Disabled
Type Trunk Access
Access policy Open
VLAN 100
Voice VLAN
RSTP Enabled Disabled
STP guard Disabled
Cancel Update

Figure 4-19 *A Lab Admin Enabling a Disabled Port*

Thanks to port-level permissions, you have successfully enabled this port, despite only having read-only access to the rest of the network (see Figure 4-20). If you try to make changes to another port that is not tagged correctly, you will receive an error, as demonstrated in Figure 4-21.

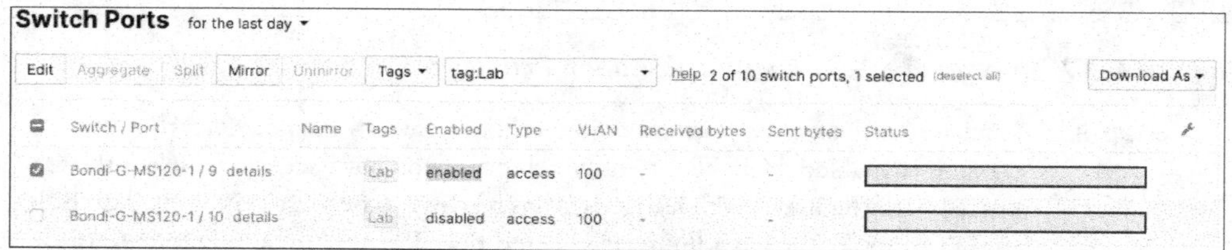

Figure 4-20 *Verifying That the Lab Admin Was Able to Enable a Port*

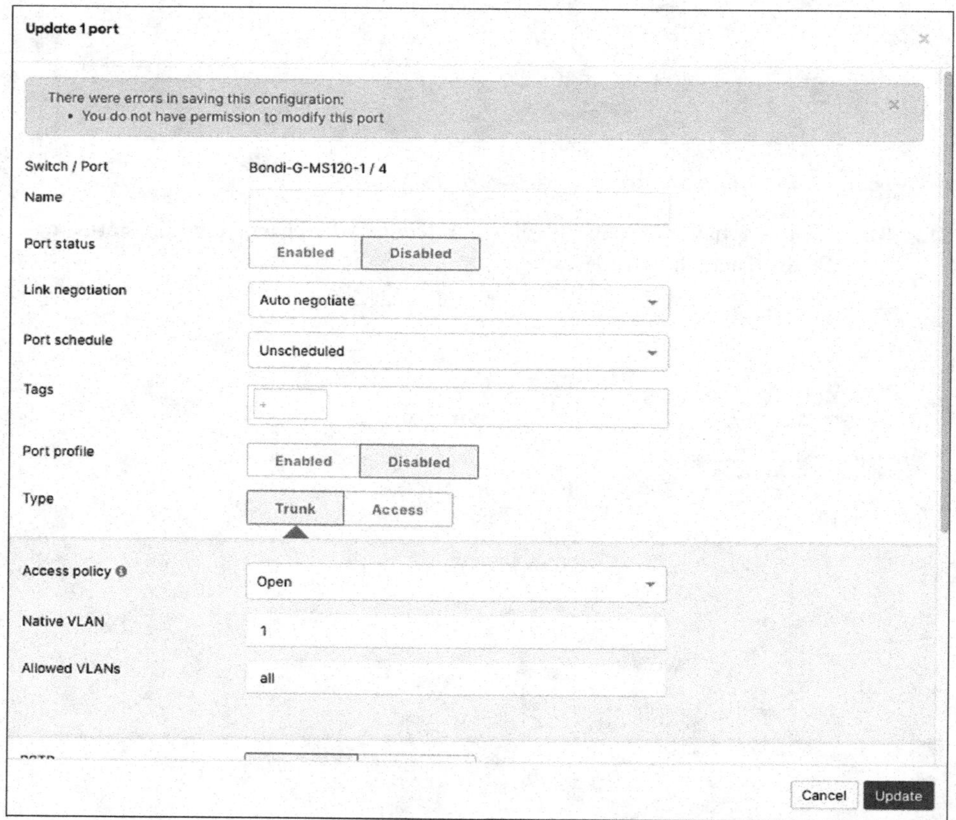

Figure 4-21 *Verifying That the Lab Admin Is Not Able to Edit Other Ports*

Role-Based Access Control for Camera-Only Administrators

The Meraki platform features multiple product lines including smart cameras (the MV series) and sensors (the MT series), creating a need for additional admin roles beyond the traditional network admins.

Camera-only roles are intentionally limited to camera-related functions. When correctly configured, local camera-only administrators can log in to both Meraki Dashboard and Meraki Vision. The Meraki Vision portal is a purpose-built CCTV portal designed for staff who need to monitor CCTV footage. Meraki Vision portal has none of the other features of Meraki Dashboard. In Meraki Dashboard, camera-only administrator access is limited to read-only access to the cameras page (other menu items are hidden), as demonstrated in Figure 4-22.

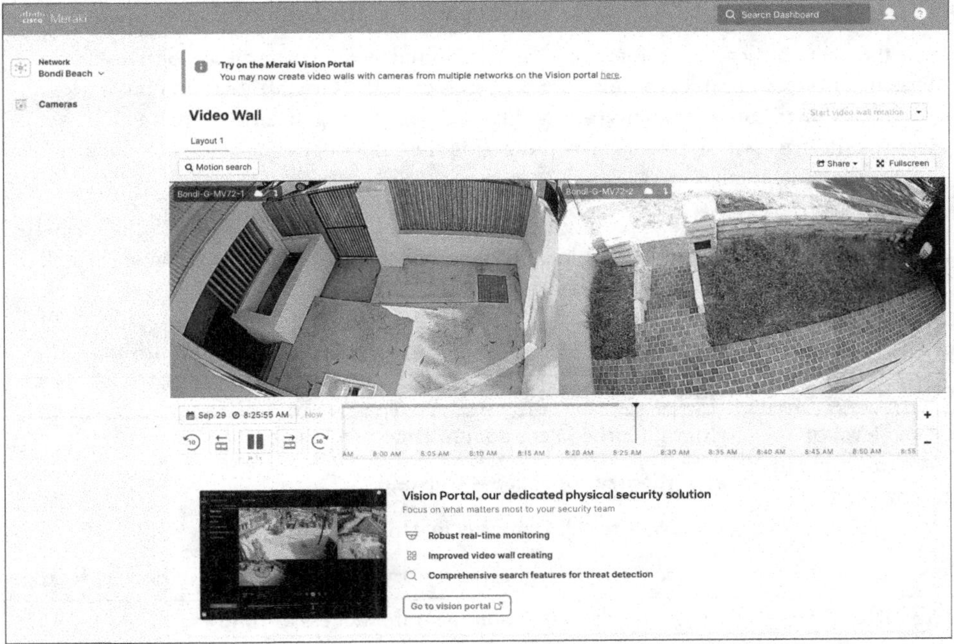

Figure 4-22 *A Camera-Only Admin's Limited View of Meraki Dashboard*

In either portal, camera-only admins cannot make changes to camera settings such as focus, zoom, or aperture, nor can they create video walls or access the network tab of cameras. A camera-only admin's access is therefore limited to performing only what is allowed by the following camera roles (see Figure 4-23):

- **No Access:** These admins do not have access to any cameras.
- **View Live Footage:** Admins with this level of access can watch live footage on a single camera or video wall.

- **View Any Footage:** Admins with this level of access can watch live and historical footage on a single camera or video wall.
- **View and Export Any Footage:** Admins with this level of access can watch all footage and manage video exports.

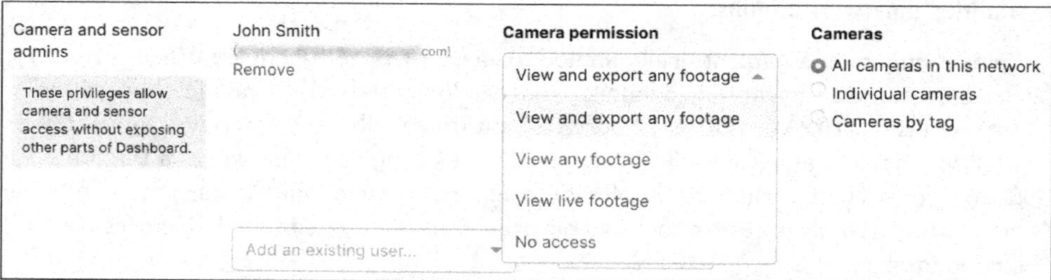

Figure 4-23 *Camera Roles for Local Administrators at the Network Level*

Local camera-only administrators can be configured at the organization or network level. Organization-wide camera admins are configured on the Organization administrators page (**Organization > Administration**). Privileges at the organization level must be set to None; otherwise, these privileges will override the camera privileges, giving users more access than intended.

Camera-only users should be configured in a purposeful way to limit their scope to what is required. You can configure the local camera-only users as outlined in Table 4-1 and Figure 4-24 to suit their job requirements.

Table 4-1 *How to Configure Camera-Only Users to Suit Their Access Requirements*

Access Required	How to Configure
The same level of access to all cameras in the organization	Configure the user's administrator access as follows: ■ **Organization Access** to **None.** ■ **Target** to **All Cameras in This Organization.** ■ **Access** to the highest necessary, such as **View and export all footage.**
Differentiated levels of access to cameras in the organization	Configure the user's administrator access as follows: ■ **Organization Access** to **None.** ■ **Target** to **All Cameras in This Organization.** ■ **Access** to the lowest access the user requires, such as **View live footage.** ■ On the network-wide administrators page (**Network-wide > Administration**), specify those cameras to which this user needs a higher level of access. For camera-only networks, you will also find this page under **Cameras > General** (under Configure) > **Camera and Sensor Only Admins**).

Access Required	How to Configure
Access to only certain cameras	The best way to restrict access within the same organization is to group the cameras into different networks. For example, create a camera-only network for common area devices and another for cameras in restricted or sensitive areas. Then configure the administrator's access as follows: ■ **Organization Access** to **None**. ■ **Target** to the appropriate network containing the cameras you want to allow access to. ■ **Access** to the lowest access the user requires, such as View live footage.
No access to any cameras while retaining access to Dashboard	The best way to configure this access would be to have all the cameras in their own organization, with another organization for all other devices, such as switches and access points. Only camera administrators would be given access to the camera organization. In this case, you would have two completely standalone instances of Meraki Dashboard, with neither team having any visibility of the other environment.

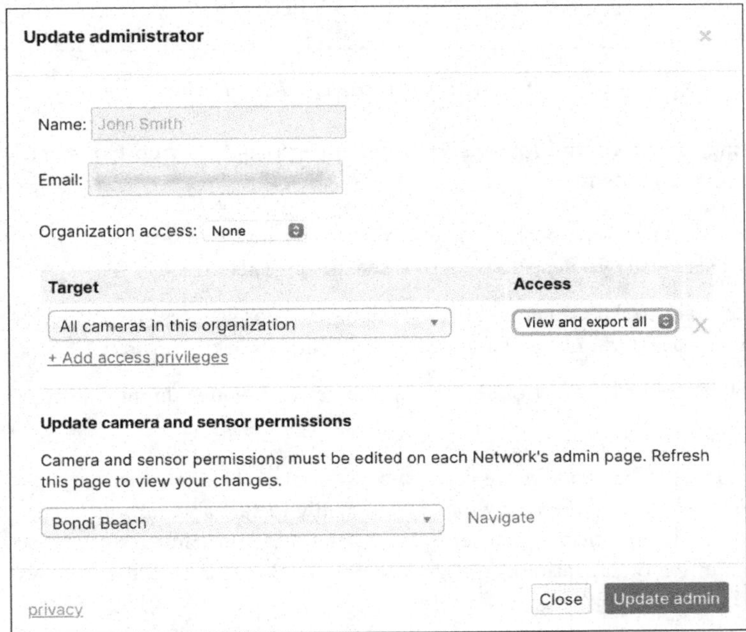

Figure 4-24 *An Example of an Administrator Configured as a Camera-Only Admin*

We cover more details on this topic in Chapter 12, "Physical Security."

Role-Based Access Control for Sensor-Only Administrators

Sensor-only administrators are admin accounts that have access to sensor devices and nothing else in Dashboard. Three additional roles apply to sensor-only admins, as illustrated in Figure 4-25:

- **No Access:** These users do not have access to any sensors.
- **Read-Only Sensor Access:** Admins with this level of access can read sensor readings and configurations but not make any changes.
- **Full Sensor Access:** Admins with this level of access can both monitor and edit sensor readings and configurations.

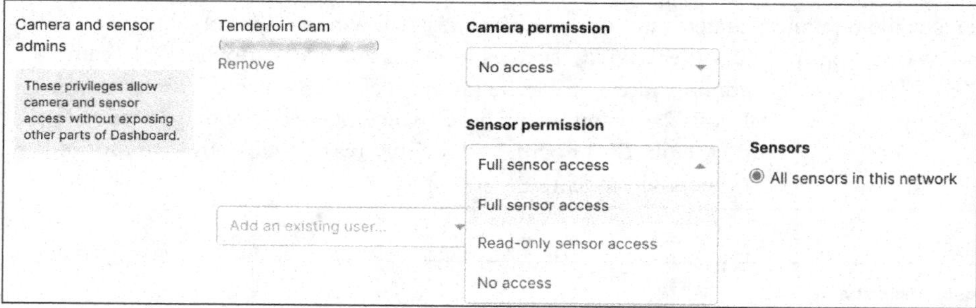

Figure 4-25 *Sensor Roles for Local Administrators at the Network Level*

At the time of writing, access control for sensors is still undergoing heavy development. It is important to note the following:

- Sensors connect via a gateway; both the gateway and the sensor need to be in the same network. This means you can't have a true sensor-only network.
- There is no equivalent to All Cameras in This Organization for sensors. This would be an elegant solution, so do not be surprised to see it added in the future.
- It is not possible to select a subset of sensors on the network-wide administration page.

It is important to remember that sensors are used to collect data such as temperature, air quality, and moisture readings, none of which is personally identifiable information. Nevertheless, to create a local sensor-only user (this user will have the same level of access for all sensors in the organization), configure their administrator profile as follows (**Organization > Administration**):

- **Organization Access** to **None**
- **Target** to the network containing the sensors and their gateways
- **Access** to the highest access the user requires, such as full access

When single sign-on is configured, permissions for camera and sensor admins can also be assigned using Security Assertion Markup Language (SAML). The organization-wide roles used by single sign-on can be defined in Dashboard by navigating to **Organization > Camera and Sensor Roles.** The permissions mapping is done at time of login, and the admin user is mapped to one of these locally configured roles. It is recommended to use single sign-on for medium to large organizations or where administrators require differentiated access. Configuring single sign-on using SAML is explained in detail in Chapter 5, "Securing Administrator Access to Meraki Dashboard."

For more information on role-based access for cameras and sensors using SAML, see https://documentation.meraki.com/MT/MT_General_Articles/Camera_and_sensor-only_admin_(IoT_Admin).

Role-Based Access Control Using Systems Manager Limited Access Roles

There are additional roles known as *limited access roles* when using Meraki Systems Manager for mobile device management (MDM). Limited access roles allow you to create roles that have defined privileges, for a defined scope of Systems Manager devices. These roles apply only to System Manager commands such as rebooting devices, requesting device check-in, and pushing out notifications. These commands are targeted at managed end-user devices such as phones, tablets, and computers. Here are some examples of use cases where this functionality could come in handy:

- A trainer wants to reboot all classroom devices at the end of a lesson.
- A store manager wants all devices in the store to check in at the start of the day (to verify they are functioning and that none have gone missing).
- You may have administrators responsible for end-user technology whom you want to give limited access to Meraki Dashboard. You could create a role that provides full access to Systems Manager, while limiting their access to the rest of Dashboard.

Limited access roles remain hidden in Meraki Dashboard until all three of these prerequisites are met:

- At least one Systems Manager Agent license has been added.
- A Systems Manager Network has been created.
- At least one device has been enrolled.

Once the prerequisites are in place, follow these steps to tag your Systems Manager devices and configure limited access roles:

Step 1. Log in to Meraki Dashboard (https://dashboard.meraki.com).

Step 2. If you want to use the built-in tags such as IOS devices or Android devices, you can go straight to Step 5. To use custom tags, navigate to **Systems Manager > Devices**, as demonstrated in Figure 4-26.

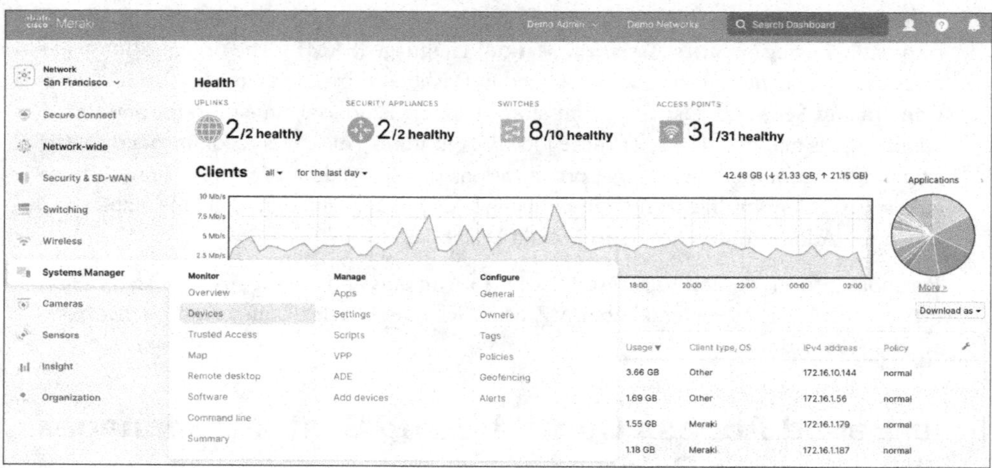

Figure 4-26 *Navigating to the Systems Manager Devices Page*

Step 3. Select the devices you want to tag, as shown in Figure 4-27, and then click the **Tag** drop-down menu.

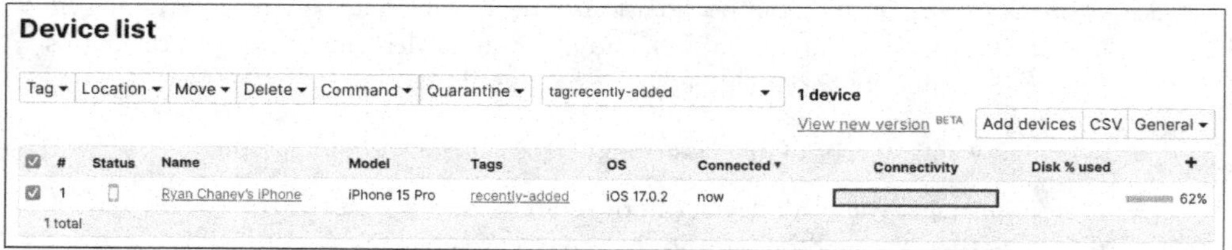

Figure 4-27 *Selecting Systems Manager Devices to Tag*

Step 4. Input the tag name in the **Add:** text input box and click **Add.** In the example in Figure 4-28, we created a tag called **Store_device** to identify all the devices that are used in retail store locations.

Device list

Tag Location Move Delete Command Quarantine

Add:

Store_device x

Add

Remove:

Choose tags to remove

Remove

Figure 4-28 *Creating a System Manager Tag and Adding It to Our Device(s)*

Step 5. Now create the limited access role by first navigating to **Systems Manager > General** (under Configure) for a standalone Systems Manager (SM) network or **Network-wide > Administration** (under Configure) in a combined network. Scroll down to Limited Access Roles (see Figure 4-29).

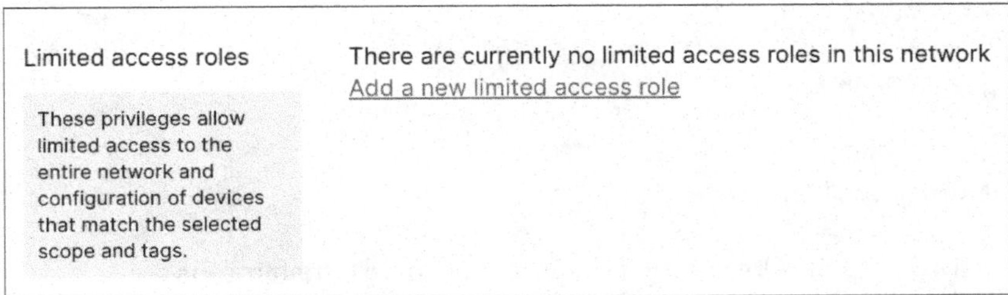

Figure 4-29 *Limited Access Roles on the Network-Wide Administration Page*

Step 6. Click **Add a New Limited Access Role.**

Enter a name for this role in the text input box under **Role Name.** Then set the appropriate scope. In the example shown in Figure 4-30, we created a role for a store manager with a scope of **With ANY of the Following Tags.**

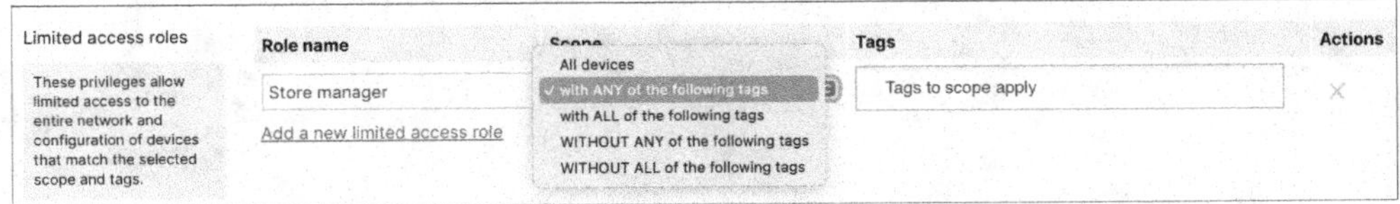

Figure 4-30 *Entering Name and Scope to Create a Limited Access Role*

Step 7. Select the tags that identify the devices that this admin should have access to. In the example in Figure 4-31, we selected the **Store_device** tag. Click **Save** in the bottom-right corner.

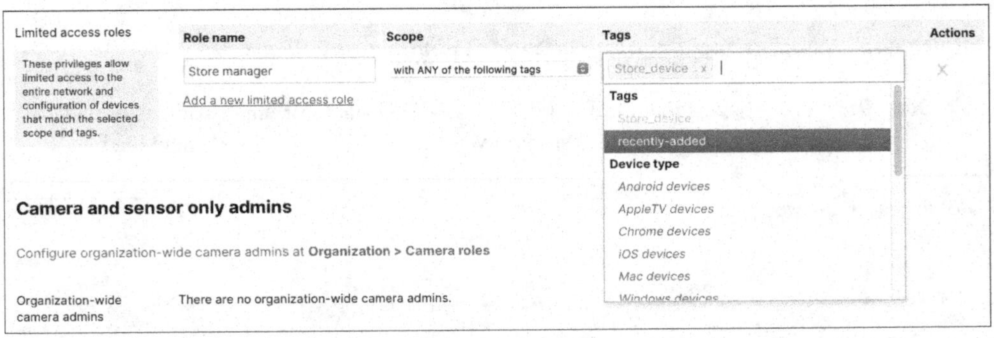

Figure 4-31 *Selecting the Tag(s) to Create a Limited Access Role*

The **Limited Access Roles** section should now look like the screen in Figure 4-32. A banner at the top of the page confirms that the changes have been saved (not shown here).

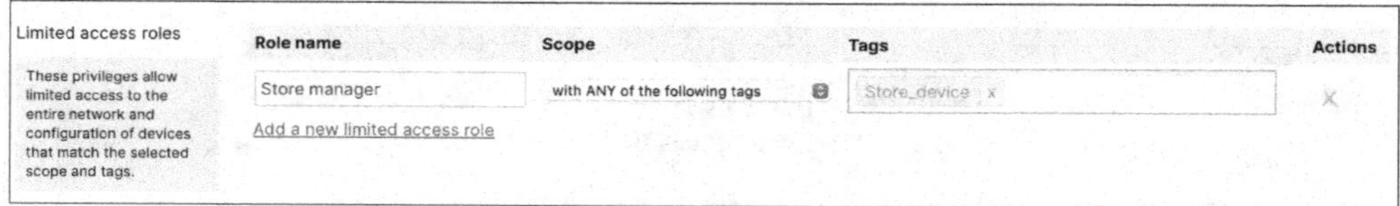

Figure 4-32 *A Completed Limited Access Role*

Step 8. Navigate to the Organization administrators page (**Organization > Administrators**), as demonstrated in Figure 4-33.

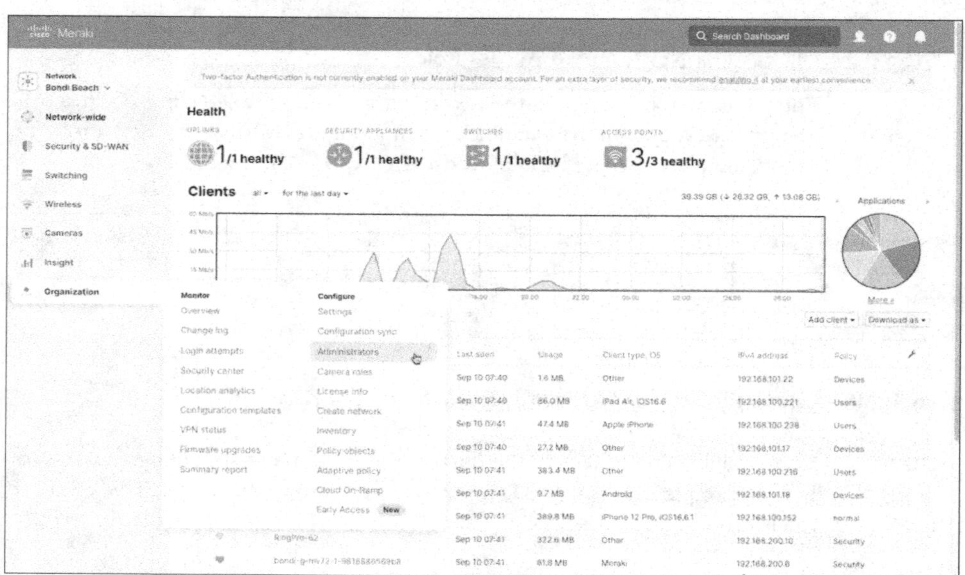

Figure 4-33 *Navigating to the Organization Administrators Page*

Step 9. From page shown in Figure 4-34, click the name or email address of an existing administrator that you want to modify (or create a new one).

Acme administrators

Force logout | Unlock | Delete   john   Add admin

Name ▲	Email address	Privilege	Account status	Authentication method	Two-factor authentication	Has API key	Last active
John Smith	[illegible]	Organization (Read)	Ok	Email	Off	No	29 Sep 2023 at AWST

1 total

Figure 4-34 *The Organization Administrators Page*

Step 10. In the dialog box shown in Figure 4-35, set the Organization access to **None.** Set the **Target** to the network containing the Systems Manager devices, and under **Access,** choose the name of the role you have just created. Here, we chose the **Store Manager** role. Finish by clicking **Update Admin.**

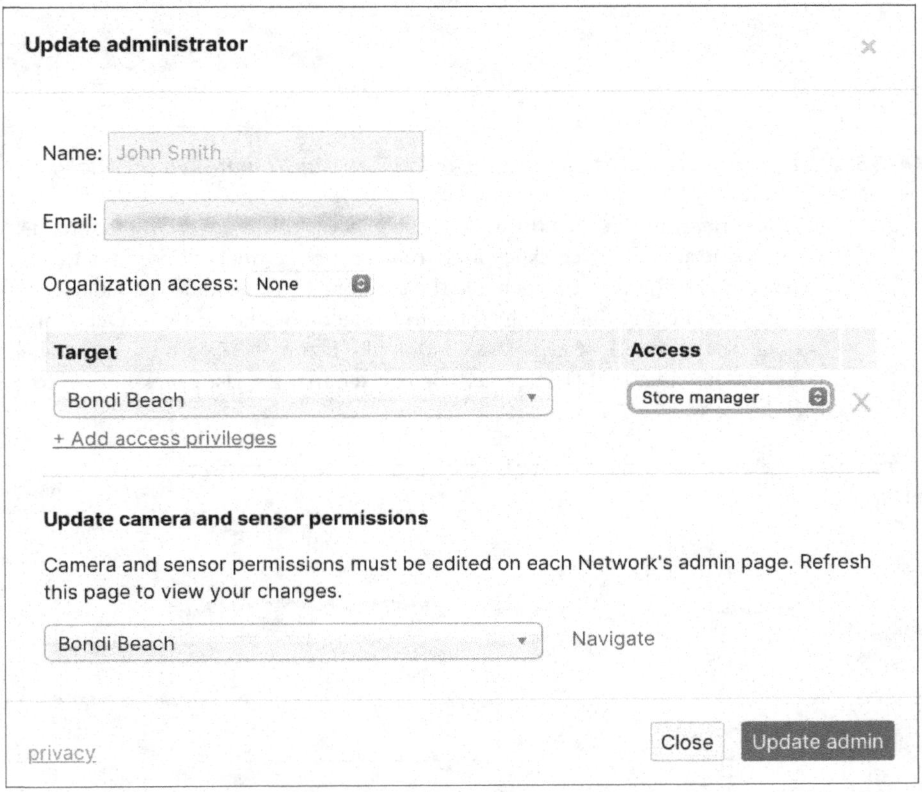

Figure 4-35 *An Example of an Administrator Configured in a Limited Access Role*

Step 11. You now return to the Organization administrators page. Click **Save Changes** for the changes to be applied.

Perform the following steps to verify that the changes are in effect:

Step 1. Log in as the user with the limited access role. Navigate to **Systems Manager > Devices.** Note the limited view of Dashboard that this user has, as demonstrated in Figure 4-36.

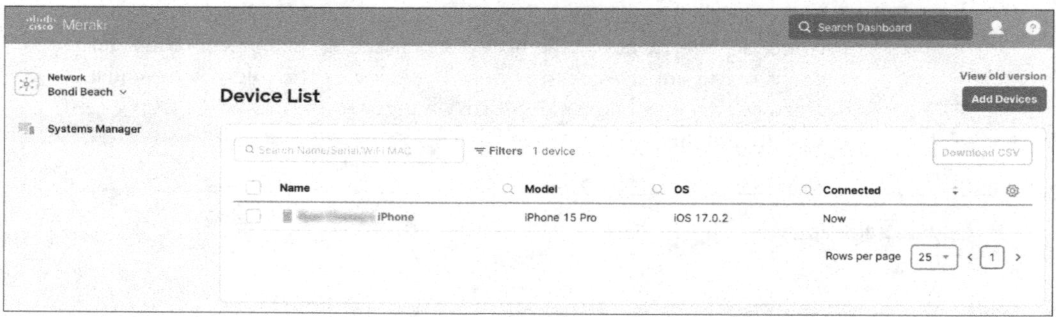

Figure 4-36 *Navigating to the Systems Manager Devices Page (Limited Access Role)*

Step 2. Test that the privileges for this new limited access role are working as intended by requesting a device check-in. Before starting, to make it possible to determine the check-in time, enable the columns for **Tags** and **Last Check-in (MDM)** by clicking the settings (or sprocket) icon on the far right. Once this is done, the **Device List** page should look like Figure 4-37 with the additional columns showing. In this example, you can see that the last check-in time for this device was 7:37 a.m.

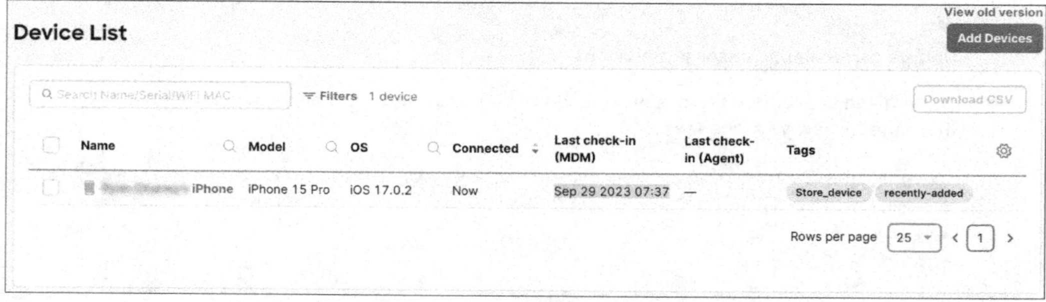

Figure 4-37 *Confirming the Most Recent Check-In Date/Time*

Step 3. Check the box on the row for the device(s) you want to check in and select **Request Check-in** from the **Command** drop-down menu, as demonstrated in Figure 4-38.

Step 4. Click **Confirm** on the pop-up window, as shown in Figure 4-39. You see the **Devices List** page again with confirmation that the check-in request has been sent, as demonstrated in Figure 4-40.

You can now see that this device has successfully completed check-in, with a new check-in time of 7:54 a.m., as demonstrated in Figure 4-41.

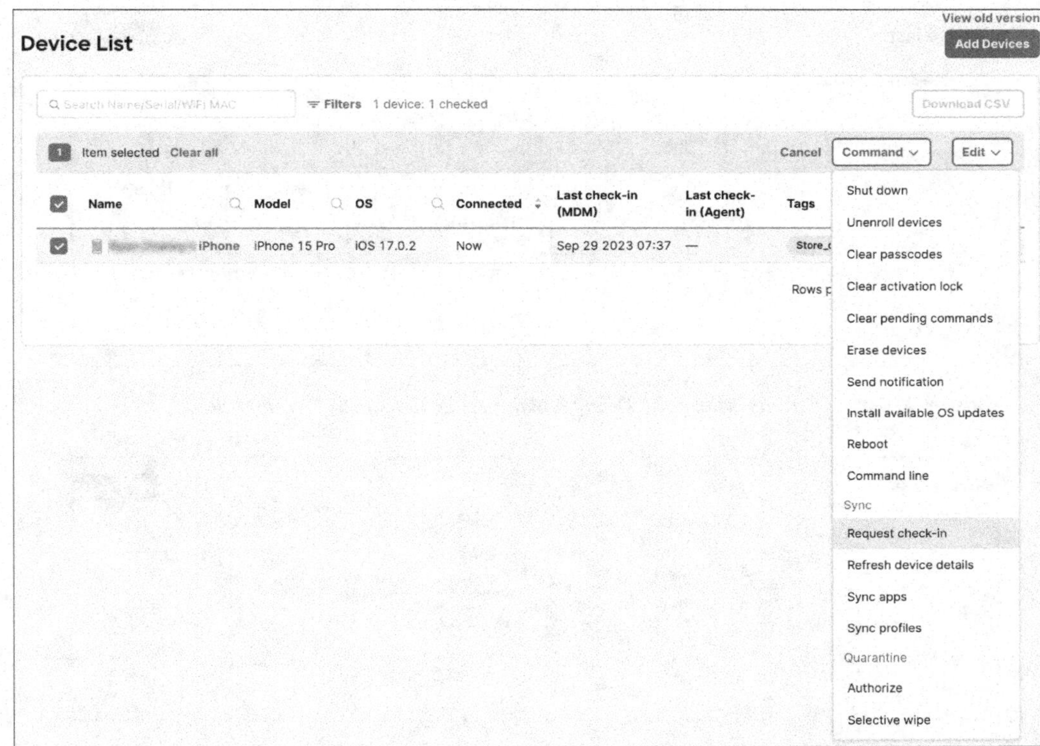

Figure 4-38 *Requesting a Device Check-In with Systems Manager*

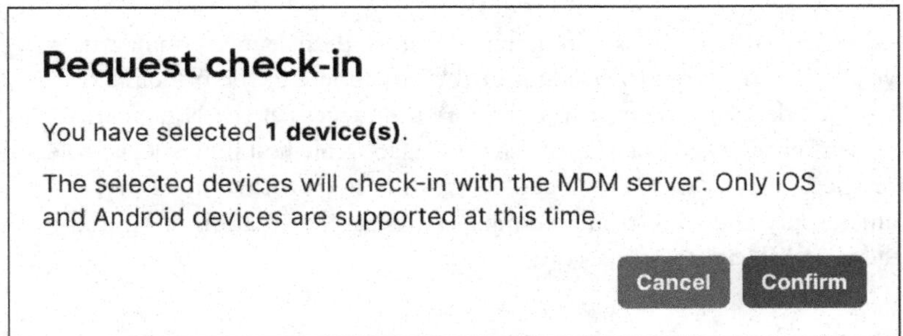

Figure 4-39 *Confirming the Check-In Request*

If you would like to know more about limited access roles, please check out https://documentation.meraki.com/SM/Other_Topics/Limited_Access_Roles. For more information on Meraki Systems Manager, refer to Chapter 11, "Securing End-User Devices."

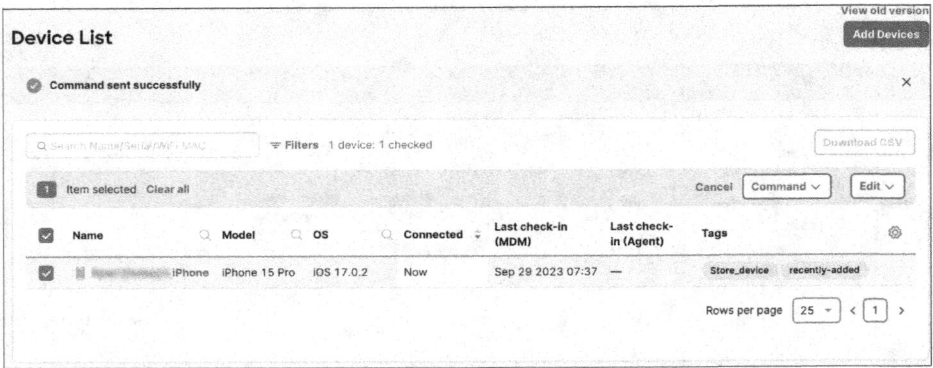

Figure 4-40 *Systems Manager Devices Page After Check-In Request Sent*

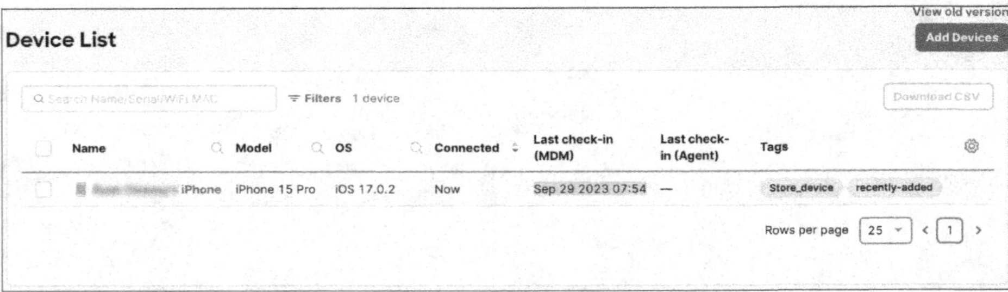

Figure 4-41 *Successful Check-In with Updated Time*

Summary

Role-based access control (RBAC) is a key requirement of modern security standards. In this chapter, we detailed the steps to configure RBAC to adhere to the principle of least privilege. This included learning how to configure user access at the organization and network levels within the Dashboard hierarchy. We also explained how special roles can be created for specific use cases. This included creating roles with control over specific ports, camera-only and sensor-only admins, as well as the creation of limited access roles for Systems Manager admins.

Further Reading

Cisco Meraki. (2023, June 8). Limited Access Roles. https://documentation.meraki.com/SM/Other_Topics/Limited_Access_Roles

Cisco Meraki. (2023, August 22). Meraki Dashboard Organizational Structure. https://documentation.meraki.com/General_Administration/Organizations_and_Networks/Meraki_Dashboard_Organizational_Structure

Cisco Meraki. (2023, November 1). Managing Dashboard Administrators and Permissions. https://documentation.meraki.com/General_Administration/Managing_Dashboard_Access/Managing_Dashboard_Administrators_and_Permissions

Chapter 5

Securing Administrator Access to Meraki Dashboard

In this chapter, you learn the following:

- Why it's important to secure administrator access to Meraki Dashboard
- How to configure Meraki Dashboard's native security features to secure administrative access according to industry best practices
- How to implement Security Assertion Markup Language (SAML)–based single sign-on (SSO) by integrating with an external identity provider
- How to implement multifactor authentication (MFA) for administrative access to Meraki Dashboard via SMS and Cisco Duo

Securing Administrative Access to Meraki Dashboard

One of the key themes from industry best practice is the requirement for strong authentication, including multifactor authentication. This is especially applicable to management interfaces. Meraki Dashboard is the primary means of administering the Meraki platform. It is analogous to a management interface or console port in a traditional network. For this reason, it is paramount that only authorized users have access to this critical management interface. Behind the key themes of strong authentication and role-based access control (RBAC), there are many specific technical requirements common across the IT security standards (see Appendix A, "A Comparison of Common Security Standards and Framework Requirements"). This chapter focuses on how to implement technical controls aimed at meeting those specific requirements. First, this chapter addresses these requirements using the native features available in Meraki Dashboard. Then this chapter contrasts the native capabilities with the expanded functionality available when utilizing SAML-based single sign-on. Read on to learn how to secure access to Meraki Dashboard.

Meraki Dashboard Local Administrator Access Controls

Cisco Talo's 2023 Year in Review report highlighted the fact that compromised login credentials accounted for nearly a quarter of initial access vectors, ranking the second highest. Administrator credentials must be resilient because they can be used to disable controls and typically have access to more sensitive data. In the following sections, we discuss how to configure local administrator accounts and harden management access using the built-in features of Meraki Dashboard.

Creating Meraki Dashboard Local Administrator Accounts

NIST 800-53 (Control IA-2), HIPAA (Technical Safeguard 164.312(a)(2)(i)), and PCI DSS 4.0 (Requirement 8.2) all require unique user IDs for administrators. It is easy to understand why this is best practice. Unique user IDs allow for administrative access to be turned on as required when new administrators join, and off as they leave the organization or change roles. More importantly, unique user IDs allow for the actions of the individual administrators to be tracked; log entries record not only what changed and when but also who made that change. This information is important for both audit and compliance.

Meraki Dashboard administrators can be configured locally or in an external directory like Microsoft's Entra ID. For now, we focus on local administrator accounts, as we cover directory integration in the SAML single sign-on (SSO) for Dashboard. You will have at least a minimal number of local administrators, regardless of whether or not you configure single sign-on for Dashboard. It's important to note that Meraki Dashboard has no default administrator accounts or default passwords. Instead, the first administrator account is created when the organization is first created in Dashboard.

User IDs for Meraki Dashboard are based on users' email addresses, ensuring that each user has their own unique user ID. You cannot add multiple users with the same email address. Trying to do this will simply overwrite the existing user ID and will require verification again.

By default, there are no technical controls to stop multiple users from sharing the same login credentials, although doing so is strongly discouraged and would be a breach of compliance if picked up by an auditor. User IDs should never be created for shared email addresses (such as a team mailbox), and credentials should never be shared. For these reasons, it is best practice to put other controls in place to prevent the sharing of accounts. This effort should include limiting simultaneous logins, requiring multifactor authentication, and requiring regular password changes. You can find guidance on how to configure these features throughout the remainder of this chapter.

Creating a New Administrator Account (Inside a New Meraki Organization)

When setting up Meraki Dashboard for the first time, you need to create a new organization (or "org"). When doing so, you create an initial administrator account. A guide to creating a new Meraki organization can be found at the following URL: https://documentation.meraki.com/General_Administration/Organizations_and_Networks/Creating_a_Dashboard_Account_and_Organization.

Creating a New Administrator Account (Inside an Existing Meraki Organization)

Follow these steps to add additional administrators to an existing Meraki organization:

Step 1. Log in to Meraki Dashboard (https://dashboard.meraki.com).

Step 2. Navigate to **Organization** and then **Administrators** (under Configure), as illustrated in Figure 5-1.

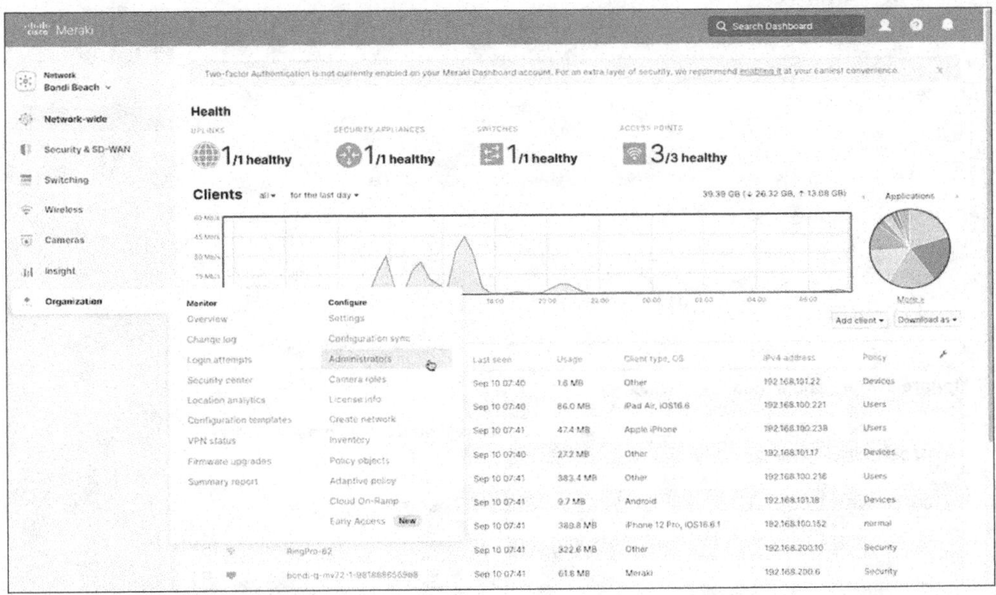

Figure 5-1 *Navigating to the Organization Administrators Page*

Step 3. Click **Add Admin** on the right side of the screen, as illustrated in Figure 5-2.

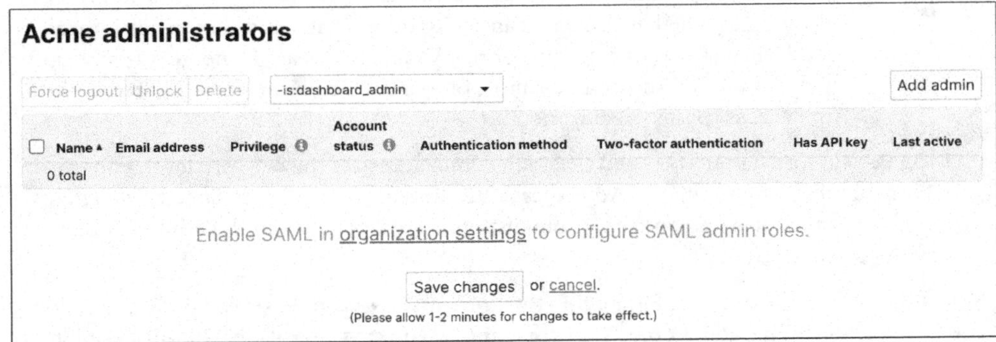

Figure 5-2 *Adding a New Administrator User*

Step 4. Fill out the pop-up form with the user's name and email address, as illustrated in Figure 5-3. The email address you use should be one under your organization's domain name, not a personal email account. Corporate email addresses have enterprise-grade email security; additionally, this ensures that admins do not retain their access if they leave the organization.

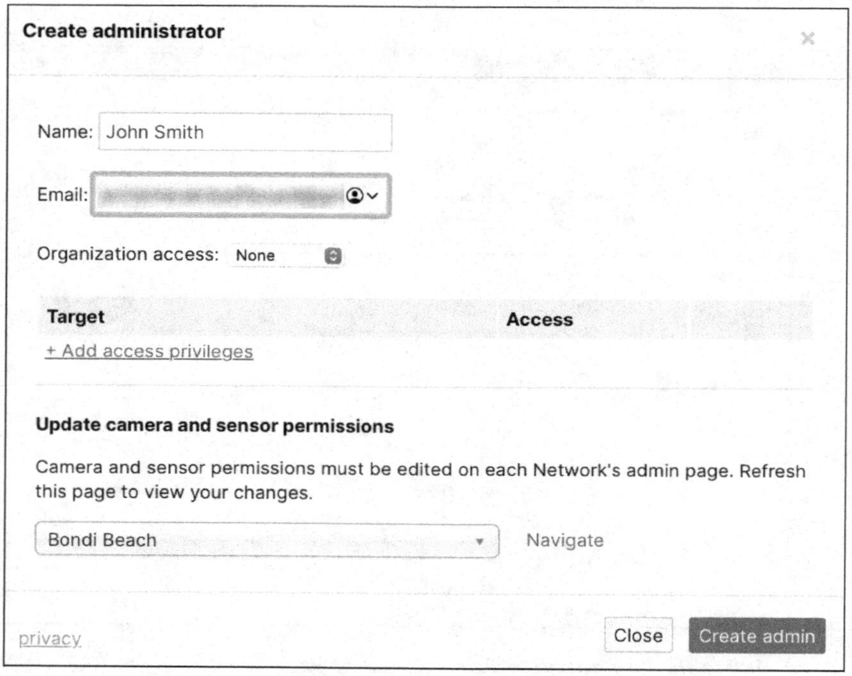

Figure 5-3 *Adding a New Administrator User's Account Details*

Step 5. Select the appropriate level of access for this user's role. **Organization Access** determines whether this user can see or make changes at the organizational level, such as creating new networks. Valid options are **None**, **Read-only**, and **Full.** Figure 5-4 shows an example of a user who has been configured with full access to this organization.

Step 6. (Optional) If you need to assign admin access at the network level, you can do so by clicking **+ Add Access Privileges** (under Target). Specify which individual networks this administrator has access to and the level of access required.

As illustrated in Figure 5-5, the level of access can be set to one of the following: **Full**, **Read-only**, **Monitor-only**, or **Guest Ambassador**. In this example, we don't require this level of granularity but instead rely on the level of access provided at the organization level. Click **Create Admin** to finish creating this new administrator account, as illustrated in Figure 5-5.

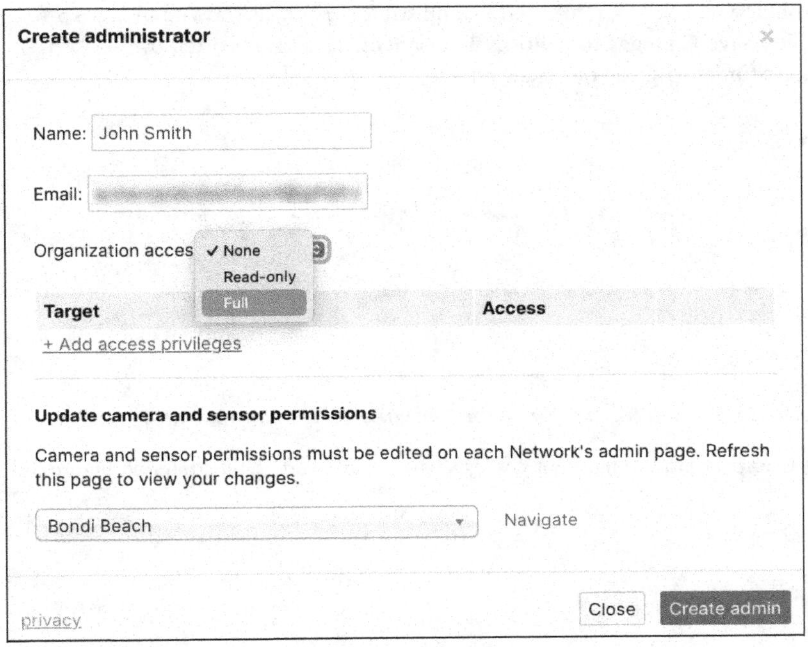

Figure 5-4 *Setting a New Administrator User's Organization Permissions*

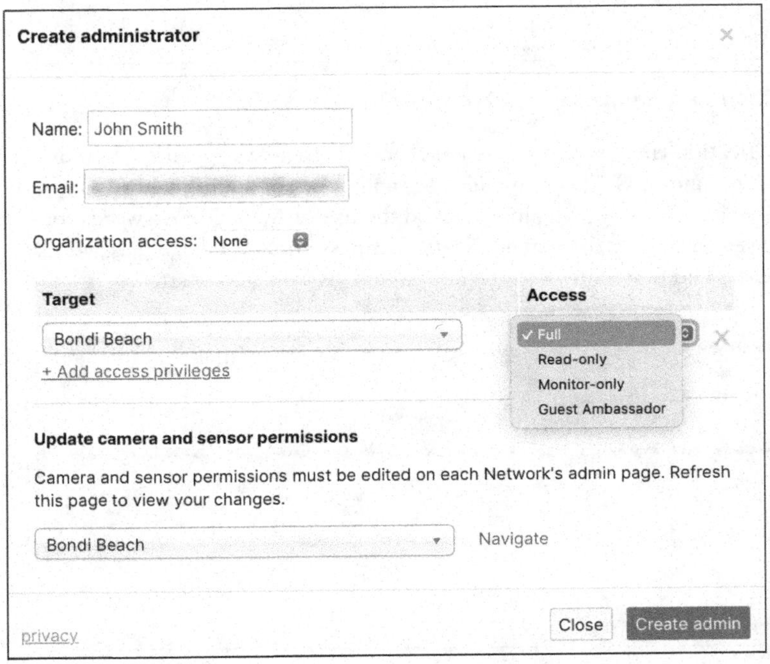

Figure 5-5 *Setting User Permissions at the Network Level*

Step 7. You now see the Organization Administrators page, as shown in Figure 5-6. Click **Save Changes** to confirm the changes. This step is often overlooked, so don't forget to save your changes!

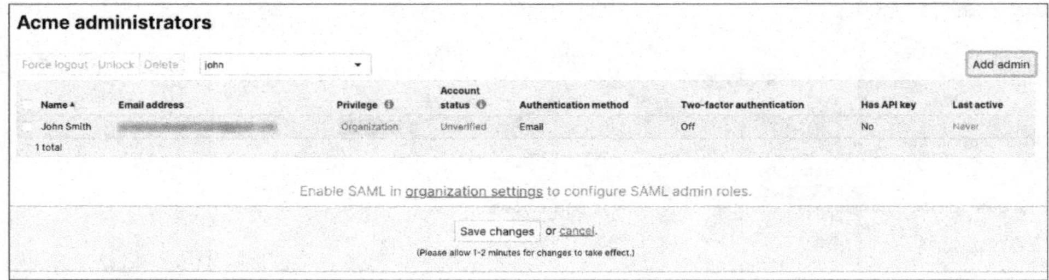

Figure 5-6 *Organization Administrators Page Showing New Administrator*

A banner confirms that your changes have been saved, as illustrated in Figure 5-7.

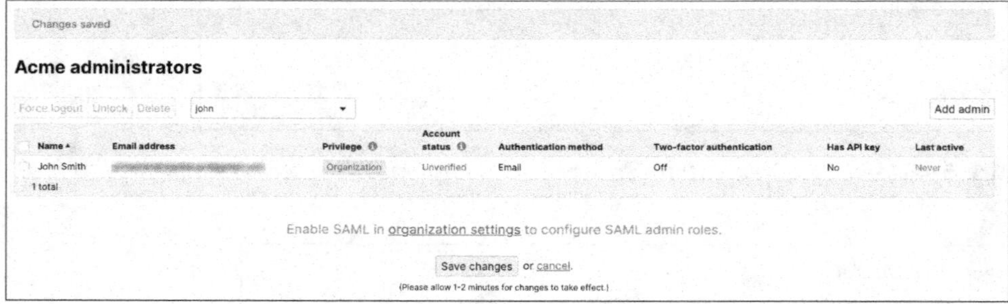

Figure 5-7 *Organization Administrators Page with Changes Saved*

A verification email is sent to the email address that was specified, as illustrated in Figure 5-8. This step addresses an important additional PCI DSS 4.0 requirement (8.3.5), which aims to avoid the use of "default" passwords for new users and avoid the communication of passwords via email. Passwords are set by and only known to the new admin, as we demonstrate.

Welcome to Cisco Meraki Inbox ×

Cisco Meraki - No Reply <noreply@meraki.com> 16:46 (0 minutes ago)

to me

You have been signed up for a Cisco Meraki account with administrator privileges to the organization "Acme". Your login email is .

Choose your password here.

Thanks,

Cisco Meraki

Reply Forward

Figure 5-8 *New Admin User Email Invitation*

Step 8. On receiving the verification email, the user must click the verification link, which will take them to a page where they need to choose an initial password for their account. They need to enter that password a second time to confirm and click **Set Password.** This password must comply with the password policy configured in Meraki Dashboard, as illustrated in Figure 5-9.

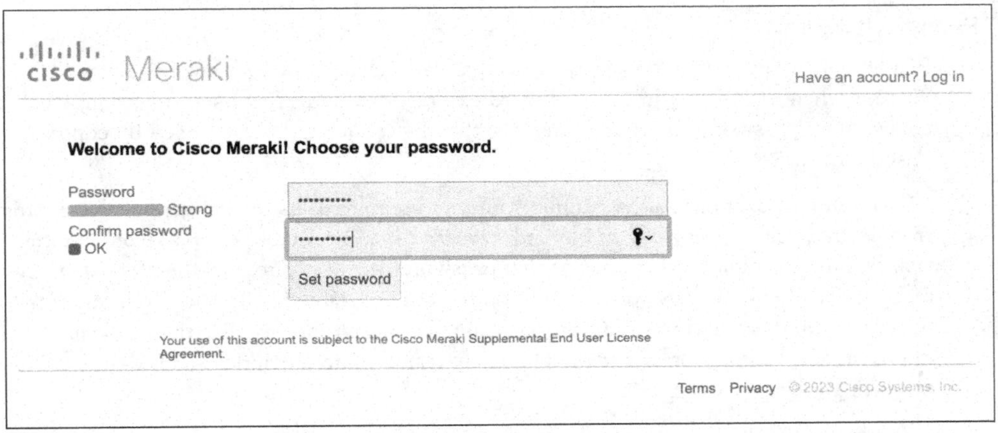

Figure 5-9 *New Admin User Choose Password Screen*

Step 9. After the password has been set, the user will receive another email with a six-digit code. They must copy and paste that code into the text box on the screen shown in Figure 5-10 and click **Verify.**

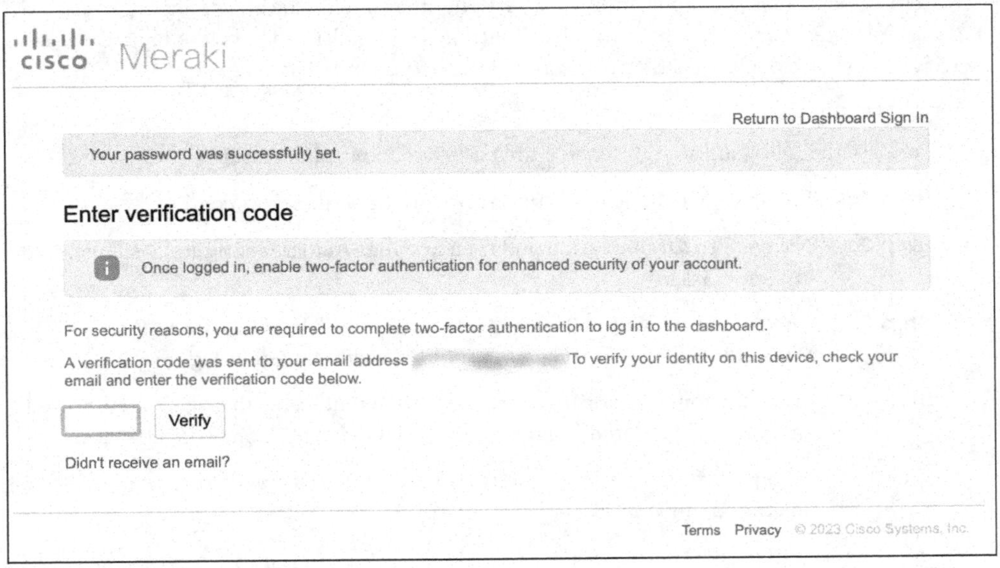

Figure 5-10 *New Admin User Verification Code Page*

Step 10. The new user now can log in to Meraki Dashboard with the specified level of access.

An administrator's access can be updated at any time by clicking their name on the Organization Administrators page (**Organization > Administrators**).

Password Age

PCI DSS 4.0 requirement 8.3.10.1 requires that users change their passwords every 90 days when MFA is not in use. Password expiration ensures that users are prompted to change their passwords at regular intervals, thereby reducing the risk posed by compromised credentials.

Cisco Meraki Dashboard allows administrators to require users to change their passwords from as frequent as every day to beyond 999,999 days. By default, the password expiration feature is disabled, which means that passwords never expire. It is therefore strongly recommended that the password expiration feature be enabled and configured for an interval of 90 days. If your organization requires a shorter interval, use that. Bear in mind, though, that a shorter interval will likely result in more helpdesk calls due to users forgetting their passwords.

Another benefit of requiring regular password changes is ensuring that increases in password complexity requirements flow through to users in a timely fashion. This reduces the period when users continue using simpler passwords that were permitted under a previous password policy.

> **Note** Follow proper change management procedures to reduce the impacts to others when enabling the password change policy for the first time. If the age of any existing passwords exceeds the new password age limit, those administrators will be logged out of Meraki Dashboard and forced to change their password immediately.

Perform the following steps to enable the password expiration feature:

Step 1. Log in to Meraki Dashboard (https://dashboard.meraki.com).

Step 2. Navigate to **Organization** and then **Settings** (under Configure), as illustrated in Figure 5-11.

Step 3. Check the box next to **Force Users to Change Their Password Every ___ Days** and enter **90** in the text input box, as illustrated in Figure 5-12.

Step 4. In the bottom right of the screen, a warning indicates that there are unsaved changes, as illustrated in Figure 5-13. Click **Save** to submit the changes.

A banner confirms that the settings have been saved and are now in effect, as illustrated in Figure 5-14.

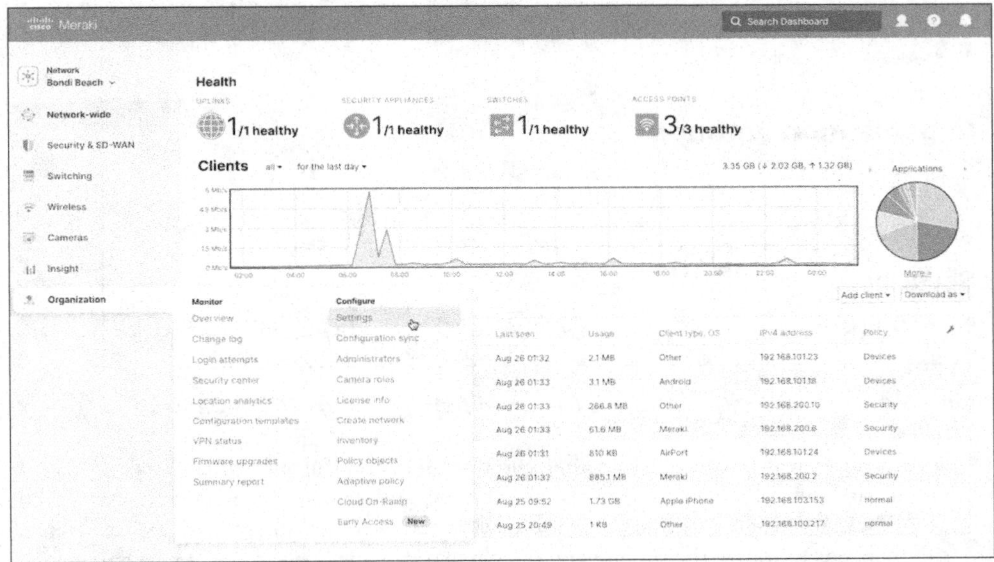

Figure 5-11 *Navigating to Organization Settings*

Security

Password expiration	☑ Force users to change their password every [90] days
Used passwords	✓ Force users to choose passwords different from their past [2] passwords
Strong passwords	☐ Force users to choose strong passwords for their accounts
Account lockout	☐ Lock accounts after [ ] consecutive failed login attempts
Idle timeout	☐ Logout users after [ ] minutes of inactivity.
Two-factor authentication	☐ Force users to set up and use two-factor authentication

Figure 5-12 *Enabling the Password Expiration Feature*

You have unsaved changes.

Save or cancel

Figure 5-13 *Submitting Unsaved Changes*

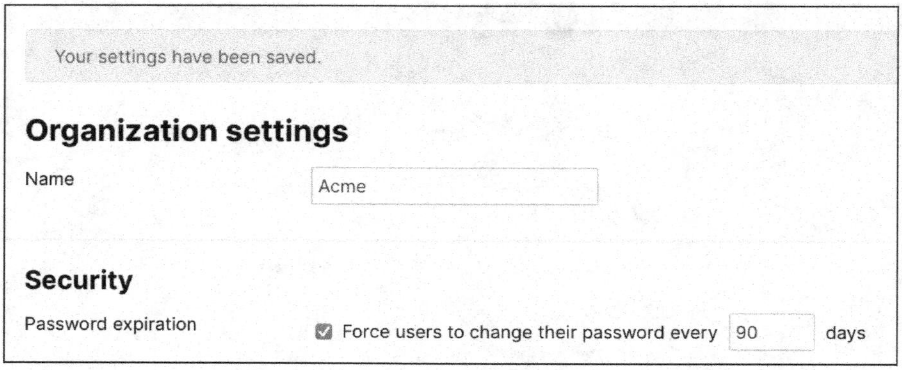

Your settings have been saved.

Organization settings

Name: Acme

Security

Password expiration: Force users to change their password every 90 days

Figure 5-14 *Confirmation That the Password Expiry Feature Has Been Enabled*

With the password expiry feature configured, after successful authentication to Dashboard, any admin user whose password age is greater than the password expiry period will be required to change their password, as illustrated in Figure 5-15. The user simply needs to follow the prompts on the password change page to set a new password.

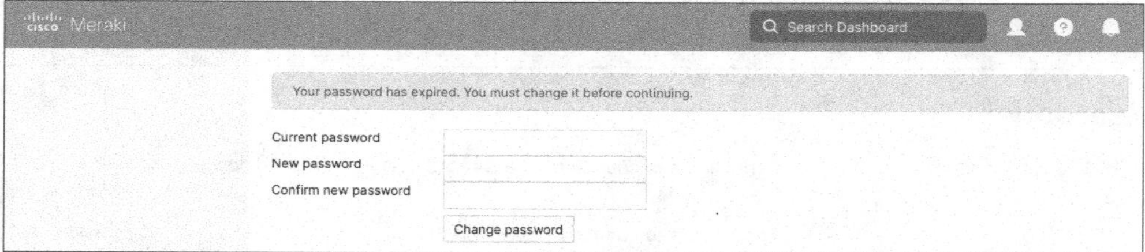

Figure 5-15 *Page Advising Admins to Change Password Due to Password Expiry*

Password Reuse

Changing passwords regularly ensures that the owner of the account is the only one using it. Password reuse policies play a vital role in mitigating the risks associated with compromised passwords and reduces the sharing of accounts. Both HIPAA and PCI DSS require controls to prevent the reuse of previously used passwords. This control works hand in hand with the password expiration policy to ensure user credentials are changed frequently.

The default password reuse policy in Dashboard prevents users from reusing a password if it's the same as their two previous passwords. If the password reuse limit is too low, users can simply reset their password multiple times and go back to using their original password. PCI DSS 4.0 requires that users are prevented from reusing a password that is the same as any of their last four passwords. The number of previous passwords can be increased to at least 999,999, effectively preventing the reuse of any previously used passwords. The password reuse policy cannot be disabled, or the quantity reduced below two.

Perform the following steps to configure the password reuse policy:

Step 1. Log in to Meraki Dashboard (https://dashboard.meraki.com).

Step 2. Navigate to **Organization** and then **Settings** (under Configure).

Step 3. Enter the number of the previous passwords to prevent their reuse in the text input box next to **Force Users to Choose Passwords Different from Their Past ___ Passwords.** In this case, we used a count of 4, as illustrated in Figure 5-16.

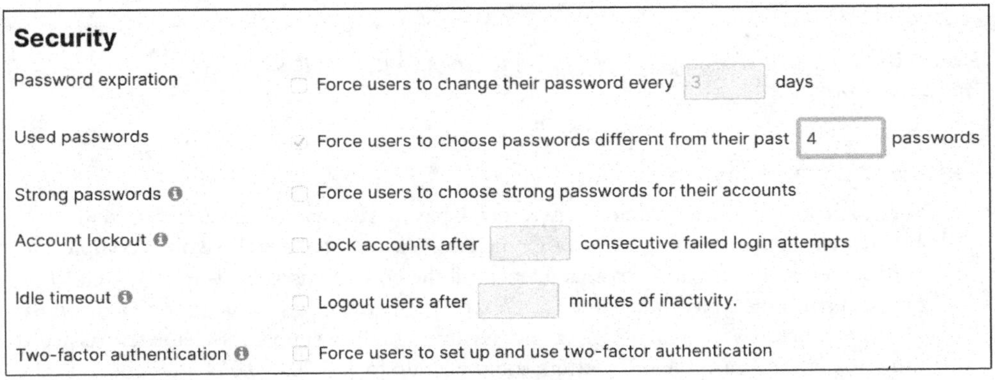

Security

Password expiration — Force users to change their password every [3] days

Used passwords — ✓ Force users to choose passwords different from their past [4] passwords

Strong passwords — Force users to choose strong passwords for their accounts

Account lockout — Lock accounts after [ ] consecutive failed login attempts

Idle timeout — Logout users after [ ] minutes of inactivity.

Two-factor authentication — Force users to set up and use two-factor authentication

Figure 5-16 *Configuring the Password Reuse Policy*

Step 4. At the bottom right of the screen, you see a warning that there are unsaved changes. Click **Save** to submit the changes. A banner confirms that the settings have been saved and are now in effect, as illustrated in Figure 5-17.

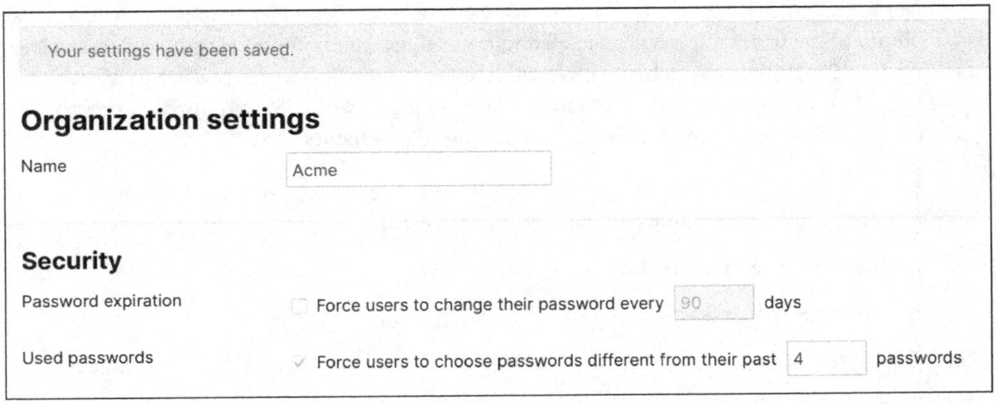

Your settings have been saved.

Organization settings

Name — Acme

Security

Password expiration — Force users to change their password every [90] days

Used passwords — ✓ Force users to choose passwords different from their past [4] passwords

Figure 5-17 *Confirmation That the Password Reuse Changes Are Now in Effect*

With the password reuse policy now configured, when a Dashboard user changes their password and tries to use a recently used password, the user will be presented with the error message shown in Figure 5-18. For the change to succeed, the user simply needs to choose a password that has not been used recently, as per the password reuse policy.

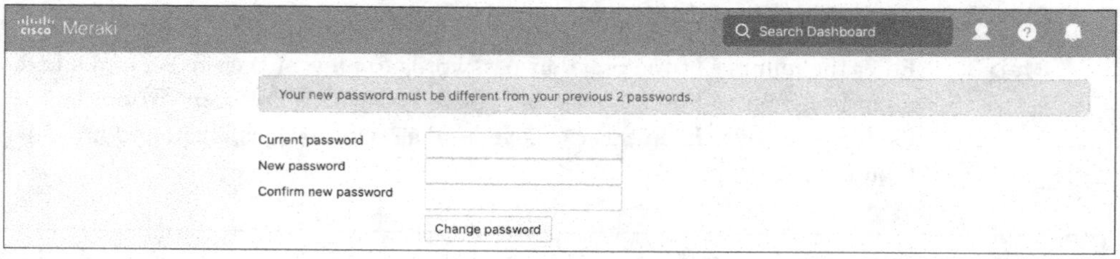

Figure 5-18 *Error Message when Trying to Reuse a Recent Password Upon Password Change*

Password Complexity

Brute-force attacks are a common way to break passwords that haven't already been obtained via a data breach or some other means. A brute-force attack involves computers trying every combination of characters until the correct password is found. Even for a computer, with the delay of sending each attempt over the Internet and getting a response back, this process is very time-consuming. As an example, a simple six-character password with numbers and case-sensitive letters could take up to 19,770,609,664 attempts to find the correct password. However, simply increasing the required password length to eight characters and allowing special characters increases the possible password combinations to 281,474,976,710,656. This equates to 14,237 times more password combinations.

Each year as technology gets more sophisticated and computers and networks get faster, the time required for a brute-force attack diminishes. As a result, industry best practice has been increasing password complexity requirements over time, as well as more recently mandating multifactor authentication. For example, PCI DSS 4.0 requires that passwords contain numeric and alphanumeric characters and have a minimum length of 8 characters (ideally 12). This can be achieved by enabling the strong passwords feature in Meraki Dashboard (it's not enabled by default). The strong passwords feature forces users to create passwords that meet *all* of the following requirements:

- Must not contain common words, to help prevent the use of easily guessable or dictionary-based passwords such as *password*
- Must be at least eight characters long
- Must contain at least three of the following character types:
  - Number
  - Lowercase letter
  - Uppercase letter
  - Symbol (for example, ! @ # $ % ^ & *)

Perform the following steps to configure the strong password policy:

Step 1. Log in to Meraki Dashboard (https://dashboard.meraki.com).

Step 2. Navigate to **Organization** and then **Settings** (under Configure).

Step 3. Check the box next to **Force Users to Choose Strong Passwords for Their Accounts.** If you place your mouse cursor over the "I" symbol at the end of **Strong Passwords**, Dashboard will show you what the strong password policy includes, as illustrated in Figure 5-19.

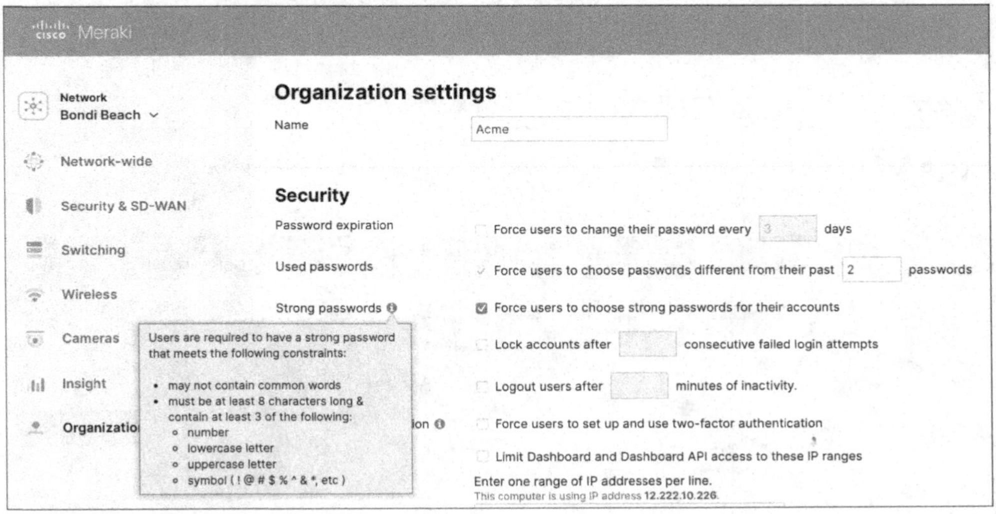

Figure 5-19 *Enabling the Strong Password Policy*

Step 4. At the bottom right of the screen, a warning indicates that there are unsaved changes, as illustrated in Figure 5-20. Click **Save** to submit the changes. A banner confirms that the settings have been saved and are now in effect, as illustrated in Figure 5-21.

Figure 5-20 *Submitting Unsaved Changes*

With the strong password policy enacted, users will need to choose a password that complies with this policy whenever resetting their password or when a new admin user is created. Any user who chooses a password that does not meet the required criteria will be presented with the error message shown in Figure 5-22.

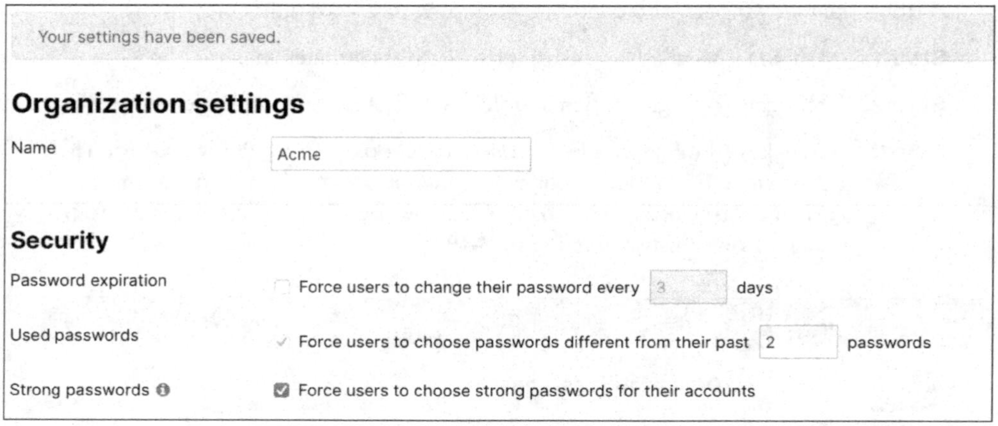

Your settings have been saved.

Organization settings

Name Acme

Security

Password expiration Force users to change their password every 3 days

Used passwords Force users to choose passwords different from their past 2 passwords

Strong passwords Force users to choose strong passwords for their accounts

Figure 5-21 *Confirmation That the Strong Password Policy Is Now in Effect*

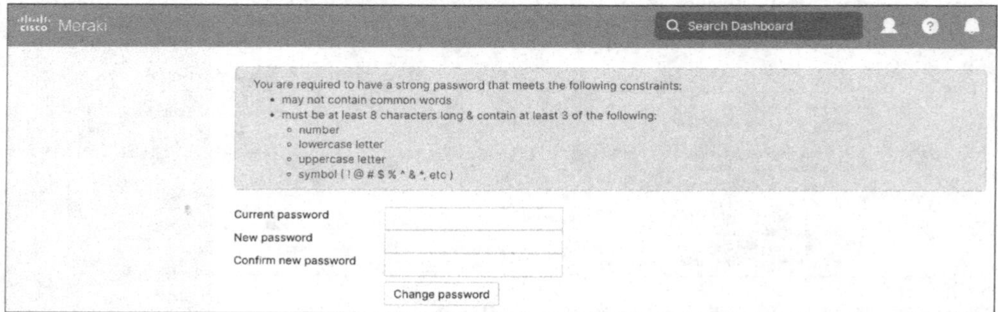

Figure 5-22 *Error Message Displayed If a New Password Does Not Match the Strong Password Policy*

Account Lockout After Invalid Login Attempts

Mitigating password compromise attempts is critical for maintaining a strong security posture. One of the most effective ways to detect and prevent brute-force attacks is by implementing a policy that locks user accounts after a certain number of failed consecutive login attempts. Both NIST 800-53 (Control AC-7) and PCI DSS 4.0 (Requirement 8.3.4) require locking out an account after a specified number of invalid authentication attempts.

You can implement this policy in Meraki Dashboard by enabling the Account lockout feature and setting a threshold for failed login attempts. This feature is not enabled by default. The number of login attempts can be any value from 1 to 999,999+ attempts. It is common for IT security standards to recommend locking out accounts after a number of invalid login attempts; however, they don't typically stipulate a suitable limit.

Thankfully, PCI DSS 4.0 does; therefore, we recommend using the PCI threshold of 10 failed attempts.

Perform the following steps to configure the account lockout policy:

Step 1. Log in to Meraki Dashboard (https://dashboard.meraki.com).

Step 2. Navigate to **Organization** and then **Settings** (under Configure).

Step 3. Check the box next to **Lock Accounts After ___ Consecutive Failed Login Attempts** and enter a value in the text input box. If you place your mouse cursor over the "I" symbol at the end of **Account Lockout**, Meraki Dashboard will explain what this policy does and also how to unlock locked accounts, as illustrated in Figure 5-23.

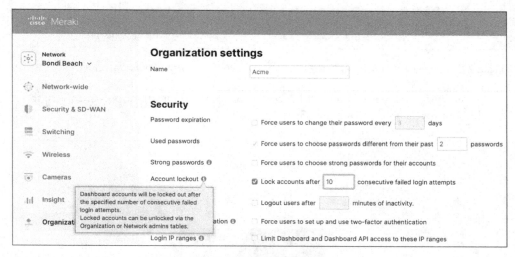

Meraki
Network
Bondi Beach
Network-wide
Security & SD-WAN
Switching
Wireless
Cameras
Insight
Organizati
Organization settings
Name
Acme
Security
Password expiration
Force users to change their password every 3 days
Used passwords
Force users to choose passwords different from their past 2 passwords
Strong passwords
Force users to choose strong passwords for their accounts
Account lockout
Lock accounts after 10 consecutive failed login attempts
Dashboard accounts will be locked out after the specified number of consecutive failed login attempts.
Locked accounts can be unlocked via the Organization or Network admins tables.
Logout users after minutes of inactivity.
ation
Force users to set up and use two-factor authentication
Login IP ranges
Limit Dashboard and Dashboard API access to these IP ranges

Figure 5-23 *Enabling the Account Lockout Policy*

Step 4. At the bottom right of the screen, a warning indicates that there are unsaved changes, as illustrated in Figure 5-24. Click **Save** to submit the changes. A banner confirms that the settings have been saved and are now in effect, as illustrated in Figure 5-25.

Figure 5-24 *Submitting Unsaved Changes*

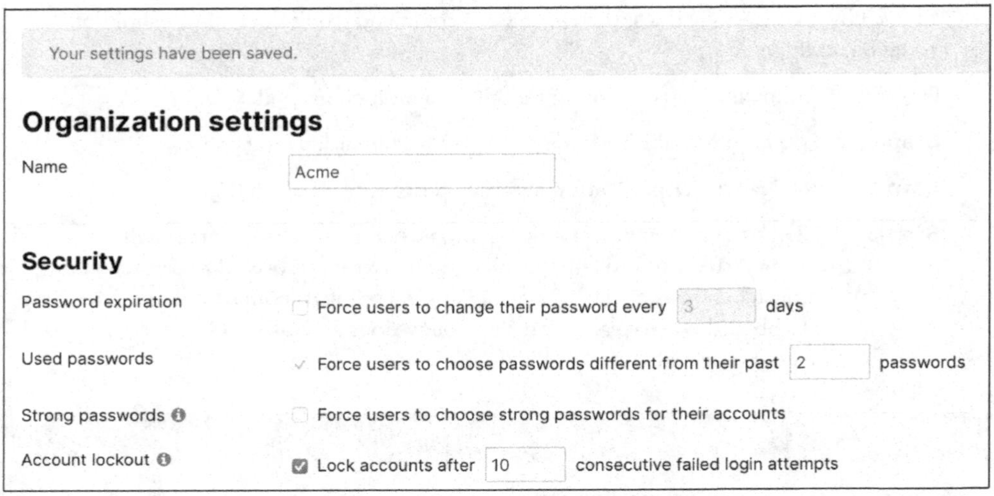

Your settings have been saved.

Organization settings

Name — Acme

Security

Password expiration — Force users to change their password every 3 days

Used passwords — Force users to choose passwords different from their past 2 passwords

Strong passwords — Force users to choose strong passwords for their accounts

Account lockout — Lock accounts after 10 consecutive failed login attempts

Figure 5-25 *Confirmation That the Account Lockout Policy Is Now in Effect*

After trying 10 times to log in with incorrect passwords, you will be presented with the lockout warning shown in Figure 5-26.

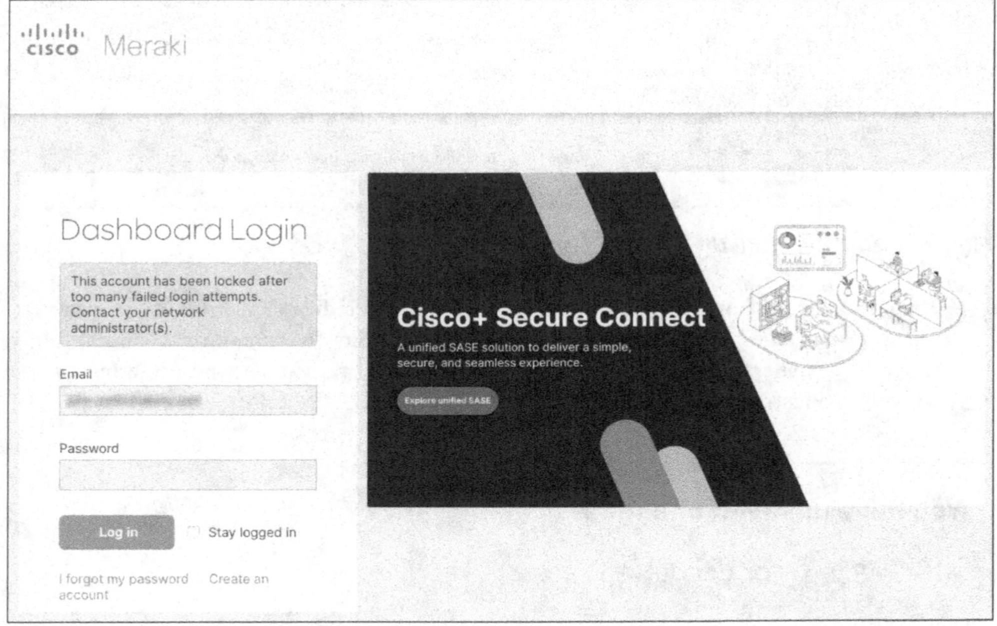

Figure 5-26 *Account Lockout Screen*

If you find yourself locked out of Dashboard due to too many login attempts, then another administrator should log in to Dashboard and unlock the account using the steps documented here: https://documentation.meraki.com/General_Administration/Managing_Dashboard_Access/Locked_Out_of_Dashboard. This applies to both network and organization level administrators.

Idle Timeout

Given the critical role of Meraki Dashboard in network and security administration, ensuring its security is paramount. An unattended console session could enable an attacker to bypass authentication controls and access this critical administration interface. For this reason, session timeouts are commonly required by industry best practice. For example, PCI DSS 4.0 requires an administrator to reauthenticate if their session has been idle for more than 15 minutes. Meraki Dashboard supports this capability through a feature known as *Idle timeout*. When a user session has been idle for close to the configured limit, Meraki Dashboard will prompt the user to continue their session or log out immediately, as illustrated in Figure 5-27.

Note The idle timeout setting applies to all active sessions, regardless of whether the account is locally configured or resides in an external directory in the case of SAML single sign-on.

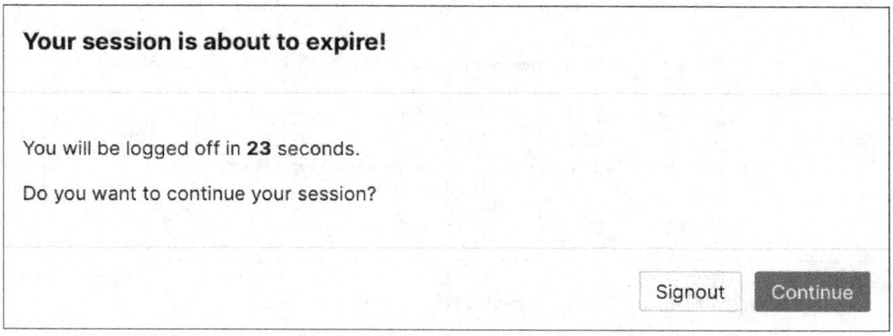

Your session is about to expire!

You will be logged off in **23** seconds.

Do you want to continue your session?

Signout Continue

Figure 5-27 *Idle Timeout Prompt*

If no action is taken, then the session will automatically time out, and the administrator will need to reauthenticate when they return, as illustrated in Figure 5-28.

Idle timeout, when enabled, automatically logs out users from the Dashboard after a configurable period of inactivity. This feature, which is disabled by default, can be configured for a timeout duration of between 1 and 2,147,483,647 minutes. It is recommended that you enable this feature and use a configured timeout of 15 minutes, which is the idle timeout value required by PCI DSS 4.0 requirement 8.2.

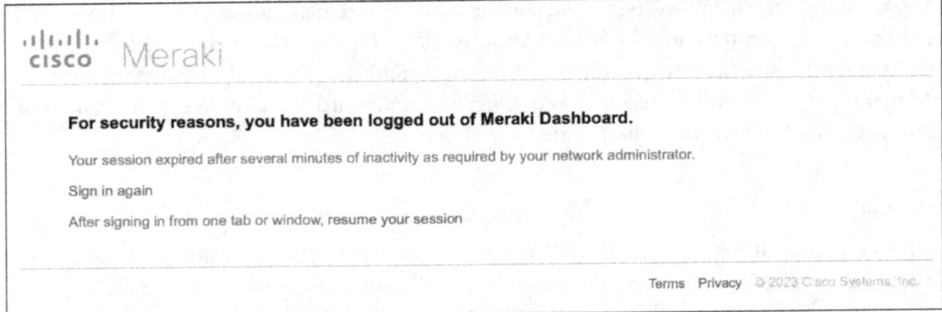

Figure 5-28 *Expired Session Logout Screen*

Perform the following steps to configure the idle timeout feature:

Step 1. Log in to Meraki Dashboard (https://dashboard.meraki.com).

Step 2. Navigate to **Organization** and then **Settings** (under Configure).

Step 3. Check the box for **Idle Timeout** next to **Logout Users After ___ Minutes of Inactivity** and enter the recommended value of **15** minutes, as illustrated in Figure 5-29.

Security

Password expiration	Force users to change their password every 90 days
Used passwords	Force users to choose passwords different from their past 2 passwords
Strong passwords	Force users to choose strong passwords for their accounts
Account lockout	Lock accounts after 10 consecutive failed login attempts
Idle timeout	Logout users after 15 minutes of inactivity.

Figure 5-29 *Configuring the Idle Timeout Feature*

Step 4. At the bottom right of the screen, a warning indicates that there are unsaved changes, as illustrated in Figure 5-30. Click **Save** to submit the changes. A banner confirms that the settings have been saved and are now in effect, as illustrated in Figure 5-31.

You have unsaved changes.

Save or cancel

Figure 5-30 *Submitting Unsaved Changes*

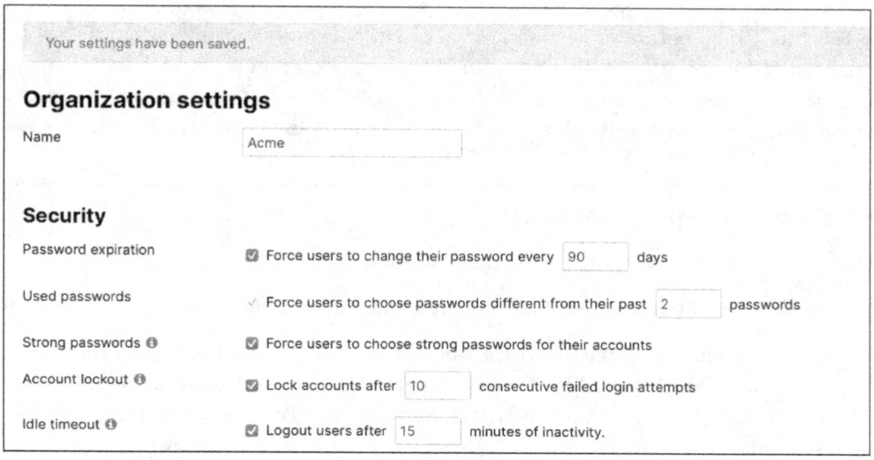

Your settings have been saved.

Organization settings

Name Acme

Security

Password expiration — Force users to change their password every 90 days

Used passwords — Force users to choose passwords different from their past 2 passwords

Strong passwords — Force users to choose strong passwords for their accounts

Account lockout — Lock accounts after 10 consecutive failed login attempts

Idle timeout — Logout users after 15 minutes of inactivity.

Figure 5-31 *Confirmation That the Idle Timeout Policy Is in Effect*

With the idle timeout feature now configured, any Dashboard session left idle for the timeout period will be logged out automatically.

IP Whitelisting

One of the most robust ways to harden administrator access is to use a *whitelist*. An IP whitelist enables an organization to limit admin access to connections originating from these trusted IP addresses. By defining your trusted IP address range, you add an extra layer of protection and reduce the risk of unauthorized access. This is analogous to configuring an access list on VTY ports on traditional Cisco devices, something that engineers have done for decades. Interestingly, Essential Eight is currently the only standard/framework that explicitly calls for an IP whitelisting capability; nevertheless, it is good practice and highly recommended.

> **Tip** Be sure to give yourself plenty of flexibility when configuring these subnets in case of unforeseen events. You don't want to tie yourself down to one jump box or ISP and then find yourself locked out of Dashboard due to an unforeseen event. If your organization owns and uses its own public IP address space, that is a good place to start, because you're likely to keep using those addresses even if you change ISP. Also, think about where you might need to access the Dashboard in an emergency; this could include public subnets used for out-of-band management access, virtual private networks (VPNs), private mobile networks that have Internet access, and the subnets of fixed consumer and mobile Internet providers used by administrators. Remember to factor this IP whitelisting into your organization disaster recovery plans.

The login IP ranges feature is disabled by default, allowing admin users to log in to the Dashboard from anywhere in the world. You can restrict this access by enabling this feature and specifying the subnets from which access to the Dashboard and/or the Dashboard API is allowed.

Note The IP whitelisting feature in Meraki Dashboard applies only when logging in with locally configured accounts. When using SAML SSO, you can configure IP whitelisting in Meraki Dashboard as well as part of your SAML SSO/MFA configuration. This will ensure that the IP whitelisting policy is applied regardless of how users log in to Dashboard.

Perform the following steps to configure the login IP ranges feature:

Step 1. Log in to Meraki Dashboard (https://dashboard.meraki.com).

Step 2. Navigate to **Organization** and then **Settings** (under Configure).

Step 3. Locate **Limit Dashboard and Dashboard API Access to These IP Ranges** and **Limit Dashboard API Access to These IP Ranges.** Meraki Dashboard conveniently lets you know which IP address you are connecting from for this session.

It is very difficult to undo these changes if you lock yourself out, so before you activate this policy, revisit this page from all the various ways you and your colleagues may need to connect to Dashboard and build up a list of suitable subnets. It is advisable to specify between 3 and 10 different subnets, rather than limiting access to a single subnet or, even worse, a single IP. Remember that there are billions of IPv4 addresses and trillions of IPv6 addresses, so limiting access to even 1 million addresses still massively reduces the attack surface.

Meraki Dashboard will accept any combination of single IPv4/IPv6 addresses, a range of IPv4 addresses, or CIDR subnets for IPv4/IPv6. It is recommended to limit both IPv4 and IPv6 subnets. As a safeguard, Meraki Dashboard will force you to include the current IP address that you are connecting from.

Step 4. Check the box next to **Limit Dashboard and Dashboard API Access to These IP Ranges** and/or **Limit Dashboard API Access to These IP Ranges,** as illustrated in Figure 5-32.

Enter the appropriate subnets and/or IP addresses that you want to allow. Multiple entries are allowed; however, each entry must be on a new line. IP addresses can be individual IPv4/IPv6 addresses, an IP range separated by the dash (–) symbol, or a subnet with CIDR (slash notation, such as /24).

Step 5. At the bottom right of the screen, a warning indicates that there are unsaved changes, as illustrated in Figure 5-33. Click **Save** to submit the changes. A banner confirms that the settings have been saved and are now in effect.

Once this configuration is activated, only administrators connecting from the allowed IP addresses will have access to your organization's Dashboard. Any user trying to access your Dashboard from a blocked IP address will receive the error message shown in Figure 5-34.

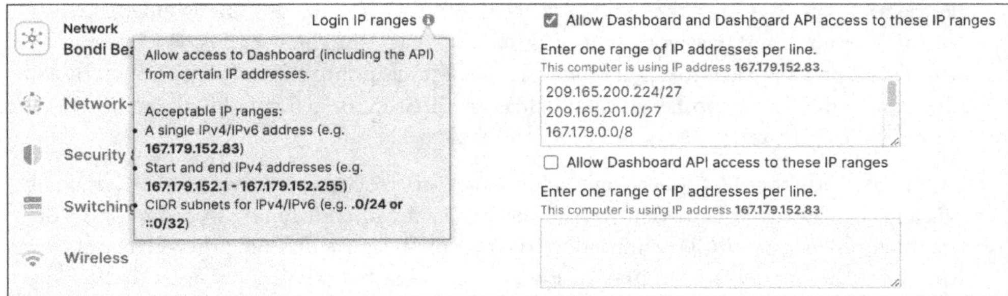

Figure 5-32 *Configuring the Login IP Ranges Feature*

Figure 5-33 *Submitting Unsaved Changes*

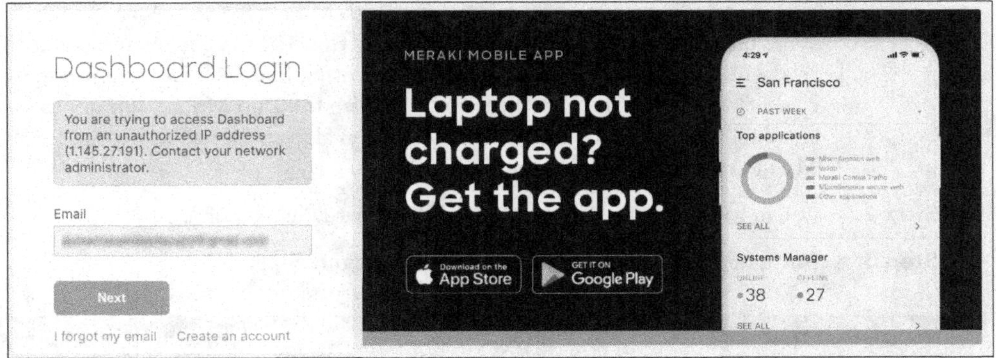

Figure 5-34 *Blocked IP Range Warning Message*

If you find yourself locked out of Meraki Dashboard due to an IP whitelist policy, you can find the recovery procedure on Meraki's website at https://documentation.meraki.com/General_Administration/Managing_Dashboard_Access/Locked_Out_of_Dashboard.

Multifactor Authentication (MFA)

As security threats continue to evolve, using multiple authentication methods is an effective way to enhance the authentication process and ensure a higher level of security. Strong authentication, including multifactor authentication, is a key requirement across all of today's security standards. Multifactor authentication, also known as two-factor authentication (2FA), refers to authenticating using something else that is independent of the username and password. This is generally something the user has. For example, this could be a physical token, a biometric like a fingerprint or facial recognition, or a code transmitted via another means such as email, SMS, or generated with an app. In this book, we use the terms *MFA* and *2FA* interchangeably.

In Meraki Dashboard two-factor authentication is controlled at the user level. Additionally, via an organization policy, admin users who haven't set up 2FA can be forced to do so during their next login. This is an important distinction, because disabling the global policy does not disable two-factor authentication for any user, but it will allow users to disable two-factor authentication on their accounts.

When you are enabling two-factor authentication for the first time, it needs to be enabled on at least one admin user account before you can enforce it globally. Meraki Dashboard supports two-factor authentication using either SMS or Cisco Duo, and either of these can be used for the initial user. Note: SMS is not available in all countries.

Configuring Two-Factor Authentication Using Cisco Duo

Perform the following steps to configure two-factor authentication using Cisco Duo.

Step 1. If you are rolling out two-factor authentication using Cisco Duo to all admin users, then now is a good time to ensure that everyone (including yourself) has the Duo Mobile app on their mobile devices. It is recommended that you manage all corporate mobile devices with Meraki Systems Manager (or some other mobile device management platform). There are many reasons for this, which we will cover in Chapter 11, "Securing End-User Devices." In this case, it provides a simple and easy way to push the Duo Mobile app out to all admin users. If you prefer, for now you can also choose to download Duo Mobile from your appropriate app store.

Step 2. Log in to Meraki Dashboard (https://dashboard.meraki.com).

Step 3. Navigate to the **My Profile** page shown in Figure 5-35.

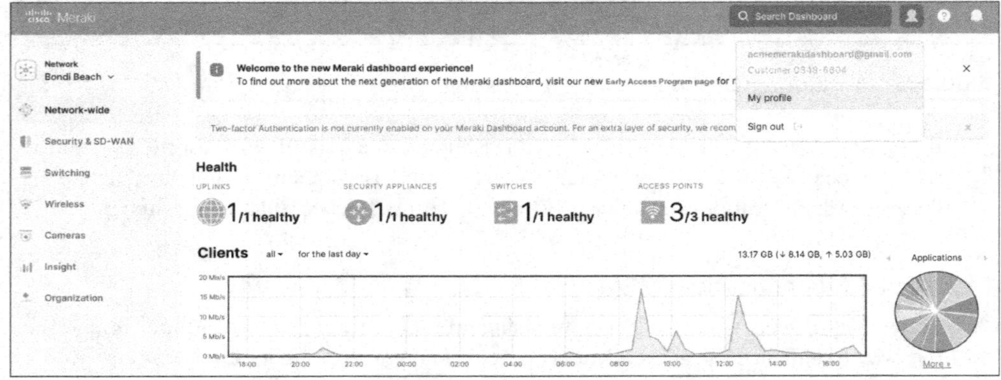

Figure 5-35 *Navigating to the My Profile Page*

Step 4. Scroll down and click **Set Up Two-Factor Authentication**, as illustrated in Figure 5-36. You are presented with a helpful page that will guide you through the 2FA enrollment process, as illustrated in Figure 5-37.

cisco Meraki

Network
Bondi Beach

Network-wide

Security & SD-WAN

Switching

Wireless

Change your password

Your new password will be synced to all Dashboard accounts with this email address.

Current password

New password

Confirm password

Change password

Two-factor authentication

Two-Factor authentication is **OFF**.

Set up two-factor authentication

Figure 5-36 *Enabling Two-Factor Authentication on a User's Profile*

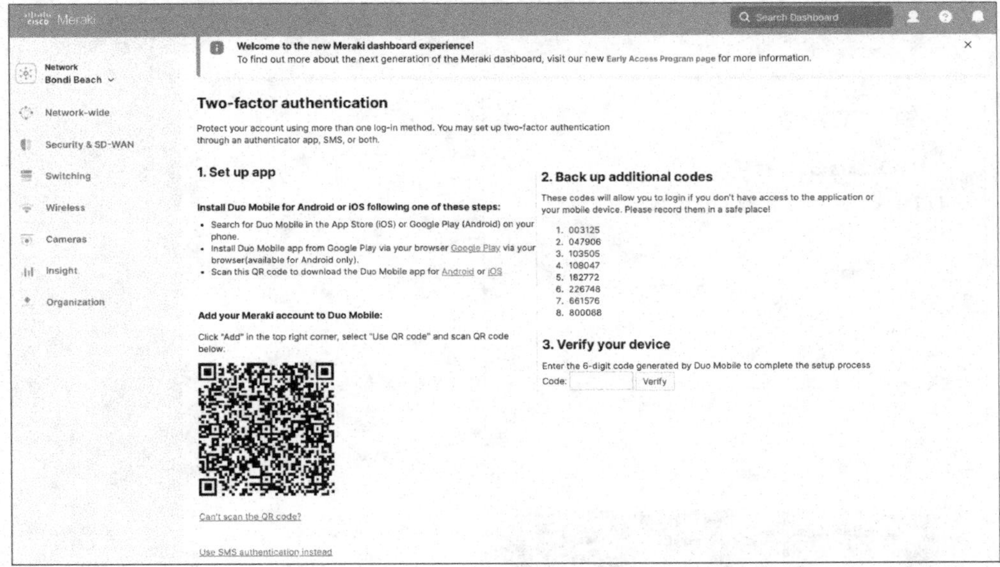

Figure 5-37 *Completing the 2FA User Enrollment Process*

Step 5. It is really important to make a note of the eight one-time-use codes on the right side of the screen, so we suggest you do this step first. These are "break glass in case of emergency" codes that you can use if, for any reason, your second authentication factor (such as your mobile device) is unavailable. Store these codes in your favorite password manager, like 1Password or LastPass, in case you ever need them.

Step 6. If you haven't already, download the Duo Mobile app to your mobile device from the appropriate app store. Open the app on your mobile device, and you should see the welcome screen shown in Figure 5-38. Click **Continue**.

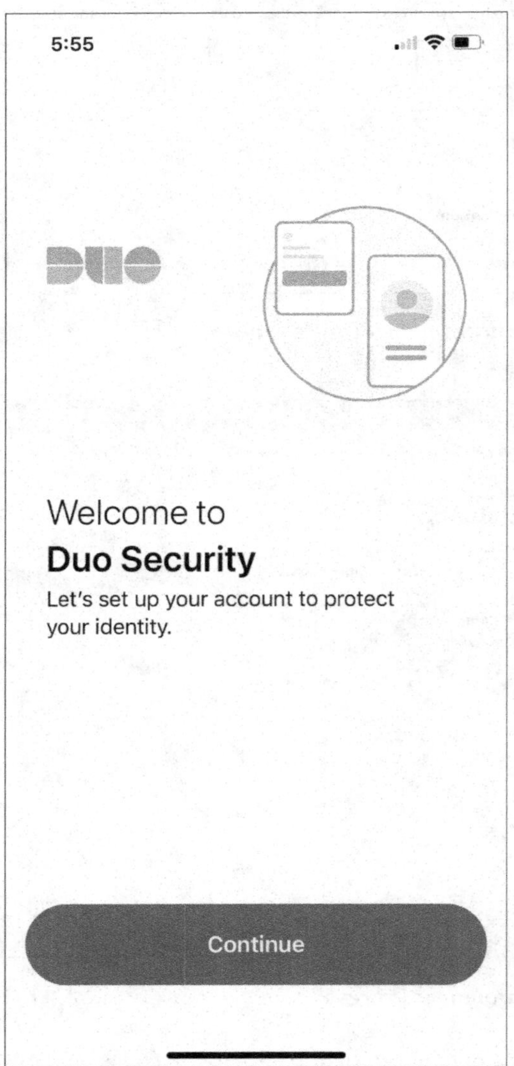

Figure 5-38 *Cisco Duo App Welcome Screen*

Step 7. In the Duo Mobile app, click **Use a QR Code**, as illustrated in Figure 5-39. Scan the QR code and point your mobile device's camera at the QR code on the Dashboard two-factor authentication enrollment page.

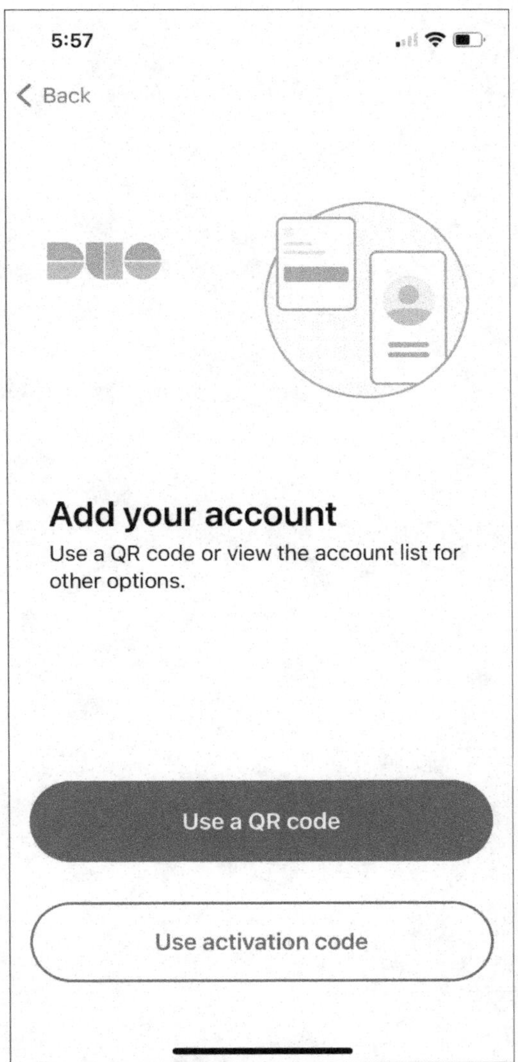

Figure 5-39 *Cisco Duo Scanning the QR Code*

Step 8. In the Duo Mobile app, give this account a name, as illustrated in Figure 5-40. Click **Save** to accept the suggested name. You can rename the account later if you want.

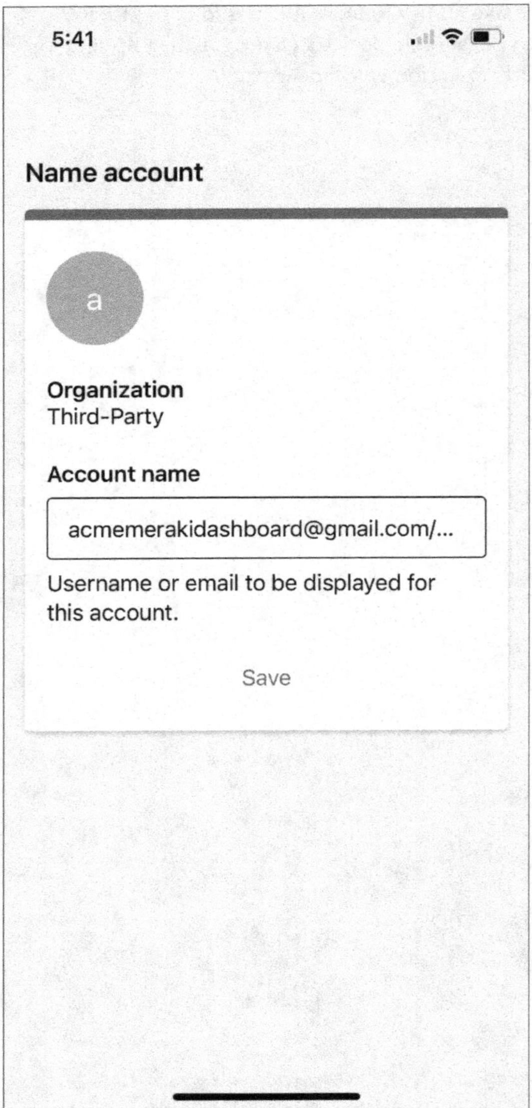

Figure 5-40 *Naming the Cisco Duo Account*

Step 9. The following steps may vary depending on whether you have used the Duo Mobile app before or previously set it up for this account. If this is your first time using Duo Mobile, you will be asked to set up a recovery password. After you've done this, the account setup will be completed, as illustrated in Figure 5-41.

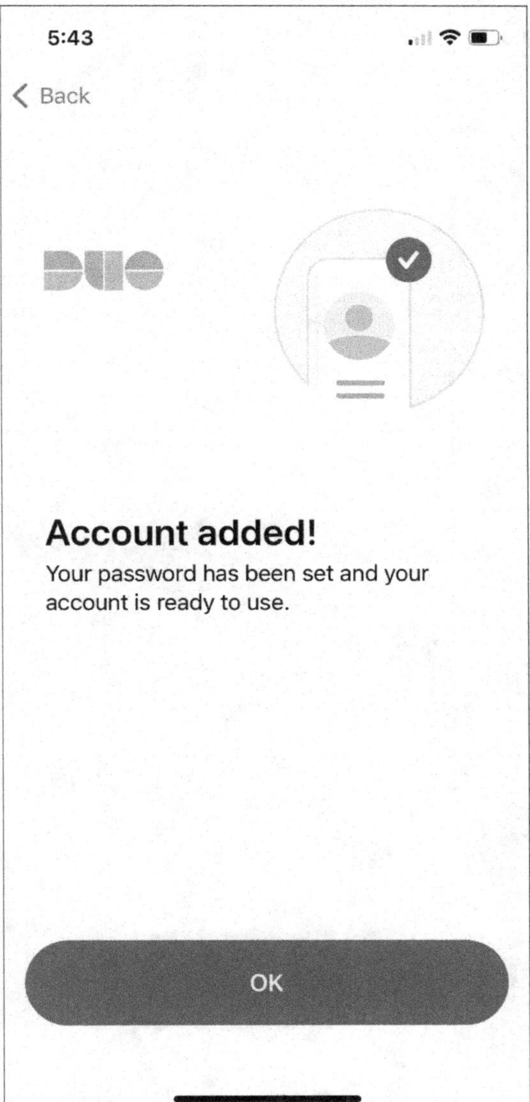

Figure 5-41 *Completion of the Cisco Duo Account Setup*

Step 10. If this is your first time using the Duo Mobile app, then you may see a privacy pop-up, as illustrated in Figure 5-42. Click either **Continue** or **Turn Off** to get to the next screen.

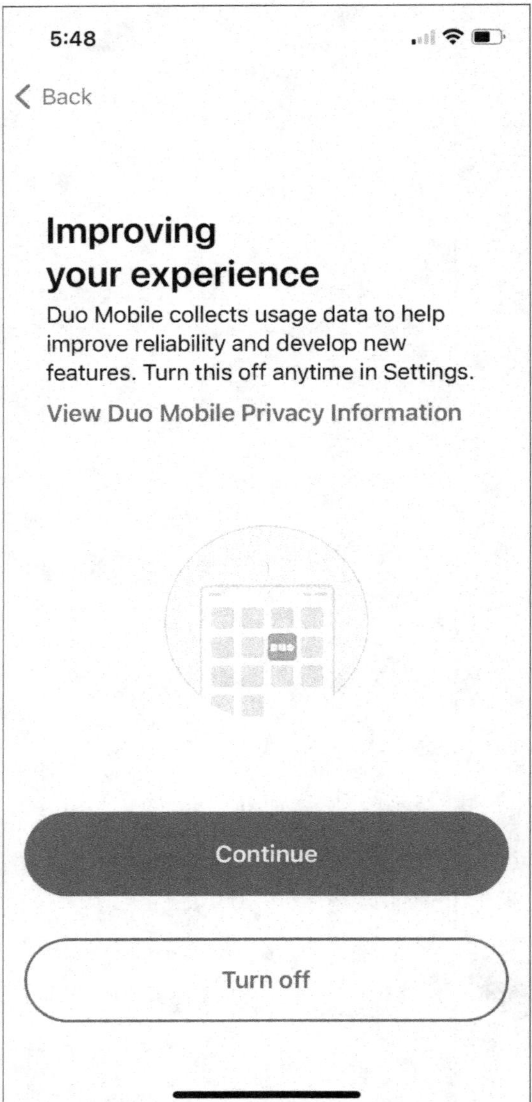

Figure 5-42 *Duo Mobile Privacy Pop-Up*

Step 11. From the screen in Figure 5-43, click **Show Password** to reveal a six-digit passcode. Then enter this code into the text box under **Verify Your Device** on the Meraki Dashboard two-factor authentication enrollment page.

Step 12. You now see confirmation that your mobile app is configured correctly, as illustrated in Figure 5-44. Click **Continue.**

5:48
Back
Almost there
Copy the passcode back into your app.
Show passcode

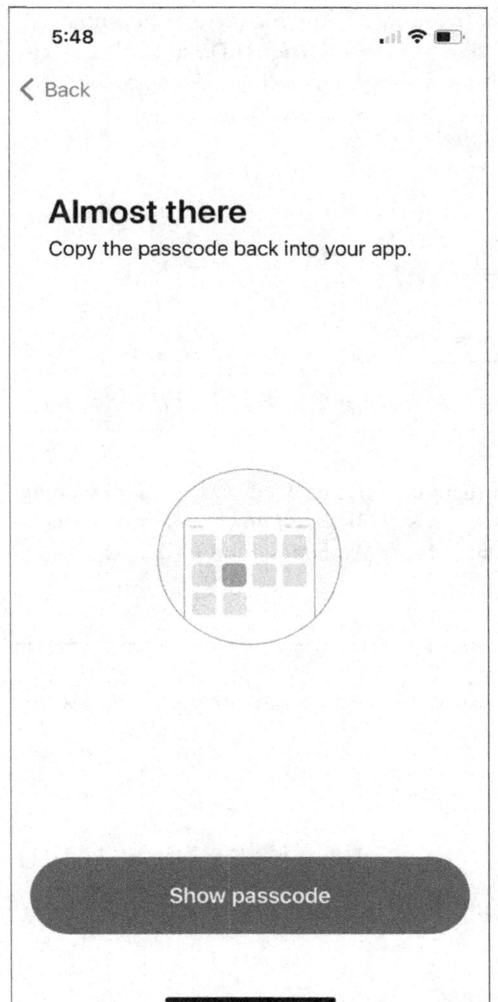

Figure 5-43 *Duo Mobile Initial Passcode Page*

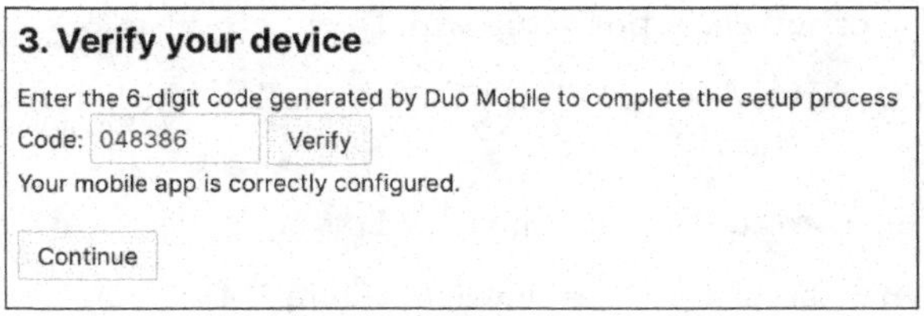

3. Verify your device
Enter the 6-digit code generated by Duo Mobile to complete the setup process
Code: 048386
Verify
Your mobile app is correctly configured.
Continue

Figure 5-44 *Duo Mobile Code Confirmation*

The two-factor authentication configuration is now complete. A pop-up message states that you will be logged out of any *additional* Dashboard sessions, as illustrated in Figure 5-45; however, you will not be logged out of this Dashboard session.

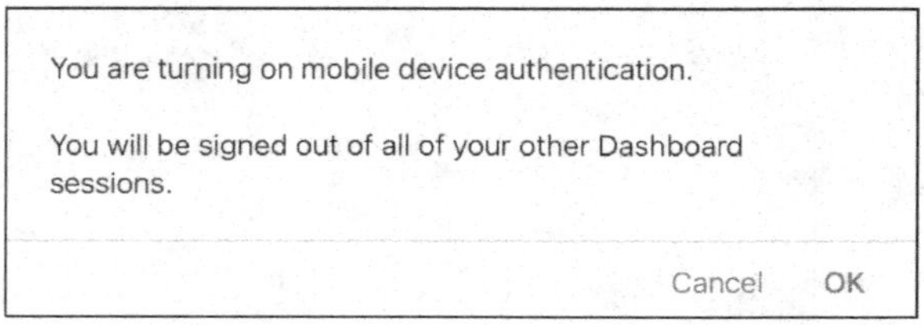

You are turning on mobile device authentication.

You will be signed out of all of your other Dashboard sessions.

Cancel OK

Figure 5-45 *Meraki Dashboard Logout Pop-Up After User Two-Factor Authentication Set Up*

Step 13. You can verify that two-factor authentication is enabled for this user by going back to the **My Profile** page (shown in Step 3). Scroll down to **Two-Factor Authentication**, where you now see **Mobile Authentication Is ON**, as illustrated in Figure 5-46.

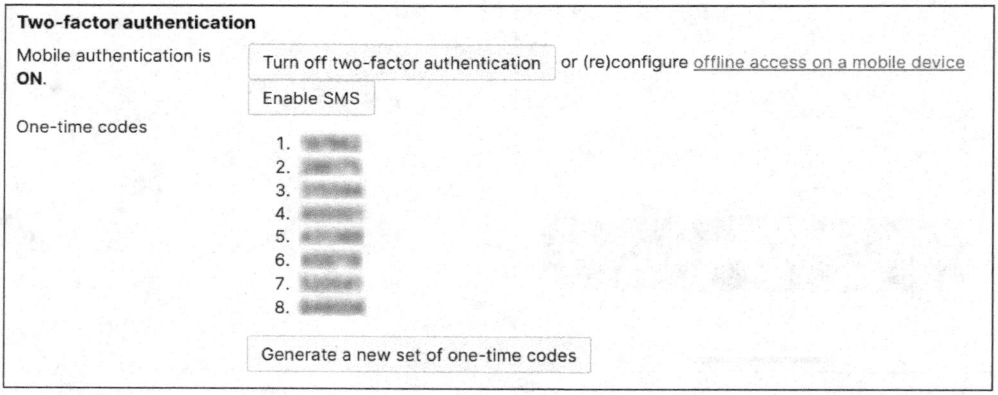

Two-factor authentication

Mobile authentication is **ON**. | Turn off two-factor authentication | or (re)configure offline access on a mobile device

Enable SMS

One-time codes

1.
2.
3.
4.
5.
6.
7.
8.

Generate a new set of one-time codes

Figure 5-46 *Verifying Two-Factor Authentication Is Enabled for an Admin Account*

Follow these steps to test the two-factor authentication setup with Duo:

Step 1. Log out of your current Dashboard session. This takes you back to the login page.

Step 2. Enter your username and password as normal and click **Log In**.

Step 3. You are presented with an additional page, as shown in Figure 5-47, requiring the passcode from Duo Mobile. Enter this and click **Verify** to log in to Meraki Dashboard.

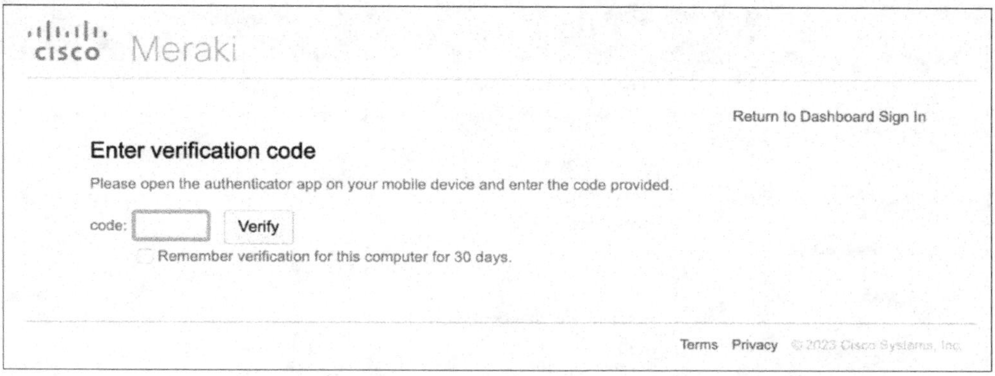

cisco Meraki

Return to Dashboard Sign In

Enter verification code

Please open the authenticator app on your mobile device and enter the code provided.

code: Verify

Remember verification for this computer for 30 days.

Terms Privacy © 2023 Cisco Systems, Inc.

Figure 5-47 *The Additional Two-Factor Verification Login Page*

Configuring Two-Factor Authentication Using SMS

Perform the following steps to configure two-factor authentication using SMS.

Step 1. Log in to Meraki Dashboard (https://dashboard.meraki.com).

Step 2. Navigate to the **My Profile** page, as shown in Figure 5-48.

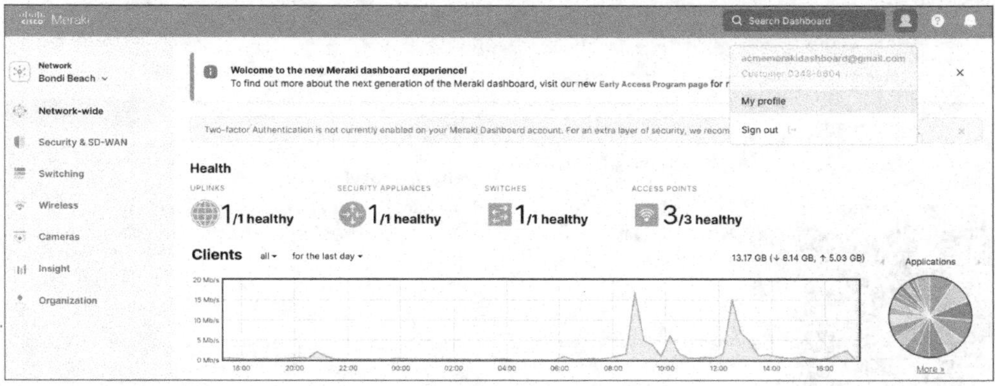

Figure 5-48 *Navigating to the My Profile Page*

Step 3. From the screen in Figure 5-49, scroll down to **Two-Factor Authentication** and click **Set Up Two-Factor Authentication.**

Step 4. It is really important to make a note of the eight one-time-use codes on the right side of the screen, so we suggest you do this step now. These are "break glass in case of emergency" codes that you can use if, for any reason, your second authentication factor (such as your mobile device) is unavailable.

Step 5. Click the link for **Use SMS Authentication Instead** toward the bottom of the page shown in Figure 5-50.

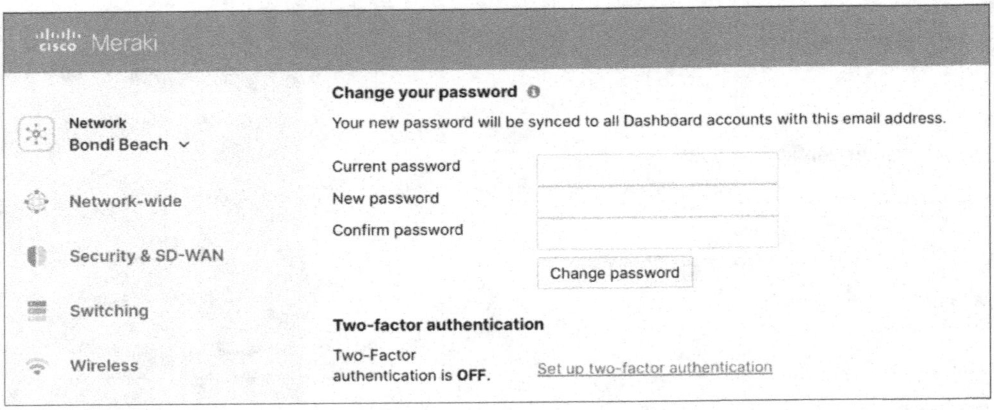

Figure 5-49 *Enabling Two-Factor Authentication on a User's Profile*

Figure 5-50 *Configuring SMS as the Second Factor of Authentication*

Step 6. From the screen in Figure 5-51, enter your mobile number in the text box next to **Phone Number** and click **Send Code.**

When you receive the SMS with the six-digit verification code, enter this code into the text box next to **Code** and click **Verify.** The Next button should now be available, so click **Next.**

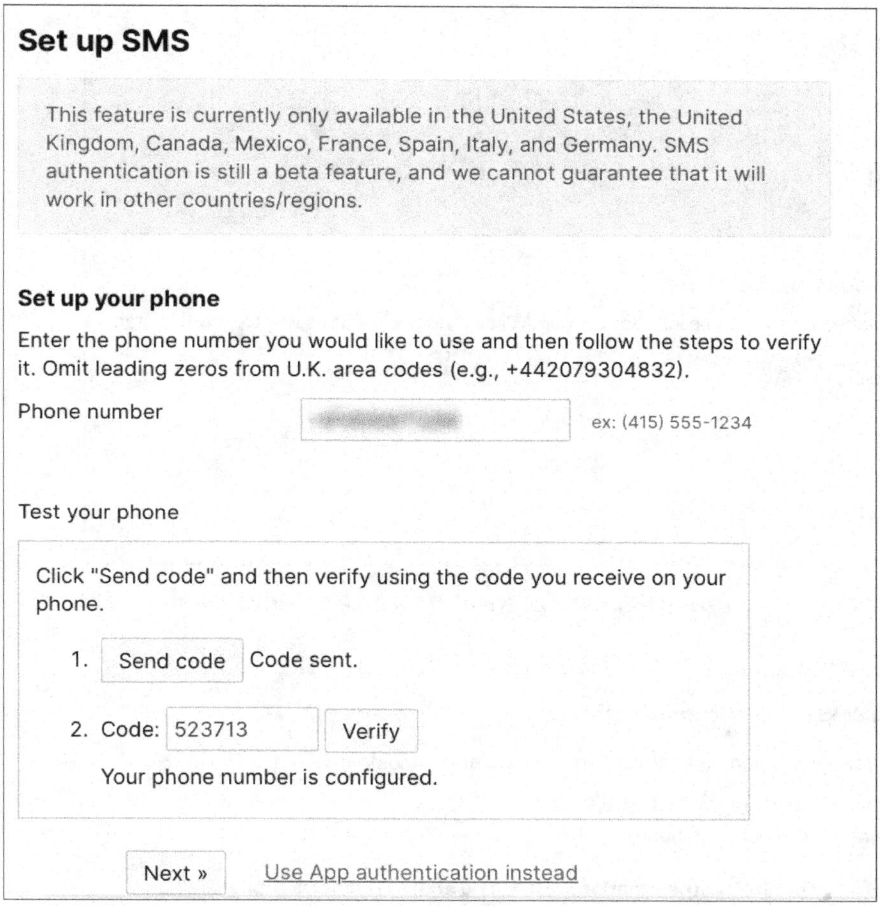

Set up SMS

This feature is currently only available in the United States, the United Kingdom, Canada, Mexico, France, Spain, Italy, and Germany. SMS authentication is still a beta feature, and we cannot guarantee that it will work in other countries/regions.

Set up your phone

Enter the phone number you would like to use and then follow the steps to verify it. Omit leading zeros from U.K. area codes (e.g., +442079304832).

Phone number ex: (415) 555-1234

Test your phone

Click "Send code" and then verify using the code you receive on your phone.

1. Send code Code sent.
2. Code: 523713 Verify

Your phone number is configured.

Next » Use App authentication instead

Figure 5-51 *Adding a Phone Number for Two-Factor Authentication Using SMS*

Step 7. (Optional) On the page shown in Figure 5-52, you can also enter a backup phone number in case your primary number is unavailable. You can also do this after SMS authentication is enabled by revisiting the **My Profile** page. If electing to add a backup number, enter this now and test it by clicking **+(Optional) Test Backup Phone.**

Click **Next** to move to the next screen.

Step 8. On the page shown in Figure 5-53, you should confirm the SMS settings are correct; then click **Turn On SMS Authentication.**

Step 9. A pop-up message warns that you will be logged out of all other Dashboard sessions, as illustrated in Figure 5-54. This will not affect this session. Click **OK.**

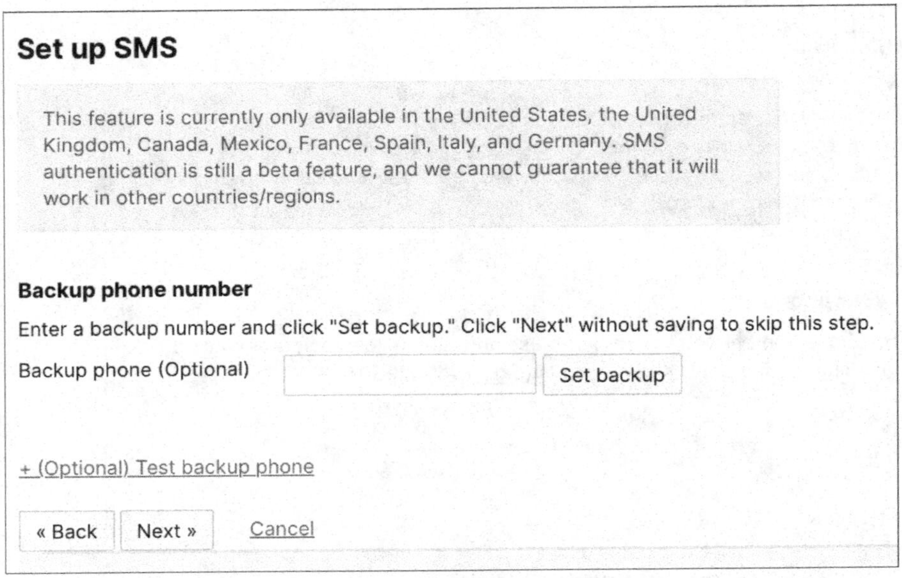

Set up SMS

This feature is currently only available in the United States, the United Kingdom, Canada, Mexico, France, Spain, Italy, and Germany. SMS authentication is still a beta feature, and we cannot guarantee that it will work in other countries/regions.

Backup phone number

Enter a backup number and click "Set backup." Click "Next" without saving to skip this step.

Backup phone (Optional) Set backup

+ (Optional) Test backup phone

« Back Next » Cancel

Figure 5-52 *Setting Up a Backup Phone Number for SMS Verification*

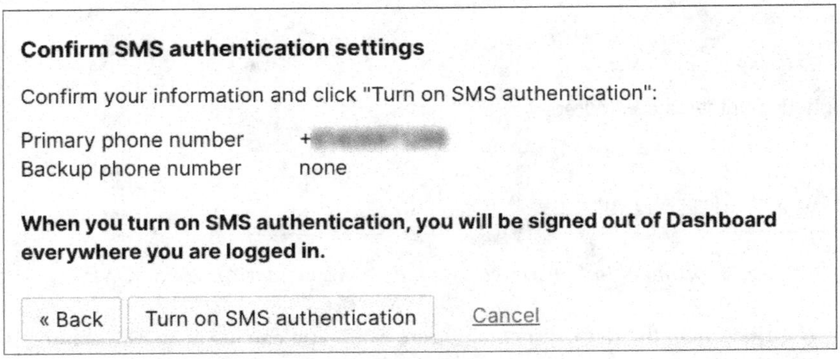

Confirm SMS authentication settings

Confirm your information and click "Turn on SMS authentication":

Primary phone number +
Backup phone number none

When you turn on SMS authentication, you will be signed out of Dashboard everywhere you are logged in.

« Back Turn on SMS authentication Cancel

Figure 5-53 *SMS Setup Confirmation Page*

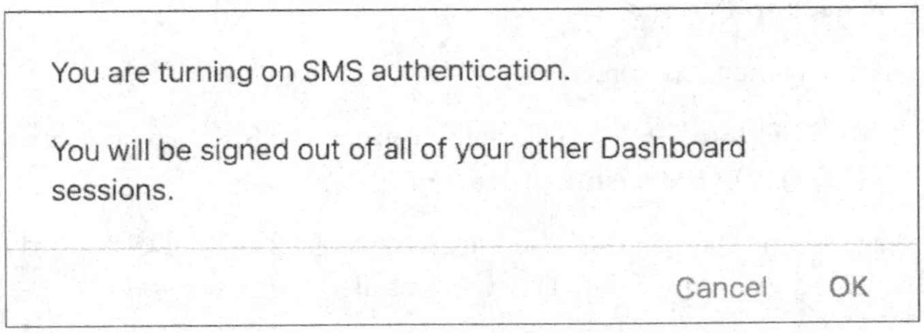

You are turning on SMS authentication.

You will be signed out of all of your other Dashboard sessions.

Cancel OK

Figure 5-54 *SMS Dashboard Logout Notification*

Step 10. You see another pop-up message, this time requesting that you verify the password for this administrator account, as illustrated in Figure 5-55. Enter your password and click **Verify**.

Verify password

To perform this action, please re-enter your password.

••••••••••

I forgot my password

Cancel Verify

Figure 5-55 *SMS Dashboard Password Verification Pop-Up*

Step 11. You now return to the **My Profile** page to verify the setup of two-factor authentication using SMS. Scroll down to **Two-Factor Authentication** and verify that you can see **Two-Factor Authentication Is ON** with your phone number displayed, as illustrated in Figure 5-56.

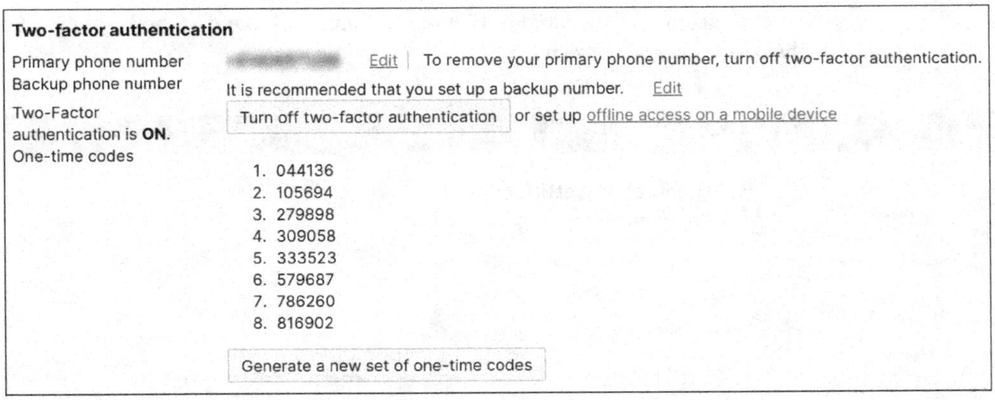

Two-factor authentication

Primary phone number — Edit | To remove your primary phone number, turn off two-factor authentication.

Backup phone number — It is recommended that you set up a backup number. Edit

Two-Factor authentication is **ON**. — Turn off two-factor authentication or set up offline access on a mobile device

One-time codes

1. 044136
2. 105694
3. 279898
4. 309058
5. 333523
6. 579687
7. 786260
8. 816902

Generate a new set of one-time codes

Figure 5-56 *Verification of SMS Two-Factor Authentication Setup on the My Profile Page*

Enabling Two-Factor Authentication at the Organization Level

Now that you have verified that two-factor authentication is working, you can safely enable it at the organization level.

It is highly recommended that you take the extra step of forcing all admin users to use two-factor authentication. Not doing so and relying on all users to implement this individually will inevitably end up in two-factor authentication being enabled for some users and not others, compromising security. Because MFA is a requirement of most of today's security standards, avoiding this step will likely also result in an audit finding.

> **Tip** Before enabling this policy, make sure you have at least two known good admin accounts that are enabled for two-factor authentication. In an emergency, the second account can be used to disable this policy again. This will be required if Meraki Support is called on to disable two-factor authentication for your account.

> **Note** Enabling two-factor authentication will not break API access. Two-factor authentication applies only to administrative access to Meraki Dashboard, not the Dashboard API.

Perform the following steps to enable two-factor authentication for all admin users in this organization:

Step 1. Log in to Meraki Dashboard (https://dashboard.meraki.com).

Step 2. Navigate to **Organization** and then **Settings** (under Configure).

Step 3. Check the box next to **Force Users to Set Up and Use Two-Factor Authentication**, as illustrated in Figure 5-57, and click **Save** in the bottom-right corner of your screen.

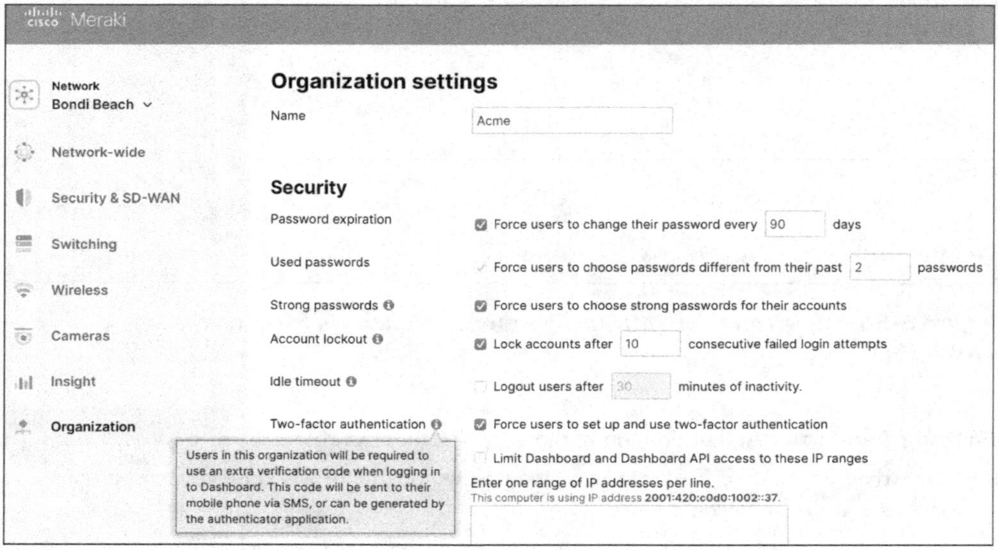

Figure 5-57 *Enabling Two-Factor Authentication Globally*

It is not possible to enable two-factor authentication globally without enabling it on at least one user. Trying to do so will generate an error, advising you of the need to carry out the enrollment steps on the **My Profile** page first, as illustrated in Figure 5-58.

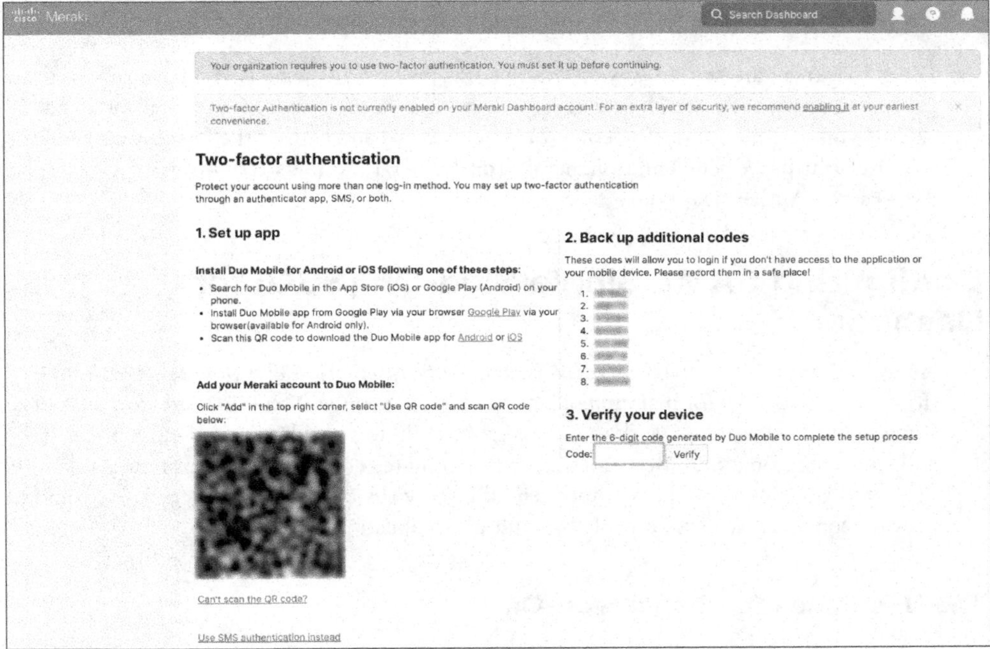

Figure 5-58 *The 2FA Setup Page at Login for Admin Accounts That Have Not Completed This Step*

As long as your account has been enabled for two-factor authentication, then you will be able to complete this step, even if all other administrator accounts have not completed their 2FA setup.

When you complete this step, user accounts that have been configured for 2FA under their **My Profile** page will be able to log in with two-factor authentication as normal. Accounts that have not done the two-factor authentication setup will be forced to complete this step at login before they can access the Dashboard.

Recovering from Being Locked Out of Meraki Dashboard Due to a Two-Factor Authentication Issue

There are a number of ways to restore Dashboard access, depending on the issue you are having:

- Use one of the backup codes that you noted earlier.
- If using SMS, use the backup mobile number to obtain the verification code.

- If using Duo, obtain a replacement mobile device and use Duo Restore to restore your Duo account settings to the new device. This will enable you to generate the verification codes to log in to Dashboard again. It is recommended that all users enable Duo Restore.
- Ask another admin to delete your admin account and re-create it again.

Given that there are several ways to resolve this problem, as long as you have followed the preceding steps, then you should never need to raise a case with Meraki Support. That said, if you do find yourself needing to raise a case, you can find the process on Meraki's website at https://documentation.meraki.com/General_Administration/Other_Topics/Two-Factor_Authentication.

Configuring SAML Single Sign-On (SSO) for Dashboard

Almost all organizations use an identity management solution like Microsoft Entra ID (formerly Azure AD) for maintaining their users and groups. Meraki Dashboard supports using Security Assertion Markup Language (SAML) to provide external authentication and single sign-on (SSO). Because this feature requires configuration, it is not enabled by default. SAML SSO should be implemented to ease the task of administering users and to provide consistent access controls for multiple applications.

The Use Cases for Single Sign-On

Leveraging SAML SSO also allows organizations to provide additional access controls for Meraki Dashboard:

- SSO prevents the sharing of accounts and helps to identify where administrator credentials may have been compromised by restricting concurrent logins to Meraki Dashboard per account.
- SSO ensures the level of access is still appropriate for admins by enforcing regular reviews. This could be done by automatically disabling administrator accounts after a specified period of time, unless they are revalidated.
- SSO ensures that administrator accounts that are no longer used are automatically disabled.
- SSO ensures that administrator accounts that are created for third parties, to provide temporary or emergency access, are automatically disabled when no longer needed. Typically, this would be after a specified period of elapsed time since creation (such as seven days).
- Managed service providers (MSPs) typically manage each customer as a separate organization and have common administrators across all customers. The easiest way for an MSP to have common administrators across multiple organizations is to use SAML-based single sign-on with a common SAML administrator role configured in each of the organizations.

SAML Single Sign-On Login Flow

The three key elements to SAML single sign-on are as follows:

- **User:** The client that is attempting to log in to a service provider.
- **Identity provider (IdP):** The authority on a user's identity. It knows the user's username, password, and any groups/attributes.
- **Service provider (SP):** The application that the user wishes to use—in this case, Meraki Dashboard.

Meraki Dashboard supports both IdP-initiated SAML and SP-initiated SAML. Both login types can be used simultaneously and are not mutually exclusive. Unless admin users only want to log in to Meraki Dashboard through their IdP's portal, then it's recommended to take the extra step to configure SP-initiated SAML. Using SP-initiated SAML will allow admin users to log directly in to Dashboard, while also supporting single sign-on with the Meraki mobile app. Figure 5-59 illustrates the IdP-initiated SAML login flow, and Figure 5-60 illustrates the SP-initiated SAML login flow.

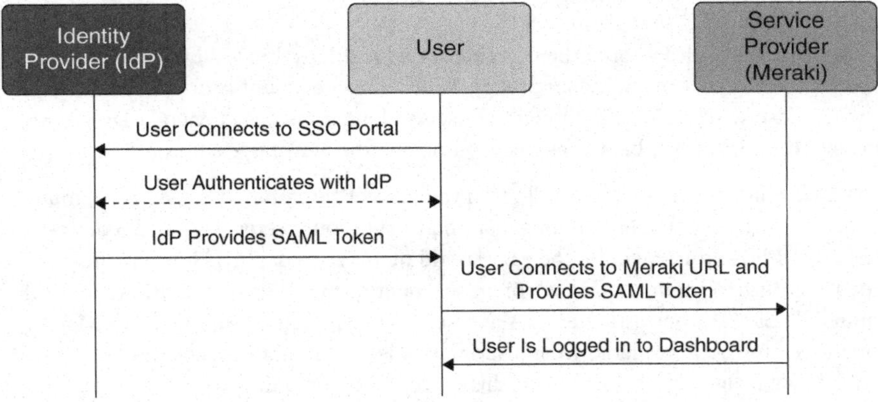

Figure 5-59 *Identity Provider-Initiated SAML Login Flow*

SAML Single Sign-On Design

SAML 2.0, which Meraki Dashboard supports, is a standard, so any product that supports it should work with Meraki Dashboard. The major differences between the various IdP and MFA solutions come down to

- How easy it is to integrate and get working
- How good the documentation is to support you
- The level of skills required and the availability of those skills
- The quality of that vendor's support
- Cost

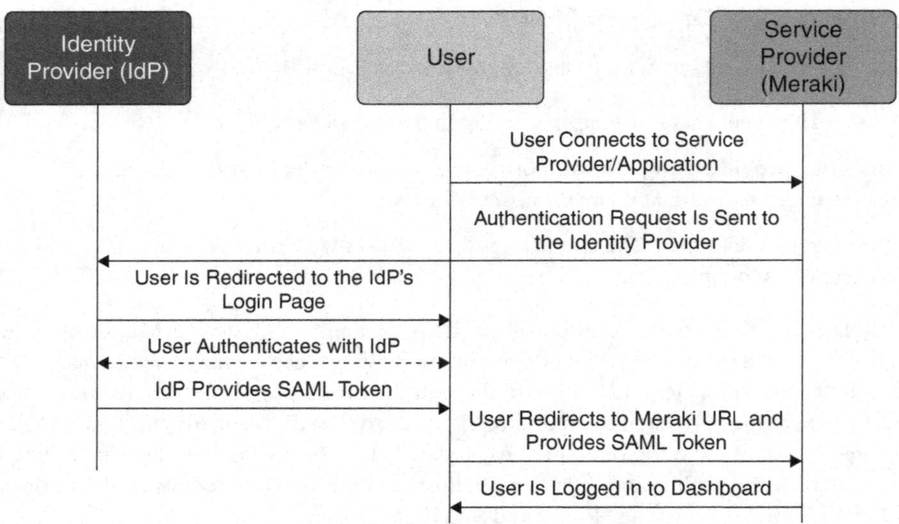

Figure 5-60 *Service Provider-Initiated SAML Login Flow*

Remember that the multifactor authentication for a local Meraki Dashboard administrator is configured as part of their user profile. When a user account is hosted externally, which is the case with SAML SSO, then the user no longer resides in Meraki Dashboard. This means that MFA must be a consideration of your SAML single sign-on design.

As you will see in the sections that follow, in the case of SP-initiated SAML SSO, multiple functions can be consolidated or separated to suit your preferences and requirements. A cloud-hosted IdP will be the easiest and quickest to deploy. However, for advanced security requirements, an on-premises identity management solution may still be required. Table 5-1 contrasts the MFA and security capabilities supported in Meraki Dashboard versus those available when used with Cisco Duo enterprise MFA and a third-party identity management solution—in this case, Microsoft Entra ID.

Table 5-1 *The Available Administrator Access Controls with Different Authentication Solutions*

	Meraki Dashboard (Native)	**Cisco Duo with Microsoft Entra ID (Formerly Azure AD)**
Solution		
Service Provider	Meraki Dashboard	Meraki Dashboard
Identity Provider	—	Cisco Duo
MFA Provider	SMS/Cisco Duo	Cisco Duo
Identity Management	Meraki Dashboard	Microsoft Entra ID
Type of MFA	Time-based one-time password (TOTP) via Cisco Duo app	Enterprise MFA with group policies

	Meraki Dashboard (Native)	**Cisco Duo with Microsoft Entra ID (Formerly Azure AD)**
Solution		
Benefits	Fast, simple, inexpensive	Inline enrollment with Duo, automatic user sync between Duo and Entra, more advanced controls
Number of steps to configure	Low (~40)	High (~100)
Level of difficulty	Easy	Medium
Password Policies		
Password age	Yes, configurable	Yes, configurable (via PowerShell)
Password reuse	Yes, configurable	Yes, most recent password can't be reused by default. For greater restrictions an on-premises Active Directory is required.
Password complexity	Yes, minimum password length limit of eight characters	Yes, minimum password length limit of eight characters. For greater restrictions an on-premises Active Directory is required.
Account lockout after invalid login attempts	Yes, configurable	Yes, configurable with automatic unlock
Security Policies		
IP whitelisting	Yes	Yes, via Duo. Geoblocking also supported
Restrictions on concurrent logins	No	Not natively. Possible via integration with on-premises Active Directory and third-party software or scripting.
Automatically disable inactive accounts	No	Yes, via access reviews
Automatically disable accounts after predetermined period of time unless revalidated	No	Yes, via access reviews
Automatically disable temporary accounts (could be time-based, usage-based, and so on)	No	Yes, via access reviews

It is common for users to not always act as they are supposed to, for temporary changes to remain in place, and for regular reviews to be put off or forgotten. The preceding capability requirements originate from NIST 800-53 and provide worthwhile additional controls targeting this human element. These capabilities are especially applicable to IT environments where access is provided on a need-to-know basis. Using system-enforced controls provides assurances that processes are functioning as they're supposed to.

Configuring Meraki SAML SSO Using Cisco Duo and Microsoft Entra ID

Logging in to Meraki Dashboard with single sign-on and enterprise MFA is recommended for all organizations. Setting this up from scratch for the first time can be quite daunting for network engineers. One of the factors that makes it hard is the fact that the configuration steps are not contained within a single configuration guide. To make this task as easy as possible, this section guides you through all the setup steps from start to finish, including those not covered in the configuration guides, such as creating users and groups in MS Entra ID and enrolling with Cisco Duo, as well as the verification steps.

Quite a number of steps are required for the initial setup of this integration. The high-level tasks are summarized in the list that follows. If you'd like to complete this setup in stages, the steps required are grouped under these headings throughout the remainder of this chapter.

1. Prerequisites:
    a. If you're not already a Microsoft Entra customer, you need to set up an account at https://www.microsoft.com/en-us/security/business/microsoft-entra-pricing. We used Microsoft Entra ID P2 for the following steps. The Microsoft Entra Governance add-on is required for some use cases, such as the automatic disabling of inactive users. Speak to your Microsoft specialist to determine the best tier for your requirements.
    b. Configure user(s) and group(s) in Microsoft Entra ID:
        i. Create an account for the directory sync between Cisco Duo and Microsoft Entra ID.
        ii. Configure a group for the Meraki Dashboard administrators in Microsoft Entra ID.
        iii. Configure at least one user and assign them to the Meraki Dashboard administrators group in Microsoft Entra ID.
    c. Configure directory sync between Cisco Duo and Microsoft Entra ID.
    d. Recommended: Reduce the administrative privileges on the directory sync account after initial sync.
    e. Configure SAML SSO between Cisco Duo and Microsoft Entra.
2. Configure IdP-initiated SAML SSO between Cisco Duo and Meraki Dashboard.

3. Take the additional steps to enable SP-initiated SAML SSO between Cisco Duo and Meraki Dashboard.

4. Verify that administrators can log in using SAML SSO.

Prerequisites

The following tasks are required before integrating Cisco Duo and Meraki Dashboard. If you are already using Cisco Duo with Microsoft Entra ID to authenticate to other applications, skip ahead to "Configuring IdP-Initiated SAML SSO between Cisco Duo and Meraki Dashboard."

Configuring the Users and Groups in Microsoft Entra ID

Step 1. Log in to Microsoft Entra admin center as an administrator user (https://entra.microsoft.com/#home), as illustrated in Figure 5-61.

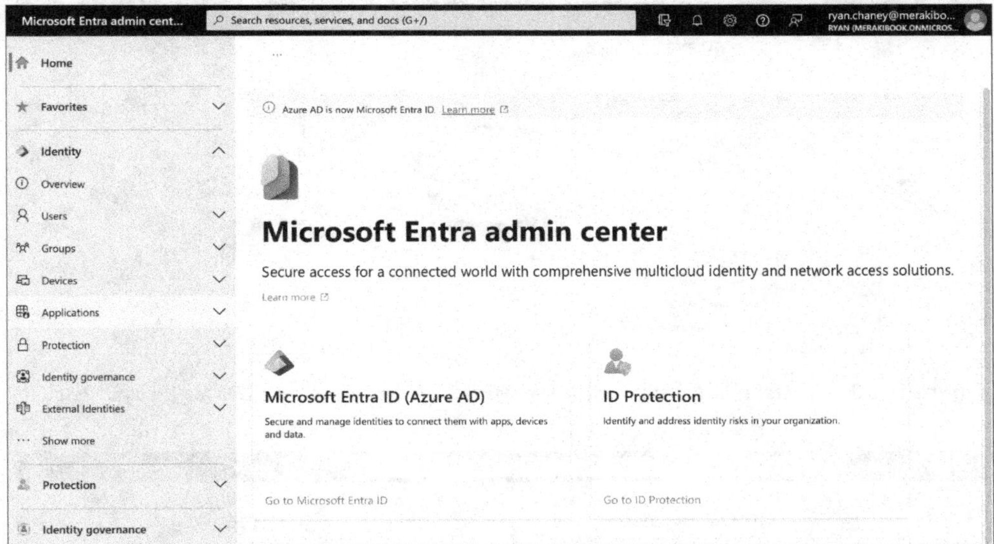

Figure 5-61 *Home Page of Microsoft Entra Admin Center*

Step 2. Click **Go to Microsoft Entra ID.**

Step 3. Navigate to **Users** > **All Users**, as illustrated in Figure 5-62.

Step 4. Create a user with the Global Administrator role for the directory sync with Cisco Duo. To start, click **+ New User**, as illustrated in Figure 5-63.

Step 5. Enter a **User Principal Name** (username) and a meaningful **Display Name.** You can choose your own values or use the values shown in Figure 5-64.

Uncheck the box for **Auto-Generate Password** and then enter a password for this user. Click **Next: Properties.**

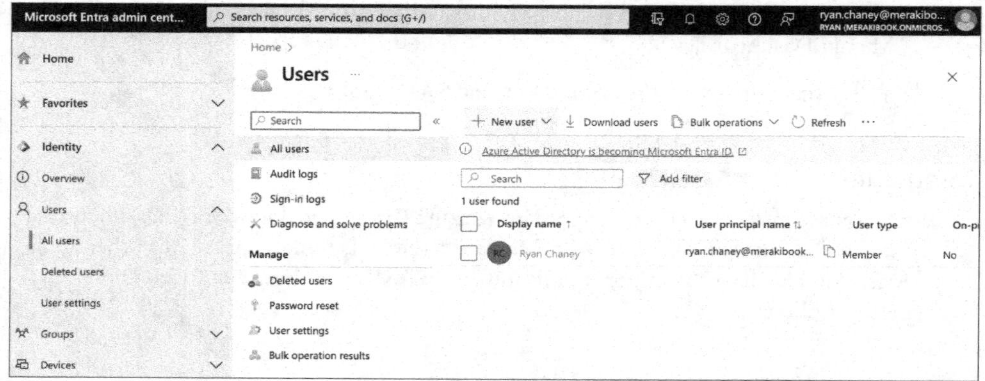

Figure 5-62 *Microsoft Entra Admin Center's Users Page*

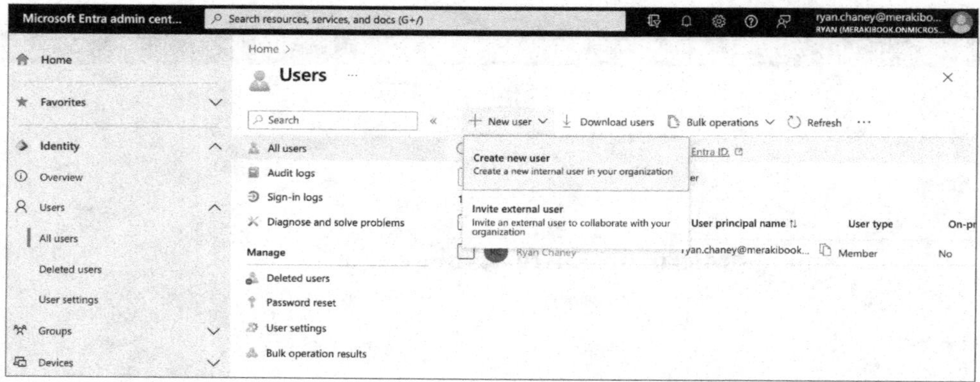

Figure 5-63 *Creating a New User on the Microsoft Entra Admin Center's Users Page*

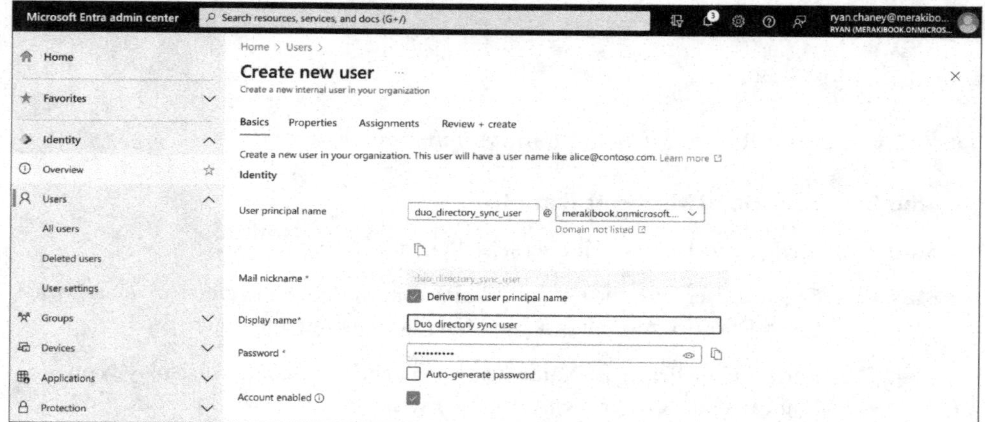

Figure 5-64 *Entering New User Basics on the Microsoft Entra Admin Center's Create New User Page*

Step 6. Click **Next: Assignments** from the screen illustrated in Figure 5-65.

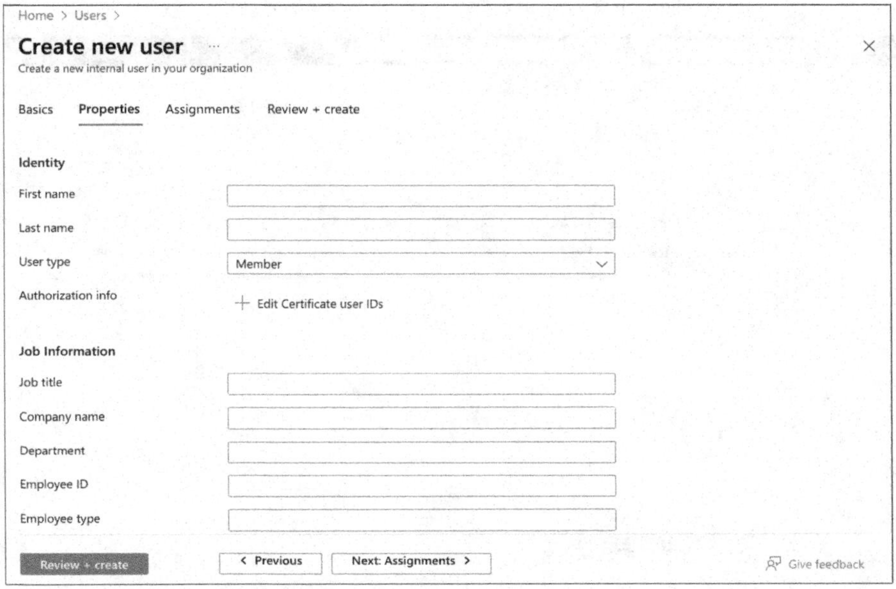

Home > Users >

Create new user ...

Create a new internal user in your organization

Basics **Properties** Assignments Review + create

Identity

First name

Last name

User type: Member

Authorization info: + Edit Certificate user IDs

Job Information

Job title

Company name

Department

Employee ID

Employee type

Review + create | < Previous | Next: Assignments > | Give feedback

Figure 5-65 *Entering New User Properties on the Create New User Page*

Step 7. Click **Add Role** from the screen shown in Figure 5-66.

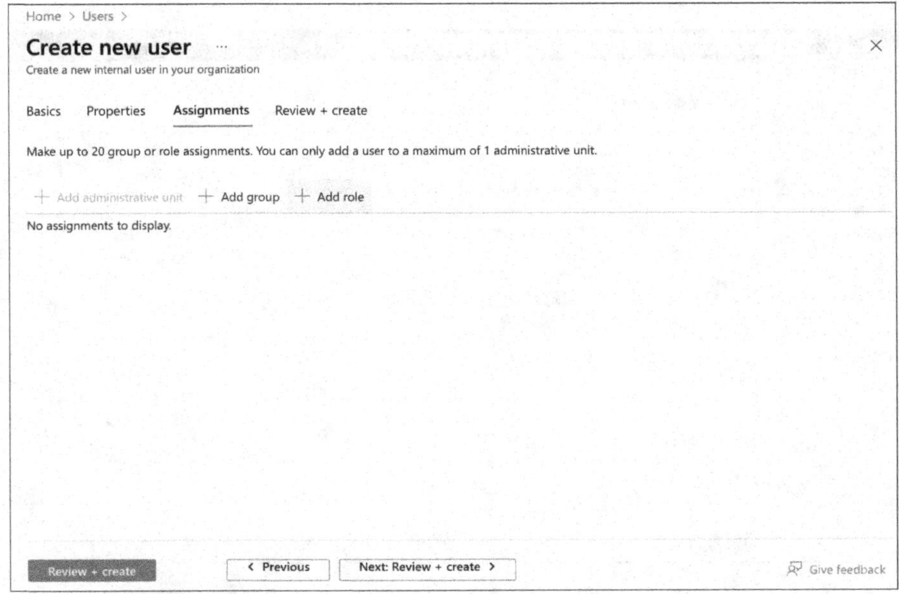

Figure 5-66 *Entering New User Assignments on the Create New User Page*

Step 8. In the search field, enter **global.** Check the box before **Global Administrator** and then click **Select** at the bottom of this panel, as illustrated in Figure 5-67.

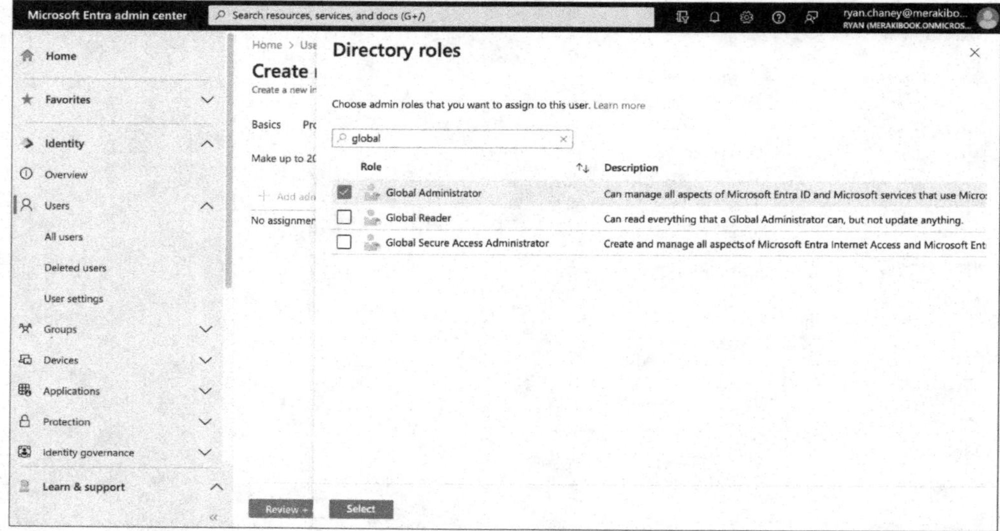

Figure 5-67 *Assigning a Role to a New User During the Create New User Process*

Step 9. You should now be back on the **Assignments** tab of the **Create New User** page with the Global Administrator role showing, as illustrated in Figure 5-68. Click **Next: Review + Create.**

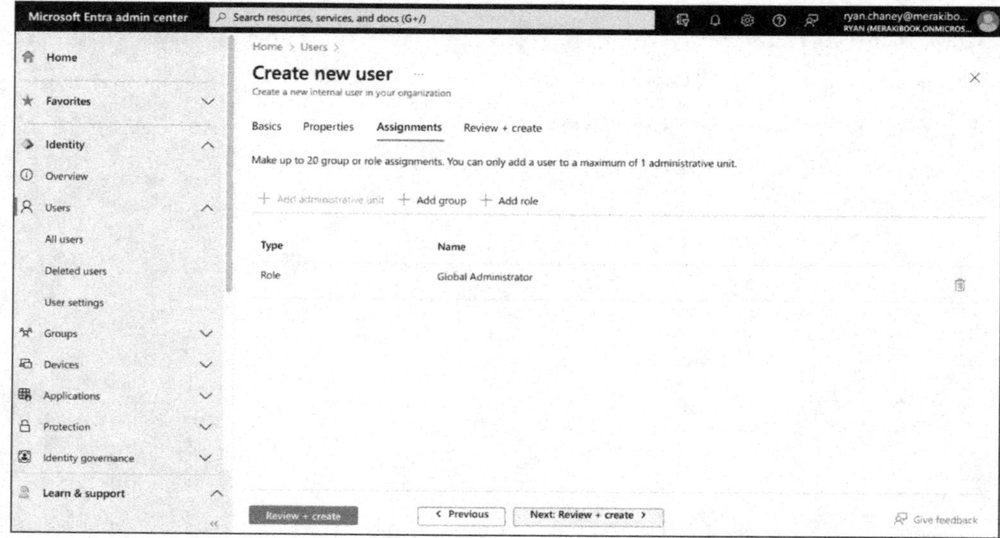

Figure 5-68 *Assignments Tab on the Create New User Page in the Microsoft Entra Admin Center*

Step 10. From the screen in Figure 5-69, click **Create** to finish creating the new user.

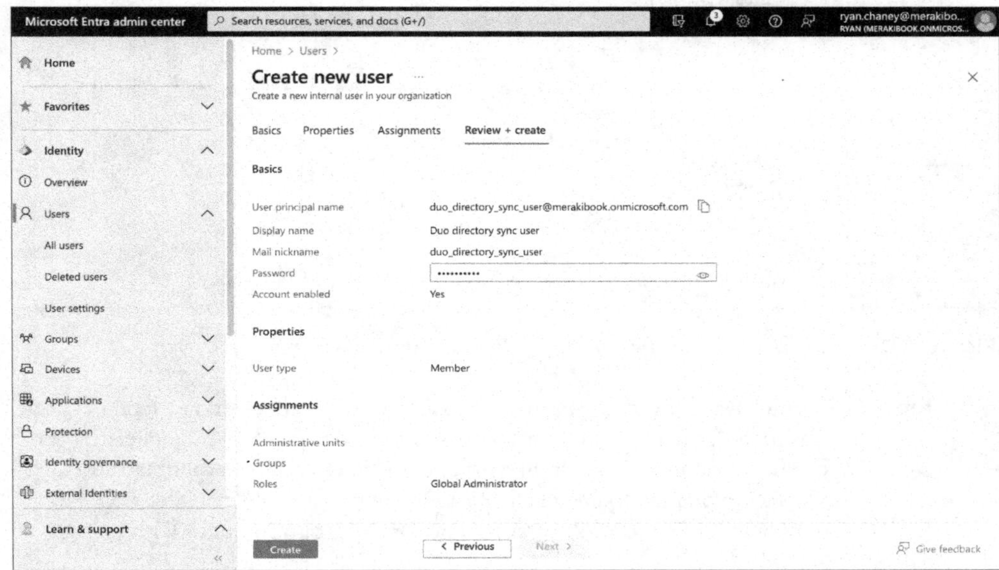

Figure 5-69 *Review + Create Tab on the Create New User Page in the Microsoft Entra Admin Center*

Step 11. Wait 30 seconds and click **Refresh** to refresh the Users page. You should see the newly created user listed, as illustrated in Figure 5-70.

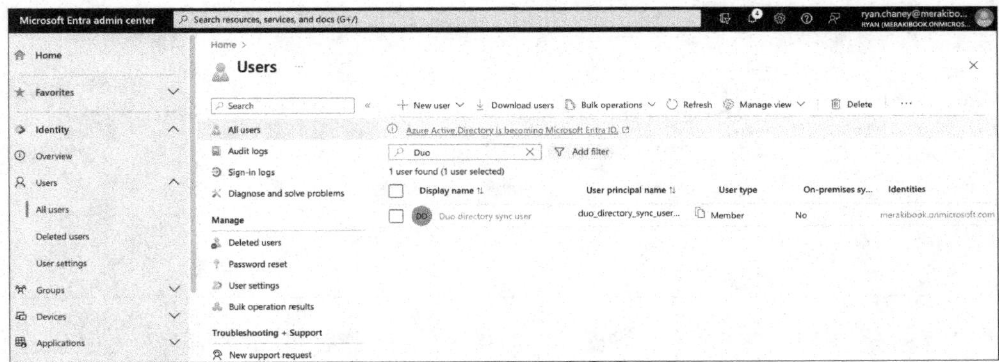

Figure 5-70 *Users Page in the Microsoft Entra Admin Center After Creating a Global Admin User*

Step 12. Next, you need to create a group for the Meraki administrators. Navigate to **Groups > All Groups** and then click **New Group**, as illustrated in Figure 5-71.

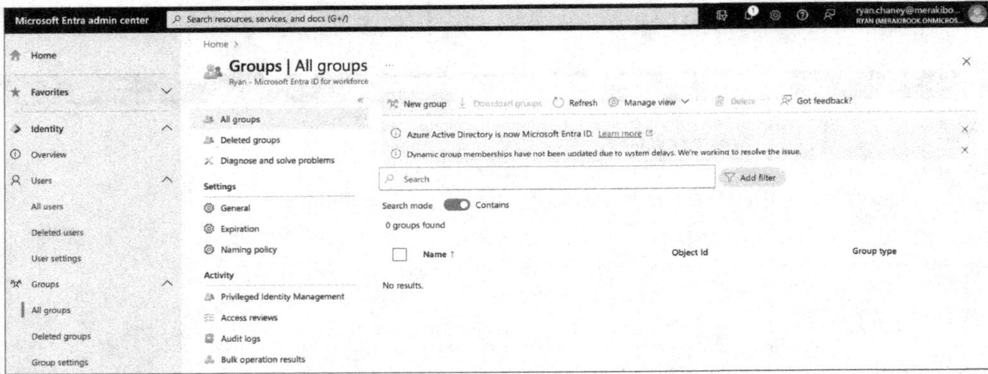

Figure 5-71 *Groups Page in the Microsoft Entra Admin Center*

Step 13. If you have an existing SAML administrator role configured in Meraki Dashboard, then this group must have the same name. SAML administrators can be found in Meraki Dashboard under **Organization > Administrators.** We show you how to create an SAML administrator role in a later step. From the screen in Figure 5-72, enter a name for the group and click **Create.**

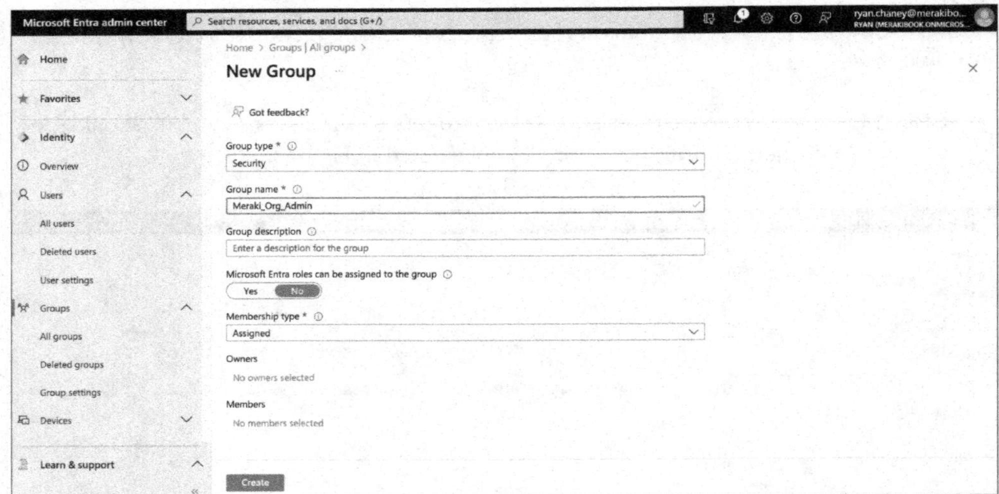

Figure 5-72 *Entering a Group Name on the New Group Page in the Microsoft Entra Admin Center*

Step 14. Next, you need to create your first Meraki Dashboard administrator user who will be a member of the group created in the previous step. From the menu on the left, navigate to the Users page by clicking **Identity > Users > All Users.**

Click **Create New User** from the **New User** drop-down menu, as illustrated in Figure 5-73.

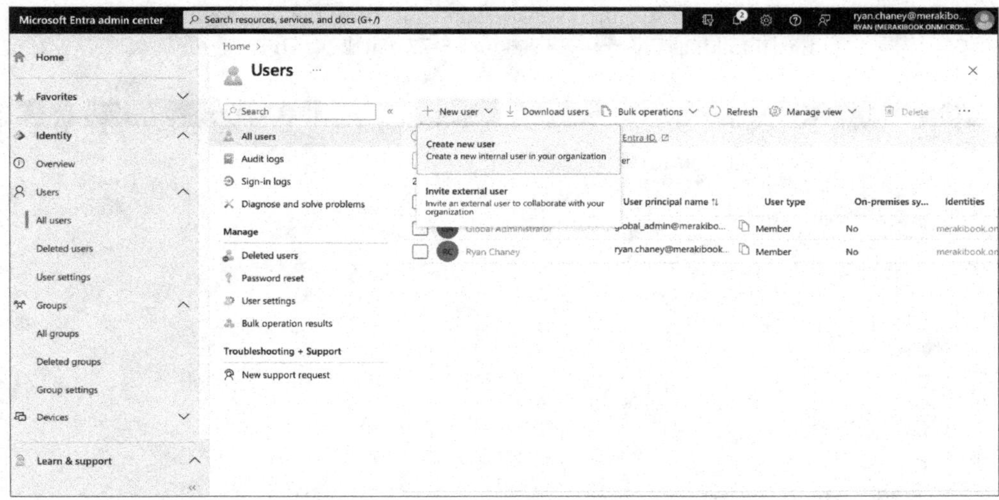

Figure 5-73 *Creating a Meraki Dashboard Admin User in the Microsoft Entra Admin Center*

Step 15. From the screen in Figure 5-74, enter a **User Principal Name** (username) and a meaningful **Display Name.**

Uncheck the box before **Auto-Generate Password** and then enter a **Password** for this user. Click **Next: Properties.**

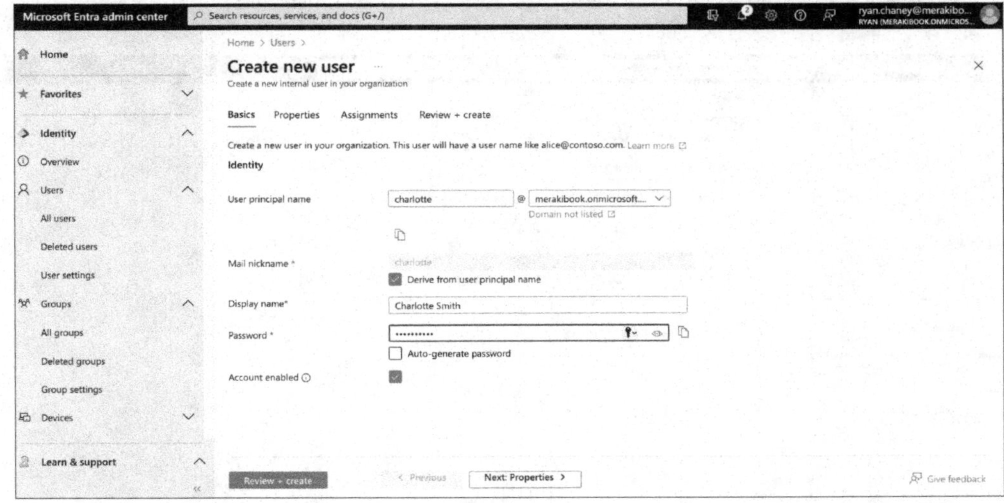

Figure 5-74 *Entering User Basics for a Meraki Dashboard Admin User on the Create New User Page*

Step 16. Scroll down to **Contact Information** and enter the user's email address in the **Email** field, as illustrated in Figure 5-75. Click **Next: Assignments.**

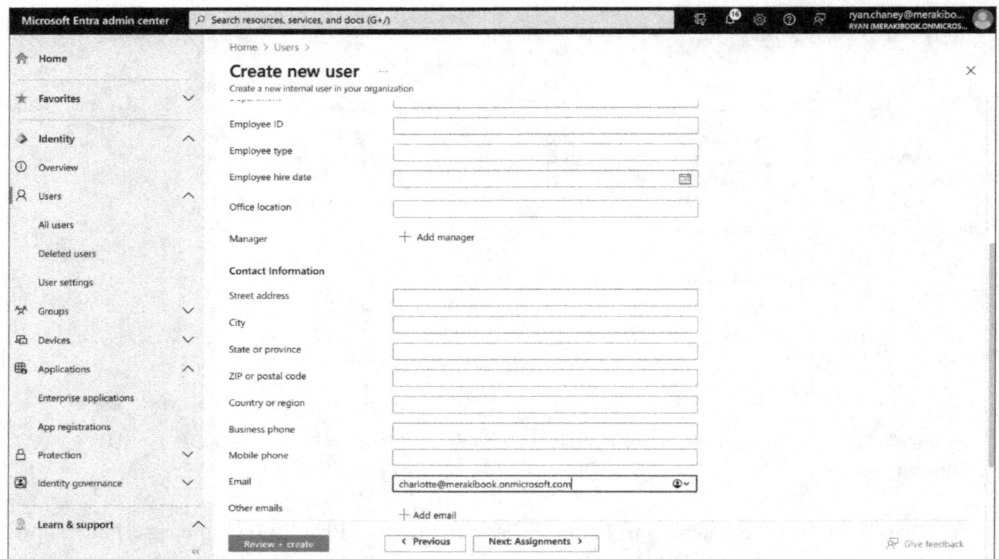

Figure 5-75 *Entering an Email Address for a Meraki Dashboard Admin User on the Create New User Page*

Step 17. On the Assignments tab, click **Add Group**, as illustrated in Figure 5-76.

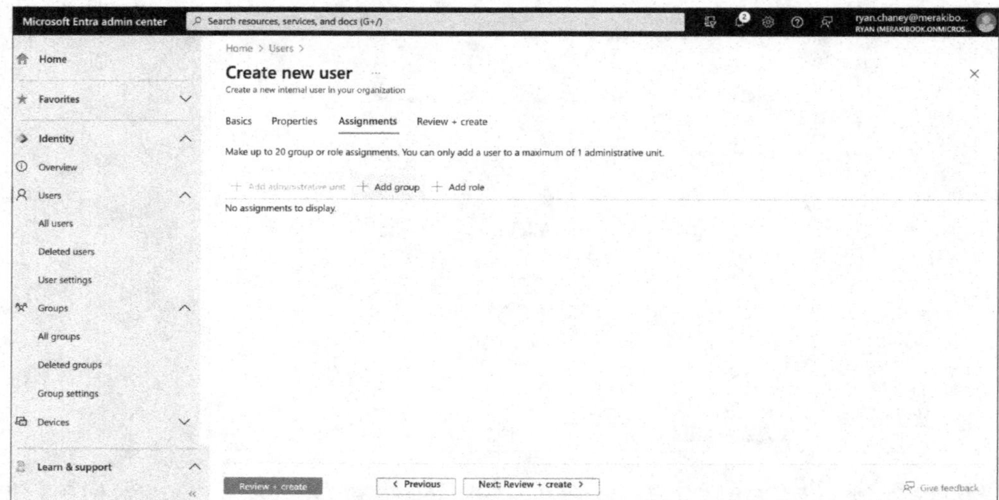

Figure 5-76 *Assigning a Group to a Meraki Dashboard Admin User on the Create New User Page*

Step 18. Check the box next to the group for the Meraki Dashboard admins (for this example, it is Meraki_Org_Admin) and click **Select**, as illustrated in Figure 5-77.

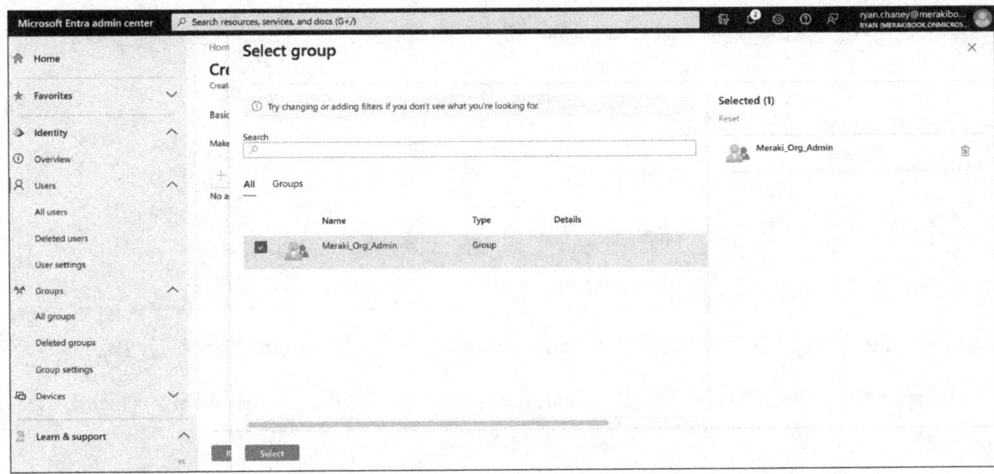

Figure 5-77 *Adding the Group for Meraki Dashboard Admins on the Create New User Page*

Step 19. On the **Assignments** tab shown in Figure 5-78, click **Next: Review + Create.**

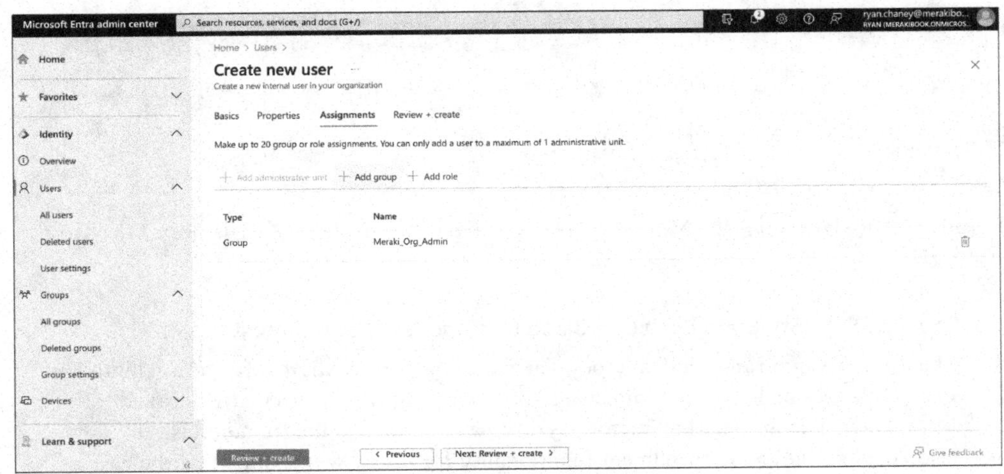

Figure 5-78 *Reviewing the Meraki Org Admin Group Assignment on the Create New User Page*

Step 20. On the **Review + Create** tab, click **Create** to finish, as illustrated in Figure 5-79.

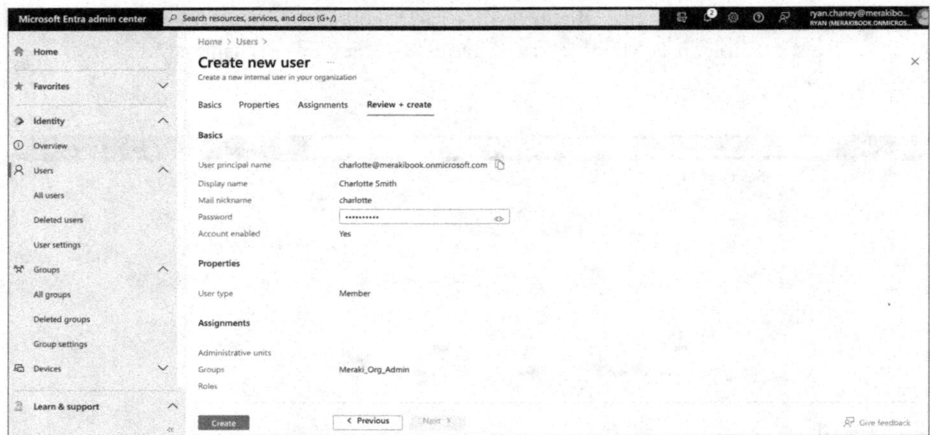

Figure 5-79 *Reviewing the New Meraki Admin User on the Create New User Page*

Step 21. Wait 30 seconds and refresh the page. You should see the new user listed, as illustrated in Figure 5-80.

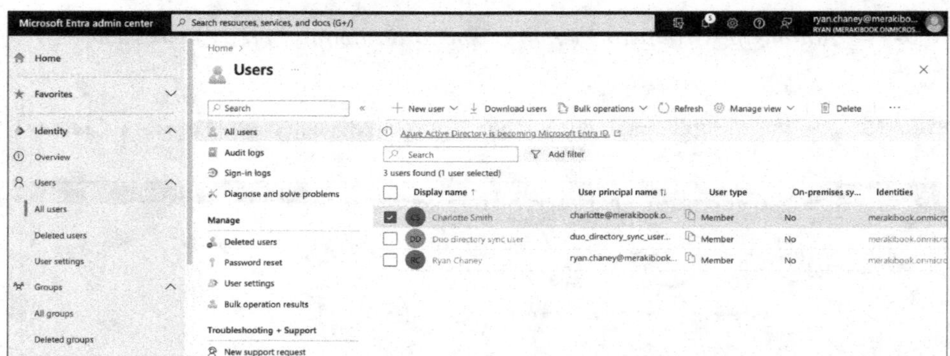

Figure 5-80 *Verifying the New Meraki Dashboard Admin User Addition in Microsoft Entra ID*

Configuring Directory Sync Between Cisco Duo and Microsoft Entra ID

The directory sync automatically populates the users from Microsoft Entra ID into Cisco Duo. Duo uses its local user database to keep track of which users have enrolled for MFA. Having an automatic directory sync greatly simplifies life for administrators, while also enabling the inline enrollment functionality for users. We demonstrate the ease of inline enrollment later in this chapter.

Follow these steps to configure directory sync between Cisco Duo and Microsoft Entra ID:

Step 1. Log in to the Cisco Duo Admin Panel (https://admin.duosecurity.com/login).

Step 2. Navigate to **Users > Directory Sync**. From the **Add New Sync** drop-down menu, click **Azure AD**, as illustrated in Figure 5-81.

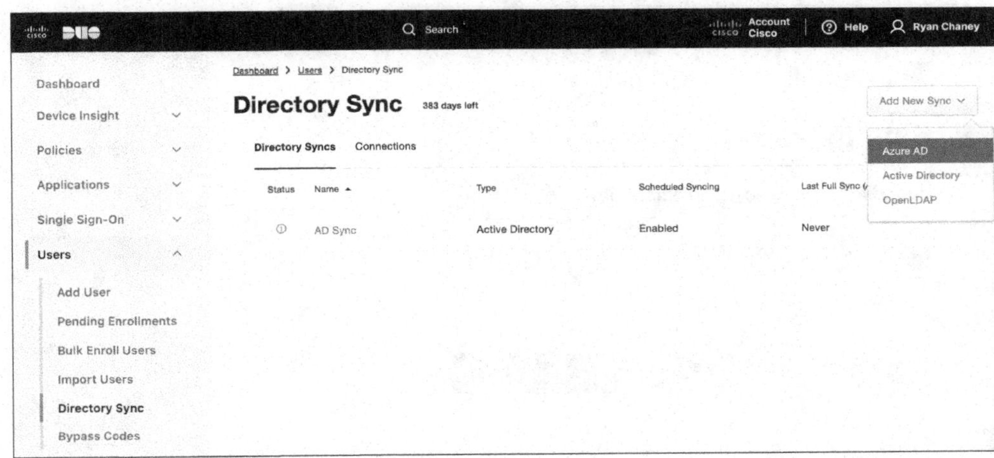

Figure 5-81 *Adding Directory Sync for Microsoft Entra ID in the Cisco Duo Admin Panel*

Step 3. From the screen in Figure 5-82, select **Add New Connection** and click **Continue.**

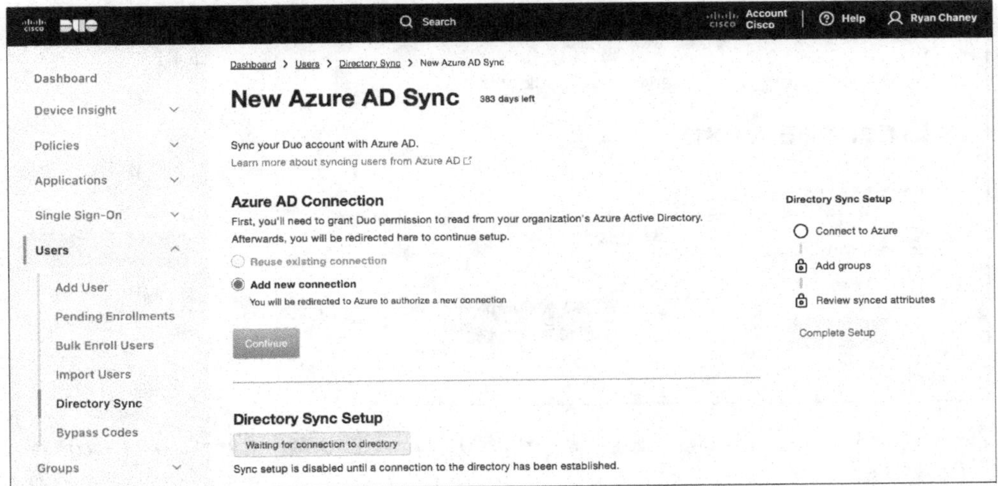

Figure 5-82 *New Directory Sync Page for Microsoft Entra ID in the Cisco Duo Admin Panel*

Step 4. On the screen in Figure 5-83, enter the username for the account with the Global Administrator role created earlier and click **Next.** You may be asked to pick the username from a list if you have signed in previously.

Step 5. From the screen in Figure 5-84, enter the password for this account and click **Sign In.** After this step, you might need to reset the password for this user. Do this so that you can proceed to the next step.

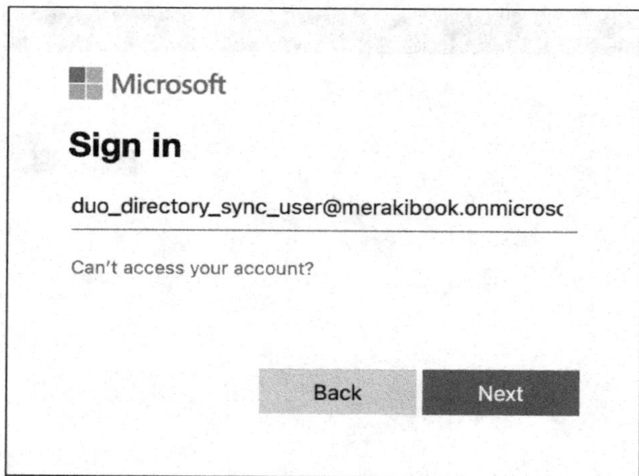

Figure 5-83 *The Username Login Page as Part of MS Entra Directory Sync in the Cisco Duo Admin Panel*

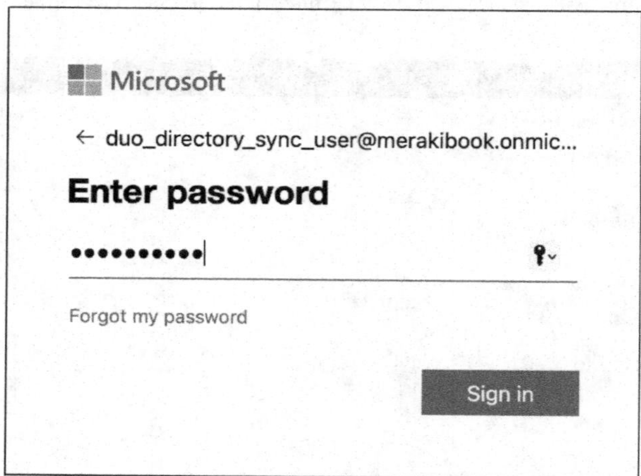

Figure 5-84 *Password Login Page as Part of MS Entra Directory Sync in the Cisco Duo Admin Panel*

Step 6. On the **Permissions Requested** page, click **Accept** to allow Duo to sync with Microsoft Entra, as illustrated in Figure 5-85.

Step 7. You will return to this page. Note the **Connect to Azure** button has a checkmark and the status under **Azure AD Connection** is **Connected.** For clarity, rename the directory sync by clicking **Rename** at the top of the page and then click **Save.** In the screenshot in Figure 5-86, we've renamed ours **Microsoft Entra.**

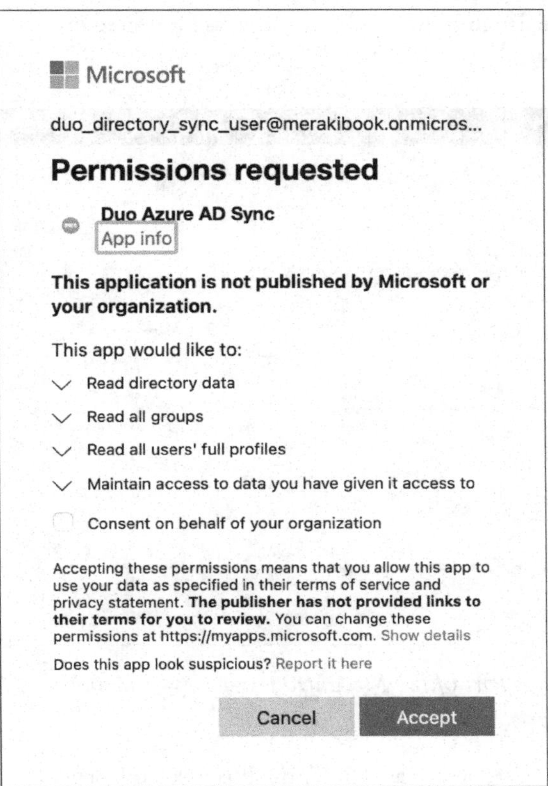

Figure 5-85 *Permissions Requested Page as Part of MS Entra Directory Sync in the Cisco Duo Admin Panel*

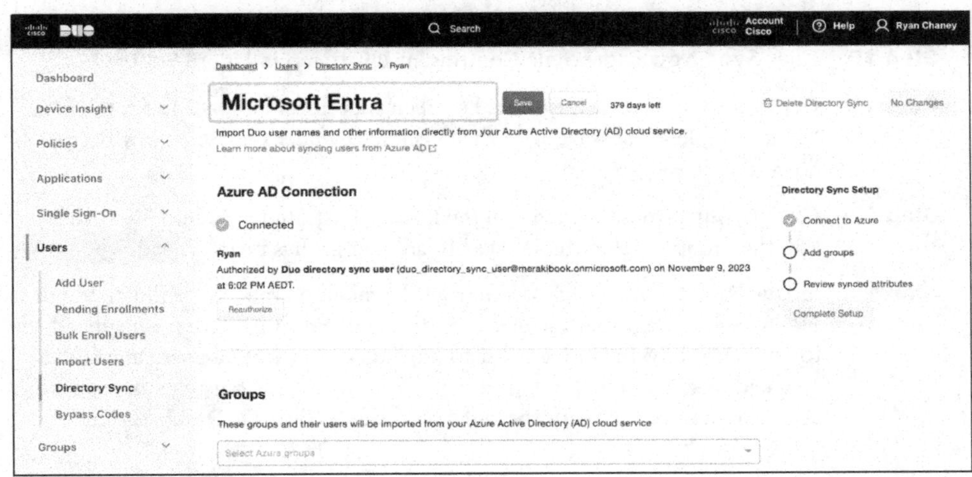

Figure 5-86 *Microsoft Entra Directory Sync After Renaming in the Cisco Duo Admin Panel*

Step 8. Select your Meraki admin group from the **Groups** box, as illustrated in Figure 5-87.

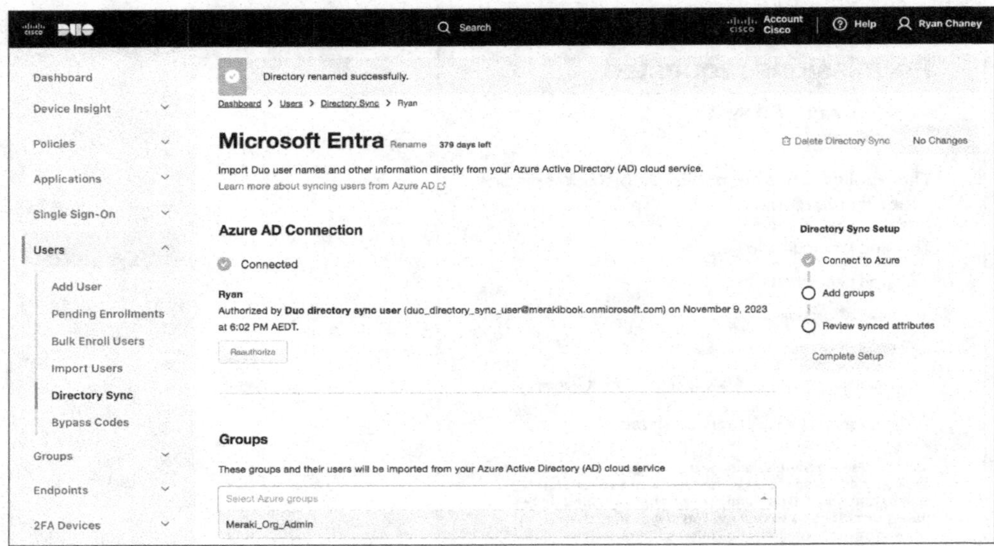

Figure 5-87 *Selecting Groups to Sync as Part of the MS Entra Directory Sync in the Cisco Duo Admin Panel*

Step 9. Scroll down to **Normalize Usernames** and check the box next to **Normalize Usernames Before Importing Them**, as illustrated in Figure 5-88. If you miss this step, the Duo user enrollment will fail.

Scroll down to the **Email** * text field and enter **userPrincipalName.** Next, click **Save** and then click **Complete Setup.**

Step 10. Click **Sync Now** under Sync Controls, as illustrated in Figure 5-89.

Step 11. Confirm that the directory sync has been successful by looking for the "Sync complete" message with the checkmark under the **Sync Now** button, as illustrated in Figure 5-90.

Step 12. Click **Groups** from the menu on the left, as illustrated in Figure 5-91. Verify that the group for the Meraki Dashboard admins has been synced.

Step 13. In Duo Admin Panel, click **Users** from the menu on the left, as illustrated in Figure 5-92. Verify that the users in Microsoft Entra ID have been synced to Duo correctly. In Duo, each account should have both a username and an email address, as shown in Figure 5-92. You should see only the username in the Username column, not the full email address. Meraki Dashboard maps the username field from the login page to the email address in Duo; therefore, without an email address for the Duo user account the admin user won't be able to log in.

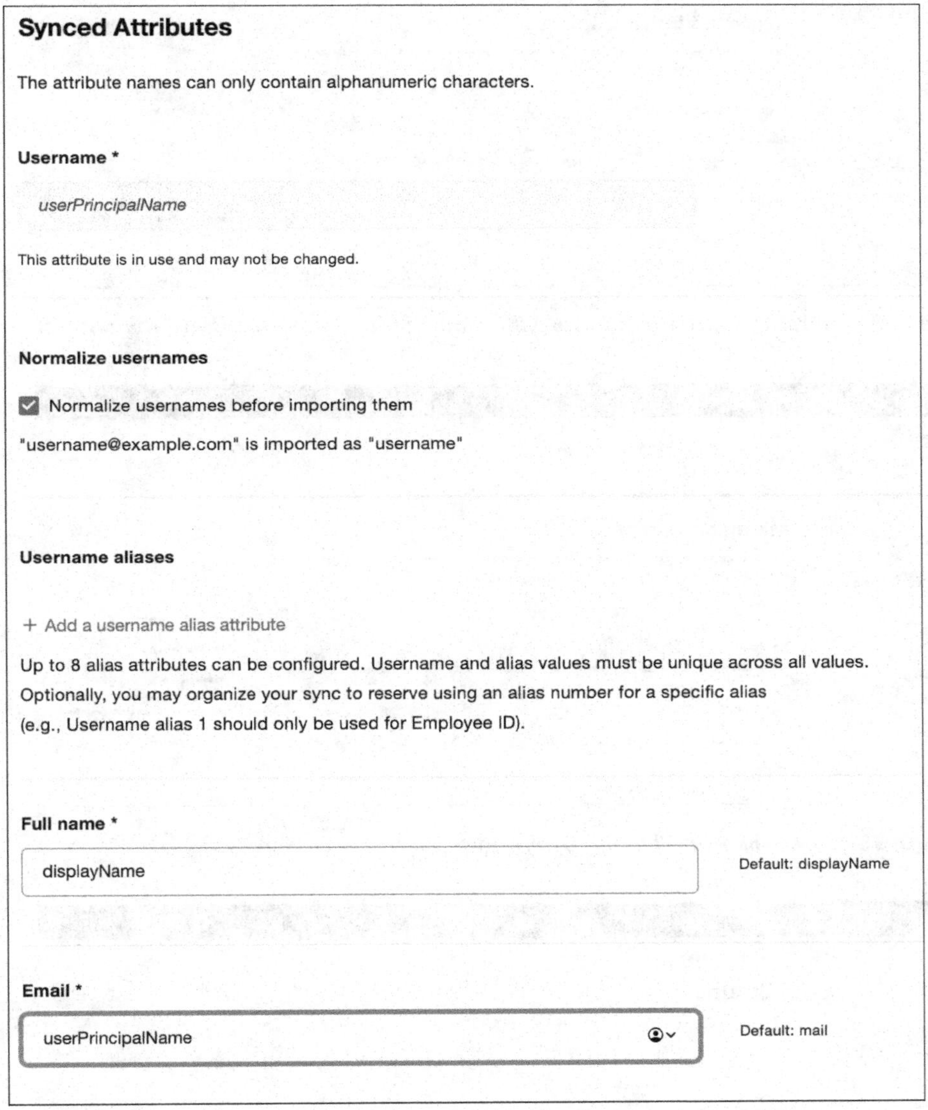

Synced Attributes
The attribute names can only contain alphanumeric characters.
Username *
userPrincipalName
This attribute is in use and may not be changed.
Normalize usernames
Normalize usernames before importing them
"username@example.com" is imported as "username"
Username aliases
+ Add a username alias attribute
Up to 8 alias attributes can be configured. Username and alias values must be unique across all values.
Optionally, you may organize your sync to reserve using an alias number for a specific alias
(e.g., Username alias 1 should only be used for Employee ID).
Full name *
displayName
Default: displayName
Email *
userPrincipalName
Default: mail

Figure 5-88 *Selecting Normalize Usernames as Part of the MS Directory Sync Setup in the Cisco Duo Admin Panel*

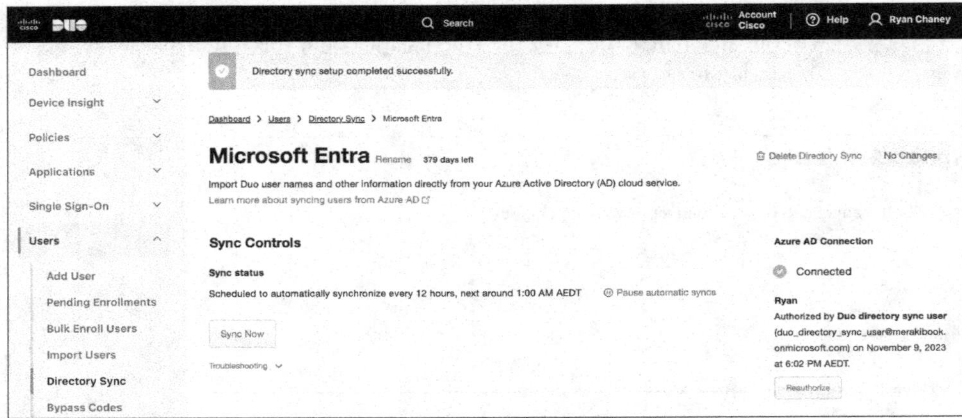

Figure 5-89 *First Directory Sync with Microsoft Entra in the Cisco Duo Admin Panel*

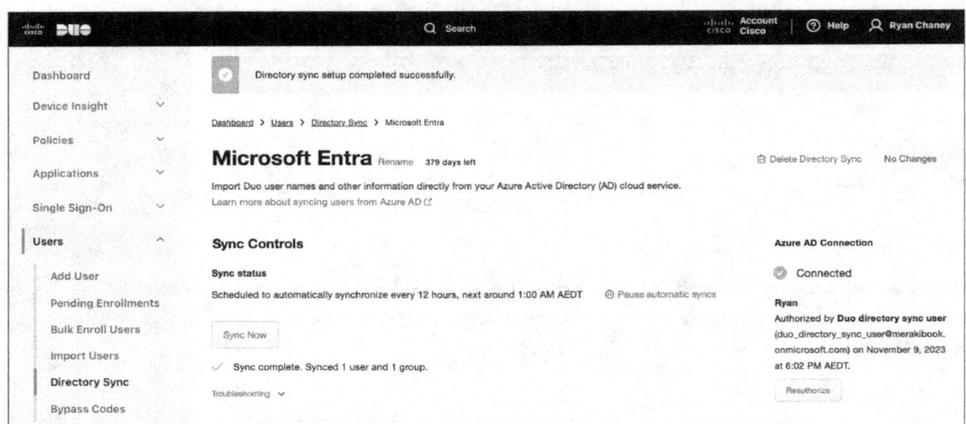

Figure 5-90 *Confirmation That the Directory Sync Has Been Successful*

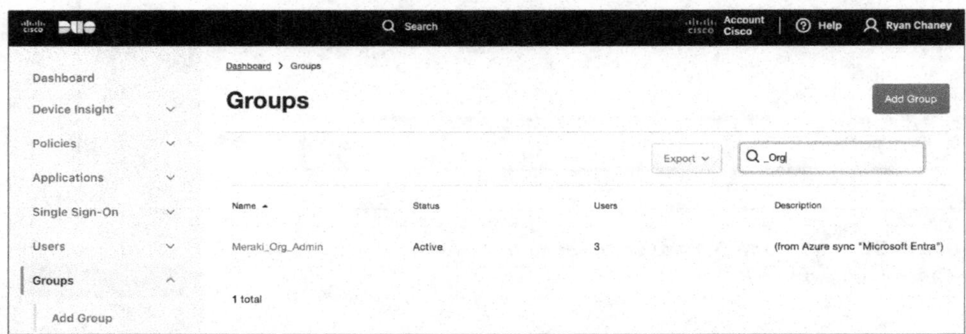

Figure 5-91 *Verifying That the Groups Have Been Imported Correctly from MS Entra to Cisco Duo*

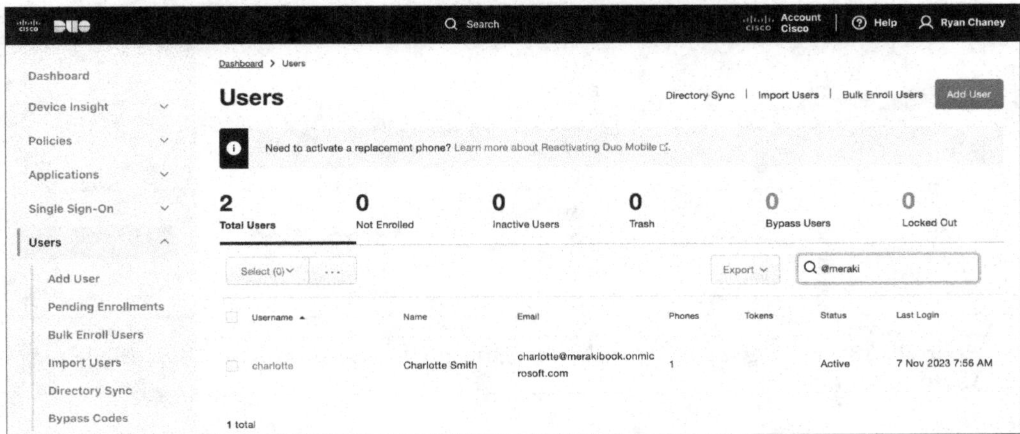

Figure 5-92 *Verifying That Users Have Been Imported Correctly from MS Entra to Cisco Duo*

> **Note** If you run into trouble with this section, Cisco Duo has published a detailed guide on setting up and troubleshooting user sync with Microsoft Entra ID (formerly Azure AD) at https://duo.com/docs/azuresync#overview.

Recommended: Reducing the Administrative Privileges on the Directory Sync Account After Initial Sync

The Global Administrator role is only required for authorization (and reauthorization). The Global Reader role, which is a read-only role, is sufficient the rest of the time. In line with the principle of least privileged access, it is recommended to change the Microsoft Entra account used for directory sync to the lesser Global Reader role after the first sync has been completed successfully.

Follow these steps to change the role on the Duo directory sync account:

Step 1. In the Microsoft Entra admin center, navigate to **Identity > Users > All Users.** From the screen shown in Figure 5-93, click the display name for the account used for syncing with Duo.

Step 2. Click **Assigned Roles** and then **+ Add Assignments** from the screen shown in Figure 5-94.

Step 3. Click **Search Role** and enter **global** in the **Search Role by Name** field. From the screen in Figure 5-95, select **Global Reader** and then click **Next.**

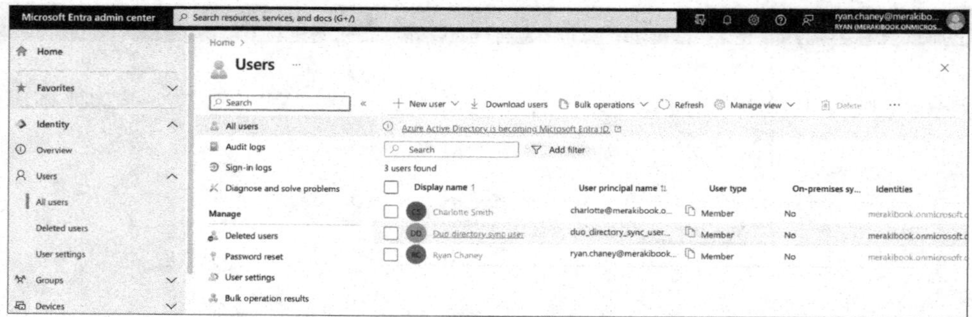

Figure 5-93 *Editing the Role for the Duo Directory Sync User on the Users Page in Microsoft Entra*

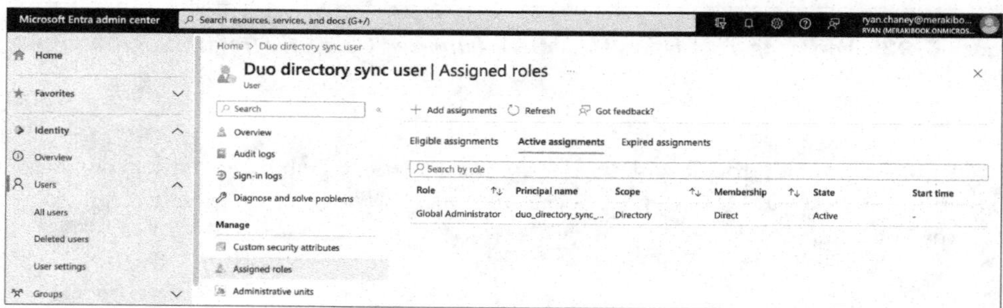

Figure 5-94 *Viewing the Assigned Roles for the Duo Directory Sync User in Microsoft Entra*

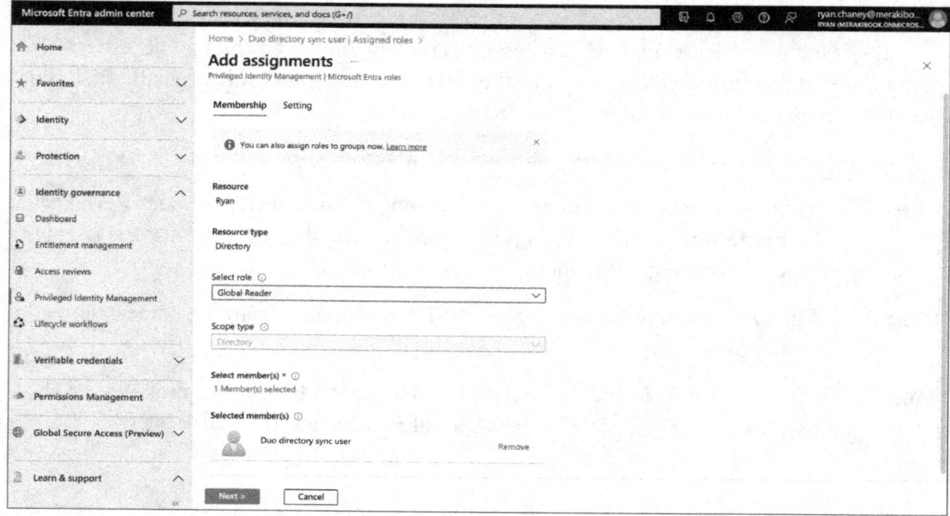

Figure 5-95 *Assigning the Global Reader Role to the Duo Directory Sync User in Microsoft Entra*

Step 4. On the **Add Assignments** page, under **Assignment Type**, select **Active.** From the screen in Figure 5-96, enter some text in the **Enter Justification** text box and then click **Assign.**

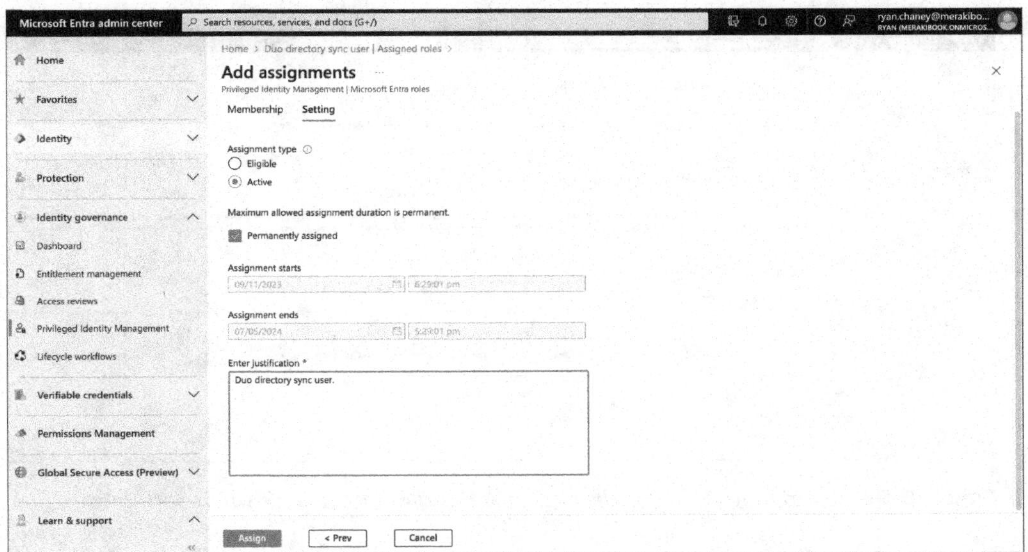

Figure 5-96 *Activating the Global Reader Role on the Duo Directory Sync User in Microsoft Entra*

Step 5. Wait 30 seconds and then click **Refresh** to refresh the **Assigned Roles** page. You should see both Global Administrator and Global Reader listed, as illustrated in Figure 5-97.

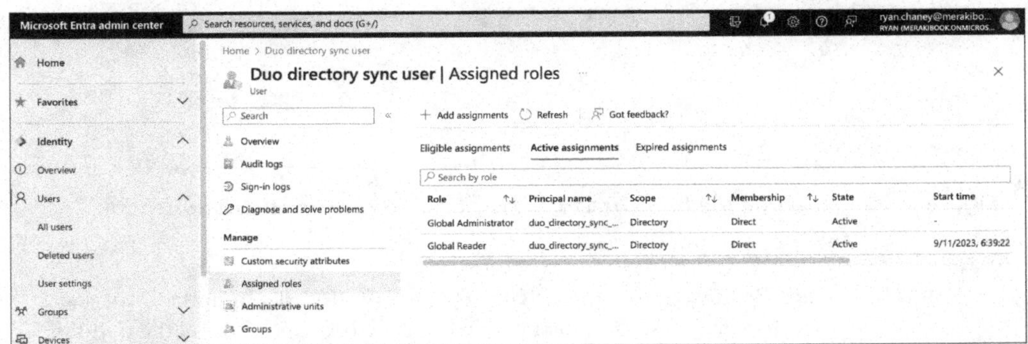

Figure 5-97 *Confirming the New Role Has Been Assigned to the Duo Directory Sync User*

Step 6. Navigate to **Roles & Admins > Roles & Admins.** In the **Search by Name or Description** field, search for **global**, as illustrated in Figure 5-98.

Click the number in the **Assignments** column for the Global Administrator role.

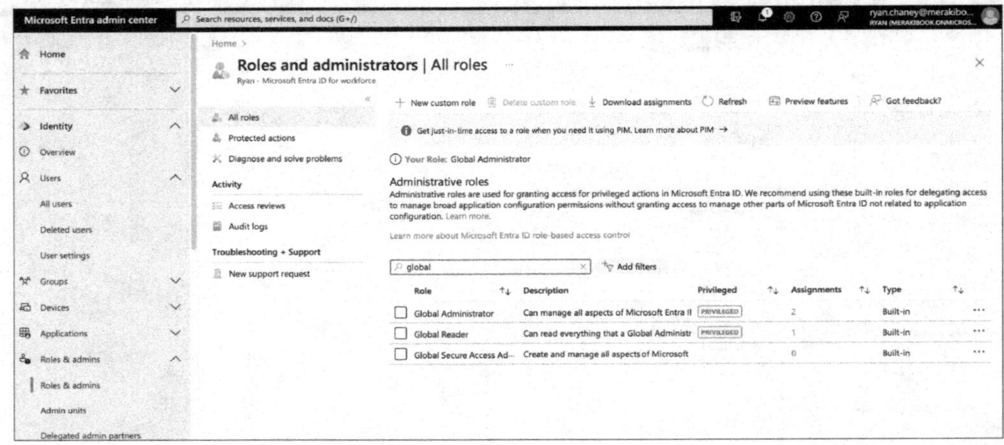

Figure 5-98 *Searching Roles for the Global Administrator Role in Microsoft Entra*

Step 7. Click the Duo directory sync user on the **Active Assignments** tab, as illustrated in Figure 5-99.

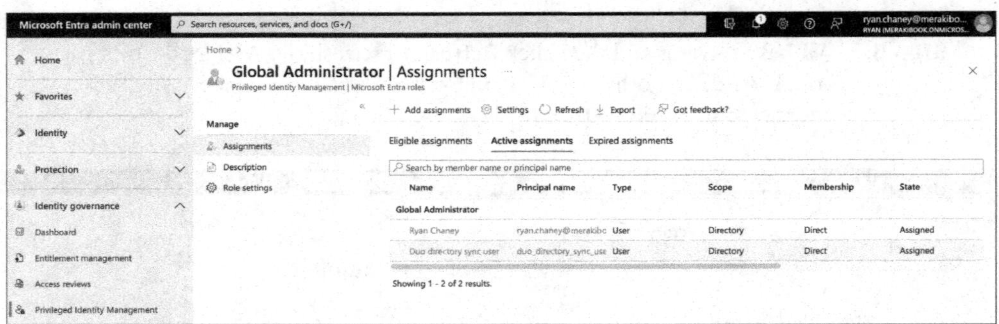

Figure 5-99 *Selecting the Duo Directory Sync User on the Global Administrator Assignments Page*

Step 8. Click **Remove** to remove the Global Administrator role from the Duo directory sync user, as illustrated in Figure 5-100. Click **Yes** on the pop-up window that asks for confirmation.

Step 9. On the **Global Administrator Assignments** page, after you refresh the page, you can see that the Duo directory sync user has been removed from the list, as illustrated in Figure 5-101.

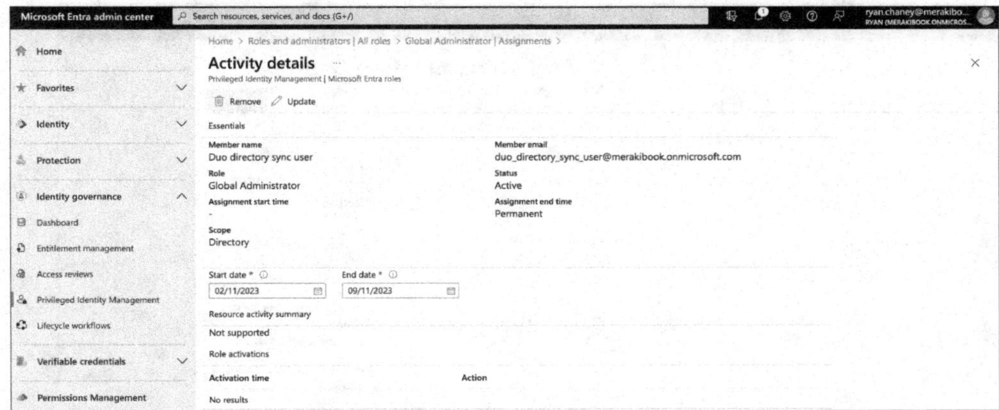

Figure 5-100 *Removing the Global Administrator Role from the Duo Directory Sync User*

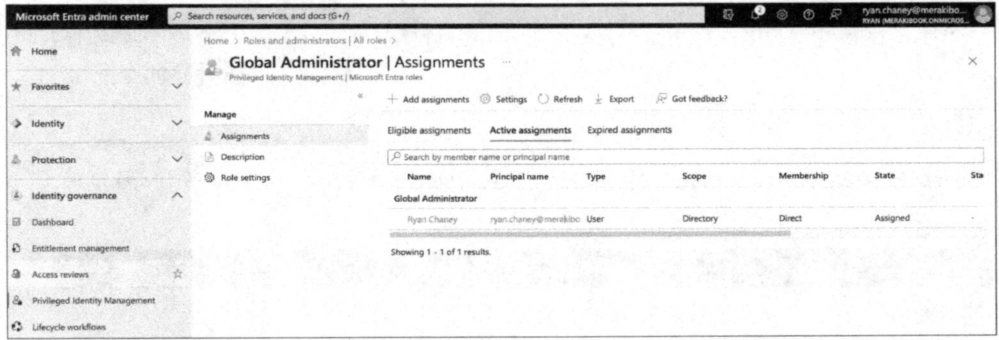

Figure 5-101 *Confirming the Role Removal on the Duo Directory Sync User in Microsoft Entra*

Configuring SAML SSO Between Cisco Duo and Microsoft Entra

When users authenticate with their username and password, these credentials are provided to Cisco Duo, which uses them to authenticate the user against Microsoft Entra using SAML. Therefore, two SAML integrations are required: one between Cisco Duo and Meraki Dashboard, as well as this integration between Cisco Duo and Microsoft Entra.

Follow these steps to configure SAML SSO between Cisco Duo and Microsoft Entra:

Step 1. Log in to the Cisco Duo Admin Panel (https://admin.duosecurity.com/login).

Step 2. Navigate to **Single Sign-on** (from the menu on the left) and click **Add SAML Identity Provider**, as illustrated in Figure 5-102.

Step 3. The **SAML Identity Provider Configuration** page opens, as illustrated in Figure 5-103. Leave this tab open because you will need to refer back to it.

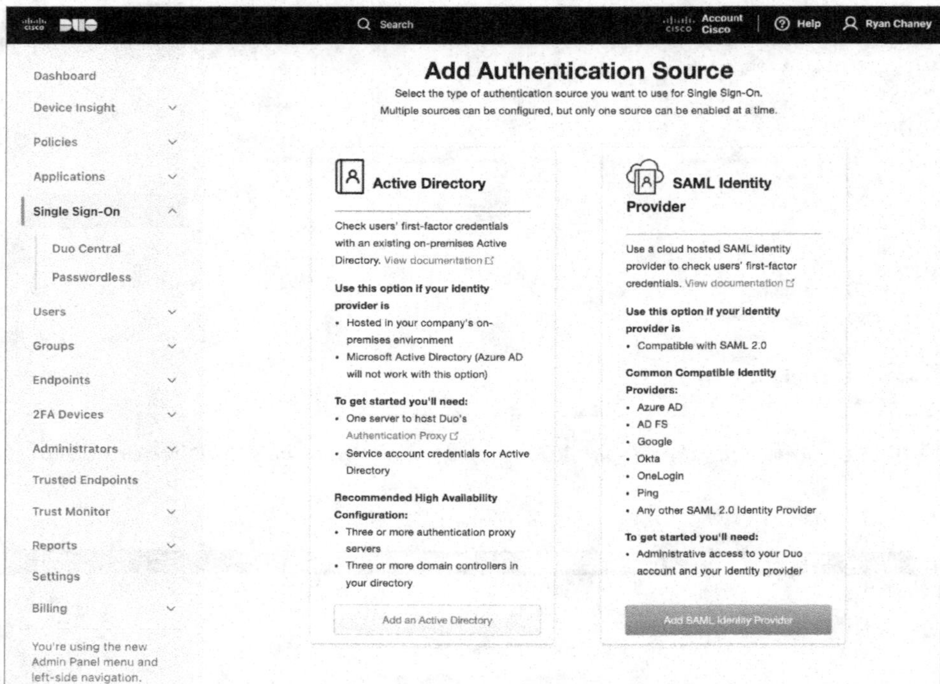

Figure 5-102 *Adding an SAML Identity Provider for Microsoft Entra in Cisco Duo*

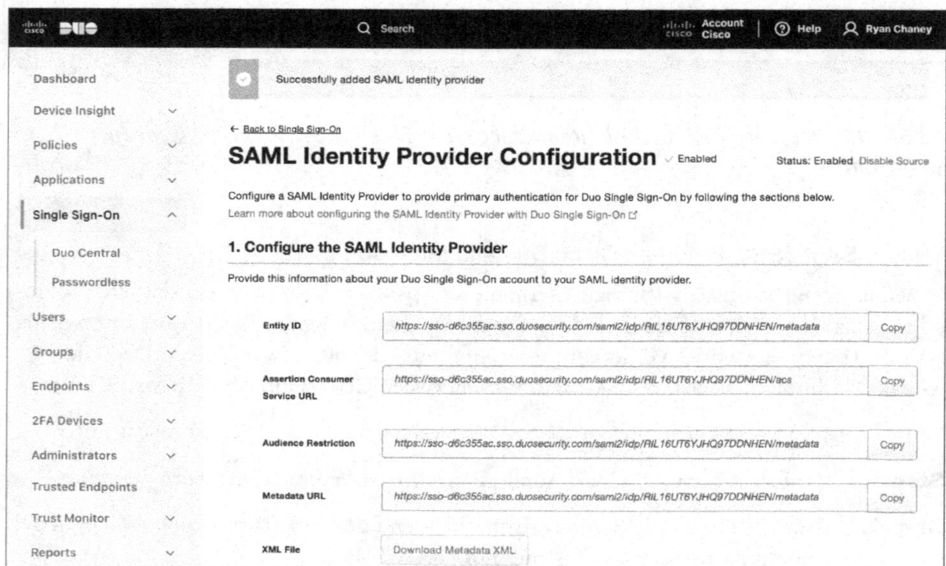

Figure 5-103 *The SAML Identity Provider Configuration Page in Cisco Duo*

Step 4. Log in to Microsoft Entra admin center as an administrator user (https://entra.microsoft.com/#home). From the home page shown in Figure 5-104, click **Go to Microsoft Entra ID**.

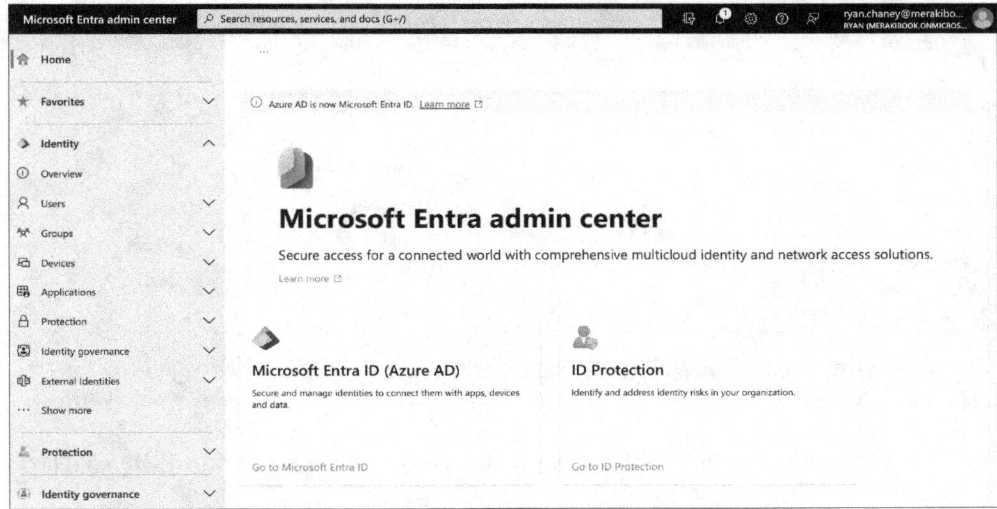

Figure 5-104 *The Microsoft Entra Admin Center Home Page*

Step 5. Navigate to **Applications > Enterprise Applications** and then click **+ New Application** from the screen in Figure 5-105.

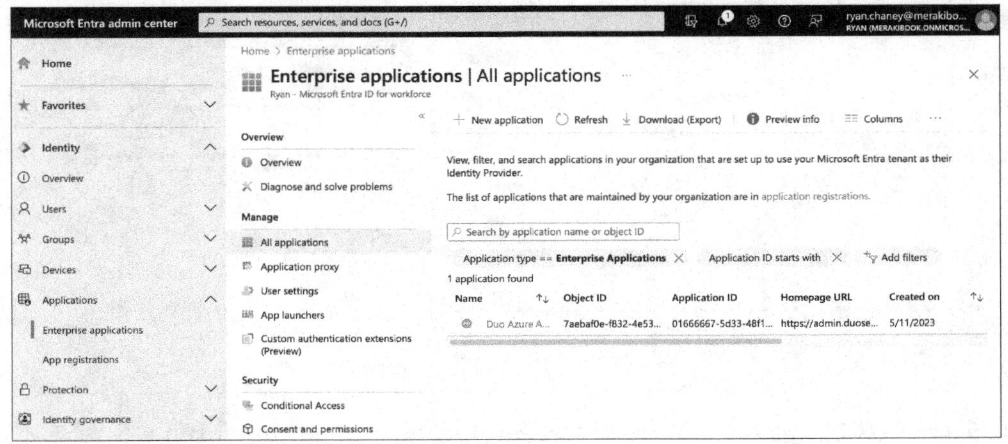

Figure 5-105 *Adding a New Application in Microsoft Entra*

Step 6. Click **+ Create Your Own Application** on top of the gallery page shown in Figure 5-106.

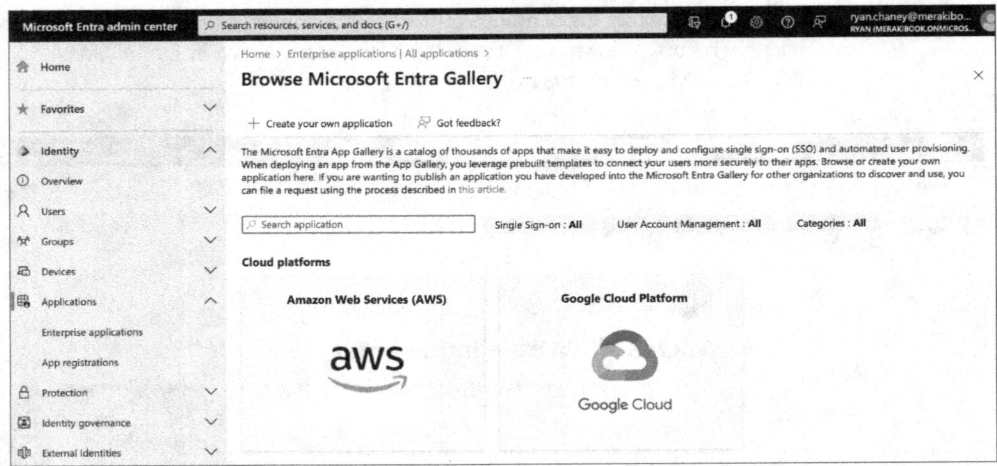

Figure 5-106 *Adding a New Application via the Microsoft Entra Gallery in Microsoft Entra*

Step 7. Enter a name for this application. In this example, we've chosen **Duo SSO**, as illustrated in Figure 5-107. Click **Create.**

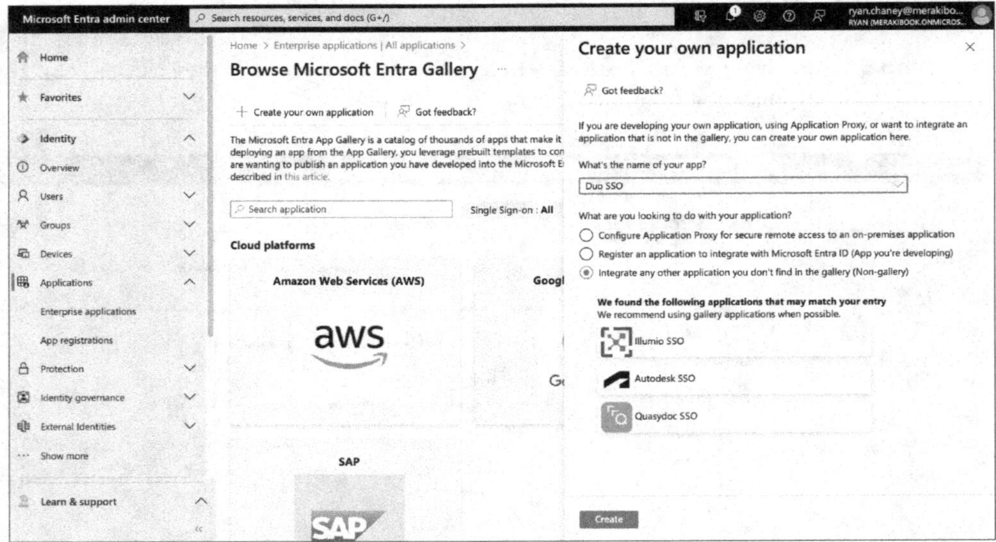

Figure 5-107 *Entering a Name for the New Application in Microsoft Entra*

Step 8. From the **Overview** page shown in Figure 5-108, click **Assign Users and Groups.**

Step 9. From the **Users and Groups** page shown in Figure 5-109, click **+ Add User/Group.**

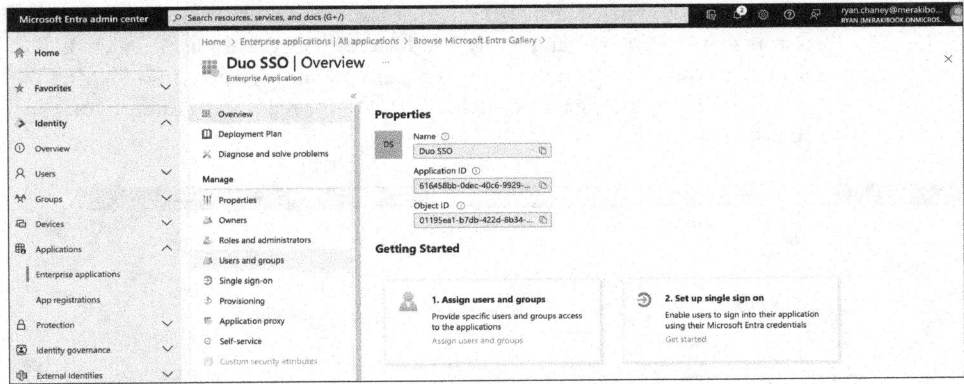

Figure 5-108 *The Overview Page for the New Duo SSO Application in Microsoft Entra*

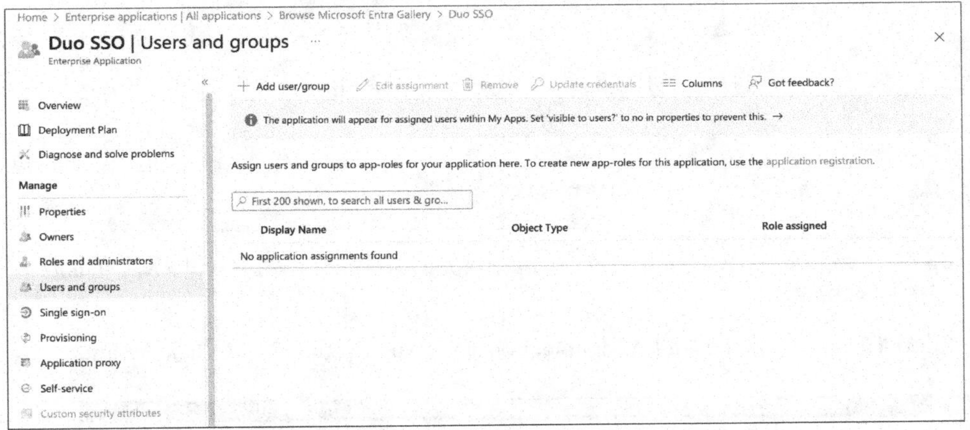

Figure 5-109 *The Users and Groups Page for the New Duo SSO Application in Microsoft Entra*

Step 10. On the **Add Assignment** page shown in Figure 5-110, click **None Selected** under **Users and Groups.**

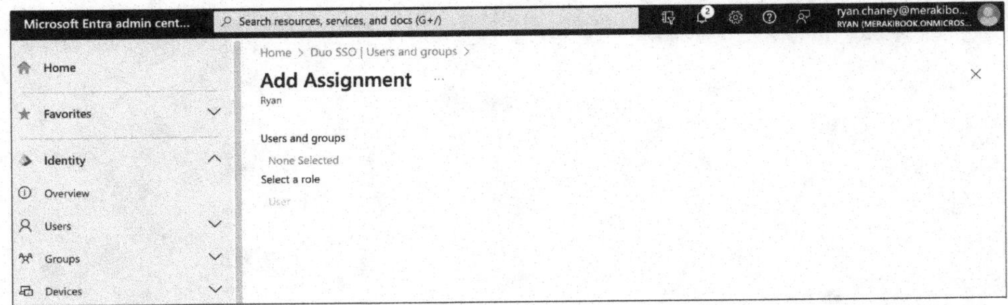

Figure 5-110 *The Add Assignment Page for the New Duo SSO Application in Microsoft Entra*

Step 11. In the screen shown in Figure 5-111, click the box next to the Meraki administrators group. In this example, we used **Meraki_Org_Admin.** Then click **Select.** This option will control which groups are authenticated via SAML SSO. If you have other groups, such as a group for read-only admins, you can also add them here.

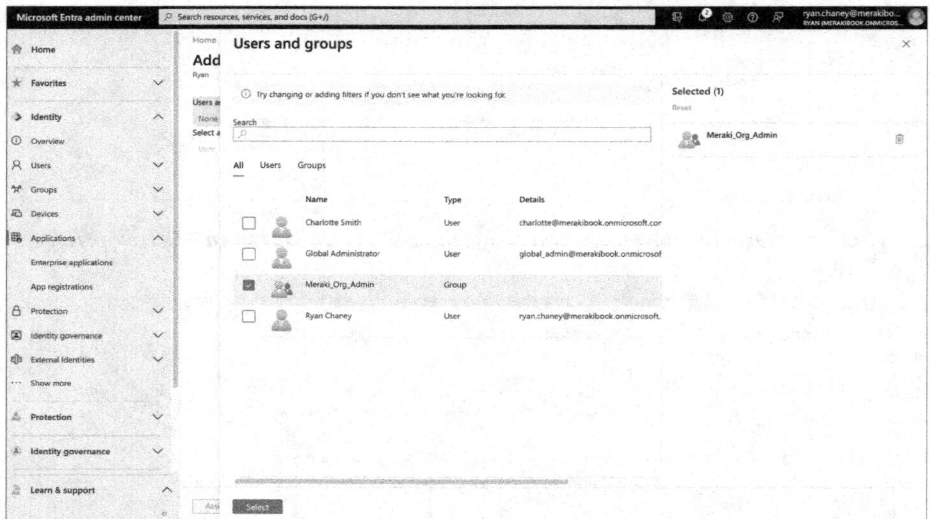

Figure 5-111 *Adding the Meraki Dashboard Administrators Group to the New Duo SSO Application*

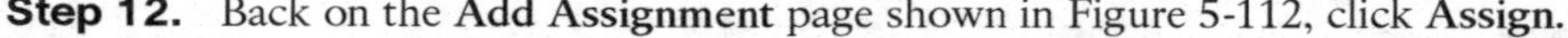

Step 12. Back on the **Add Assignment** page shown in Figure 5-112, click **Assign.**

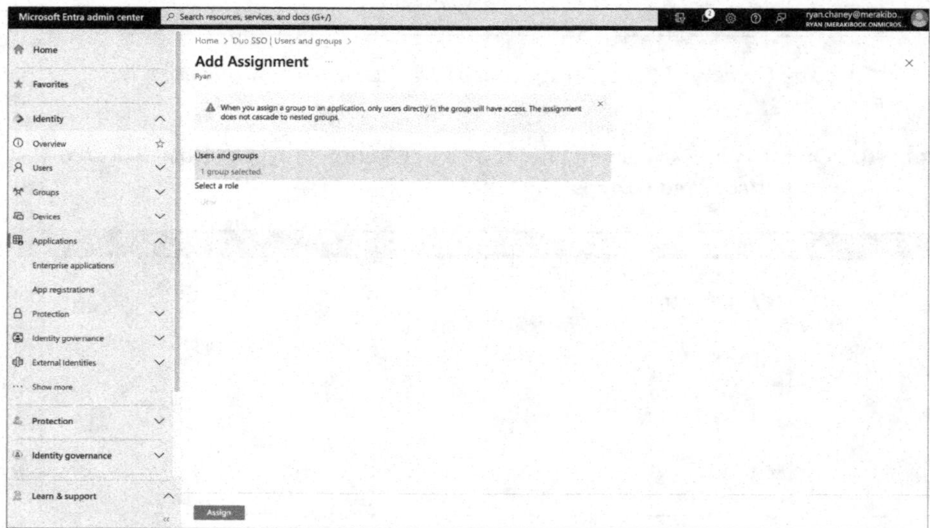

Figure 5-112 *Finalizing the New Group Assignments for the New Duo SSO Application*

Step 13. Back on the **Users and Groups** page for the Duo SSO application, you can see the Meraki administrators group has been assigned, as illustrated in Figure 5-113. Click **Single Sign-On** under **Users and Groups.**

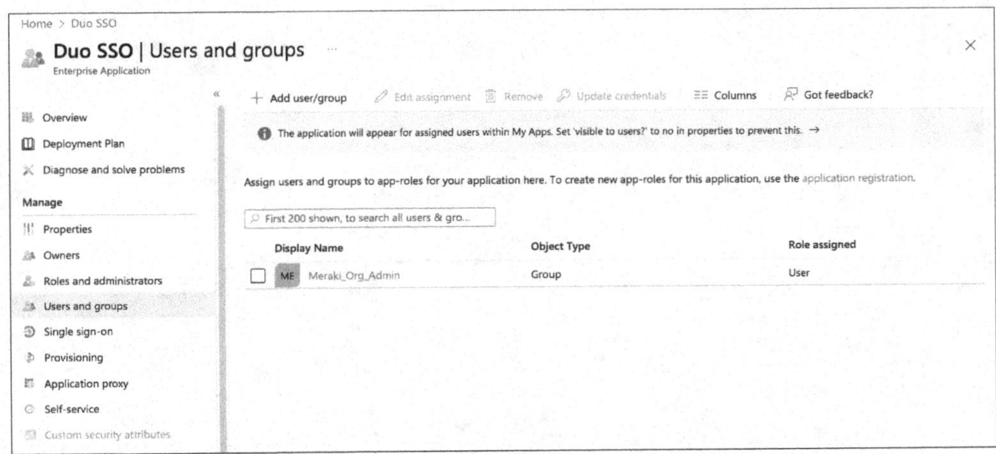

Figure 5-113 *Confirming the Group Assignment on the New Duo SSO Application*

Step 14. On the **Single Sign-On** page for the Duo SSO application shown in Figure 5-114, click the **SAML** box under **Select a Single Sign-On Method.**

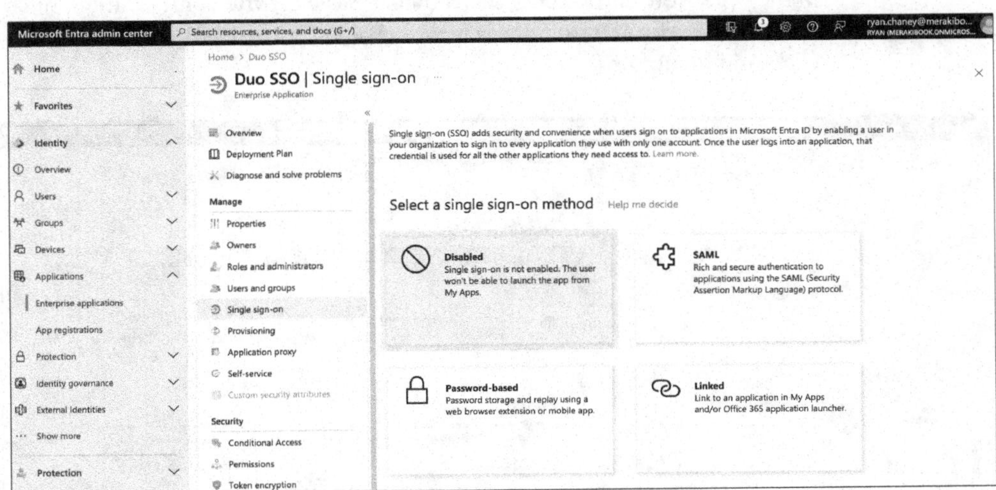

Figure 5-114 *Configuring SAML on the New Duo SSO Application in Microsoft Entra*

Step 15. On the **SAML-Based Sign-on** page shown in Figure 5-115, under **Set Up Single Sign-On with SAML,** click **Edit** across from **Basic SAML Configuration.**

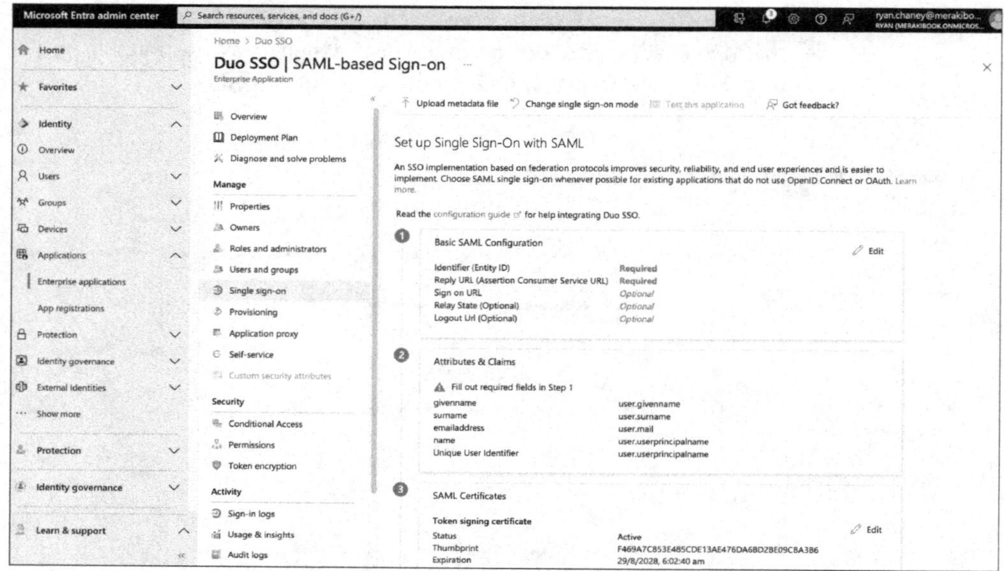

Figure 5-115 *Editing the Basic SAML Configuration on the New Duo SSO*

Step 16. Now copy across the values from the **SAML Identity Provider Configuration** page in the Cisco Duo Admin Panel (from Step 3).

In the Microsoft Entra admin center, under **Basic SAML Configuration**, find **Identifier (Entity ID)** from the screen shown in Figure 5-116. Under that, click **Add Identifier**.

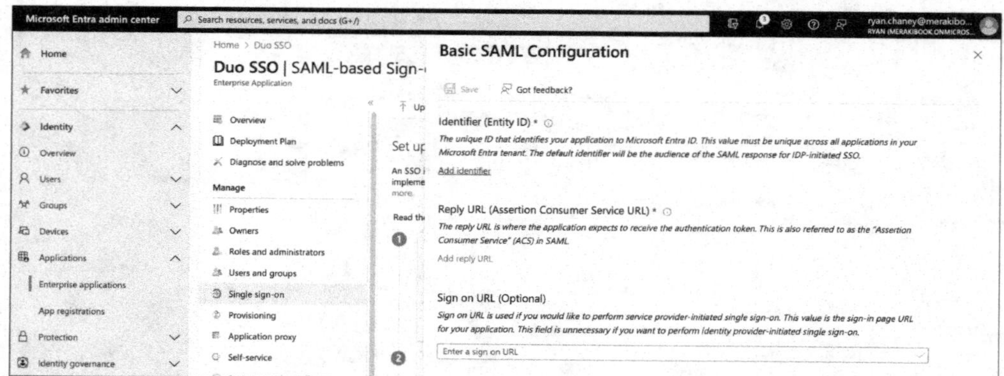

Figure 5-116 *Adding an Identifier Under Basic SAML Configuration for the Duo SSO Application*

Step 17. From the **SAML Identity Provider Configuration** page in the Cisco Duo Admin Panel, copy the **Entity ID** and paste it into the new, empty field under

Identifier (Entity ID) on the **Basic SAML Configuration** page, as illustrated in Figure 5-117.

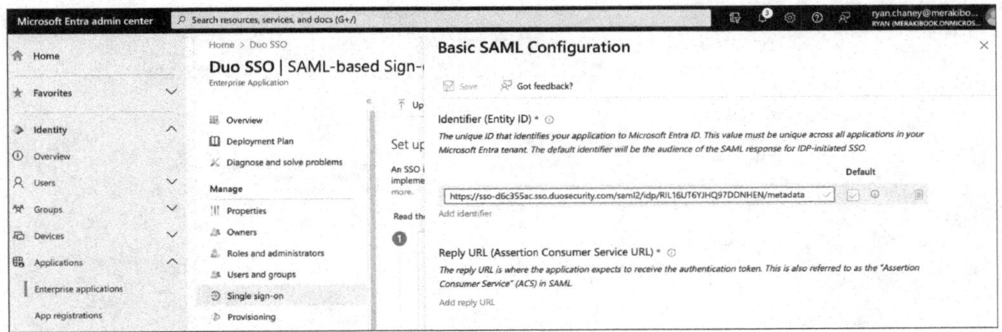

Figure 5-117 *Pasting the Entity ID into the Basic SAML Configuration for the Duo SSO Application*

Step 18. In Microsoft Entra, click **Add Reply URL** under **Reply URL (Assertion Consumer Service URL).**

From the **SAML Identity Provider Configuration** page in the Cisco Duo Admin Panel, copy the **Assertion Consumer Service URL** and paste it into the new field under **Reply URL (Assertion Consumer Service URL)** on the **Basic SAML Configuration** page, as illustrated in Figure 5-118.

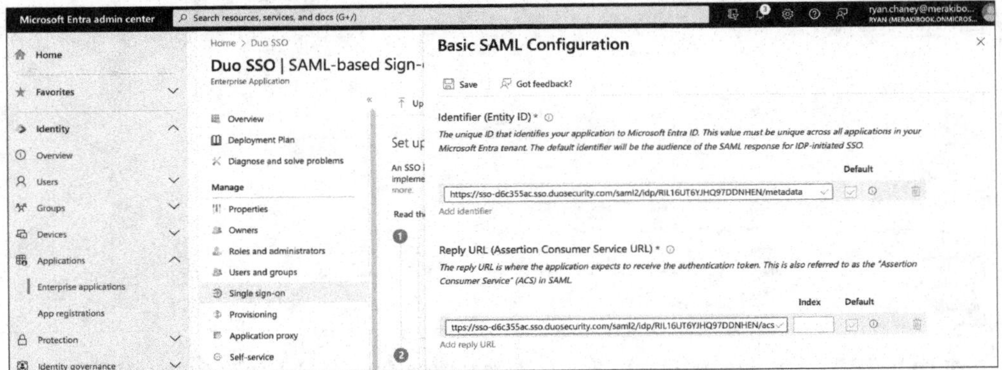

Figure 5-118 *Pasting the Reply URL into the Basic SAML Configuration for the Duo SSO Application*

Step 19. Click **Save** (top middle of the page) and then close this page using the **X** in the top right. You will return to the page illustrated in Figure 5-119.

Click **Edit** next to **Attributes & Claims.**

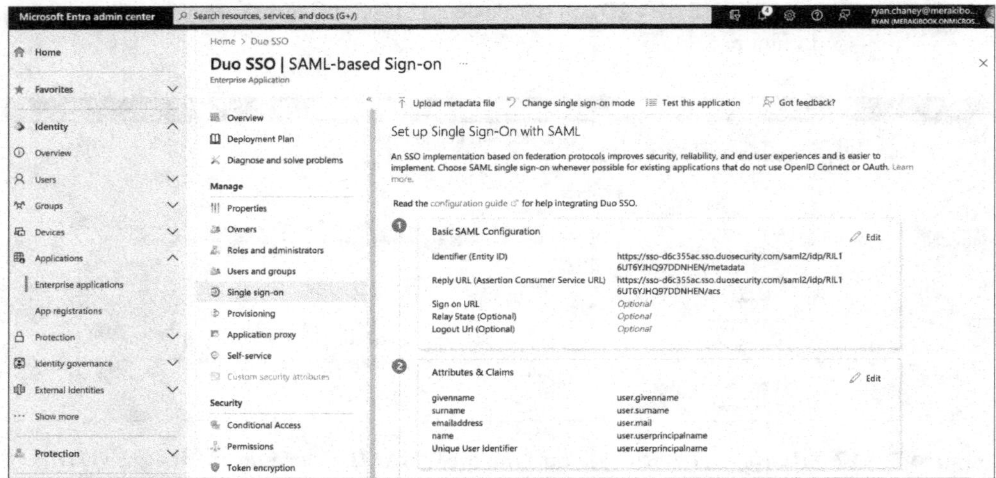

Figure 5-119 *The SAML SSO Page After Completing Changes to the Duo SSO Application in Microsoft Entra*

Step 20. Delete all four of the **Additional Claims** using the three dots (...) on the right of their value and clicking **Delete**, as illustrated in Figure 5-120. Click **OK** to confirm each deletion.

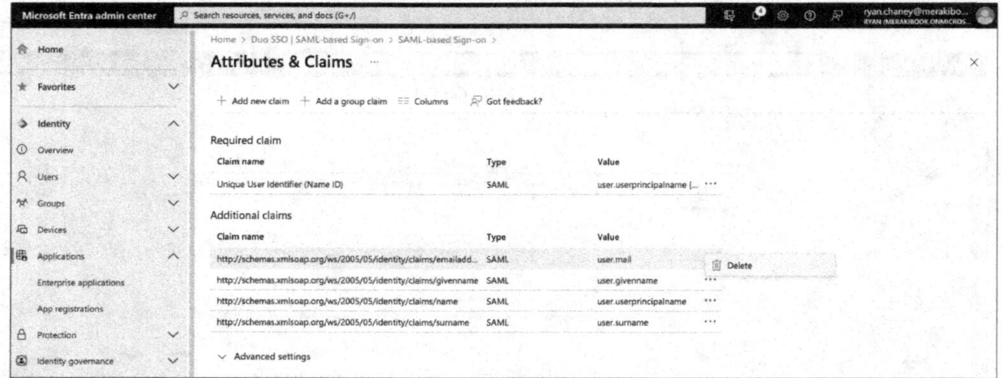

Figure 5-120 *The Attributes & Claims Page for the Duo SSO Application in Microsoft Entra*

Step 21. Click **Add New Claim** at the top of the **Attributes & Claims** page illustrated in Figure 5-121.

Step 22. In the **Name** field, enter **Email.**

For the **Source Attribute**, enter **user.mail**, as illustrated in Figure 5-122. Click **Save.**

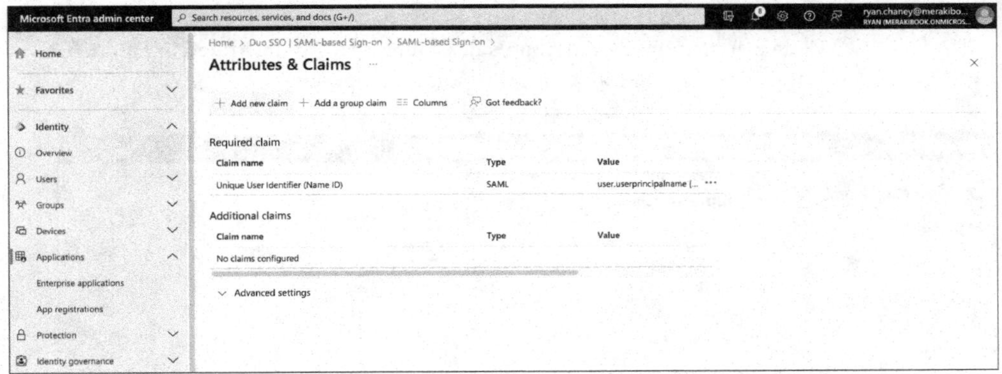

Figure 5-121 *Adding a New Claim to the Duo SSO Application on the Attributes & Claims Page*

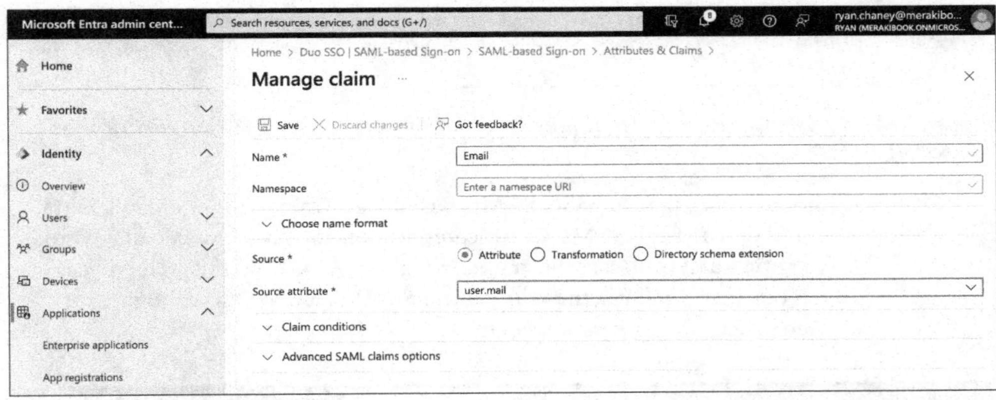

Figure 5-122 *Configuring a New Claim on the Duo SSO Application in Microsoft Entra*

Step 23. Add four more claims, one at a time, by repeating the previous two steps for **Username**, **FirstName**, **LastName**, and **DisplayName** as per Table 5-2. Leave **Namespace** empty for each of these claims.

Table 5-2 *Additional Claims to Be Added to the Duo SSO Application in Microsoft Entra*

Name	Source	Source Attribute
Username	Attribute	user.userprincipalname
FirstName	Attribute	user.givenname
LastName	Attribute	user.surname
DisplayName	Attribute	user.displayname

Step 24. After all the additional claims have been added, confirm that the **Additional Claims** appear on the **Attributes & Claims** page, as illustrated in Figure 5-123. If the claims are all there, click the **X** in the top right.

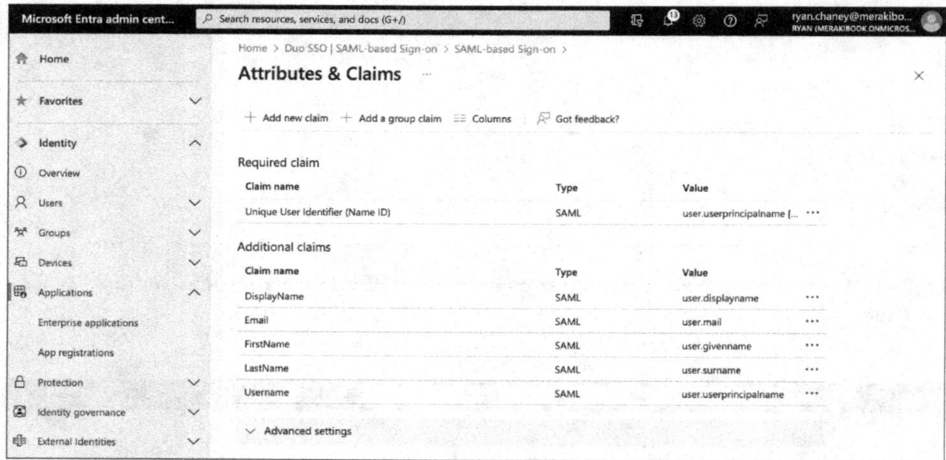

Figure 5-123 *The Completed Attributes and Claims for the Duo SSO Application in Microsoft Entra*

Step 25. You return to the Duo SSO **SAML-Based Sign-On** page in Microsoft Entra. Scroll down to the **SAML Certificates** section and click **Download** next to **Certificate (Base64)**, as illustrated in Figure 5-124. Keep this web browser tab open; you will use the values under **Set Up Duo SSO** to configure the Duo side of this integration next.

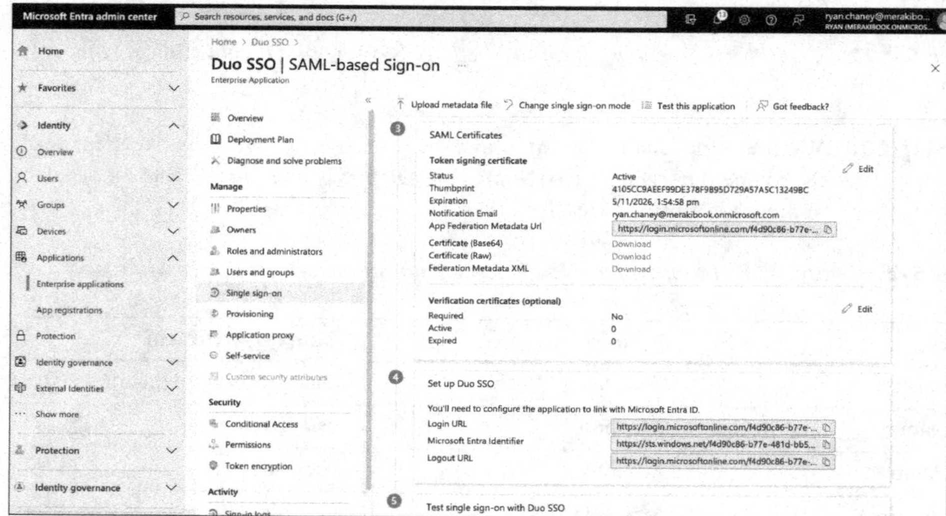

Figure 5-124 *The SAML Certificates Section on the Duo SSO SAML-Based Sign-On Page*

Step 26. Switch to your web browser tab that is open to the Duo Admin Panel **SAML Identity Provider Configuration** page (from Step 3). Scroll down to **Configure Duo Single Sign-On.** In the **Display Name** field, enter a name that will identify the integration with Microsoft Entra. As you can see in Figure 5-125, we used **Microsoft Entra SAML IdP.**

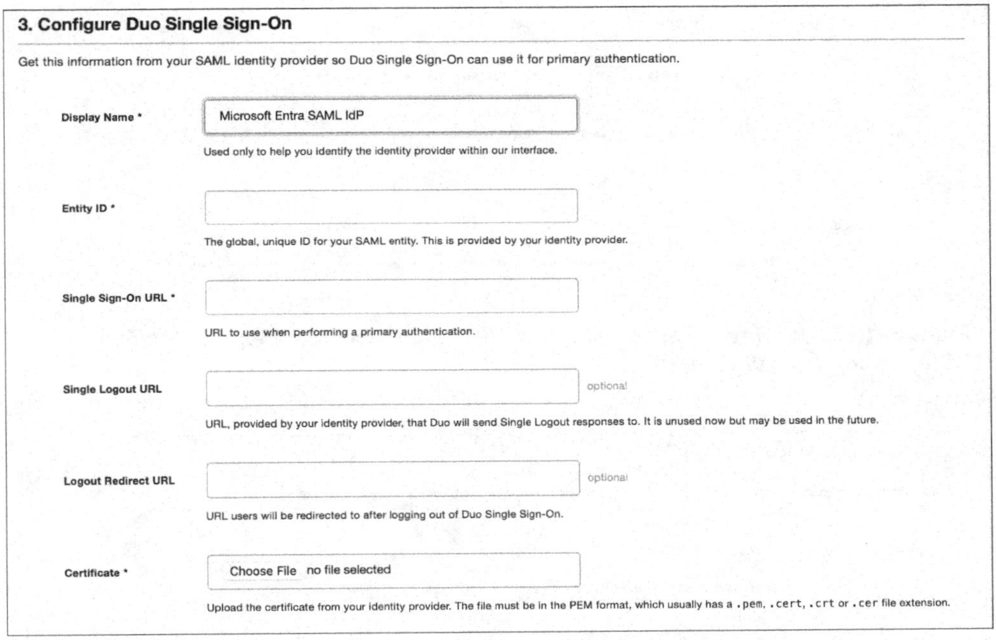

Figure 5-125 *Configuring SAML SSO with Microsoft Entra in the Duo Admin Panel*

Step 27. From the **Set Up Duo SSO** section of the **SAML-Based Single Sign-On** page in Microsoft Entra, copy the **Login URL** and paste this into the **Single Sign-On URL** field on the **SAML Identity Provider Configuration** page in the Duo Admin Panel, as illustrated in Figure 5-126.

Step 28. From the **Set Up Duo SSO** section of the **SAML-Based Single Sign-on** page in Microsoft Entra, copy the **Microsoft Entra Identifier** and paste this into the **Entity ID** field on the **SAML Identity Provider Configuration** page in the Duo Admin Panel, as illustrated in Figure 5-127. Leave the rest of the fields as they are.

Step 29. Next, upload the certificate you downloaded earlier from the **SAML-Based Single Sign-On** page in Microsoft Entra to the **Certificate** section on the **SAML Identity Provider Configuration** page in the Duo Admin Panel, illustrated in Figure 5-128. To do this, scroll down to **Certificate** and click **Choose File.** From the pop-up window, locate the certificate downloaded from Microsoft Entra earlier and click **Upload.**

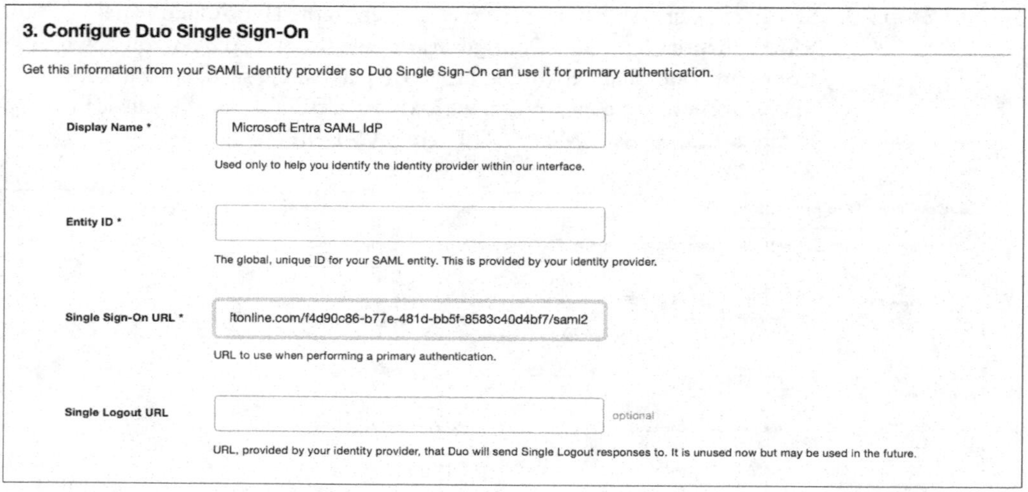

3. Configure Duo Single Sign-On

Get this information from your SAML identity provider so Duo Single Sign-On can use it for primary authentication.

Display Name * Microsoft Entra SAML IdP

Used only to help you identify the identity provider within our interface.

Entity ID *

The global, unique ID for your SAML entity. This is provided by your identity provider.

Single Sign-On URL * ftonline.com/f4d90c86-b77e-481d-bb5f-8583c40d4bf7/saml2

URL to use when performing a primary authentication.

Single Logout URL optional

URL, provided by your identity provider, that Duo will send Single Logout responses to. It is unused now but may be used in the future.

Figure 5-126 *Pasting the Single Sign-On URL into the SAML Identity Provider Configuration Page in Duo*

3. Configure Duo Single Sign-On

Get this information from your SAML identity provider so Duo Single Sign-On can use it for primary authentication.

Display Name * Microsoft Entra SAML IdP

Used only to help you identify the identity provider within our interface.

Entity ID * https://sts.windows.net/f4d90c86-b77e-481d-bb5f-8583c40d

The global, unique ID for your SAML entity. This is provided by your identity provider.

Single Sign-On URL * https://login.microsoftonline.com/f4d90c86-b77e-481d-bb5f-

URL to use when performing a primary authentication.

Single Logout URL optional

URL, provided by your identity provider, that Duo will send Single Logout responses to. It is unused now but may be used in the future.

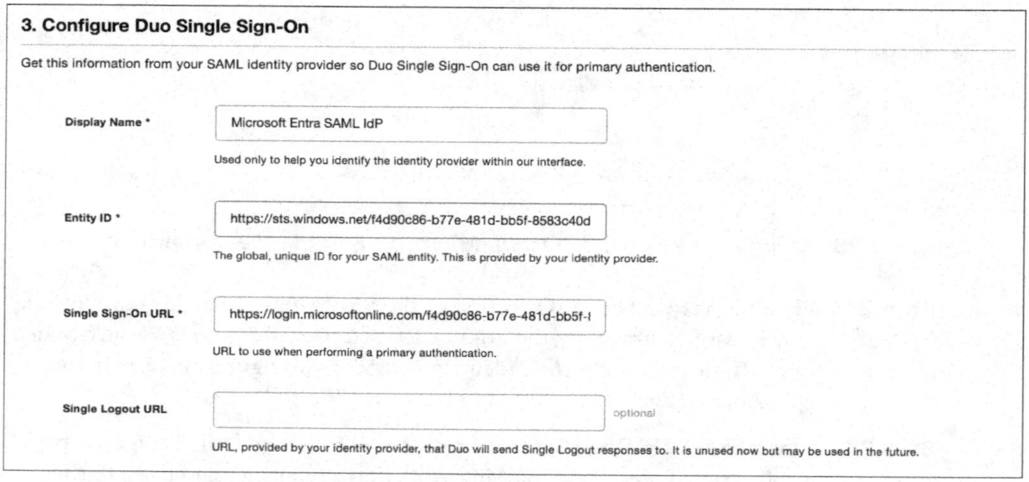

Figure 5-127 *Pasting the Entity ID into the SAML Identity Provider Configuration Page in Duo*

Step 30. On the **SAML Identity Provider Configuration** page in the Duo Admin Panel, scroll down and check **Require Encrypted Assertion.** Ensure the values for **Assertion Encryption Algorithm** and **Key Transport Encryption Algorithm** match the screenshot in Figure 5-129. Click **Download Certificate**, and then click **Save.**

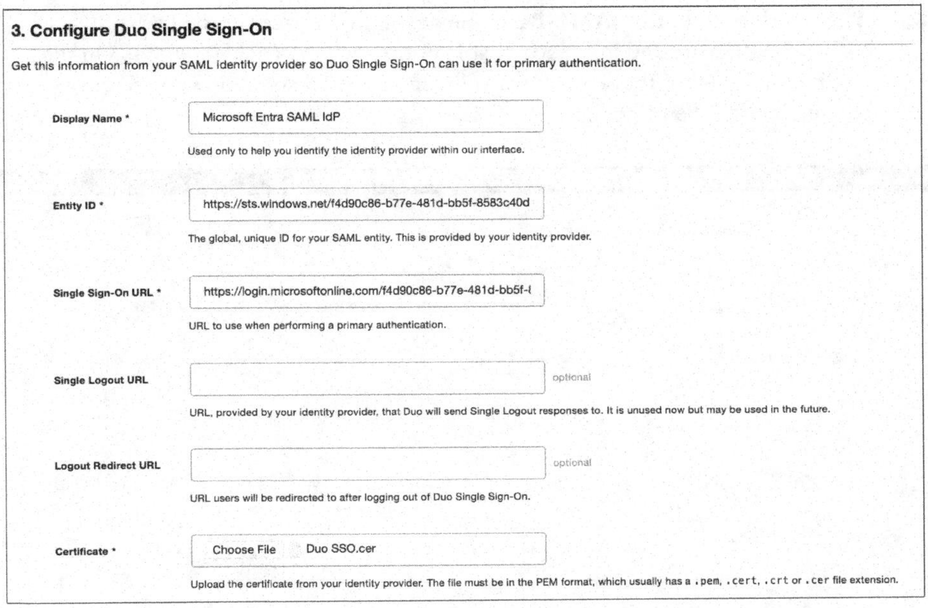

3. Configure Duo Single Sign-On

Get this information from your SAML identity provider so Duo Single Sign-On can use it for primary authentication.

Display Name * Microsoft Entra SAML IdP

Used only to help you identify the identity provider within our interface.

Entity ID * https://sts.windows.net/f4d90c86-b77e-481d-bb5f-8583c40d

The global, unique ID for your SAML entity. This is provided by your identity provider.

Single Sign-On URL * https://login.microsoftonline.com/f4d90c86-b77e-481d-bb5f-(

URL to use when performing a primary authentication.

Single Logout URL optional

URL, provided by your identity provider, that Duo will send Single Logout responses to. It is unused now but may be used in the future.

Logout Redirect URL optional

URL users will be redirected to after logging out of Duo Single Sign-On.

Certificate * Choose File Duo SSO.cer

Upload the certificate from your identity provider. The file must be in the PEM format, which usually has a .pem, .cert, .crt or .cer file extension.

Figure 5-128 *Uploading the Certificate on the SAML Identity Provider Configuration Page in Duo*

Existing Certificate * CN=Microsoft Azure Federated SSO Certificate - 2026-11-05 02:54:58+00:00

Choose File no file selected

Upload the certificate from your identity provider. The file must be in the PEM format, which usually has a .pem, .cert, .crt or .cer file extension.

Username normalization * None

Simple

"DOMAIN\username", "username@example.com", and "username" are treated as the same user.

Controls if a username should be altered before trying to match them with a Duo user account.

Assertion encryption Require encrypted assertion

Early Access

Assertion encryption algorithm

AES256-CBC

Key transport encryption algorithm

RSA-OAEP (with fixed SHA mask)

Certificate

Download Certificate

Save ✓ Successfully saved. Go back to Single Sign-On or protect an application

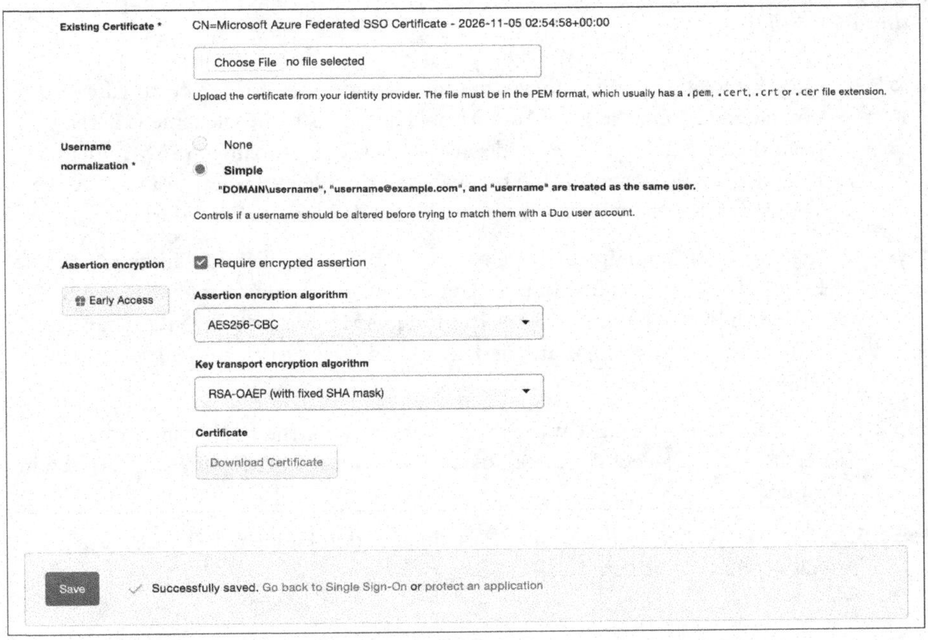

Figure 5-129 *Assertion Encryption Settings on the SAML Identity Provider Configuration Page in Duo*

Step 31. Switch back to the **SAML-Based Single Sign-On** page for the Duo SSO application created in the Microsoft Entra admin console (Step 24). On the middle panel of the screen shown in Figure 5-130, scroll down to **Security** and click **Token Encryption.**

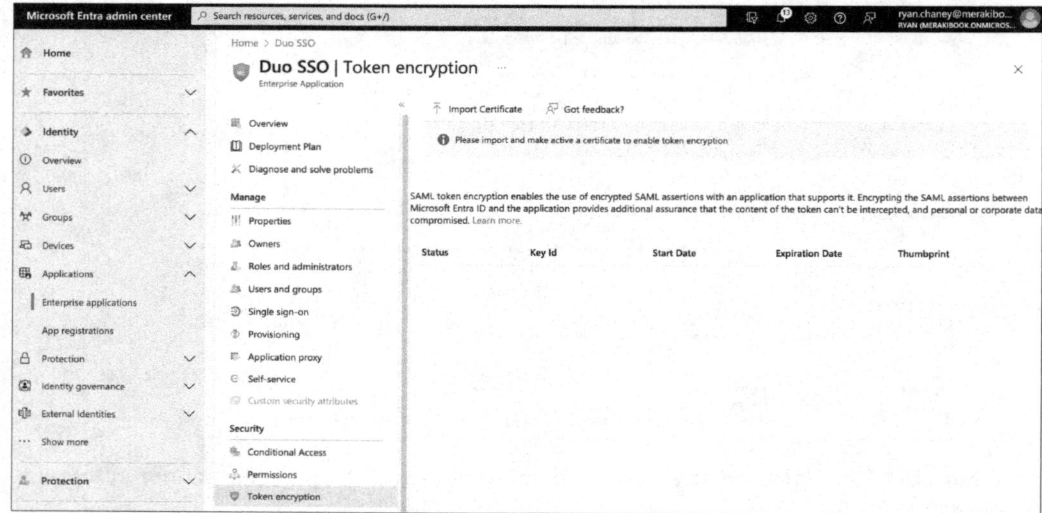

Figure 5-130 *The Token Encryption Tab of the Duo SSO Application in the Microsoft Entra Admin Console*

Step 32. On your local computer, locate the file ending in .crt for the certificate you downloaded from the Duo Admin Panel in Step 30. The filename is derived from the SAML Identity Provider name, so the file is named [SAML Identity Provider].crt. Rename this file by changing the file extension from .crt to .cer. The certificate file will now be named **[SAML Identity Provider].cer.**

Step 33. On the **Token Encryption** page for the Duo SSO application in the Microsoft Entra admin center, click **Import Certificate** at the top of the page. From the screen shown in Figure 5-131, select the **[SAML Identity Provider].cer** certificate file from your computer and click **Add.** The certificate will be imported with the status **Inactive.**

Step 34. Click the three dots (...) at the right of the row for the freshly imported certificate and select **Activate Token Encryption Certificate**, as illustrated in Figure 5-132.

Step 35. Click **Yes** on the pop-up window, as illustrated in Figure 5-133. The certificate's status will now be listed as **Active.**

Figure 5-131 *Importing the Duo Certificate into the Token Encryption Page in Microsoft Entra*

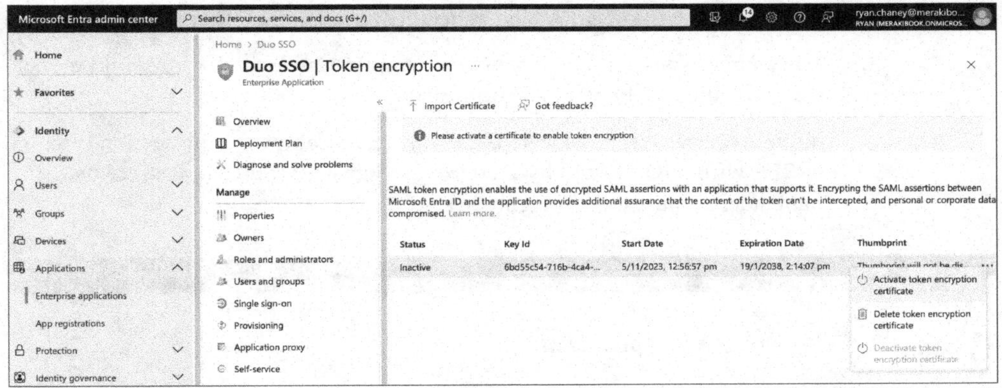

Figure 5-132 *Activating the Duo Certificate on the Token Encryption Page in Microsoft Entra*

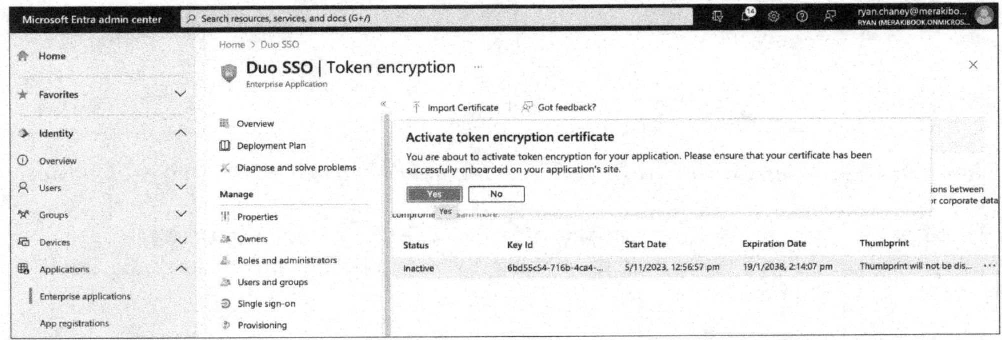

Figure 5-133 *Pop-Up Window when Activating the Duo Certificate on the Token Encryption in Microsoft Entra*

Note If you run into trouble with this section, Cisco Duo has published a detailed guide on setting up and troubleshooting SAML with Microsoft Entra ID (formerly Azure AD) at https://duo.com/docs/sso#saml.

Now that you've configured SAML SSO between Cisco Duo and Microsoft Entra, you can continue on to the next section.

Configuring IdP-Initiated SAML SSO Between Cisco Duo and Meraki Dashboard

IdP-initiated single sign-on typically involves first logging in to a portal and then launching applications from there. These applications use single sign-on with the credentials derived from the initial portal login. To log in directly to Meraki Dashboard using single sign-on, referred to as SP-initiated SAML SSO, you must complete these IdP-initiated SAML SSO steps first, followed by a couple of extra steps shown in the next section.

Step 1. Log in to the Cisco Duo Admin Panel (https://admin.duosecurity.com/login).

Step 2. Navigate to **Applications > Protect an Application.** Search for **Meraki** in the search field under **Protect an Application.**

In the **Applications** list, locate the entry for **Meraki** with a protection type of **2FA with SSO Hosted by Duo (Single Sign-On)** and click **Protect** on the right side, as illustrated in Figure 5-134.

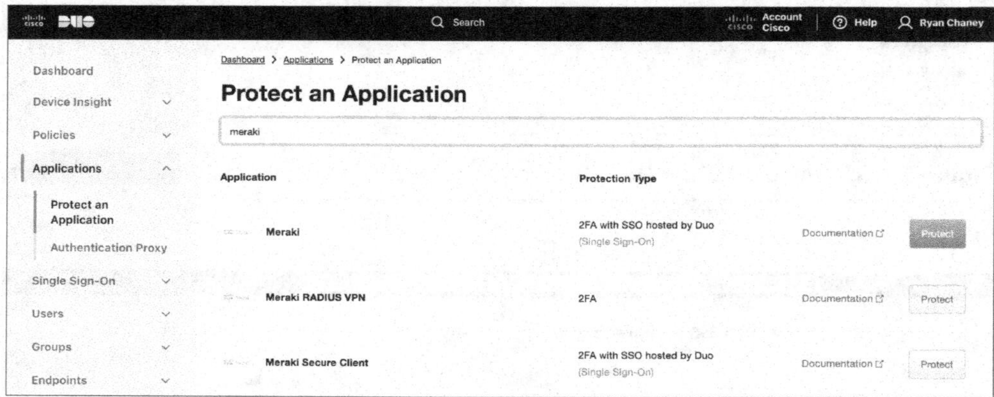

Figure 5-134 *Configuring SAML SSO with Meraki Dashboard in the Duo Admin Panel*

Step 3. You now see the page shown in Figure 5-135. Keep this browser tab open. You will be copying these values to Meraki Dashboard as part of the SAML SSO setup.

Step 4. Log in to Meraki Dashboard (https://dashboard.meraki.com).

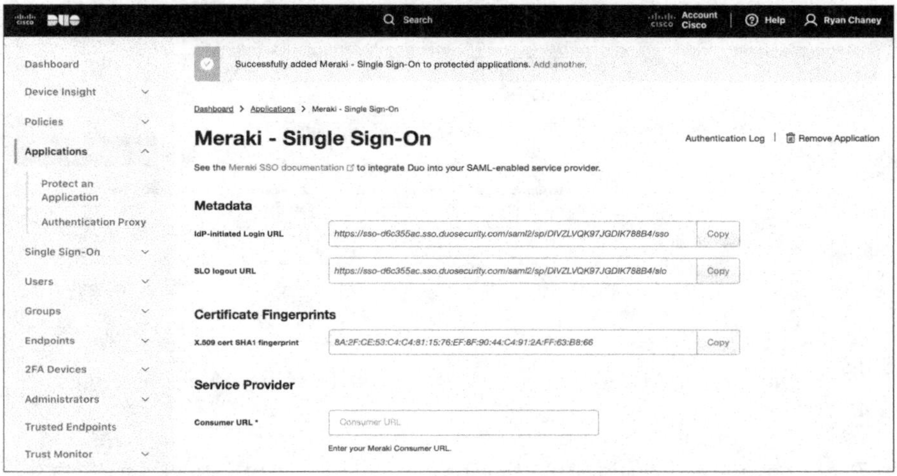

Figure 5-135 *The Meraki Single Sign-On Application Page in Cisco Duo*

Step 5. Navigate to **Organization > Settings** (under Configure), as illustrated in Figure 5-136.

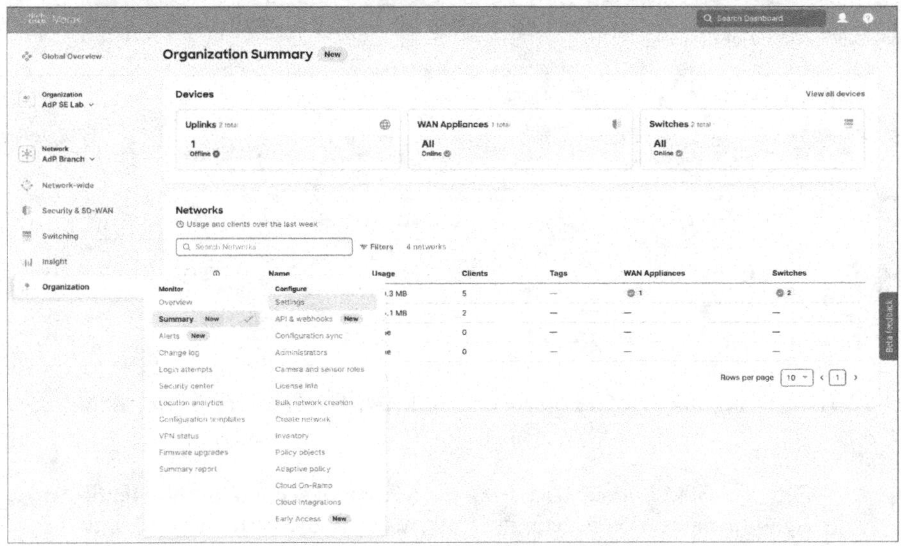

Figure 5-136 *Navigating to the Organization Settings in Meraki Dashboard to Set Up SAML SSO*

Step 6. Scroll down to **Authentication** and change the **SAML SSO** drop-down menu to **SAML SSO Enabled**, as illustrated in Figure 5-137.

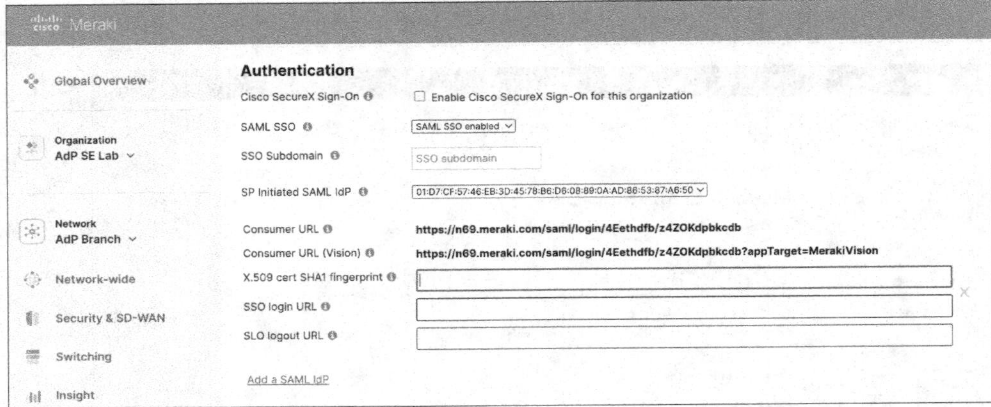

Figure 5-137 *Enabling SAML SSO in Meraki Dashboard as Part of the Duo SSO Integration*

Step 7. Copy the X.509 cert SHA1 fingerprint from the **Certificate Fingerprints** section on the **Meraki Single Sign-On** application page in the Duo Admin Panel (from Step 3). Paste this fingerprint into the **X509 Cert SHA1 Fingerprint** field under **Authentication**, as shown in Figure 5-138.

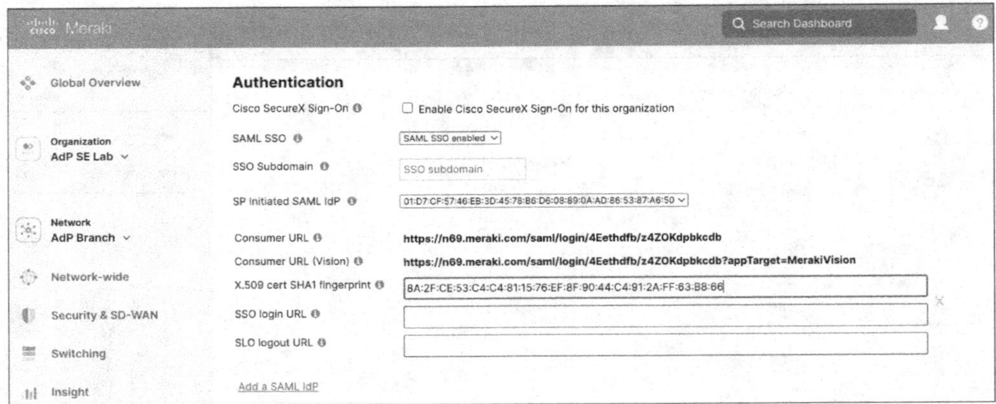

Figure 5-138 *Copying the x.509 Fingerprint to Meraki Dashboard for Duo SAML SSO Integration*

Step 8. Copy the **SLO Logout URL** from the **Metadata** section on the **Meraki Single Sign-On** application page in the Duo Admin Panel. Paste this URL into the **SLO Logout URL** field you see in Figure 5-139.

Step 9. You now need to add the SAML role(s) that users will be mapped to when they log in. In Meraki Dashboard, navigate to **Organization > Administrators.** Scroll down to **SAML Administrator Roles** and click **Add SAML Role.**

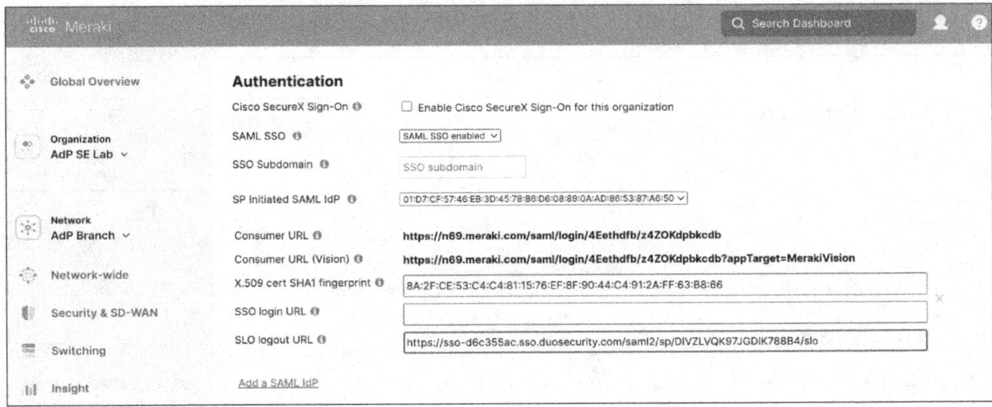

Figure 5-139 *Copying the SLO Logout URL to Meraki Dashboard for Duo SSO Integration*

For clarity, it's strongly recommended to use the same group names in Microsoft Entra as the names of the SAML administrator roles in Meraki Dashboard. Enter the **Role** and set the **Organization Access.** In the example shown in Figure 5-140, the intention is for members of the **Meraki_Org_Admin** group in Microsoft Entra to have full organizational access in Meraki Dashboard.

Click **Create Role** to finish.

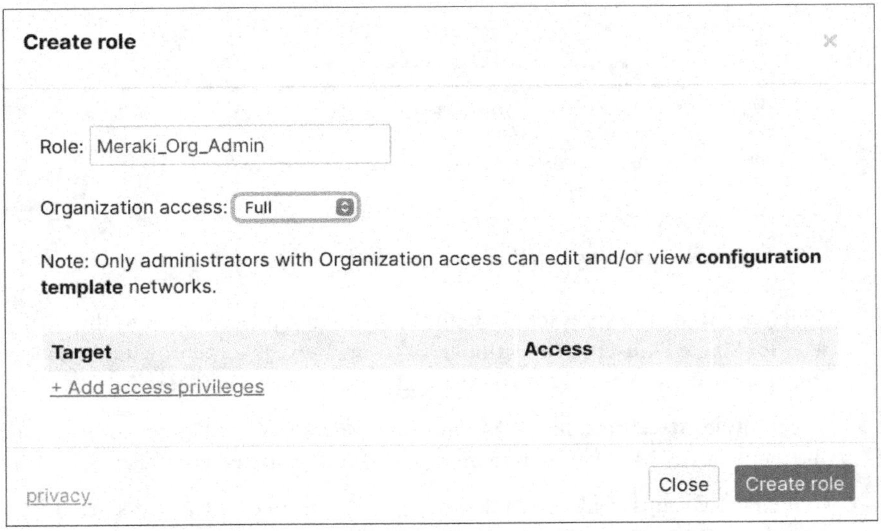

Create role

Role: Meraki_Org_Admin

Organization access: Full

Note: Only administrators with Organization access can edit and/or view **configuration template** networks.

Target	Access
+ Add access privileges	

privacy

Close | Create role

Figure 5-140 *Adding an SAML Administrator Role in Meraki Dashboard for the Duo SSO Integration*

Step 10. On the **Organization > Administrators** page, click **Save Changes**, as illustrated in Figure 5-141.

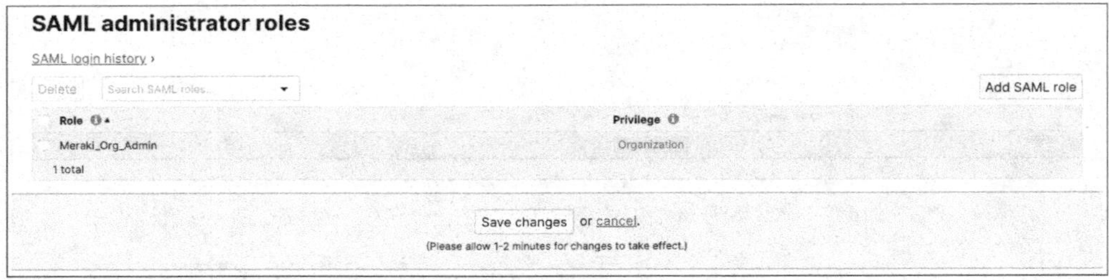

Figure 5-141 *Saving Changes to the SAML Administrator Roles in Meraki Dashboard*

Step 11. Navigate to **Organization > Settings** and scroll down to **Authentication.** From the screen shown in Figure 5-142, copy the **Consumer URL** to the clipboard or a text editor. Do not copy the Consumer URL (Vision) URL.

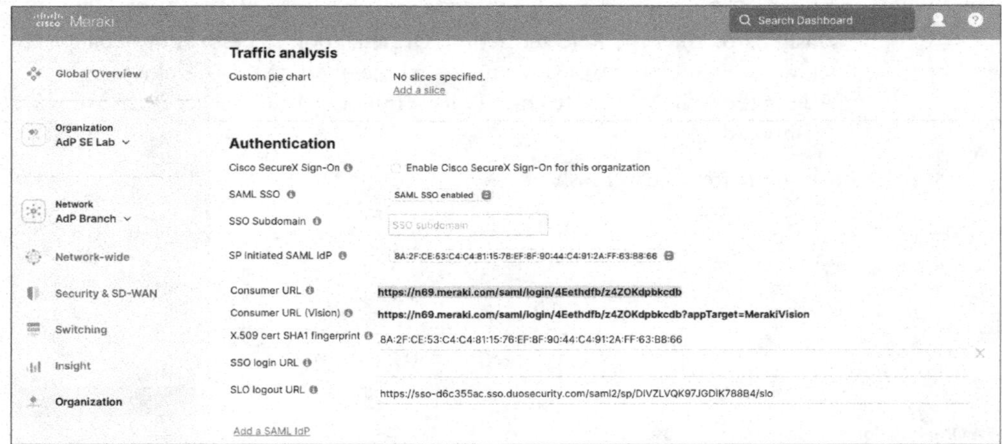

Figure 5-142 *Copying the Consumer URL from Meraki Dashboard*

Step 12. Switch back to your browser tab with the Duo Admin Panel open to the **Meraki Single Sign-On** application page (from Step 3). Scroll down to **Service Provider** and paste in the **Consumer URL**, as illustrated in Figure 5-143.

Step 13. Locate **Role Attributes.** In the **Meraki Role** field shown in Figure 5-144, enter the name of the Meraki SAML administrator role you created in Step 9.

In the **Duo Groups** field, match this group to the name of the group synced from Microsoft Entra. Members of the Duo group will be assigned the matching SAML administrator role in Meraki Dashboard. You can have multiple lines if you have multiple roles for read-only admins, camera admins, and so on.

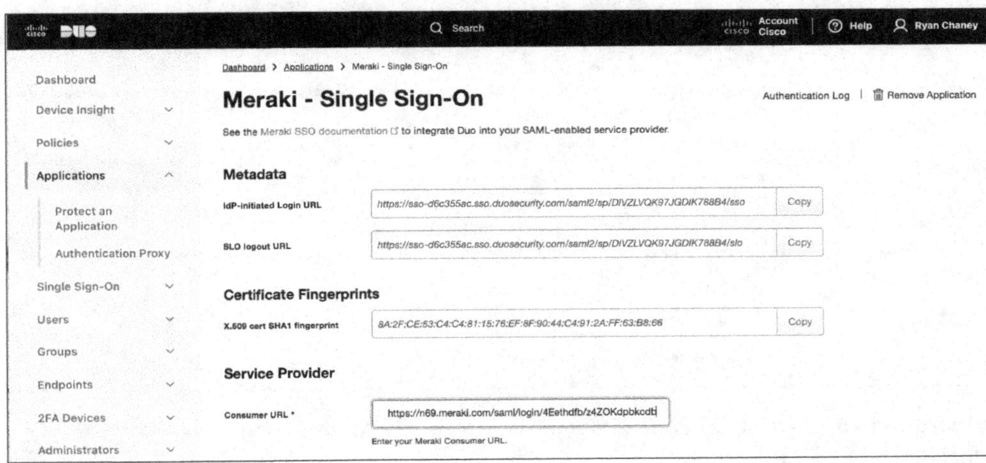

Figure 5-143 *Adding the Consumer URL to Duo as Part of the SAML SSO with Meraki Dashboard*

Figure 5-144 *Matching the SAML Administrator Roles to Duo Groups*

Step 14. Staying on the same page, scroll down to **Mail Attribute** and select **<Email Address>** from the drop-down menu, as illustrated in Figure 5-145.

Step 15. Still on the same page, scroll down to the bottom of the page and click **Save**. This page now appears with the **Application Modified Successfully** banner at the top of the screen, as illustrated in Figure 5-146.

Now that you've completed the IdP-initiated SAML portion of the configuration, you can continue on to make the additional changes necessary for the SP-initiated SAML login.

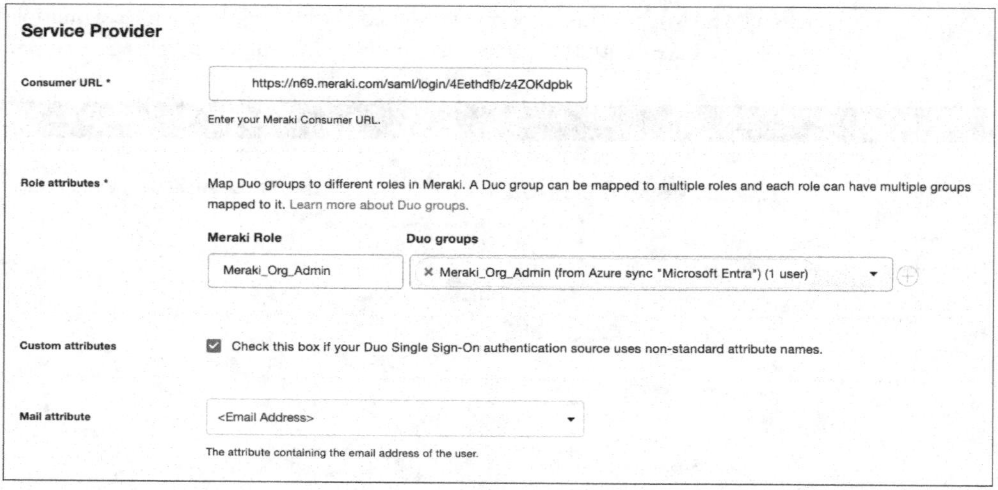

Service Provider

Consumer URL * https://n69.meraki.com/saml/login/4Eethdfb/z4ZOKdpbk
Enter your Meraki Consumer URL.

Role attributes * Map Duo groups to different roles in Meraki. A Duo group can be mapped to multiple roles and each role can have multiple groups mapped to it. Learn more about Duo groups.

Meraki Role | Duo groups
Meraki_Org_Admin | × Meraki_Org_Admin (from Azure sync "Microsoft Entra") (1 user)

Custom attributes ☑ Check this box if your Duo Single Sign-On authentication source uses non-standard attribute names.

Mail attribute <Email Address>
The attribute containing the email address of the user.

Figure 5-145 *Setting the Mail Attribute as Part of the Meraki Single Sign-On Setup in Duo*

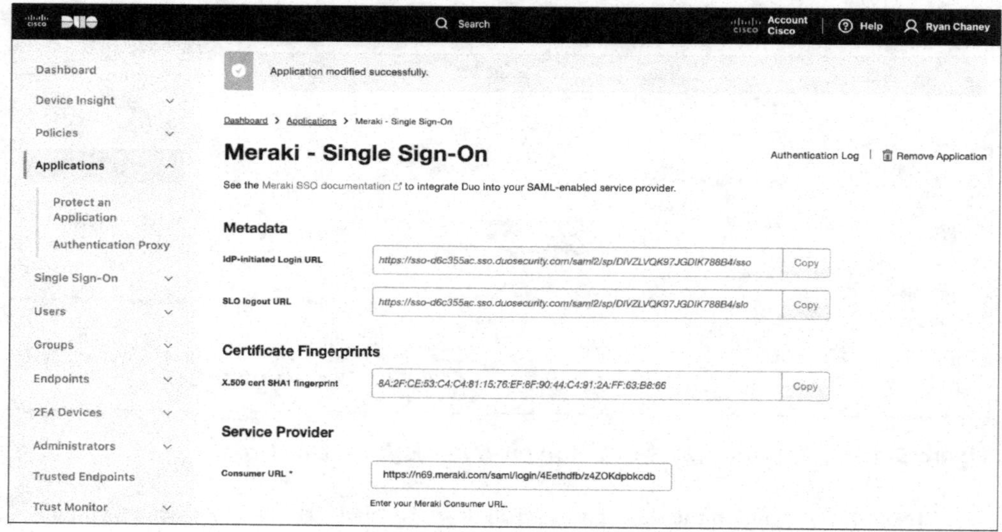

Figure 5-146 *Successful Completion of the Meraki Single Sign-On Integration in Duo*

Adding SP-Initiated SAML SSO

Step 1. Log in to the Cisco Duo Admin Panel (https://admin.duosecurity.com/login).

Step 2. Navigate to **Applications > Meraki Single Sign-On.** Copy the **IdP-Initiated Login URL** to the clipboard or a text editor, as illustrated in Figure 5-147.

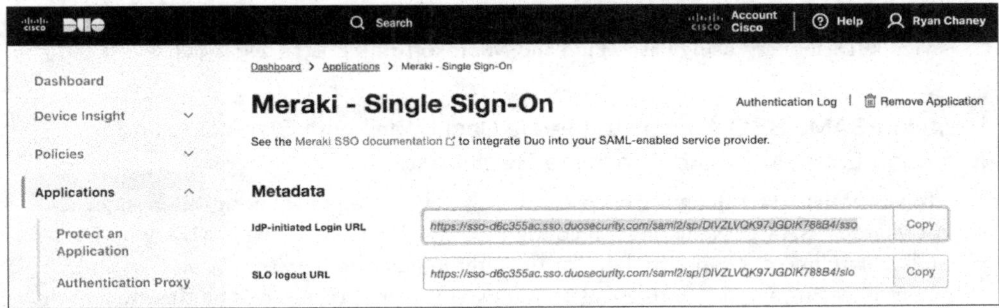

Figure 5-147 *Navigating to the Meraki – Single Sign-On Application in the Cisco Duo Admin Panel*

Step 3. Log in to Meraki Dashboard (https://dashboard.meraki.com).

Step 4. Navigate to **Organization > Settings** and scroll down to **Authentication.** Paste the **IdP-Initiated Login URL** into the **SSO Login URL** field.

The last step required on this page is to configure an SSO subdomain. The SSO subdomain forms part of the URL used to log in to Meraki Dashboard when using single sign-on—for example, https://<SSO_Subdomain>.sso.meraki.com. Add the prefix you would like to use in the **SSO Subdomain** field. Here, we used **adp_se_lab**, which is taken from our org name, as illustrated in Figure 5-148.

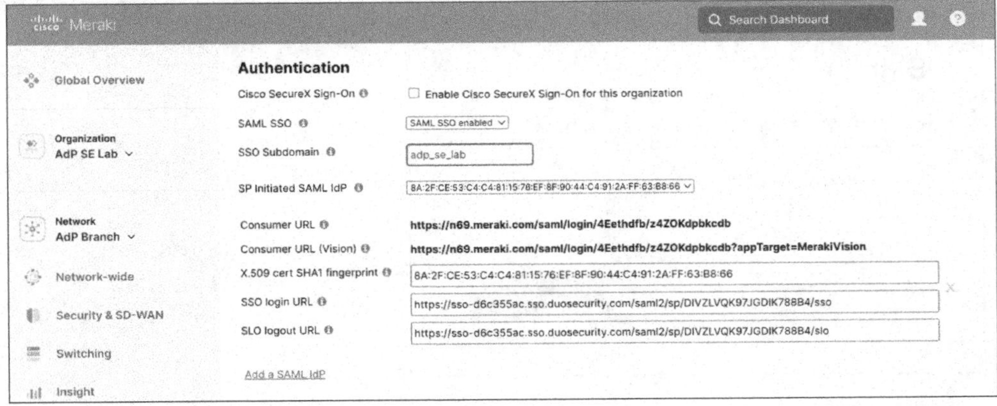

Figure 5-148 *Adding the Configuration for SP-Initiated SAML SSO with Duo in Meraki Dashboard*

> **Note** If you run into trouble with this section, Cisco Duo has published a detailed guide on setting up and troubleshooting SAML single sign-on between Meraki Dashboard and Cisco Duo at https://duo.com/docs/sso-meraki.

At this point, you've completed the configuration necessary to enable SAML SSO with Meraki Dashboard using Cisco Duo and Microsoft Entra. Let's test it out.

Verifying SAML SSO Access to Meraki Dashboard with Cisco Duo and Microsoft Entra (Including Duo Inline Enrollment)

To verify that everything is working, you now need to log in via both IdP-initiated and SP-initiated SAML. No additional configuration is required to enable MFA with Duo. Inline enrollment is supported due to the tight integration between Cisco Duo and Microsoft Entra. Inline enrollment allows users to enroll themselves on their first login, which also means that users do not need to receive an enrollment email. We demonstrate this next.

Verifying IdP-Initiated SAML SSO Administrator Access

Step 1. In Duo Admin Panel, copy the **IdP-Initiated Login URL** from the **Meraki – Single Sign-On** application page shown in Step 14 (Figure 5-145) from the previous section, "Configuring IdP-Initiated SAML SSO Between Cisco Duo and Meraki Dashboard."

Paste this URL into your web browser to open it. When the page opens, you will be asked for your username. Enter the email address of a user in the Meraki administrators group in Microsoft Entra, as illustrated in Figure 5-149.

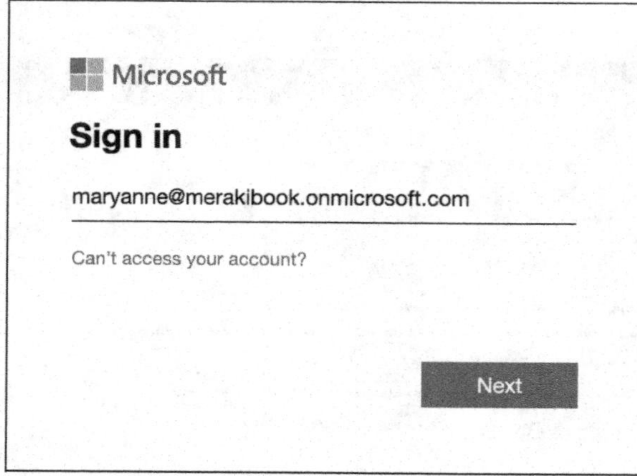

Figure 5-149 *Username Prompt During IdP-Initiated SAML SSO to Meraki Dashboard Using Duo*

Step 2. From the screen in Figure 5-150, enter your password and click **Sign In**.

Step 3. Because this is this user's first time logging in, a password change is required. Enter a new password, confirm it, and then click **Sign In**.

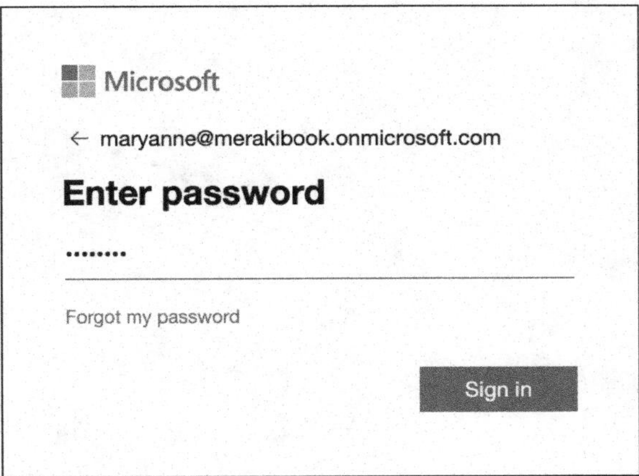

Figure 5-150 *Password Prompt During IdP-Initiated SAML SSO to Meraki Dashboard Using Duo*

Step 4. On the page shown in Figure 5-151, which asks if you would like to stay signed in, you can click either option.

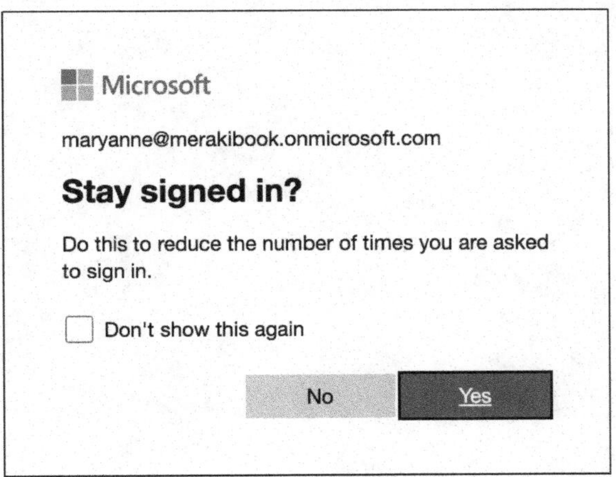

Figure 5-151 *Stay Signed In Page During IdP-Initiated SAML SSO to Meraki Dashboard Using Duo*

Step 5. This is the step where the Cisco Duo inline enrollment starts. Because this is the first time logging in as this user, you need to set up a preferred MFA method. From the screen in Figure 5-152, click **Next** to start the enrollment process.

Step 6. Click **Next** until you get to the screen shown in Figure 5-153 and then select one of the MFA methods available. The next steps will vary based on the MFA method chosen.

Figure 5-152 *Duo Inline Enrollment as Part of IdP-Initiated SAML SSO to Meraki Dashboard*

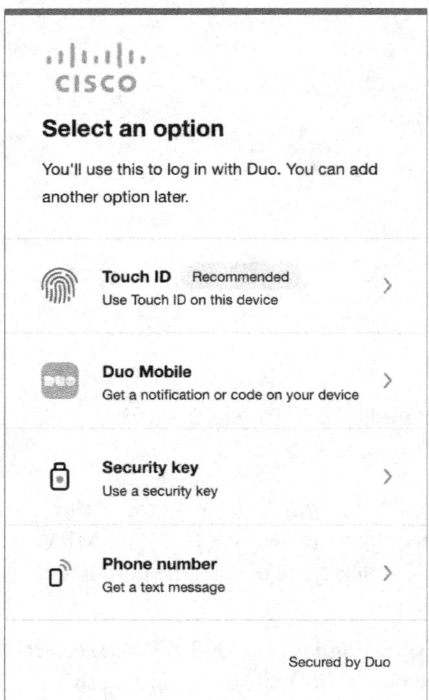

Figure 5-153 *Choosing a Preferred MFA Method as Part of Duo Inline Enrollment*

Step 7. After you have completed the setup of one MFA method, you see the page shown in Figure 5-154. You can add an extra authentication method if you like. When done, click **Skip for Now**.

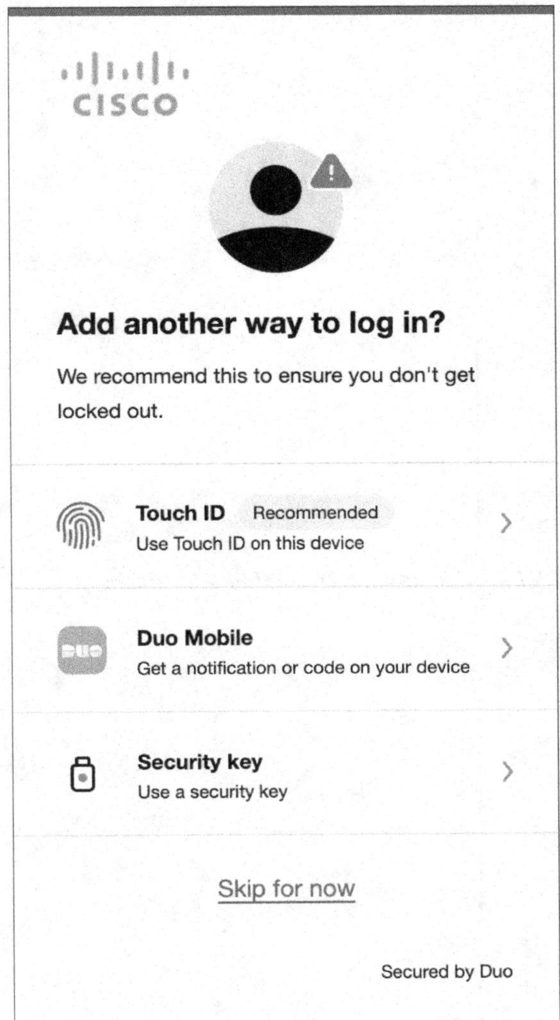

Figure 5-154 *Enrolling in Additional MFA Methods as Part of Duo Inline Enrollment*

Step 8. The Duo MFA enrollment is now complete. On the page shown in Figure 5-155, click **Log In with Duo** to start the MFA login.

Step 9. If you set up SMS as your MFA method, click **Send a Passcode** from the screen shown in Figure 5-156. Otherwise, follow the prompts appropriate for your enrolled MFA method until you get to the success page.

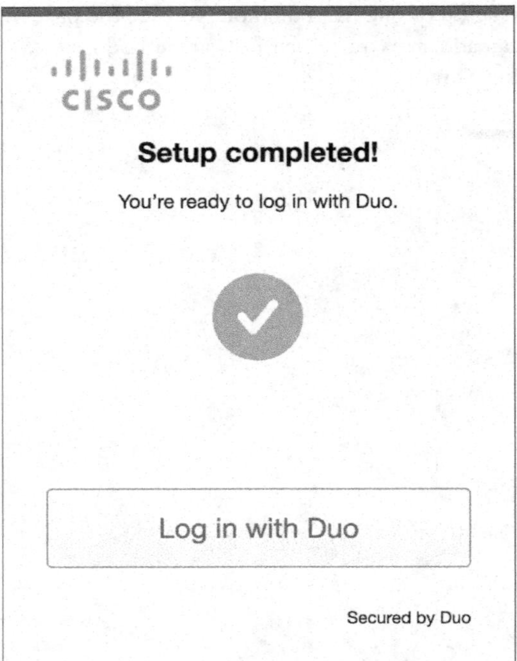

Figure 5-155 *Completing the Duo MFA Enrollment via a Duo Inline Enrollment*

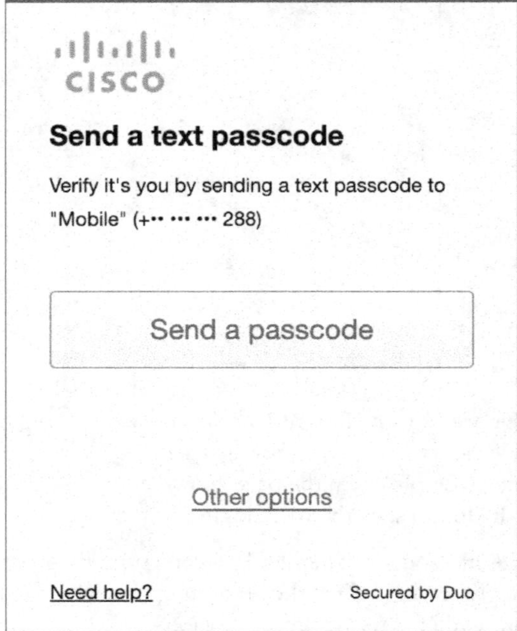

Figure 5-156 *MFA Authentication Using SMS with Cisco Duo*

Step 10. Enter the code received via SMS and click **Verify**, as illustrated in Figure 5-157. You briefly see a success message, as illustrated in Figure 5-158.

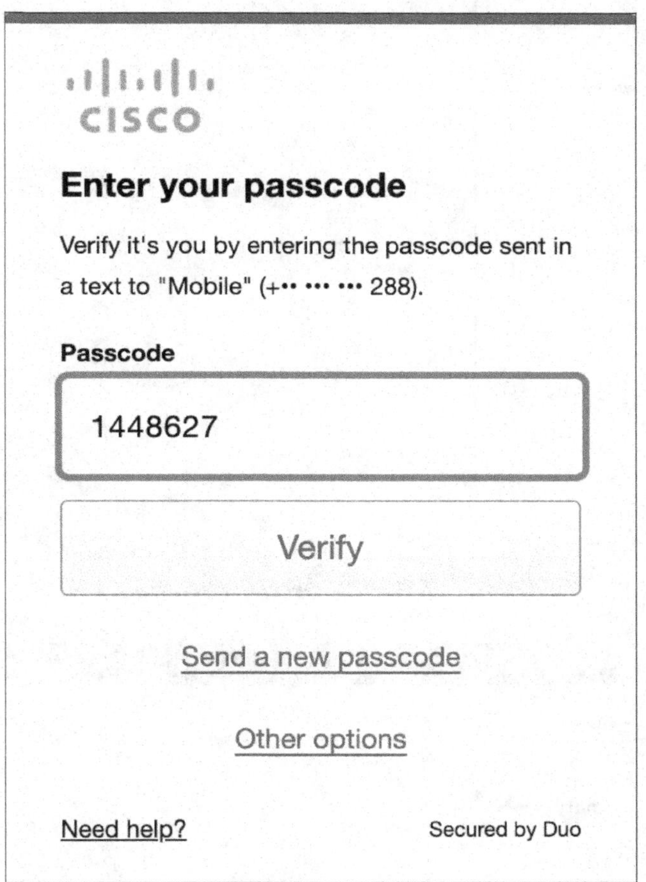

Figure 5-157 *Entering a One-Time Passcode Received via SMS as Part of Multifactor Authentication*

Finally, you are delivered into Meraki Dashboard. Here, we clicked on the profile icon to verify the logging-in user, as illustrated in Figure 5-159.

Step 11. When you click **Sign Out** on the Profile menu to log out of Meraki Dashboard, the session ends, and you see the Duo page in Figure 5-160 advising you to close your browser tab.

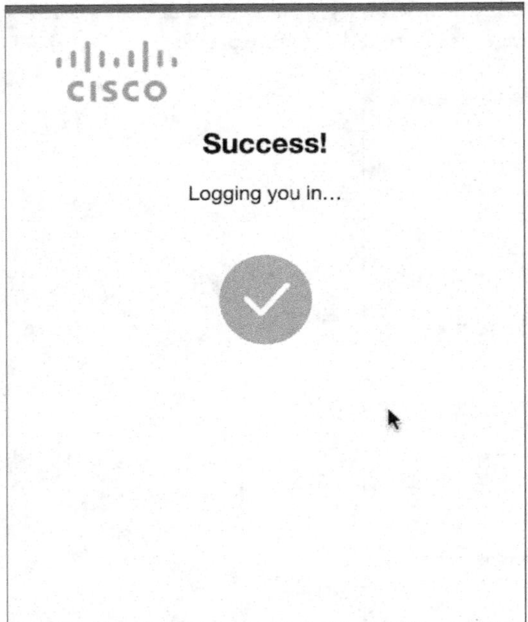

Figure 5-158 *Success Message as Part of MFA Login with Cisco Duo*

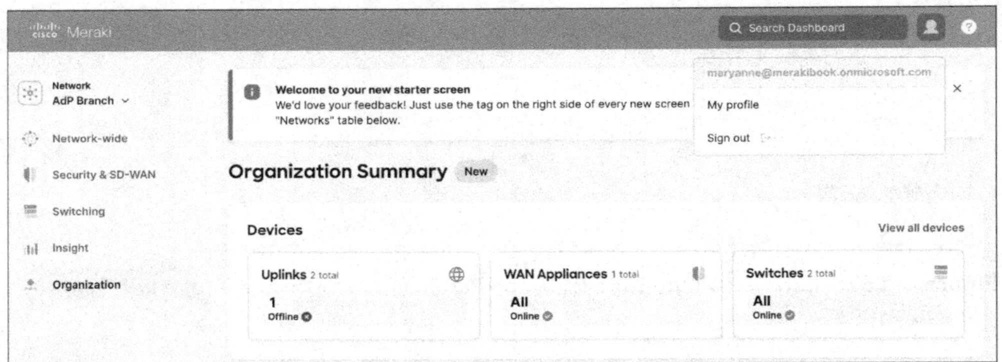

Figure 5-159 *Successful IdP-Initiated SAML SSO to Meraki Dashboard Using Cisco Duo*

Verifying SP-Initiated SAML SSO Administrator Access

Step 1. Log out of Microsoft Entra admin center or use a different web browser. Enter your SP-initiated single sign-on URL in your web browser. The format once again is <SSO subdomain>.sso.meraki.com; in this case we used https://adp_se_lab.sso.meraki.com (see Figure 5-161).

You'll be testing with a user who is already enrolled in Duo, so this time you don't need to complete the inline enrollment steps.

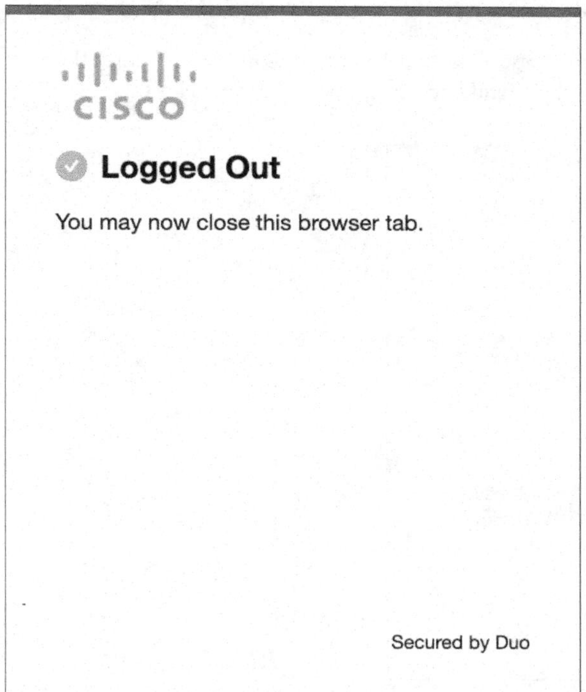

Figure 5-160 *Duo Logout Page After Logging Out of Meraki Dashboard*

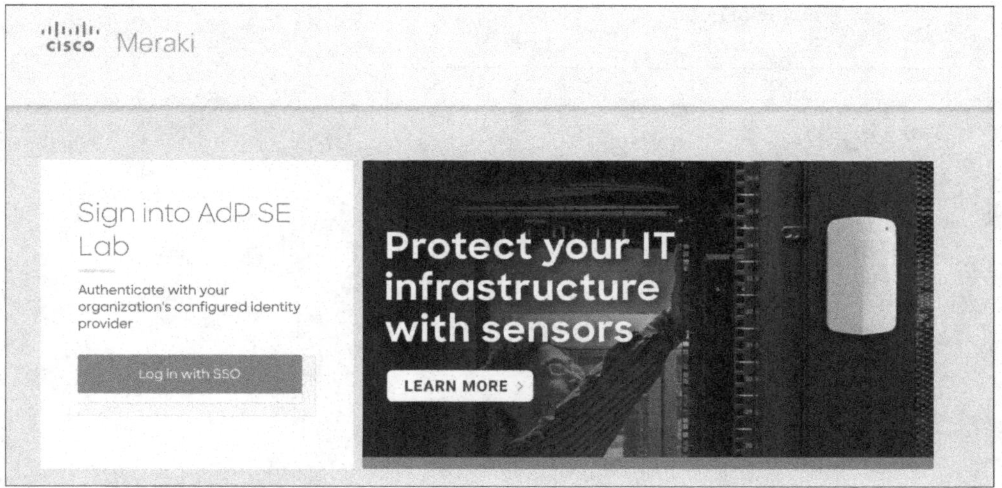

Figure 5-161 *The Meraki Single Sign-On Login Page (Duo Integration with Microsoft Entra)*

Step 2. Click **Log In with SSO.**

Step 3. A Microsoft Sign In page appears, as illustrated in Figure 5-162. Enter the email address of one of the Meraki administrators and click **Next.**

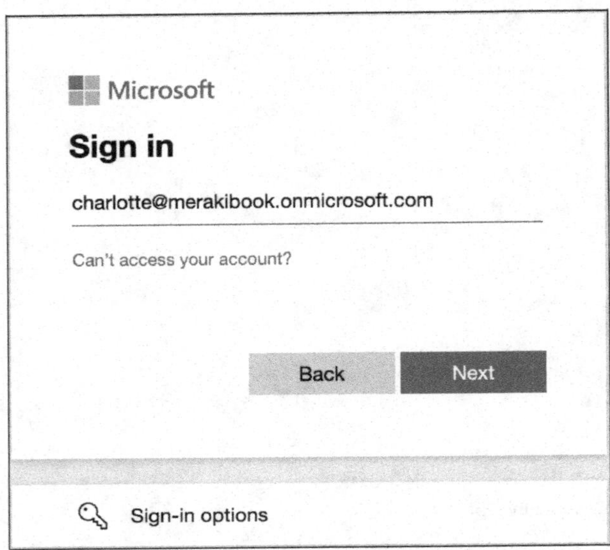

Figure 5-162 *Entering Username During the SP-Initiated SAML SSO*

Step 4. Enter the password for this account and click **Sign In**, as illustrated in Figure 5-163.

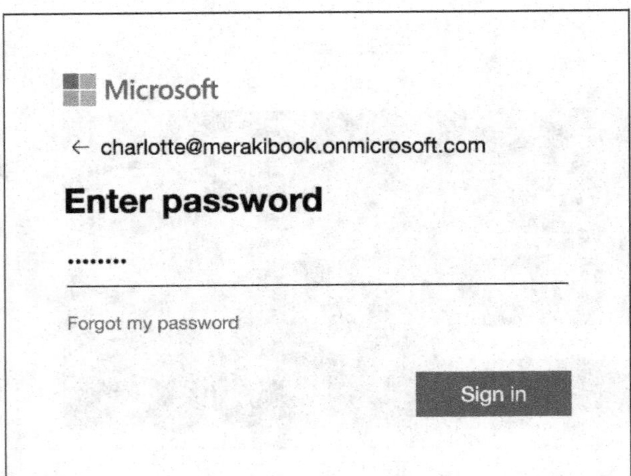

Figure 5-163 *Entering a Password During the SP-Initiated SAML SSO*

Step 5. You are redirected to a Cisco Duo login page for multifactor authentication. There you are presented with the method(s) that you're enrolled with. If you enrolled with SMS for MFA like we did, click **Send a Passcode** to receive the passcode via SMS, as illustrated in Figure 5-164. If you enrolled with another method, follow the prompts onscreen until you're successfully logged in to Meraki Dashboard.

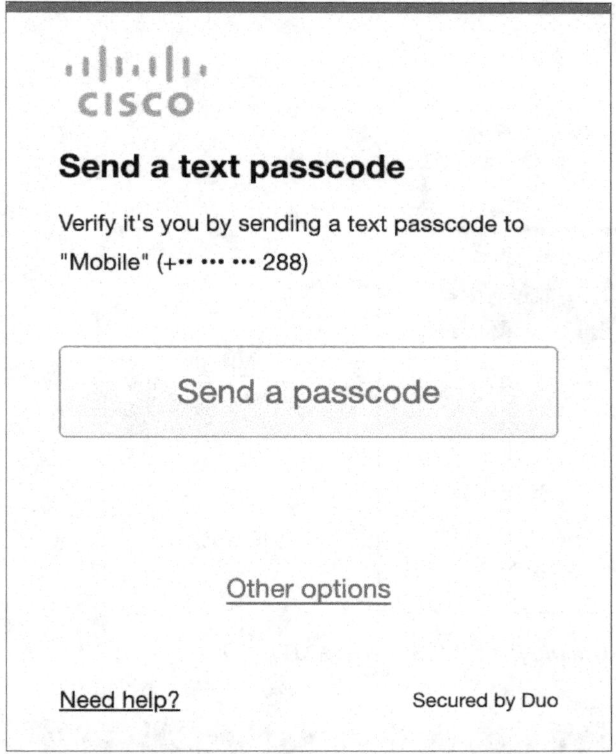

Figure 5-164 *Sending a Passcode via SMS During the SP-Initiated SAML SSO*

Step 6. To complete multifactor authentication using SMS, enter the passcode received via SMS and click **Verify**, as illustrated in Figure 5-165.

Step 7. Once authentication is complete, you're delivered into Meraki Dashboard. Here, we confirmed the username we used to log in by clicking on the **Profile** menu, as illustrated in Figure 5-166.

Step 8. When you sign out, you're taken to a Duo sign-out page, which is the same as the one you saw when using IdP-initiated SAML SSO, as illustrated in Figure 5-167.

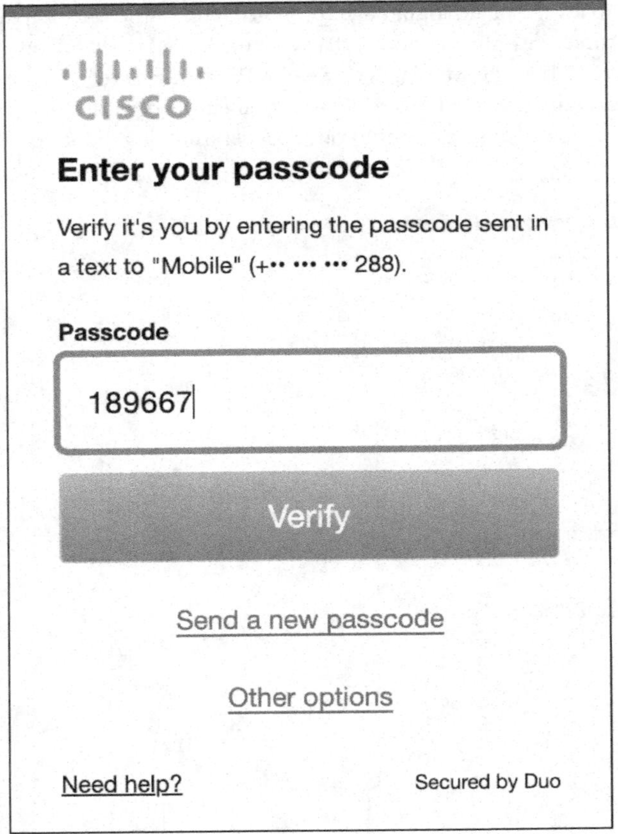

Figure 5-165 *Completing MFA During the SP-Initiated SAML SSO*

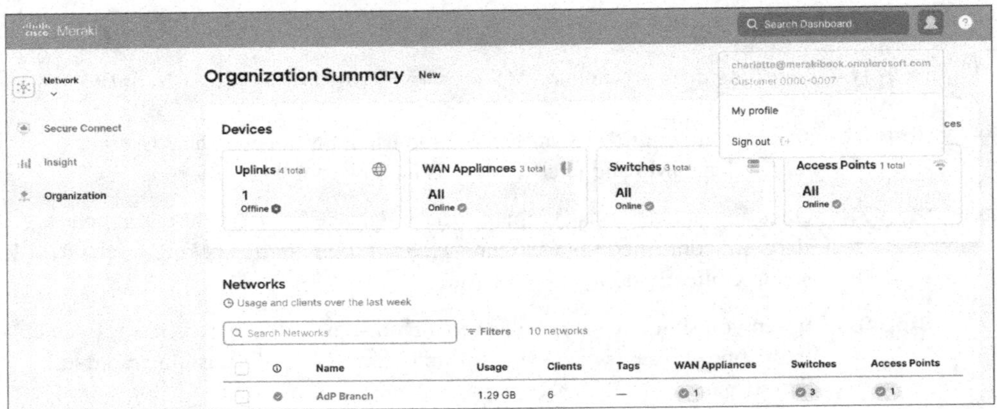

Figure 5-166 *Successful SP-Initiated SAML SSO to Meraki Dashboard*

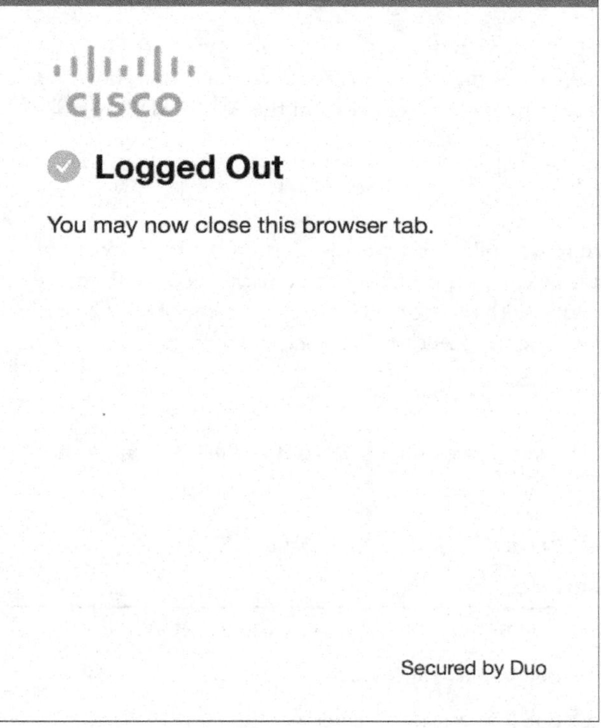

Figure 5-167 *Duo Logout Page After Logging Out of Meraki Dashboard*

Implementing Additional Access Controls Using Cisco Duo and Microsoft Entra ID

The first portion of this chapter took you through the steps to secure administrative access to Meraki Dashboard when using its native capabilities. Now that you're using SAML single sign-on and the user no longer resides in Meraki Dashboard, these controls shift to the identity management and MFA solutions being used. The remainder of this chapter shows how to configure these controls. Additionally, we discuss how to extend the native capabilities of Meraki Dashboard to provide advanced controls required by some IT security standards.

Password Policies

As mentioned previously, strong authentication features heavily in IT security industry best practices. The security of administrative interfaces is paramount, and key to that are password controls and MFA. Read on to learn how common password requirements can be met when using Cisco Duo and Microsoft Entra ID for SAML single sign-on.

Password Age

The default password expiry duration (maximum password age) in Microsoft Entra ID is 90 days. This setting cannot be changed in the Microsoft Entra admin center; however, it can be changed via the **Set-MsolPasswordPolicy** cmdlet from the Azure AD PowerShell module.

Password Reuse

Microsoft Entra's default password reuse policy prevents the reuse of the most recent password. At present, this policy cannot be changed for cloud-based user accounts. If you need something different, such as complying with the PCI DSS 4.0 requirement of four, this can be done by synchronizing with an on-premises Active Directory environment.

Password Complexity

Microsoft Entra's default password complexity policy, outlined in Table 5-3, allows for strong passwords as standard.

Table 5-3 *Microsoft Entra's Default Password Complexity Policy*

<table>
<tr><th>Property</th><th>Requirements</th></tr>
<tr><td>Complexity</td><td>Passwords require three out of four of the following:
■ At least one uppercase character
■ At least one lowercase character
■ At least one number
■ At least one special character</td></tr>
<tr><td>Password length</td><td>Minimum of 8 characters and no more than 175 characters</td></tr>
<tr><td>Characters allowed</td><td>Uppercase characters (A–Z)
Lowercase characters (a–z)
Numbers (0–9)
Special characters (including space):
@ # $ % ^ & * ( ) _ + ! + = [ ] { } | \ , . ? / ` ~ ‘ “ ; < ></td></tr>
<tr><td>Characters not allowed</td><td>Unicode characters</td></tr>
</table>

Microsoft Entra's password complexity policy cannot be changed for cloud-hosted user accounts. If you need something different, such as a minimum password length of 12 characters, this is possible by synchronizing with an on-premises Active Directory environment.

Account Lockout After Invalid Login Attempts

With Microsoft Entra, by default, user accounts are locked out after 10 failed attempts. This setting is configurable to a value between 1 and 50.

To change the number of attempts before account lockout in the Microsoft Entra admin center, navigate to **Protection > Authentication Methods**, as illustrated in Figure 5-168. Adjust the value in the field next to **Lockout Threshold** and click **Save**.

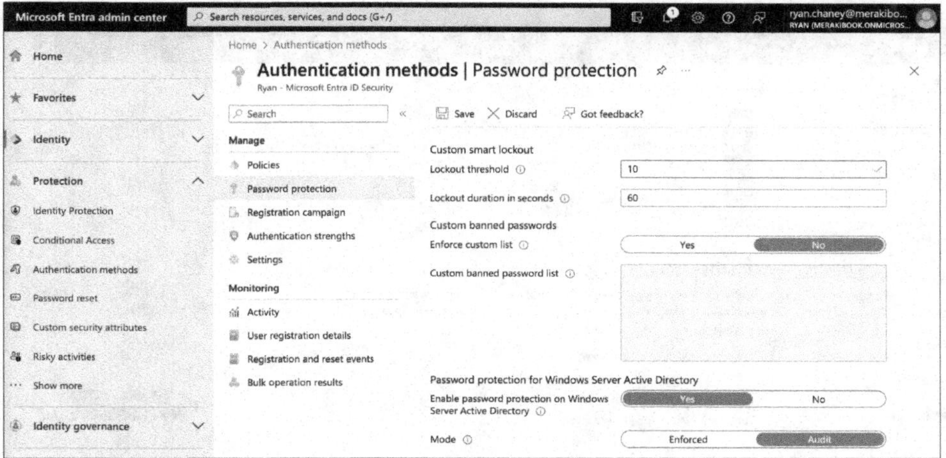

Figure 5-168 *Changing the Account Lockout Settings, Microsoft Entra Admin Center*

By default, locked-out accounts are unlocked after a minimum duration of 60 seconds. Valid duration values are between 5 and 18,000 seconds (5 hours).

To change the lockout duration in the Microsoft Entra admin center, navigate to **Protection > Authentication Methods.** Adjust the value in the field next to **Lockout Duration** in seconds and click **Save.**

Security Policies

Some IT security standards, such as NIST 800-53, require advanced security practices above and beyond password policies. Read on to learn how these advanced security policies can be implemented when using Cisco Duo and Microsoft Entra ID for SAML single sign-on.

IP Whitelisting

It is important to note that the IP whitelisting feature in Meraki Dashboard applies only to logins using local accounts. IP whitelisting must also be supported by either the SAML SSO or MFA solution to apply to all Dashboard logins. In our case, we're using Cisco Duo, which supports both IP whitelisting and geoblocking.

Follow these steps to configure IP whitelisting as part of the Duo MFA configuration:

Step 1. Log in to the Duo Admin Panel (https://admin.duosecurity.com/login).

Step 2. Navigate to **Policies** (located on the left-side menu) and click **Edit Global Policy**, as illustrated in Figure 5-169. The Global Policy will apply to all applications. If you want to make this change just for the Meraki single sign-on application, open the Meraki single sign-on application from the **Applications** page. Scroll down to **Policy** and click either **Apply a Policy to Groups of Users** or **Apply a Policy to All Users.**

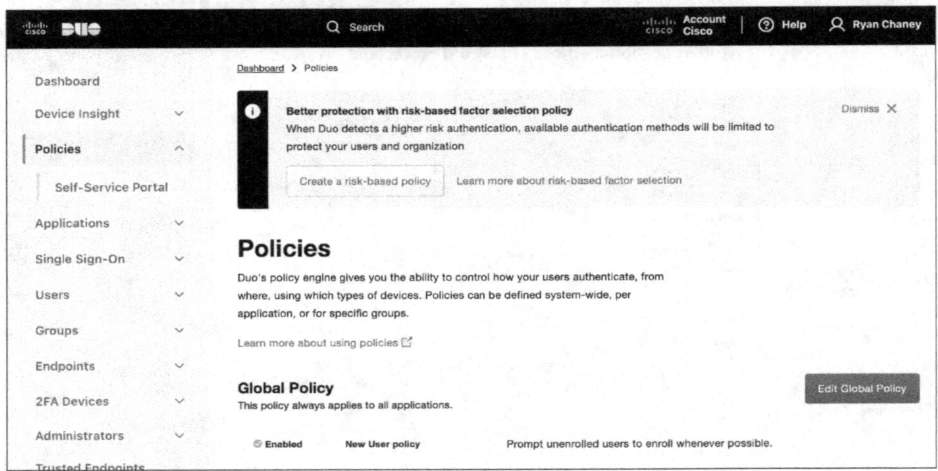

Figure 5-169 *Navigating to the Policies in the Duo Admin Panel*

Step 3. On the **Edit Policy** window for the Global Policy, click **Authorized Networks.**

To create an IP whitelist, enter the subnets you wish to permit in the box labeled **Require 2FA from These Networks** and check the box next to **Deny Access from All Other Networks**, as illustrated in Figure 5-170. Click **Save Policy** at the bottom of this window to save the changes.

Depending on what you're trying to achieve, you may prefer to just list the countries where users are allowed to log in from (geoblocking). To configure geoblocking in Duo Admin Panel as part of the global policy, navigate to **Policies** and click **Edit Global Policy.** Geoblocking is configured under **User Location** in the **Users** section of the Global Policy.

Restricting Concurrent Logins

Restrictions on concurrent logins are not supported natively in Microsoft Entra ID. However, restrictions are possible when you are synchronizing with an on-premises Active Directory environment via third-party applications or scripting. Speak to your Microsoft specialist or partner for the best way to achieve these restrictions.

Automatically Disabling Inactive Accounts

In Microsoft Entra, a user is deemed to be inactive if that user has not logged in for 30 days. Microsoft Entra ID's access reviews feature enables admins to identify and disable inactive accounts, as illustrated in Figure 5-171. This process typically relies on human interaction, but it can be automated through automatic actions.

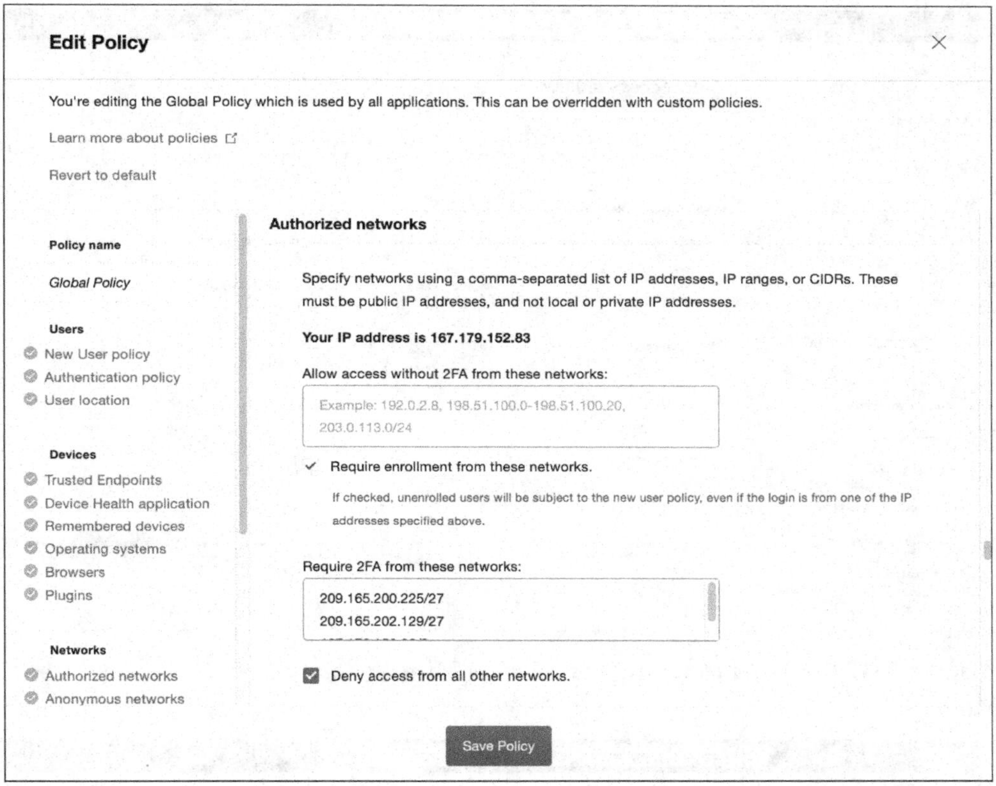

Edit Policy

You're editing the Global Policy which is used by all applications. This can be overridden with custom policies.

Learn more about policies

Revert to default

Policy name

Global Policy

Users

New User policy

Authentication policy

User location

Devices

Trusted Endpoints

Device Health application

Remembered devices

Operating systems

Browsers

Plugins

Networks

Authorized networks

Anonymous networks

Authorized networks

Specify networks using a comma-separated list of IP addresses, IP ranges, or CIDRs. These must be public IP addresses, and not local or private IP addresses.

Your IP address is 167.179.152.83

Allow access without 2FA from these networks:

Example: 192.0.2.8, 198.51.100.0-198.51.100.20, 203.0.113.0/24

Require enrollment from these networks.

If checked, unenrolled users will be subject to the new user policy, even if the login is from one of the IP addresses specified above.

Require 2FA from these networks:

209.165.200.225/27
209.165.202.129/27

Deny access from all other networks.

Save Policy

Figure 5-170 *Configuring IP Whitelisting in the Duo Admin Panel*

The access review feature can be configured to

- Routinely look for inactive users in the Meraki administrator groups
- Review whether access is still required
- Specify which users are authorized to make access decisions
- Determine what automatic actions to take if there is no human intervention

Microsoft has published an excellent guide on how to configure access reviews. It is available at https://learn.microsoft.com/en-us/entra/id-governance/create-access-review.

Automatically Disabling Accounts After a Predetermined Period of Time Unless Revalidated

An access review should be configured where administrative access needs to be revalidated. Both the frequency of reviews and the users who are authorized to reapprove access are configurable, as illustrated in Figure 5-172. Default actions can remove access automatically if no action is taken by reviewers.

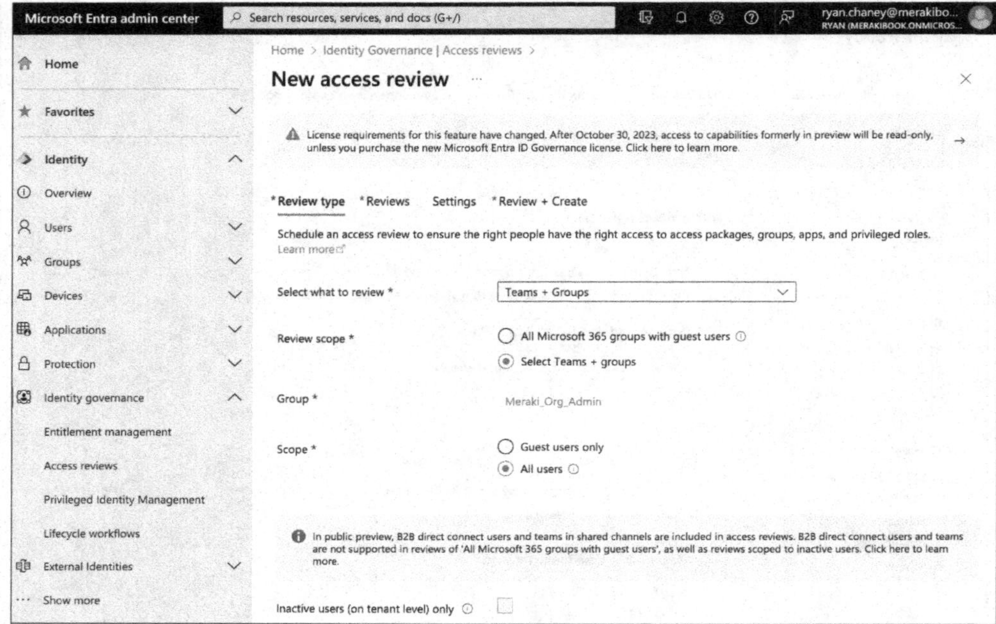

Figure 5-171 *Configuring Access Reviews in Microsoft Entra*

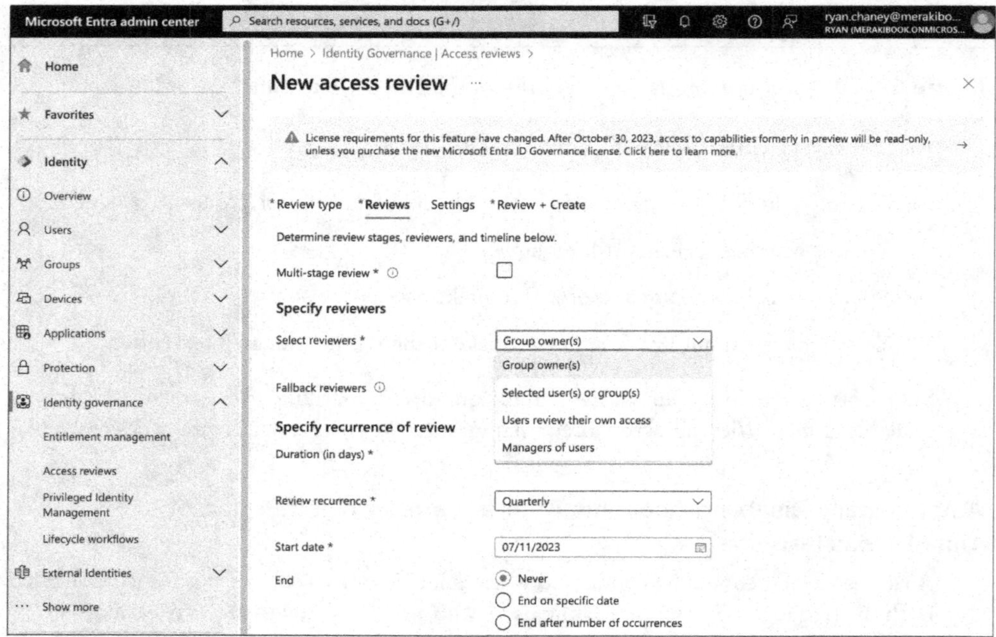

Figure 5-172 *Configuring Reviewers with Revalidation Authority as Part of Access Reviews*

You can find more information on access reviews via this handy guide published by Microsoft at https://learn.microsoft.com/en-us/entra/id-governance/create-access-review.

Automatically Disabling Temporary Accounts

Last, access reviews can also be used to disable temporary accounts. You can place these temporary users in their own group and configure an access review of that group with an automatic action to remove access, as illustrated in Figure 5-173.

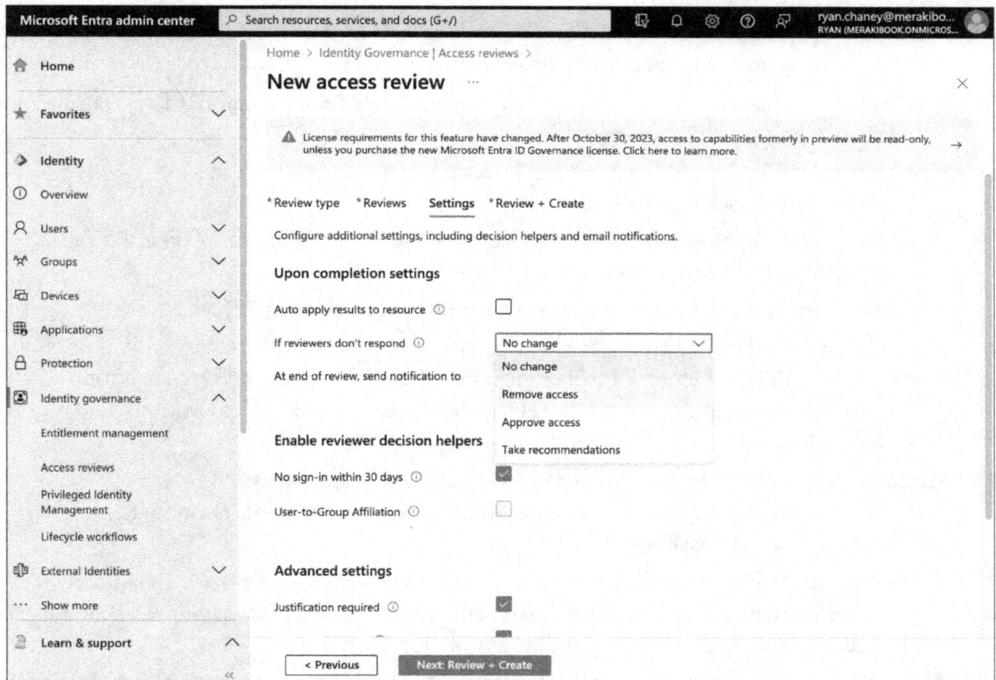

Figure 5-173 *Configuring Automatic Actions on an Access Review in Microsoft Entra*

Summary

Strong authentication and multifactor authentication are key requirements of modern security standards. Meraki Dashboard has a range of easy-to-configure controls out of the box, including policies for minimum password complexity, IP whitelisting, and idle timeout. In this chapter, we detailed how to implement strong administrative access controls using the native capabilities of Dashboard. Despite IT security standards requiring them, these features tend to be disabled by default; therefore, it is recommended to enable them.

In addition, we also detailed the steps to integrate Meraki Dashboard with Cisco Duo and Microsoft Entra for single sign-on, while using Cisco Duo for multifactor authentication. In this scenario, Cisco Duo functioned as both an identity provider and MFA provider. Meraki Dashboard's capability to integrate with other identity providers brings about enhanced capabilities such as geoblocking, access reviews, and the ability to automatically disable admin accounts.

Further Reading

Cisco Duo. (2022, September 7). Azure AD Sync for Duo Users and Admins. https://duo.com/docs/azuresync#overview.

Cisco Duo. (2022, October 11). Duo Single Sign-On for Meraki Dashboard. https://duo.com/docs/sso-meraki

Cisco Duo. (2023a, November 16). User Deletion. https://duo.com/docs/administration-settings#user-deletion

Cisco Duo. (2023b, November 16). Configure the Duo Single Sign-On App in Entra ID. https://duo.com/docs/sso#saml

Cisco Duo. (n.d.). How Does the Inactive User Expiration Setting Affect Users? https://help.duo.com/s/article/4111

Cisco Meraki. (2023, August 24). Creating a Dashboard Account and Organization. https://documentation.meraki.com/General_Administration/Organizations_and_Networks/Creating_a_Dashboard_Account_and_Organization

Cisco Meraki. (2023, October 9). Locked Out of Dashboard. https://documentation.meraki.com/General_Administration/Managing_Dashboard_Access/Locked_Out_of_Dashboard

Cisco Meraki. (2023, October 12). Configuring SAML Single Sign-On for Dashboard. https://documentation.meraki.com/General_Administration/Managing_Dashboard_Access/Configuring_SAML_Single_Sign-on_for_Dashboard

Cisco Meraki. (2023, October 23). SP-Initiated SAML SSO Configuration Guide. https://documentation.meraki.com/General_Administration/Managing_Dashboard_Access/SP-Initiated_SAML_SSO_Configuration_Guide

Cisco Meraki. (2023, November 1). Managing Dashboard Administrators and Permissions. https://documentation.meraki.com/General_Administration/Managing_Dashboard_Access/Managing_Dashboard_Administrators_and_Permissions

Cisco Meraki. (2023, November 15). Two-Factor Authentication. https://documentation.meraki.com/General_Administration/Other_Topics/Two-Factor_Authentication

Cisco Talos. (2023, December). Cisco Talos Year In Review. https://blog.talosintelligence.com/content/files/2023/12/2023_Talos_Year_In_Review.pdf

Microsoft. (2023a, October 24). Combined Password Policy and Check for Weak Passwords in Microsoft Entra ID. https://learn.microsoft.com/en-us/entra/identity/authentication/concept-password-ban-bad-combined-policy

Microsoft. (2023b, October 24). Review Access to Groups and Applications in Access Reviews. https://learn.microsoft.com/en-us/entra/id-governance/perform-access-review

Microsoft. (2023c, October 24). Create an Access Review of Groups and Applications in Microsoft Entra ID. https://learn.microsoft.com/en-us/entra/id-governance/create-access-review

Chapter 6

Security Operations

In this chapter, you learn the following:

- What logging and monitoring capabilities exist in Meraki Dashboard and how to configure them
- How to integrate Meraki Dashboard with the Splunk Cloud Platform for advanced monitoring use cases
- How to automate incident responses using Meraki Dashboard and solutions like ServiceNow
- How to reduce the time required for compliance reporting by integrating Meraki Dashboard with solutions like AlgoSec

Logging and monitoring are two of the key themes seen across industry best practices, as identified in Chapter 2, "Security Frameworks and Industry Best Practices." The NIST Cybersecurity Framework, as an example, requires that networks be continuously monitored for cybersecurity events and that events be recorded. It is critical that both activities are occurring; without monitoring, you will miss the opportunity to prevent a data breach, ransomware, or some other negative event. You don't want to be the organization that first finds out about a cybersecurity event after a ransom request arrives or by reading about it in the news headlines.

This chapter focuses on the capabilities required by security operations teams, namely logging, monitoring, and incident response. This data provides a critical forensic trail; however, security is quickly becoming a big data problem. The Meraki platform helps to solve this problem by allowing data to be collected in a number of ways, both internally and externally, enabling insights to be derived, and actions to be taken faster. Organizations must ensure that their logging and monitoring capabilities are fit for purpose. An ability to pull together the complete picture, across various technology domains, is required to answer obvious questions such as

- When did this incident start? Is it still occurring?
- Where did it start? What was the entry point?
- How did this spread (lateral movement)?
- What has been affected?

Read on to learn about the logging, monitoring, and incident response capabilities in Meraki Dashboard and how to configure them.

Centralized Logging Capabilities

Meraki makes logging easy through its built-in logging capabilities. Having a reliable log of all events occurring to and on the network is not only vital for monitoring and troubleshooting but may also be required as evidence. By default, logging is enabled as soon as an organization is created in Dashboard and no configuration is required.

Meraki Dashboard maintains three types of logs:

- **Login attempts:** A login event is generated any time an organization or network administrator attempts to log in to Dashboard. This includes regular Dashboard login attempts and SAML logins. Log entries are created for all organizations that an administrator has access to.
- **Change log:** This log tracks changes made to an organization (including associated networks) since it was created. Information includes changes made via Dashboard and those made via the Dashboard API.
- **Event log:** This log tracks events that have occurred in a network such as client VPN logins and port up/down.

Meraki has tight audit controls in relation to logging. All logs are read-only and cannot be modified or deleted by an administrator (via Dashboard or API). Access to view these logs requires Dashboard admin access, which is controlled using role-based access control (RBAC). Logging for all devices is on by default. There are no settings that can be configured (other than time zone), and logging cannot be turned off. This means, for example, that it is not possible for an administrator to turn off logging temporarily and make changes without these changes being recorded. Likewise, it is not possible for someone to make changes in Dashboard and then cover up those actions by deleting or altering logs. The one exception to this relates to organizations hosted in Europe. The instance of Dashboard for the EU region has extra capabilities that allow for the handling of data privacy requests, including data deletion. For more information on the EU GDPR features, refer to the guide at https://documentation.meraki.com/General_Administration/Privacy_and_Security/Meraki_Data_Privacy_and_Protection_Features/.

Timestamps are vital because they make it possible for events to be correlated and the sequence of events understood. All log entries in Meraki Dashboard are timestamped. For these timestamps to be useful, there needs to be consistent time across the Meraki infrastructure (PCI DSS 4.0 requirement 10.6.1). The Meraki Cloud takes care of all time synchronization, meaning that you do not need to configure NTP nor maintain your own NTP servers. You only need to select the correct time zone for your network. Time zones cannot be set at the organization level. An easy way to ensure that all devices in Dashboard have their time zone configured consistently is by using configuration templates (**Organization > Configuration Templates**, under Monitor).

The default time zone is **America – Los Angeles (UTC -7.0 DST)**, so if this is what you require, you're all set. Otherwise, follow these steps to set the time zone:

Step 1. Log in to Meraki Dashboard (https://dashboard.meraki.com).

Step 2. Navigate to **Network-wide > General** (under Configure).

Step 3. Scroll down to **Local Time Zone.** Select the correct time zone from the drop-down menu (see Figure 6-1) and click **Save** in the bottom-right corner of the page.

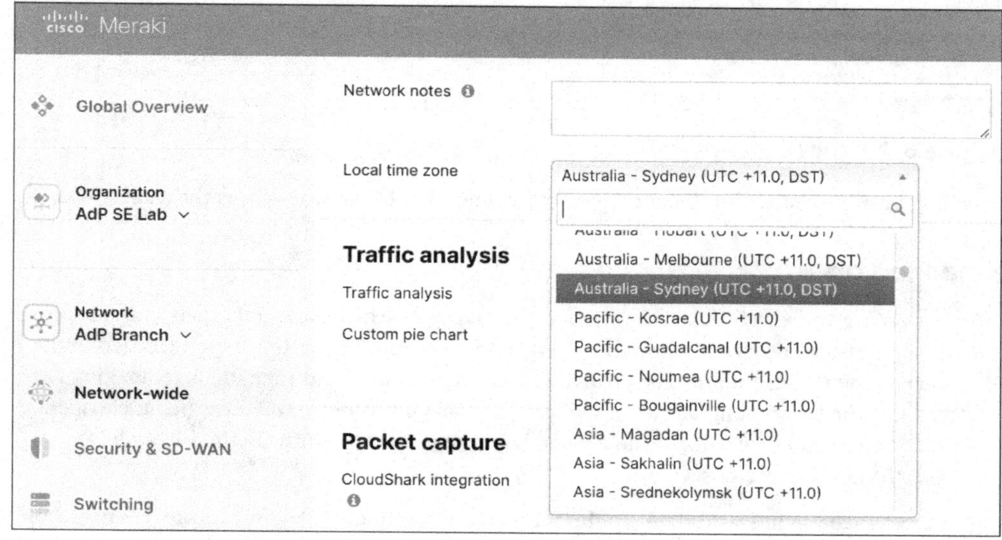

Figure 6-1 *Setting the Local Time Zone in Meraki Dashboard*

The time zone for the change log and login attempts pages default to UTC and GMT, respectively. Although UTC is technically a time standard and GMT is a time zone, in practical terms they are the same, because the time in UTC is always the same in GMT, and vice versa. The event log is displayed using the respective time zone configured for that network.

Meraki uses a storage retention period rather than an actual storage limit, so you don't have to worry about warnings related to running out of capacity. All logs are retained for at least 12 months in compliance with PCI DSS 4.0 requirement 10.5.1. If required, logs can also be exported for longer retention or for advanced audit use cases. We cover how to configure this later in this chapter.

Login Attempts

Privileged access events, such as when an administrator tries to log in to Dashboard, are recorded on the login attempts page. The login attempts page captures all login attempts, whether successful or unsuccessful, and can be found in Meraki Dashboard by navigating to **Organization > Login Attempts** (under Monitor). Use the search field at the top of the page (see Figure 6-2) to filter the results based on a keyword or IP address. You can also sort using the column headings. Figure 6-2 shows login attempts using IPv6 addresses, demonstrating how Dashboard's existing logging supports both IPv6 and IPv4.

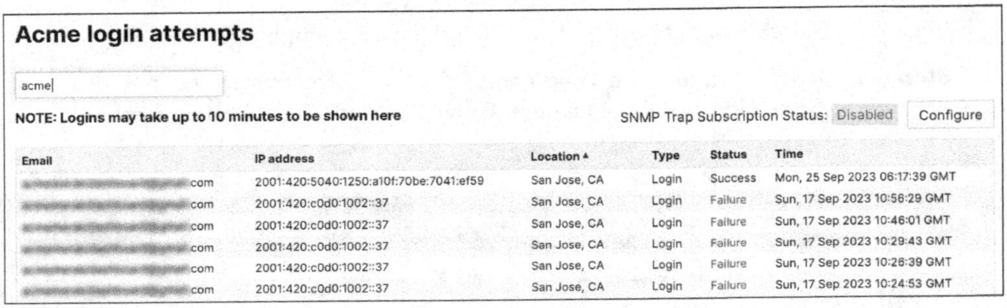

Acme login attempts

acme

NOTE: Logins may take up to 10 minutes to be shown here SNMP Trap Subscription Status: Disabled Configure

Email	IP address	Location ▲	Type	Status	Time
.com	2001:420:5040:1250:a10f:70be:7041:ef59	San Jose, CA	Login	Success	Mon, 25 Sep 2023 06:17:39 GMT
.com	2001:420:c0d0:1002::37	San Jose, CA	Login	Failure	Sun, 17 Sep 2023 10:56:29 GMT
.com	2001:420:c0d0:1002::37	San Jose, CA	Login	Failure	Sun, 17 Sep 2023 10:46:01 GMT
.com	2001:420:c0d0:1002::37	San Jose, CA	Login	Failure	Sun, 17 Sep 2023 10:29:43 GMT
.com	2001:420:c0d0:1002::37	San Jose, CA	Login	Failure	Sun, 17 Sep 2023 10:26:39 GMT
.com	2001:420:c0d0:1002::37	San Jose, CA	Login	Failure	Sun, 17 Sep 2023 10:24:53 GMT

Figure 6-2 *The Login Attempts Page in Dashboard*

Log entries related to login attempts are retained for 14 months; this is the same globally.

Change Log

In accordance with industry best practice, privilege escalation events, such as changes to an administrator's permissions and changes to configuration settings, are recorded in the change log in Dashboard. The change log records the date and time, the user making the change, the location in Dashboard where the change was made, the item being changed, and the old and new values. The change log is kept for 12 months in the EU and 24 months in other regions.

The change log in Dashboard can be found by navigating to **Organization > Change Log** (under Monitor). Figure 6-3 shows an example of change log entries relating to an administrator whose role was changed from a store admin to a camera admin.

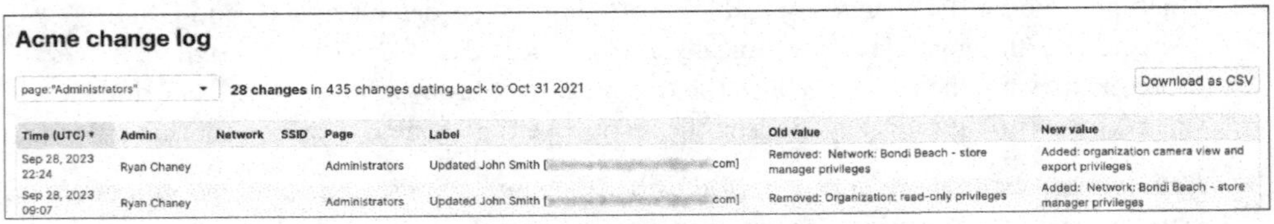

Acme change log

page:"Administrators" **28 changes** in 435 changes dating back to Oct 31 2021 Download as CSV

Time (UTC) ▾	Admin	Network	SSID	Page	Label	Old value	New value
Sep 28, 2023 22:24	Ryan Chaney			Administrators	Updated John Smith [com]	Removed: Network: Bondi Beach - store manager privileges	Added: organization camera view and export privileges
Sep 28, 2023 09:07	Ryan Chaney			Administrators	Updated John Smith [com]	Removed: Organization: read-only privileges	Added: Network: Bondi Beach - store manager privileges

Figure 6-3 *Change Log Showing Changes to Administrator Privileges*

It is possible to both search and filter the change log. To search the change log, type your search criteria in the search field, as shown in Figure 6-3. You can search for any number or text you see on the change log page except time and date. You can even search for multiple criteria by putting a space between each, as shown in Figure 6-4. Search is not case sensitive.

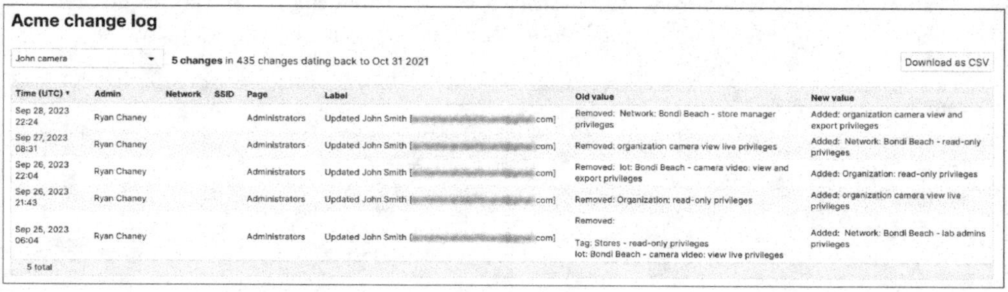

Figure 6-4 *Change Log Showing a Search for Multiple Criteria*

The change log can be sorted by the Time, Admin, Network, SSID, or Page columns simply by clicking the column headings. To filter the change log, use the drop-down menu on the right side of the search box, as shown in Figure 6-5. In addition, if you move your mouse cursor over any value in the Admin, Network, SSID, Page, or Label columns, a filter icon will appear. Click this icon to filter based on that value. Network names appear as hyperlinks; clicking them filters based on the network name.

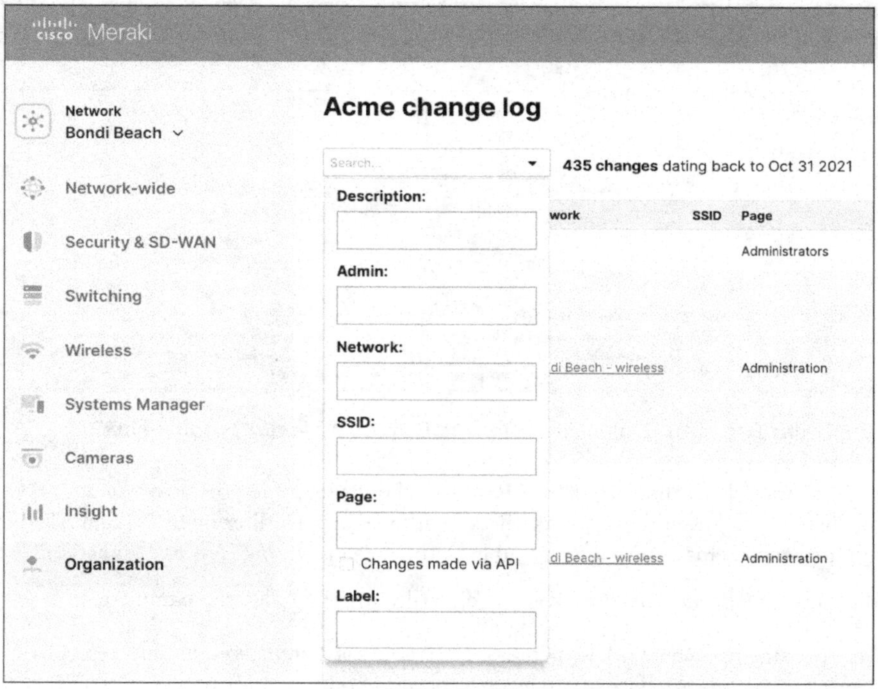

Figure 6-5 *Change Log Search Drop-Down Menu Showing the Filtering Options*

Event Log

The event log captures everything that happens on the network, such as wireless clients associating, VPN clients connecting, port state changes, and dot1x, as shown in Figure 6-6. The event log does not capture administrator logins, however. The event log shows configuration updates received from Dashboard; however, for the details of those changes, refer to the change log. Event logs are retained for 12 months; this is the same globally.

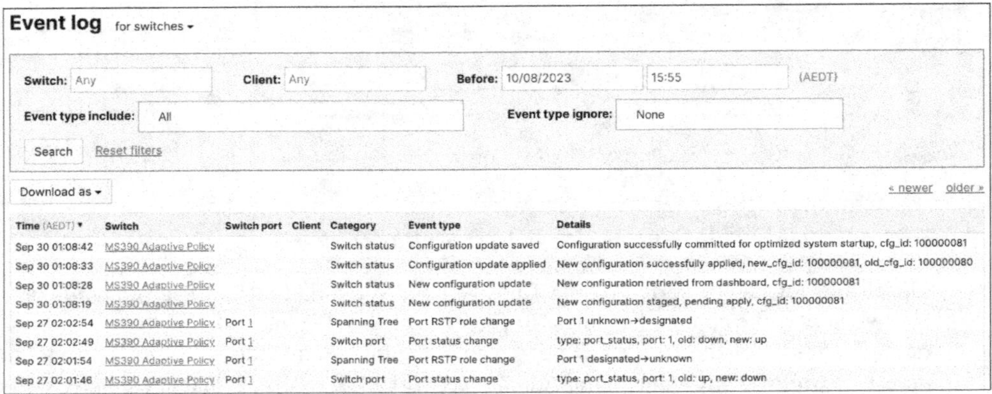

Figure 6-6 *Event Log Showing Switching-Related Events*

For combined networks, you can filter by device type using the drop-down menu next to **Event Log**, as shown in Figure 6-7.

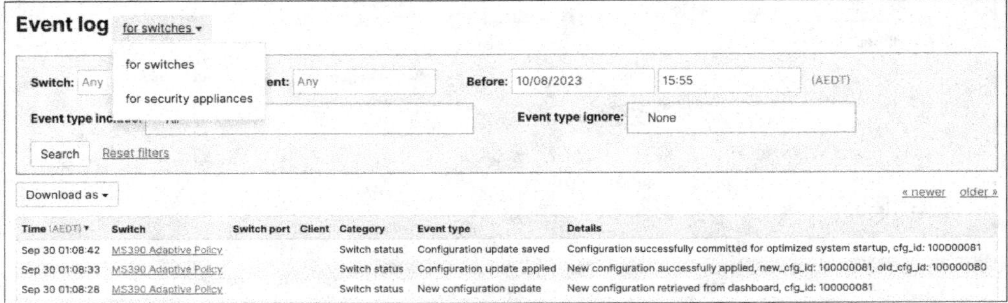

Figure 6-7 *Event Log Drop-Down Menu for the Different Meraki Product Families*

The criteria available to filter on change based on the device type you have selected. For example, when you have access points selected, it's possible to filter on individual APs; when you have cameras selected, you're able to filter on individual cameras; and so on.

In addition to Meraki device type, you can also filter by the following parameters:

- Client: Using hostname, MAC address, or IP address. *Client*, in this case, refers to connected end-user devices such as laptops and phones.

- Event type to include
- Event type to exclude
- Date
- Time

There are many event types, and they are specific to the product family selected. Refer to the following URL for the latest list of available event types and more detail on what they include: https://documentation.meraki.com/General_Administration/Cross-Platform_Content/Meraki_Event_Log.

On the event log page, it is only possible to sort based on time. However, you can export the event log output in CSV format using the **Download As** button, and sort or filter however you like. Finally, the event log is also available via the Dashboard API using the operation ID, getNetworkEvents. For more information, refer to Meraki's Developer Hub page at https://developer.cisco.com/meraki/api-v1/get-network-events/.

Creating API Keys

Meraki Dashboard has an API that makes it quick and easy to integrate with modern, typically cloud-based applications. When you're setting up an integration with applications such as Splunk, ServiceNow, and many others, the first task is to generate an API key. This API key is then used to authenticate that application to your Meraki Dashboard organization.

API keys are attached to user accounts. SAML users cannot generate API keys, so accounts with API keys need to be created in Dashboard. In this case, the use of Dashboard accounts with API keys is synonymous with a traditional service account in Active Directory. Therefore, it is recommended to create accounts with API keys as standalone Dashboard users and to not use these accounts for Dashboard administration. This approach is recommended for three reasons:

1. If an API key is attached to a staff member's account and that person leaves the organization, disabling or removing their account would also break the application integration.
2. The purpose of the account is clearer, making it easier to monitor its behavior for anomalies or turn off individual applications, if required.
3. It adheres to the principle of least privilege.

Some applications using API integration do not restrict themselves to a single organization by default. Therefore, it is also recommended that the email address used for these accounts is not added as an administrator in another Meraki organization. This ensures that applications have access to only the intended Meraki organization.

Before creating the API key, ensure that API access is enabled for your organization in Dashboard (**Organization > Settings**). Scroll down to **Dashboard API Access** and ensure that **Enable Access to the Meraki Dashboard API** is checked, as shown in Figure 6-8.

Figure 6-8 *Enabling API Access at the Organization Level in Meraki Dashboard*

Follow these steps to create a Dashboard user account to be used for API access:

Step 1. Log in to Meraki Dashboard (https://dashboard.meraki.com).

Step 2. Navigate to **Organization** > **Administrators** (under Configure), as shown in Figure 6-9.

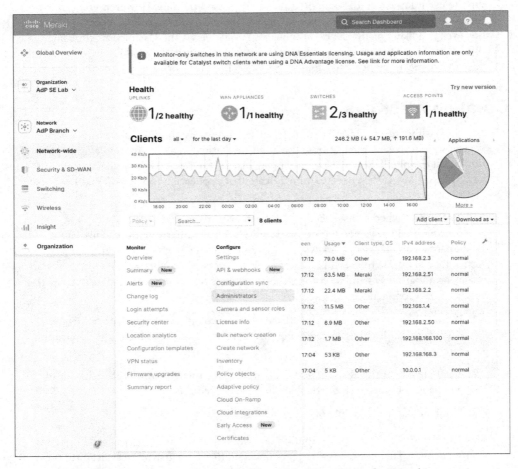

Figure 6-9 *Adding a User in Meraki Dashboard for Accessing the Meraki Dashboard API*

Step 3. Click **Add Admin** in the top right.

Step 4. Enter a name that describes the purpose of this account and set Organization Access to **Read-only**, as shown in Figure 6-10.

An email address is required for verification purposes, so ensure there is a mailbox on your corporate email domain for this user. Enter the user's email address in the **Email** field. Click **Create Admin.**

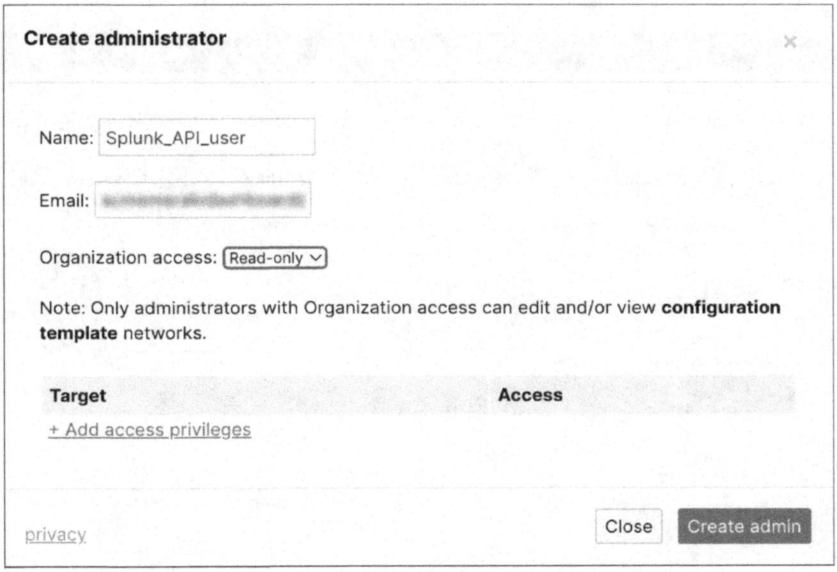

Figure 6-10 *Entering the User Account Details to Be Used for API Access*

Step 5. Log in to the email account for this user and click the link that says **Choose Your Password Here**, as shown in Figure 6-11.

Figure 6-11 *The Meraki Verification Email Sent to the Account to Be Used for API Access*

Step 6. Log out of Meraki Dashboard. Then log in again using the username and password created in the preceding steps. If prompted for a security code as part of the two-factor authentication process, use the code emailed to this user.

Step 7. Once logged in, navigate to **Organization > API & Webhooks**, as shown in Figure 6-12.

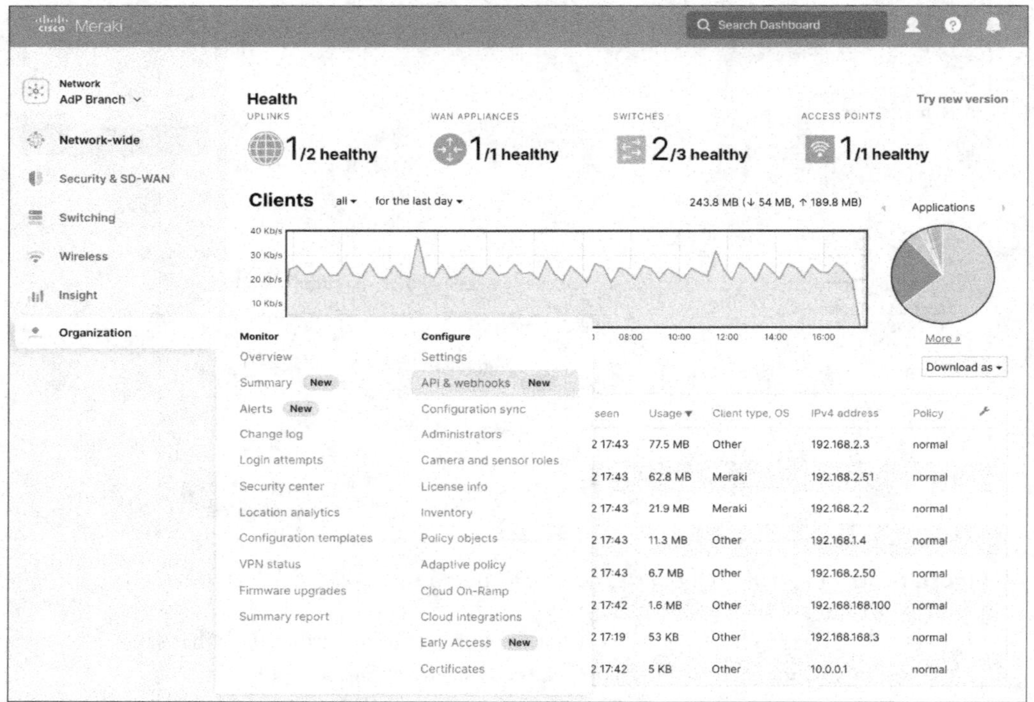

Figure 6-12 *Navigating to the API & Webhooks Page in Meraki Dashboard*

Step 8. Click **Generate API Key**, as shown in Figure 6-13.

Step 9. You then go to the **API Keys and Access** page. Click **Generate API Key**, as shown in Figure 6-14. You can do this even though this account has only read-only access.

Step 10. On the pop-up window, click **Copy** to copy your API key to the clipboard. Record this key securely somewhere because this is the only time you will see it in plaintext. You will need this API key again when configuring the application integration.

Check the box next to **I've Stored My API Key** and then click **Done** to close this window.

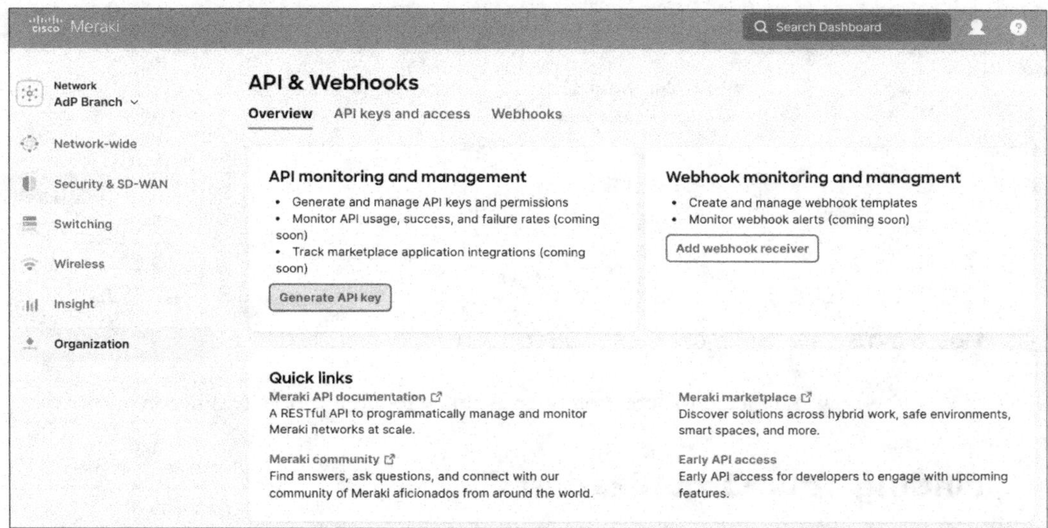

Figure 6-13 *The API Keys and Access Page in Meraki Dashboard*

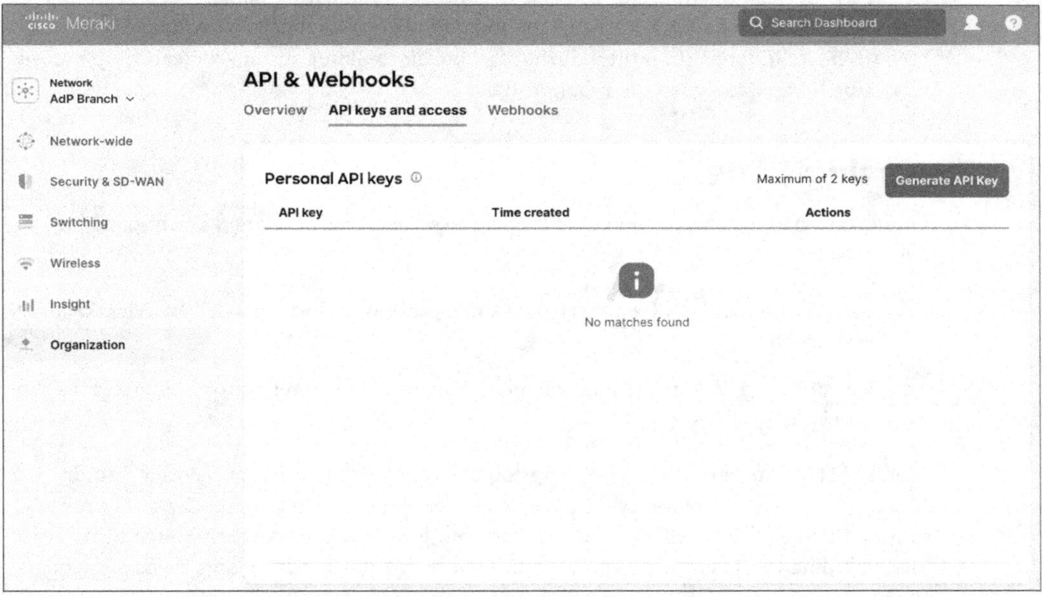

Figure 6-14 *Generating an API Key in Meraki Dashboard*

Step 11. You return to the **API & Webhooks** page, where you see that an API key has been created, as shown in Figure 6-15.

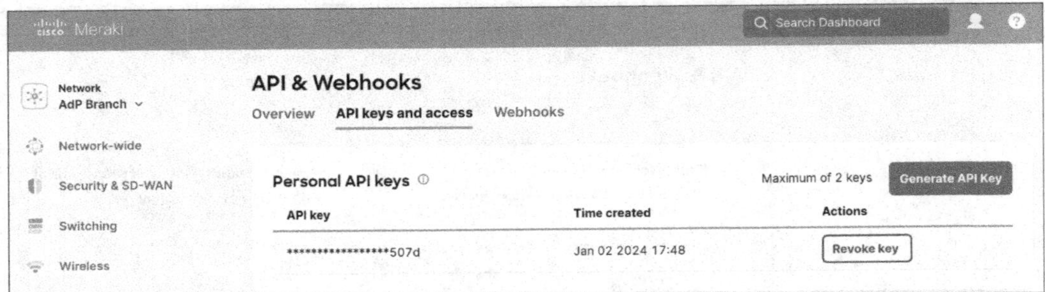

Figure 6-15 *Successful Creation of an API Key in Meraki Dashboard*

You've now completed the creation of an API key for application integration purposes.

Finding Your Organization ID

Another credential that is often required when setting up an application integration is the organization ID. You can find it on the bottom of every page in Meraki Dashboard (a sample figure is shown in Chapter 3, "Meraki Dashboard and Trust"). Scroll down, and at the bottom of the page, you see "Data for [Organization name] (organization ID: XXXXXXXXXXXXXXXXXX) is hosted in [Region name]." Now that you know how to locate it, when prompted during an application integration, you can simply copy this value and paste it into the required field.

Exporting Logs

Organizations might want to export log and flow data out of Meraki Dashboard for reasons such as

- A need to retain logs for longer than the retention period provided by Meraki Dashboard
- A desire to store logs for multiple platforms in a central repository, such as for event correlation purposes

Meraki Dashboard events can be exported via syslog or via integrations that use the Meraki API, such as Splunk. When you're comparing these two methods, it is important to note that syslog is configured at the network level. Therefore, when you're using syslog, including the syslog configuration in your configuration templates is recommended. In comparison, the API keys on which application integrations rely are configured once and cover the entire organization. The other major difference between using syslog and the API is that syslog traffic is sourced directly from devices, whereas logs collected using the API are pulled from Meraki Dashboard itself. Read on to learn how to configure Meraki Dashboard to export log data.

Exporting Logs to Splunk

If you've been working in IT for any amount of time, you've likely already heard of Splunk. Splunk, which is now part of Cisco, is a company that is known for its big data platform. Splunk's platform is able to ingest data from multiple systems and derive insights from it. Figure 6-16 illustrates Splunk's Unified Security and Observability Platform, including event sources, as well as the tools that derive insights and enable actions to be taken.

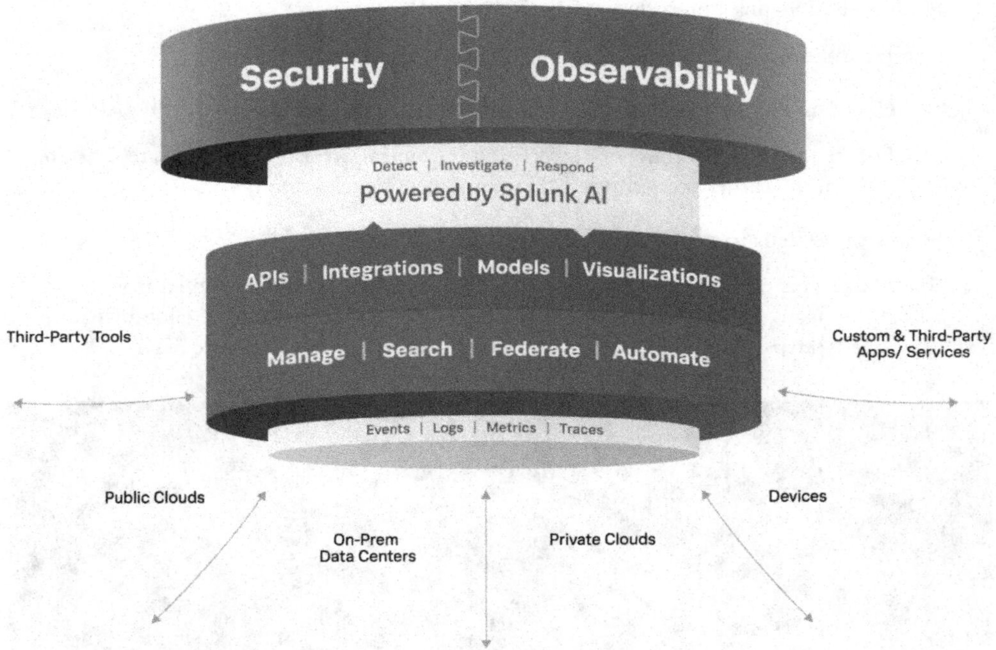

Figure 6-16 *Graphical Overview of How Splunk Ingests and Processes Data*

Using Splunk enables enterprises to address advanced audit, analysis, and reporting requirements, such as the audit and accountability controls required by NIST 800-53 AU-6. Splunk helps to address these requirements by providing the capability to

- Ingest and store audit records from multiple systems in a central location
- Analyze and correlate these audit records to gain organization-wide awareness

Splunk has published a supported add-on for Cisco Meraki, making it easy to pull data from Meraki Dashboard into Splunk. The Cisco Meraki add-on for Splunk uses the Meraki Dashboard API to collect data on audit events (including organization config changes), device statuses, alerts, changes, and authentication events for access points, cameras, switches, and security appliances.

Splunk can also be used to ingest syslog data from Meraki Dashboard. If doing this, refer to the "Syslog" section later in this chapter for instructions on how to configure syslog in Meraki Dashboard. You can send syslog data to Splunk, but it is more time-consuming to set up than using the API-based add-on described previously. If you're sending syslog data to Splunk, the recommended way is to use the Splunk Connect for Syslog–supported add-on. Refer to the following link to learn how to set up Splunk Connect for Syslog: https://splunkbase.splunk.com/app/4740.

Splunk is available in both cloud and on-premises versions, known as Splunk Cloud Platform and Splunk Enterprise, respectively.

Complete these steps before starting the Splunk integration:

- Create an API key. Refer to the steps in the earlier section titled "Creating API Keys."
- Ensure that you how know to locate your organization ID. If you don't, refer to the steps in the earlier section titled "Finding Your Organization ID."

Follow these steps to configure the Meraki add-on for Splunk:

Step 1. This example uses Splunk Cloud, but the steps should be similar if you are using Splunk Enterprise. Log in to your personalized Splunk Cloud URL (https://XXXXXXXX.splunkcloud.com), as shown in Figure 6-17.

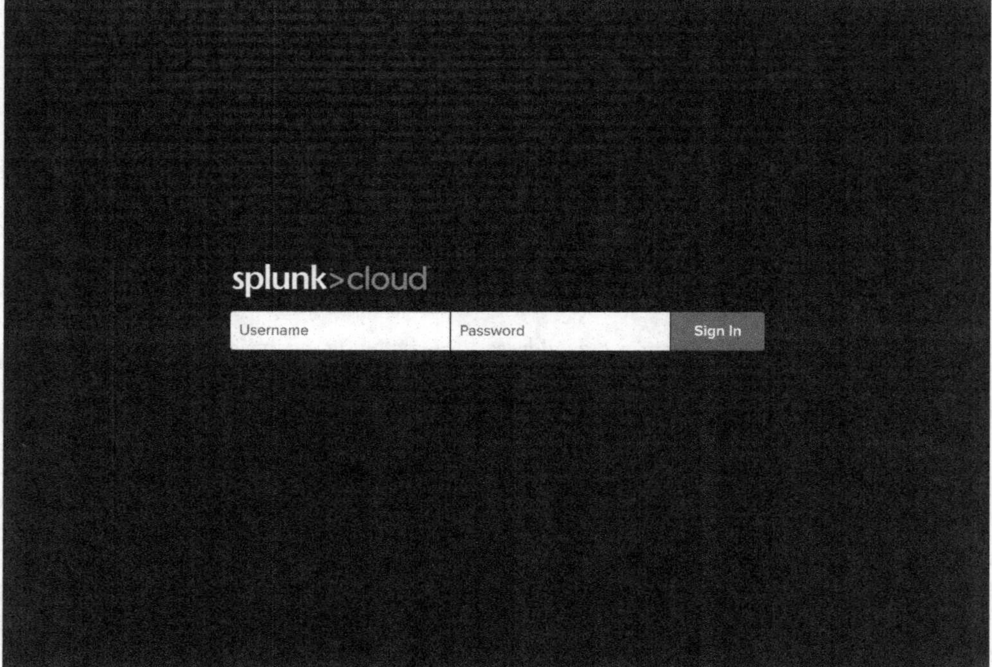

Figure 6-17 *The Splunk Cloud Login Page*

Step 2. Add the Splunk add-on for Cisco Meraki. To do so, click the **Find More Apps** link on the left side of the screen, as shown in Figure 6-18.

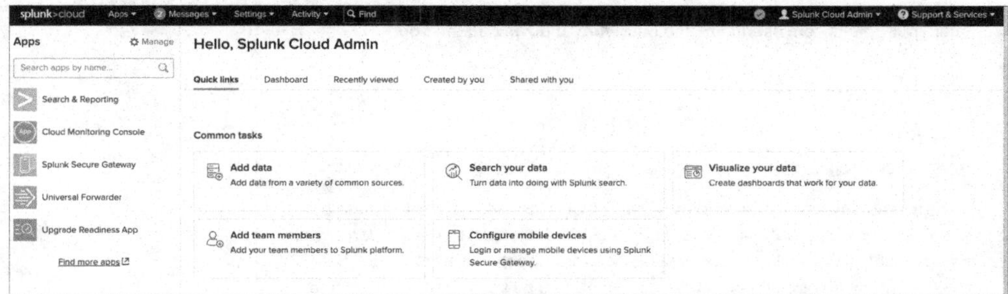

Figure 6-18 *Navigating to Find More Apps in Splunk Cloud*

Step 3. On this new page, in the search field under **Browse More Apps**, enter **meraki**, and press **Enter**.

Next to **Splunk Add-on for Cisco Meraki**, click **Install**, as shown in Figure 6-19.

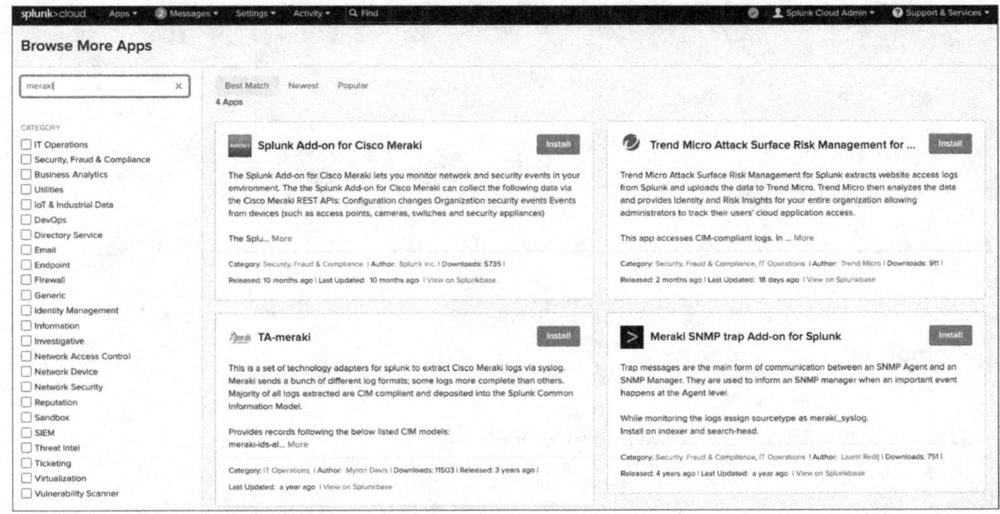

Figure 6-19 *Searching for the Splunk Add-on for Cisco Meraki in Splunk Cloud*

Step 4. On the pop-up window, enter your Splunk.com administrator username and password (not the sc_admin details); then click **Agree and Install**, as shown in Figure 6-20.

Step 5. On the following pop-up window, click **Open the App**, as shown in Figure 6-21.

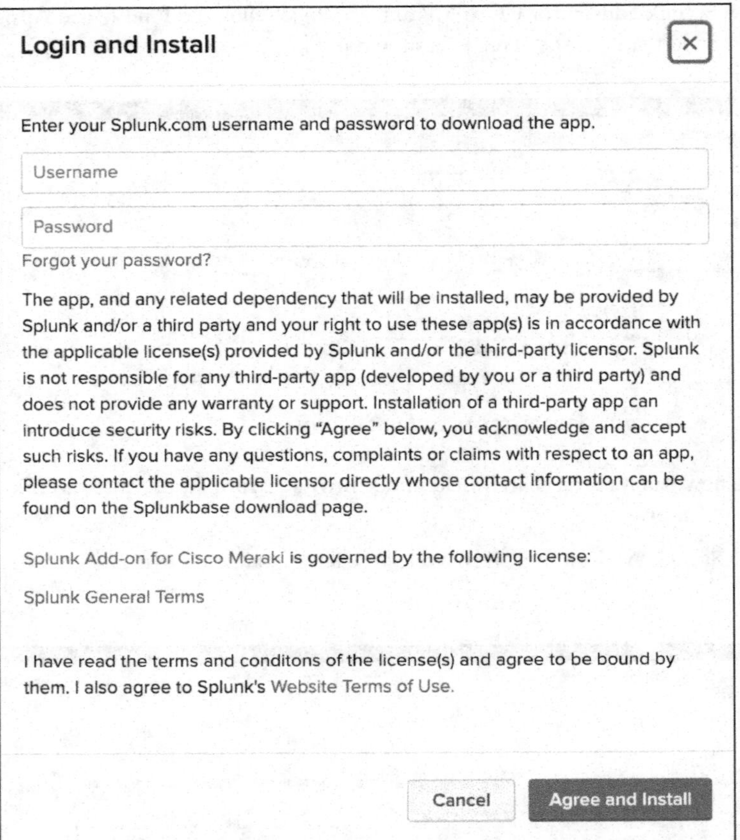

Figure 6-20 *Entering Splunk Administrator Details to Install the Meraki App*

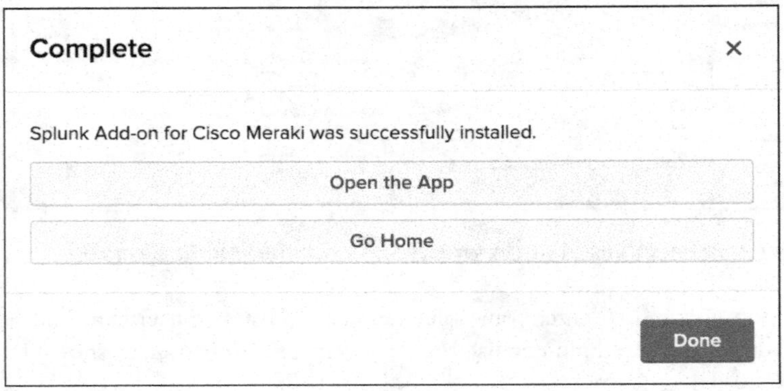

Complete

Splunk Add-on for Cisco Meraki was successfully installed.

Open the App

Go Home

Done

Figure 6-21 *Notification of the Successful Installation of the Splunk Add-on for Cisco Meraki*

Step 6. The **Configuration** page appears. On the **Organization** tab, click the **Add** button on the far right, as shown in Figure 6-22.

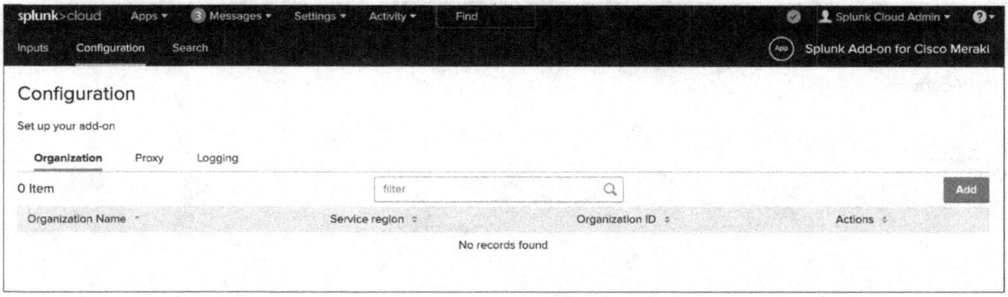

Figure 6-22 *The Configuration Tab of the Splunk Add-On for Cisco Meraki Page in Splunk Cloud*

Step 7. On the **Add Organization** pop-up window shown in Figure 6-23, enter the following:

- **Organization Name:** This is intended to match your Meraki organization name. This field does not allow spaces, so if you have spaces in your organization name, replace them with underscores.
- **Service Region:** Unless your Meraki Dashboard region is China, you can leave this as is.
- **Organization API Key:** Paste in your Meraki API key.
- **Organization ID:** Paste in your Meraki organization ID.

Click **Add**.

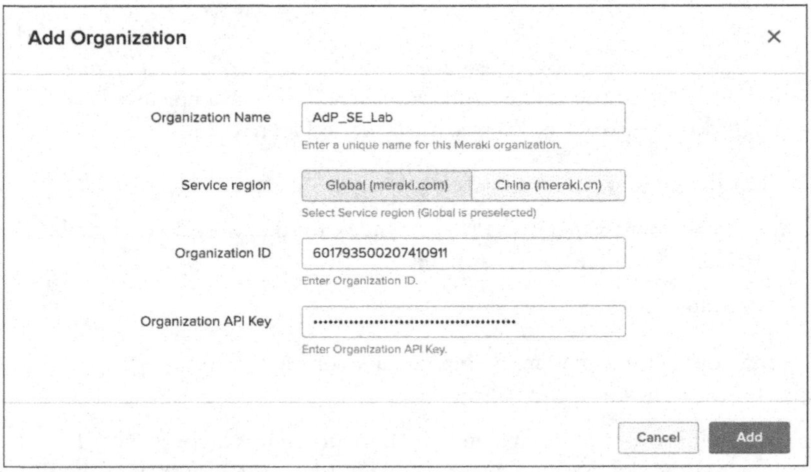

Figure 6-23 *Adding the Organization Details in the Splunk Add-On for Cisco Meraki App*

Step 8. You then return to the **Configuration** page. Click the **Inputs** tab in the top left, as shown in Figure 6-24.

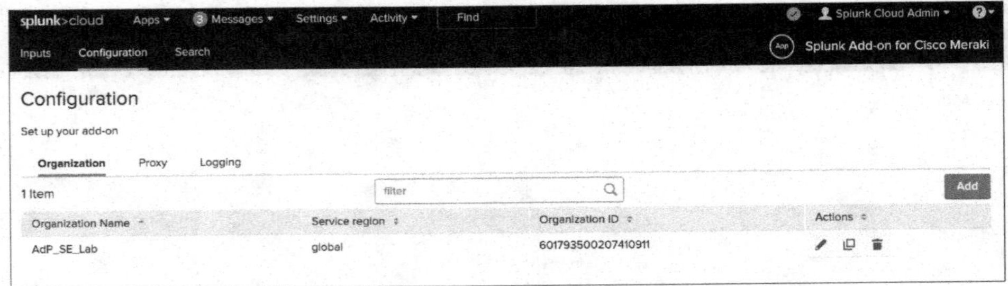

Figure 6-24 *The Splunk Add-on for Cisco Meraki Configuration Page After Adding the Organization Details*

Step 9. On the **Inputs** page, click **Create New Input**. From the drop-down menu, select the input to add. In this example, add all of them starting with Security Appliances, as shown in Figure 6-25.

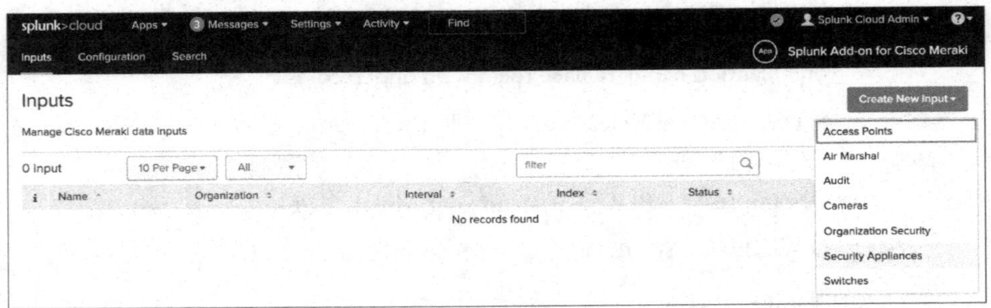

Figure 6-25 *Adding New Inputs on the Inputs Page of the Cisco Meraki Add-On in Splunk Cloud*

Step 10. On the **Add Security Appliances** page, in the **Name** field, enter a unique name for this input. You cannot use spaces here. In this example, we have used **Meraki_Security_Appliances**, as shown in Figure 6-26.

a. Select the **Organization** name from the drop-down menu.

b. You might want to specify a different **Index** for the Meraki events to be stored in. For now, leave this as **main**.

c. Click **Add**.

You can now see an entry on the **Inputs** page for Meraki_Security_Appliances, as shown in Figure 6-27.

Step 11. To ensure all events are available in Splunk Cloud, repeat Steps 9 and 10 for the remaining available inputs. When you're finished, the **Inputs** page should look similar to Figure 6-28.

Add Security Appliances ×

Name: Meraki_Security_Appliances
Enter a unique name for the input.

Organization: AdP_SE_Lab
Select the organization using which you want to collect the events.

Interval: 360
Interval for this Input (in seconds).

Index: main
An Index is a type of data repository. Select the index in which you want to collect the events.

Cancel | Add

Figure 6-26 *Adding the Security Appliances Input to the Splunk Add-On for Cisco Meraki*

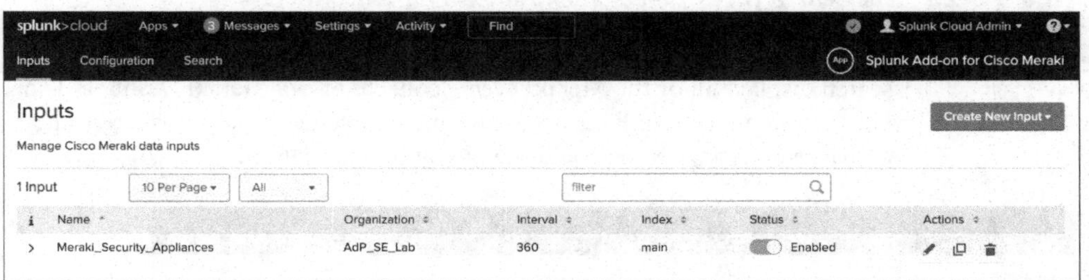

Figure 6-27 *The Inputs Tab of the Splunk Add-On for Cisco Meraki After Adding a New Input*

splunk>cloud Apps Messages Settings Activity Find Splunk Cloud Admin

Inputs Configuration Search Splunk Add-on for Cisco Meraki

Inputs

Manage Cisco Meraki data inputs

Create New Input

7 Inputs 10 Per Page All filter

Name	Organization	Interval	Index	Status	Actions
Meraki_Access_Points	AdP_SE_Lab	360	main	Enabled	
Meraki_Air_Marshall	AdP_SE_Lab	360	main	Enabled	
Meraki_Audit	AdP_SE_Lab	360	main	Enabled	
Meraki_Cameras	AdP_SE_Lab	360	main	Enabled	
Meraki_Organization_Security	AdP_SE_Lab	360	main	Enabled	
Meraki_Security_Appliances	AdP_SE_Lab	360	main	Enabled	
Meraki_Switches	AdP_SE_Lab	360	main	Enabled	

Figure 6-28 *The Inputs Tab of the Splunk Add-On for Cisco Meraki After Adding All the Available Inputs*

Now that you've completed the configuration required for the Splunk add-on for Cisco Meraki, you can find more information about the add-on at https://docs.splunk.com/Documentation/AddOns/released/Meraki/AboutAddon.

Follow these steps to verify that the Splunk integration is working:

Step 1. In the **Splunk Add-on for Cisco Meraki** app, navigate to the **Search** page (see Figure 6-29) by clicking **Search** to the right of **Configuration.**

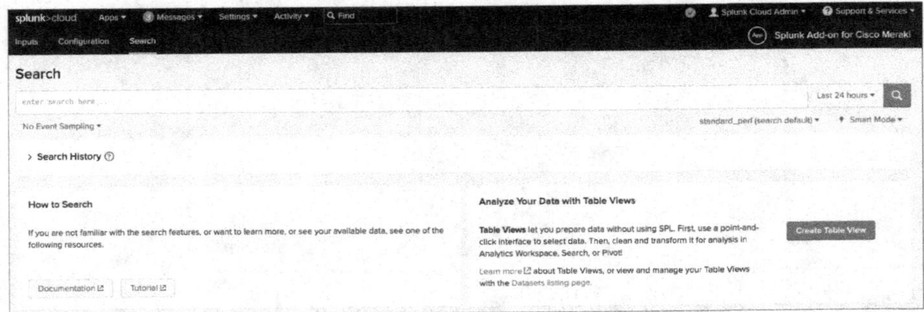

Figure 6-29 *The Search Page of the Splunk Add-On for Cisco Meraki*

Step 2. Under **Search**, in the **Enter Search Here** input field, type **index="main"**. This search displays all of the Meraki events collected from Meraki Dashboard so far, as demonstrated in Figure 6-30. Because some of the inputs, such as audit, go back seven days, you should see plenty of events listed.

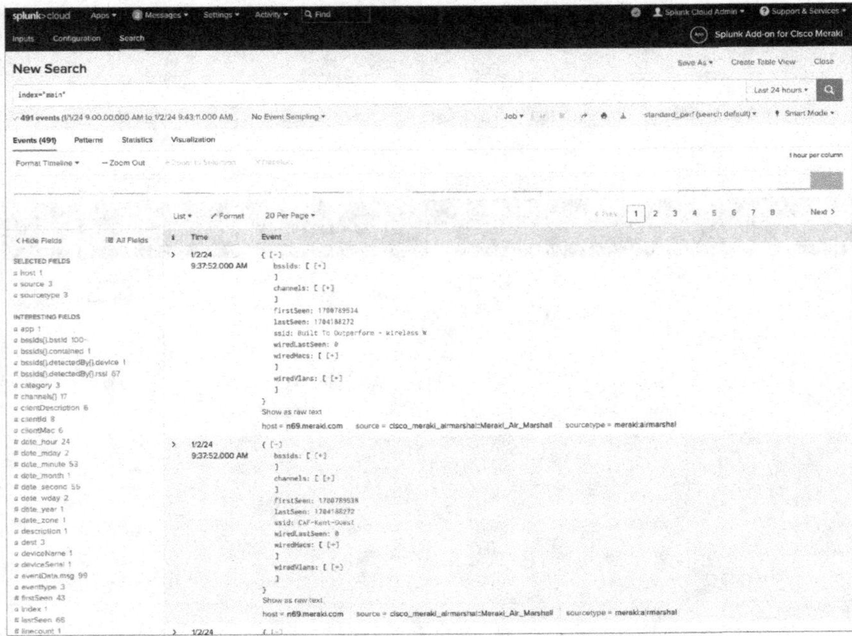

Figure 6-30 *Searching for All Meraki Events in the Splunk Add-On for Cisco Meraki App*

Step 3. These events can be filtered further using the links under **Interesting Fields** on the left side of the results. In the example shown in Figure 6-31, we have filtered the logs by clicking **eventtype** (under **Interesting Fields**) and then **meraki_api_audit** (on the **eventtype** pop-up window under **Values**).

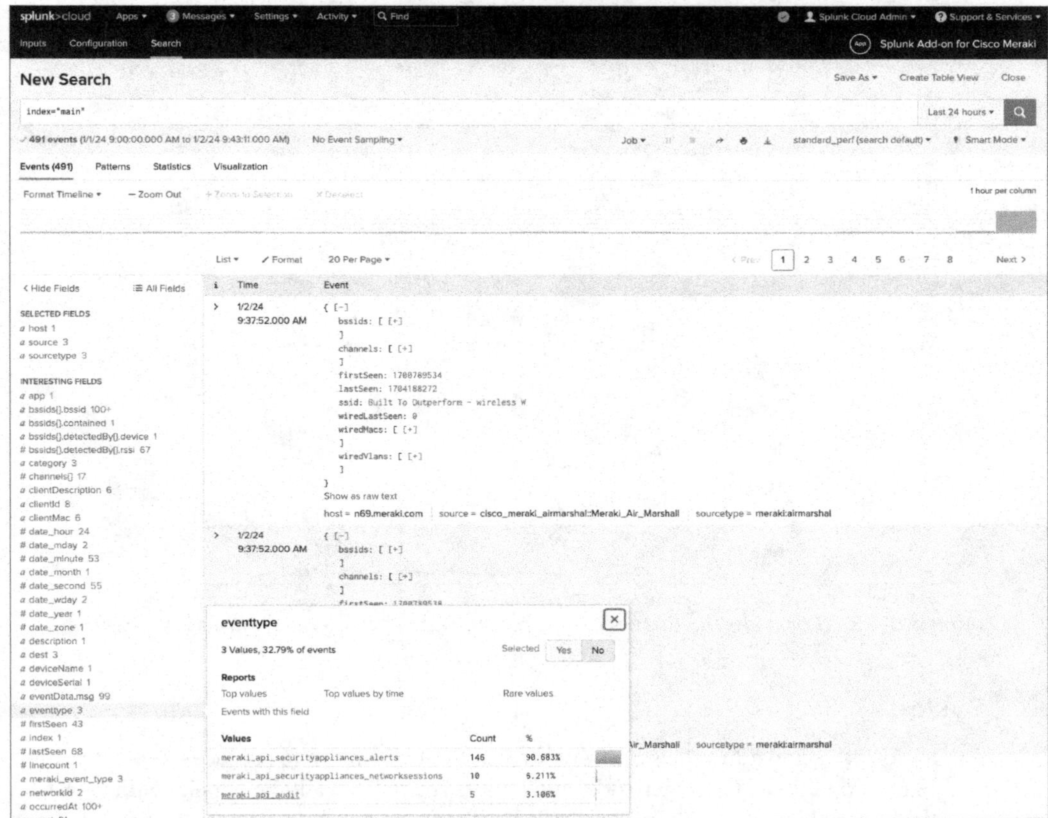

Figure 6-31 *Filtering Results in the Splunk Add-On for Cisco Meraki App*

We had recently disabled and then re-enabled a switchport. Using the filter from the previous step, we have successfully located these events. This result shows that we have been able to successfully export events from Meraki Dashboard to Splunk (see Figure 6-32).

At this point, you have completed the setup and verification of the integration between Meraki Dashboard and Splunk Cloud.

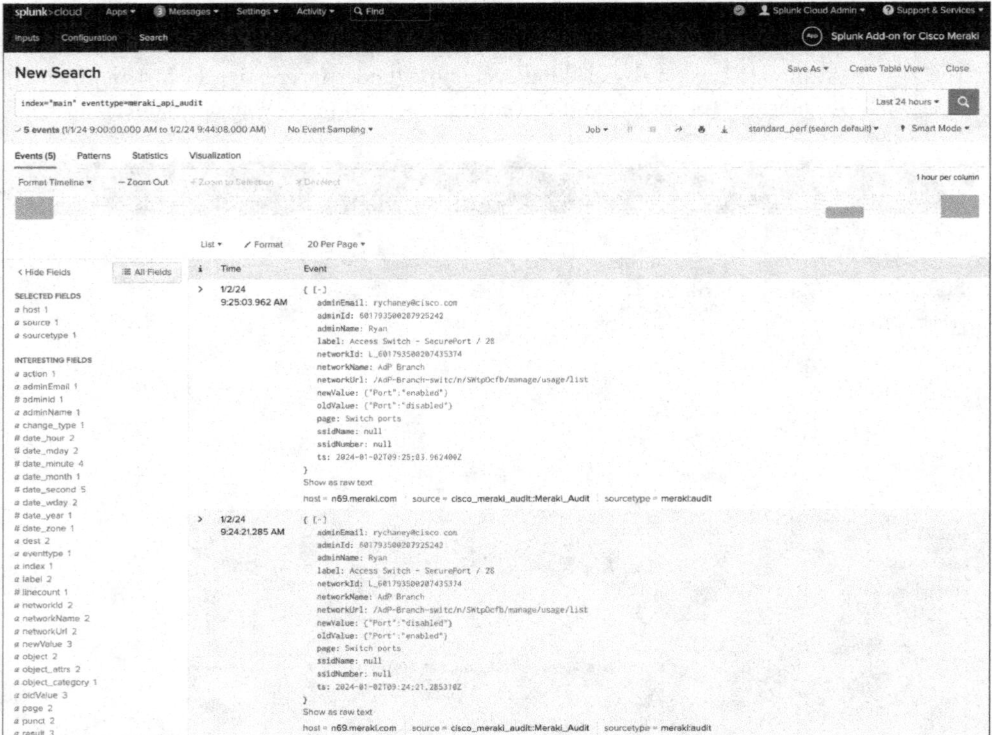

Figure 6-32 *Locating the Events of Interest in the Splunk Add-On for Cisco Meraki*

Syslog

Syslog is a standard for message logging that has been in use for decades. If you've configured traditional Cisco networks in the past, you will already be familiar with it. While the built-in logging capabilities are sufficient for a lot of organizations, syslog is also supported if there is a use case for it. The logs in Dashboard continue to function as normal, regardless of whether syslog is configured or not.

When configuring a syslog server, you must specify one or more categories of log messages to be sent to this syslog server. Meraki refers to these categories as *roles*. They include

- **URL:** Details of all client web requests on the network.
- **Flows:** Details of all attempted connections matching firewall rules, whether permitted or denied. Logging can be enabled or disabled per firewall rule. This is done using the check box in the Syslog column on the **Security & SD-WAN > Firewall** page in Meraki Dashboard.
- **Event logs:** The same as what you see in the built-in event log. These are split into appliance, switch, and wireless roles.

- **Security events:** These are generated by Meraki MX appliances for events such as a malicious file being blocked or an IDS rule being triggered.
- **Air Marshall events:** These relate to the wireless IPS functionality and include such events as the detection of rogue access points.

You can find an explanation of all the various syslog messages generated by Meraki at https://documentation.meraki.com/General_Administration/Monitoring_and_Reporting/Syslog_Event_Types_and_Log_Samples.

Syslog traffic is originated from Meraki devices themselves; therefore, the syslog server needs to be reachable from each of the networks where syslog is configured. In the case of a Meraki MX appliance, the shortest route to the syslog server could be through a LAN interface, the WAN interface (non-VPN), or inside a site-to-site AutoVPN. In the AutoVPN example, this traffic is subject to the outbound firewall, so if this traffic is restricted, a rule will need to be added to allow UDP traffic to the IP address of the syslog server on port 514. To configure this, navigate to **Security Appliance > Site-to-Site VPN** (under Configure) > **Organization-wide Settings** and click **Add a Rule.**

Follow these steps to configure the exporting of log data using syslog in Meraki Dashboard:

Step 1. Log in to Meraki Dashboard (https://dashboard.meraki.com).

Step 2. Navigate to **Network-wide > General** (under Configure).

Step 3. Scroll down to **Reporting.** In network types other than Combined, syslog servers are added under the **Logging** section instead of **Reporting.** Click **Add a Syslog Server**, as shown in Figure 6-33.

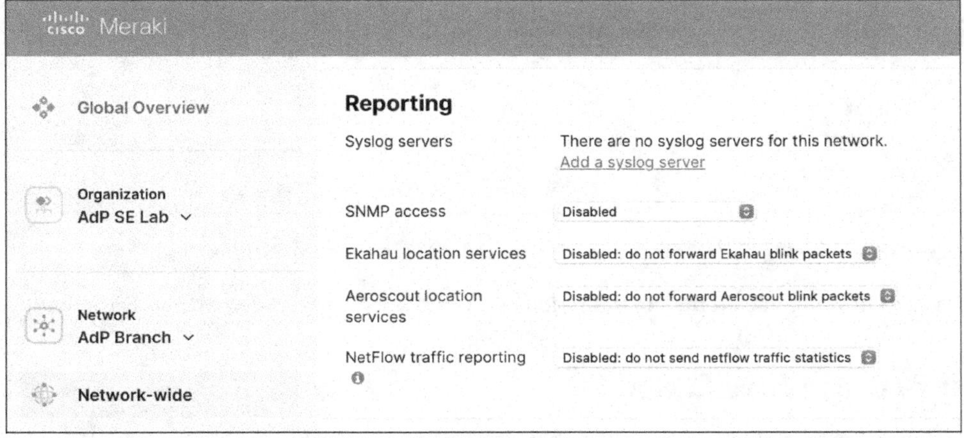

Figure 6-33 *Adding a Syslog Server in Meraki Dashboard*

Step 4. Enter the syslog server IP address in the field shown and choose at least one role from the **Roles** input field, as shown in Figure 6-34. Click **Save** at the bottom right of the screen to save the changes.

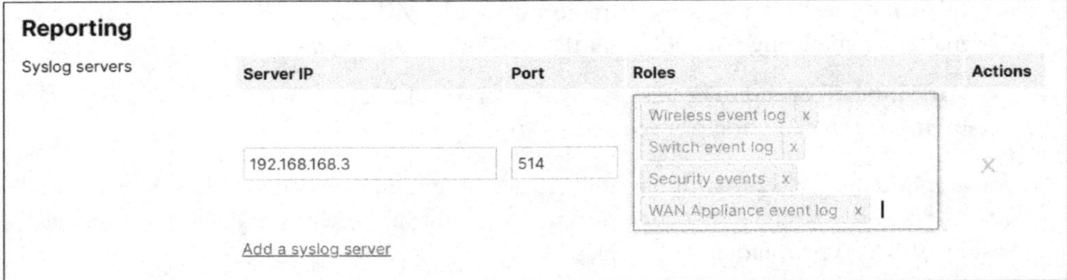

Figure 6-34 *Entering the Details for a New Syslog Server in Meraki Dashboard*

At this point, you've completed the configuration of syslog in Meraki Dashboard.

Follow these steps to verify that syslog is working:

Step 1. If you haven't already, install a syslog application on the host you specified in Step 4 of the preceding list.

Step 2. Take an action that will generate an event matching a role that has been configured for this syslog server.

To verify the configuration was working, we installed Kiwi Syslog Server (available at https://www.solarwinds.com/free-tools/kiwi-free-syslog-server) and kicked off a client VPN connection to generate a syslog message. In Figure 6-35, you can see the AnyConnect VPN log entry on the syslog server (in blue).

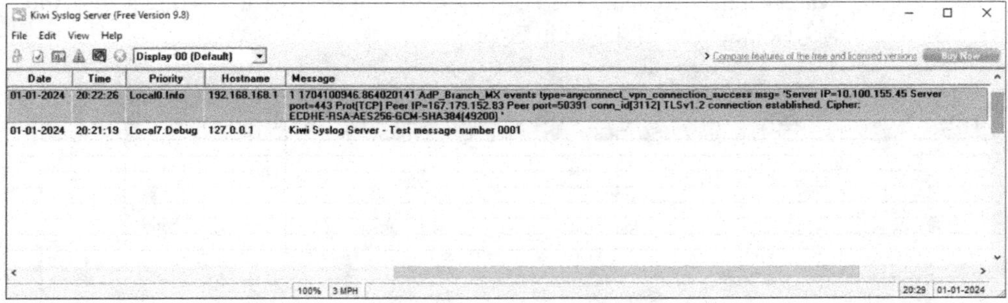

Figure 6-35 *Syslog Entry for an AnyConnect VPN Connection Attempt*

You've now completed the configuration and verification of syslog in Meraki Dashboard.

Exporting Flow Data

Threats are becoming increasingly sophisticated and fast moving. A typical incident today starts with a user receiving an email with a malicious link (phishing). Clicking that link opens a website that downloads malware onto their machine. When the malware is inside the organization, it then spreads laterally, infecting other hosts before phoning home, ready for the next stage of the attack. This is known as the *cyber kill chain*.[1] Each of these interactions crisscrosses the network, making the network an invaluable source of data. Having a complete picture of all flow data is required before meaningful analysis can be done. Flow data from the network becomes actionable once it is analyzed by an extended detection and response (XDR) system. Fundamentally, XDR systems provide three key functions:

- **Visibility:** Providing the ability to ingest vast amounts of raw telemetry data, even if sessions are encrypted, and to correlate that into a picture of what is occurring inside the organization. This includes the ability to display real-time graphical views of network traffic (in accordance with PCI DSS 4.0 requirement 1.2.4) and creating a complete audit trail for effective forensic investigations.
- **Detection:** Taking this knowledge of what's occurring inside the organization and combining that with threat intelligence to reveal indicators of compromise. This capability can reveal complex multistage attacks, command-and-control (C&C) networks, ransomware, distributed-denial-of-service (DDoS) attacks, illicit crypto mining, and more.
- **Quicker response:** Enabling security operations center (SOC) staff to work more effectively by filtering out the noise, prioritizing incidents, reducing manual effort, and providing best-practice guided workflows. XDR systems help identify what is affected so that SOC operators can quickly understand and remediate incidents.

Cisco's XDR solution, simply named Cisco XDR, is a cloud-hosted SaaS platform that supports multivendor environments. Cisco XDR supports a wide range of data sources, including

- Cloud, including Amazon Web Services (AWS), Microsoft Azure, and Google Cloud Platform (GCP)
- On-premises networks, including Meraki, via Cisco Telemetry Broker
- Identity, including Meraki Systems Manager
- Email, firewall, endpoint, and cloud security solutions

Refer to the following link for more information on Cisco XDR: https://www.cisco.com/site/au/en/products/security/xdr/index.html.

NetFlow, IPFIX, and Encrypted Traffic Analytics

It is critical to know what is happening on the network before, during, and after an incident. NetFlow provides a way to understand what is occurring on the network through its ability to create records of all IP flows and export that data to a collector for analysis.

NetFlow was originally created by Cisco in the late '90s. The latest version is NetFlow v9. IPFIX is based on NetFlow and is in the process of being standardized by the IETF. The Meraki MS390, Catalyst 9300-M, 9300L-M, and 9300X-M switches all support both NetFlow v9 and IPFIX for IPv4 and IPv6 traffic. The Meraki MX and Z platforms support NetFlow v9. Encrypted Traffic Analytics is currently supported only on the MS390, Catalyst 9300-M, 9300L-M, and 9300X-M switches, because these have the required UADP ASIC.

In this section, we walk you through how to configure NetFlow in Meraki Dashboard. NetFlow traffic is sourced directly from Meraki devices rather than the Meraki Cloud, meaning that it does not require any NAT or firewall rules to allow this into the network.

Follow these steps to configure the export of NetFlow data:

Step 1. Log in to Meraki Dashboard (https://dashboard.meraki.com).

Step 2. Navigate to **Network-wide > General** (under Configure), as shown in Figure 6-36.

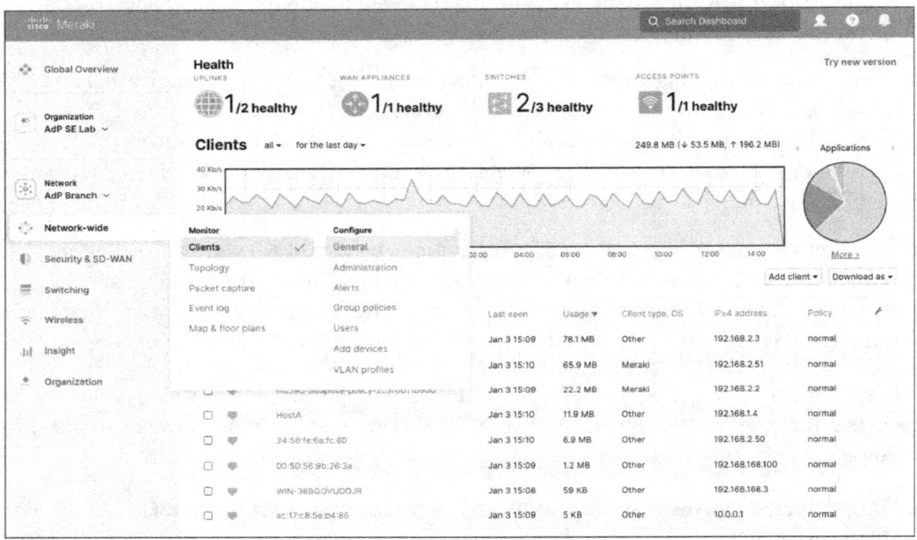

Figure 6-36 *Navigating to the Network-Wide General Page in Meraki Dashboard*

Step 3. Scroll down to **Reporting**. From the NetFlow traffic reporting drop-down menu, select **Enabled: Send NetFlow Traffic Statistics**, as shown in Figure 6-37.

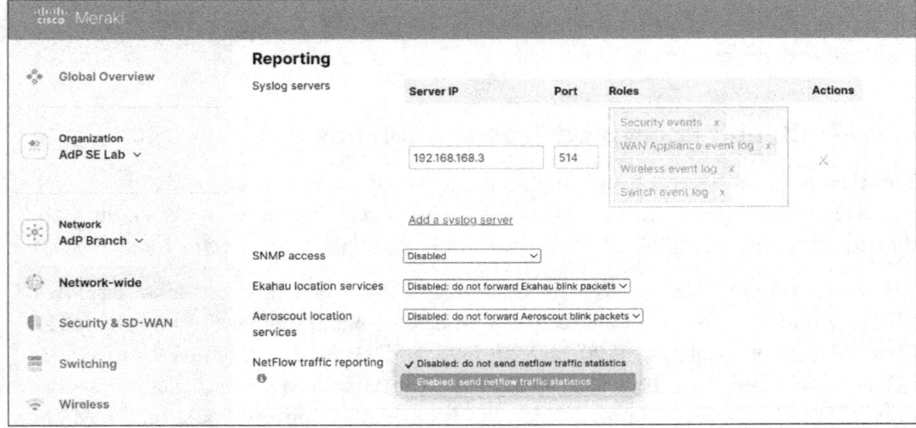

Figure 6-37 *Enabling NetFlow Traffic Reporting in Meraki Dashboard*

Step 4. In the page shown in Figure 6-38, enter the following details:

- **NetFlow Collector IP:** This is the IP address of the NetFlow collector.
- **NetFlow Collector Port:** This is the UDP port on which the NetFlow collector is listening. In the example, the NetFlow collector is configured to use port 2055.
- **Encrypted Traffic Analytics:** If you have Meraki MS390 switches in your environment and you wish to use the Encrypted Traffic Analytics (ETA) feature, check this box. This feature also requires a collector such as Cisco Secure Network Analytics, Cisco Secure Cloud Analytics, or similar that supports ETA. For this demonstration, we have left this option unchecked.
- **ETA Collector Port (if ETA feature is checked):** This is the UDP port used by the NetFlow collector for Encrypted Traffic Analytics information.

Click **Save** at the bottom of the page.

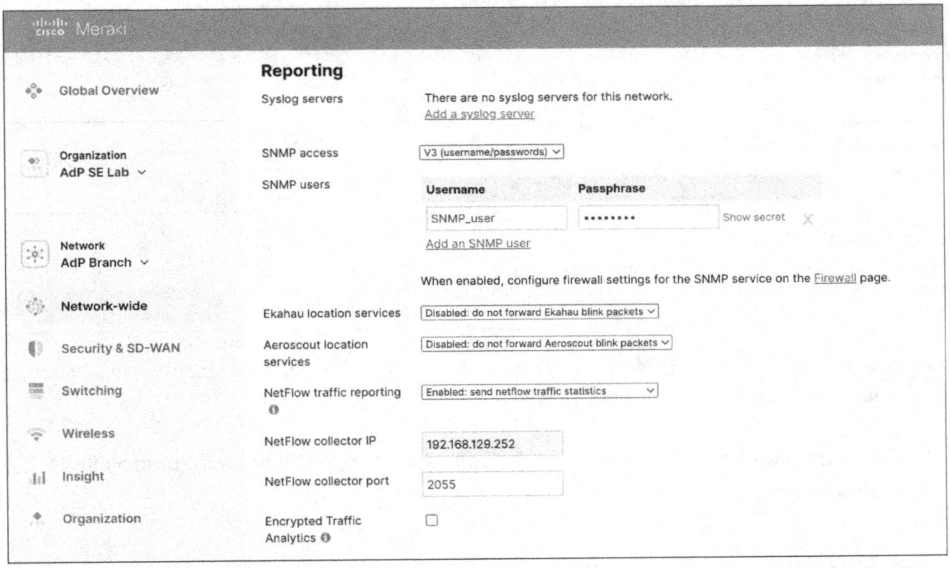

Figure 6-38 *Configuring NetFlow Traffic Reporting in Meraki Dashboard*

The NetFlow configuration in Meraki Dashboard is now complete.

To verify that NetFlow traffic is now being sent, you can use the Cisco Telemetry Broker (CTB). Cisco Telemetry Broker is an appliance that collects, filters, translates, and shares flow-based telemetry in the following formats:

- NetFlow v5, v9, and IPFIX
- VPC Flow Logs
- NSG Flow Logs

In this example, Cisco Telemetry Broker is configured to export the NetFlow telemetry to Secure Cloud Analytics, where it can be viewed. Secure Cloud Analytics, which is now part of Cisco XDR, performs the incident correlation function and sends the results onto the Cisco XDR portal for investigation. In the Secure Cloud Analytics event viewer shown in Figure 6-39, you can see DNS traffic that is traversing the network. This event viewer confirms that the NetFlow configuration is working.

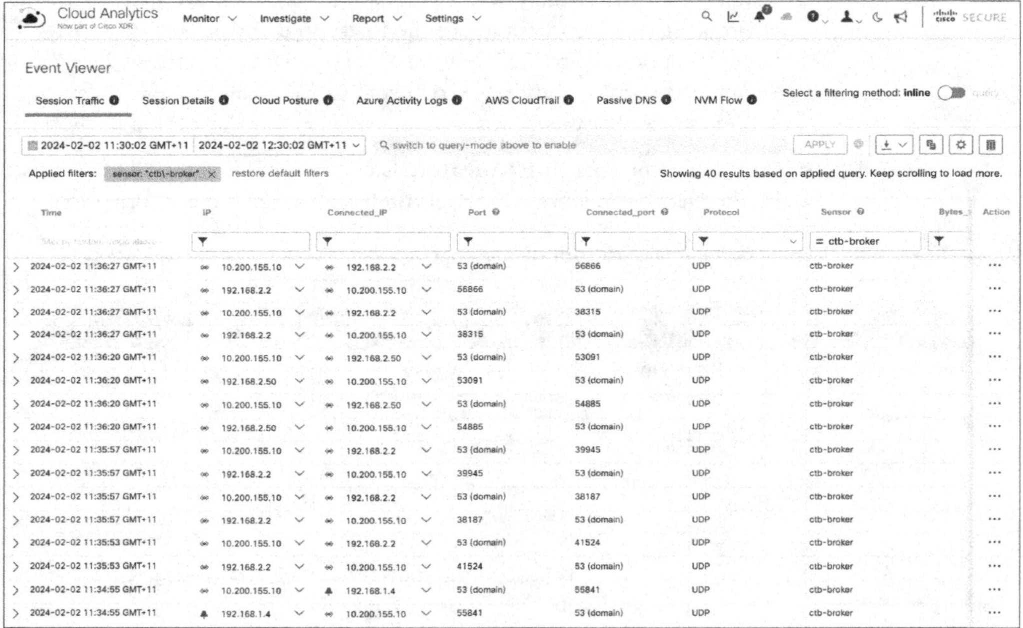

Figure 6-39 *Verifying That NetFlow Data Is Being Sent by Meraki and Received Using Cisco Secure Analytics*

At this point, you have completed the verification of the NetFlow configuration in Meraki Dashboard.

Syslog Flows

As previously mentioned in the "Syslog" section, one of the roles available when configuring syslog is flows. The term *flows* here refers to hits on firewall rules for traffic traversing Meraki MX security appliances. This can be tailored per rule so that some connections are logged while others aren't. Some flow collectors can ingest syslog data, making it a rather exotic, though valid, way to communicate flow information. The major downside of using syslog, rather than NetFlow, is that any sessions that do not traverse a firewall would not be logged (for example, between two clients on the same switch). For the steps to configure the syslog flows role, refer to the preceding section on syslog.

Compliance Reporting with AlgoSec

As highlighted in Chapter 2, industry best practice requires organizations to regularly monitor their compliance with security standards. AlgoSec is a multivendor, network security management platform that provides centralized management of security policies, optimizes firewall rules, and automates policy deployment. As part of their solution, AlgoSec also provides multivendor compliance reporting across both cloud and on-premises networks. This massively reduces the effort required for compliance reporting. Supported standards include PCI DSS, ISO/IEC 27001, NIST 800-53, HIPAA, ASD-ISM, and many more.

AlgoSec is a Cisco SolutionsPlus partner. SolutionsPlus partners offer a select set of tested Cisco-compatible products on the Cisco global price list. This means AlgoSec can be purchased as part of a complete solution, from the same authorized Cisco partner that you purchase Meraki from today. For more information on AlgoSec, refer to the AlgoSec page on the Meraki Marketplace at https://apps.meraki.io/en-US/apps/380640/algosec.

Prerequisites

Before starting the AlgoSec setup, ensure you have completed these two steps:

- AlgoSec integrates with Meraki using the Dashboard API and therefore requires an API key. If you haven't already created an API key, then complete the steps in the earlier section titled "Creating API Keys."
- You also need your AlgoSec license file. This file is sent to you when you order AlgoSec. If you have not received it yet, get in touch with your Partner Account Manager or your AlgoSec Account Manager.

Integrating AlgoSec with Meraki Dashboard for Compliance Reporting

Follow these steps to install and configure AlgoSec on VMware and integrate it with Meraki:

Step 1. Register and log in to the AlgoSec Portal at https://portal.algosec.com/login/index.php. You can use either the Partner Portal or the Customer Portal for these steps.

Step 2. Navigate to **Downloads > Software** and then click **AlgoSec Security Management Suite**, as shown in Figure 6-40.

Step 3. Select **New Installation – Select Deployment Type**, as shown in Figure 6-41. Software images are available for AWS, Azure, Linux, VMware, and physical appliances. Select **VMware** and then click **Next**.

Step 4. Click **Download** to start the download of AlgoSec Security Management Suite (ASMS), as shown in Figure 6-42. Leave this browser tab open because you come back to it in a later step.

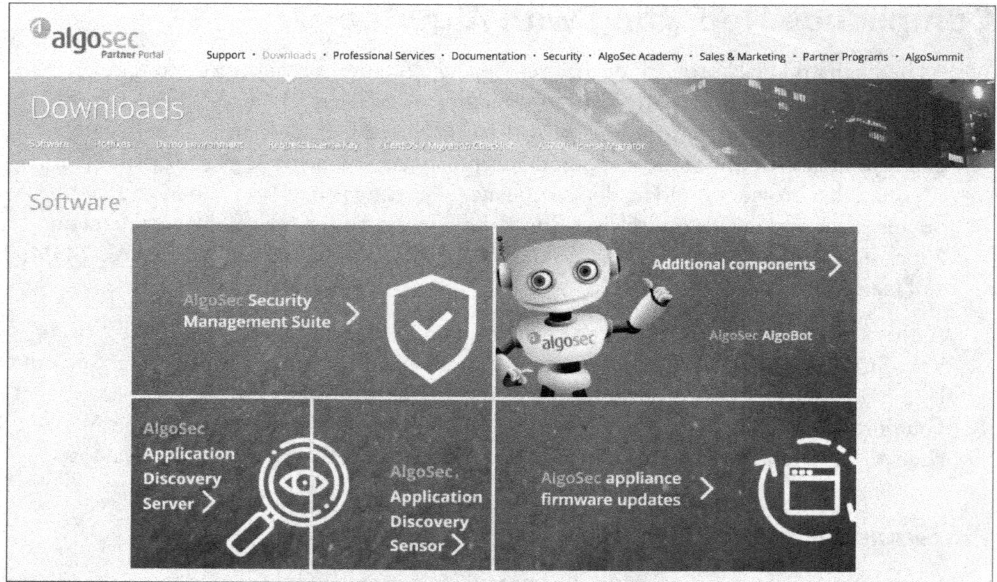

Figure 6-40 *Navigating to the Downloads Page in the AlgoSec Partner Portal*

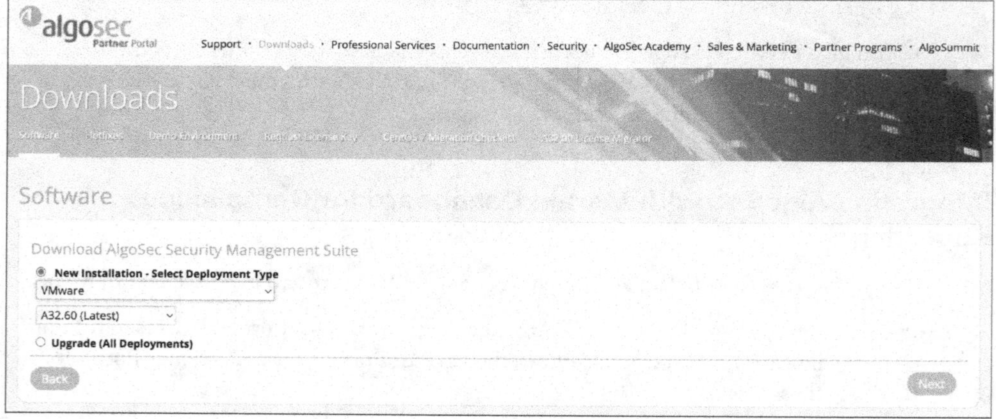

Figure 6-41 *The Software Downloads Page in the AlgoSec Partner Portal*

Step 5. When the download is complete, in VMware, create a new VM using the OVF file and boot it up. You can find the system requirements for ASMS at https://www.algosec.com/docs/en/asms/a32.60/asms-help/content/install-guide/prerequisites.htm.

Step 6. AlgoSec boots to a CLI login page. Log in using the username **root** and the password **algosec**.

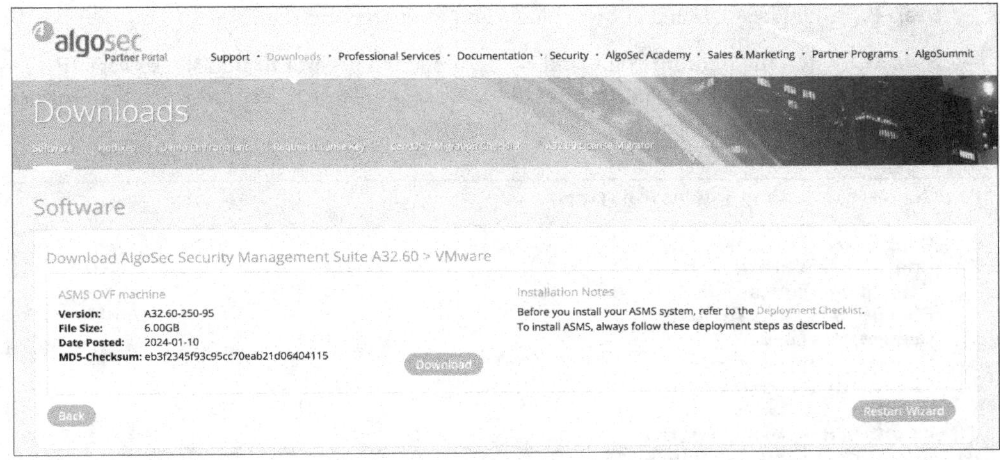

Figure 6-42 *Downloading AlgoSec Security Management Suite from the AlgoSec Portal*

Step 7. To select the menu items, enter the number relating to the menu item and then press Enter (or Return, if using a Mac). For example, enter **1** and then press Enter to configure the IP address, as shown in Figure 6-43. By default, AlgoSec uses an IP address and DNS servers received via DHCP. Use this menu to check and, if necessary, set an IP address, time zone, and DNS servers.

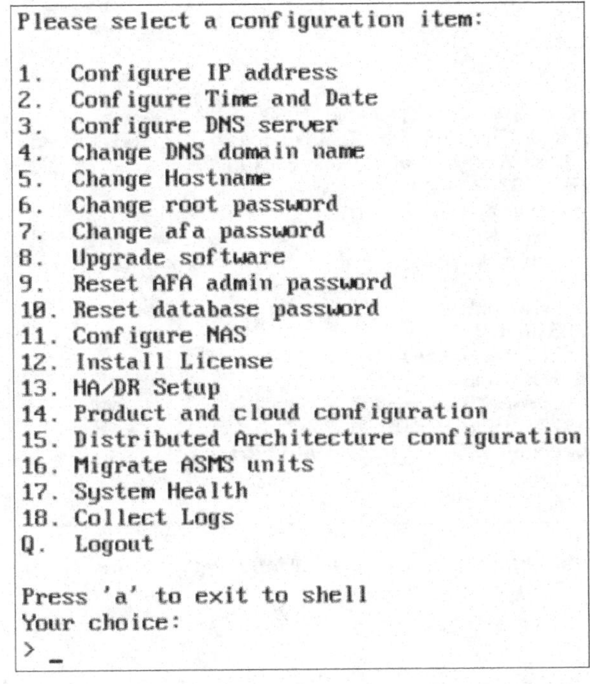

Figure 6-43 *The AlgoSec CLI Menu*

Step 8. Quit the CLI menu by typing **a** and then pressing Enter.

Step 9. Run the **ifconfig** command at the command prompt to find the server's IP address, as shown in Figure 6-44. Make a note of this address in a text editor because you need it in a following step.

```
Please select a configuration item:

1.  Configure IP address
2.  Configure Time and Date
3.  Configure DNS server
4.  Change DNS domain name
5.  Change Hostname
6.  Change root password
7.  Change afa password
8.  Upgrade software
9.  Reset AFA admin password
10. Reset database password
11. Configure NAS
12. Install License
13. HA/DR Setup
14. Product and cloud configuration
15. Distributed Architecture configuration
16. Migrate ASMS units
17. System Health
18. Collect Logs
Q.  Logout

Press 'a' to exit to shell
Your choice:
> a
[root@algosec ~]#
[root@algosec ~]# ifconfig
eth0: flags=4163<UP,BROADCAST,RUNNING,MULTICAST>  mtu 1500
        inet 192.168.100.193  netmask 255.255.255.0  broadcast 192.168.100.255
        ether 00:0c:29:92:f9:4d  txqueuelen 1000  (Ethernet)
        RX packets 167  bytes 33543 (32.7 KiB)
        RX errors 0  dropped 0  overruns 0  frame 0
        TX packets 67  bytes 7145 (6.9 KiB)
        TX errors 0  dropped 0 overruns 0  carrier 0  collisions 0

lo: flags=73<UP,LOOPBACK,RUNNING>  mtu 65536
        inet 127.0.0.1  netmask 255.0.0.0
        loop  txqueuelen 1000  (Local Loopback)
        RX packets 1877  bytes 549728 (536.8 KiB)
        RX errors 0  dropped 0  overruns 0  frame 0
        TX packets 1877  bytes 549728 (536.8 KiB)
        TX errors 0  dropped 0 overruns 0  carrier 0  collisions 0

[root@algosec ~]# _
```

Figure 6-44 *Confirming the IP Address for AlgoSec Security Management Suite*

Step 10. Open a web browser and navigate to https://[*IP address of the AlgoSec VM*]. At this point, you are prompted to create an administrator account. Enter the required information, as shown in Figure 6-45, and then click **Next**.

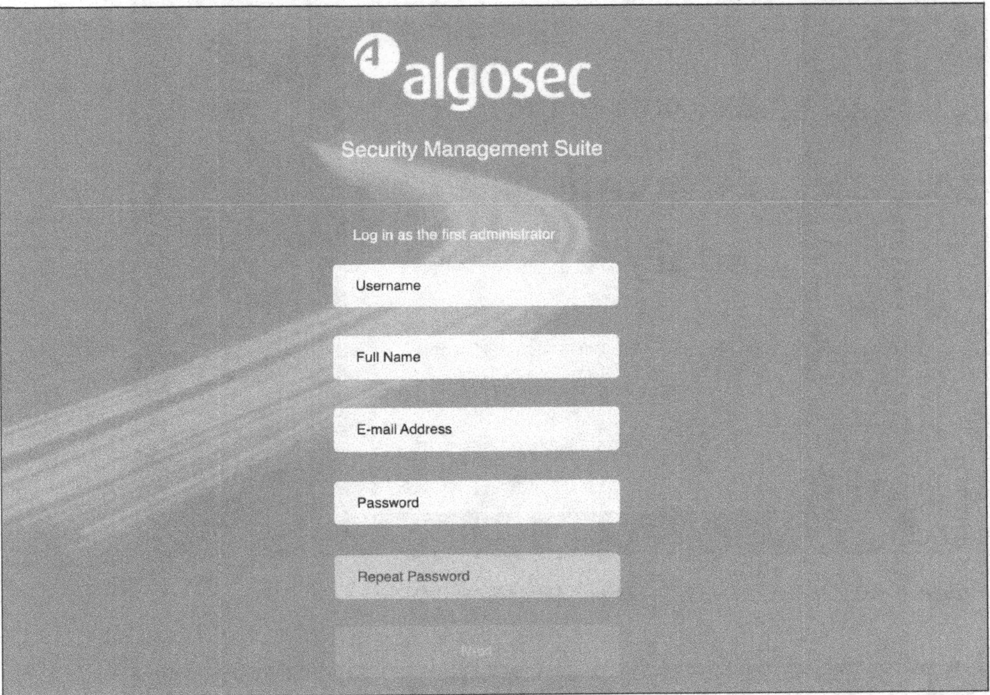

Figure 6-45 *Creating an Admin Account on First Login to AlgoSec Security Management Suite*

Step 11. You are logged in to AlgoSec Security Management Suite, where you will see a series of pop-up windows about having no devices, and so on. Close these windows until you see the pop-up window with **Welcome to the Firewall Analyzer.** Then click **Install License**, as shown in Figure 6-46.

Step 12. You are presented with the terms and conditions page. Click **Accept**.

Step 13. On the License installation window, click **Select a File**, locate the license file from AlgoSec, and click **Open**. On returning to this window, click **Install**, as shown in Figure 6-47.

Step 14. To integrate with Meraki, first ensure you see **Firewall Analyzer** in the top left of the AlgoSec Security Management Suite (ASMS). Click the logged-in user in the top right and select **Administration** from the drop-down menu, as shown in Figure 6-48.

Figure 6-46 *Install License Welcome Page in ASMS*

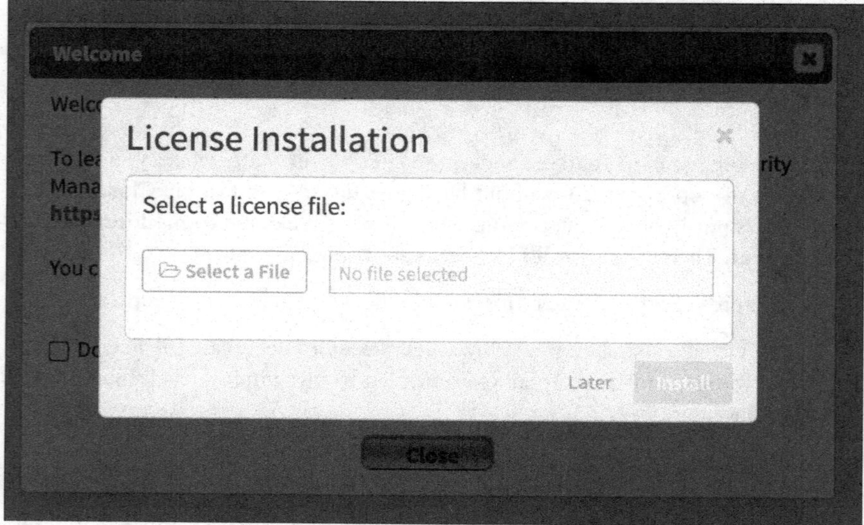

Figure 6-47 *Installing the License File in ASMS*

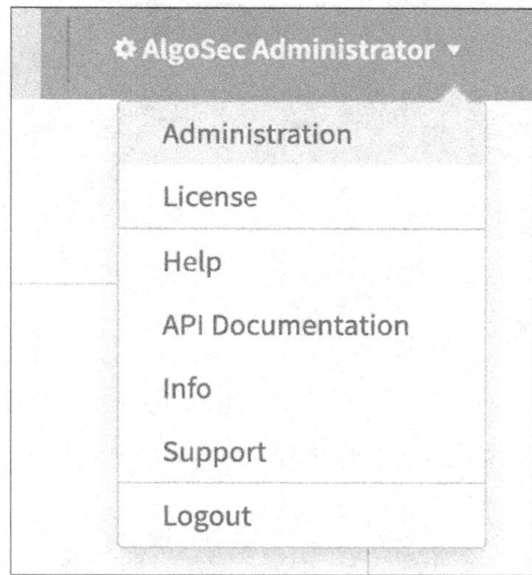

Figure 6-48 *Navigating to the Administration Page in ASMS*

Step 15. On the **Administration** page, click the **Devices Setup** tab.

Step 16. Click the **New** drop-down menu and then click **Devices**, as shown in Figure 6-49.

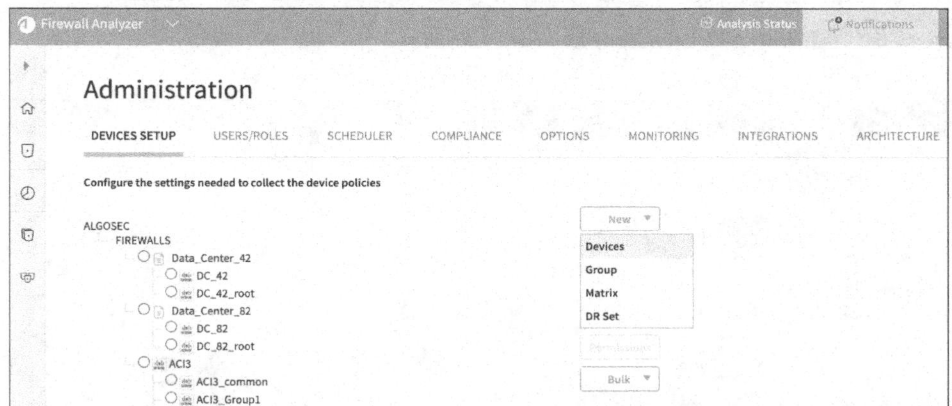

Figure 6-49 *Adding a New Device on the Administration Page in ASMS*

Step 17. Click the **Cisco** button to reveal a drop-down menu and then click **Meraki**, as shown in Figure 6-50.

Step 18. Enter a **Display Name.** We recommend using your Meraki organization name. You can't use spaces in the display name; however, you can use underscores in addition to numbers and letters.

In the **Authentication key** field, paste in the Meraki Dashboard API key created in the prerequisite step, as shown in Figure 6-51.

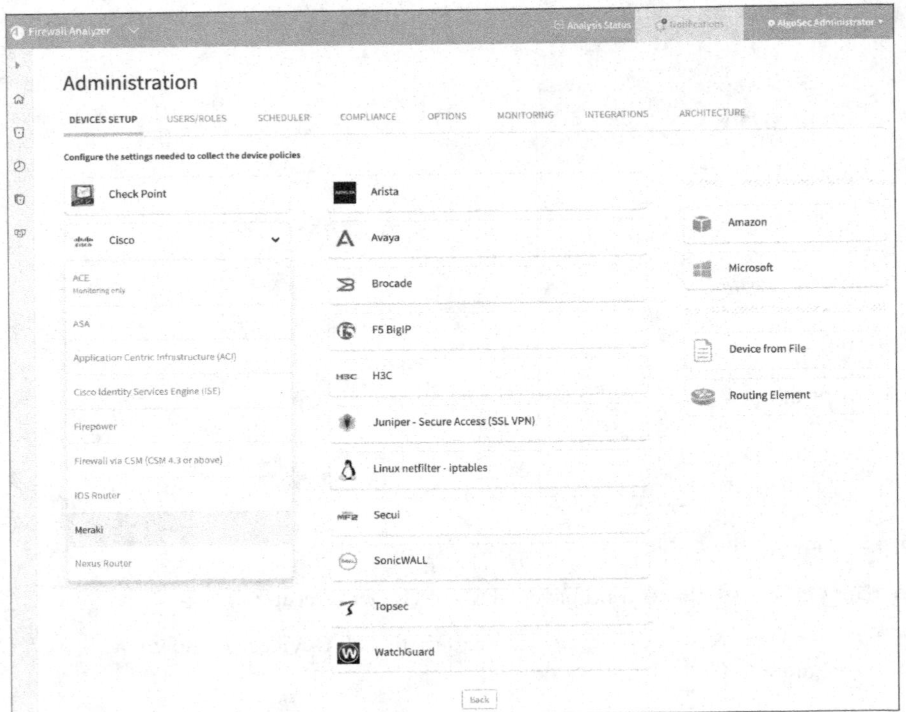

Figure 6-50 *Adding a New Meraki Device in ASMS*

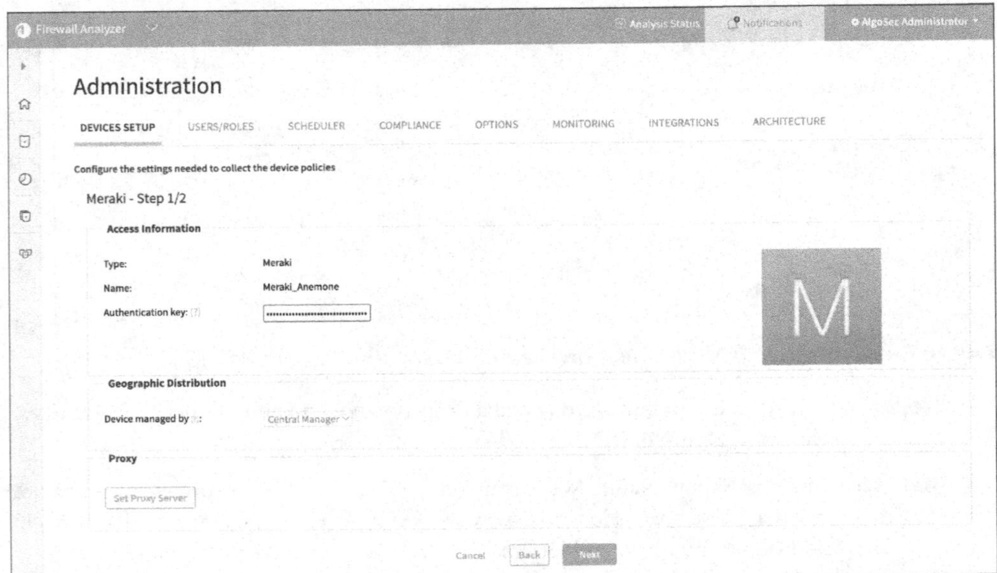

Figure 6-51 *Entering the API Key in ASMS to Integrate with Meraki Dashboard*

Step 19. On the following page, ensure the right Meraki organizations are selected and then click **Finish.** For more information on these steps, refer to the AlgoSec guide at https://www.algosec.com/docs/en/asms/a32.60/asms-help/content/afa-admin/adding-a-csm-managed-cisco.htm#Meraki.

Step 20. Devices need to be analyzed before the compliance reports can be generated. To do this, navigate to the device tree by clicking **Firewall Analyzer** (top left) > **Devices.** Select the display name for the recently added Meraki organization shown in the list on the left. On the page that opens on the right, click **Analysis**, as shown in Figure 6-52.

Note AlgoSec recommends setting up a scheduled task to analyze all your devices daily to capture changes and have a history of the devices.

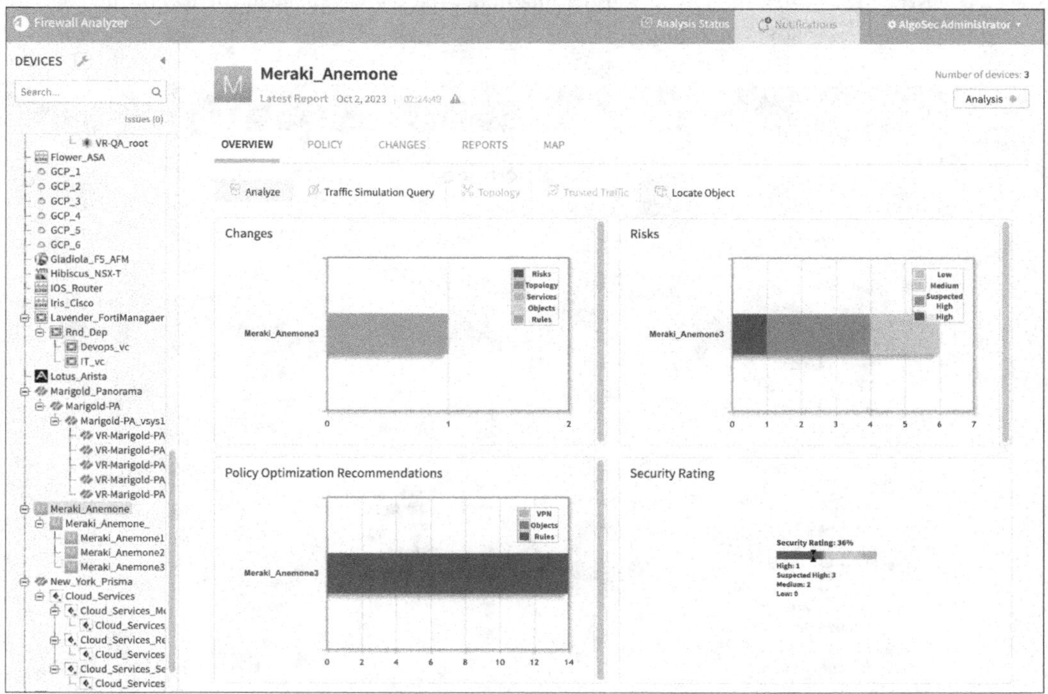

Figure 6-52 *Analyzing Meraki Devices in AlgoSec Security Management Suite*

Step 21. On the pop-up window, click **Start Analysis**, as shown in Figure 6-53.

Step 22. A progress bar labeled **Analysis in Progress** appears in the top right of the page. Wait until this analysis completes.

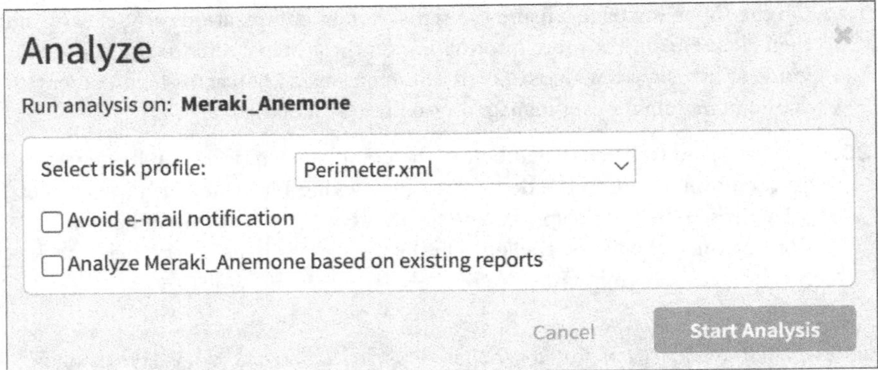

Figure 6-53 *Starting the Analyze Process for the Newly Imported Meraki Org*

Step 23. Click the **Latest Report** link under the display name at the top of the page, as shown in Figure 6-54.

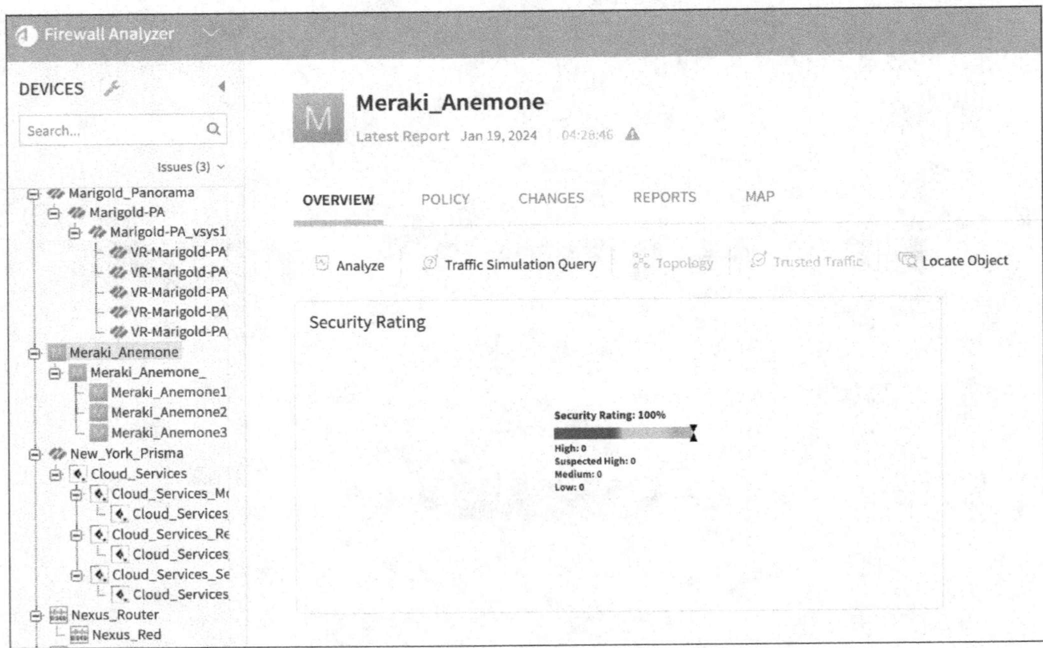

Figure 6-54 *Navigating to the Compliance Reporting Page in ASMS*

Step 24. Clicking this link opens a new tab. Click **Regulatory Compliance** from the menu on the left. A summary page with links to the enabled regulatory compliance reports then appears, as shown in Figure 6-55.

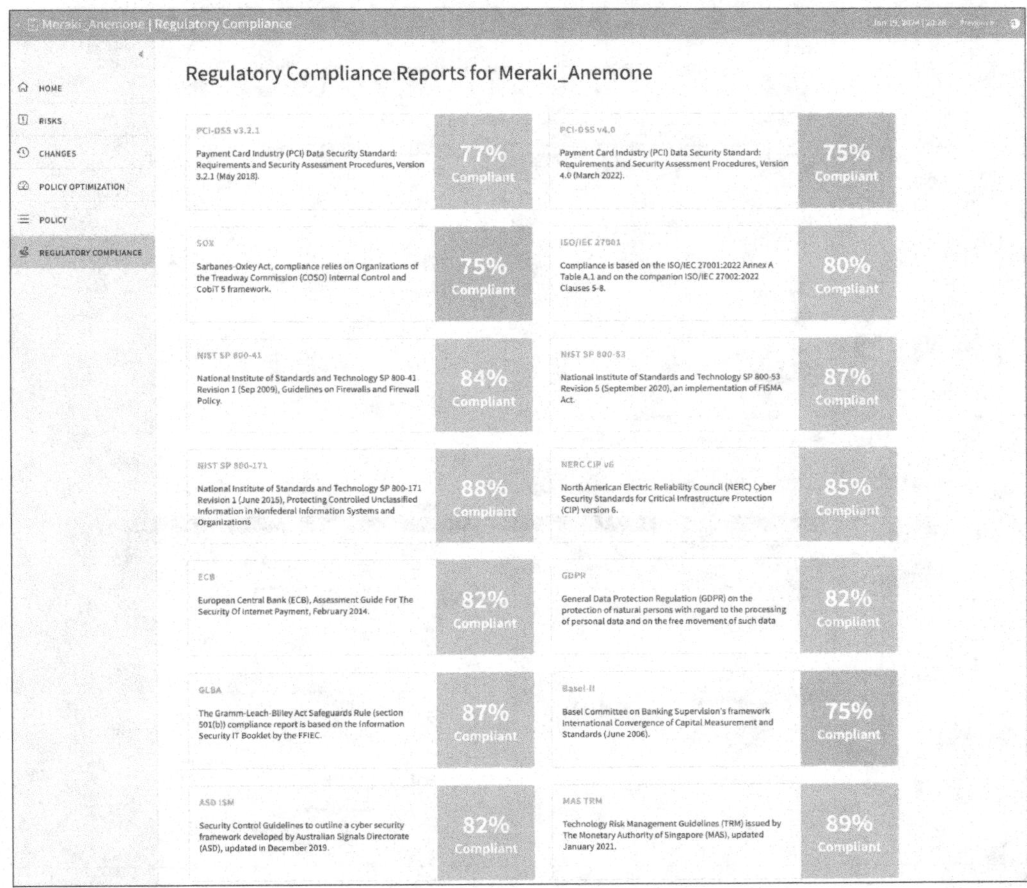

Figure 6-55 *The Available Regulatory Compliance Reports in AlgoSec Security Management Suite*

Step 25. Click either the report score or the standard name (such as PCI-DSS v4.0). Doing so opens a new tab with a report detailing the requirements of that standard and how AlgoSec is or can be configured to enable automatic data collection for each requirement, as shown in Figure 6-56. Scroll down to see the full report.

The available reports and the reports themselves can be customized. Refer to the following URL for further details: https://www.algosec.com/docs/en/asms/a32.60/asms-help/content/afa-admin/customizing-risk-and-compliance.htm.

You've now completed the setup and demonstration of compliance reporting with AlgoSec.

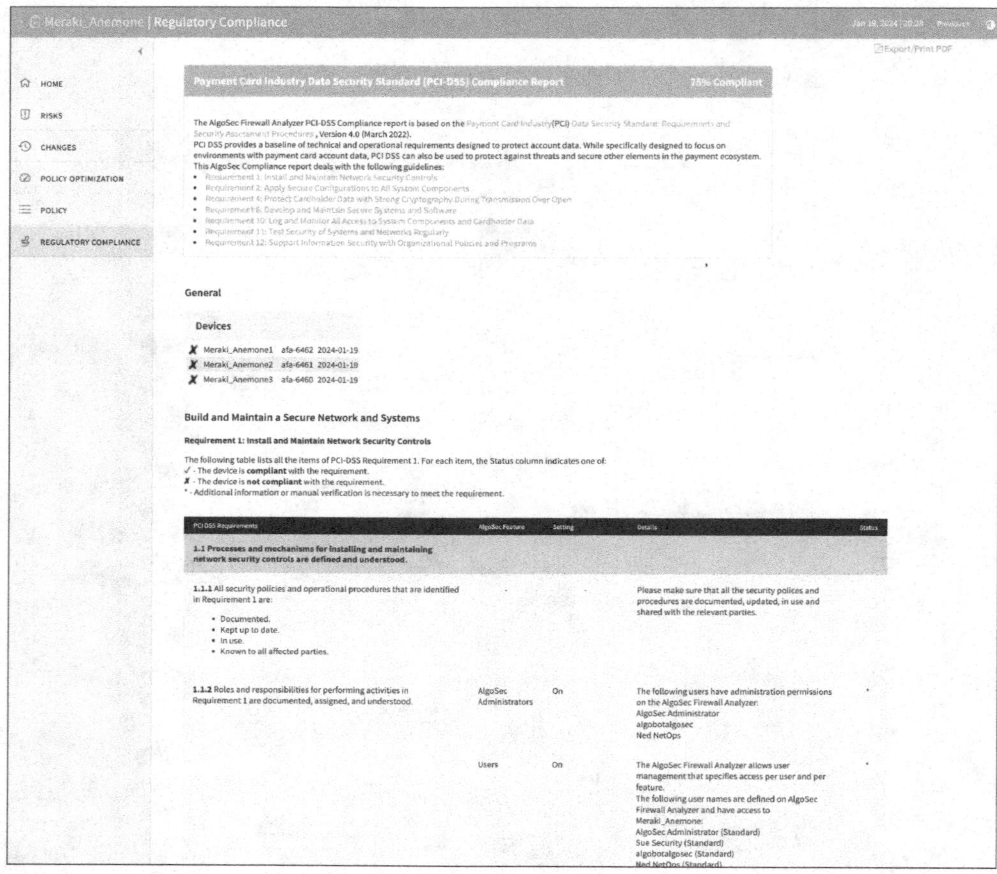

Figure 6-56 *A Sample PCI DSS 4.0 Compliance Report in AlgoSec Security Management Suite*

Monitoring and Incident Response

Monitoring and incident response is a key theme of industry best practice. IT environments need to be monitored 24×7 to ensure prompt action in response to cybersecurity incidents. In this section, we introduce the dashboards within Meraki Dashboard that are most useful to network operations center (NOC) and security operations center (SOC) staff. Additionally, this section also describes the steps to integrate Meraki Dashboard with third-party monitoring systems using webhooks, SNMP, and the Meraki Dashboard API. Responding quickly to security incidents is key to reducing risk. To address this need, this chapter also shows how organizations can build a prompt incident response capability using Meraki Dashboard. To achieve this, we demonstrate how Meraki can be integrated with incident management systems like ServiceNow and incident response solutions like PagerDuty.

Security Center

Security Center is a dashboard that provides a centralized view of security events seen by Meraki MX appliances in your organization. You can think of this as your SOC portal. The security events displayed include those detected by IDS/IPS rules as well as Advanced Malware Protection (AMP) events. You can find Security Center in Meraki Dashboard by navigating to **Organization > Security Center**, as shown in Figure 6-57.

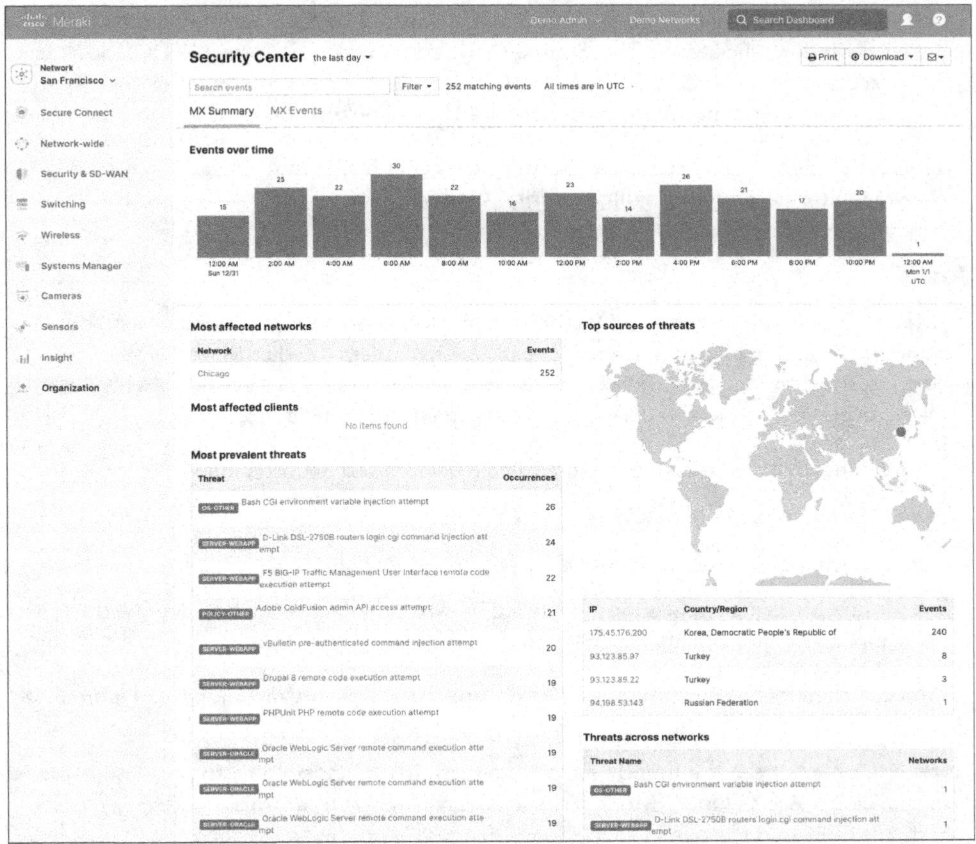

Figure 6-57 *Security Center in Meraki Dashboard*

Security Center is an easy way to understand the top threats targeting your organization. Here, you can learn more about the threats being seen and the common vulnerabilities and exposures (CVEs) being targeted. To do this, click a threat listed in the **Most Prevalent Threats** table and then click **Rule Details.**

The Security Center page can be filtered in the following ways:

- **By individual threats:** Click the threat listed in the **Most Prevalent Threats** table and then click **Show This Signature Only.**

- **By time period:**
  - Click the drop-down menu next to **Security Center** at the top of the page.
  - Click one of the columns on the **Events over Time** chart to filter on a particular day or hour.
- **By network:** Click the Network name under **Most Affected Networks** and select **Show This Network Only.**
- **By source IP:** Click an IP listed under **Top Sources of Threats**, and then on the pop-up window, click **Show This Source Only.** You can also perform a WHOIS lookup on a source IP. To do this, click the IP address listed under **Top Sources of Threats**, and then on the pop-up window, click **WHOIS Lookup.**

You can find more information on Security Center at https://documentation.meraki.com/MX/Monitoring_and_Reporting/Security_Center.

Alerts

Meraki Dashboard features an Organizational Alerts page to aid in more proactive and quicker resolution of issues. Alerts appear here regardless of whether you have configured alerting on the **Network-wide > Alerts** page. The Alerts page covers a wide range of alerts occurring across any network in your organization, including

- Connectivity issues, such as unreachable devices and 802.1x failures
- Configuration issues, such as VLAN mismatch
- Device health issues, such as fan or power supply failures
- Issues affecting applications identified by Meraki Insights, such as degraded application performance or ISP issues

You can think of the alerts page as the NOC page for your organization (see Figure 6-58).

> **Note** The Alerts page is currently in early preview. If you are not able to access **Organization > Alerts** (under Monitor), instead navigate to **Organization > Early Access** and enable **Opt-in** to view and manage alerts in a new centralized Alerts page.

Active alerts can be sorted by time by clicking the **Time (UTC)** column heading. They can also be filtered by

- Date range, using the drop-down menu at the top of the screen
- Criticality, by clicking the Critical, Warning, or Information buttons
- Network, Alert Type, Device Type, or Device Tags, using the drop-down menus just above the entries in the alerts table

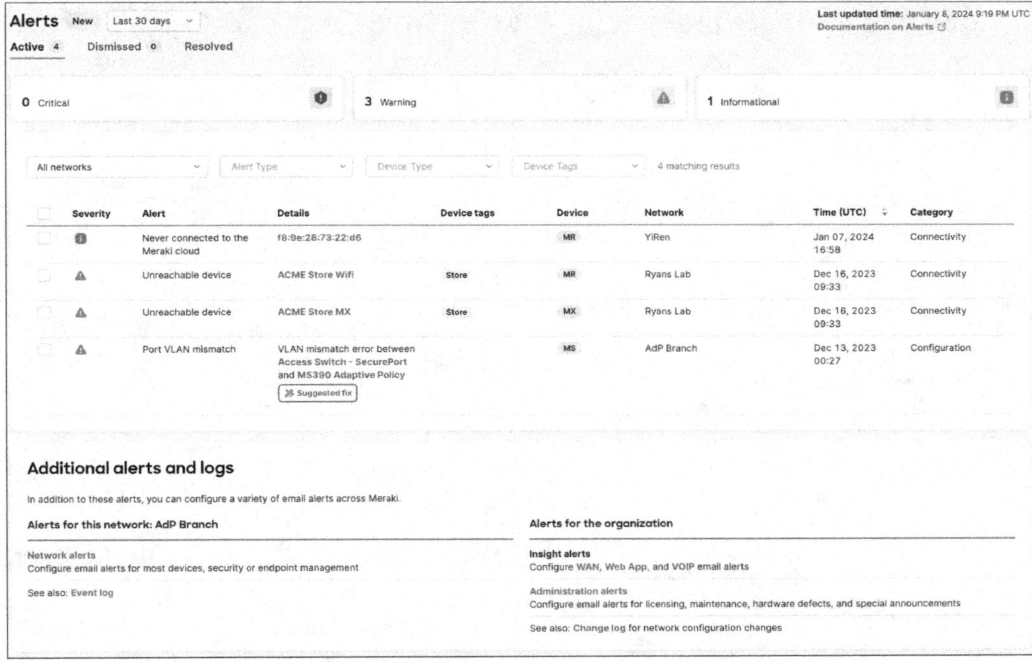

Figure 6-58 *The Organization Alerts Page in Meraki Dashboard*

To get more context on an alert, click the device hostname link in the **Details** column. Doing so opens the device summary page. Here, you can see more information about the alert, as shown in Figure 6-59.

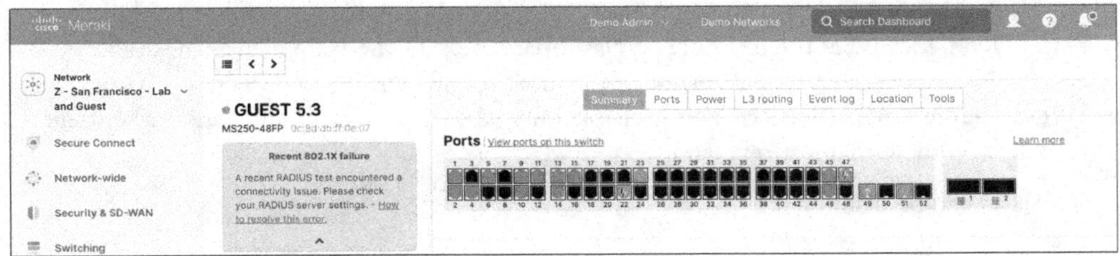

Figure 6-59 *Additional Details on an Alert as Seen on the Device Summary Page in Meraki Dashboard*

The Alerts page can also suggest fixes for faster issue resolution. You can see an example of this with the warning for VLAN mismatch in Figure 6-60. Clicking **Suggested Fix** pops out a sidebar explaining the issue and allowing an admin to implement the suggested fix.

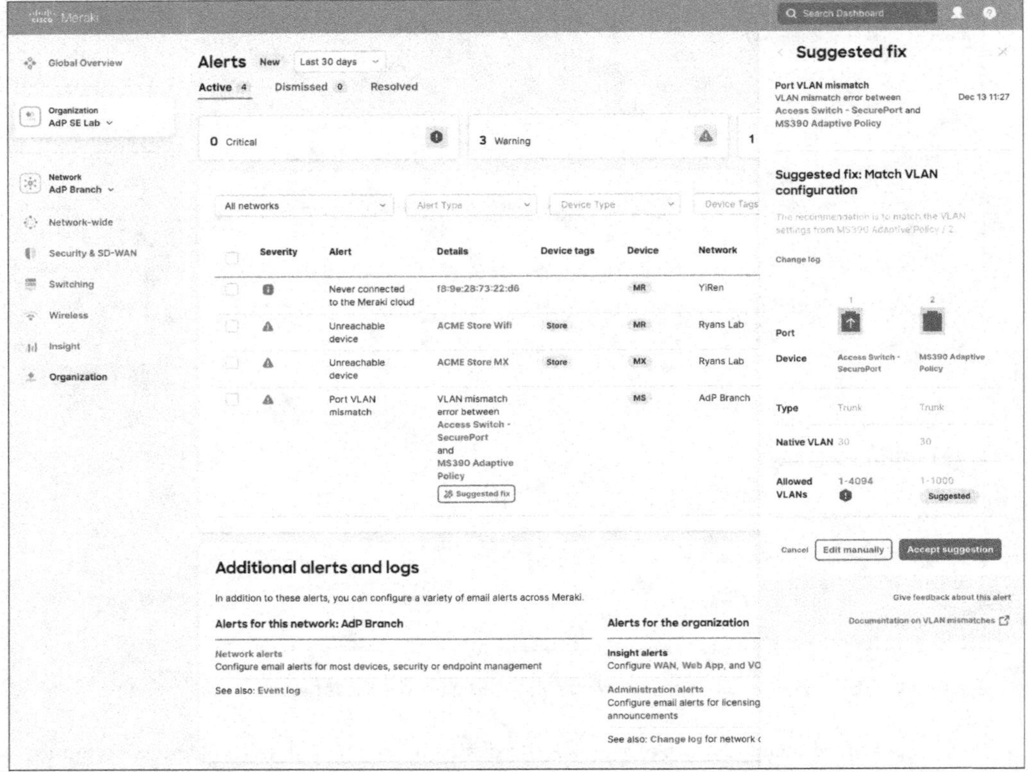

Figure 6-60 *The Suggested Fix Sidebar on the Alerts Page in Meraki Dashboard*

Also available with the new Alerts page is the alerts hub, which is represented by the bell icon, located at the top right of Dashboard, next to the Help menu. This hub provides easy access to a snapshot of the most recent alerts for the current network (see Figure 6-61). The alerts hub is visible only when you're accessing pages other than those on the Organization menu.

Alerts can be dismissed by

- **Alerts page:** Select the alerts to dismiss using the check boxes and then clicking the **Dismiss Alert** button.
- **Alerts hub:** Click the icon of the circle with a small x to the right of the alert.

Dismissed alerts are visible on the **Dismissed** tab on the **Organization > Alerts** page. Once alerts are resolved, they can be found on the **Resolved** tab.

For more information on the alerts page and alerts hub, go to https://documentation.meraki.com/General_Administration/Cross-Platform_Content/Global_Alerts_Widget.

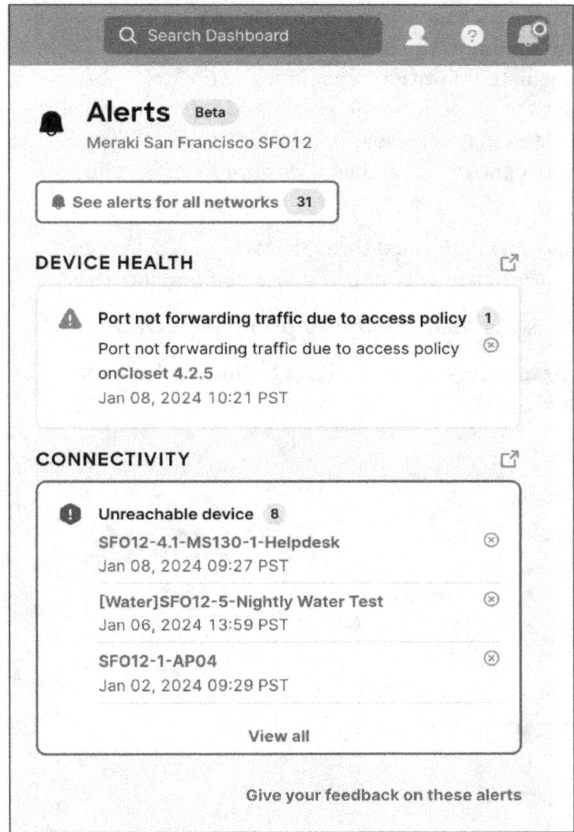

Figure 6-61 *Alerts Hub in Meraki Dashboard*

External Alerting

Many large organizations have centralized operations centers that monitor all infrastructure, not just the network. Meraki environments support integration through standard interfaces such as webhooks and SNMP traps for alerting and the Dashboard API and SNMP for polling. As we move into this next section, consider how best to tie Meraki into your organization's existing operations support systems (OSS).

Webhooks

Meraki Dashboard features the ability to configure webhooks for external alerting. Webhooks can be seen as a modern, and arguably more secure, alternative to SNMP traps. Webhooks work by sending an HTTPS POST to a unique URL. The receiving service, which is listening on this URL, is preconfigured to perform an action such as notifying support teams or updating a status page. Webhooks can be triggered by the same alerts available to email and SNMP traps. Many platforms support webhook integration; some of the more common ones include ServiceNow, Cisco Webex, PagerDuty, and Jira.

In this example, we use PagerDuty as the receiving service. PagerDuty is an easy-to-use operations cloud platform, which aims to reduce the mean time to resolution (MTTR) through its event management and human mobilization capabilities. Webhooks trigger incidents in PagerDuty, which then notifies responders via phone, SMS, push notifications, or email. Incidents can be acknowledged, resolved, or reassigned directly from a mobile device, and if incidents are not acknowledged, then escalations can be triggered automatically.

PagerDuty can also keep staff and customers informed through status pages. Service statuses shown on a status page can be automatically updated in case of an incident.

Follow these steps to configure webhooks in Meraki Dashboard with PagerDuty:

Step 1. Log in to Pager Duty (app.pagerduty.com). Navigate to **Integrations** > **Service Integrations**, as shown in Figure 6-62.

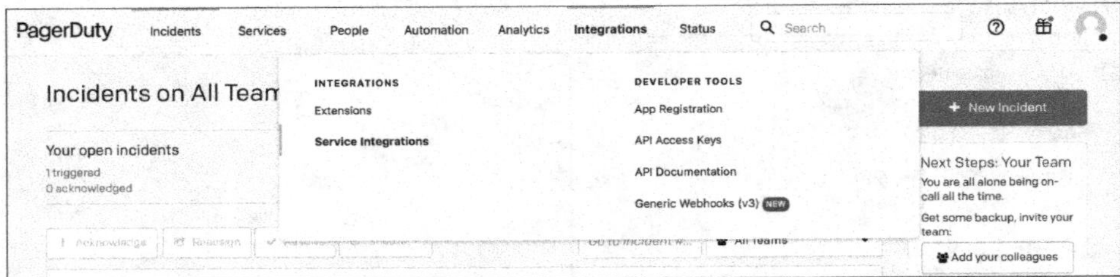

Figure 6-62 *Navigating to Service Integrations in PagerDuty*

Step 2. Click **+ New Service**, as shown in Figure 6-63.

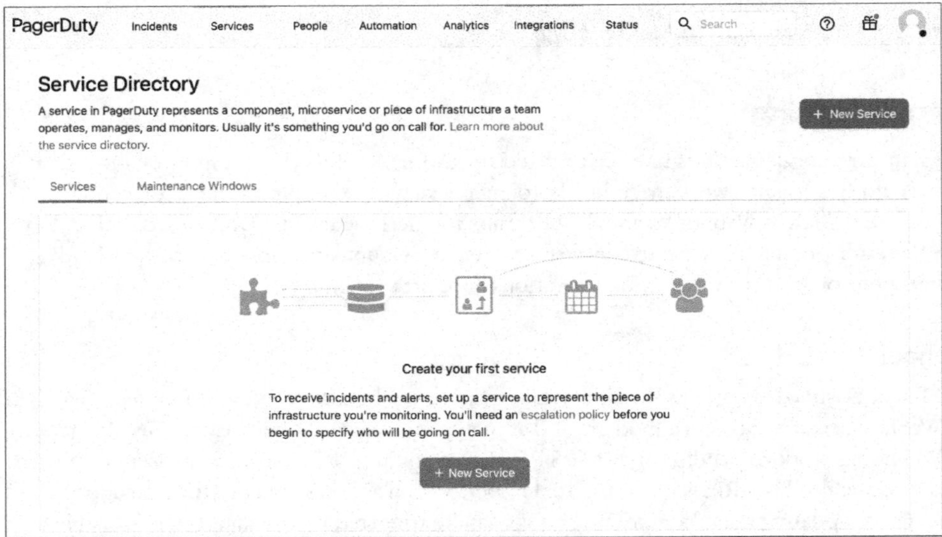

Figure 6-63 *Creating a New Service in Service Directory PagerDuty*

Step 3. Enter a description for this integration in the **Name*** field. In Figure 6-64, we've used **Meraki Alerts with Webhooks.** Click **Next.**

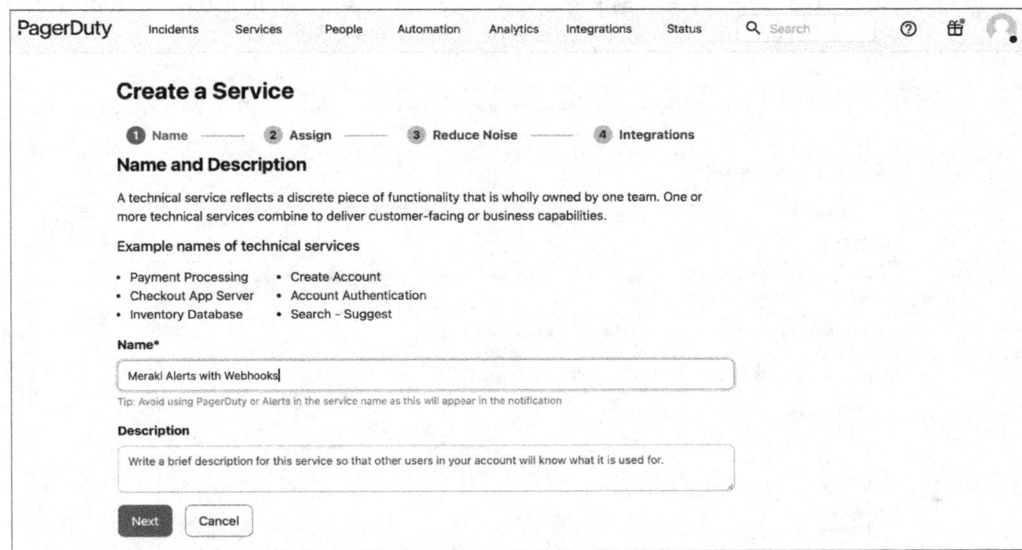

Figure 6-64 *Adding a Name for the New Service in PagerDuty*

Step 4. The **Assign** page then appears, as shown in Figure 6-65. This page can be updated at a later date after you know the webhook is functioning correctly. Click **Next**.

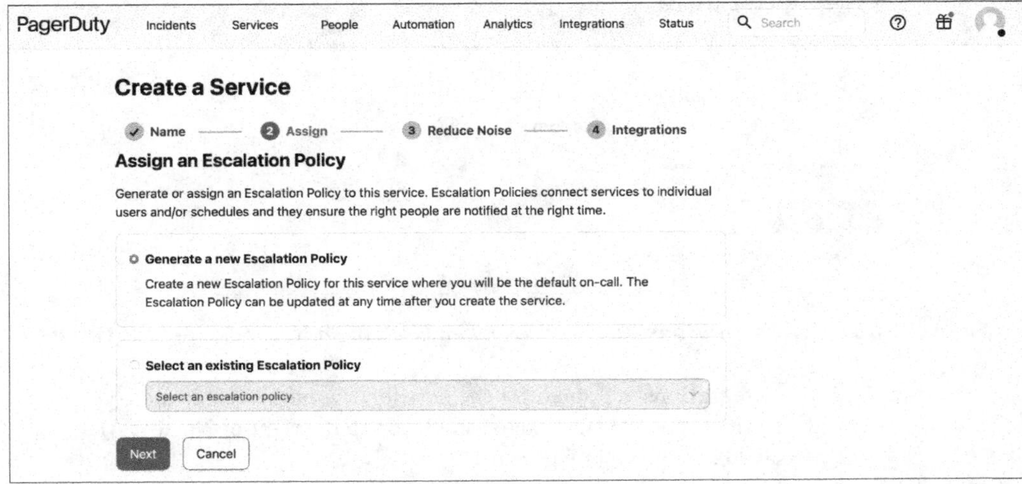

Figure 6-65 *The Assign Page when Creating a New Service in PagerDuty*

Step 5. On the **Reduce Noise** page, click **Next** again to get to the **Integrations** page. If necessary, you can come back and configure this page at a later date.

Step 6. On the **Integrations** page, search for "Custom Event Transformer" and click to select it, as shown in Figure 6-66. Click **Create Service.**

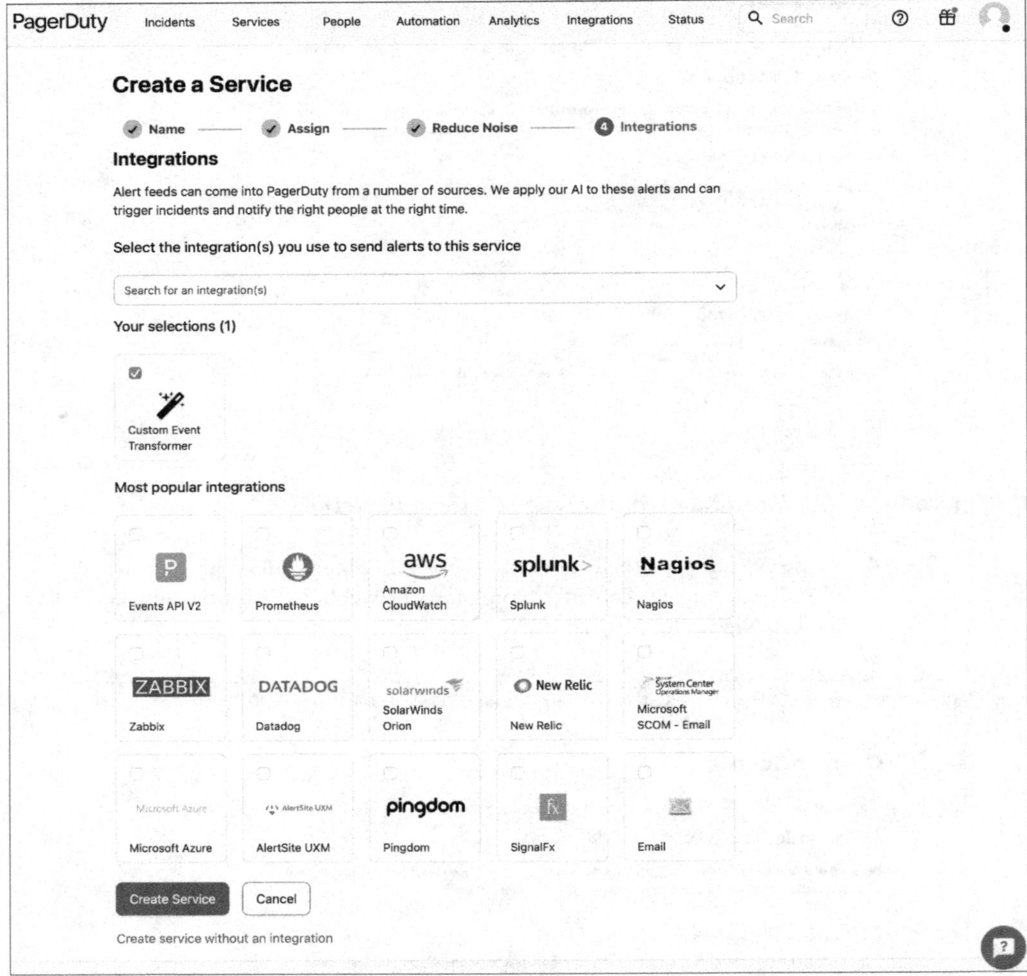

Figure 6-66 *The Integrations Page as Seen when Creating a New Service in PagerDuty*

Step 7. The **Integrations** tab opens for the new service that's been created. Click the settings icon (the sprocket-shaped icon to the right of **No Test Alert Received**), as shown in Figure 6-67.

Step 8. Click the **Show JavaScript** button. Click the **Edit Integration** button in the top right, as shown in Figure 6-68.

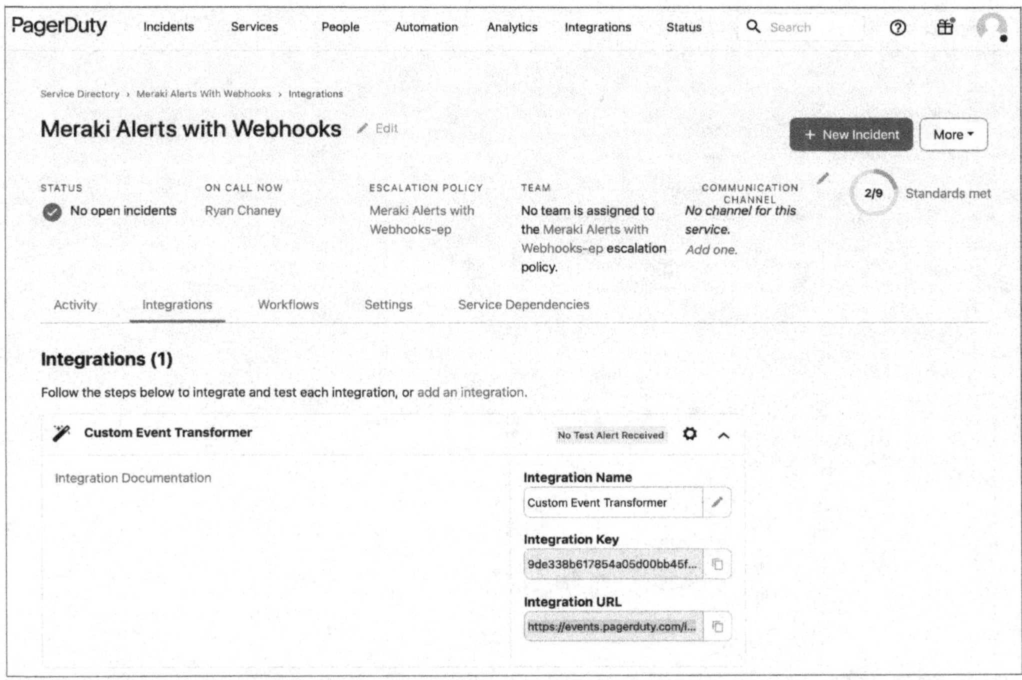

Figure 6-67 *The Meraki Alerts with Webhooks Page in the Service Directory*

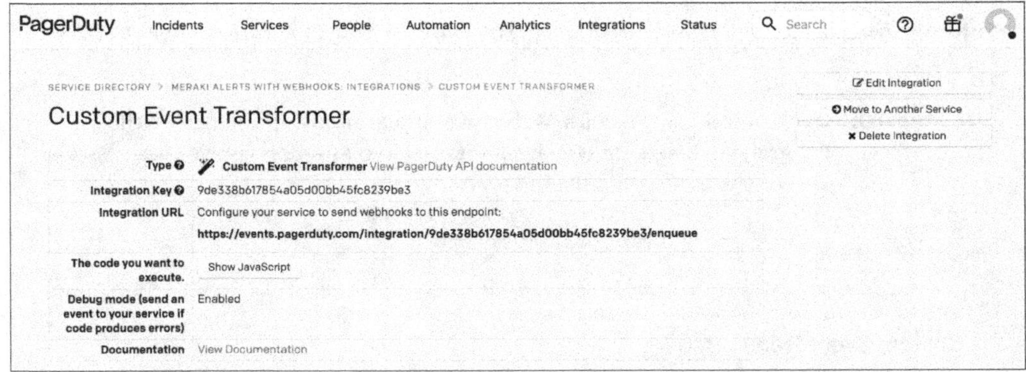

Figure 6-68 *Navigating to the Edit Integration Page in PagerDuty*

Step 9. Replace the code in the text field under the **Show JavaScript** button with the code starting with **// Consume Meraki Alert via Webhook** (see Figure 6-69) from the following URL: https://developer.cisco.com/meraki/build/meraki-alerts-with-pagerduty/. Click **Save Changes.**

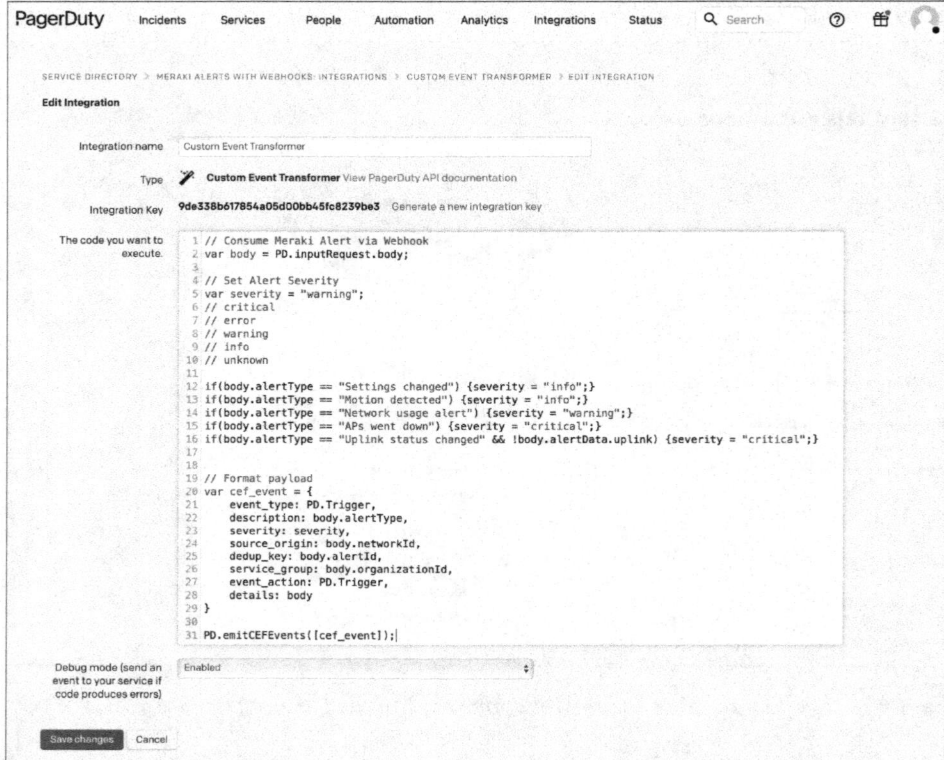

Figure 6-69 *Inserting the Required JavaScript into the Edit Integration Page in PagerDuty*

Step 10. Click **Meraki Alerts with Webhooks: Integrations.** If you named the integration something else, click the name you used; it appears after **Service Directory**, as shown in Figure 6-70.

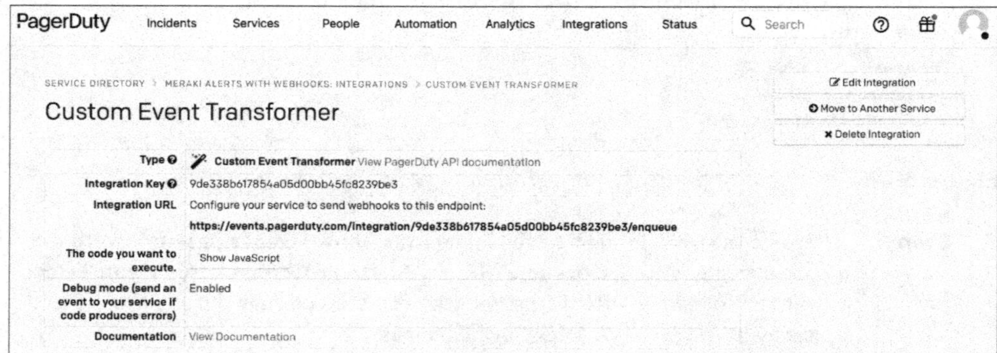

Figure 6-70 *The Custom Event Transformer Page for the Meraki Integration in PagerDuty*

Step 11. Using the expand icon, expand the **Custom Event Transformer** box under the **Integrations** heading. Doing so reveals the **Integration Name**, **Integration Key**, and **Integration URL**, as shown in Figure 6-71. Keep this browser tab open because you need to copy **Integration Key** and **Integration URL** in a later step.

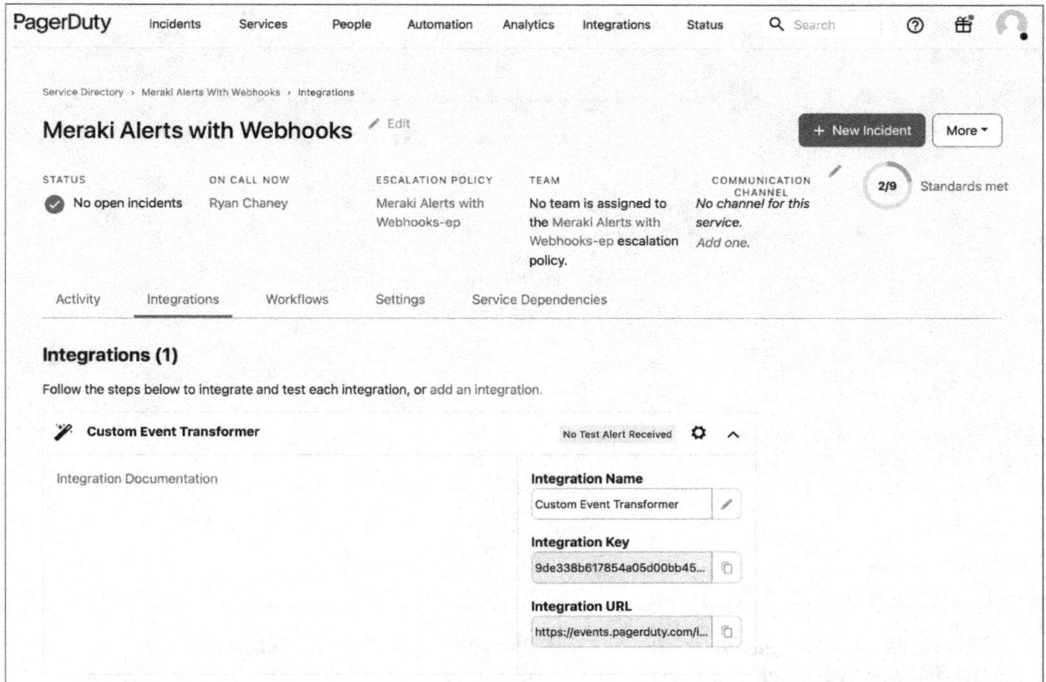

Figure 6-71 *The Integration Key and Integration URL for the Meraki Service in PagerDuty*

Step 12. It's time to switch gears now and move onto configuring Meraki Dashboard. Open a new tab in your web browser and log in to Meraki Dashboard (https://dashboard.meraki.com).

Step 13. Navigate to **Organization > API & Webhooks** (under Configure), as shown in Figure 6-72.

Step 14. Click **Add Webhook Receiver**, as shown in Figure 6-73.

Step 15. Click **Add Receiver**, as shown in Figure 6-74.

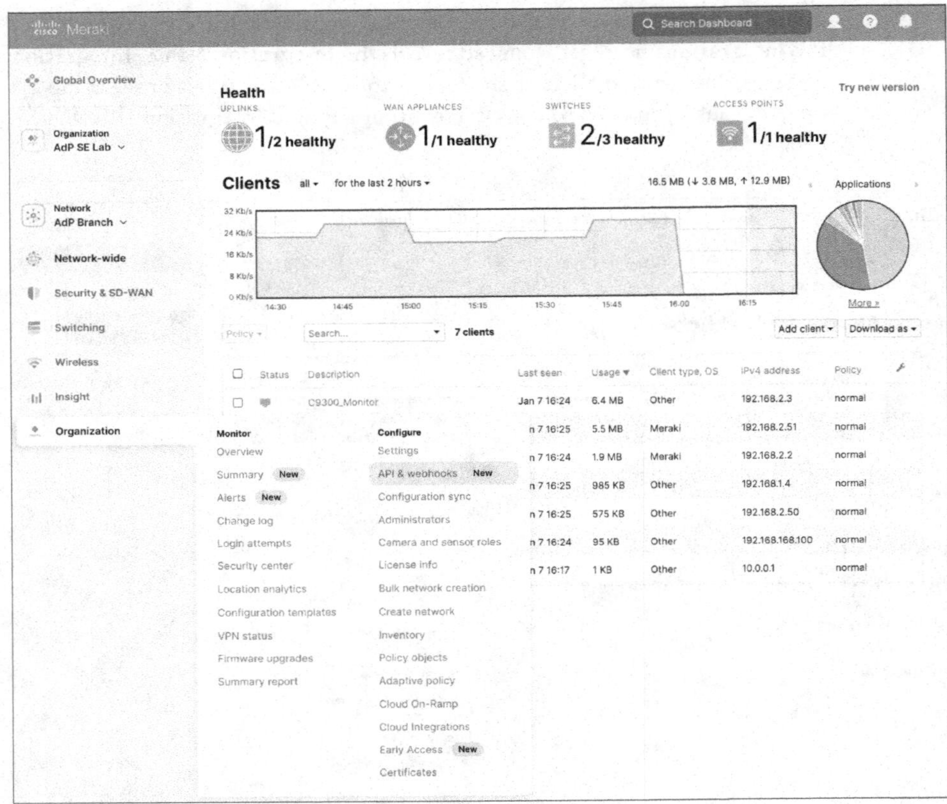

Figure 6-72 *Navigating to the API & Webhooks Page in Meraki Dashboard (Webhooks Example)*

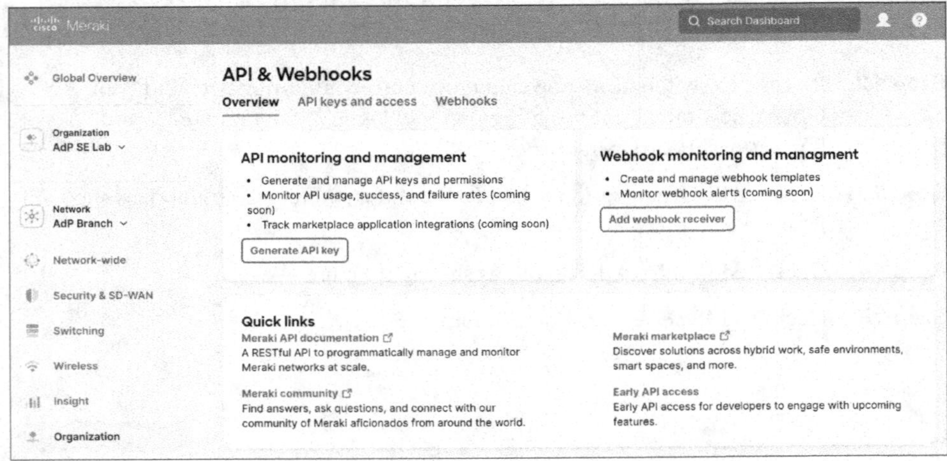

Figure 6-73 *Navigating to the Webhook Receiver Page in Meraki Dashboard*

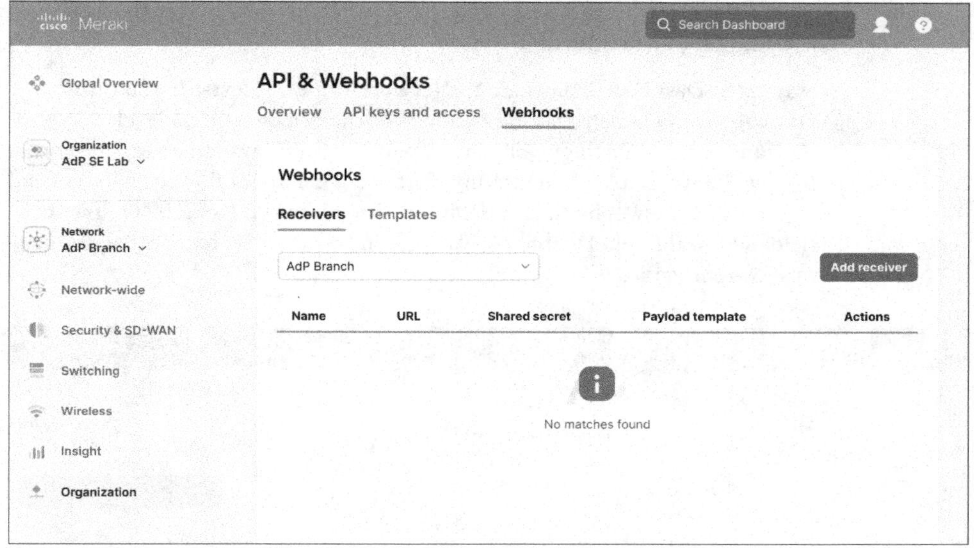

Figure 6-74 *Adding a Webhook Receiver in Meraki Dashboard*

Step 16. On the screen shown in Figure 6-75, enter the following:

- **Name:** This name describes this webhook receiver. In this case, we've used **PagerDuty**.
- **URL:** This is the URL where the webhook messages are sent. In PagerDuty, copy the URL from the **Integration URL** field on the **Meraki Alerts with Webhooks Integrations** page from Step 11.
- **Shared Secret:** In PagerDuty, copy the key from the **Integration Key** field on the **Meraki Alerts with Webhooks Integrations** page from Step 11.

Click **Save.**

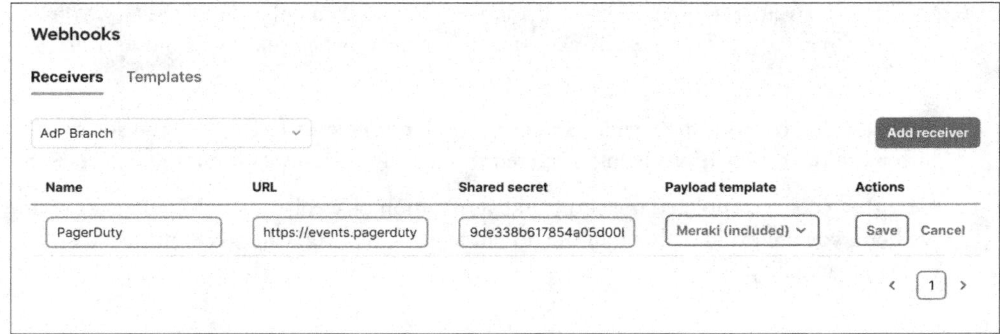

Figure 6-75 *Entering the Configuration Parameters for the PagerDuty Webhook in Meraki Dashboard*

Step 17. The final required step is to configure the alerts that will trigger the webhook notification to PagerDuty.

Staying in Dashboard, navigate to **Network-wide > Alerts.** In the future, you will also be able to configure alerts at the organizational level (**Organization > Settings**), but this capability is not available yet. For now, trigger the webhook whenever any alert is triggered. To do this, all you need to do is add the webhook as a default recipient. In the **Default Recipients** field, add **Webhook: [Webhook Name]**—in this case **Webhook: PagerDuty**, as shown in Figure 6-76.

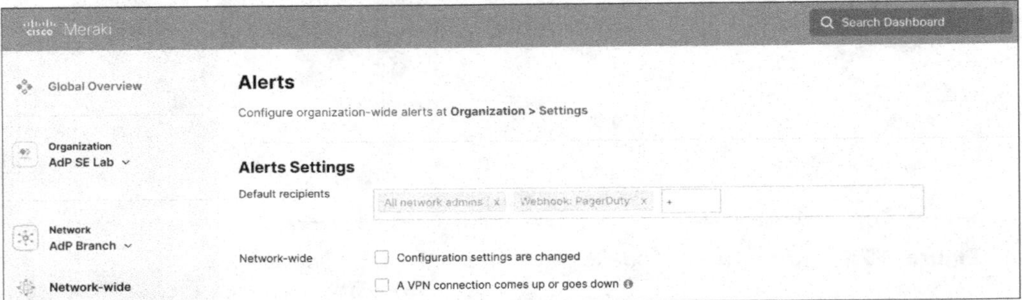

Figure 6-76 *Adding a Webhook Receiver as a Default Recipient for Alerts in Meraki Dashboard*

At this point, you've completed the configuration of alerting using a webhook in Meraki Dashboard.

To verify this webhook is working, you can either trigger an alert that notifies the default recipients or scroll down to **Webhooks** and click **Send Test Webhook.** You also can send webhook tests by navigating to **Organization > API & Webhooks > Webhooks** and clicking **Send Test** from the **Options** drop-down menu, as shown in Figure 6-77. Sending a test from either location displays a success message if the test is successful.

Note If you have configured your email address and mobile number in PagerDuty, you will receive an automated phone call, an SMS, and an email when the test is successful.

In PagerDuty, on both the **Service Integrations** and **Incidents** pages, you can see the history of the notifications being triggered through the API integration (see Figure 6-78).

Now that you've completed the setup and verification of webhooks in Meraki Dashboard, we hope you are excited about all the potential use cases you can dream up for this modern capability.

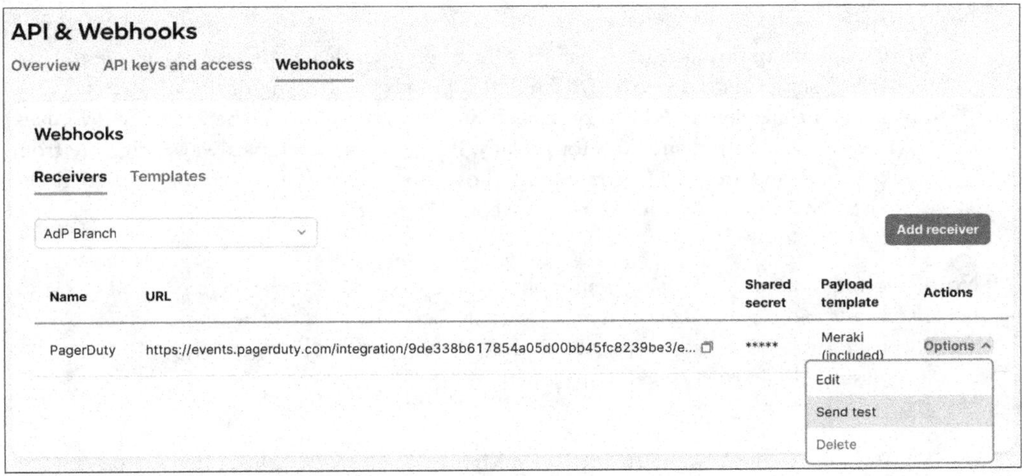

Figure 6-77 *Sending a Test Alert to a Webhook Receiver on the API & Webhooks Page in Meraki Dashboard*

Activity over last 7 days

Service	Title	Time	Activity
Meraki Alerts with Webhooks	[#5] Settings changed	at 7:21 PM	Resolved by Ryan Chaney by phone.
Meraki Alerts with Webhooks	[#5] Settings changed	at 7:19 PM	Triggered through the API. **Description:** Settings changed (View Message)
Meraki Alerts with Webhooks	[#4] Settings changed	at 7:19 PM	Resolved by Ryan Chaney by phone.
Meraki Alerts with Webhooks	[#3] Power supply went down	at 7:19 PM	Resolved by Ryan Chaney by phone.
Meraki Alerts with Webhooks	[#2] Power supply went down	at 7:19 PM	Resolved by Ryan Chaney by phone.
Meraki Alerts with Webhooks	[#4] Settings changed	at 7:18 PM	Triggered through the API. **Description:** Settings changed (View Message)
Meraki Alerts with Webhooks	[#3] Power supply went down	at 7:13 PM	Triggered through the API. **Description:** Power supply went down (View Message)
Meraki Alerts with Webhooks	[#2] Power supply went down	at 6:56 PM	Triggered through the API. **Description:** Power supply went down (View Message)
Default Service	[#1] Example Incident	at 6:51 PM	Resolved by Ryan Chaney through the website.
Default Service	[#1] Example Incident	at 4:40 PM	Triggered by Ryan Chaney through the website. **Description:** Example Incident (View Message)

Per Page: 25 < 1-10 >

Figure 6-78 *The Activity Log on the Incidents Page in PagerDuty Showing Events Being Triggered by the Webhook*

SNMP Traps

SNMP traps are outbound alerts that are sent when specific events take place, such as an interface state change. Meraki Dashboard supports the sending of SNMP v2c and v3 traps for real-time alerts. SNMP v2c packets are sent in clear text, whereas SNMP v3 uses SHA1 for authentication and AES for privacy. Because SNMP traps always originate from Meraki Cloud, and are therefore transmitted over the Internet, it is recommended that you use SNMP v3 or, even better, to use webhooks instead.

Note Meraki recommends using webhooks instead of SNMP traps where possible because webhooks have greater coverage. Another benefit is that traffic on port 443, which is used by webhooks, is typically allowed through firewalls, whereas SNMP is not, requiring more initial effort to get it working.

SNMP traps use the same alert settings in Meraki Dashboard as those that are used for email alerts. This means that email alerts, as well as SNMP traps, will be sent when any of the configured alerts are seen.

Follow these steps to configure SNMP Traps in Meraki Dashboard:

Step 1. Log in to Meraki Dashboard (https://dashboard.meraki.com).

Step 2. Navigate to **Network-wide > Alerts** (under Configure), as shown in Figure 6-79.

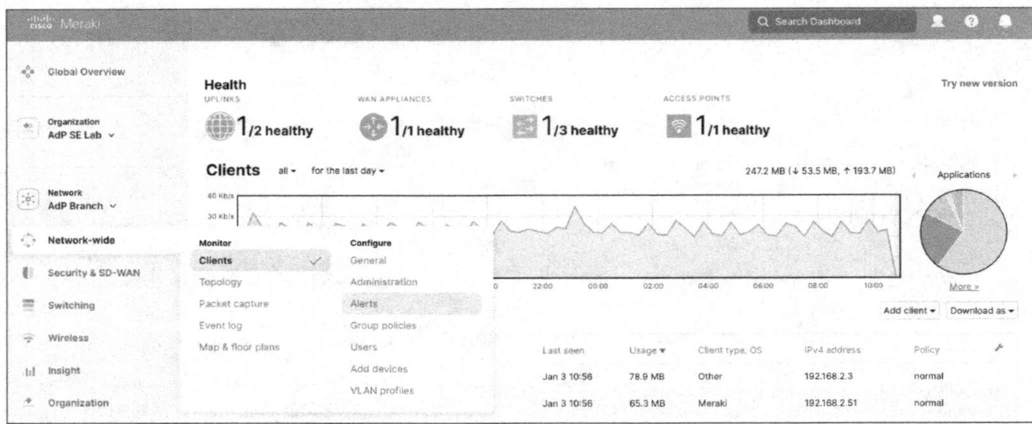

Figure 6-79 *Navigating to the Network-Wide Alerts Page in Meraki Dashboard*

Step 3. Scroll down to **SNMP Traps.** Click the drop-down menu next to **Access** and choose the version of SNMP you need. In this case (see Figure 6-80), we used SNMP v3 because this option offers authentication and encryption.

Step 4. Click **Add an SNMP User**, as shown in Figure 6-81.

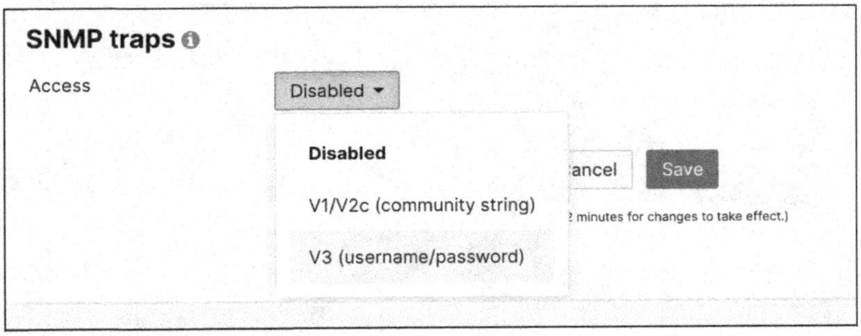

Figure 6-80 *Enabling SNMP Traps in Meraki Dashboard*

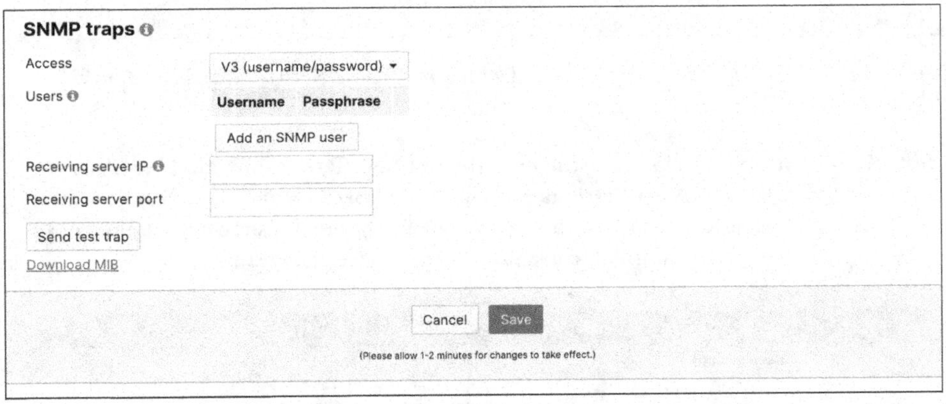

Figure 6-81 *Adding an SNMP User as Part of the SNMP Traps Configuration in Meraki Dashboard*

Step 5. On the screen in Figure 6-82, enter the following details:

- **Username and Passphrase:** These must be the same as configured on your SNMP server. The same passphrase is used for authentication and privacy.
- **Receiving Server IP:** This is the IP address of your SNMP server. Because SNMP traps are sent from Meraki Cloud, it must be a public IP address.
- **Receiver Server Port:** This port needs to match your SNMP server. For IPv4, the standard port for SNMP traps is 162.

Use the **Send Test Trap** button to ensure that SNMP traps are reaching your SNMP server. To ensure they do so, this will likely require firewall and NAT rules in other parts of your network.

Depending on your SNMP server, it might not natively understand the SNMP trap format that Meraki sends. If this is the case, use the **Download MIB** link to download the MIB file and install it on your SNMP server.

Click **Save**.

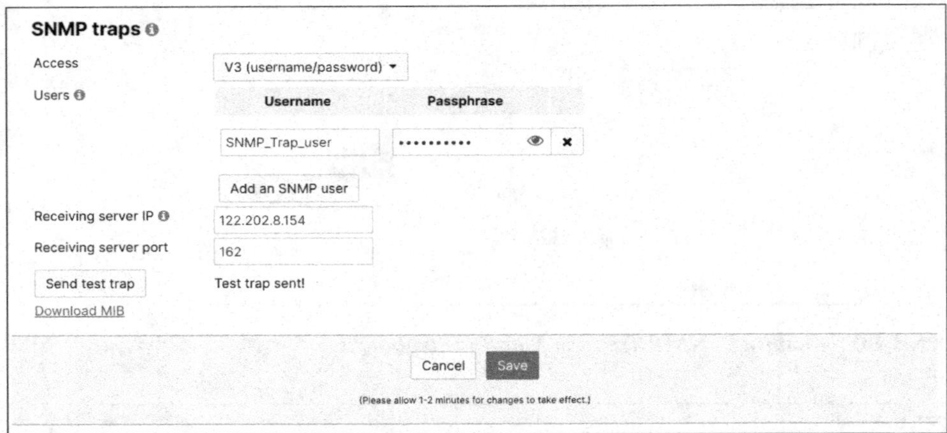

Figure 6-82 *Entering the Configuration Details to Enable SNMP Traps in Meraki Dashboard*

Step 6. When you can successfully see the test SNMP traps on your SNMP server, scroll up to **Alert Settings** and check the boxes for the alerts that you want to generate traps for (a subset of available options is shown in Figure 6-83). When you're finished, click **Save** to save these changes.

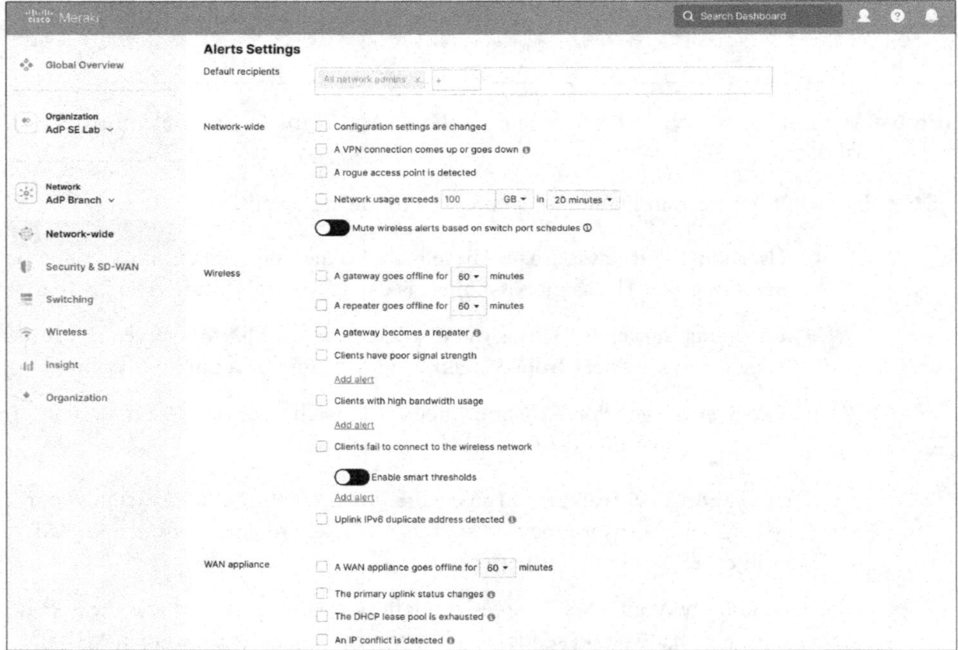

Figure 6-83 *Configuring the Network-Wide Alert Settings in Meraki Dashboard*

Step 7. SNMP traps can also be sent for events related to login attempts. To configure these traps, navigate to **Organization > Login Attempts** and click the **Configure** button next to **SNMP Trap Subscription Status**, as shown in Figure 6-84.

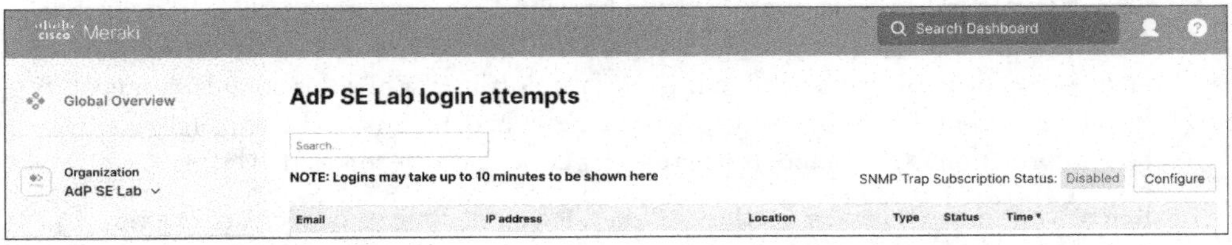

Figure 6-84 *Configuring SNMP Traps on the Login Attempts Log*

Step 8. On the pop-up window, select **V3 (Username/Password)** and click **Save**, as shown in Figure 6-85.

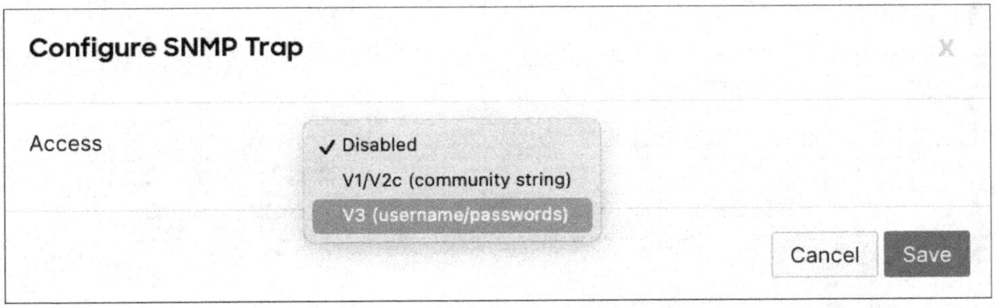

Figure 6-85 *Configuring SNMP v3 Traps on the Login Attempts Log*

You've completed the configuration for sending SNMP traps from Meraki Dashboard. For more information on this process, refer to https://documentation.meraki.com/General_Administration/Monitoring_and_Reporting/SNMP_Overview_and_Configuration.

External Polling

Polling has been traditionally used for reporting (such as interface utilization or errors) and monitoring (such as interface up/down). While reporting and monitoring are available out of the box through Meraki Dashboard, larger organizations with centralized operations support systems (OSS) will require the capability to poll the network. Fortunately, Meraki supports external polling through the use of both its Meraki Dashboard API and traditional SNMP. The sections that follow provide more detail.

Meraki Dashboard API

Meraki Dashboard has an application programming interface (API) that can be used to run queries and return data about your Meraki organization. This API provides the foundational building blocks that enable you to create your own monitoring scripts. In the context of monitoring, the API could be used as an alternative to SNMP polling or SNMP traps. For example, you can use the Dashboard API to query the status of Meraki devices and then take some action if devices are offline. While this sounds rudimentary, the ability to build on this with follow-up queries and actions, and completely control how information is presented, is where using code really becomes powerful.

Before you start, you again need an API key. If you don't have one, create one now by referring to the "Creating API Keys" section earlier in the chapter. Meraki has published a library for Python, which makes it incredibly easy to write your own code; we demonstrate this shortly. The Meraki Python library requires Python 3.7 or higher. To install the Meraki Python library using the pip package manager, use the following command to yield the results demonstrated in Figure 6-86:

```
pip3 install meraki
```

```
ryanchaney — -zsh — 168×21
ryanchaney@RYCHANEY-M-6X1J ~ % pip3 install meraki
Collecting meraki
  Downloading meraki-1.46.0-py3-none-any.whl.metadata (10 kB)
Requirement already satisfied: requests in /Library/Frameworks/Python.framework/Versions/3.9/lib/python3.9/site-packages (from meraki) (2.31.0)
Requirement already satisfied: aiohttp in /Library/Frameworks/Python.framework/Versions/3.9/lib/python3.9/site-packages (from meraki) (3.9.1)
Requirement already satisfied: attrs>=17.3.0 in /Library/Frameworks/Python.framework/Versions/3.9/lib/python3.9/site-packages (from aiohttp->meraki) (23.2.0)
Requirement already satisfied: multidict<7.0,>=4.5 in /Library/Frameworks/Python.framework/Versions/3.9/lib/python3.9/site-packages (from aiohttp->meraki) (6.0.4)
Requirement already satisfied: yarl<2.0,>=1.0 in /Library/Frameworks/Python.framework/Versions/3.9/lib/python3.9/site-packages (from aiohttp->meraki) (1.9.4)
Requirement already satisfied: frozenlist>=1.1.1 in /Library/Frameworks/Python.framework/Versions/3.9/lib/python3.9/site-packages (from aiohttp->meraki) (1.4.1)
Requirement already satisfied: aiosignal>=1.1.2 in /Library/Frameworks/Python.framework/Versions/3.9/lib/python3.9/site-packages (from aiohttp->meraki) (1.3.1)
Requirement already satisfied: async-timeout<5.0,>=4.0 in /Library/Frameworks/Python.framework/Versions/3.9/lib/python3.9/site-packages (from aiohttp->meraki) (4.0.3)
Requirement already satisfied: charset-normalizer<4,>=2 in /Library/Frameworks/Python.framework/Versions/3.9/lib/python3.9/site-packages (from requests->meraki) (3.3.2)
Requirement already satisfied: idna<4,>=2.5 in /Library/Frameworks/Python.framework/Versions/3.9/lib/python3.9/site-packages (from requests->meraki) (3.6)
Requirement already satisfied: urllib3<3,>=1.21.1 in /Library/Frameworks/Python.framework/Versions/3.9/lib/python3.9/site-packages (from requests->meraki) (1.26.12)
Requirement already satisfied: certifi>=2017.4.17 in /Library/Frameworks/Python.framework/Versions/3.9/lib/python3.9/site-packages (from requests->meraki) (2023.11.17)
Downloading meraki-1.46.0-py3-none-any.whl (280 kB)
   ---------------------------------------- 280.9/280.9 kB 4.0 MB/s eta 0:00:00
Installing collected packages: meraki
Successfully installed meraki-1.46.0
ryanchaney@RYCHANEY-M-6X1J ~ %
```

Figure 6-86 *Installing the Meraki Library Using pip*

Next, we demonstrate the Meraki Python library, using a simple Python script to query the Meraki Dashboard API and return the details of any Meraki devices that are offline. For our integrated development environment (or IDE), we use PyCharm (https://www.jetbrains.com/pycharm/). There are a few basic steps to set up the PyCharm IDE, but if you choose to use the same project for all your Meraki scripts, this is just a one-time process.

Follow these steps to set up the PyCharm IDE environment:

Step 1. Open PyCharm and create a new project (**File > New Project**). Update **Location** with your chosen project name by replacing pythonProject (highlighted in Figure 6-87). In this example, we'll be using **Meraki** as our project name. Click **Create**.

Step 2. You need to add the Meraki library to the Python Interpreter by selecting **Pycharm > Settings > Project:** [Project Name] **> Python Interpreter**, as shown in Figure 6-88. Click the **+** symbol at the top of the table.

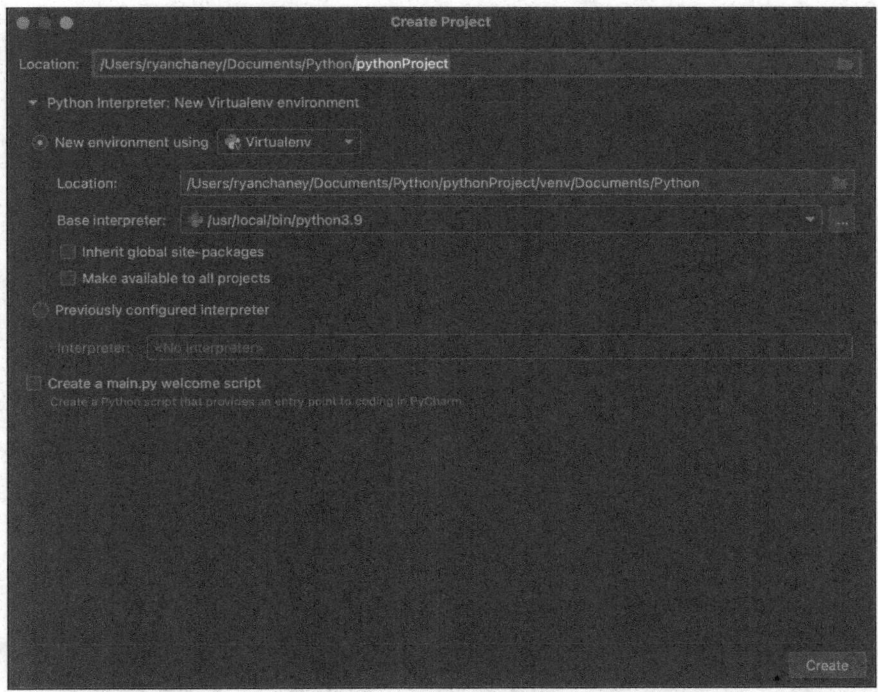

Figure 6-87 *Creating a New Project in PyCharm*

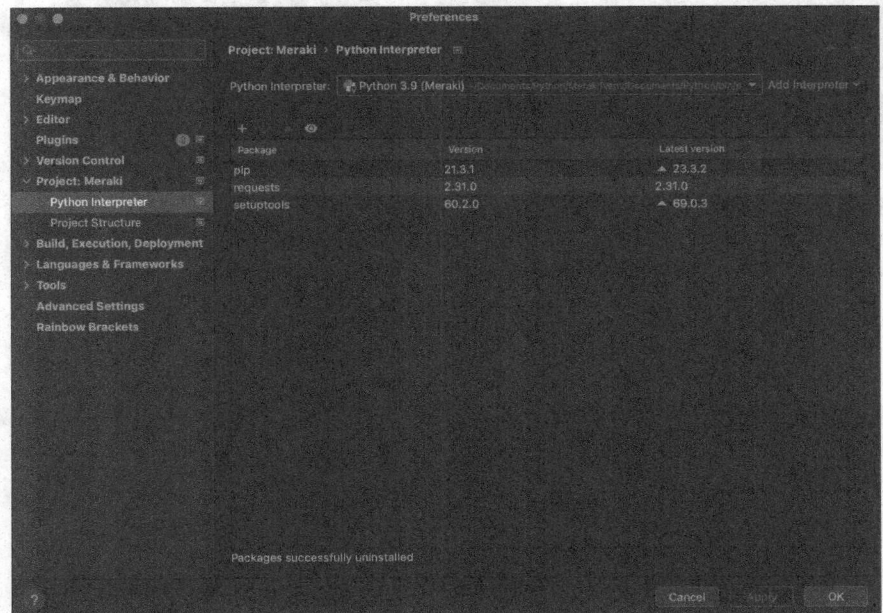

Figure 6-88 *Adding a New Library to the PyCharm Project Interpreter*

Step 3. Search for "meraki."

a. Click **Install Package** at the bottom of the screen shown in Figure 6-89.

b. When you see package "meraki" installed successfully (as shown in Figure 6-89), close this window.

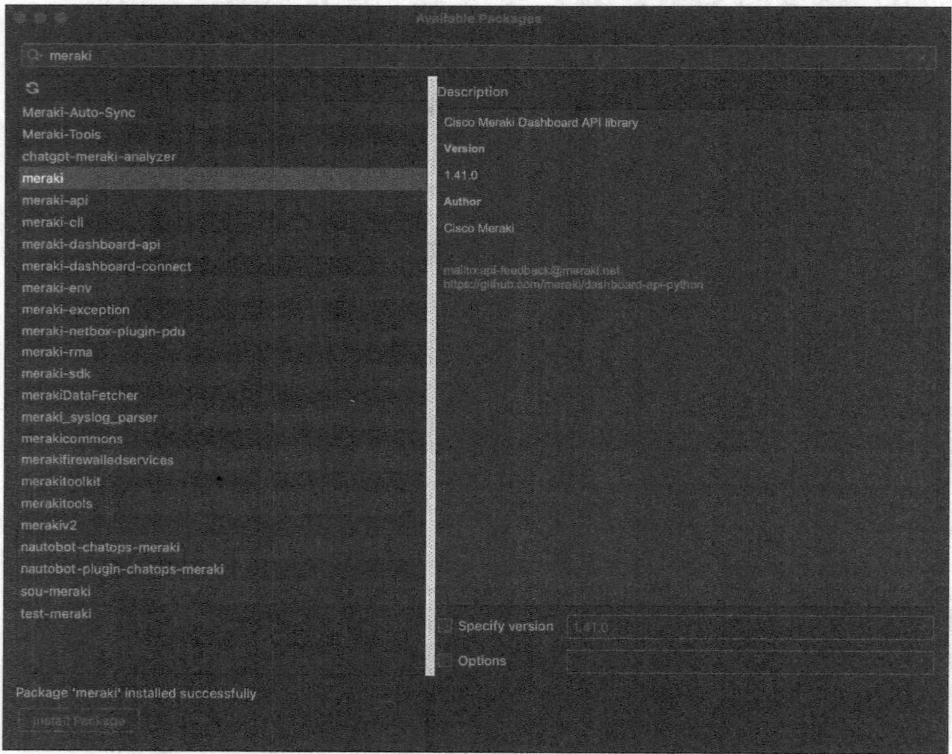

Figure 6-89 *Installing the Meraki Library in PyCharm*

Step 4. Click **OK** to exit **Preferences** and return to the main PyCharm window.

Step 5. Navigate to **File > New**. Select **New Python File**, and on the window shown in Figure 6-90, enter a name for this file. Here, we have used **scratch.py**.

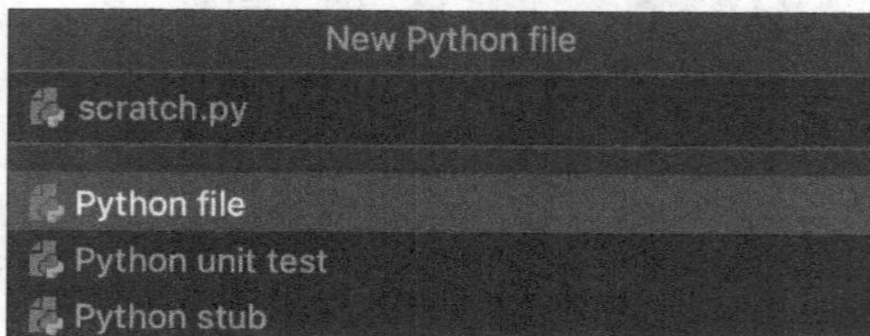

Figure 6-90 *Creating a New Python File in PyCharm*

Step 6. It's recommended that you do not hardcode credentials like passwords and API keys into your code. This is best practice—not only because they are displayed in clear text but also because if the code is shared, then those credentials are shared also. Here, we use environment variables in PyCharm to keep these variables private.

Note When it's time to run the code outside of the IDE (such as when moving the script to a server used for network monitoring), these environment variables need to be migrated also.

To create an environment variable for the API key in PyCharm, navigate to **Run > Edit Configurations.**

Under **Environment Variables**, click the **Edit Environment Variables** icon (the one that looks like a clipboard) on the far right of **PYTHONUNBUFFERED=1**, as shown in Figure 6-91.

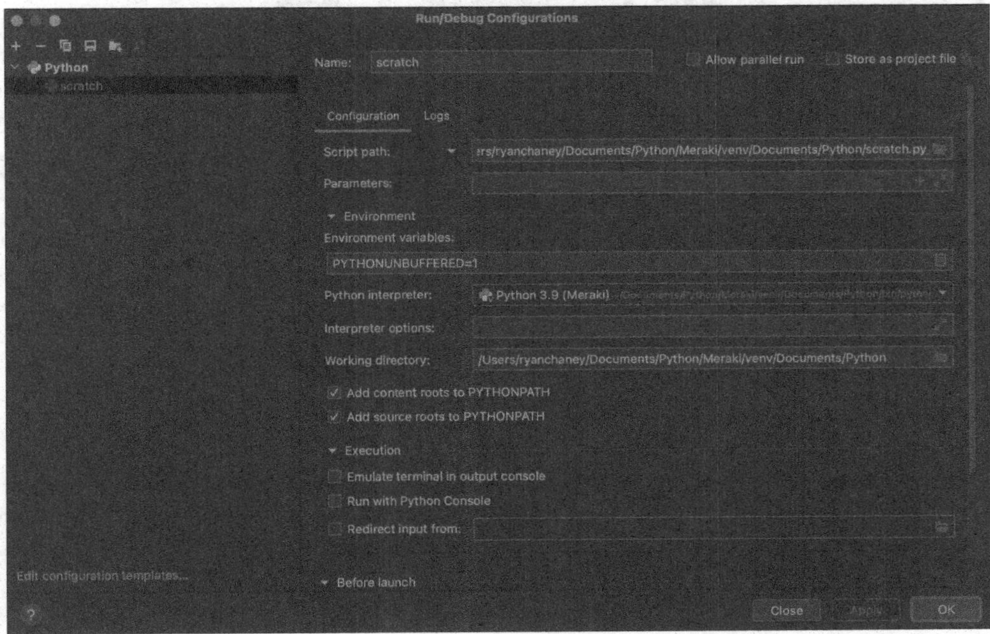

Figure 6-91 *Navigating to Environment Variables in PyCharm*

Step 7. Click the + icon under **User Environment Variables**, as shown in Figure 6-92.

a. Enter a **Name** for the environment variable. We recommend using **MERAKI_DASHBOARD_API_KEY** for the environment variable name. This is the environment variable name commonly used in Cisco's documentation, as well as the scripts posted on Cisco DevNet.

b. Click into the **Value** field and paste in the API key that you generated earlier in Meraki Dashboard.

c. Click **OK** to close the **Environment Variables** window.

d. Click **OK** again to close the **Run/Debug Configurations** window to return to the main PyCharm window.

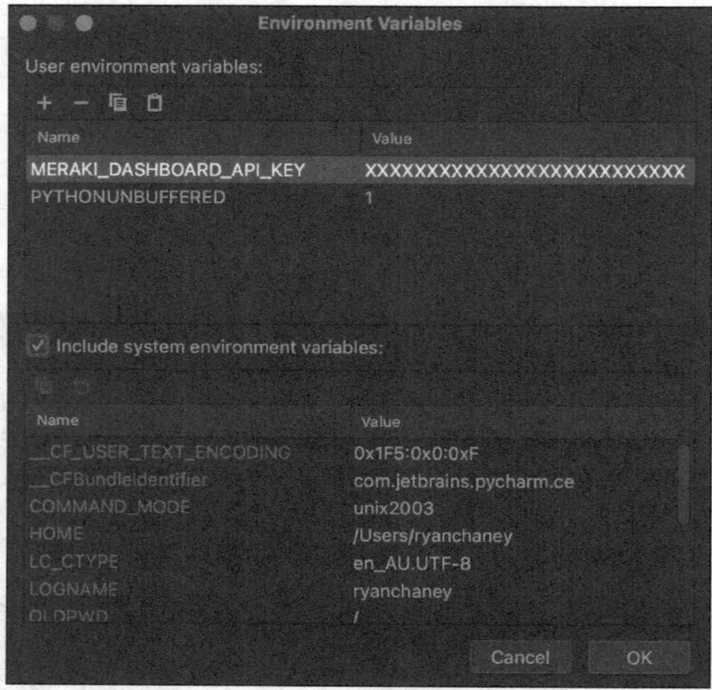

Figure 6-92 *Adding an Environment Variable for the API Key in PyCharm*

Now that you've completed the setup of PyCharm, you can get started with your first Python script using the Meraki Dashboard API. For this, you also need your organization ID, if you don't know where to find it, refer to the "Finding Your Organization ID" section earlier in the chapter.

All of the queries available as part of the Meraki Dashboard API are documented on the Meraki Developer Hub. You can access the Meraki Developer Hub at https://developer.cisco.com/meraki/api/. The API call used in this example is "Get Organization Devices Availabilities," which is explained in detail at https://developer.cisco.com/meraki/api/get-organization-devices-availabilities/.

The short script shown in Example 6-1 uses the Meraki Python library to query the Meraki Dashboard API and returns the status of Meraki devices tagged with "Store."

To start the script, click the green play button on the menu bar in PyCharm. The result, displayed as an easy-to-read table (see Figure 6-93), tells us that all the store devices are dormant. The dormant status means that they are offline and have been offline for more than a week. If this was a production environment, someone would be in serious trouble for not picking this up earlier!

Note To use this sample code, an additional Python library was added to the project interpreter called Pandas. You can add it in the same way you added the Meraki one earlier.

Example 6-1 *Sample Python Script to Query Device Availability Using the Dashboard API*

```
""" This script uses the Meraki Python library to query the Meraki Dashboard API """

# Import required libraries
import os
import meraki
import pandas as pd

# Import API Key from environment variable rather than hardcoding it
MERAKI_DASHBOARD_API_KEY = os.environ['MERAKI_DASHBOARD_API_KEY']

# Authenticate to the Meraki Dashboard API
dashboard = meraki.DashboardAPI(MERAKI_DASHBOARD_API_KEY)

# Create variable for the Organization ID
org_ID = 601793500207410911 # Replace with your own Organization ID

# Make Dashboard API calls - This one checks for the availabilities of devices with
  the tag "Store"
response = dashboard.organizations.getOrganizationDevicesAvailabilities(org_ID,
  total_pages='all', tags="Store")

# Output formatted pandas dataframe with just desired columns
meraki_dataframe = pd.DataFrame(response)
print(meraki_dataframe[['name', 'tags', 'productType', 'status']])
```

You've now completed this brief introduction on how to use the Meraki Dashboard API to monitor Meraki infrastructure. With this helpful starter and a bit of Python knowledge, you'll be writing your own code in no time! For further examples of Python scripts using the Meraki Dashboard API, check out those available on Cisco DevNet at https://developer.cisco.com/codeexchange/search/?q=meraki&languages=Python.

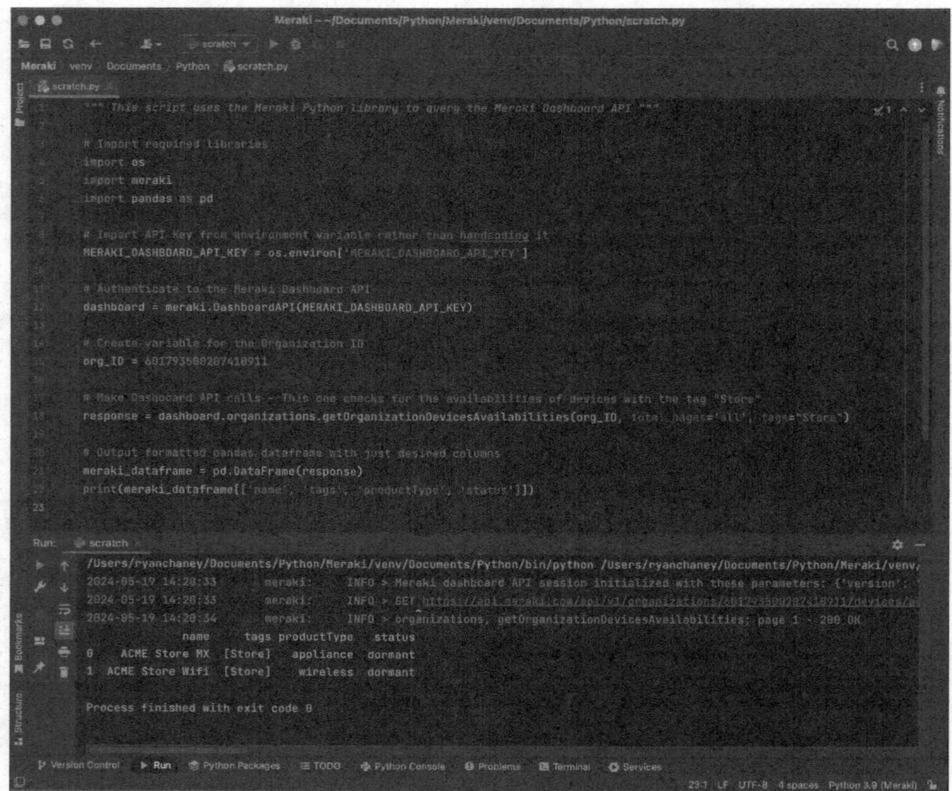

Figure 6-93 *PyCharm Screenshot Showing the Code to Return Device Status and the Status of Store Devices*

SNMP

Network engineers have used SNMP for decades to poll devices and report back things like interface error counters, interface utilization, memory usage, CPU usage, and so on. With SNMP polling, information of interest is first requested by the network management system (NMS) or SNMP application. In contrast, SNMP traps are preconfigured and sent by devices when an event occurs, without any interaction with other applications. Data collected via SNMP polling has typically been used by monitoring systems for reporting and issue resolution in traditional CLI-based networks. Because Meraki provides reporting and monitoring out of the box via Meraki Dashboard, most organizations do not need to set up SNMP polling, except when needing to integrate with existing OSSs.

Meraki supports both SNMP version 2c and version 3. The big difference between the two is that SNMP v2c uses a community string for authentication and transmits packets in clear text. SNMP v3, on the other hand, features strong authentication and data encryption for privacy. When using SNMP v2c, Meraki provides a complex community string to use. You can enable both SNMP v2c and v3 at the same time, but if you're using SNMP, it is recommended that you use only SNMP v3.

Meraki Dashboard and Meraki devices can be polled using SNMP. By default, Meraki devices cannot be polled from outside of the local IP network; however, this can be allowed with a whitelist (**Organization > Settings** [under Configure] > **SNMP**). Meraki devices support the majority of the object identifiers (OIDs) in the common SNMPv2 (.1.3.6.1.2.1.1) and interface (.1.3.6.1.2.1) MIBs. When polling the Meraki Cloud, an additional MIB—MERAKI-CLOUD-CONTROLLER-MIB—is used for Meraki-specific information. A download link for this MIB becomes available when SNMP is enabled in Meraki Dashboard. Installing this MIB is covered in the following steps.

> **Note** Meraki SNMP access supports only get requests. No changes to the Dashboard configuration can be made using SNMP.

Follow these steps to configure SNMP in Meraki Dashboard:

Step 1. Log in to Meraki Dashboard (https://dashboard.meraki.com).

Step 2. Navigate to **Organization** > **Settings** (under Configure), as shown in Figure 6-94.

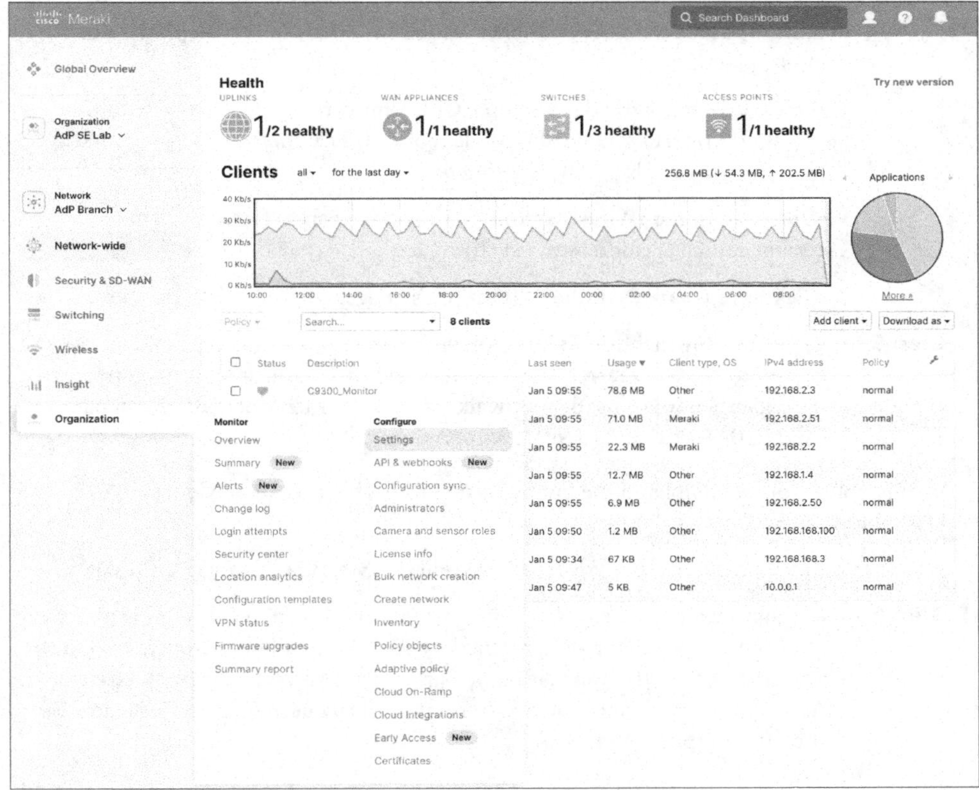

Figure 6-94 *Navigating to Organization Settings in Meraki Dashboard*

Step 3. Scroll down to **Settings**, as shown in Figure 6-95.

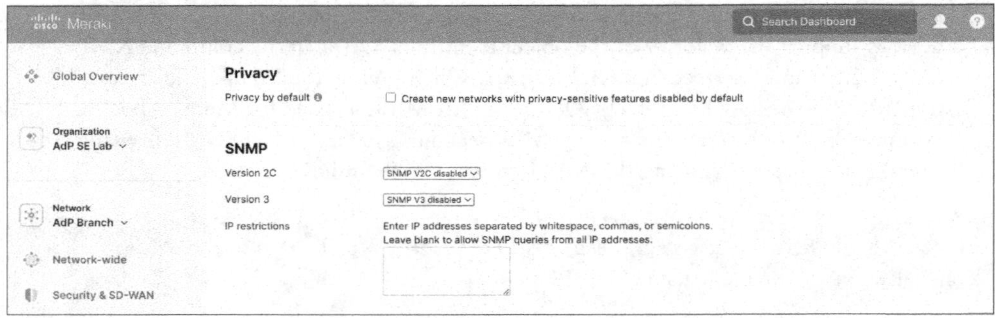

Figure 6-95 *SNMP Settings at the Organization Level in Meraki Dashboard*

Step 4. In this example, we configure SNMP v3. From the **Version 3** drop-down menu, select **SNMP V3 Enabled.**

The **Authentication Mode** and **Privacy Mode** preselect the stronger SHA and AES128 standards.

Enter a password in the **Authentication Password** and **Privacy Password** input boxes.

Handily, Meraki provides a sample CLI command for you to use with this configuration. All you need to do is replace *<auth pass>* and *<priv pass>* with the passwords you have defined.

(Optional) In the **IP Restrictions** field, if you wish to restrict polling to certain source IP addresses, list them here.

Click **Save Changes** at the bottom of the page.

Step 5. Click the **Download MIB** link shown in Figure 6-96. This file needs to be copied to the MIB search path for the application you are querying from. In this example, we've used **snmpwalk** on MacOS 14.2; the MIB search path used in this setup is /usr/share/snmp/mibs.

At this point, you've completed the configuration to enable SNMP in Meraki Dashboard.

Follow these steps to verify that you're able to poll the Meraki Cloud using SNMP:

Step 1. Use **snmpwalk** to query the Meraki Cloud. As shown in Figure 6-97, we've used the sample command provided by Meraki Dashboard from Step 5 in the preceding list, with the addition of our authentication and privacy passwords. As you can see, this test begins to return OID values, which we use later for specific **snmpget** requests.

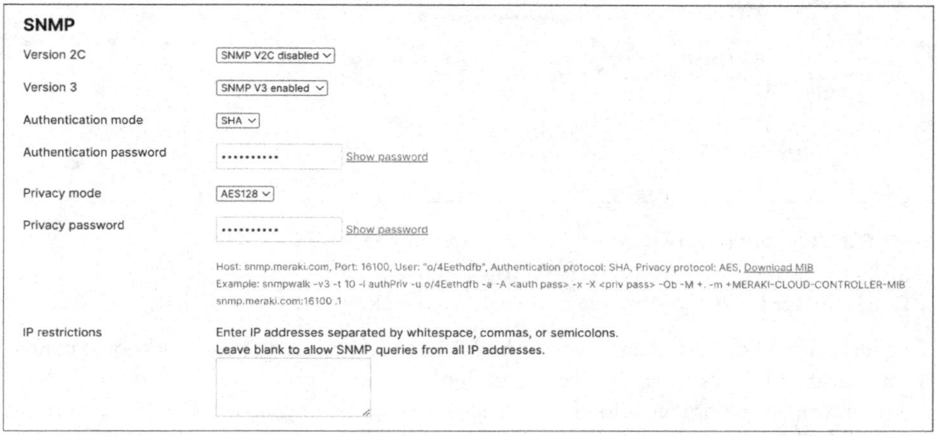

SNMP

Version 2C — SNMP V2C disabled

Version 3 — SNMP V3 enabled

Authentication mode — SHA

Authentication password — •••••••••• Show password

Privacy mode — AES128

Privacy password — •••••••••• Show password

Host: snmp.meraki.com, Port: 16100, User: "o/4Eethdfb", Authentication protocol: SHA, Privacy protocol: AES, Download MIB
Example: snmpwalk -v3 -t 10 -l authPriv -u o/4Eethdfb -a -A <auth pass> -x -X <priv pass> -Ob -M +. -m +MERAKI-CLOUD-CONTROLLER-MIB snmp.meraki.com:16100 .1

IP restrictions — Enter IP addresses separated by whitespace, commas, or semicolons.
Leave blank to allow SNMP queries from all IP addresses.

Figure 6-96 *Configuring the Organization SNMP Settings in Meraki Dashboard*

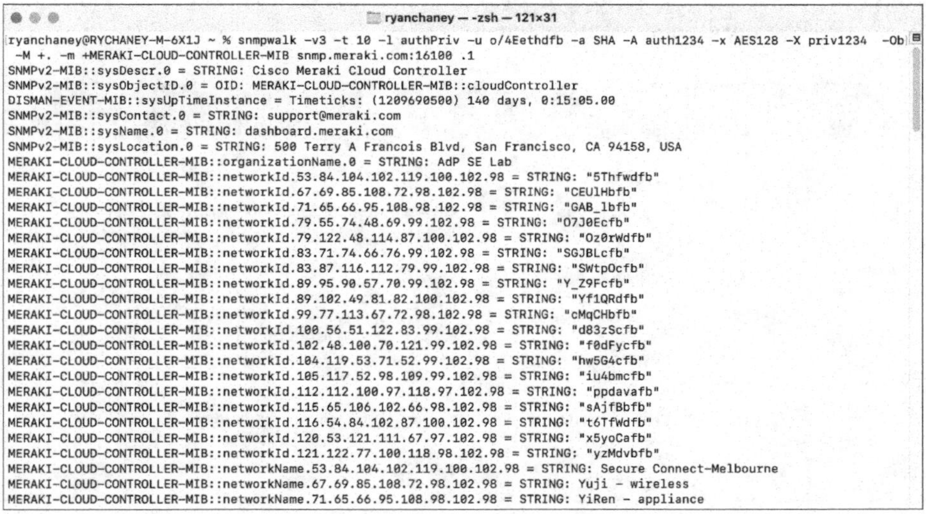

```
ryanchaney — -zsh — 121×31
ryanchaney@RYCHANEY-M-6X1J ~ % snmpwalk -v3 -t 10 -l authPriv -u o/4Eethdfb -a SHA -A auth1234 -x AES128 -X priv1234  -Ob
 -M +. -m +MERAKI-CLOUD-CONTROLLER-MIB snmp.meraki.com:16100 .1
SNMPv2-MIB::sysDescr.0 = STRING: Cisco Meraki Cloud Controller
SNMPv2-MIB::sysObjectID.0 = OID: MERAKI-CLOUD-CONTROLLER-MIB::cloudController
DISMAN-EVENT-MIB::sysUpTimeInstance = Timeticks: (1209690500) 140 days, 0:15:05.00
SNMPv2-MIB::sysContact.0 = STRING: support@meraki.com
SNMPv2-MIB::sysName.0 = STRING: dashboard.meraki.com
SNMPv2-MIB::sysLocation.0 = STRING: 500 Terry A Francois Blvd, San Francisco, CA 94158, USA
MERAKI-CLOUD-CONTROLLER-MIB::organizationName.0 = STRING: AdP SE Lab
MERAKI-CLOUD-CONTROLLER-MIB::networkId.53.84.104.102.119.100.102.98 = STRING: "5Thfwdfb"
MERAKI-CLOUD-CONTROLLER-MIB::networkId.67.69.85.108.72.98.102.98 = STRING: "CEUlHbfb"
MERAKI-CLOUD-CONTROLLER-MIB::networkId.71.65.66.95.108.98.102.98 = STRING: "GAB_lbfb"
MERAKI-CLOUD-CONTROLLER-MIB::networkId.79.55.74.48.69.99.102.98 = STRING: "O7J0Ecfb"
MERAKI-CLOUD-CONTROLLER-MIB::networkId.79.122.48.114.87.100.102.98 = STRING: "Oz0rWdfb"
MERAKI-CLOUD-CONTROLLER-MIB::networkId.83.71.74.66.76.99.102.98 = STRING: "SGJBLcfb"
MERAKI-CLOUD-CONTROLLER-MIB::networkId.83.87.116.112.79.99.102.98 = STRING: "SWtpOcfb"
MERAKI-CLOUD-CONTROLLER-MIB::networkId.89.95.90.57.70.99.102.98 = STRING: "Y_Z9Fcfb"
MERAKI-CLOUD-CONTROLLER-MIB::networkId.89.102.49.81.82.100.102.98 = STRING: "Yf1QRdfb"
MERAKI-CLOUD-CONTROLLER-MIB::networkId.99.77.113.67.72.98.102.98 = STRING: "cMqCHbfb"
MERAKI-CLOUD-CONTROLLER-MIB::networkId.100.56.51.122.83.99.102.98 = STRING: "d83zScfb"
MERAKI-CLOUD-CONTROLLER-MIB::networkId.102.48.100.70.121.99.102.98 = STRING: "f0dFycfb"
MERAKI-CLOUD-CONTROLLER-MIB::networkId.104.119.53.71.52.99.102.98 = STRING: "hw5G4cfb"
MERAKI-CLOUD-CONTROLLER-MIB::networkId.105.117.52.98.109.99.102.98 = STRING: "iu4bmcfb"
MERAKI-CLOUD-CONTROLLER-MIB::networkId.112.112.100.97.118.97.102.98 = STRING: "ppdavafb"
MERAKI-CLOUD-CONTROLLER-MIB::networkId.115.65.106.102.66.98.102.98 = STRING: "sAjfBbfb"
MERAKI-CLOUD-CONTROLLER-MIB::networkId.116.54.84.102.87.100.102.98 = STRING: "t6TfWdfb"
MERAKI-CLOUD-CONTROLLER-MIB::networkId.120.53.121.111.67.97.102.98 = STRING: "x5yoCafb"
MERAKI-CLOUD-CONTROLLER-MIB::networkId.121.122.77.100.118.98.102.98 = STRING: "yzMdvbfb"
MERAKI-CLOUD-CONTROLLER-MIB::networkName.53.84.104.102.119.100.102.98 = STRING: Secure Connect-Melbourne
MERAKI-CLOUD-CONTROLLER-MIB::networkName.67.69.85.108.72.98.102.98 = STRING: Yuji - wireless
MERAKI-CLOUD-CONTROLLER-MIB::networkName.71.65.66.95.108.98.102.98 = STRING: YiRen - appliance
```

Figure 6-97 *Output of an **snmpwalk** Request Against Meraki Cloud*

Step 2. Use the **snmpget** command to retrieve a value for a specific OID from Meraki Cloud—in this case, the organization name. The command is quite lengthy, but it is essentially the same as the preceding one, with **snmpget** instead of **snmpwalk** and a specific OID on the end rather than .1. For example:

```
snmpget -v3 -t 10 -l authPriv -u o/4Eethdfb -a SHA
-A <auth pass> -x AES128 -X <priv pass> -Ob -M +. -m
+MERAKI-CLOUD-CONTROLLER-MIB snmp.meraki.com:16100
.1.3.6.1.4.1.29671.1.1.1.0
```

A string is returned with the organization name, AdP SE Lab, as demonstrated in Figure 6-98.

```
ryanchaney — -zsh — 120×10
ryanchaney@RYCHANEY-M-6X1J ~ % snmpget -v3 -t 10 -l authPriv -u o/4Eethdfb -a SHA -A auth1234 -x AES128 -X priv1234 -Ob
-M +. -m +MERAKI-CLOUD-CONTROLLER-MIB snmp.meraki.com:16100 .1.3.6.1.4.1.29671.1.1.1.0
MERAKI-CLOUD-CONTROLLER-MIB::organizationName.0 = STRING: AdP SE Lab
ryanchaney@RYCHANEY-M-6X1J ~ %
```

Figure 6-98 *Output of an **snmpget** Request Against Meraki Cloud*

These steps verify that you're able to query the Meraki Cloud using SNMP.

To query Meraki devices themselves with SNMP, you need to do some additional configuration at the network level. This configuration is completely independent of the SNMP configuration at the organization level. Follow these steps to enable SNMP for devices in your network:

Step 1. In Meraki Dashboard, navigate to **Network-wide > General.**

Step 2. Scroll down to **Reporting.** Next to SNMP access, select **V3 (Username/ Password)**, as shown in Figure 6-99.

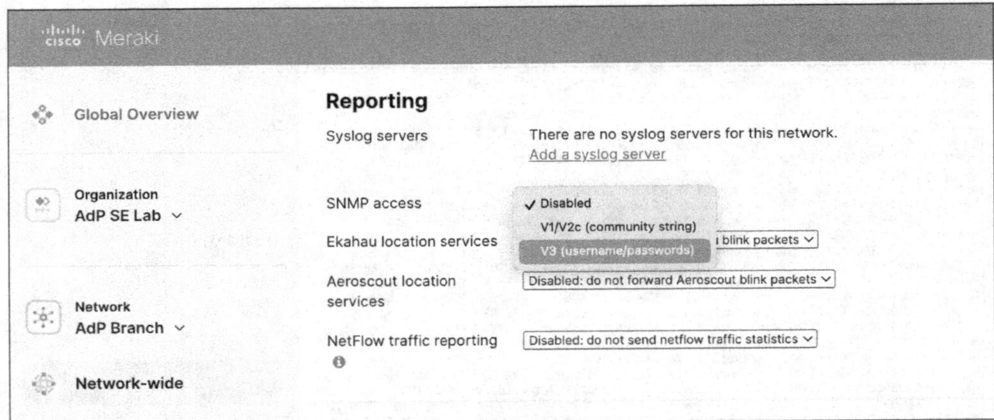

Figure 6-99 *Enabling SNMP at the Network Level*

Step 3. Click **Add an SNMP User.** Enter a **Username** and **Passphrase** that you would like to use to query devices in this network, as shown in Figure 6-100. If you have special characters in the Username field here (like / or #), the changes will not save properly. You can use underscores, however. Click **Save.**

Step 4. Open the **Firewall** link in a new tab. Create a new inbound firewall rule to allow inbound traffic on port 161. In Figure 6-101, we have specified the

Server VLAN (which equates to subnet 192.168.168.0/24) to restrict the hosts that can poll this device.

Click **Finish Editing** and then **Save** at the bottom of the page.

Reporting

Syslog servers — There are no syslog servers for this network.
Add a syslog server

SNMP access — V3 (username/passwords)

SNMP users

Username	Passphrase	
SNMP_user	•••••••••	Show secret

Add an SNMP user

When enabled, configure firewall settings for the SNMP service on the Firewall page.

Ekahau location services — Disabled: do not forward Ekahau blink packets

Aeroscout location services — Disabled: do not forward Aeroscout blink packets

NetFlow traffic reporting — Disabled: do not send netflow traffic statistics

Figure 6-100 *Configuring an SNMP User at the Network Level in Meraki Dashboard*

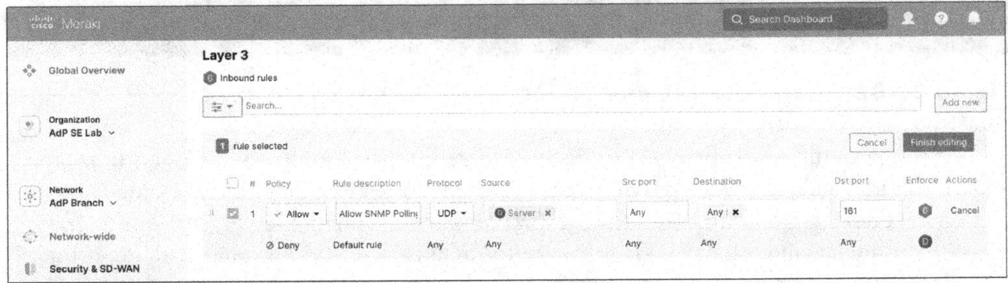

Figure 6-101 *Configuring a Firewall Rule to Allow SNMP Requests to Devices*

You've now completed the configuration to allow devices in this network to be queried with SNMP.

To verify this configuration is working, carry out an SNMP walk of a device in this network from another host inside your environment. In this example, we used the **snmpwalk** tool (available at https://ezfive.com/snmpsoft-tools/snmp-walk/) to test from a local Windows Server.

> **Note** The following was required for this test to work:
>
> 1. The password for this Dashboard user must be used for both authentication and privacy, i.e., the same password for both.
> 2. DES had to be specified as the privacy protocol. This would not work when any other privacy protocol was specified, such as AES128.

In Figure 6-102, you can see the successful SNMPwalk of a Meraki MX67C device.

```
Command Prompt
C:\Users\Administrator\Downloads\SnmpWalk>snmpwalk -r:192.168.168.1 -v:3 -sn:SNMP_user -ap:SHA -aw:auth1234 -pp:DES -pw:auth1234
SnmpWalk v1.01 - Copyright (C) 2009 SnmpSoft Company
[ More useful network tools on http://www.snmpsoft.com ]

OID=.1.3.6.1.2.1.1.1.0, Type=OctetString, Value=Meraki MX67C LTE Router/Security Appliance - Worldwide
OID=.1.3.6.1.2.1.1.2.0, Type=OID, Value=1.3.6.1.4.1.29671.2.120
OID=.1.3.6.1.2.1.1.5.0, Type=OctetString, Value=AdP Branch MX
OID=.1.3.6.1.2.1.1.9.1.2.1, Type=OID, Value=1.3.6.1.6.3.1
OID=.1.3.6.1.2.1.1.9.1.2.2, Type=OID, Value=1.3.6.1.6.3.16.2.2.1
OID=.1.3.6.1.2.1.1.9.1.2.3, Type=OID, Value=1.3.6.1.2.1.31
OID=.1.3.6.1.2.1.1.9.1.3.1, Type=OctetString, Value=The MIB module for SNMPv2 entities
OID=.1.3.6.1.2.1.1.9.1.3.2, Type=OctetString, Value=View-based Access Control Model for SNMP.
OID=.1.3.6.1.2.1.1.9.1.3.3, Type=OctetString, Value=The MIB module to describe generic objects for network interface sub-layers
OID=.1.3.6.1.2.1.1.9.1.4.1, Type=TimeTicks, Value=0:00:00.00
OID=.1.3.6.1.2.1.1.9.1.4.2, Type=TimeTicks, Value=0:00:00.00
OID=.1.3.6.1.2.1.1.9.1.4.3, Type=TimeTicks, Value=0:00:00.01
OID=.1.3.6.1.2.1.2.1.0, Type=Integer, Value=5
OID=.1.3.6.1.2.1.2.2.1.1.1, Type=Integer, Value=1
OID=.1.3.6.1.2.1.2.2.1.1.2, Type=Integer, Value=2
OID=.1.3.6.1.2.1.2.2.1.1.3, Type=Integer, Value=3
OID=.1.3.6.1.2.1.2.2.1.1.4, Type=Integer, Value=4
OID=.1.3.6.1.2.1.2.2.1.1.5, Type=Integer, Value=5
OID=.1.3.6.1.2.1.2.2.1.2.1, Type=OctetString, Value=port1
OID=.1.3.6.1.2.1.2.2.1.2.2, Type=OctetString, Value=port2
OID=.1.3.6.1.2.1.2.2.1.2.3, Type=OctetString, Value=port3
OID=.1.3.6.1.2.1.2.2.1.2.4, Type=OctetString, Value=port4
OID=.1.3.6.1.2.1.2.2.1.2.5, Type=OctetString, Value=port5
OID=.1.3.6.1.2.1.2.2.1.3.1, Type=Integer, Value=6
OID=.1.3.6.1.2.1.2.2.1.3.2, Type=Integer, Value=6
OID=.1.3.6.1.2.1.2.2.1.3.3, Type=Integer, Value=6
OID=.1.3.6.1.2.1.2.2.1.3.4, Type=Integer, Value=6
OID=.1.3.6.1.2.1.2.2.1.3.5, Type=Integer, Value=6
OID=.1.3.6.1.2.1.2.2.1.4.1, Type=Integer, Value=1500
OID=.1.3.6.1.2.1.2.2.1.4.2, Type=Integer, Value=1500
OID=.1.3.6.1.2.1.2.2.1.4.3, Type=Integer, Value=1500
OID=.1.3.6.1.2.1.2.2.1.4.4, Type=Integer, Value=1500
OID=.1.3.6.1.2.1.2.2.1.4.5, Type=Integer, Value=1500
```

Figure 6-102 *Successful snmpwalk of a Meraki MX Appliance*

At this point in the chapter, you've completed your verification for SNMP. SNMP is now configured and ready for your monitoring systems to begin polling Meraki Cloud and Meraki devices. Refer to the following link for more information on SNMP with Meraki: https://documentation.meraki.com/General_Administration/Monitoring_and_Reporting/SNMP_Overview_and_Configuration.

Automated Incident Response with ServiceNow

An incident response capability is a common requirement of security standards. For example, FIPS 200 requires that

> Organizations must: (i) establish an operational incident handling capability for organizational information systems that includes adequate preparation, detection, analysis, containment, recovery, and user response activities; and (ii) track, document, and report incidents to appropriate organizational officials and/or authorities.[2]

Likewise, NIST 800-53 (requirement 10.7.2) requires that the failure of critical security control systems be detected, alerted, and addressed promptly. Regardless of the security standard, incident response systems are found in every organization simply because organizations must have a way to record and manage incidents in order to operate.

ServiceNow is a platform commonly used by organizations to manage incidents and maintain an inventory of the devices it owns. This is typically referred to as a configuration management database (CMDB). Meraki provides a Now Certified app, named Service Graph Connector for Meraki, which allows organizations to

- Automatically import their Meraki organizations, networks, and devices into ServiceNow
- Create incidents based on webhook alerts from Meraki Dashboard

Version 1.3.3 of the Service Graph Connector for Meraki, which is the latest at the time of writing, supports the latest versions of ServiceNow, including Vancouver, Utah, and Tokyo. The latest compatibility information is shown on the Service Graph Connector for Meraki page on the ServiceNow Store (store.servicenow.com). To find this page, search for "meraki" and click on **Service Graph Connector For Meraki.**

The Service Graph Connector for Meraki features a guided setup process to make this integration as easy as possible. Similar to the integration with Splunk described previously, this ServiceNow integration also requires a Meraki Dashboard API key. If you haven't already created an API key for ServiceNow, complete the steps in the "Creating API Keys" section earlier in this chapter.

By default, the guided setup process imports all organizations. If you have attached the API key to an admin who has access to multiple organizations, you might need to filter based on organization ID. Refer to the "Finding Your Organization ID" section earlier in the chapter for help on how to locate the organization ID. If you have followed the recommendations in the "Creating API Keys" section, and you wish to limit ServiceNow's view to one Meraki organization, no other configuration is required.

Follow these steps to enable Meraki Dashboard to raise incidents automatically in ServiceNow:

Step 1. Log in to your ServiceNow instance.

Step 2. The first task is to install the Service Graph Connector for Meraki application from the ServiceNow Store. Navigate to **All > Search for Store** and click **Available to Obtain from Store** under System Applications, as shown in Figure 6-103.

Step 3. In the search field, type **meraki**. On the resulting page for Service Graph Connector For Meraki, click **View Details**, as shown in Figure 6-104.

Step 4. Click **Request Install** in the upper right, as shown in Figure 6-105.

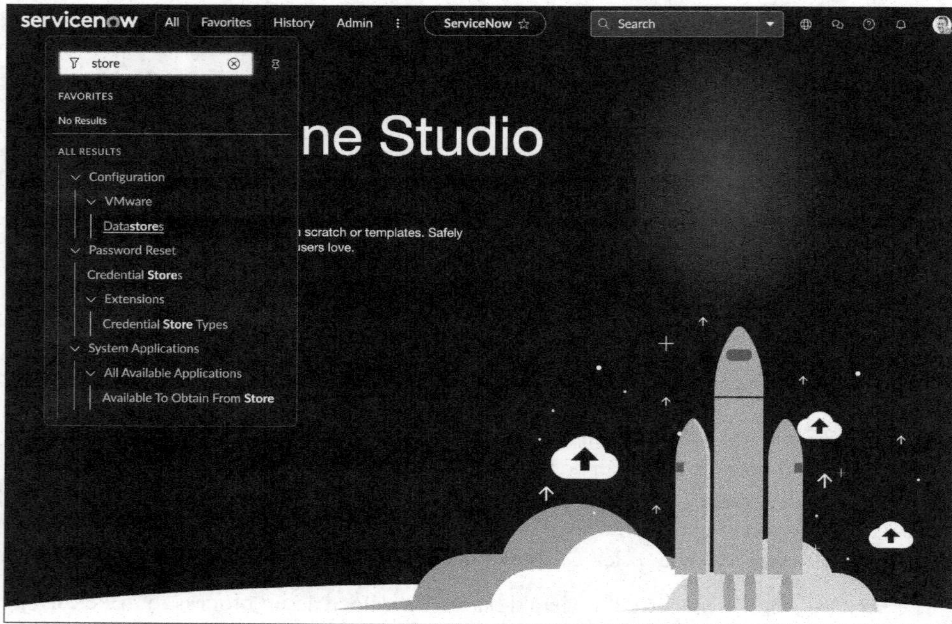

Figure 6-103 *Navigating to the ServiceNow Store in ServiceNow*

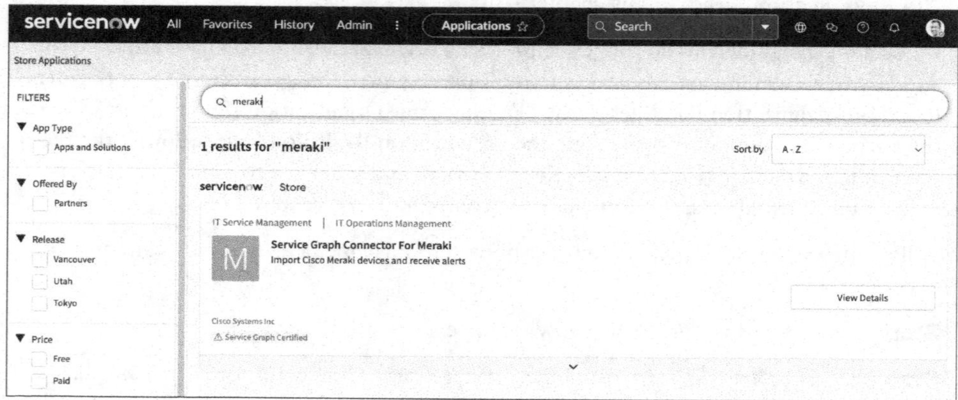

Figure 6-104 *Searching for the Service Graph Connector for Meraki in the ServiceNow Store*

Step 5. With the Service Graph Connector for Meraki installed, it's now time to run through the guided setup. Navigate to **All** > **Service Graph Connectors** > **Meraki** > **Setup**, as shown in Figure 6-106.

Step 6. On the **Service Graph Connector for Meraki** page, click the **Get Started** button on the right to start the guided setup. In our case, the button says **Review** because this integration was completed previously (see Figure 6-107).

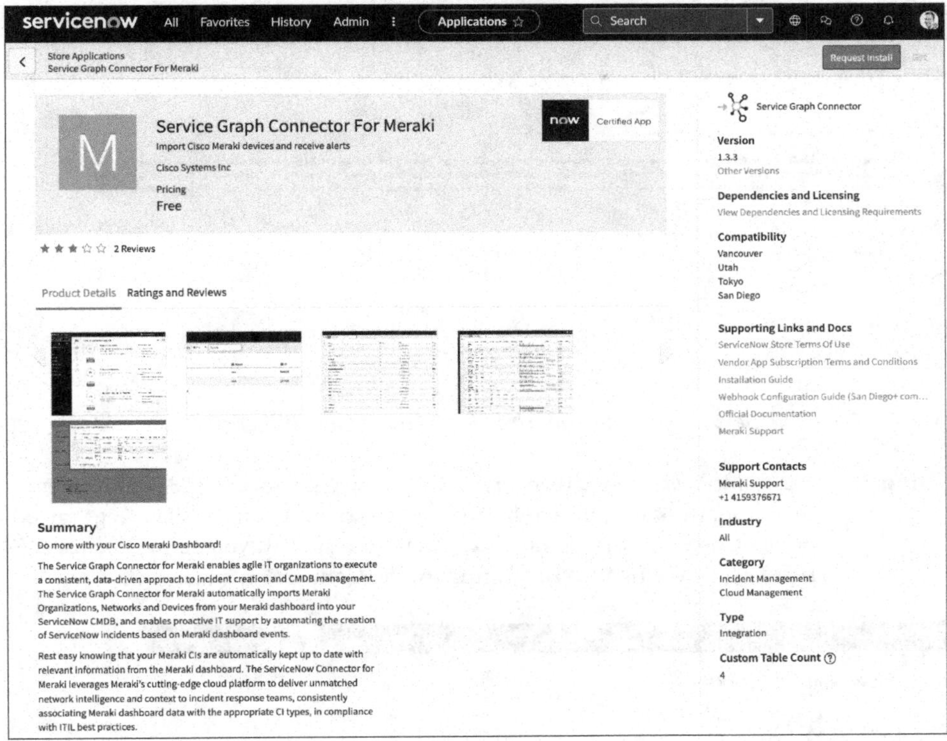

Figure 6-105 *Installing the Meraki Connector from the ServiceNow Store*

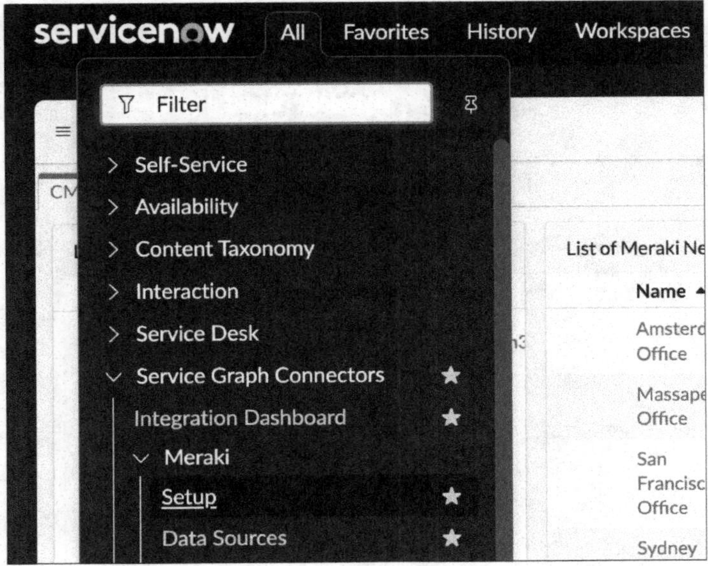

Figure 6-106 *Navigating to the Meraki Connector Guided Setup Page in ServiceNow*

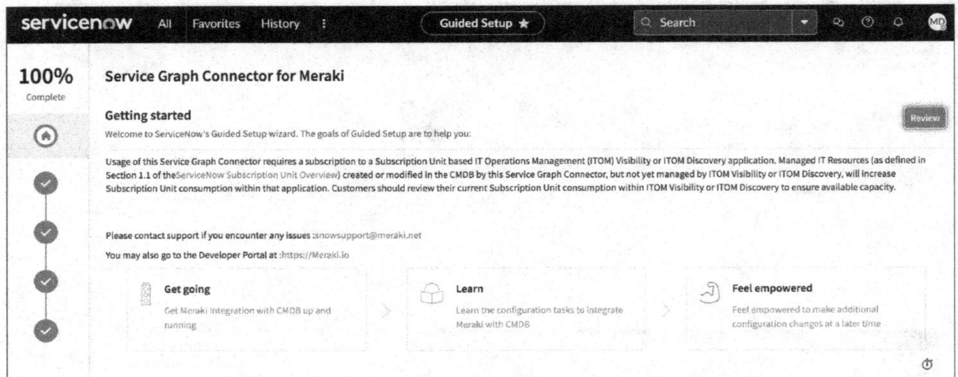

Figure 6-107 *The Service Graph Connector for Meraki Page in ServiceNow*

Step 7. The guided setup page then appears, as shown in Figure 6-108. To complete the setup, work from top to bottom, completing each step. Click **Get Started** on the **Configure the Connection** pane. Alternatively, you may also click the first task on the right of the **Configure the Connection** pane.

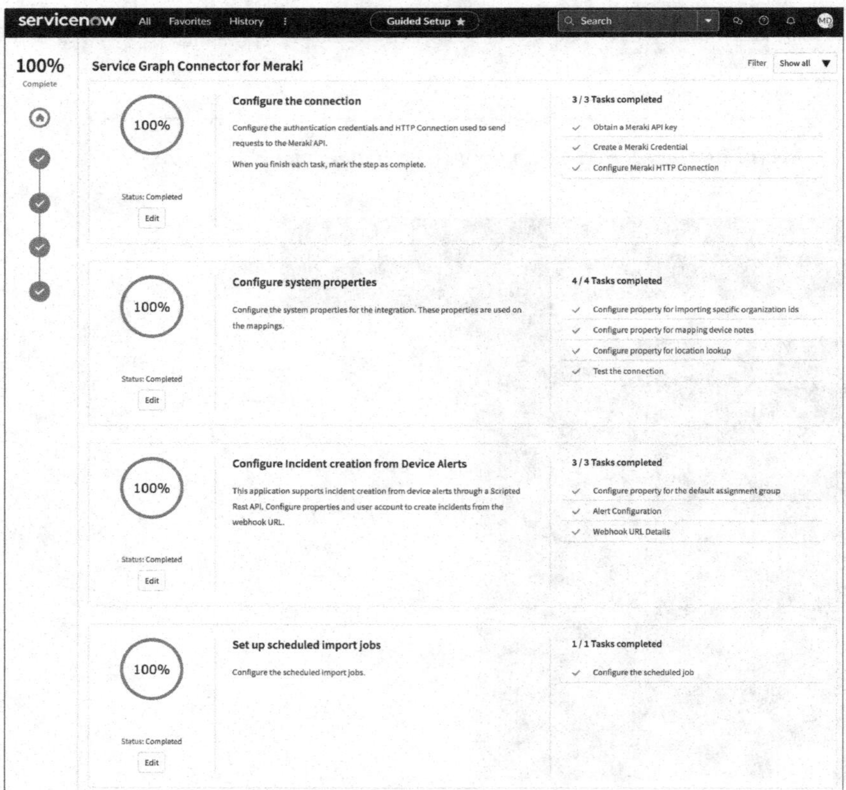

Figure 6-108 *Starting the Guided Setup for the Meraki Connector in ServiceNow*

Step 8. Next, each step is clearly explained with links to documentation to assist you. You can also find instructions at the Service Graph Connector for Meraki on Developer Hub at https://developer.cisco.com/meraki/build/servicenowgetting-started/#guided-setup-instructions. When all the tasks have been successfully completed, you will see the **100% Complete** status message in the top left, as shown in Figure 6-109.

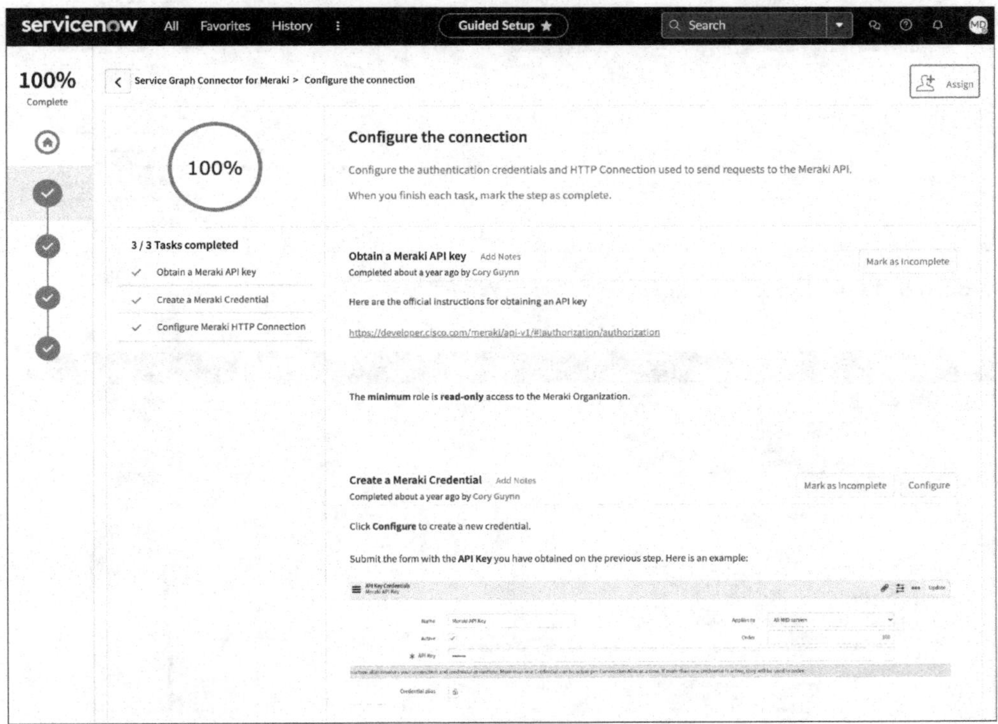

Figure 6-109 *Guided Setup Showing the Steps and How to Complete Them in ServiceNow*

With the service graph connector fully configured, ServiceNow is able to display incidents (navigate to **All > Incidents > All**), as illustrated in Figure 6-110.

By clicking an incident number, you can see all the details of the incident, including the device affected, nature of the incident, and time of incident, as shown in Figure 6-111.

This description completes this section on the integration between ServiceNow and Meraki using the Service Graph for Meraki Connector. ServiceNow is an entire topic just by itself, but we hope that this section has given you both the confidence and the information to get started. For more information on ServiceNow, contact your ServiceNow specialist.

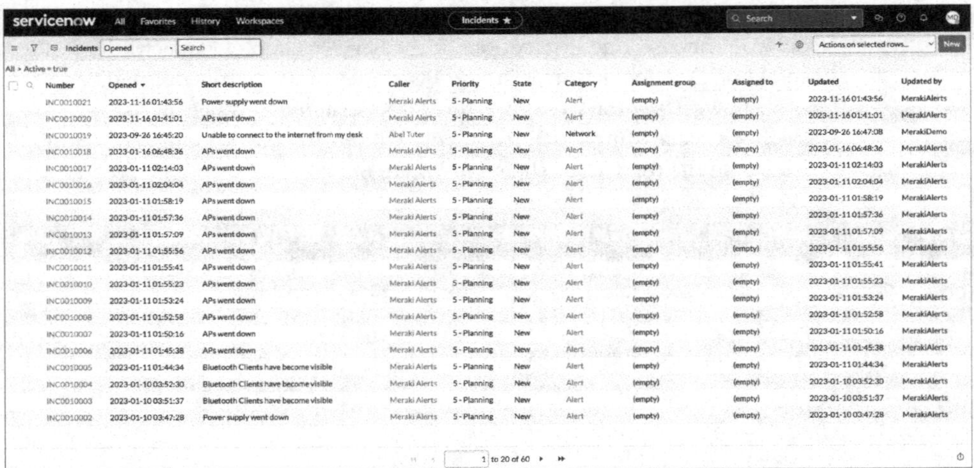

Figure 6-110 *The Incidents Page in ServiceNow*

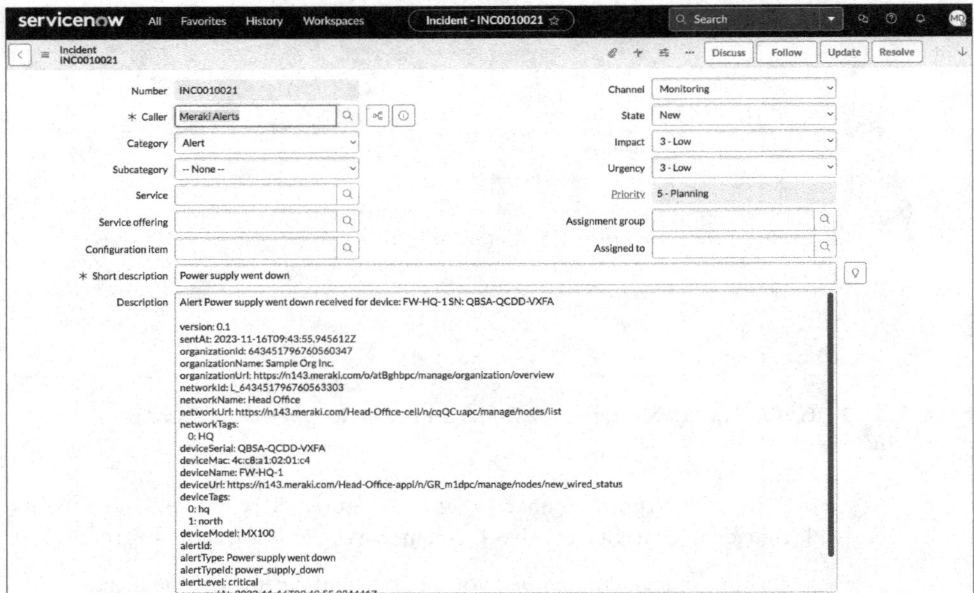

Figure 6-111 *The Incidents Page Showing the Details of a Specific Incident in ServiceNow*

Security Management

Meraki Dashboard helps operators to understand the make-up of the IT infrastructure and how clients and network devices are connected. For example, Dashboard makes it easy to understand whether devices are running up-to-date software that includes patches for known vulnerabilities. To demonstrate the benefit of this, imagine a scenario where a security advisory has come out identifying a high-risk vulnerability, potentially affecting network devices in your organization. Meraki Dashboard, through its software inventory capabilities, can identify any devices needing to be upgraded, and those upgrades can be scheduled to occur without additional operator effort. Likewise, if there is a configuration change that can mitigate this threat, an operator can quickly update a configuration template and push this out. In addition, an audit can be done to identify any devices not using a configuration template, which is used to ensure best practice and bring these devices back into compliance. These are real-world everyday tasks that are fundamental to a strong security posture. In a traditional network, without these tools, or managing box-by-box, this requires a lot of manual effort. Fortunately, Meraki Dashboard provides these capabilities, without requiring any effort to stand them up or maintain them.

Inventory

Industry best practice, including NIST CSF and PCI DSS 4.0, requires organizations to maintain an inventory of their information systems, including hardware models and associated operating system and firmware versions. This is important to ensure that

- Only authorized infrastructure is being used.
- Only approved software versions are in use.
- Devices are able to receive the latest security patches because they are still supported by the vendor.
- Configuration baselines are consistent across the entire infrastructure.

With traditional networks, it's possible to have devices in the network that no one knows are there. This can happen when companies merge or when key staff leave the organization. If there are devices in the network that you don't know about, it is highly likely that they will have out-of-date software and insecure configurations (such as weak or default admin logins and weak network access controls).

Hardware

Because all devices must appear in the inventory (**Organization > Inventory**) to connect to Meraki Dashboard, Dashboard always has an accurate picture of the organization's installed base. From the inventory page (see Figure 6-112), an administrator can see

- **Devices:** Total count by product family and device type; which country devices are deployed in; their MAC address, IP address, tags, serial number, and order number
- **Licenses:** All licensing, including what's in use and expiration dates
- **Networks:** All the networks configured (including their names and total number) and number of devices and licenses per network

Figure 6-112 *Devices Inventory Page in Dashboard*

The inventory can be exported in CSV format by clicking the **Export** button or via the Dashboard API.

If you have a keen eye, you will notice the Cisco Catalyst switch in Figure 6-112. Select Cisco Catalyst models can also be added to Meraki Dashboard, in either Monitoring or Managed modes. For more on cloud monitoring for Catalyst devices, refer to https://documentation.meraki.com/Cloud_Monitoring_for_Catalyst/Onboarding/Cloud_Monitoring_for_Catalyst_Eligibility_and_Requirements_for_Onboarding.

For information on how to add Catalyst 9300 switches into Dashboard in Meraki managed mode, please visit https://documentation.meraki.com/MS/Deployment_Guides/Getting_started%3A_Cisco_Catalyst_9300_with_Meraki_Dashboard.

Meraki publishes a list of platforms that have been announced end of sale/end of life on its website: https://documentation.meraki.com/General_Administration/Other_Topics/Meraki_End-of-Life_(EOL)_Products_and_Dates. All organizations must plan to migrate off end-of-life platforms before they reach their end-of-support date. When devices reach end of support, no more patches for security vulnerabilities will be released, but the device will typically still function. Choosing to run end-of-life hardware platforms will likely result in an audit finding.

Software

The best place to see an inventory of all the software versions that your Meraki devices are running is on the **Schedule Upgrades** page (**Organization > Firmware Upgrades > Schedule Upgrades**), as shown in Figure 6-113. On this page you can

- Sort by firmware type to ensure that you are not running any beta firmware.

- Sort by status to ensure that all devices are running the latest firmware (status is Good). The status can also be
  - **Critical**, meaning that the firmware version is out of date and may have security vulnerabilities and/or lack key performance improvements.
  - **Warning**, meaning that there is a newer stable major firmware or newer minor beta firmware available that may contain security fixes, new features, and performance improvements.
- Check the availability of any minor releases (shown in the **Availability** column).
- Take any remedial action, such as scheduling software upgrades.

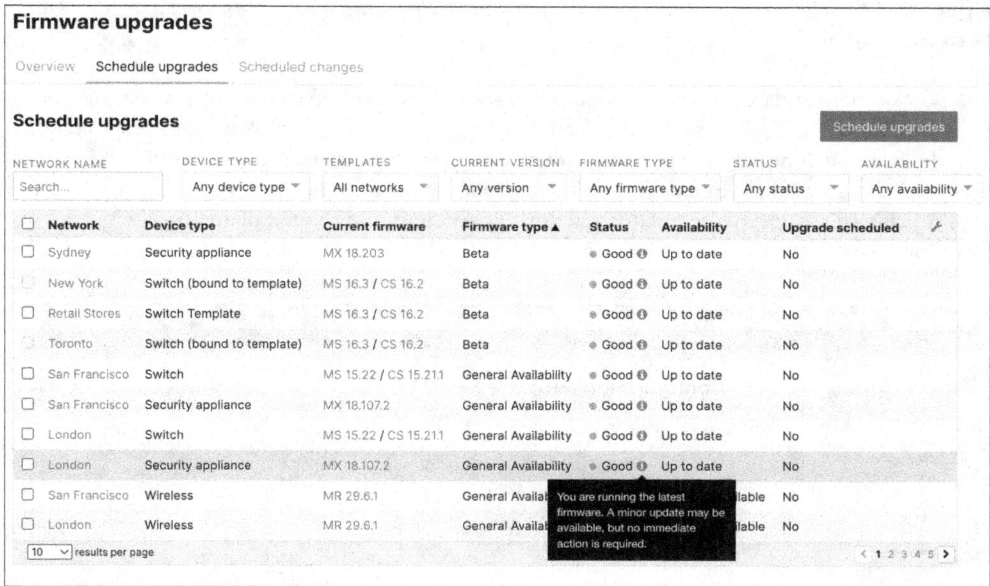

Figure 6-113 *Software Inventory Shown on the Firmware Upgrade Page*

Configuration

The best way to maintain an inventory of your configurations is to use configuration templates (**Organization > Configuration Templates**), as shown in Figure 6-114. A configuration template (or simply template for short) contains all of the settings for a network. These templates enable you to have a standard configuration for a site type such as a teleworker or retail store. With a bit of thought, a handful of templates can manage the configurations for thousands of locations.

> **Tip** Apply version control to your configuration templates by adopting a simple naming convention.

Configuration templates

Create a new template | Delete | Combine | Split

	#	Name	# of bound networks	Network type
☐	1	Data center - version 1.1	0	Combined
☐	2	Retail store - version 2.2	0	Combined
☐	3	Teleworker - version 3.0	0	Combined

3 total

Figure 6-114 *The Configuration Templates Page Showing Templates for Three Different Location Types*

To see the templates in your organization, click the down arrow next to the current network name (on the left side in Dashboard). Here, you see the templates grouped under the heading **Templates.** You open a template in Dashboard just like you would change between networks—by clicking its name from the network list (shown in Figure 6-115). When you switch to a template, you are able to configure the template just like you would a network.

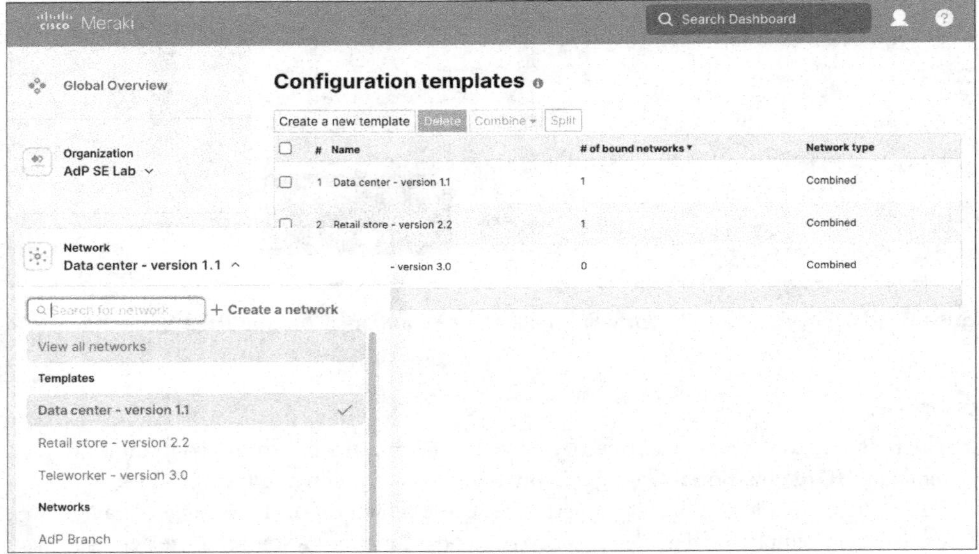

Figure 6-115 *Choosing a Template to Configure via the Network Drop-Down Menu*

Configuration templates are applied to one or more networks by binding those networks to the template. To bind a template to a network, navigate to the **Configuration Templates** page (**Organization > Configuration Templates**) and click the template name. If this template has not been bound to any networks yet, you will see a pop-up window asking you to bind the template to a network. If this template has networks bound to it already, you can add more by clicking the **Bind Additional Networks** button, as shown in Figure 6-116.

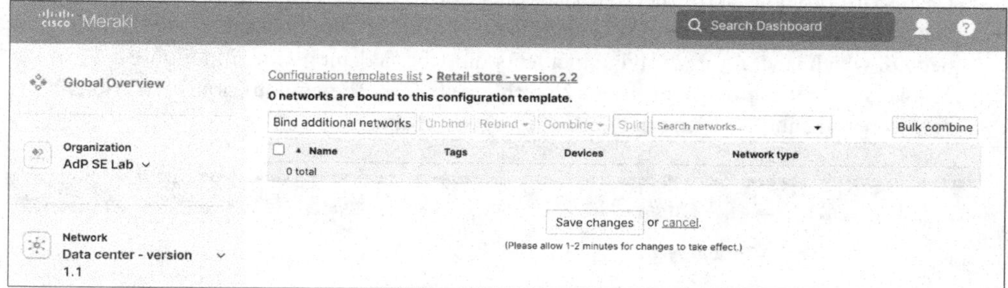

Figure 6-116 *A Configuration Template with the Options to Bind Additional Networks*

For more information on managing networks with configuration templates, visit https://documentation.meraki.com/General_Administration/Templates_and_Config_Sync/Managing_Multiple_Networks_with_Configuration_Templates.

Client Devices

While we're on the topic of inventory, it's also worthwhile to note that Meraki Dashboard can also keep a detailed inventory of all managed client devices. This includes all phones, tablets, PCs, and Apple TVs managed by Systems Manager, Meraki's mobile device management (MDM) product. To see the device inventory, navigate to **Systems Manager > Devices** in Meraki Dashboard, as shown in Figure 6-117.

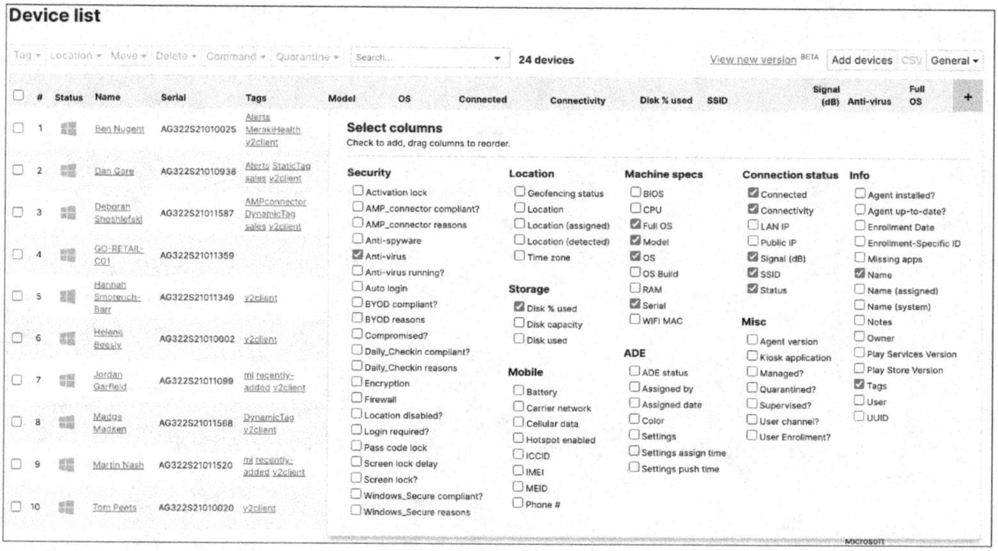

Figure 6-117 *The Options Available to Display on the Systems Manager Devices List*

Topology

Industry standards require organizations to understand how their networks are connected and the data flows running across them. To assist in meeting this requirement, Meraki Dashboard provides autogenerated, network-wide topology diagrams. These topology views (**Network-wide > Topology**) enable staff to quickly see how the network is connected, which is vital for resolving incidents quickly, as demonstrated in Figure 6-118. Meraki's built-in topology diagrams also free staff from the copious hours traditionally spent creating and updating network diagrams by hand.

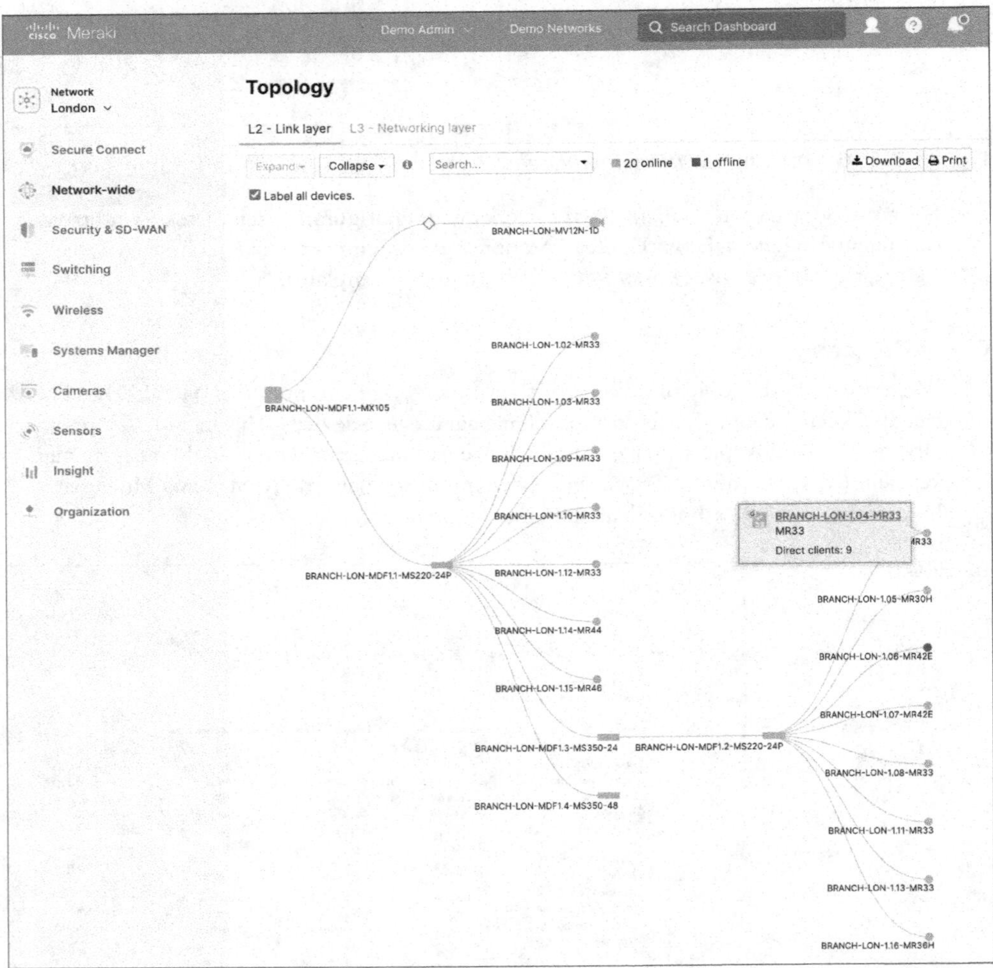

Figure 6-118 *Viewing the Layer 2 Topology of a Network in Dashboard*

The topology page displays

- All the Meraki devices at a site, their hostnames, and their health, which is depicted using a traffic light system (red = down, orange = error, green = OK)
- A Layer 2 network diagram showing the ports used to connect devices and how many clients are connected to switches and APs
- A Layer 3 network diagram including the subnets used, non-Meraki next hops, and VPN tunnels

On this page, an admin can

- Expand or collapse branches of the diagram based on level or device type
- Search for devices
- Filter devices using the drop-down menu to the right of the search box

For more details on the network topology page in Meraki Dashboard, refer to https://documentation.meraki.com/MS/Monitoring_and_Reporting/Network_Topology.

Summary

Meraki has extensive logging, monitoring, and incident response capabilities, both out of the box and via integrations with popular third-party platforms. Out of the box, Meraki provides visibility of alerts, changes to or on the network, login attempts, security events, and application performance. At the same time, Meraki also provides quick and easy integration with a vast range of platforms providing advanced visibility, threat detection, compliance reporting, and incident response capabilities (to name a few). In addition, Meraki Dashboard supports both modern and traditional ways to export logs, flows, and alerts. Furthermore, Meraki Dashboard can also be polled via both the Dashboard API and SNMP. Lastly, to speed up incident resolution and ease compliance, Meraki Dashboard maintains an inventory of software, hardware, end devices, and configurations, as well as a self-generated, interactive network topology. As demonstrated, Meraki truly leverages the power of its platform to provide a best-in-class security operations capability.

Notes

[1] Lockheed Martin. (2024). Cyber Kill Chain. https://www.lockheedmartin.com/en-us/capabilities/cyber/cyber-kill-chain.html

[2] National Institute of Standards and Technology. (2006, March). *FIPS PUB 200, Minimum Security Requirements for Federal Information and Information Systems*. https://nvlpubs.nist.gov/nistpubs/FIPS/NIST.FIPS.200.pdf

Further Reading

AlgoSec. (2024). Network Security FAQs: Answered by AlgoSec Experts. https://www.algosec.com/resources/network-security-faqs/#what-is-algosec

Cisco Meraki. (2021, October 25). MS NetFlow and Encrypted Traffic Analytics. https://documentation.meraki.com/MS/Monitoring_and_Reporting/MS_NetFlow_and_Encrypted_Traffic_Analytics

Cisco Meraki. (2023, September 27). Meraki Device Reporting – Syslog, SNMP, and API. https://documentation.meraki.com/General_Administration/Monitoring_and_Reporting/Meraki_Device_Reporting_-_Syslog%2C_SNMP%2C_and_API

Cisco Meraki. (2023, October 19). Syslog Server Overview and Configuration. https://documentation.meraki.com/General_Administration/Monitoring_and_Reporting/Syslog_Server_Overview_and_Configuration

Cisco Meraki. (2023, October 23). Security Center. https://documentation.meraki.com/MX/Monitoring_and_Reporting/Security_Center

Cisco Meraki. (2023, November 8). SNMP Overview and Configuration. https://documentation.meraki.com/General_Administration/Monitoring_and_Reporting/SNMP_Overview_and_Configuration

Cisco Meraki. (2023, November 14). NetFlow Overview. https://documentation.meraki.com/MX/Monitoring_and_Reporting/NetFlow_Overview

Cisco Meraki. (2023, December 20). Cisco Meraki Dashboard API. https://documentation.meraki.com/General_Administration/Other_Topics/Cisco_Meraki_Dashboard_API#Enable_API_access

Cisco Meraki. (2024a). Meraki Dashboard API Python Library. Developer Hub. https://developer.cisco.com/meraki/api/python/#meraki-dashboard-api-python-library

Cisco Meraki. (2024b). Webhooks. Developer Hub. https://developer.cisco.com/meraki/webhooks/introduction/#overview

Cisco Meraki. (2024, January 12). Alerts and Notifications. https://documentation.meraki.com/General_Administration/Cross-Platform_Content/Alerts_and_Notifications

Cisco Meraki. (2024, February 2). Alerts. https://documentation.meraki.com/General_Administration/Cross-Platform_Content/Global_Alerts_Widget

Cisco Meraki. (2024, March 9). Meraki Data Privacy and Protection Features. https://documentation.meraki.com/General_Administration/Privacy_and_Security/Meraki_Data_Privacy_and_Protection_Features

Cisco Meraki. (2024, April 16). MS NetFlow and Encrypted Traffic Analytics. https://documentation.meraki.com/MS/Monitoring_and_Reporting/MS_NetFlow_and_Encrypted_Traffic_Analytics

National Institute of Standards and Technology (NIST). (2020, September). *NIST 800-53 Rev. 5: Security and Privacy Controls for Information Systems and Organizations.* https://nvlpubs.nist.gov/nistpubs/SpecialPublications/NIST.SP.800-53r5.pdf

PagerDuty. (2023, September 8). "PagerDuty 101 Series, Part 1: Introduction to the Power of PagerDuty" YouTube Video. https://www.youtube.com/watch?v=DKLZPo6RUr4

Splunk. (2024a). Splunk Add-on for Cisco Meraki. https://docs.splunk.com/Documentation/AddOns/released/Meraki/AboutAddon

Splunk. (2024b). Source types for the Splunk Add-on for Cisco Meraki. https://docs.splunk.com/Documentation/AddOns/released/Meraki/Sourcetypes

Wikipedia. (2024, February). Syslog. https://en.wikipedia.org/wiki/Syslog

Chapter 7

User Authentication

In this chapter, you learn the following:

- The supported methods of authenticating network and VPN access in a Meraki network and how to determine the best authentication method for your use case
- How to configure Meraki Cloud authentication, SAML, RADIUS, and Active Directory to authenticate user access
- How to integrate Cisco Duo to enable multifactor authentication (MFA) for users accessing the network

Chapter 2, "Security Frameworks and Industry Best Practices," identified Zero Trust and strong authentication (including MFA) as key themes prevalent across industry security standards. This extends not just to the administration of IT infrastructure, as was addressed in Chapter 5, "Securing Administrator Access to Meraki Dashboard," but also to the users accessing the network. An example of this is NIST 800-53 IA-2, which requires that organizations have the capability to uniquely identify and authenticate users prior to accessing the network.

This chapter focuses on various solutions for authenticating user access to the network, whether wired, wireless, or VPN, in support of Zero Trust. With a suitable authentication solution in place, employees and guests can be challenged prior to accessing the network. Depending on your requirements, users can be authenticated by Meraki Cloud authentication or via an integration with an identity and access management (IAM) solution. MFA goes hand in hand with strong authentication and should also be included in your authentication solution design. The remainder of this chapter covers how to configure Meraki Dashboard to authenticate users and how to leverage third-party identity and MFA solutions to provide even stronger controls.

Meraki supports the most commonly used industry authentication protocols including RADIUS, SAML, and Active Directory. Because both RADIUS and SAML are standards-based, this means Meraki Dashboard can integrate with pretty much anything on the market. This application support is extended again by the integration capabilities of IAM solutions such as Cisco Duo and Cisco ISE. In addition, Meraki Dashboard has its own built-in authentication, however this is really suitable only for small networks.

Table 7-1 provides a comparison of the authentication solutions that we show you how to configure in this chapter.

Table 7-1 *Comparison of the Authentication Solutions as Implemented in This Chapter*

	Meraki Cloud Authentication	**SAML Using Cisco Duo and Microsoft Entra**	**RADIUS Using Cisco ISE, Duo, and Microsoft Active Directory**	**Microsoft Active Directory**
Solution				
Identity Provider (IdP)	—	Cisco Duo	—	—
Identity and Access Management (IAM)	—	—	Cisco Identity Services Engine (ISE)	—
MFA	—	Cisco Duo	Cisco Duo	—
Identity Management (Users and groups reside here)	Meraki Dashboard	Microsoft Entra	Microsoft Active Directory	Microsoft Active Directory
Type of MFA	N/A	Enterprise MFA with group policies	Enterprise MFA with group policies	N/A
Suitable for	Wi-Fi guest users or small networks where the administrators are also the users, such as a home network, small business, or lab.	Networks and enterprises of all sizes, especially if they're already using Microsoft Entra.	Networks and enterprises of all sizes that want to use Active Directory and need strong controls, including MFA.	Networks and enterprises of all sizes with existing Active Directory and strong Microsoft skills.

	Meraki Cloud Authentication	**SAML Using Cisco Duo and Microsoft Entra**	**RADIUS Using Cisco ISE, Duo, and Microsoft Active Directory**	**Microsoft Active Directory**
Benefits	Fast, simple, no additional charge.	Same authentication solution can be leveraged for users and administrators. Full-featured MFA with inline enrollment, one solution for IDP and MFA, advanced password and security controls.	Same solution for on-premises, cloud, or hybrid deployments. Leverages existing Active Directory while supporting many other identity solutions, including Entra. Greatest capabilities in terms of password and security controls.	Less infrastructure to deploy if you have Active Directory on site already.
Points to Consider	Not recommended for enterprise use. Labor intensive if users are connecting via VPN, wired, and wireless.	No support for wired and wireless access methods today (only AnyConnect VPN supported).	Does not support Duo inline enrollment.	Direct Active Directory user authentication is supported on Meraki MX only, not MS (wired) or MR (wireless) access policies. Lacks the excellent troubleshooting tools available with Cisco ISE. More Microsoft configuration required, such as certificates, which can be tricky for inexperienced users. Consider SAML or RADIUS if MFA is a requirement.
Number of Steps to Configure	Low	Low (~20 additional, when Dashboard SAML SSO already in place)	Medium (~60)	Low
Level of Difficulty	Easy	Easy	Medium	Medium, but hard if you need to troubleshoot

You might be asking why has Cisco Duo been categorized as an identity provider (IdP) in the SAML use case? Isn't it just an MFA solution? No, Cisco Duo, through its Duo Single Sign-On feature, is also a cloud-hosted SAML 2.0 identity provider. To support inline enrollment, we leverage this capability throughout the chapter, configuring Meraki MX in Meraki Dashboard to point to Duo for SAML authentication.

This chapter also introduces Cisco Identity Services Engine (ISE), which is a feature-rich and mature identity and access management solution. *Identity and access management* is a widely used industry term to describe solutions that provide authentication and authorization—in this case, for user access. Although the users themselves can be configured locally, this would be rare in an enterprise use case. This directory function, where user accounts are configured, has therefore been separated out and is referred to here as identity management. Cisco ISE, used as the IAM in the RADIUS example, is therefore utilized as a policy engine to implement MFA, assign SGTs and ACLs, and operate as a certificate authority. Cisco ISE is required in order to meet the most technically challenging requirements, such as restricting access based on time of day or limiting concurrent logins.

Our intention with this book is to show you how to configure all cloud or all on-premises identity solutions. The combination of Cisco ISE, Cisco Duo, and your desired identity management solution provides either an all-cloud or a hybrid solution. If you require an authentication solution that meets the highest industry security standards and supports both SAML and RADIUS authentication, we highly recommend you deploy Cisco ISE and Cisco Duo together. For a comparison of the password and security policy capabilities, refer to Chapter 5.

Configuring Meraki Cloud Authentication

Meraki Cloud authentication is a simple solution included with Meraki Dashboard. It is suitable for small networks where the administrators are also the users, such as a home network, small business, or lab. For enterprises, it is highly recommended to integrate with an external identity provider for the following reasons:

- Meraki Cloud users are configured per access method (wired/wireless/VPN). If you have more than a few users and you need to authenticate access via more than one access method (such as when using dot1x for wired and wireless), this requires a lot of manual effort to administer.
- Unlike Dashboard administrators, which are configured at the organization or network level, Meraki Cloud users can be configured only at the network level. If you have more than a couple of networks, again, administering users will require a lot of manual effort.
- Passwords are generated by admins (not hidden) and by default are sent via email, which is not best practice.
- It is not possible for 802.1X users to reset their own passwords.

Follow these steps to configure Meraki Cloud authentication:

Step 1. Log in to Meraki Dashboard (https://dashboard.meraki.com).

Step 2. To be able to configure users, you must first enable Meraki Cloud authentication for each access method (wired/wireless/VPN). Follow these steps for each of the access methods where users will be authenticating using Meraki Cloud:

- **VPN:** Navigate to **Security & SD-WAN > Client VPN**. On the Client VPN page, set **Client VPN Server** to **Enabled**, as shown in Figure 7-1, and **Authentication Type** to **Meraki Cloud Authentication.** Then click **Save Changes.**

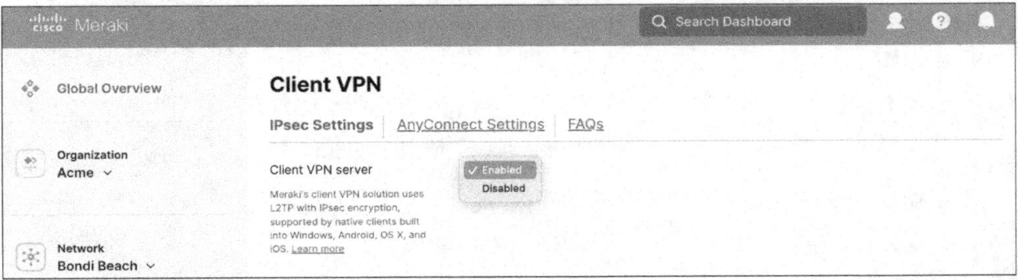

Figure 7-1 *Enabling the Client VPN Server in Meraki Dashboard*

- **Wired:** Navigate to **Switching > Access Policies** (under Configure). Meraki authentication is already selected by default (see Figure 7-2). Click **Add an Access Policy** and then click **Save Changes.**

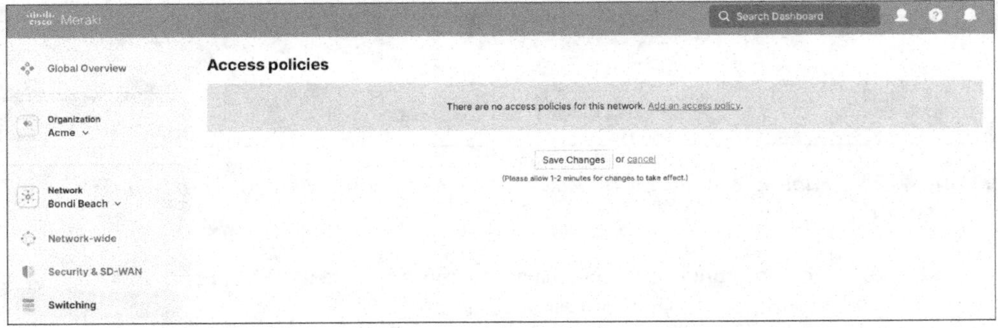

Figure 7-2 *Adding a Wired Access Policy in Meraki Dashboard*

- **Wireless:** Navigate to **Wireless > Access Control** (under Configure). Select an SSID. Under **Security**, select **Enterprise With** and ensure **Meraki Cloud Authentication** is selected from the drop-down menu, as shown in Figure 7-3. Click **Save** in the bottom-right corner.

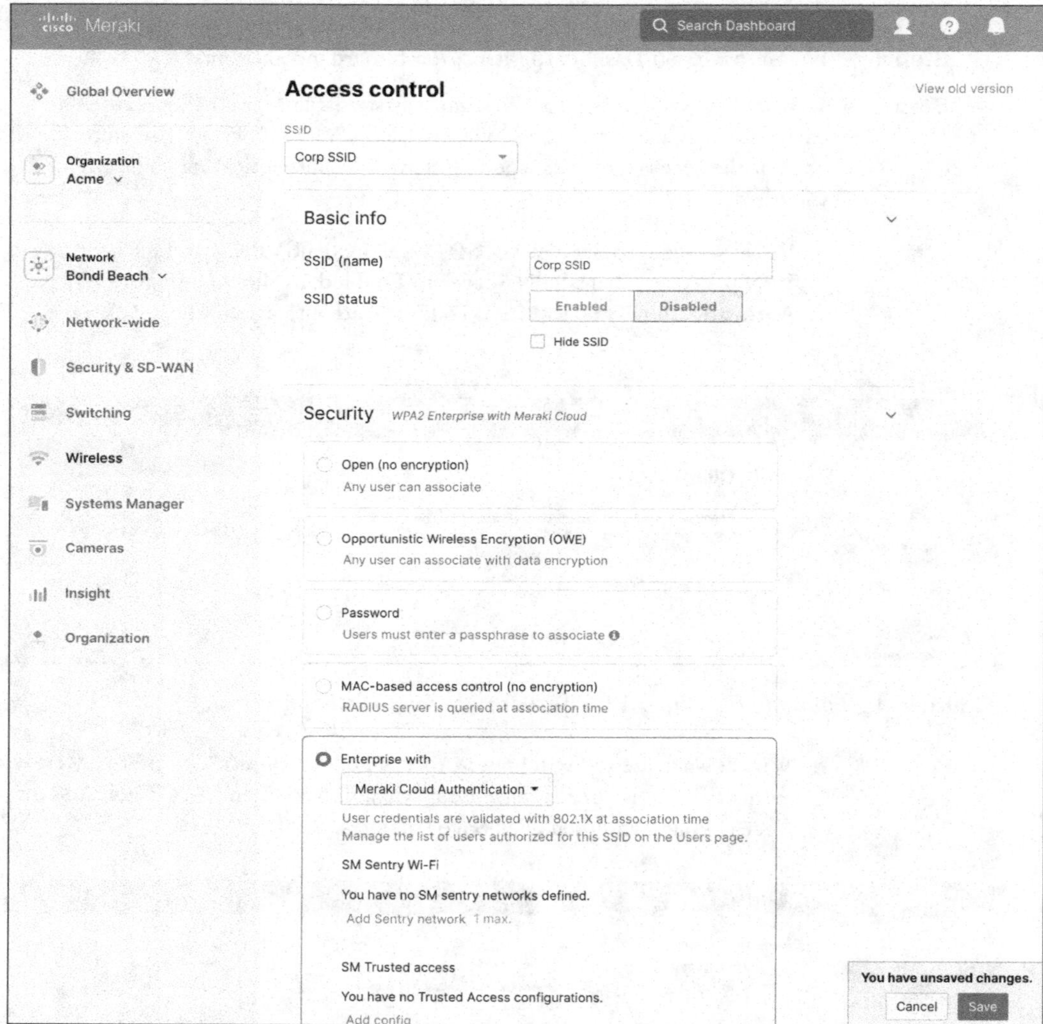

Figure 7-3 *Enabling Meraki Cloud Authentication on a Wireless SSID in Meraki Dashboard*

Step 3. To configure user access, navigate to **Network-wide > Users** (under Configure), as shown in Figure 7-4.

Step 4. On the **User Management Portal** page (see Figure 7-5), choose the access method from the **Zone** drop-down menu. Click **Add New User.**

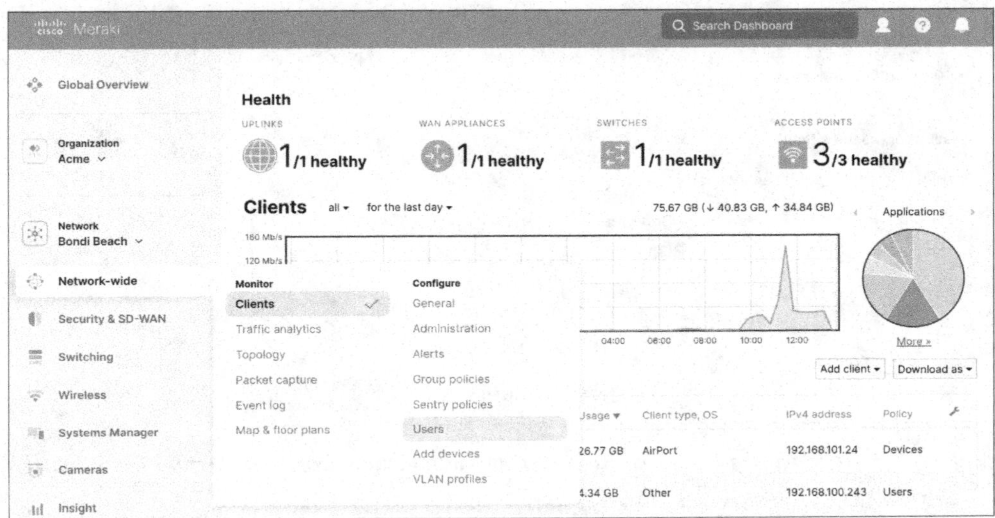

Figure 7-4 *Navigating to the Network-Wide Users Page in Meraki Dashboard*

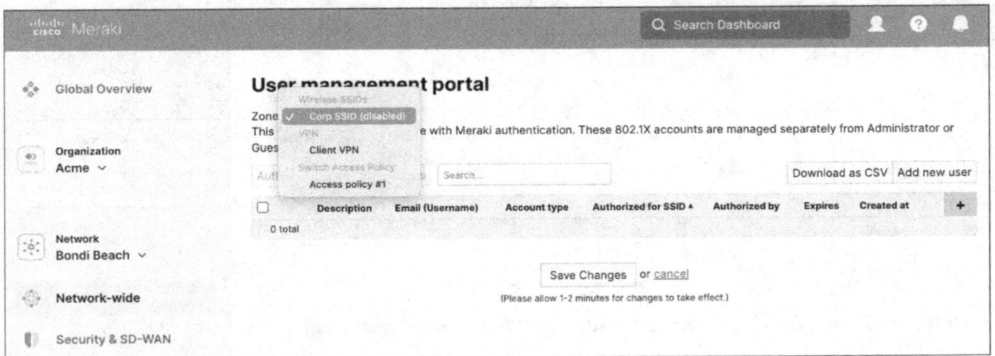

Figure 7-5 *Selecting the Zone on the User Management Portal*

Step 5. On the **Create User** pop-up window, as shown in Figure 7-6, do the following:

- Enter the user's first and last name in the **Description** field.
- Enter their email address in the **Email (Username)** field.
- Either enter a password or click **Generate** to generate a random password.
- Select **Yes** from the **Authorized** drop-down menu.
- Optional: Set an expiry.
- Click **Create User.**

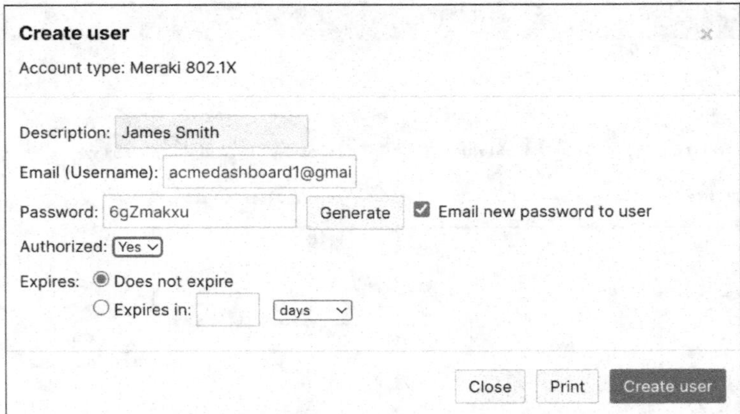

Figure 7-6 *Creating a New User in the User Management Portal in Meraki Dashboard*

Step 6. Back on the User management portal (see Figure 7-7), click **Save Changes.**

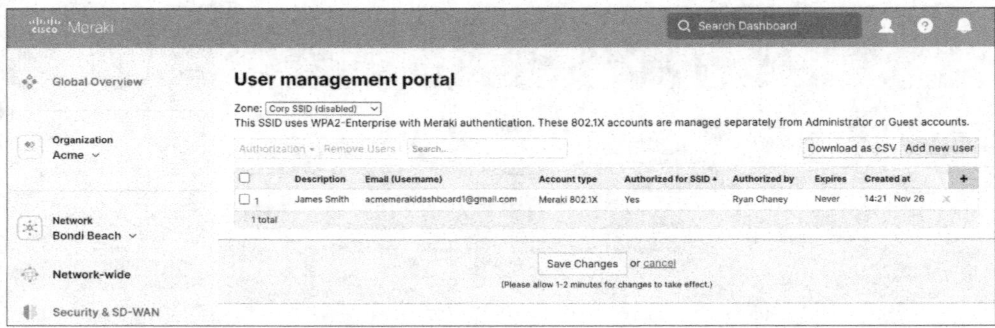

Figure 7-7 *A New User on the User Management Portal Page in Meraki Dashboard*

This user is now configured and ready to access the network. To configure the network so that this user can connect via wired or wireless, refer to Chapter 8, “Wired and Wireless LAN Security.” For configuring VPN access, refer to Chapter 9, “Meraki MX and WAN Security.”

Configuring SAML with Cisco Duo and Microsoft Entra

For organizations of all sizes, it is recommended to have a centralized identity management system for managing users and groups. Regardless of the number of users, this approach eases the burden of controlling access to the numerous applications your enterprise will be using.

In Chapter 5, we configured SAML SSO between Meraki Dashboard and Cisco Duo. One of the key reasons you would use SAML for authenticating user network access is that you are already using it for administrator access to Dashboard. Following are some benefits of using SAML with Cisco Duo for user access:

- It provides multifactor authentication and identity and access management via the same platform.
- SAML supports Duo inline enrollment, a key usability feature.
- If users have had temporary passwords assigned in Microsoft Entra, they are able to reset their passwords when logging in.

In this example, we explain the additional steps required to support the authentication of user access using SAML. Here, we'll configure AnyConnect VPN in Meraki Dashboard to authenticate users using Cisco Duo and SAML. Microsoft Entra is used for identity management. If you haven't completed the steps in the Chapter 5 section titled "Configuring Meraki SAML SSO Using Cisco Duo and Microsoft Entra ID," complete those steps now. When configuring the users and groups in Microsoft Entra, create an additional group called **Network Access** and add at least one user to this group.

> **Note** Currently, native SAML-based user authentication is supported only with AnyConnect VPN. SAML is not supported with Meraki's IPsec client VPN or 802.1X (wired or wireless).

Follow these steps to configure SAML-based authentication for AnyConnect VPN:

Step 1. Log in to Meraki Dashboard (https://dashboard.meraki.com).

Step 2. Navigate to **Security & SD-WAN > Client VPN > AnyConnect Settings.**

Under **Client Connection Details**, copy the Hostname URL.

Ensure the **AnyConnect Port** is 443.

Under **Authentication and Access**, click the **Authentication Type** drop-down menu and select **SAML**, as shown in Figure 7-8.

Step 3. Next to **SAML Configuration**, in the text field under **AnyConnect Server URL**, type **https://** and then paste in the hostname URL, as shown in Figure 7-9.

Copy the **AnyConnect Server URL** to the clipboard or a text editor. You need it for Duo in the following steps.

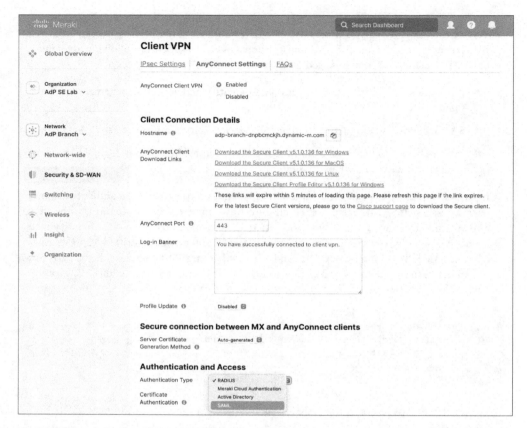

Figure 7-8 *Selecting SAML as the Authentication Type for AnyConnect VPN in Meraki Dashboard*

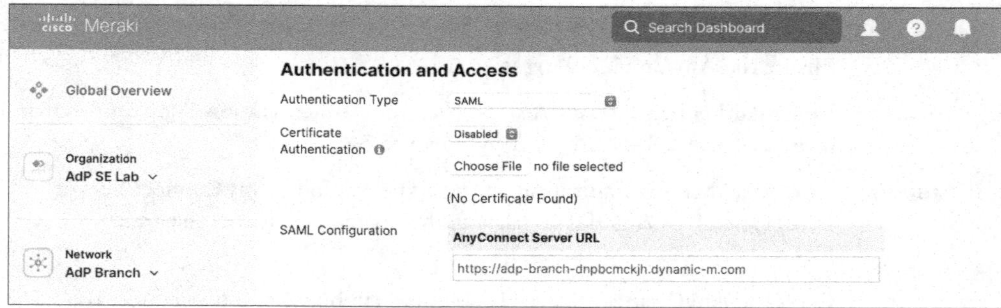

Figure 7-9 *Adding the AnyConnect Server URL into the AnyConnect VPN Settings in Meraki Dashboard*

Step 4. In another tab in your web browser, log in to the Cisco Duo Admin Panel (https://admin.duosecurity.com/login).

Step 5. You need to ensure that Duo is syncing the Network Access group. Navigate to **Users > Directory Sync** and click the directory sync for Microsoft Entra.

Find **Groups** and add the **Network Access** group if it is not listed. Click **Save** and then **Sync Now** (see Figure 7-10). You can choose to have separate groups for VPN and on-premises access for more granular control. If doing this, add any extra groups here.

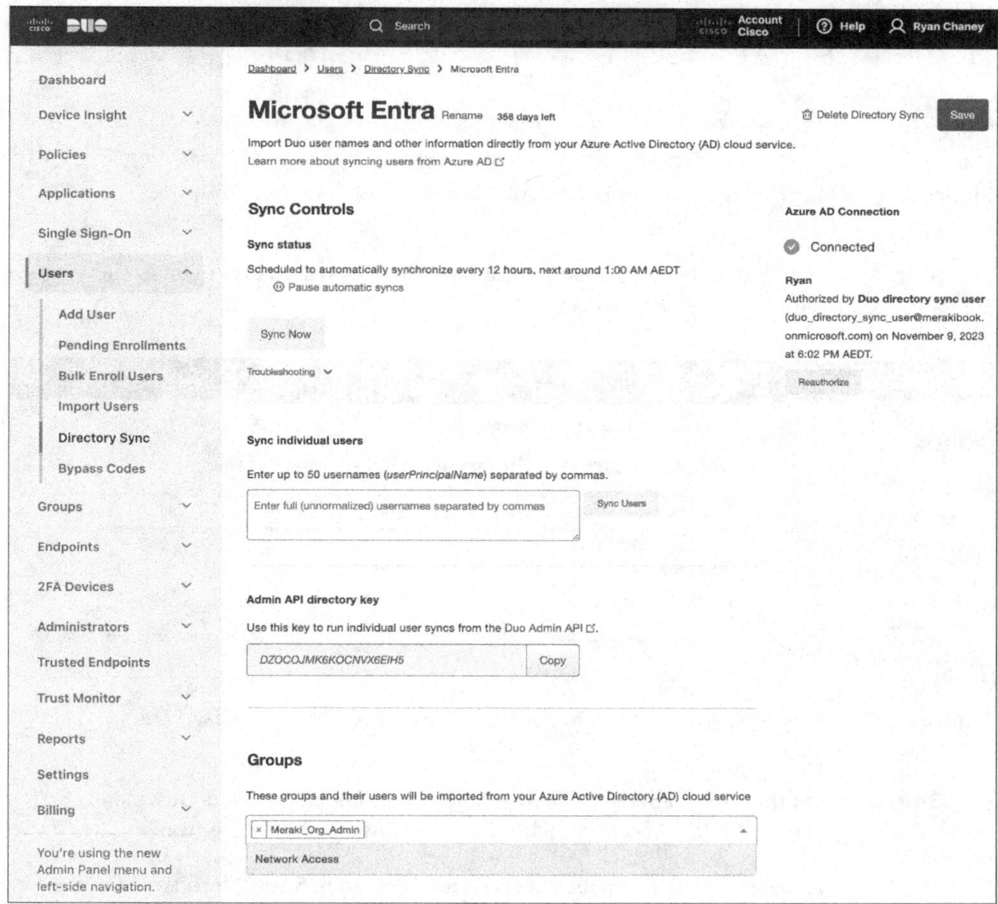

Figure 7-10 *Adding a New Group to the Directory Sync Page for Microsoft Entra*

Step 6. Select **Applications** from the menu on the left. Then, click **Protect an Application,** as shown in Figure 7-11.

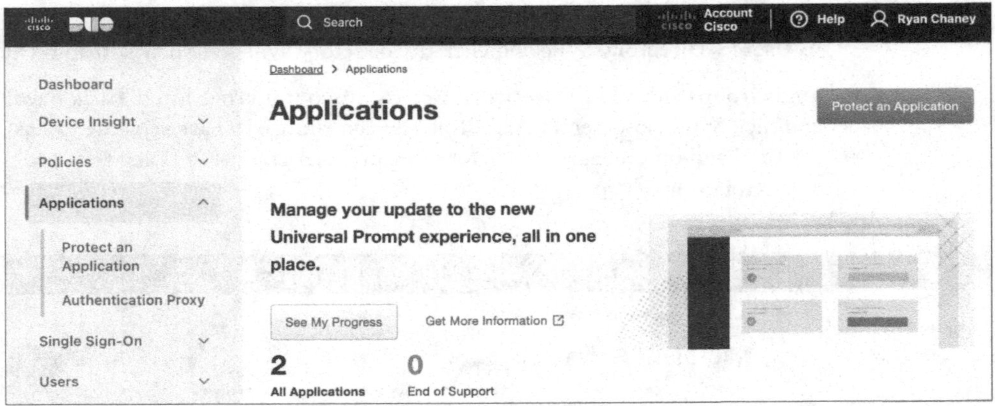

Figure 7-11 *Adding an Application for AnyConnect VPN in Cisco Duo*

Step 7. Search for "meraki secure" in the **Filter by Keywords** text field, as shown in Figure 7-12. Click **Protect.**

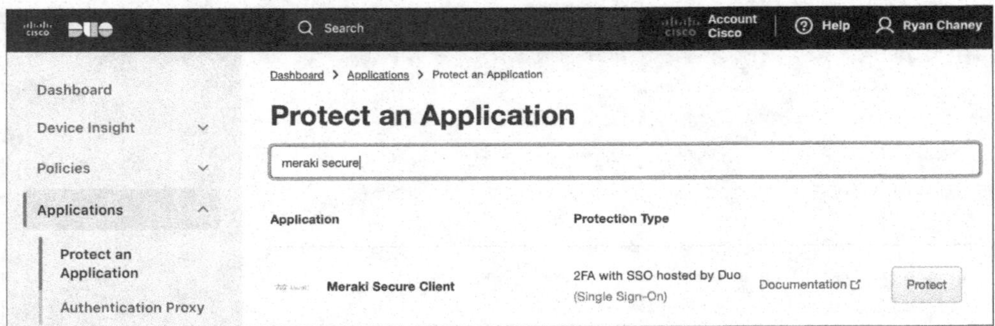

Figure 7-12 *Searching for the Meraki Secure Client Application in Cisco Duo*

Step 8. On the **Meraki Secure Client – Single Sign-On** page, under **Downloads** and next to **SAML Metadata File**, click the **Download XML** button.

a. Paste the **AnyConnect Server URL** (copied in Step 3) into the **AnyConnect Server URL** * field, as shown in Figure 7-13.

b. Scroll down to **Settings**, next to **Permitted Groups**, check the box for **Only Allow Authentication from Users in Certain Groups**, and select the Network Access group.

c. Scroll to the bottom of the page and click **Save.**

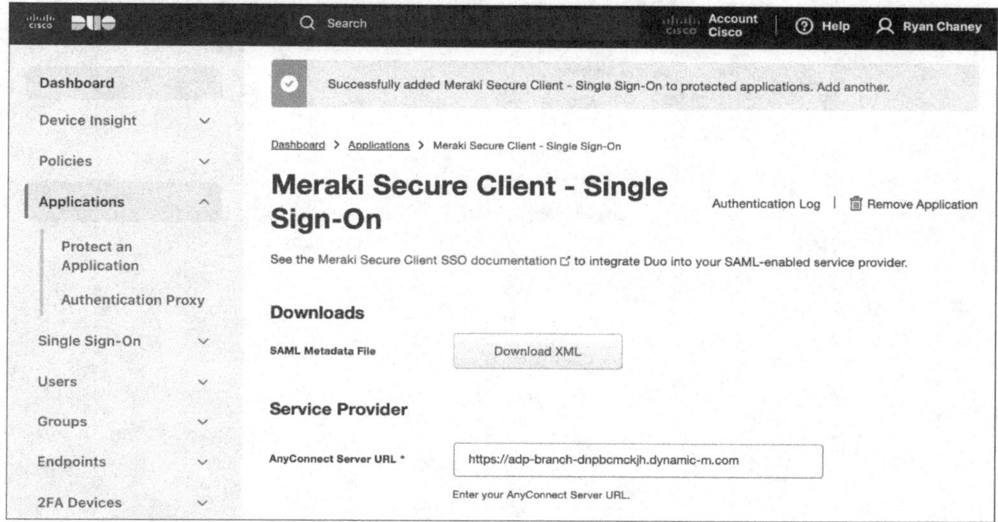

Figure 7-13 *Successful Addition of the Meraki Secure Client Application in Cisco Duo*

Step 9. Switch back to the tab in your web browser that is open to the **AnyConnect Settings** page in Meraki Dashboard (see Figure 7-14).

a. Under **Authentication and Access**, click **Choose File** and upload the SAML metadata XML file downloaded in the preceding step.

b. In the **AnyConnect VPN Subnet** field, enter a subnet to be assigned to VPN users when they connect. This can be any spare subnet in one of your existing IP address ranges.

c. We have specified a custom nameserver. If you have one in your network, you can specify that. Otherwise, use the default **Use Google Public DNS.**

d. Click **Save Changes.**

Step 10. Because this example uses Microsoft Entra for identity management, you need to make one more change for it to work. Log in to the Microsoft Entra admin center (https://entra.microsoft.com).

Step 11. Navigate to **Applications > Enterprise Applications.** Click the name, **Duo SSO**, as shown in Figure 7-15.

Step 12. On the **Duo SSO** enterprise application page, click **Users and Groups.** Then click **+ Add User/Group**, as shown in Figure 7-16.

Step 13. On the **Add Assignment** page, under **Users and Groups**, click **None Selected**, as shown in Figure 7-17.

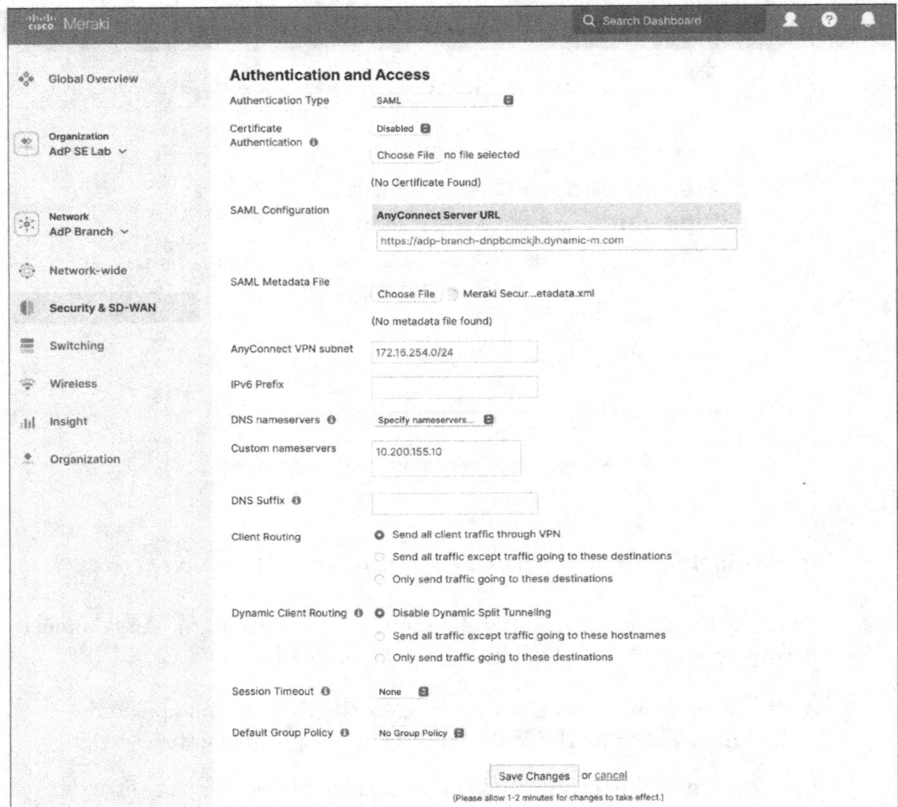

Figure 7-14 *Completing the SAML Authentication Configuration on the AnyConnect Settings Page*

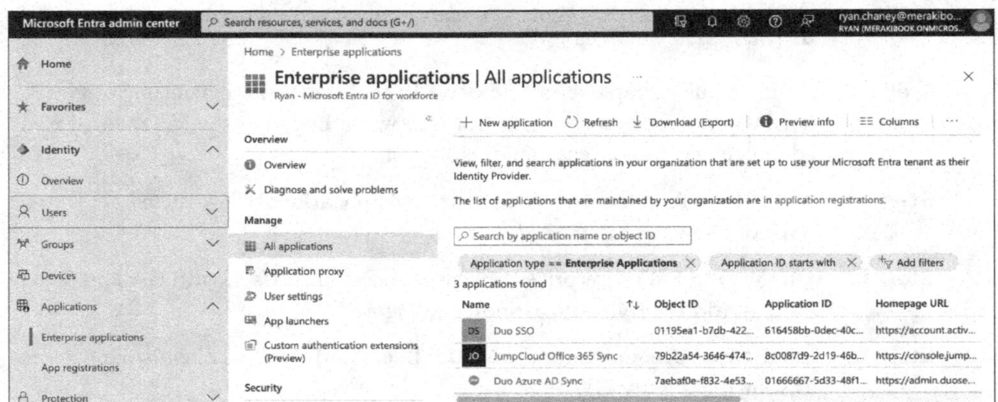

Figure 7-15 *Locating the Duo SSO Application in the Microsoft Entra Admin Center*

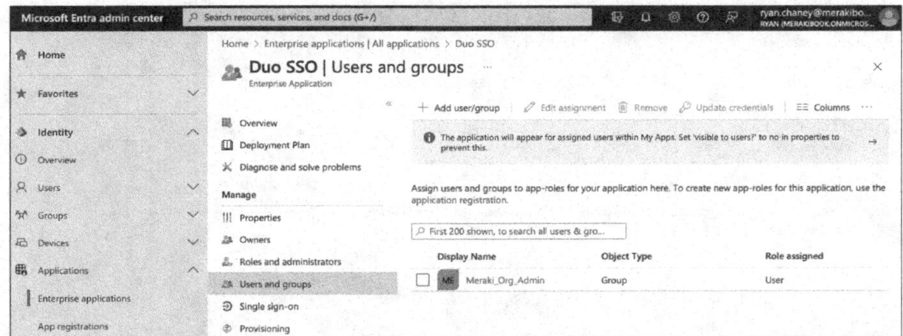

Figure 7-16 *Adding a Group to the Duo SSO Application in the Microsoft Entra Admin Center*

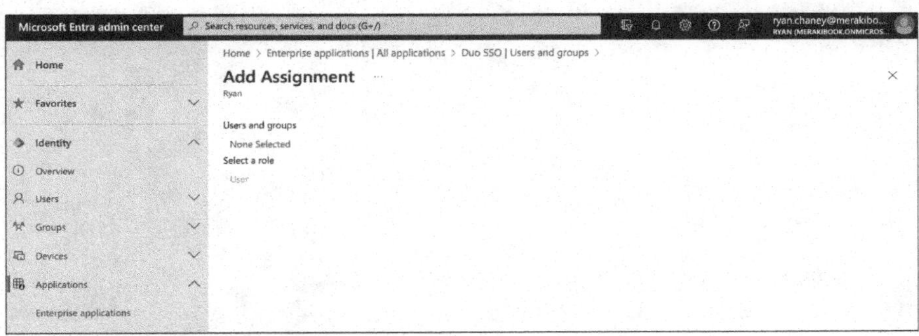

Figure 7-17 *Group Assignment Page on the Duo SSO Application in the Microsoft Entra Admin Center*

Step 14. On the **Users and Groups** page, search for the **Network Access** group, select the check box next to its name, and then click the **Select** button, as shown in Figure 7-18.

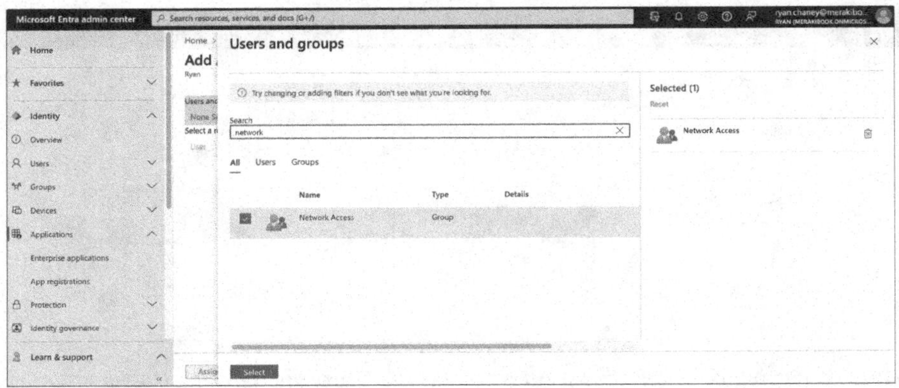

Figure 7-18 *Adding the Network Access Group to the Duo SSO Application in the Microsoft Entra Admin Center*

Step 15. Back on the **Add Assignment** page, click **Assign**, as shown in Figure 7-19.

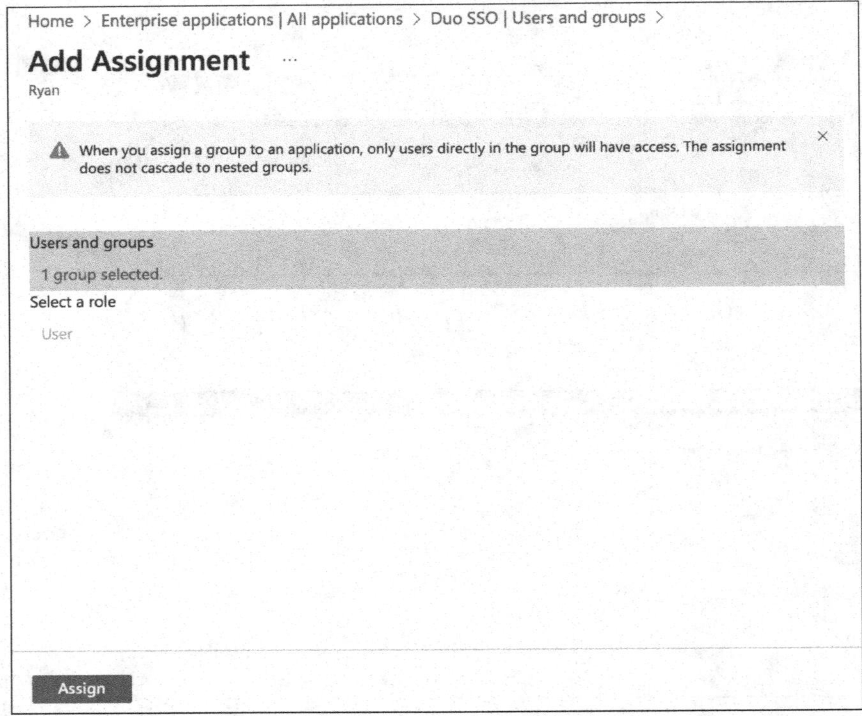

Figure 7-19 *Assigning the New Group on the Add Assignment Page for the Duo SSO Application*

Step 16. Back on the **Duo SSO** enterprise application page, you can see the Network Access group that you've just added, as shown in Figure 7-20. If you are using different groups for network and VPN access, be sure to add any others here.

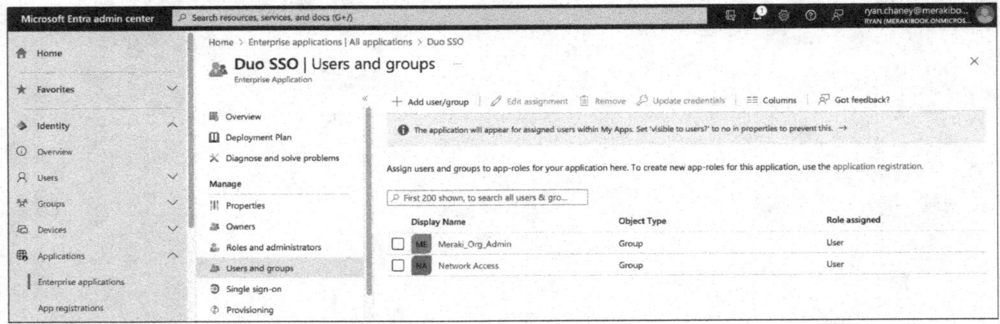

Figure 7-20 *Verifying the New Group Addition on the Users and Groups Page for the Duo SSO Application*

At this point, you've completed the steps required for basic SAML authentication.

Confirming Functionality of SAML Configuration Using AnyConnect VPN

Follow these steps to verify that the SAML configuration is working using AnyConnect VPN:

Step 1. Download and install the Cisco Secure Client application. You can download it from the **AnyConnect Settings** page in Meraki Dashboard.

Step 2. Copy the **AnyConnect Server URL** from the **AnyConnect Settings** page in Meraki Dashboard. Paste this URL into the field under **AnyConnect VPN**, as shown in Figure 7-21.

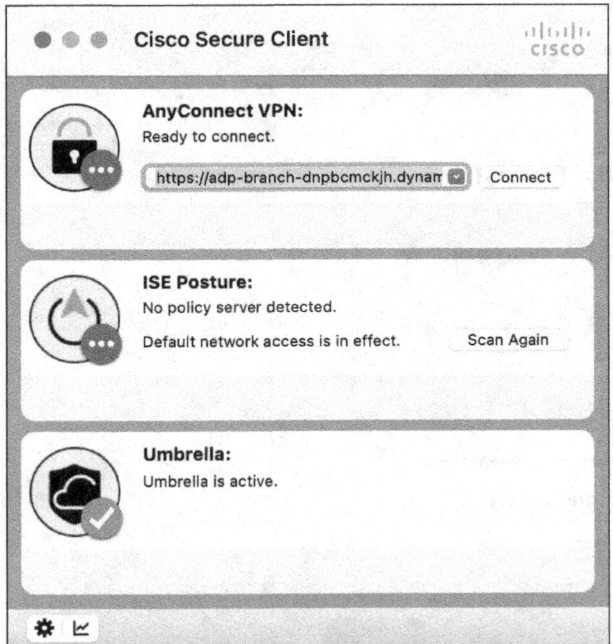

Figure 7-21 *Entering the AnyConnect Server URL into the Cisco Secure Client*

Step 3. Enter the username for a user in the Network Access group and click **Next**, as shown in Figure 7-22.

Step 4. Enter the password for a user in the Network Access group and click **Sign In**, as shown in Figure 7-23. If the next page is a **Stay Signed In?** window, click either **Yes** or **No** to move to the next page.

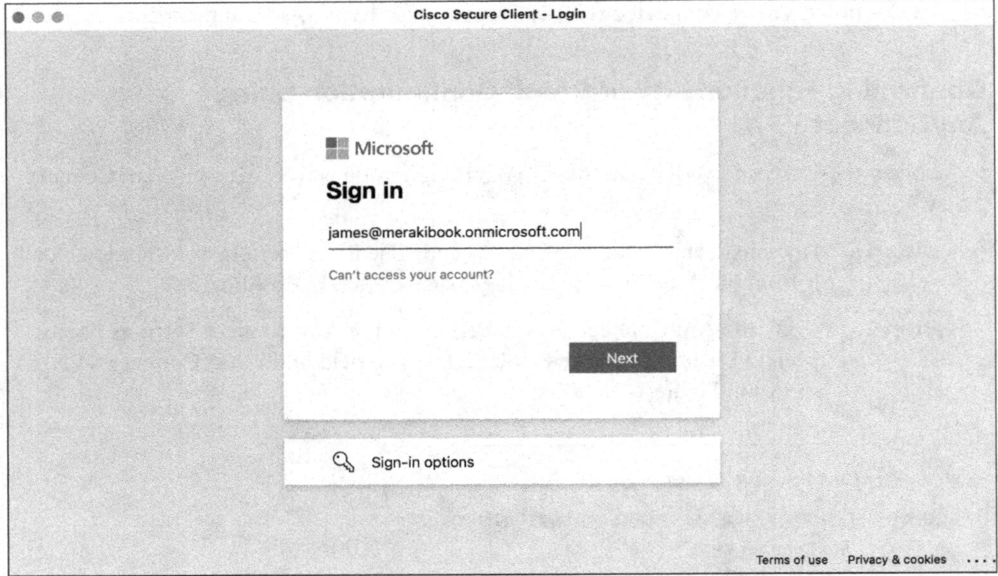

Figure 7-22 *Entering the Username for AnyConnect VPN Using the Cisco Secure Client*

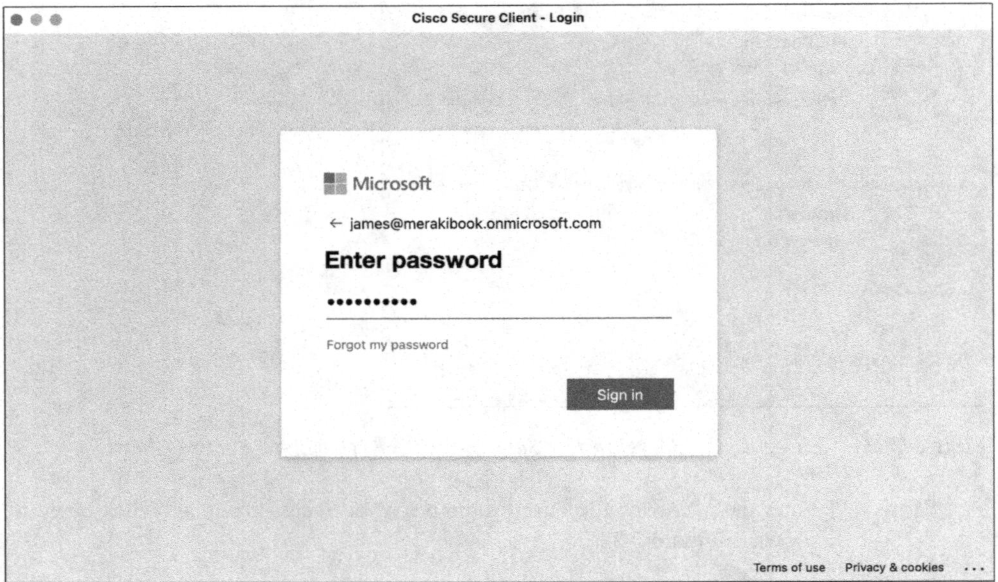

Figure 7-23 *Entering the Password for AnyConnect VPN Using the Cisco Secure Client*

Step 5. Because this user has not enrolled with Duo, the inline enrollment now begins. The enrollment steps are shown in Chapter 5, so we won't show these again here. Click **Next** from the screen shown in Figure 7-24. Complete the Duo enrollment and multifactor authentication.

Figure 7-24 *Duo Welcome Page for a New User Using the Cisco Secure Client*

Step 6. After the Duo inline enrollment and MFA authentication have been completed, a banner message appears, as shown in Figure 7-25. This banner is configurable in case you want to display your own policy, acceptable use information, or the like here. Click **Accept**.

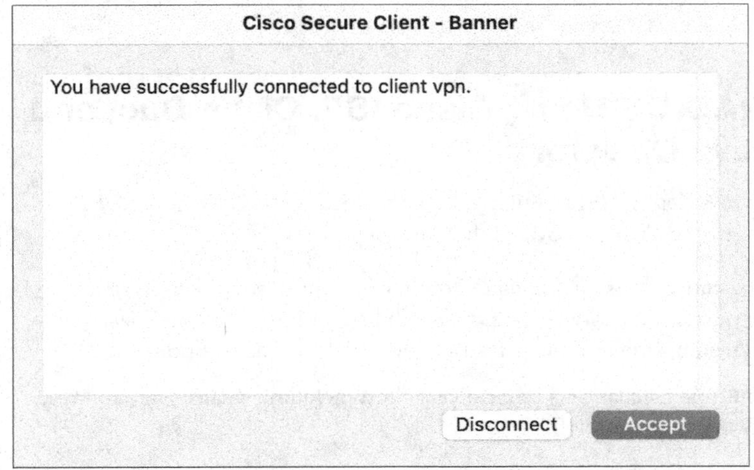

Figure 7-25 *Banner Message During AnyConnect VPN Login Using the Cisco Secure Client*

The Cisco Secure Client now shows the VPN **Connected** status with a connection timer incrementing, as shown in Figure 7-26.

Figure 7-26 *Cisco Secure Client After Successfully Connecting to AnyConnect VPN on Meraki MX*

At this point, you've completed the configuration and verification of SAML for user authentication. To learn more details about wired or wireless access, refer to Chapter 8. For configuring VPN access, refer to Chapter 9.

Configuring RADIUS Using Cisco ISE, Cisco Duo, and Microsoft Active Directory

Cisco Identity Services Engine (ISE) is highly recommended when utilizing RADIUS to control network access because it provides the following:

- Strong profiling capabilities, including contextual attributes such as user, time, device, device posture, location, threat, vulnerability, and access type. These attributes provide important context for flexible, risk-based access policies.
- Support for multiple mechanisms to enforce policy, including security group tags (SGTs) for network segmentation.
- Greatly simplified administration of PKI infrastructure and certificates that are required for 802.1X. This includes its own certificate authority (CA), while also

supporting a wide range of certificate authorities. In Chapter 8, we demonstrate how to deploy 802.1X utilizing Cisco ISE's policy and CA functions.

- Great troubleshooting tools, including
  - Incredibly detailed logging showing, in one record, all the authentication details, every step of the authentication and authorization flow, and the root cause in case of an authentication failure. Examples of Cisco ISE's authentication detail reports are shown in the following chapter.
  - The ability to test user authentication directly from ISE. This test also reports back the user's group memberships and their account attributes.
  - A diagnostics tool for testing/troubleshooting joining ISE to an Active Directory domain. This invaluable tool enables network engineers to troubleshoot what can otherwise be an overwhelming integration.

When thinking about deploying Cisco ISE, consider the following:

- Cisco ISE can be deployed as a virtual machine. This means it can be hosted on-premises or in the cloud.
- Cisco ISE supports Microsoft Active Directory and Microsoft Entra, enabling authentication solutions that are purely on-premises, purely cloud, or hybrid. This makes ISE perfect for enterprises whose identity management infrastructure is on-premises today but may be planning to shift to the cloud in the future.
- Cisco ISE supports a wide range of identity repositories, including Lightweight Directory Access Protocol (LDAP), RADIUS, and SAML IdPs. This means you can support other, potentially lower-cost, directory solutions.
- Hardware ISE appliances incorporate a trusted platform module (TPM), meaning they share the same hardware trust model as network infrastructure (as discussed in Chapter 3, "Meraki Dashboard and Trust").

Prerequisites

To ensure that the setup goes as smoothly as possible, first ensure the following requirements are met for Cisco Identity Services Engine (ISE), Microsoft Active Directory, and Cisco Duo:

- **Cisco Identity Services Engine (ISE):**
  - Must be version 3.2 patch 1 or later. In this example, we run version 3.2.0.542 patch 1. To check the version, log in to ISE and navigate to **Settings** (sprocket icon in top right) > **About ISE and Server.**
  - Ensure that ISE can resolve the domain name for your Active Directory server and has IP reachability to Active Directory and the devices that will be sending it RADIUS requests.

- **Microsoft Active Directory:**
  - Ensure you are running a supported version of Windows Server. Meraki supports any version that is still supported by Microsoft. Currently, that means any version later than Windows Server 2016. You can refer to the following link to see whether your release is still supported by Microsoft: https://learn.microsoft.com/en-us/deployoffice/endofsupport/windows-server-support.
  - Ensure the AD DS and DNS roles are installed and the services are running. On your Windows Server, run the command **dcdiag /test:dns /v /e /dnsbasic /dnsrecordregistration** and ensure that all the tests are successful. This command needs to be run as administrator. To do this, navigate to **Windows Server > Search Windows.** Then enter **cmd.** In the search results, right-click **Command Prompt** and select **Run as Administrator.** Figure 7-27 shows the summary output from a Windows 2016 Server when running the **dcdiag** command.

```
   Summary of test results for DNS servers used by the above domain controllers:

      DNS server: 10.200.155.100 (WIN-38BGOVUDOJR)
         All tests passed on this DNS server
         Name resolution is functional._ldap._tcp SRV record for the forest root domain is registered

      DNS server: 192.168.168.3 (WIN-38BGOVUDOJR)
         All tests passed on this DNS server
         Name resolution is functional._ldap._tcp SRV record for the forest root domain is registered

   Summary of DNS test results:

                                  Auth Basc Forw Del  Dyn  RReg Ext
      _________________________________________________________________
      Domain: lab.local
         WIN-38BGOVUDOJR          PASS WARN n/a  n/a  n/a  PASS n/a

   ........................ lab.local passed test DNS
Test omitted by user request: LocatorCheck
Test omitted by user request: Intersite
```

Figure 7-27 *Output of the dcdiag Test on Windows Server 2016*

  - Pay special attention to the SRV records in your DNS server. No default port is specified when you're creating the SRV records for _kerberos and _kpasswd. If the ports are not entered, this will lead to the Kerberos checks failing when testing from ISE (**Menu > Administration > External Identity Sources > Active Directory > Advanced Tools > Diagnostics Tool**). Table 7-2, Figure 7-28, and Figure 7-29 outline the SRV records required in DNS.

Table 7-2 *SRV Records Required on the DNS Server to Enable Integration with Cisco ISE*

Service	Protocol	Port
_kerberos	_tcp	88
_ldap	_tcp	389
_kpasswd	_tcp	416

Service	Protocol	Port
_gc	_tcp	3268
_kerberos	_udp	88
_kpasswd	_udp	416

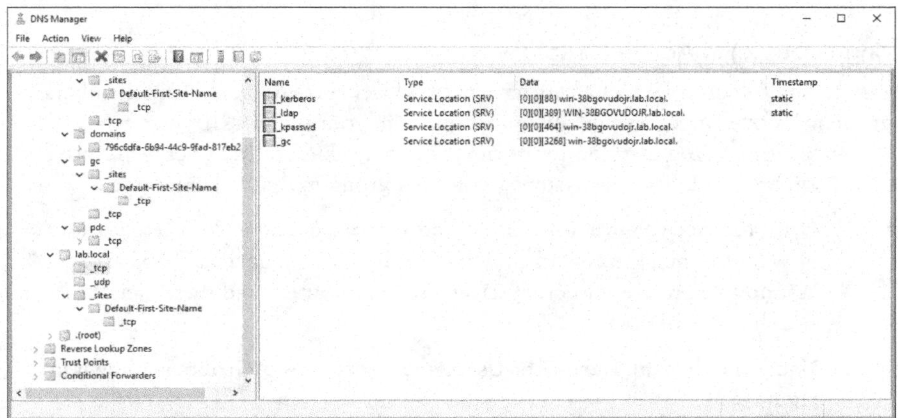

Figure 7-28 *The TCP-Related SRV Records Created in DNS Manager on Windows Server 2016*

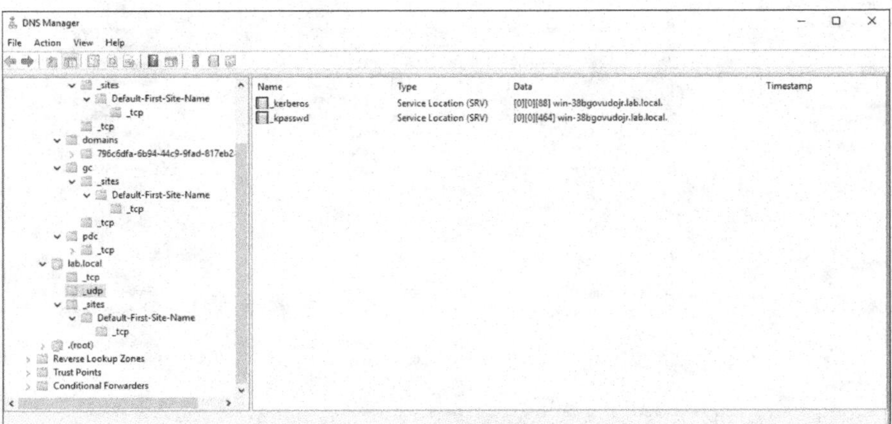

Figure 7-29 *The UDP-Related SRV Records Created in DNS Manager on Windows Server 2016*

- Ensure at least one user and one domain admin account are configured in Active Directory.

- **Cisco Duo:** Download and install the latest version of the Duo Authentication Proxy application. This application can be co-located on your Active Directory server. Our example runs version 6.2.0, and is co-located on our Active Directory server.

Configuring Users and Groups in Microsoft Active Directory

Authenticating user access to the network, whether wired, wireless, or VPN, will require user accounts and groups to be configured in an identity management solution. These steps are the same regardless of the access type, so we show them separately here rather than repeat them multiple times. Follow the instructions in the next two sections to create at least one user and at least one group to be used for authenticating network access.

Configuring Group(s) in Active Directory

The easiest way to control which users have network access is to make them members of a group in Active Directory and allow that group in your policies. If you already have a suitable group, you can skip to the next section, "Configuring User(s) in Active Directory"; otherwise, follow these steps to create a group in Active Directory:

Step 1. Open the **Active Directory Users and Computers** console. There are lots of ways to open the console; my preferred way is to navigate to **Search Windows > Active Directory Users and Computers** and then click the search result to open.

Under the domain, right-click **Users** and select **New > Group**, as shown in Figure 7-30.

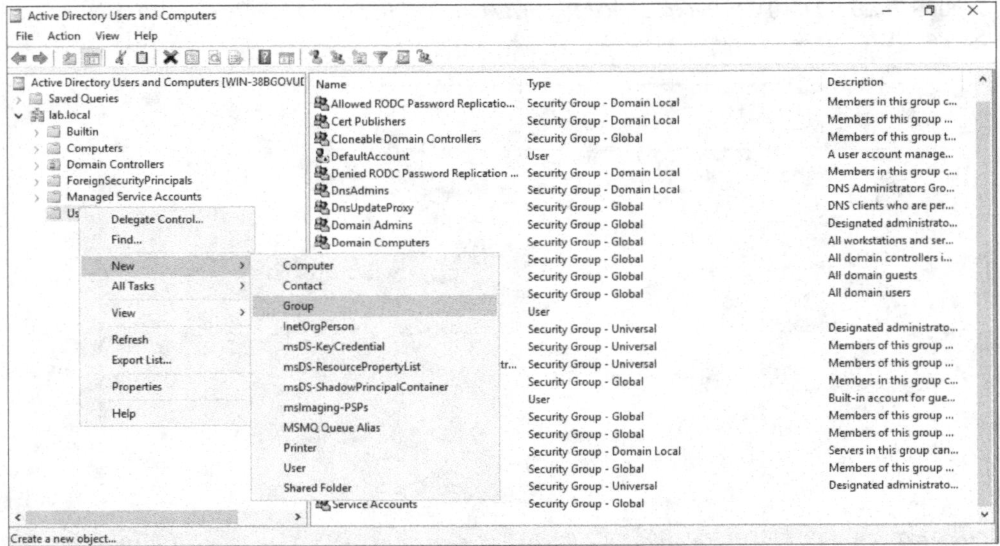

Figure 7-30 *Adding a New Group in Active Directory Users and Computers*

Step 2. Enter the **Group** name. In this example, we've used the name **Network Access** (see Figure 7-31). Click **OK**.

You've now completed the process of adding a new group in Active Directory.

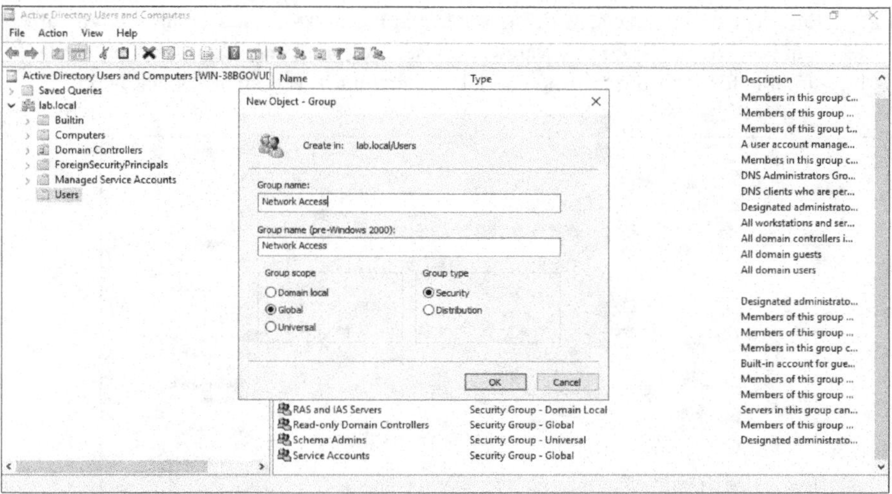

Figure 7-31 *Entering a Name for the New Group in Active Directory Users and Computers*

Configuring User(s) in Active Directory

For users to authenticate to the network, they need to have an account in Active Directory and be members of the correct group. Follow these steps to create a user account in Active Directory and add the necessary group memberships:

Step 1. Open the **Active Directory Users and Computers** console. Right-click **Users** and select **New > User**, as shown in Figure 7-32.

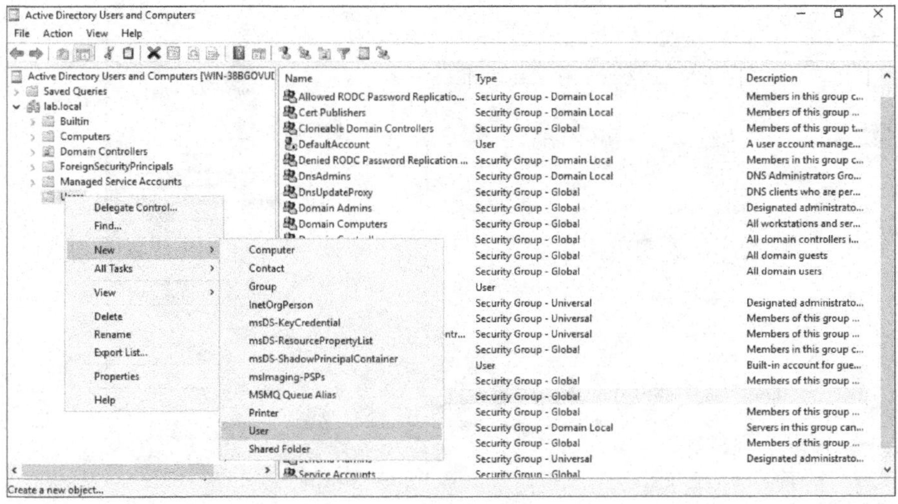

Figure 7-32 *Adding a New User in Active Directory Users and Computers*

Step 2. Enter the user's details, as demonstrated in Figure 7-33. At a minimum, you are required to enter the **First Name** and **User Logon Name.** Consider the standards suitable for your organization and try to maintain consistency. Click **Next.**

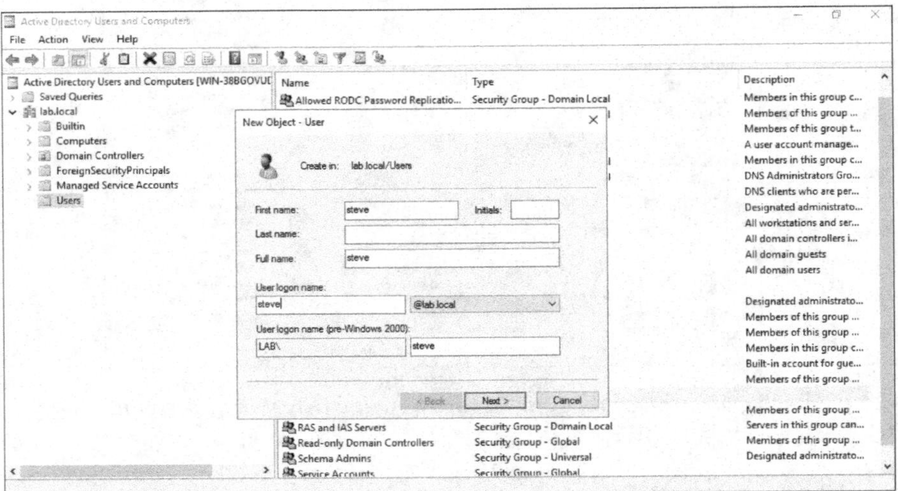

Figure 7-33 *Entering the Username Details for a New User in Active Directory Users and Computers*

Step 3. Enter a **Password** for this user and re-enter the same password in the **Confirm Password** field, as shown in Figure 7-34. Click **Next.**

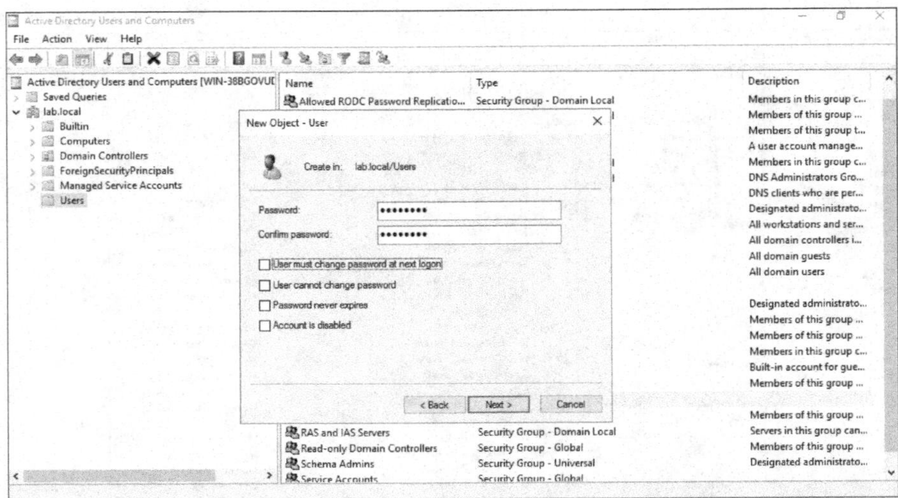

Figure 7-34 *Entering the Password Details for a New User in Active Directory Users and Computers*

Step 4. Click **Finish** to create this user (see Figure 7-35).

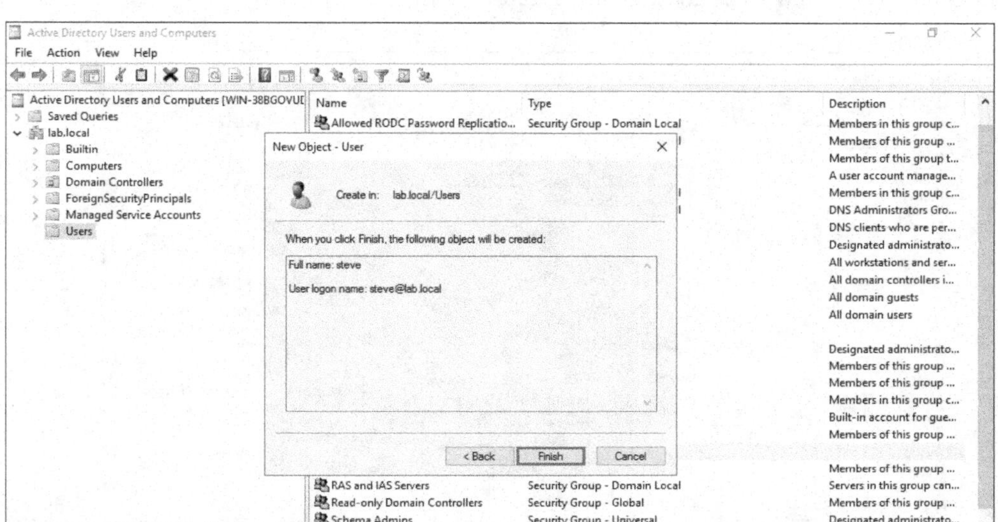

Figure 7-35 *Completing the Addition of a New User in Active Directory Users and Computers*

Step 5. Back on the **Users** pane, right-click the new user and click **Properties**, as shown in Figure 7-36.

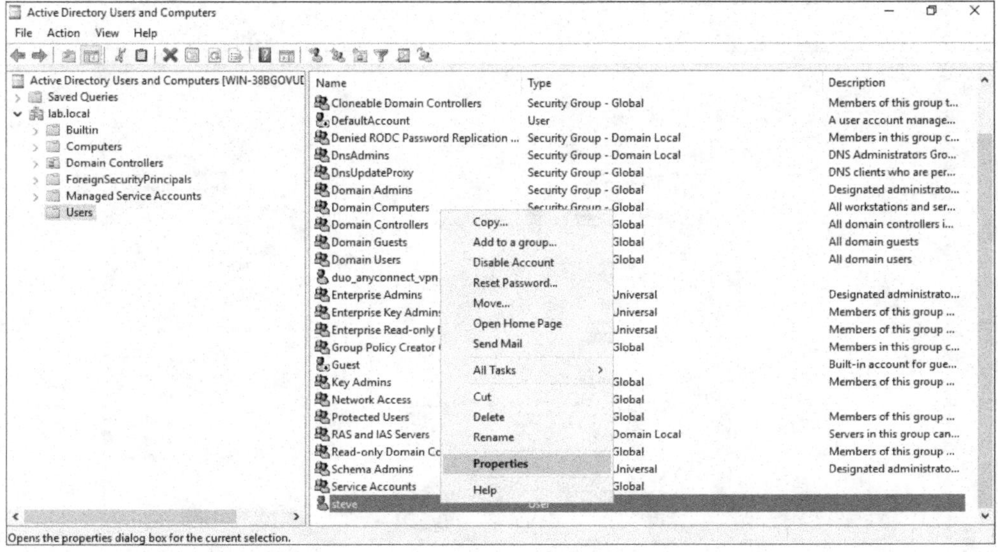

Figure 7-36 *Opening User Properties on an Account in Active Directory Users and Computers*

Step 6. On the user's properties window, click the **Member Of** tab and then click **Add**, as demonstrated in Figure 7-37.

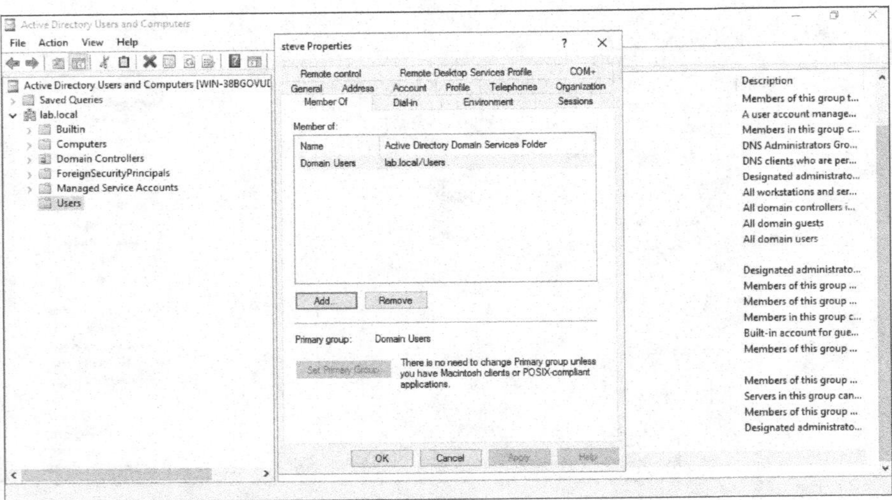

Figure 7-37 *The Member Of Tab on the User Properties Page in Active Directory Users and Computers*

Step 7. In the text box under **Enter the Object Names to Select**, enter the name of the group created. In this example, the name is Network Access (see Figure 7-38).

Click **Check Names** to search for this group and underline the group name, indicating that the group has been found in Active Directory. Click **OK** to finish.

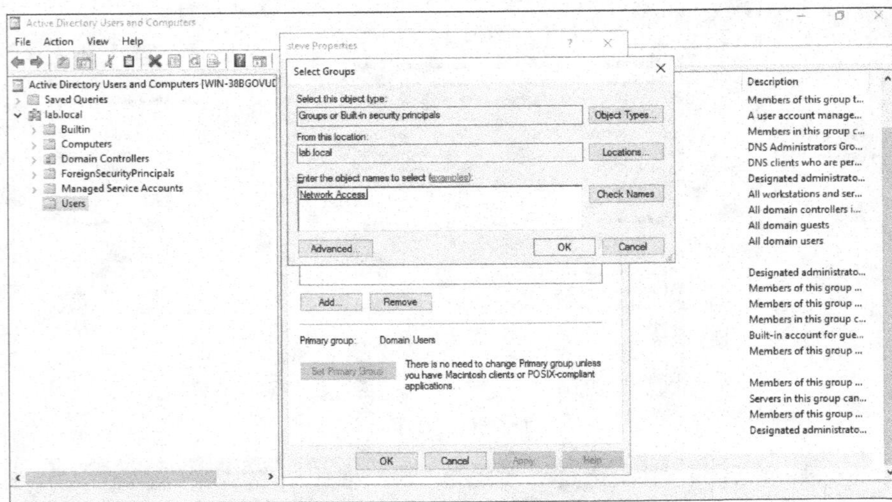

Figure 7-38 *Adding the Network Access Group to a User on Active Directory Users and Computers*

At this point, you've completed the process of creating a new user and adding that user to a group in Active Directory.

Configuring Cisco Identity Services Engine (ISE)

This section covers how to configure Cisco ISE to accept RADIUS requests from devices and how to integrate Cisco ISE with Microsoft Active Directory. Enabling staff to use the same credentials they use for other corporate applications not only makes the network more user-friendly, but it also reduces helpdesk calls. These steps are applicable to all access types including wired, wireless, and VPN.

Adding Network Access Devices (NADs) to Cisco ISE

Cisco ISE uses a whitelist-like behavior to decide which devices to accept RADIUS requests from. This section covers how to add authenticators (switches, access points, and MX security appliances) to Cisco ISE so that ISE responds to their RADIUS requests and knows these are authorized devices. Cisco ISE refers to such devices as network access devices (NADs).

Meraki MS Switches and MR Access Points

If your Meraki devices are sitting behind an MX appliance that is not participating in a site-to-site VPN, the source IP address used for RADIUS traffic will be the public IP address of the MX appliance at that site.

Alternatively, if your Meraki devices are sitting behind an MX appliance that is participating in a site-to-site VPN, the source IP address used for RADIUS traffic will use the Meraki device's local IP address.

You can find the public and local IPs for all access points in Meraki Dashboard by navigating to **Wireless** > **Access Points** (under Monitor) > **List**. You can find the public and local IPs for all switches in Meraki Dashboard by navigating to **Switching** > **Switches** (under Monitor). On either page, if the Public IP or the Local IP column is not showing, click the sprocket icon on the right and ensure their respective box is checked.

Keep these pages open because you need the IP addresses in the steps that follow. You can also use the **Download** drop-down menu to export this data in CSV format.

Meraki MX Security Appliances

The source IP address used for RADIUS traffic from a Meraki MX is typically the IP address of its Internet interface.

You can find the management IP addresses for all your MX devices in **Meraki Dashboard** > **Organization** > **Overview** > **Devices**, as shown in Figure 7-39.

Keep this tab open because you need the IP addresses in the steps that follow. You can also use the **Download** drop-down menu to export this data in CSV format.

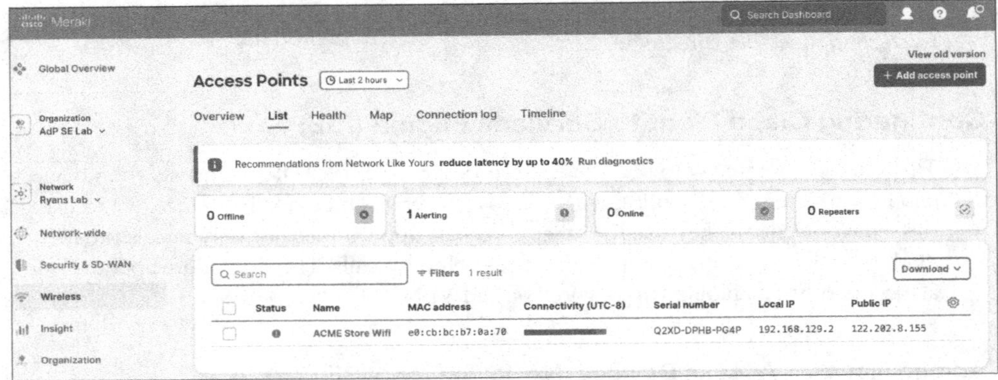

Figure 7-39 *Access Point Public and Local IPs on the Access Points Page in Meraki Dashboard*

Step 1. Log in to your instance of Cisco Identity Services Engine (ISE).

Step 2. In Cisco ISE, navigate to **Menu > Administration > Network Resources > Network Devices**, as shown in Figure 7-40.

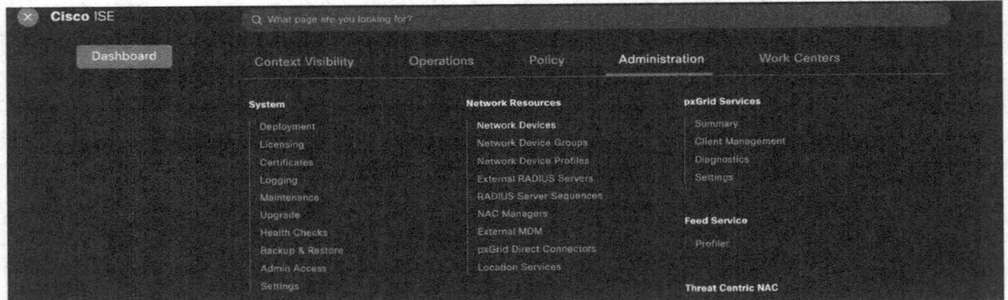

Figure 7-40 *Navigating to the Network Devices Page in Cisco ISE*

Step 3. Click **+ Add** to add a new device on the **Network Devices** navigation pane, as shown in Figure 7-41.

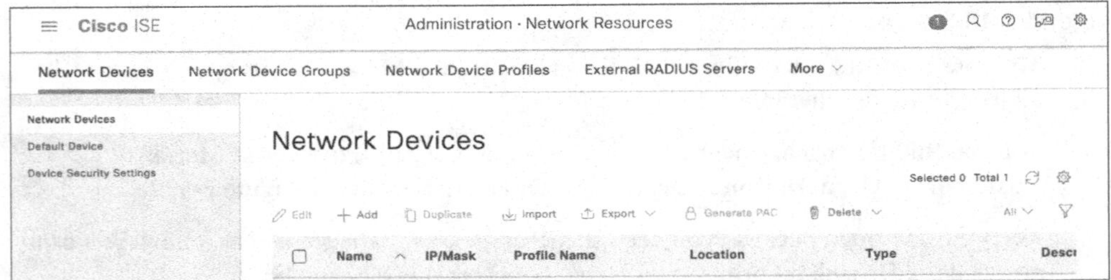

Figure 7-41 *Adding a New Device on the Network Devices Page in Cisco ISE*

Step 4. On the **Network Devices** page (see Figure 7-42), enter the following:

- **Name:** Here, we have used the hostname of our Meraki device. This field doesn't allow spaces, so we have used underscores instead. If you will be adding a subnet or wildcard in the following step, we recommend using something other than the hostname (such as the network name) that better reflects the purpose of this entry.
- **IP Address and subnet mask:** This is the source IP address(es) or subnet(s) from which RADIUS traffic originates. You can add an IP range, multiple rows, or a wildcard of 0.0.0.0/0 to reduce the amount of effort required here.
- **IPSEC:** Set this to **No.**
- Tick and expand **RADIUS Authentication Settings.** Then enter the shared secret that will be configured on the Meraki device(s).

Last, scroll down and click **Submit.**

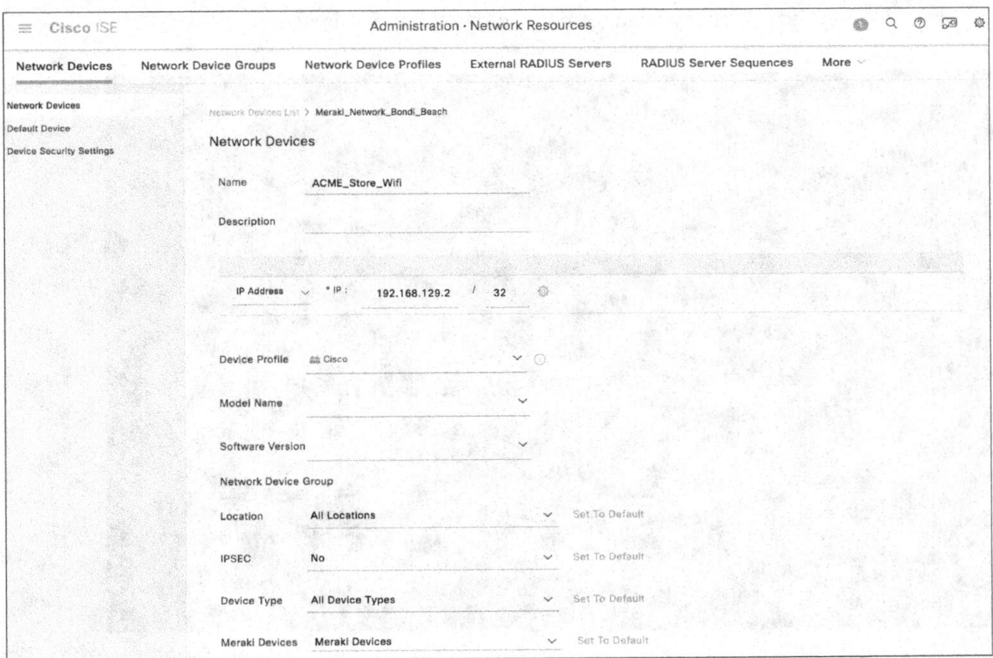

Figure 7-42 *Configuring a New Network Access Device in Cisco ISE*

The new network device is then listed on the **Network Devices** page, as demonstrated in Figure 7-43.

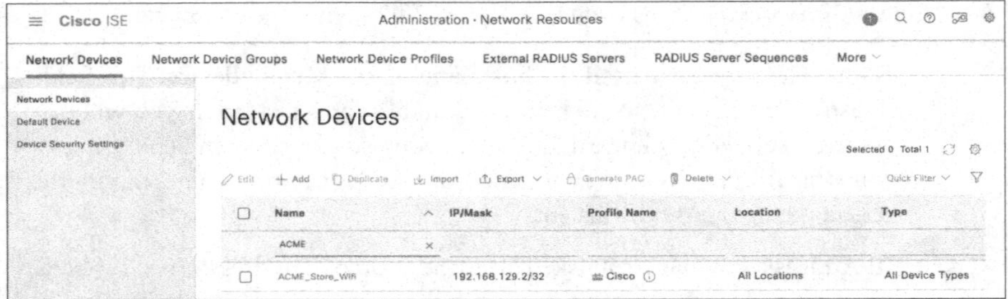

Figure 7-43 *The Network Devices Page in Cisco ISE After Adding a New Device*

Adding Active Directory as an External Identity Source

With Active Directory now configured, the next task is to integrate AD with Cisco ISE. This allows ISE policy in the following sections to verify user credentials against Active Directory:

Step 1. In ISE, navigate to **Menu > Administration > External Identity Sources** (under Identity Management), as shown in Figure 7-44.

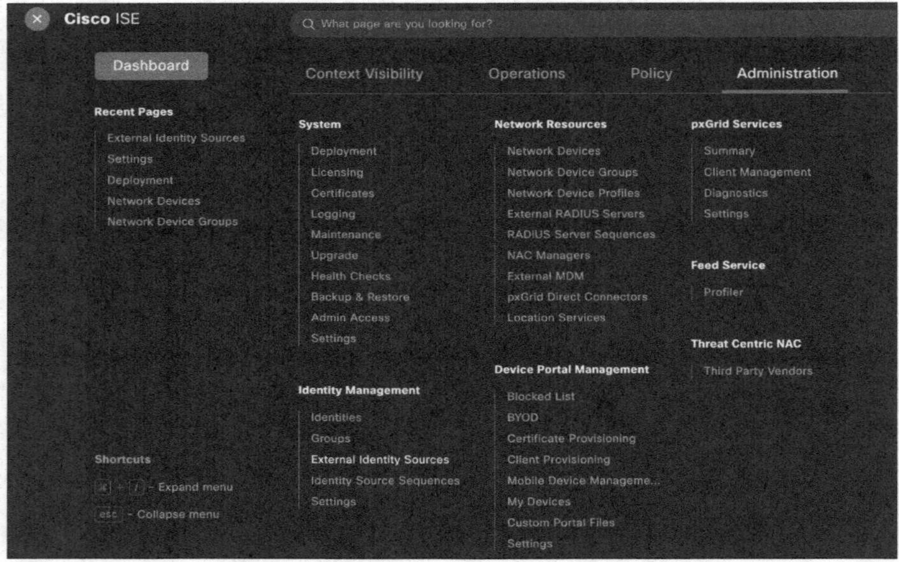

Figure 7-44 *Navigating to the External Identity Sources Page in Cisco ISE*

Step 2. You need to add the Active Directory server to ISE.

a. Click **Active Directory** from the menu on the left.

b. Click **+ Add** on the Active Directory pane (see Figure 7-45).

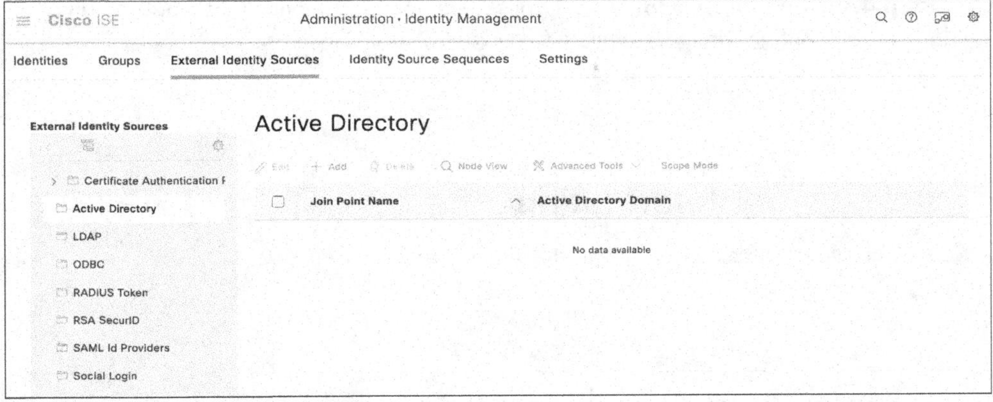

Figure 7-45 *The Active Directory Pane in Cisco ISE*

Step 3. Enter a description for this in the **Join Point Name.**

a. Enter the domain you have configured in Active Directory into the **Active Directory Domain** field, as shown in Figure 7-46.

b. Click **Submit.**

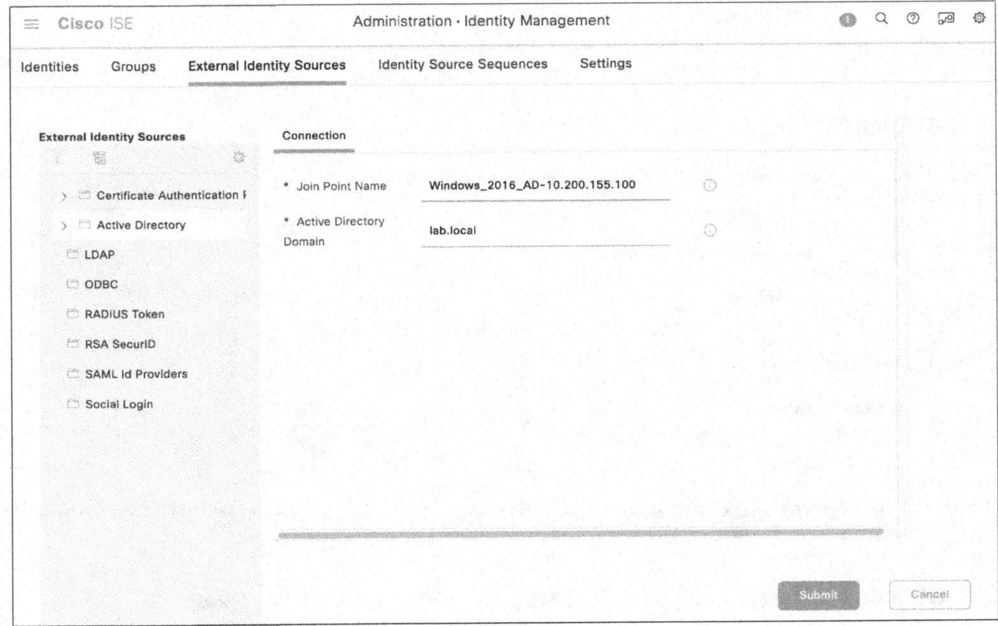

Figure 7-46 *Adding a New Active Directory Server to Cisco ISE*

Step 4. A pop-up window asks if you would you like to join all ISE nodes to this Active Directory domain (see Figure 7-47). Click **Yes.**

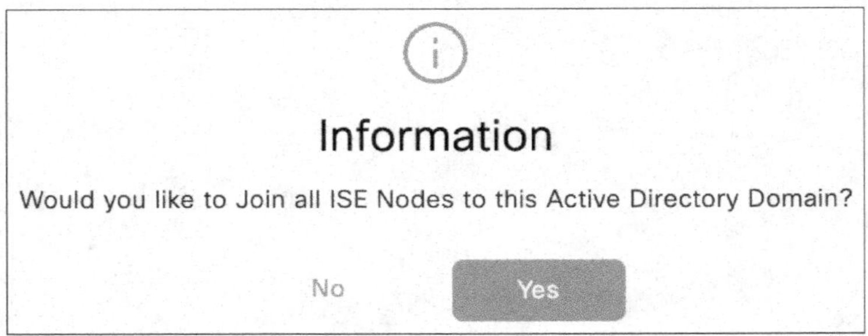

Figure 7-47 *Pop-Up Window Asking You to Join All ISE Nodes to This Active Directory Domain*

Step 5. On the **Join Domain** window (see Figure 7-48), do the following:

- Enter **AD User Name.**
- Enter the **Password.** This is the password for the preceding account.
- Check **Store Credentials** to save admin login credentials.

Click **OK.**

Join Domain

Please specify the credentials required to Join ISE node(s) to the Active Directory Domain.

* AD User Name Administrator

* Password ··········

Specify Organizational Unit

Store Credentials

Cancel OK

Figure 7-48 *Entering Credentials Required to Join the ISE Node to the AD Domain in Cisco ISE*

Step 6. If successful, you see the window in Figure 7-49. Click **Close.**

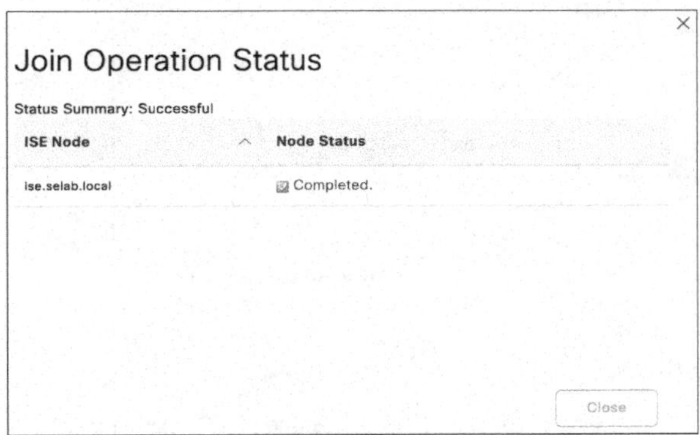

Figure 7-49 *Join Operation Status Window Upon Successfully Joining ISE to the AD Domain*

If unsuccessful, head back to the Active Directory pane, and from the **Advanced Tools** drop-down menu, select **Diagnostics Tool.** Ensure the AD server you have just added is selected from the **Join Point** drop-down menu, and then from the **Run Tests** drop-down menu, select **Run All Tests,** as shown in Figure 7-50. This output helps you to understand why the join operation is failing.

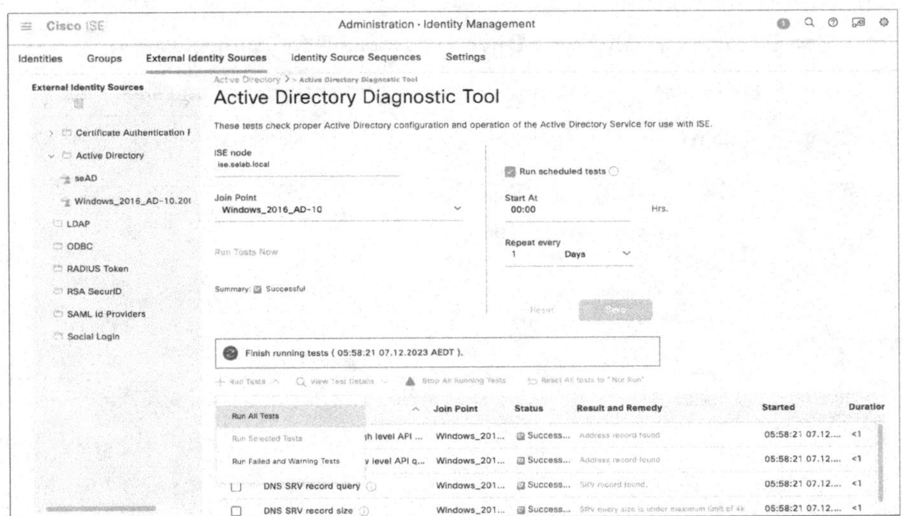

Figure 7-50 *The Active Directory Diagnostic Tool in Cisco ISE*

Step 7. Back on the Active Directory pane (**Menu > Administration > Identity Management > External Identity Sources > Active Directory**), click the name of the AD server that has just been added. On the new pane, click the **Allowed Domains** tab, as shown in Figure 7-51.

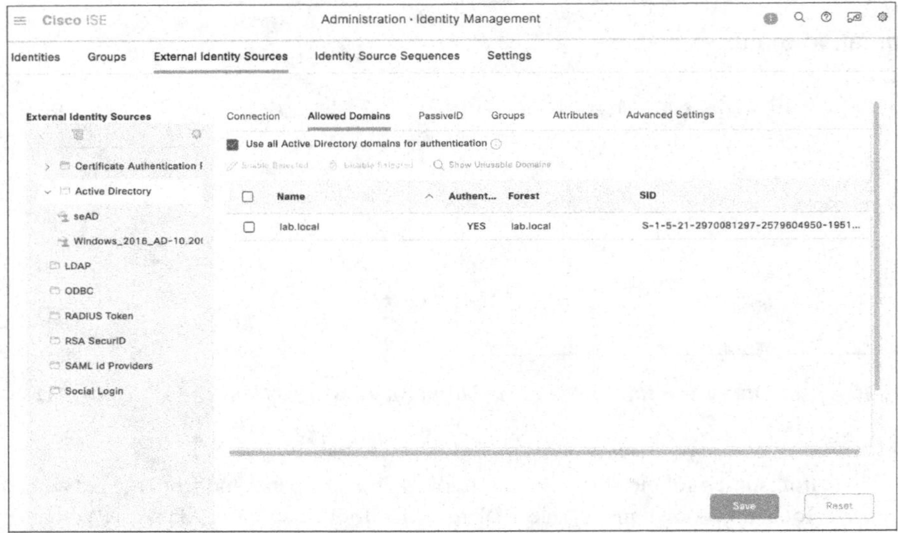

Figure 7-51 *The Allowed Domains Tab for an Active Directory Server in Cisco ISE*

Step 8. Check the box next to the domain you want to authenticate users against (see Figure 7-52).

a. Uncheck **Use All Active Directory Domains for Authentication.**

b. Click **Enable Selected** and ensure the **Authenticate** column shows **YES.**

c. Click **Save.**

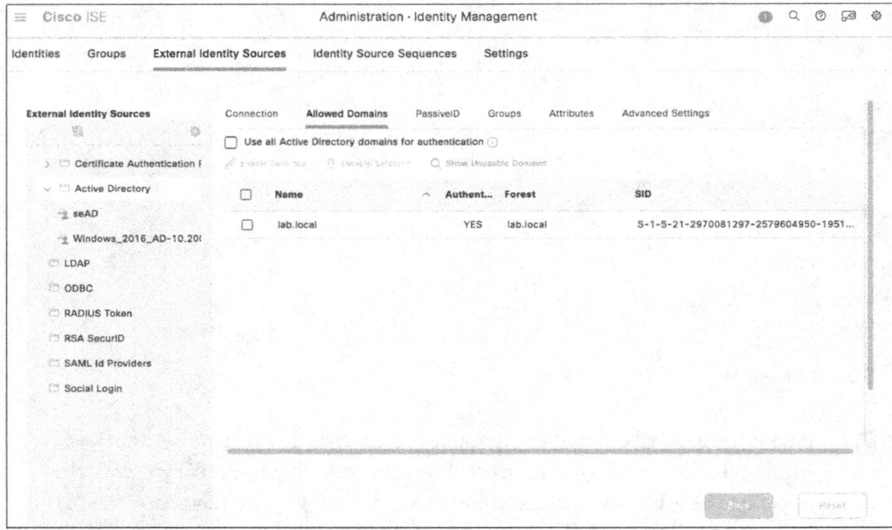

Figure 7-52 *Configuring the Allowed Domains on the Active Directory Server in Cisco ISE*

Step 9. Click the **Groups** tab. Click the **+ Add** drop-down menu and choose **Select Groups From Directory**, as shown in Figure 7-53.

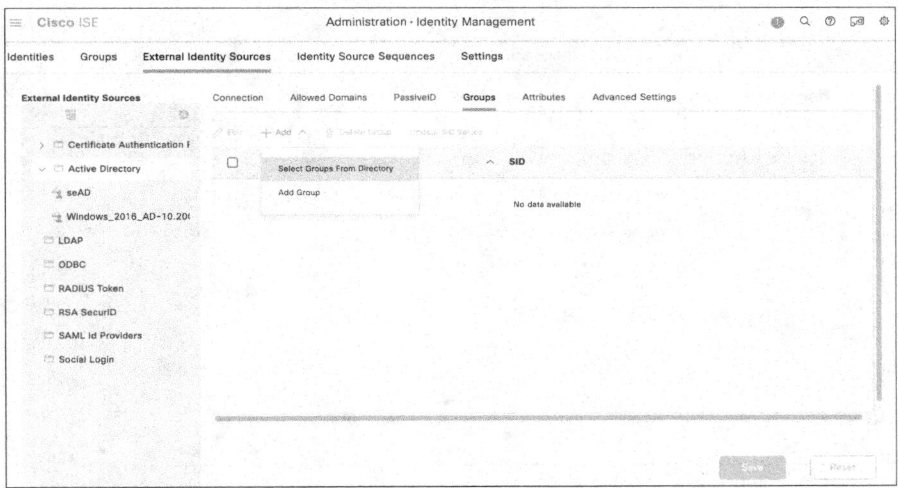

Figure 7-53 *The Groups Tab for an Active Directory Server in Cisco ISE*

Step 10. On the **Select Directory Groups** pane, click **Retrieve Groups.** If you know the name of the group, you can enter this in the **Name Filter** field and then click **Retrieve Groups.** In our case, we want to see the Network Access group listed, as shown in Figure 7-54.

a. Check the box for this group.

b. Click **OK.**

c. Back on the **Groups** tab, click **Save.**

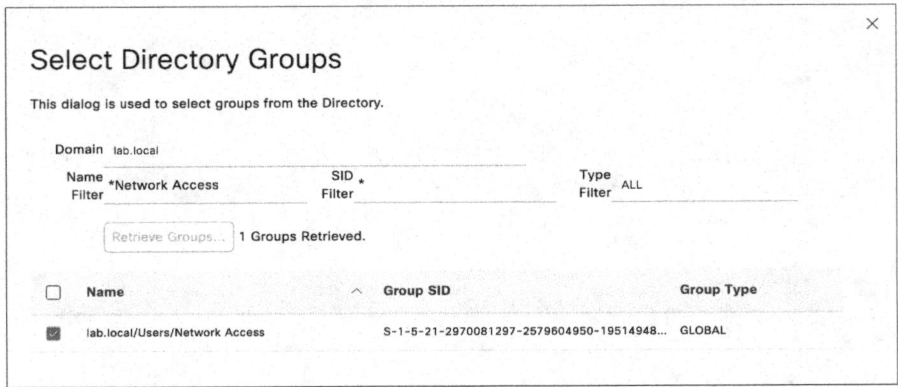

Figure 7-54 *Selecting the Active Directory Groups to Be Used for Authentication in Cisco ISE*

Step 11. Now, you can test that user authentication is working, which is possible directly from ISE. On the Active Directory pane, click the **Advanced Tools** drop-down menu and select **Test User for All Join Points**, as shown in Figure 7-55.

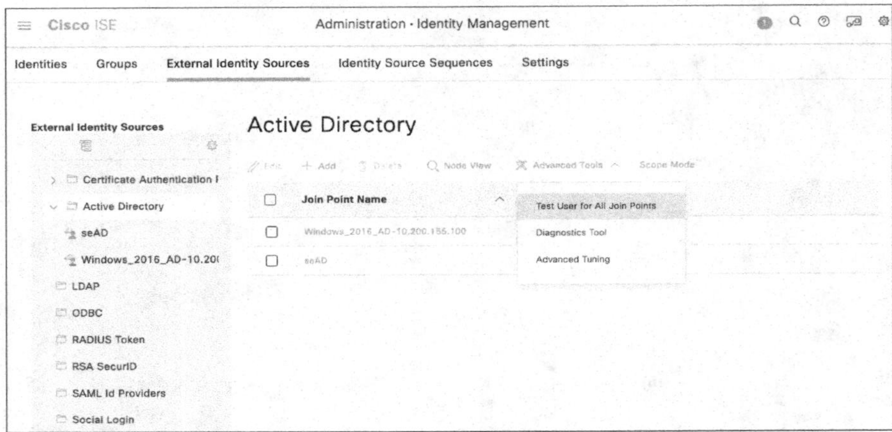

Figure 7-55 *Navigating to the Active Directory User Test Tool in Cisco ISE*

Step 12. On the **Test User Authentication** page, enter the username (including the domain) and the user's password and click **Test**. The **Authentication Result** provides detailed insight into how the AD is performing (see Figure 7-56). If your test was unsuccessful, it will tell you why it failed.

Figure 7-56 *The Test User Authentication Tool in Cisco ISE*

You've now completed the necessary steps in Cisco ISE to

1. Accept authentication RADIUS requests from Meraki devices.
2. Integrate Cisco ISE with Microsoft Active Directory to authenticate users and groups.

RADIUS Configuration for Wired and Wireless 802.1X

Industry best practice requires that users be authenticated before being granted access to the network. The common way to achieve this is using 802.1X, which requires RADIUS. In this section, we show you how to configure RADIUS in Meraki Dashboard for wired and wireless access. In this example we use the Cisco Identity Services Engine for access management and Microsoft Active Directory for identity management. Cisco ISE provides the certificates necessary for Protected EAP (PEAP) out of the box. PEAP uses one-way trust where ISE uses a certificate to identify itself, but clients do not need a certificate. In Chapter 8, we also show you how to implement EAP-TLS, which is a common EAP mechanism utilizing both client and server certificates. Cisco ISE greatly simplifies the setup and troubleshooting of RADIUS and certificates; therefore, it is highly recommended to deploy Cisco ISE when implementing 802.1X.

A number of tasks are required to configure RADIUS for wired and wireless access. They have been summarized into the high-level tasks outlined in the following list. If you'd like to complete this setup in stages, then the required steps have also been grouped under these headings throughout the remainder of this section.

Meraki

1. Configuring organization-wide RADIUS

Cisco Identity Services Engine (ISE)

2. Adding network access devices (NADs) in Cisco ISE. This step was previously covered in the section titled "Configuring Cisco Identity Services Engine (ISE)."
3. Creating a policy set
4. Configuring an authentication policy
5. Configuring an authorization policy

Configuring Organization-Wide RADIUS in Meraki Dashboard

The organization-wide RADIUS server is a new feature that is currently in Early Access Preview. Early Access Preview allows administrators to selectively opt in to new Dashboard features before they become Generally Available (GA). This feature allows RADIUS servers to be defined at the organization level and applied to your RADIUS configuration elsewhere in Dashboard. Organization-wide RADIUS cuts down on the number of times RADIUS server details need to be entered into Dashboard, reducing the chance of errors. Administrators can reuse known-good RADIUS server configurations again and again, and far less effort is required if RADIUS passwords (secrets) need to be updated.

Today, organization-wide RADIUS servers can be applied only to wired configurations, but you can expect to see support for wireless and VPN in the future.

Follow these steps to configure organization-wide RADIUS servers:

Step 1. Log in to Meraki Dashboard (https://dashboard.meraki.com).

Step 2. Because this feature is in Early Access Preview, it first needs to be enabled. This task needs to be done only once. Navigate to **Organization > Early Access**, as shown in Figure 7-57.

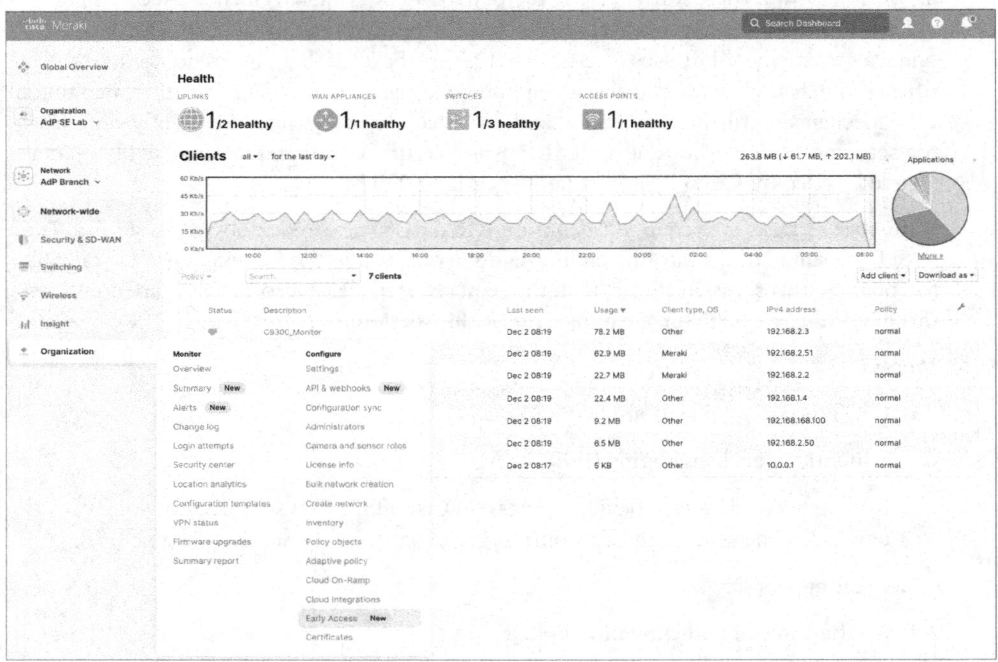

Figure 7-57 *Navigating to the Early Access Page in Meraki Dashboard*

Step 3. Scroll down to **Organization-wide RADIUS Server** (see Figure 7-58) and move the slider across to the right to enable it.

Step 4. An Opt In Settings pop-up window then appears (see Figure 7-59). Select **Opt in Entire Organization** and click **Save**.

Step 5. You then return to the **Meraki Early Access Program** page. The slider for **Organization-wide RADIUS Server** is now blue and across to the right, which indicates that it is enabled (see Figure 7-60).

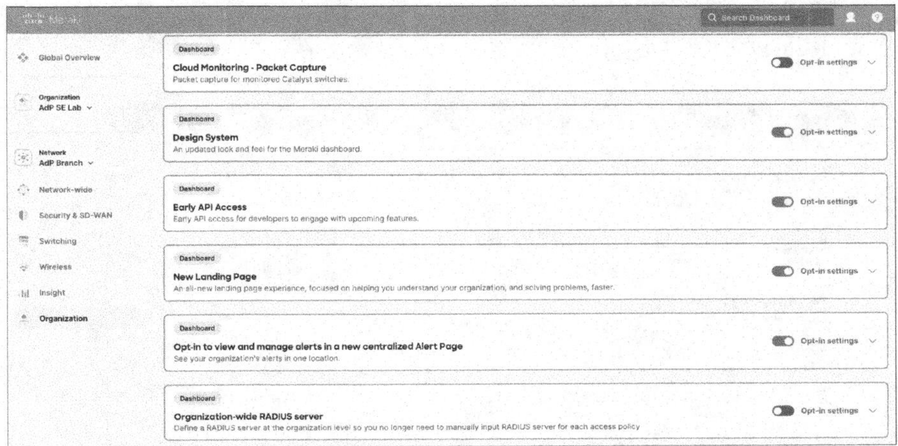

Figure 7-58 *Enabling the Organization-Wide RADIUS Feature in Meraki Dashboard*

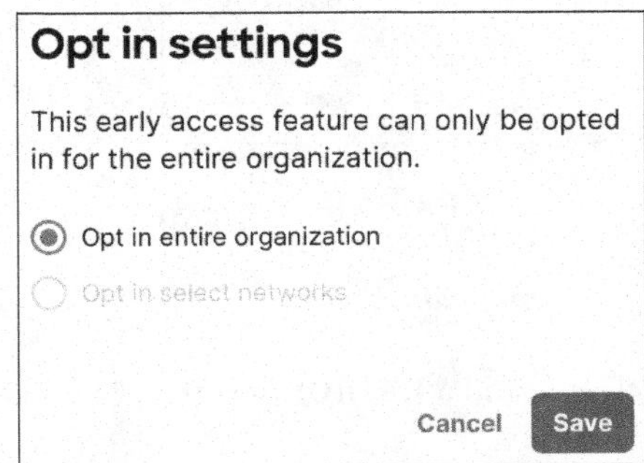

Figure 7-59 *Pop-Up Window when Enabling the Organization-Wide RADIUS Feature*

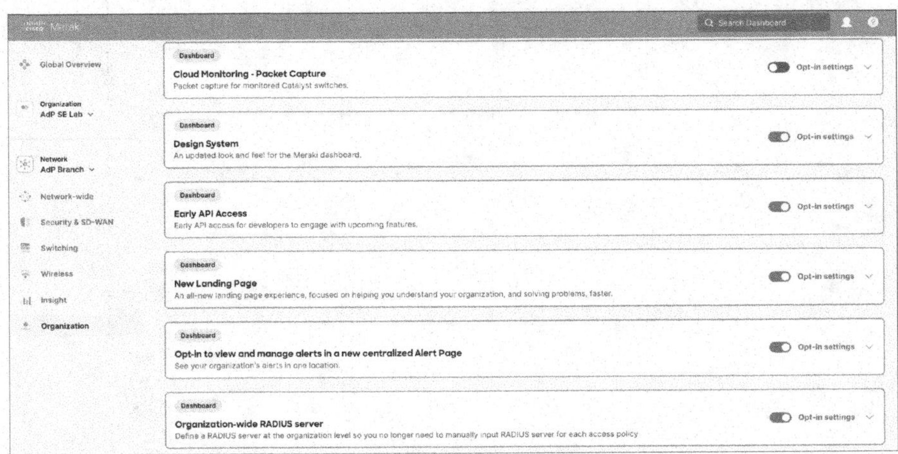

Figure 7-60 *Meraki Early Access Program Page with Organization-Wide RADIUS Enabled*

Step 6. Navigate to **Organization** > **Settings** (under Configure), as shown in Figure 7-61.

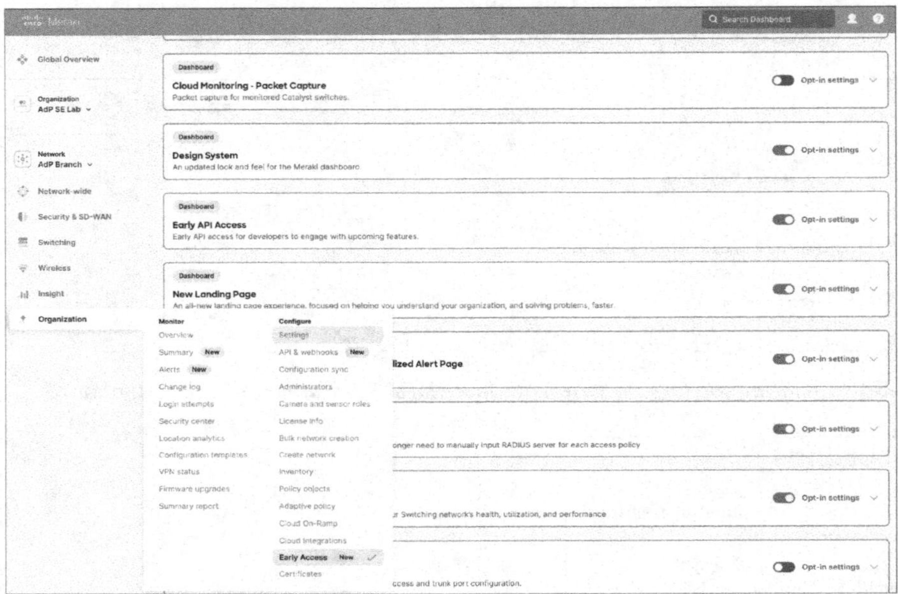

Figure 7-61 *Navigating to Organization Settings in Meraki Dashboard*

Step 7. Scroll down to **RADIUS Servers** and click **+ Add a RADIUS Server**, as shown in Figure 7-62.

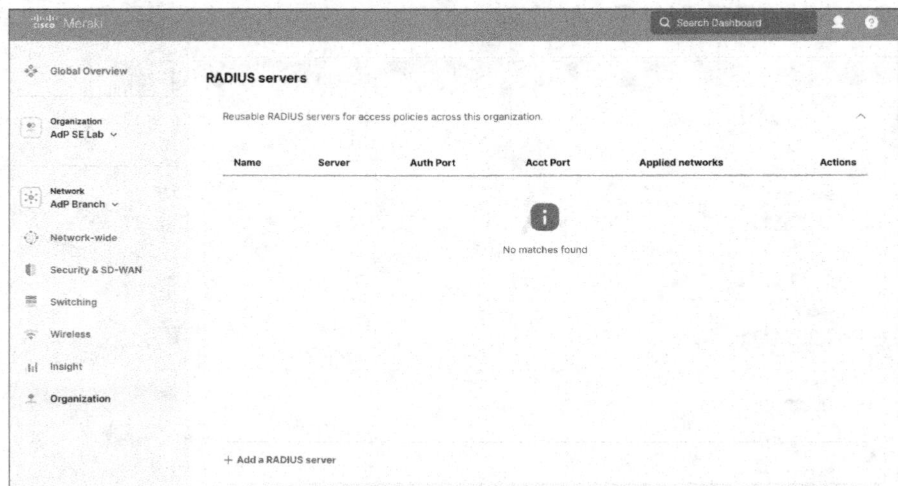

Figure 7-62 *Adding an Organization-Wide RADIUS Server in Meraki Dashboard*

Step 8. The **Add RADIUS Server** pop-up window then appears (see Figure 7-63).

a. In the **Address** field, enter the IP address for your Cisco ISE server.

b. Enter a meaningful name in the **Name** field. Here, we have used **Cisco ISE.**

c. Enter the password being used for the RADIUS secret in the **Secret** field.

d. Leave the remainder of this page at their default settings.

e. Click **Save.**

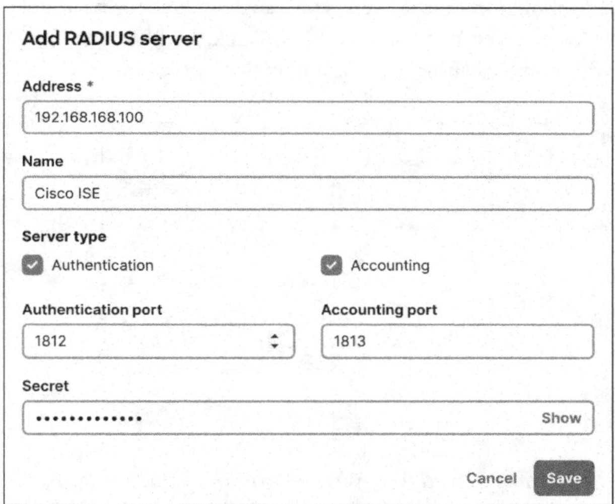

Figure 7-63 *Entering Configuration Details for Organization-Wide RADIUS Server in Meraki Dashboard*

Step 9. You then return to the **Organization Settings** page. Under **RADIUS servers,** a banner confirms that the organization-wide RADIUS server has been added successfully, as shown in Figure 7-64.

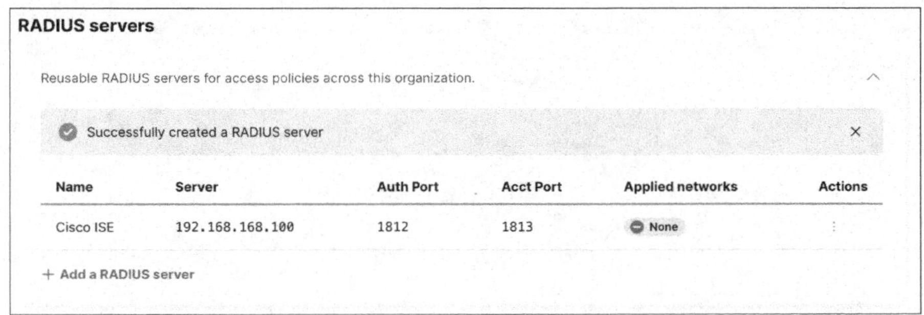

Figure 7-64 *Successful Addition of an Organization-Wide RADIUS Server in Meraki Dashboard*

The addition of the organization-wide RADIUS server is now complete.

Creating a Policy Set for Wired and Wireless 802.1X in Cisco ISE

Policy sets allow administrators to have different access policies for different use cases. In our example, we use policy sets to independently control each of the access methods: wired, wireless, and AnyConnect VPN.

Follow these steps to add a policy set for Meraki wireless:

Step 1. In Cisco ISE, navigate to **Menu > Policy > Policy Sets.**

On the **Policy Sets** page shown in Figure 7-65, you can see a default policy and an existing policy for Meraki AnyConnect VPN. Click the blue **+** to the left of **Status** (leftmost column heading) to add a new policy set.

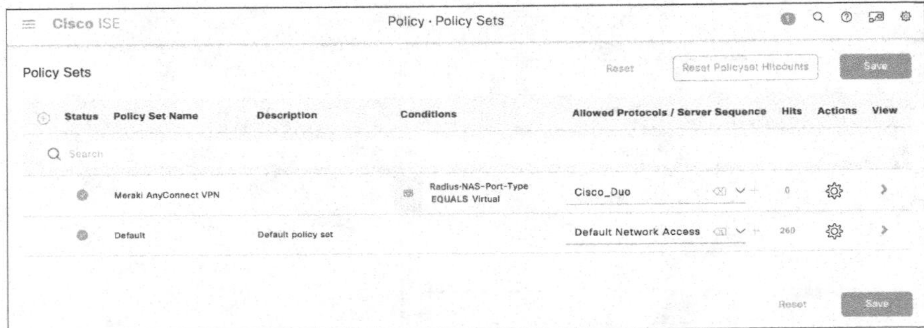

Figure 7-65 *Adding a Policy Set for Meraki Wired and Wireless on the Policy Sets Page in Cisco ISE*

Step 2. Select the policy set name that's just been added (**New Policy Set 1**), press the Delete key, and enter a name that is meaningful to you. In the example shown in Figure 7-66, we've added a policy set called **Meraki Wired and Wireless.**

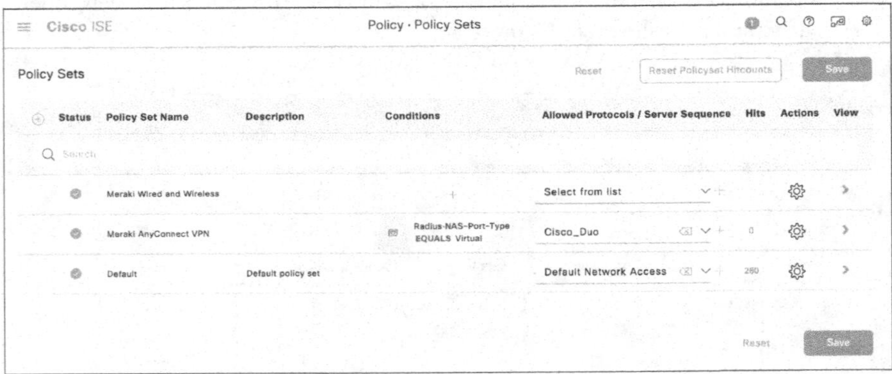

Figure 7-66 *Renaming the Meraki Wireless Policy Set Name in Cisco ISE*

Step 3. Click the **+** under **Conditions** for the new row that's been added. This brings up the **Conditions Studio** window (see Figure 7-67 and Figure 7-68). Click the **X** top-right corner to close the help screen.

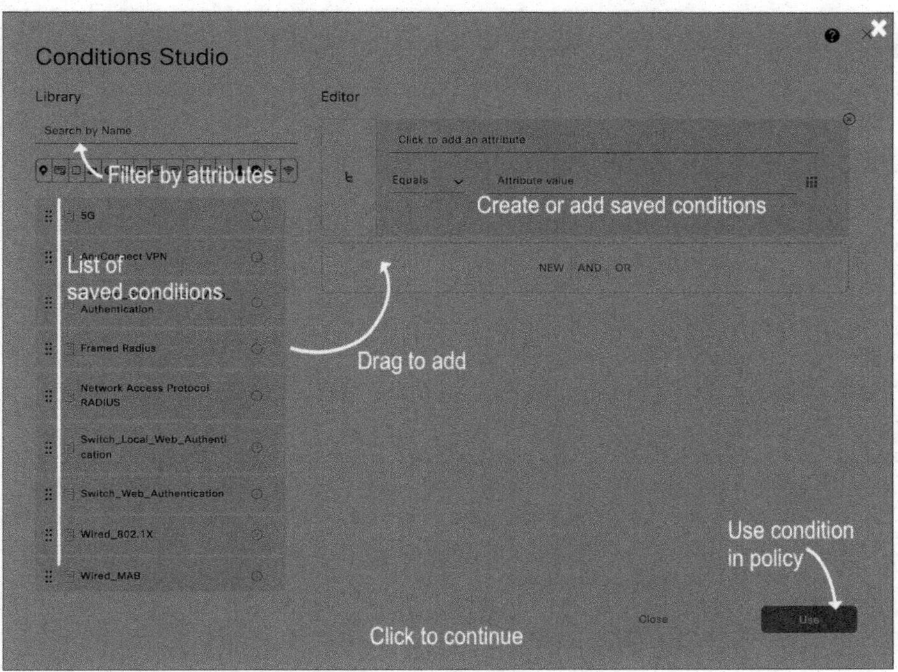

Figure 7-67 *The Conditions Studio Help Page in Cisco ISE*

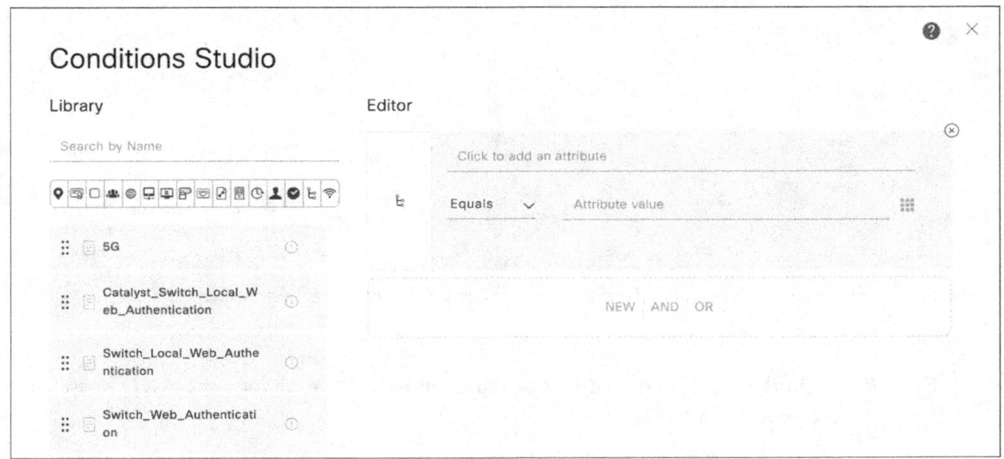

Figure 7-68 *The Conditions Studio Window in Cisco ISE*

Step 4. In the **Search by Name** field, type **wireless**. Drag the **Wireless_802.1X** condition to where you can see **NEW | AND | OR** on the right side, as shown in Figure 7-69.

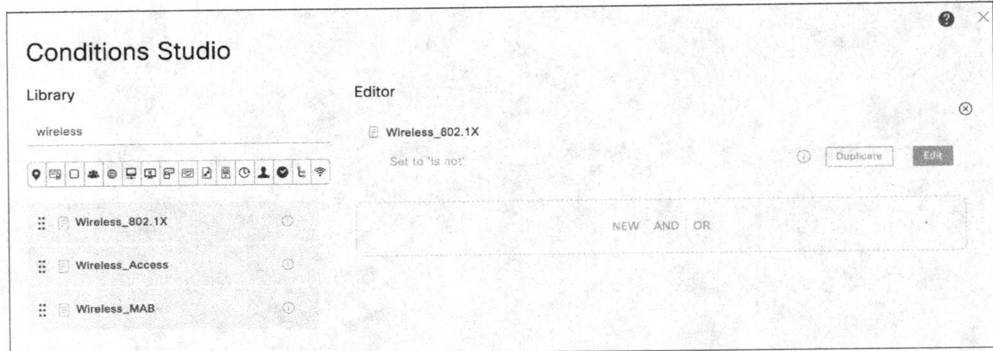

Figure 7-69 *Selecting the Wireless_802.1X Condition in the Conditions Studio*

Step 5. If two access methods are authenticated in the same way, they can share a policy set, simplifying the overall ISE policy. You need to add another library object to this condition so that the same policy set can be used for wired and wireless. On the **Editor** pane on the right (see Figure 7-70), where you can see **NEW | AND | OR**, click **OR**.

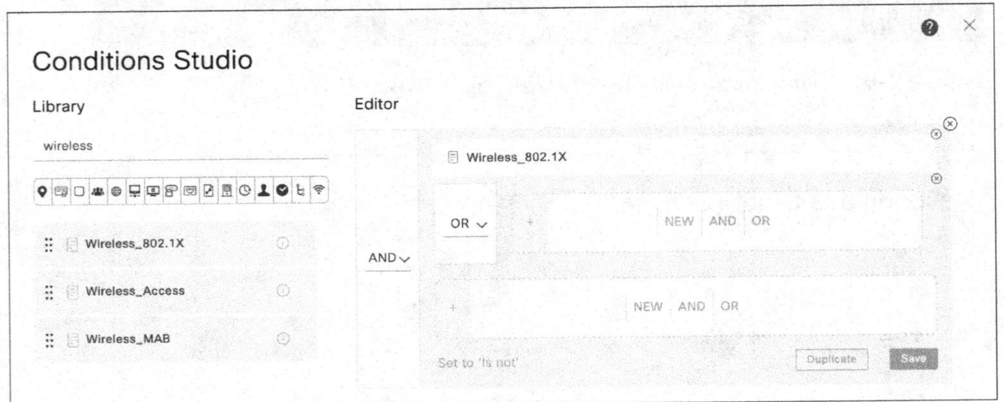

Figure 7-70 *Preparing to Add a Second Library Object to the New Condition in Cisco ISE*

Step 6. On the left side of the **Editor** pane, under **Editor**, change the **AND** drop-down menu to **OR**.

The top **NEW | AND | OR** box now has a red dotted line around it. You need to remove it, so click the circle with an x closest to the right corner of the top

NEW | AND | OR box. The Conditions Studio window should now look like Figure 7-71.

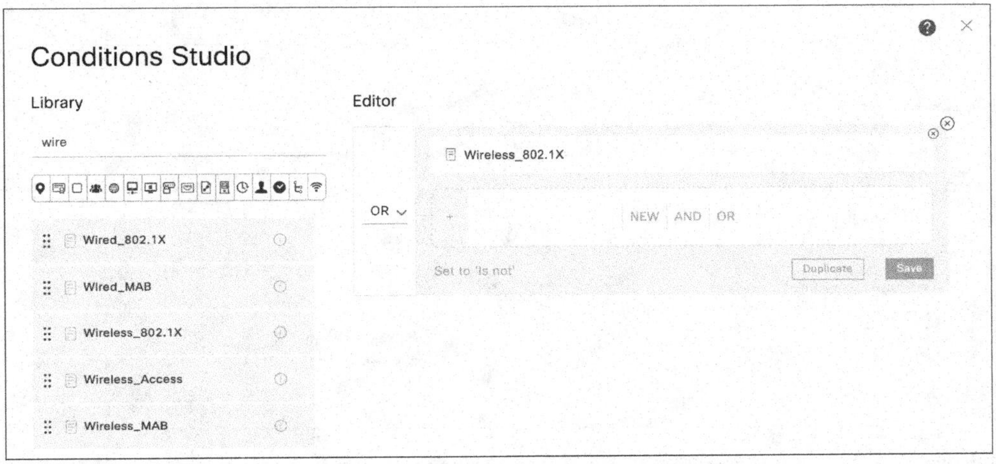

Figure 7-71 *Adding the OR Logic to the New Condition in Cisco ISE*

Step 7. Drag the **Wired_802.1X** condition to where you can see **NEW | AND | OR** just above **Save** on the right side.

The Conditions Studio page should now look like Figure 7-72. If so, scroll down and click **Use.**

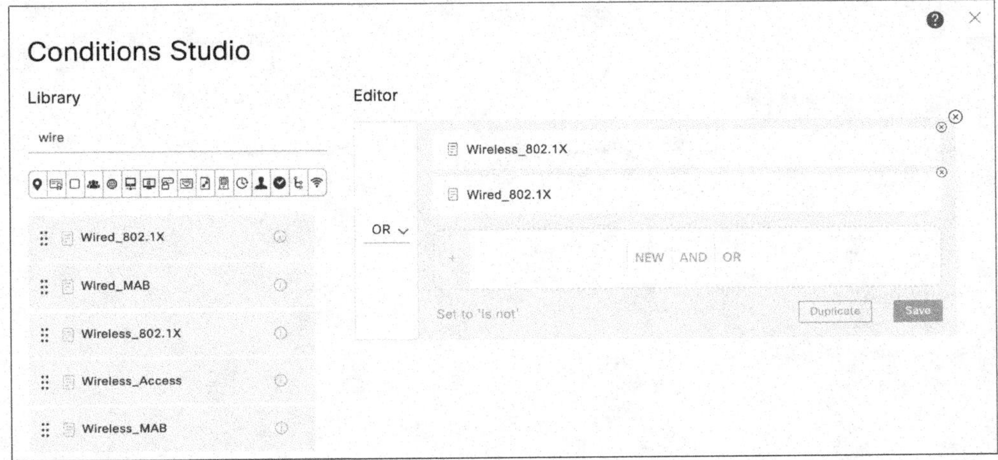

Figure 7-72 *Adding the Wired_802.1X Condition in the Conditions Studio*

Step 8. Back on the **Policy Sets** page, the Meraki Wired and Wireless policy set should look like Figure 7-73. From the **Allowed Protocols / Server Sequence** drop-down menu, select **Default Network Access.** Click **Save.**

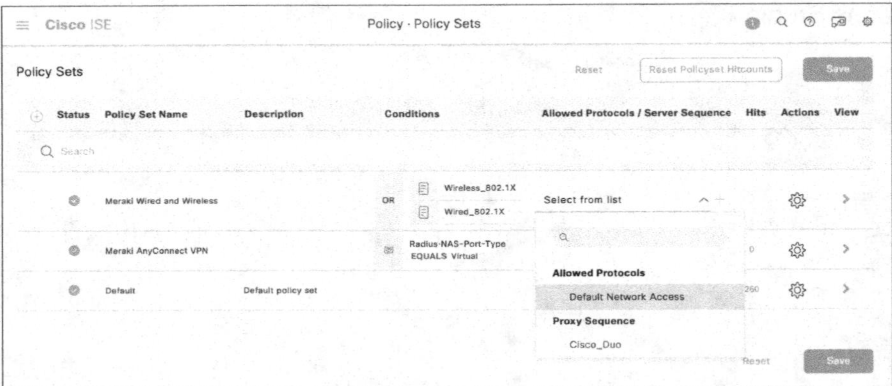

Figure 7-73 *Configuring the Allowed Protocols for Wired and Wireless on the Policy Sets Page in Cisco ISE*

Configuring an Authentication Policy in Cisco ISE

Step 1. If you're not already on the Policy Sets page in ISE, navigate to **Menu > Policy > Policy Sets.** Find the policy set for Meraki Wired and Wireless and click the > icon under the **View** column to see the results shown in Figure 7-74.

Figure 7-74 *Navigating to the Authentication Policy on the Wired and Wireless Policy in Cisco ISE*

Step 2. Expand **Authentication Policy (1).**

a. In the **Use** column, select the Active Directory server added earlier from the drop-down menu, as shown in Figure 7-75.

b. Click **Save.**

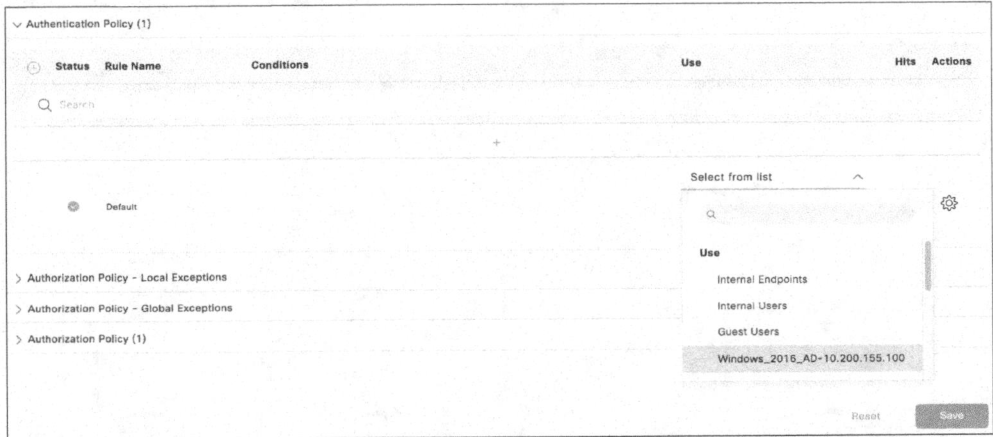

Figure 7-75 *Adding an Active Directory Server to the Wired and Wireless Authentication Policy in Cisco ISE*

You've now completed the configuration of the authentication policy on the wired and wireless policy set. You can find out more about Cisco ISE authentication policies from the configuration guide at https://www.cisco.com/c/en/us/td/docs/security/ise/3-2/admin_guide/b_ise_admin_3_2/b_ISE_admin_32_segmentation.html#c_auth_overview.

Configuring an Authorization Policy in Cisco ISE

Step 1. The default authorization policy is to deny access. Therefore, the next step is to configure an authorization policy that will permit authenticated users to connect.

a. Still on the same Policy Sets page as in Figure 7-74, expand **Authorization Policy (1).**

b. Click the sprocket icon on the right side of the **Default** row and select **Insert New Row Above**, as shown in Figure 7-76.

Step 2. Click the **+** icon in the **Conditions** column to open the **Conditions Studio**, as shown in Figure 7-77.

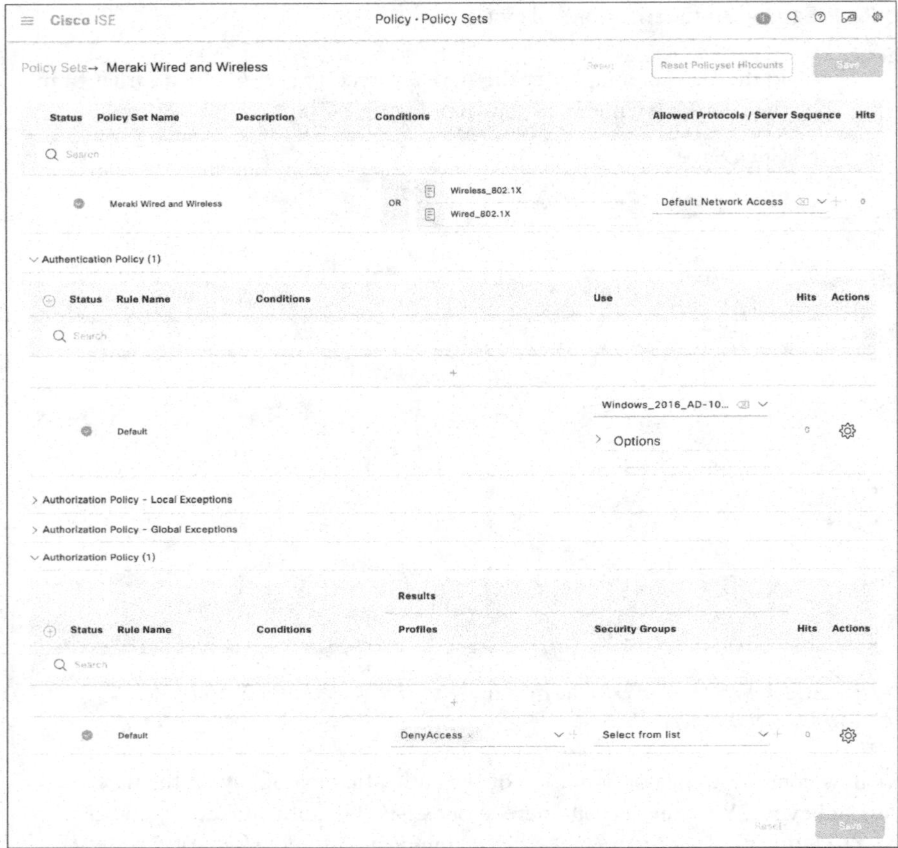

Figure 7-76 *Adding a New Authorization Policy to the Meraki Wired and Wireless Policy Set*

Figure 7-77 *Adding a Condition to a New Wired and Wireless Authorization Rule in Cisco ISE*

Step 3. In the **Editor** pane, click the **Click to Add an Attribute** line, and then click the icon for **Identity Group**, as shown in Figure 7-78.

In the **Dictionary** column, click the name of Active Directory server added earlier. In this case, it is the one with the name starting with **Windows_2016_AD-10.20...** with the Attribute **ExternalGroups**.

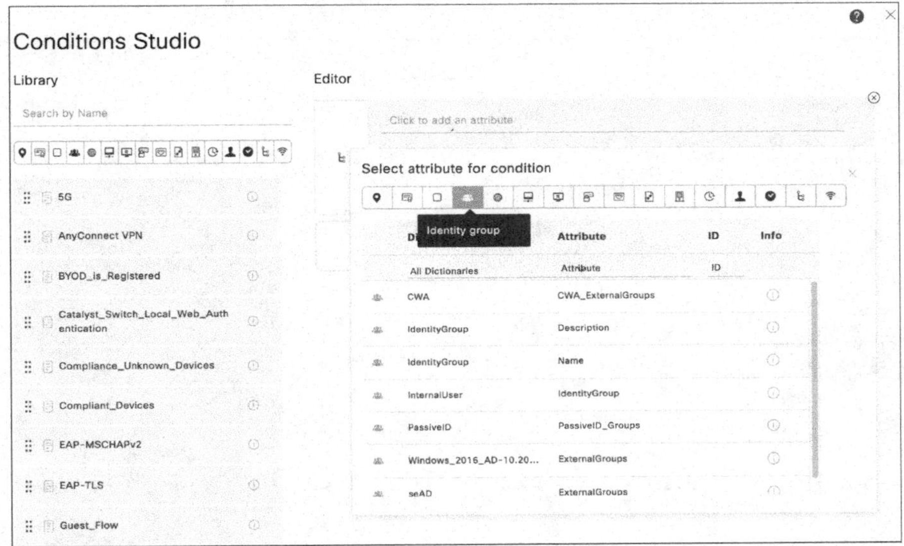

Figure 7-78 *Adding an Identity Group as a Condition on an Authorization Rule in Cisco ISE*

Step 4. To the right of **Equals**, click **Choose from List or Type** and select the **Network Access** group from the drop-down menu. Figure 7-79 shows what the Editor pane should look like after you have made this selection. Scroll down and click **Use**.

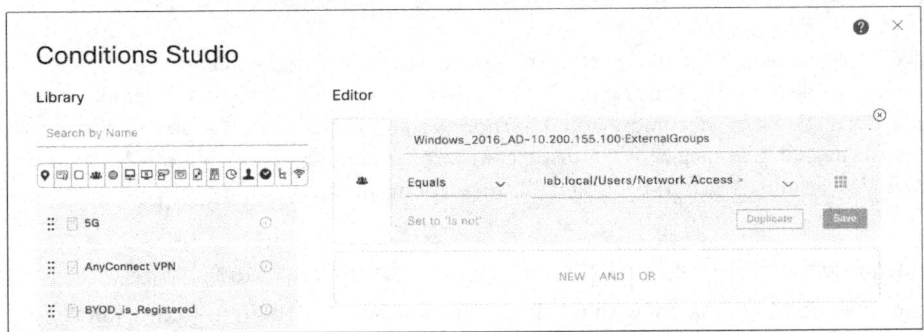

Figure 7-79 *Adding an AD Group as a Condition on an Authorization Rule in Cisco ISE*

Step 5. Back on the **Policy Sets > Meraki Wired and Wireless** page, select **PermitAccess** from the **Profiles** drop-down menu for the new authorization rule, as shown in Figure 7-80.

   a. If you want to, you can rename this rule to something more meaningful.

   b. Click **Save**.

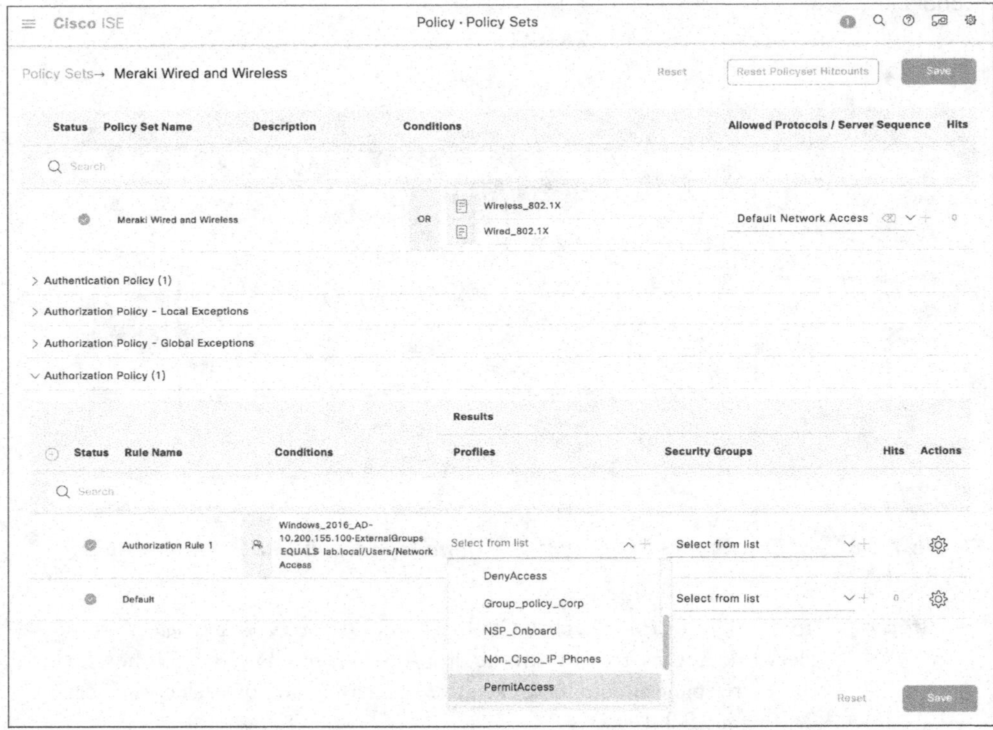

Figure 7-80 *Setting Permit Access on the New Authorization Rule in Cisco ISE*

You've now completed the basic setup of RADIUS for wired and wireless 802.1X. This setup is suitable for 802.1X using the PEAP authentication protocol, as we demonstrate in Chapter 8. You can learn more about authorization policies in the Cisco ISE configuration guide available at https://www.cisco.com/c/en/us/td/docs/security/ise/3-2/admin_guide/b_ise_admin_3_2/b_ISE_admin_32_segmentation.html#c_authz_policy.

Confirming Functionality of RADIUS Authentication on Wireless

Unlike other access methods, with wireless you can test RADIUS right from within Dashboard without the need for a wireless client. You need to have at least one access point configured because Dashboard will check that the access point can reach the RADIUS server, which in this case is Cisco ISE. If you have multiple access points in your network, Dashboard will test that each of them can reach the RADIUS server.

In Chapter 8, we guide you through how to configure the network side of this configuration and how to test against an SSID using a wireless client. For now, we just want to verify that the RADIUS infrastructure can authenticate users with minimal network infrastructure deployed.

Follow these steps to verify that RADIUS authentication is functioning correctly:

Step 1. In Meraki Dashboard, navigate to **Wireless > Access Control**, as shown in Figure 7-81.

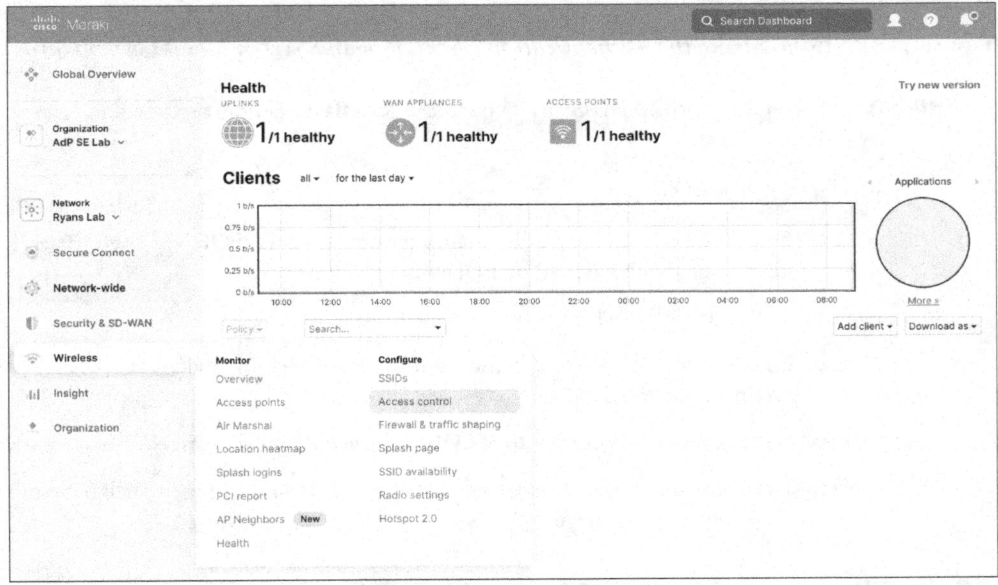

Figure 7-81 *Navigating to Wireless Access Control in Meraki Dashboard*

Step 2. Select an SSID from the **SSID** drop-down menu at the top of the **Access Control** page. This SSID must have Layer 2 (L2) connectivity to the neighboring device. Typically, this means a matching VLAN configuration between the AP and the switch it is connected to. Scroll down to **Security** and select **Enterprise With**. Underneath **Enterprise With**, ensure **My RADIUS Server** is selected, as shown in Figure 7-82.

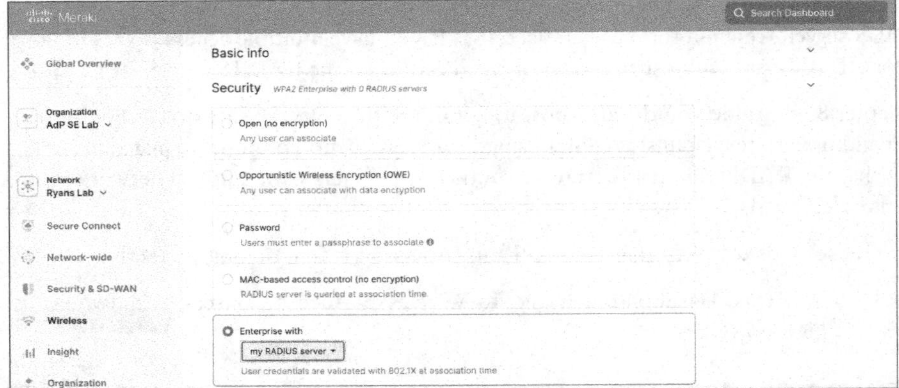

Figure 7-82 *Configuring the Authentication Method on an SSID in Meraki Dashboard*

Step 3. Scroll down to **RADIUS** and expand the **RADIUS** section, as shown in Figure 7-83.

a. Click **Add Server.**

b. Enter the IP address or fully qualified domain name (FQDN) of the Cisco ISE server in the **Host IP or FQDN** field.

c. Set the **Port** to 1812.

d. Enter the RADIUS secret being used between Meraki devices and Cisco ISE in the **Secret** field.

e. Under **Test Connectivity to RADIUS Server At**, click **Cancel.**

f. The **Done** button then becomes visible. Click **Done**, and then click **Save** at the bottom of the page.

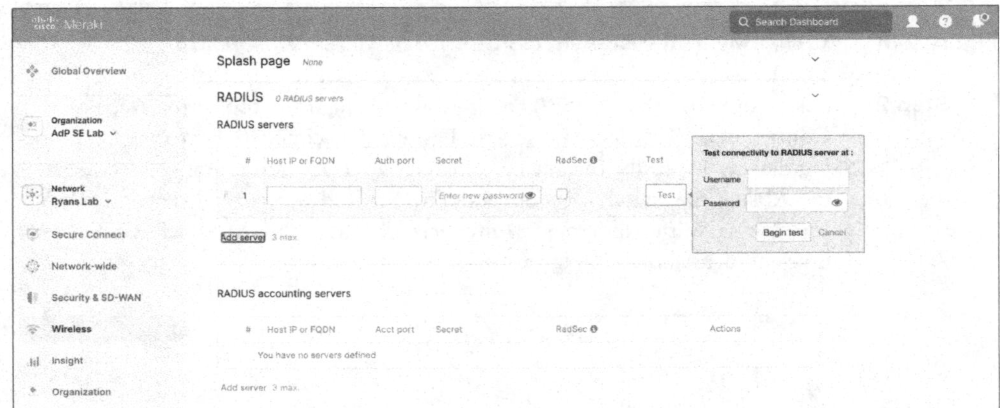

Figure 7-83 *Adding a RADIUS Server on an SSID in Meraki Dashboard*

Step 4. You're now ready to test the RADIUS setup.

a. Click **Test**, as shown in Figure 7-84.

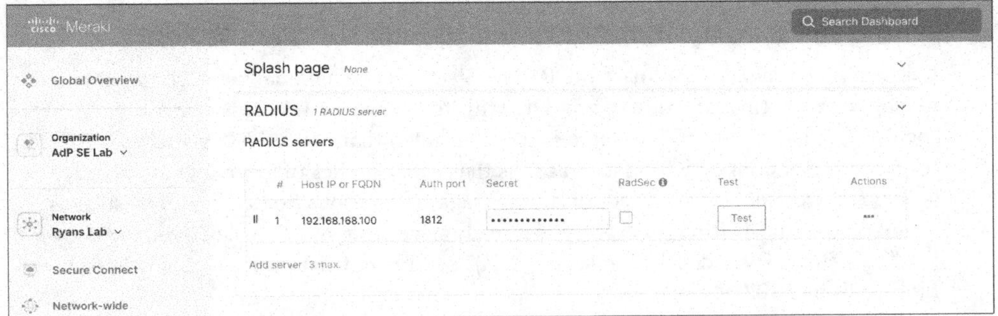

Figure 7-84 *Configuring a RADIUS Server on an SSID in Meraki Dashboard*

b. Enter the username and password in their respective fields; then click **Begin Test**, as shown in Figure 7-85.

Figure 7-85 *Conducting a RADIUS Test on a Wireless SSID in Meraki Dashboard*

Voila! The test was successful, confirming that you're able to authenticate wireless users against RADIUS, as Figure 7-86 illustrates.

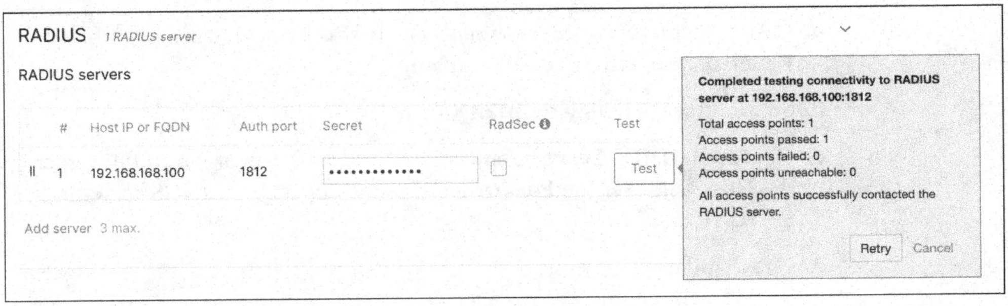

Figure 7-86 *A Successful RADIUS Test in Meraki Dashboard*

You've completed the basic RADIUS configuration for wireless. In addition, you successfully verified that you're able to authenticate wireless users. For more information on how to configure the Meraki wireless network, refer to Chapter 8.

Confirming Functionality of RADIUS Authentication for Wired 802.1X

Our aim here is again to validate the RADIUS setup with minimal network infrastructure deployed. With this intention in mind, for this test we use a LAN port on a Meraki MX security appliance. In production, it is recommended that Meraki MS switches are used for all end-user connectivity. The reason is that MS switches offer greater support for access features such as PoE, security group tags, and various 802.1X features, such as Change of Authorization (CoA). If you already have your switches deployed, head over to the "Zero Trust (Wired and Wireless Dot1X)" section in Chapter 8 to learn how to configure and test 802.1X.

> **Note** In the Meraki MX range, 802.1X is supported only on the MX64/65(W), MX67/68(C/W), and Z3(C) teleworker gateways.

In this example, we utilize Protected EAP (PEAP) between the supplicant (client) and the RADIUS server. Follow these steps to test RADIUS for wired access:

Step 1. RADIUS servers must be configured at the port level on Meraki MX. Organization-wide RADIUS servers are not currently supported.

   a. In Meraki Dashboard, navigate to **Security & SD-WAN** > **Configure** > **Addressing & VLANs** (see Figure 7-87).

   b. Ensure that this MX is in the default **Routed** mode.

   c. Under **Routing**, ensure that the **LAN Setting** is set to **VLANs**.

Step 2. Under **Per-port VLAN Settings**, select the port(s) where 802.1X is required for testing and click **Edit**.

Step 3. On the **Configure MX LAN ports** pop-up window, ensure the configuration is as follows (see Figure 7-88):

   a. Ensure that the ports are enabled. The first option, confusingly labeled **Enabled**, needs to be set to **Enabled**.

   b. Set the **Access Policy** to **802.1X**.

   c. Next to **RADIUS Servers**, enter the IP address of your Cisco ISE server in the **Host** field. Set the **Port** to **1812** and enter your RADIUS secret in the **Secret** field.

   d. Click **Update**.

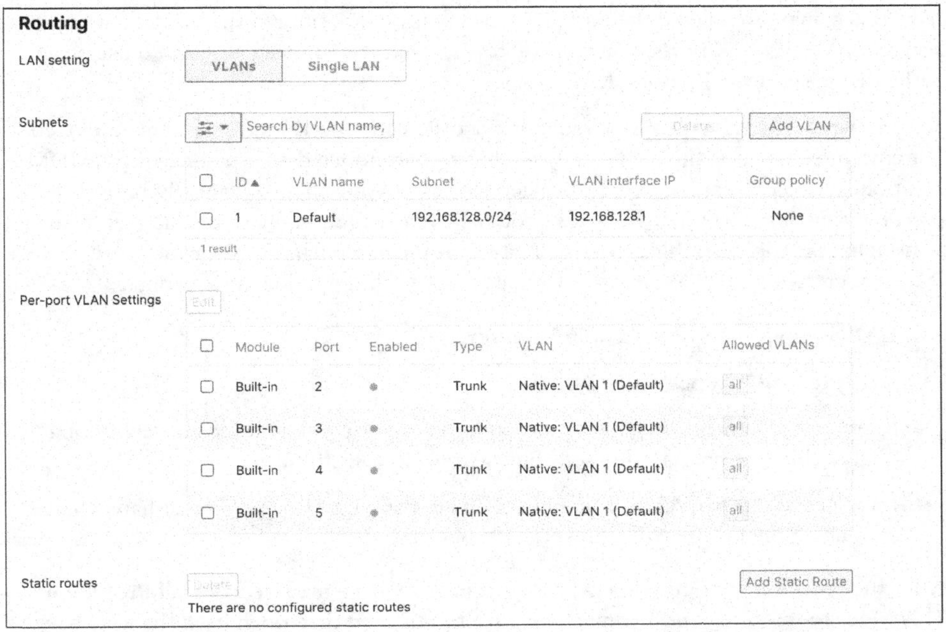

Figure 7-87 *The Routing Section of the Addressing & VLANs Page for a Cisco MX Appliance*

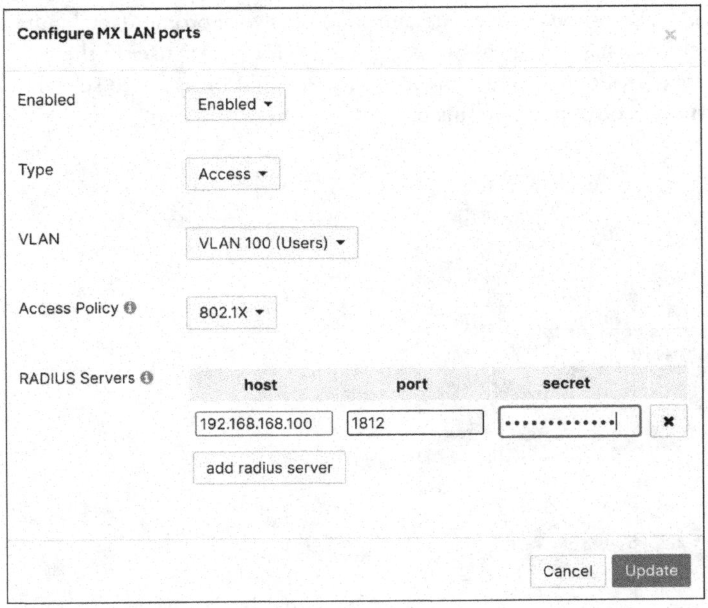

Figure 7-88 *Editing the 802.1X Port Configuration on a Cisco MX Security Appliance*

Now that you've completed the basic RADIUS configuration for authenticating wired access on Meraki MX ports, you're ready for the next step: testing that wired users can authenticate successfully using RADIUS.

Testing wired 802.1X with a Mac requires a profile with 802.1X settings to be imported. For enterprise devices, this is typically a job for your mobile device management (MDM) solution, such as Meraki Systems Manager. However, you can also manually import the profile for testing purposes. To test without an MDM solution, use a profile editor, such as iMazing or Apple Configurator, to create a profile and push it to your local device. In iMazing, create an 802.1X Ethernet: Global policy with the following attributes:

- **EAP Setup Modes** set to **Login Window.**
- **Accepted EAP Types** set to **PEAP.**
- (Optional) Username and password. Under **Password,** you will see an alert stating "This field must have a value set," but the profile will still work.
- **Interface** set to **No Value.** You will see an alert stating "This field must have a value set," again the profile will still work without this.

After the profile is configured in iMazing, from the **File** menu, select **Install Profile on This Mac.** To install on another machine, save the file and then open it on the Mac where you'll be testing 802.1X.

Follow these steps to verify that wired RADIUS authentication is functioning correctly:

Step 1. Connect the test PC or laptop to an Ethernet port on the MX that is configured for 802.1X. You should see a username and password prompt (see Figure 7-89). Enter the username and password credentials for an AD user in the Network Access group. If you're using a Mac, you might be asked to select a certificate to use; you can ignore this prompt.

Figure 7-89 *The Login Prompt on macOS for a Client Connecting to the LAN Using 802.1X Authentication*

Step 2. If you are prompted to accept the Cisco ISE server-side certificate, accept this by clicking **Continue** (see Figure 7-90). You should now be connected to the network. In Figure 7-91, the event log entries from Meraki Dashboard show a user physically connecting to a port, completing the EAP authentication to RADIUS, and then being allowed onto the network.

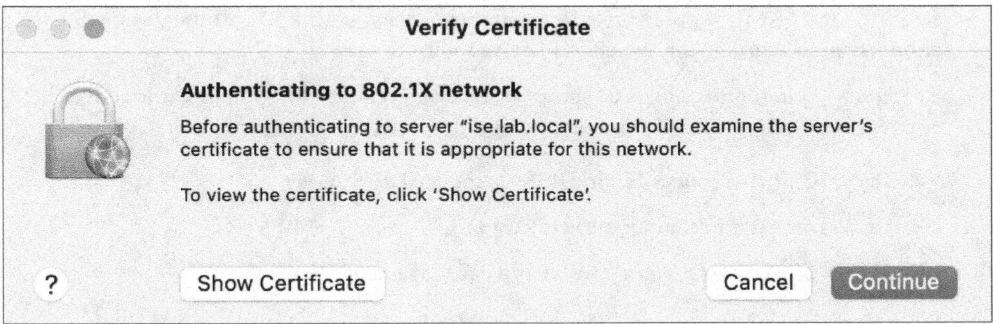

Figure 7-90 *The Verify Certificate Prompt to Accept the Server-Side Certificate for Wired 802.1X on macOS*

Event log for security appliances ▾

Client: Any Before: 03/17/2024 10:43 (AEDT)

Event type include: All Event type ignore: None

Search Reset filters

Download as ▾ « newer older »

Time (AEDT) ▾	Client	Category	Event type	Details
Mar 17 10:42:57		Status	Ethernet port carrier change	device: port3, carrier: false
Mar 17 10:42:10	RYCHANEY-M-6X1J	802.1X	802.1X authentication	port: 4, identity: hayden@lab.local
Mar 17 10:42:10	RYCHANEY-M-6X1J	802.1X	Successful authentication (EAP success)	port: 4, identity: hayden@lab.local
Mar 17 10:42:10	RYCHANEY-M-6X1J	802.1X	RADIUS response	port: 4, rtt: 0.064 ms

Figure 7-91 *Event Log Showing Successful 802.1x Connection to a Meraki Wired Network*

Now that you've completed the tasks required to verify that RADIUS authentication is working for wired users, you can learn more about how to configure security on the wired network in Chapter 8.

RADIUS Configuration for AnyConnect VPN with Duo MFA

Industry standards are shifting to require stronger controls in relation to remote network access. This can be seen in the changes going from PCI DSS 3.2.1 to version 4.0. In PCI version 4.0, MFA is now required for all remote access, and not just access to sensitive areas. Therefore, it is highly recommended to use multifactor authentication when deploying a remote access solution.

Like wired and wired access, RADIUS can also be used to authenticate VPN users. Earlier in this chapter, we showed you how to configure SAML for authenticating AnyConnect users. In Meraki Dashboard, RADIUS is supported for both client VPN and AnyConnect VPN, whereas SAML currently is supported only with AnyConnect. Both RADIUS and SAML support multifactor authentication with VPN, although only SAML supports inline enrollment, which is a key usability feature.

The intention in this section is to show what an on-premises solution might look like. The applications used as part of this solution and the functions they provide are

- Cisco Identity Services Engine (ISE) as the RADIUS server
- Cisco Duo for multifactor authentication
- Microsoft Active Directory for identity management

When using RADIUS for authentication, Cisco Duo requires an on-premises application called Duo Authentication Proxy. Duo Authentication Proxy receives RADIUS requests, queries AD, and syncs the users and groups with Active Directory. Duo Authentication Proxy can be deployed at various parts of the authentication chain. However, this does have a bearing on the features that can be supported (such as Change of Authorization, or CoA). We recommend deploying Duo Authentication Proxy, as shown in Figure 7-92, to maximize the capabilities supported.

> **Note** In this example, LDAP is used as the protocol to communicate with Active Directory.

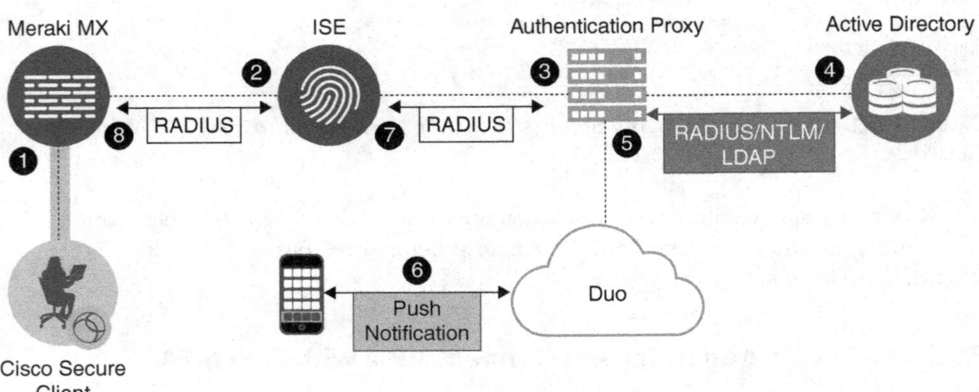

Figure 7-92 *AnyConnect VPN on Meraki MX with Cisco ISE, Cisco Duo, and Active Directory*

A number of tasks are required to configure RADIUS for VPN access. They have been summarized into the high-level tasks in the following list. If you'd like to complete this setup in stages, we have also grouped the steps required under these headings throughout the remainder of this section.

Cisco Duo

1. Configuring Duo Authentication Proxy
2. Configuring AD Sync in Duo Admin Panel
3. Encrypting passwords in Duo Authentication Proxy (Optional, but recommended)
4. Enrolling users with Cisco Duo

Cisco Identity Services Engine (ISE)

5. Configuring Cisco Duo as an external RADIUS server in Cisco ISE
6. Adding network access devices (NADs) in Cisco ISE. This step was previously covered in the "Configuring Cisco Identity Services Engine (ISE)" section.
7. Creating a policy set

Meraki Dashboard

8. Configuring RADIUS for AnyConnect VPN

Configuring Duo Authentication Proxy

Step 1. Log in to Cisco Duo Admin Panel (https://admin.duosecurity.com/login).

Step 2. Navigate to **Applications** and click **Protect an Application**, as shown in Figure 7-93.

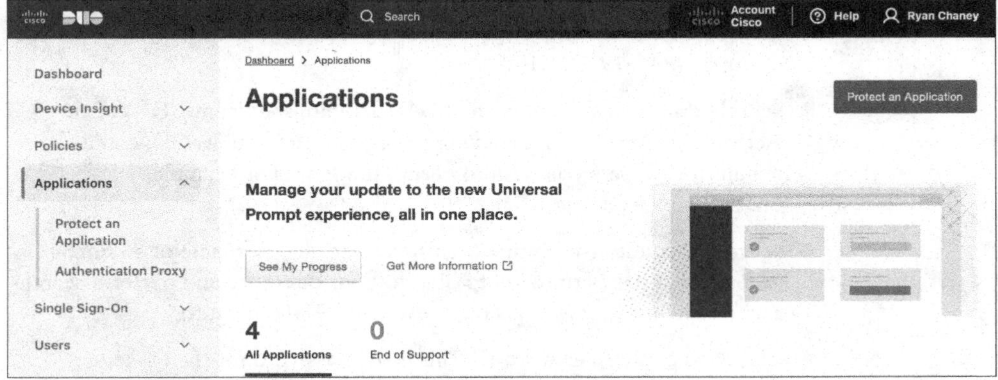

Figure 7-93 *Adding a New Application for Cisco ISE in Cisco Duo Admin Panel*

Step 3. In the **Filter by Keywords** field, search for "Cisco ISE RADIUS."

a. Click the **Protect** button corresponding to this application, as shown in Figure 7-94.

b. The **Cisco ISE RADIUS** application page opens. Leave this web browser tab open because you need the values under **Details** for configuring the Duo Authentication Proxy in the next step.

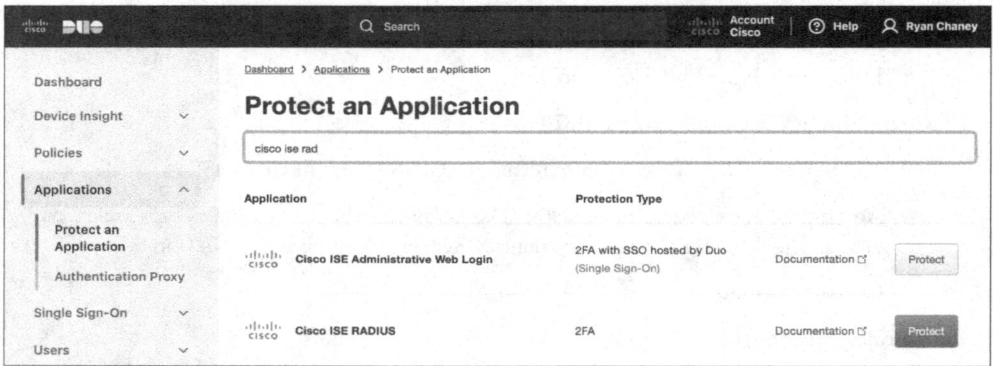

Figure 7-94 *Searching for the Cisco ISE RADIUS Application in Cisco Duo Admin Panel*

Step 4. Open the **Duo Authentication Proxy Manager** application that you installed as part of the prerequisite steps.

In the **Configure: Authproxy.cfg** pane on the left, configure the following:

Under **[ad_client]**, add/edit the following:

- **host=** This refers to the IP address of your Active Directory server. For example, host=192.168.168.3.
- **search_dn=** This refers to the LDAP distinguished name (DN) of the Active Directory/LDAP container or organizational unit (OU) containing all of the users you wish to permit to log in. For example, search_dn=DC=lab,DC=local.
- **search_account_username=** This refers to the username of a domain account that has permission to bind to your directory and perform searches. For example, service_account_username=Administrator.
- **search_account_password=** This is the password for the preceding account. For example, search_account_password=XXXXXXXX.

Under **[radius_server_auto]**, add/edit the following:

- **ikey=** Copy the **Integration Key** from the **Cisco ISE RADIUS** application page here.
- **skey=** Copy the **Secret Key** from the **Cisco ISE RADIUS** application page here.
- **api_host=** Copy the **API Hostname** from the **Cisco ISE RADIUS** application page here.
- **radius_ip_1=** This is the IP address for your Cisco ISE server.
- **radius_secret_1=** This is the RADIUS secret that you will configure in Cisco ISE.
- **failmode=** This determines the behavior if Duo Cloud is unavailable. This is either **safe**, which allows users if primary authentication succeeds, or **secure**, which rejects authentication attempts if Duo is unavailable.
- **client=ad_client** This links the RADIUS server config with the Active Directory configuration.
- **port=1812** The port on which to listen for incoming RADIUS access requests.

Note If you need to know more about configuring Duo Authentication Proxy, we strongly recommend that you refer to the guide at https://duo.com/docs/authproxy-reference.

Step 5. Still in the **Duo Authentication Proxy Manager** application, click **Validate** and scroll down to the bottom of the output on the right pane. Under **SUMMARY**, you should see "No issues detected," as shown in Figure 7-95. Click **Save**.

If Authentication Proxy is not already running, click the **Start Service** button.

You might notice that the passwords in the following figures are masked; we show you how to do this in a later step.

Configuring AD Sync in Duo Admin Panel

Configuring Automatic Directory syncing (AD Sync) is highly recommended; otherwise, users and groups in Duo would need to be managed manually, taking up a lot of unnecessary effort.

Step 1. To configure AD Sync, in **Duo Admin Panel**, navigate to **Users > Directory Sync.**

Click the **Add New Sync** drop-down menu and select **Active Directory**, as shown in Figure 7-96.

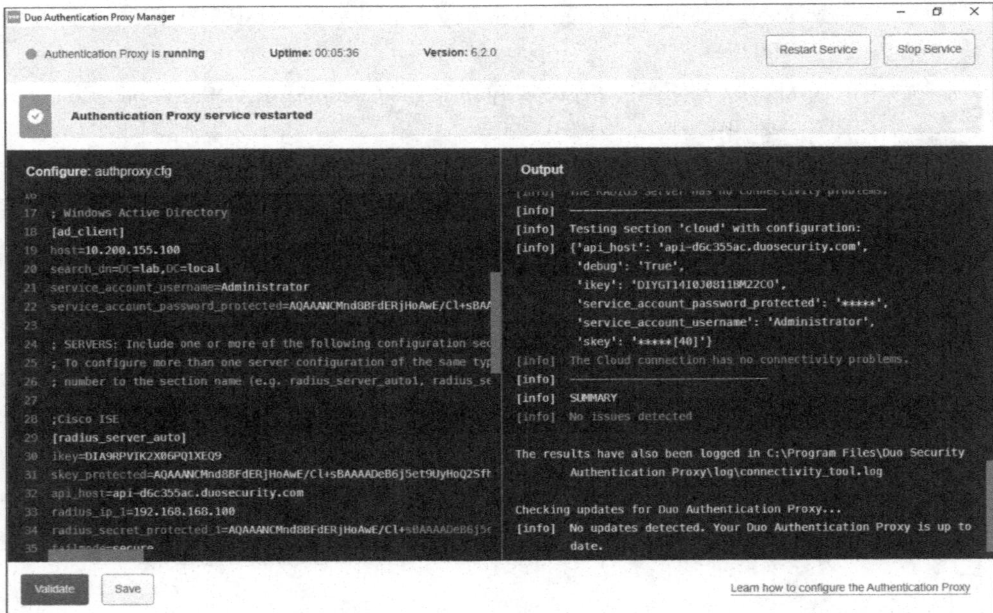

Figure 7-95 *AD and RADIUS Configuration in Duo Authentication Proxy Manager*

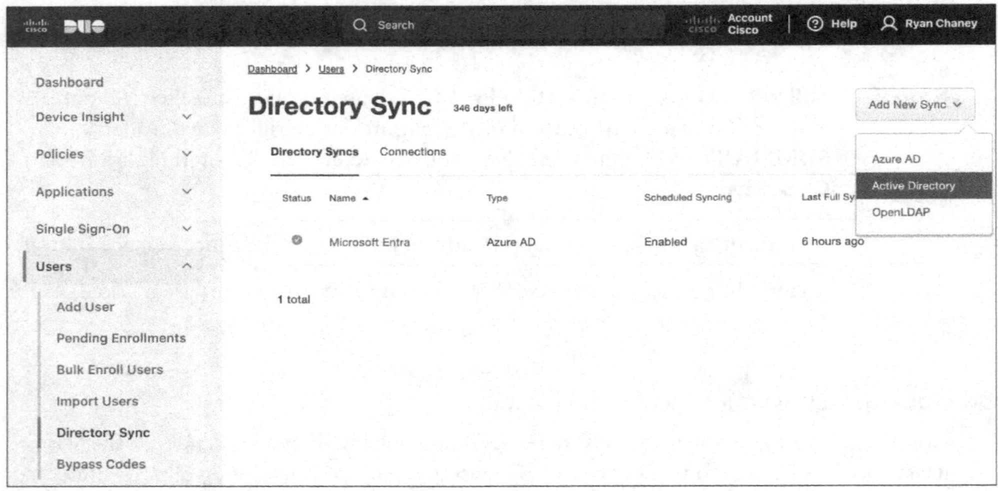

Figure 7-96 *Adding a New AD Sync in Cisco Duo Admin Panel*

Step 2. On the **New Active Directory Sync** page, click **Add New Connection** and then click **Continue**, as shown in Figure 7-97.

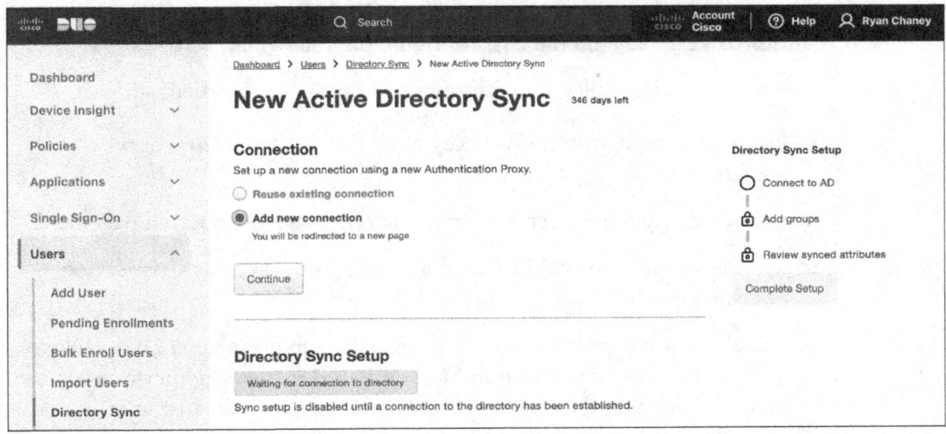

Figure 7-97 *Starting the Configuration of a New AD Sync in Cisco Duo Admin Panel*

Step 3. On the **AD Sync Connection** page, you see an additional integration and secret keys, as shown in Figure 7-98. These keys are used for AD sync. Keep this web browser tab open because you need to copy and paste the values to a new section in the Duo Authentication Proxy (authproxy) configuration.

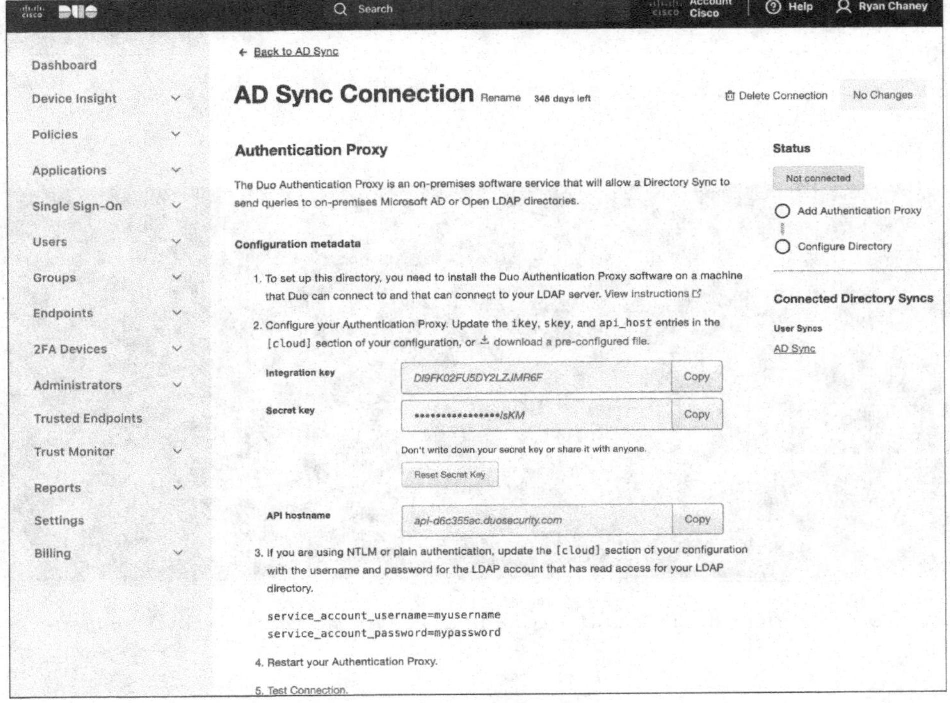

Figure 7-98 *The AD Sync Connection Page in Cisco Duo Admin Panel*

Step 4. Switch back to Duo Authentication Proxy Manager. In the **Configure: Authproxy.cfg** pane on the left, configure the following:

Add a new section called **[cloud]**, and underneath that heading, add

- **ikey=** Copy the **Integration Key** from the **AD Sync Connection** page here.
- **skey=** Copy the **Secret Key** from the **AD Sync Connection** page here.
- **api_host=** Copy the **API Hostname** from the **AD Sync Connection** page here.
- **search_account_username=** This refers to the username of a domain account that has permission to bind to your directory and perform searches. For example, service_account_username=Administrator.
- **search_account_password=** This is the password for the preceding account. For example, search_account_password=XXXXXXXX.

Click **Validate**, then **Save**, and then **Restart Service**. Once again, you should see "No issues detected" under **SUMMARY** in the **Output** pane, as shown in Figure 7-99.

You might notice that the passwords in the figures are masked; we show you how to do this in a later step.

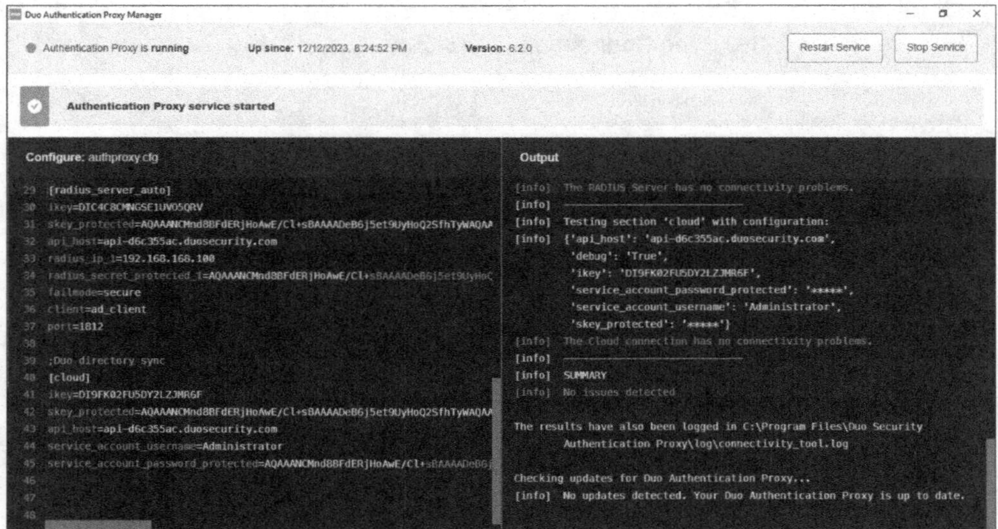

Figure 7-99 *Configuring the Cloud Section in Duo Authentication Proxy Manager*

Step 5. Switch back to the web browser tab open at the **AD Sync Connection** page in Duo Admin Panel (from Step 3). From the screen shown in Figure 7-100, do the following:

a. In the **Hostname or IP Address** field, enter the IP address for your Active Directory domain controller. This is the IP address the Duo Authentication Proxy talks to locally, you do not need to worry about reachability from the cloud to this IP address. You can add additional domain controllers by clicking **+ Add Domain Controller.**

b. In the **Port** field, enter the port that your Active Directory server is listening on. In the example, we've used LDAP on port 389.

c. Check the **Base DN** * is present and correct.

d. Click **Save** in the top right.

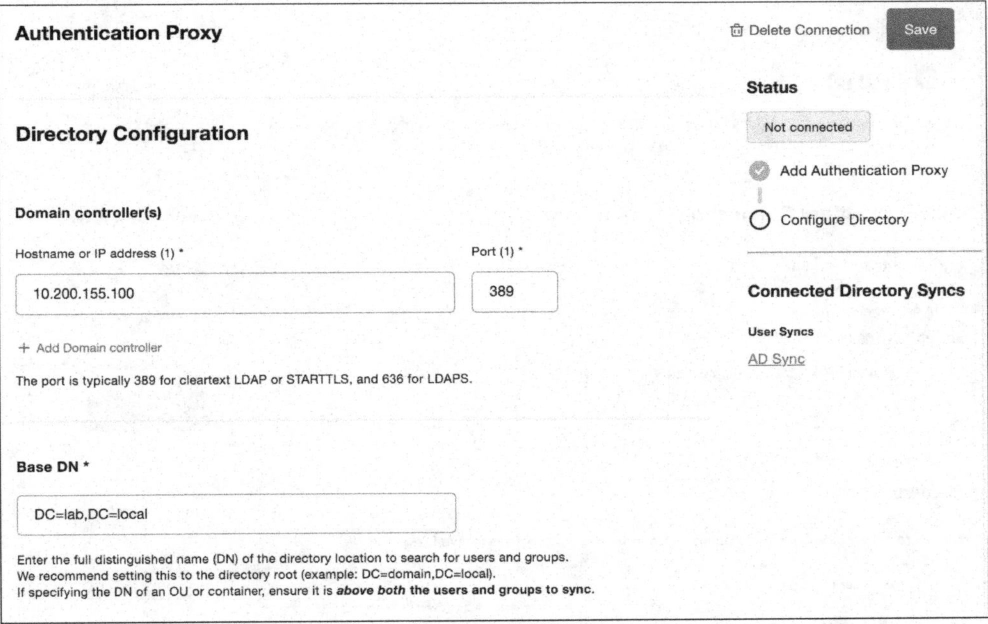

Figure 7-100 *Configuring the AD Sync Connection Page in Cisco Duo Admin Panel*

Step 6. Duo now checks that the values you have provided are correct. Then you should see the **Status** change to **Connected**, as shown in Figure 7-101.

Click **Back to AD Sync** at the top of the page.

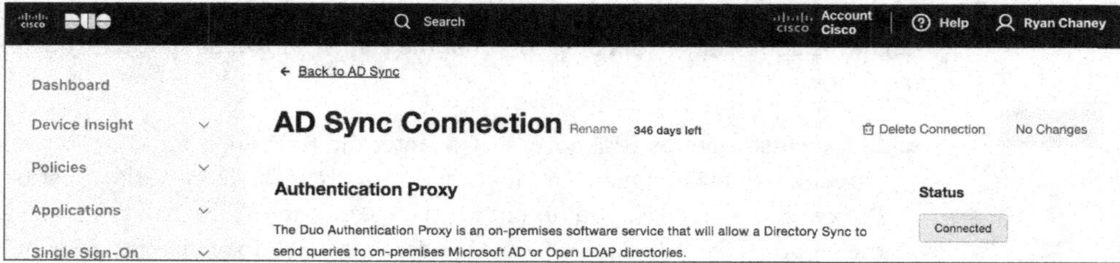

Figure 7-101 *Successful AD Connection in Cisco Duo Admin Panel*

Step 7. On the **AD Sync** page, under **Groups**, click into the **Select AD Groups** field and search for the **Network Access** group added earlier in Active Directory (or the group name you're using instead), as shown in Figure 7-102. Click the group name to select it.

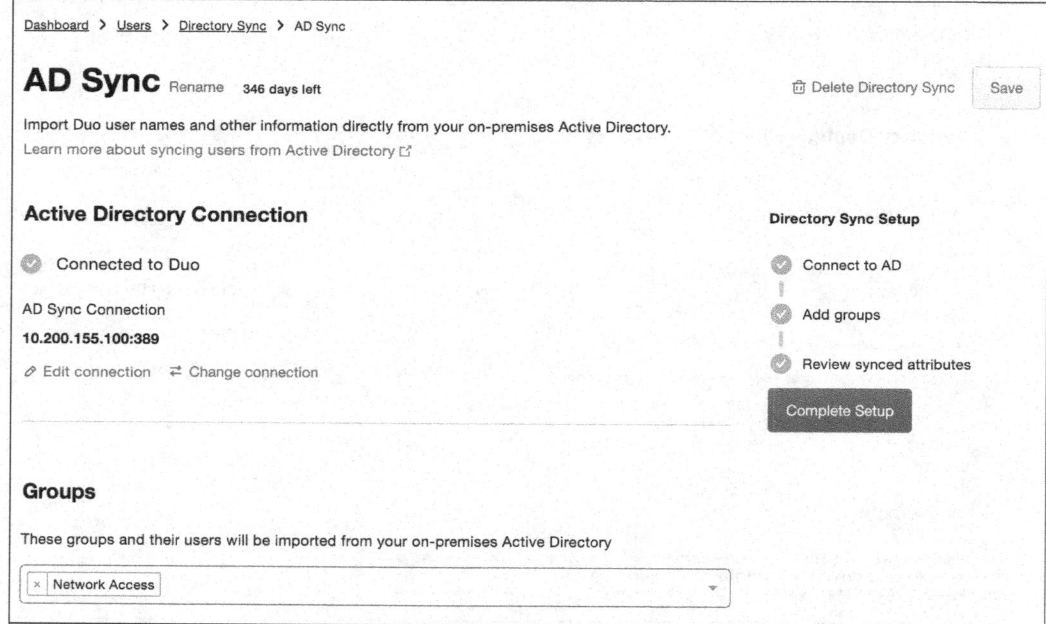

Figure 7-102 *Selecting the Groups to Sync on the AD Sync Page in Cisco Duo Admin Panel*

Step 8. Staying on the **AD Sync** page, scroll down to **Email** * and enter **userprincipalname**, as shown in Figure 7-103. Doing this avoids having to configure an email address for each user account in the Active Directory. Click **Save**.

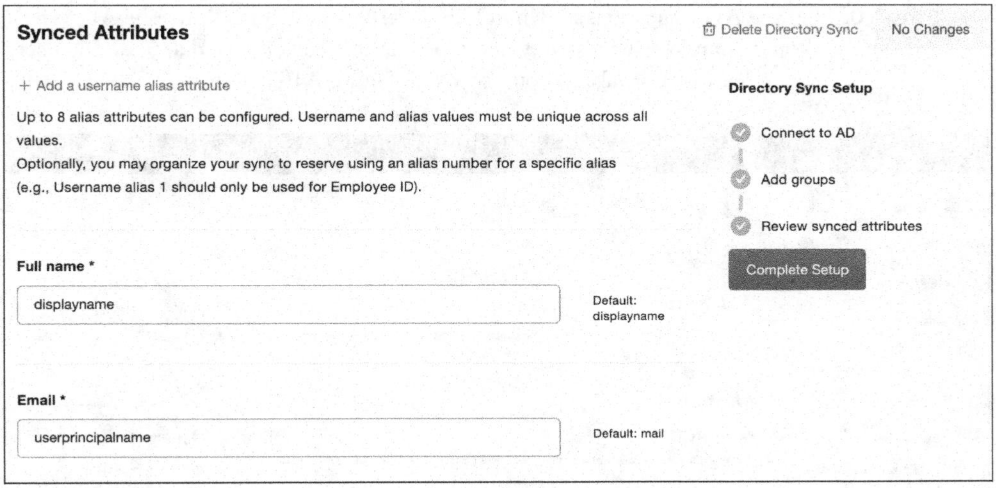

Figure 7-103 *Editing the Email Attribute on the AD Sync Page in Cisco Duo Admin Panel*

Step 9. You should now see the screen shown in Figure 7-104, indicating you're ready to complete the setup of the AD Sync. Click **Complete Setup**.

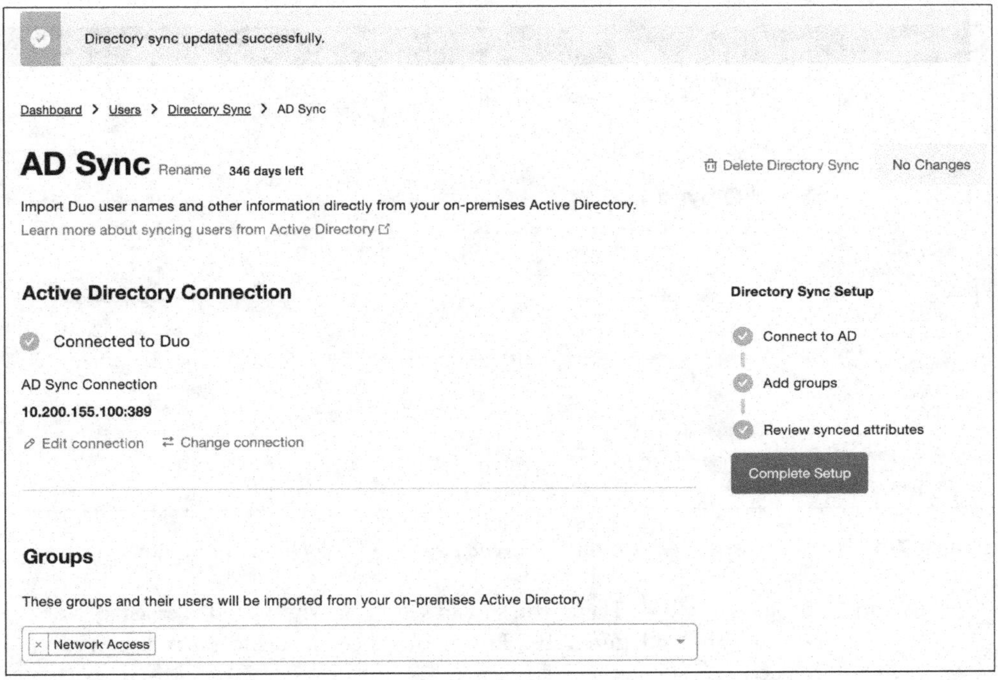

Figure 7-104 *Completing the AD Sync Setup in Cisco Duo Admin Panel*

Step 10. On the **AD Sync** page shown in Figure 7-105, click **Sync Now.** The AD Sync should complete successfully and report that it has imported at least one user and at least one group, as you can see in Figure 7-106.

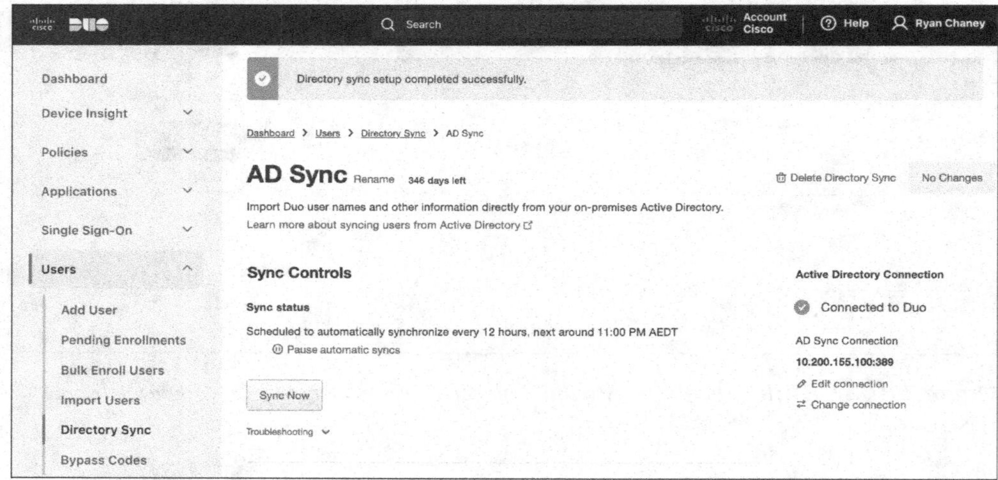

Figure 7-105 *Starting the Sync on the AD Sync Page in Cisco Duo Admin Panel*

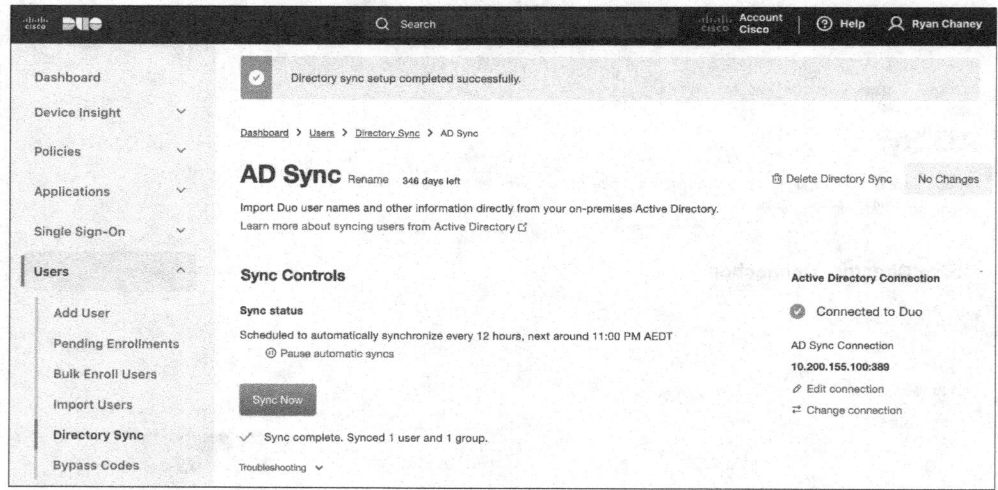

Figure 7-106 *Successful Sync on the AD Sync Page in Cisco Duo Admin Panel*

Step 11. Navigate to **Users.** There, you should see the newly synced user listed, as demonstrated in Figure 7-107. Ensure that their email address is displayed correctly.

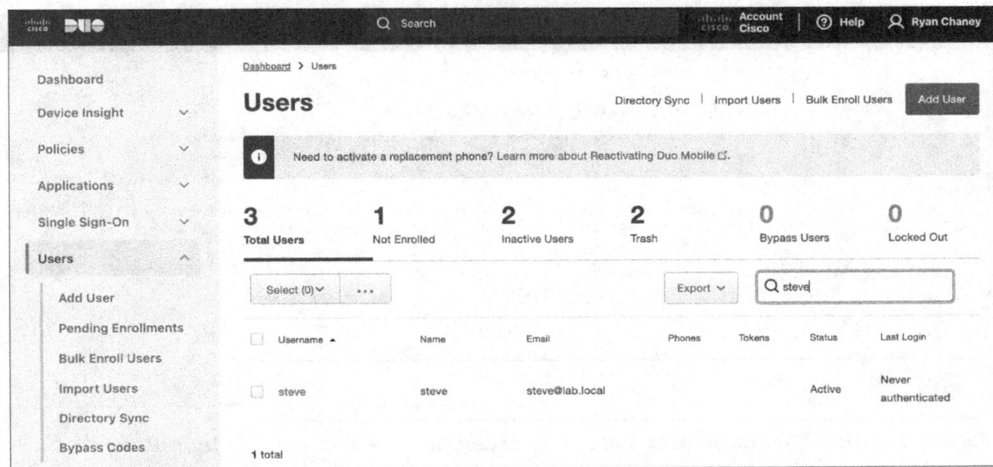

Figure 7-107 *Confirming That the AD Synced Users Are Present in Cisco Duo Admin Panel*

Step 12. Navigate to **Groups**. There, you should see the newly synced group listed, as demonstrated in Figure 7-108.

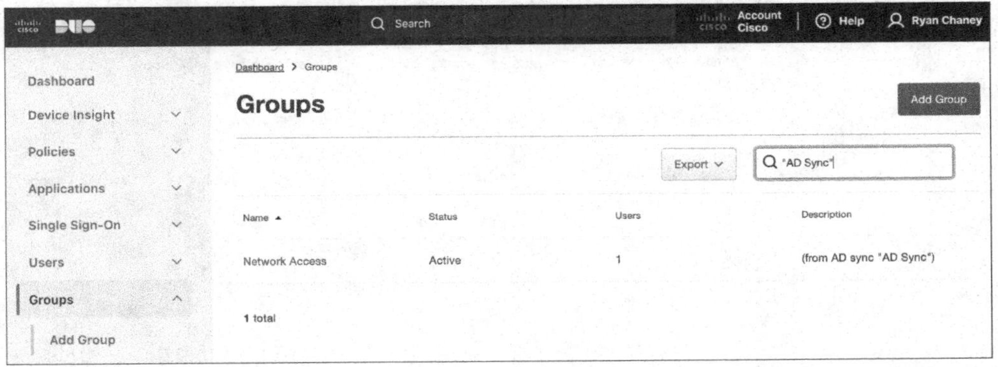

Figure 7-108 *Confirming That the AD Synced Group Is Present in Cisco Duo Admin Panel*

Step 13. Navigate to **Applications > Authentication Proxy**. You should see the Duo Authentication Proxy application listed with the status **Connected to Duo**, as shown in Figure 7-109. Click the **Name** that corresponds to the hostname of your server.

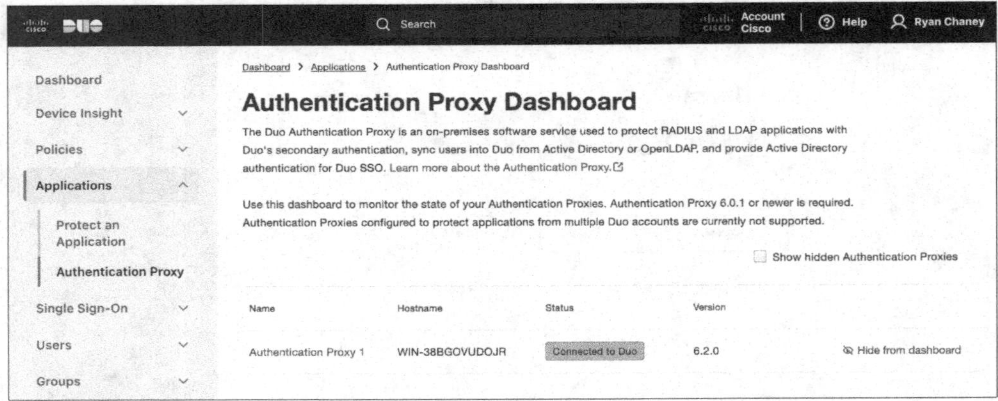

Figure 7-109 *The Authentication Proxy Dashboard in Cisco Duo Admin Panel*

Step 14. Scroll down on the **Authentication Proxy** page, and you should see that it is linked to both the **AD Sync** and the **Cisco ISE RADIUS** applications configured earlier (see Figure 7-110). The verification of the directory syncing with Duo Authentication Proxy is now complete.

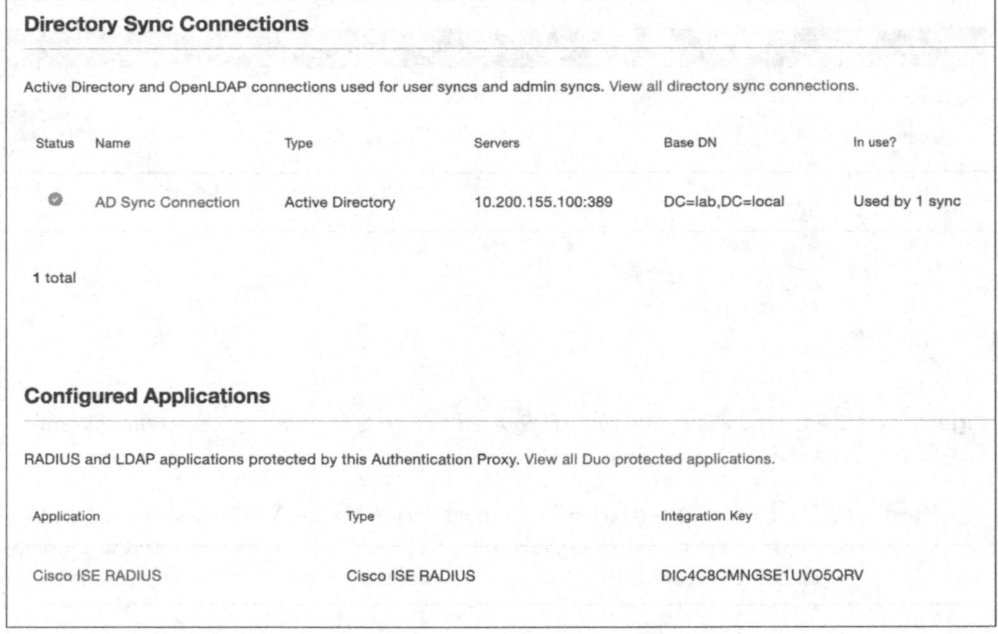

Figure 7-110 *The Authentication Proxy Directory Sync and Configured Applications in Cisco Duo Admin Panel*

Step 15. In Duo Admin Panel, navigate to **Applications > Cisco ISE RADIUS.**

a. Scroll down to **Settings.** From the screen shown in Figure 7-111, under **Username Normalization**, select **Simple.**

b. Under **Permitted Groups**, check **Only Allow Authentication from Users in Certain Groups** and select the Network Access group.

c. Click **Save.**

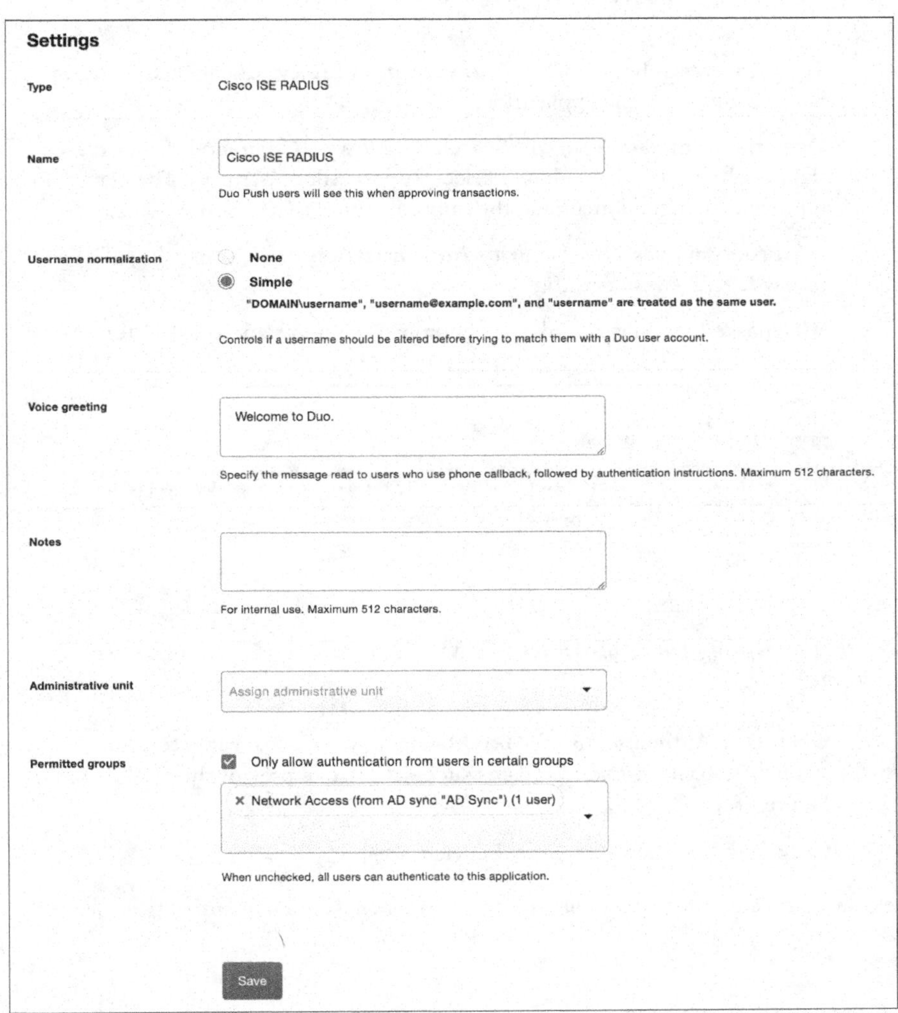

Figure 7-111 *Final Configuration Changes to the Cisco ISE RADIUS Application in Duo*

You've now completed the process of setting up Duo Authentication Proxy and Cisco Duo.

Encrypting Passwords in Duo Authentication Proxy

If you are running Duo Authentication Proxy on Windows, encrypting the passwords and secrets to keep them private is recommended. This functionality is analogous to the service password encryption command on IOS. Once encrypted, passwords are no longer visible as plain text, preventing someone from obtaining them by simply glancing over at your screen.

Step 1. To begin, switch back to **Duo Authentication Proxy Manager.** Click **Stop Service** and close the application.

Open the **Command Prompt** (**Search Windows > Command Prompt**; then right-click the search result and select **Run as Administrator**). Then enter the following command including the quotation marks (see Figure 7-112):

"C:\Program Files\Duo Security Authentication Proxy\bin\authproxy_passwd.exe" --whole-config

When asked "Would you like to continue?" enter **yes** and press Enter.

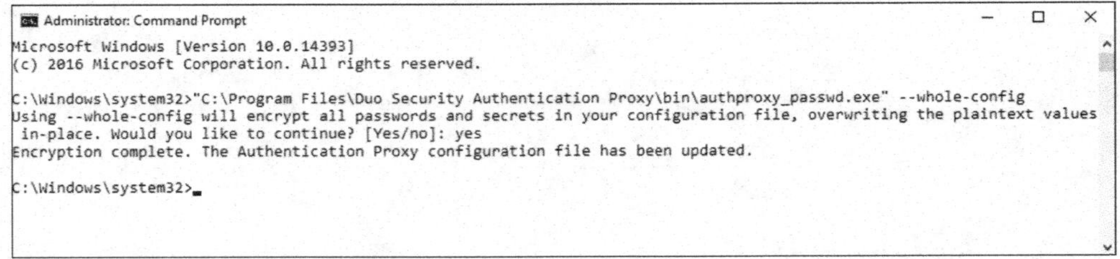

Figure 7-112 *Encrypting Duo Authentication Manager Passwords via Windows Command Prompt*

Step 2. Open **Duo Authentication Proxy Manager** again, click **Validate**, and ensure the configuration validates successfully like previously, as shown in Figure 7-113.

Click **Save** and then click **Start Service.**

You've now completed the process of encrypting passwords in Duo Authentication Proxy.

Enrolling Users with Cisco Duo

Step 1. In Duo Admin Panel, navigate to **Users.**

As demonstrated in Figure 7-114, you see the new users listed with a **Status** of **Active** and a **Last Login** of **Never Authenticated.** These users need to enroll with Cisco Duo before they can connect to the network using Duo MFA. This step is required because Duo inline enrollment is not supported with RADIUS.

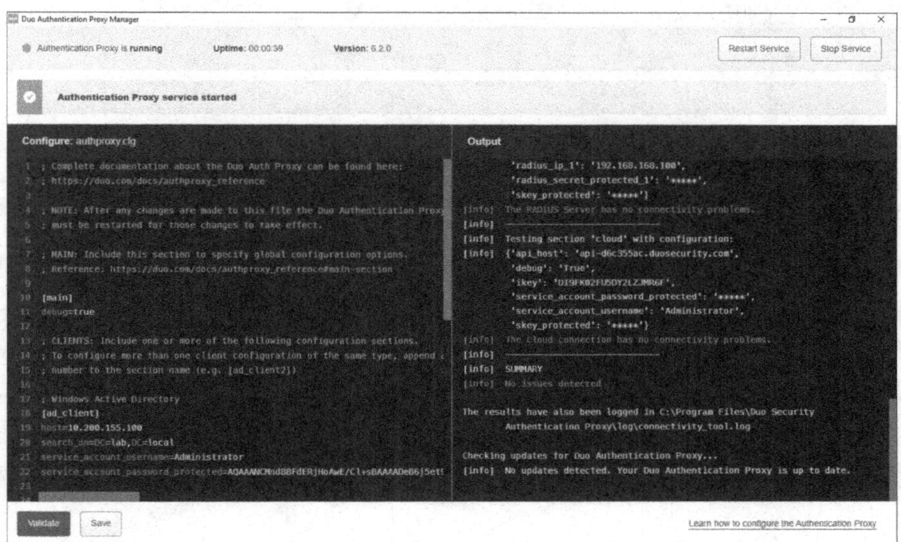

Figure 7-113 *Completed Restart of Duo Authentication Proxy Manager After Encrypting Passwords*

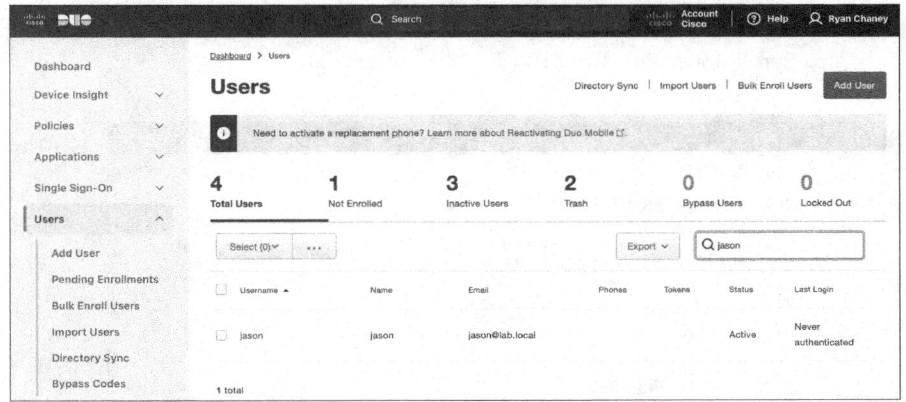

Figure 7-114 *The Users Page in Cisco Duo Admin Panel*

Step 2. To enroll individual users, click the user's username on the **Users** page (shown in Figure 7-114) and then click **Send Enrollment Email** located in the top-right corner of the user's page, as shown in Figure 7-115.

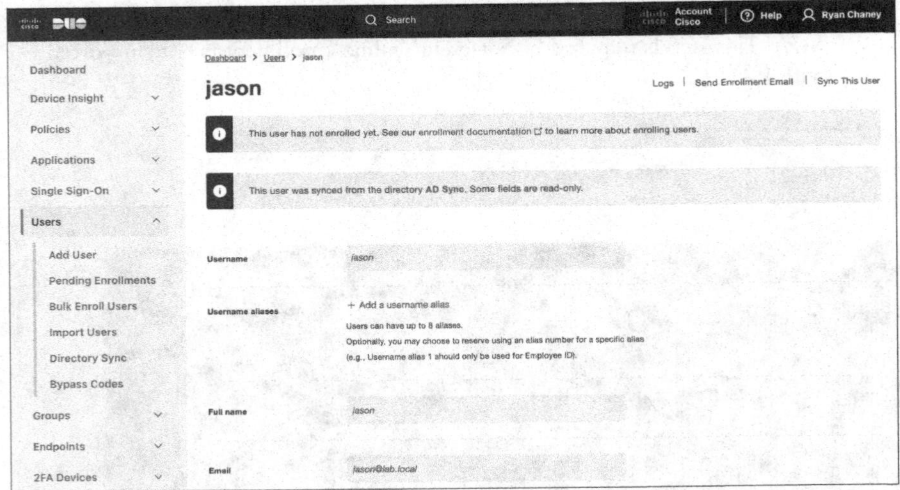

Figure 7-115 *The Users Page for an Individual User in Cisco Duo*

Step 3. If you need to enroll many users, use the Bulk Enroll Users tool instead. Navigate to **Users > Bulk Enroll Users.**

a. You need the usernames and email addresses in a CSV file. These can be exported from Active Directory, using the **Filter** and **Export List** tools on the menu bar in **Active Directory Users and Computers.**

b. Paste the list of usernames and email addresses in the format *username1,email1* into the **Users CSV** text field, as shown in Figure 7-116.

c. Scroll down and click **Send Enrollment Links.**

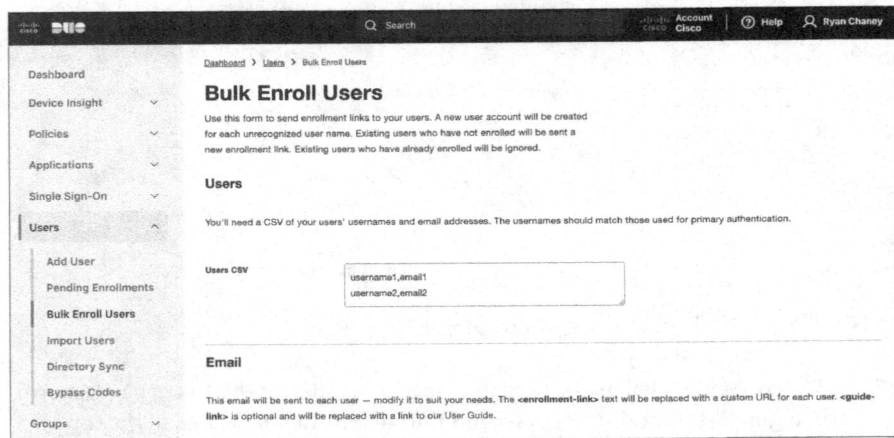

Figure 7-116 *The Bulk Enroll Users Page in Cisco Duo Admin Panel*

Step 4. Users will receive an email, like that shown in Figure 7-117. Each user will need to click the URL underneath **To begin, click this link to enroll a phone, tablet or other device** to start the Duo enrollment process.

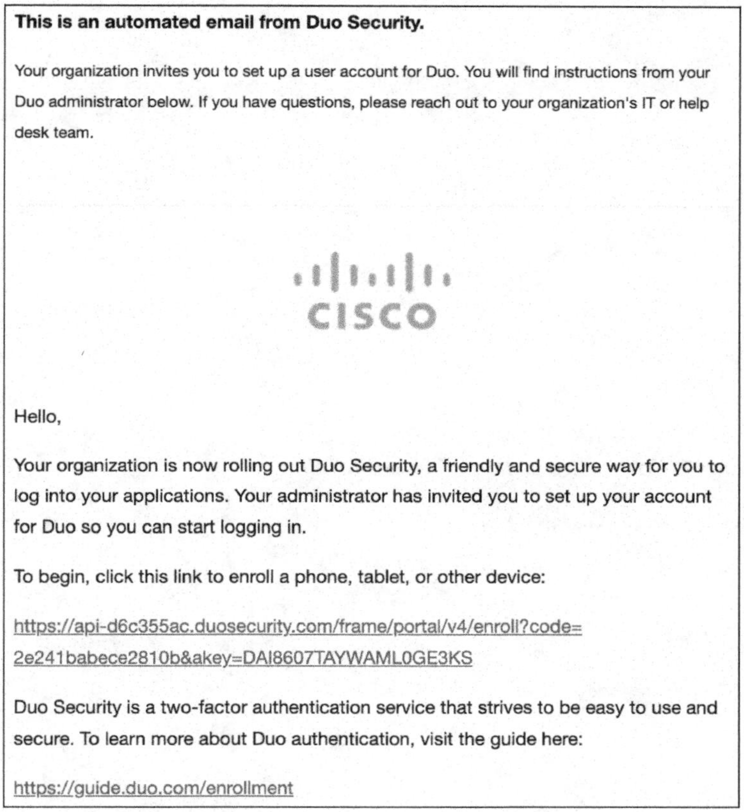

This is an automated email from Duo Security.

Your organization invites you to set up a user account for Duo. You will find instructions from your Duo administrator below. If you have questions, please reach out to your organization's IT or help desk team.

CISCO

Hello,

Your organization is now rolling out Duo Security, a friendly and secure way for you to log into your applications. Your administrator has invited you to set up your account for Duo so you can start logging in.

To begin, click this link to enroll a phone, tablet, or other device:

https://api-d6c355ac.duosecurity.com/frame/portal/v4/enroll?code=
2e241babece2810b&akey=DAI8607TAYWAML0GE3KS

Duo Security is a two-factor authentication service that strives to be easy to use and secure. To learn more about Duo authentication, visit the guide here:

https://guide.duo.com/enrollment

Figure 7-117 *An Enrollment Email from Cisco Duo*

Step 5. Clicking the link on the page in Figure 7-117 will bring the user to the page shown in Figure 7-118. The user needs to click **Next** until they get to the page where they can choose their preferred MFA method.

Step 6. Now the user needs to choose the MFA method they would like to enroll with. They will be given the option to enroll with more than one. The options can be reduced based on what an administrator allows. The steps from here differ slightly based on the MFA method chosen. In the example here, we have chosen Duo Mobile, which sends out a push notification to the Duo Mobile app, as shown in Figure 7-119. Once the enrollment process has been completed, the user can close this page.

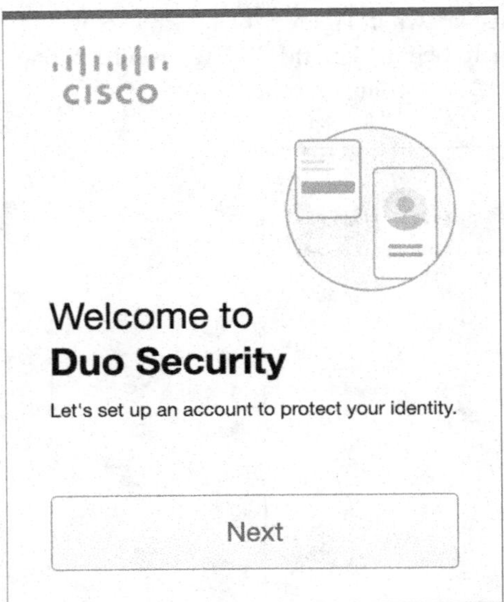

Figure 7-118 *The Duo Welcome Page as Part of User Enrollment*

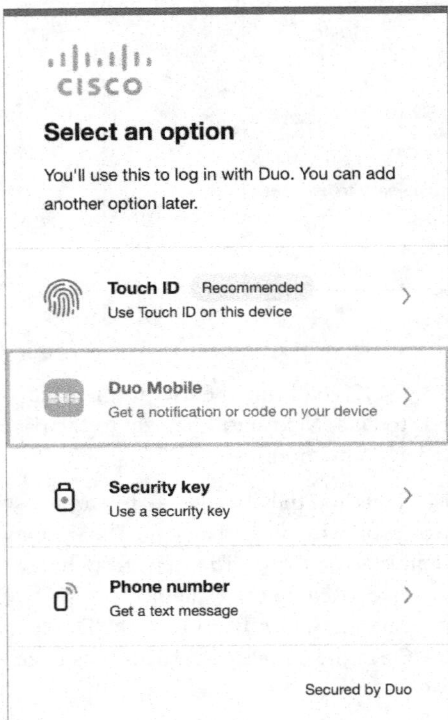

Figure 7-119 *Choosing the Preferred MFA Method as Part of Enrolling a User with Cisco Duo*

At this point, you've completed the process of enrolling a user with Cisco Duo.

Configuring Cisco Duo as an External RADIUS Server in Cisco ISE

Step 1. Log in to your instance of Cisco Identity Services Engine (ISE).

Step 2. In Cisco ISE, navigate to **Menu > Administration > Network Resources > External RADIUS Servers**, as shown in Figure 7-120.

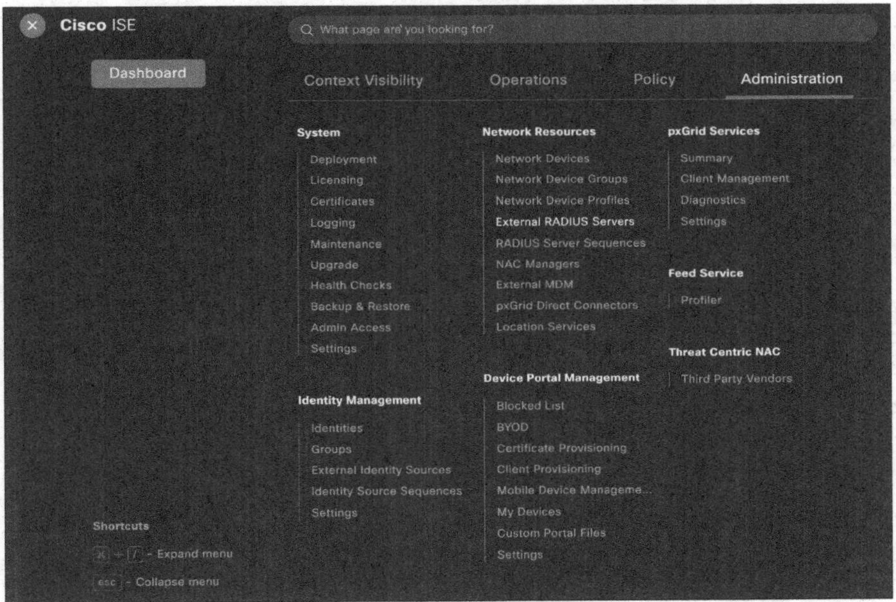

Figure 7-120 *Navigating to the External RADIUS Servers Page in Cisco ISE*

Step 3. On the **External RADIUS Servers** page, click **+ Add**, as shown in Figure 7-121.

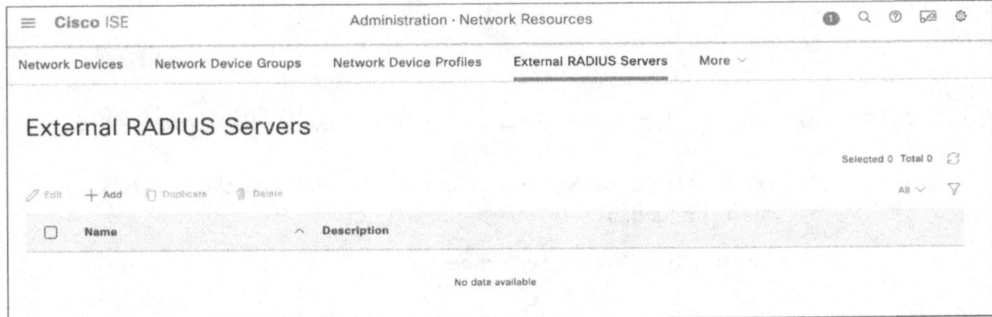

Figure 7-121 *Adding a RADIUS Server on the External RADIUS Servers Page in Cisco ISE*

Step 4. On the **New External RADIUS Servers** page, enter a **Name** for this RADIUS server. In the example (see Figure 7-122), we have called this entry **Cisco_Duo.** This field does not accept full stops or spaces.

a. Enter the IP address for Cisco Duo in the **Host IP** field.

b. Enter the RADIUS secret in the **Shared Secret** field.

c. Click **Submit.** If you are editing an existing RADIUS server you will have a **Save** button instead of **Submit.**

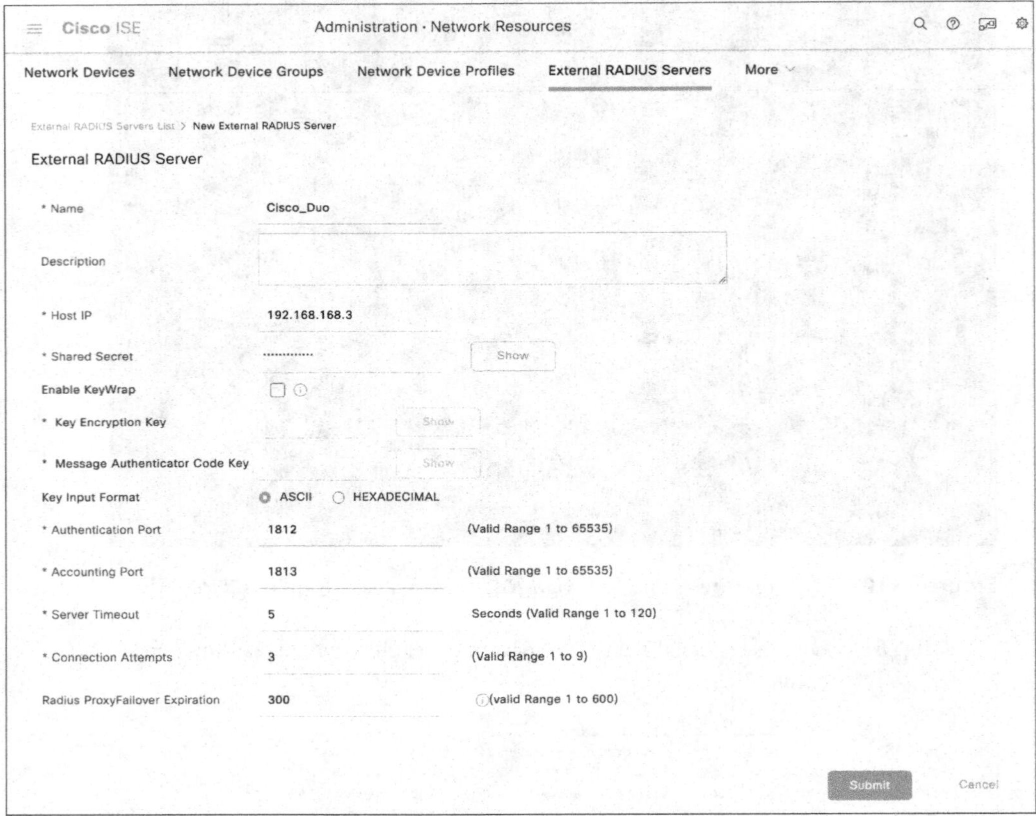

Figure 7-122 *Entering Configuration Details for a New RADIUS Server in Cisco ISE*

Step 5. The **External RADIUS Servers** page opens again, listing the RADIUS server that was just added, as shown in Figure 7-123.

Click the **RADIUS Server Sequences** tab.

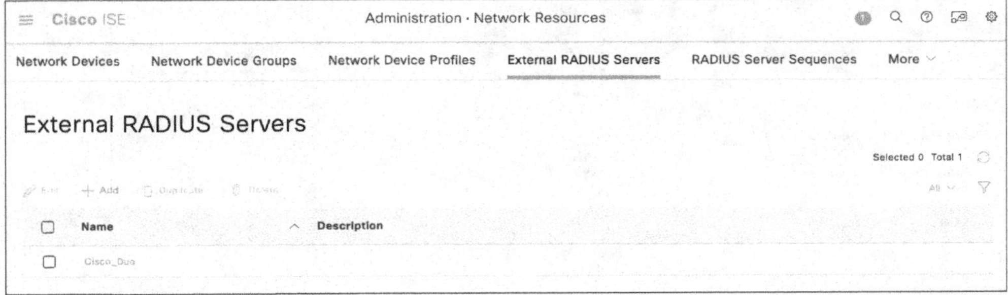

Figure 7-123 *The External RADIUS Servers Page in Cisco ISE After Adding Cisco Duo*

Step 6. On the **RADIUS Server Sequences** page (see Figure 7-124), click **+ Add.**

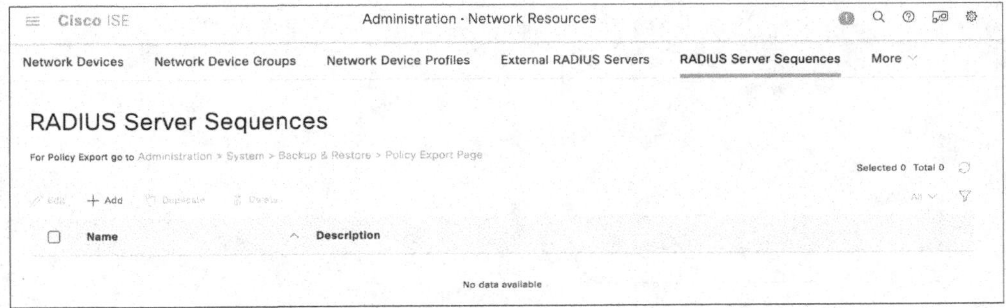

Figure 7-124 *The RADIUS Server Sequences Page in Cisco ISE*

Step 7. On the **RADIUS Server Sequences** page, enter a **Name.** In this example, we've used **Cisco_Duo** again (see Figure 7-125).

a. Under **User Selected Service Type**, you need to move the RADIUS server configured in the earlier steps from the **Available** column to the * **Selected** column. Select **Cisco_Duo** and click the > button to move it to the * **Selected** column as shown.

b. Click **Submit.**

Now, you've completed the process of configuring Cisco Duo as a RADIUS server in Cisco ISE.

Creating the Policy Set for AnyConnect VPN in Cisco ISE

Policy sets allow administrators to have different access policies for different use cases. In this example, we use policy sets to independently control each of the access methods: AnyConnect VPN and wired and wireless access.

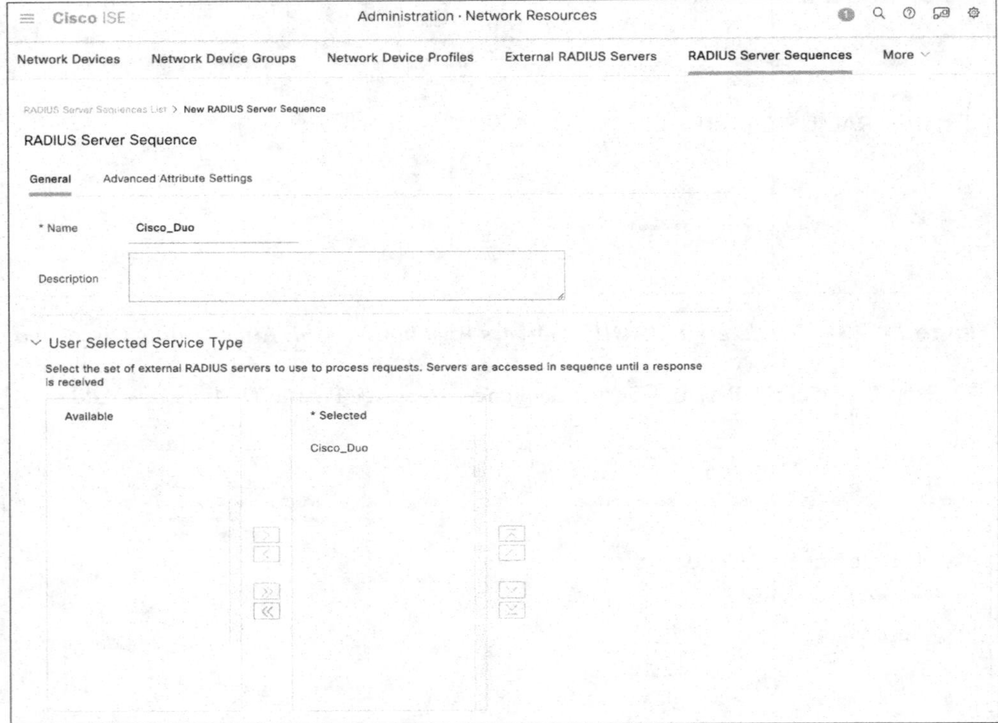

Figure 7-125 *Adding a RADIUS Server Sequence for Duo in Cisco ISE*

Follow these steps to add a policy set for AnyConnect VPN:

Step 1. In Cisco ISE, navigate to **Menu > Policy > Policy Sets.**

Step 2. On the **Policy Sets** page shown in Figure 7-126, you can see a default policy and two existing policies for wired and wireless access.

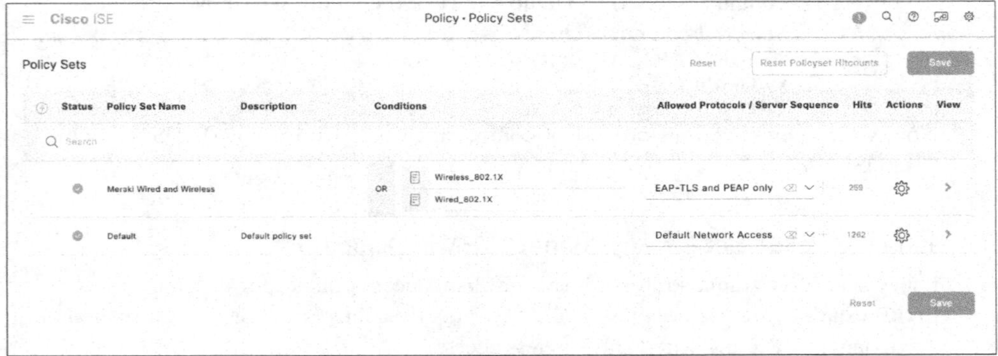

Figure 7-126 *The Policy Sets Page in Cisco ISE*

Click the blue **+** to the left of **Status** to add a new policy set (to the left of the column headings), as shown in Figure 7-127.

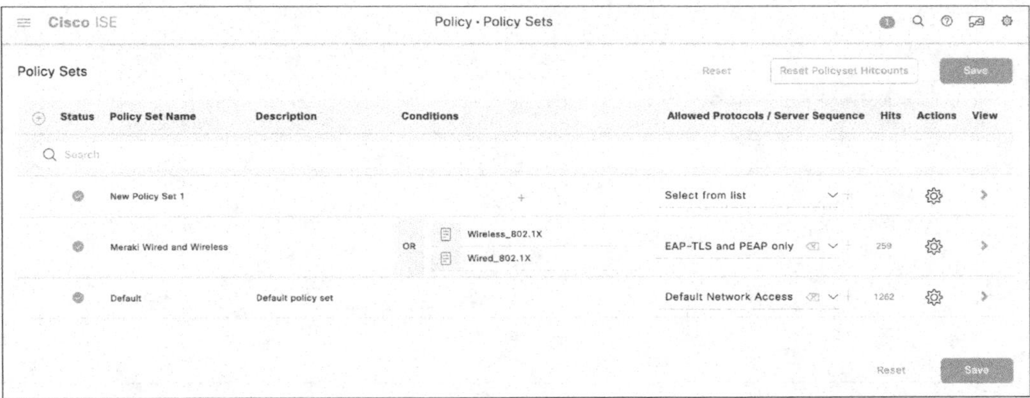

Figure 7-127 *Adding a New Policy Set on the Policy Sets Page in Cisco ISE*

Step 3. Highlight the policy set name for the row you've just added (**New Policy Set 1**). Then press the Delete key to remove the existing name and enter a name that is meaningful for you. In this example, we've added a policy set called **Meraki AnyConnect VPN** (see Figure 7-128).

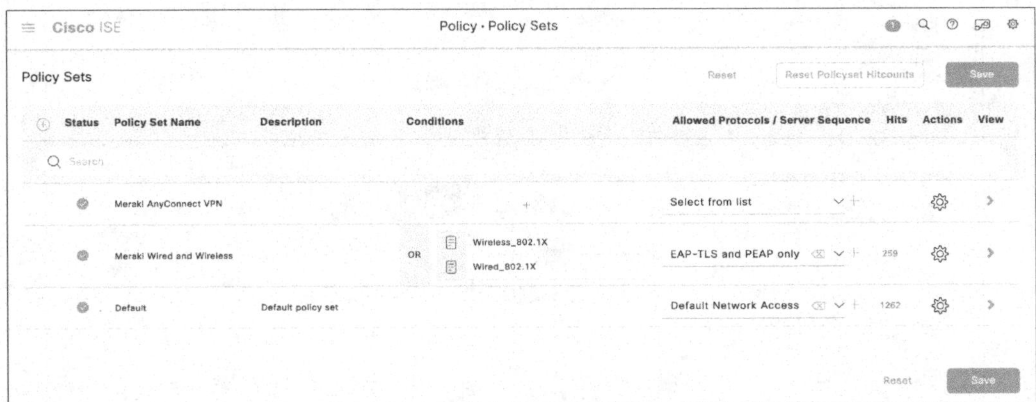

Figure 7-128 *Renaming the Policy Set Name in Cisco ISE*

Step 4. Click the **+** under **Conditions** for the new row that's been added. This brings up the **Conditions Studio** window, as shown in Figure 7-129.

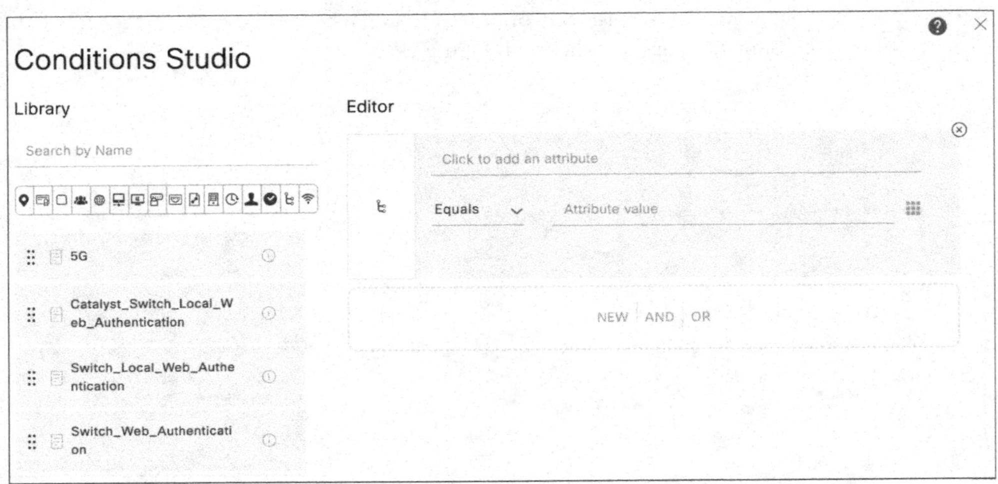

Figure 7-129 *The Conditions Studio Window in Cisco ISE*

Step 5. Click the **Click to Add an Attribute** line. On the Editor pane on the right, click the **Port** icon, as shown in Figure 7-130, and select **NAS-Port-Type**.

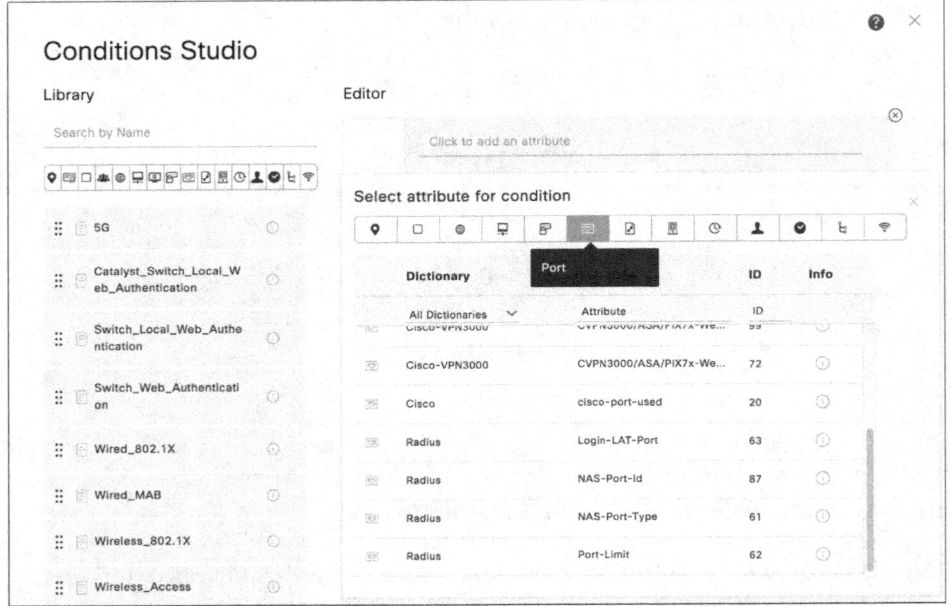

Figure 7-130 *Selecting NAS-Port-Type in Conditions Studio*

Step 6. Set **Choose from List or Type** to **Virtual**, as shown in Figure 7-131. Click **Save**.

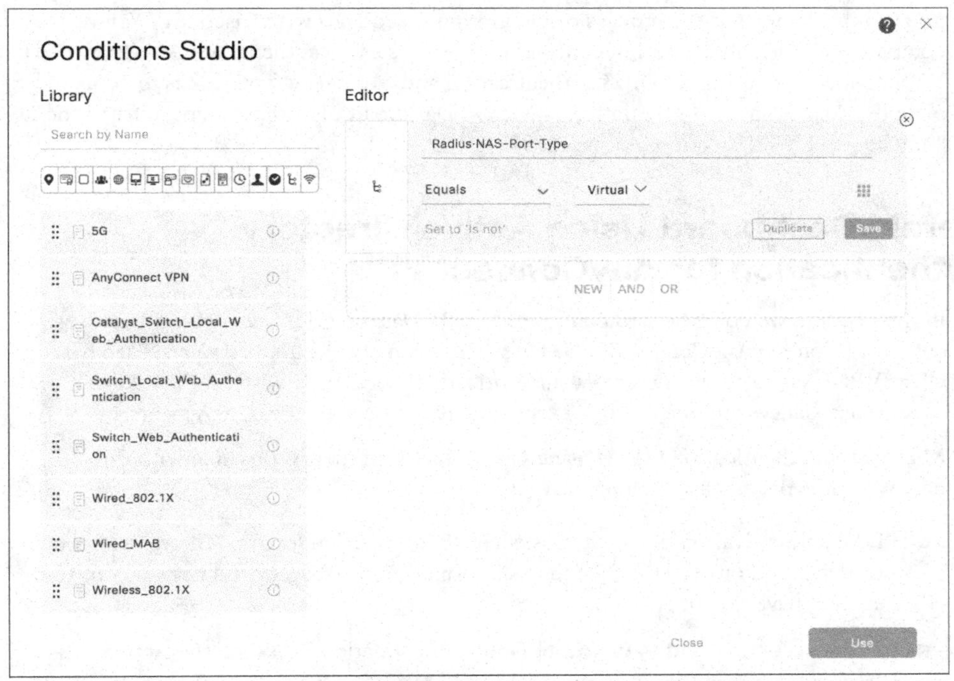

Figure 7-131 *Selecting the NAS Port Type Virtual in Conditions Studio*

Step 7. Back on the **Policy Sets** page, set the **Allowed Protocols / Server Sequence** to **Cisco_Duo** (under Proxy Sequence), as shown in Figure 7-132. This now references the external RADIUS server created earlier for Cisco Duo. Click **Save.**

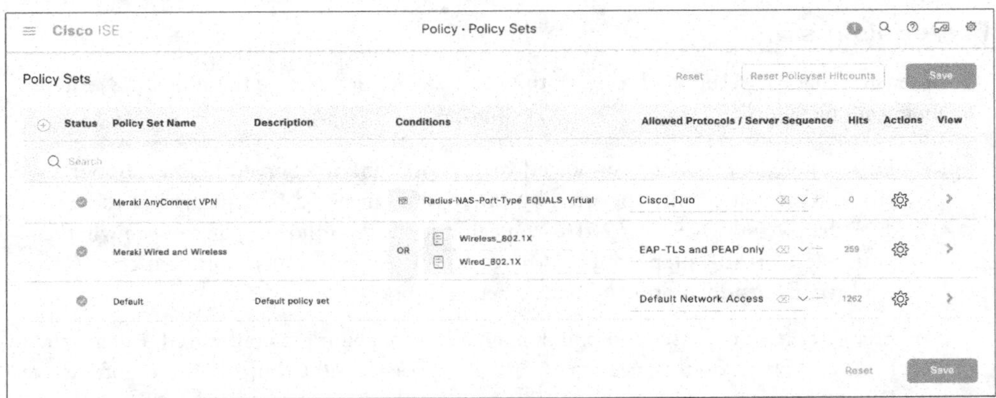

Figure 7-132 *Configuring the Proxy Sequence for Duo on the Policy Sets Page in Cisco ISE*

You've now completed the process of integrating Cisco Duo with Cisco ISE. You've also completed all the authentication configuration necessary to authenticate AnyConnect VPN connections using RADIUS authentication and MFA. The final task is to complete the AnyConnect configuration in Meraki Dashboard. For these steps, refer to the "AnyConnect VPN" section in Chapter 9.

Meraki Dashboard Using Active Directory Authentication for AnyConnect VPN

In this section, we cover how to configure Meraki Dashboard using Active Directory authentication for AnyConnect VPN. These steps can also be applied to an IPsec-based client VPN. Native Active Directory authentication works only with the Meraki MX security appliances and feels as if it exists only to support legacy deployments.

Multifactor authentication (MFA) using Cisco Duo is, in theory, possible with this deployment type, albeit with a few caveats:

- LDAP authentication does not pass client IP information to Duo. Therefore, policy settings based on available IP address information, like authorized networks or user location, have no effect.
- It is not recommended to co-locate Duo Authentication Proxy on the Active Directory server in this scenario. This would result in a port conflict that would need to be managed.
- There is a distinct lack of documentation on this deployment type.

If you are looking to secure user access with MFA, and you should be, then it is recommended that you deploy SAML- or RADIUS-based authentication instead. The configuration of both SAML, RADIUS, and the pros and cons of each are covered earlier in this chapter.

Prerequisites

To ensure that the setup goes as smoothly as possible, first ensure the following requirements are met:

- Ensure you are running a supported version of Windows Server. Meraki supports any version that is still supported by Microsoft; currently, that means any version later than Windows Server 2016. You can refer to the following link to see whether your release is still supported by Microsoft: https://learn.microsoft.com/en-us/deployoffice/endofsupport/windows-server-support.
- Ensure at least one user and one domain admin account are configured. For instructions on how to do this, see the "Configuring Users and Groups in Microsoft Active Directory" section as part of configuring RADIUS authentication using Cisco ISE, Cisco Duo, and Microsoft earlier in the chapter.

- Unlike RADIUS, when using Active Directory authentication, the server must be on a subnet local to the MX, or a remote subnet on the VPN. You can get around this issue by using a static route if required.
- A certificate must be created for each Active Directory server, as specified in Table 7-3.

Table 7-3 *TLS Certificate Requirements for Active Directory Authentication*

Requirement	Certreq key or Powershell New-SelfSignedCertificate Parameter
The Subject value must contain the fully qualified domain name of the Active Directory server.	New-SelfSignedCertificate, example: Subject = 'CN=WIN-38BGOVUDOJR.lab.local' Certreq example: Subject = CN=WIN-38BGOVUDOJR.lab.local
The purpose must include "Proves your identity to a remote computer." This means that the Enhanced Key Usage of the certificate needs to include client authentication.	New-SelfSignedCertificate: TextExtension = @("2.5.29.37={text}1.3.6.1.5.5.7.3.2") Certreq: 2.5.29.37={text} continue = 1.3.6.1.5.5.7.3.2
The certificate must have an expiry date beyond today's date.	New-SelfSignedCertificate example: NotAfter = (Get-Date).AddMonths(36) Certreq, example: NotAfter = 9/23/2027 10:31 AM
The Version value must contain "v3," indicating that it is an X.509 Version 3 certificate.	Nothing required, default.
The Enhanced Key Usage value must contain the Server Authentication certificate purpose.	New-SelfSignedCertificate: TextExtension = @("2.5.29.37={text}1.3.6.1.5.5.7.3.1") Certreq: 2.5.29.37={text} continue = 1.3.6.1.5.5.7.3.1
The Public key value should be set to "RSA (2048 Bits)."	KeyAlgorithm = 'RSA' KeyLength = 2048
The Subject Alternative Name value must contain the syntax "DNS Name=myserver.mydomain.com," where the DNS name is the fully qualified domain name of your server.	New-SelfSignedCertificate example: DnsName = 'CN=WIN-38BGOVUDOJR.lab.local'

Requirement	Certreq key or Powershell New-SelfSignedCertificate Parameter
	Certreq, requires request format to be CMC and attribute san:dns=dns.name. See https://learn.microsoft.com/en-us/troubleshoot/windows-server/windows-security/add-san-to-secure-ldap-certificate.
The Key usage must contain the Digital Signature and Key Encipherment values.	Nothing required, default.

Refer to the following URL for more information on certreq on Windows Server: https://learn.microsoft.com/en-us/windows-server/administration/windows-commands/certreq_1.

- To verify a certificate in Windows Server, open the Certificate Manager tool (**Search Windows > certmgr**) or search for "manage computer certificates" in the Control Panel. Expand **Personal** and then **Certificates**, right-click the certificate, and click **Open**. Confirm the preceding on the **General** and **Details** tabs.

  Additionally, the server must have the corresponding private key. To verify that the private key exists, view the **General** tab of the certificate and verify that you see the following message: "You have a private key that corresponds to this certificate." In Certificate Manager, the private key is located in the **Trusted Root Certification Authorities > Certificates** folder, as shown in Figure 7-133.

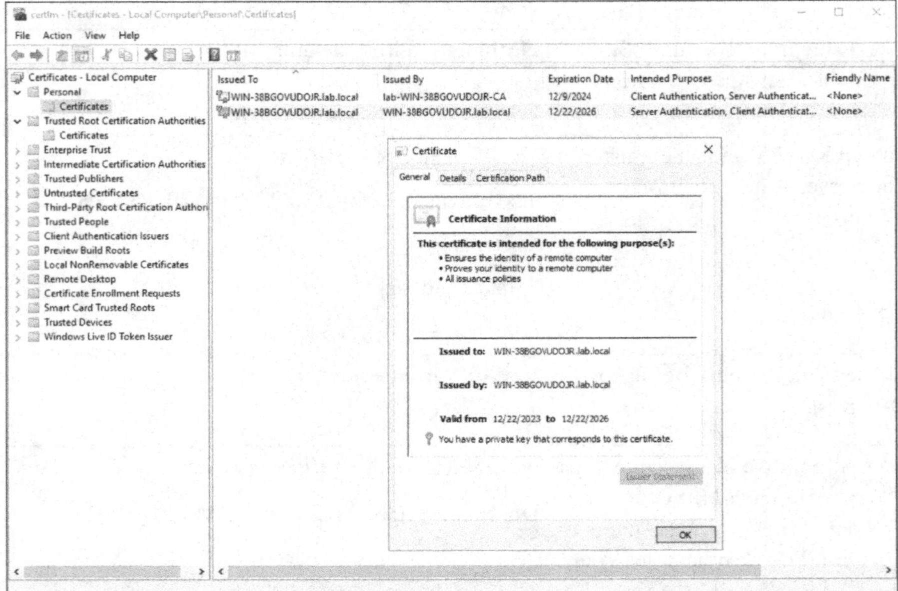

Figure 7-133 *Certificate Properties in Certificate Manager on Windows Server*

You can verify the certificate details used when Meraki Dashboard connects to Active Directory by using a packet capture. In Meraki Dashboard (**Network-wide > Packet capture**), capture the packets being sent to the Active Directory server when a user authenticates. Open the resulting pcap file with Wireshark and look for the entry shown in Figure 7-134.

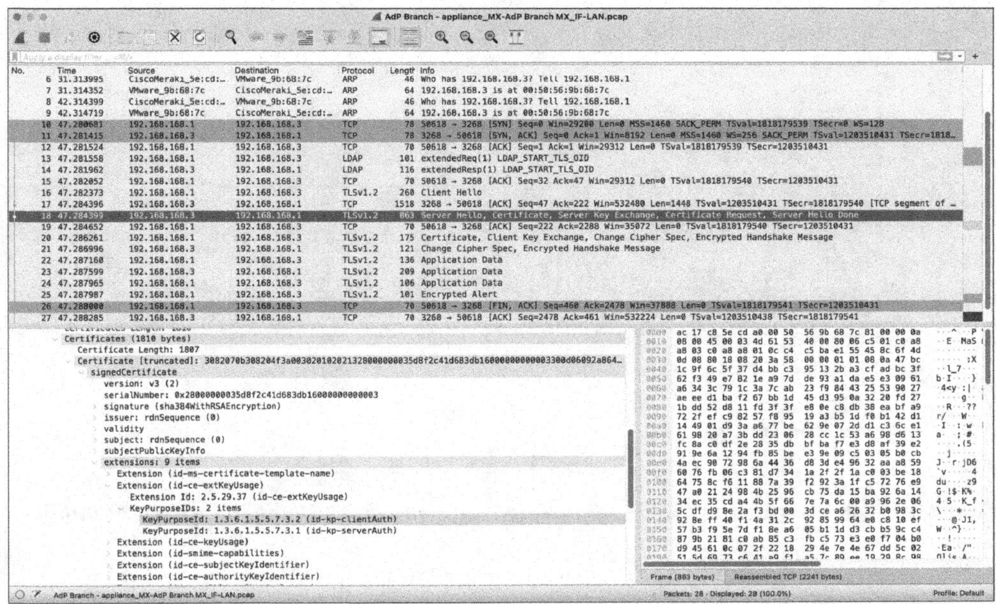

Figure 7-134 *Examining Certificate Details Seen in a Packet Capture from Meraki Dashboard in Wireshark*

- Ensure the AD DS role is installed and the service is running. You can test this using the **dsquery** command at the Command Prompt in Windows Server. In the example shown in Figure 7-135, we've queried AD for a user with the name **steve** for the domain **lab.local**. The username and password used as the credentials for this query are specified using the username (**-u**) and password (**-p**); these are the same credentials that will be used by Meraki Dashboard.

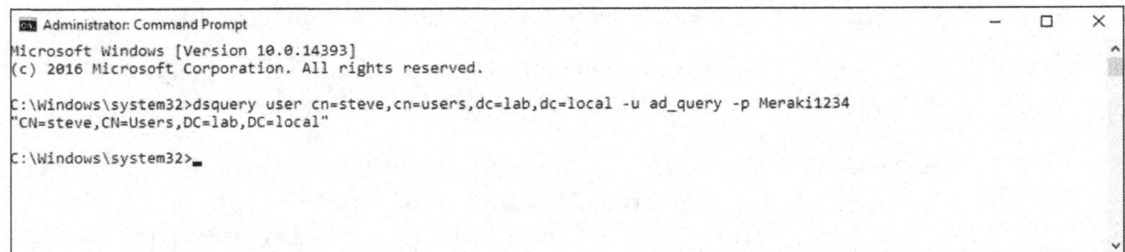

Figure 7-135 *Testing LDAP Using the* ***dsquery*** *Command in the Windows Command Prompt*

- Another way to test that LDAP is functioning correctly is to run the **ldp.exe** command (**Search Windows > ldp.exe**). Use the **Connect** option from the **Connection** menu to ensure the LDAP service is available. Use port 3268 to test without SSL and port 3269 to test with SSL. Once that's successful, use **Bind** (**Connection > Bind**), to test the Domain Admin credentials that will be configured in Meraki Dashboard, as shown in Figure 7-136.

Figure 7-136 *Testing the LDAP Service and Authentication Using* ***ldp.exe*** *on Windows Server*

With the prerequisites in place, you're ready to configure Active Directory authentication in Meraki Dashboard.

Configuring Active Directory Authentication

Follow these steps to configure Active Directory authentication:

Step 1. Log in to Meraki Dashboard (https://dashboard.meraki.com).

Step 2. Navigate to **Security & SD-WAN > Client VPN > AnyConnect Settings.** If you want to use the traditional IPsec-based client VPN, stay on the **IPsec Settings** tab and adapt the following steps.

Step 3. Set **AnyConnect Client VPN** to **Enabled**, as shown in Figure 7-137.

Step 4. Scroll down to **Authentication and Access.** Set **Authentication Type** to **Active Directory**. Enter the following (see Figure 7-138):

  a. Short Domain: This refers to the domain portion of the pre-Windows 2000 user logon name. You can check this on the properties page of any user account in Active Directory Users and Computers. In our case, this is **LAB.**

  b. IP Address: This is the IP address of the Active Directory server.

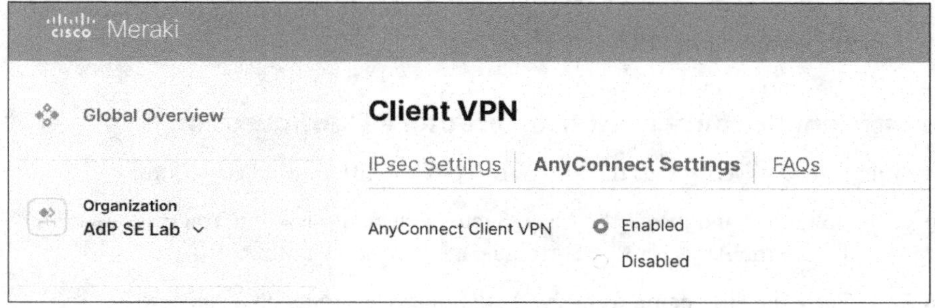

Figure 7-137 *Enabling AnyConnect Client VPN in Meraki Dashboard*

c. **Domain Admin:** This is the username of the domain administrator account the MX should use to query the Active Directory server.

d. **Password:** This is the password for the preceding domain admin account.

e. In the **AnyConnect VPN Subnet** field, enter a subnet to be assigned to VPN users when they connect. This can be any spare subnet in one of your existing IP address ranges.

f. We have specified a custom nameserver. If you have one in your network, you can specify that; otherwise, use the default **Use Google Public DNS**.

g. Click **Save Changes**.

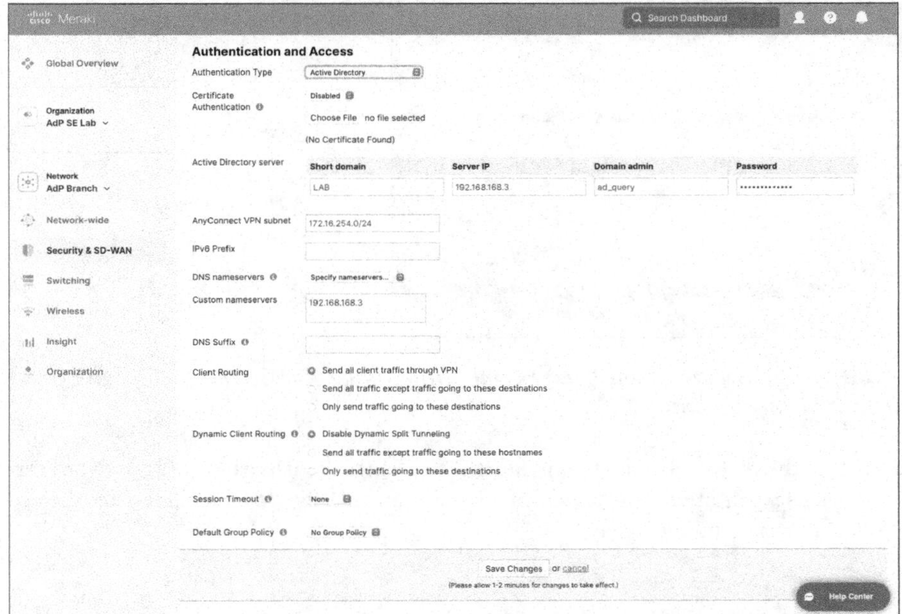

Figure 7-138 *Configuring Active Directory Authentication for VPN Access in Meraki Dashboard*

You've now completed the initial steps required to enable the authentication of users via Active Directory on Meraki MX.

Confirming Functionality of Active Directory Configuration

Follow these steps to verify that the Active Directory configuration is working:

Step 1. Download and install the Cisco Secure Client application. You can download it from the **AnyConnect Settings** page in Meraki Dashboard.

Step 2. Copy the **Hostname** from the **AnyConnect Settings** page in Meraki Dashboard.

Paste this URL into the field under **AnyConnect VPN**, as shown in Figure 7-139.

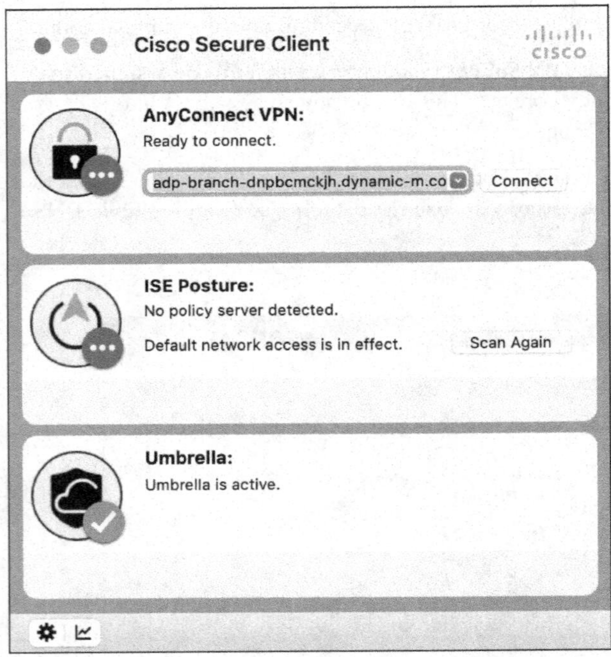

Figure 7-139 *Cisco Secure Client Before Connecting Using AnyConnect VPN with Active Directory Authentication*

Step 3. In the dialog box shown in Figure 7-140, enter the username and password for a user in Active Directory. Note: Do not include the domain name after the username in this case.

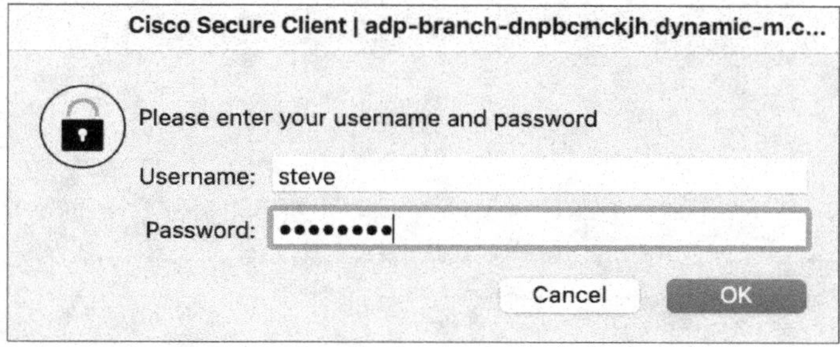

Figure 7-140 *Entering the Username and Password for AnyConnect VPN (Active Directory Authentication)*

Step 4. Once authentication has been completed, a banner message appears. Click **Accept**.

Step 5. The Cisco Secure Client now shows the VPN status **Connected** with a connection timer incrementing (see Figure 7-141). You can also verify this connectivity in the logs in Meraki Dashboard, as shown in Figure 7-142.

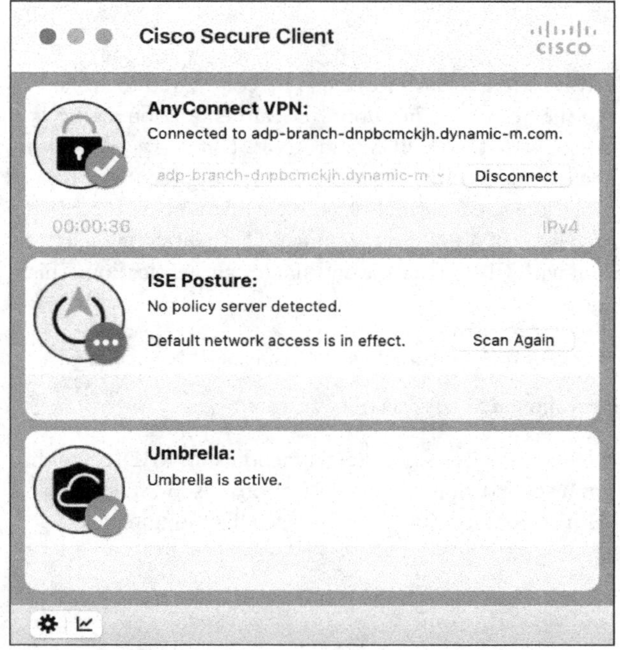

Figure 7-141 *A Successful Connection to AnyConnect VPN Using Active Directory Authentication*

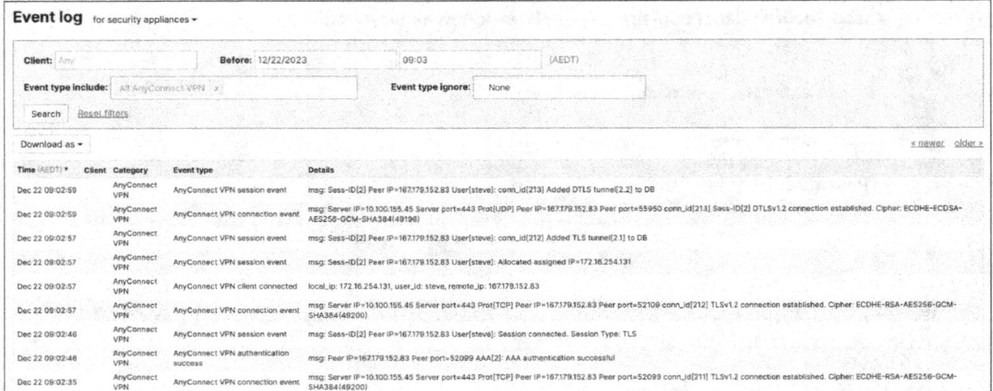

Figure 7-142 *Event Log Showing AnyConnect Successful User Logon Using Active Directory Authentication*

You've now completed the setup and verification of Active Directory for user authentication. For more information on configuring VPN access, refer to Chapter 9.

Summary

This chapter detailed the various ways Meraki Dashboard can be configured to authenticate users who are connecting to the network. The supported authentication methods include Meraki Cloud authentication, SAML, RADIUS, and Active Directory, each with their own pros and cons. Cloud-based multifactor authentication (MFA), identity provider, and identity management solutions are a natural fit with Meraki and are the easiest to integrate. In the case of AnyConnect VPN, we recommend authenticating user access using SAML in combination with Cisco Duo for multifactor authentication. This approach has two major advantages:

- SAML supports both admin access to Dashboard as well as user VPN access.
- SAML supports Duo inline enrollment, a key usability feature.

For authenticating client VPN, wired, and wireless, we recommend using RADIUS with Cisco ISE and client certificates as a second form of authentication. Cisco ISE greatly eases the challenges of dealing with certificates (PKI) and has excellent logging and troubleshooting tools.

Further Reading

Abbott, T., Burger A., Cho, V., and Carmichael, T. (2016) How To: Integrate Meraki Networks with ISE. Cisco Community. https://community.cisco.com/t5/security-knowledge-base/how-to-integrate-meraki-networks-with-ise/ta-p/3618650

AlKurdi, Z. (2020, July 16). Duo Integration Options for Cisco AnyConnect VPN with ASA and FTD. https://community.cisco.com/t5/security-knowledge-base/duo-integration-options-for-cisco-anyconnect-vpn-with-asa-and/ta-p/4114832

Cisco Duo. (2022, May 23). Duo Two-Factor Authentication for Meraki Client VPN (SAML). https://duo.com/docs/meraki-radius#configure-your-meraki-client-vpn

Cisco Duo. (2022, June 9). Duo Two-Factor Authentication for Cisco ISE. https://duo.com/docs/ciscoise-radius#install-the-duo-authentication-proxy

Cisco Duo. (2022, October 19). Duo Two-Factor Authentication for LDAP Applications. https://duo.com/docs/ldap

Cisco Duo. (2023, August 9). Duo Single Sign-On for Meraki Secure Client. https://duo.com/docs/sso-meraki-secure-client

Cisco Duo. (2023, November 30). Authentication Proxy – Reference. https://duo.com/docs/authproxy-reference#encrypting-passwords

Cisco Meraki. (2023, February 11). Resetting Passwords for Network Users. https://documentation.meraki.com/General_Administration/Cross-Platform_Content/Resetting_Passwords_for_Network_Users

Cisco Meraki. (2023, August 25). AnyConnect Authentication Methods. https://documentation.meraki.com/MX/Client_VPN/AnyConnect_on_the_MX_Appliance/Authentication

Cisco Meraki. (2023, September 20). MX Access Policies (802.1X). https://documentation.meraki.com/MX/Access_Control_and_Splash_Page/MX_Access_Policies_(802.1X)

Cisco Meraki. (2023, October 12). Change of Authorization with RADIUS (CoA) on MR Access Points. https://documentation.meraki.com/MR/Encryption_and_Authentication/Change_of_Authorization_with_RADIUS_(CoA)_on_MR_Access_Points

Cisco Meraki. (2023, October 19). Client VPN Overview. https://documentation.meraki.com/MX/Client_VPN/Client_VPN_Overview

Cisco Meraki. (2023, October 27). Access Control. https://documentation.meraki.com/MR/Access_Control

Cisco Meraki. (2023, November 3). Meraki MS Switch Access Policies (802.1X). https://documentation.meraki.com/MS/Access_Control/MS_Switch_Access_Policies_(802.1X)

Cisco Meraki. (2023, November 16). Configuring Active Directory with MX Security Appliances. https://documentation.meraki.com/MX/Content_Filtering_and_Threat_Protection/Configuring_Active_Directory_with_MX_Security_Appliances

Cisco Systems. (2023, April 18). Configure Duo Integration with Active Directory and ISE for Two-Factor Authentication on Anyconnect/Remote Access VPN Clients. https://www.cisco.com/c/en/us/support/docs/security/duo/217739-configure-duo-integration-with-active-di.html

Cisco Systems. (2023, July 10). Cisco Identity Services Engine Data Sheet. https://www.cisco.com/c/en/us/products/security/identity-services-engine/ise-ds.html

Cisco Systems. (2023, July 13). Configure EAP-TLS Authentication with ISE. https://www.cisco.com/c/en/us/support/docs/security/identity-services-engine/214975-configure-eap-tls-authentication-with-is.html

National Institute of Standards and Technology (NIST). (2020, August). *NIST 800-207 Zero Trust Architecture*. https://nvlpubs.nist.gov/nistpubs/SpecialPublications/NIST.SP.800-207.pdf

National Institute of Standards and Technology (NIST). (2020, September). *NIST 800-53 Rev. 5: Security and Privacy Controls for Information Systems and Organizations*. https://nvlpubs.nist.gov/nistpubs/SpecialPublications/NIST.SP.800-53r5.pdf

PCI Security Standards Council. (2022, May). *Summary of Changes from PCI DSS Version 3.2.1 to 4.0 Revision 1*. https://listings.pcisecuritystandards.org/documents/PCI-DSS-v3-2-1-to-v4-0-Summary-of-Changes-r1.pdf

PCI Security Standards Council. (2022, December). PCI DSS: v4.0. https://www.pcisecuritystandards.org/document_library/

Chapter 8

Wired and Wireless LAN Security

In this chapter, you learn the following:

- How to implement a zero trust architecture (ZTA) utilizing 802.1X on wired and wireless networks
- How to implement Layer 3 and Layer 7 firewalling on Meraki MR access points (APs)
- How to implement security features on Meraki MS switches such as port isolation, rogue DHCP server detection, and Secure Port
- How to implement a security policy using group policies and adaptive policies with security group tags

Today's IT security standards, including NIST 800-207, call for a shift away from simply building networks to building secure networks. This move has been in the making for many years with remote access; however, it is now at the forefront with the prevalence of cloud-hosted applications. The fact that a user or device connects to a trusted network is no longer sufficient to infer trust.[1] Zero trust, a key theme from industry best practices, recognizes the need to shift away from implicitly trusting users and devices based solely on their physical or network location. Instead, today's networks must implement authentication and authorization to protect resources and data, and not just network segments.

In addition to implementing 802.1X, Meraki's MS switches and MR access points include other enterprise security capabilities required for building secure networks, such as segmentation and encryption. This includes features that network engineers will be familiar with, such as firewalling, access control lists, MAC filtering, and port isolation. Meraki Dashboard also makes it simple to implement advanced security features like group policies and security group tags. The examples in this chapter show IPv4, but when configuring controls, you should consider IPv6 also. Many government organizations are mandated to support IPv6, and some operating systems prefer IPv6 over IPv4 if both are available. If you implement IPv4-only controls, yet run IPv6 in your network, then these controls will be ineffective. Read on to learn more about these critical security capabilities.

Access Control Lists and Firewalls

Meraki MS switches support basic access control lists, whereas Meraki MR access points support more advanced Layer 3 and Layer 7 application firewalling and rate-limiting. Having the ability to configure a firewall directly on the AP is quite unique and provides granular control, even with limited infrastructure.

Access Control Lists (Meraki MS)

Meraki MS switches support access control lists (ACLs), enabling administrators to control traffic between hosts. Because these are switches, it is understandable that the default policy is to allow all traffic. ACL entries are evaluated sequentially from top to bottom. ACL entries are stateless, meaning that you will need a rule to permit the return traffic if you have a *deny any* rule configured. Access control lists are fairly basic. Consider using group policies where greater functionality is required. Figure 8-1 shows the default switching ACL as seen in Meraki Dashboard.

> **Note** Configured ACLs apply to all switches in a network.

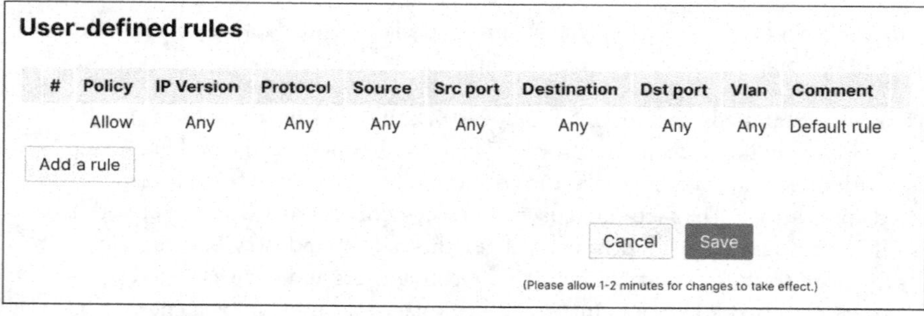

Figure 8-1 *The Default Switching ACL in Meraki Dashboard*

Follow these steps to configure an ACL in Meraki Dashboard:

Step 1. Log in to Meraki Dashboard (https://dashboard.meraki.com).

Step 2. Navigate to **Switching > ACL** (see Figure 8-2).

Step 3. In this example we configure a simple policy to block traffic between two hosts connected to the same switch. Click **Add a Rule** under **User-Defined Rules.**

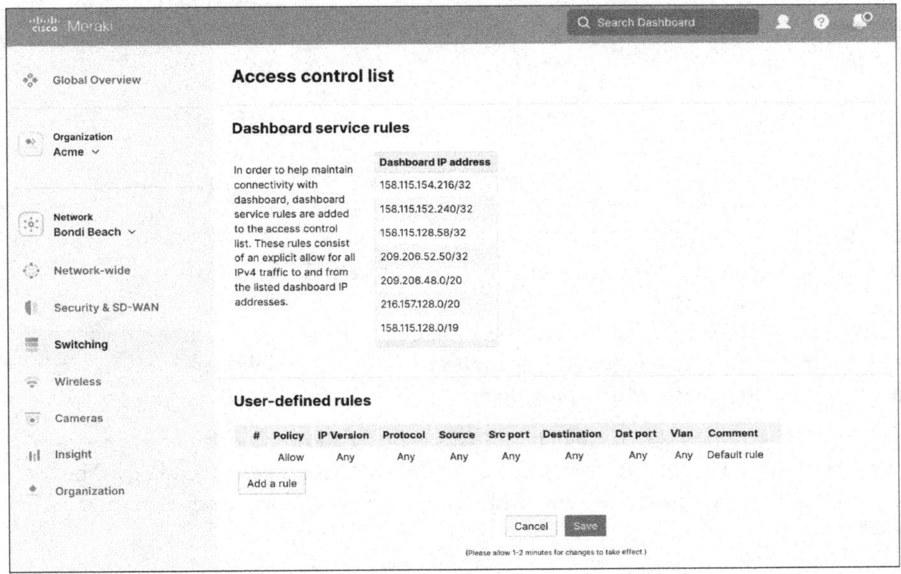

Figure 8-2 *Configuring Access Control Lists in Meraki Dashboard*

Step 4. A new row appears above the default *allow any to any* rule. Select the appropriate **IP Version** and **Protocol**; then enter the **Source** and **Destination** IP addresses to filter. IPv4 or IPv6 addressing can be used in the source and destination fields. Meraki Dashboard automatically adds a /32 subnet mask when an IPv4 host IP address is entered. To block traffic to or from subnets, also include the subnet mask in CIDR notation (e.g. /24). Leave the remaining fields as their defaults (Any) (see Figure 8-3).

Click **Save.** The user-defined rules now look like Figure 8-4.

Figure 8-3 *Adding a Rule to an Access Control List in Meraki Dashboard*

You would typically not need to specify a VLAN in the VLAN column when configuring an ACL. One use case for which you would specify a VLAN is to blackhole traffic on a VLAN. This would be akin to an old-school VACL (VLAN ACL) on a Cisco switch.

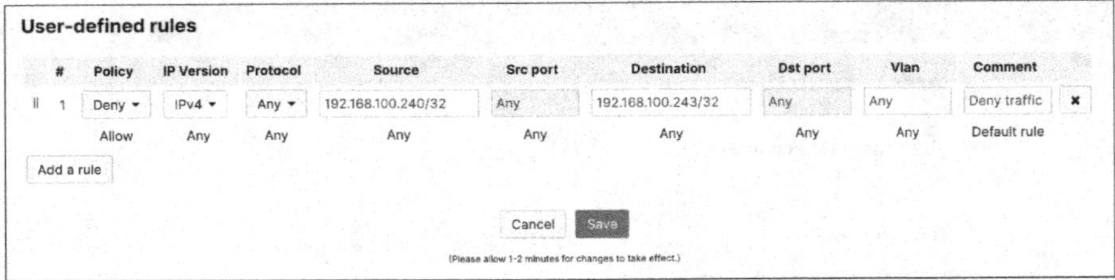

Figure 8-4 *Successful Addition of a New Rule to an Access Control List*

At this point, you've completed the process of adding a simple ACL rule to Meraki switches. Rules can be edited at any time. Where there are multiple rules, you can reorder them simply by dragging and dropping them.

It's possible to verify that traffic matching ACLs is being allowed or denied appropriately by using the ACL Hit Counter. To find the ACL Hit Counter in Meraki Dashboard, navigate to **Switching > Switches** (under Monitor). Then click the switch name and select **Tools.**

Ensure the traffic you want to monitor is running. In this case, we've used a simple ping. To kick off the ACL Hit Counter tool, simply set the **Duration** and click **Run.** The ACL Hit Counter returns a table, as shown in Figure 8-5. Note that you can have multiple pages if there are lots of ACL entries. The second-to-last line confirms that traffic matches are being made on the rule configured in Figure 8-4.

ACL Hit Counter Duration: 1 min Run

ACL Hit Counter Table - 1 min

Search...

Policy	IP Version	Protocol	Source	Src port	Destination	Dst port	Vlan	Hits	IPV4	IPV6
allow	ipv4	any	158.115.154.216/32	Any	Any	Any	Any	181	181	-
allow	ipv4	any	Any	Any	158.115.154.216/32	Any	Any	169	169	-
allow	ipv4	any	158.115.152.240/32	Any	Any	Any	Any	29	29	-
allow	ipv4	any	Any	Any	158.115.152.240/32	Any	Any	29	29	-
allow	ipv4	any	158.115.128.58/32	Any	Any	Any	Any	0	0	-
allow	ipv4	any	Any	Any	158.115.128.58/32	Any	Any	0	0	-
allow	ipv4	any	209.206.52.50/32	Any	Any	Any	Any	0	0	-
allow	ipv4	any	Any	Any	209.206.52.50/32	Any	Any	0	0	-
allow	ipv4	any	209.206.48.0/20	Any	Any	Any	Any	0	0	-
allow	ipv4	any	Any	Any	209.206.48.0/20	Any	Any	0	0	-
allow	ipv4	any	216.157.128.0/20	Any	Any	Any	Any	374	374	-
allow	ipv4	any	Any	Any	216.157.128.0/20	Any	Any	141	141	-
allow	ipv4	any	158.115.128.0/19	Any	Any	Any	Any	0	0	-
allow	ipv4	any	Any	Any	158.115.128.0/19	Any	Any	0	0	-
allow	ipv6	any	2620:12F:C000::/44	Any	Any	Any	Any	0	-	0
allow	ipv6	any	Any	Any	2620:12F:C000::/44	Any	Any	0	-	0
deny	ipv4	any	192.168.100.240/32	Any	192.168.100.243/32	Any	Any	51	51	-
allow	both	any	Any	Any	Any	Any	Any	987247	987243	4

100 results per page 1

Figure 8-5 *Monitoring Traffic Using the ACL Hit Counter Tool in Meraki Dashboard*

To confirm that the ACL rule is working in practice, conduct a ping test before and after the changes. As you can see in Figure 8-6, after the deny rule was applied, all pings were blocked.

```
ryanchaney — -zsh — 77×18
ryanchaney@RYCHANEY-M-6X1J ~ % ping -c 3 192.168.100.243
PING 192.168.100.243 (192.168.100.243): 56 data bytes
64 bytes from 192.168.100.243: icmp_seq=0 ttl=64 time=12.347 ms
64 bytes from 192.168.100.243: icmp_seq=1 ttl=64 time=6.128 ms
64 bytes from 192.168.100.243: icmp_seq=2 ttl=64 time=4.726 ms

--- 192.168.100.243 ping statistics ---
3 packets transmitted, 3 packets received, 0.0% packet loss
round-trip min/avg/max/stddev = 4.726/7.734/12.347/3.312 ms
ryanchaney@RYCHANEY-M-6X1J ~ % ping -c 3 192.168.100.243
PING 192.168.100.243 (192.168.100.243): 56 data bytes
Request timeout for icmp_seq 0
Request timeout for icmp_seq 1

--- 192.168.100.243 ping statistics ---
3 packets transmitted, 0 packets received, 100.0% packet loss
ryanchaney@RYCHANEY-M-6X1J ~ %
```

Figure 8-6 *Using ping to Test That an Access Control List Is Working as Expected*

Now that you've completed the configuration of ACLs on Meraki MS switches, if you want more information on configuring ACLs, refer to https://documentation.meraki.com/MS/Layer_3_Switching/Configuring_ACLs.

Meraki MR Firewall

Meraki MR access points support per-SSID Layer 3 and Layer 7 firewalling for both IPv4 and IPv6. Both Layer 3 and Layer 7 firewall rules are stateless, meaning that you need a rule to permit the return traffic if you have a deny any rule configured. The default policy is to deny traffic between the wireless network and the local LAN, while allowing all other traffic, as illustrated in Figure 8-7. A *local LAN* is defined here as IP addresses in the RFC 1918 private IP address space (such as 10/8, 172.16/12, and 192.168/16). This default makes sense for:

- Guest Wi-Fi
- When Layer 2 switches are being used and traffic between different VLANs is being controlled by a local Meraki MX

Depending on your use case, you may or may not need to change this default.

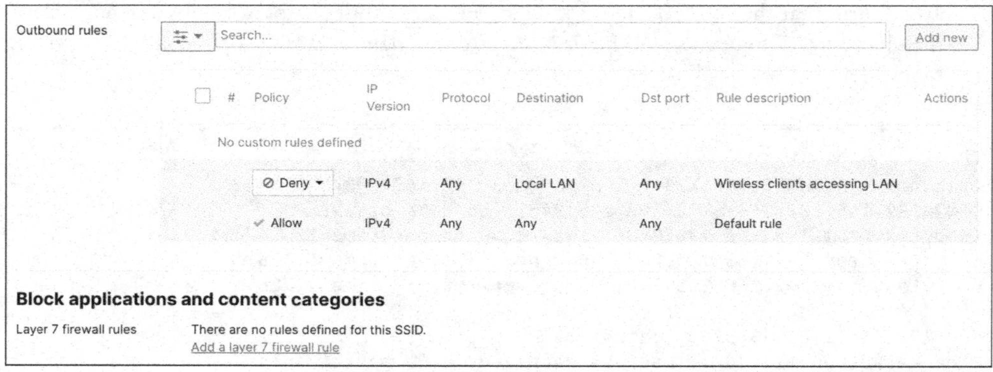

Figure 8-7 *The Default Wireless Firewall and Traffic Shaping Policy in Meraki Dashboard*

> **Note** On Meraki MR, flows permitted by nondefault Layer 3 firewall rules are not reevaluated against the Layer 7 firewall rules. It's important to understand this capability because it is different to Meraki MX, which does reevaluate traffic at Layer 7.

Layer 3 Firewall

Follow these steps to configure a Layer 3 firewall rule on a Meraki SSID:

Step 1. Log in to Meraki Dashboard (https://dashboard.meraki.com).

Step 2. Navigate to **Wireless > Firewall & Traffic Shaping** (see Figure 8-8).

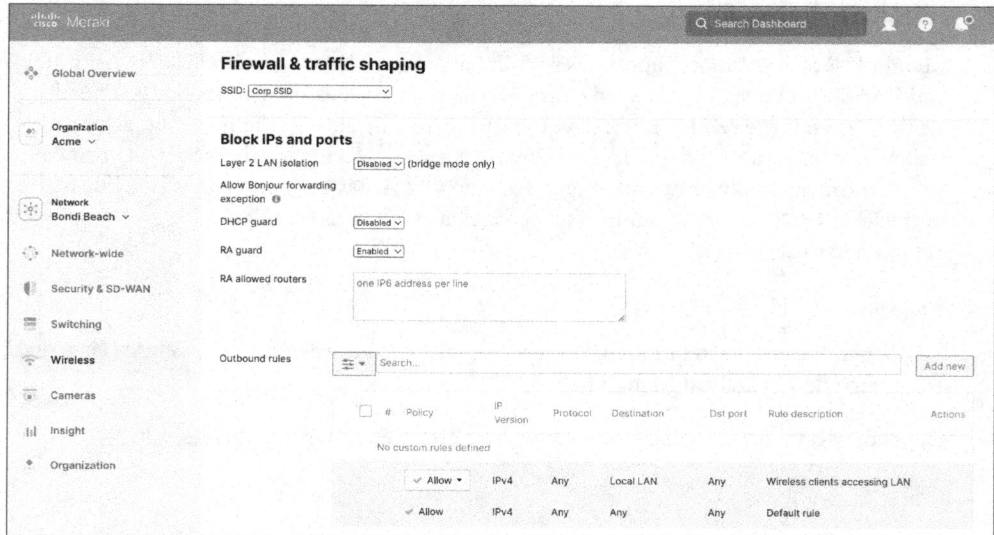

Figure 8-8 *The Firewall & Traffic Shaping Page for Wireless in Meraki Dashboard*

Step 3. Under **Outbound Rules**, click **Add New.**

In terms of the protocol, you can now specify ICMP, which was not available with ACLs on switches. Because our intention in this example is to block ICMP between two hosts, we have configured the policy as shown in Figure 8-9. Again, Dashboard will add a /32 subnet mask if you don't specify one.

Click **Finish Editing** when done. Don't forget to also click **Save** in the bottom right of the page to apply these changes.

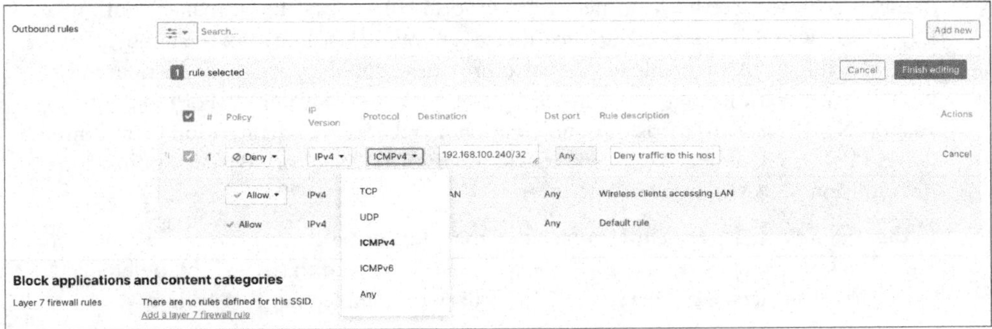

Figure 8-9 *Configuring a Wireless Layer 3 Firewall Rule in Meraki Dashboard*

Step 4. With the Layer 3 firewall rule in place, you can verify that it is working as expected. There is no equivalent of the ACL traffic monitor in this case, so instead you can use the packet capture tool to verify this (**Network-wide > Packet Capture**). The outbound packet capture on the AP's wired interface (see Figure 8-10) confirms that only one-way traffic is being seen. ICMP echo requests are reaching the wireless host, but the return ICMP echo reply packets are being dropped by the Layer 3 firewall policy.

Packet capture for access points

Access point: All Access Points

Interface: Wired

Output: View output below

Duration (secs): 600

Ignore: broadcast packets, multicast packets

Filter expression: host 192.168.100.243 and icmp

clear output or Start capture

Sample filter expressions

host 10.1.27.253
packets to and from ip address 10.1.27.253
host 10.1.27.253 and port 53
packets to and from ip address 10.1.27.253 and TCP or UDP port 53 (DNS)
icmp[icmptype] != icmp-echo and icmp[icmptype] != icmp-echoreply
all ICMP packets that are not echo requests/replies (i.e., not ping packets):
ether host 11:22:33:44:55:66
packets to and from ethernet host 11:22:33:44:55:66
See more examples.

The maximum packet capture duration is 3600 seconds.
This capture will stop after 600 seconds, or when 5000 packets have been captured.

Packet capture logs

```
--- Start Of Stream ---
05:27:54.905927 IP 192.168.100.240 > 192.168.100.243: ICMP echo request, id 24183, seq 0, length 64
05:27:55.908808 IP 192.168.100.240 > 192.168.100.243: ICMP echo request, id 24183, seq 1, length 64
05:27:56.910849 IP 192.168.100.240 > 192.168.100.243: ICMP echo request, id 24183, seq 2, length 64
05:27:57.914138 IP 192.168.100.240 > 192.168.100.243: ICMP echo request, id 24183, seq 3, length 64
--- End Of Stream ---
```

Figure 8-10 *Using the Packet Capture Tool in Meraki Dashboard to Verify That the Firewall Rule Is Working*

You've now completed the configuration and verification of Layer 3 firewalling on Meraki access points. You can find more information on this feature at https://documentation.meraki.com/MR/Firewall_and_Traffic_Shaping/MR_Firewall_Rules.

Layer 7 Firewall (Including NBAR Content Filtering)

All Meraki Wi-Fi 6 or later access points running at least MR firmware 27 support Network-Based Application Recognition, also referred to as NBAR. NBAR is a powerful application recognition engine that supports more than 1,500 applications. It is highly recommended that your network supports NBAR, because it makes configuring Layer 7 firewall rules to block applications as simple as just knowing the application name. Having NBAR-capable devices also provides administrators with far richer visibility of applications on the Clients page (**Network-wide > Clients**). For more information on NBAR, refer to https://documentation.meraki.com/General_Administration/Cross-Platform_Content/Next-gen_Traffic_Analytics_-_Network-Based_Application_Recognition_(NBAR)_Integration.

In this example, management have decided that staff are spending too much time watching Patrick Boyle episodes on YouTube and have requested that YouTube be blocked until further notice. We use a Layer 7 firewall rule to implement this policy.

> **Note** Blocking HTTPS websites using a Layer 7 firewall rule does not provide a block page to the users. If one is required (recommended), use Secure Connect instead.

Follow these steps to configure a Layer 7 firewall policy on a Meraki SSID:

Step 1. Log in to Meraki Dashboard (https://dashboard.meraki.com).

Step 2. Navigate to **Wireless > Firewall & Traffic Shaping.** Scroll down to **Block Applications and Content Categories** (see Figure 8-11).

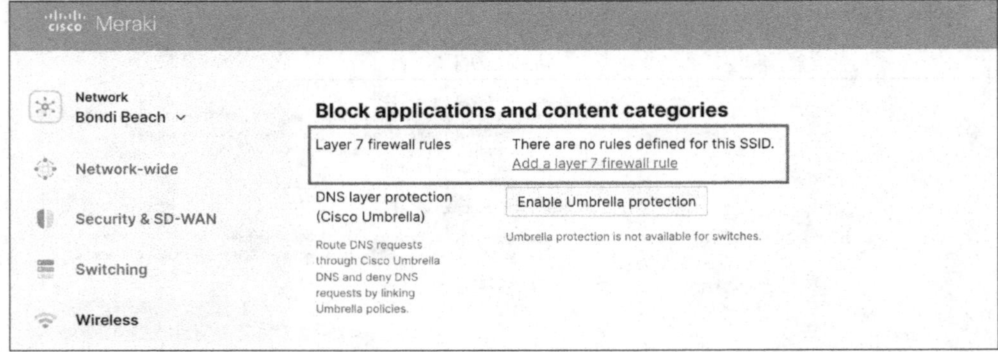

Figure 8-11 *Adding a Wireless Layer 7 Firewall Rule in Meraki Dashboard*

Step 3. Click **Add a Layer 7 Firewall Rule.**

Step 4. It is possible to block applications using any of the following from the **Application** drop-down menu:

- A content category, such as Gaming or Peer-to-Peer (P2P). Once a category is selected, it's possible to block all available subcategories or to specify an individual application within that category.
- **HTTP hostname:** This enables you to deny traffic based on a URL.
- **Port, Remote IP Range, or Remote IP Range & Port:** Similar to the Layer 3 firewall policy.

The example shown in Figure 8-12 blocks YouTube using a Layer 7 firewall rule. To block YouTube in this way, start by selecting **Video & Music** from the **Application** drop-down menu. In the adjacent drop-down menu for the subcategory, select **YouTube.**

Click **Save.**

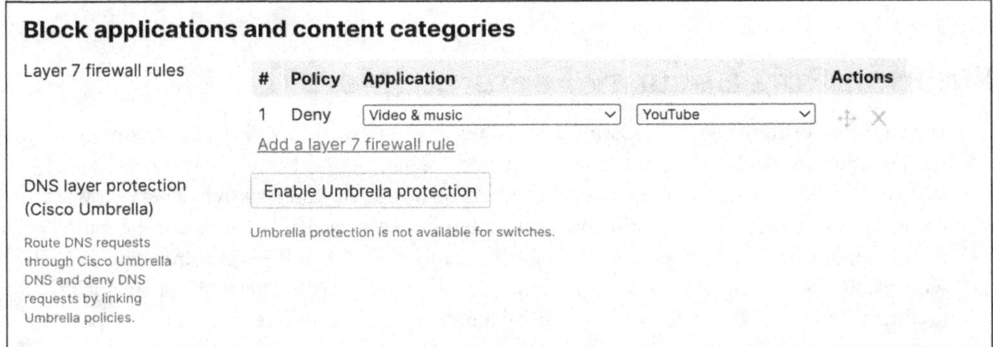

Figure 8-12 *Configuring a Wireless Layer 7 Firewall Rule in Meraki Dashboard*

This Layer 7 firewall policy is now configured. To verify that the policy is working, simply try opening YouTube with a web browser while connected to this SSID. You should get results similar to Figure 8-13. The site may still load if cached, so clear the browser cache before you test.

For more information on Layer 7 firewall rules, refer to https://documentation.meraki.com/General_Administration/Cross-Platform_Content/Creating_a_Layer_7_Firewall_Rule.

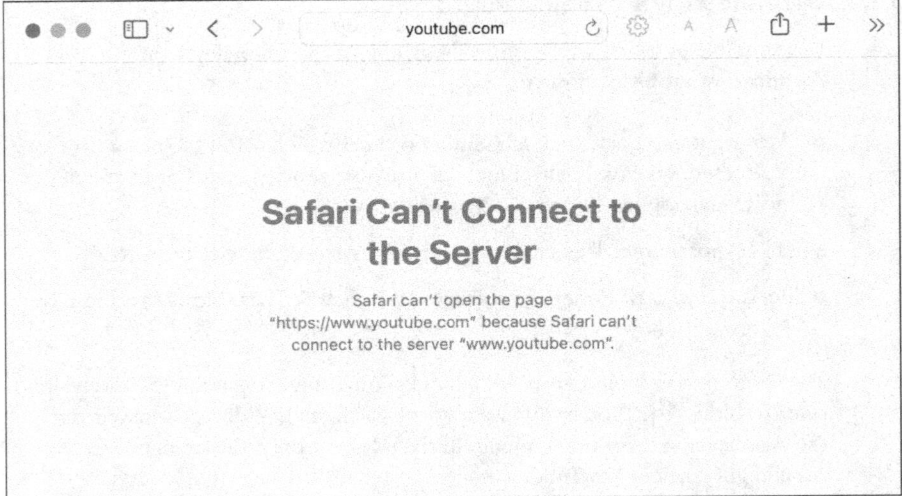

Figure 8-13 *Successfully Blocking YouTube Access Using a Wireless Layer 7 Firewall Policy*

Ethernet Port Security Features (Meraki MS)

If you have configured Cisco Catalyst switches in the past, you will recognize many of the capabilities available on Meraki switch ports. This section focuses on the subset of features that can be used to secure your wired network. Because switches serve a wide range of use cases, it's good to know that a plethora of security features can be called on. An example of a requirement from a security standard is NIST 800-53 requirement 9.2.2, which calls for a control to restrict the use of publicly accessible network jacks within facilities. This could be a hallway in a data center with an IP phone attached or a patched but unused port in an airport or shopping center. The features described here are all valid ways to restrict a port to its intended purpose. If a port does not have a legitimate reason for being enabled, simply disable it.

MAC Allow Lists

MAC allow lists are exactly that—they enable you to limit the hosts that can use a switch port to those with a MAC address on a predefined whitelist. The one downside of MAC allow lists is the need to manually configure them and keep them updated. Say you have a MAC allow list configured to restrict a port to just the office printer. When that printer is replaced, the new printer won't work until the port is reconfigured. Up to 20 MAC addresses can be added to a MAC allow list, and MAC allow lists are not configured by default.

Follow these steps to configure a MAC allow list on a Meraki switch port:

Step 1. Log in to Meraki Dashboard (https://dashboard.meraki.com).

Step 2. Navigate to **Switching > Switch Ports.** Click the name of the port you wish to edit. Alternatively, if editing multiple ports, select them by checking the boxes next to their names and then click **Edit.**

Step 3. Make sure the port **Type** is set to **Access.** From the **Access Policy** drop-down menu, select **MAC Allow List** (see Figure 8-14).

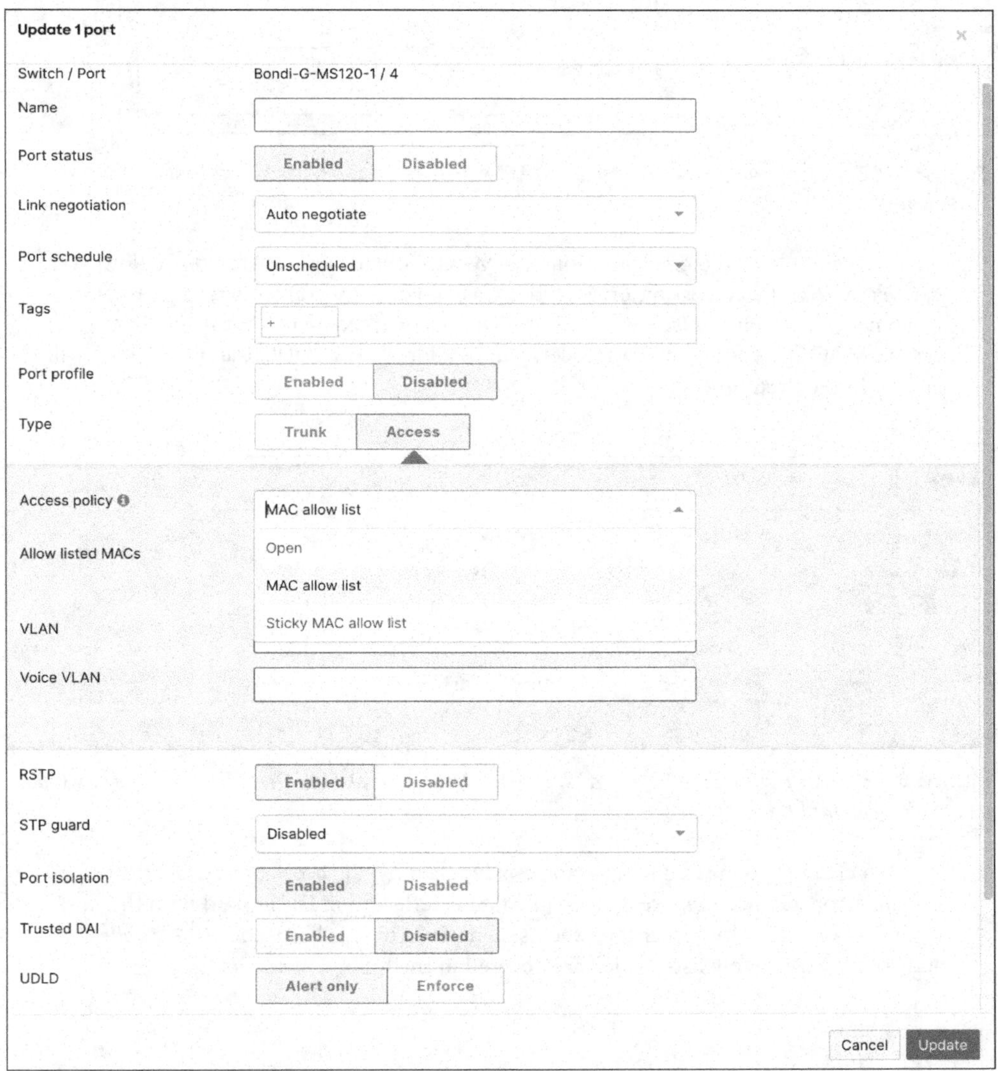

Figure 8-14 *Configuring a MAC Allow List in Meraki Dashboard*

Step 4. Enter the MAC address you want to allow in the **Allow Listed MACs** text field (see Figure 8-15). When adding multiple MAC addresses, separate them using a space or comma or by entering a new MAC address on each line. In this example, we have entered an incorrect MAC address to see what happens when a host that is not on a MAC allow list tries to connect to the network. Click **Update**.

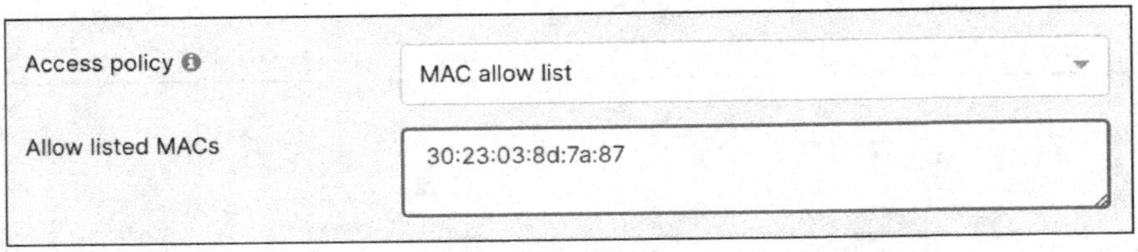

Access policy: MAC allow list

Allow listed MACs: 30:23:03:8d:7a:87

Figure 8-15 *Configuring an Allowed MAC Address on a MAC Allow List in Meraki Dashboard*

This step completes the configuration of a MAC allow list on a switch port. Now, you can verify that the configuration is working as intended by connecting the host and examining the event log (see Figure 8-16). The port will come up, but if the host is not on the MAC allow list, it will not receive an IP address from DHCP, and a warning will appear in the event log.

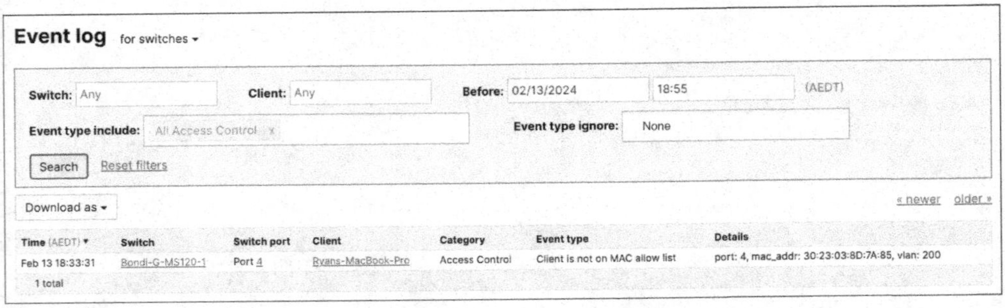

Event log for switches

Switch: Any Client: Any Before: 02/13/2024 18:55 (AEDT)

Event type include: All Access Control Event type ignore: None

Search Reset filters

Download as « newer older »

Time (AEDT)	Switch	Switch port	Client	Category	Event type	Details
Feb 13 18:33:31	Bondi-G-MS120-1	Port 4	Ryans-MacBook-Pro	Access Control	Client is not on MAC allow list	port: 4, mac_addr: 30:23:03:8D:7A:85, vlan: 200

1 total

Figure 8-16 *An Event Log Message Warning That a Host Has Been Denied Access Due to a MAC Allow List*

When a client is connected to a port and is blocked by an access policy, the port goes into an error state (see Figure 8-17). This state is reflected in Dashboard with the port having an orange color rather than the usual green. This applies to both MAC allow lists and sticky MAC allow lists, which are covered in the following section.

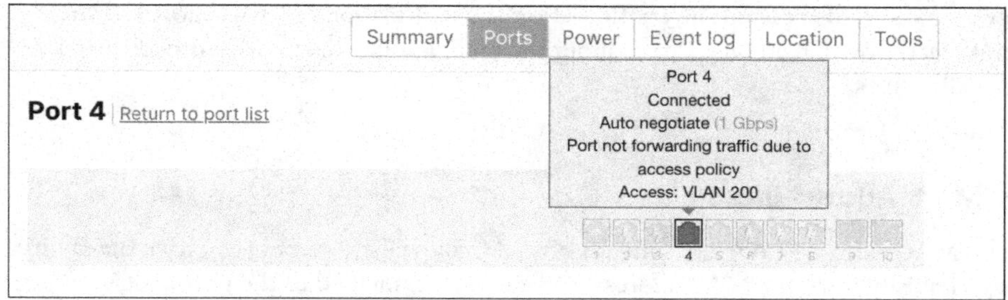

Figure 8-17 *The Port Details Page Showing a Port Dropping Traffic Due to a MAC Allow List Policy*

If the host is on the allow list, it will connect as normal, and an event log entry will not be generated. From the **Switch Ports** page (**Switching > Switch Ports**), click **Details** next to the respective port name. This opens the details page for the respective switch port (see Figure 8-18). Scroll down to **Status** and click **Ping** to verify that the host is reachable (see Figure 8-19).

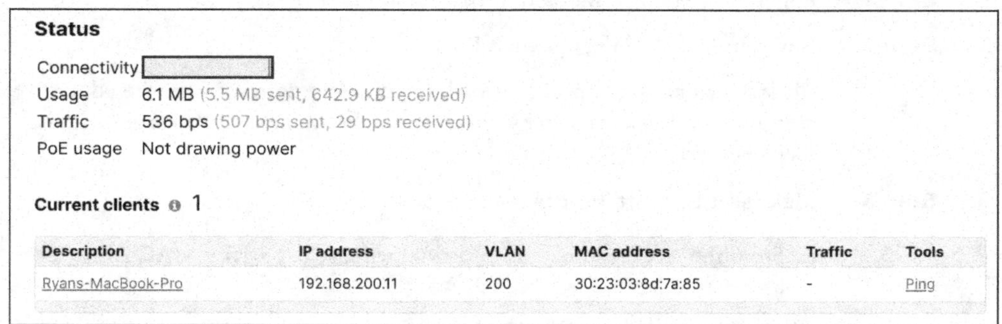

Figure 8-18 *Displaying the Port Status Showing the Details of a Connected Client and the ping Tool*

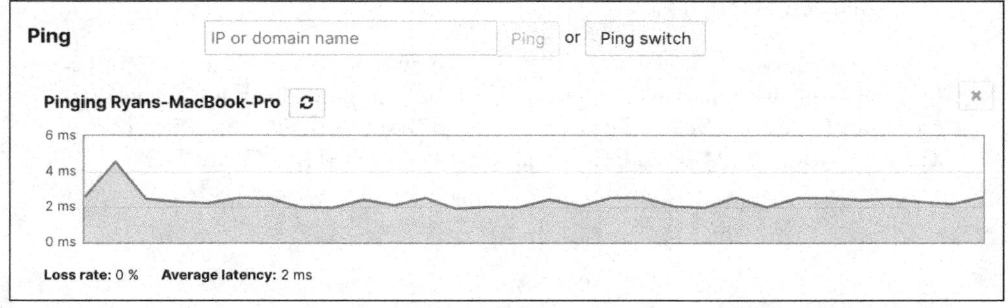

Figure 8-19 *Verifying a Client's Connectivity Using the ping Tool in Meraki Dashboard*

Now that you've completed the configuration and verification of MAC allow lists in Meraki Dashboard, read on to learn about the more advanced, and user-friendly, sticky MAC allow lists.

Sticky MAC Allow Lists

Sticky MAC allow lists operate similarly to MAC allow lists, except they have the ability to dynamically learn the MAC addresses of devices connected to the port and save those addresses in the MAC whitelist. Administrators just need to specify a limit—as little as 1 and no more than 20. When this list is full, all subsequent devices will be denied access to the network. It can take up to 5 minutes for the learned MAC address to appear in Dashboard. When you are listing multiple MAC addresses on a sticky MAC allow list, the addresses can be separated by a space or comma, or you can enter each MAC address on a new line. Sticky MAC allow lists persist through a device reboot, but administrators can also clear them to resume learning new MAC addresses.

Follow these steps to configure a sticky MAC allow list on a Meraki switch port:

Step 1. Log in to Meraki Dashboard (https://dashboard.meraki.com).

Step 2. Navigate to **Switching > Switch Ports.**

Click the name of the port you wish to edit. Alternatively, if you're editing multiple ports, select them by checking the boxes next to their names and then click **Edit**.

Step 3. Make sure the port **Type** is set to **Access**.

a. From the **Access Policy** drop-down menu, select **Sticky MAC Allow List** (see Figure 8-20).

b. Set the **Allow List Size Limit**; it must be a minimum of 1 and no more than 20. For this example, we have specified a limit of 1. In this case, the first MAC address will be learned and allowed, and all remaining devices that connect to this port will not be able to access the network.

c. Click **Update**.

The configuration of a sticky MAC allow list is now complete. You can verify this setup by connecting different devices up to and past the configured limit. It can take up to 5 minutes for learned MAC addresses to show in Dashboard. Edit the switch port again, and you will see the MAC addresses that have been learned (see Figure 8-21).

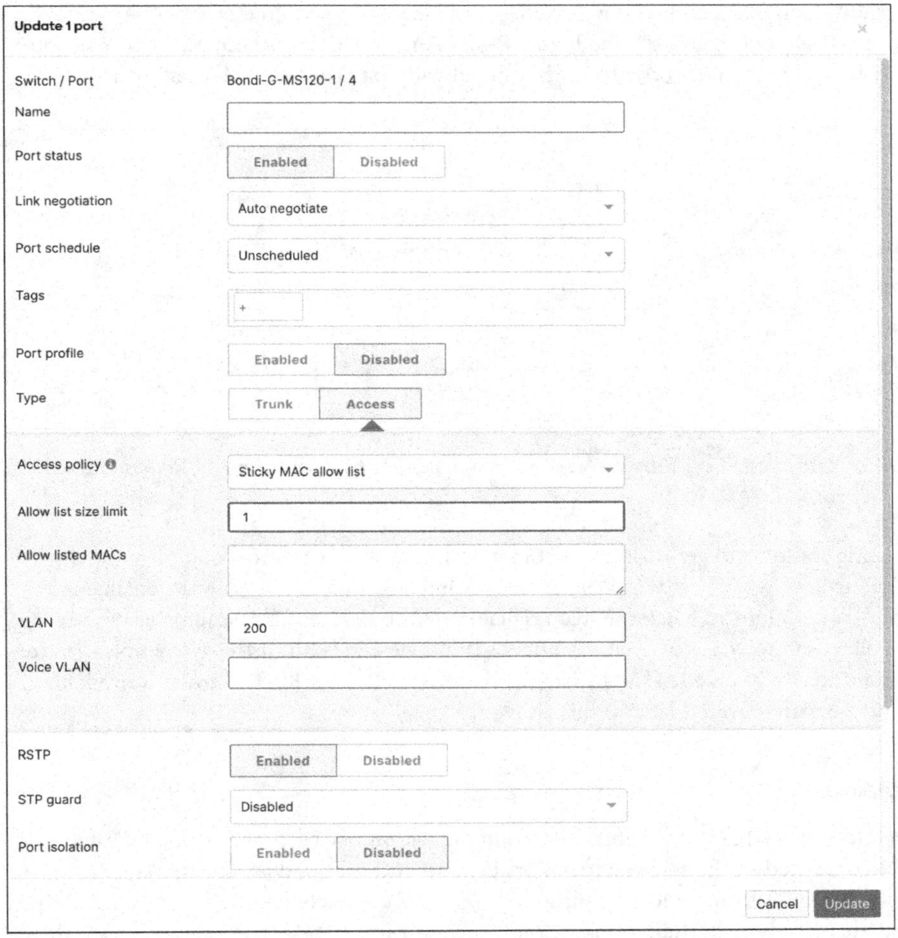

Figure 8-20 *Enabling a Sticky MAC Allow List on a Switch Port*

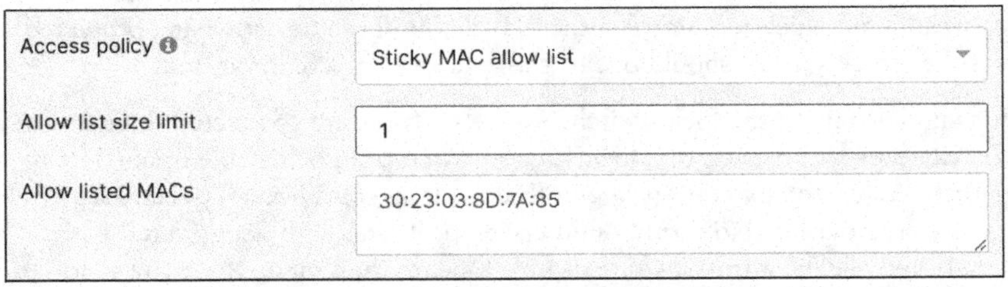

Figure 8-21 *Displaying Learned MAC Addresses on a Port Configured with a Sticky MAC Allow List*

After the limit is exceeded, you will see an event log entry with the event type "Sticky MAC allow list limit reached" (see Figure 8-22). Any new devices connected now will not be able to access the network unless they are already on the sticky MAC allow list.

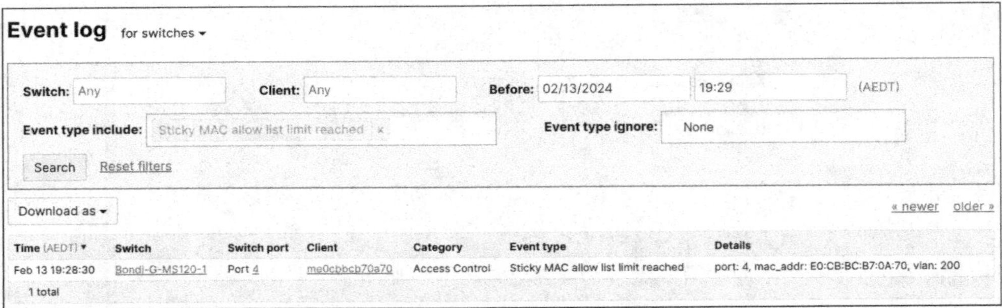

Figure 8-22 *An Event Log Entry Showing a Warning when the Limit Is Reached on a Sticky MAC Allow List*

The configuration and verification of sticky MAC allow lists are now complete. Sticky MAC allow lists work best when the devices being attached to the network change infrequently—even more so when the team replacing these devices also administer the network, such as in the case of access points or IP phones. In both of these examples, better tools that don't rely on MAC addresses such as SecurePort or 802.1X are now available. Both of them are covered later in this chapter.

Port Isolation

Port isolation is a feature that prevents communication between devices in the same VLAN connected to the same switch. Port isolation can be used as an extra layer of security. Port isolation could be configured for ports connected to devices that need to communicate only with the Internet (cloud) such as Meraki MV smart cameras. Another use case might be to reduce the threat of lateral movement between IOT devices in the same VLAN or devices in a DMZ. Devices may coexist in the same VLAN because they are similar in terms of their function or security level; however, there may still be no need to allow east-west communication between them. Isolating these devices using protected ports reduces the attack surface should one of those devices be compromised.

Port isolation applies only to the local switch. Where switches are connected to upstream switches, you can prevent hosts on the downstream switch from being able to connect to hosts on an upstream switch by configuring both downlink (southbound) ports and all host ports with port isolation. No northbound uplink ports should be configured with port isolation; otherwise, host traffic won't be able to leave the switch. Refer to the following guide for further explanation: https://documentation.meraki.com/MS/Port_and_VLAN_Configuration/Restricting_Traffic_with_Isolated_Switch_Ports.

Follow these steps to configure a port isolation on a Meraki switch port:

Step 1. Log in to Meraki Dashboard (https://dashboard.meraki.com).

Step 2. Navigate to **Switching > Switch Ports.** Port isolation works between two or more ports on the same switch. Select at least two ports by checking the boxes next to their names and then click **Edit.**

Step 3. Next to **Port Isolation**, select **Enabled** (see Figure 8-23).

Click **Update.**

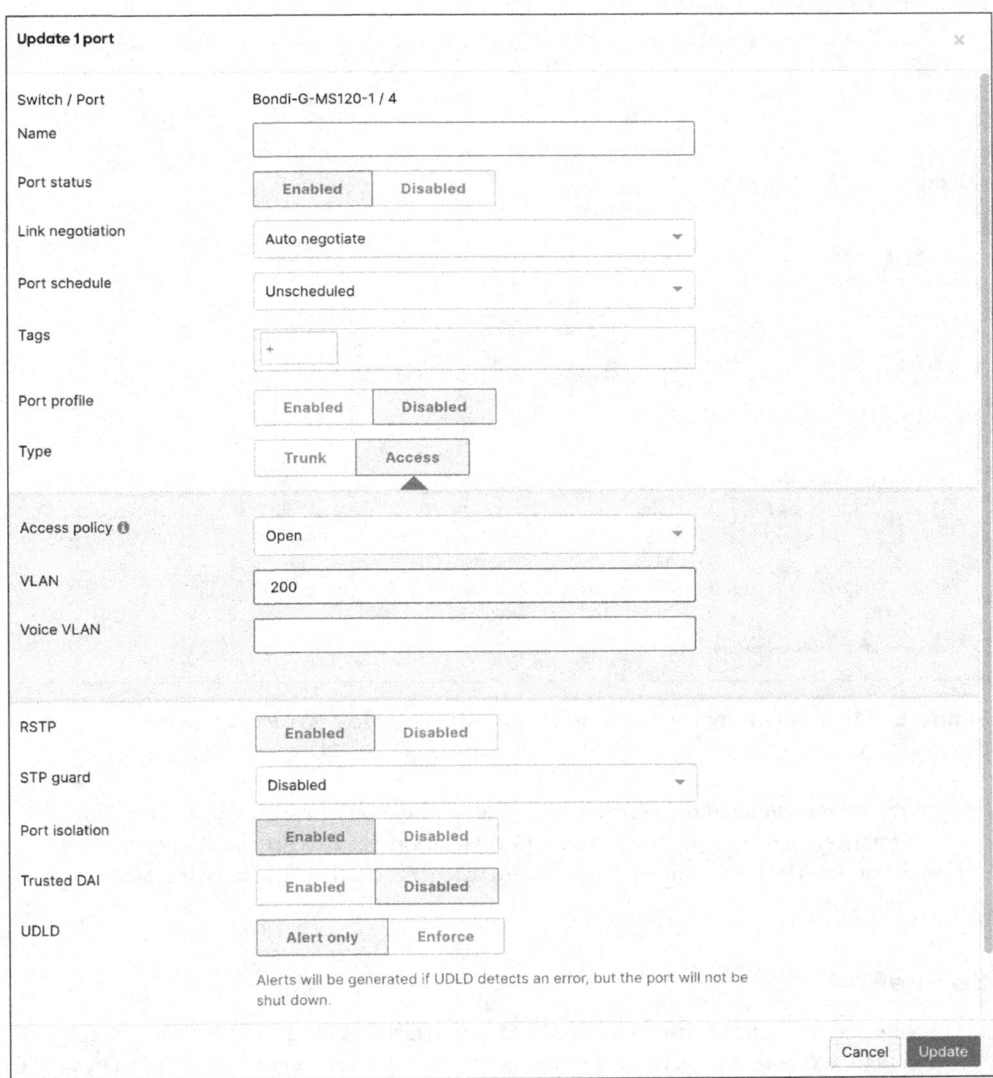

Figure 8-23 *Configuring the Port Isolation Feature on a Switch Port in Meraki Dashboard*

In this example, port isolation has been used to restrict reachability between two Meraki MV cameras in the same subnet. With port isolation now configured, you can use the ping tool in Dashboard to test that the policy is working as intended (**Meraki Dashboard > Cameras > Cameras** [under Monitor]; then click the name of the camera and then select the **Network** tab). Figure 8-24 proves that the camera (192.168.200.2) has connectivity to the Internet (8.8.8.8). However, it no longer has IP reachability to 192.168.200.6, which is in the same subnet and VLAN, confirming that port isolation is working as expected.

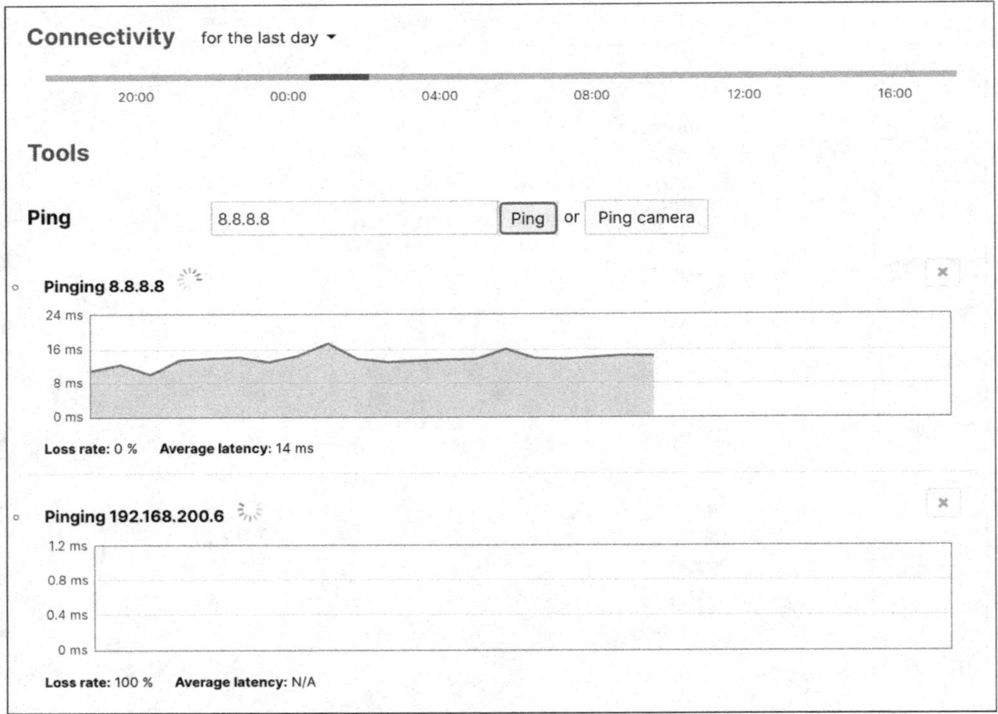

Figure 8-24 *Using ping to Demonstrate the Port Isolation Feature Working Successfully*

You've now completed the configuration and verification of isolated ports. For more information on restricting traffic using port isolation, refer to https://documentation.meraki.com/MS/Port_and_VLAN_Configuration/Restricting_Traffic_with_Isolated_Switch_Ports.

SecurePort

SecurePort is a smart feature on Meraki MS switches that enables Meraki MR access points to authenticate themselves to the network. With SecurePort enabled, when an MR access point is first connected, the only traffic allowed on the switch port is traffic to Meraki Dashboard. After the AP has downloaded its certificate and configuration, it then initiates an 802.1X authentication to the switch port. The switch checks the authenticity of this certificate against the Meraki Cloud and confirms that this MR access point belongs to the same Meraki organization. In doing so, SecurePort builds on the existing hardware trust model, ensuring that only genuine and authorized Meraki access points are operating on your network. When the AP has authenticated, the connected switch port is automatically configured, enabling devices to authenticate to SSIDs configured on the AP as usual. If a non-Meraki MR device were to be connected to this switch port now, such as a user's PC, the switch port would revert to its original configuration. By enabling the easy authentication of network infrastructure devices, in effect, SecurePort becomes part of the zero trust architecture. The major benefit for operations staff is removing the need to manage certificates or manually configure switch ports for APs. Watch this space to see what the future holds for SecurePort and what other Meraki infrastructure could be authenticated in this way.

To use SecurePort, your network must meet the following requirements:

- Both the switch and the access point must reside in the same Meraki organization.
- The switch model must be an MS210 or better running firmware 14.15 or later.
- Access points must support 802.11ac Wave 2 or later.
- The access point must be directly connected to the switch port on the switch that supports SecurePort.
- The management VLAN, as seen when editing an APs LAN IP, should not be configured on the MR access point. SecurePort will automatically place the AP in the same management VLAN as the switch.

If SecurePort is enabled, but devices in your network do not support it, the network will continue to function as if SecurePort was disabled.[2]

Follow these steps to configure SecurePort:

Step 1. Log in to Meraki Dashboard (https://dashboard.meraki.com).

Step 2. With all the prerequisites in place, all that is required is to enable SecurePort on this network. Navigate to **Network-wide > General** and scroll down to **SecurePort**.

Step 3. From the drop-down menu adjacent to **SecurePort**, select **Enabled** (see Figure 8-25).

Click **Save** at the bottom of the page.

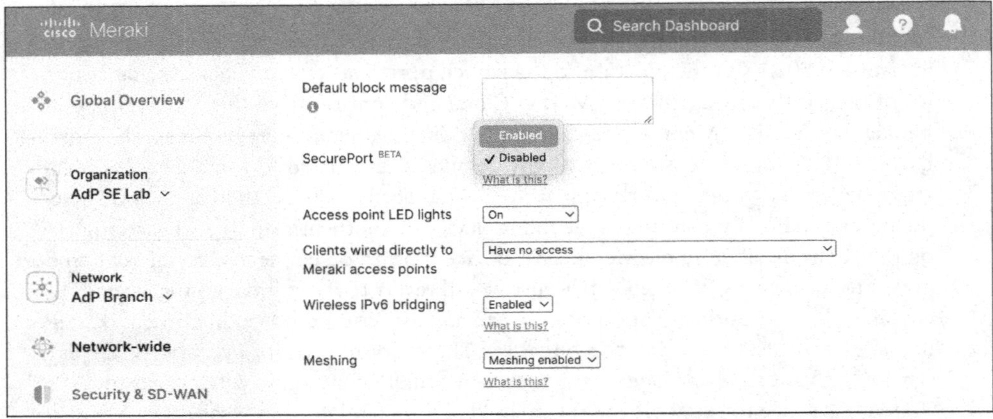

Figure 8-25 *Enabling SecurePort on a Network in Meraki Dashboard*

You've now completed the configuration of SecurePort. To verify that SecurePort is in effect, navigate to the details page of a port connected to an MR access point (**Switching > Switch Ports**; then click **Details** for the port connected to an AP). As shown in Figure 8-26, a new banner in green states that the AP was authenticated using SecurePort.

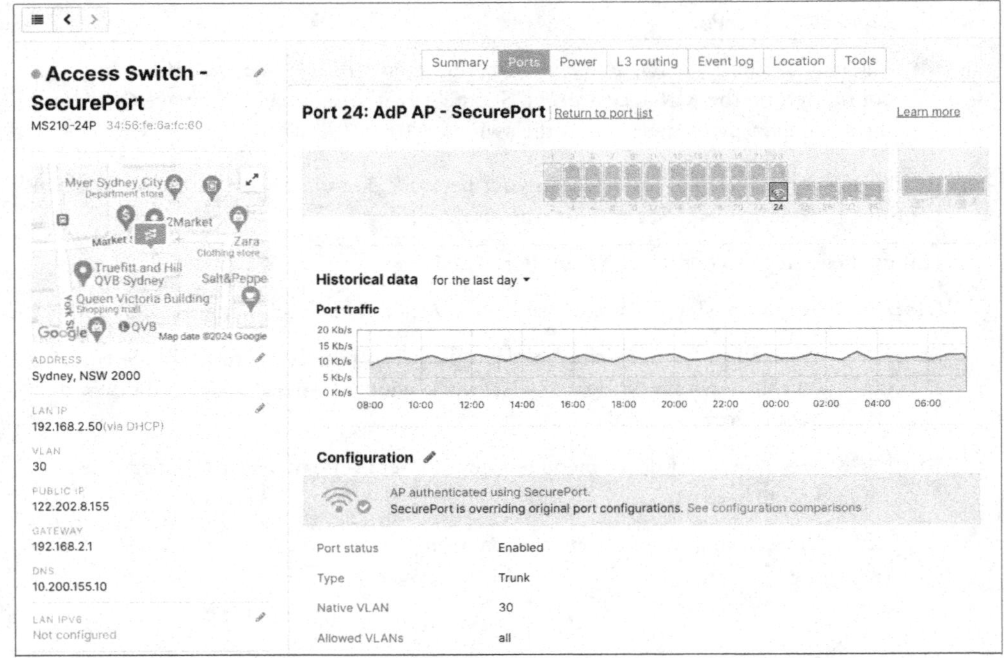

Figure 8-26 *Verifying that SecurePort Is in Operation on a Switch Port in Meraki Dashboard*

You've now completed the configuration and verification of SecurePort. For more details, refer to https://documentation.meraki.com/MS/Access_Control/SecurePort_(formerly_known_as_SecureConnect).

Dynamic ARP Inspection

Address Resolution Protocol (ARP) is susceptible to man-in-the-middle attacks, also known as on-path attacks. Here a host fraudulently updates a switch's ARP table so that a nefarious host receives traffic intended for another legitimate host. The intention could be either to masquerade as a valid host or to simply disrupt a host by blackholing its traffic. Dynamic ARP Inspection (DAI) prevents these types of attacks by inspecting ARP traffic on untrusted ports. ARP traffic is dropped if it does not correspond with the DHCP snooping table. When these ARP packets are dropped, the local ARP cache is not updated, thereby maintaining its integrity.

Dynamic ARP Inspection associates a trust state with every switch port. Switch ports marked as trusted are excluded from DAI validation checks, and all ARP traffic is permitted. By default, switch ports are untrusted.

Dynamic ARP Inspection is supported on the majority of MS switches running the latest firmware releases. Refer to the following guide for the exact supported models and the required minimum software versions: https://documentation.meraki.com/MS/Other_Topics/Dynamic_ARP_Inspection.

Dynamic ARP Inspection is a simple precaution against spoofed MAC and IP addresses. It is recommended that you trust only ports connected to known and trusted devices, such as uplinks to other Meraki switches and trusted devices using static IP addresses. Leave the remaining switch ports as their defaults so that ARP traffic is inspected.

Follow these steps to configure a Dynamic ARP Inspection on a Meraki switch port:[3]

Step 1. Log in to Meraki Dashboard (https://dashboard.meraki.com).

Step 2. Navigate to **Switching > Switch Ports.**

By default, all ports are untrusted (**Trusted DAI** set to **Disabled**), so it's recommended that you configure all uplinks and any ports attached to devices with static IP addresses as trusted (**Trusted DAI** set to **Enabled**) before enabling Dynamic ARP Inspection. Click the name of the port you wish to edit. Alternatively, if editing multiple ports, select them by checking the boxes next to their names and then click **Edit**.

Step 3. Locate **Trusted DAI**, set this to **Enabled**, and click **Update** (see Figure 8-27).

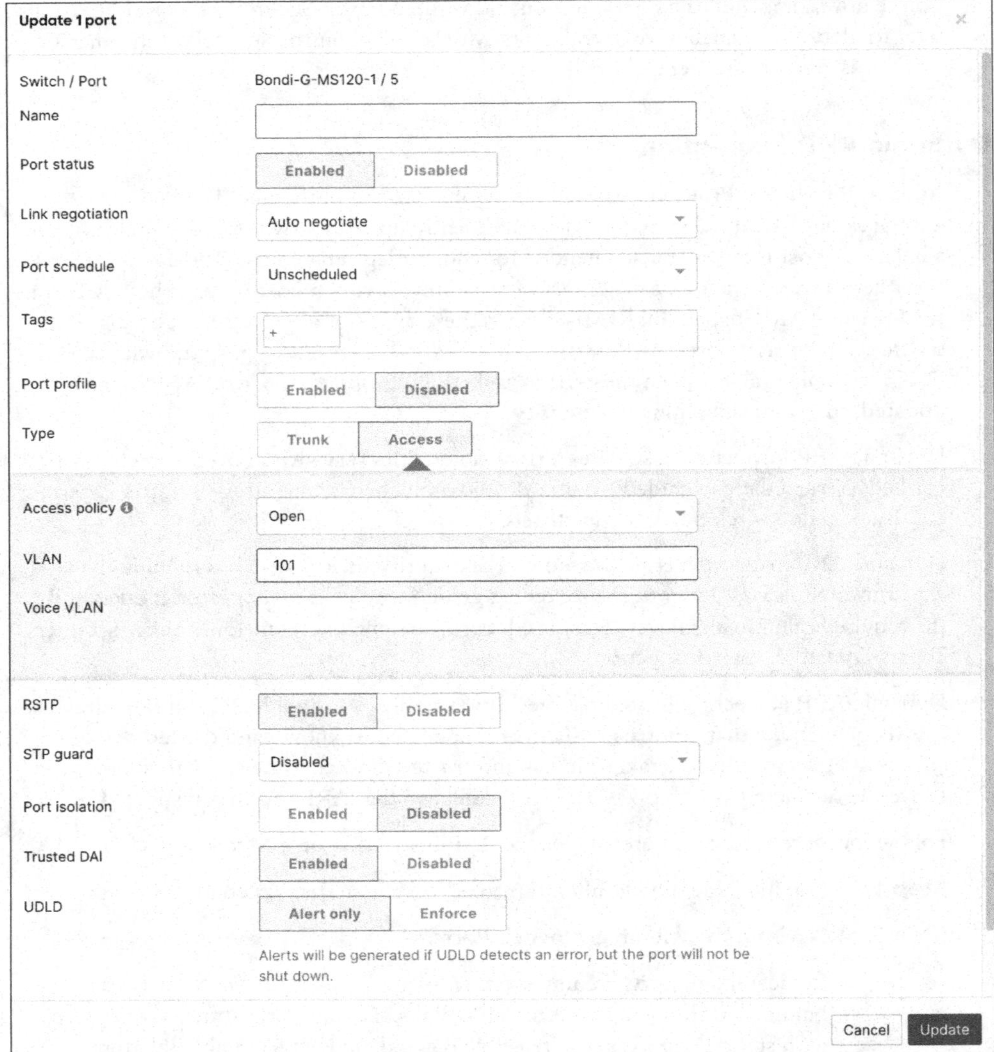

Figure 8-27 *Configuring the Dynamic ARP Inspection Trusted Status on a Switch Port in Meraki Dashboard*

Step 4. Navigate to **Switching > DHCP Servers & ARP** (under Monitor).

  a. Scroll down to **Dynamic ARP Inspection.**

  b. From the **DAI status** drop-down menu (see Figure 8-28), select **Enabled** and click **Save Changes.**

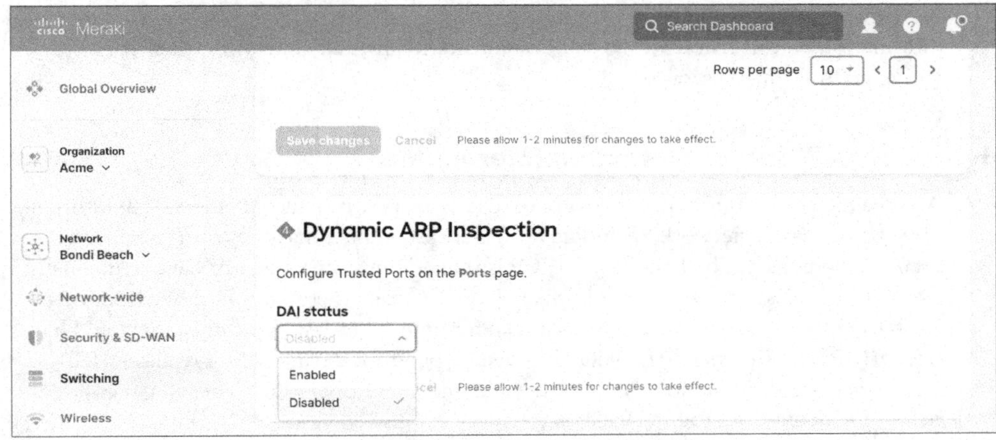

Figure 8-28 *Enabling Dynamic ARP Inspection in Meraki Dashboard*

The configuration to enable Dynamic ARP Inspection is now complete.

To verify the setup is working, simply configure a host with a static IP address and connect it to an untrusted port (**Trusted DAI** set to **Disabled**). The event log displays entries with an event type of **DAI Blocked** for the host that is trying to access the network (see Figure 8-29). Clients blocked by DAI inspection can also be seen on the **DHCP Servers, RA Guard, and DAI** page under **DAI Blocked Events (Switching > DHCP Servers & ARP)**.

Time (AEDT)	Switch	Switch port	Client	Category	Event type	Details
Feb 15 08:19:44	Bondi-G-MS120-1			Access Control	DAI blocked	mac: 30:23:03:8D:7A:85, ip: 192.168.200.55, vlan: 200
Feb 15 08:19:42	Bondi-G-MS120-1			Access Control	DAI blocked	mac: 30:23:03:8D:7A:85, ip: 192.168.200.55, vlan: 200
Feb 15 08:19:40	Bondi-G-MS120-1			Access Control	DAI blocked	mac: 30:23:03:8D:7A:85, ip: 192.168.200.55, vlan: 200
Feb 15 08:19:38	Bondi-G-MS120-1			Access Control	DAI blocked	mac: 30:23:03:8D:7A:85, ip: 192.168.200.55, vlan: 200
Feb 15 08:19:36	Bondi-G-MS120-1			Access Control	DAI blocked	mac: 30:23:03:8D:7A:85, ip: 192.168.200.55, vlan: 200
Feb 15 08:19:34	Bondi-G-MS120-1			Access Control	DAI blocked	mac: 30:23:03:8D:7A:85, ip: 192.168.200.55, vlan: 200
Feb 15 08:19:32	Bondi-G-MS120-1			Access Control	DAI blocked	mac: 30:23:03:8D:7A:85, ip: 192.168.200.55, vlan: 200
Feb 15 08:19:30	Bondi-G-MS120-1			Access Control	DAI blocked	mac: 30:23:03:8D:7A:85, ip: 192.168.200.55, vlan: 200
Feb 15 08:19:28	Bondi-G-MS120-1			Access Control	DAI blocked	mac: 30:23:03:8D:7A:85, ip: 192.168.200.55, vlan: 200
Feb 15 08:19:26	Bondi-G-MS120-1			Access Control	DAI blocked	mac: 30:23:03:8D:7A:85, ip: 192.168.200.55, vlan: 200
Feb 15 08:19:24	Bondi-G-MS120-1			Access Control	DAI blocked	mac: 30:23:03:8D:7A:85, ip: 192.168.200.55, vlan: 200
Feb 15 08:19:21	Bondi-G-MS120-1			Access Control	DAI blocked	mac: 30:23:03:8D:7A:85, ip: 192.168.200.55, vlan: 200
Feb 15 08:19:20	Bondi-G-MS120-1			Access Control	DAI blocked	mac: 30:23:03:8D:7A:85, vlan: 200

13 total

Figure 8-29 *Log Entries in the Event Log Showing a Host Blocked by Dynamic ARP Inspection*

Now that you've completed the setup of Dynamic ARP Inspection, you can find more information on this feature at https://documentation.meraki.com/MS/Other_Topics/Dynamic_ARP_Inspection.

Rogue DHCP Server Detection (Meraki MS)

A Dynamic Host Configuration Protocol (DHCP) server provides IP addressing information for hosts on a network, including an IP address, subnet mask, gateway, and DNS server IP addresses. The benefit of DHCP is that administrators do not have to manually assign IP addresses to every host in the network. Clients therefore can move from network to network—something we often take for granted today. Typically, you would have one DHCP server per subnet. DHCP has been around for decades. As a result, DHCP servers are prevalent in most network devices and client operating systems, increasing the risk of incidents from rogue DHCP servers.

DHCP is easy to disrupt simply by adding another DHCP server to a subnet. I (Ryan) once worked for a large company in London that had 200 developers working in an office. It was a common occurrence for a developer to spin up a virtual machine to do some testing, and that virtual machine would often have DHCP server turned on. Before long, 200 developers were not able to do any work, and the IT team were running around trying to get to the bottom of the problem. The result was an enormous amount of lost productivity and time wasted troubleshooting. In another instance, an organization had severely limited their guest Wi-Fi, which resulted in staff members and contractors bringing in their own APs and connecting them to the network. These APs would serve out IP addresses using DHCP, and once again users were impacted. With these real-world examples in mind, we highly recommend that you take steps to block and detect rogue DHCP servers on your network.

Fortunately, Meraki Dashboard makes it easy for administrators to implement controls to block untrusted DHCP servers. This feature supports both IPv4 and IPv6 DHCP servers. In this example, IPv4 addresses are provided by a DHCP server on a Meraki MX. This MX is directly connected to a Meraki MS switch, and IPv6 is not used. The aim is to protect the current DHCP server and ensure that no other DHCP servers can disrupt the network. To this end, we demonstrate how to configure a policy to trust the current DHCP server and block all unknown DHCP servers.

Follow these steps to protect against rogue DHCP servers in your network:

Step 1. Log in to Meraki Dashboard (https://dashboard.meraki.com).

Step 2. Navigate to **Switching > DHCP Servers and DHCP** (under Monitor). Meraki Dashboard keeps track of DHCP servers it has seen on the network, as shown in the **DHCP Servers** table in Figure 8-30.

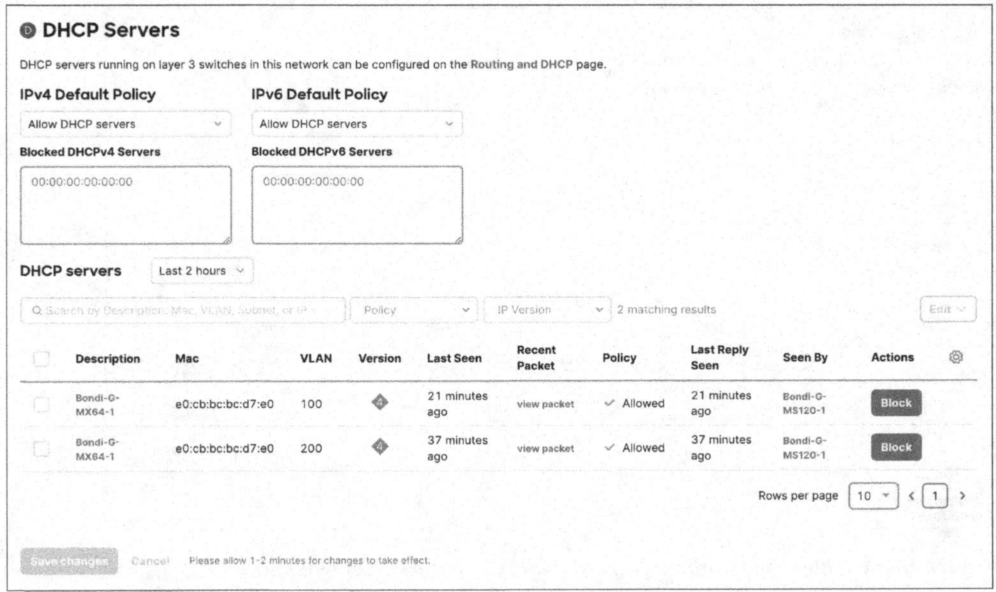

Figure 8-30 *The DHCP Servers and ARP Page in Meraki Dashboard*

Step 3. Set **IPv4 Default Policy** to **Block DHCP Servers.**

a. Copy the MAC address from the **Mac** column in the table shown in Figure 8-31 that corresponds to the DHCP server in your network. Paste this into the **Allowed DHCPv4 Servers** text box.

b. Click **Save Changes.**

c. If you are running DHCPv6 in your network, you could similarly block rogue DHCPv6 servers here also.

At this point, you've completed the configuration to block rogue DHCP servers on your network.

Follow these steps to verify the setup is working:

Step 1. Ensure that there is at least one client in the same VLAN as your rogue DHCP server and ensure that the clients have IP reachability to the rogue DHCP server.

Step 2. Renew the DHCP lease on your clients. For the Mac, you can find instructions on how to do this at https://support.apple.com/en-au/guide/mac-help/mchlp1545/mac. At the Windows command prompt, enter the **ipconfig /release** command, followed by the **ipconfig /renew** command.

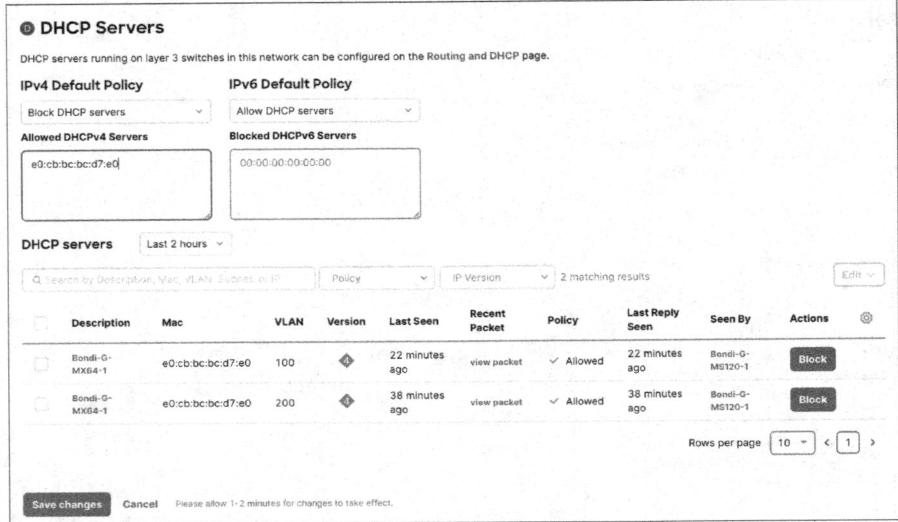

Figure 8-31 *Blocking Unknown DHCP Servers in Meraki Dashboard*

Step 3. In Meraki Dashboard, you see an event log message with the event type **DHCP Blocked (Network-wide > Event Log)**, as shown in Figure 8-32. This window also displays details of the rogue DHCP server, such as its IP address, VLAN, and MAC address.

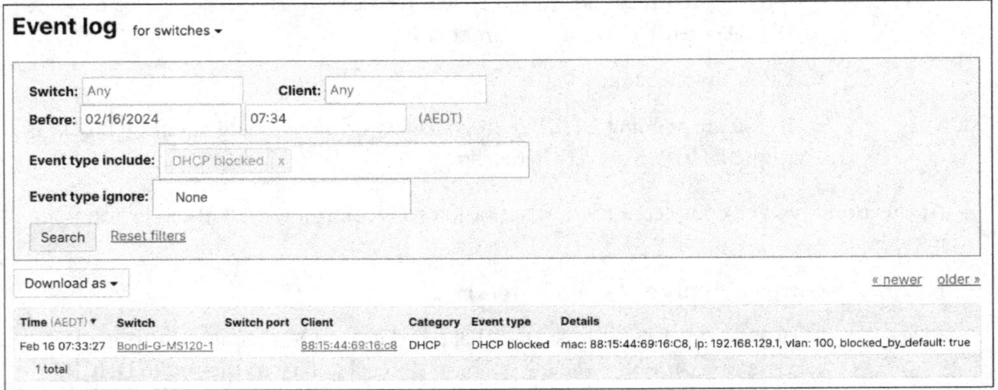

Figure 8-32 *The DHCP Block Log Message in the Event Log in Meraki Dashboard*

Step 4. Click the MAC address in the **Client** column to launch the **Client** page in Dashboard, showing exactly how this rogue DHCP server is connected to the network. In Figure 8-33, the rogue DHCP server is connected to port 4 on a Meraki switch at the Bondi branch with the hostname Bondi-G-MS120-1.

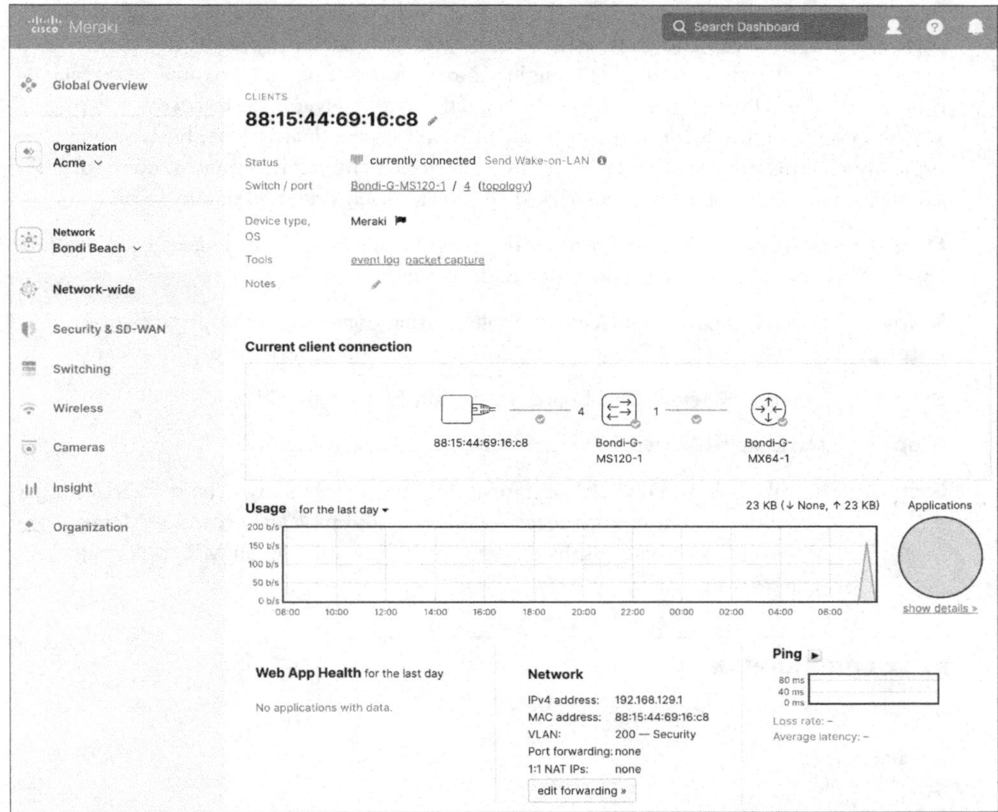

Figure 8-33 *Identifying How a Rogue DHCP Server Is Connected to the Network in Meraki Dashboard*

You've now completed the configuration to block untrusted DHCP servers, as well as the steps to verify that this feature is working correctly. For more information on the DHCP servers and ARP page in Meraki Dashboard, refer to https://documentation.meraki.com/MS/Monitoring_and_Reporting/MS_DHCP_Servers.

Hardening Meraki MR and MS Devices (Local Status Page)

Security best practice requires that administrators change all default passwords; this includes those that protect the local management interfaces on devices. As an example, PCI DSS 4.0 requirement 2.2.2 has the following requirements:

- If the vendor default accounts will be used, the default password is changed per Requirement 8.3.6 (password complexity requirement).
- If the vendor default accounts will not be used, the account is removed or disabled.

Even though Meraki devices are cloud managed, each Meraki device has a local status page where basic setup and diagnostic information is available. Typically, this page is accessed only once to configure the minimum required settings for the device to reach Dashboard. For APs, you would typically use DHCP and never need to access this page. What is visible on the local status page varies based on the device type, but you would typically use this page to see details of the interfaces including their status, configure IP address and cellular settings, check that devices can reach Dashboard, and so on.

Once devices are connected to Dashboard, access to the local status page should be hardened with a complex password or disabled altogether.

Follow these steps to harden devices by implementing controls in relation to their local status page:

Step 1. Log in to Meraki Dashboard (https://dashboard.meraki.com).

Step 2. Navigate to **Network-wide > General** (under Configure).

Step 3. Scroll down to **Device Configuration.** Figure 8-34 shows the default settings. You can see that remote access is disabled and physical access to Meraki access points is also disabled (typically, you would get an MR status page using Wi-Fi).

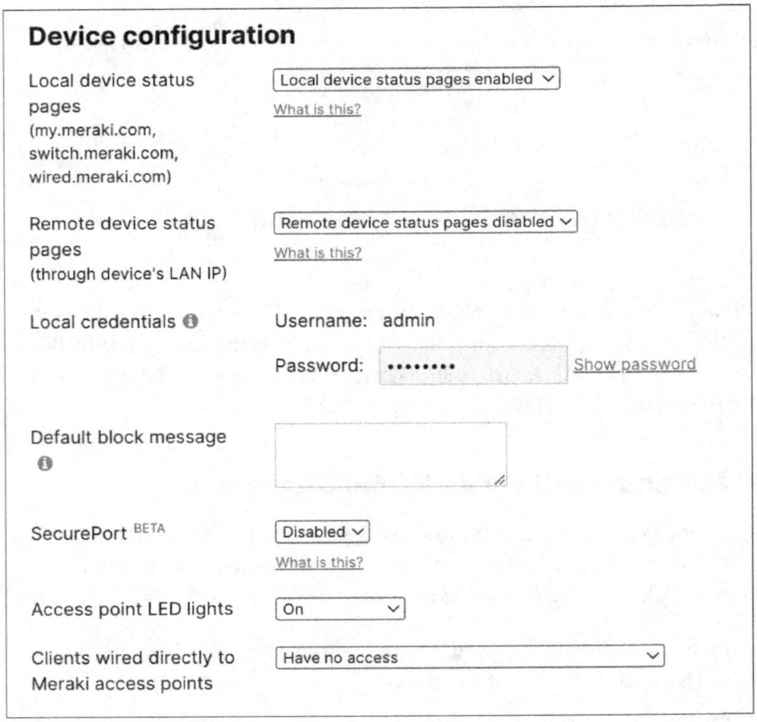

Figure 8-34 *The Device Configuration Section of the Network-Wide General Page in Meraki Dashboard*

Step 4. Here, you should set a strong password that complies with your organization's password policy.

The local status page can be disabled if your network is already set up and functioning correctly (see Figure 8-35). Do this by selecting **Local Devices Status Pages Disabled** from the **Local Device Status Pages** drop-down menu. Note that the local status page remains available when connecting to physical management ports on devices that have them. Therefore, it is important to still set a strong password even if disabling the local status page.

To finish, click **Save** in the bottom right corner of the page.

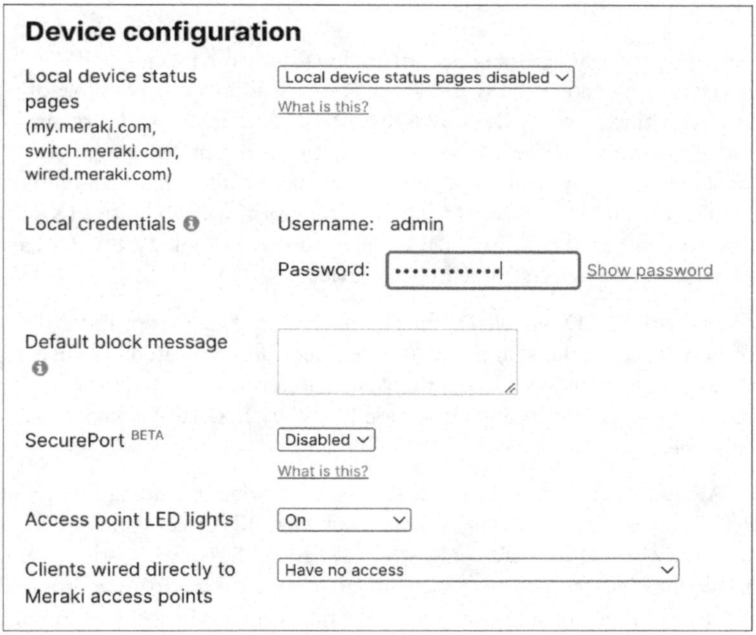

Device configuration

Local device status pages (my.meraki.com, switch.meraki.com, wired.meraki.com) — Local device status pages disabled — What is this?

Local credentials — Username: admin — Password: •••••••••••• — Show password

Default block message

SecurePort BETA — Disabled — What is this?

Access point LED lights — On

Clients wired directly to Meraki access points — Have no access

Figure 8-35 *Setting a Strong Password for the Local Status Page in Meraki Dashboard*

You've completed the hardening of the local device status page for a network. In larger deployments, it is recommended that you use templates so that these settings are applied everywhere. If you want to verify that these settings are in effect, try connecting to the LAN IP addresses of your Meraki devices using HTTP or the following URLs:

- **Meraki MR devices:** http://ap.meraki.com
- **Meraki MS devices:** http://switch.meraki.com
- **Meraki MX devices:** http://mx.meraki.com or http://wired.meraki.com
- **Meraki MG devices:** http://mg.meraki.com
- **All devices:** http://setup.meraki.com or http://my.meraki.com

For more information on the local status page, including how to access it and examples from the various Meraki products, refer to https://documentation.meraki.com/General_Administration/Tools_and_Troubleshooting/Using_the_Cisco_Meraki_Device_Local_Status_Page.

Zero Trust (Wired and Wireless Dot1x)

The term *zero trust* was coined by Forrester analyst John Kindervag in 2010 and refers to an information security model that denies access to applications and data by default. Under this model, users and devices are granted access based on policy informed by "continuous, contextual, risk-based verification across users and their associated devices."[4]

Zero trust is a key theme prevalent across IT security standards. More recently, NIST published their zero trust architecture, NIST SP 800-207, which adopts this principle of zero trust. Another practical example is NIST SP 800-53 IA-3's requirement for organizations to identify and authenticate devices, before allowing them to establish a network connection. The most common way to authenticate devices before allowing them onto the network is to implement 802.1X. Once referred to as Network Access Control (NAC), 802.1X is an IEEE standard drafted back in 2001. Being a mature technology, 802.1X has broad support both in Meraki products and end-user devices.

SSIDs and switch ports with 802.1X enabled typically block all traffic, except Extensible Authentication Protocol (EAP) packets, until a device has been authenticated. The user's device is referred to as a *supplicant*, the access point or switch is referred to as the *authenticator*, and the server doing the authentication (typically RADIUS) is known as the *authentication server*.

Over time various EAP authentication methods have been developed, including Protected EAP (PEAP), EAP-TLS, EAP-TTLS, and many others. Each method differs slightly. For example, PEAP uses server-side certificates only, whereas EAP-TLS requires both server-side and client-side certificates. Because each authentication method has its own pros and cons, ultimately the decision on which to use comes down to which is best suited to your organization's requirements. Read on to learn more about PEAP and EAP-TLS, which are the two most commonly used EAP methods.

The following sections detail how to configure 802.1X on Meraki MR access points and MS switches. These sections build on the steps from Chapter 7, "User Authentication," which show how to configure Cisco Identity Services Engine (ISE) to support 802.1X authentication for wired and wireless access. The Meraki side of the configuration is simple and involves only a few steps. In combination, the aim is to show you a simple and reliable way to get started with 802.1X. This includes EAP-TLS, which is often thought of as an advanced topic because it requires client-side certificates. Generating client-side certificates requires a certificate authority and, typically, a mobile device management solution like Meraki Systems Manager to distribute them. Read on to learn how to deploy 802.1X on your Meraki network.

802.1X with Protected EAP (PEAP) on Wired and Wireless Networks

This section focuses on the tasks required to enable basic 802.1X on your wireless network. Out of the box, a minimal RADIUS setup typically results in PEAP being negotiated as the authentication protocol. Using PEAP, an authentication server uses a certificate to authenticate itself to the client only. The client (supplicant) does not need to provide its own certificate to the authentication server for it to verify. This makes PEAP easy to roll out because an administrator does not have to manage certificates on client devices. It is still recommended that you use EAP-TLS, which can be enabled easily using Sentry policies. We cover Sentry policies, as well as how to configure traditional EAP-TLS, later in this chapter.

Configuring Wireless 802.1X with Protected EAP (PEAP)

Two high-level tasks need to be completed for users to successfully authenticate to the wireless network using 802.1X. An administrator must

1. Configure a policy on the RADIUS infrastructure to permit authorized users to connect to the network. For these steps, refer to the "RADIUS Configuration for Wired and Wireless 802.1X" section in Chapter 7.
2. Configure the wireless network to forward the authentication requests onto the RADIUS authentication server, which in this example is Cisco ISE. These steps are covered in the list that follows.

Follow these steps to configure 802.1X authentication with PEAP on a wireless SSID:

Step 1. Log in to Meraki Dashboard (https://dashboard.meraki.com).

Step 2. Navigate to **Wireless** > **Access Control** (under Configure).

Step 3. Select the correct SSID from the **SSID** drop-down menu (see Figure 8-36).

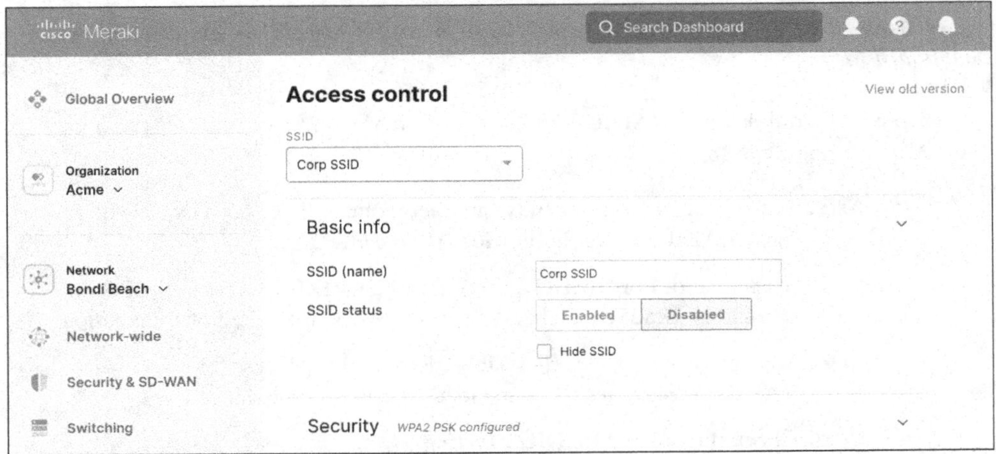

Figure 8-36 *The Wireless Access Control Page in Meraki Dashboard*

Step 4. Scroll down to **Security** and select the **Enterprise With** option. From the drop-down menu under **Enterprise With**, select **My RADIUS Server** (see Figure 8-37).

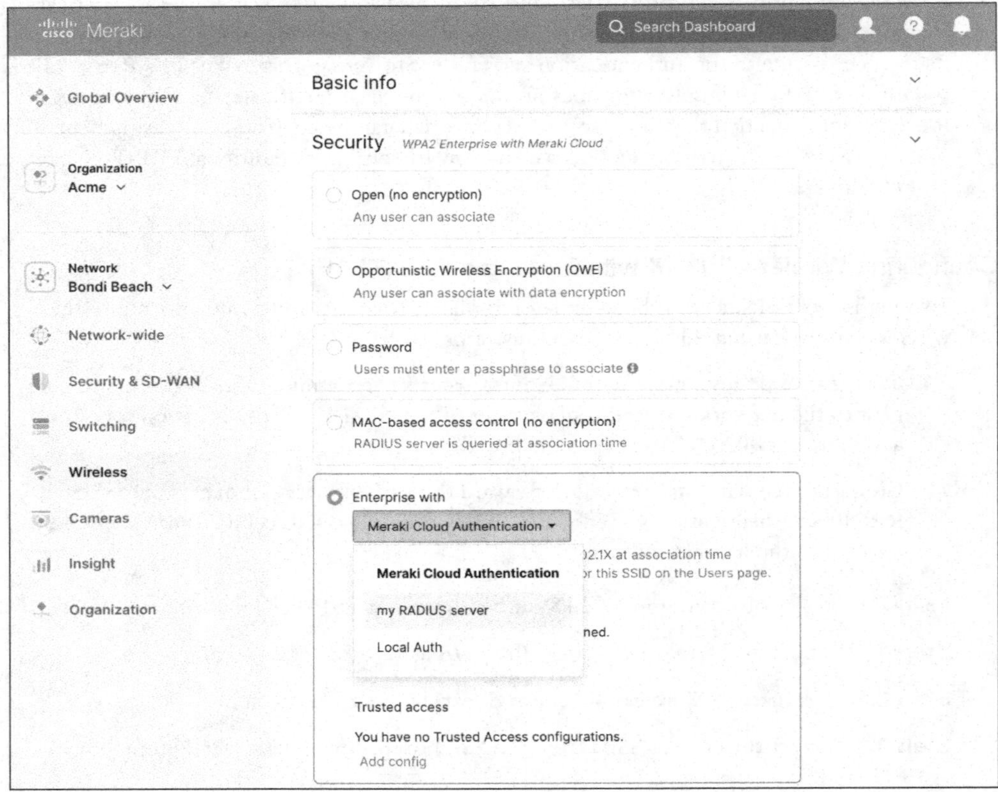

Figure 8-37 *Configuring RADIUS as the Authentication Method on an SSID in Meraki Dashboard*

Step 5. Scroll down to **RADIUS**, and then click **RADIUS** to expand this panel (see Figure 8-38).

a. Enter the IP address or fully qualified domain name (FQDN) for the primary RADIUS server in the **Host IP or FQDN** field.

b. Set the **Auth Port** to **1812** and enter the RADIUS secret in the **Secret** field. Leave **RadSec** unchecked; we discuss it at the end of this section.

c. When you're finished, click **Done.** Repeat this process for any other RADIUS servers (it's recommended to have a minimum of two).

d. Check the box for **RADIUS Testing.**

e. Scroll down to **RADIUS Accounting Servers.**

f. Click **Add Server**, and then click **Cancel** if you see a RADIUS test pop-up message.

g. In the **Host IP or FQDN** field, enter the IP address or FQDN for your Cisco ISE server.

h. Set the **Acct Port** to **1813.**

i. Enter the password being used for the RADIUS secret in the **Secret** field. Again, leave RadSec unchecked.

j. Later in this chapter we use this policy to assign group policies. If you are already planning to assign group policies using ISE, select **Filter-ID** from the **RADIUS Attribute Specifying Group Policy Name** drop-down menu.

k. Finish by clicking **Save** at the bottom of the page.

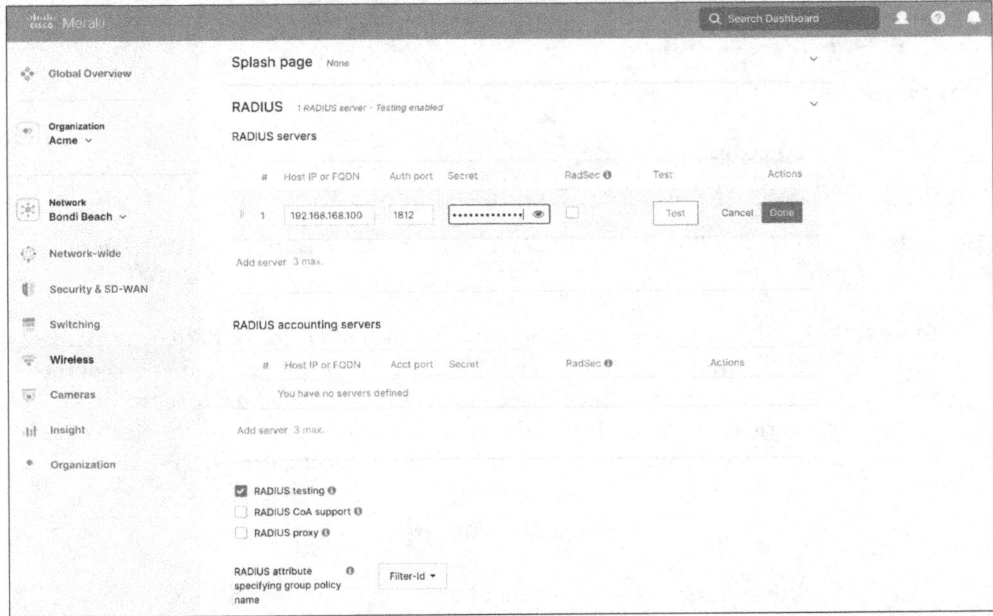

Figure 8-38 *Configuring RADIUS Servers for Wireless Access Control in Meraki Dashboard*

At this point, you've completed the configuration of the wireless network necessary for 802.1X authentication. Before trying to connect to the wireless network, ensure you have completed the setup of the RADIUS servers, as detailed in the "RADIUS Configuration for Wired and Wireless 802.1X" section in Chapter 7.

With both the wireless network and the RADIUS infrastructure configured, follow these steps to verify that 802.1X is functioning:

Step 1. Using a client device such as a laptop or mobile device, try associating to the SSID on which you just configured the wireless access control. In this example, shown in Figure 8-39, we've used a Mac to connect to **Corp SSID**. When you are prompted for a username and password, enter the credentials for a user you configured in Active Directory in Chapter 7.

Figure 8-39 *The Login Prompt on macOS for a Client Connecting to an SSID with 802.1X Authentication*

Step 2. PEAP uses a certificate to authenticate the server side of this connection. Because this is the first connection, the client might be asked to accept the certificate. In this example (see Figure 8-40), we've used a Mac, so click **Continue** to accept the certificate. This step occurs only on the first connection; on subsequent connections, devices connect automatically.

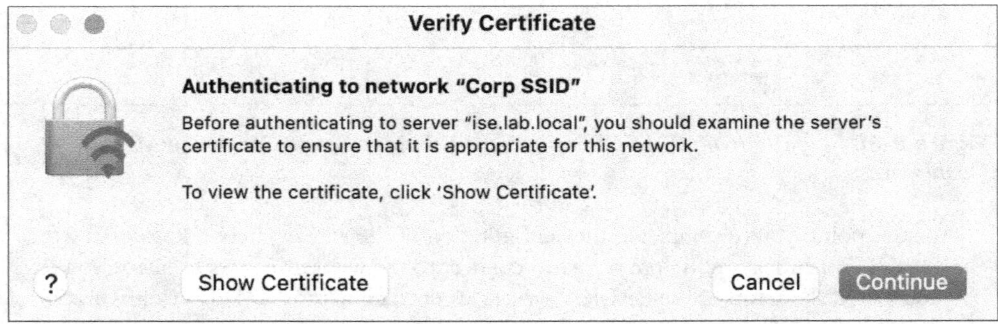

Figure 8-40 *The Verify Certificate Prompt to Accept the Server-Side Certificate on macOS*

Step 3. The user has now been successfully connected to the network. You can verify this by referring to the authentication detail report found in Cisco ISE (**Menu > Operations > Live Logs**). As per the excerpt shown in Figure 8-41, using this report, an administrator can easily verify that a user was successfully authenticated, and the authentication protocol was indeed PEAP.

Authentication Details	
Source Timestamp	2024-04-06 12:15:37.981
Received Timestamp	2024-04-06 12:15:37.981
Policy Server	ise
Event	5200 Authentication succeeded
Username	hayden@lab.local
Endpoint Id	F8:FF:C2:0E:84:38
Calling Station Id	F8-FF-C2-0E-84-38
Endpoint Profile	Apple-Device
Authentication Identity Store	Windows_2016_AD-10.200.155.100
Identity Group	Profiled
Authentication Method	dot1x
Authentication Protocol	PEAP (EAP-MSCHAPv2)
Service Type	Framed
Network Device	ACME_Store_Wifi
Device Type	All Device Types
Location	All Locations
NAS IPv4 Address	192.168.129.2
NAS Port Type	Wireless - IEEE 802.11
Authorization Profile	PermitAccess
Response Time	111 milliseconds

Figure 8-41 *Authentication Detail Report Excerpt from Cisco ISE Showing a Successful Wireless 802.1X Connection*

Step 4. Last, you also can use the event log in Meraki Dashboard to verify that this connection used 802.1X. As shown in Figure 8-42, the event log shows this client's association to the Corp SSID and the subsequent successful RADIUS and 802.1X authentication.

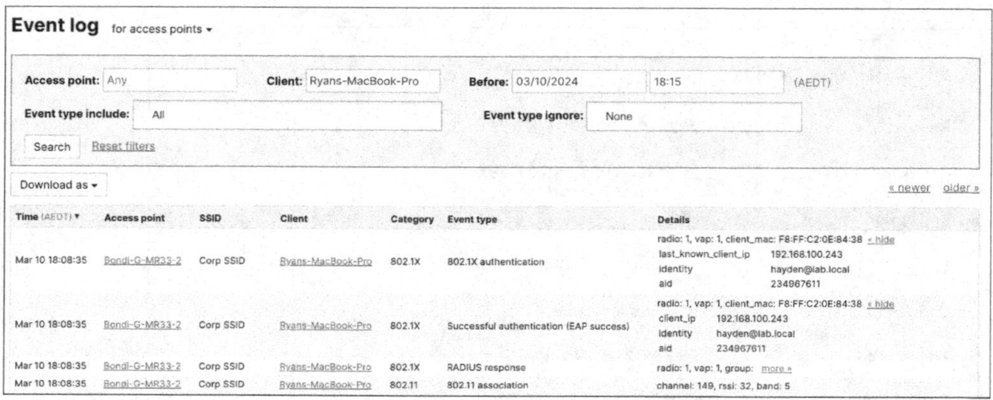

Figure 8-42 *The Event Log in Meraki Dashboard Showing a Successful Wireless 802.1X Authentication*

The configuration and verification of wireless 802.1X using PEAP are now complete. To learn more about access control on Meraki wireless networks, check out Meraki's Access Control guide available at https://documentation.meraki.com/MR/Access_Control.

Eagle-eyed readers might have noticed the check box for RadSec on Figure 8-38. RadSec improves on traditional RADIUS through the addition of certificates and strong encryption between the APs and the RADIUS server. RadSec support was introduced with MR firmware 30.X and is supported with Cisco ISE. If you wish to deploy RadSec with Meraki MR access points, check out https://documentation.meraki.com/MR/Encryption_and_Authentication/MR_RADSec.

Configuring Wired 802.1X with Protected EAP (PEAP)

With 802.1X with PEAP already configured and working on the wireless network, only a tiny tweak is needed to get it working on the wired network as well.

Let's recap the prerequisite steps already completed in Chapter 7:

1. An organization-wide RADIUS server was configured in Meraki Dashboard.
2. A policy set matching wired 802.1X RADIUS requests was configured on Cisco ISE.
3. The wired 802.1X setup established in the previous section was verified using a client connected to a LAN port on a Meraki MX security appliance.

Now, the only remaining steps are to configure an access policy, apply it to the required switch ports, and verify that users are able to authenticate onto the network.

Follow these steps to configure 802.1X authentication on switch ports:

Step 1. Log in to Meraki Dashboard (https://dashboard.meraki.com).

Step 2. Navigate to **Switching > Access Policies** (under Configure), as shown in Figure 8-43.

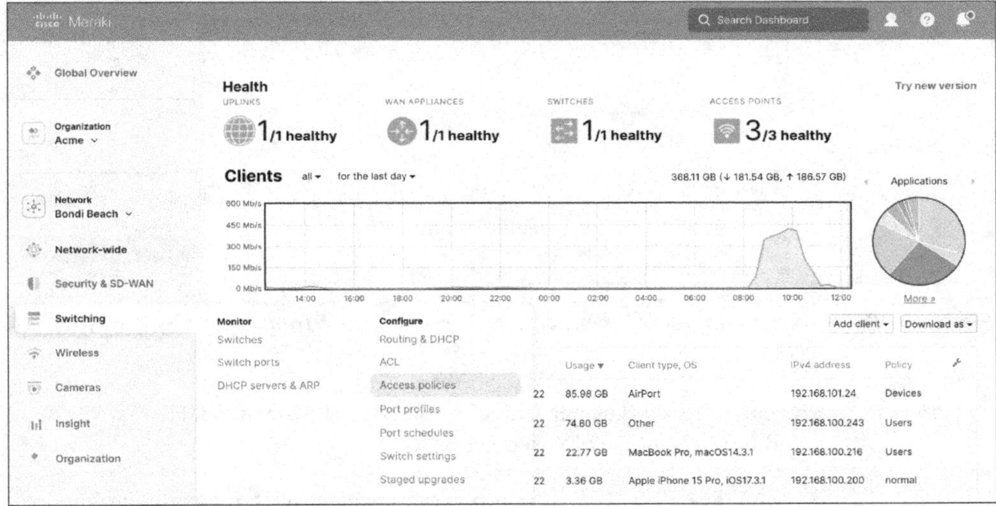

Figure 8-43 *Navigating to the Switching Access Policies Page in Meraki Dashboard*

Step 3. Click **Add an Access Policy.** This access policy, once configured, allows you to implement a consistent 802.1X policy across any switches in this network (see Figure 8-44).

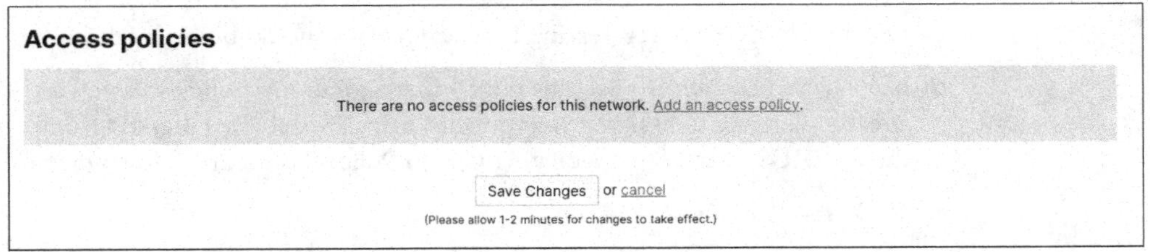

Figure 8-44 *Adding a Wired Access Policy in Meraki Dashboard (Organization-Wide)*

Step 4. Select **My RADIUS Server** from the **Authentication Method** drop-down menu, as shown in Figure 8-45.

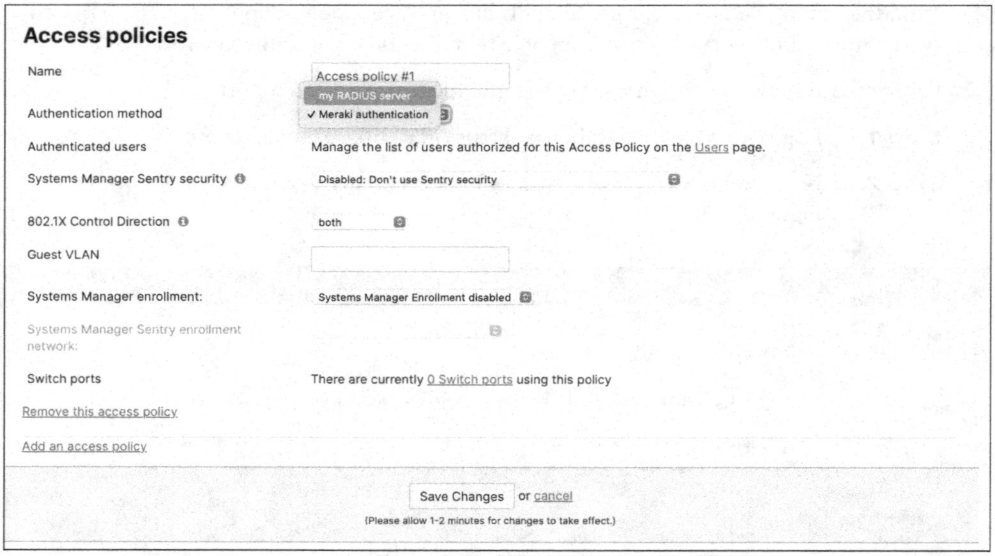

Figure 8-45 *Configuring the Authentication Method on a Wired Access Policy in Meraki Dashboard*

Step 5. Give this access policy a meaningful name in the **Name** field. Here, we have called ours **Wired 802.1X** (see Figure 8-46).

  a. From the **Select RADIUS** drop-down menu, check the box next to the **Organization-wide RADIUS Server** that was added in Chapter 7. This automatically adds it into the list of RADIUS servers above and under **RADIUS Accounting Servers** below.

  b. If you like, you can add multiple RADIUS servers here for resiliency. These servers can be configured manually or as additional organization-wide RADIUS servers.

  c. Ensure **RADIUS Server Testing** is checked. This should be on by default.

  d. Later in this chapter we use this policy to assign group policies. If you are already planning to assign group policies using ISE, select **Filter-ID** from the **RADIUS Attribute Specifying Group Policy Name** drop-down menu.

  e. Click **Save Changes**.

Step 6. With the access policy configured, the next step is to apply it to the switch ports. Navigate to **Switching > Switch Ports**.

Step 7. From the **Switch Ports** page, select the ports to enable 802.1X on and click **Edit**.

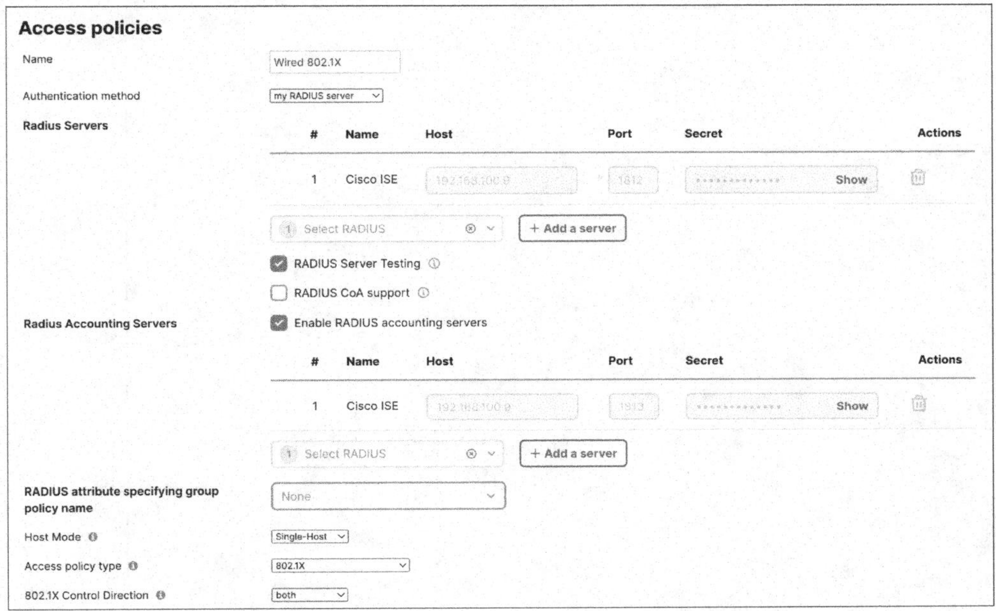

Figure 8-46 *Adding an Organization-Wide RADIUS Server to a Wired Access Policy in Meraki Dashboard*

Step 8. From the **Access Policy** drop-down menu, select the name of the access policy configured previously. In this example, we've selected the access policy named **Wired 802.1X** (see Figure 8-47).

Click **Update.**

Now that you've completed the configuration of 802.1X on switch ports, it's time to connect a client to test. If testing on a Mac, then, just like in Chapter 7, this requires a profile to be added to your Mac to enable 802.1X. Refer to the "Confirming Functionality of RADIUS Authentication for Wired 802.1X" section in Chapter 7 for guidance on how to create this profile.

With both the switching and the RADIUS infrastructure configured, follow these steps to verify that wired 802.1X is functioning:

Step 1. Connect a laptop to a switch port that has been configured with the 802.1X access policy. You might be prompted to select the profile to use for this connection if you have multiple 802.1X profiles applied. In this case, the iMazing profile that needed to be chosen was called **802.1X Ethernet: Global.**

Next, when you see a prompt asking for an account name and password (see Figure 8-48), enter the credentials for a user configured in Active Directory in Chapter 7. Upon successfully authenticating to the network, these credentials are saved, and next time the user will connect automatically.

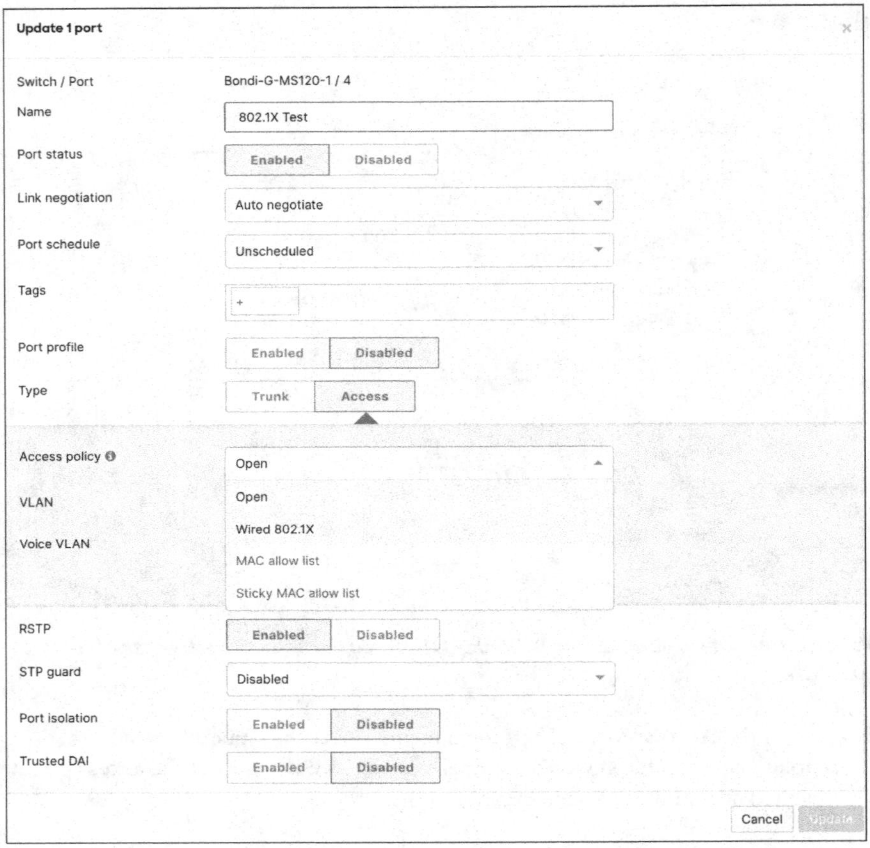

Figure 8-47 *Configuring a Switch Port with an 802.1X Access Policy in Meraki Dashboard*

Figure 8-48 *The Login Prompt on macOS for a Client Connecting to the LAN Using 802.1X Authentication*

Step 2. Because this is the first time connecting, the user is prompted to accept the server-side certificate from Cisco ISE (see Figure 8-49). As with the username and password shown in Figure 8-48, the user needs to do this only once. Before you click **Continue**, it is good practice to first verify the details of the certificate by clicking **Show Certificate**.

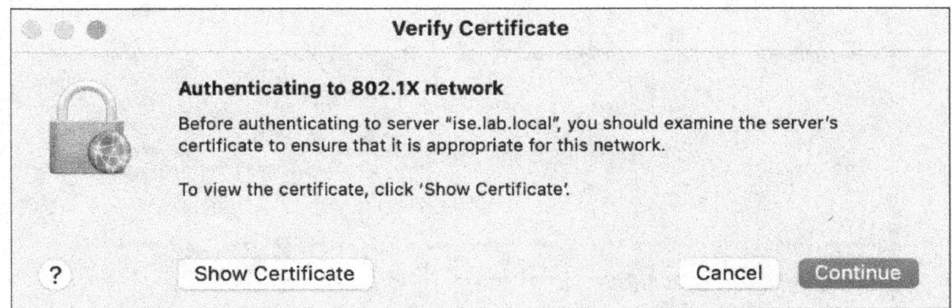

Figure 8-49 *The Verify Certificate Prompt to Accept the Server-Side Certificate for Wired 802.1X on macOS*

Step 3. The user now receives an IP address and is connected to the network. Figure 8-50 shows an excerpt from System Settings confirming that this client was authenticated using 802.1X with PEAP. You can find this page by navigating to **System Settings > Network**; then click the name of your LAN adapter before selecting **Details > 802.1X**.

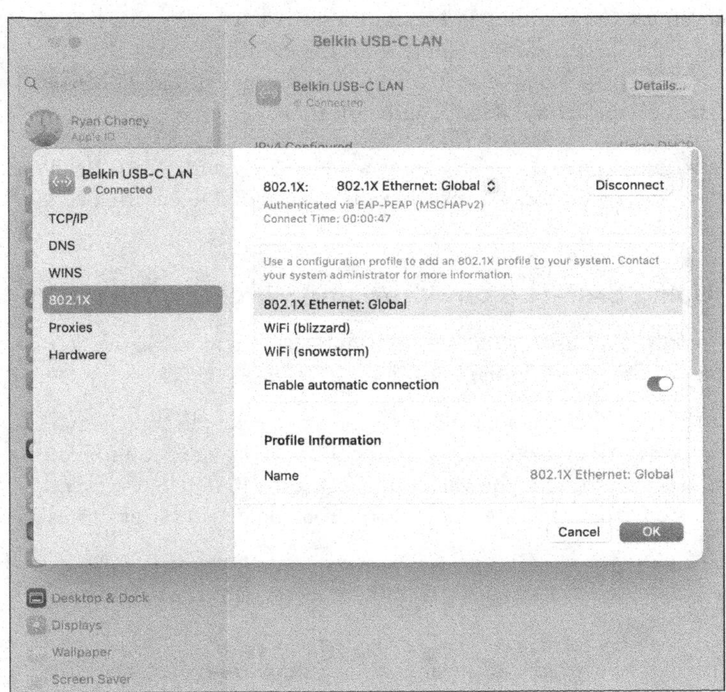

Figure 8-50 *Verifying 802.1X and the Authentication Protocol in macOS System Settings*

Step 4. As with wireless 802.1X earlier, you can confirm the successful connection on the Live Logs page, as shown in Figure 8-51.

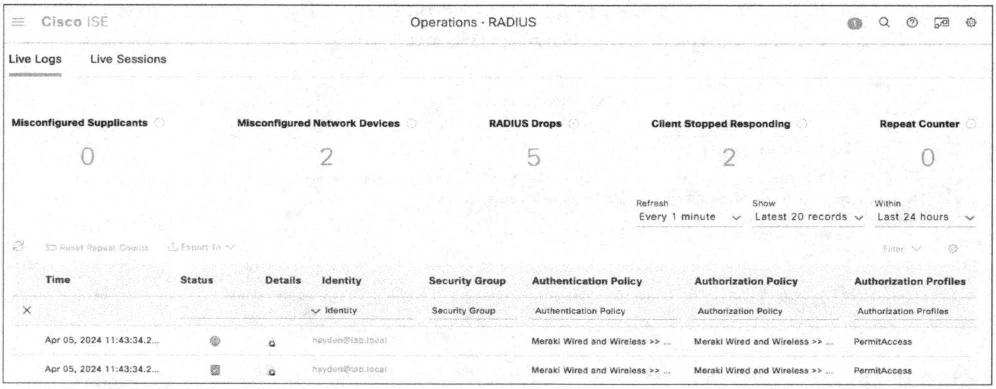

Figure 8-51 *Verifying a Successful Wired 802.1X Client Authentication on the Live Logs Page in Cisco ISE*

Step 5. You can use the authentication detail report to verify everything in relation to this 802.1X request, including the username, authenticator, and authentication protocol (see Figure 8-52).

Step 6. Finally, you can use the event log in Meraki Dashboard to verify that this connection used 802.1X. As shown in Figure 8-53, the event log shows this client's association to port 4 on the switch with the hostname Bondi-G-MS120-1 and the subsequent successful 802.1X authentication.

You've completed the configuration and verification of wired 802.1X with PEAP. Read on to learn how to configure your wired and wireless networks with 802.1X and the EAP-TLS authentication protocol.

Configuring 802.1X Using EAP-TLS on Wired and Wireless Networks

Six high-level tasks are required for users to successfully authenticate to the network using EAP-TLS. An administrator must do the following:

1. Ensure that there is IP reachability among all three parties: the supplicant (client device), the authenticator (AP or switch management IP address), and the authentication servers (in this case, Cisco ISE). You can do this using the RADIUS test function on the wireless access control page for each network. You could also script this using the API.
2. Configure these networks to forward authentication requests onto the RADIUS servers (in this case, Cisco ISE):
   - **a.** On wireless networks, you achieve this using an access control policy. The configuration steps are the same as those shown in the "Configuring Wireless 802.1X with Protected EAP (PEAP)" section earlier.

b. On wired networks, you achieve this using an access policy. The configuration steps are the same as those shown in the "Configuring Wired 802.1X with Protected EAP (PEAP)" section.

Authentication Details

Source Timestamp	2024-03-16 13:15:51.137
Received Timestamp	2024-03-16 13:15:51.137
Policy Server	ise
Event	5200 Authentication succeeded
Username	hayden@lab.local
User Type	User
Endpoint Id	80:69:1A:56:FB:23
Calling Station Id	80-69-1A-56-FB-23
Authentication Identity Store	Windows_2016_AD-10.200.155.100
Identity Group	Profiled
Audit Session Id	6c602b060001040165f500cc
Authentication Method	dot1x
Authentication Protocol	PEAP (EAP-MSCHAPv2)
Service Type	Framed
Network Device	All
Device Type	All Device Types
Location	All Locations
NAS IPv4 Address	192.168.101.2
NAS Port Type	Ethernet
Authorization Profile	PermitAccess
Response Time	155 milliseconds

Figure 8-52 *Part of an Authentication Detail Report from Cisco ISE for a Successful Wired 802.1X Connection*

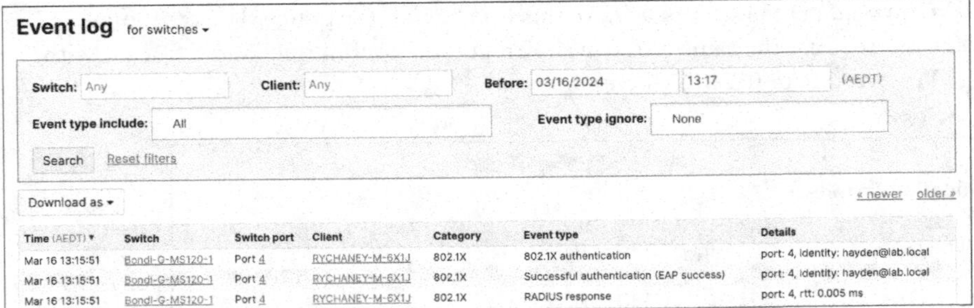

Figure 8-53 *The Event Log in Meraki Dashboard Showing a Successful Wired 802.1X Authentication*

3. Configure a policy on the RADIUS infrastructure to authenticate users connecting to the network using EAP-TLS. In this section, Cisco ISE is reconfigured to support client certificate authentication, which is needed for EAP-TLS. Achieving this outcome requires changes to the default identity source sequence and the existing policy set created in Chapter 7. These steps are covered in the following sections.

4. Generate a device certificate using your public key infrastructure (PKI). For this example, we use Cisco ISE's built-in Certificate Provisioning Portal to generate a client certificate. These steps are covered in the subsequent sections.

5. Export the CA certificate. When the trusted CA certificate is on the client, the server-side certificate can be validated automatically, meaning users are not prompted to accept certificates. In turn, this improves the user experience and makes connecting to the network more seamless. In this example, we use the self-signed server certificate used by ISE for EAP authentication as the CA certificate. These steps are covered in the following sections.

6. Push both the device certificate and the CA certificate to the client and configure an 802.1X profile on the client. In this example, we use Meraki Systems Manager to push both the certificates and the network settings to the client. For these steps, refer to the steps in the "Certificate Settings Payload" and "Wi-Fi Settings Payload" section in Chapter 11, "Securing End-User Devices." For testing on Macs, you could also do this with a profile editor like iMazing.

Configuring the Identity Source Sequence in Cisco ISE

Let's start with a fresh install of Cisco ISE. The default identity source sequence requires a configuration change to enable client authentication using certificates.

Follow these steps to learn how to enable certificate-based authentication in Cisco ISE:

Step 1. In Cisco ISE, navigate to **Menu > Administration > Identity Source Sequences** (under Identity Management), as shown in Figure 8-54.

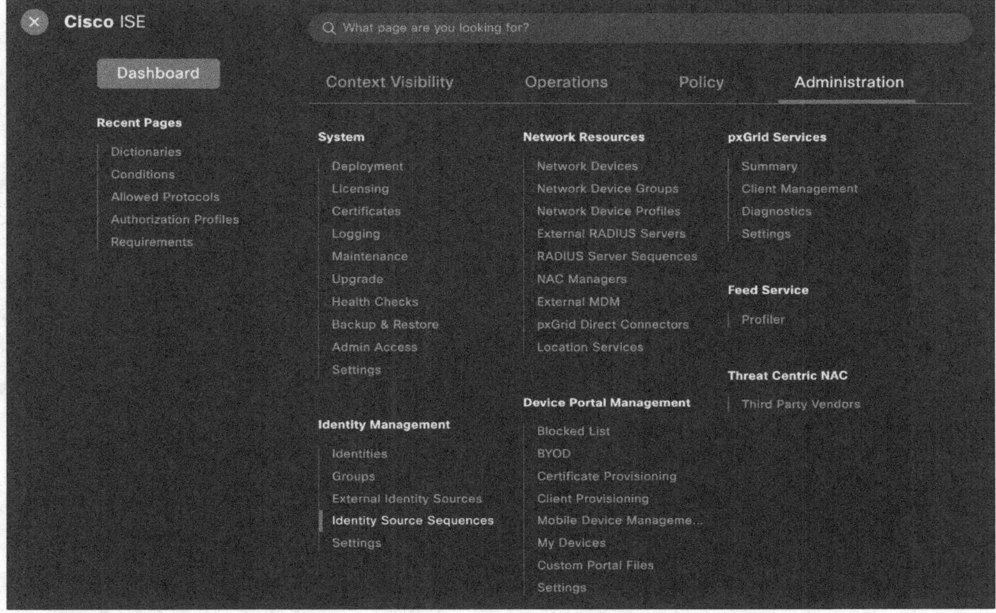

Figure 8-54 *Navigating to Identity Source Sequences in Cisco ISE*

Step 2. On the **Identity Source Sequences** page (see Figure 8-55), click **Certificate_Request_Sequence.**

Cisco ISE Administration · Identity Management

Identities | Groups | External Identity Sources | Identity Source Sequences | Settings

Identity Source Sequences

For Policy Export go to Administration > System > Backup & Restore > Policy Export Page

Selected 0 Total 5

Edit + Add Duplicate Delete All

Name	Description	Identity Stores
All_User_ID_Stores	A built-in Identity Sequence to include all Use...	Preloaded_Certificate_Profile,Internal Users,A...
Certificate_Request_Sequence	A built-in Identity Sequence for Certificate Re...	Internal Users,All_AD_Join_Points
Guest_Portal_Sequence	A built-in Identity Sequence for the Guest Portal	Internal Users,Guest Users,All_AD_Join_Points
MyDevices_Portal_Sequence	A built-in Identity Sequence for the My Device...	Internal Users,All_AD_Join_Points
Sponsor_Portal_Sequence	A built-in Identity Sequence for the Sponsor P...	Internal Users,All_AD_Join_Points

Figure 8-55 *The Default Identity Source Sequences Page in Cisco ISE*

Step 3. Under **Certificate Based Authentication**, check **Select Certificate Authentication Profile**, and from the drop-down menu, select **Preloaded_Certificate_Profile** (see Figure 8-56).

Scroll down and click **Save**.

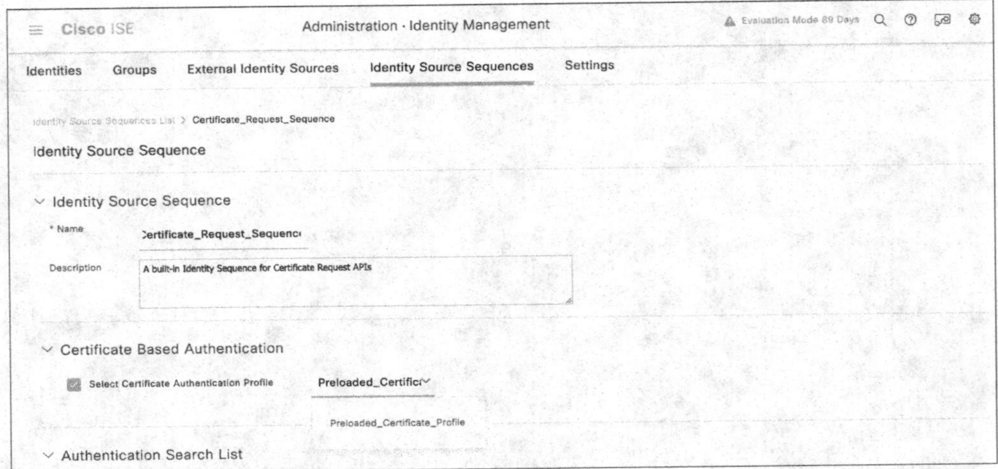

Figure 8-56 *Enabling Certificate-Based Authentication on the Default Identity Source Sequence in Cisco ISE*

You've completed the necessary changes to the default identity source sequence list in Cisco ISE. Continue reading for further steps needed to enable 802.1X with EAP-TLS using Cisco ISE.

Configuring the Policy Set in Cisco ISE

Follow these steps to reconfigure the existing ISE policy set to support EAP-TLS:

Step 1. Log in to your instance of Cisco Identity Services Engine (ISE).

Step 2. For tight control over the authentication protocol, first create an allowed protocols list that prefers EAP-TLS, while offering fallback to PEAP.

a. Navigate to **Menu > Policy > Results** (under Policy Elements).

b. Select **Default Network Access** and click **Duplicate** (see Figure 8-57).

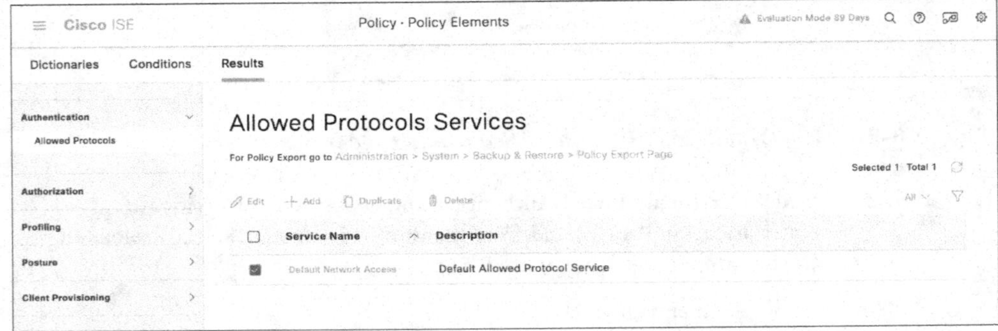

Figure 8-57 *Duplicating the Existing Allowed Protocols List in Cisco ISE*

Step 3. Change **Name** to **EAP-TLS and PEAP Only** (see Figure 8-58).

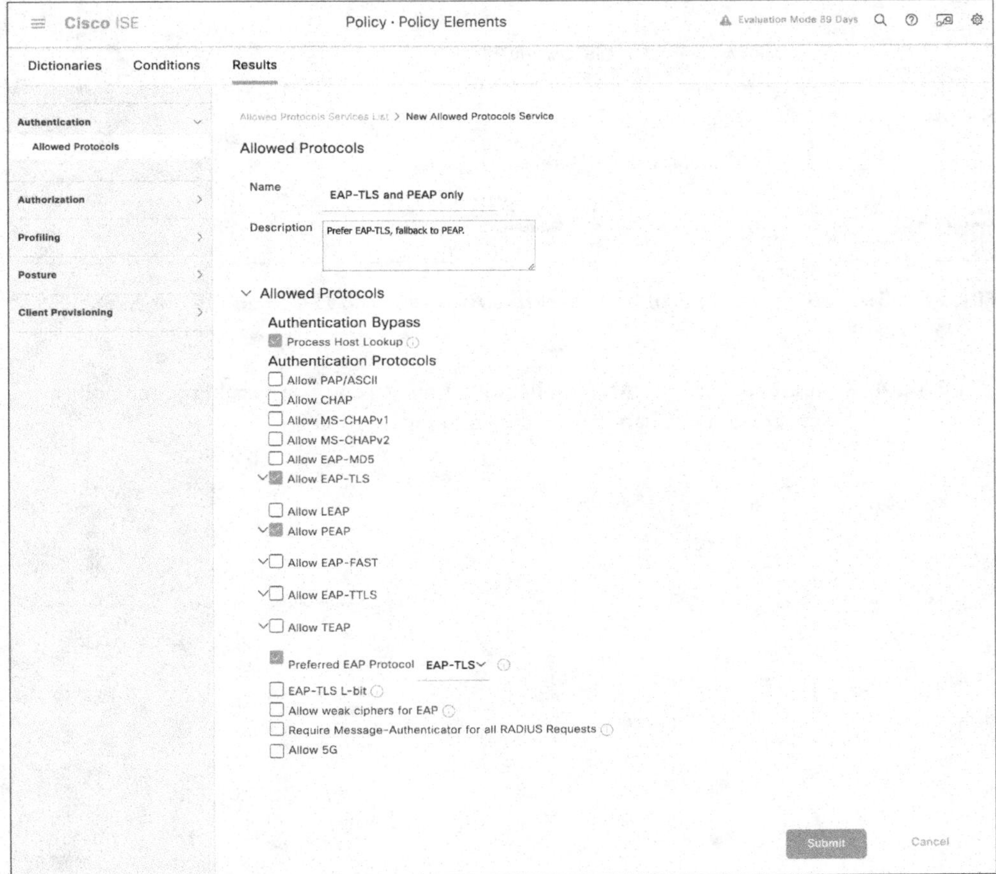

Figure 8-58 *Configuring the New Allowed Protocols List in Cisco ISE*

a. (Optional) Add a **Description**. Here, we have added **Prefer EAP-TLS, Fallback to PEAP.**

b. Under **Authentication Protocols**, collapse the options until the screen is displayed like Figure 8-58.

c. Under **Authentication Protocols**, leave only **Allow EAP-TLS** and **Allow PEAP** checked. Uncheck the remaining authentication protocols.

d. Check **Preferred EAP Protocol** and select **EAP-TLS** from the drop-down menu.

e. Click **Submit** (you might also use **Save** if you have been to this page before). You should now see the page shown in Figure 8-59.

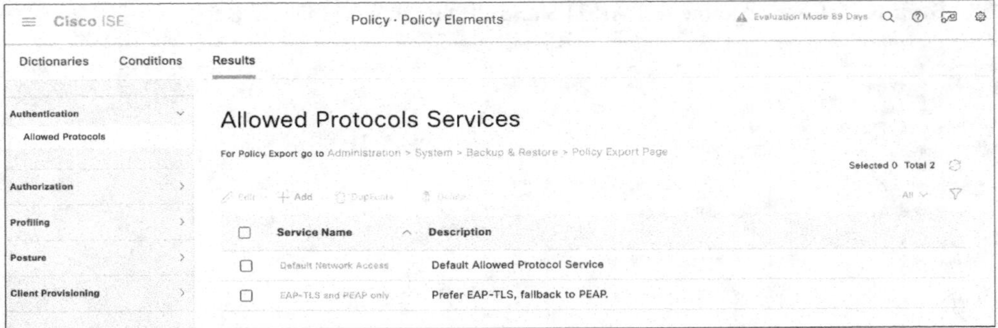

Figure 8-59 *The Allowed Protocols Services Page in Cisco ISE Showing the Newly Created List*

Step 4. In ISE, navigate to **Menu > Policy > Policy Sets.** You should see the policy sets created in Chapter 7, as shown in Figure 8-60.

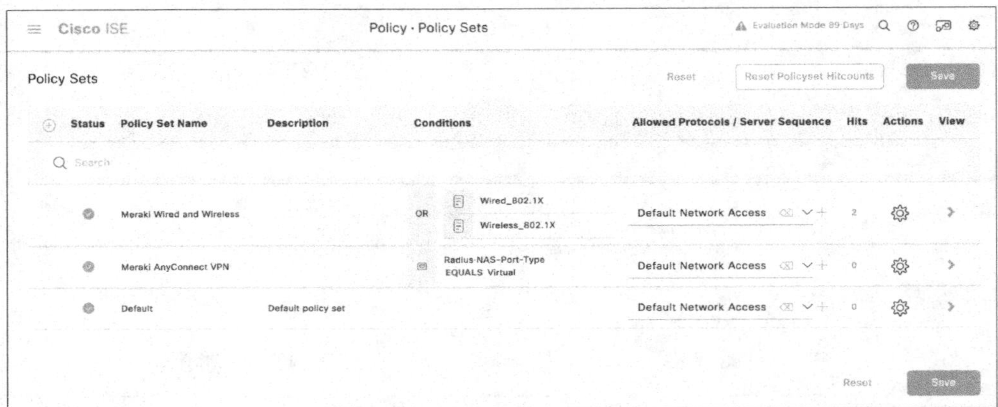

Figure 8-60 *The Policy Sets Page in Cisco ISE Showing the Policy Sets Created in Chapter 7*

Step 5. For the policy set, **Meraki Wired and Wireless**, under **Allowed Protocols/ Server Sequence** (see Figure 8-61), select the **EAP-TLS and PEAP Only** allowed protocols list created in the previous step.

Click **Save.**

Step 6. On the right side of the **Meraki Wired and Wireless** row, click the > icon under the **View** heading.

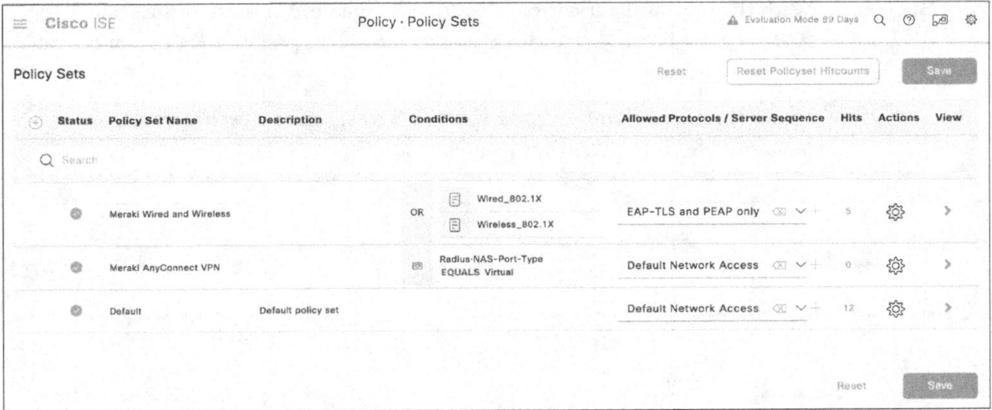

Figure 8-61 *Configuring a New Allowed Protocols List on the Wired and Wireless Policy Set in Cisco ISE*

Step 7. On the **Meraki Wired and Wireless** policy set page, expand the **Authentication Policy** pane. Click the sprocket icon on the right and select **Insert New Row Above**, as shown in Figure 8-62.

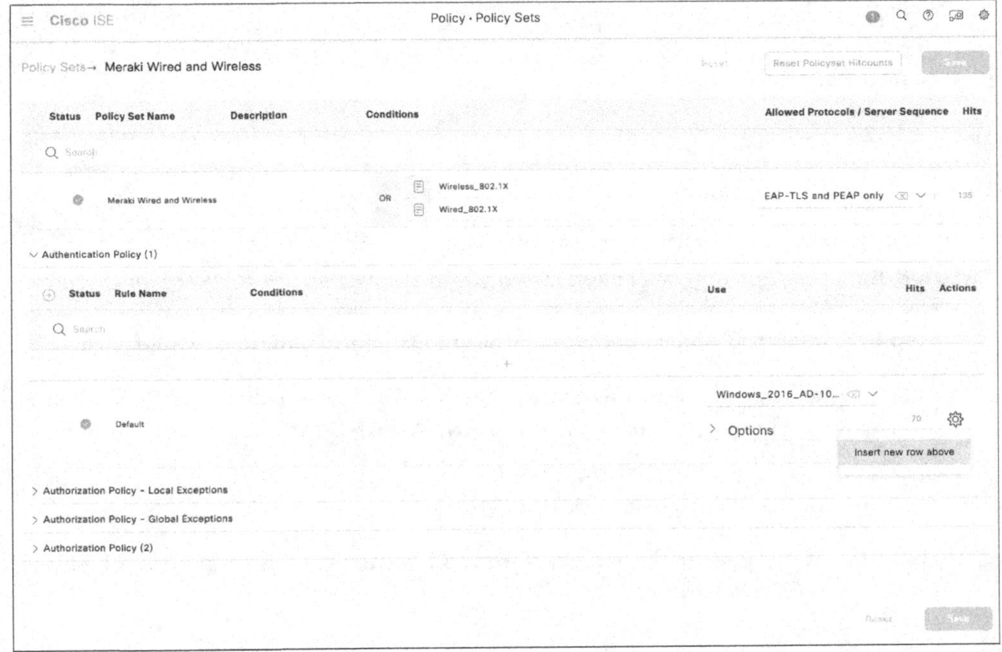

Figure 8-62 *Adding a New Row to an Authentication Policy on a Policy Set in Cisco ISE*

Step 8. With the new authentication rule added, rename **Authentication Rule 1** to **EAP-TLS** by highlighting the existing rule name, pressing **Delete**, and entering the new name.

Under the **Use** column, for the **EAP-TLS** row, select **Certificate_Request_Sequence** from the drop-down menu (see Figure 8-63).

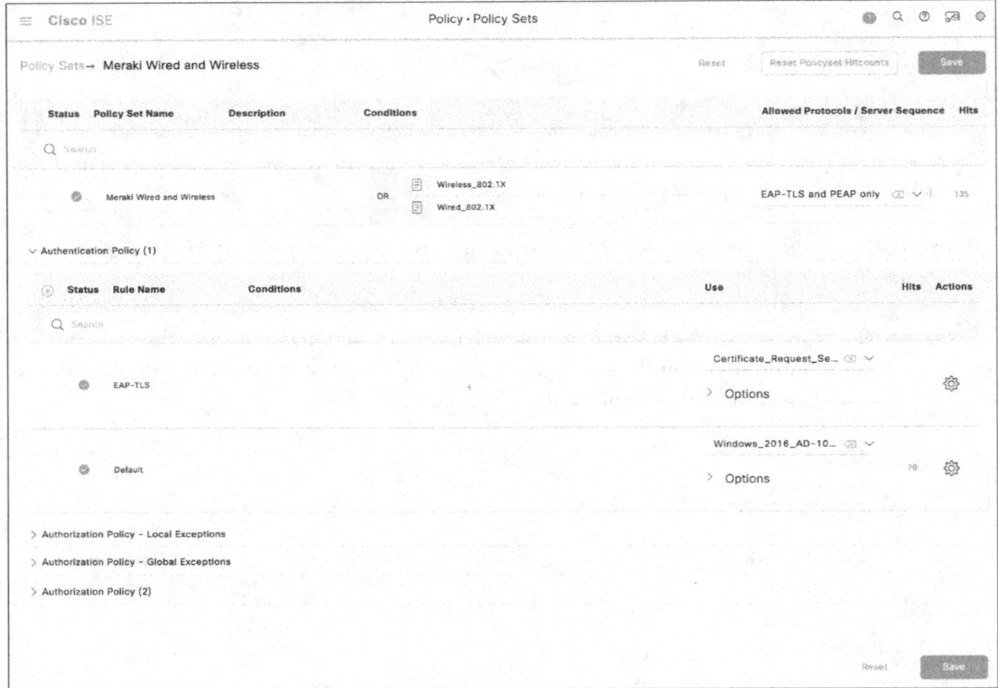

Figure 8-63 *Configuring the New Authentication Policy Rule for EAP-TLS in Cisco ISE*

Step 9. Click the **+** icon under **Conditions** to open the **Conditions Studio** page.

a. On the **Conditions Studio** page (see Figure 8-64), drag **EAP-TLS** from the **Library** pane on the left to the **NEW | AND | OR** box on the **Editor** pane on the right.

b. Scroll down and click **Use.**

Step 10. When you see the **Meraki Wired and Wireless** policy set page (see Figure 8-65), click **Save.**

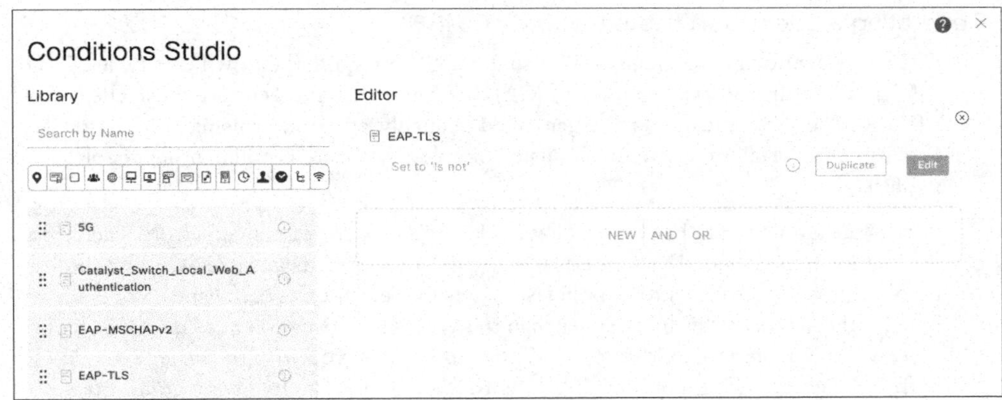

Figure 8-64 *Adding a Condition to the EAP-TLS Authentication Rule in Cisco ISE*

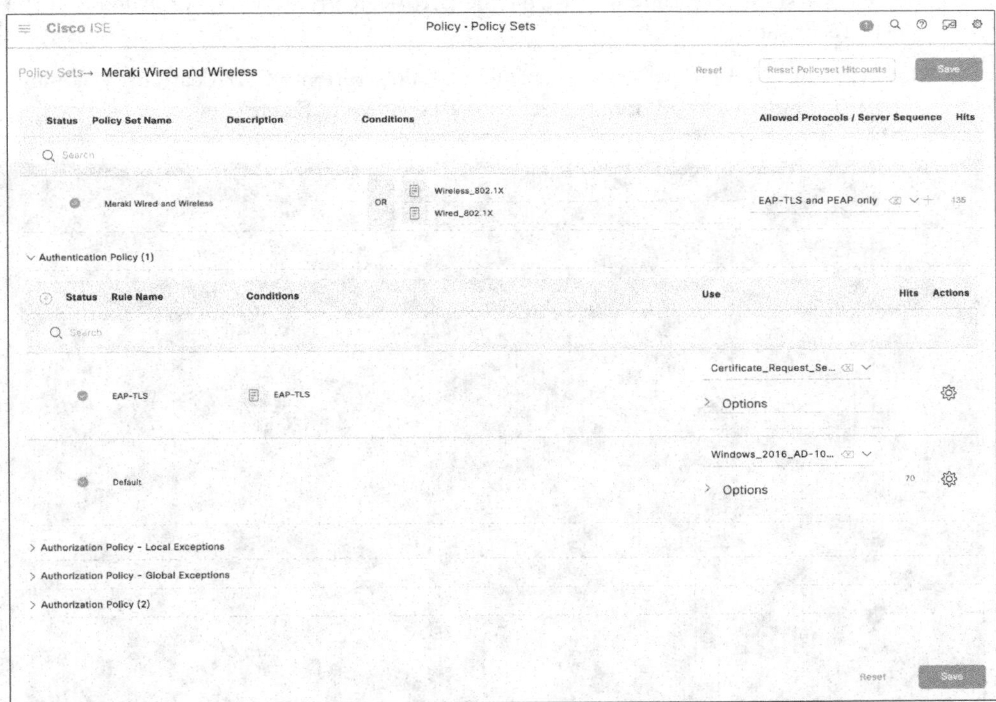

Figure 8-65 *The Meraki Wired and Wireless Policy Set Page After the Authentication Policy Changes*

At this point, you've completed the changes to the original policy set created in Chapter 7. This policy set can now authenticate wired and wireless EAP-TLS clients, with fallback to PEAP on clients without certificates.

Generating a Client Certificate Using Cisco ISE

Clients authenticating to the network using EAP-TLS require their own certificate. Cisco ISE has a built-in certificate authority (CA) that can be used to generate these client certificates. These certificates can be generated manually, as we show using the Certificate Provisioning Portal, or automatically using Simple Certificate Enrollment Protocol (SCEP).

Certificate administration, even at a low scale, requires a lot of manual effort. Therefore, it is highly recommended that enterprises use an automated means like SCEP, or auto-enrollment via Microsoft group policies, to generate certificates for clients. SCEP is beyond the scope of this book other than to say it is supported on Systems Manager profiles; we encourage you to learn more about this topic. If you wish to use an external CA with ISE, instead of ISE's built-in CA, refer to Steps 1–3 in the following guide: https://www.cisco.com/c/en/us/support/docs/security/identity-services-engine/214975-configure-eap-tls-authentication-with-is.html.

Follow these steps to learn how to enable the Certificate Provisioning Portal and generate a client certificate:

Step 1. In Cisco ISE, navigate to **Menu > Administration > Certificate Provisioning** (under Device Portal Management), as shown in Figure 8-66.

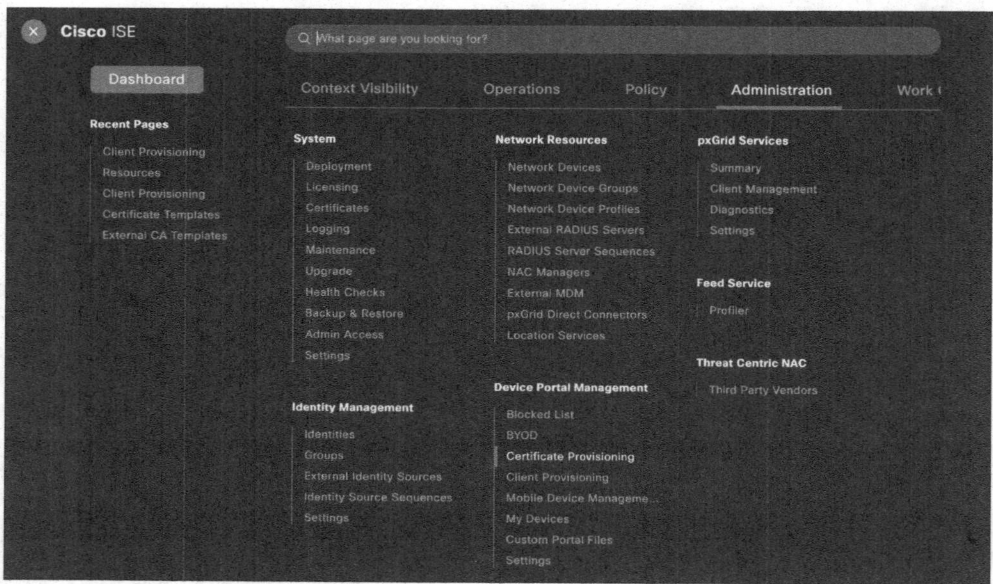

Figure 8-66 *Navigating to the Certificate Provisioning Page in Cisco ISE*

Step 2. Click **Certificate Provisioning Portal (Default)**, as shown in Figure 8-67.

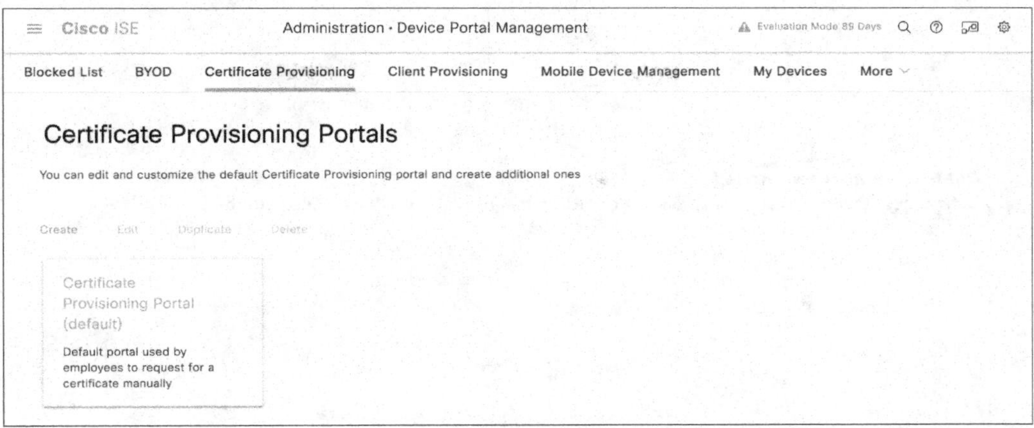

Figure 8-67 *Opening the Certificate Provisioning Portal Configuration Page in Cisco ISE*

Step 3. Because this is the first time the Certificate Provisioning Portal is being used, it requires some initial setup before being accessible.

a. Expand **Portal Settings.** From the **Authentication Method** drop-down menu, select **All_User_ID_Stores.**

b. Under **Configure Authorized Groups**, move the user groups that will be allowed access to the Certificate Provisioning Portal from the **Available** box to the **Chosen** box on the right. You achieve this by selecting the groups and using the arrow buttons to move them across to the right or clicking the **Choose All** button (see Figure 8-68).

Step 4. Scroll down to **Acceptable Use Page (AUP) Settings** and uncheck **Include an AUP Page.**

Step 5. Scroll down to **Certificate Portal Settings.** From the **Certificate Templates** drop-down menu, select **EAP_Authentication_Certificate_Template** (see Figure 8-69).

Step 6. Scroll up to the top of the page and click **Save.**

Finally, click **Portal Test URL** to launch the Certificate Provisioning Portal (see Figure 8-70).

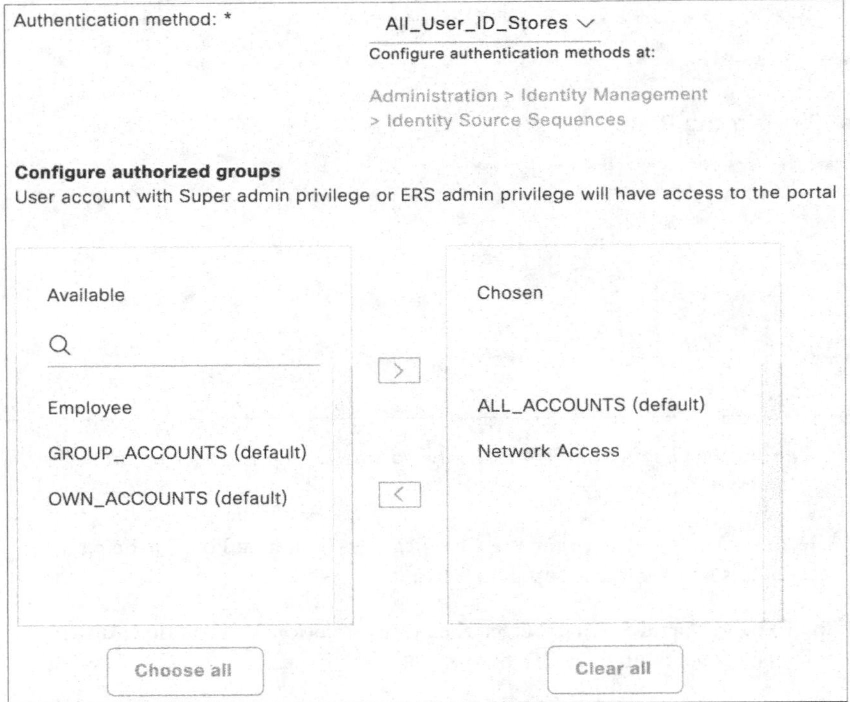

Figure 8-68 *Choosing the User Groups That Will Have Access to the Certificate Provisioning Portal in Cisco ISE*

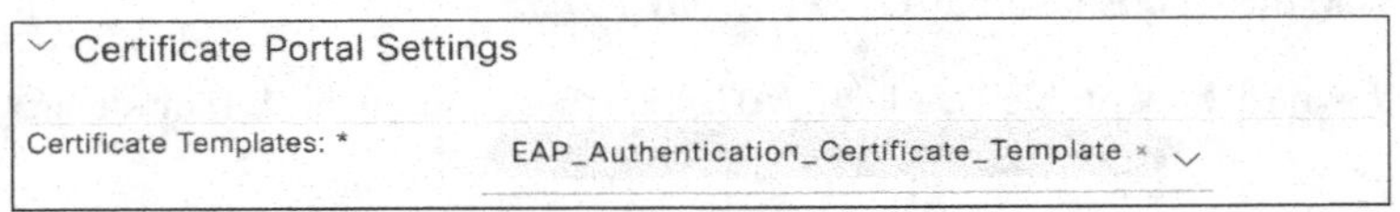

Figure 8-69 *Configuring the Certificate Template to Use on the Certificate Provisioning Portal in Cisco ISE*

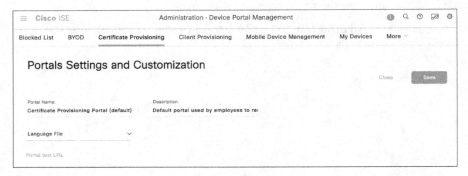

Figure 8-70 *Launching the Certificate Provisioning Portal in Cisco ISE*

Step 7. You can now see the **Certificate Provisioning Portal** login page, as shown in Figure 8-71. Log in using a user account that will be used for network access.

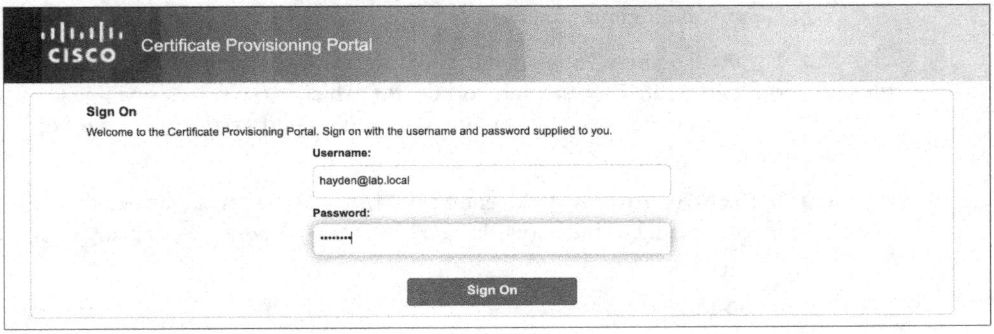

Figure 8-71 *The Certificate Provisioning Portal Login Page in Cisco ISE*

Step 8. If presented with the **Post Access** page, click **Continue.** You should now see the **Certificate Provisioning Portal** page shown in Figure 8-72.

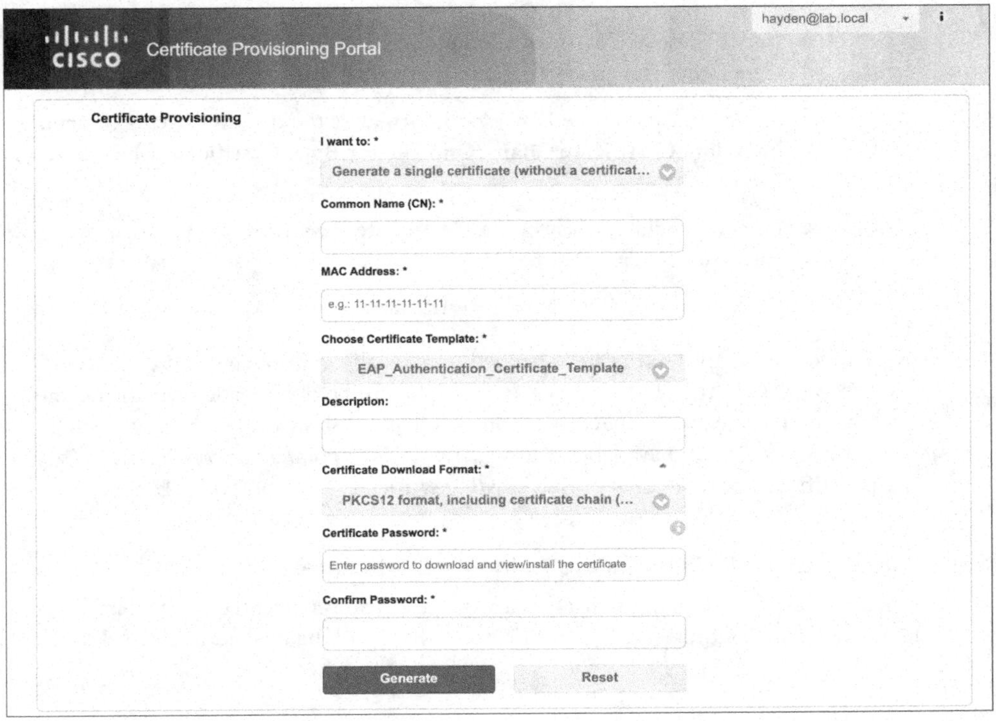

Figure 8-72 *The Certificate Provisioning Portal Page in Cisco ISE*

Step 9. On the page shown in Figure 8-73, do the following:

- Leave **I Want To:** set to **Generate a Single Certificate (Without a Certificate Signing Request).**
- For the **Common Name (CN),** enter the username that you logged in to the Certificate Provisioning Portal with (which is the same as will be used for network access). Only admin users can request certificates for other users.
- In the **MAC Address** field, enter the MAC address for the device that will be connecting to the network. You can enter this address using any of the following syntaxes:
  - 00-11-22-33-44-55
  - 00:11:22:33:44:55
  - 0011.2233.4455
  - 001122-334455
  - 001122334455
- Under **Choose Certificate Template**, ensure the **EAP_Authentication_Certificate_Template** is selected; this should be default.
- Leave the **Certificate Download Format** as the default: **PKCS12 Format, Including Certificate Chain (One File for Both Certificate Chain and Key).**
- Enter a matching password in **Certificate Password** and **Confirm Password** fields.
- Click **Generate** to create the certificate and download it as a zip file.

Now that you've completed the steps needed to manually generate a client certificate using Cisco ISE's Certificate Provisioning Portal, unzip the downloaded certificate and keep it handy for later. If you have questions relating to ISE's Certificate Provisioning Portal, check out the FAQ available at https://www.cisco.com/c/en/us/td/docs/security/ise/3-1/certificate_provisioning_portal_faqs/b_certificate_prov_portal_3_1.html.

Exporting the Cisco ISE Certificate Authority Certificate

As mentioned earlier, to automatically trust the certificates presented by ISE, an administrator must export the CA certificate so that it can be pushed to client devices.

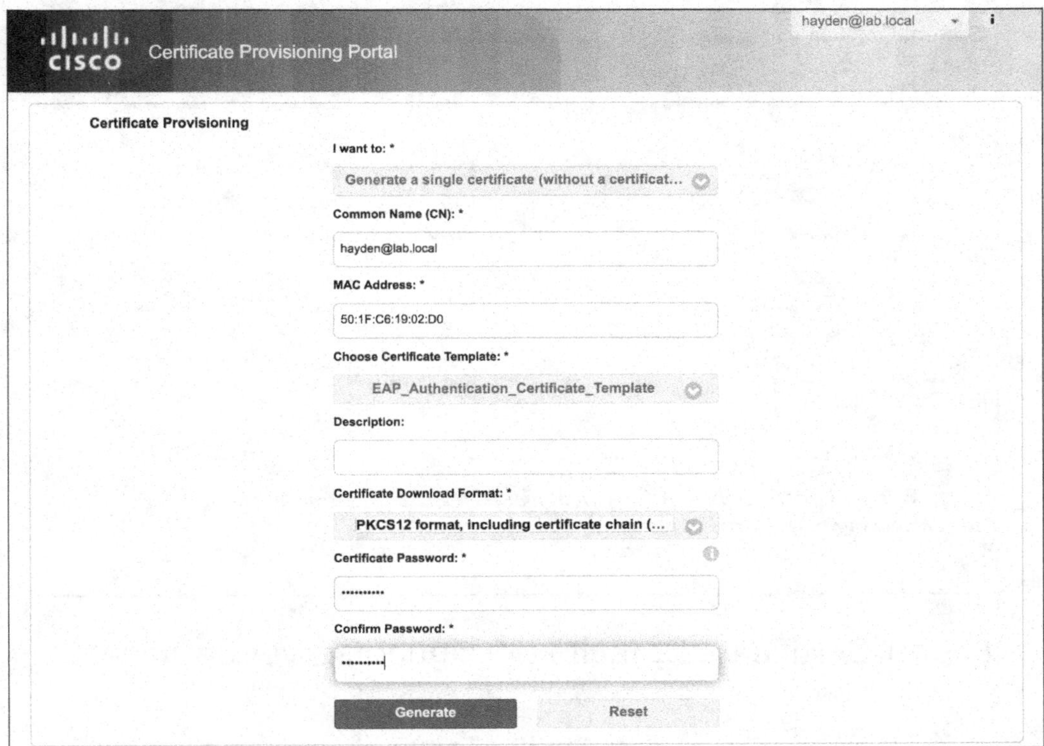

Figure 8-73 *Completing the Certificate Provisioning Form in the Certificate Provisioning Portal*

Follow these steps to learn how to export the relevant system certificate from Cisco ISE:

Step 1. The certificate that must be exported is the ISE EAP certificate, which is the certificate that ISE presents to clients during 802.1X authentication.

a. In Cisco ISE, navigate to **Menu > System > Certificates.**

b. Check the box next to the certificate that is used by EAP Authentication, as shown in Figure 8-74.

c. Click **Export.**

Step 2. On the **Export Certificate** pop-up window, leave **Export Certificate Only** selected and click **Export** (see Figure 8-75). Clicking this button downloads the CA certificate to your local machine in PEM format. Keep this certificate handy because it will be required in a subsequent step.

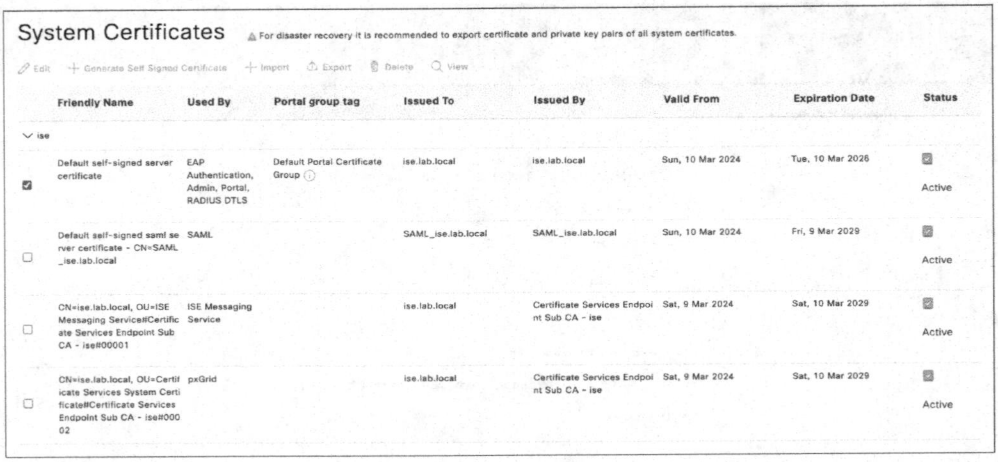

System Certificates ⚠ For disaster recovery it is recommended to export certificate and private key pairs of all system certificates.

Edit + Generate Self Signed Certificate + Import Export Delete View

	Friendly Name	Used By	Portal group tag	Issued To	Issued By	Valid From	Expiration Date	Status
ise								
☑	Default self-signed server certificate	EAP Authentication, Admin, Portal, RADIUS DTLS	Default Portal Certificate Group	ise.lab.local	ise.lab.local	Sun, 10 Mar 2024	Tue, 10 Mar 2026	Active
☐	Default self-signed saml server certificate - CN=SAML_ise.lab.local	SAML		SAML_ise.lab.local	SAML_ise.lab.local	Sun, 10 Mar 2024	Fri, 9 Mar 2029	Active
☐	CN=ise.lab.local, OU=ISE Messaging Service#Certificate Services Endpoint Sub CA - ise#00001	ISE Messaging Service		ise.lab.local	Certificate Services Endpoint Sub CA - ise	Sat, 9 Mar 2024	Sat, 10 Mar 2029	Active
☐	CN=ise.lab.local, OU=Certificate Services System Certificate#Certificate Services Endpoint Sub CA - ise#00002	pxGrid		ise.lab.local	Certificate Services Endpoint Sub CA - ise	Sat, 9 Mar 2024	Sat, 10 Mar 2029	Active

Figure 8-74 *Locating the CA Certificate Used by ISE for Generating and Authenticating EAP Certificates*

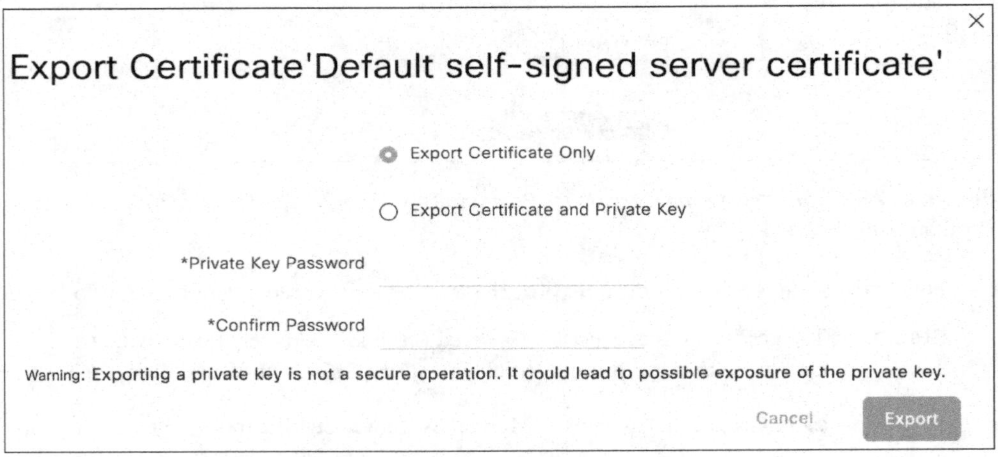

Export Certificate'Default self-signed server certificate'

Export Certificate Only

Export Certificate and Private Key

*Private Key Password

*Confirm Password

Warning: Exporting a private key is not a secure operation. It could lead to possible exposure of the private key.

Cancel Export

Figure 8-75 *Exporting the CA Certificate from Cisco ISE*

You've now completed the steps necessary to export the Cisco ISE CA certificate. The device certificate, the CA certificate, and an 802.1X profile need to be pushed to a client to test. In this book we demonstrate how to do this using Meraki Systems Manager. For these required steps, see the examples in the "Certificate Settings Payload" and "Wi-Fi Settings Payload" sections in Chapter 11. Figure 8-76 shows an example of a Systems Manager profile with the device certificate, CA certificate, and Wi-Fi payload with EAP-TLS configured.

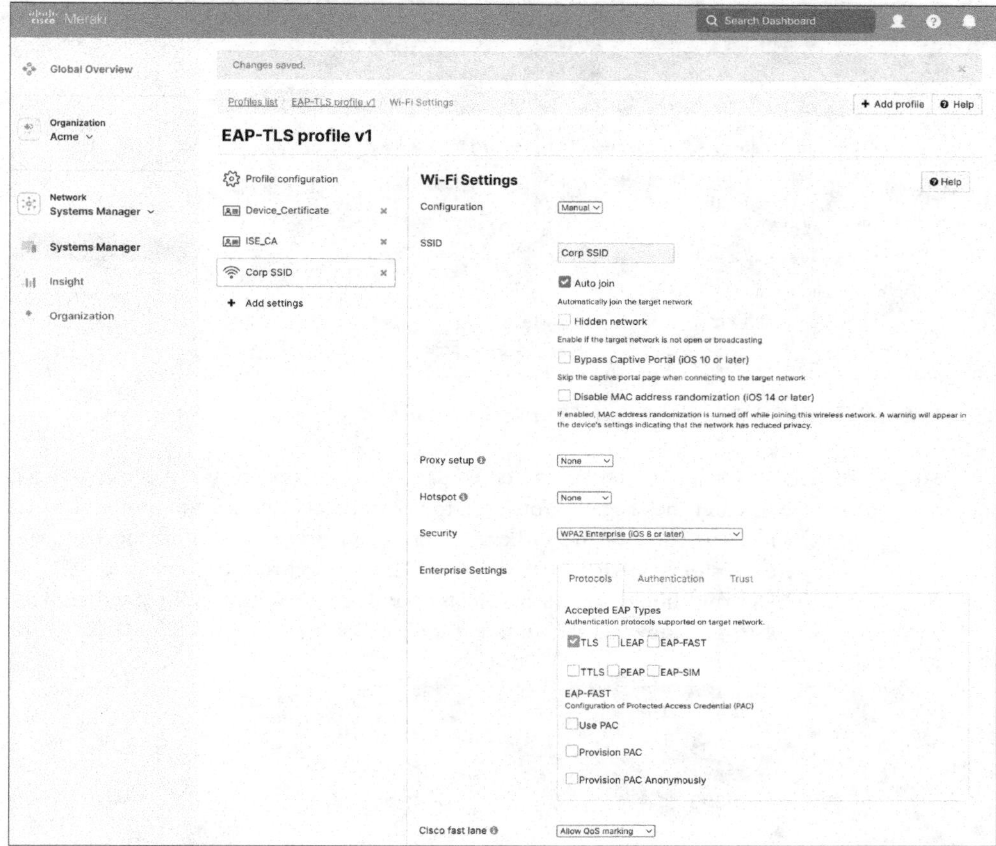

Figure 8-76 *A Systems Manager Profile with the Device and CA Certificates and Wi-Fi Payload*

Testing Wireless 802.1X with EAP-TLS

With the 802.1X profile and the required certificates pushed to the client, testing is as simple as trying to associate to the same SSID configured in the "Configuring Wireless 802.1X with Protected EAP (PEAP)" section earlier. The ISE policy attempts to authenticate the user with EAP-TLS and fall back to PEAP if needed.

Follow these steps to test that wireless 802.1X with EAP-TLS is now functioning correctly:

Step 1. Connect to your 802.1X SSID; in this case, this is the SSID called **Corp SSID**.

Step 2. Depending on how your 802.1X profile was created, you may be asked to confirm the certificate to use with a username and password, or your device may simply connect without any further interaction required. Figure 8-77 shows the login prompt that you are presented with.

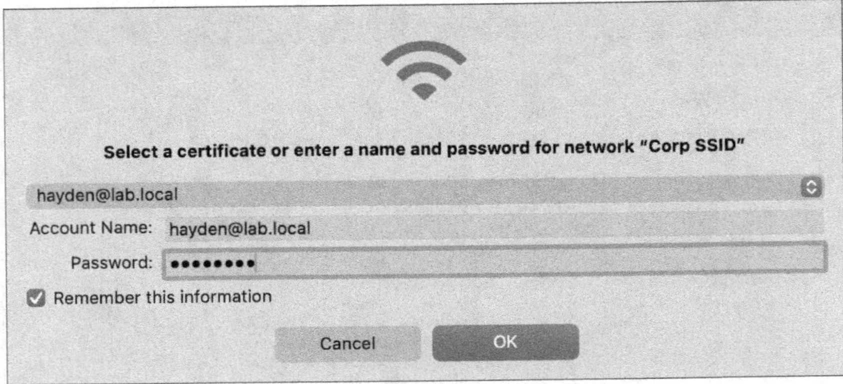

Figure 8-77 *macOS Wireless 802.1X Login Window*

Step 3. After the right credentials are entered, they will be saved, and the user won't have to enter these again. You need to verify the authentication protocol either on the client or the authentication server. To verify this in macOS, navigate to **Systems Settings** > **Wireless** > **Details** (next to the Connected SSID) > **802.1X**. You should see **Authenticated via EAP-TLS** clearly displayed at the top of this window (as shown in Figure 8-78).

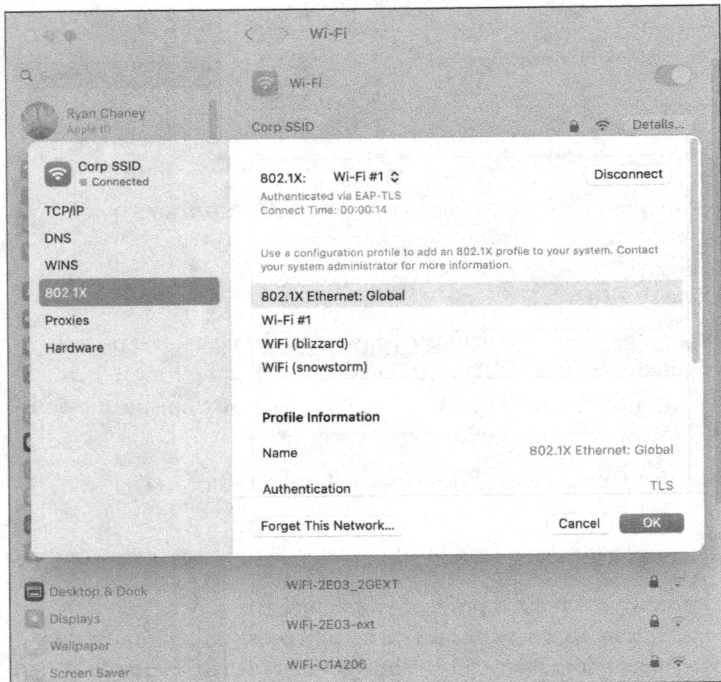

Figure 8-78 *Verifying That EAP-TLS Is Being Used for the Wi-Fi Authentication Protocol in macOS*

Step 4. You also can verify EAP-TLS as the authentication protocol in the authentication details reports in Cisco ISE. Figure 8-79 shows an excerpt of a sample report.

Authentication Details	
Source Timestamp	2024-03-21 20:30:22.962
Received Timestamp	2024-03-21 20:30:22.962
Policy Server	ise
Event	5200 Authentication succeeded
Username	hayden@lab.local
Endpoint Id	C8:89:F3:C9:F8:64
Calling Station Id	C8-89-F3-C9-F8-64
Endpoint Profile	Apple-Device
Authentication Identity Store	Windows_2016_AD-10.200.155.100
Authentication Method	dot1x
Authentication Protocol	EAP-TLS
Service Type	Framed
Network Device	All
Device Type	All Device Types
Location	All Locations
NAS IPv4 Address	192.168.101.5
NAS Port Type	Wireless - IEEE 802.11
Authorization Profile	PermitAccess
Response Time	100 milliseconds

Figure 8-79 *Verifying That EAP-TLS Is Being Used for the Wi-Fi Authentication Protocol in Cisco ISE*

You've now completed the verification of wireless 802.1X access using EAP-TLS.

Testing Wired 802.1X with EAP-TLS

The steps for verifying 802.1X with EAP-TLS on wired are similar to those for wireless. Follow these steps to test that wired 802.1X with EAP-TLS is now functioning correctly:

Step 1. Connect your client device's Ethernet port to a switch port configured for 802.1X on a Meraki switch.

Step 2. Depending on how your 802.1X profile was created, you may be asked to confirm the certificate to use with a username and password, or your device may simply connect without any further interaction required. Figure 8-80 shows the login prompt that you are presented with.

Figure 8-80 *macOS Wired 802.1X Login Window*

Step 3. After the right credentials are entered, they will be saved, and the user won't have to enter them again. As stated earlier, you need to verify the authentication protocol either on the client or the authentication server. To verify this in macOS, navigate to macOS **Systems Settings > Network.** Then click the name of the connected LAN interface and select **Details > 802.1X.** You should see **Authenticated via EAP-TLS** clearly displayed at the top of this window (as shown in Figure 8-81).

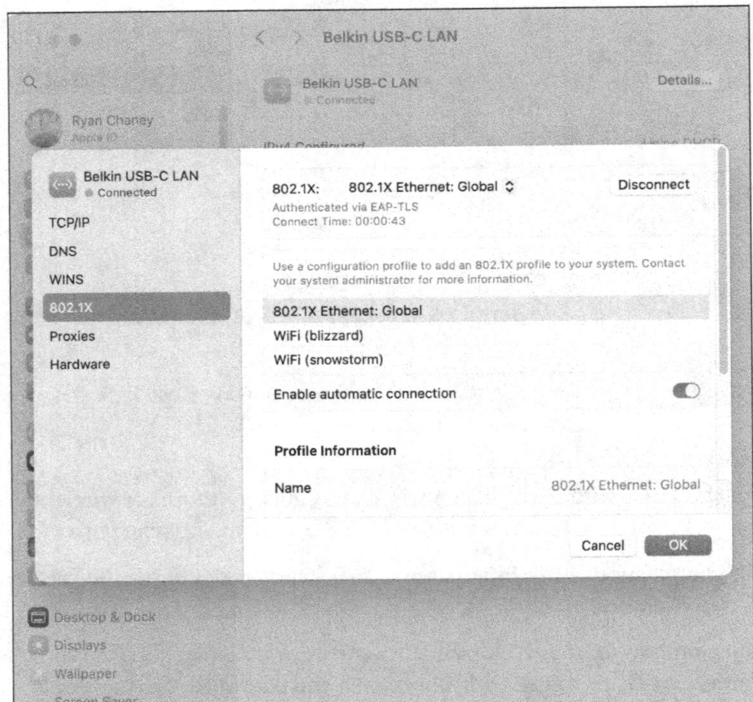

Figure 8-81 *Verifying That EAP-TLS Is Being Used for the Wired Authentication Protocol in macOS*

Step 4. You also can verify EAP-TLS as the authentication protocol in the authentication details reports in Cisco ISE. Figure 8-82 shows an excerpt of a sample report.

Authentication Details

Source Timestamp	2024-03-21 20:49:41.483
Received Timestamp	2024-03-21 20:49:41.483
Policy Server	ise
Event	5200 Authentication succeeded
Username	hayden@lab.local
Endpoint Id	80:69:1A:56:FB:23
Calling Station Id	80-69-1A-56-FB-23
Endpoint Profile	Apple-Device
Authentication Identity Store	Windows_2016_AD-10.200.155.100
Audit Session Id	6c602b060001040965fc019b
Authentication Method	dot1x
Authentication Protocol	EAP-TLS
Service Type	Framed
Network Device	All
Device Type	All Device Types
Location	All Locations
NAS IPv4 Address	192.168.101.2
NAS Port Type	Ethernet
Authorization Profile	PermitAccess
Response Time	109 milliseconds

Figure 8-82 *Verifying That EAP-TLS Is Being Used for the Wired Authentication Protocol in Cisco ISE*

At this point, you've completed the verification of 802.1X with EAP-TLS on wired networks. With EAP-TLS deployed the traditional way, continue on to the following section, where we show a far quicker way to roll out EAP-TLS to devices enrolled with Meraki Systems Manager.

Sentry-Based 802.1X with EAP-TLS on Wired and Wireless Networks

Sentry Wi-Fi is a Meraki feature that provides a simple and easy way to push out a Wi-Fi profile and certificates to devices enrolled with Meraki Systems Manager. It provides managed devices with instant access to your organization's Wi-Fi network. To learn how to enroll devices with Meraki Systems Manager, refer to Chapter 11.

Sentry Wi-Fi

Sentry Wi-Fi is compatible with Meraki wireless SSIDs using certificate-based device authentication (EAP-TLS) and either WPA1 or WPA2 encryption. This is by far the easiest way to enable EAP-TLS. Although Sentry Wi-Fi can be enabled using a Wi-Fi profile, the easiest way to enable Sentry Wi-Fi is directly on the SSID.

Follow these steps to configure Sentry Wi-Fi:

Step 1. Log in to Meraki Dashboard (https://dashboard.meraki.com).

Step 2. Navigate to **Wireless > Access Control** (under Configure).

Step 3. On the **Access Control** page, select an appropriate SSID from the **SSID** drop-down menu. You can rename an unconfigured SSID on this page by changing the name in the **SSID (Name)** field under **Basic Info**.

Step 4. Scroll down to **Security** and select **Enterprise With** (see Figure 8-83). Sentry Wi-Fi is available only when the authentication is Meraki Cloud Authentication. Select this option if it is not already selected; it is the default on new SSIDs.

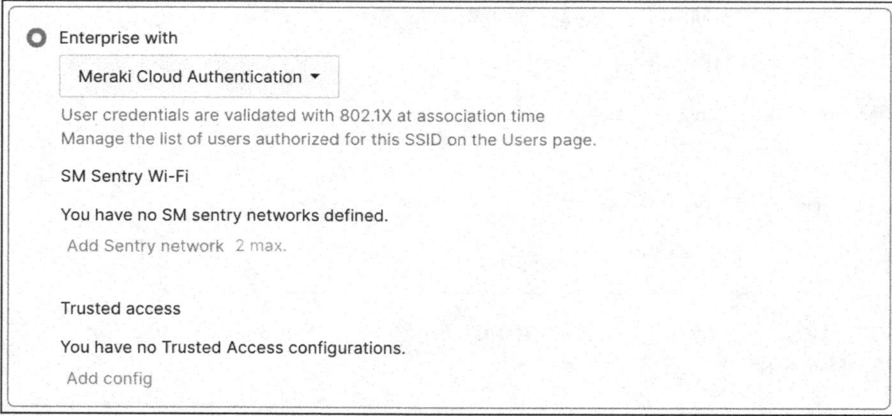

Figure 8-83 *Configuring Sentry Wi-Fi on an SSID in Meraki Dashboard*

Step 5. Click **Add Sentry Network.**

a. Under **Network**, select your Systems Manager network. The network we've used in this example is named **Systems Manager.**

b. If necessary, use the **Scope** drop-down menu items in conjunction with **Tags** to match the required endpoints (see Figure 8-84).

c. Click **Save** in the bottom-right corner.

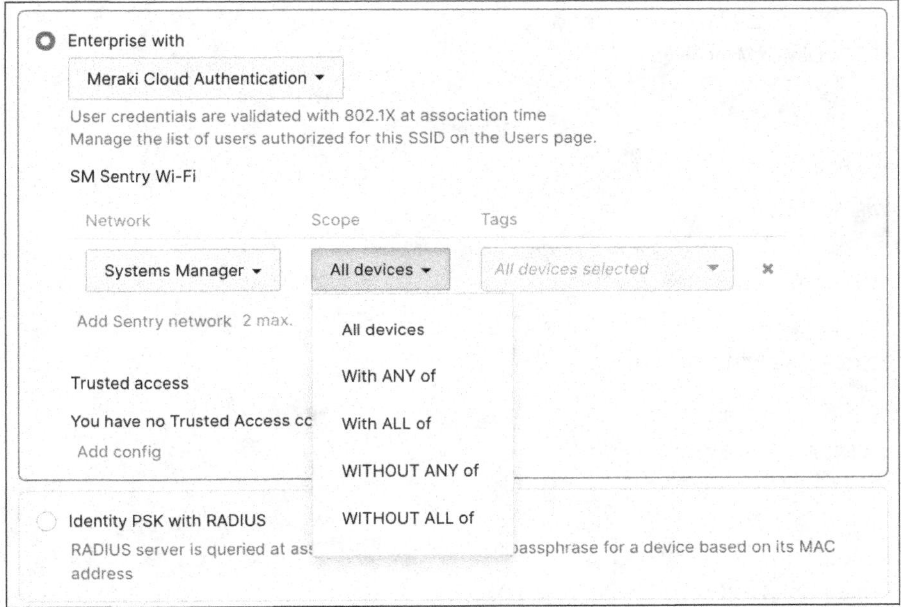

Figure 8-84 *Configuring the Scope for Sentry Wi-Fi on an SSID in Meraki Dashboard*

After you complete the configuration of Sentry Wi-Fi, it will take some time for the devices to check in and receive their updates. In the meantime, perform any additional network configuration required on the SSID and ensure this SSID is enabled. To push out the profile faster, navigate to the Devices list (**Systems Manager > Devices**). From there, select the devices that need updating and then select **Sync Profiles** from the **Command** menu.

Follow these steps to verify that the Sentry Wi-Fi profile is working correctly:

Step 1. Check the profiles received by your devices. In this example, we demonstrate this using an Apple iOS device. For other operating systems, check the support documentation from the device manufacturer.

On iOS 17, navigate to **Settings > General > VPN & Device Management > Meraki Systems Manager** (under MOBILE DEVICE MANAGEMENT) >

More Details (under Profile). The iOS devices in this example run iOS 17.2.

Figure 8-85 shows the **Sentry SSID** under **WI-FI NETWORK** as well as the device and CA certificates that have been pushed to the device.

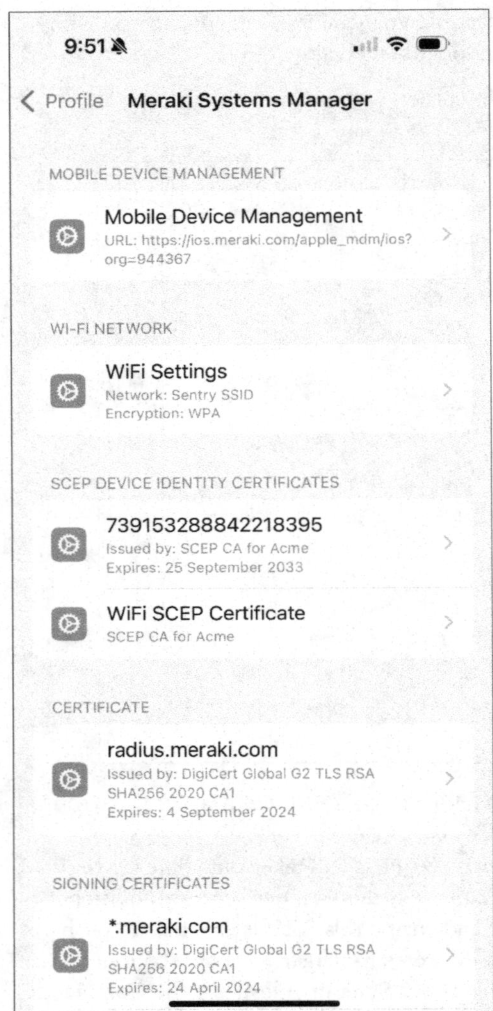

Figure 8-85 *A Profile Pushed by Systems Manager to an Apple iOS Device*

Step 2. Still on your iOS device, navigate to **Settings > Wi-Fi** and connect to the SSID whose network name was shown in the **WiFi Settings** profile in Figure 8-85. In this example, the SSID name is **Sentry SSID.** You should be able to connect to this network without entering any credentials.

The event log in Meraki Dashboard shows the enrolled device using a certificate to authenticate, as illustrated in Figure 8-86.

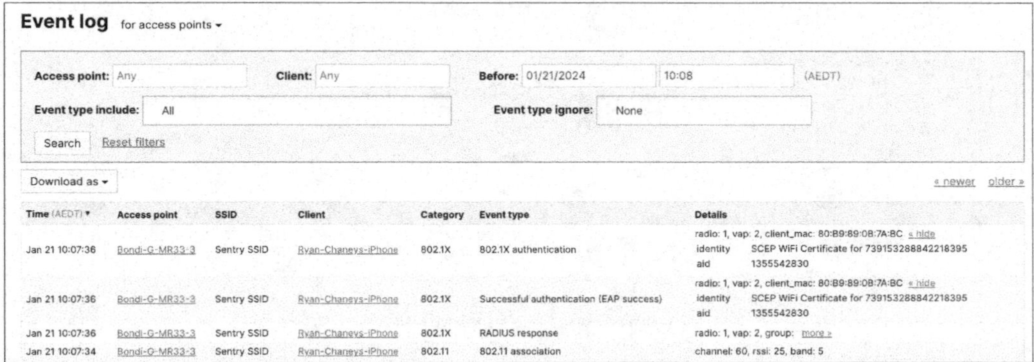

Figure 8-86 *The Event Log in Meraki Dashboard Showing a Sentry Wi-Fi Connection Using EAP-TLS*

You've now completed the setup and verification of Sentry Wi-Fi. We hope that you're impressed with how quick and easy that was to set up.

On the same SSID, it is also possible to enable Systems Manager self-enrollment. Doing so enables users to enroll with System Manager, receive the Wi-Fi profile and certificates, and then connect to the enterprise Wi-Fi. To enable this, navigate to **Wireless > Access Control** and select the Sentry Wi-Fi-enabled SSID. Next, scroll down to **Splash Page**, select **Endpoint Management Enrollment**, and finish by clicking **Save**.

Sentry LAN

While researching this book, we noticed a number of people asking online if there was a wired equivalent of Sentry Wi-Fi. What they were asking for was an easier way to authenticate devices enrolled with Meraki Systems Manager to the LAN using 802.1X (EAP-TLS). Although such a feature is not documented and doesn't have an official name, this is actually possible using an access control policy. For the purposes of this book, we have named this feature *Sentry LAN*. This section demonstrates this feature using a Mac laptop running macOS 14.5, connecting to an MS 120 switch running 16.7 firmware. Because this is an undocumented feature, be sure to test it thoroughly in your environment before deploying it.

Follow these steps to configure Sentry LAN on switch ports:

Step 1. Log in to Meraki Dashboard (https://dashboard.meraki.com).

Step 2. Navigate to **Switching > Access Policies** (under Configure).

Step 3. On the **Access Policies** page, click the **Add an Access Policy** link. You then see the screen in Figure 8-87.

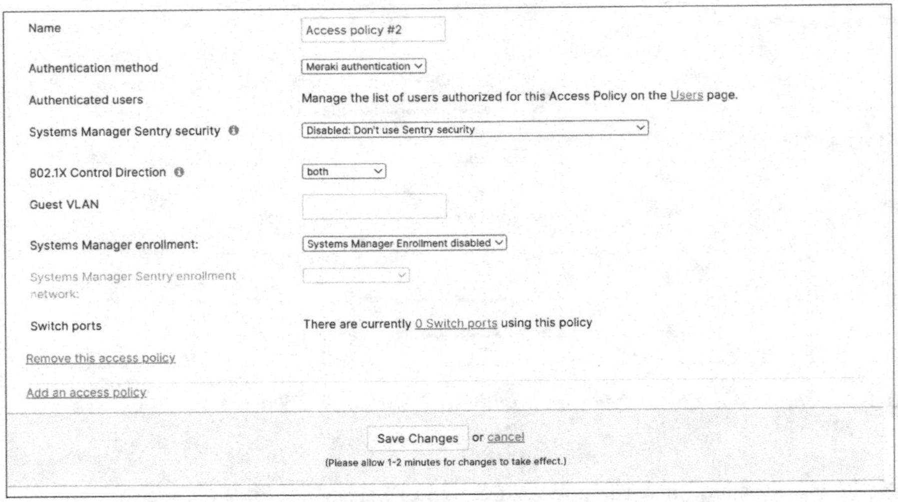

Figure 8-87 *Creating a New Access Policy for Sentry-Based LAN Authentication in Meraki Dashboard*

Step 4. Enter a meaningful **Name** for this access policy. Here, we have used the name **Sentry LAN.**

Ensure the **Authentication Method** is **Meraki Authentication.** Users do not need to be defined and authorized when using Sentry-based policies.

From the **Systems Manager Sentry Security** drop-down menu, select **Enabled: Allow Devices with the Following Tag Scopes Access to Network,** as illustrated in Figure 8-88.

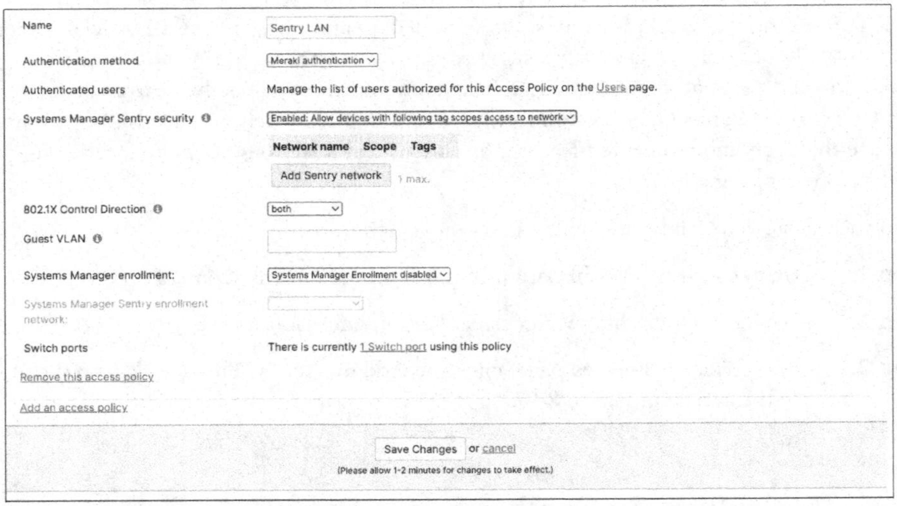

Figure 8-88 *Configuring Sentry-Based LAN Authentication in Meraki Dashboard*

Step 5. Click **Add Sentry Network** and select the **Network Name** in which your Systems Manager devices reside. In this book, we've used a dedicated network called **Systems Manager**.

a. Set the **Scope** as required. This can be all devices or some devices based on a tag. In this example, we've used the tag **Sentry_LAN** (see Figure 8-89), which we assigned earlier. If you're using a custom tag like this, add it to at least one device on the **Systems Manager > Devices** page first.

b. Click **Save Changes.** As well as saving the changes to the access policy, this step also creates a profile in **Systems Manager > Settings** and applies it to devices with the scope specified here.

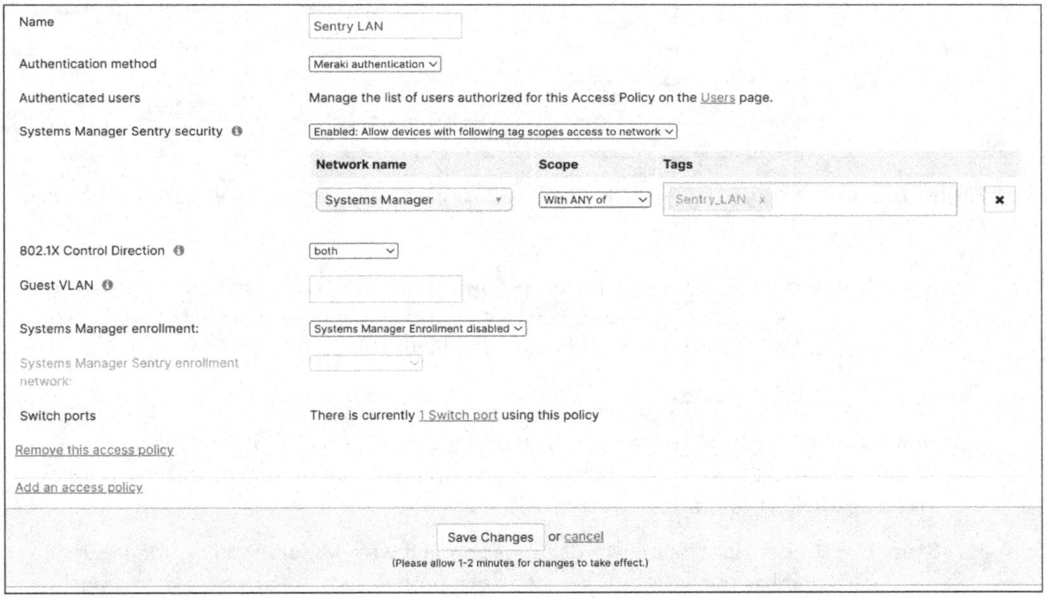

Figure 8-89 *Configuring the Scope for Sentry-Based LAN Authentication in Meraki Dashboard*

Step 6. Just like with a regular 802.1X access policy, the Sentry LAN access policy needs to be assigned to switch ports to be effective.

a. In Dashboard, navigate to **Switching > Switch Ports.**

b. Select the ports where you want to enable Sentry LAN and click the **Edit** button at the top, as shown in Figure 8-90.

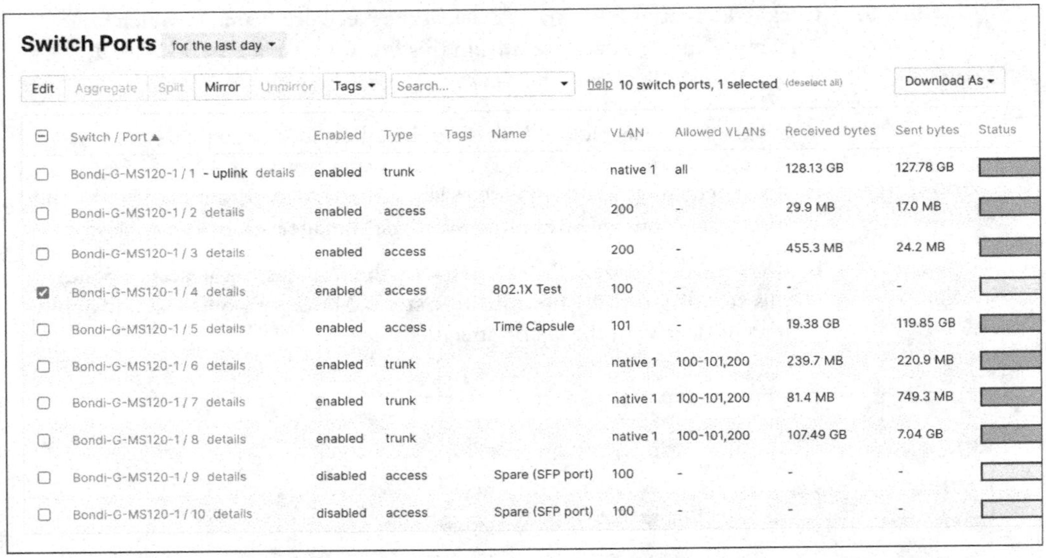

Switch Ports for the last day ▾

Edit | Aggregate | Split | Mirror | Unmirror | Tags ▾ | Search... ▾ | help 10 switch ports, 1 selected (deselect all) | Download As ▾

☐	Switch / Port ▲	Enabled	Type	Tags	Name	VLAN	Allowed VLANs	Received bytes	Sent bytes	Status
☐	Bondi-G-MS120-1 / 1 - uplink details	enabled	trunk			native 1	all	128.13 GB	127.78 GB	
☐	Bondi-G-MS120-1 / 2 details	enabled	access			200	-	29.9 MB	17.0 MB	
☐	Bondi-G-MS120-1 / 3 details	enabled	access			200	-	455.3 MB	24.2 MB	
☑	Bondi-G-MS120-1 / 4 details	enabled	access		802.1X Test	100	-	-	-	
☐	Bondi-G-MS120-1 / 5 details	enabled	access		Time Capsule	101	-	19.38 GB	119.85 GB	
☐	Bondi-G-MS120-1 / 6 details	enabled	trunk			native 1	100-101,200	239.7 MB	220.9 MB	
☐	Bondi-G-MS120-1 / 7 details	enabled	trunk			native 1	100-101,200	81.4 MB	749.3 MB	
☐	Bondi-G-MS120-1 / 8 details	enabled	trunk			native 1	100-101,200	107.49 GB	7.04 GB	
☐	Bondi-G-MS120-1 / 9 details	disabled	access		Spare (SFP port)	100	-	-	-	
☐	Bondi-G-MS120-1 / 10 details	disabled	access		Spare (SFP port)	100	-	-	-	

Figure 8-90 *Selecting the Ports to Enable Sentry LAN–Based Authentication in Meraki Dashboard*

Step 7. From the **Access Policy** drop-down menu, select the name for the access policy that was created in Step 4. In this example, we have selected the **Sentry LAN** access policy, as illustrated in Figure 8-91.

Click **Update.**

Now that you've completed the configuration required to enable Sentry-based authentication using 802.1X with EAP-TLS on wired ports, you can follow these steps to verify that everything is working correctly:

Step 1. Check that your client device is enrolled with Meraki Systems Manager and has the Meraki Ethernet profile pushed to it. As mentioned previously, we've used a Mac for this testing. On macOS, navigate to **System Settings > Privacy & Security > Profiles** and double-click the profile called **Meraki Ethernet (***assigned Systems Manager tag***)** to display the screen shown in Figure 8-92. Refer to Chapter 11 for the steps on enrolling a device with Meraki Systems Manager.

Step 2. Connect this device's Ethernet port to a port on your Meraki switch that has the Sentry LAN access policy applied. If you have multiple 802.1X profiles, you might be asked to confirm the certificate to use for authentication. This choice is saved, so in the future, this device will connect automatically.

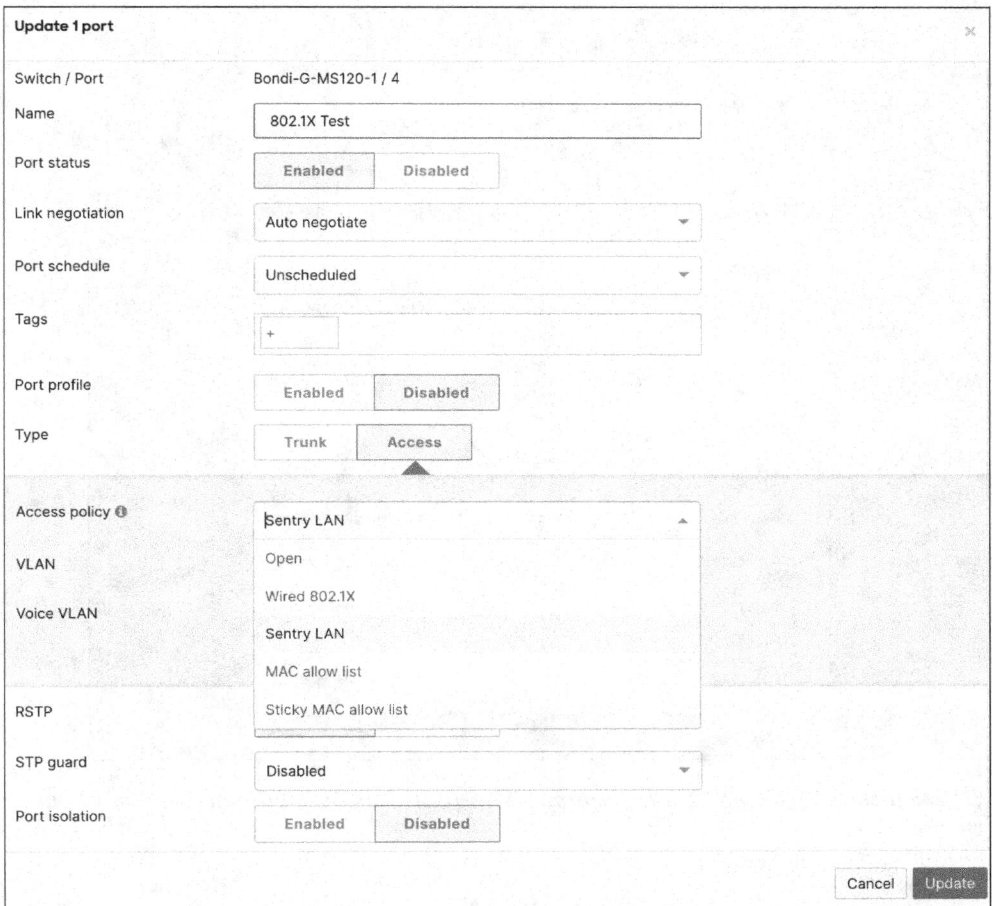

Figure 8-91 *Enabling the Sentry LAN Access Policy on a Switch Port in Meraki Dashboard*

On the screen shown in Figure 8-93, you do not need to enter an **Account Name.** If the correct certificate is selected, simply click **OK.**

Step 3. You should now be connected to the network. You can verify this on macOS by navigating to **Systems Settings > Network.** Then click the LAN adapter and select **Details > 802.1X.** In Figure 8-94, you can see confirmation that the authentication protocol used here is indeed EAP-TLS.

Step 4. The Meraki Dashboard event log records the successful 802.1X authentication (see Figure 8-95); however, you need to verify the authentication protocol itself on the client.

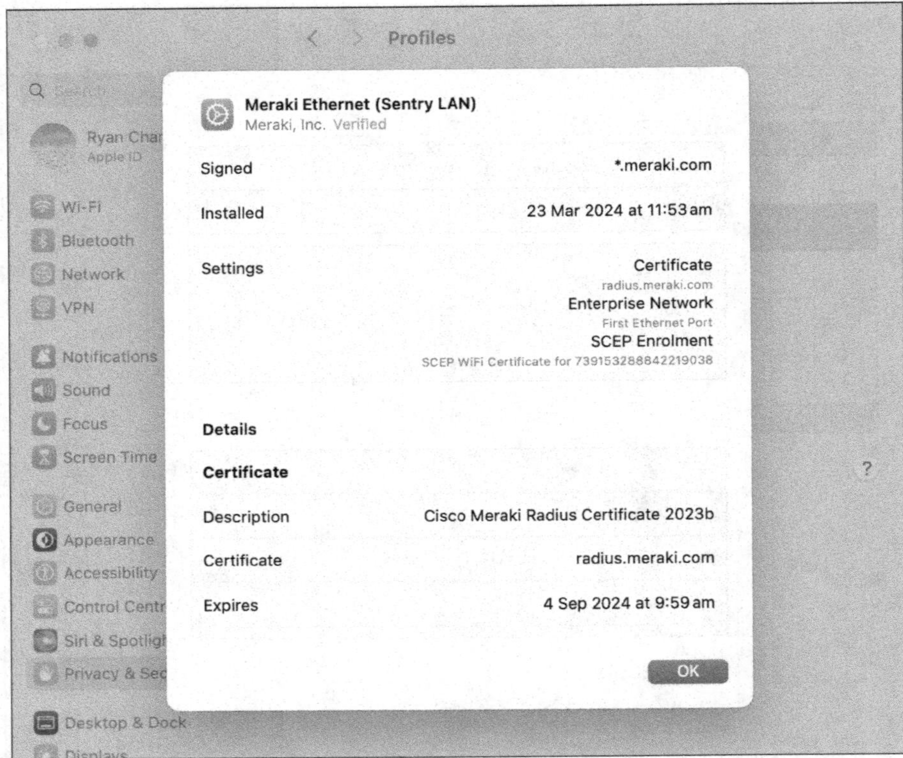

Figure 8-92 *Verifying That the Sentry LAN Profile Has Been Pushed to a Mac Client Device*

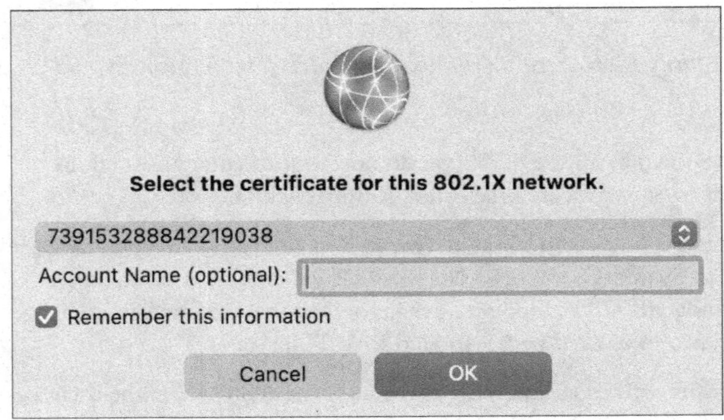

Figure 8-93 *Authenticating to the LAN on macOS with Sentry-Based 802.1X*

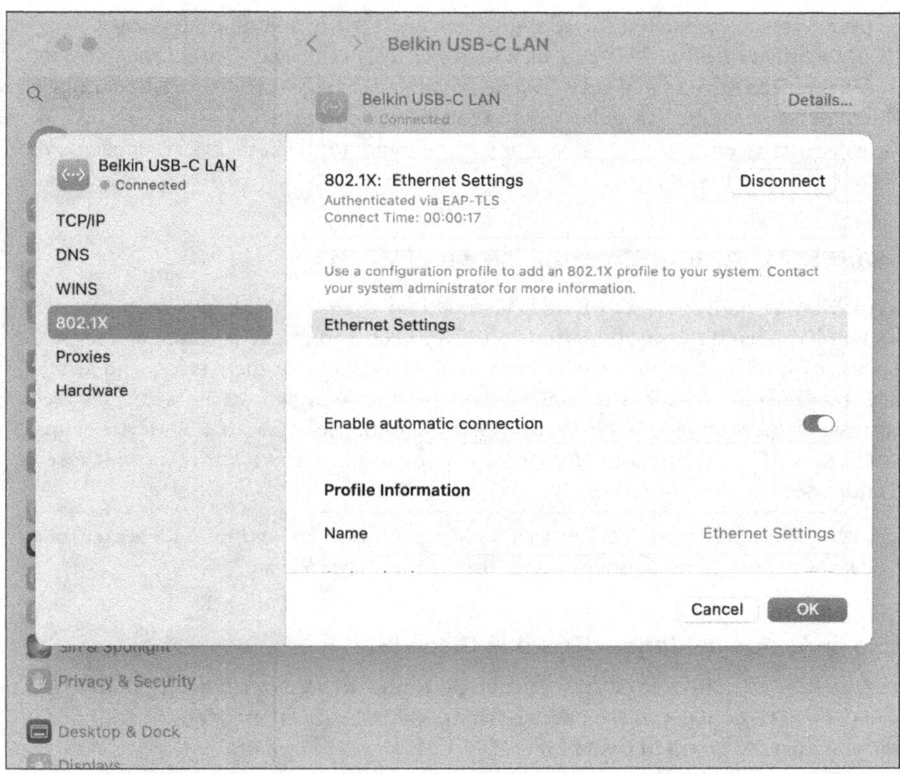

Figure 8-94 *Verifying EAP-TLS as the Authentication Protocol on a Sentry-Based 802.1X Connection in macOS*

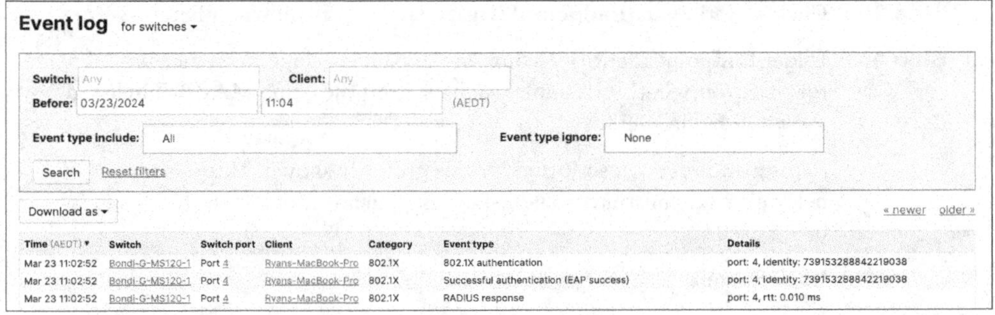

Figure 8-95 *The Event Log in Meraki Dashboard Showing a Successful Sentry-Based Wired 802.1X Authentication*

At this point, you've completed the configuration and verification of Sentry-based 802.1X authentication with EAP-TLS, aka Sentry LAN. Compared to 802.1X deployments utilizing RADIUS, seeing EAP-TLS deployed in this way often surprises people just how much easier it can be. Given how easy Sentry LAN and Sentry Wi-Fi are to deploy, there's really no reason why networks of any size should not be authenticating clients on both wired and wireless now.

Configuring MAC Authentication Bypass (MAB)

MAC Authentication Bypass, or MAB, is intended for devices that do not support 802.1X and has been traditionally used for devices such as printers. As more and more devices improve their capabilities in relation to network security, there is less and less justification to deploy MAB. That said, MAB does provide organizations with a way to authenticate any remaining devices on the network, until such time that all devices support 802.1X. MAC Authentication Bypass should be used only as a last resort because MAC addresses can be spoofed easily.

MAC Authentication Bypass requires Cisco ISE, specifically an endpoint identity group and a new policy set, as we demonstrate in the section that follows.

Configuring an Endpoint Identity Group in Cisco ISE

For this use case, the endpoint identity group performs the role of a whitelist, authorizing selected devices to connect to the network using MAB. Follow these steps to configure an endpoint identity group in Cisco ISE:

Step 1. Log in to your instance of Cisco ISE.

Step 2. Navigate to **Menu > Work Centers > Id Groups** (under Network Access), as illustrated in Figure 8-96.

Step 3. Click **+ Add** under **Endpoint Identity Groups**, as shown in Figure 8-97.

Step 4. Under **Endpoint Identity Group**, in the **Name** field, enter a meaningful name for this group. In this example, we have used the name **MAB-Whitelist**, as shown in Figure 8-98.

(Optional) Enter a description for this group as shown. This description will help other administrators understand the purpose for which this group is being used.

Click **Submit**.

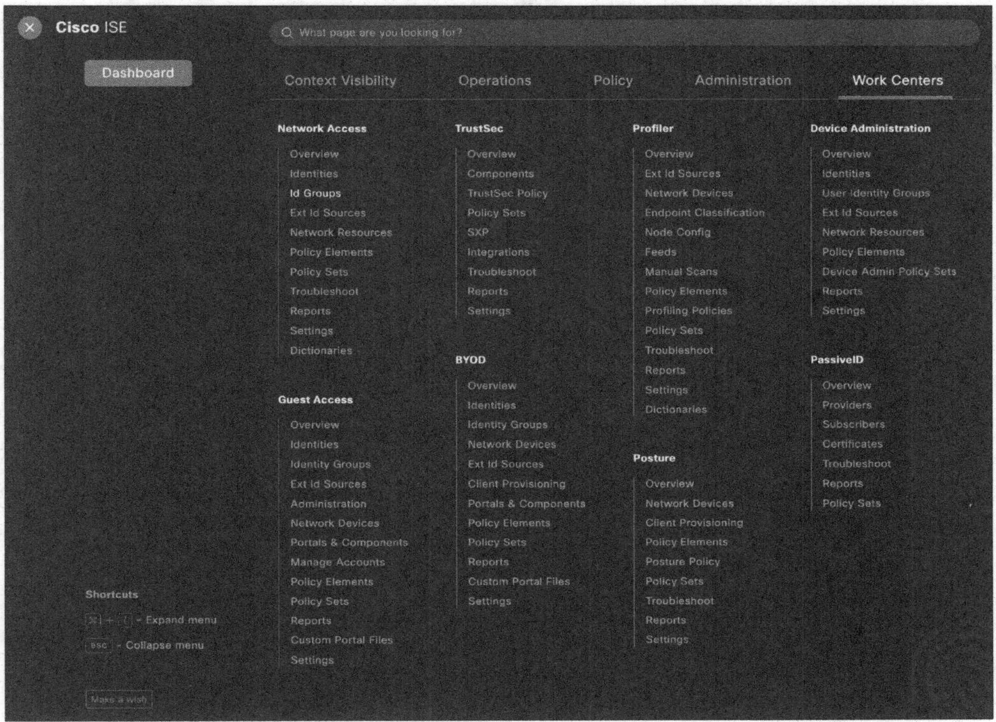

Figure 8-96 *Navigating to Id Groups in Cisco ISE*

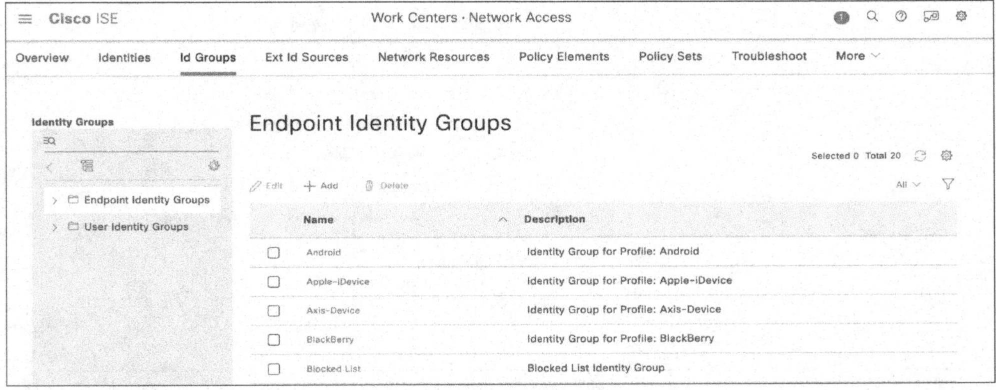

Figure 8-97 *Creating a New Endpoint Identity Group in Cisco ISE*

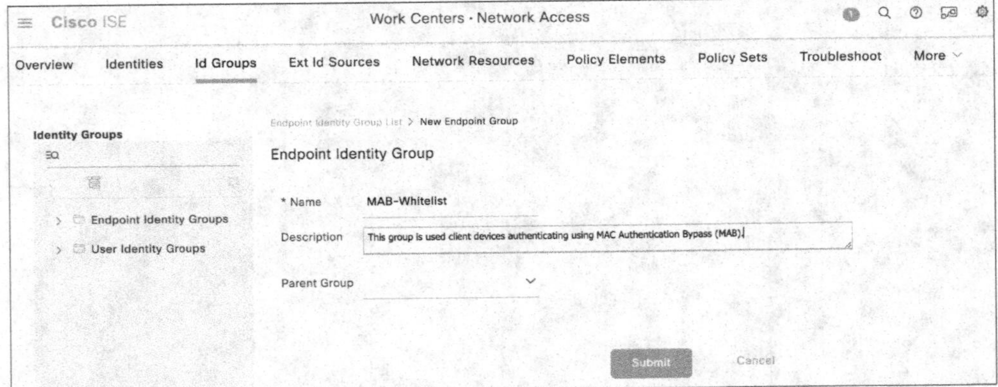

Figure 8-98 *Configuring a New Endpoint Identity Group in Cisco ISE*

Step 5. You should see the **Endpoint Identity Groups** page again with the new group listed, as shown in Figure 8-99. Click the **Identities** tab at the top of the page.

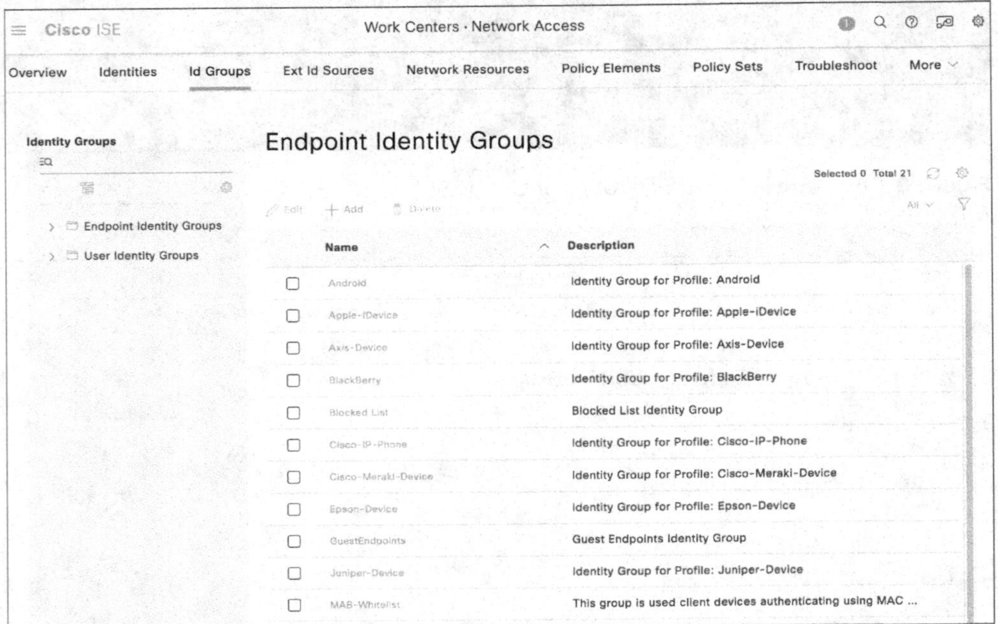

Figure 8-99 *The Endpoint Identity Groups Listing in Cisco ISE Showing the New Addition*

Step 6. If your devices have already connected to the network, they will be listed in the table on this page, as shown in Figure 8-100. Click the MAC address to open it and then click the pencil icon to edit. Otherwise, click **Add**.

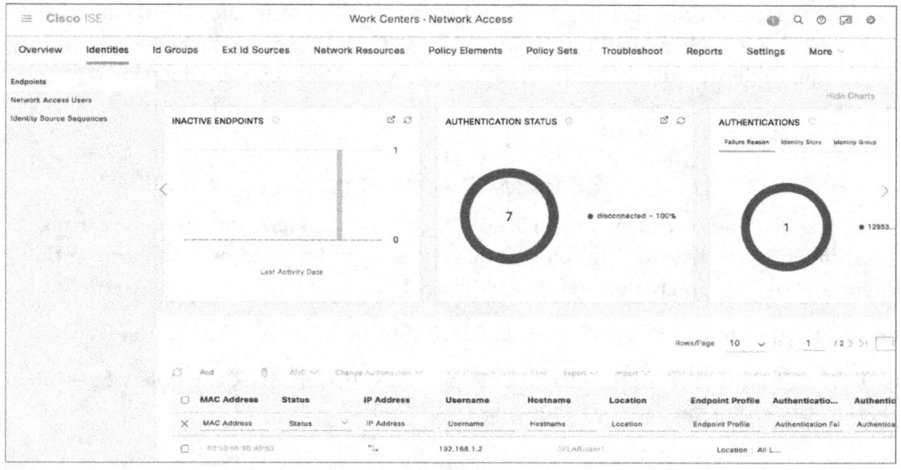

Figure 8-100 *Selecting a MAC Address to Add to the Endpoint Identity Group in Cisco ISE*

Step 7. On the pop-up window with the heading **Add Endpoint**, enter the MAC address for the end device in the **Mac Address** field (see Figure 8-101).

a. Check the box in front of **Static Group Assignment.** From the **Identity Group Assignment** drop-down menu, select the endpoint identity group created in the previous steps.

b. Click **Save.**

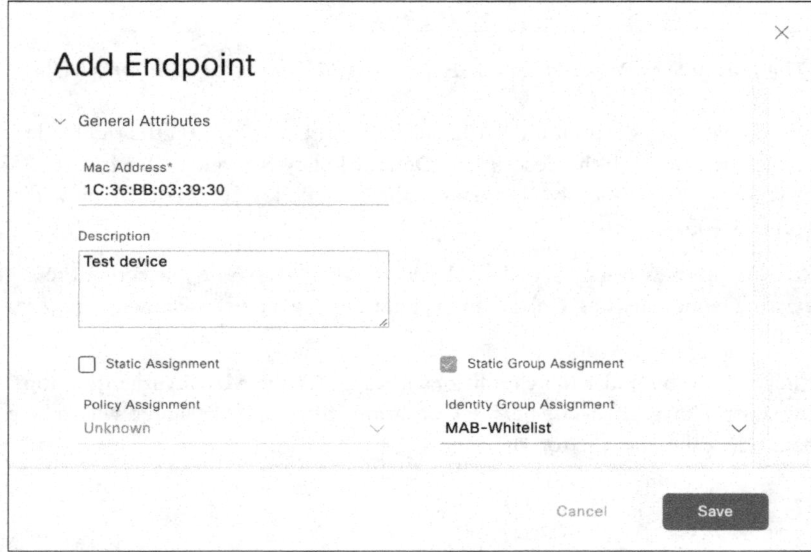

Figure 8-101 *Adding a MAC Address to the Endpoint Identity Group in Cisco ISE*

You've now completed the creation of an endpoint identity group and added client MAC addresses to it. Remember to add any additional MAC addresses to the endpoint identity group if required in the future. Read on to learn how to reference this group via a policy set in Cisco ISE.

Creating a Policy Set in Cisco ISE for MAC Authentication Bypass

The next step is to add a policy set in Cisco ISE to match devices authenticating using MAC Authentication Bypass. This checks that a device's MAC address is present in the endpoint identity group created (refer to Figure 8-101).

Follow these steps to create a policy set in Cisco ISE for MAC Authentication Bypass:

Step 1. Continuing on from Step 7 in the previous section, click the **Policy Sets** tab at the top of the page, as shown in Figure 8-102.

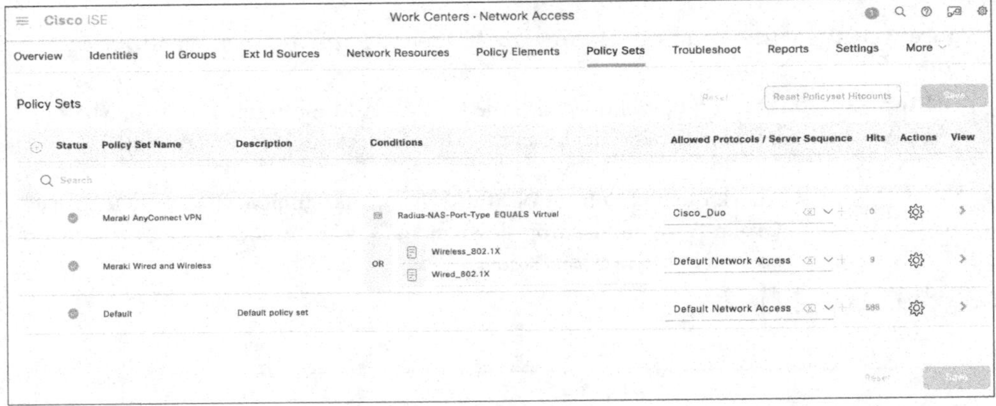

Figure 8-102 *The Policy Sets Page in Cisco ISE Before Adding a Policy Set for MAB*

Step 2. On the page shown in Figure 8-102, click the sprocket icon on the right side of the last row (with the description **Default Policy Set**) and select **Insert New Row Above.** You should now see the **New Policy Set 1** row, as shown in Figure 8-103.

Step 3. Rename this new policy set **MAC Authentication Bypass** by selecting the existing name, pressing **Delete**, and typing the new name, as shown in Figure 8-104.

Step 4. Click the **+** icon under the **Conditions** heading for the **MAC Authentication Bypass** policy set. This opens the **Conditions Studio.** If presented with a help page, click the **X** in the top right.

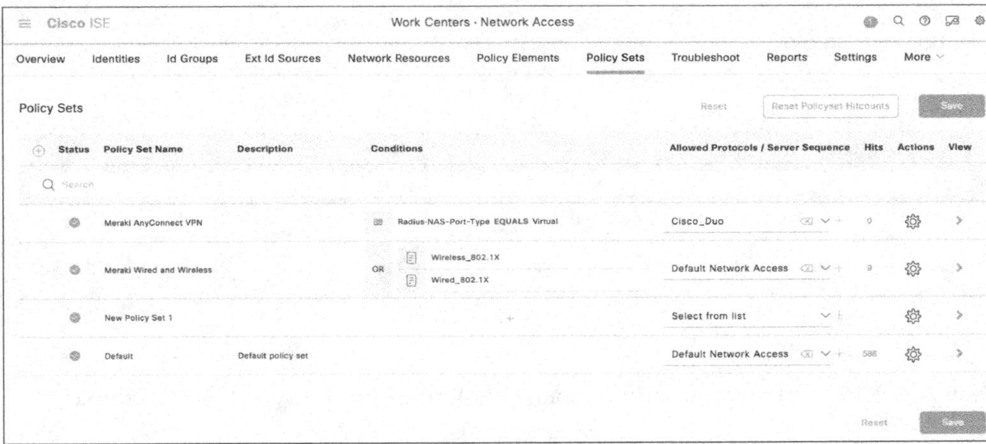

Figure 8-103 *Creating a New Policy Set to Be Used for MAB Authentication*

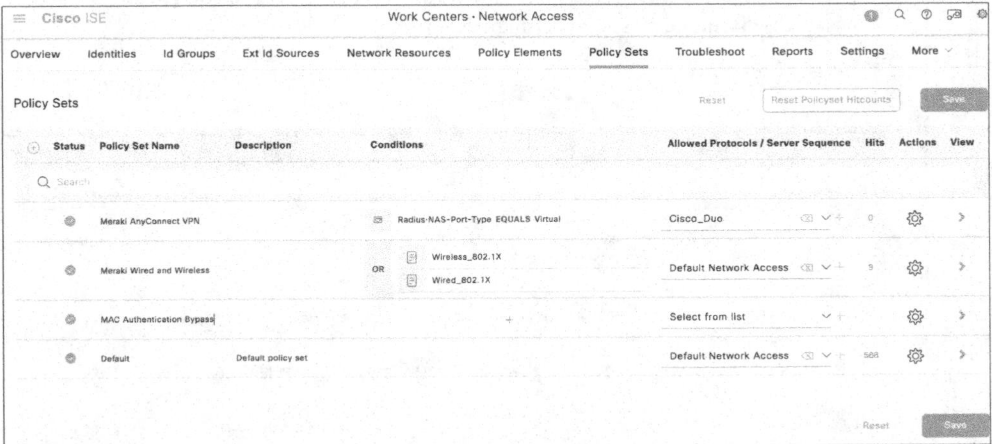

Figure 8-104 *Renaming the New Policy Set in Cisco ISE*

Step 5. Drag **Wired_MAB** from the **Library** pane on the left to the **NEW | AND | OR** box in the **Editor** pane on the right.

a. Drag **Wireless_MAB** from the **Library** pane on the left to the **NEW | AND | OR** box in the **Editor** pane on the right.

b. Change the **AND** drop-down to the left of **Wired_MAB** and **Wireless_MAB** to **OR**. The **Conditions Studio** window should now look the same as Figure 8-105.

c. Scroll down and click **Use**.

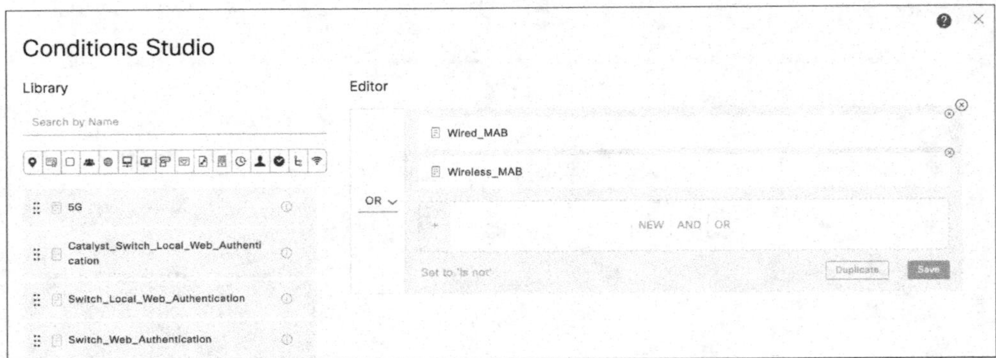

Figure 8-105 *Creating a Condition Matching Wired and Wireless MAB in Cisco ISE*

Step 6. You should be back on the **Policy Sets** page now.

a. On the **MAC Authentication Bypass** policy set row, select **Default Network Access** from the **Allowed Protocols / Server Sequence** drop-down menu, as shown in Figure 8-106.

b. Click **Save.**

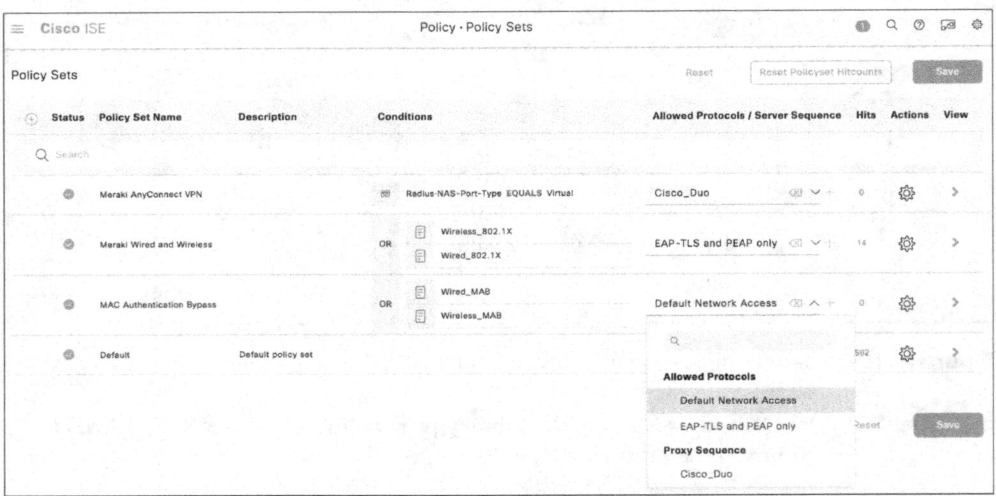

Figure 8-106 *Setting the Allowed Protocols on the MAB Policy Set in Cisco ISE*

Step 7. Click the > icon under the **View** column heading for the **MAC Authentication Bypass** policy set.

Step 8. Expand the **Authentication Policy**.

For the **Default** authentication rule, from the **Use** drop-down menu, select **Internal Endpoints**, as shown in Figure 8-107.

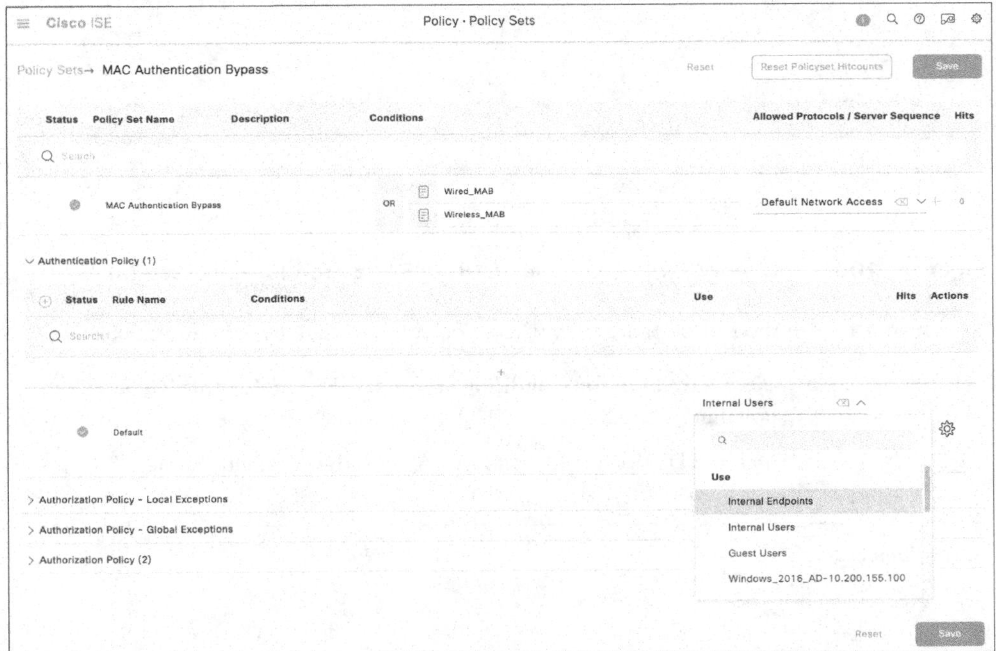

Figure 8-107 *Configuring the Authentication Policy for the MAB Policy Set in Cisco ISE*

Step 9. Expand the **Authorization Policy**. Click the sprocket icon on the right side and click **Insert New Row Above**, as shown in Figure 8-108.

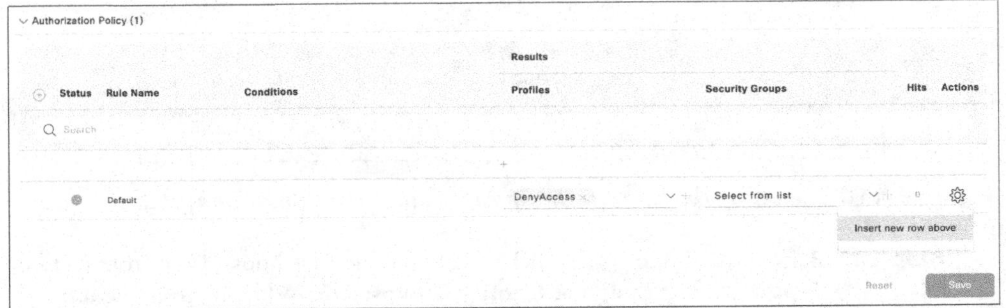

Figure 8-108 *Adding a New Rule on the MAB Authorization Policy in Cisco ISE*

Step 10. Click the **+** icon under the **Conditions** heading (see Figure 8-109) to open the **Conditions Studio**.

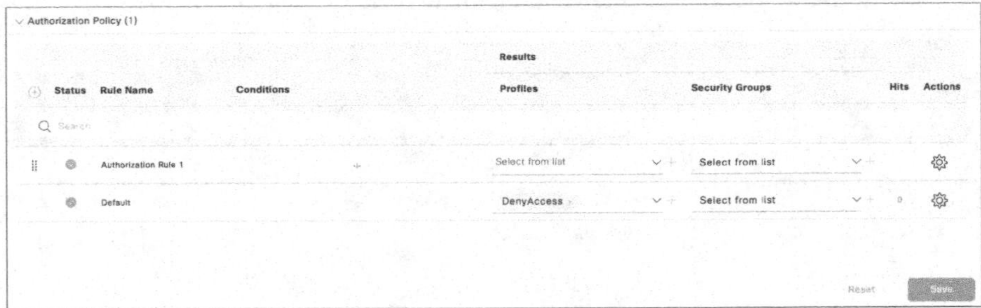

Figure 8-109 *Adding a Condition to the MAB Authorization Rule in Cisco ISE*

Step 11. On the **Editor** pane, click where you can see **Click to Add an Attribute.**

a. **Select Attribute for Condition** appears. Click the **Identity Group** icon, as shown in Figure 8-110.

b. Click the Dictionary **IdentityGroup** with the Attribute **Name.**

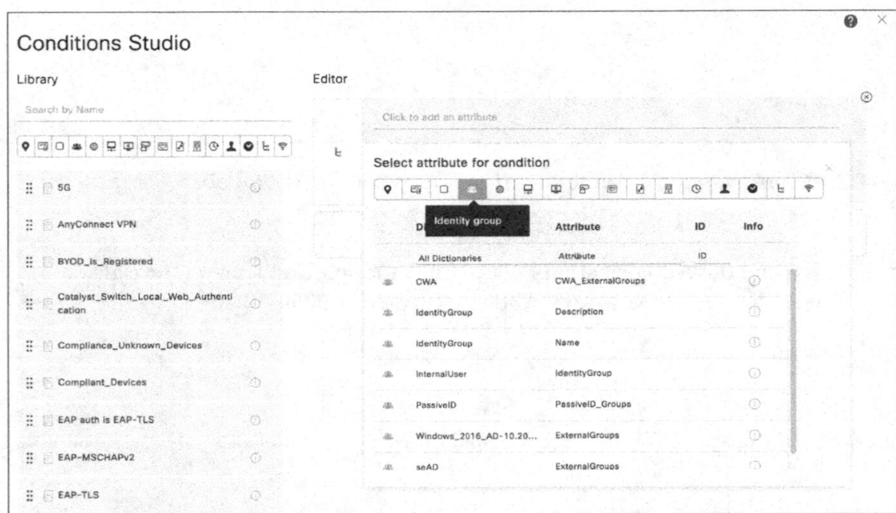

Figure 8-110 *Selecting the Identity Group Attribute in the Conditions Studio*

Step 12. Back on the **Editor** pane, click where you can see **Choose Type from List or Type** and select **Endpoint Identity Groups:MAC-Whitelist** from the drop-down menu, as shown in Figure 8-111. Scroll down and click **Use.**

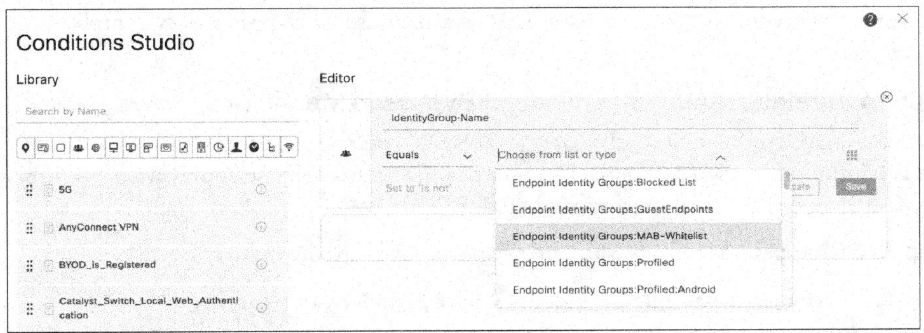

Figure 8-111 *Configuring the Endpoint Identity Group on a Condition for MAB Authorization in Conditions Studio*

Step 13. Back on the **MAC Authentication Bypass** policy set page, select **PermitAccess** from the **Profiles** drop-down menu, as shown in Figure 8-112.

Click **Save** to finish.

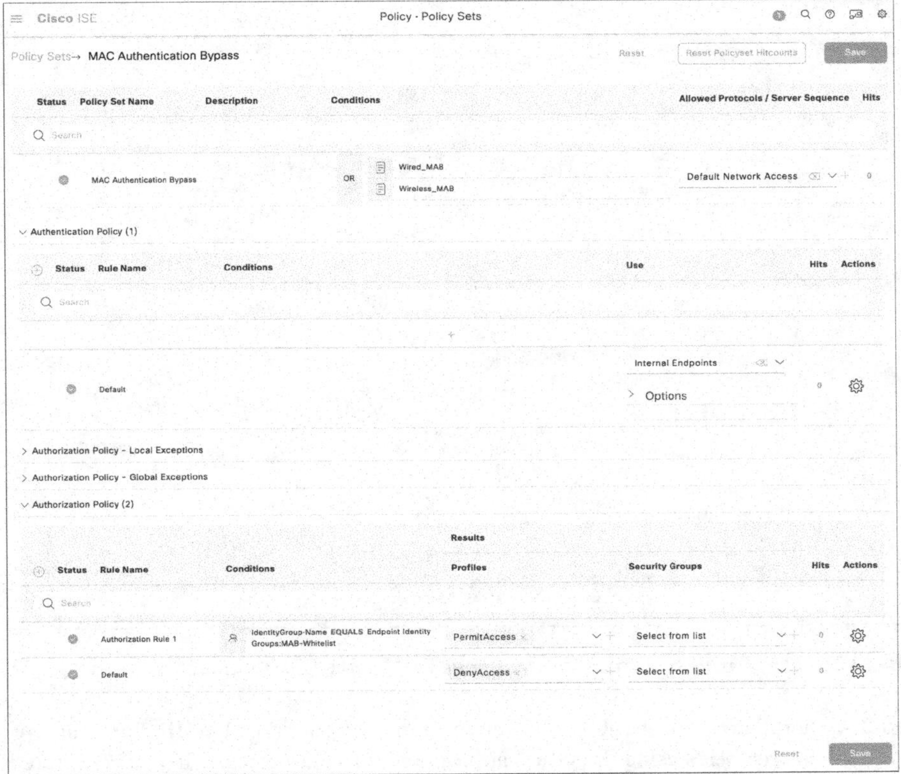

Figure 8-112 *The Completed Policy Set for MAB in Cisco ISE*

The configuration of the policy set for MAC Authentication Bypass is now complete.

Configuring Wireless MAC Authentication Bypass in Meraki Dashboard

To enable MAC Authentication Bypass on an SSID, you apply an access control policy that is configured for MAB. Follow these steps to learn how to configure an access policy for MAC Authentication Bypass in a wireless SSID:

Step 1. Log in to Meraki Dashboard (https://dashboard.meraki.com).

Step 2. Navigate to **Wireless > Access Control** (under Configure).

a. Select the **SSID** at the top of the page.

b. Under Security, select **MAC-Based Access Control (No Encryption)**, as shown in Figure 8-113.

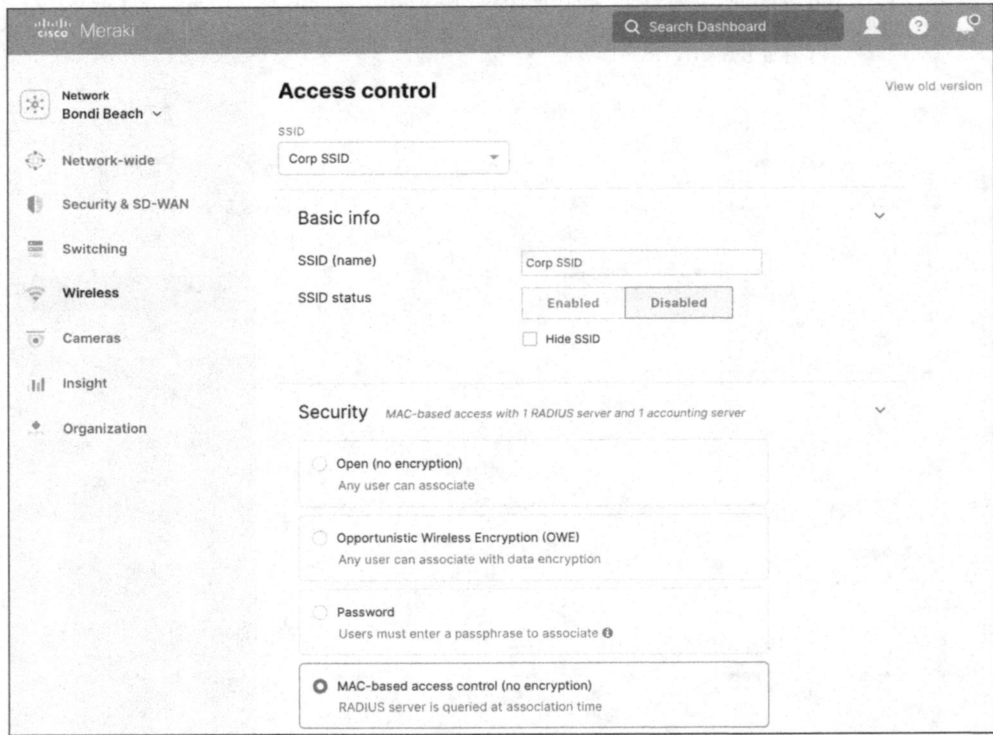

Figure 8-113 *The Wireless Access Control Page in Meraki Dashboard*

Step 3. Scroll down to the **RADIUS** section and configure the **Host IP**, **Ports**, and **Secret** fields using the values appropriate for your network. If you configured RADIUS previously for 802.1X, you can use the same values again here. It is recommended that you check **RADIUS Testing** and set **RADIUS Attribute Specifying Group Policy Name** to **Filter-Id**, as shown in Figure 8-114.

Click **Save**.

RADIUS 1 RADIUS server, 1 accounting server - Testing enabled

RADIUS servers

#	Host IP or FQDN	Auth port	Secret	RadSec	Test	Actions
1	192.168.100.9	1812	••••••••••••••	☐	Test	•••

Add server 3 max.

RADIUS accounting servers

#	Host IP or FQDN	Acct port	Secret	RadSec	Actions
1	192.168.100.9	1813	••••••••••••••	☐	•••

Add server 3 max.

Accounting interim interval: 10 minutes

☑ RADIUS testing
☐ RADIUS CoA support
☐ RADIUS proxy

RADIUS attribute specifying group policy name: Filter-Id

Figure 8-114 *Configuring RADIUS Settings on an Access Control Policy for MAC Authentication Bypass*

Now that you've completed the configuration for MAC Authentication Bypass on a wireless SSID, follow these steps to verify that the MAC Authentication Bypass is working correctly:

Step 1. Ensure that the device being used for this test has its MAC address specified in the endpoint identity group configured in Cisco ISE. Be aware that on an iOS device, if Private Wi-Fi Address is turned on (default), the MAC address being used can change and may prevent MAB from working correctly. For this reason, it is recommended that you disable Private Wi-Fi Address on the iOS device before testing.

Step 2. Connect to the SSID configured for MAB earlier as per normal. The device should connect automatically without any prompts for a username, password, or certificate.

Step 3. To verify that the device was authenticated via the MAB policy and not some other policy, check the live log in Cisco ISE (**Menu > Operations > Live Logs** [under RADIUS]). Figure 8-115 shows an excerpt from an authentication detail report for a successful Wi-Fi association using MAB.

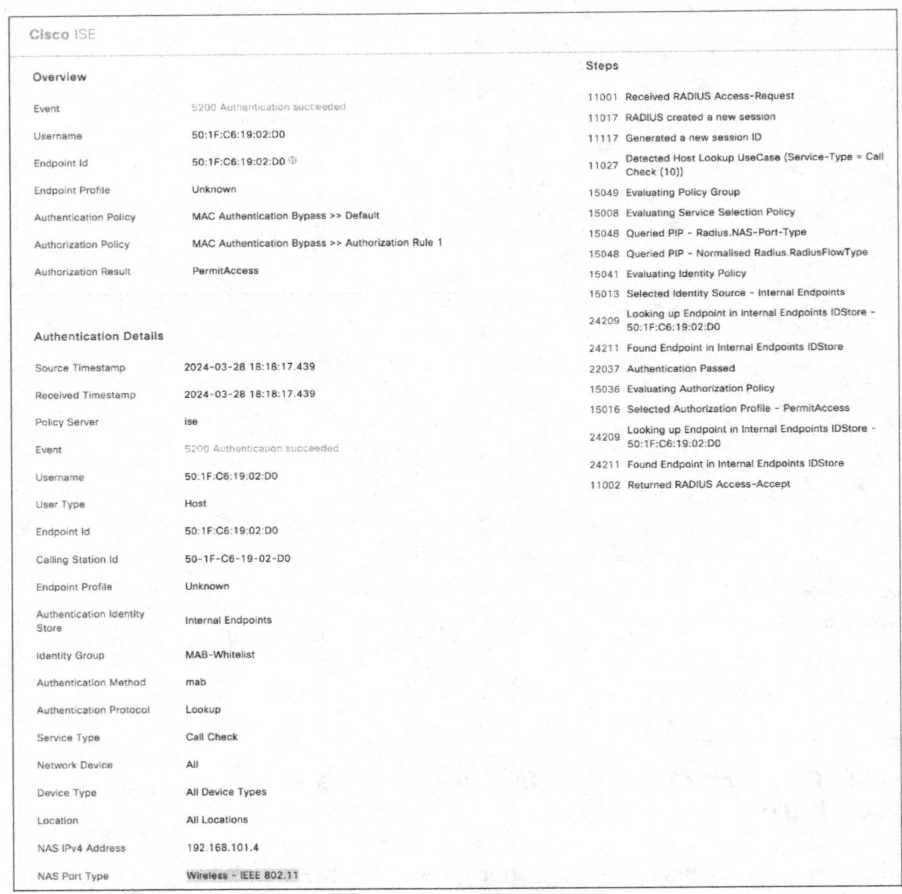

Figure 8-115 *An Authentication Detail Report in Cisco ISE Showing a Successful Authentication Using MAB*

Step 4. You also can verify the use of MAC Authentication Bypass by using the event log in Meraki Dashboard, as shown in Figure 8-116.

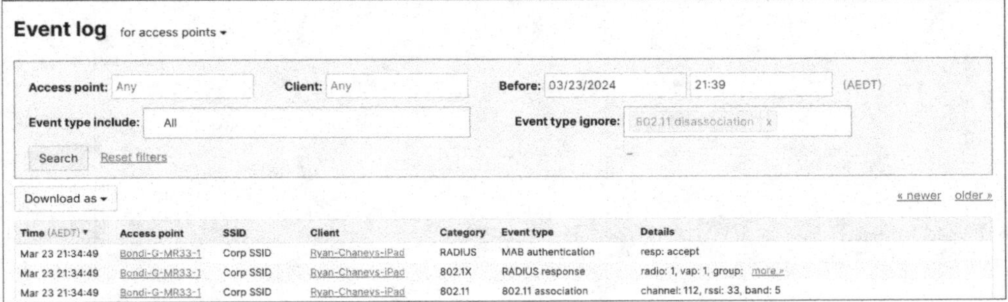

Figure 8-116 *Verifying MAC Authentication Bypass Using the Event Log in Meraki Dashboard*

You've completed the configuration for MAC Authentication Bypass on a wireless SSID. To learn more about MAB on Meraki MR access points, refer to the following guide: https://documentation.meraki.com/MR/Encryption_and_Authentication/MAC-Based_Access_Control_Using_Cisco_ISE_-_MR_Access_Points.

Configuring Wired MAC Authentication Bypass in Meraki Dashboard

MAC Authentication Bypass is enabled on switch ports by applying an access policy that is configured for MAB. Follow these steps to learn how to configure an access policy for MAC Authentication Bypass on Meraki switch ports:

Step 1. Log in to Meraki Dashboard (https://dashboard.meraki.com).

Step 2. Navigate to **Switching > Access Policies** (under Configure). Click **Add an Access Policy.**

Step 3. On the new access policy, configure the following (see Figure 8-117):

- Give the policy a meaningful name in the **Name** field.
- Enter the **Host**, **Port**, and **Secret** details for both the RADIUS Servers and RADIUS Accounting Servers. In this example, we're using Cisco ISE for RADIUS and RADIUS accounting. You can select organization-wide RADIUS servers from the **Select RADIUS** drop-down menu.
- It is recommended that you check **RADIUS Server Testing** and set **RADIUS Attribute Specifying Group Policy Name** to **Filter-ID.**
- Set **Access Policy Type** to **MAC Authentication Bypass.**
- Leave all other settings as their defaults.

Click **Save** to save these changes.

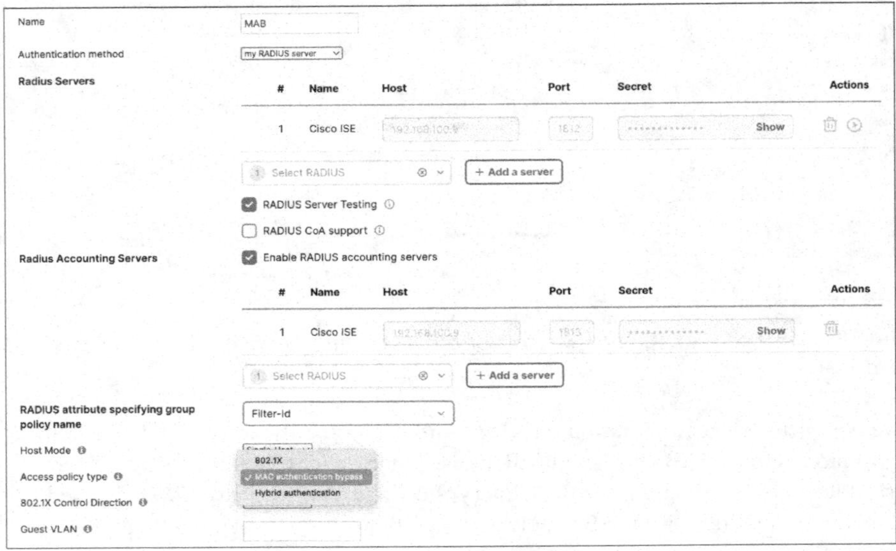

Figure 8-117 *Configuring the RADIUS Servers for Wired MAB Authentication in Meraki Dashboard*

Step 4. This access policy needs to be applied to your switch ports. Navigate to **Switching > Switch Ports**.

Step 5. On the **Switch Ports** page (see Figure 8-118), select the ports to configure and click **Edit**.

Meraki

Network
Bondi Beach

Network-wide
Security & SD-WAN
Switching
Wireless
Cameras
Insight
Organization

Switch Ports for the last day

Edit | Aggregate | Split | Mirror | Unmirror | Tags | Search... | help 10 switch ports, 1 selected (deselect all)

	Switch / Port ▲	Enabled	Type	Access policy	VLAN	Allowed VLANs	Received bytes	Sent bytes
☐	Bondi-G-MS120-1 / 1 - uplink details	enabled	trunk	Open	native 1	all	125.42 GB	125.41 GB
☐	Bondi-G-MS120-1 / 2 details	enabled	access	Open	200	-	29.0 MB	16.9 MB
☐	Bondi-G-MS120-1 / 3 details	enabled	access	Open	200	-	462.5 MB	24.4 MB
☐	Bondi-G-MS120-1 / 4 details	enabled	access	Open	100	-	761.6 KB	1.1 MB
☑	Bondi-G-MS120-1 / 5 details	enabled	access	Open	101	-	21.55 GB	110.90 GB
☐	Bondi-G-MS120-1 / 6 details	enabled	trunk	Open	native 1	100-101,200	15.29 GB	2.35 GB
☐	Bondi-G-MS120-1 / 7 details	enabled	trunk	Open	native 1	100-101,200	6.27 GB	4.31 GB
☐	Bondi-G-MS120-1 / 8 details	enabled	trunk	Open	native 1	100-101,200	81.69 GB	7.60 GB
☐	Bondi-G-MS120-1 / 9 details	disabled	access	Open	100	-	-	-
☐	Bondi-G-MS120-1 / 10 details	disabled	access	Open	100	-	-	-

Figure 8-118 *Selecting Switch Ports to Edit on the Switch Ports Page in Meraki Dashboard*

Step 6. From the **Access Policy** drop-down menu (see Figure 8-119), select the name of the MAC Authentication Bypass access policy created in Step 3. Click **Update**.

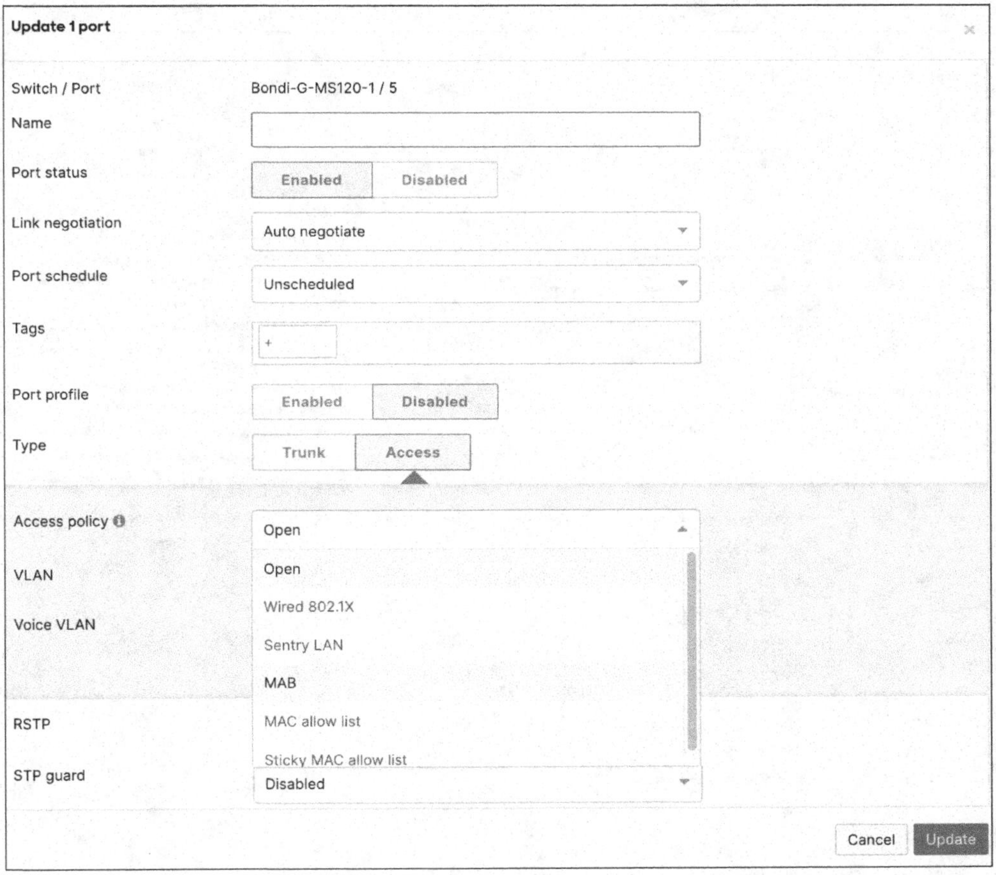

Figure 8-119 *Applying the MAB Access Policy to a Switch Port in Meraki Dashboard*

Now that you've completed the configuration of MAC Authentication Bypass on a switch port in Meraki Dashboard, follow these steps to verify that MAC Authentication Bypass is working correctly:

Step 1. Ensure that the client device being used for this test has its MAC address specified in the endpoint identity group configured in Cisco ISE.

Step 2. Connect the Ethernet port of the client device to a switch port configured with the MAB access policy. The device should connect automatically without any prompts for a username, password, or certificate.

Step 3. To verify that the device was authenticated via the MAB policy and not some other policy, check the live log in Cisco ISE (**Menu > Operations > Live Logs** [under RADIUS]). Figure 8-120 shows an excerpt from an authentication detail report for a successful wired association using MAB.

Cisco ISE

Overview

Event	5200 Authentication succeeded
Username	1C:36:BB:03:39:30
Endpoint Id	1C:36:BB:03:39:30
Endpoint Profile	Apple-Device
Authentication Policy	MAC Authentication Bypass >> Default
Authorization Policy	MAC Authentication Bypass >> Authorization Rule 1
Authorization Result	PermitAccess

Authentication Details

Source Timestamp	2024-03-28 18:23:55.708
Received Timestamp	2024-03-28 18:23:55.708
Policy Server	ise
Event	5200 Authentication succeeded
Username	1C:36:BB:03:39:30
User Type	Host
Endpoint Id	1C:36:BB:03:39:30
Calling Station Id	1C-36-BB-03-39-30
Endpoint Profile	Apple-Device
Authentication Identity Store	Internal Endpoints
Identity Group	MAB-Whitelist
Audit Session Id	6c602b060001040b66051b0b
Authentication Method	mab
Authentication Protocol	Lookup
Service Type	Call Check
Network Device	All
Device Type	All Device Types
Location	All Locations
NAS IPv4 Address	192.168.101.2
NAS Port Type	Ethernet

Steps

11001	Received RADIUS Access-Request
11017	RADIUS created a new session
11027	Detected Host Lookup UseCase (Service-Type = Call Check (10))
15049	Evaluating Policy Group
15008	Evaluating Service Selection Policy
15048	Queried PIP - Radius.NAS-Port-Type
15048	Queried PIP - Normalised Radius.RadiusFlowType
15041	Evaluating Identity Policy
15013	Selected Identity Source - Internal Endpoints
24209	Looking up Endpoint in Internal Endpoints IDStore - 1C:36:BB:03:39:30
24211	Found Endpoint in Internal Endpoints IDStore
22037	Authentication Passed
15036	Evaluating Authorization Policy
15016	Selected Authorization Profile - PermitAccess
24209	Looking up Endpoint in Internal Endpoints IDStore - 1C:36:BB:03:39:30
24211	Found Endpoint in Internal Endpoints IDStore
11002	Returned RADIUS Access-Accept

Figure 8-120 *An Authentication Detail Report Showing a Successful MAB Authentication*

Step 4. You also can verify successful wired MAB authentication in the event log in Meraki Dashboard, as shown in Figure 8-121.

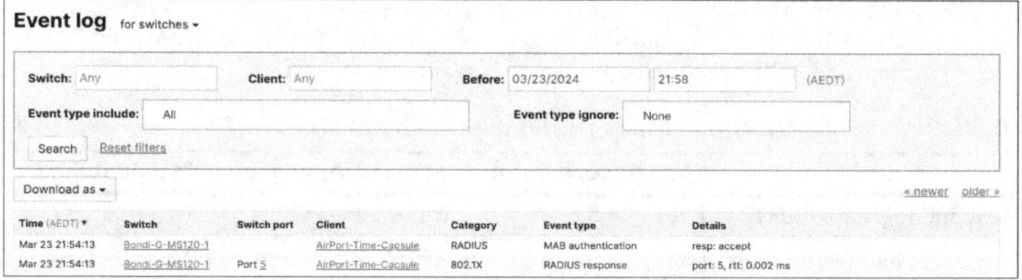

Figure 8-121 *The Event Log in Meraki Dashboard Showing a Successful MAB Authentication*

At this point, you've completed the configuration for MAC Authentication Bypass on Meraki switch ports. You can learn more about access policies (including MAB) at https://documentation.meraki.com/MS/Access_Control/MS_Switch_Access_Policies_(802.1X).

Group Policies

Group policies are exactly that—they are security policies that can be applied to a group of users or devices. The policy settings that can be applied include

- When the network can be accessed
- What VLAN the client is assigned to
- What firewall rules are applied

In the future, you will also be able to assign adaptive policy groups using group policies (we cover adaptive policies later in this chapter).

NIST 800-53 AC-4(21) requires that organizations have a way to separate information flows logically or physically. Separating traffic is easy to do physically, but what about where this is not practicable? For example, in a small retail footprint, how would you separate card payments traffic from all other traffic, without changing how users interact with the network? Group policies allow administrators to advertise one SSID at that location while dropping users and devices into different VLANs based on the group they're assigned to. There are many other use cases for group policies such as staff and students, staff and guests, users and devices—basically anywhere you have differentiated access requirements.

Creating a Group Policy

Group policies are configured at the network level. No group policies are created by default; they must be configured by administrators.

Pay attention to the features supported on each platform because support does vary (see Table 8-1). It is recommended that you deploy the full Meraki "stack" (Meraki Wi-Fi, switching, and MX) for the widest range of capabilities.

Table 8-1 *Supported Group Policy Features by Meraki Device Type*[5]

	MR Access Point	MX or Z Appliance	MS Switches
Scheduling (time of day)	Yes	Yes	No
Per-client bandwidth limit	Yes	Yes	No
Hostname visibility	Yes	Yes	No
VLAN tagging	Yes	No	No
Splash page authorization	Yes	No	No
Layer 3 firewall rules	Yes	Yes	Yes
Layer 7 firewall rules	Yes	Yes	No
Traffic shaping rules	Yes	Yes	No
Security filtering (AMP, IPS)	No	Yes, with Advanced Security License	No
Content filtering	No	Yes, with Advanced Security License	No

Follow these steps to create a group policy in Meraki Dashboard:

Step 1. Log in to Meraki Dashboard (https://dashboard.meraki.com).

Step 2. Navigate to **Network-wide > Group Policies** (under Configure). From the screen shown in Figure 8-122, click **Add a Group.**

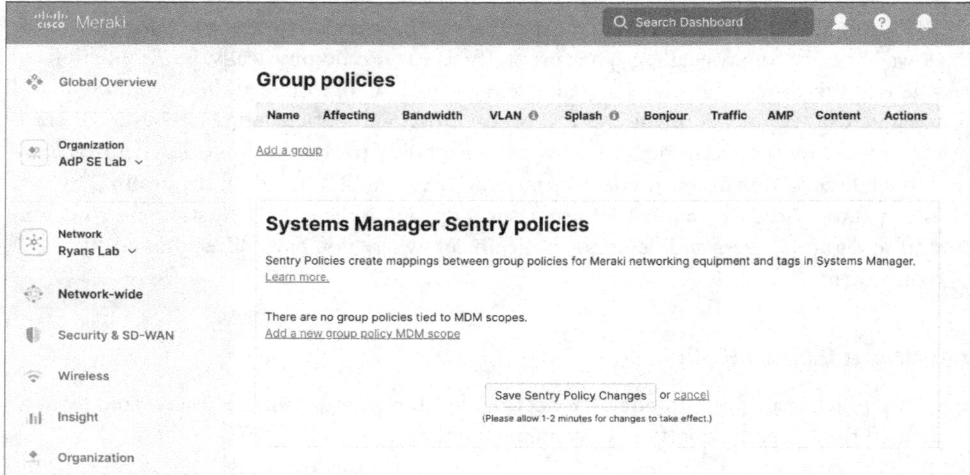

Figure 8-122 *The Group Policies Page in Meraki Dashboard*

Step 3. Figure 8-123 shows some of the settings available in a group policy:

- Start by giving the policy a **Name** that reflects its intended use. In this example, we have used the name **Staff** because our policy will be applied to employees.
- Under **Wireless Only**, users in this group are assigned to VLAN 127.
- The only other policy applied is a Layer 7 firewall rule blocking access to eBay.
- Configure your policy as required; then click **Save Changes** at the bottom of the page.

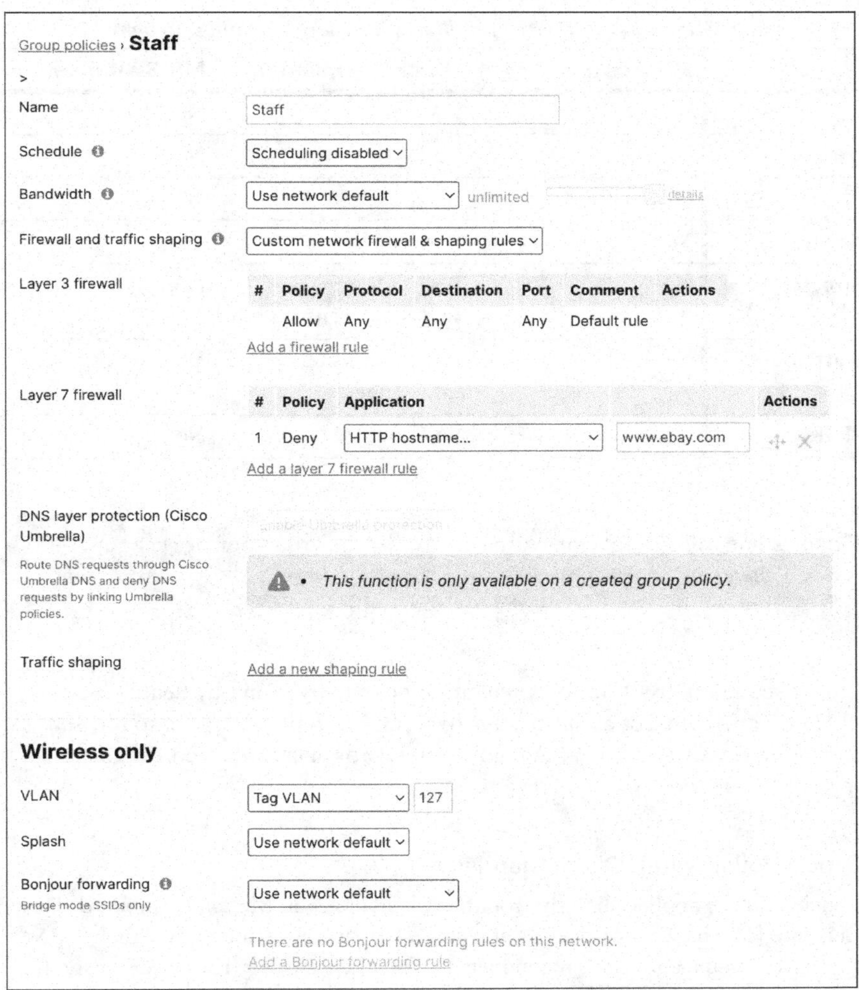

Figure 8-123 *Configuring a Group Policy for Staff in Meraki Dashboard*

Now that you've completed the configuration of a basic group policy, be sure to create a group policy for each use case relevant to your environment. For more information on creating group policies, refer https://documentation.meraki.com/General_Administration/Cross-Platform_Content/Creating_and_Applying_Group_Policies. Read on to learn the various ways group policy can be applied.

Applying Group Policies

Group policies can be applied in numerous ways, but not all ways are available on all Meraki devices. For example, applying a group policy by device type is available only on Meraki MR access points. Table 8-2 provides a summary of the supported ways to apply group policies using the various Meraki devices.

Table 8-2 *Supported Ways to Apply Group Policies by Meraki Device Type*

	MR Access Point	MX or Z Appliance	MS Switches
By client	Yes	Yes	No
By device type	Yes	No	No
By VLAN	No	Yes	No
By Sentry policy	Yes	Yes	Yes
By Active Directory group	No	Yes, with Advanced Security License	No
By RADIUS attribute	Yes	Yes, when using AnyConnect	Yes
By Identity PSK	Yes	No	No

Note Although some Meraki documentation states that the group policies cannot be assigned to wired clients using Sentry policies, we have tested this and can confirm that this does indeed work.

The following sections cover how to assign group policies by client, by Sentry policy, and by RADIUS attribute. For all other ways to apply group policies, refer to https://documentation.meraki.com/General_Administration/Cross-Platform_Content/Creating_and_Applying_Group_Policies.

Applying Group Policies to a Client Manually

Group policies can be applied directly from the Clients page in Meraki Dashboard. This approach is fine for a handful of devices at a single site or for testing in the lab, but this approach is not scalable and is not recommended for an enterprise. The major reason for this is that group policies recognize clients based on their MAC address. Modern mobile operating systems (both iOS and Android) implement MAC randomization. This means a group policy can be applied once; however, if that device reconnects with a different MAC address, the group policy would need to be manually reapplied. Although you can turn off randomization on devices you control, either manually or using a Systems Manager profile (see Chapter 11), there are still more efficient ways to apply group policies at scale.

Follow these steps in Meraki Dashboard to apply a group policy to a client manually:

Step 1. Log in to Meraki Dashboard (https://dashboard.meraki.com).

Step 2. Navigate to **Network-wide > Clients** (under Monitor). Select the devices where you want to apply a group policy by using the check box to the left of the table. In this example shown in Figure 8-124, one client in VLAN 130 is selected. This client has a group policy of normal—that is, no group policy applied.

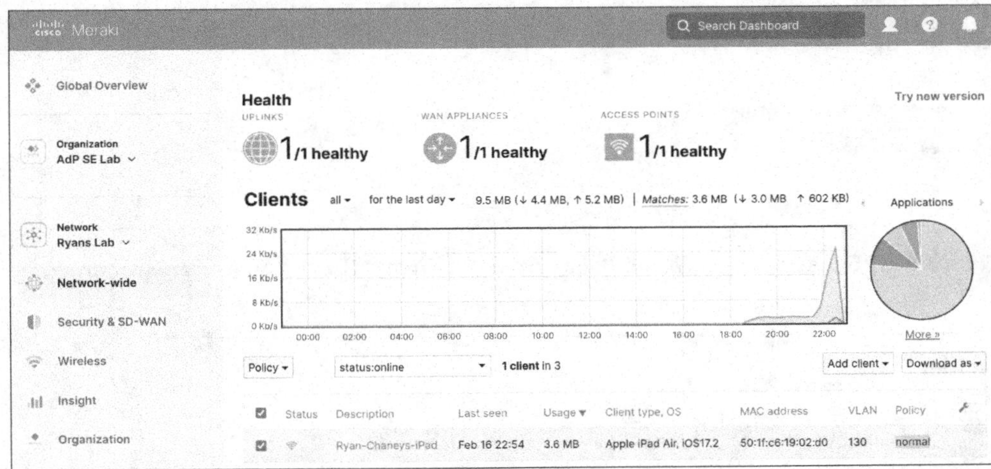

Figure 8-124 *The Clients Page in Meraki Dashboard*

Step 3. From the **Policy** drop-down menu, select **Group Policy.** Ensure that the group policy name is the desired one, in this case **Staff** (see Figure 8-125), and then click **Apply Policy.**

You've completed the steps to manually assign a group policy to a host. When Meraki Dashboard updates, you can verify that the changes are now in effect by returning to the Clients page (**Network-wide > Clients**). In this example, you can see that the group policy name has updated to **Staff** and the VLAN is now the staff VLAN, **127**, as shown in Figure 8-126.

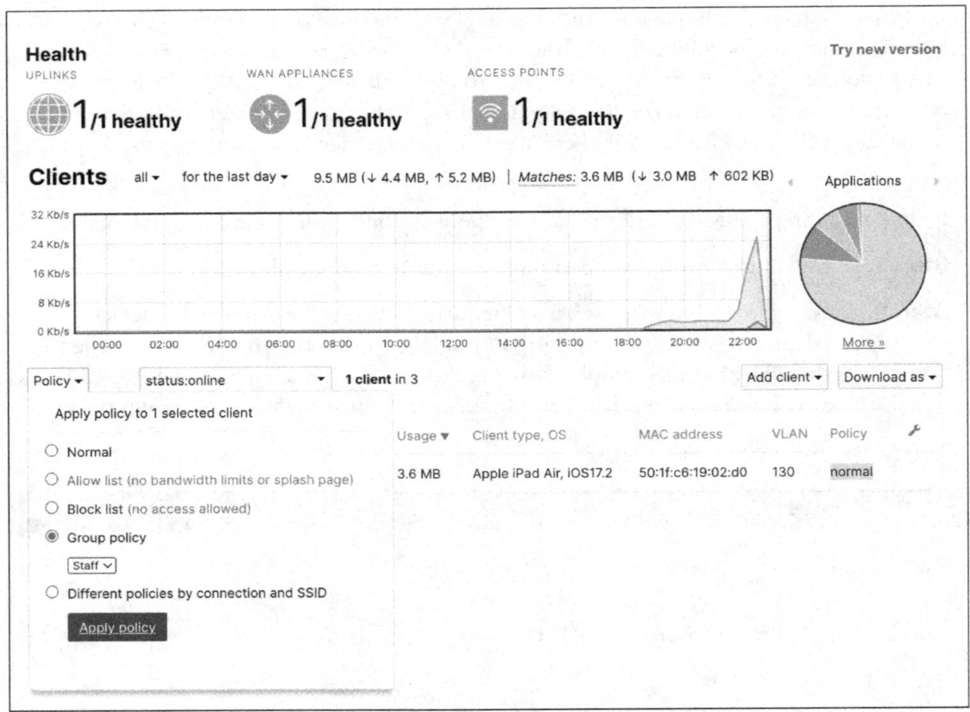

Figure 8-125 *Applying a Group Policy from the Clients Page in Meraki Dashboard*

Figure 8-126 *Verifying the Group Policy Is Now Applied Using the Clients Page in Meraki Dashboard*

Also, when testing from this device's web browser, you can no longer access www.ebay.com (see Figure 8-127). This restriction is configured on the Staff group policy, confirming that the policy is applied and working as expected.

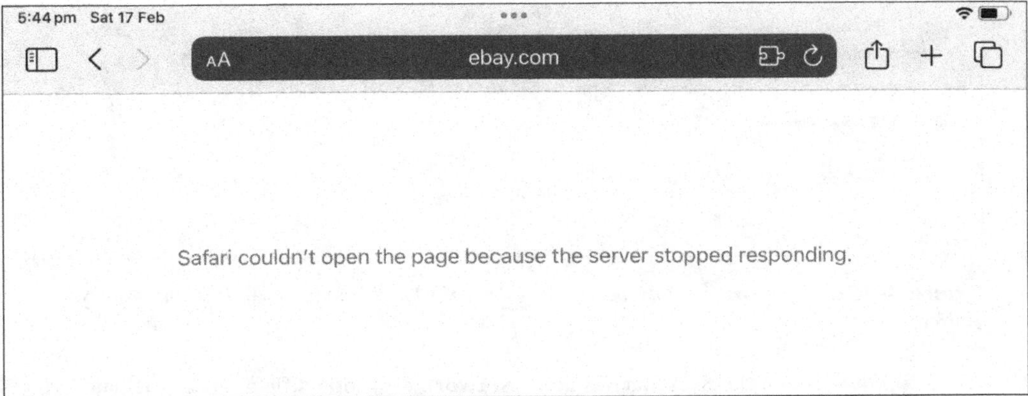

Figure 8-127 *Verifying That the Group Policy Is Successfully Blocking Access to ebay.com*

You've completed the steps needed to manually assign a group policy to a client and verify it is functioning correctly. The next section describes how to automatically assign group policies to devices enrolled with Meraki Systems Manager.

Applying Group Policies Using a Sentry Policy

Meraki has its own mobile device management (MDM) platform called Systems Manager, which you learn more about in Chapter 11. A group policy applied based on Systems Manager enrollment is referred to as a *Sentry policy*. Applying a group policy to Systems Manager devices is easy and persists whether MAC address randomization is on or not.

Follow these steps to apply a group policy using a Sentry policy:

Step 1. Log in to Meraki Dashboard (https://dashboard.meraki.com).

Step 2. Navigate to **Network-wide > Group Policies** (under Configure) to display the screen shown in Figure 8-128.

Step 3. Click **Add a New Group Policy MDM Scope.** It's possible to add multiple rows to assign different group policies to devices with different Systems Manager tags.

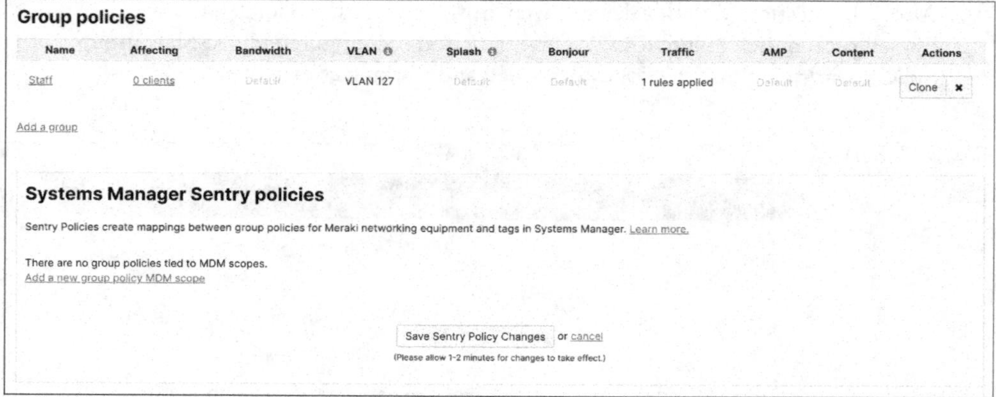

Figure 8-128 *The Group Policies Page in Meraki Dashboard Showing the Sentry Policies*

Step 4. From the **Systems Manager Network** drop-down field, select the name of your Systems Manager network. In our case, it is simply called **Systems Manager.**

a. Set the **Tag Scope.** In this example, we have simply selected **All Devices.**

b. From the **Policy** drop-down menu, select the name of the group policy. In this example, our group policy is named **Staff**, as shown in Figure 8-129.

c. Click **Save Sentry Policy Changes** to finish.

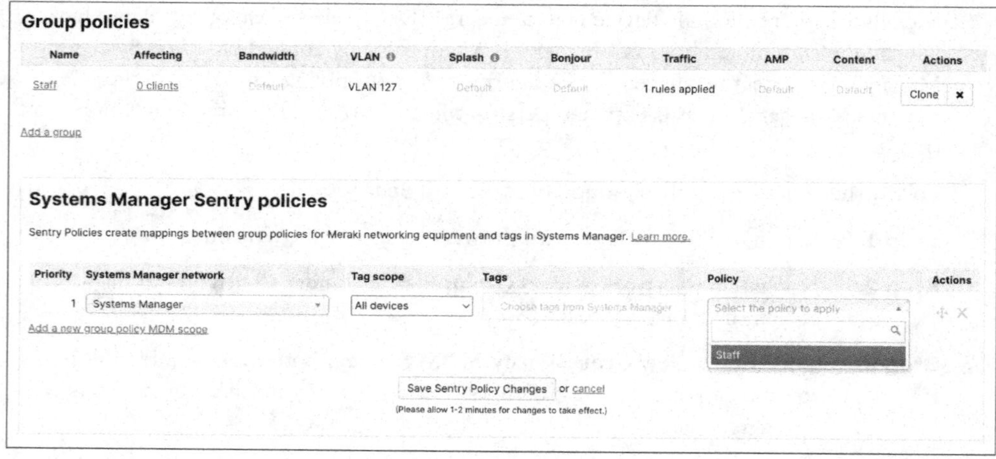

Figure 8-129 *Configuring a Sentry Policy in Meraki Dashboard*

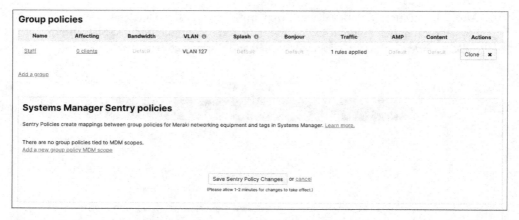

You've now completed the steps to apply a group policy to devices enrolled with Systems Manager. Before verifying that this configuration is working, remove any previous group policy from the device. Additionally, if this is an iOS device, and you had previously disabled Private Wi-Fi Address, you can reenable it. Figure 8-130 shows the Clients page in Meraki Dashboard before enrolling an iPad device with Meraki Systems Manager.

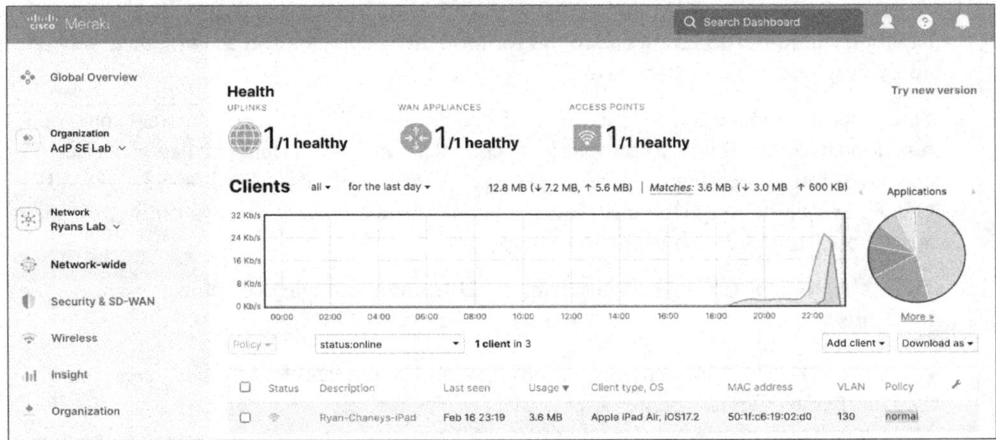

Figure 8-130 *The Clients Page Before Enrolling the iPad with Systems Manager*

As demonstrated in Figure 8-131, after this device was enrolled with Meraki Systems Manager, the group policy was applied automatically. This is another great example of how Systems Manager makes life easy for administrators.

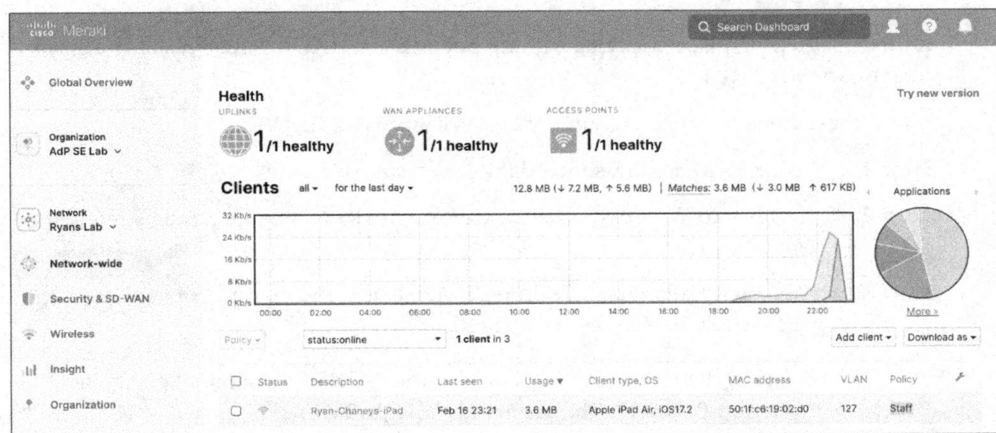

Figure 8-131 *The Clients Page After Enrolling the iPad with Systems Manager*

You've completed the steps to apply a group policy using a Sentry policy and verify that it is working. For more information on Sentry policies, refer to the following guide: https://documentation.meraki.com/SM/Other_Topics/Configuring_Sentry_Policies.

Applying Group Policies Using RADIUS Attributes and Cisco ISE

Group policies can also be applied using the Filter-ID attribute in RADIUS. The Filter-ID capability in RADIUS has been around for more than 20 years and is a common way to apply downloadable ACLs to hosts.

One practical application for this capability is the Essential Eight requirement that organizations have the ability to prevent privileged accounts (excluding privileged service accounts) from accessing the Internet, email, and web services. NIST 800-53 and SWIFT CSCF have similar requirements. This goal could be achieved by using a group policy to apply an ACL based on a user's AD group.

To be able to apply group policies using RADIUS, the following prerequisites are required:

- Ensure RADIUS authentication for wired and/or wireless 802.1X has been configured, as shown in Chapter 7.
- Ensure the wired and/or wireless network has been configured for 802.1X, as shown in the "Zero Trust" section earlier in this chapter.
- Ensure that the device you will test with later can connect to the network using 802.1X.
- Ensure that a group policy has already been configured, as per the earlier section "Creating a Group Policy."

With these steps in place, applying a group policy using RADIUS requires only a small configuration change to get working.

Follow these steps to apply a group policy to clients using RADIUS:

Step 1. Log in to Meraki Dashboard (https://dashboard.meraki.com).

Step 2. Navigate to **Wireless > Access Control** (under Configure), as illustrated in Figure 8-132.

Step 3. (Wireless) From the **SSID** drop-down menu at the top of the page, select the SSID that is configured for 802.1X.

   a. Scroll down to **RADIUS** and look for **RADIUS Attribute Specifying Group Policy Name.** Ensure this is set to **Filter-ID**.

   b. Click **Save.**

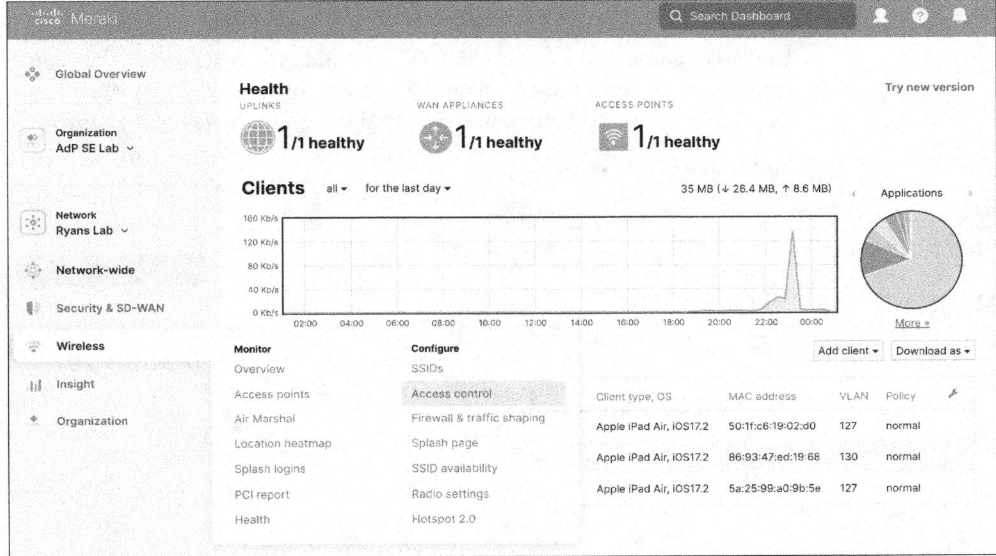

Figure 8-132 *Navigating to the Wireless Access Control Page in Meraki Dashboard*

c. (Wired) To also configure this setting for wired 802.1X networks, navigate to **Switching > Access Policies.**

d. On the applicable access policy, scroll down to **RADIUS** and ensure that **RADIUS Attribute Specifying Group Policy Name** is set to **Filter-Id**, as shown in Figure 8-133.

e. Click **Save.**

Step 4. Log in to your instance of Cisco ISE.

Step 5. Navigate to **Policy > Policy Elements > Results.** From the menu on the left, click **Authorization Profiles**, as shown in Figure 8-134.

Step 6. On the **Standard Authorization Profiles** page, click **+ Add** to create a new authorization profile.

Step 7. The key settings that need to be configured here (see Figure 8-135) are as follows:

a. Enter a meaningful name in the **Name** field. If you'll be assigning multiple group policies, it is recommended that you reference the group policy name in the authorization policy name.

b. Set **Access Type** to **ACCESS_ACCEPT**.

c. Under Common Tasks, check **ACL (Filter-Id).** In the text field to the right, type in the name of the group policy exactly how it appears in Meraki Dashboard. In our example, we have used the group policy name **Staff**.

d. To finish, click **Save**.

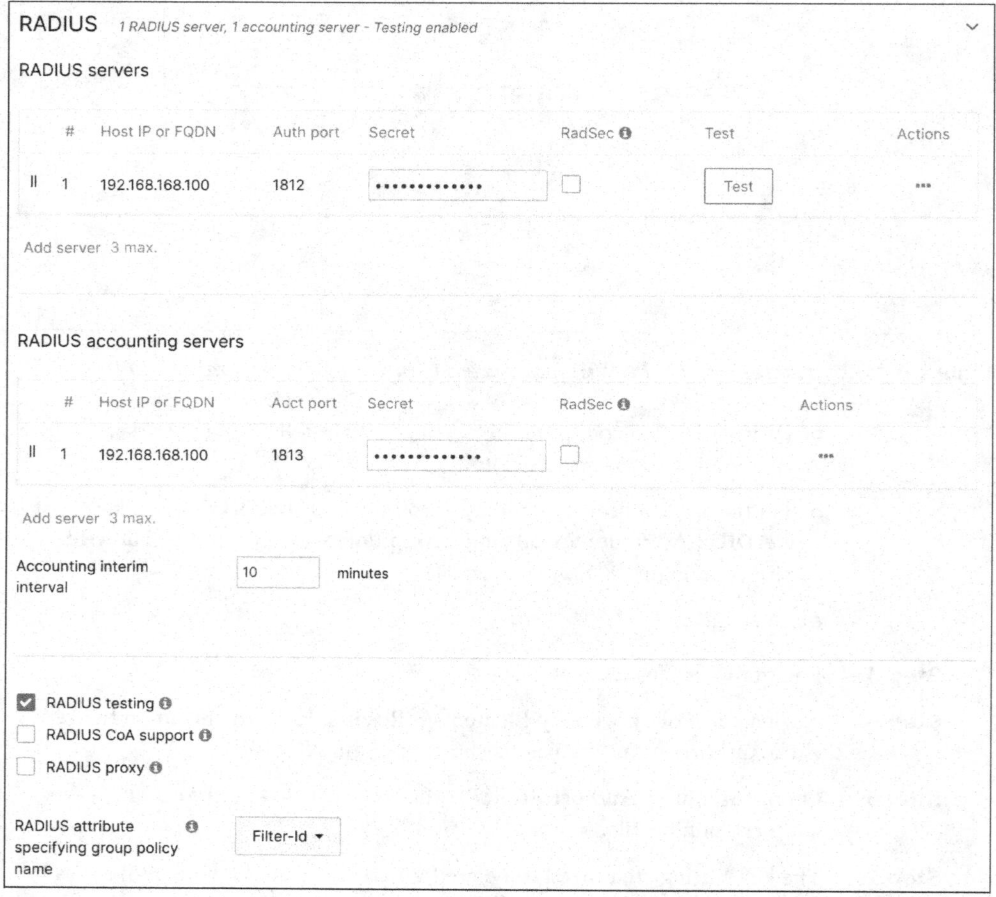

Figure 8-133 *Configuring the RADIUS Attribute Specifying the Group Policy Name in Meraki Dashboard*

Step 8. Navigate to **Policy > Policy Sets.** Expand the policy set for wired and wireless 802.1X by clicking the > icon under the **View** column, as shown in Figure 8-136.

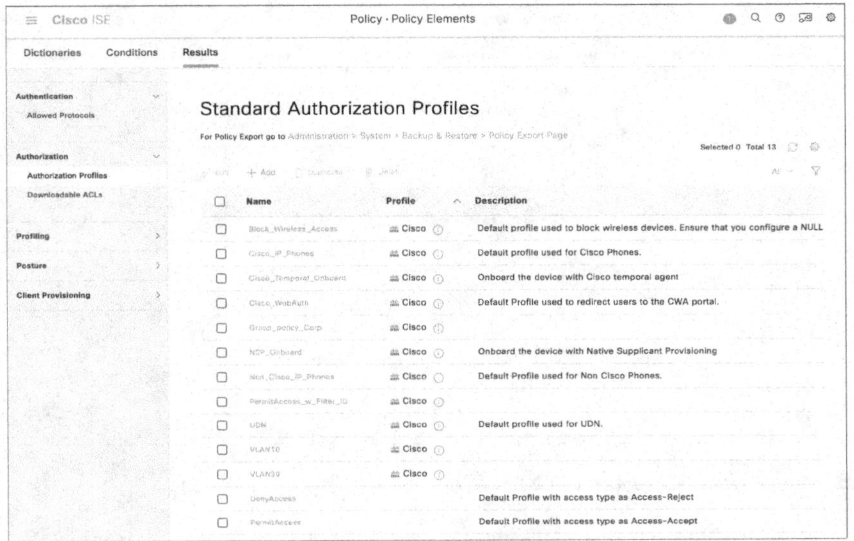

Figure 8-134 *The Authorization Profiles Page in Cisco ISE*

Authorization Profiles > PermitAccess_w_Filter_ID

Authorization Profile

* Name	PermitAccess_w_Filter_ID
Description	
* Access Type	ACCESS_ACCEPT
Network Device Profile	Cisco
Service Template	☐
Track Movement	☐
Agentless Posture	☐
Passive Identity Tracking	☐

Common Tasks

☐ DACL Name

☐ IPv6 DACL Name

☑ ACL (Filter-ID) Staff

Figure 8-135 *Adding the Group Policy Name to an Authorization Policy in Cisco ISE*

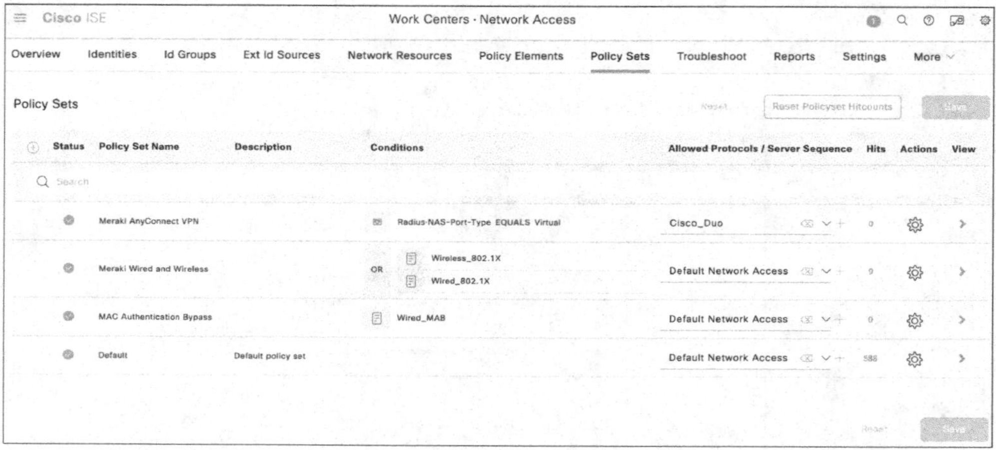

Figure 8-136 *The Policy Sets Page in Cisco ISE*

Step 9. Expand **Authorization Policy.** From the screen shown in Figure 8-137, replace the existing profile with the profile with the filter ID configured in Step 7.

Click **Save.**

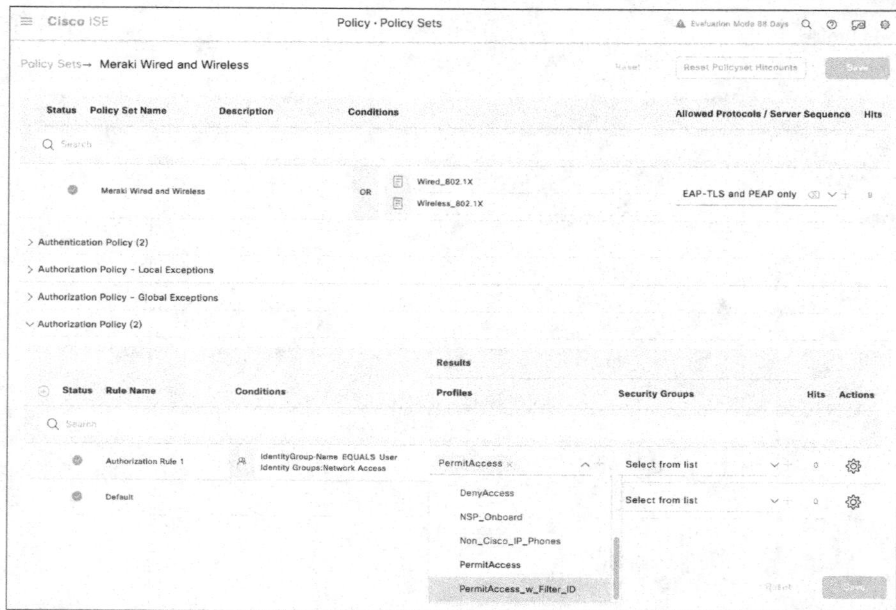

Figure 8-137 *Applying the New Authorization Profile with the Group Policy Name to a Policy Set in Cisco ISE*

You've completed the changes required to Meraki Dashboard and Cisco ISE. Before verifying the changes are working, have a quick look at your event log and an earlier RADIUS response message (see Figure 8-138). There should be nothing next to **Group** in the Details column.

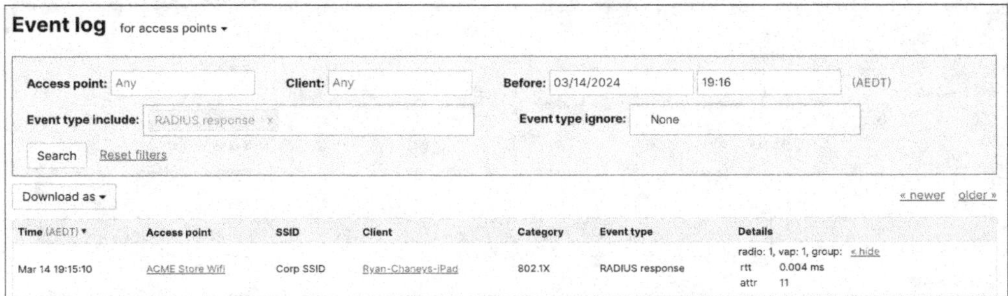

Figure 8-138 *The Event Log Showing RADIUS Messages Without the Filter-ID Attribute in Meraki Dashboard*

Tip Filter ID is also known as RADIUS attribute type 11. In the log entry in Figure 8-138, Attr is short for attribute, and the number 11 refers to the type.

Now that the authorization profile has been updated to supply a filter-ID with the group policy name, connect to the wireless network again. Once connected, check the event log. This time you should notice the group name listed in the RADIUS response. In this example (see Figure 8-139), you can see the group policy name **Staff**.

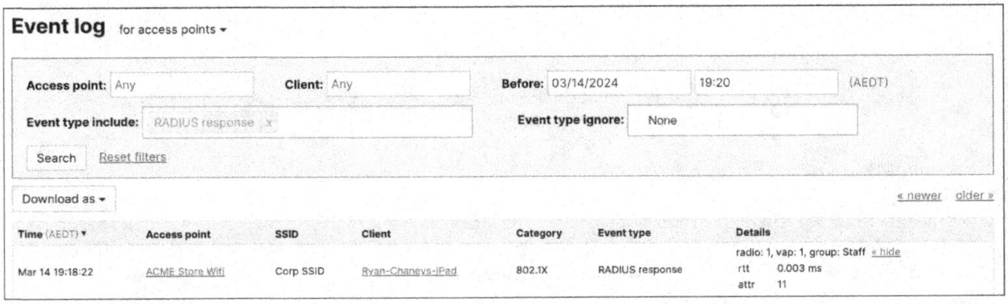

Figure 8-139 *The Event Log Showing RADIUS Messages with the Filter-ID Attribute in Meraki Dashboard*

This client is now unable to access ebay.com while having access to all other sites, proving the group policy is in effect. On the Clients page in Meraki Dashboard (**Network-wide > Clients**), you can see that this client is in the Staff VLAN (127) and the Staff group policy is being applied (see Figure 8-140). When using 802.1X, the group policy name is shown under the column heading **802.1X Policy**. To enable visibility of the 802.1X Policy column, use the spanner icon on the right side of the table headings.

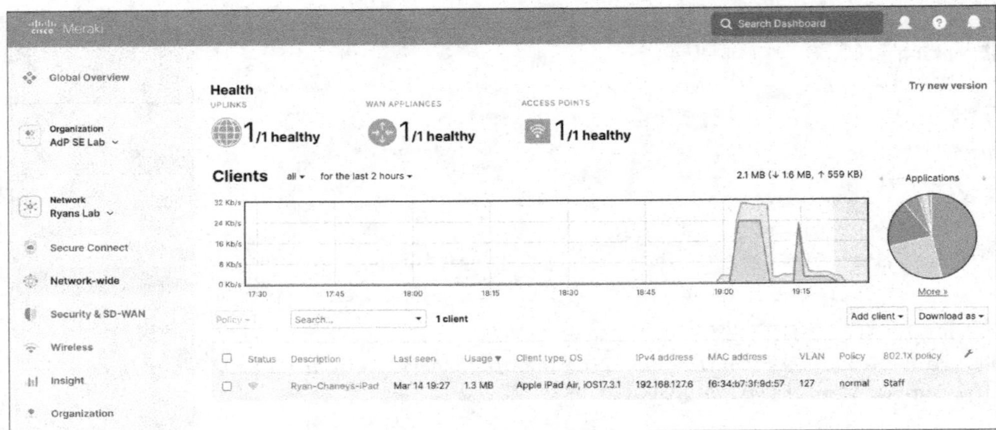

Figure 8-140 *The Clients Page in Meraki Dashboard Showing That the Group Policy Is Now Applied (Filter-ID)*

Finally, Cisco ISE authentication detail reports available on the Live Logs page also record the Filter-ID attribute being sent and the group policy name. Figure 8-141 provides an excerpt of the authentication detail report showing the Filter-ID **Staff**.

Result	
Filter-ID	Staff
Class	CACS:c0a8a864QdE0n7Mpeu5XlfwT1YVv1dBue_8kM0fH4/wlvGWTmq8:ise/499484190/175
MS-MPPE-Send-Key	****
MS-MPPE-Recv-Key	****
LicenseTypes	Essential license consumed.

Figure 8-141 *The Authentication Detail Report in Cisco ISE Showing the Filter-ID with the Group Policy Name*

At this point, you've completed the configuration steps to assign group policies using a RADIUS filter-ID attribute. In this section, we also covered how to verify this setup using the event log in Meraki Dashboard and the authentication detail reports in Cisco ISE.

This section covered the most commonly used ways to assign group policies on a Meraki network. For more information on creating group policies and other ways to assign them, refer to the following guide: https://documentation.meraki.com/General_Administration/Cross-Platform_Content/Creating_and_Applying_Group_Policies.

Adaptive Policy and Security Group Tags (SGTs)

Segmentation is another key requirement from industry best practice. Examples include isolating cardholder data environments (CDEs) from the rest of the organization in the case of PCI DSS, or the separation of privileged and unprivileged environments in the case of NIST 800-53. Segmentation could be achieved in numerous ways, as you've already seen, including the use of VLANs and group policies. However, the most recent—and arguably most elegant—way to provide segmentation is by using security group tags.

Security group tags (SGTs, sometimes referred to in Cisco documentation as scalable group tags) are used to identify traffic and enforce security policy. SGTs are analogous to Quality of Service (QoS) markings or MPLS labels in that they are typically applied close to the source, and decisions on how packets are handled are made based on a quick lookup of a tag, rather than a full inspection of the packet at every hop. The SGT is added to the IP header of a packet within an EtherType called Cisco MetaData (CMD).

Security group tags can be used pervasively to enforce segmentation for both wired and wireless clients, both locally and over the WAN. To use SGTs effectively, all network infrastructure must support this feature. All devices require a minimum of advanced licenses. Security group tags are supported on the following Meraki MR wireless access points, MS switches, and MX security appliances:

- **Wireless access points:** All Wi-Fi 5 Wave 2, Wi-Fi 6, and Wi-Fi 6E MR and CW access points running MR27+.
- **Switches:**
  - MS390 running MS14.33.1 firmware or later.
  - C9300-M running firmware version CS15.21.1 or later.
  - C9300\L\X-M running firmware version CS16.7 or later.
  - Switches that do not support CMD EtherType may still forward the tagged packets if the switch is operating as L2 only.
- **Security Appliances:** MX/Z3+, includes all models capable of running at least MX18.1 firmware. The one exception is MX84, which is not supported due to a hardware limitation. It is recommended that you run the latest stable release to maximize feature support. Refer to the following guide for complete details on the software versions and licenses required to support the various adaptive policy features on Meraki MX: https://documentation.meraki.com/General_Administration/Cross-Platform_Content/Adaptive_Policy_for_MX%2F%2FZ_Platforms#Functionality_Breakdown.

For the remainder of this section on adaptive policy, we examine its usage from the real-life use case of an enterprise trying to stay PCI compliant. It's best practice to segment payment and nonpayment traffic to reduce the scope of PCI compliance audits. By doing this, organizations need to audit only the part of the network carrying PCI traffic, massively reducing the compliance burden. Security group tags are a great fit for this requirement, which we now demonstrate as we step through how to configure adaptive policies.

Enabling Adaptive Policy

Adaptive policy is enabled per network. Once adaptive policy is enabled on a network, you will see the option to configure peer SGT capable and adaptive policy groups on your switch ports.

Follow these steps to create an adaptive policy in Meraki Dashboard:

Step 1. Log in to Meraki Dashboard (https://dashboard.meraki.com).

Step 2. Navigate to **Organization > Adaptive Policy** (under Configure). Under the **Networks** tab, select any networks that will have SGT-tagged traffic and currently have **Adaptive Policy Disabled** and click **Enable** (see Figure 8-142).

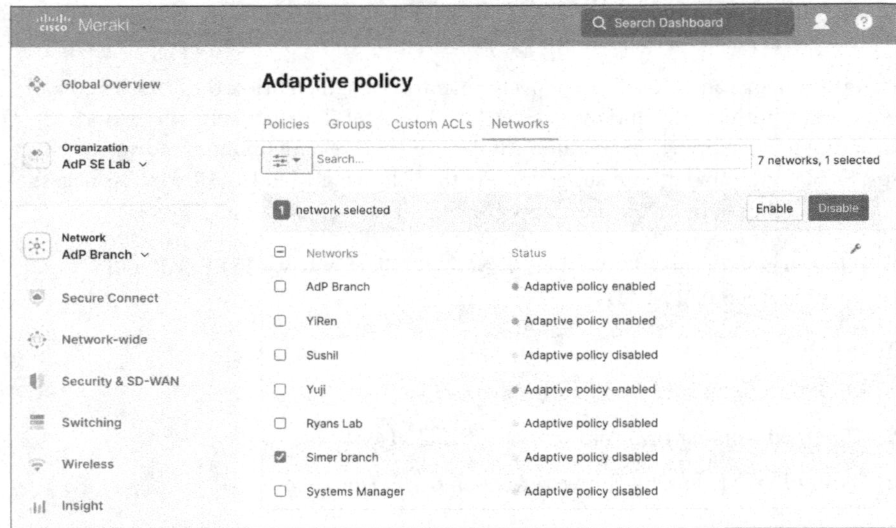

Figure 8-142 *Enabling Adaptive Policy on Networks in Meraki Dashboard*

Step 3. On the pop-up window shown in Figure 8-143, click **Enable.** On the following window, click **Done** to return to the **Adaptive Policy** page.

You've completed the steps to enable adaptive policy on a network in Dashboard. You can also find these steps in the following guide: https://documentation.meraki.com/General_Administration/Cross-Platform_Content/Adaptive_Policy_Configuration_Guide#Enabling_or_disabling_Adaptive_Policy_in_a_Network.

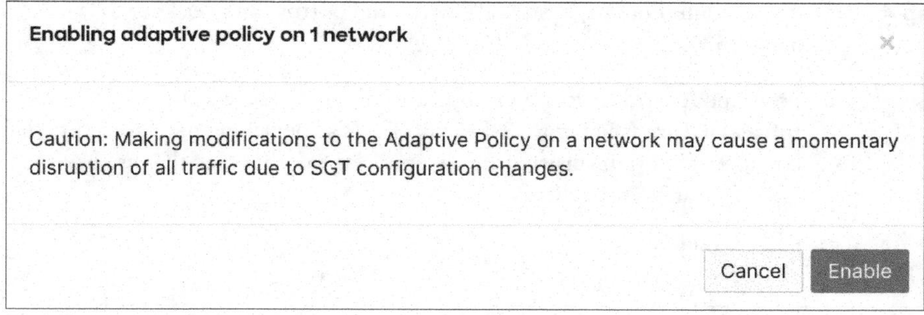

Figure 8-143 *Enabling Adaptive Policy Pop-Up Window in Meraki Dashboard*

Configuring Security Group Tag Propagation

MX security appliances can preserve and propagate SGTs over the WAN. This is supported today using Auto VPN on MX security appliances in Routed mode (default). The propagation of SGTs over LAN ports and VPNs needs to be enabled but is not enabled by default.

Enabling SGT Propagation on Meraki MS Switches

Follow these steps to enable the propagation of security group tags when using Meraki MS switches:

Step 1. Log in to Meraki Dashboard (https://dashboard.meraki.com).

Step 2. Navigate to **Switching > Switch Ports** (under Monitor).

Step 3. Select the ports connected to Meraki APs, MS switches, or MXs that will carry traffic tagged with SGTs and click **Edit.** A good way to identify these ports is to turn on the CDP/LLDP column using the spanner icon on the right, as shown in Figure 8-144.

Figure 8-144 *Selecting the Switch Ports to Configure in Meraki Dashboard*

Step 4. On the **Update Port** page, scroll down to the bottom and set **Peer SGT Capable** to **Enabled.**

a. From the **Adaptive Policy Group** drop-down menu, select **2: Infrastructure** (see Figure 8-145). SGT 2 is a special tag used for ports that connect network infrastructure, as opposed to other tags that are used to identify traffic from clients.

b. Click **Update.**

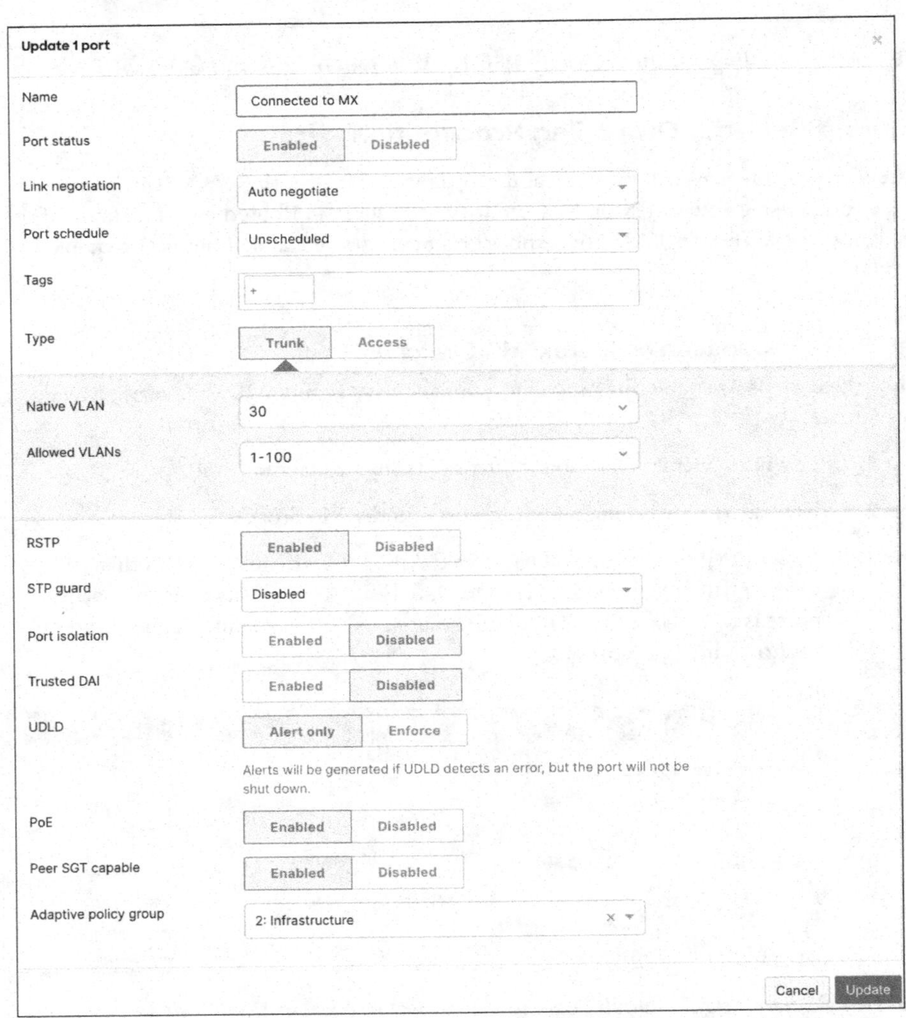

Figure 8-145 *Setting Peer SGT Capable on a Switch Port in Meraki Dashboard*

Step 5. Back on the **Switch Ports** page, you can see that port 1 now has **Peer SGT Capable** enabled (see Figure 8-146). Repeat these steps for any other switch ports connected to Meraki APs, switches, or MXs that will carry traffic tagged with SGTs.

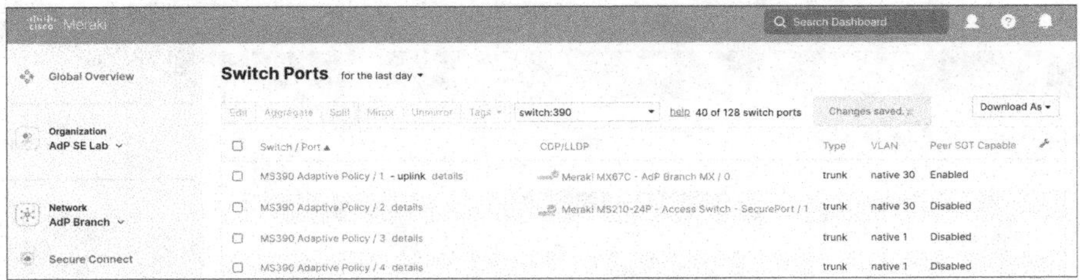

Figure 8-146 *The Switch Ports Page in Meraki Dashboard Showing which Ports Have Peer SGT Capable Enabled*

You've completed the steps required to enable SGT propagation on Meraki MS switches. You also can find these steps in the following guide: https://documentation.meraki.com/General_Administration/Cross-Platform_Content/Adaptive_Policy_MS_Configuration_Guide.

Enabling SGT Propagation on Meraki MX Security Appliances

Follow these steps to enable SGT propagation over Auto VPN site-to-site VPNs:

Step 1. Log in to Meraki Dashboard (https://dashboard.meraki.com).

Step 2. Navigate to **Security & SD-WAN > Site-to-Site VPN** (under Configure), as shown in Figure 8-147.

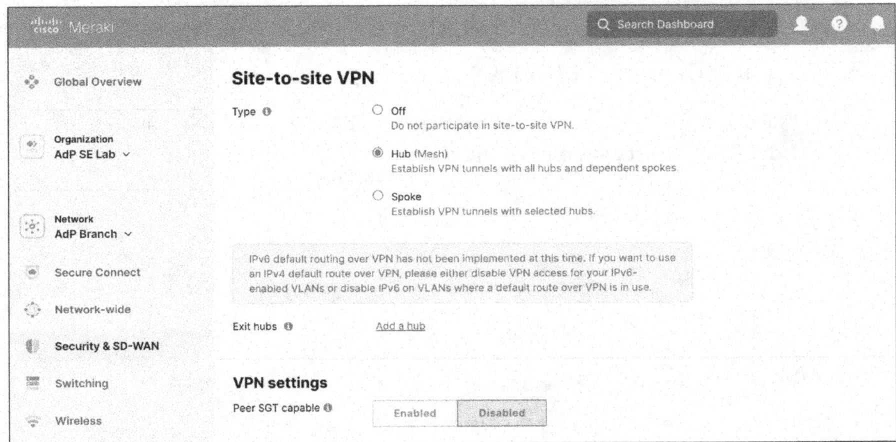

Figure 8-147 *The Peer SGT Capable Setting on the Site-to-Site VPN Page in Meraki Dashboard*

Step 3. From the screen shown in Figure 8-148, under **VPN Settings**, change **Peer SGT Capable** to **Enabled.**

Click **Save.**

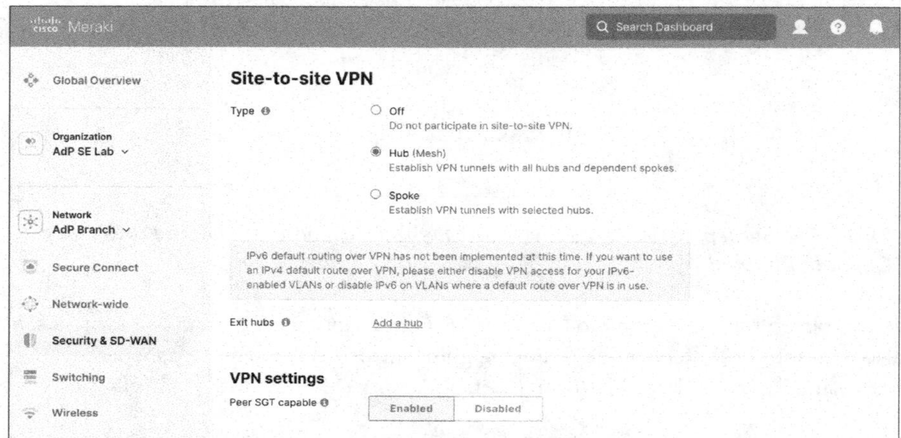

Figure 8-148 *Configuring Peer SGT Capable on the Site-to-Site VPN Page in Meraki Dashboard*

Step 4. In addition to propagating SGTs to VPN peers, you must also enable SGT propagation for any MX LAN ports connected to Meraki APs and switches that support SGTs.

a. Navigate to **Security & SD-WAN > Addressing & VLANs.**

b. Ensure **LAN Setting** is set to **VLANs.**

c. Scroll down to **Per-Port VLAN Settings** (see Figure 8-149).

d. Select any ports that do not have **Peer SGT Capable** enabled and click **Edit.** These ports must be trunk ports.

Per-port VLAN Settings   Edit

☐	Module	Port	Enabled	Type	VLAN	Allowed VLANs	Access Policy	Peer SGT Capable
☑	Built-in	2	•	Trunk	Native: VLAN 30 (Management)	all	-	Disabled
☐	Built-in	3	•	Trunk	Native: VLAN 30 (Management)	all	-	Enabled
☐	Built-in	4	•	Access	VLAN 10 (Server)	-	Open	-
☐	Built-in	5	•	Trunk	Native: VLAN 30 (Management)	all	-	Enabled

Figure 8-149 *The Per-Port VLAN Settings Section of the Addressing & VLANs Page in Meraki Dashboard*

Step 5. Set **Peer SGT Capable** to **Enabled** and click **Update** (see Figure 8-150). Later versions of MX firmware (18.210+) may display an **Adaptive Policy** drop-down menu. If you see this, select **2: Infrastructure**.

Figure 8-150 *The Configure MX LAN Ports Window in Meraki Dashboard*

Step 6. All ports connected to SGT-capable switches should now show as **Enabled** under the **Peer SGT Capable** column, as shown in Figure 8-151. Click **Save**.

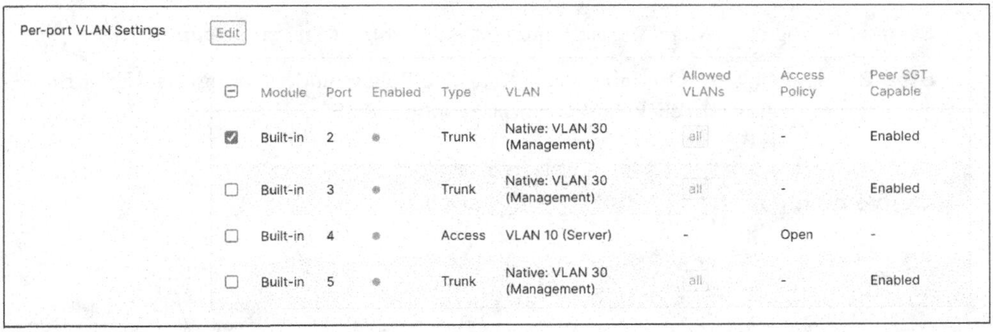

Figure 8-151 *The Per-Port VLAN Settings Pane on the Addressing & VLANs Page Showing Peer SGT Enabled Ports*

You've completed the steps to enable SGT propagation on VPN peers and LAN ports on Meraki MX security appliances. These steps and more information regarding configuring SGTs on Meraki MXs can be found in the following guide: https://documentation.meraki.com/General_Administration/Cross-Platform_Content/Adaptive_Policy_for_MX%2F%2FZ_Platforms.

Creating Security Group Tags

Security group tags can be defined in Meraki Dashboard manually or synced from Cisco ISE. This is a one-way sync from Cisco ISE today; however, it's expected that you will be able to sync SGTs in both directions in the future. In addition to the SGTs themselves, this sync also includes the policies and the SGACLs. If you're running a purely Meraki network, Cisco ISE is not essential for adaptive policy; however, if you are running a hybrid network with Meraki and traditional Cisco devices, integrating with Cisco ISE would be desirable. Cisco has published a short YouTube video showing how to set up this functionality, which you can find at https://www.youtube.com/watch?v=zLZjyV9dMVI. I (Ryan) also encourage you to search this topic on www.ciscolive.com, because there is some great content there.

Due to the caveats with the syncing of ISE's TrustSec policies and Meraki adaptive policies at present, this chapter focuses on the creation of adaptive policy in Meraki Dashboard itself. That said, we show the creation of SGTs in Cisco ISE because administrators may want to use ISE to assign SGTs to users as part of their existing 802.1X policy.

In Meraki Dashboard, SGTs are defined as part of adaptive policy groups, which have both a name and a value. This value can be any number between 1 and 65,519, excluding 2, which is used by the built-in Infrastructure tag. When you're defining SGTs manually in both Meraki Dashboard and Cisco ISE, it is highly recommended that you use the same name-to-value mappings.

Creating Adaptive Policy Groups in Meraki Dashboard

Follow these steps to create adaptive policy groups in Meraki Dashboard:

Step 1. Log in to Meraki Dashboard (https://dashboard.meraki.com).

Step 2. Navigate to **Organization > Adaptive Policy** (under Configure). Under the **Groups** tab, click **Add Group** (see Figure 8-152).

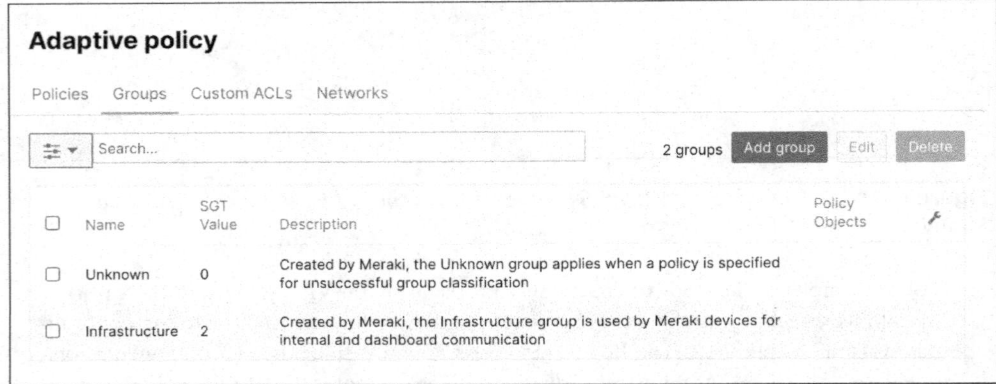

Figure 8-152 *The Groups Tab on the Adaptive Policy Page in Meraki Dashboard*

Step 3. Create the adaptive policy group for staff and their corporate devices. From the screen shown in Figure 8-153, enter the following:

- **Name:** Enter a meaningful name. In this example, we've used **Staff.**
- **SGT Value:** This is the number used to identify traffic in this group. It can be any available value between 1 and 65,519. In this example, we've used a value of **10.**
- **(Optional) Description:** Enter a short description that explains the purpose of this adaptive policy group.
- **Policy Object Binding:** This is the IP address of the incoming traffic used as a last resort to tag packets. It is optional, and because the staff and POS devices will be in the same subnet, you can leave this blank.

Click **Review Changes.**

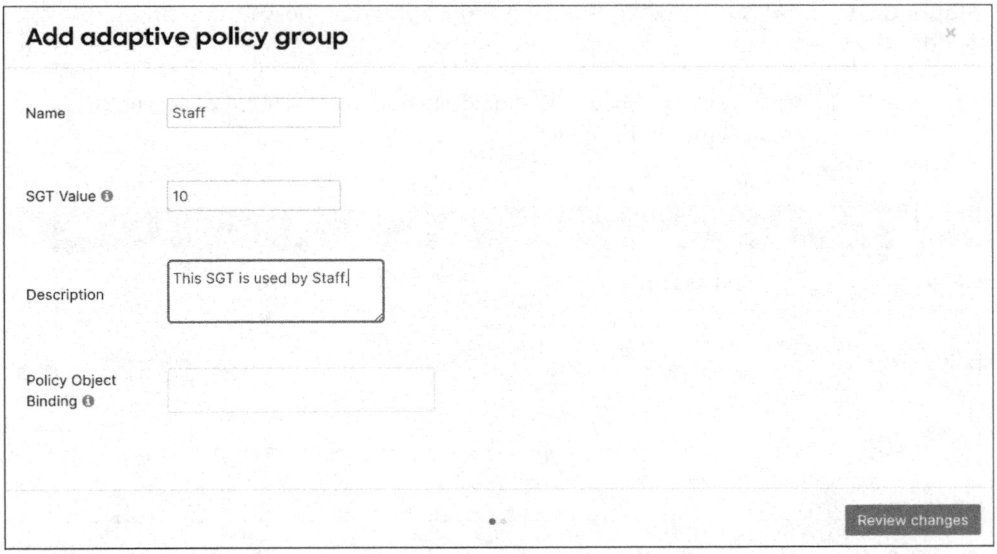

Figure 8-153 *Adding an Adaptive Policy Group in Meraki Dashboard*

Step 4. On the **Summary** page (see Figure 8-154), click **Submit** and then close this window.

Step 5. Repeat the preceding steps for any other groups that need to be added. In this example, another group is required for point-of-sale devices. Repeat Steps 2 to 4 with the following attributes:

- **Name:** POS
- **SGT Value:** 20

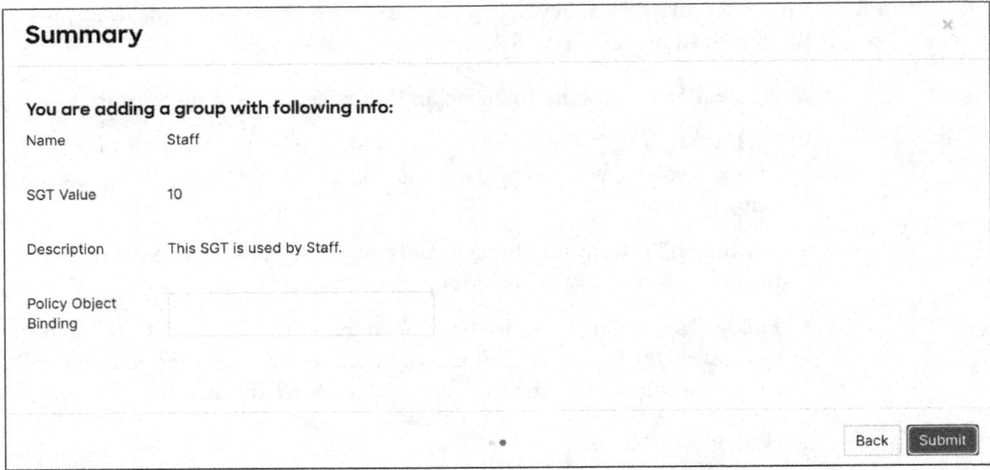

Figure 8-154 *The Summary Page when Adding a New Adaptive Policy Group in Meraki Dashboard*

When you're finished, you should see both groups listed under the **Groups** tab (as shown in Figure 8-155).

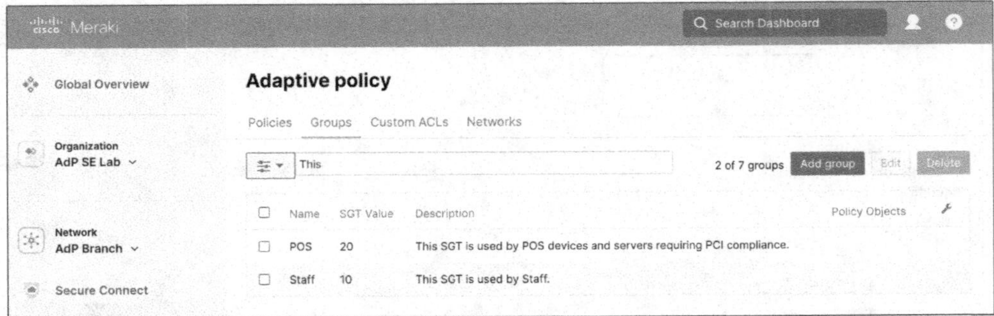

Figure 8-155 *The Adaptive Policy Page in Meraki Dashboard Showing the Staff and Point-of-Sale Groups*

You've now completed the steps to add adaptive policy groups and their associated security group tags in Meraki Dashboard. You can find more information on creating adaptive policy groups in the following guide: https://documentation.meraki.com/General_Administration/Cross-Platform_Content/Adaptive_Policy_Configuration_Guide#Creating_or_editing_user_groups.

Creating Security Group Tags in Cisco ISE

Because Cisco ISE will be used to assign SGTs to users authenticating via 802.1X, SGTs also need to be created there. To ease troubleshooting, be sure to mirror the names and values with those used in Meraki Dashboard.

Follow these steps to create security group tags in Meraki Dashboard:

Step 1. Log in to your instance of Cisco Identity Services Engine (ISE).

Step 2. Navigate to **Menu > Work Centers > Settings** (under TrustSec), as shown in Figure 8-156.

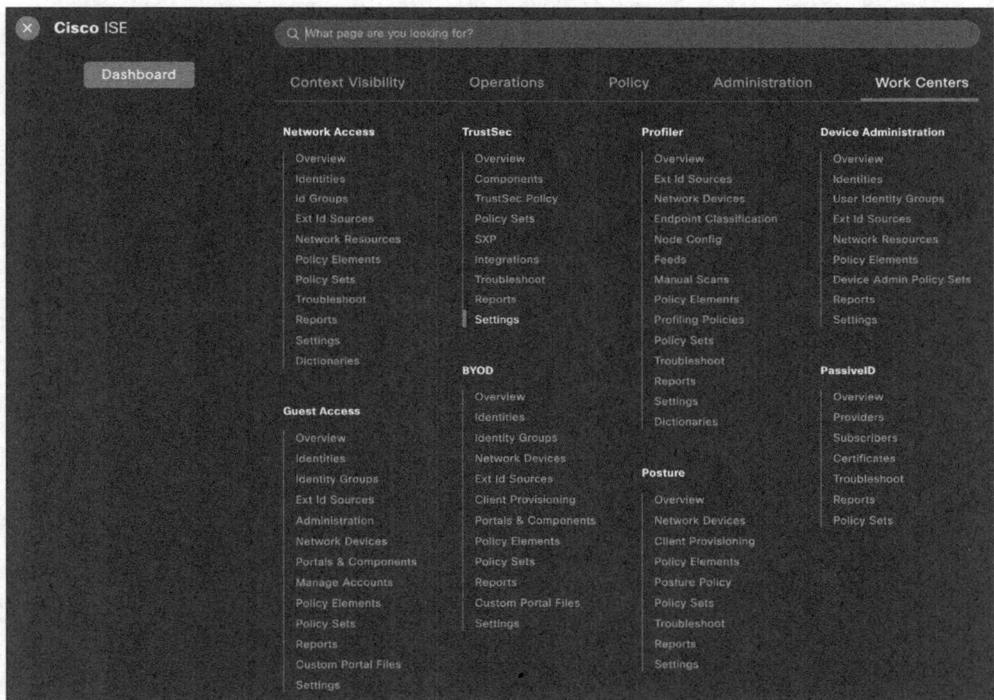

Figure 8-156 *Navigating to the Settings Tab in the TrustSec Work Center in Cisco ISE*

Step 3. Under **Security Group Tag Numbering**, select **User Must Enter SGT Numbers Manually** (see Figure 8-157). Scroll down and click **Save**.

Step 4. Click the **Components** tab. Just above the table containing the existing security groups, click **+ Add** (see Figure 8-158).

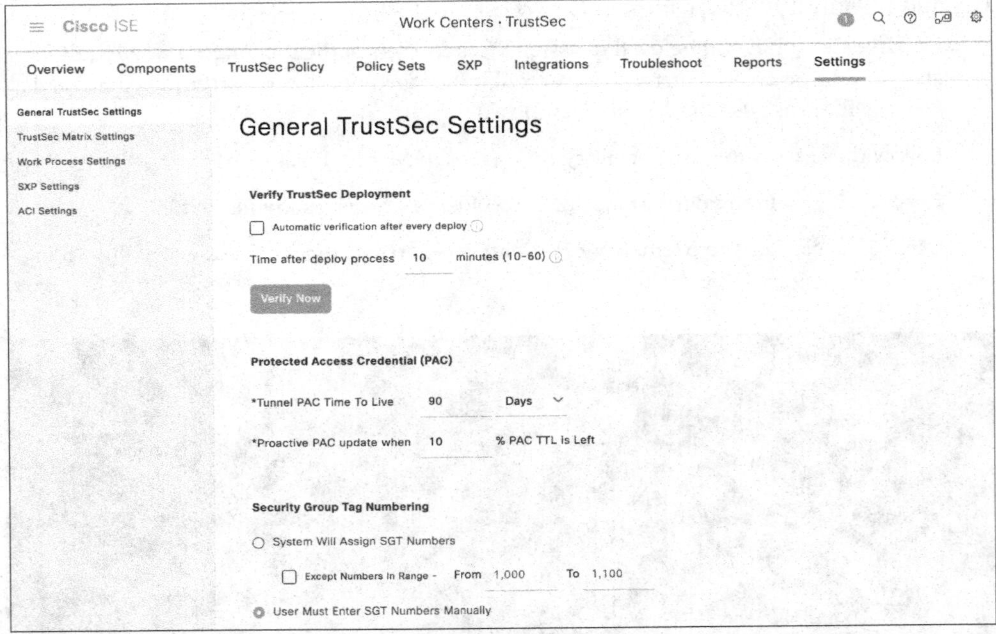

Figure 8-157 *Enabling User-Assigned SGTs in Cisco ISE*

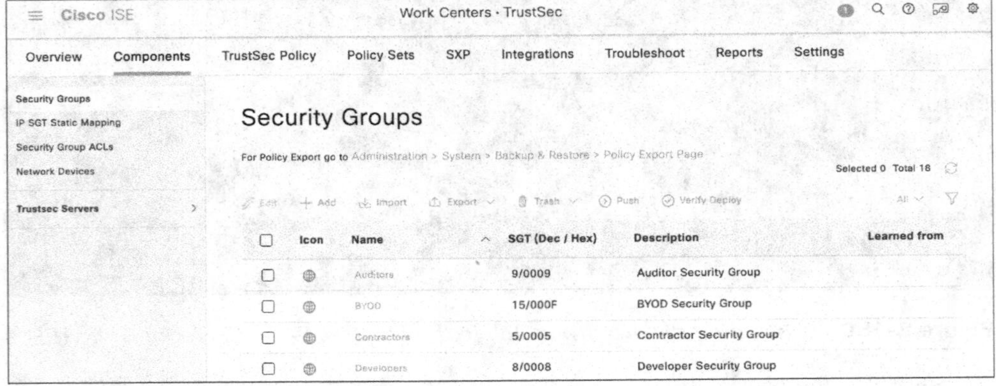

Figure 8-158 *The Components Tab in the TrustSec Work Center in Cisco ISE*

Step 5. On the screen shown in Figure 8-159, enter the following:

- **Name:** This is a meaningful name for this security group. Ensure that it matches the adaptive policy group name used in Meraki Dashboard.

- **Tag Value:** This is the number used to identify traffic in this group. Ensure that it matches the SGT Value used for this adaptive policy group in Meraki Dashboard.

Click **Submit.**

Repeat Steps 4 and 5 for all remaining security groups. For this example, we have created groups for **Staff** (10) and **POS** (20).

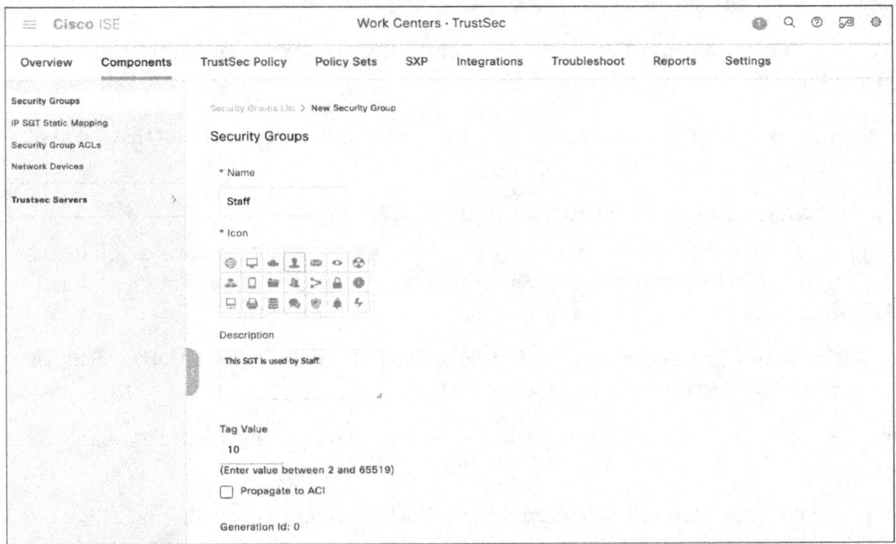

Figure 8-159 *Creating a Security Group in Cisco ISE*

Step 6. After all the required security groups have been created, they should be listed on the **Security Groups** page in Cisco ISE, as shown in Figure 8-160.

Security Groups

For Policy Export go to Administration > System > Backup & Restore > Policy Export Page

Selected 0 Total 2

Edit | Add | Import | Export | Trash | Push | Verify Deploy | Quick Filter

	Icon	Name	SGT (Dec / Hex)	Description	Learned from
			Dec. Value	This	
		POS	20/0014	This SGT is used by POS devices and servers requiring PCI compl...	
		Staff	10/000A	This SGT is used by Staff.	

Figure 8-160 *The Security Groups Page in Cisco ISE After Successfully Creating the Required Groups*

You've now completed the steps to create security groups in Cisco ISE. You can find these steps documented in the following guide: https://documentation.meraki.com/General_Administration/Cross-Platform_Content/Adaptive_Policy_and_Cisco_ISE.

Assigning Security Group Tags

Security group tags can be assigned either

- Statically, in the case of SSIDs and switch ports, or
- Dynamically, using RADIUS attributes, commonly used when authenticating clients using 802.1X

We show the configuration steps for each of these methods in the sections that follow.

Statically Assigning Security Group Tags to SSIDs

To assign adaptive group policies statically to an SSID, you must first have enabled adaptive policy on the network in which the access point resides. If this has not been done, the **Adaptive Policy Group** drop-down menu will not be visible.

The adaptive policy group can be assigned only to SSIDs enabled for RADIUS, such as those previously configured for PEAP or EAP-TLS.

Follow these steps to assign SGTs statically on wireless SSIDs using adaptive policy groups:

Step 1. Log in to Meraki Dashboard (https://dashboard.meraki.com).

Step 2. Navigate to **Wireless > Access Control** (under Configure).

Step 3. Select an existing SSID that is enabled for RADIUS authentication from the SSID drop-down menu at the top of the page.

Step 4. Scroll down to **Client IP and VLAN.** From the **Adaptive Policy Group** drop-down menu (see Figure 8-161), select the SGT you want to statically assign to all traffic on this SSID.

Click **Save.**

You've completed the steps necessary to statically assign SGTs to all client traffic on an SSID. You can find more details about configuring adaptive policy on Meraki MR access points using the following guide: https://documentation.meraki.com/General_Administration/Cross-Platform_Content/Adaptive_Policy_MR_Configuration_Guide.

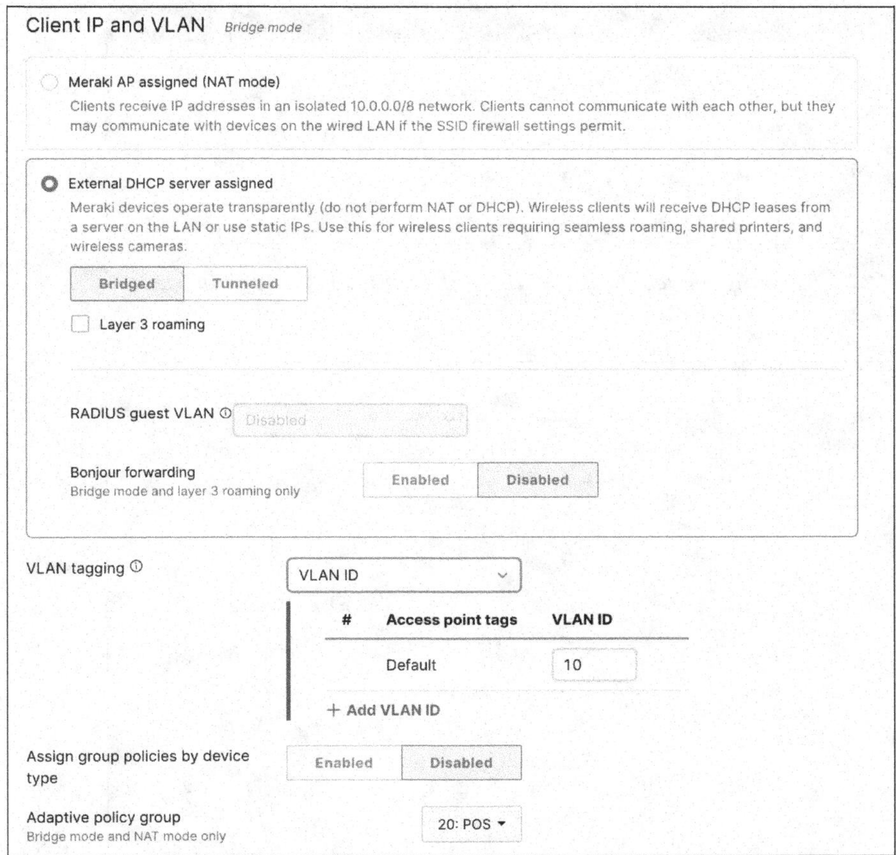

Figure 8-161 *Enabling Static SGT Assignment for All Client Traffic on an SSID in Meraki Dashboard*

Statically Assigning Security Group Tags to Switch Ports

Follow these steps to assign SGTs on switch ports using adaptive policy groups:

Step 1. Log in to Meraki Dashboard (https://dashboard.meraki.com).

Step 2. Navigate to **Switching > Switch Ports** (under Monitor).

Step 3. Similar to Figure 8-162, select the access switch ports where SGTs will be statically assigned and click **Edit.**

Step 4. From the **Adaptive Policy Group** drop-down menu, select the group required. In the example, the point-of-sale server will connect here, so we have assigned the **POS** group with a tag of **20**, as shown in Figure 8-163. Click **Update.**

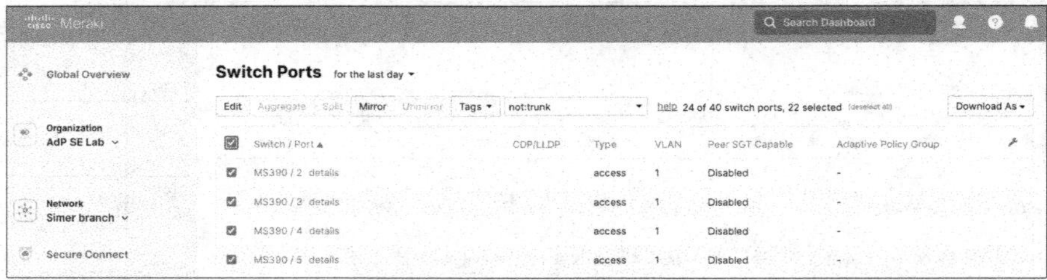

Figure 8-162 *Selecting Switch Ports to Edit on the Switch Ports Page in Meraki Dashboard*

Update 22 ports

Name

Port status: Enabled | Disabled

Link negotiation: Auto negotiate

Port schedule: Unscheduled

Tags: +

Type: Trunk | Access

Access policy: Open

VLAN: 1

Voice VLAN

RSTP: Enabled | Disabled

STP guard: Disabled

Port isolation: Enabled | Disabled

Trusted DAI: Enabled | Disabled

UDLD: Alert only | Enforce

Alerts will be generated if UDLD detects an error, but the port will not be shut down.

PoE: Enabled | Disabled

Adaptive policy group: 20: POS

Cancel | Update

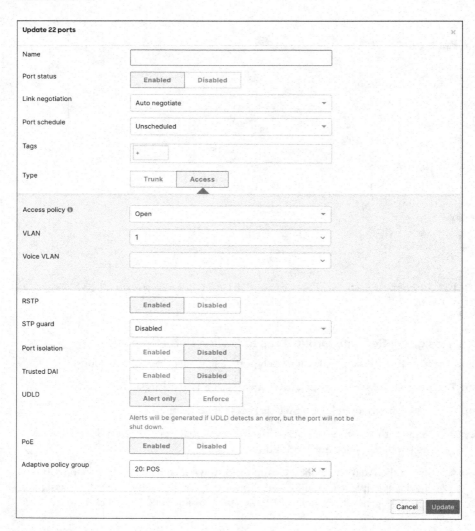

Figure 8-163 *Configuring the Adaptive Policy Group on Switch Ports in Meraki Dashboard*

Back on the **Switch Ports** page, you can see that the access ports now have the adaptive policy group **POS** configured, as shown in Figure 8-164.

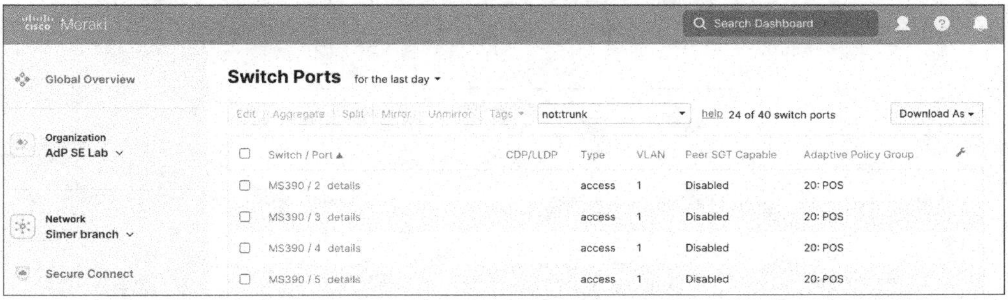

Figure 8-164 *The Switch Ports Page in Meraki Dashboard Showing Ports with Adaptive Policy Group Configured*

Now that you've completed the steps to statically assign SGTs to traffic on switch ports, you can find more information about configuring adaptive policy on Meraki MR switches using the following guide: https://documentation.meraki.com/General_Administration/Cross-Platform_Content/Adaptive_Policy_MS_Configuration_Guide#Static_assignment_of_Adaptive_Policy_Group_by_switchport.

Assigning Security Group Tags Using Cisco ISE

If you are not using group policies or want to use adaptive policy for wired *and* wireless access, you can assign SGTs using Cisco ISE directly. With the network already configured for 802.1X, the existing ISE policy can be easily adapted to return an SGT. Before starting, ensure you have the following prerequisites in place:

- The adaptive policy is enabled. If it is not, complete the steps in the earlier section "Enabling Adaptive Policy."
- The SGT propagation is configured. If it is not, complete the steps in the earlier section "Configuring Security Group Tag Propagation."
- 802.1X is already configured. If it is not, configure 802.1X using PEAP, EAP-TLS, or MAB from the relevant sections earlier in this chapter.
- The security group tag must be configured in Cisco ISE. If it is not, refer to the earlier section "Creating Security Group Tags in Cisco ISE."

Follow these steps to update Cisco ISE to assign a security group tag as part of 802.1X authentication:

Step 1. Log in to your instance of Cisco Identity Services Engine (ISE).

Step 2. Navigate to **Menu > Policy > Policy Sets** (see Figure 8-165).

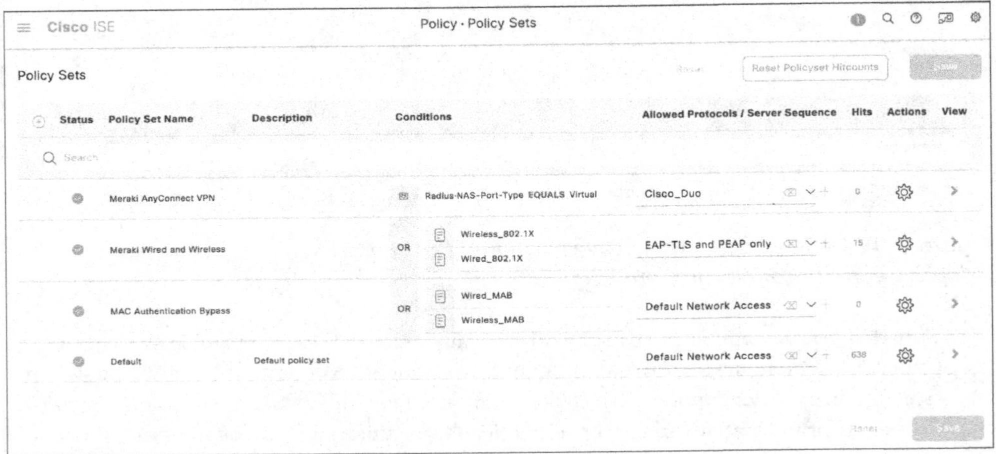

Figure 8-165 *The Policy Sets Page in Cisco ISE*

Step 3. Find the **Meraki Wired and Wireless** policy set and click the > icon under the **View** column.

Step 4. Expand the Authorization Policy. On the existing rule used to permit user access, from the **Security Group** drop-down menu, select the name that relates to the appropriate SGT/Adaptive Policy Group. In this example, we've used 802.1X to authenticate employees, so we have chosen the **Staff** security group, as shown in Figure 8-166.

Click **Save.**

At this point, you've completed the simple task of adapting an existing 802.1X ISE policy set to also assign security group tags. Read on as we move on to creating and testing the adaptive policy.

Creating an Adaptive Policy

Adaptive policies are analogous to an access list, except instead of using IP addresses, rules are created based on security group tags. Adaptive policies are configured at the organization level, unlike group policies, which are configured at the network level. Security policy is enforced at egress by examining the source and destination tag and then taking the desired action (allow or deny). It is recommended that all clients connect to switches or access points because SGT enforcement currently is not supported on the MX itself. By default, an adaptive policy permits all traffic.

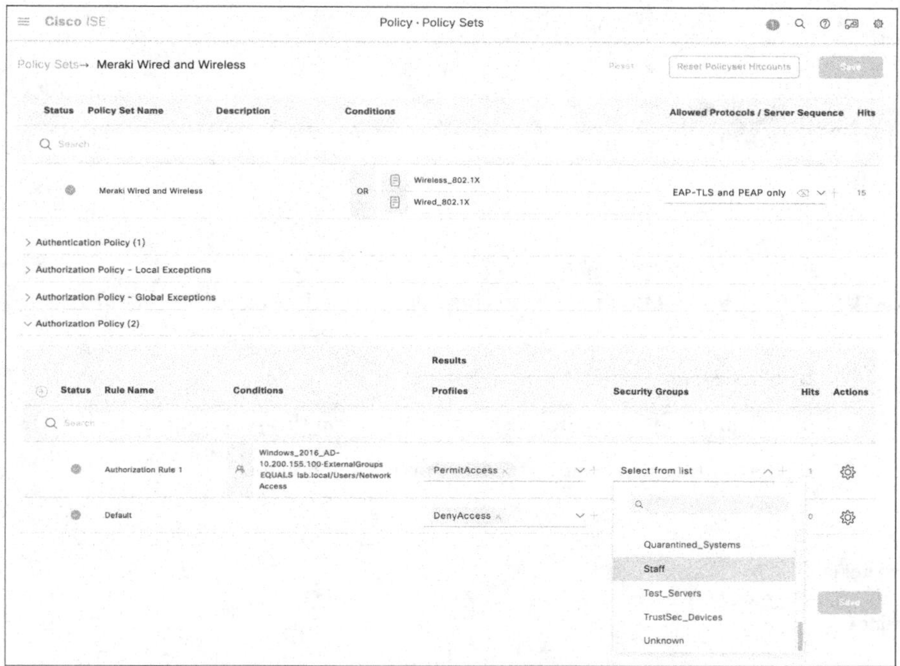

Figure 8-166 *Adding a Security Group to an Existing Authorization Rule on the Wired and Wireless 802.1X Policy Set*

> **Note** Meraki's vision is to have end-to-end segmentation on all parts of the platform. Being able to leverage adaptive policy groups more broadly, such as in firewall policies for external traffic, would be very exciting. Expect to see this vision come to life with each upcoming release.

Follow these steps to create an adaptive policy:

Step 1. Log in to Meraki Dashboard (https://dashboard.meraki.com).

Step 2. Navigate to **Organization-wide > Adaptive Policy** (under Configure). Click the **Policies** tab.

Click **Add Policies** (see Figure 8-167).

Step 3. In this example, the Adaptive Policy group staff (tag 10) should not be able to talk to point-of-sale devices (tag 20).

a. To achieve this, select the **Staff** group under **Source Groups** and the **POS** group under **Destination Groups** (see Figure 8-168).

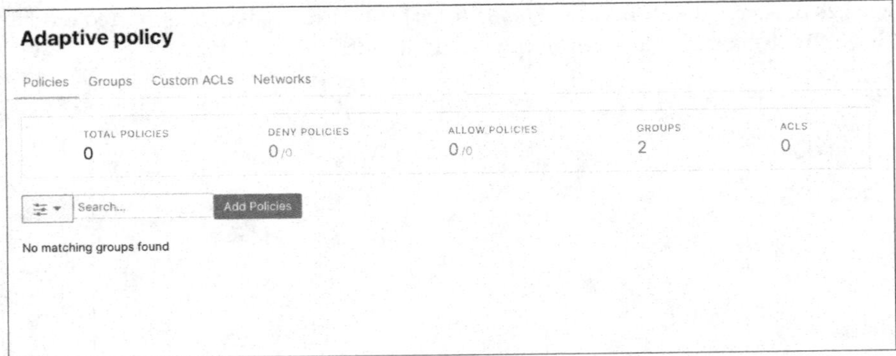

Figure 8-167 *The Policies Tab on the Adaptive Policy Page in Meraki Dashboard*

b. Click **Deny**.

c. When a pop-up window asks you to confirm this policy change, click **OK**.

d. Repeat this step to add any other policies you need.

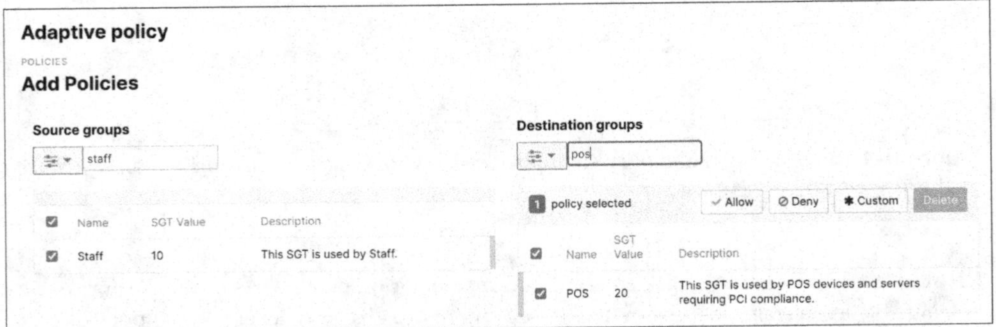

Figure 8-168 *Configuring an Adaptive Policy in Meraki Dashboard*

Step 4. Figure 8-169 shows the final adaptive policy. This policy segments staff and point-of-sale traffic, even when on the same IP subnet.

You've now completed the configuration of a basic adaptive policy. You test this configuration in the next section. Refer to the following guide to learn more about configuring adaptive policy: https://documentation.meraki.com/General_Administration/Cross-Platform_Content/Adaptive_Policy_Configuration_Guide.

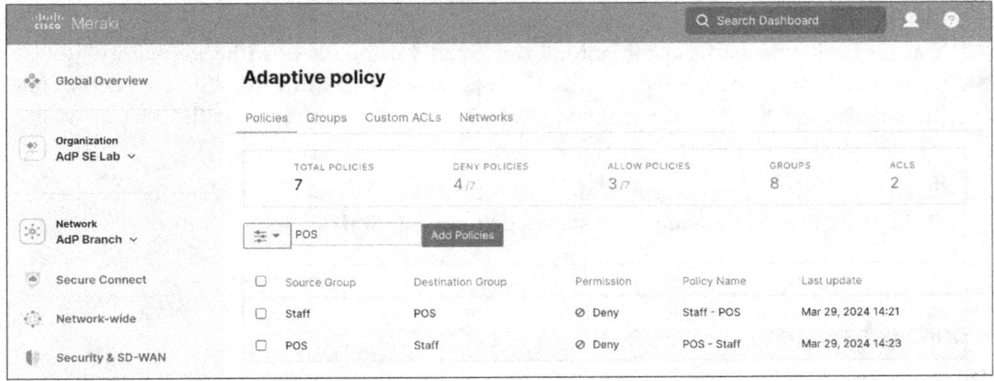

Figure 8-169 *The Adaptive Policy Page Showing the Final Policy for the PCI Use Case*

Testing Adaptive Policy

Now it's time to bring all the preceding configuration together and demonstrate the adaptive policy in effect. Figure 8-170 illustrates the topology used.

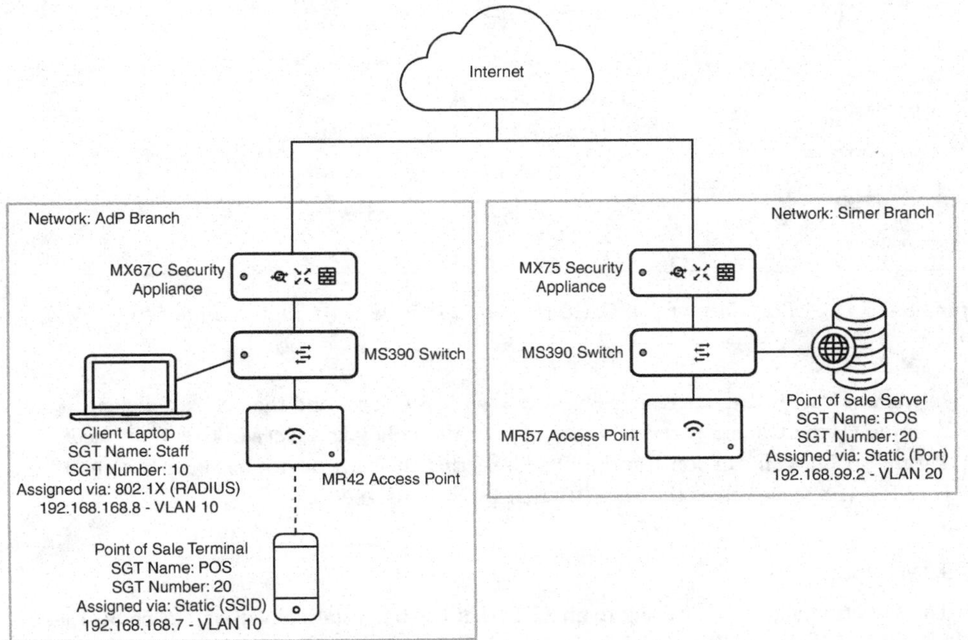

Figure 8-170 *Network Diagram Depicting the Lab Used for Demonstrating the PCI Compliance Use Case*

Client Laptop

You can authenticate the client laptop using 802.1X using PEAP with the security group tag assigned by Cisco ISE. Figure 8-171 shows the log entry in Cisco ISE. This entry confirms that the same Meraki wired and wireless policy set configured earlier is used and the staff SGT is assigned.

Figure 8-172 shows an excerpt of the authentication detail report highlighting the details of the 802.1X login, including the security group tag (**Staff**).

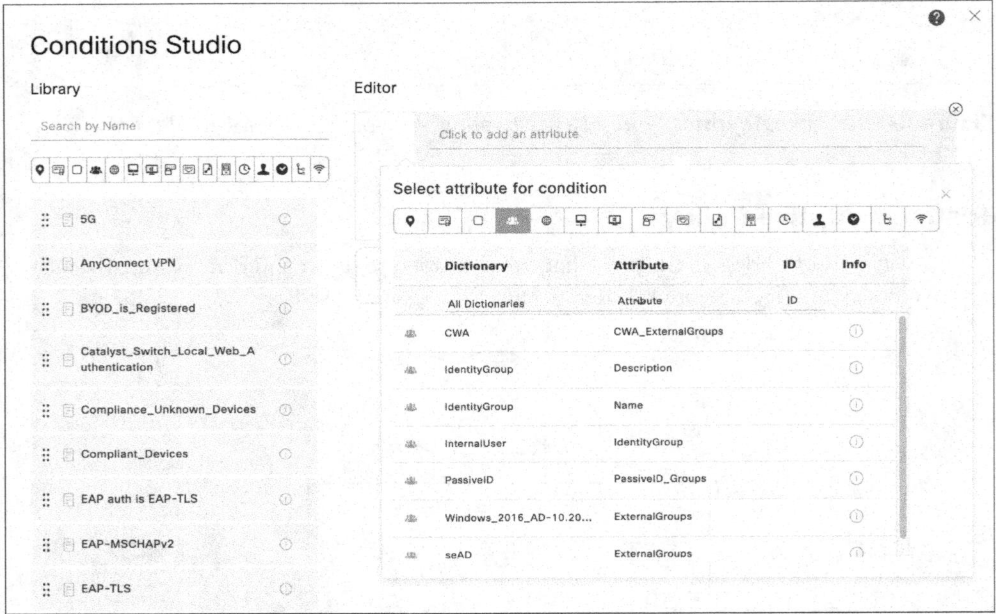

Figure 8-171 *A Log Entry from Cisco ISE Showing the Staff Tag Assigned to the Staff Device*

In Meraki Dashboard, navigate to **Network-wide > Clients** and then click the client to bring up the **Clients Overview** page. Under the **Policy** and **Network** sections (see Figure 8-173), you can confirm the IP address that the staff device has been assigned (192.168.168.8) as well as the SGT (10) that ISE has assigned.

POS Terminal

The POS terminal is connecting to an SSID that has been statically assigned on SGT (see Figure 8-174). This SSID is bridged into the same VLAN as the staff laptop.

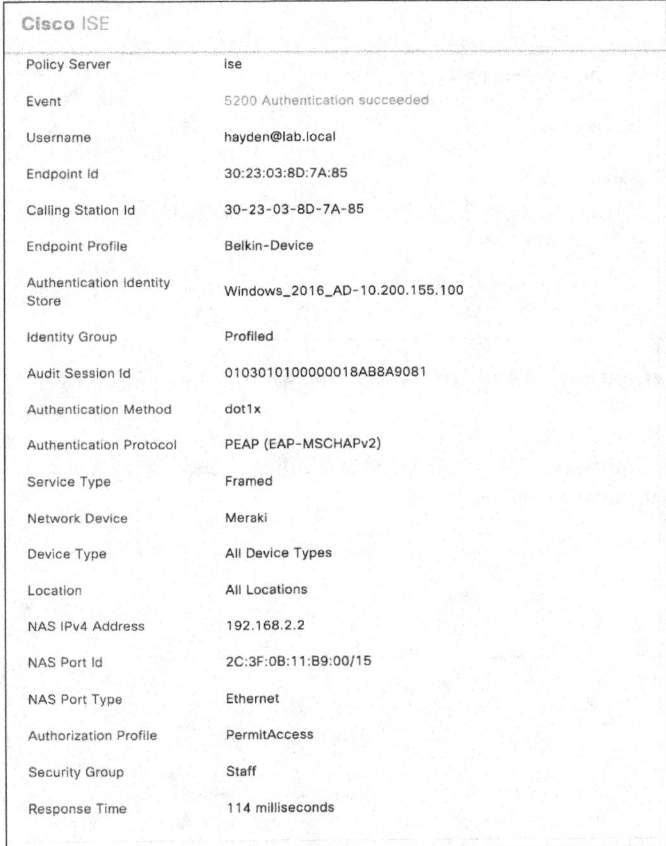

Cisco ISE
Policy Server ise
Event 5200 Authentication succeeded
Username hayden@lab.local
Endpoint Id 30:23:03:8D:7A:85
Calling Station Id 30-23-03-8D-7A-85
Endpoint Profile Belkin-Device
Authentication Identity Store Windows_2016_AD-10.200.155.100
Identity Group Profiled
Audit Session Id 0103010100000018AB8A9081
Authentication Method dot1x
Authentication Protocol PEAP (EAP-MSCHAPv2)
Service Type Framed
Network Device Meraki
Device Type All Device Types
Location All Locations
NAS IPv4 Address 192.168.2.2
NAS Port Id 2C:3F:0B:11:B9:00/15
NAS Port Type Ethernet
Authorization Profile PermitAccess
Security Group Staff
Response Time 114 milliseconds

Figure 8-172 *An Excerpt of an Authentication Detail Report Showing the Security Group Tag (Staff) Being Assigned*

Policy

Device policy: normal ▾
Adaptive Policy: 10: Staff
Bandwidth: unlimited
Layer 3 firewall: 0 rules
Layer 7 firewall: 0 rules
Traffic shaping: 0 rules
show details »

Network

IPv4 address: 192.168.168.8 dynamic ▾
MAC address: 30:23:03:8d:7a:85
VLAN: 10 — Server
Port forwarding: none
1:1 NAT IPs: none
edit forwarding »

Figure 8-173 *An Excerpt from the Clients Page Showing the Staff Device's SGT and IP Address*

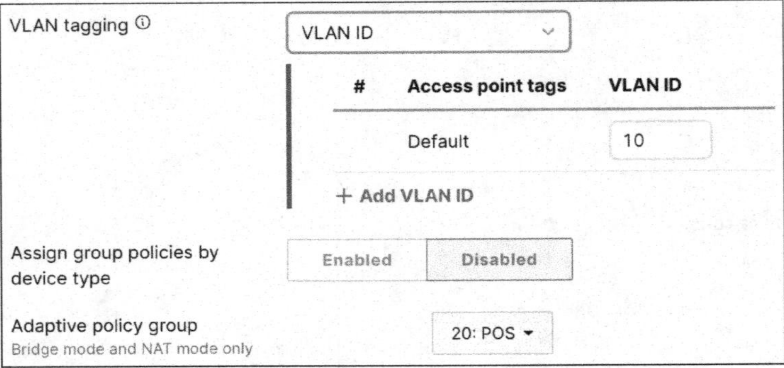

Figure 8-174 *The SSID Configuration Showing the Manually Assigned Adaptive Policy Group*

You can confirm that Cisco ISE has not assigned the SGT by the absence of a security group name in the log entry shown in Figure 8-175.

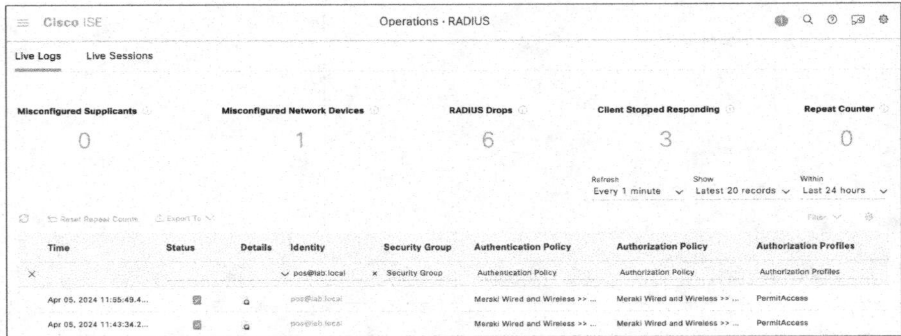

Figure 8-175 *The Log Entry from Cisco ISE Showing That an SGT Has Not Been Assigned During Authentication*

On the Overview tab of the Clients page once again, you can confirm the IP address (192.168.168.7) and SGT (20) used for this POS terminal, as demonstrated in Figure 8-176.

Policy

Device policy: normal ▾
Adaptive Policy: 20: POS
Bandwidth: unlimited
Layer 3 firewall: 0 rules
Layer 7 firewall: 0 rules
Traffic shaping: 0 rules
show details »

Network

IPv4 address: 192.168.168.7 dynamic ▾
IPv6 address (link-local): fe80:0:0:0:c70:2e49:c87a:704a
MAC address: c8:89:f3:c9:f8:64
VLAN: 10 — Server
Port forwarding: none
1:1 NAT IPs: none
edit forwarding »

Figure 8-176 *An Excerpt from the Overview Tab on the Clients Page Showing the Staff Device's SGT and IP Address*

POS Server

At another site, you can see the POS server. This device connects to a switch port that has its SGT (20) statically assigned, as shown in Figure 8-177.

Switch Ports for the last day ▾

Edit | Aggregate | Split | Mirror | Unmirror | Tags ▾ | switch:390 AND port:19 | help 1 of 40 switch ports | Download As ▾

☐	Switch / Port ▲	Name	Link	Peer SGT Capable	Adaptive Policy Group	Access policy	Type	VLAN	Enabled
☐	MS390 / 19 details	POS Server	Auto negotiate (100 Mbps)	Disabled	20: POS	Open	access	20	enabled

Figure 8-177 *The Switch Port Configuration for the Port Connecting to the POS Server Shown in Meraki Dashboard*

On the Overview tab of the Clients page once again, you can confirm the IP address (192.168.98.2) and SGT (20) for this POS server, as shown in Figure 8-178.

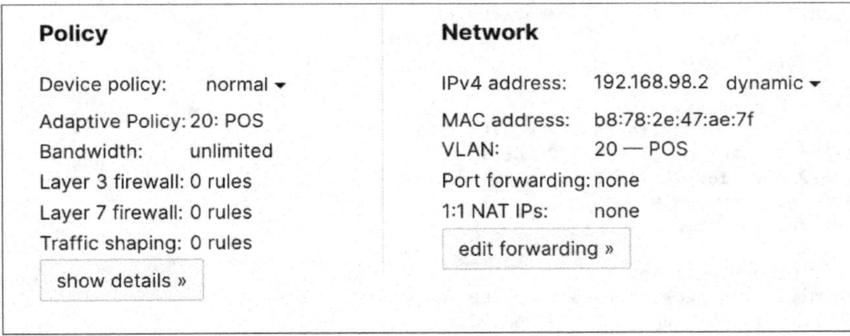

Figure 8-178 *An Excerpt from the Overview Tab on the Clients Page Showing the POS Server's SGT and IP Address*

Testing

With all the host network configuration verified, you can now test to see whether the adaptive policy is working as desired. To recap, devices with the tag **Staff** should not be able to communicate with devices with the tag **POS**, which includes the POS terminal and the POS server. Inversely, the POS terminal should be able to communicate with the remote POS server, but it should not be able to communicate with devices with the **Staff** tag.

First, let's verify this from the staff laptop using a simple ping (see Figure 8-179). Let's start by confirming the IP address the device is using (192.168.168.8) and that it has reachability to the device's default gateway (192.168.168.1). Next, confirm that communication with the POS terminal (192.168.168.7) is blocked. It is, proving that microsegmentation is working. Even though the staff laptop and POS terminal are in the same VLAN and subnet, the adaptive policy prevents them from communicating. Next, confirm that the adaptive policy is also working over the WAN by verifying that communication with the POS server (192.168.98.2) is blocked, which it is. Last, you can verify that connectivity over the WAN is working by successfully pinging the default gateway for the 192.168.98.0/24 subnet (192.168.98.1).

```
ryan — -bash — 87×36
Ryans-MacBook-Pro:~ ryan$ ifconfig | grep 192
        inet 192.168.168.8 netmask 0xffffff00 broadcast 192.168.168.255
Ryans-MacBook-Pro:~ ryan$ ping -c 3 192.168.168.1
PING 192.168.168.1 (192.168.168.1): 56 data bytes
64 bytes from 192.168.168.1: icmp_seq=0 ttl=64 time=115.390 ms
64 bytes from 192.168.168.1: icmp_seq=1 ttl=64 time=3.047 ms
64 bytes from 192.168.168.1: icmp_seq=2 ttl=64 time=9.454 ms

--- 192.168.168.1 ping statistics ---
3 packets transmitted, 3 packets received, 0.0% packet loss
round-trip min/avg/max/stddev = 3.047/42.630/115.390/51.515 ms
Ryans-MacBook-Pro:~ ryan$ ping -c 3 192.168.168.7
PING 192.168.168.7 (192.168.168.7): 56 data bytes
Request timeout for icmp_seq 0
Request timeout for icmp_seq 1

--- 192.168.168.7 ping statistics ---
3 packets transmitted, 0 packets received, 100.0% packet loss
Ryans-MacBook-Pro:~ ryan$ ping -c 3 192.168.98.2
PING 192.168.98.2 (192.168.98.2): 56 data bytes
Request timeout for icmp_seq 0
Request timeout for icmp_seq 1

--- 192.168.98.2 ping statistics ---
3 packets transmitted, 0 packets received, 100.0% packet loss
Ryans-MacBook-Pro:~ ryan$ ping -c 3 192.168.98.1
PING 192.168.98.1 (192.168.98.1): 56 data bytes
64 bytes from 192.168.98.1: icmp_seq=0 ttl=64 time=7.666 ms
64 bytes from 192.168.98.1: icmp_seq=1 ttl=64 time=9.185 ms
64 bytes from 192.168.98.1: icmp_seq=2 ttl=64 time=7.030 ms

--- 192.168.98.1 ping statistics ---
3 packets transmitted, 3 packets received, 0.0% packet loss
round-trip min/avg/max/stddev = 7.030/7.960/9.185/0.904 ms
Ryans-MacBook-Pro:~ ryan$
```

Figure 8-179 *ping Test Results from the Staff Laptop*

Next, let's conduct a similar test from the device emulating the POS terminal (see Figure 8-180). Let's begin by verifying the IP address of the POS terminal (192.168.168.7) and confirm that it has reachability to the default gateway (192.168.168.1). Following this, you can confirm that communication with the Staff device (192.168.168.8) is blocked. Last, you can confirm that the POS terminal can talk to the remote POS server (192.168.98.2) and the default gateway for the subnet on which the POS server sits (192.168.98.1).

```
ryanchaney — -zsh — 81×38
ryanchaney@RYCHANEY-M-6X1J ~ % ifconfig | grep 192
        inet 192.168.168.7 netmask 0xffffff00 broadcast 192.168.168.255
ryanchaney@RYCHANEY-M-6X1J ~ % ping -c 3 192.168.168.1
PING 192.168.168.1 (192.168.168.1): 56 data bytes
64 bytes from 192.168.168.1: icmp_seq=0 ttl=64 time=6.490 ms
64 bytes from 192.168.168.1: icmp_seq=1 ttl=64 time=6.196 ms
64 bytes from 192.168.168.1: icmp_seq=2 ttl=64 time=3.916 ms

--- 192.168.168.1 ping statistics ---
3 packets transmitted, 3 packets received, 0.0% packet loss
round-trip min/avg/max/stddev = 3.916/5.534/6.490/1.150 ms
ryanchaney@RYCHANEY-M-6X1J ~ % ping -c 3 192.168.168.8
PING 192.168.168.8 (192.168.168.8): 56 data bytes
Request timeout for icmp_seq 0
Request timeout for icmp_seq 1

--- 192.168.168.8 ping statistics ---
3 packets transmitted, 0 packets received, 100.0% packet loss
ryanchaney@RYCHANEY-M-6X1J ~ % ping -c 3 192.168.98.2
PING 192.168.98.2 (192.168.98.2): 56 data bytes
64 bytes from 192.168.98.2: icmp_seq=0 ttl=63 time=90.798 ms
64 bytes from 192.168.98.2: icmp_seq=1 ttl=63 time=103.570 ms
64 bytes from 192.168.98.2: icmp_seq=2 ttl=63 time=21.767 ms

--- 192.168.98.2 ping statistics ---
3 packets transmitted, 3 packets received, 0.0% packet loss
round-trip min/avg/max/stddev = 21.767/72.045/103.570/35.932 ms
ryanchaney@RYCHANEY-M-6X1J ~ % ping -c 3 192.168.98.1
PING 192.168.98.1 (192.168.98.1): 56 data bytes
64 bytes from 192.168.98.1: icmp_seq=0 ttl=64 time=5.503 ms
64 bytes from 192.168.98.1: icmp_seq=1 ttl=64 time=6.241 ms
64 bytes from 192.168.98.1: icmp_seq=2 ttl=64 time=5.477 ms

--- 192.168.98.1 ping statistics ---
3 packets transmitted, 3 packets received, 0.0% packet loss
round-trip min/avg/max/stddev = 5.477/5.740/6.241/0.354 ms
ryanchaney@RYCHANEY-M-6X1J ~ %
```

Figure 8-180 *ping Test Results from the POS Terminal (Simulated)*

Next, you can confirm that traffic between the POS terminal and the Staff devices is indeed being dropped using the packet capture tool in Meraki Dashboard (**Network-wide > Packet Capture**), as shown in Figure 8-181.

Repeating the packet capture, this time with a ping from the staff device to the POS terminal, you can see a similar one-way flow of ICMP packets (see Figure 8-182). This confirms that traffic is being dropped by the adaptive policy as intended.

At this point, you've completed this section on the adaptive policies using security group tags. To learn more about adaptive policies, we recommend reading the following guide as well as the MS, MX, and MR configuration guides referred to within it: https://documentation.meraki.com/General_Administration/Cross-Platform_Content/Adaptive_Policy_Overview.

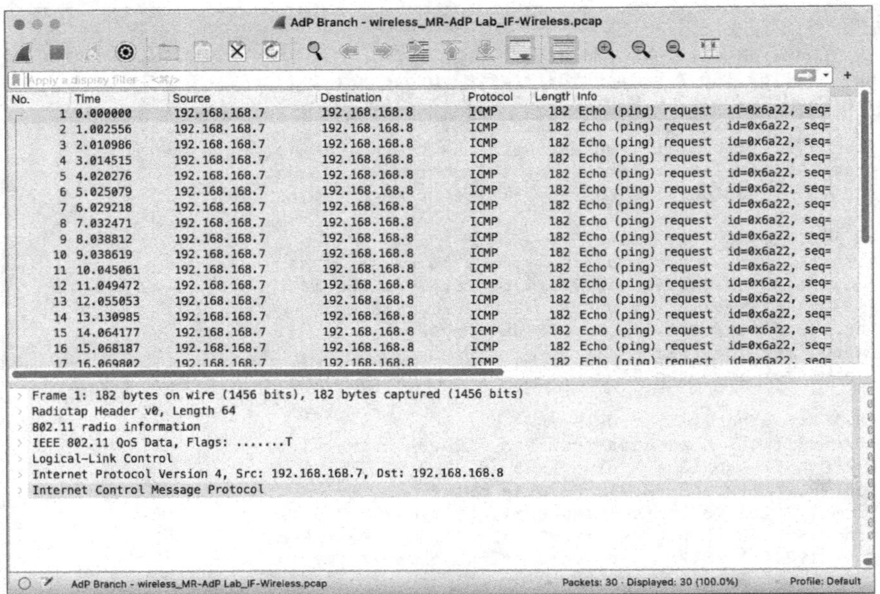

Figure 8-181 *Packet Capture Output Showing One-Way Traffic from the POS Terminal Toward the Staff Device*

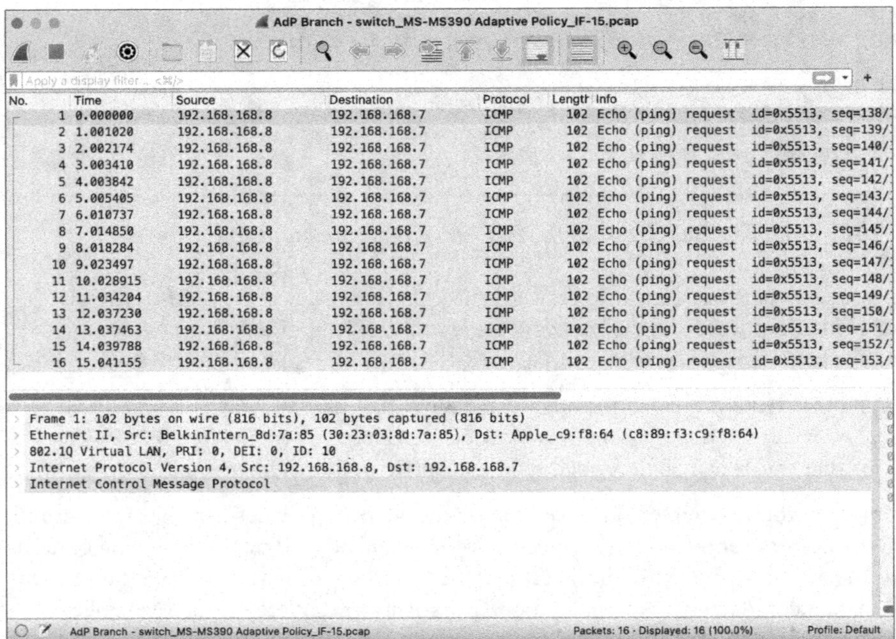

Figure 8-182 *Packet Capture Output Showing One-Way Traffic from the POS Terminal Toward the Staff Device*

Wireless Security

In this final section, we tackle the last remaining common wireless security requirements. First, PCI DSS 4.0 requirement 4.2.1.2 requires that industry best practice must be used to protect cardholder data, including the implementation of strong cryptography for authentication and transmission. Meraki supports the latest standard in wireless security, WPA3, including WPA3 with 192-bit security. WPA3 provides the highest capabilities in terms of security protocols and cryptography, including

- **Authentication:** Extensible Authentication Protocol–Transport Layer Security (EAP-TLS) using Elliptic Curve Diffie-Hellman (ECDH) exchange and Elliptic Curve Digital Signature Algorithm (ECDSA) using a 384-bit elliptic curve.
- **Authenticated encryption:** 256-bit Galois/Counter Mode Protocol (GCMP-256).
- **Key derivation and confirmation:** 384-bit Hashed Message Authentication Mode (HMAC) with Secure Hash Algorithm (HMAC-SHA384).
- **Robust management frame protection:** 256-bit Broadcast/Multicast Integrity Protocol Galois Message Authentication Code (BIP-GMAC-256).[6]

To support WPA3, Meraki APs must have hardware that is at least 802.11ac Wave-2 capable and be able to run MR firmware version 27 or later. To configure the WPA3 encryption method on an SSID in Meraki Dashboard, navigate to **Wireless > Access Control > WPA Encryption** (see Figure 8-183).

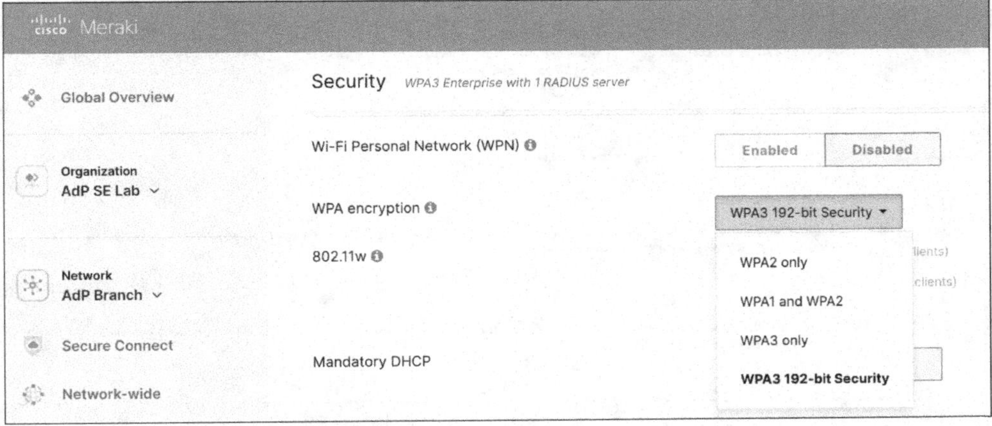

Figure 8-183 *Configuring WPA Encryption on an SSID in Meraki Dashboard*

To find out more about configuring WPA3, refer to the following guide: https://documentation.meraki.com/MR/Wi-Fi_Basics_and_Best_Practices/WPA3_Encryption_and_Configuration_Guide/.

Next, PCI DSS 4.0 requirement 11.2.1 calls for the ability to regularly detect the presence of, and distinguish between, authorized and unauthorized wireless access points. Administrators should also be notified of unauthorized APs. Meraki's Air Marshal wireless IPS capability has been created for exactly this purpose and can alert administrators of the following:

- Rogue APs connected to the network
- Access points spoofing your SSIDs or access points
- Malicious broadcasts and packet floods

Air Marshal is enabled by default and can be located in Meraki Dashboard by navigating to **Wireless > Air Marshal** (under Monitor), as shown in Figure 8-184. It is recommended that you deploy Meraki APs that have dedicated scanning radios to maintain the best wireless performance. Access points without dedicated scanning radios need to go "off channel" briefly—that is, to stop serving clients—to scan for rogue APs.

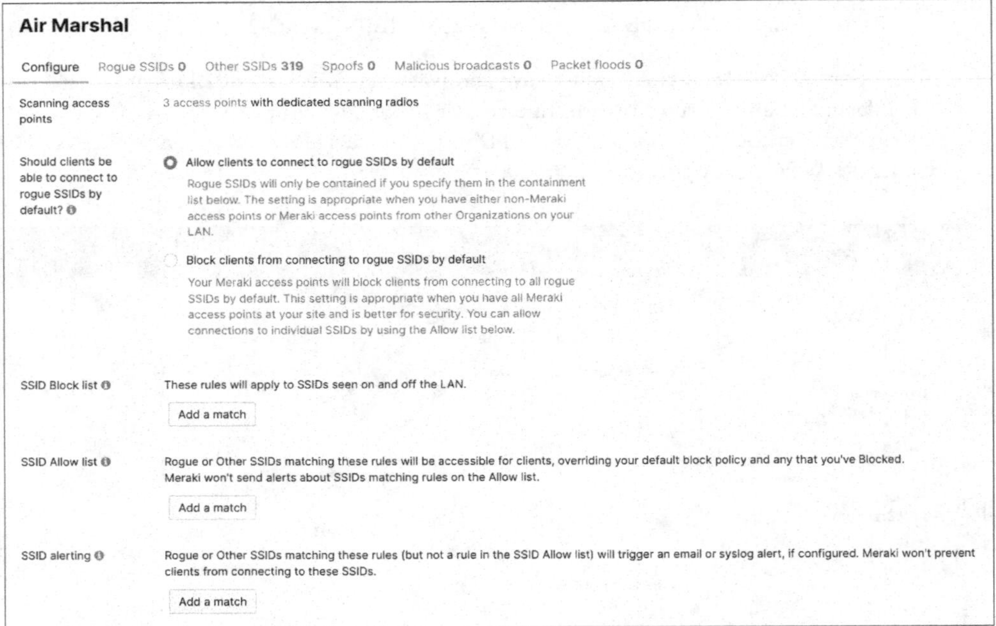

Figure 8-184 *The Air Marshal Configuration Page in Meraki Dashboard*

You can find further information on Meraki's Air Marshal capability at https://documentation.meraki.com/MR/Monitoring_and_Reporting/Air_Marshal.

Finally, NIST 800-53 AC-18(5) requires that organizations take action to limit unauthorized use of wireless communications outside of organization-controlled boundaries. This includes the ability to calibrate transmission power levels and to choose suitable radio antennas. Meraki has both indoor and outdoor APs available with external antennas, allowing for the signal to be directed, and signal strength tailored, to suit the environment. In addition, all APs can have their RF signal customized as needed using RF profiles (**Wireless > Radio Settings**). It is recommended that you hire a wireless specialist to conduct a site survey for each site before and after deployment. This helps to ensure that the wireless network doesn't inadvertently extend further than required. For more information on configuring RF profiles, refer to https://documentation.meraki.com/MR/Radio_Settings/RF_Profiles.

Summary

This chapter covered a broad range of topics related to securing Meraki wired and wireless networks. The chapter opened with traditional IP and port-based security features such as ACLs, Layer 3 and 7 firewalling, port isolation, Dynamic ARP Inspection, and the very handy, rogue DHCP server detection feature. Next, we discussed zero trust and how users must now have their identity verified, rather than being implicitly trusted. To achieve this, we described how to implement 802.1X on wired and wireless networks, building on the foundations from Chapter 7. This included showing the "easy button" that allows any administrator to deploy EAP-TLS using Sentry-based access. Finally, this chapter covered how to implement segmentation and control using both group policies and adaptive policies. Both of these were demonstrated operating natively in Meraki and with Cisco ISE. Once again, we highly recommend Cisco ISE be deployed when 802.1X is being deployed or where RADIUS is required. We hope that you have a greater appreciation now of just how capable the Meraki platform is when it comes to securing the network at the access layer.

Notes

[1] National Institute of Standards and Technology (NIST). (2020, August). *NIST 800-207 Zero Trust Architecture*. https://nvlpubs.nist.gov/nistpubs/SpecialPublications/NIST.SP.800-207.pdf

[2] Cisco Meraki. (2023, June 27). SecurePort (Formerly Known as SecureConnect). https://documentation.meraki.com/MS/Access_Control/SecurePort_(formerly_known_as_SecureConnect)

[3] Cisco Meraki. (2023, November 15). Dynamic ARP Inspection. https://documentation.meraki.com/MS/Other_Topics/Dynamic_ARP_Inspection

[4] Holmes, D. & Burn, J. (2022, January 24). The Definition of Modern Zero Trust. *Forrester*. https://www.forrester.com/blogs/the-definition-of-modern-zero-trust/

[5] Cisco Meraki. (2024, January 13). Creating and Applying Group Policies. https://documentation.meraki.com/General_Administration/Cross-Platform_Content/Creating_and_Applying_Group_Policies

[6] WiFi Alliance. (n.d.). Discover Wi-Fi Security. https://www.wi-fi.org/discover-wi-fi/security

Further Reading

Abbott, T., Burger, A., Cho, V., et al. (2016, June 20). Integrate Meraki Networks with ISE. Cisco Community. https://community.cisco.com/t5/security-knowledge-base/how-to-integrate-meraki-networks-with-ise/ta-p/3618650

AllThingsNetworking. (2022, April 10). ISE MAB Configuration. https://www.allthingsnetworking.net/ise-mab-wired-configuration/

Australian Cyber Security Centre. (ACSC). (2022, November 24). Essential Eight Maturity Model. https://www.cyber.gov.au/resources-business-and-government/essential-cyber-security/essential-eight/essential-eight-maturity-model

Cisco Meraki. (2022, April 22). Switch ACL Operation. https://documentation.meraki.com/MS/Other_Topics/Switch_ACL_Operation

Cisco Meraki. (2022, November 19). Using RADIUS Attributes to Apply Group Policies. https://documentation.meraki.com/MR/Group_Policies_and_Block_Lists/Using_RADIUS_Attributes_to_Apply_Group_Policies

Cisco Meraki. (2023, July 7). IPv6 Support on MR Access Points. https://documentation.meraki.com/MR/Other_Topics/IPv6_Support_on_MR_Access_Points

Cisco Meraki. (2023, July 19). Meraki MS Group Policy Access Control Lists. https://documentation.meraki.com/MS/Access_Control/Meraki_MS_Group_Policy_Access_Control_Lists

Cisco Meraki. (2023, August 23). Layer 3 and 7 Firewall Processing Order. https://documentation.meraki.com/General_Administration/Cross-Platform_Content/Layer_3_and_7_Firewall_Processing_Order

Cisco Meraki. (2023, September 23). MR Firewall Rules. https://documentation.meraki.com/MR/Firewall_and_Traffic_Shaping/MR_Firewall_Rules

Cisco Meraki. (2023, October 5). Adaptive Policy MR Configuration Guide. https://documentation.meraki.com/General_Administration/Cross-Platform_Content/Adaptive_Policy/Adaptive_Policy_MR_Configuration_Guide

Cisco Meraki. (2023, October 13). Adaptive Policy Overview. https://documentation.meraki.com/General_Administration/Cross-Platform_Content/Adaptive_Policy/Adaptive_Policy_Overview

Cisco Meraki. (2023, October 14). Adaptive Policy MS Configuration Guide. https://documentation.meraki.com/General_Administration/Cross-Platform_Content/Adaptive_Policy/Adaptive_Policy_MS_Configuration_Guide

Cisco Meraki. (2023, October 25). Adaptive Policy and Cisco ISE. https://documentation.meraki.com/General_Administration/Cross-Platform_Content/Adaptive_Policy/Adaptive_Policy_and_Cisco_ISE

Cisco Meraki. (2024, January 13). Creating and Applying Group Policies. https://documentation.meraki.com/General_Administration/Cross-Platform_Content/Creating_and_Applying_Group_Policies

Cisco Meraki. (2024a, January 23). "Deny Local LAN" Settings in Cisco Meraki MR Firewall. https://documentation.meraki.com/MR/Firewall_and_Traffic_Shaping/'Deny_Local_LAN'_settings_in_Cisco_Meraki_MR_firewall

Cisco Meraki. (2024b, January 23). MAC-Based Access Control Using Cisco ISE – MR Access Points. https://documentation.meraki.com/MR/Encryption_and_Authentication/MAC-Based_Access_Control_Using_Cisco_ISE_-_MR_Access_Points

Cisco Meraki. (2024, January 24). Configuring ACLs. https://documentation.meraki.com/MS/Layer_3_Switching/Configuring_ACLs

Cisco Meraki. (2024a, January 31). Adaptive Policy MX/Z Configuration Guide. https://documentation.meraki.com/General_Administration/Cross-Platform_Content/Adaptive_Policy/Adaptive_Policy_MX_Configuration_Guide

Cisco Meraki. (2024b, January 31). Adaptive Policy for MX/Z Platforms. https://documentation.meraki.com/General_Administration/Cross-Platform_Content/Adaptive_Policy_for_MX%2F%2FZ_Platforms

Cisco Meraki. (2024, February 6). MS Switch Access Policies (802.1X). https://documentation.meraki.com/MS/Access_Control/MS_Switch_Access_Policies_(802.1X)

Cisco Meraki. (2024, February 14). Tracking Down Rogue DHCP Servers. https://documentation.meraki.com/MX/DHCP/Tracking_Down_Rogue_DHCP_Servers

Cisco Meraki. (2024, March 20). WPA3 Encryption and Configuration Guide. https://documentation.meraki.com/MR/Wi-Fi_Basics_and_Best_Practices/WPA3_Encryption_and_Configuration_Guide

Cisco Systems. (2018, April 23). Configure ISE 2.0 Certificate Provisioning Portal. https://www.cisco.com/c/en/us/support/docs/security/identity-services-engine/200534-ISE-2-0-Certificate-Provisioning-Portal.html#anc8

Cisco Systems. (2021, August 11). Certificate Provisioning Portal FAQs, Release 3.1. https://www.cisco.com/c/en/us/td/docs/security/ise/3-1/certificate_provisioning_portal_faqs/b_certificate_prov_portal_3_1.html

Cisco Systems. (2023, July 31). Configure EAP-TLS Authentication with ISE. https://www.cisco.com/c/en/us/support/docs/security/identity-services-engine/214975-configure-eap-tls-authentication-with-is.html

CSF Tools. (n.d.a.). AC-4(21): Physical/Logical Separation of Information Flows. https://csf.tools/reference/nist-sp-800-53/r4/ac/ac-4/ac-4-21/

CSF Tools. (n.d.b.). AC-18(5) Antennas and Transmission Power Levels. https://csf.tools/reference/nist-sp-800-53/r5/ac/ac-18/ac-18-5/

CSF Tools. (n.d.c.). IA-3: Device Identification and Authentication. https://csf.tools/reference/nist-sp-800-53/r4/ia/ia-3/

Lee, F. [faylee]. (2020, September 18). Group Based Policy Fundamentals. Cisco Community. https://community.cisco.com/t5/security-knowledge-base/group-based-policy-fundamentals/ta-p/3764433

National Institute of Standards and Technology (NIST). (2020, August). *NIST 800-207 Zero Trust Architecture*. https://nvlpubs.nist.gov/nistpubs/SpecialPublications/NIST.SP.800-207.pdf

Pan, M. [Minyi]. (2022, November 30). New Name, Same Great Feature—MS and MR SecurePort. *Cisco Meraki Community.* https://community.meraki.com/t5/Feature-Announcements/New-name-same-great-feature-MS-and-MR-SecurePort/ba-p/174080

PCI Security Standards Council. (2022, December). *PCI DSS: v4.0.* https://www.pcisecuritystandards.org/document_library/

Wikipedia. (2024, March 14). IEEE 802.1X. https://en.wikipedia.org/wiki/IEEE_802.1X

Chapter 9

Meraki MX and WAN Security

In this chapter, you learn the following:

- How to encrypt site-to-site WAN traffic to Meraki and non-Meraki devices using Meraki MX
- The differences between the various remote-access technologies, including client VPN, Sentry VPN, and AnyConnect VPN, as well as how to configure them
- How to deploy Meraki's vMX security appliance in public cloud environments, such as Amazon Web Services (AWS)

Meraki MX Introduction

Meraki MX combines firewall, VPN, SD-WAN, content, and threat filtering into a single easy-to-deploy, cloud-managed device. Today, Meraki's MX appliance range offers a versatile lineup tailored to meet customers' diverse networking needs, including physical and virtual offerings. Virtual MX (vMX) is designed to be deployed in public cloud environments, including Amazon Web Services (AWS), Google Cloud Platform (GCP), Azure, and Alibaba Cloud. While technically its own product line, the Z series teleworker gateways incorporate the majority of the functionality of Meraki MX. For the purposes of this chapter, the Z series should be considered part of the MX family. Figure 9-1 shows Meraki's full lineup across the MX and Z series.

Encryption is another of the key themes common across IT security standards and security best practices. For example, NIST CSF requirement PR.DS-02 requires that confidentiality, integrity, and availability of data-in-transit be protected. In another example, PCI DSS 4.0 requirement 4.2.1 mandates that strong cryptography and security protocols be implemented to safeguard data transmitted over public networks. This includes ensuring that communications are authenticated, use appropriate encryption, and do not fall back to insecure versions, algorithms, key sizes, and so on. Read on to learn how Meraki's site-to-site and remote-access VPN solutions help organizations maintain compliance with industry best practices. Please note that firewall, IPS, content filtering, and other Internet security features are covered in Chapter 10, "Securing User Traffic."

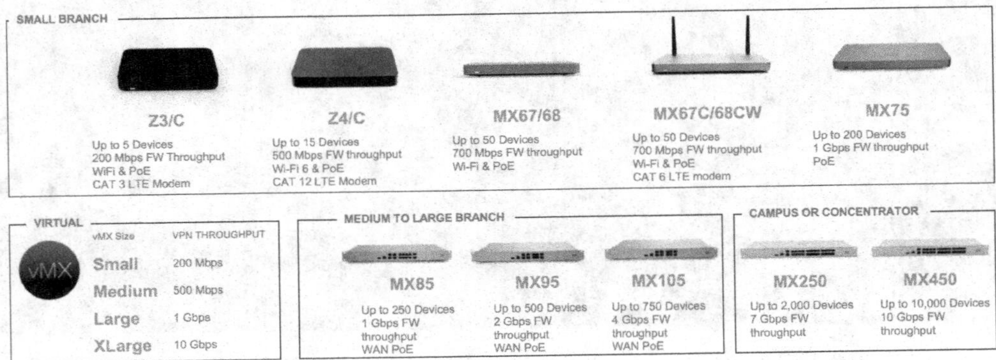

Figure 9-1 *Meraki's MX and Z Series Product Lineup*

Site-to-Site VPN (Auto VPN)

Site-to-site VPN is an always-on VPN between two or more, traditionally static, sites. Historically, site-to-site VPNs have been time-consuming to set up due to manual configuration and the need for matching pre-shared keys, authentication mechanisms, encryption protocols, and security associations. Meraki has made this easy with the Auto VPN feature. In terms of how it operates, Auto VPN is most similar to DMVPN in traditional Cisco networks; however, Auto VPN is far simpler to configure because it leverages the existing IP connectivity with Meraki Cloud. As a result, administrators only need to elect the site-to-site VPN type and nominate subnets to advertise over the VPN. This means that site-to-site VPNs can be established with only a couple of clicks. Configuration templates can also be utilized to further speed up VPN deployments with large numbers of sites.

Meraki Cloud records the IP reachability information for all MXs in what is known as the VPN Registry. To establish the VPN, MX appliances send a Register Request message to their VPN registry. This encrypted communication occurs over sessions established using NexTunnel on TCP port 443. The Register Request message contains the IP address and the UDP port that the MX communicates on. The Register Request message also requests the reachability information for its VPN peers. The contact information for this new VPN participant is propagated to any existing site-to-site VPN participants. In reply, the VPN registry sends Register Response messages back to this new MX with the contact information for its VPN peers. This also includes two 16-character keys, one per direction, required to establish the tunnels. With these exchanges complete, the VPN tunnels are now able to be established and routes propagated.

Site-to-site VPN is configurable as mesh or hub and spoke or a combination of the two. All hubs will form a full mesh of VPN tunnels between them. A typical use case for a hub site is a site that provides access to corporate applications and/or aggregates connections such as a data center. Offices or branch sites are typically configured as spokes. Spokes establish VPN tunnels only to hub sites, meaning traffic between spoke sites is routed via hub sites. If there is a lot of traffic between branch sites, it might make more sense to have these sites also configured as hubs. Configuring all sites as hubs results in a full-mesh topology.

MXs can have multiple WAN uplinks and can be deployed as an HA pair, allowing for automatic failover. For maximum scalability, it is recommended that you use dedicated MXs as hubs configured in VPN Concentrator mode (**Security & SD-WAN > Addressing & VLANs**) and to use a hub-and-spoke topology because this minimizes the number of tunnels required.

Follow these steps to configure a site-to-site VPN using Meraki MX:

Step 1. Log in to Meraki Dashboard (https://dashboard.meraki.com).

Step 2. You need at least one site configured as a hub. Ensure the hub site network is selected from the **Network** drop-down menu on the left, and navigate to **Security & SD-WAN > Site-to-Site VPN** (under Configure).

Step 3. From the options listed in Figure 9-2, next to **Type**, select **Hub (Mesh).** An exit hub is not required in this example. Exit hubs are used as the default gateway in a full-mesh topology. You may see this referred to in Meraki documentation as *full-tunneling*.

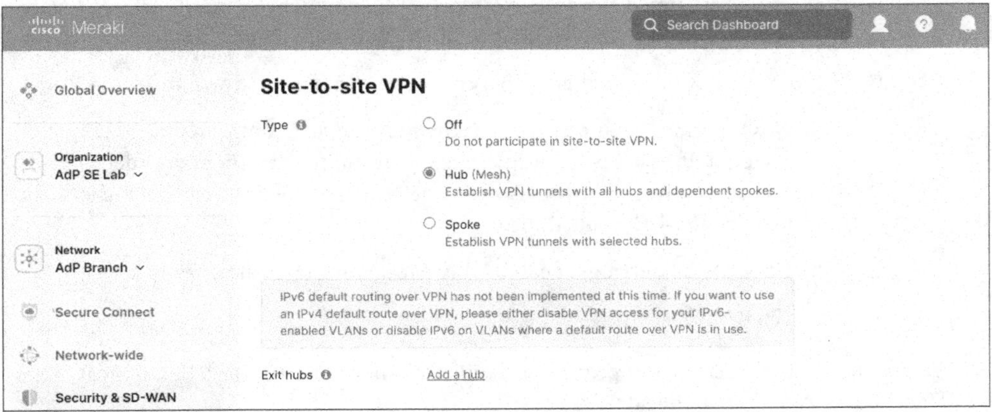

Figure 9-2 *Configuring a Site-to-Site VPN Hub Site in Meraki Dashboard*

Step 4. Scroll down and enable **VPN Mode** on any subnets that need to be advertised over the VPN, as demonstrated in Figure 9-3. Typically, all subnets would be part of the VPN. Leave all other settings as their defaults and click **Save** to save these changes.

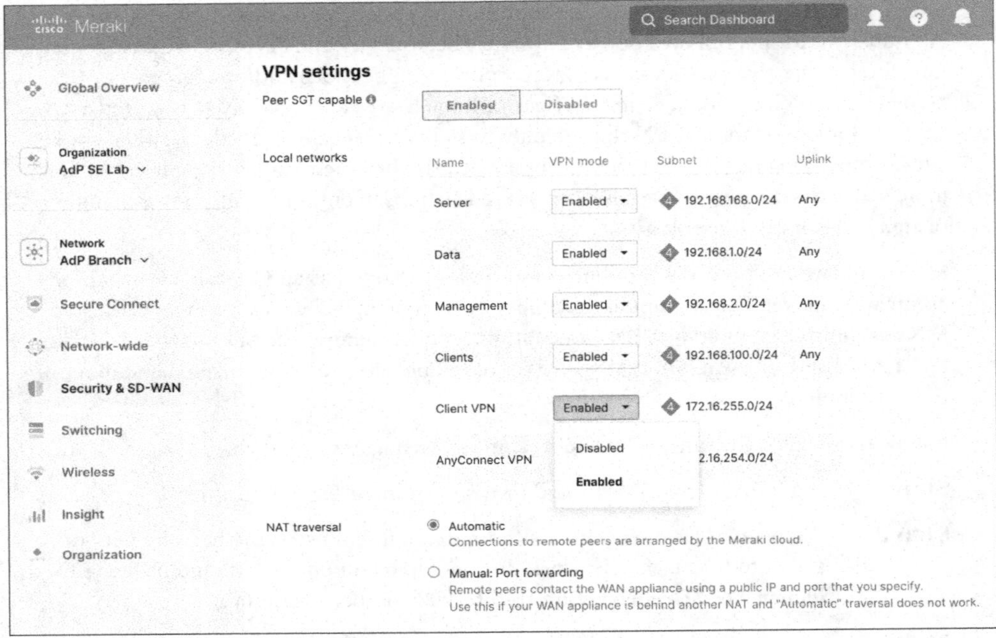

Figure 9-3 *Enabling VPN Mode on Subnets for the Site-to-Site VPN Hub Site in Meraki Dashboard*

Step 5. Next, we demonstrate how to configure a spoke site. Ensure the spoke site network is selected from the **Network** drop-down menu on the left. Navigate to **Security & SD-WAN > Site-to-Site VPN** (under Configure).

Step 6. From the options listed next to **Type**, select **Spoke**, as shown in Figure 9-4.

a. Next to **Hubs**, you can see that the hub site just configured is already selected. If you have multiple hubs, you can reorder them in order of preference. If a hub site will also provide access to the Internet, then check the box for **IPv4 Default Route.**

b. Under **VPN Settings**, enable **VPN Mode** on the local networks.

c. Click **Save.**

You've now completed the setup of a basic hub-and-spoke site-to-site VPN. Repeat Steps 5 and 6 for any other spoke sites.

Follow these steps to verify that the site-to-site VPN is working:

Step 1. In Meraki Dashboard, navigate to **Security & SD-WAN > VPN Status** (under Monitor).

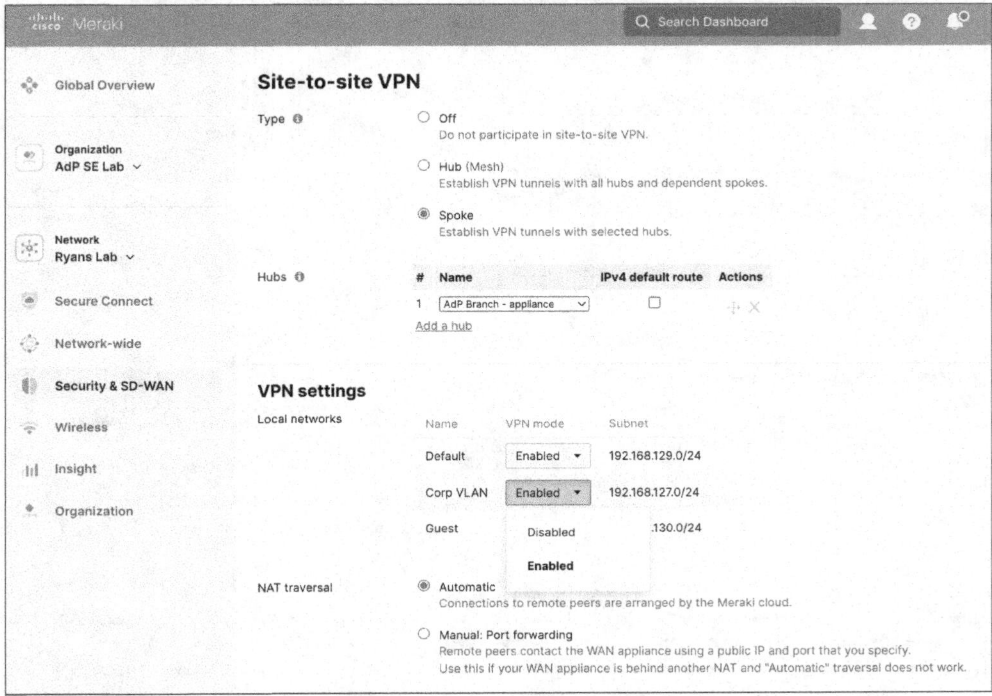

Figure 9-4 *Configuring a Site-to-Site VPN Spoke Site in Meraki Dashboard*

Step 2. On the **VPN Status** page, you can confirm that the VPN tunnel is up, as shown in Figure 9-5. By placing your mouse pointer over the network name under the **Description** column, you can see the latency and usage over that particular VPN tunnel. On the **Exported Subnets** tab, you can confirm the subnets that this site is advertising to the hub site.

Step 3. The next task is to confirm that routes are being received from the hub site. In Meraki Dashboard, navigate to **Security & SD-WAN** > **Route Table** (under Monitor).

Step 4. On the **Route Table** page, under **Destination**, use the **Search by Destination** field to filter on the name of the MX at the hub site. You should see routes listed, as shown in Figure 9-6.

Step 5. Navigate to **Security & SD-WAN** > **Appliance Status** > **Tools**. Next to **Ping**, enter the default gateway address for a subnet received from the hub and click the **Ping** button. As you can see from Figure 9-7, you are able to verify that connectivity to this subnet over the VPN is working.

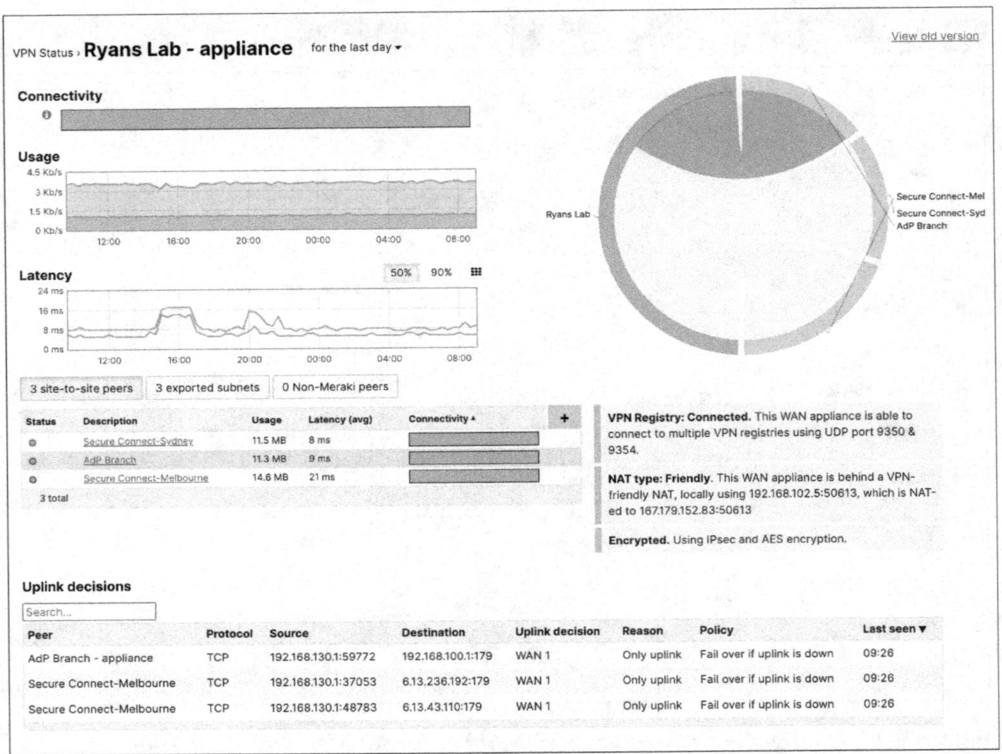

Figure 9-5 *The VPN Status Page in Meraki Dashboard*

Route table Rebuild

Looking for the previous version?

Routes updated as of Today at 10:08 AM.

IP VERSION	SUBNET/PREFIX	NAME	VLAN	NEXT HOP	DESTINATION	TYPE	REPORTED
All	Search by subnet/prefix	Search by name	Search by VLAN ID	Search by network	AdP	All	Current

Stat	Version	Subnet	Name	VLAN	Next hop	Destination	Type
—		172.16.254.0/24	AdP Branch - appliance: AnyConnect VPN	—	AdP Branch - appliance	AdP Branch - appliance	Meraki VPN: VLAN
—		172.16.255.0/24	AdP Branch - appliance: Client VPN	—	AdP Branch - appliance	AdP Branch - appliance	Meraki VPN: VLAN
•		192.168.1.0/24	AdP Branch - appliance: Data	20	AdP Branch - appliance	AdP Branch - appliance	Meraki VPN: VLAN
•		192.168.2.0/24	AdP Branch - appliance: Management	30	AdP Branch - appliance	AdP Branch - appliance	Meraki VPN: VLAN
•		192.168.100.0/24	AdP Branch - appliance: Clients	100	AdP Branch - appliance	AdP Branch - appliance	Meraki VPN: VLAN
•		192.168.168.0/24	AdP Branch - appliance: Server	10	AdP Branch - appliance	AdP Branch - appliance	Meraki VPN: VLAN

6 results

Figure 9-6 *The VPN Routes Being Received from the Hub Site Over a Site-to-Site VPN*

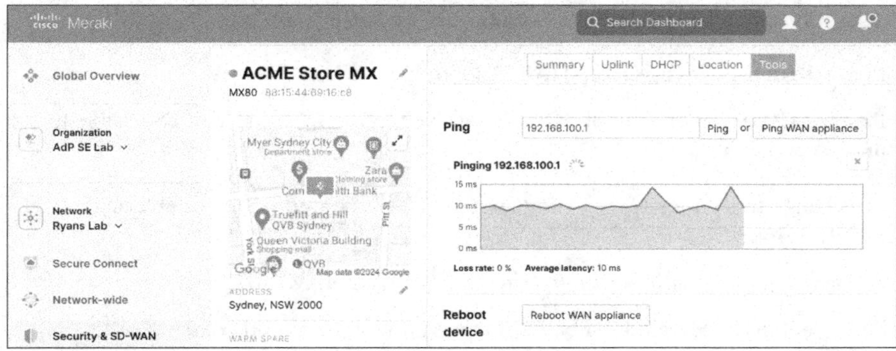

Figure 9-7 *Verifying Connectivity to the Hub Site Over a Site-to-Site VPN*

At this point, you've completed the configuration and verification of site-to-site VPN. For a great guide on Auto VPN best practices, refer to https://documentation.meraki.com/Architectures_and_Best_Practices/Cisco_Meraki_Best_Practice_Design/Best_Practice_Design_-_MX_Security_and_SD-WAN/Meraki_Auto_VPN_General_Best_Practices.

Site-to-Site VPN with Non-Meraki Devices

Meraki MX security appliances can also connect to non-Meraki devices using IPsec. This feature might be required in the following scenarios:

- You need to interconnect Meraki with Cisco devices such as ISR routers and Firepower security appliances.
- You are connecting to cloud providers like AWS and Azure.
- Two Meraki MXs in different organizations need to establish a VPN.
- You are connecting to SASE solutions. Cisco Umbrella, like other SASE solutions, traditionally relied on IPsec tunnels to shift user traffic to the cloud for policy to be applied to it. This is no longer required with Cisco Secure Connect, which natively integrates with Meraki using Auto VPN. You can learn about Cisco Secure Connect in the following chapter.

> **Note** Non-Meraki VPN peers have an organization-wide scope. This means that if multiple MXs connect to the same non-Meraki VPN peer, they will use the same shared secret.

VPN connections to non-Meraki peers have the following requirements:

- Preshared keys are required. Certificates are not supported today.
- There must be IP reachability between local and remote peers over UDP ports 500 and 4500.

The default IPsec policy for new non-Meraki VPN peers is as follows:

- **Phase 1 (IKE Policy):** 3DES, SHA1, DH Group2, lifetime 8 hours
- **Phase 2 (IPsec Rule):** Any of 3DES or AES; either MD5 or SHA1; PFS disabled; lifetime 8 hours

You can change this policy by selecting another preconfigured policy or creating a custom IPsec policy.

Follow these steps to configure site-to-site VPN with a non-Meraki peer:

Step 1. Log in to Meraki Dashboard (https://dashboard.meraki.com).

Step 2. Navigate to **Security & SD-WAN > Site-to-Site VPN** (under Configure).

Step 3. Under **Site-to-Site VPN**, next to **Type**, select **Hub (Mesh)**, as shown in Figure 9-8.

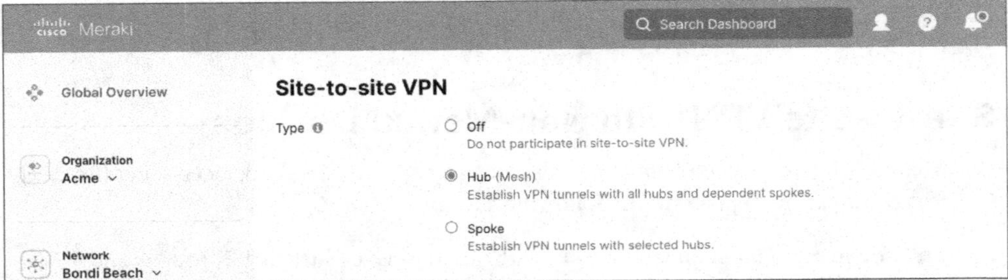

Figure 9-8 *Configuring a Site-to-Site VPN Hub Site for a Non-Meraki Peer in Meraki Dashboard*

Step 4. Scroll down to **VPN Settings** and set **VPN Mode** to **Enabled** for all subnets that need to use this VPN (see Figure 9-9). In this example, these are existing subnets. You can create new subnets in Meraki Dashboard by navigating to **Security & SD-WAN > Addressing & VLANs.**

Step 5. Scroll down to **Organization-wide** settings.

Step 6. To the right of **Non-Meraki VPN Peers**, click **Add a Peer**, as shown in Figure 9-10.

Step 7. A pane slides out from the right with a range of fields to be completed. You need to scroll down to see all of the fields. Let's first focus on the fields shown in Figure 9-11. Enter the following:

- **Name:** Enter a meaningful name for this VPN peer. Here, we have used **Non-Meraki Peer.**

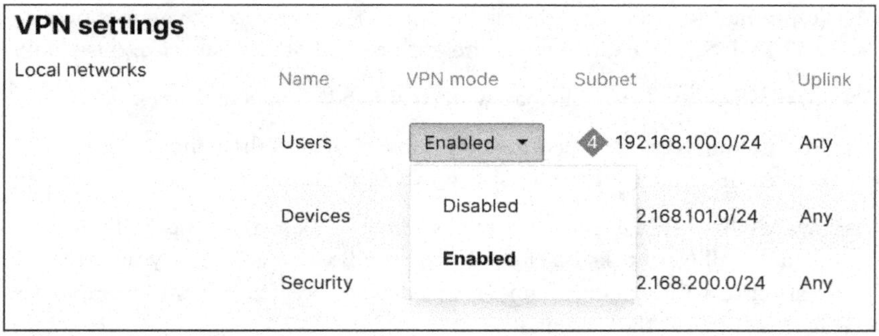

Figure 9-9 *Enabling VPN Mode on Subnets for a Non-Meraki Site-to-Site VPN Peer*

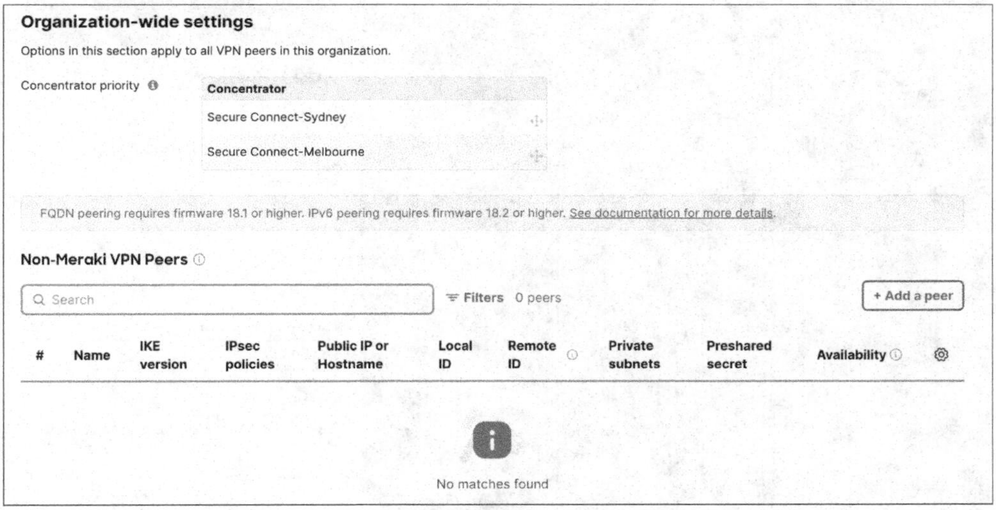

Figure 9-10 *Adding a Non-Meraki VPN Peer in Meraki Dashboard*

- **IKE Version:** Set this to the Internet Key Exchange version required; it must match the remote peer. In this example, we have selected **IKEv2.**
- **Public IP or Hostname:** Enter the IP address or fully qualified domain name (FQDN) of the remote peer.
- **Local ID:** This is what the remote peer will receive as the remote ID for this MX. If this field is left blank, which is the default, then the uplink IP of the MX will be used, not the public IP as you might assume. Some peers may expect this to match the public IP of the MX, a user FQDN (for example, user@domain.com), or FQDN (for example, www.example.com) based on their configuration.[1]

- **(Optional) Remote ID:** You can configure this to match the remote peer's user FQDN, FQDN, or IPv4 address if needed; otherwise, leave this blank.
- **Shared Secret:** This is the password that needs to match the remote peer.
- **Private Subnets:** This identifies the subnets behind the remote peer. You can list individual subnets or specify 0.0.0.0/0 for all subnets.
- **Availability:** This setting determines which MXs can use this VPN. By default, **All Networks** is selected. Tags can be entered where you want to restrict this VPN peer to only certain devices or sites. For this example, we have left this as the default.

Scroll down to **IPSec Policy.**

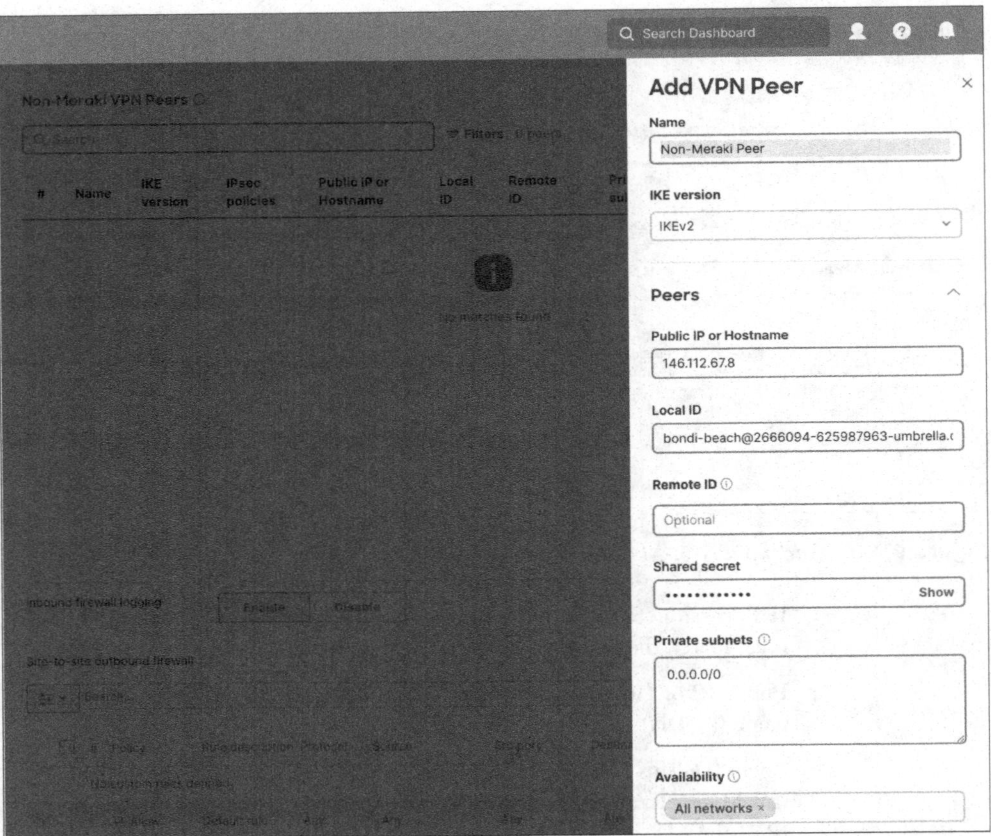

Figure 9-11 *Configuring the Peer Details for a Non-Meraki VPN Peer in Meraki Dashboard.*

Step 8. From the **Preset** drop-down menu, select the one that best meets your use case (see Figure 9-12). These presets populate all the IPsec settings required.

If a suitable preset is not listed, select **Custom** and adjust the IPsec options to match the remote peer.

Click **Add**.

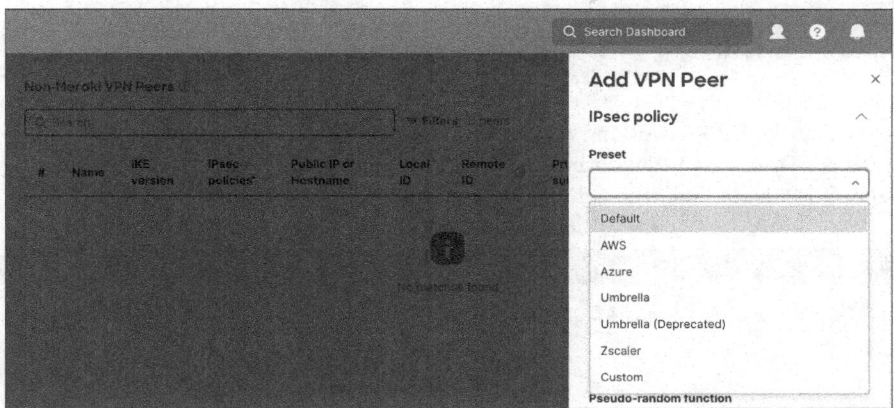

Figure 9-12 *Selecting the IPsec Policy for a Non-Meraki Site-to-Site VPN Peer in Meraki Dashboard*

Step 9. You then return to the **Non-Meraki VPN Peers** section on the **Site-to-Site VPN** page (see Figure 9-13). Click **Save Changes.**

When you use a default route for the private subnets, a pop-up window warns that the most specific routes will be used. Click **Confirm Changes.**

Figure 9-13 *Completing the Configuration of a Non-Meraki VPN Peer in Meraki Dashboard*

You've now completed the configuration of a site-to-site VPN to a non-Meraki peer.

> **Note** Unlike Auto-VPN, which automatically establishes tunnels over both primary and secondary WAN interfaces, non-Meraki VPN connections are established using the primary Internet uplink only. An enhancement has been planned for this, so check with your Meraki specialist if this is something you require.

To verify that the VPN is working correctly, in Meraki Dashboard, navigate to **Security & SD-WAN > VPN Status**; then click the **Non-Meraki Peers** tab (as shown in Figure 9-14). Note the green light under **Status** indicating that the VPN is up.

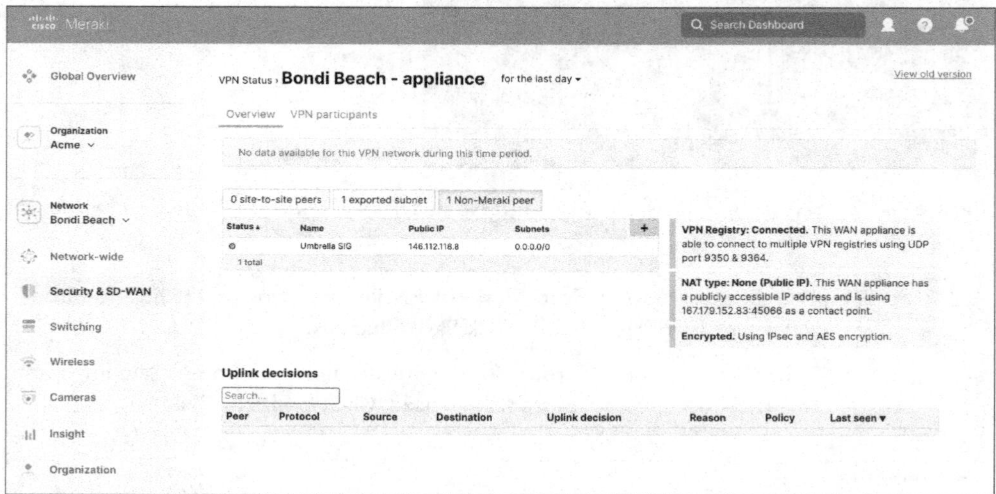

Figure 9-14 *The VPN Status Page in Meraki Dashboard Showing a Non-Meraki VPN Peer*

> **Note** Administrators might need to further restrict IP traffic going over a VPN, especially when VPNs are used to connect to third parties. This restriction is achieved using a site-to-site outbound firewall rule, configured on the Site-to-Site VPN page in Meraki Dashboard (**Security & SD-WAN > Site-to-Site VPN**), as shown in Figure 9-15. Be aware that these are *outbound* firewall rules. This means that if the intention is to deny traffic to a subnet, this subnet should be used as the **Source** in the firewall rule. You are in effect blocking the return traffic; however, this restriction still achieves the same outcome. Site-to-site VPN rules are organization-wide and apply to all VPN peers. If you want the policy to apply only to certain remote sites, specify the local networks for the remote site in the **Destination** field. To learn more about outbound site-to-site firewall rules, refer to https://documentation.meraki.com/MX/Site-to-site_VPN/Site-to-site_VPN_Firewall_Rule_Behavior.

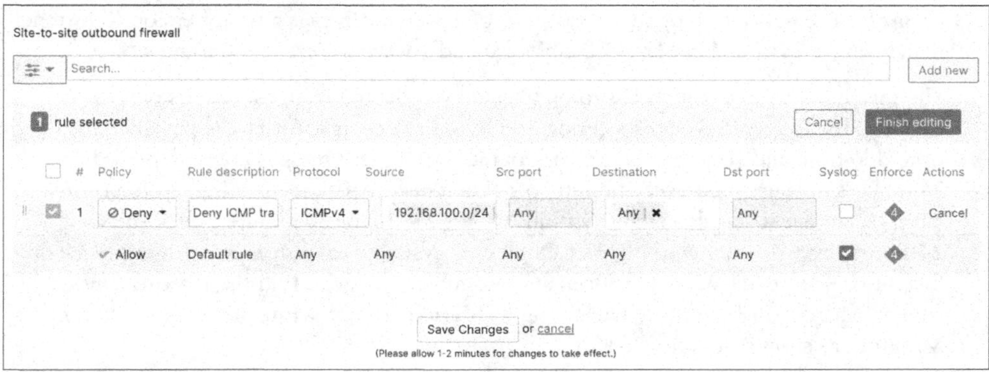

Figure 9-15 *Configuring a Site-to-Site Outbound Firewall Rule in Meraki Dashboard*

You've now completed the configuration and verification of site-to-site VPNs to non-Meraki peers. For more information on this feature, refer to https://documentation.meraki.com/MX/Site-to-site_VPN/Site-to-Site_VPN_Settings#Non-Meraki_VPN_Peers.

ThousandEyes

Not so long ago the majority of business-to-business communication occurred over private WANs, over which organizations had complete control. ThousandEyes began life as a San Francisco startup that believed that the Internet would replace these private networks over time. This would create a problem because businesses would have no visibility into, and no control over, the Internet. The need for an Internet visibility platform has only increased with the shift to the public cloud. Today, businesses rely on Software as a Service (SaaS) and the public cloud heavily for internal and external digital services, all of which exist outside of the organization's control. Mohit Lad and Ricardo Oliveira, former Ph.D. students and founders, describe ThousandEyes as the "Google Maps for the Internet." By being able to map out the path that services traverse over the Internet and into public clouds, organizations can ensure the highest level of digital experience.

Having this level of visibility is something that is encouraged by IT security best practices. The NIST Cybersecurity Framework recommends that organizations monitor external service providers for adverse cybersecurity events (Requirement DE.CM-06). Outages and events like distributed denial-of-service (DDoS) attacks are common occurrences on the Internet. They impact an organization's operations, whether they know it or not. ThousandEyes can detect these events, making administrators aware and enabling them to take corrective actions.

ThousandEyes works by running synthetic tests, tests that are independent of any customer traffic, between agents embedded in networks and in the public cloud. This, in turn, allows ThousandEyes to create a dashboard showing how end-to-end networks are performing. Additionally, ThousandEyes provides a global view of ongoing and historical Internet disruptions in service providers around the world; this is known as *Internet*

Insights. The first phase of the integration of ThousandEyes is a basic version of Internet Insights, now available in Meraki Dashboard and known as *Internet Outages*.

The Internet Outages page is based on telemetry collected from thousands of ThousandEyes agents. The tests conducted by these agents identify the provider, location, duration, and scale of the network outages. Internet Outages covers a period of 24 hours and is updated every minute, providing near real-time visibility. To focus on more recent events, such as those within the last 15, 30, or 60 minutes, click the **Last 24 hours** drop-down menu. Internet Outages is available to customers with either Meraki Insight or Secure SD-WAN Plus licensing. Administrators can find the Internet Outages page in Meraki Dashboard by navigating to **Meraki Insight > Internet Outages** (under Monitor), as shown in Figure 9-16.

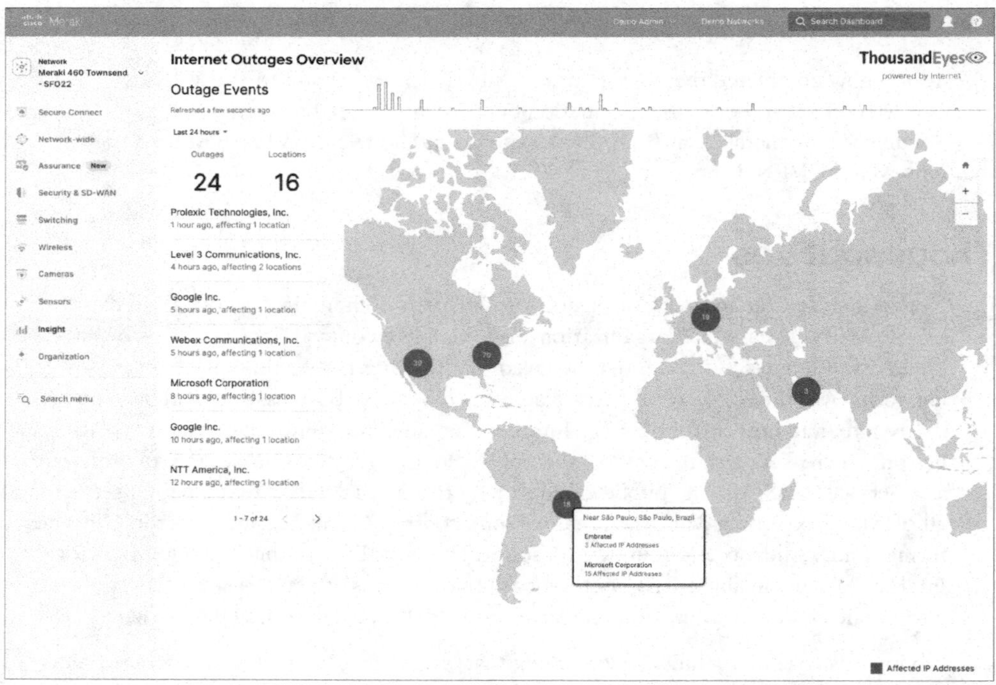

Figure 9-16 *ThousandEyes Internet Outages Dashboard*

It's important to note that the Internet Outages page today is in its first iteration and is relatively basic. Customers who have their own ThousandEyes agents deployed will have access to the full Internet Insights capabilities via the ThousandEyes portal. For more information on the Internet Outages page, refer to https://documentation.meraki.com/MI/Internet_Outages/MI_Internet_Outages_Overview. For the full ThousandEyes experience, including deploying agents on MX appliances and conducting your own continuous, synthetic testing, refer to https://documentation.meraki.com/MI/ThousandEyes/Meraki_MX_ThousandEyes_Configuration_Guide.

Remote-Access VPN

Staff working offsite, whether road warriors or those engaged in hybrid work, need a secure way to access enterprise applications. Meraki MX security appliances support both client VPN and AnyConnect VPN, both of which enable staff on laptops and mobile devices to work remotely. Cisco Secure Connect, which we introduce in the next chapter, also supports client and client-less cloud-hosted VPN access. All of the various Cisco VPN solutions feature encryption to protect the confidentiality of data being transmitted over untrusted networks. For more details on remote access using Secure Connect, refer to https://documentation.meraki.com/CiscoPlusSecureConnect/Cisco__Secure_Connect_Now_Remote_Access, and for client-less remote access, refer to https://documentation.meraki.com/CiscoPlusSecureConnect/Cisco__Secure_Connect_-_Client-less_Remote_Access_(ZTNA).

The sections that follow cover the configuration of client VPN, Sentry VPN, and AnyConnect VPN. Sentry VPN is not actually a different type of VPN, as you will find out; it is just a simple way to roll out client VPN access to your organization. Table 9-1 highlights the differences between client VPN and AnyConnect VPN to help administrators decide which to deploy.

Table 9-1 *Comparison of Available Meraki Remote-Access VPN Types*

	Meraki MX Client VPN	Meraki MX AnyConnect VPN
Feature Support		
Tunnel Protocol	L2TP	TLS/DTLS
Encryption	AES-128/3DES-SHA1	AES-256 & 3DES-168
Authentication methods supported	Meraki Cloud Authentication, RADIUS, Active Directory	SAML, Meraki Cloud Authentication, RADIUS, Active Directory
License required	Any MX license	Requires an additional Cisco AnyConnect license
Sentry VPN support	Yes	No
Split Tunnel support	No	Yes
Requires Cisco AnyConnect or Cisco Secure Client	No	Yes
AnyConnect Network Visibility Module (NVM) supported	No	Yes

Client VPN

Client VPN is Meraki's original remote-access VPN offering and has been available for many years. Client VPN connects clients using an encrypted L2TP tunnel. Client VPN uses Triple Data Encryption Standard (3DES) encryption with Secure Hash Algorithm 1 (SHA1) hashing algorithms for Phase 1 and Advanced Encryption Standard 128 (AES-128)/3DES encryption with SHA1 hashing algorithms for Phase 2. Client VPN is available on all current Meraki MX appliances with any tier of license. Client VPN is supported on a wide range of operating systems, including Mac, Windows, and Linux. This includes support for the native VPN client built into macOS, iOS, and iPadOS.

Client VPN is quick and simple to configure, as we now demonstrate.

Follow these steps to configure client VPN on Meraki MX:

Step 1. Log in to Meraki Dashboard (https://dashboard.meraki.com).

Step 2. Navigate to **Security & SD-WAN > Client VPN** (under Configure).

Step 3. Figure 9-17 shows the default **Client VPN** page. Staying on the **IPsec Settings** tab, select **Enabled** from the **Client VPN Server** drop-down menu.

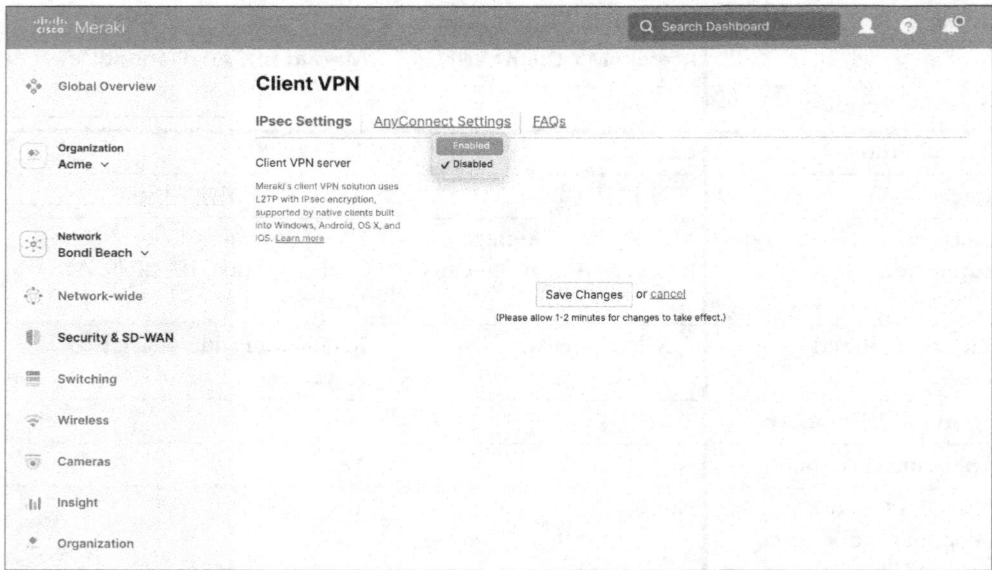

Figure 9-17 *Enabling the Client VPN Server in Meraki Dashboard*

Step 4. All the settings available for the client VPN are then exposed (see Figure 9-18).

- **Hostname:** This is generated automatically. Meraki operates a dynamic DNS server that automatically updates the IP address this resolves to.
- **Subnet:** This is the subnet from which IP addresses will be allocated to users. This subnet needs to be one that is not already used elsewhere in the network. Do a lookup on the **Security & SD-WAN > Route Table** page to confirm that the subnet is available.

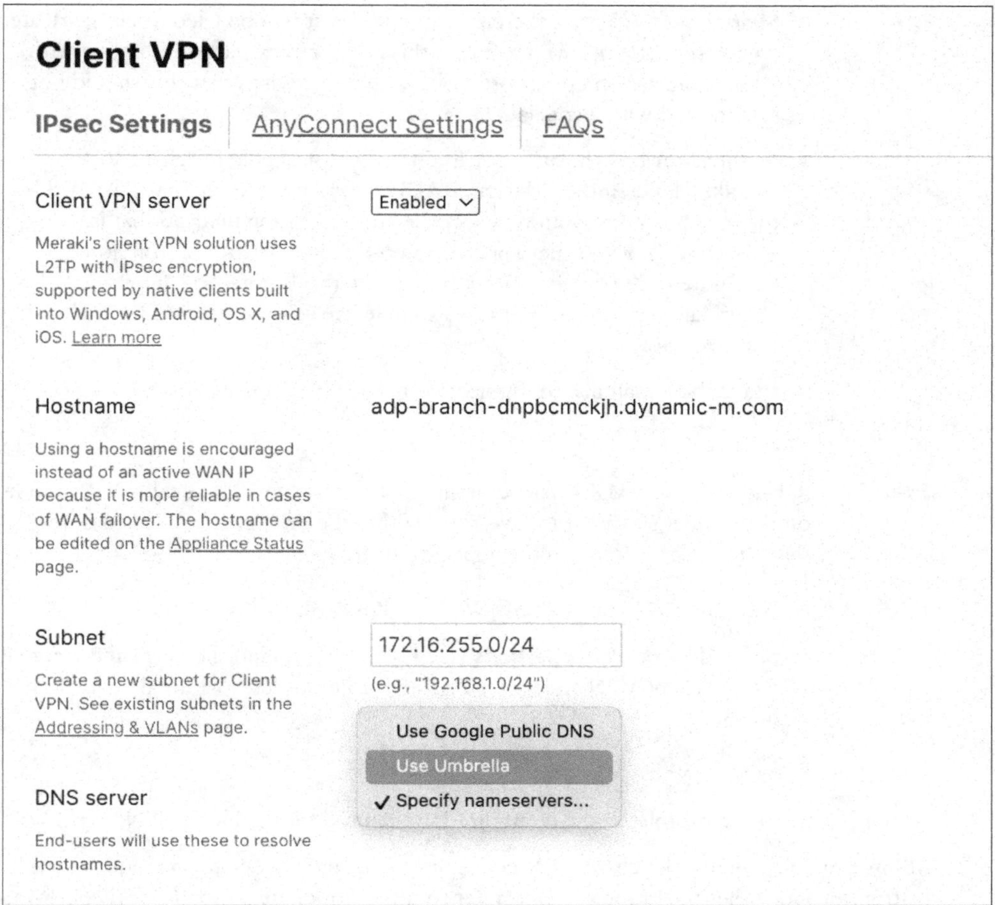

Figure 9-18 *Configuring Client VPN Settings in Meraki Dashboard (Part 1)*

- **DNS Server:** This decides the DNS server IP addresses that will be assigned to client VPN users. Without this, users will not be able to resolve hostnames. The available options are shown in the figure. In this example, we've chosen **Use Umbrella** to assign Cisco's Umbrella DNS servers. Select **Specify Nameservers** if your organization has its own DNS servers and then enter their IP addresses in the **Custom Nameservers** field.

Step 5. Scroll down to **WINS Server** (see Figure 9-19).

- **WINS Server:** Leave as **No WINS Servers.** WINS is not required because DNS will be used instead.
- **Shared Secret:** This is the pre-shared key that will be used to authenticate connection attempts. Ensure that this is a complex password in line with your organization's password policy. Meraki advises that this should not start or end with a special character.
- **Authentication:** The authentication options available for client VPN are Meraki Cloud Authentication, RADIUS, or Active Directory; RADIUS is the recommended option. Select the authentication method that is appropriate for your network. For step-by-step instructions on how to configure each of these authentication methods, refer to Chapter 7, "User Authentication." For this example, we've used **Meraki Cloud Authentication.**
- Leave the remaining configuration options as their defaults.

Click **Save.**

Step 6. (Optional) If this MX is participating in a site-to-site VPN, enable VPN mode on this subnet so that it is advertised within the organization. This ensures that VPN users can reach the applications they need.

a. Navigate to **Security & SD-WAN > Site-to-Site VPN.**

b. Scroll down to **VPN Settings** (see Figure 9-20). Find the new subnet added for the client VPN and select **Enabled** from the **VPN Mode** drop-down menu.

c. Click **Save.**

At this point, you've completed the configuration required for the client VPN.

In this example, we test the client VPN configuration using macOS. If you require instructions for other operating systems, refer to https://documentation.meraki.com/MX/Client_VPN/Client_VPN_OS_Configuration. Follow these steps to verify that the client VPN is now functioning.

Step 1. Navigate to **System Settings > VPN.**

Step 2. Click the **Add VPN Configuration** drop-down menu and select **L2TP over IPSec...** to show the window in Figure 9-21.

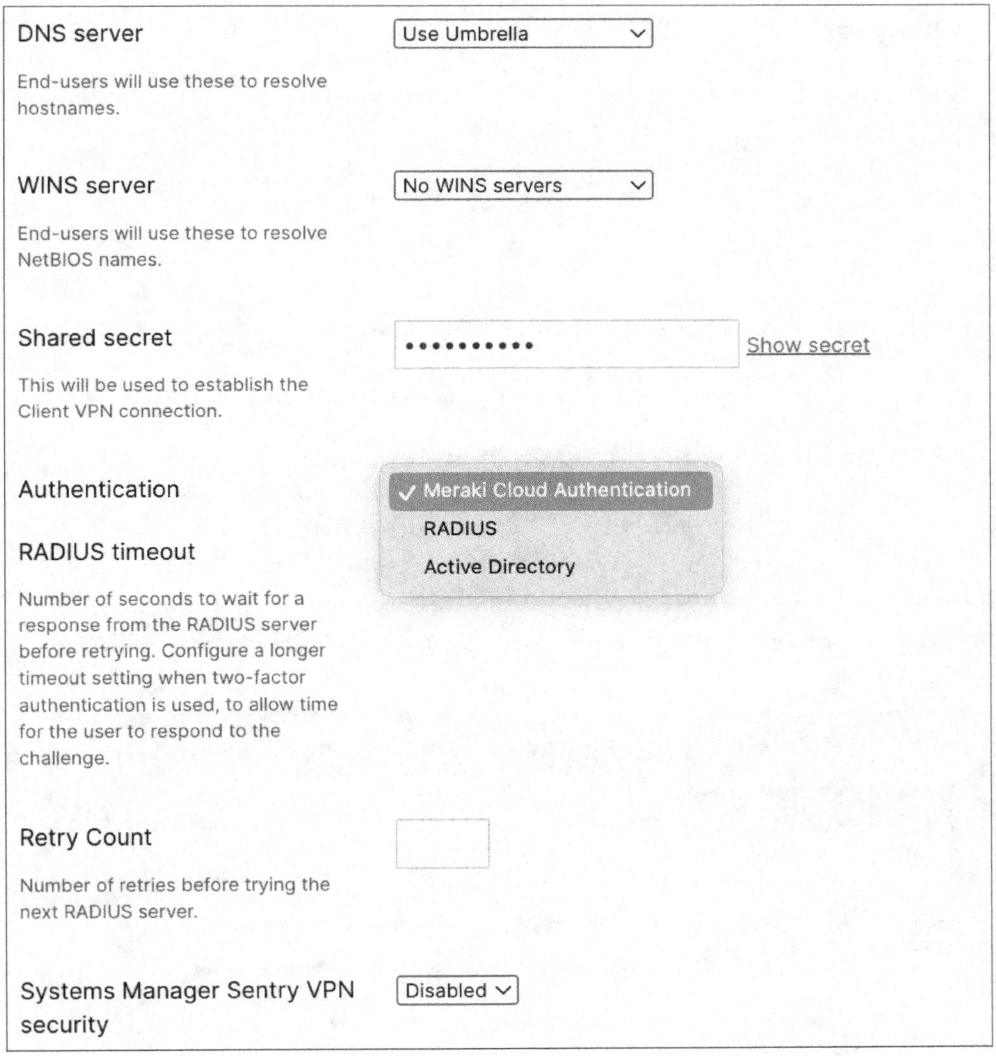

DNS server
Use Umbrella

End-users will use these to resolve hostnames.

WINS server
No WINS servers

End-users will use these to resolve NetBIOS names.

Shared secret
•••••••••• Show secret

This will be used to establish the Client VPN connection.

Authentication
✓ Meraki Cloud Authentication
RADIUS
Active Directory

RADIUS timeout

Number of seconds to wait for a response from the RADIUS server before retrying. Configure a longer timeout setting when two-factor authentication is used, to allow time for the user to respond to the challenge.

Retry Count

Number of retries before trying the next RADIUS server.

Systems Manager Sentry VPN security
Disabled

Figure 9-19 *Configuring Client VPN Settings in Meraki Dashboard (Part 2)*

Step 3. Enter the following details:

- **Display Name:** This is a meaningful name that identifies this VPN. It is recommended that you use the Meraki MX hostname or network name here.
- **Server Address:** This needs to match the **Hostname** from the **Client VPN** page. It is recommended that you copy and paste this address to avoid typos.

Figure 9-20 *Enabling VPN Mode on a New Client VPN Subnet in Meraki Dashboard*

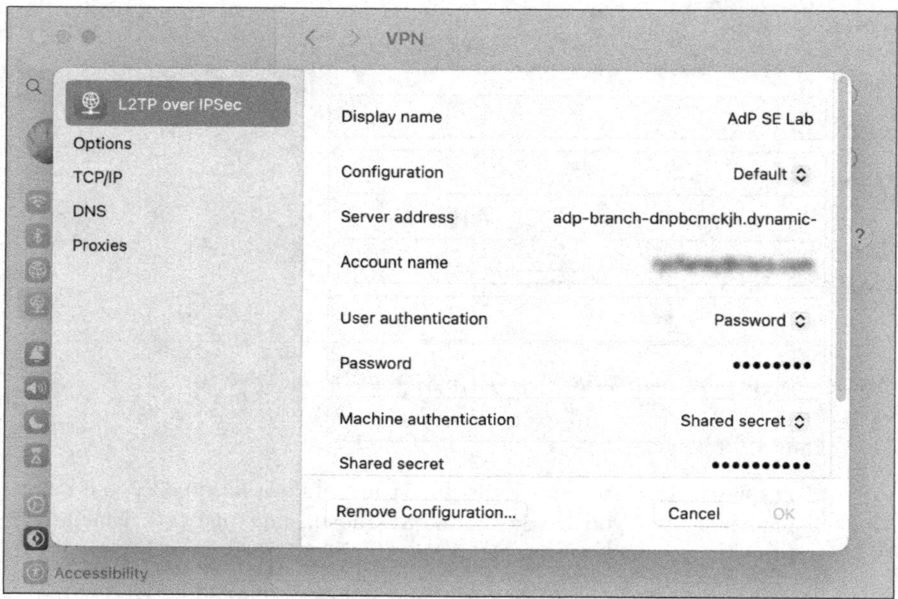

Figure 9-21 *Configuring a VPN Profile on macOS*

- **Account Name:** This is the username to use when authenticating. If you are using Meraki Cloud Authentication, this is the username that has been authorized for client VPN access. If using RADIUS, this typically is a user that is configured in your identity management solution, like Active Directory or Microsoft Entra ID.
- **User Authentication:** Leave as **Password.**
- **Password:** Enter the password for the user entered in the **Account Name** field.
- **Machine Authentication:** Leave as **Shared Secret.**
- **Shared Secret:** Enter the **Shared Secret** that was used on the **Client VPN** page.
- **Group Name:** This field can be left blank.

Click **OK.**

Step 4. Back on the VPN pane, to connect, click the slider to the right of the VPN profile just added, as shown in Figure 9-22. A green icon with **Connected** and a connection timer appear after the connection has been successfully established.

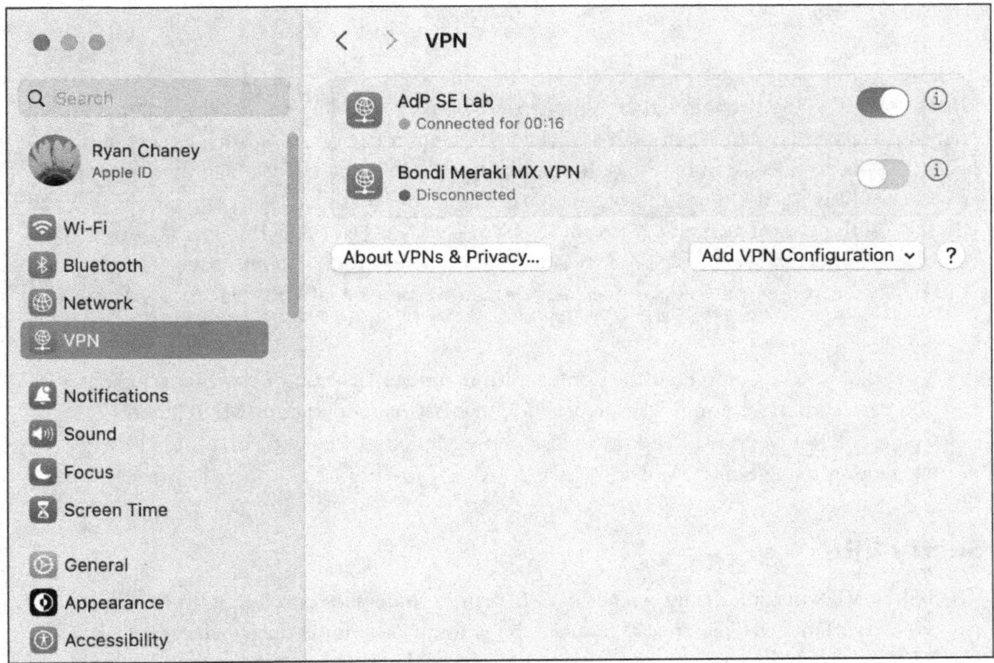

Figure 9-22 *Successfully Connecting to a Client VPN Using macOS*

Step 5. Administrators can see which users are connected using the **Clients** page in Meraki Dashboard (**Network-wide > Clients**). Filter on client VPN users by clicking the **Search...** drop-down menu. Set the **Client Type** to **Client VPN**, as shown in Figure 9-23.

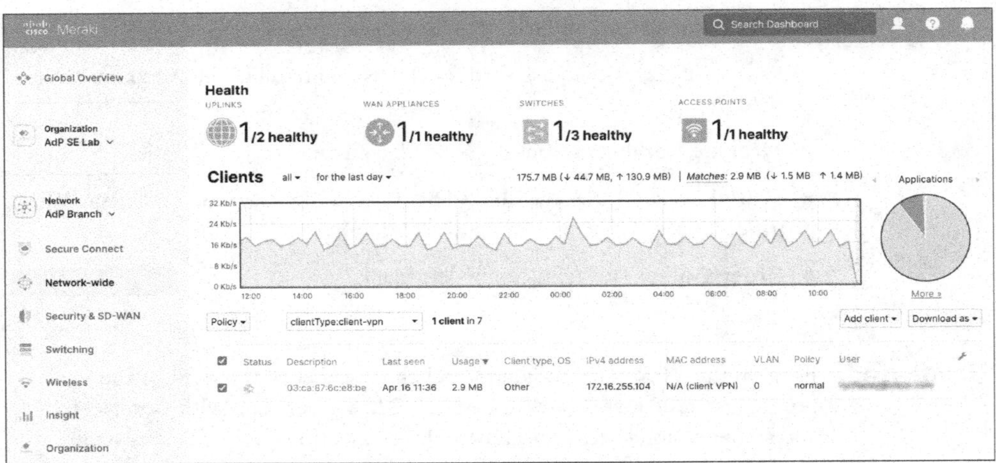

Figure 9-23 *The Clients Page in Meraki Dashboard Showing the Successfully Connected Client*

> **Note** NIST 800-53 requires that administrators have the ability to disconnect or disable remote access to systems. This can be achieved in a number of ways, such as setting the client VPN server back to disabled. Individual user access can be disabled wherever the user account is hosted. For example, if you're using Meraki Cloud Authentication, you can do this on the User management portal (**Network-wide > Users**). If the user is currently online, their access can be blocked by selecting the user on the **Clients** page. Then, from the **Policy** drop-down menu (see Figure 9-24), select **Block List** and then **Apply Policy**.

Now that you've completed the configuration and verification of the Meraki client VPN, you can learn more about it at https://documentation.meraki.com/MX/Client_VPN/Client_VPN_Overview. Read on to learn how Meraki makes implementing client VPN even easier using Sentry VPN.

Sentry VPN

Sentry VPN automatically pushes a VPN profile to devices enrolled with Meraki Systems Manager. This greatly reduces the amount of administrative effort to roll out VPN access. Note that to use Sentry VPN, the authentication type must be Meraki Cloud Authentication. Currently, Sentry VPN is supported only with client VPN, not

AnyConnect VPN. If you are using AnyConnect VPN on Meraki MX or a non-Meraki VPN solution, use a VPN settings payload in a Systems Manager profile instead.

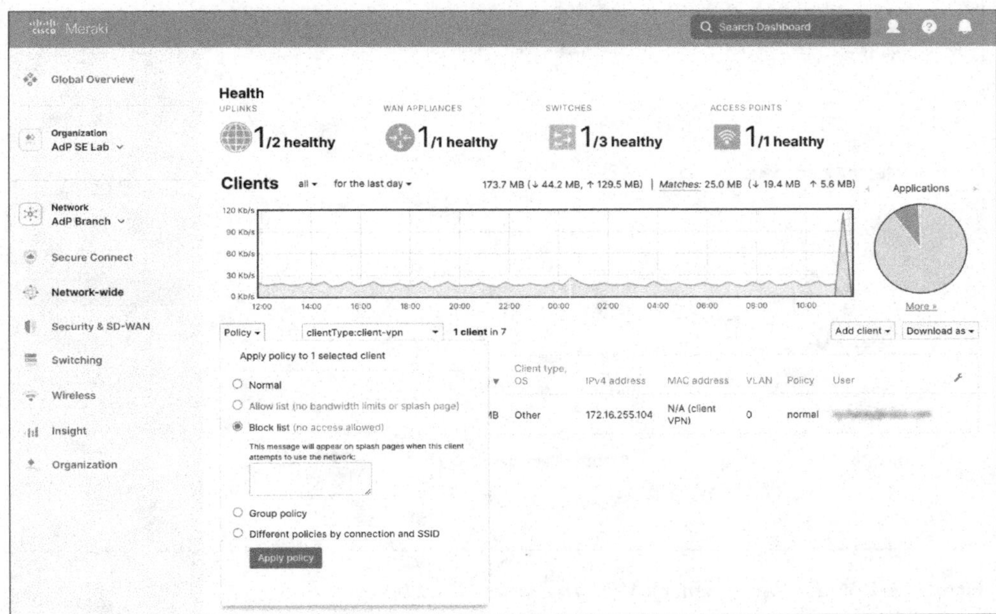

Figure 9-24 *Blocking a Client VPN User*

As a prerequisite, complete the steps in the earlier "Client VPN" section. Only a slight change is then required to enable Sentry VPN. Refer to Chapter 11, "Securing End-User Devices," for the steps to configure Systems Manager and enroll devices.

Follow these steps to configure Sentry VPN:

Step 1. Log in to Meraki Dashboard (https://dashboard.meraki.com).

Step 2. Navigate to **Security & SD-WAN > Client VPN** (under Configure).

Step 3. Staying on the **IPsec Settings** tab, scroll down to **Systems Manager Sentry VPN Security** and select **Enabled** from the drop-down menu, as shown in Figure 9-25. This exposes the **Systems Manager Sentry VPN Security** section.

Step 4. Scroll down to **Systems Manager Sentry VPN Security** (see Figure 9-26).

a. Under **Network Name**, click **Add Sentry Network** to select the Meraki network containing the Systems Manager devices. In this example, the Systems Manager devices are in a network called **Systems Manager**.

b. Customize the **Scope** and **Tags** to suit. In this example, we've set the scope to **All Devices**.

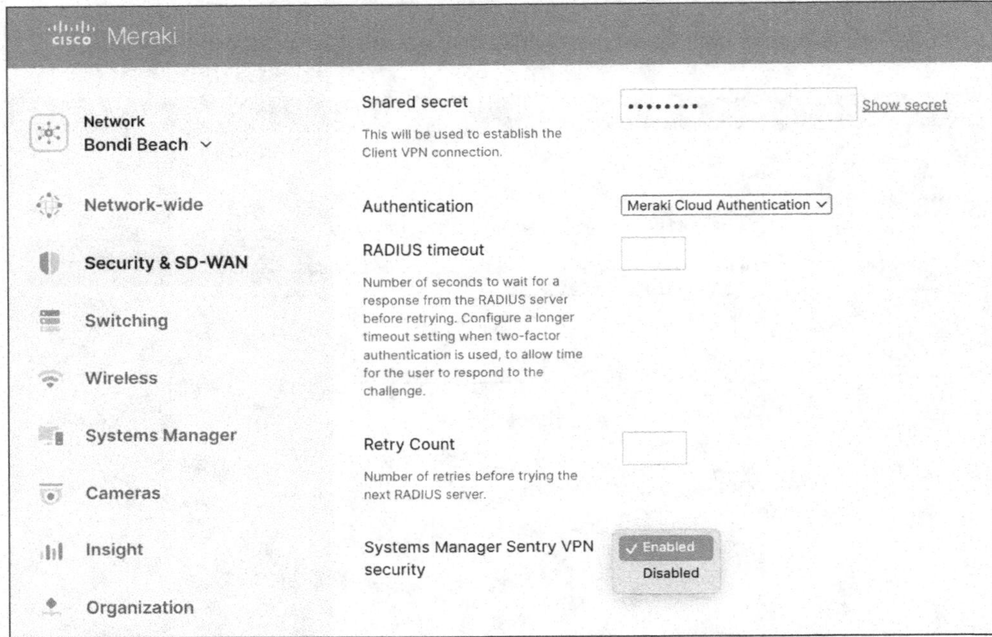

Figure 9-25 *Enabling Sentry VPN in Meraki Dashboard*

c. Check **Send All Traffic.**

d. Typically, a proxy server would not be required. Configure this setting if necessary.

e. Click **Save Changes.**

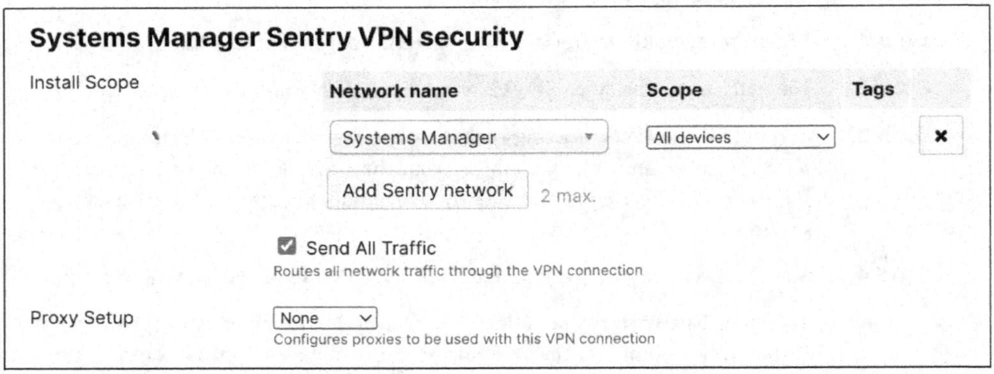

Systems Manager Sentry VPN security
Install Scope
Network name
Scope
Tags
Systems Manager
All devices
Add Sentry network
2 max.
Send All Traffic
Routes all network traffic through the VPN connection
Proxy Setup
None
Configures proxies to be used with this VPN connection

Figure 9-26 *Configuring Sentry VPN on the Client VPN Page in Meraki Dashboard*

You've now completed the configuration of Sentry VPN. It will take a little while for the devices to check in and receive their profile updates. You can speed up this process by navigating to **Systems Manager > Devices**, selecting **All Devices**, and then selecting **Sync Profiles** from the **Command** menu.

Follow these steps to verify Sentry VPN:

Step 1. Start by checking the profiles received by your devices. We demonstrate this using Apple iOS 17. Navigate to **Settings > General > VPN & Device Management > Meraki Systems Manager** (under MOBILE DEVICE MANAGEMENT). In the list next to **Contains**, you should see **VPN Settings** listed, as shown in Figure 9-27.

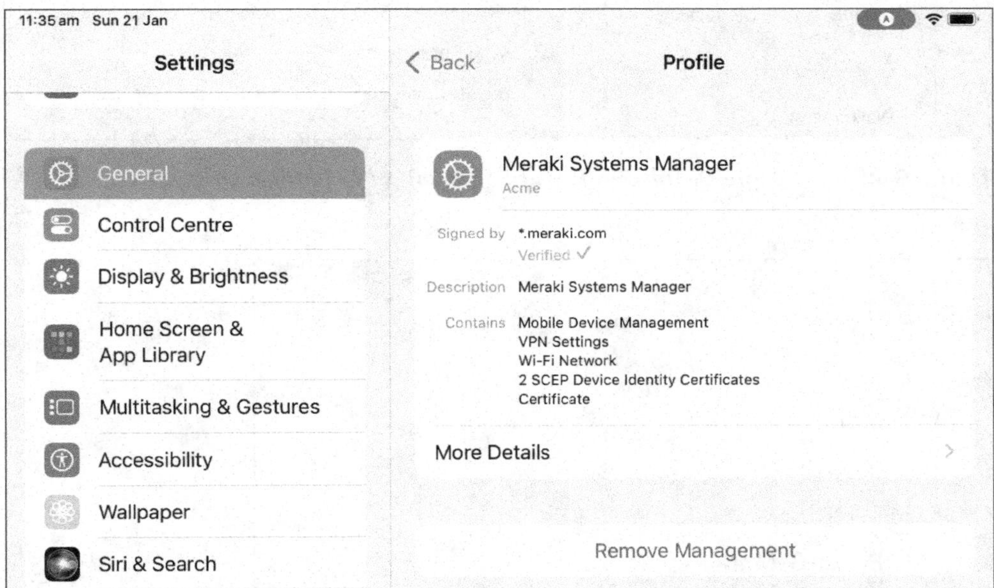

Figure 9-27 *A Meraki Systems Manager Profile with VPN Settings on an iOS Device*

Step 2. Staying on the **Profile** page, click **More Details**.

Under **VPN SETTINGS**, you can see the VPN profile with the hostname of the Meraki MX security appliance in brackets, as shown in Figure 9-28.

Step 3. Navigate to **Settings > General > VPN & Device Management.** Then click **VPN** (see Figure 9-29).

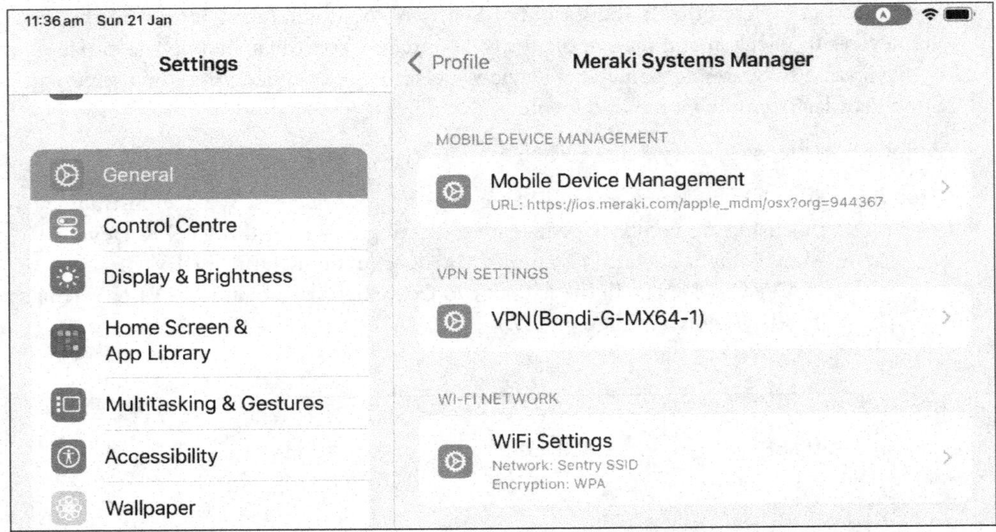

Figure 9-28 *The More Details Profile Page Showing VPN Settings on an iOS Device*

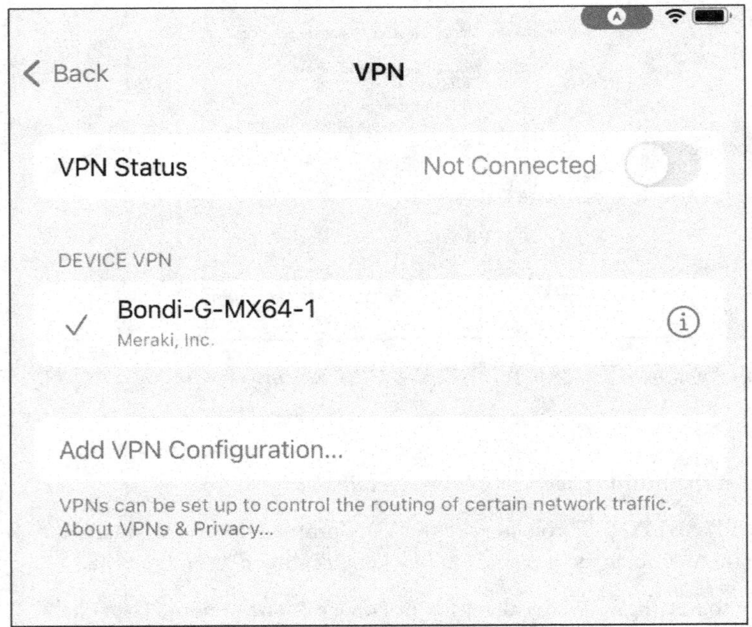

Figure 9-29 *VPN Settings Pane on an iOS Device Showing a Preconfigured Meraki VPN*

Step 4. Before testing, ensure that you are not connected to the Wi-Fi at the same location as the Meraki MX appliance where the VPN terminates. To connect, swipe the **VPN Status** slider to the right. The VPN will connect without any user intervention.

Once you're successfully connected, the **VPN Status** will change to **Connected**, as shown in Figure 9-30. Additionally, you will see **VPN** displayed in the top right next to the battery status.

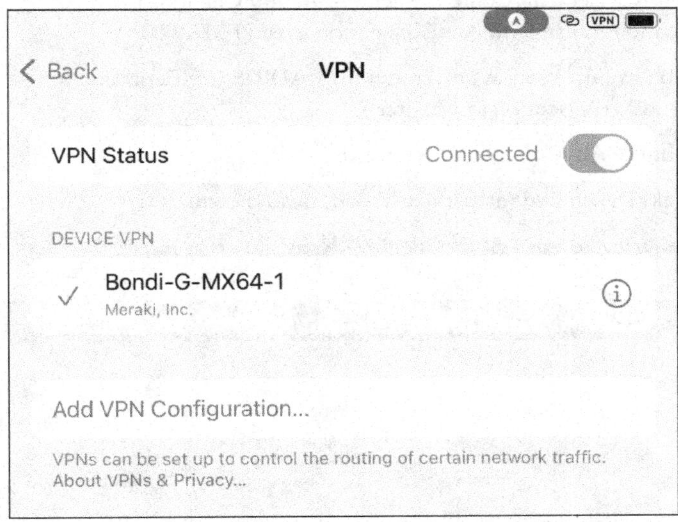

Figure 9-30 *VPN Settings Pane on an iOS Device Showing a Successful VPN Connection*

The configuration and verification of Sentry VPN are now complete. To connect to a VPN using an Android device (9.0+), navigate to **Settings > Network & Internet > VPN**; then tap the VPN name and tap **Connect**. To learn more about Meraki Systems Manager, refer to Chapter 11.

AnyConnect VPN

Cisco AnyConnect is Cisco's more modern SSL/DTLS-based VPN solution. AnyConnect has existed for over a decade and is used by over 400 million people globally. Cisco introduced AnyConnect VPN on the Meraki MX in 2022. Cisco AnyConnect offers a number of improvements to the original client VPN, as highlighted previously in Table 9-1. An additional practical benefit for customers running a mix of Cisco (Cisco Secure Firewall, ISR) and Meraki (Z, MX, or Secure Connect) is the ability to run a common VPN client on all end-user devices. For customers considering a Meraki MX–based remote-access VPN solution, Cisco's recommendation is to deploy AnyConnect VPN.

AnyConnect VPN is supported on all current MX platforms, including vMX running at least firmware version 16.16. This excludes MX64(W) and MX65(W), which require at least firmware version 17.6.

AnyConnect cannot be enabled on the same WAN uplink as the NAT exceptions (No NAT) feature and is not supported on the cellular interface. If VPN is required over a cellular connection, the recommendation is to add a Meraki MG cellular gateway in IP Passthrough mode.

Cisco Secure Client (formerly Cisco AnyConnect Secure Mobility Client) is the recommended VPN client application to use with AnyConnect on Meraki MX.

The following configuration example follows on from the "RADIUS Configuration for AnyConnect VPN with Duo MFA" section in Chapter 7.

Follow these steps to configure AnyConnect VPN access:

Step 1. Log in to Meraki Dashboard (https://dashboard.meraki.com).

Step 2. Navigate to **Security & SD-WAN > Client VPN**, as shown in Figure 9-31.

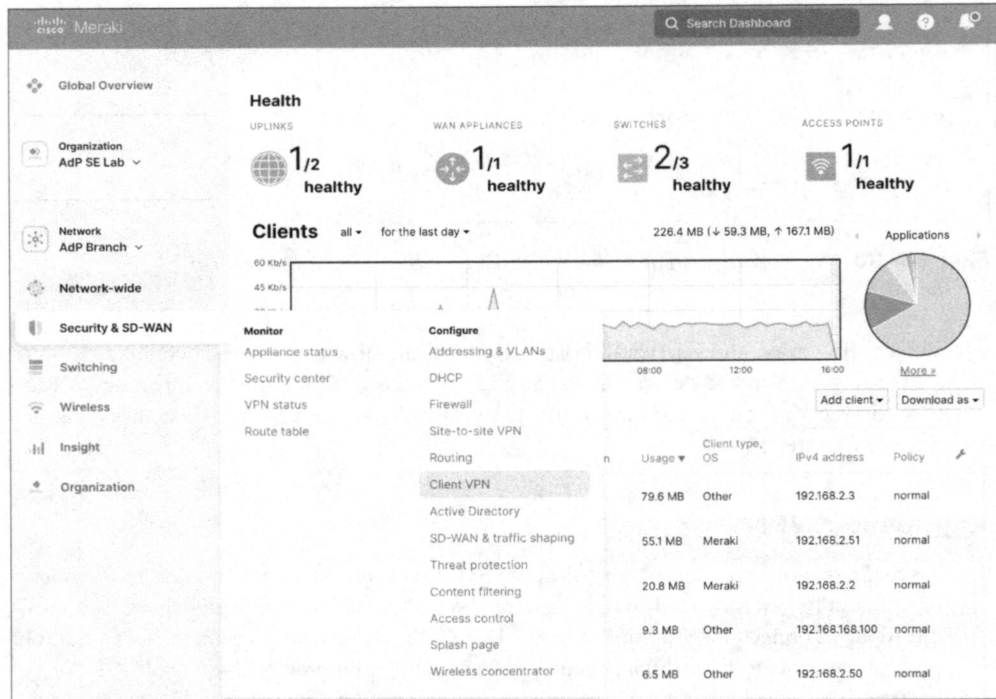

Figure 9-31 *Navigating to the Client VPN Page in Meraki Dashboard*

Step 3. On the **Client VPN** page, click the **AnyConnect Settings** tab. If you are prompted to accept the license agreement, do this. This is a reminder that you need AnyConnect licenses to use this feature.

Step 4. On the **AnyConnect Settings** page, set **AnyConnect Client VPN** to **Enabled**, as shown in Figure 9-32. This exposes the AnyConnect settings.

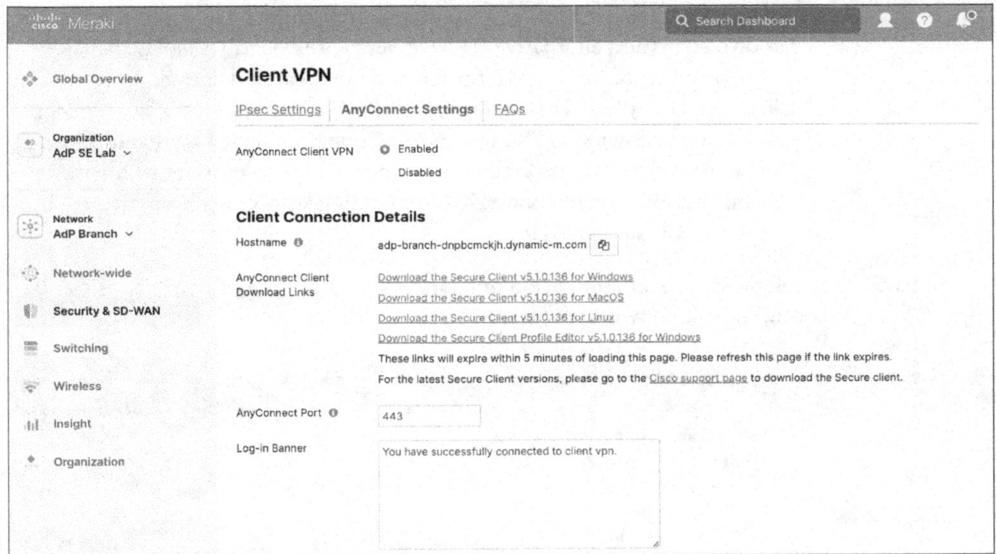

Figure 9-32 *Enabling AnyConnect Client VPN in Meraki Dashboard*

Things to note and/or configure on this page:

- **Hostname:** This is a dynamic DNS hostname to use when connecting and is derived from the MX appliance's hostname. This is the same as we had previously for the client VPN. Note that on this page the URL can be copied using the icon of two overlapping pages on the right.
- **AnyConnect Client Download Links:** Even though it says AnyConnect, this is where you can download the newer Secure Connect Client for the various operating systems. You use these links later in the verification part.
- **AnyConnect Port:** This specifies the port the AnyConnect server will accept and negotiate tunnels on. Leave this setting as the default (443). If other web services need to use port 443 on this MX, it's recommended that you terminate the VPN users on another MX. This way, users don't have to remember to change the port when configuring their VPN client.
- **Log-in Banner:** This pop-up message is displayed to users after they have successfully connected. Tailor this message to suit your organization's

requirements. In this example, we leave this as the default. To disable the log-in banner, simply leave the banner field blank.

- **Profile Update:** Administrators have the option of pushing an AnyConnect profile to clients after they have authenticated. A number of things can be part of the AnyConnect profile, including always-on VPN, start before logon, and certificate enrollment. Perhaps the most common reason to deploy AnyConnect profiles is so that administrators can preconfigure the list of backup and alternative VPN servers with friendly display names. These profiles are in an XML format and are created using the Secure Client Profile Editor. The Secure Client Profile Editor can be downloaded using the last download link under **AnyConnect Client Download Links.** For more information on creating AnyConnect profiles, refer to https://documentation.meraki.com/MX/Client_VPN/AnyConnect_on_the_MX_Appliance/Client_deployment.

Step 5. Scroll down to **Authentication and Access.** Again, a lot of parameters can be configured, as shown in Figure 9-33.

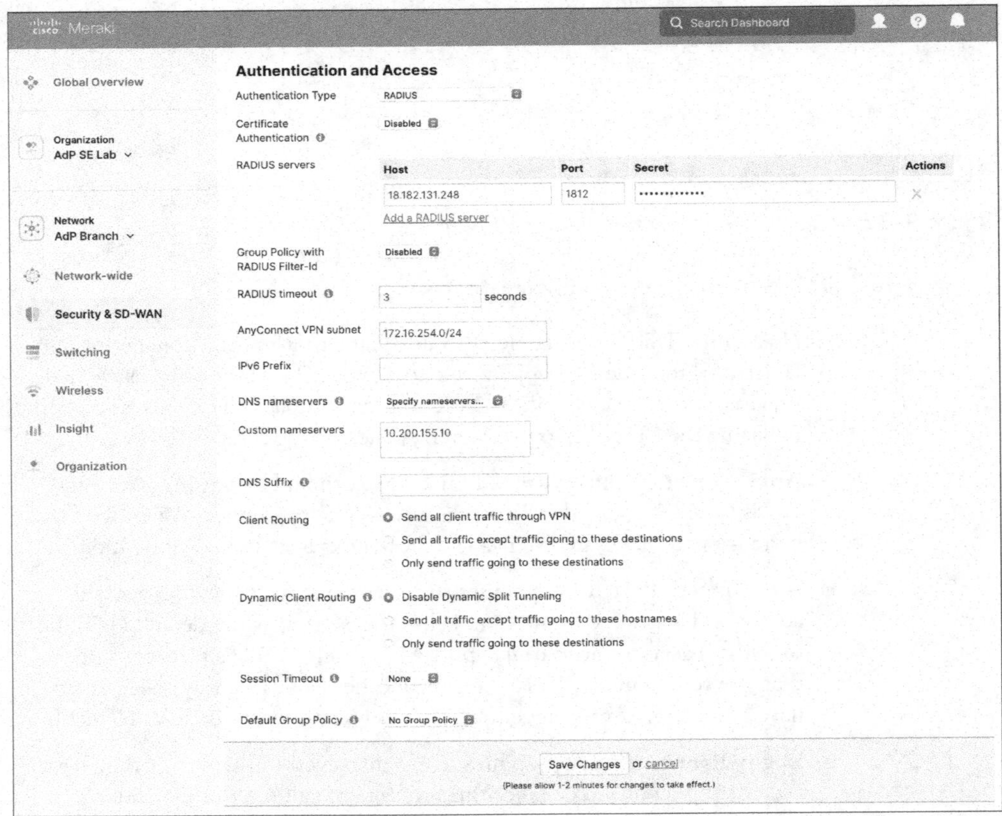

Figure 9-33 *Configuring AnyConnect Authentication and Access Settings for RADIUS*

a. Set the **Authentication Type** to the type required. In this example, we use **RADIUS.** Other supported options include SAML, Meraki Cloud Authentication, and Active Directory. Once selected, the available options on this page will update.

b. If using a third-party CA to issue client certificates, set **Certificate Authentication** to **Enabled** and attach the trusted certificate authority (CA) certificate. CA certificates must be in PEM format. For this example, we have left this as **Disabled** (default).

c. For the RADIUS server, in the **Host** field, enter the IP address or FQDN for Cisco Identity Services Engine (ISE).

d. Enter **1812** in the **Port** field.

e. Enter the RADIUS secret in the **Secret** field. In this example, this is the secret configured for the Meraki MX during the ISE network access device configuration in Chapter 7.

f. **Group Policy with RADIUS Filter-ID** (Optional): Visible when the authentication type is RADIUS, this allows Meraki group policies to be applied based on the filter-ID assigned by the RADIUS servers. For more information on this feature, refer to the "Applying Group Policies Using RADIUS Attributes and Cisco ISE" section in Chapter 8, "Wired and Wireless LAN Security." Enable this setting if using this feature; otherwise, leave disabled.

g. **AnyConnect VPN subnet:** This is the subnet from which IP addresses will be allocated to VPN users when connecting. As for client VPN, ensure this subnet is not used elsewhere already and enable **VPN Mode** on the **Site-to-Site VPN** page after the AnyConnect VPN is configured. In this example, we've used **172.16.254.0/24**. Remember to include the subnet mask in CIDR notation.

h. **IPv6 Prefix** (Optional): This specifies the IPv6 prefix that AnyConnect will use for both terminating VPN tunnels as well as IPv6 traffic inside the tunnel. It requires MX firmware version 18.104 or later.

i. **DNS Nameservers:** The options here are **Use Google Public DNS**, **Use Umbrella**, and **Specify Nameservers.** If your organization has its own DNS servers, specify those like we have here. Otherwise, use the default **Use Google Public DNS.**

j. **Client Routing:** This relates to what has traditionally been referred to as *split tunneling* and controls what client traffic is sent over VPN. Typically, all client traffic is sent over the VPN; this is the default, and the setting we use for this example. These exceptions are useful if users need to connect to local devices, such as home printers, while being connected to AnyConnect.

k. **Dynamic Client Routing:** Dynamic client routing allows for the specification of traffic that should be included or excluded in the VPN tunnel based on domain name rather than subnet. In this example, we leave this as default (Disabled). Configuring Dynamic Client Routing would allow users to directly access cloud services, rather than routing this traffic over the VPN.

l. **Session Timeout** (Optional): The default is **None**; other options are 8 hours, 1 day, 7 days, and Custom. Custom allows for a timeout to be specified (in hours) up to 256 hours.

m. **Default Group Policy** (Optional): If not using filter-ID, use this setting to assign group policies to VPN users. For this example, we've left this as the default (No Group Policy).

Click **Save Changes.**

For more details on any of these options, refer to https://documentation.meraki.com/MX/Client_VPN/AnyConnect_on_the_MX_Appliance.

Now that you've completed the configuration of AnyConnect VPN, follow the next steps to verify that the AnyConnect VPN configuration is working correctly.

Confirming Functionality of AnyConnect VPN Access

Follow these steps to verify that the AnyConnect VPN configuration is working:

Step 1. Download and install the Cisco Secure Client application. You can download this from the **AnyConnect Settings** page in Meraki Dashboard.

Step 2. Copy the **Hostname** from the **AnyConnect Settings** page in Meraki Dashboard. Paste this into the field under **AnyConnect VPN**, as shown in Figure 9-34. Notice how there is no https:// at the beginning like there was for SAML authentication.

Step 3. In the dialog box shown in Figure 9-35, enter the username and password for a user in the Network Access group who has enrolled with Duo and click **OK.**

Step 4. As long as the username and password are correct, Duo will prompt the user to verify their identity using multifactor authentication on their enrolled device. If the login was unsuccessful but the username and password credentials are correct, examine the authproxy.log file on the Active Directory server because this file may explain why. You can find the authproxy.log file in C:\Program Files\Duo Security Authentication Proxy\log.

In this case, everything is functioning as expected. This user is configured with Duo Mobile as the MFA method, so you receive a notification on your mobile device. Here, you need to select the green **Approve** button to approve this access, as shown in Figure 9-36.

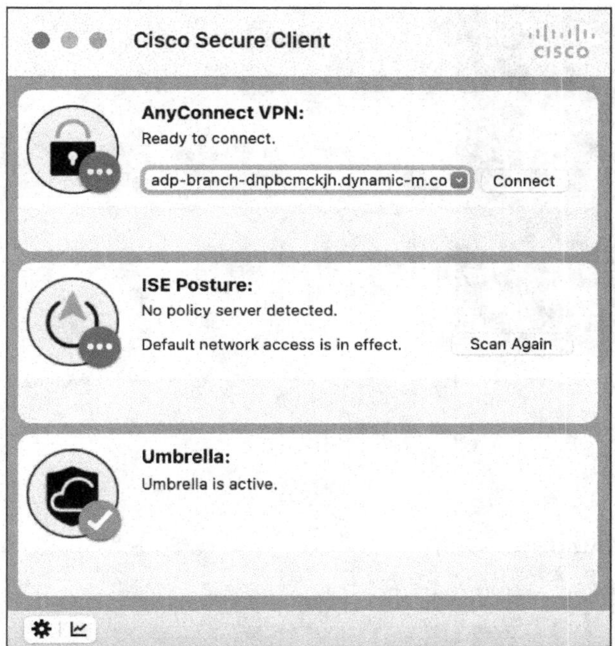

Figure 9-34 *Entering the AnyConnect Server Hostname into the Cisco Secure Client*

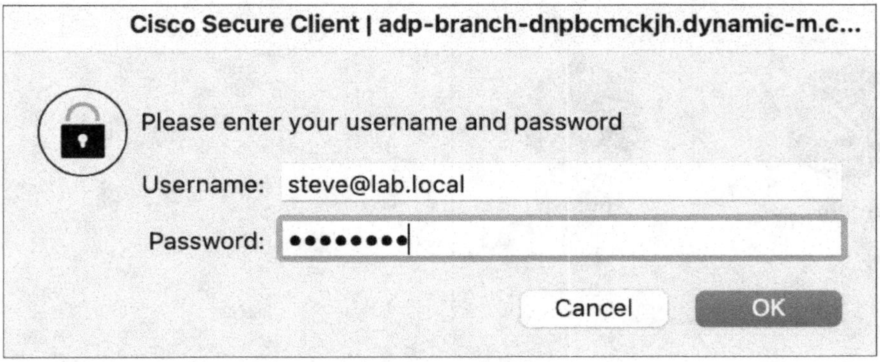

Cisco Secure Client | adp-branch-dnpbcmckjh.dynamic-m.c...

Please enter your username and password

Username: steve@lab.local

Password: ••••••••

Cancel OK

Figure 9-35 *Entering the Username and Password for AnyConnect VPN Using RADIUS*

This approach also works with the Duo app on the Apple Watch, allowing users to approve push notifications directly from their wrist. For a guide on using your Apple Watch with Cisco Duo, refer to https://guide.duo.com/apple-watch.

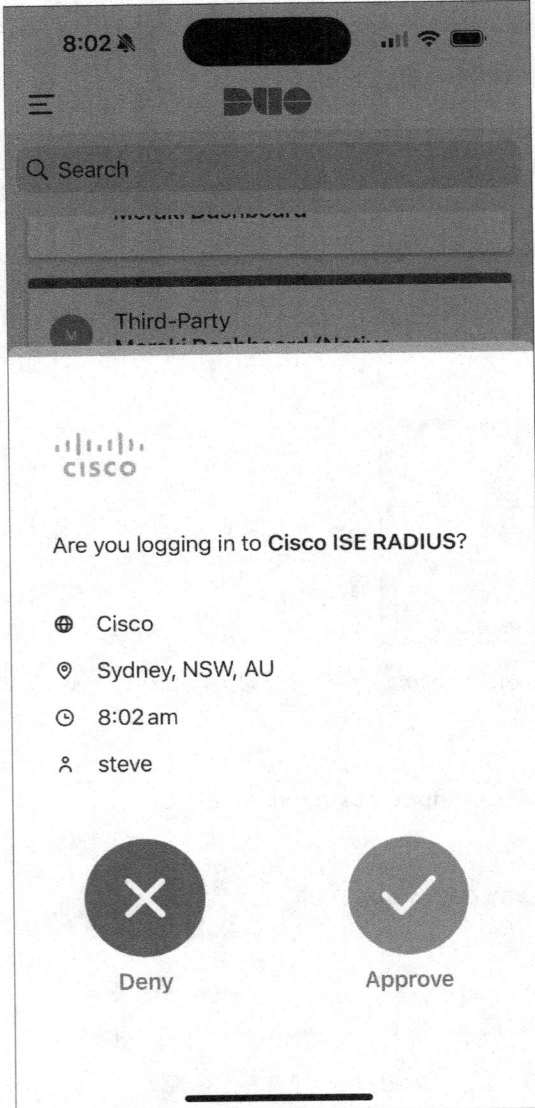

Figure 9-36 *Performing Cisco Duo Multifactor Authentication on a User's Mobile Device*

Step 5. When authentication has been completed, the user will see the configurable banner message shown in Figure 9-37. Click **Accept**.

The Cisco Secure Client now shows the VPN status **Connected** with a connection timer incrementing, as shown in Figure 9-38.

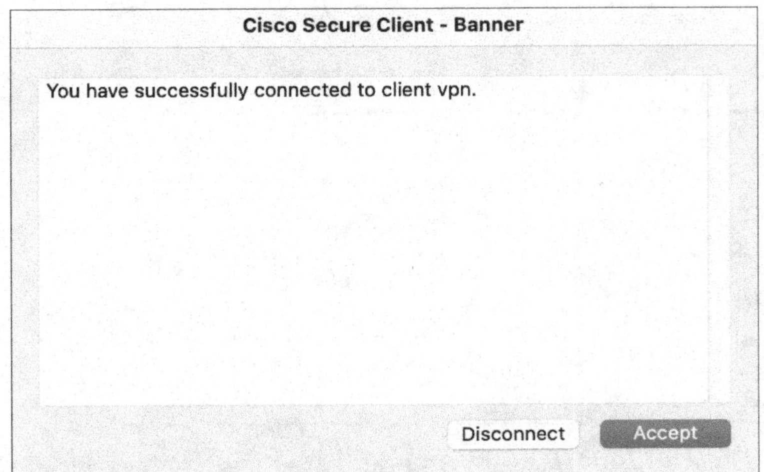

Figure 9-37 *Banner Message During AnyConnect VPN Login Using the Cisco Secure Client*

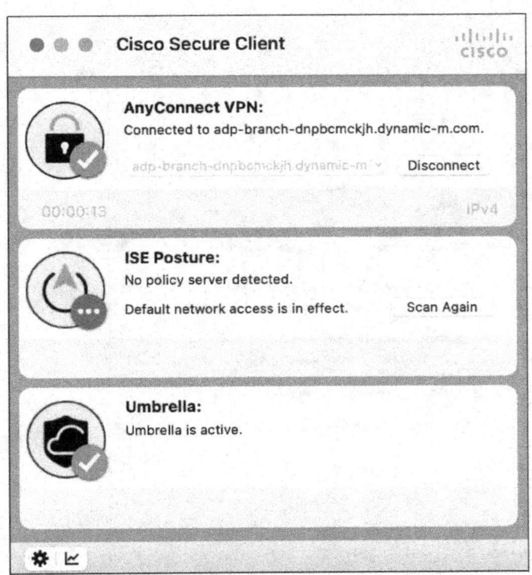

Figure 9-38 *Cisco Secure Client After Successfully Connecting to AnyConnect VPN Using RADIUS*

Step 6. You can also verify this connectivity in Cisco ISE on the RADIUS page (**Menu > Operations > RADIUS**). Under the **Details** column, click the icon for the **Authentication Detail Report**, as highlighted in Figure 9-39.

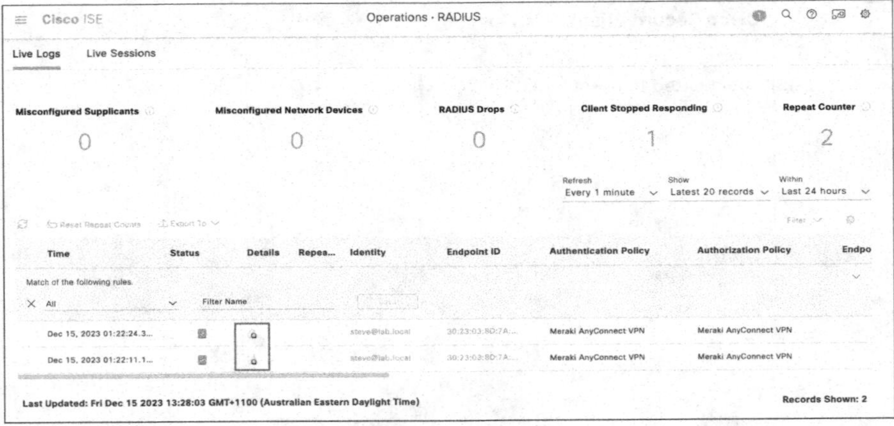

Figure 9-39 *RADIUS Page in Cisco ISE*

Step 7. The **Authentication Detail Report** shows you extensive details about the client and the authentication chain. The report is more than a page; we've shown just the first half of a sample report in Figure 9-40.

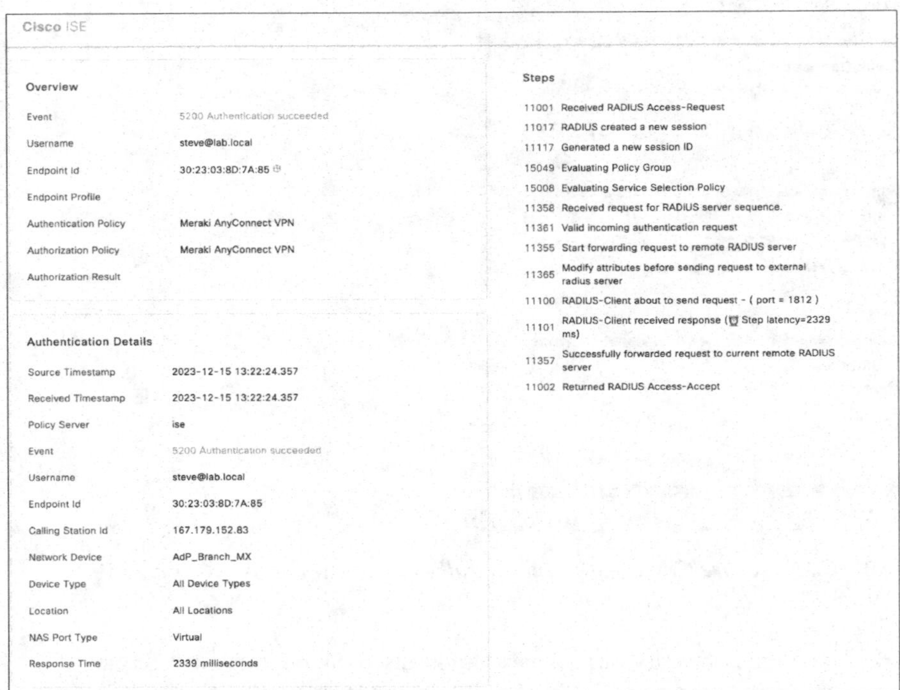

Figure 9-40 *Cisco ISE Authentication Detail Report After a Successful AnyConnect VPN Login*

At this point, you've completed the configuration and verification of AnyConnect on Meraki MX. In addition, in this example, you also verified that RADIUS and Duo MFA are also functioning correctly. To learn more about AnyConnect VPN, refer to the configuration guide available at https://documentation.meraki.com/MX/Client_VPN/AnyConnect_on_the_MX_Appliance.

Restricting Client VPN Traffic

Administrators may wish to restrict what users can access when connecting via a remote-access VPN. This is possible in a number of ways:

- By using the Client Routing feature (see Step 5 of the configuration steps in the "AnyConnect VPN" section). With this feature, which equates to split tunneling, administrators can limit inbound VPN traffic to only certain target subnets.
- By specifying a default group policy on the AnyConnect settings page (see Step 5 of the configuration steps in the "AnyConnect VPN" section).
- By assigning a group policy via the Filter-ID RADIUS attribute when using RADIUS authentication. Refer to Chapter 8 for more details on creating and assigning group policies using RADIUS.
- By using a Sentry policy to assign a group policy (**Network-wide > Group Policies**).
- By using an *Outbound* Layer 3 firewall policy on the Meraki MX (**Security & SD-WAN > Firewall**). This method works for both a client VPN and AnyConnect VPN. It's important to remember that these rules are applied in the outbound direction, meaning that the source will be the local VPN subnet. To learn more about how to configure an outbound firewall rule for this use case, refer to https://documentation.meraki.com/MX/Client_VPN/Restricting_Client_VPN_access_using_Layer_3_firewall_rules.

The following steps use group policies and assume that a group policy has already been created. To learn how to create a group policy, refer to the "Creating a Group Policy" section in Chapter 8 first. Then follow these steps to restrict AnyConnect VPN traffic using a group policy:

Step 1. Log in to Meraki Dashboard (https://dashboard.meraki.com).

Step 2. Navigate to **Security & SD-WAN > Client VPN** (under Configure).

Step 3. Click the **AnyConnect Settings** tab.

Step 4. Scroll down to **Default Group Policy.**

a. From the **Default Group Policy** drop-down menu, select the group policy that you want to apply to all VPN users, as shown in Figure 9-41. In this example, the group policy we've applied is called **Remote_access_VPN_users.** This policy has a Layer 3 firewall rule preventing ICMP traffic from reaching a host with the IP address 10.200.155.10.

b. Click **Save Changes.**

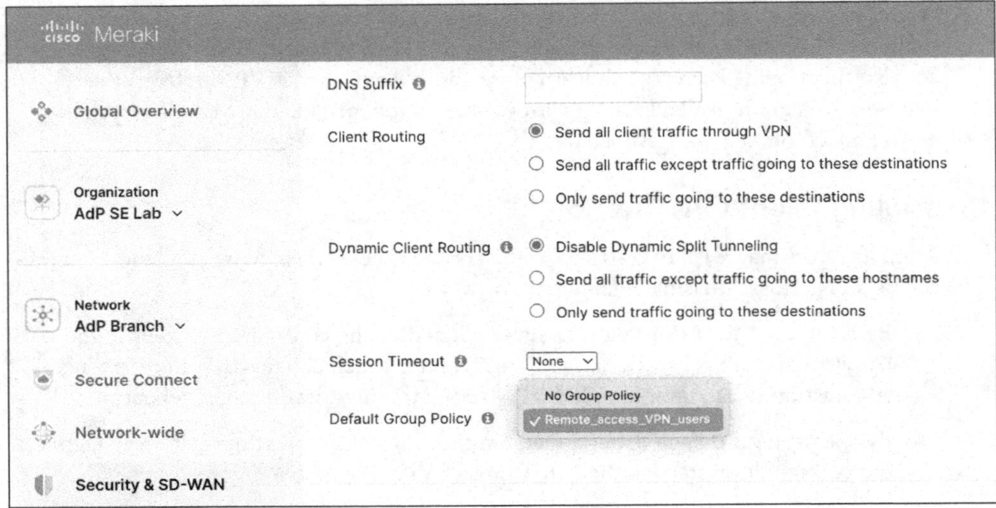

Figure 9-41 *Applying a Default Group Policy to an AnyConnect VPN*

Now that you've completed the steps to apply a group policy to AnyConnect VPN users, you can verify that this policy is working. Prior to this configuration change, users were able to connect via AnyConnect and ping host 10.200.155.10, as shown in Figure 9-42.

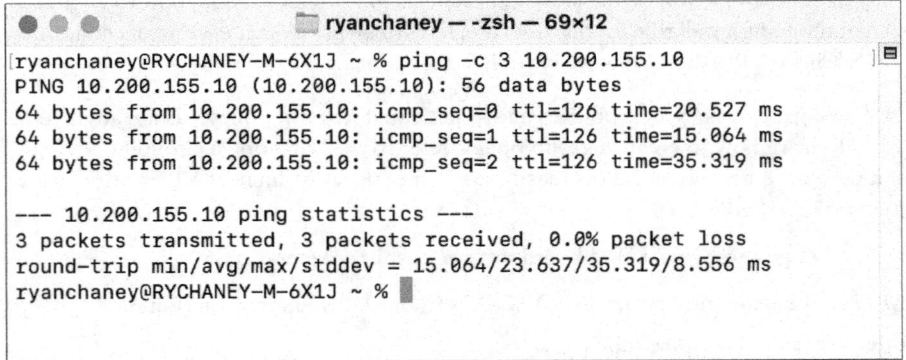

ryanchaney — -zsh — 69×12
ryanchaney@RYCHANEY-M-6X1J ~ % ping -c 3 10.200.155.10
PING 10.200.155.10 (10.200.155.10): 56 data bytes
64 bytes from 10.200.155.10: icmp_seq=0 ttl=126 time=20.527 ms
64 bytes from 10.200.155.10: icmp_seq=1 ttl=126 time=15.064 ms
64 bytes from 10.200.155.10: icmp_seq=2 ttl=126 time=35.319 ms
--- 10.200.155.10 ping statistics ---
3 packets transmitted, 3 packets received, 0.0% packet loss
round-trip min/avg/max/stddev = 15.064/23.637/35.319/8.556 ms
ryanchaney@RYCHANEY-M-6X1J ~ %

Figure 9-42 *A ping Test by an AnyConnect VPN User Before the Application of the Group Policy*

With the group policy applied, users can still ping the default gateway for this subnet (10.200.155.1), as shown in Figure 9-43. However, they can no longer ping this host (10.200.155.10), proving that the firewall policy is being enforced as required.

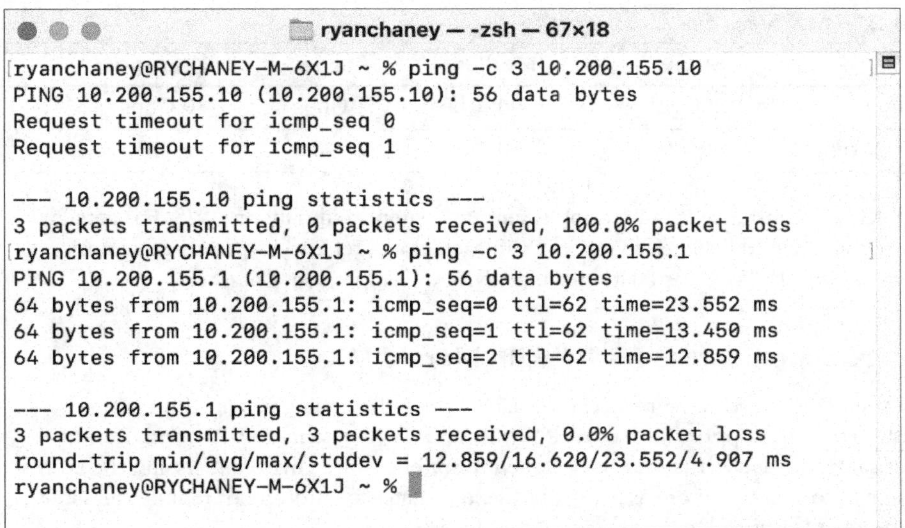

Figure 9-43 *A ping Test by an AnyConnect VPN User After the Application of the Group Policy*

This section completes the discussion of the various ways to apply controls to client VPN traffic.

Virtual MX (vMX)

Virtual MX (vMX) is a virtual instance of the Meraki MX security appliance designed for the public cloud. Often people assume that because vMX is virtual, it will run on VMware, but this is not the case currently. vMX does, however, support all the major cloud platforms, including Amazon Web Services (AWS), Microsoft Azure, Google Cloud Platform (GCP), and Alibaba Cloud. Virtual MX is also supported on Cisco's Enterprise NFV Infrastructure Software (NFVIS) platform. NFVIS is designed to host virtual networking functions at branch locations and on-premises data centers. Please note that Meraki is shifting development from NFVIS to other private cloud platforms and is planning to support AWS Outposts, VMware, and KVM in the future. Check with your Meraki specialist on the latest developments.

Sizing a Virtual MX

Virtual MX comes in a range of t-shirt sizes, as outlined in Table 9-2. Selecting the correct size is dependent on two key variables: the required throughput and the number of site-to-site VPN tunnels required.

Table 9-2 *vMX Sizes and Capabilities*

Auto VPN	Small	Medium	Large	X-Large
Throughput	200 Mbps	500 Mbps	1 Gbps	10 Gbps
Number of tunnels	50	250	1,000	10,000

The XL vMX instance is in beta and is currently supported only on AWS. For details on the required cloud instance to run vMX in each cloud, refer to https://documentation.meraki.com/MX/MX_Installation_Guides/vMX_Comparison_Datasheet.

Understanding Feature Parity with Meraki MX

vMX shares a lot with the physical appliances, including being managed by Meraki Dashboard, and support for Auto VPN, client VPN, AnyConnect VPN, and firewall. That said, because virtual MX is designed for public cloud environments and therefore designed to function more as a VPN headend or gateway, it does not require the same user-facing features that an MX appliance does.

The most prominent MX features not supported on vMX are

- Advanced Malware Protection (AMP)
- Intrusion detection/prevention (IDS/IPS)
- Geo IP Layer 7 firewall rules
- 802.1X Port Auth
- MX splash pages
- Dual WAN or LAN ports

The features supported by vMX are common across the different t-shirt sizes, with the exception of X-Large, which is currently in beta. Today, vMX-XL, which is designed for better processing of encrypted traffic, supports Passthrough or VPN Concentrator mode only, hence the limited feature support outlined in Table 9-3.

Table 9-3 *Feature Support on the Various Sizes of vMX*

Feature	Small	Medium	Large	X-Large
Auto VPN	Yes	Yes	Yes	Yes
One-armed concentrator mode	Yes	Yes	Yes	Yes
VPN firewall	Yes	Yes	Yes	Yes
Client VPN	Yes	Yes	Yes	No
AnyConnect VPN	Yes	Yes	Yes	No
BGP and OSPF	Yes	Yes	Yes	No

Feature	Small	Medium	Large	X-Large
NAT mode vMX	Yes	Yes	Yes	No
IPv6 capable	Yes	Yes	Yes	N/A
AWS Transit Gateway	Yes	Yes	Yes	N/A
AWS Cloud WAN	Yes	Yes	Yes	N/A
Azure RouteServer	Yes	Yes	Coming soon	N/A
Azure vWAN	Yes	Yes	Coming soon	N/A
Google Network Connectivity Center	Yes	Yes	Yes	N/A

Refer to the following URL for the latest feature support: https://documentation.meraki.com/MX/MX_Installation_Guides/vMX_Comparison_Datasheet.

Deploying Virtual MX in Amazon Web Services (AWS)

Deploying vMX requires configuration in Meraki Dashboard and in the public cloud provider's management console. In this example, we demonstrate how to deploy vMX in AWS, but the steps in Meraki Dashboard are the same for all public cloud providers. For other cloud providers, refer to the appropriate guide here:

- **vMX Setup Guide for Microsoft Azure:** https://documentation.meraki.com/MX/MX_Installation_Guides/vMX_Setup_Guide_for_Microsoft_Azure
- **vMX Setup Guide for Google Cloud Platform (GCP):** https://documentation.meraki.com/MX/MX_Installation_Guides/vMX_Setup_Guide_for_Google_Cloud_Platform_(GCP)
- **vMX Setup Guide for Alibaba Cloud:** https://documentation.meraki.com/MX/MX_Installation_Guides/vMX_Setup_Guide_for_Alibaba_Cloud

The configuration starts with the setup in Meraki Dashboard; then we move on to the AWS management console. Just as with any other Meraki device, a license is required for each vMX instance. Before starting these deployment steps, ensure that adequate licenses are present in your Meraki Dashboard inventory (**Organization > License Info**). If you require more licenses, contact your Meraki, Cisco, or Partner Account Manager.

Creating a New vMX Network in Meraki Dashboard

Follow these steps to create a new network for the vMX in Meraki Dashboard:

Step 1. Log in to Meraki Dashboard (https://dashboard.meraki.com).

Step 2. Click the **Network** drop-down menu on the left and then click **+ Create a Network**, as shown in Figure 9-44.

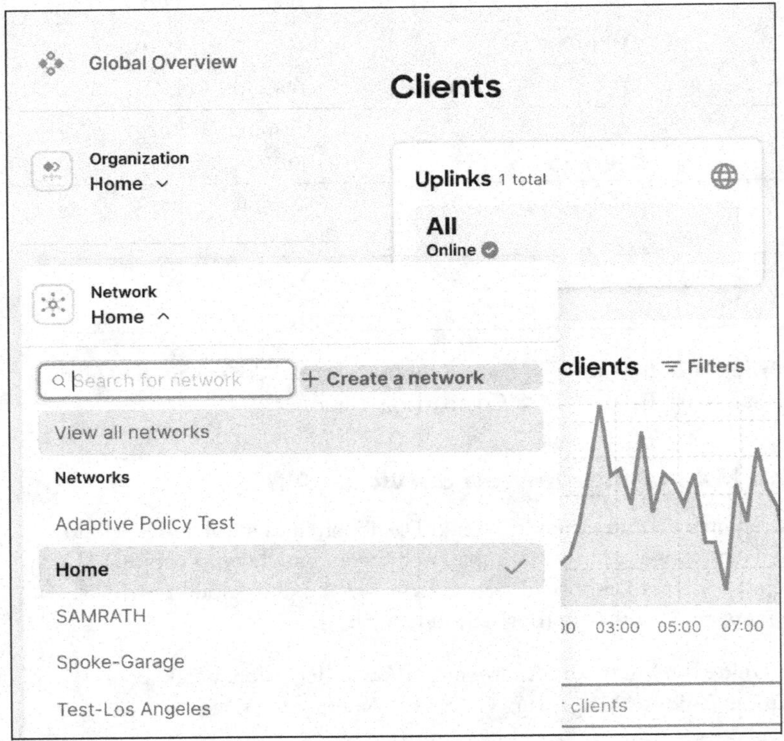

Figure 9-44 *Adding a New Network in Meraki Dashboard*

Step 3. On the **Create Network** page (see Figure 9-45), enter a meaningful name in the **Network Name** field.

a. From the **Network Type** drop-down menu, select **Security Appliance.**

b. Next to **Network Configuration, Default Meraki Configuration** should already be selected. Leave this setting as is.

c. From the **Select Devices from Inventory** table, select a vMX license. In this example, we have used a small vMX instance. If you do not select a device from the inventory table, you will be prompted to add a vMX on the following screen.

d. Click **Create Network.**

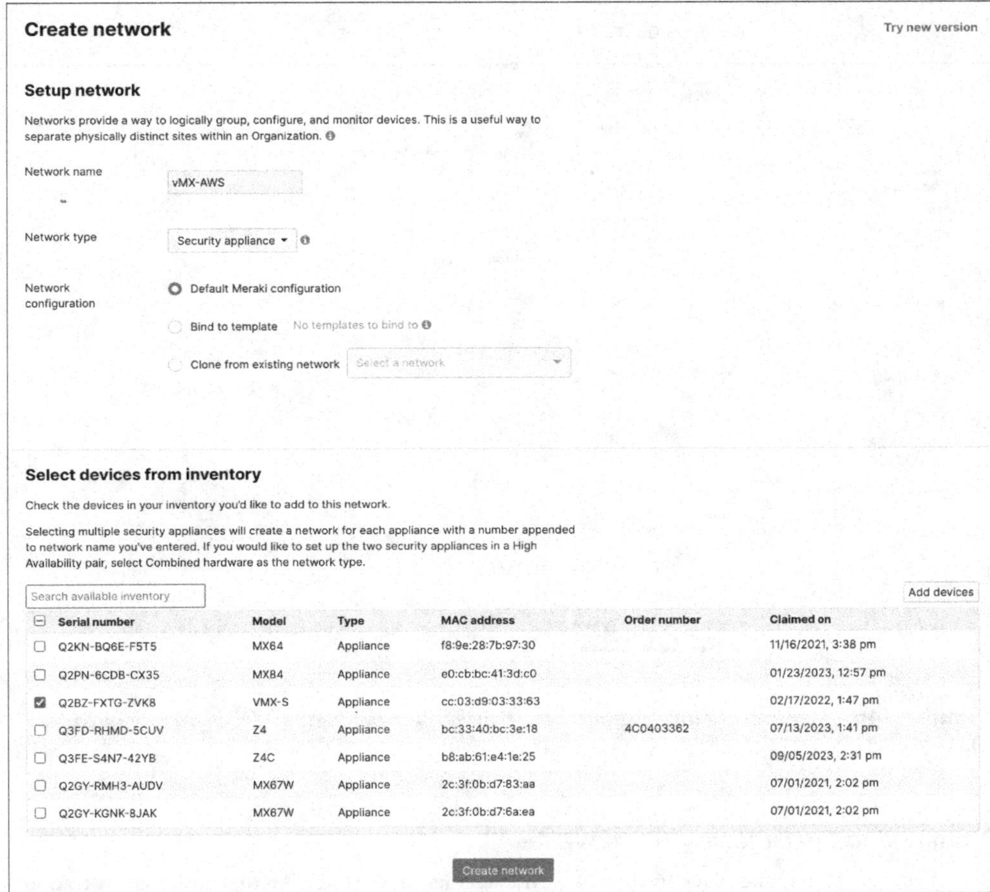

Figure 9-45 *Configuring the New vMX Network in Meraki Dashboard*

Step 4. Before continuing with this step, make sure that you have your AWS Management Console login details on hand because the token you're about to generate will expire in one hour.

a. You should already see the **Appliance Status** page for the new network created in Step 3, as shown in Figure 9-46. If not, navigate to **Security & SD-WAN > Appliance Status** (under Monitor).

b. Click **Generate Authentication Token….**

Step 5. A **vMX Authentication Token** pop-up window appears. Leave this browser tab open; you need to come back to copy it later.

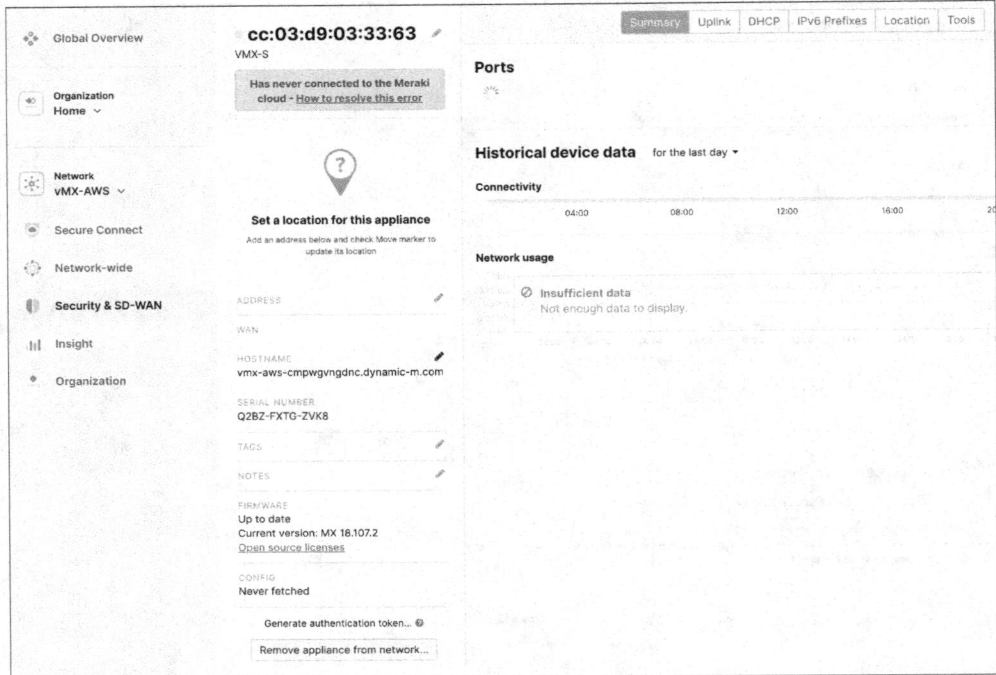

Figure 9-46 *Generating an Authentication Token for the New vMX Network in Meraki Dashboard*

Configuring the Default VPC in AWS

The next steps take place in the AWS Management Console. The first task here is to add an Internet gateway and a default route. Here, you use the default VPC and its existing (default) subnets. If you have an existing VPC and have already configured an Internet gateway and a default route, jump ahead to the section "Deploying vMX in AWS."

Step 1. Log in to AWS Management Console (https://aws.amazon.com/console/).

Step 2. In the search bar, type **vpc**, as shown in Figure 9-47. In the results, under **Services**, click **VPC**.

Step 3. On the menu to the left, click **Internet Gateways** under **Virtual Private Cloud.**

Step 4. On the **Internet Gateways** pane, click the orange **Create Internet Gateway** button, as shown in Figure 9-48.

Step 5. In the **Name Tag** field, assign a meaningful name to this Internet gateway, as shown in Figure 9-49. Click **Create Internet Gateway** to finish.

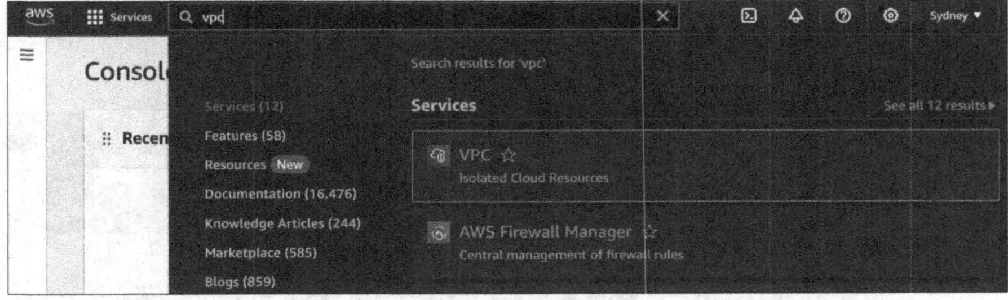

Figure 9-47 *Searching for VPC in the AWS Management Console*

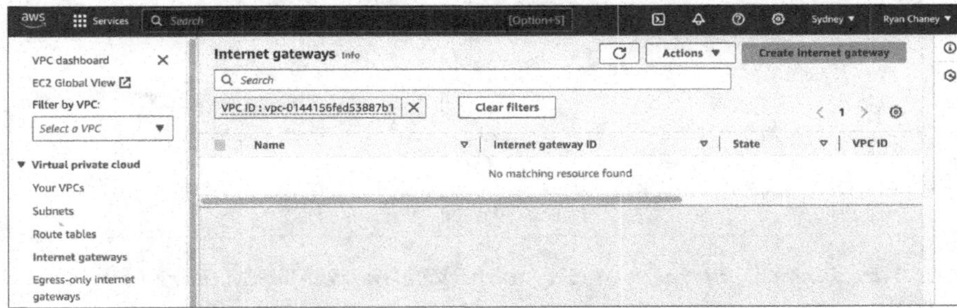

Figure 9-48 *The Default Internet Gateways Pane in the AWS Management Console*

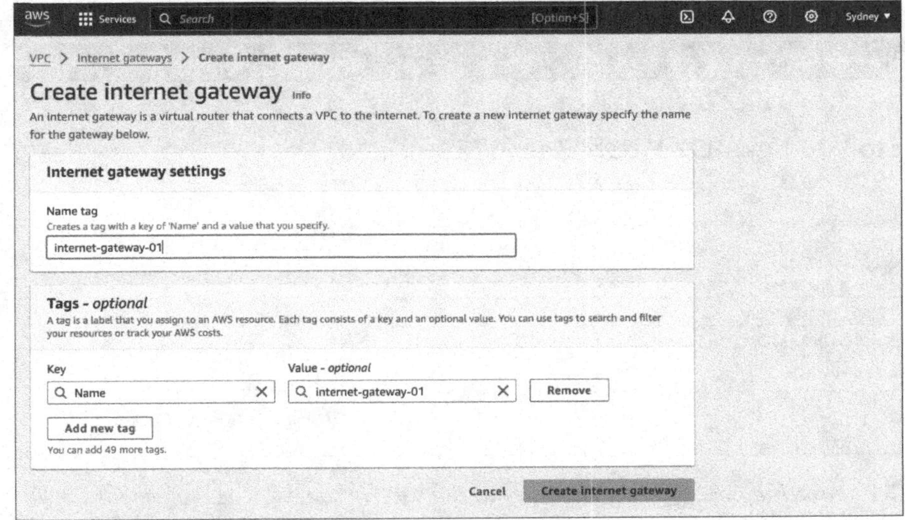

Figure 9-49 *Creating an Internet Gateway in the AWS Management Console*

Step 6. The **Details** page for the newly created Internet gateway appears, as shown in Figure 9-50. From the **Actions** menu, select **Attach to VPC**.

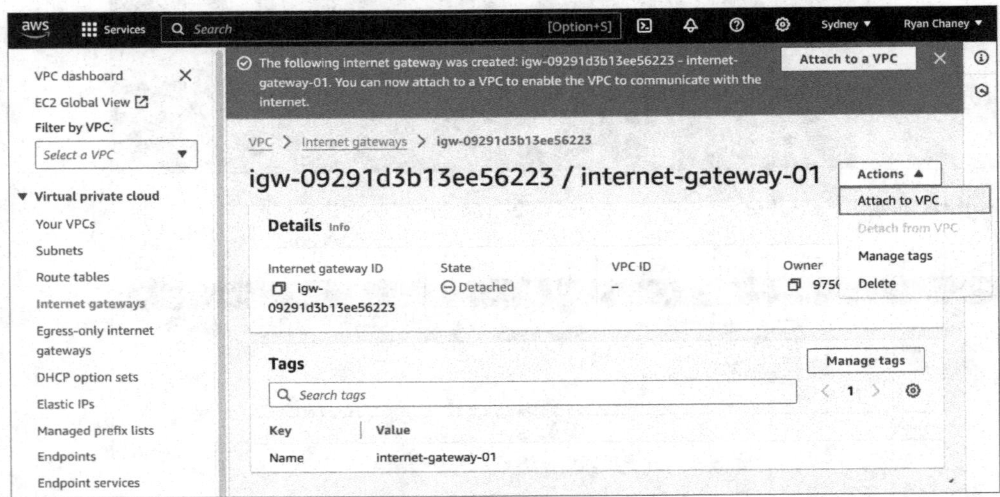

Figure 9-50 *Attaching the Internet Gateway to the VPC in the AWS Management Console (Part 1)*

Step 7. On the **Attach to VPC** page, select the default VPC from the **Available VPCs** drop-down menu, as shown in Figure 9-51. Click **Attach Internet Gateway.**

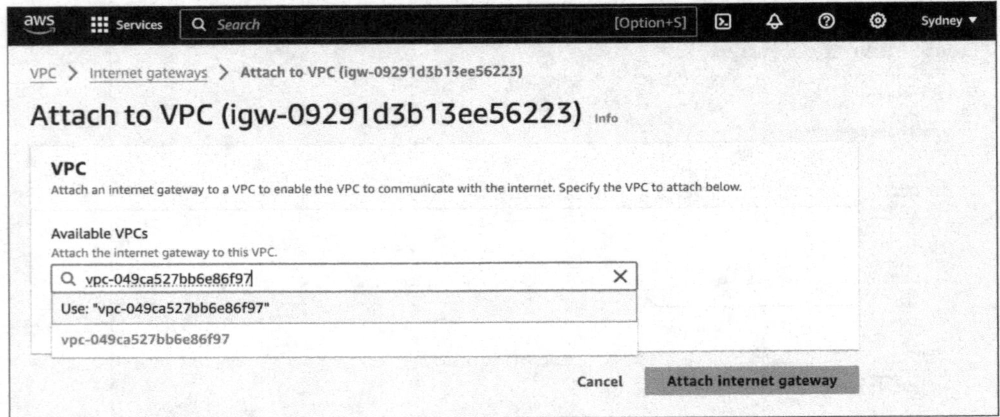

Figure 9-51 *Attaching the Internet Gateway to the VPC in the AWS Management Console (Part 2)*

Step 8. You then return to the Internet gateway details page, as shown in Figure 9-52.

Notice that the **State** has changed from **Detached**, as seen in Step 6, to **Attached.**

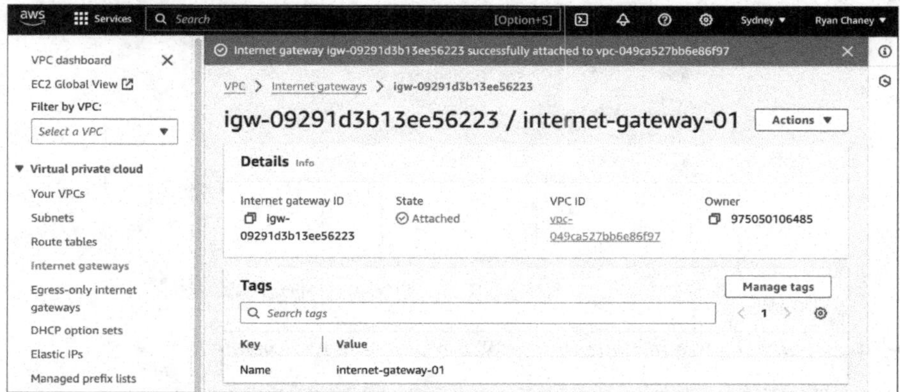

Figure 9-52 *The Internet Gateways Pane After Attaching the Internet Gateway to the VPC*

Step 9. The next task is to add a default route that points to the Internet gateway. From the menu on the left side, click **Route Tables.** On the **Route Tables** pane (see Figure 9-53), click the **Route** tab and click **Edit Routes.**

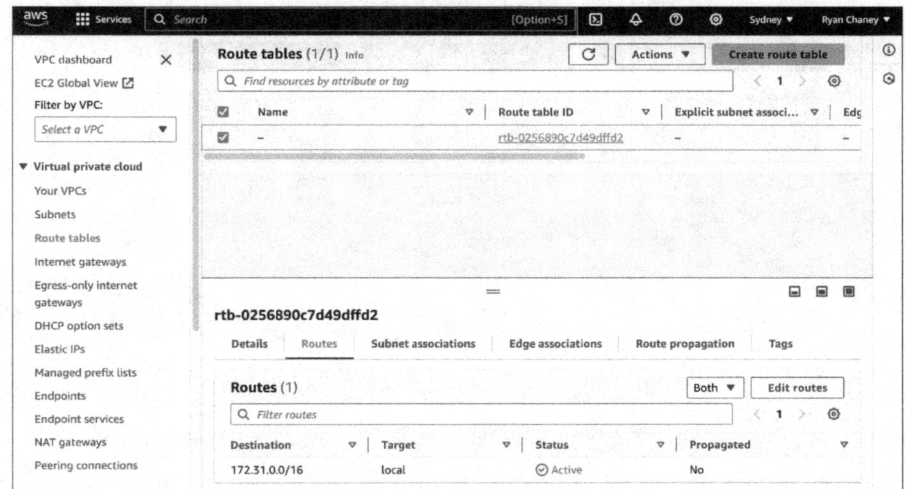

Figure 9-53 *The Route Tables Pane in the AWS Management Console*

Step 10. On the **Edit Routes** page (see Figure 9-54), click **Add Route.**

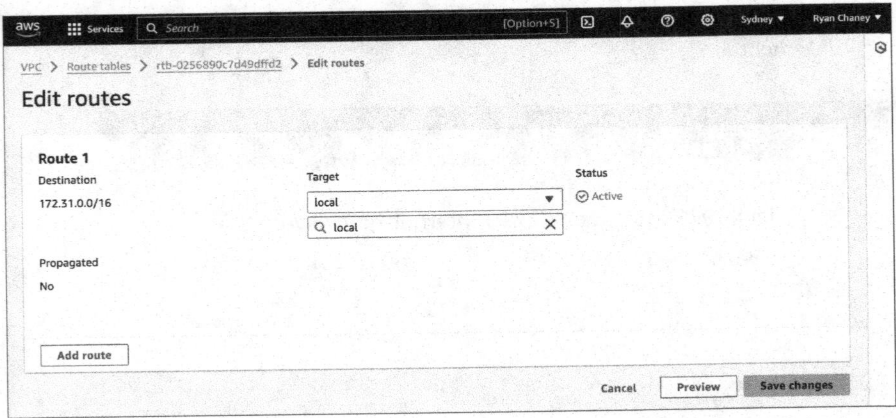

Figure 9-54 *Creating a Route Table in the AWS Management Console*

Step 11. From the **Destination** drop-down menu, select **0.0.0.0/0.**

a. From the **Target** drop-down menu (see Figure 9-55), select **Internet Gateway.**

b. From the drop-down menu under **Target**, select the Internet gateway you just created.

c. Click **Save Changes.**

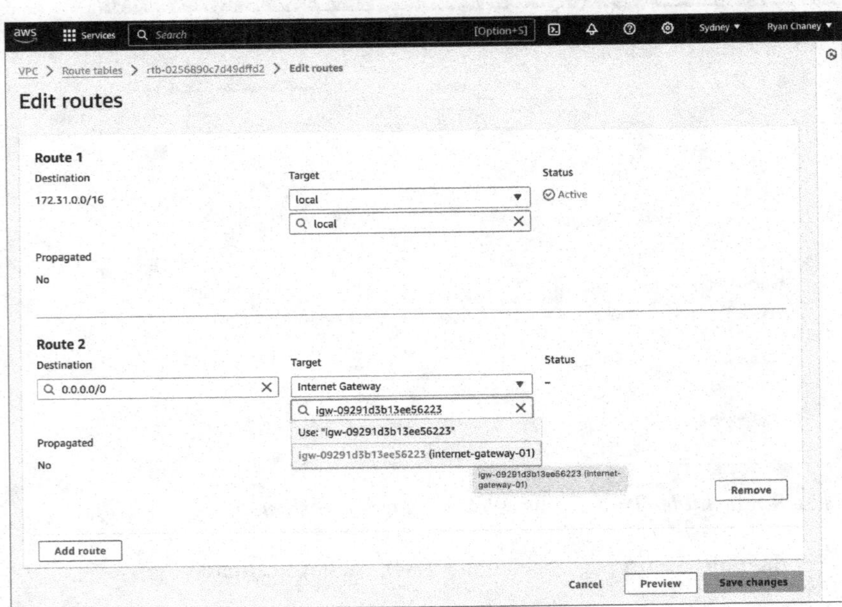

Figure 9-55 *Selecting Edit Routes on the Route Tables Pane in the AWS Management Console*

You've now completed the creation of an Internet gateway and a default route inside the default VPC. Read on to learn how to deploy a Meraki vMX instance in Amazon EC2.

Deploying vMX in AWS

As with anything that has to do with the public cloud, there are costs involved related to storage, compute, and other services. Ensure that you're aware of and comfortable with these costs before proceeding.

Follow these steps to deploy vMX from the AWS Marketplace:

Step 1. If you're not already logged in, log in now to the AWS Management Console (https://aws.amazon.com/console/).

Step 2. In the **Search** field, enter **vMX**, as shown in Figure 9-56.

In the search results, under **Marketplace**, scroll down and click **Cisco Meraki vMX** to open it. Alternatively, use the following link: https://aws.amazon.com/marketplace/server/procurement?productId=37f4eb71-a53a-4667-ab90-d23c10916415.

> **Note** The search results also show Cisco Meraki Next-Gen vMX. This is for the X-Large image; if this is what you're after, select this option.

Figure 9-56 *Search Results for Cisco Meraki vMX on the AWS Marketplace*

Step 3. The page for Cisco Meraki vMX then appears, shown in Figure 9-57. Click the **Continue to Subscribe** button.

Step 4. You then see the **Subscribe to This Software** page (see Figure 9-58). If available, click the **Continue to Configuration** button.

If you have not already accepted the terms and conditions, click **Accept Terms.** After the request has been processed, the **Continue to Configuration** button will change from gray to orange. When it is available, click the **Continue to Configuration** button.

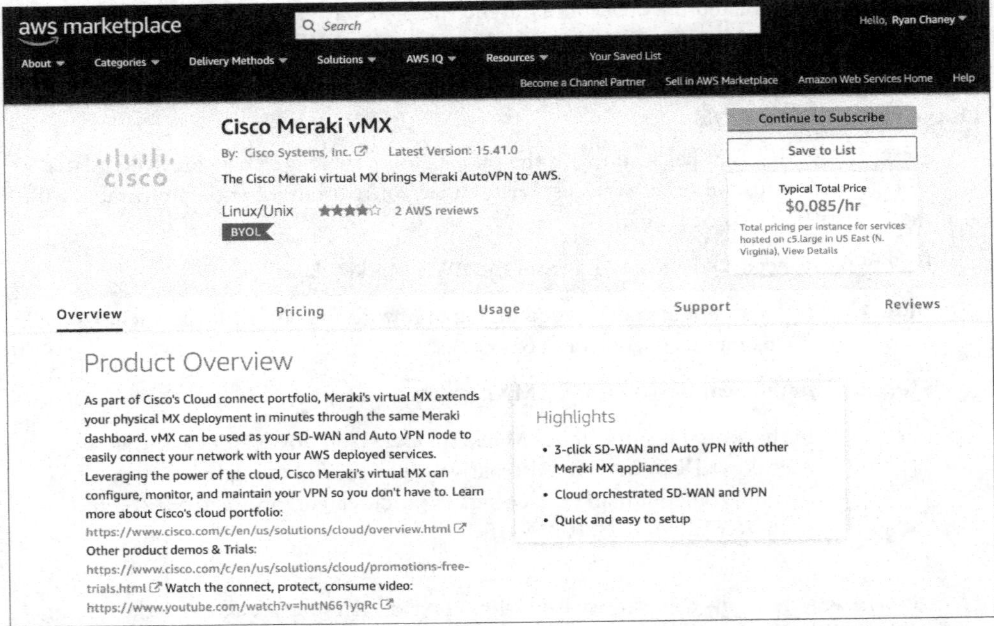

Figure 9-57 *The Cisco Meraki vMX on the AWS Marketplace*

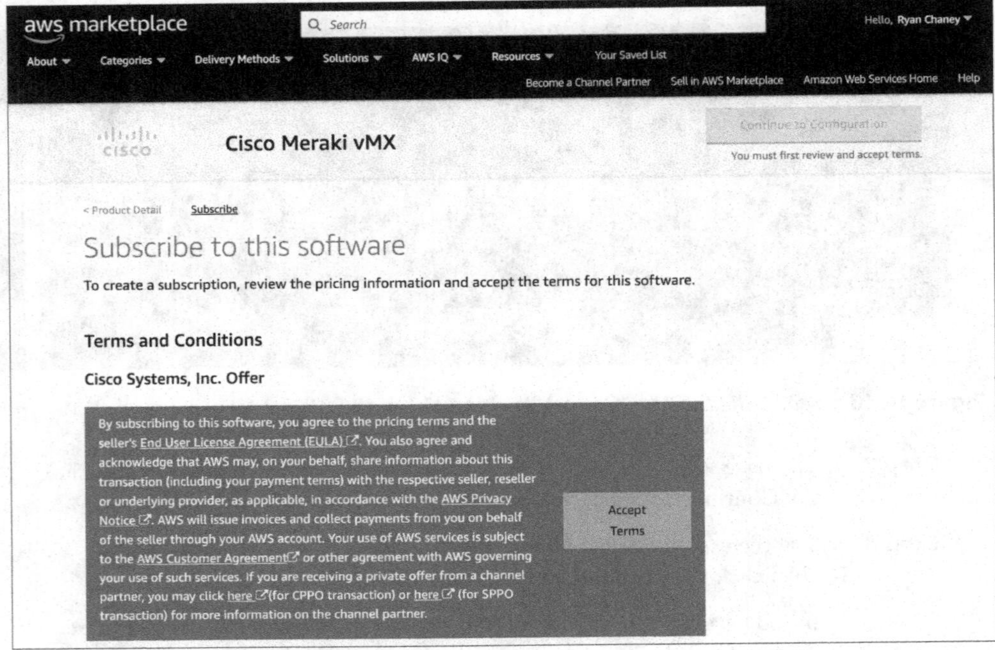

Figure 9-58 *Accepting the Cisco Meraki vMX Terms and Conditions on the AWS Marketplace*

Step 5. Here, you are prompted to select the EC2 instance settings, as shown in Figure 9-59.

The default **Region** is US East (N. Virginia). If you would like to specify a different location, from the **Region** drop-down menu, select the region in which you want to host this image. This should match the availability zone where your VPC resides (**VPC Dashboard > Your VPCs**, then click **Your VPC ID**; the availability zones are listed under Subnets). Click **Continue to Launch**.

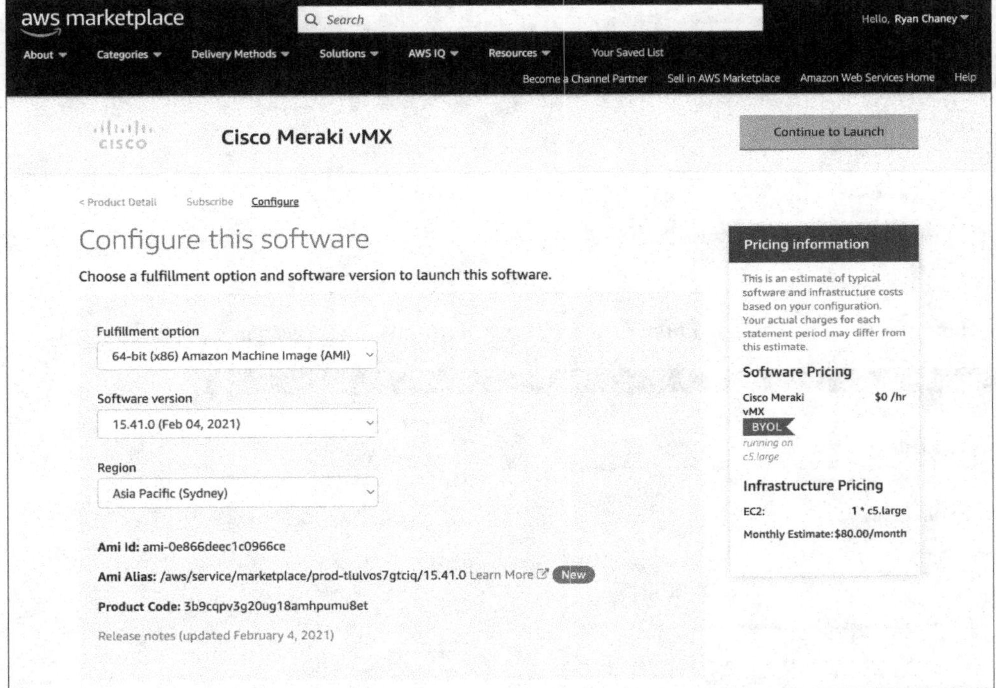

Figure 9-59 *Selecting the Region for the vMX on the AWS Marketplace*

Step 6. On the **Launch This Software** page (see Figure 9-60), from the **Choose Action** drop-down menu, click **Launch through EC2**.

Step 7. You should now see the **Launch an Instance** page (see Figure 9-61).

In the **Name** field, enter a meaningful name for this vMX. It's recommended that you use the same hostname as you will use for this device in Meraki Dashboard.

Under **Instance Type**, confirm that the instance type selected from the drop-down menu is correct. For vMX-S and vMX-M, it must be c5.large; for vMX-L, it needs to be c5.xlarge; and for vMX-XL, the instance must be c6in.2xlarge.

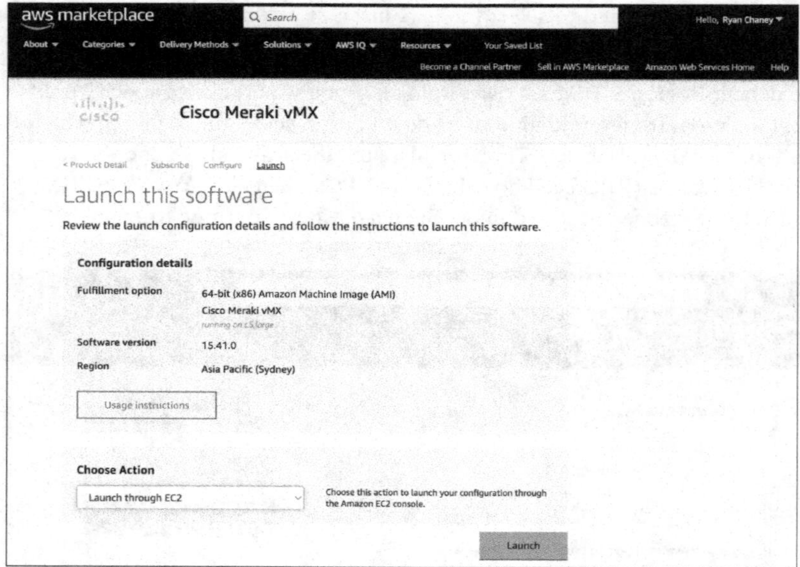

Figure 9-60 *The Launch This Software Page on the AWS Marketplace*

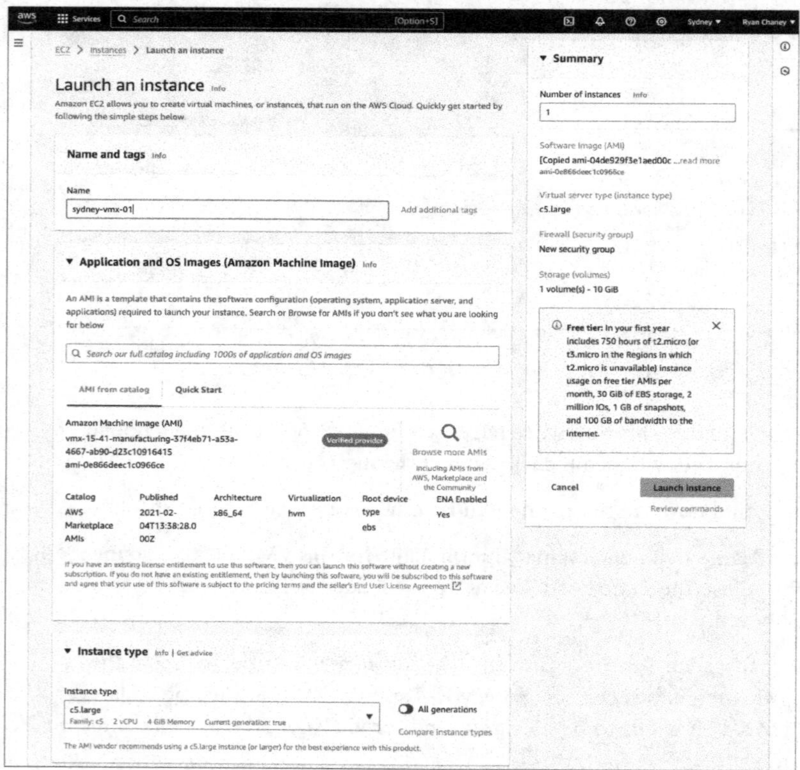

Figure 9-61 *The Launch an Instance Page on the AWS Marketplace*

Step 8. Scroll down to **Key Pair (Login).** If a key pair has already been created, select it from the drop-down menu and proceed to the next step. Otherwise, click **Create New Key Pair.** On the pop-up window (see Figure 9-62), enter a meaningful name in the **Key Pair Name** field and click **Create Key Pair.**

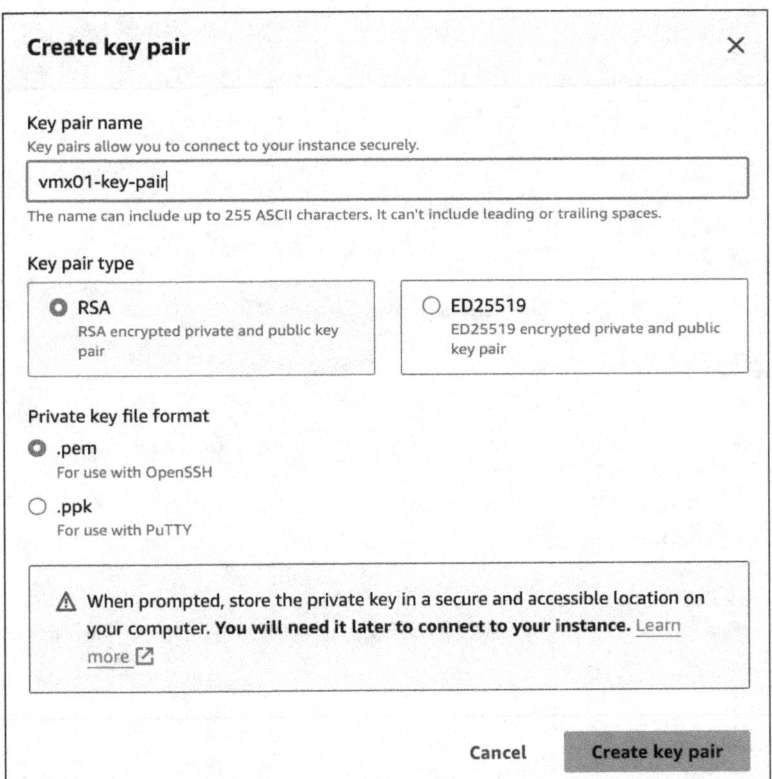

Figure 9-62 *Creating a Key Pair for the vMX Instance*

Step 9. Back on the **Launch an Instance** page, under **Network Settings,** click **Edit.**

a. From the **VPC** drop-down menu, the default VPC should already be selected (see Figure 9-63). If so, leave this setting as is.

b. From the **Subnet** drop-down menu, select the subnet where you wish to deploy the vMX.

c. From the **Auto-assign Public IP** drop-down menu, select **Enable.**

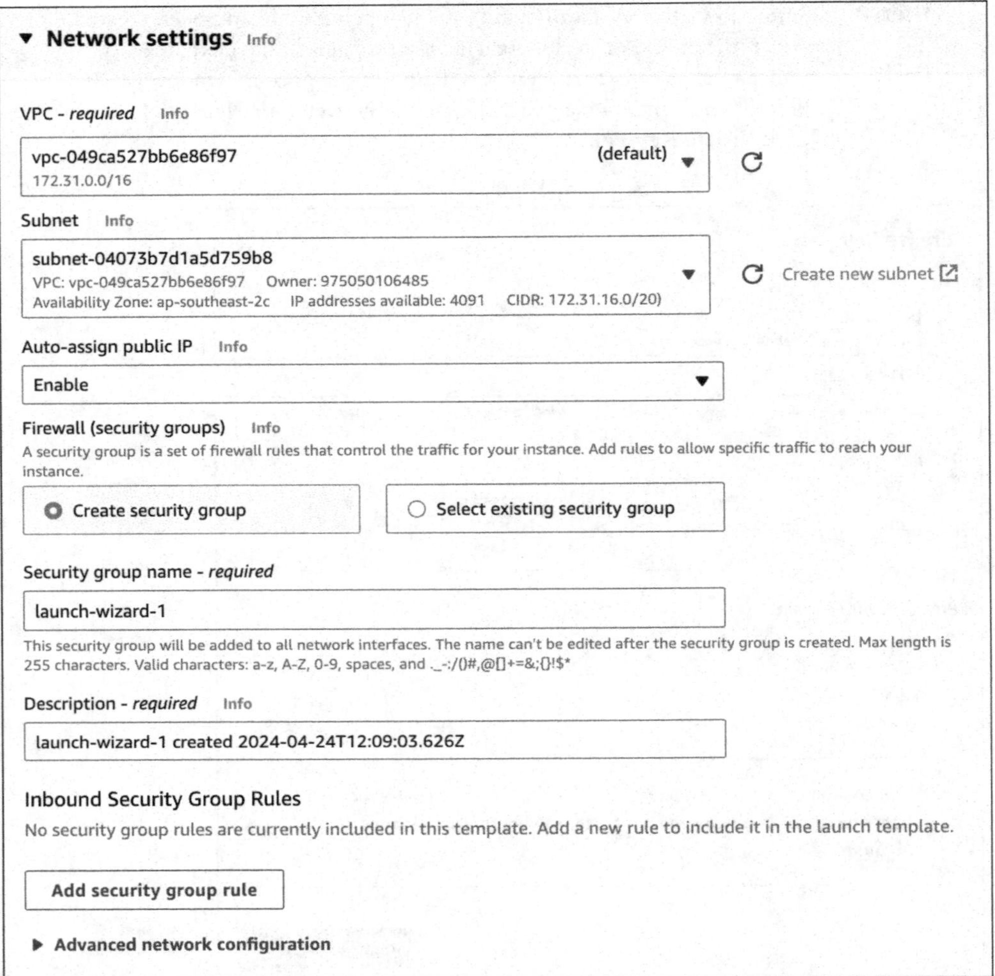

Figure 9-63 *Associating the VPC and Subnet with the New vMX Instance*

Step 10. Staying on the **Launch an Instance** page, expand the **Advanced Details** section and scroll down to the bottom (see Figure 9-64).

- **a.** Set **Metadata Accessible** to **Enabled.**
- **b.** Set **Metadata Version** to **V1 and V2 (Token Optional).**
- **c.** In the **Metadata Response Hop Limit**, enter **1**.
- **d.** Enter the vMX authentication token generated in Meraki Dashboard into the **User Data** field.

e. If it has been more than one hour since that key was generated, generate a new authentication token before pasting it into the **User Data** field. You can do this in Meraki Dashboard by clicking the **Generate Authentication Token** button on the **Appliance Status** page (**Security & SD-WAN > Appliance Status**).

f. Scroll down and click **Launch Instance**.

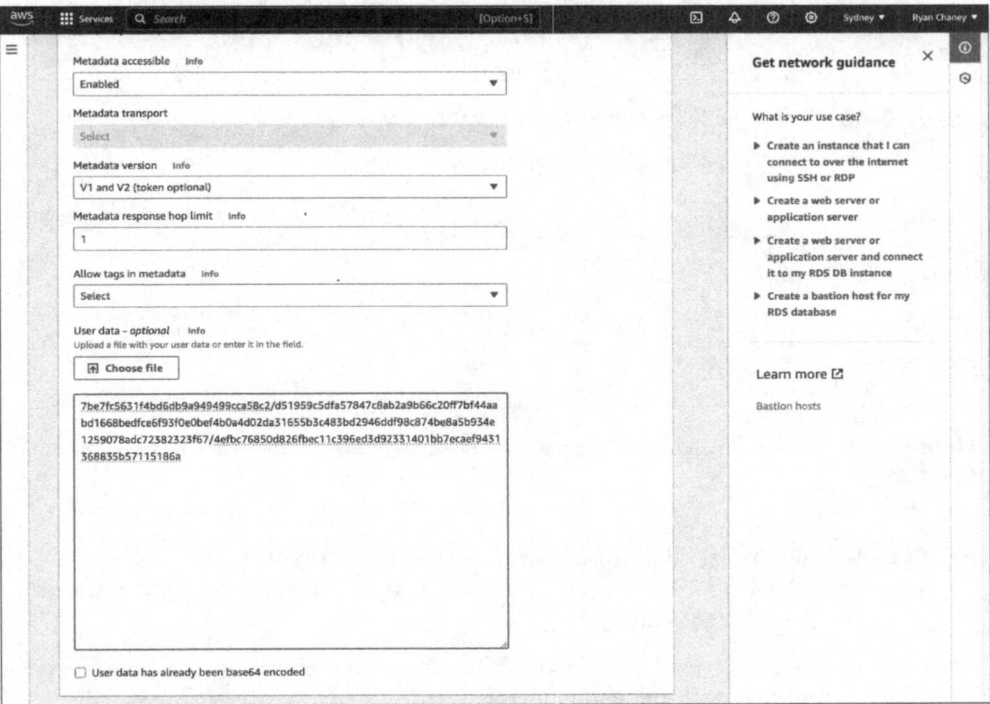

Figure 9-64 *Entering the Authentication Token to Deploy the New vMX Instance*

Step 11. You should now see the success message, as shown in Figure 9-65; however, there are still two more tasks to complete. Click the instance ID in brackets just after **Successfully Initiated Launch of Instance ([Instance ID]).** This will take you to the **Instances** page.

Step 12. On the **Instances** page, click the check box to the left of the vMX name. This opens a new pane on the lower half of the screen, as shown in Figure 9-66.

Tip You can drag the lower pane up to make it larger.

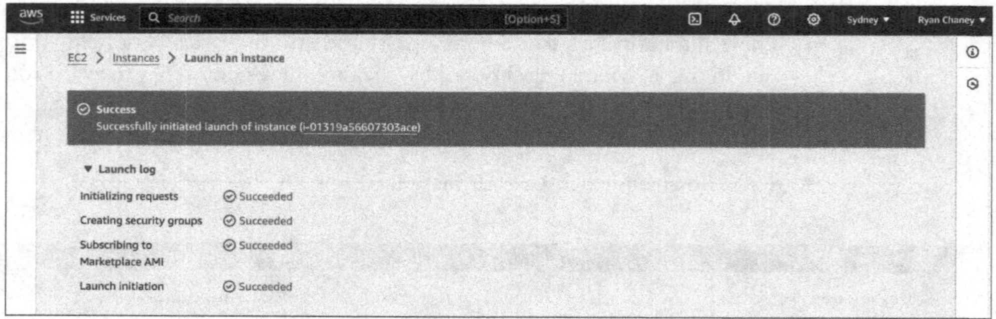

Figure 9-65 *The Launch an Instance Success Message in AWS*

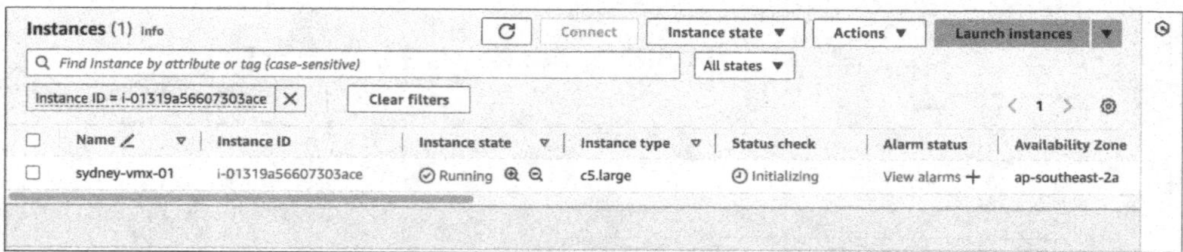

Figure 9-66 *The New vMX Instance on the Instances Page in the AWS Management Console*

Step 13. Remaining on the **Instances** page, click the **Networking** tab, as shown in Figure 9-67. Make a note of the **Public IPv4 Address** so that you can send a test ping to it later.

In the **Network Interfaces** table at the bottom of the page, click the hyperlink starting with **eni-** under **Interface ID.**

Step 14. On the **Network Interface Summary** page, from the **Actions** drop-down menu, select **Change Source/Dest. Check**, as shown in Figure 9-68.

Step 15. On the **Change Source/Destination Check** pop-up window, as shown in Figure 9-69, uncheck **Enable** and click **Save.**

Step 16. The final task is to add a route pointing to the vMX for the VPN subnets. This allows AWS applications to talk to the LAN subnets at remote sites and remote-access VPN users. Search for "vpc" in the **Search** field (see Figure 9-70), and under **VPC**, click **Route Table.**

Step 17. On the **Route Tables** page, select the route table in the **Route Tables** table. This should expose the Details tab shown in Figure 9-71. In the lower pane of the page, click the **Routes** tab; then click the **Edit Routes** button, as shown in Figure 9-71.

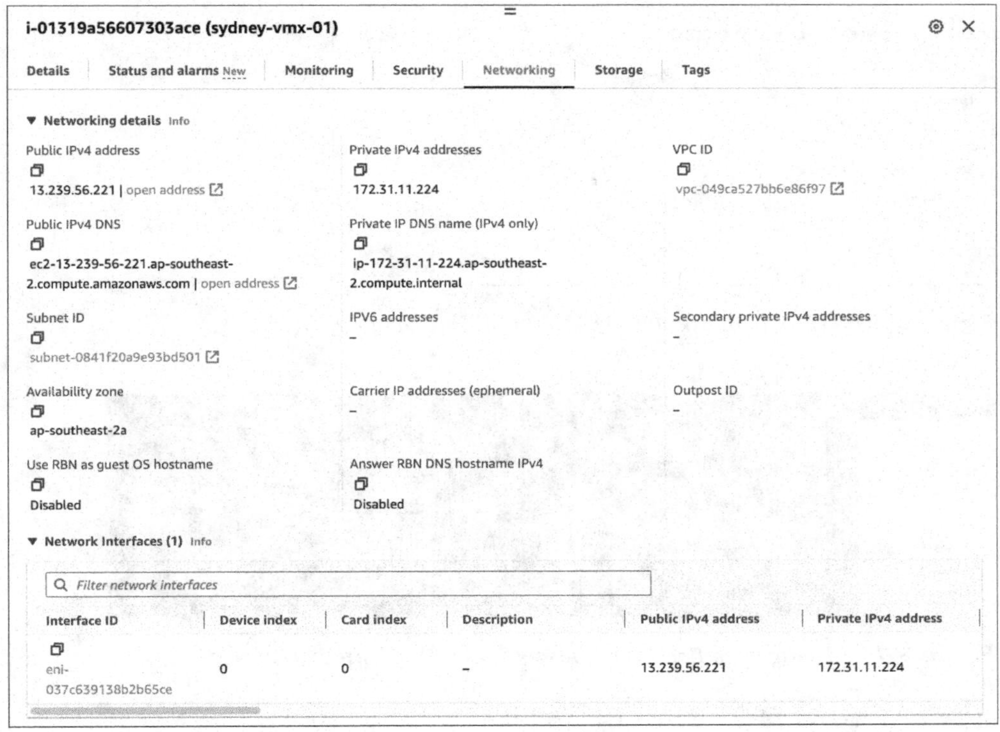

Figure 9-67 *The Networking Tab on the Instances Page in the AWS Management Console*

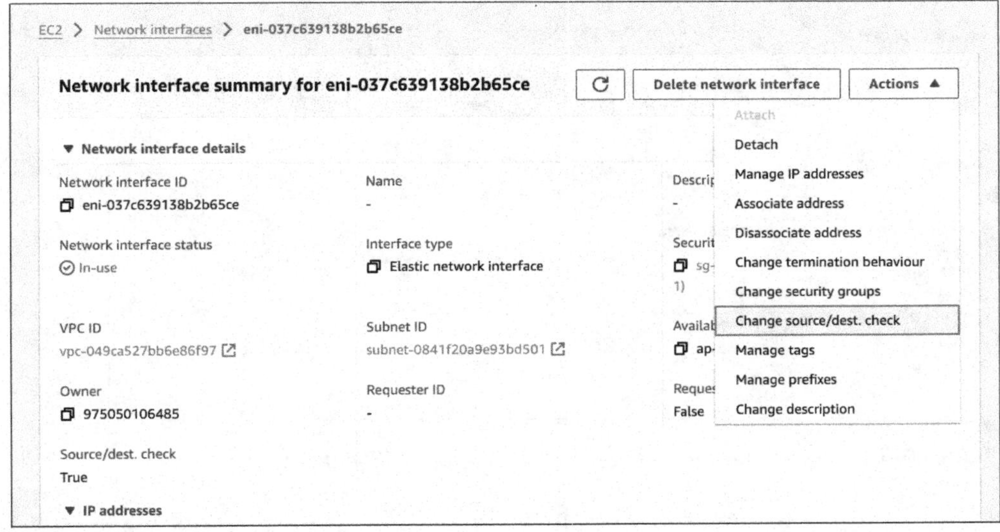

Figure 9-68 *Disabling the Source/Dest. Check on the vMX Network Interface*

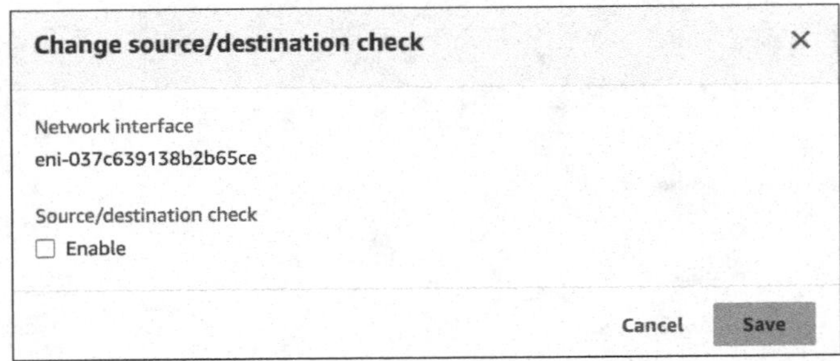

Figure 9-69 *The Change Source/Destination Check Pop-Up Window*

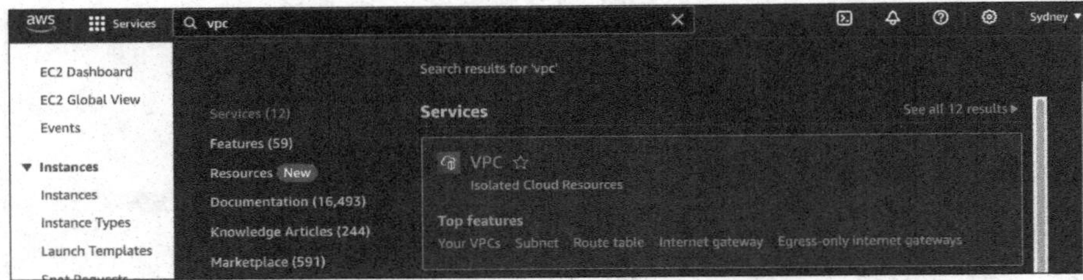

Figure 9-70 *Navigating Back to the Route Tables Page After Creating the vMX Instance*

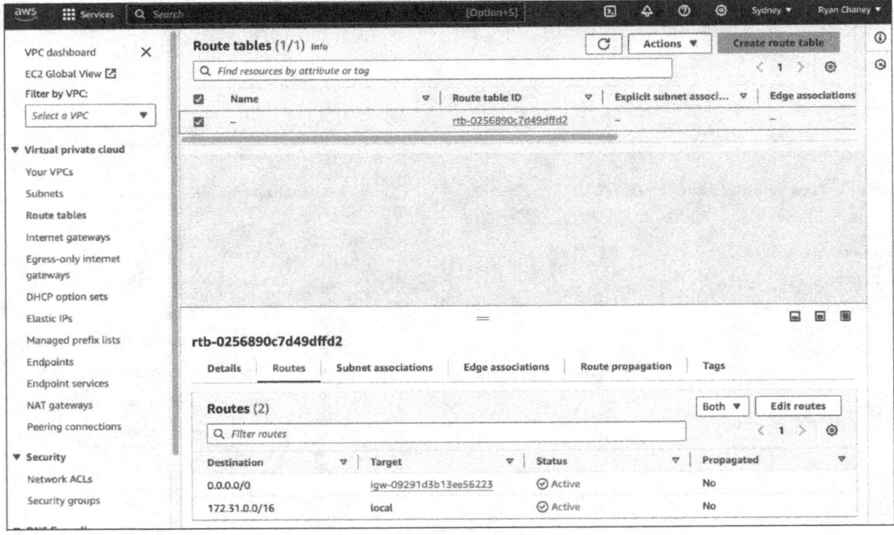

Figure 9-71 *The Route Tables Page Before Adding the Summary Route*

Step 18. On the **Edit Routes** page, click **Add Route.** Ideally, enter a summary route here to cover all the LAN subnets at remote sites and any client VPN subnets. Alternatively, add a route for each subnet required. Set the **Target** as **Instance**, and from the drop-down menu underneath **Target**, select the vMX that's just been added, as shown in Figure 9-72.

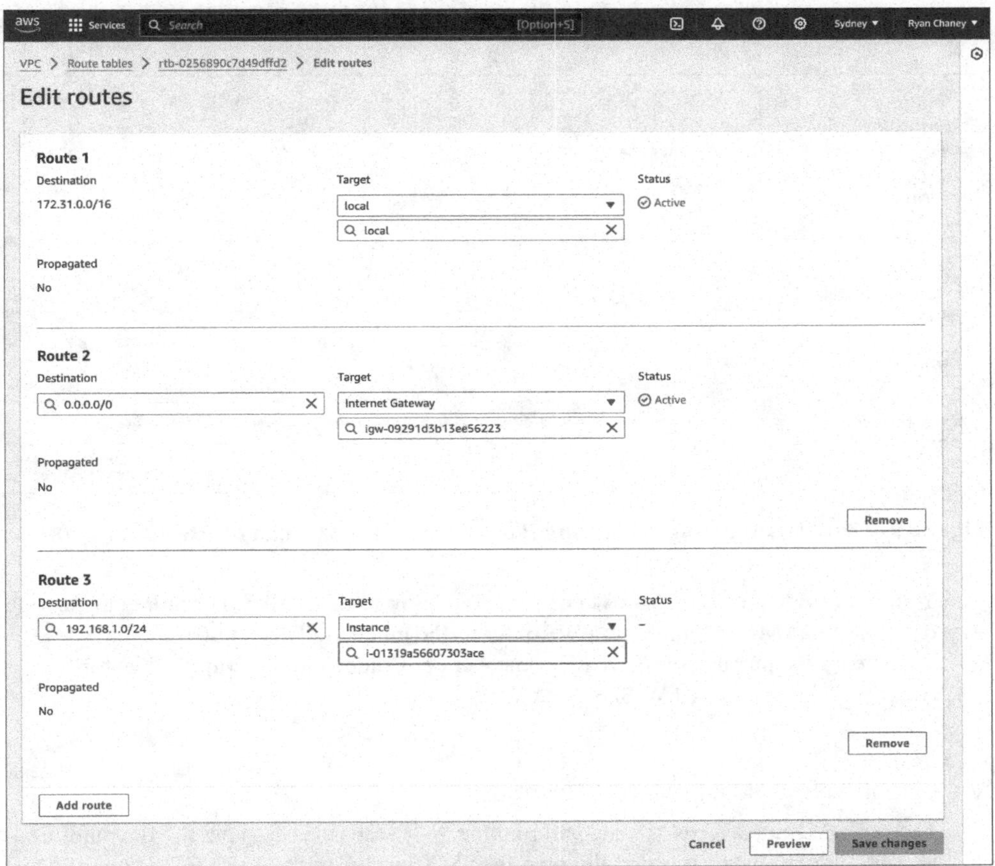

Figure 9-72 *Adding a Route to the Route Table for a VPN Subnet*

Tip The default security group attached to this vMX instance will block ping. It's highly recommended that you allow ping so that you can easily test that the vMX is reachable. To achieve this, follow these steps:

1. In the AWS Management Console, navigate to **EC2 > Instances** and click the Instance ID for vMX.
2. Click the **Security** tab at the bottom and then the hyperlink under **Security Groups**.

3. On the **Inbound Rules** tab, click **Edit Inbound Rules.**
4. On the **Edit Inbound Rules** page (see Figure 9-73), click **Add Rule.**
5. For the new rule, under **Type**, select **All ICMP – IPv4.** Under **Source**, select **Anywhere-IPv4** and then click **Save Rules.**

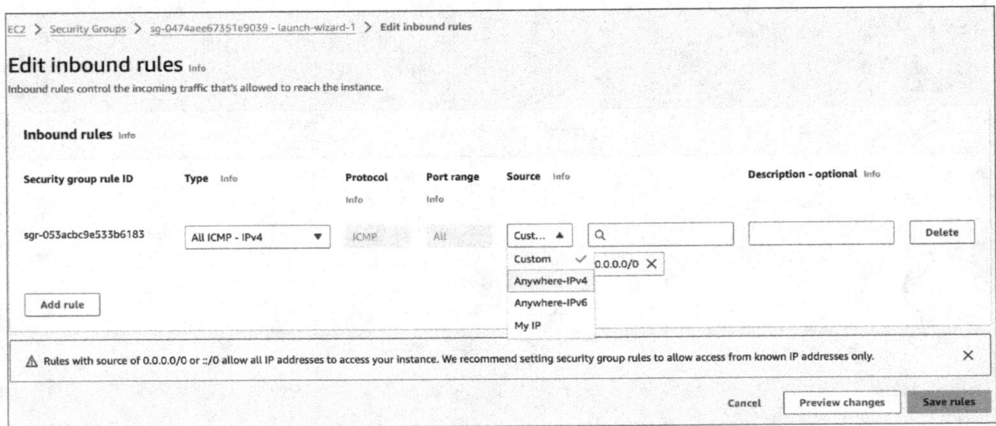

Figure 9-73 *Allowing ping for Testing Purposes on the vMX Instance Security Group*

You've now completed the steps necessary to deploy vMX in AWS. For more information on deploying vMX instances on AWS, refer to the guide available at https://documentation.meraki.com/MX/MX_Installation_Guides/vMX_Setup_Guide_for_Amazon_Web_Services_(AWS).

Viewing the New vMX in Meraki Dashboard

The new vMX instance is now up and running. With the rules to allow ICMP configured in AWS, you're able to successfully ping the vMX instance from Meraki Dashboard. On the **Appliance Status** page in Meraki Dashboard, you should see that it has a green status light and that the WAN IP is updated to the one assigned earlier in the AWS Management Console. A virtual MX looks similar to a physical MX in Dashboard, as shown in Figure 9-74. The only changes are fewer menu options under the **Security & SD-WAN > Monitor** and **Security & SD-WAN > Configure** menus.

You've now completed the steps to set up a virtual MX hosted in AWS.

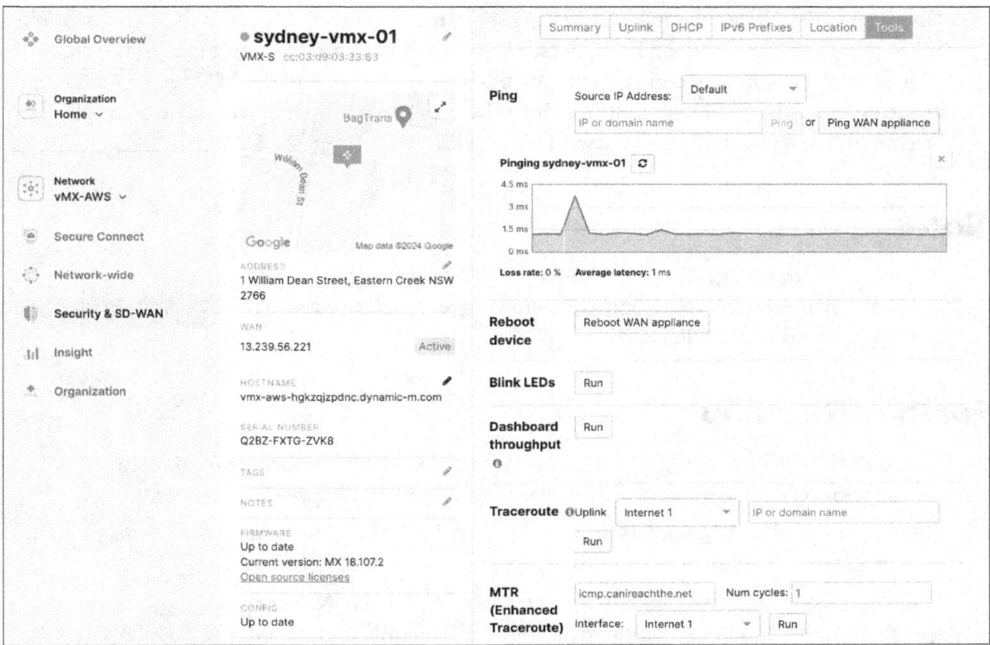

Figure 9-74 *The Meraki Dashboard Appliance Status Page for a New Meraki vMX Hosted in AWS*

Summary

This chapter focused on the capabilities of Meraki MX security appliances to protect the confidentiality, integrity, and availability of traffic carried over external links. This includes site-to-site VPNs, typically used for branch offices, which are handled with a feature known as Auto VPN. Auto VPN significantly reduces the effort, and propensity for errors, when setting up large WANs. In addition, Meraki MX also supports two flavors of remote-access VPN: client VPN and AnyConnect VPN. In addition to showing how to configure both VPN types, we also showed the benefit of Sentry VPN, which provides an easy way to turn on client VPN for all devices enrolled with Meraki Systems Manager. AnyConnect VPN, the recommended remote-access VPN solution, supports authenticating users with SAML, allowing VPN users to use the same credentials as used for Dashboard and other enterprise applications. AnyConnect VPN is a must-have for organizations that require SAML and multifactor authentication.

This chapter also introduced Cisco ThousandEyes, which provides a unique capability to detect adverse events in the external environment. The integration of ThousandEyes with Meraki MX provides vital visibility into the performance of the external telco and cloud infrastructure.

Finally, we introduced virtual MX (vMX), a virtual version of Meraki MX security appliances designed for cloud environments. This chapter also guided you through the steps to deploy a vMX instance in Amazon Web Services (AWS). Virtual MX is an excellent way to extend the WAN environment into the public cloud, while still using Meraki Dashboard to manage the full networking stack.

Notes

[1] Cisco Meraki. (2024, April 8). Site-to-Site VPN Settings. https://documentation.meraki.com/MX/Site-to-site_VPN/Site-to-Site_VPN_Settings#Non-Meraki_VPN_Peers

Further Reading

Android. (2024). Connect to a Virtual Private Network (VPN) on Android. https://support.google.com/android/answer/9089766?hl=en#zippy=%2Cconnect

Cisco Meraki. (2020, June). *Cisco Meraki Auto VPN*. https://meraki.cisco.com/product-collateral/auto-vpn-whitepaper

Cisco Meraki. (2023, June 17). AnyConnect on ASA vs. MX. https://documentation.meraki.com/MX/Client_VPN/AnyConnect_on_the_MX_Appliance/AnyConnect_on_ASA_vs._MX

Cisco Meraki. (2023, September 20). AnyConnect Licensing on the MX Appliance. https://documentation.meraki.com/MX/Client_VPN/AnyConnect_on_the_MX_Appliance/AnyConnect_Licensing_on_the_MX

Cisco Meraki. (2023, November 2). Restricting Client VPN Access Using Layer 3 Firewall Rules. https://documentation.meraki.com/MX/Client_VPN/Restricting_Client_VPN_access_using_Layer_3_firewall_rules

Cisco Meraki. (2024). *vMX – Security and SD-WAN in the Cloud*. https://meraki.cisco.com/wp-content/uploads/2023/05/vMX-datasheet-20230421-english.pdf

Cisco Meraki. (2024a, January 31). vMX Setup Guide for Alibaba Cloud. https://documentation.meraki.com/MX/MX_Installation_Guides/vMX_Setup_Guide_for_Alibaba_Cloud

Cisco Meraki. (2024b, January 31). vMX Setup Guide for NFVIS. https://documentation.meraki.com/MX/MX_Installation_Guides/vMX_Setup_Guide_for_NFVIS

Cisco Meraki. (2024, February 1). MX and Umbrella SIG IPSec Tunnel. https://documentation.meraki.com/MX/Site-to-site_VPN/MX_and_Umbrella_SIG_IPSec_Tunnel

Cisco Meraki. (2024, March 4). Meraki MX ThousandEyes Configuration Guide. https://documentation.meraki.com/MI/ThousandEyes/Meraki_MX_ThousandEyes_Configuration_Guide

Cisco Meraki. (2024, March 9). SD-WAN Internet Policies (SD-Internet). https://documentation.meraki.com/Architectures_and_Best_Practices/Cisco_Meraki_Best_Practice_Design/Best_Practice_Design_-_MX_Security_and_SD-WAN/SD-WAN_Internet_Policies_(SD-Internet)

Cisco Meraki. (2024a, March 16). vMX Comparison Datasheet. https://documentation.meraki.com/MX/MX_Installation_Guides/vMX_Comparison_Datasheet

Cisco Meraki. (2024b, March 16). vMX Setup Guide for Amazon Web Services (AWS). https://documentation.meraki.com/MX/MX_Installation_Guides/vMX_Setup_Guide_for_Amazon_Web_Services_(AWS)

Cisco Meraki. (2024, March 22). Meraki MX/Z Security and SD-WAN Licensing. https://documentation.meraki.com/General_Administration/Licensing/Meraki_MX_Security_and_SD-WAN_Licensing

Cisco Meraki. (2024, April 2). Client VPN Overview. https://documentation.meraki.com/MX/Client_VPN/Client_VPN_Overview

Cisco Meraki. (2024, April 5). Meraki Auto VPN – Configuration and Troubleshooting. https://documentation.meraki.com/MX/Site-to-site_VPN/Meraki_Auto_VPN_-_Configuration_and_Troubleshooting

Cisco Meraki. (2024, April 6). Auto VPN Hub Deployment Recommendations. https://documentation.meraki.com/Architectures_and_Best_Practices/Auto_VPN_Hub_Deployment_Recommendations

Cisco Meraki. (2024, April 8). Site-to-Site VPN Settings. https://documentation.meraki.com/MX/Site-to-site_VPN/Site-to-Site_VPN_Settings#Non-Meraki_VPN_Peers

Cisco Meraki. (2024, April 11). Site-to-Site VPN Firewall Rule Behavior. https://documentation.meraki.com/MX/Site-to-site_VPN/Site-to-site_VPN_Firewall_Rule_Behavior

Cisco Meraki. (2024, April 12). AnyConnect Client Download and Deployment. https://documentation.meraki.com/MX/Client_VPN/AnyConnect_on_the_MX_Appliance/Client_deployment

Cisco Meraki. (2024, April 15). MG IP Passthrough. https://documentation.meraki.com/MG/General_Configuration/MG_IP_Passthrough

Cisco Meraki. (2024, April 16). vMX Setup Guide for Microsoft Azure. https://documentation.meraki.com/MX/MX_Installation_Guides/vMX_Setup_Guide_for_Microsoft_Azure

Cisco Meraki. (2024a, April 17). AnyConnect on the MX Appliance. https://documentation.meraki.com/MX/Client_VPN/AnyConnect_on_the_MX_Appliance

Cisco Meraki. (2024b, April 17). Meraki Auto VPN General Best Practices. https://documentation.meraki.com/Architectures_and_Best_Practices/Cisco_Meraki_Best_Practice_Design/Best_Practice_Design_-_MX_Security_and_SD-WAN/Meraki_Auto_VPN_General_Best_Practices

Cisco Meraki. (2024, April 18). Border Gateway Protocol (BGP). https://documentation.meraki.com/MX/Networks_and_Routing/Border_Gateway_Protocol_(BGP)

Cisco Systems. (2023, December). *Configure Tunnels with Meraki MX – Option 1.* https://docs.umbrella.com/umbrella-user-guide/docs/manual-meraki-mx

Cisco ThousandEyes. (2024a). Internet Insights. https://www.thousandeyes.com/product/internet-insights/

Cisco ThousandEyes. (2024b). Our Story. https://www.thousandeyes.com/about/our-story

Lad, M. (2020, May 28). ThousandEyes + Cisco = A Thousand Times ThousandEyes. *Cisco ThousandEyes*. https://www.thousandeyes.com/blog/cisco-announces-intent-to-acquire-thousandeyes

National Institute of Standards and Technology (NIST). (2023). Public Draft: The NIST Cybersecurity Framework 2.0. https://csrc.nist.gov/pubs/cswp/29/the-nist-cybersecurity-framework-20/ipd

PCI Security Standards Council. (2022, December). PCI DSS: v4.0. https://www.pcisecuritystandards.org/document_library/

Chapter 10

Securing User Traffic

In this chapter, you learn the following:

- The breadth of the network-based controls available to protect users and data, and ensure compliance with industry best practice.
- The use cases for features such as firewalling, Geo-IP firewalling, IDS/IPS, and content filtering. This chapter also shows how to implement these features.
- The security capabilities available as part of Meraki MX security appliances, MR access points, and Secure Connect. The intention here is to help administrators decide where best to implement these controls.
- How to create a unified Secure Access Service Edge (SASE) using Cisco Secure Connect. This includes how to configure DNS, firewall, Web, and Data Loss Prevention (DLP) policies for best-in-class enterprise security.

Chapter 8, "Wired and Wireless LAN Security," and Chapter 9, "Meraki MX and WAN Security," detailed how to authenticate wired, wireless, and VPN users and associate IP-based security policy. This chapter covers additional available controls, regardless of network access and whether or not users are authenticated. This makes the controls relevant, regardless of where organizations might be on their zero trust journey.

Cisco Secure Connect, which we introduce in this chapter, is the name given to Meraki's tightly integrated unified Secure Access Service Edge (SASE) solution. Cisco Secure Connect is powered by Cisco Umbrella, Cisco's cloud-based, multifunction security service. When combined with SD-WAN on Meraki MX, Cisco Secure Connect provides a powerful, distributed, and fully featured SASE security capability. Secure Connect not only simplifies the deployment of Meraki networks but also uplifts the security capabilities, as we demonstrate in this chapter. As a result, it is highly recommended that all organizations deploy Cisco Secure Connect. Read on to learn how to configure the security functions of both Meraki MX and Cisco Secure Connect.

Comparison of Meraki's Native Security Capabilities and Cisco Secure Connect

Because security features, such as firewalls, can be deployed in different places in the network, we start this chapter with a comparison of the security features in Meraki MR, MX, and Cisco Secure Connect. The aim here is to help those designing Meraki networks to decide where best to locate these security functions.

When navigating Meraki Dashboard, you may have noticed how similar the configuration of firewalls is between Meraki MR and Meraki MX. Although the interface is similar, it's important to note that there are some key differences. Table 10-1 outlines these differences and provides a side-by-side comparison of Meraki MX, MR, and Secure Connect. As you can see, Cisco Secure Connect includes additional capabilities such as Data Loss Prevention (DLP).

Table 10-1 *Security Feature Comparison Between Meraki MR, Meraki MX, and Secure Connect*

Feature Support	Meraki MR Access Point	Meraki MX Security Appliance	Cisco Secure Connect
Can firewall policy be applied to remote access VPN clients which terminate here?	N/A	No	Yes
Layer 3 Firewall	Yes, stateless	Yes, stateful	Yes, using Cloud Firewall
Layer 7 Firewall	Yes, stateless	Yes, stateless	Yes, using Cloud Firewall
Geo-IP Firewall	No	Yes	No
URL Filtering	Yes, using L7 firewall	Yes	Yes, using Web policy
Content Filtering by Category	Yes, using L7 firewall	Yes	Yes, using Web policy
Advanced Malware Protection (AMP)	No	Yes. This is only enabled for HTTP by default to maximize performance. HTTPS can be enabled by raising a case with Meraki support.	Yes, using Web policy. Advanced sandboxing, file inspection, and file block supported.
Intrusion Detection and Prevention (IDS/IPS)	No	Yes, HTTP only	Yes, using Cloud Firewall

Feature Support	Meraki MR Access Point	Meraki MX Security Appliance	Cisco Secure Connect
Data Loss Prevention (DLP)	No	No	Yes, using DLP policy
Cloud Access Security Broker (CASB) function	No	No	Yes, using Web policy
Granular reporting	No, logging only	No, logging only	Yes, filterable by identity, location, device, date and time, blocked vs. allowed, destination, security category, threat type, and more

Note Firewall rules, of any type, apply only to traffic that traverses the security appliance. This means that firewall rules do not apply to traffic originating from or terminating at the security appliance, similar to traditional Cisco devices. For more information, see https://documentation.meraki.com/General_Administration/Cross-Platform_Content/Layer_3_and_7_Firewall_Processing_Order. VPN traffic can be filtered using split tunnel, controlling which subnets are part of the VPN, outbound rules for client VPN, or site-to-site VPN outbound firewall rules. Refer to Chapter 9 for more information on configuring site-to-site VPN and remote-access VPN.

Native Meraki MX Capabilities

Meraki MX security appliances are Meraki's range of cloud-managed, multifunction security and SD-WAN appliances. These appliances come with native security capabilities such as firewall, IDS/IPS, and content filtering. This section details these functions and how to configure them.

Layer 3 Firewall

A key theme across security standards includes various controls, such as the ability to restrict traffic between different network segments. For example, PCI DSS 4.0 requirement 1.3.1 requires that traffic into the cardholder data environment be denied by default, with only permitted flows allowed. NIST 800-53 has a similar requirement, referring instead to the need to restrict traffic between different security domains. Similarly, PCI DSS 4.0 requires network security controls (NSCs) to be implemented between trusted and untrusted networks. Firewalling has been providing this capability for decades. While it is complemented by newer features such as group policies and adaptive policies, firewalling is typically still deployed where there is external connectivity such as the Internet.

Meraki MX security appliances feature the ability to configure both Layer 3 and Layer 7 firewalling independently.

Following are some important points to note about firewalling on Meraki MX:

- By default, all inbound traffic is blocked, and all outbound traffic is allowed.
- Firewall rules are processed in a top-down order, similar to other platforms.
- There is a difference in terms of how firewall rules are processed on Meraki MX versus Meraki MR access points. On Meraki MR access points, traffic that is allowed by custom (as opposed to default) Layer 3 firewall rules is permitted and bypasses any Layer 7 firewall rules. On Meraki MX, traffic that is allowed by custom Layer 3 firewall rules is reevaluated against any Layer 7 firewall rules. Refer to the following document for more details: https://documentation.meraki.com/General_Administration/Cross-Platform_Content/Layer_3_and_7_Firewall_Processing_Order.
- On Meraki MX, Layer 3 rules configured on the Firewall page (**Security & SD-WAN > Firewall**) are stateful, meaning they do not need a rule permitting return traffic, which is part of the same connection. Layer 7 rules are stateless, as are both L3 and L7 firewall rules configured as part of a group policy (**Network-wide > Group Policies**) or wireless firewall (**Wireless > Firewall & Traffic Shaping**).
- Inbound IPv4 traffic requires either port forwarding or a Network Address Translation (NAT) rule to permit and translate traffic from the WAN IP address to an internal IP address. Refer to this guide for more information on how to configure NAT: https://documentation.meraki.com/MX/Firewall_and_Traffic_Shaping/MX_Firewall_Settings. NAT is not applicable to IPv6 traffic; therefore, inbound IPv6 traffic is controlled entirely by inbound firewall rules. It is recommended to avoid using **Any** as the source or destination for inbound IPv6 firewall rules.
- If you are using a security appliance with a cellular interface, any outbound rules configured also apply to the cellular interface. In case you want to preserve bandwidth for critical applications, Meraki Dashboard provides the ability to further restrict traffic on the backup cellular interface using cellular firewall rules.

Follow these steps to configure a Layer 3 firewall rule in Meraki Dashboard:

Step 1. Log in to Meraki Dashboard (https://dashboard.meraki.com).

Step 2. Navigate to **Security & SD-WAN > Firewall** (see Figure 10-1).

Step 3. The process to configure Layer 3 firewall rules is the same for both inbound and outbound traffic. Under the appropriate heading, either **Inbound Rules** or **Outbound Rules**, click the **Add New** button on the right side.

Step 4. A new row is added above the default rule for you to edit (see Figure 10-2). The options under **Policy** are **Permit** or **Deny**.

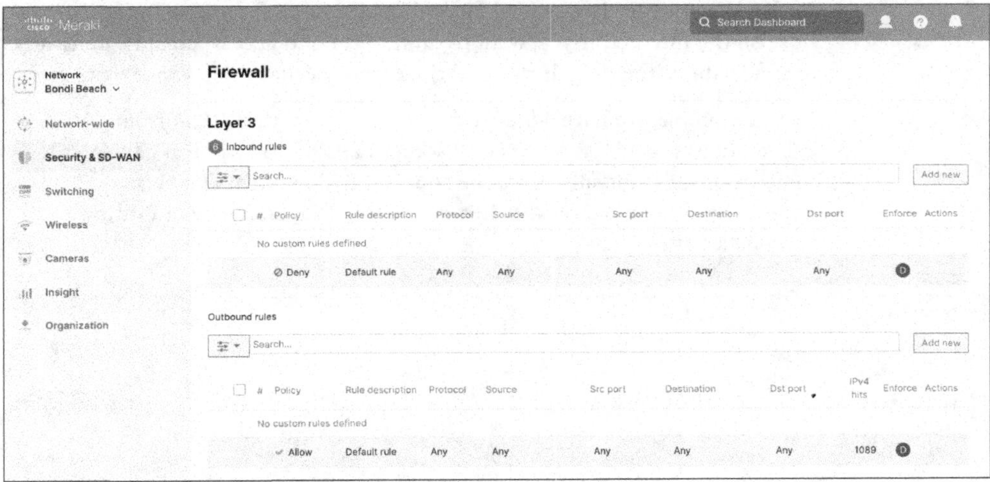

Figure 10-1 *The Meraki MX Firewall Page in Meraki Dashboard*

The **Rule** description is simply a text field that describes the purpose of this rule.

The available **Protocol** options are **TCP**, **UDP**, **ICMPv4**, **ICMPv6**, or **Any**.

The **Source** field specifies the expected source IP or subnet for this rule. The **Source** field accepts an IP address, VLAN name, CIDR subnets, or Any. Multiple IP addresses or subnets can be entered as long as they are separated with a comma. When you enter a value here, Meraki Dashboard provides an autocomplete function, which is helpful if you are

- Selecting VLANs or subnets that are local to the MX.
- Selecting policy objects that have already been configured in Dashboard (**Organization > Policy Objects**).
- Adding a host IP address. Meraki Dashboard automatically adds a /32 suffix to convert this to CIDR notation.

The **Destination** field specifies the destination IP, VLAN name, subnet, or fully qualified domain name (FQDN) for this rule. Except for the addition of FQDN and domain names, this field accepts the same values as the Source field described earlier.

The **Src Port** and **Dst Port** fields support port numbers or port ranges. Ports can be specified individually (e.g., 80), in multiples (e.g., 22, 80), or as ranges (e.g., 80–81). Multiple port ranges cannot be entered on a single rule. Therefore, create a new firewall policy each time a port range is required.

In this example, we have added an outbound rule to deny ICMP traffic to a host on the Internet. If you want to limit outbound access, create a **deny any any** rule above the default rule and the **create permit** rules above that.

In this example, we have added a simple rule to deny ICMPv4 from a VLAN called **Guests** to a host with the IP address 20.76.201.171. You can enter the same details, except substitute the source VLAN with a VLAN or subnet applicable to your network. When you're finished, click **Finish Editing** and then click **Save.**

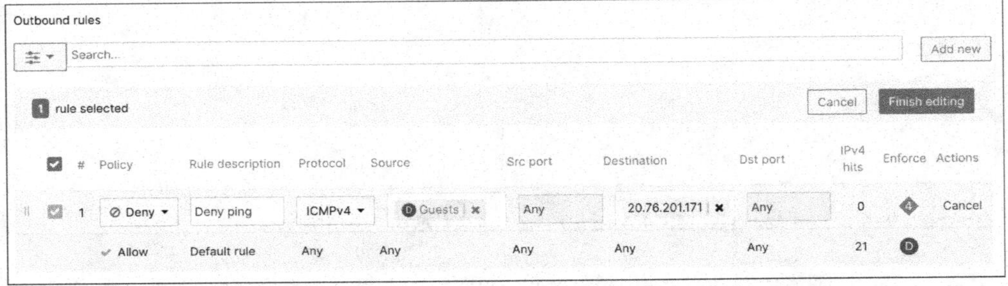

Figure 10-2 *Configuring an Outbound Layer 3 Firewall Rule on Meraki MX in Meraki Dashboard*

You've completed the steps to add a Layer 3 firewall rule on Meraki MX. To verify that this rule is working, we conducted a ping test from a host behind the MX, before and after the rule change. As you can see, traffic is now being blocked. Run a ping test from your network to verify that your rule is working, as illustrated in Figure 10-3.

```
ryanchaney — -zsh — 73×19
ryanchaney@RYCHANEY-M-6X1J ~ % ping -c 3 20.76.201.171
PING 20.76.201.171 (20.76.201.171): 56 data bytes
64 bytes from 20.76.201.171: icmp_seq=0 ttl=106 time=298.154 ms
64 bytes from 20.76.201.171: icmp_seq=1 ttl=106 time=292.845 ms
64 bytes from 20.76.201.171: icmp_seq=2 ttl=106 time=293.493 ms

--- 20.76.201.171 ping statistics ---
3 packets transmitted, 3 packets received, 0.0% packet loss
round-trip min/avg/max/stddev = 292.845/294.831/298.154/2.365 ms
ryanchaney@RYCHANEY-M-6X1J ~ % ping -c 3 20.76.201.171
PING 20.76.201.171 (20.76.201.171): 56 data bytes
Request timeout for icmp_seq 0
Request timeout for icmp_seq 1

--- 20.76.201.171 ping statistics ---
3 packets transmitted, 0 packets received, 100.0% packet loss
ryanchaney@RYCHANEY-M-6X1J ~ %
```

Figure 10-3 *Traffic Before and After the Layer 3 Firewall Rule Addition Showing Traffic Being Blocked*

Traffic matches on firewall rules can also be verified by using the hit counter on the firewall policy. We have confirmed that traffic is hitting this rule by witnessing that the **IPv4 Hits** counter, shown in Figure 10-4, is incrementing.

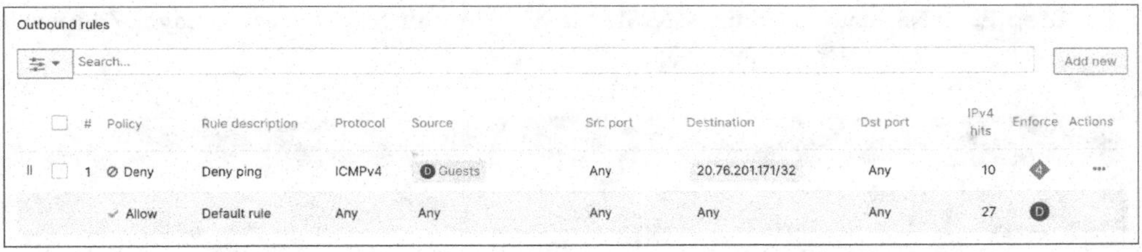

Outbound rules

Search... Add new

#	Policy	Rule description	Protocol	Source	Src port	Destination	Dst port	IPv4 hits	Enforce	Actions
1	Deny	Deny ping	ICMPv4	Guests	Any	20.76.201.171/32	Any	10		...
	Allow	Default rule	Any	Any	Any	Any	Any	27	D	

Figure 10-4 *The IPv4 Hits Counter Shown on the Meraki MX Firewall Page in Meraki Dashboard*

For more information on configuring firewall rules on Meraki MX, refer to https://documentation.meraki.com/MX/Firewall_and_Traffic_Shaping/MX_Firewall_Settings.

Layer 7 Firewall

Both Meraki MX security appliances and MR access points support Layer 7 firewalling. By employing Layer 7 firewalling, administrators can block specific web-based services, websites, or categories of websites without having to specify IP addresses or port ranges. The application classification engine in Meraki networks with current hardware utilizes Cisco Network-Based Application Recognition (NBAR). This deep packet inspection technology detects applications based on the first packet in a flow. This technology enables security to be implemented right at the start of a connection attempt. It is recommended that all devices in your network support NBAR for the widest application support and best visibility.

NBAR requires

- Meraki MX security appliances running MX16 firmware or later
- Wi-Fi 6 capable (or better) APs running MR 27.1 or later

For more information on NBAR, refer to https://documentation.meraki.com/General_Administration/Cross-Platform_Content/Next-gen_Traffic_Analytics_-_Network-Based_Application_Recognition_(NBAR)_Integration.

From the Firewall page (**Security & SD-WAN > Firewall**), it is possible to block applications by category (for example, "All video & music sites") or for a specific type of application within a category (for example, only iTunes within the Video & music category).[1] In this example, management has identified that staff are spending too much time working on their side hustles during work hours. As a result, management has decided that access to blogging sites must be banned.

Follow these steps to achieve this result using a Layer 7 firewall rule in Meraki Dashboard:

Step 1. Log in to Meraki Dashboard (https://dashboard.meraki.com).

Step 2. Navigate to **Security & SD-WAN > Firewall.** Scroll down to **Layer 7 Firewall Rules** (see Figure 10-5).

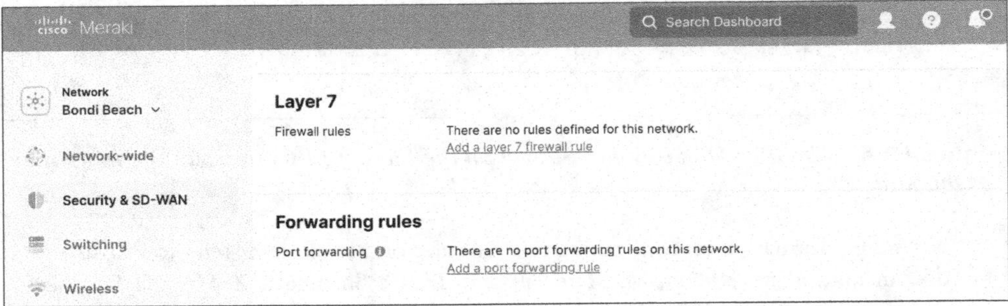

Figure 10-5 *The Layer 7 Firewall Rules on the Security & SD-WAN Page in Meraki Dashboard*

Step 3. Start by clicking **Add a Layer 7 Firewall Rule** (see Figure 10-6).

a. **Policy** is already set to **Deny** and cannot be changed. From the **Application** drop-down menu, you can choose from a large range of categories, including email, gaming, social media, peer-to-peer, video, and music. Select **Blogging** from the **Application** drop-down menu.

b. Next to **Application** is another drop-down menu where you can choose an individual site to block. Figure 10-6 shows the options available under **All Blogging.** Use multiple rules if you want to select multiple sites from this list.

c. Leave **All Blogging** selected and click **Save Changes** at the bottom of the page.

Now that you've completed the configuration of a Layer 7 firewall rule, you can verify this policy by simply using a web browser and trying to navigate to wordpress.com. As shown in Figure 10-7, access to WordPress, which is categorized as a blogging site, is now blocked. You may be wondering why a block page is not displayed, as you might expect. For HTTP requests matching a blocked category, MX redirects the client to a block page. If the website you are trying to reach is using HTTPS, the MX will reset the connection. As a result, the web browser will display an error page rather than a Meraki block page.[2] Cisco Secure Connect, which is covered later in this chapter, is able to decrypt HTTPS and present a block page.

Layer 7
Firewall rules
Policy Application Actions
1 Deny Blogging
Add a layer 7 firewall rule
✓ All Blogging
Ameba
Blogger
Destructoid
FC2
Jimdo
Sina Weibo
Tianya
TypePad
WordPress
Forwarding rules
Port forwarding
There are no port forwarding rules on this network.
Add a port forwarding rule
1:1 NAT
There are no 1:1 NAT mappings.
Add a 1:1 NAT mapping

Figure 10-6 *Configuring Layer 7 Firewall Rules on the Security & SD-WAN Page in Meraki Dashboard*

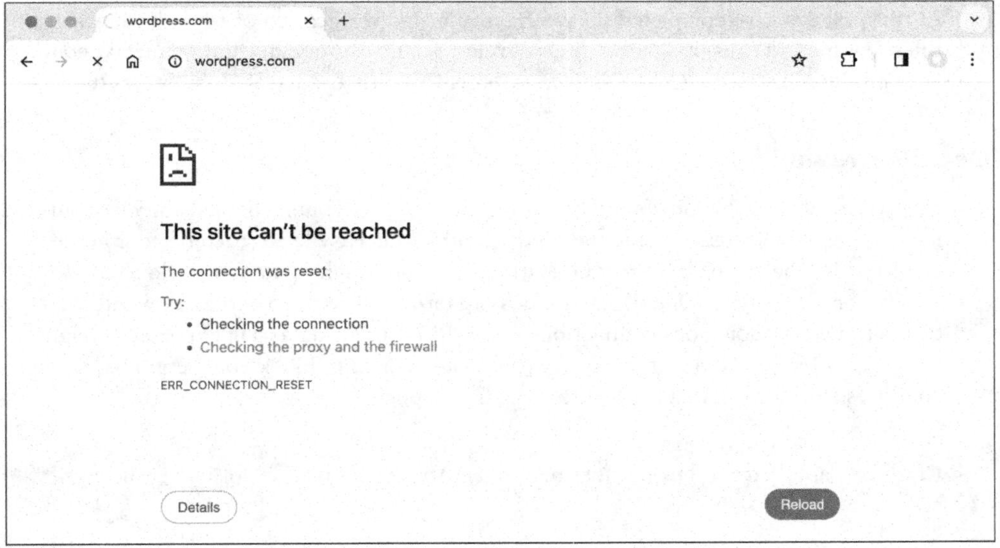

Figure 10-7 *Verifying That Layer 7 Firewall Rules Configured on Meraki MX Are in Effect*

Traffic that is denied by a Layer 7 firewall rule is recorded in the Dashboard event log with an event type of **Layer 7 Firewall Rule.** Figure 10-8 shows the log entries from the testing. NBAR ID 3444 corresponds to WordPress. You can find a full record of all NBAR IDs at https://documentation.meraki.com/General_Administration/Cross-Platform_Content/Mapping_Layer_7_Firewall_Rules_to_NBAR_IDs.

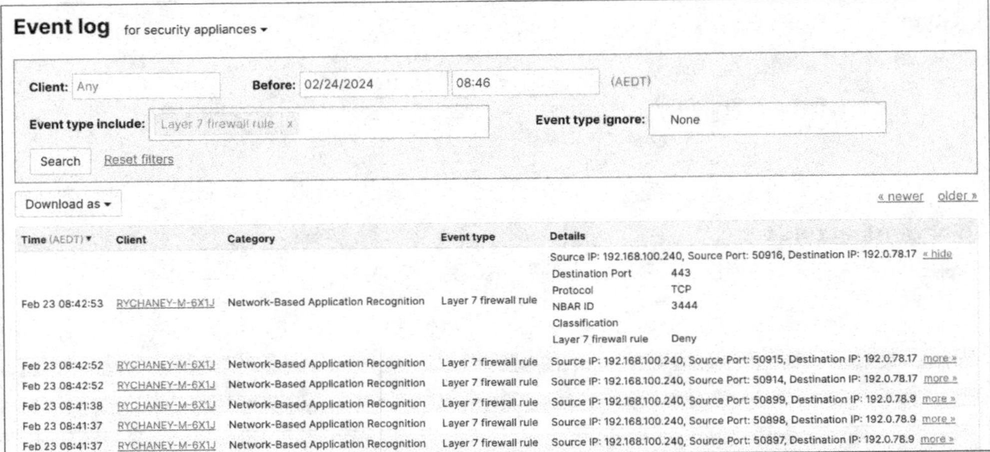

Figure 10-8 *The Event Log in Meraki Dashboard Showing the Layer 7 Firewall Rule in Effect*

At this point, you've completed the configuration and verification of Layer 7 firewall rules. For more details on Layer 7 firewall rules, see https://documentation.meraki.com/General_Administration/Cross-Platform_Content/Creating_a_Layer_7_Firewall_Rule.

Geo-IP Firewall

Many critical security threats today rely on the ability to "phone home," thereby communicating with servers outside the borders and within easy legal reach of your home country.[3] In Chapter 6, "Security Operations," we showed how to export flow data to a collector for analysis. One of the reasons organizations want to export flow information is to detect anomalous connections and exfiltration of data to unexpected foreign countries. Meraki's Geo-IP firewall is a tool that can help to block connections to foreign countries that don't have a legitimate business purpose.

> **Note** Geography-based firewall rules require an Advanced Security (or higher) license.

Enabling Detailed Traffic Analysis

Meraki Dashboard provides basic geographic visibility into flows on your network via the Traffic Analytics page (**Network-wide > Traffic Analytics**). For the Traffic Analytics page to be visible, you must have detailed traffic analysis enabled. Follow these steps to enable the Traffic Analytics page:

Step 1. Log in to Meraki Dashboard (https://dashboard.meraki.com).

Step 2. Navigate to **Network-wide > General** (under Configure). Scroll down to **Traffic Analysis.**

From the **Traffic Analysis** drop-down menu, select **Detailed: Collect Destination Hostnames** (see Figure 10-9). Click **Save.**

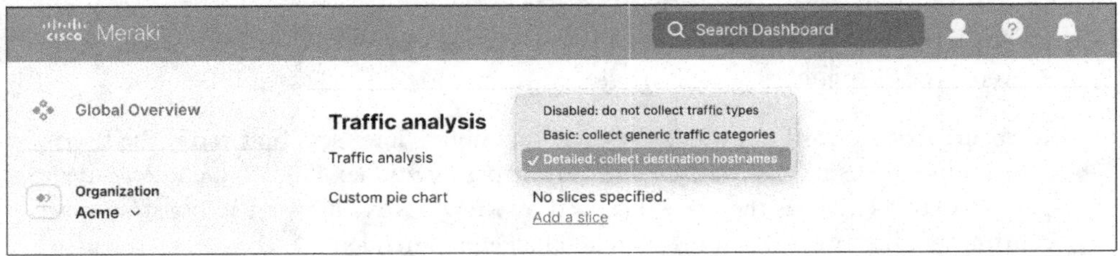

Figure 10-9 *Enabling Detailed Traffic Analysis in Meraki Dashboard*

Meraki Dashboard now begins collecting this data. It will take a few minutes for the Traffic Analytics page to be visible in Meraki Dashboard, but you should give it 24 hours to have enough data to start providing insights.

Figure 10-10 shows an example of the **Traffic Analytics** page, showing traffic to various countries or regions. Below we have highlighted a destination in the Netherlands.

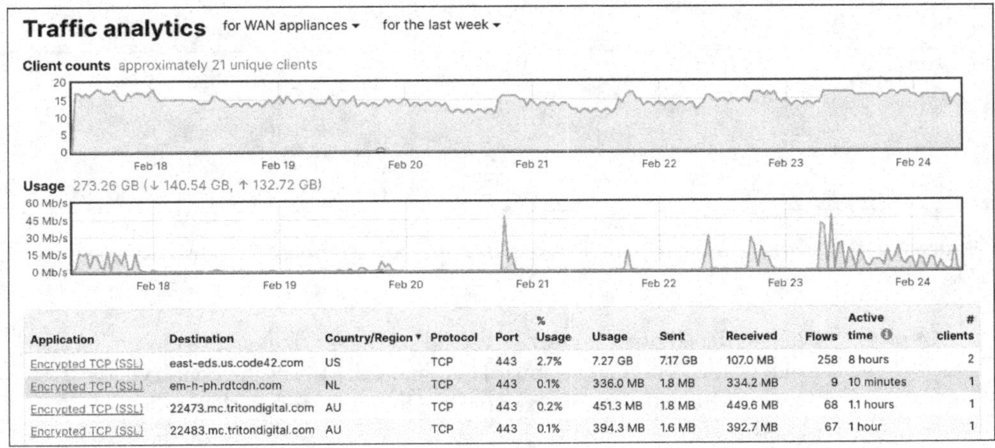

Application	Destination	Country/Region	Protocol	Port	% Usage	Usage	Sent	Received	Flows	Active time	# clients
Encrypted TCP (SSL)	east-eds.us.code42.com	US	TCP	443	2.7%	7.27 GB	7.17 GB	107.0 MB	258	8 hours	2
Encrypted TCP (SSL)	em-h-ph.rdtcdn.com	NL	TCP	443	0.1%	336.0 MB	1.8 MB	334.2 MB	9	10 minutes	1
Encrypted TCP (SSL)	22473.mc.tritondigital.com	AU	TCP	443	0.2%	451.3 MB	1.8 MB	449.6 MB	68	1.1 hours	1
Encrypted TCP (SSL)	22483.mc.tritondigital.com	AU	TCP	443	0.1%	394.3 MB	1.6 MB	392.7 MB	67	1 hour	1

Figure 10-10 *The Traffic Analytics Page in Meraki Dashboard*

Configuring Geo-IP Firewall

Imagine that the traffic to the Netherlands (highlighted in Figure 10-10) is unexpected and appears to be nefarious. Because it has no legitimate business purpose, it's determined that all traffic destined to the Netherlands should be blocked until further notice.

Although it would be unusual to block an entire country, this goal can be achieved with Geo-IP firewall rules. Geo-IP rules are based on subnet-to-country mappings, meaning that they can be circumvented in situations where

- Sites are hosted by third parties, such as content delivery networks (CDNs), in countries different to the site's top-level domain.
- Users are routed to an instance of the target site closest to them, rather than in the country of origin.

To ensure that a Geo-IP firewall policy will function as intended, first verify the IP-to-country lookup using the MaxMind tool at https://www.maxmind.com/en/geoip-demo. The MaxMind engine is the same one used by Meraki MX, allowing administrators to confirm that the target IP address will be blocked as intended.

Follow these steps to configure a Geo-IP firewall policy:

Step 1. Log in to Meraki Dashboard (https://dashboard.meraki.com).

Step 2. Navigate to **Security & SD-WAN > Firewall** (under Configure). Scroll down to **Layer 7 Firewall Rules**, and click **Add a Layer 7 Firewall Rule.**

Step 3. From the **Application** drop-down menu, select **Countries.**

From the drop-down menu to the right of **Application**, select **Traffic To/From** (see Figure 10-11).

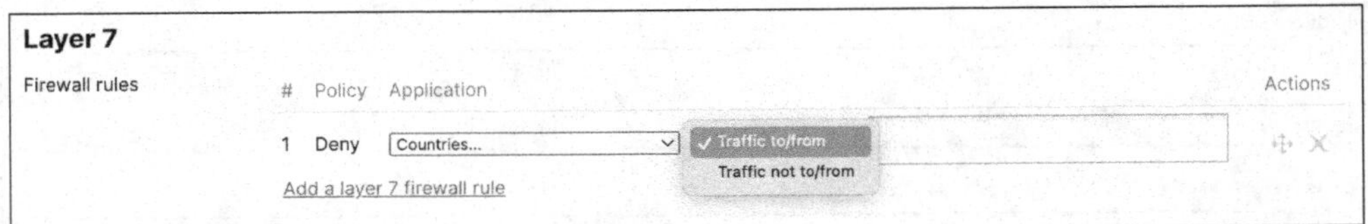

Figure 10-11 *Configuring a Geo-IP Firewall Policy on Meraki MX in Meraki Dashboard*

Step 4. Click in the **Choose Countries…** field on the far right and begin typing the name of the country. Dashboard automatically filters the country list based on what you enter. In this example, we have selected **Netherlands** (see Figure 10-12).

You can also select a country by scrolling down and selecting the country of interest. Multiple countries can be added to this field, meaning it's possible to filter multiple countries using a single L7 firewall rule.

Click **Save Changes** at the bottom of the page.

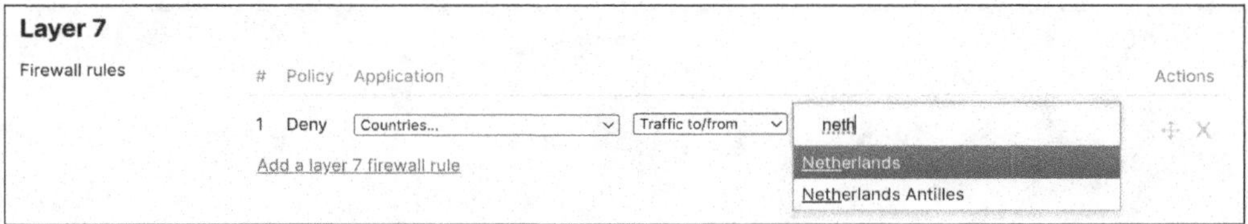

Figure 10-12 *Selecting Countries as Part of Configuring a Geo-IP Firewall Policy on Meraki MX*

You've completed the configuration of a Geo-IP firewall rule.

To verify the filtering is indeed working, we picked a Dutch website (www.iamsterdam.nl) and verified that its IP address was hosted in the Netherlands using the MaxMind tool. We then tested whether we were able to connect to this website, as shown in Figure 10-13 (note that we were automatically redirected to the .com domain; however, this didn't affect our testing).

Figure 10-13 *Demonstrating That the Test Site Is Accessible Prior to Configuring a Geo-IP-Based Firewall Policy*

After configuring the Geo-IP firewall policy, we could no longer connect to this website, as demonstrated in Figure 10-14. Because this site uses HTTPS, Meraki MX blocked access to the site by resetting the connection.

At this point, the configuration and verification of Geo-IP firewall rules are complete. To learn more about Geo-IP firewalling, refer to https://documentation.meraki.com/MX/Firewall_and_Traffic_Shaping/MX_Firewall_Settings.

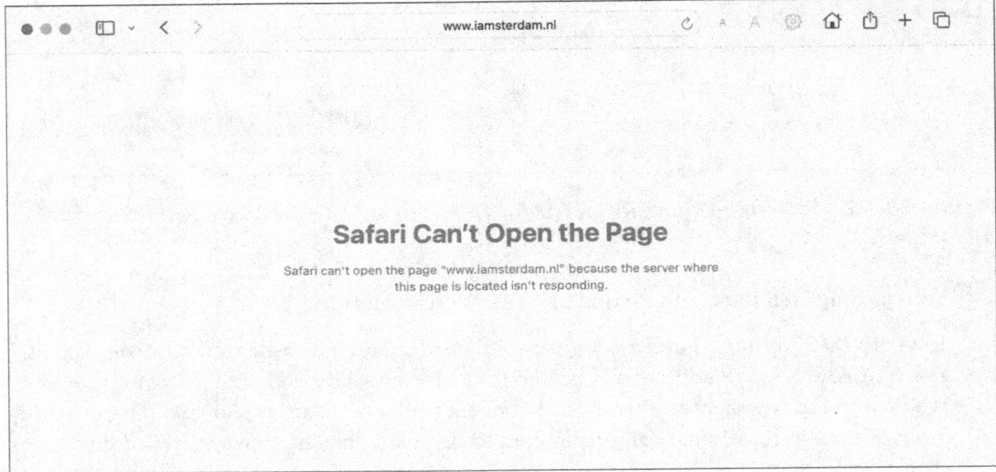

Figure 10-14 *Verifying That Dutch Sites Are Now Being Blocked with a Geo-IP Firewall Policy*

Content Filtering

Content filtering on Meraki MX refers to the ability to block selected web traffic using either a URL or a content or threat classification. Layer 7 firewall rules and content filtering are both able to block websites based on category, such as blogging. However, only content filtering can block threats, such as sites known to be hosting malware, botnets, or spam.

URL Filtering

Follow these steps to configure URL filtering using Meraki MX security appliances.

Step 1. Log in to Meraki Dashboard (https://dashboard.meraki.com).

Step 2. Navigate to **Security & SD-WAN > Content Filtering** (under Configure). Scroll down to **URL Filtering** (see Figure 10-15).

Step 3. Concerned about a wave of Taylor Swift mania impacting office productivity, management has asked IT to block access to www.taylorswift.com. Because this URL does not fall into one of the existing threat content categories, the easiest way to filter this URL is to use URL filtering.

Enter the URL you would like to block in the **Blocked URL List** field and then click **Save** (see Figure 10-16). You can enter multiple URLs by inserting them one under another. The allow list always supersedes the blocked URL list. The allow list is intended to allow access to part of a site while blocking the rest.

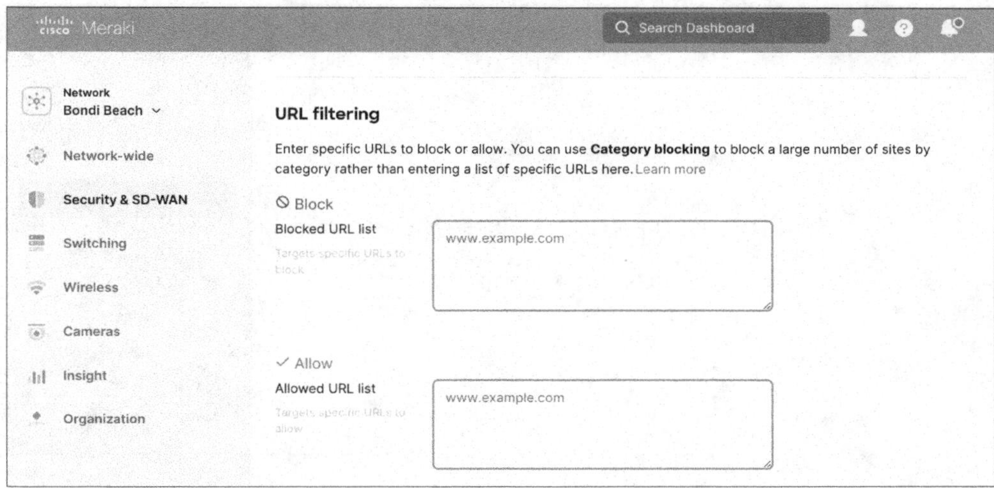

Figure 10-15 *The URL Filtering Section of the Content Filtering Page for Meraki Security Appliances in Meraki Dashboard*

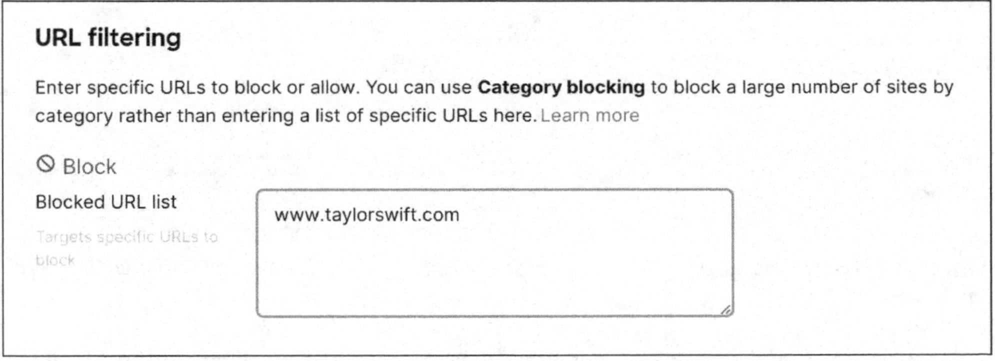

Figure 10-16 *Configuring URL Filtering on Meraki MX in Meraki Dashboard*

Now that you've completed the URL filtering configuration, to verify that the filtering is working, simply test the URL from a web browser on a client sitting behind the MX (see Figure 10-17). This site also uses HTTPS, so Meraki MX has reset the connection.

Attempts to access blocked sites are also recorded in the event log in Dashboard with an event type of **Content Filtering Blocked URL.** Figure 10-18 shows the event log entries related to the testing reflected in Figure 10-17.

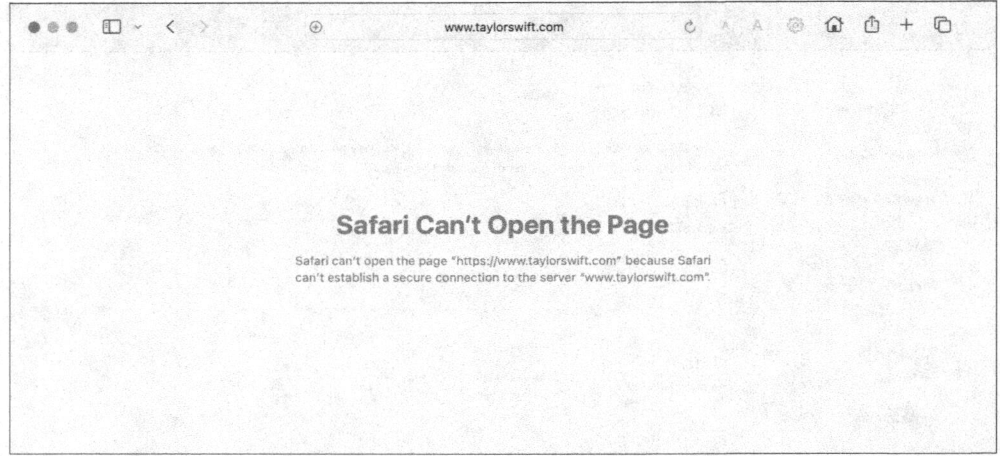

Figure 10-17 *Verifying That the URL Filter Is Working as Intended*

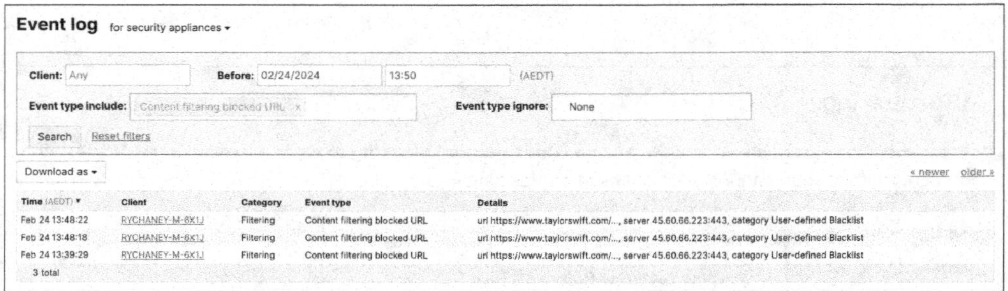

Figure 10-18 *Event Log Showing Attempts to Access a Site Blocked Using a URL Filter on Meraki MX*

You've now completed the configuration and verification of URL filtering using Meraki MX. For more information on URL filtering, refer to https://documentation.meraki.com/MX/Content_Filtering_and_Threat_Protection/Content_Filtering.

Category Blocking with Cisco Talos Intelligence

Cisco Talos is the largest, nongovernment threat intelligence research organization in the world. Talos's security researchers provide up-to-date classification of content and the identification of threats. This intelligence enables Meraki MX content filtering to block both regular content categories such as gaming and adult, as well as threat categories such as sites hosting malware, controlling botnets, sending spam, and more.

To take advantage of the threat intelligence from Cisco Talos, you must be running MX17 firmware or later. Prior to MX17, content filtering relied on services from BrightCloud.

Note Category blocking requires an Advanced Security (or higher) license.

PCI DSS 4.0, HIPAA, and NIST 800-53 all require that organizations have the capability to block malware. In addition, the Essential Eight framework requires that organizations have the capability to block Internet advertisements. Although none of the categories are blocked by default, many of the threat categories probably should be blocked. It's hard to imagine a legitimate business requirement for users to need to access phishing sites, the dark web, and the like. Read on to learn more about how to block malicious sites using content filtering on Meraki MX.

If you have an example of a URL that you want to block along with all other similar sites, enter it into Talos's IP and Domain Reputation Center at https://www.talosintelligence.com/reputation_center. This site will identify the correct content category to block. In the example of adforce.com in Figure 10-19, the correct content category is Advertisements.

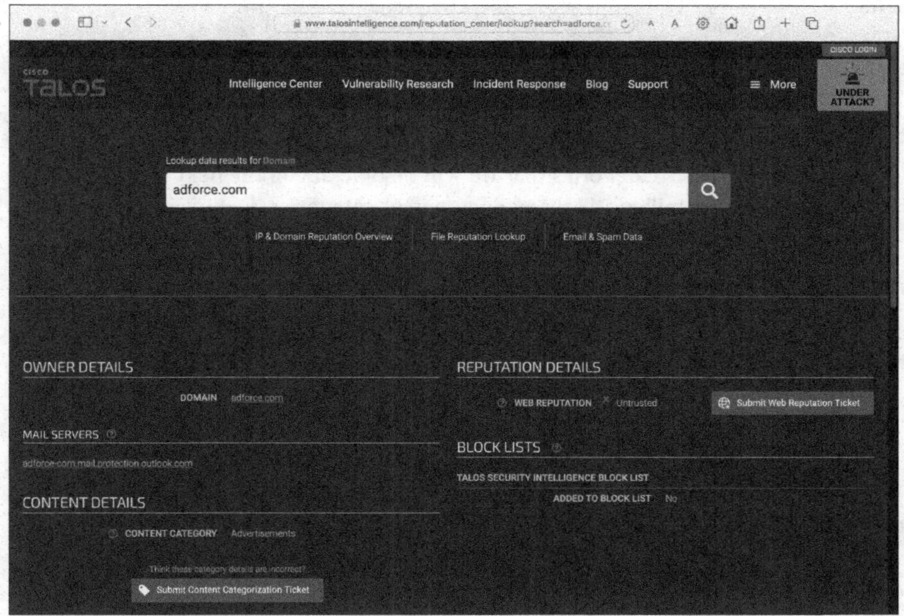

Figure 10-19 *The Talos Domain Reputation Center Website*

Follow these steps to configure content filtering:

Step 1. Log in to Meraki Dashboard (https://dashboard.meraki.com).

Step 2. Navigate to **Security & SD-WAN > Content Filtering** (under Configure), as shown in Figure 10-20.

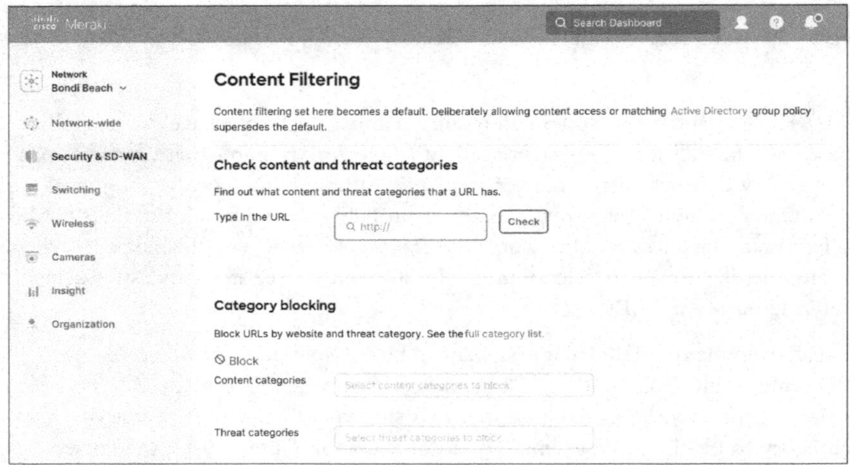

Figure 10-20 *The Content Filtering Page for Meraki Security Appliances in Meraki Dashboard*

Step 3. Under **Category Blocking**, click **See the Full Category List** to bring up a description of the content and threat categories.

In Figure 10-21, you can see the description for the **Advertisements** and **Malware Sites** categories that we will be blocking in the next step. You can find more detail on the threat and content categories, including sample URLs, on the Talos website at https://www.talosintelligence.com/categories.

Click **Back** to go back to the **Content Filtering** page.

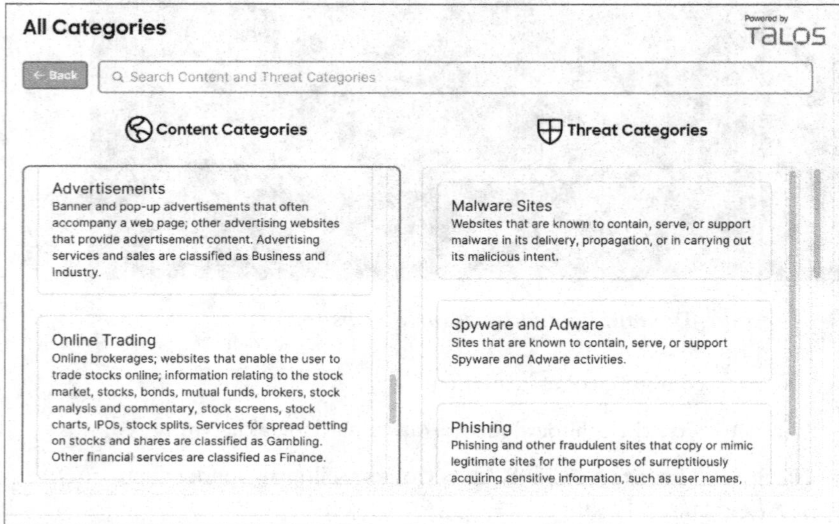

Figure 10-21 *The Cisco Talos Content and Threat Category Descriptions in Meraki Dashboard*

Step 4. From the drop-down menu next to **Content Categories** (see Figure 10-22), select **Advertisements.**

From the drop-down menu next to **Threat Categories**, select **Malware Sites.**

Click **Save.**

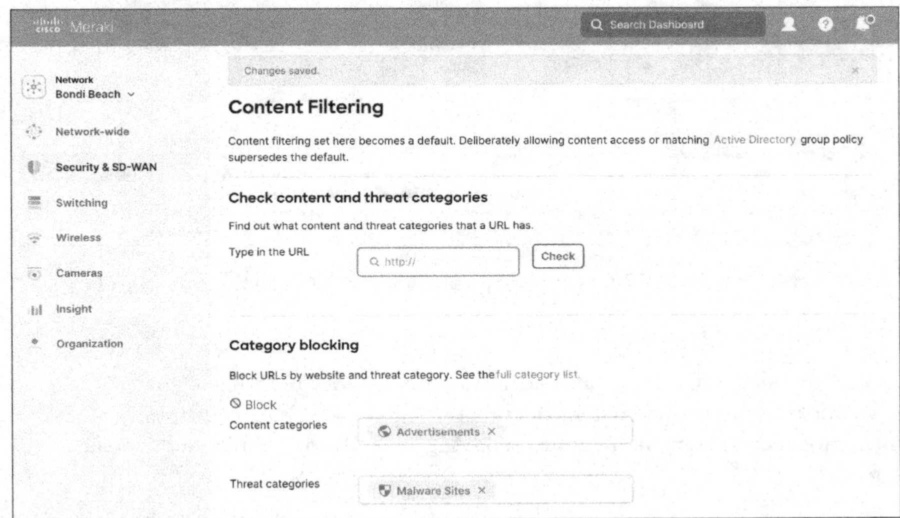

Figure 10-22 *Successfully Configuring Content and Threat Content Filters in Meraki Dashboard*

Now that you've completed the configuration of category blocking, you can verify that the blocking of sites in the advertisement content category is working—in this case, www.adforce.com. As you can see from Figure 10-23, access to this site is being blocked.

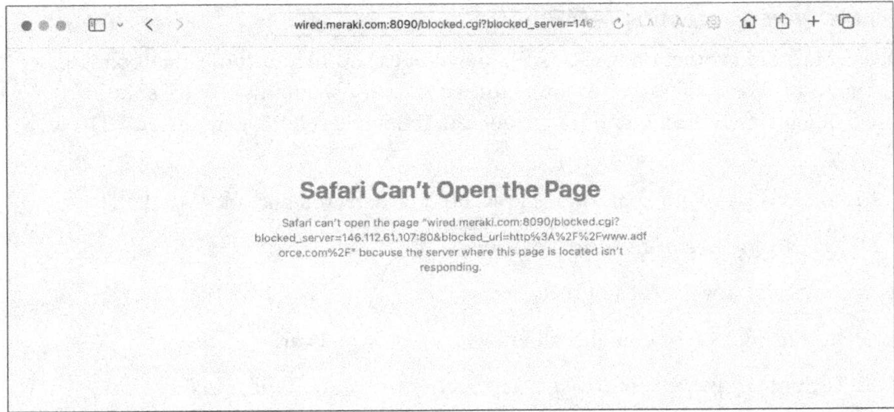

Figure 10-23 *The adforce.com Page Now Being Blocked by Using Content Filtering on Meraki MX*

Similar to URL filtering, the event log in Dashboard also records each attempt to access a URL that is denied due to category blocking, as shown in Figure 10-24.

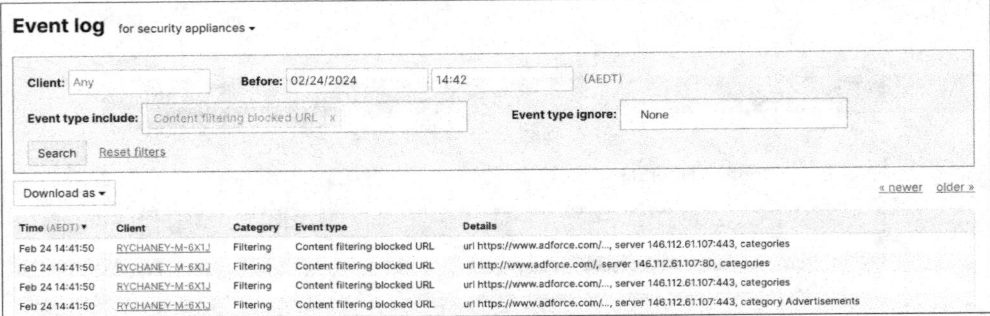

Figure 10-24 *The Event Log in Meraki Dashboard Showing Category Blocking Log Entries*

This section on the configuration and verification of category blocking is now complete. For more details on content filtering on Meraki MX, refer to https://documentation.meraki.com/MX/Content_Filtering_and_Threat_Protection/Content_Filtering.

Threat Protection

Industry best practice requires that organizations have the capability to block known threats. Basic Advanced Malware Protection and IDS/IPS functionality are available natively on Meraki MX. Both of these features require Advanced Security (or higher) licensing.

Advanced Malware Protection (AMP)

Advanced Malware Protection inspects file downloads and blocks those that contain known malware. The majority of today's modern security standards require solutions to protect against malware. Examples include the following requirements from PCI DSS 4.0:

- 5.2 Malicious software (malware) is prevented or detected and addressed.
- 5.2.2 The deployed anti-malware solution(s):
    - Detects all known types of malware.
    - Removes, blocks, or contains all known types of malware.
- 5.3.1 The anti-malware solution(s) is kept current via automatic updates.

- 5.3.2 The anti-malware solution(s) performs periodic scans and active or real-time scans.
- 5.3.5 Anti-malware mechanisms cannot be disabled or altered by users.

Note Cisco Secure Connect, which is covered later in this chapter, is highly recommended for organizations that require protection from malware due to its native ability to inspect HTTPS, as well as its configurable file block and sandboxing capabilities.

On Meraki MX, files are categorized into one of three dispositions by Cisco's AMP Cloud: Clean, Malicious, or Unknown. Meraki MX's Advanced Malware Protection function protects users by preventing HTTP-based downloads of files with a known disposition of Malicious. Advanced Malware Protection is able to inspect the following file types to determine their disposition:

- MS OLE2 (.doc, .xls, .ppt)
- XML-based Microsoft Office file types (.docx, .xlsx, and so on)
- MS Cabinet (Microsoft compression type)
- MS EXE (Microsoft executable)
- ELF (Linux executable)
- Mach-O/Unibin (OSX executable)
- DMG (Apple Disk Image)
- Java (class/bytecode, jar, serialization)
- PDF
- ZIP (regular and spanned)
- EICAR (standardized test file)
- SWF (Shockwave Flash 6, 13, and uncompressed)[4]

In accordance with the PCI requirements stated earlier, updates are handled automatically, and the solution runs in the network, meaning it cannot be disabled by users.

Advanced Malware Protection is disabled by default and relies on Traffic Analysis to function. Refer to the earlier section "Enabling Detailed Traffic Analysis" for the steps to enable Traffic Analysis.

Follow these steps to enable AMP:

Step 1. Log in to Meraki Dashboard (https://dashboard.meraki.com).

Step 2. Navigate to **Security & SD-WAN > Threat Protection** (under Configure), as shown in Figure 10-25.

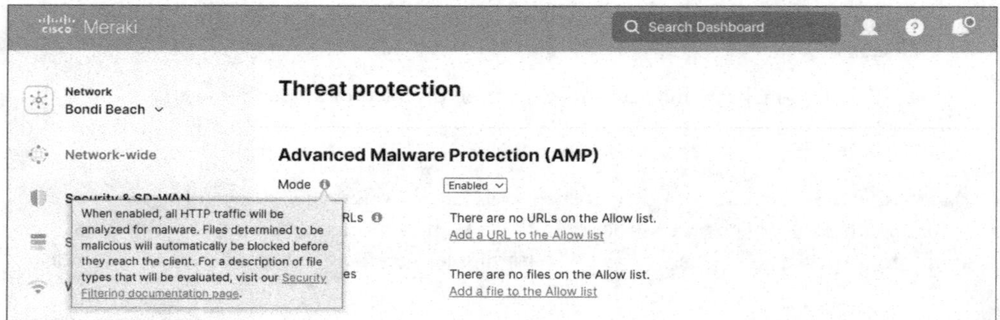

Figure 10-25 *The Security & SD-WAN Threat Protection Page in Meraki Dashboard*

Step 3. Under the heading **Advanced Malware Protection**, select **Enabled** from the **Mode** drop-down menu (see Figure 10-26) and click **Save Changes.**

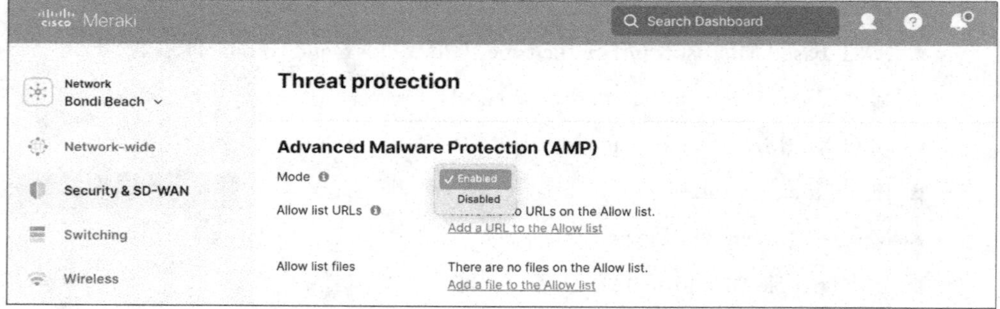

Figure 10-26 *Enabling Advanced Malware Protection on Meraki MX in Meraki Dashboard*

At this point you might be thinking, How do I test this functionality on my production network without the risk of downloading actual malware? To provide a solution to this, the European Institute for Computer Antivirus Research (EICAR) developed a file format that can be used for testing purposes. Most importantly, these files do not contain actual malware; they simply contain an ASCII string that AMP's engine matches. You can download test EICAR files using either HTTP or HTTPS from https://eicar.eu.

To verify that the AMP feature is working, simply attempt to download EICAR files over HTTP:

Step 1. Open https://eicar.eu in your web browser.

Step 2. Click the HTTP download link for **eicarcom2.zip** (see Figure 10-27).

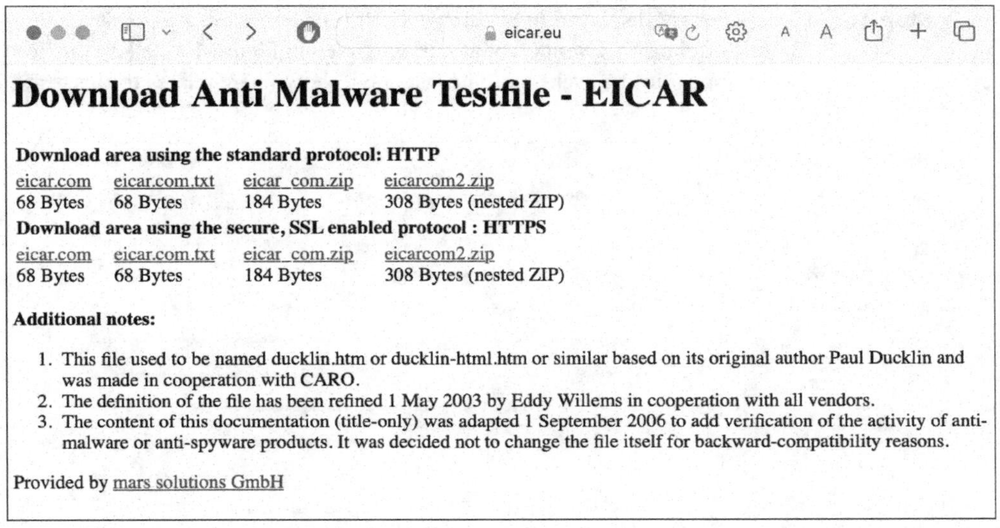

Figure 10-27 *The eicar.eu Website, Which Hosts EICAR Files for Testing Anti-Malware Functionality*

Step 3. The Advanced Malware Protection feature blocks the download of this file and resets the HTTP session (see Figure 10-28).

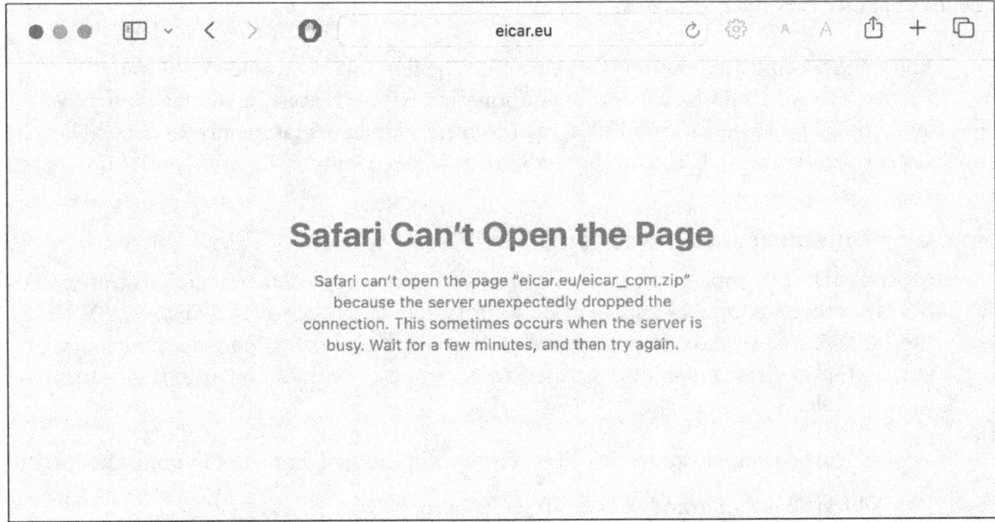

Figure 10-28 *The Web Page a User Sees After AMP Successfully Blocks a Malicious File*

Step 4. Log entries are displayed in Security Center (**Organization > Security Center**) on the **MX Events** tab, as demonstrated in Figure 10-29. Log entries do not appear in the event log. The last entry shown here relates to this test.

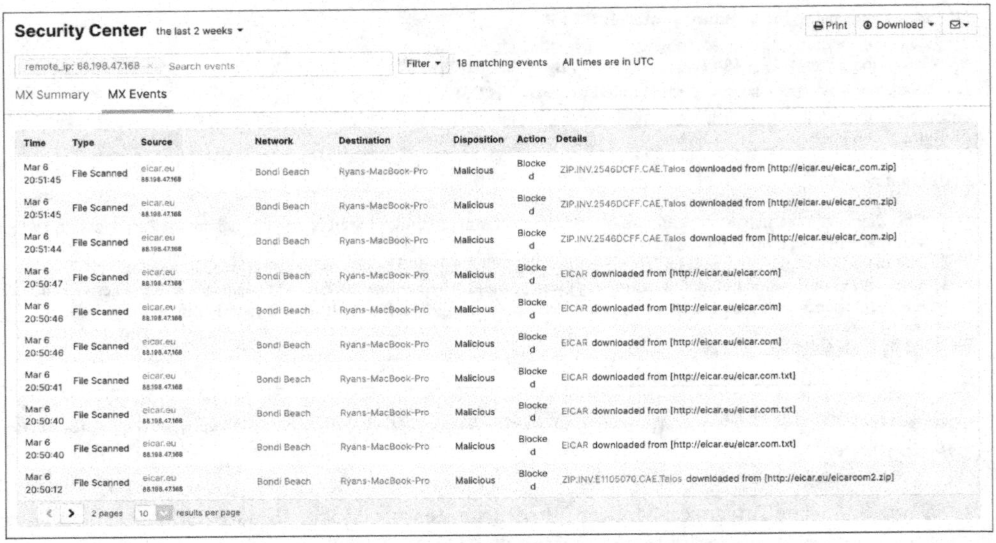

Security Center the last 2 weeks

remote_ip: 88.198.47.168 Search events | Filter | 18 matching events | All times are in UTC

Print | Download

MX Summary | MX Events

Time	Type	Source	Network	Destination	Disposition	Action	Details
Mar 6 20:51:45	File Scanned	eicar.eu 88.198.47.168	Bondi Beach	Ryans-MacBook-Pro	Malicious	Blocked	ZIP.INV.2546DCFF.CAE.Talos downloaded from [http://eicar.eu/eicar_com.zip]
Mar 6 20:51:45	File Scanned	eicar.eu 88.198.47.168	Bondi Beach	Ryans-MacBook-Pro	Malicious	Blocked	ZIP.INV.2546DCFF.CAE.Talos downloaded from [http://eicar.eu/eicar_com.zip]
Mar 6 20:51:44	File Scanned	eicar.eu 88.198.47.168	Bondi Beach	Ryans-MacBook-Pro	Malicious	Blocked	ZIP.INV.2546DCFF.CAE.Talos downloaded from [http://eicar.eu/eicar_com.zip]
Mar 6 20:50:47	File Scanned	eicar.eu 88.198.47.168	Bondi Beach	Ryans-MacBook-Pro	Malicious	Blocked	EICAR downloaded from [http://eicar.eu/eicar.com]
Mar 6 20:50:46	File Scanned	eicar.eu 88.198.47.168	Bondi Beach	Ryans-MacBook-Pro	Malicious	Blocked	EICAR downloaded from [http://eicar.eu/eicar.com]
Mar 6 20:50:46	File Scanned	eicar.eu 88.198.47.168	Bondi Beach	Ryans-MacBook-Pro	Malicious	Blocked	EICAR downloaded from [http://eicar.eu/eicar.com]
Mar 6 20:50:41	File Scanned	eicar.eu 88.198.47.168	Bondi Beach	Ryans-MacBook-Pro	Malicious	Blocked	EICAR downloaded from [http://eicar.eu/eicar.com.txt]
Mar 6 20:50:40	File Scanned	eicar.eu 88.198.47.168	Bondi Beach	Ryans-MacBook-Pro	Malicious	Blocked	EICAR downloaded from [http://eicar.eu/eicar.com.txt]
Mar 6 20:50:40	File Scanned	eicar.eu 88.198.47.168	Bondi Beach	Ryans-MacBook-Pro	Malicious	Blocked	EICAR downloaded from [http://eicar.eu/eicar.com.txt]
Mar 6 20:50:12	File Scanned	eicar.eu 88.198.47.168	Bondi Beach	Ryans-MacBook-Pro	Malicious	Blocked	ZIP.INV.E1105070.CAE.Talos downloaded from [http://eicar.eu/eicarcom2.zip]

2 pages 10 results per page

Figure 10-29 *The MX Events Tab in Security Center with Logs Reporting That a Malicious File Has Been Blocked*

You've now completed the simple steps to enable and verify Advanced Malware Protection on Meraki MX. For more information on this feature, including configuring allowed URLs and allowed files, refer to https://documentation.meraki.com/MX/Content_Filtering_and_Threat_Protection/Advanced_Malware_Protection_(AMP).

Intrusion Detection and Prevention (IDS/IPS)

Meraki's IDS/IPS implementation uses SNORT signatures to detect malicious traffic. IDS/IPS is another common requirement of security standards such as PCI DSS 4.0, SWIFT, and HIPAA. PCI DSS 4.0 requirement 11.5.1 requires "that intrusion-detection and/or intrusion-prevention techniques be used to detect and/or prevent intrusions into the network as follows:

- All traffic is monitored at the perimeter of the Cardholder Data Environment (CDE).
- All traffic is monitored at critical points in the CDE.
- Personnel are alerted to suspected compromises.
- All intrusion-detection and prevention engines, baselines, and signatures are kept up to date."[5]

IDS/IPS on Meraki MX inspects all traffic between the internal and external networks, as well as all traffic between VLANs. Traffic between hosts within the same VLAN is not inspected, which is normal for network-based IDS/IPS solutions; host-based IDS/IPS solutions should be utilized if this is a requirement. IDS/IPS should be used in conjunction with network segmentation. Chapter 8 covers the various ways to isolate network traffic such as port isolation, group policies, and adaptive policies.

It's highly recommended that Meraki MX support Snort version 3, which requires Meraki MX67 and above, running firmware release 17.6 or later (MX64/65 will continue to run Snort 2 regardless of the firmware version). The Snort engine receives regular automatic updates independent of the software release and can be upgraded with no user impact. Snort updates appear in the event log with the event type **Intrusion Detection Rules Update.** Snort recently introduced a new machine learning–based detection engine known as *SnortML*. For more on this recent update, refer to the following Snort blog post: https://blog.snort.org/2024/03/talos-launching-new-machine-learning.html.

Intrusion detection and prevention are disabled by default, so follow these steps to configure IDS/IPS:

Step 1. Log in to Meraki Dashboard (https://dashboard.meraki.com).

Step 2. Navigate to **Security & SD-WAN > Threat Protection** (under Configure). Scroll down to **Intrusion Detection and Prevention.**

Step 3. The **Mode** shown here can be set to **Disabled**, **Detection**, or **Prevention.** Detection refers to IDS mode, which alerts but doesn't block. Prevention switches to IPS mode, which blocks malicious traffic.

Vulnerabilities are graded according to the Common Vulnerability Scoring System (CVSS), which is a standardized and repeatable way to rank vulnerabilities. A score of less than 4 is low, less than 7 is medium, 7–8.9 is high, and 9 and above is critical. By selecting the **Ruleset**, you're telling the IDS/IPS the severity of vulnerabilities to look for. There are three levels:

- **Connectivity** looks for recent vulnerabilities with a CVSS score of 10.
- **Balanced** looks for a CVSS score of 9 and above; this is the default setting.
- **Security** looks for vulnerabilities with a CVSS score of 8 and above.

As you can see in Figure 10-30, we have set the **Mode** to **Prevention** and left the **Ruleset** as **Balanced.**

Remember to click **Save Changes** when finished.

Verifying that the IDS/IPS is functioning can be a little tricky, because you need to find a test tool or website that causes one of the signature rules to fire. While researching online tools, we noticed that http://www.cpcheckme.com/checkme would reliably trigger the IDS alert shown in Figure 10-31. These alerts can be found on the MX Events tab in Security Center (**Organization > Security Center**).

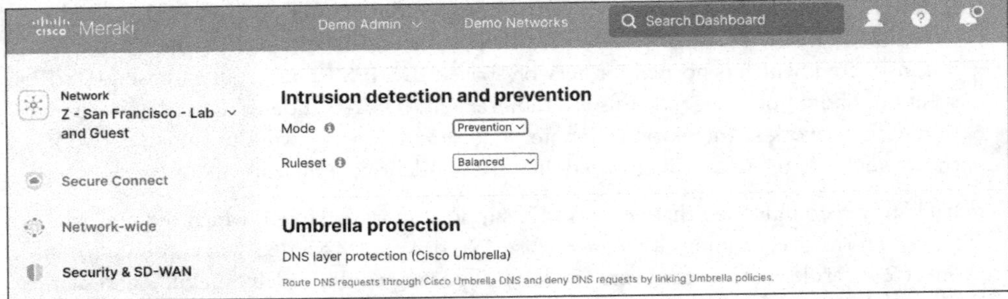

Figure 10-30 *Configuring IDS/IPS on the Security & SD-WAN Page in Meraki Dashboard*

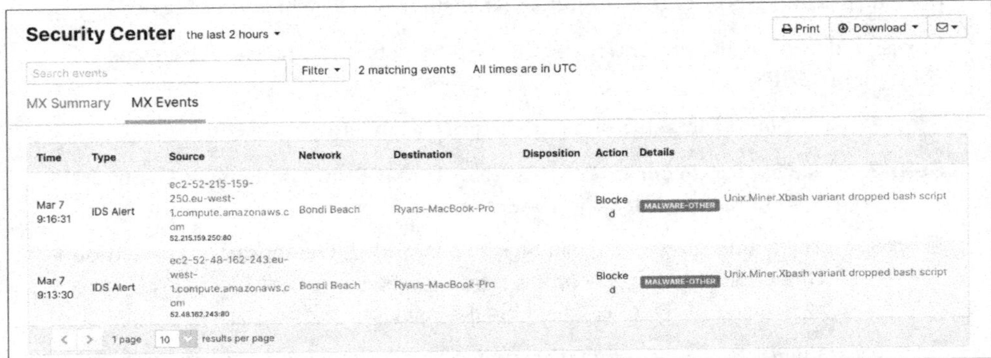

Figure 10-31 *An IDS Alert Shown on the MX Events Tab in Security Center*

You've completed the configuration and verification of IDS/IPS on Meraki MX. Note that signatures can be tuned further using allow list rules. For more information on allow list rules and configuring IDS/IPS, refer to https://documentation.meraki.com/MX/Content_Filtering_and_Threat_Protection/Threat_Protection.

Cisco Secure Connect

Cisco Secure Connect, also referred to as Secure Connect, is a complementary suite of industry-leading security capabilities that are designed to address the following three use cases:

- **Secure Internet Access (SIA):** Enhances Internet security for users, private applications, and Internet of Things (IoT) devices with cloud-based advanced protection from malware, phishing attacks, and other threats for both in-office and remote workers. Enforces Internet usage policies and manages access to public SaaS-based applications.

- **Site Interconnect:** Interconnects sites, users, and applications with native Cisco Meraki Secure SD-WAN and Cisco SD-WAN (vManage) integration, standard IPsec VPN support, and direct SaaS and IaaS Peering.
- **Secure Remote Access:** Securely connects remote workers to your private applications that are hosted in your data centers or private clouds through client-based or clientless (browser-based) remote access services.[6]

Secure Connect is a broad topic, worthy of a book just by itself. In this chapter, we focus on those capabilities most relevant to the Secure Internet Access use case:

- DNS Security
- Cloud Firewall (CDFW)
- Secure Web Gateway (SWG)
- Cloud Access Security Broker (CASB)
- Data Loss Prevention (DLP)

Figure 10-32 illustrates the elements of the Secure Connect solutions relevant to the Secure Internet Access use case.

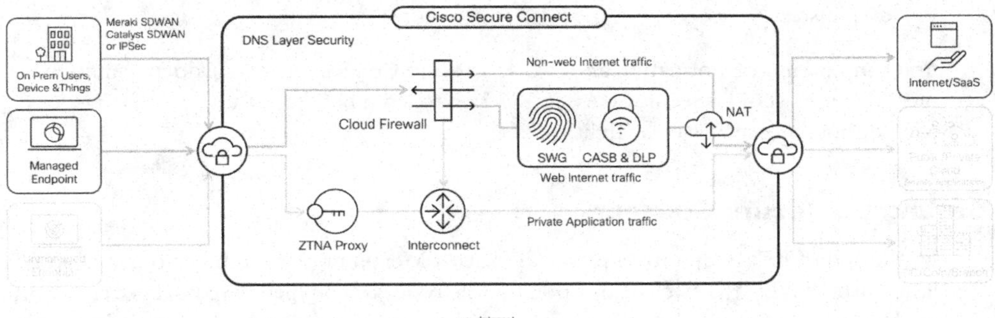

Figure 10-32 *Diagram Representing Secure Connect's Secure Internet Access Architecture*

It was previously possible to integrate Umbrella with a Meraki organization to provide some of these capabilities. What is new, however, is the deeper integration with Meraki Dashboard; adding Secure Connect feels just like adding any other Meraki product line. Today, the Cloud Firewall functionality is configurable natively in Meraki Dashboard, while other functions cross-launch into the Umbrella GUI. In the future, you can expect all capabilities to be configurable natively in Meraki Dashboard, further improving the ease of administration.

In addition, Secure Connect brings additional functionality, such as Data Loss Prevention and Cloud Access Security Broker (CASB). These products were previously separate and have now been merged to create the Secure Connect cloud.

Secure Connect improves on the native security capabilities of Meraki MX in a number of ways:

- Policy can be implemented at the DNS layer before clients establish a TCP/UDP connection to the destination. This means access can be blocked without having to decrypt the traffic. Likewise, policy can be implemented for sites that use protocols that cannot be inspected today, such as QUIC.
- Secure Connect supports HTTPS inspection, a critical capability for the modern Internet. A key requirement of NIST 800-83 is AC-4(4), requiring organizations to have the capability to inspect encrypted traffic. Because the majority of web traffic these days is encrypted, this means you cannot protect sensitive data or users without the ability to inspect HTTPS traffic.
- Secure Connect adds new CASB and DLP functions to prevent the exfiltration of sensitive data. This covers popular websites, webmail, file uploads, and the use of generative AI services.
- Security policy is now centralized, making security policy quicker and easier to administer.

You can find more information about Cisco Secure Connect at https://documentation.meraki.com/CiscoPlusSecureConnect. Read on to learn how to set up Secure Connect and configure its security capabilities.

Setting Up Secure Connect

By the end of this setup process, you will have a Meraki org, an Umbrella org, and an API integration linking the two. At this point in the process, you may have none, one, or both of these accounts pre-existing. You need to purchase Secure Connect before you can get started. To purchase Secure Connect, contact an authorized Cisco Partner or your Cisco Account Manager.

Secure Connect availability varies from country to country. You can find the latest availability at the following URL under Data Center Availability: https://documentation.meraki.com/CiscoPlusSecureConnect/Cisco__Secure_Connect_Now-_Sites/Cisco__Secure_Connect_Foundation_Meraki_SD-WAN_Integration.

The Secure Connect functions are applied in the following order (the order of operations):

1. DNS
2. Cloud Firewall
3. Secure Web Gateway (SWG)

4. CASB
5. DLP

Intuitively, we cover the configuration of these features in the same order. Some features are common to more than one function, such as HTTPS inspection, which is common to both DNS and Web. It's best practice to avoid targeting the same identities with the same feature in policies for different functions. We have tried to demonstrate a policy that aligns with best practice; however, we do recommend reading up on Umbrella when you understand the basics taught here.

Before starting the configuration, you need to purchase Secure Connect and receive the welcome email, as shown in Figure 10-33.

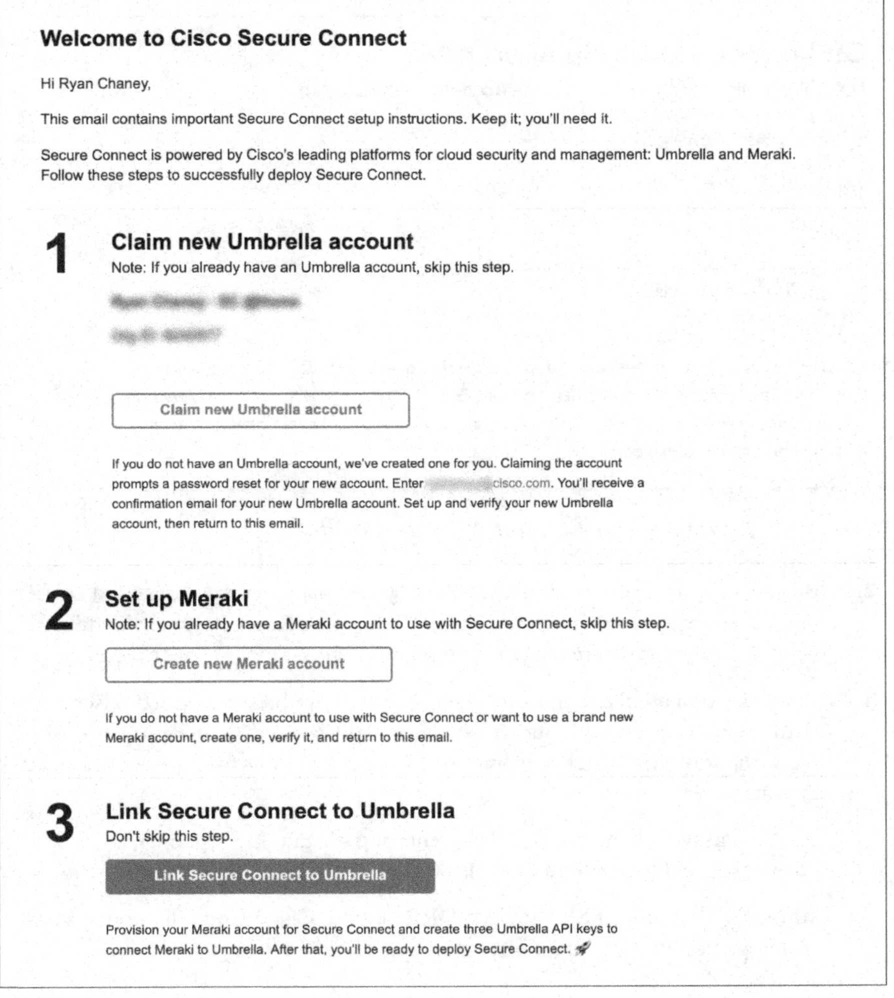

Figure 10-33 *The Cisco Secure Connect Welcome Email*

Initial Setup and Integration with Cisco Umbrella

In this example, we show the setup steps that an administrator with an existing Meraki account and a new Umbrella account would follow. We expect this scenario to be the one that would apply to the majority of readers. You must follow the setup steps in the welcome email in order (top to bottom). If you have an existing Umbrella account, you can skip Step 1. Because we have an existing Meraki account, we skip Step 2. If you do not have an existing Meraki account, you need to complete Step 2 before moving on to Step 3.

Follow these steps to complete the integration between Umbrella and Secure Connect:

Step 1. Open the Secure Connect welcome email and click the link **Claim New Umbrella Account** (see Figure 10-34).

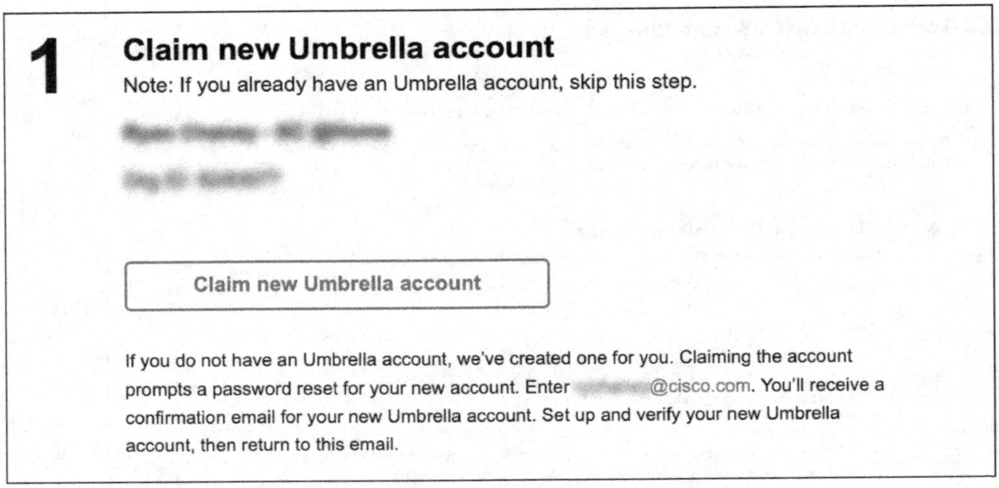

Figure 10-34 *Step 1 on the Secure Connect Welcome Email*

Step 2. Because this is a new Umbrella account, you must set a new password on first use. From the screen shown in Figure 10-35, click **Reset Password**, and an email is sent to your email address with a link to reset your password.

Step 3. Open your email client and find the email from umbrella-support@cisco.com with the subject "Reset your Cisco Umbrella Password" (see Figure 10-36). Click the link titled **click this link**, which opens the **Password Recovery** page in your web browser.

Step 4. Enter a **Password** and confirm it by entering it again in the **Confirm Password** field (see Figure 10-37).

To finish, click the **RESET PASSWORD** button. Cisco Umbrella updates and then logs you in to the administration page.

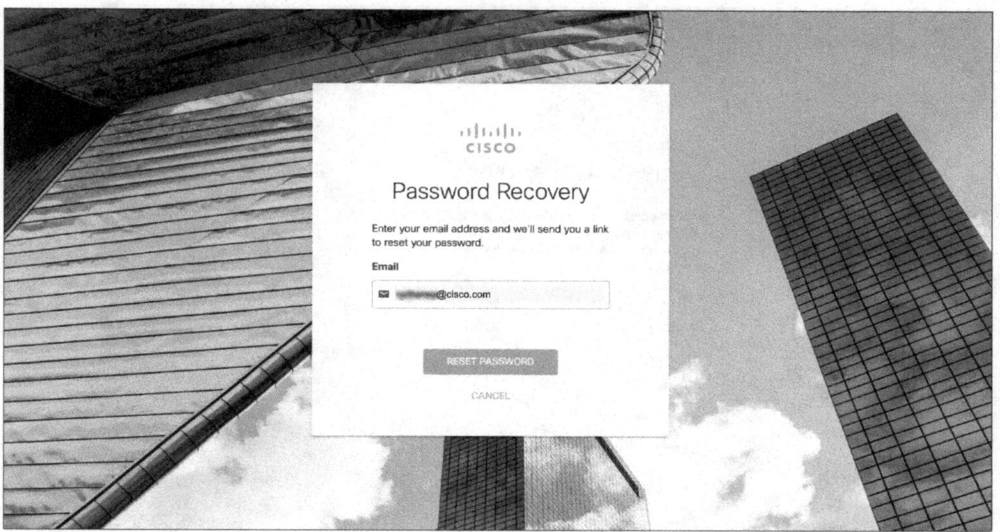

Figure 10-35 *The Cisco Umbrella Password Recovery Page*

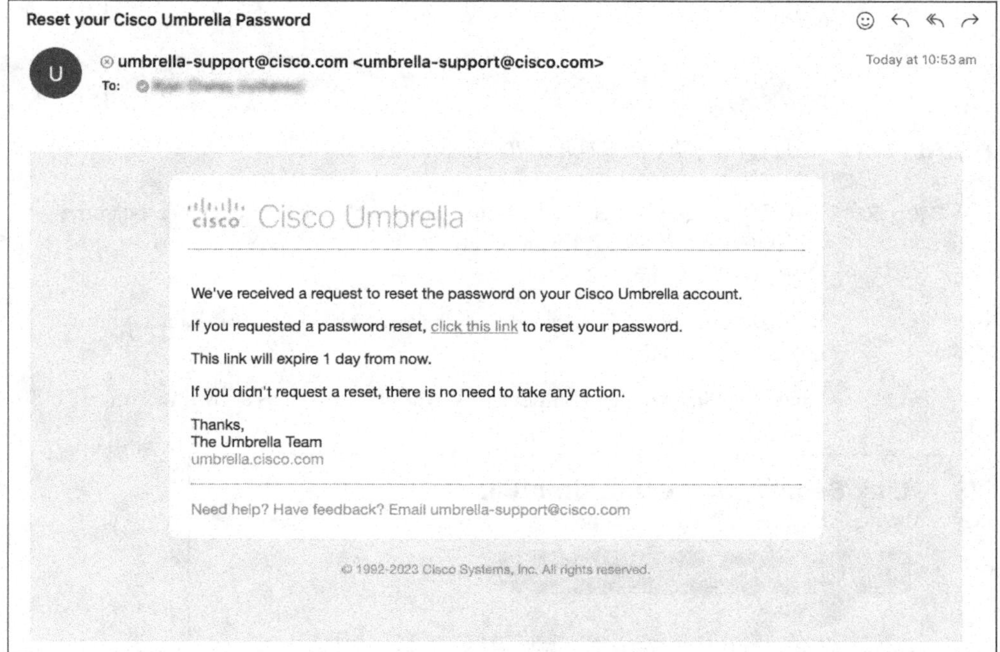

Figure 10-36 *The Cisco Umbrella Password Reset Email*

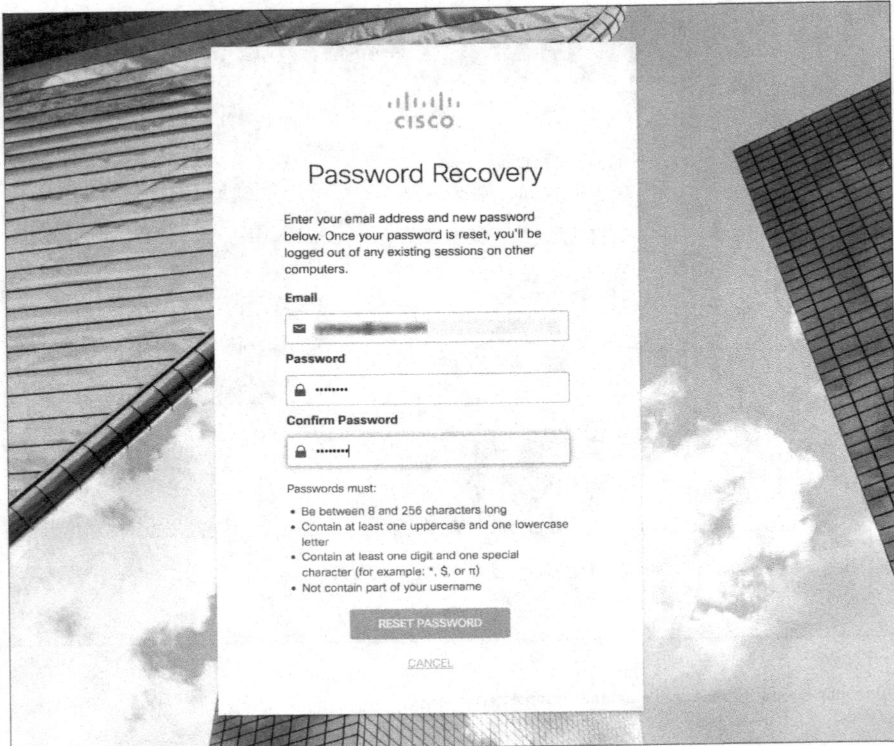

Figure 10-37 *Changing the Cisco Umbrella Account Password*

Step 5. Switch back to your email client and reopen the Secure Connect welcome email. Complete Step 2 (from Figure 10-33) if you don't already have a Meraki Dashboard account.

In this example, because we already have a Meraki Dashboard account, we move onto Step 3.

Click the **Link Secure Connect to Umbrella** button, as shown in Figure 10-38.

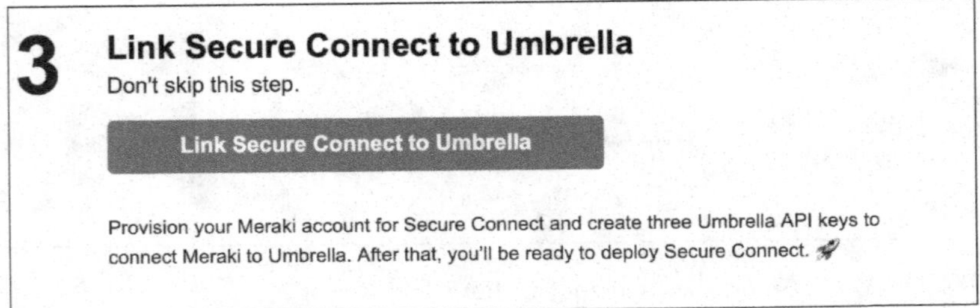

Figure 10-38 *Step 3 on the Secure Connect Welcome Email*

Step 6. After you get to the Meraki Dashboard sign-in page, log in using your existing credentials.

Step 7. If you have multiple Meraki orgs attached to this login, switch to the correct one and then click the link in the email again to open the **Cisco Plus Secure Connect** page again.

You should see the page shown in Figure 10-39 requesting Umbrella network device credentials. The first task is to generate these credentials in Cisco Umbrella and then copy the API Key and API Secret to the fields on this page. To start, click the link **Create Umbrella API Keys.**

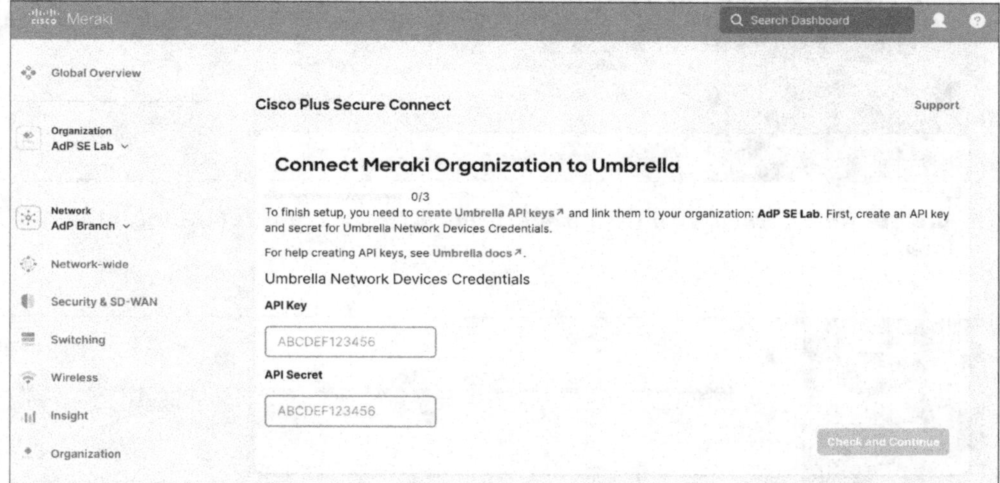

Figure 10-39 *The Connect Meraki Organization to Umbrella Page in Meraki Dashboard*

Step 8. A new tab in your web browser opens at the Cisco Umbrella login page. Log in using your Umbrella username and the password created earlier.

If you have more than one Umbrella organization linked to the same login, check that you are logged in to the correct one by expanding the panel underneath the admin name. If the Umbrella org you wish to integrate with Meraki Dashboard is listed under **Other Organizations**, click its name to switch to it (see Figure 10-40). If this doesn't apply to you, continue on to the next step.

Step 9. In Cisco Umbrella, navigate to **Admin > API Keys** from the menu on the left side.

a. Click the box labeled **Legacy Keys** (see Figure 10-41).

b. Expand the **Umbrella Network Devices** panel and click **Generate Token.**

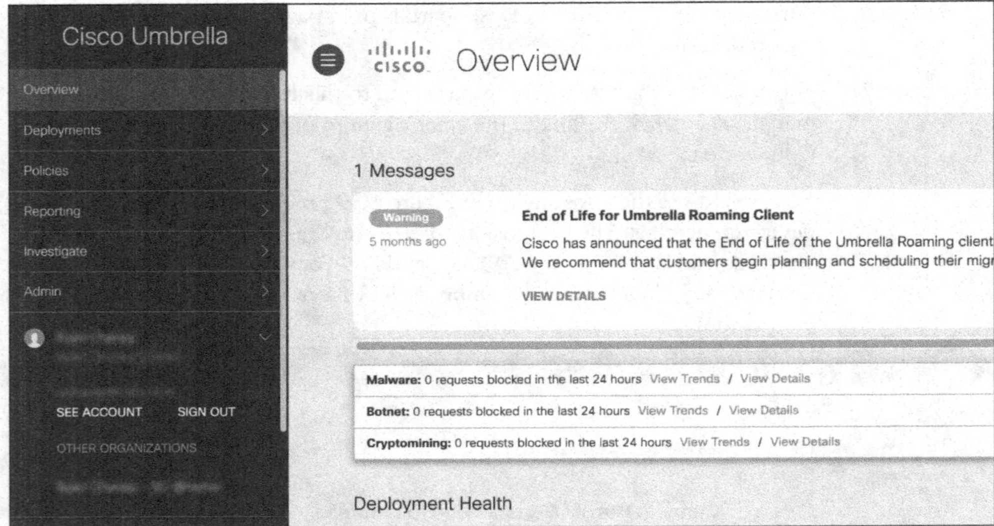

Figure 10-40 *Checking That the Correct Umbrella Organization Is Selected in Cisco Umbrella*

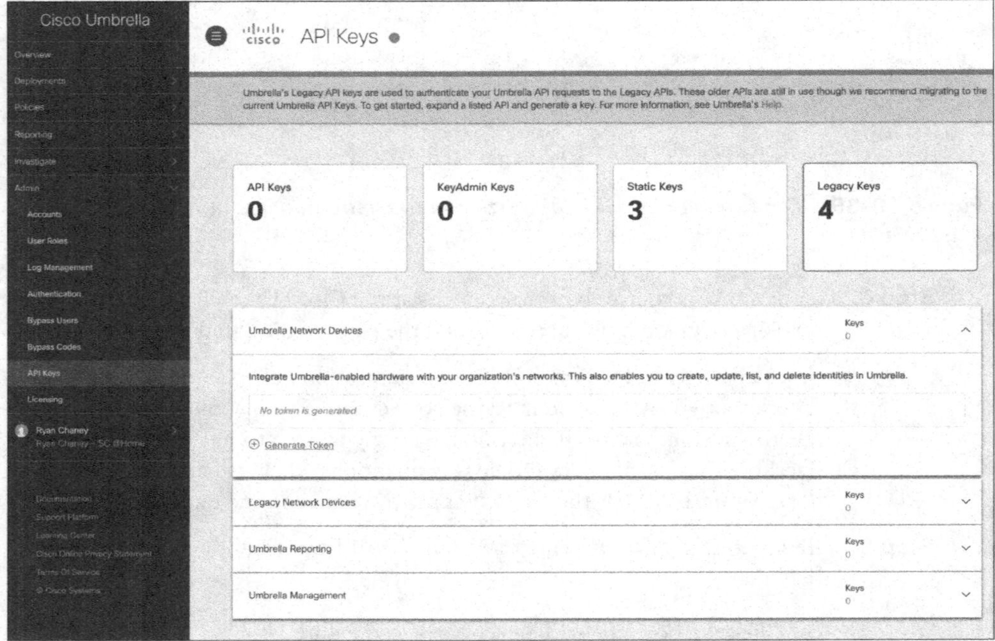

Figure 10-41 *Generating the Umbrella Network Devices API Key and Secret in Cisco Umbrella*

Step 10. As the warning states (see Figure 10-42), these credentials are displayed only once; therefore, it is highly recommended that you copy and paste the key and secret into a text editor while you complete the setup process. With all the switching between tabs, it can be easy to copy and paste the wrong credentials.

a. In Umbrella, copy the Umbrella Network Devices **Key** and paste this into the **API Key** field under **Umbrella Network Devices** in Meraki Dashboard.

b. For an easy way to copy the API key to the clipboard, click the blue icon of the two overlapping pages highlighted in Figure 10-42.

c. Similarly, copy the Umbrella Network Devices **Secret** and paste this into the **API Secret** field under **Umbrella Network Devices** in Meraki Dashboard.

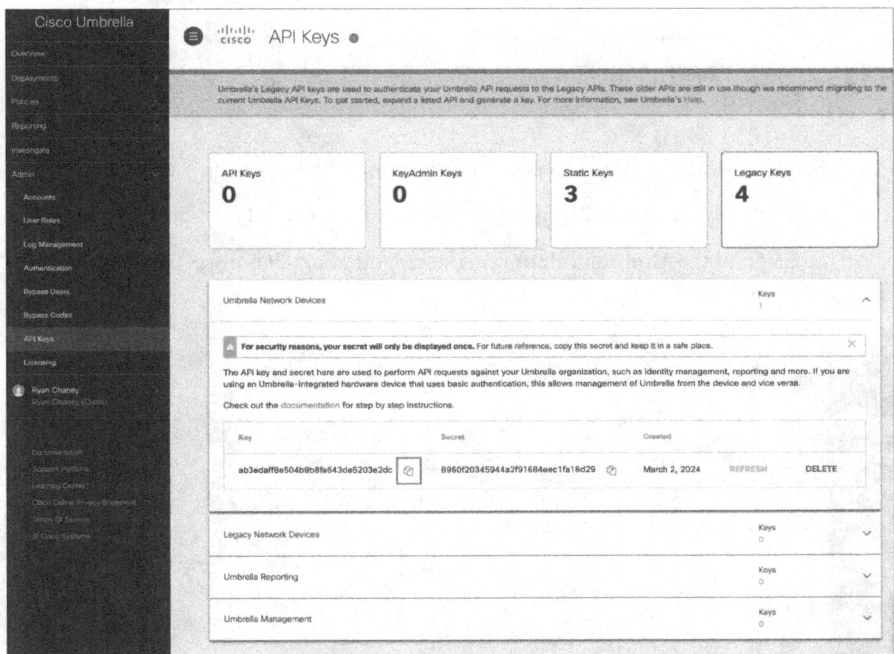

Figure 10-42 *Copying the Umbrella Network Devices API Key and Secret in Cisco Umbrella*

Step 11. Back on the **Connect Meraki Organization to Umbrella** page in Meraki Dashboard, you should see both the **API Key** and **API Secret** populated under **Umbrella Network Devices Credentials**, as shown in Figure 10-43.

a. Confirm the organization name in bold is correct.

b. Click **Check and Continue.**

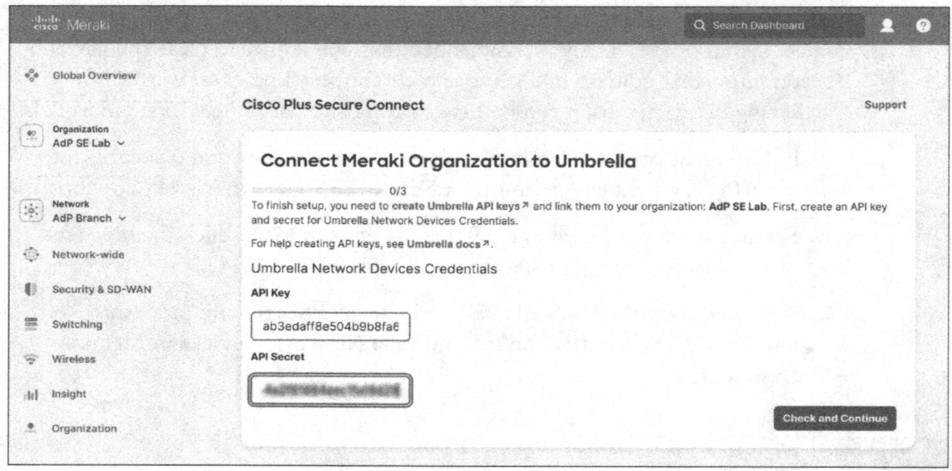

Figure 10-43 *Entering the Umbrella Network Devices Credentials in Meraki Dashboard*

Step 12. Follow a similar process to populate the Umbrella Reporting Credentials:

a. Switch back to the **Cisco Umbrella** tab in your web browser.

b. Expand the **Umbrella Reporting** pane and click **Generate Token** (see Figure 10-44).

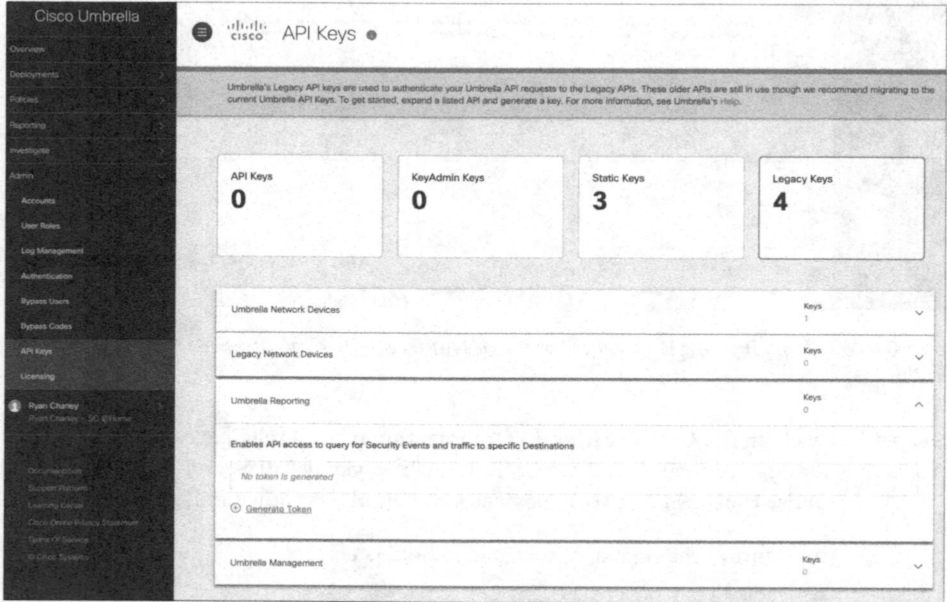

Figure 10-44 *Generating the Umbrella Reporting API Key and Secret in Cisco Umbrella*

Step 13. As the warning states, these credentials are displayed only once; therefore, it is highly recommended that you copy and paste the key and secret into a text editor while you complete the setup process (see Figure 10-45).

a. In Umbrella, copy the Umbrella Reporting **Key** and paste this into the **API Key** field under **Umbrella Reporting Credentials** in Meraki Dashboard.

b. Similarly, copy the Umbrella Reporting **Secret** and paste this into the **API Secret** field under **Umbrella Reporting Credentials** in Meraki Dashboard.

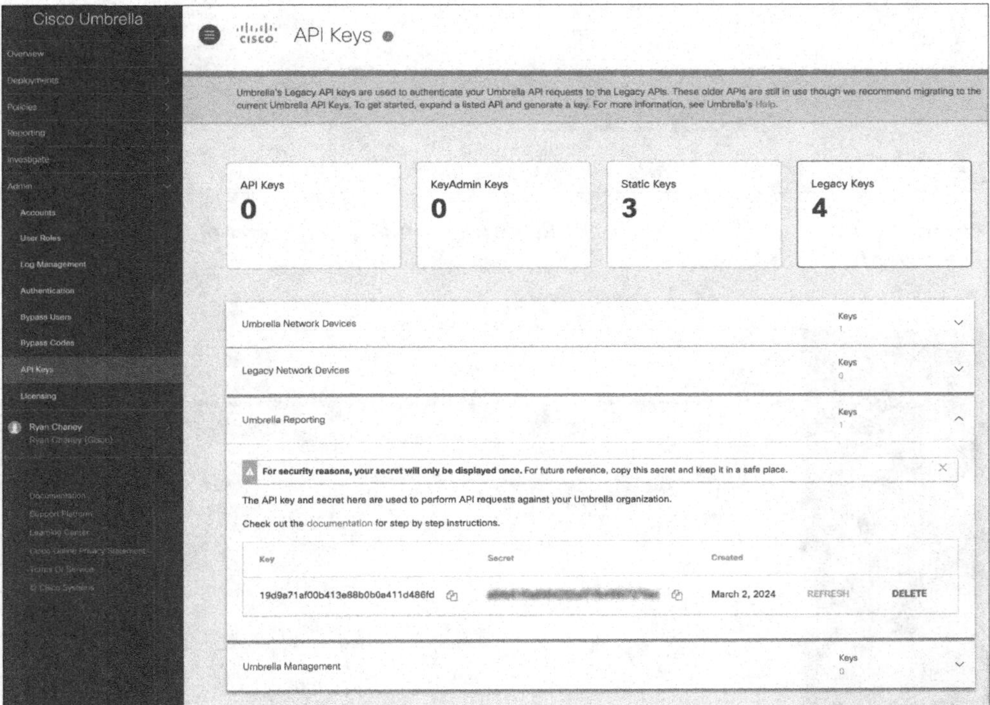

Figure 10-45 *Copying the Umbrella Reporting API Key and Secret in Cisco Umbrella*

Step 14. Back on the **Connect Meraki Organization to Umbrella** page in Meraki Dashboard, you should see both the **API Key** and **API Secret** populated under **Umbrella Reporting Credentials**, as illustrated in Figure 10-46. Click **Check and Continue.**

Step 15. Follow a similar process to populate the Umbrella Management Credentials. Switch back to the **Cisco Umbrella** tab in your web browser. Expand the **Umbrella Management** pane and click **Generate Token**, as shown in Figure 10-47.

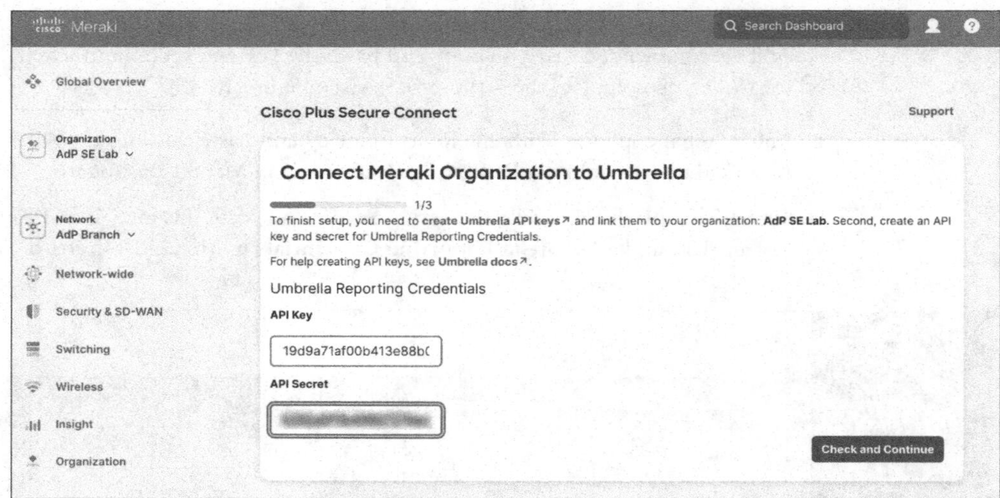

Figure 10-46 *Entering the Umbrella Reporting API Key and Secret in Meraki Dashboard*

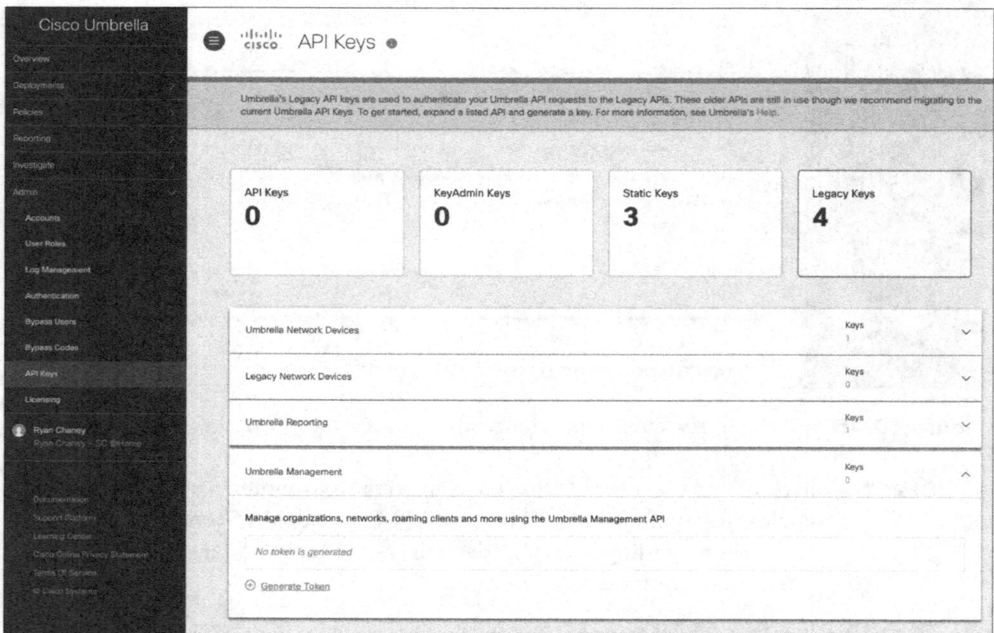

Figure 10-47 *Generating the Umbrella Management API Key and Secret in Cisco Umbrella*

Step 16. Once again, these credentials are displayed only once; therefore, it is highly recommended that you copy and paste the key and secret into a text editor until you complete the setup process shown in Figure 10-48.

a. In Umbrella, copy the Umbrella Management **Key** and paste this into the **API Key** field under **Umbrella Management Credentials** in Meraki Dashboard.

b. Similarly, copy the Umbrella Management **Secret** and paste this into the **API Secret** field under **Umbrella Management Credentials** in Meraki Dashboard.

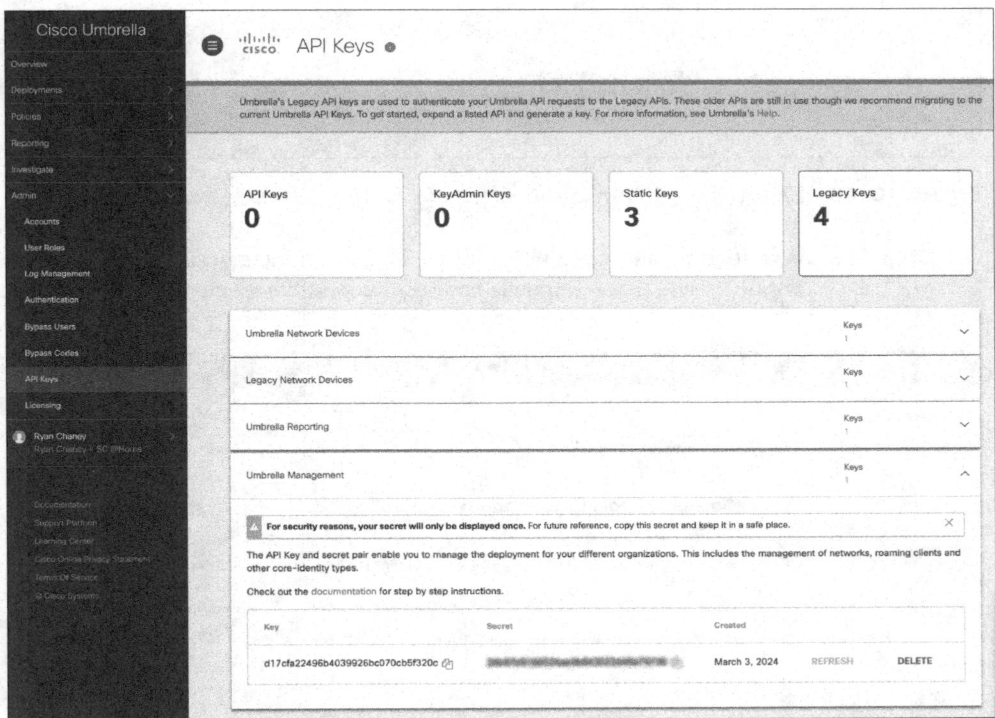

Figure 10-48 *Copying the Umbrella Management API Key and Secret in Cisco Umbrella*

Step 17. Back on the **Connect Meraki Organization to Umbrella** page in Meraki Dashboard, you should see both the **API Key** and **API Secret** populated under **Umbrella Management Credentials**, as demonstrated in Figure 10-49.

Click **Check and Continue.**

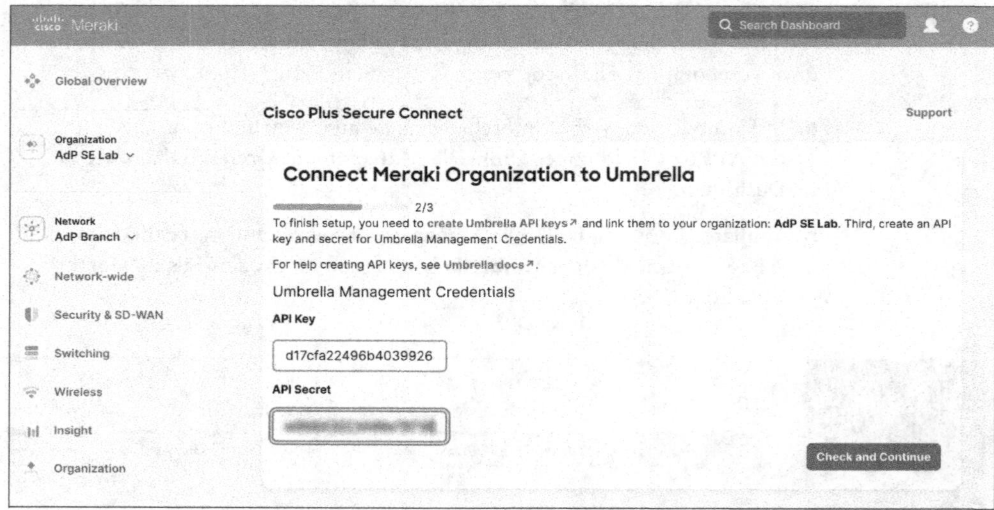

Figure 10-49 *Entering the Umbrella Management Credentials in Meraki Dashboard*

Step 18. As verified by the screen in Figure 10-50, the API integration between Meraki Dashboard and Cisco Umbrella has been successfully completed. Click **Finish.**

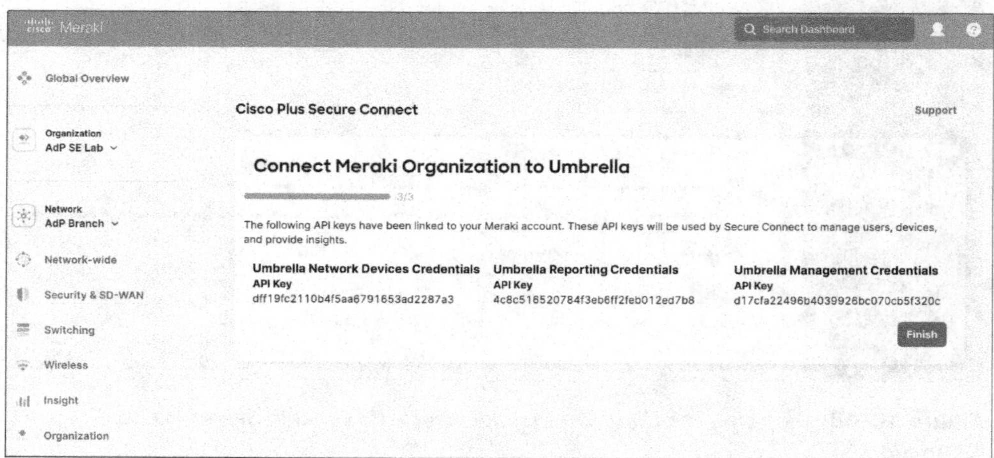

Figure 10-50 *The Final Page of the Connect Meraki Organization to Umbrella Wizard*

The API integration between Meraki Dashboard and Cisco Umbrella is now complete. If, at this point, you realize that you have used the wrong API key or secret, in Meraki Dashboard navigate to **Secure Connect > License & API Keys** and click **Replace API Credentials** to correct them (see Figure 10-51). If you have mistakenly integrated with the wrong Umbrella organization or have any other issue, raise a case with Meraki support.

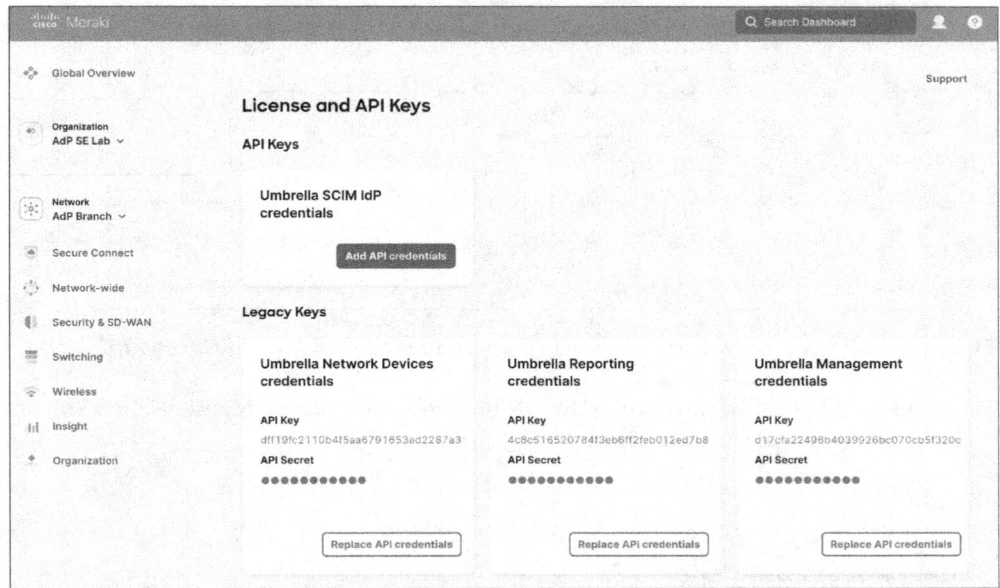

Figure 10-51 *Updating the Umbrella API Keys Used by Secure Connect*

Read on as we enable sites and demonstrate the advanced security capabilities of Secure Connect.

Adding Meraki SD-WAN Sites to Secure Connect

Meraki networks, referred to as *sites* in Secure Connect, need to be attached to Secure Connect regions to route traffic via the Secure Connect cloud. Using site-to-site VPN, Meraki MX will connect to Secure Connect as if it were a regular Auto VPN hub. Both hub-and-spoke sites can receive a default route. Spoke sites receive a default route automatically, whereas this is configurable on hub sites.

For more information on connecting hub sites to Secure Connect, refer to https://documentation.meraki.com/CiscoPlusSecureConnect/Cisco__Secure_Connect_Now-_Sites/Meraki_SD-WAN_Hub_Integration_with_Secure_Connect.

Follow these steps to attach sites to the Secure Connect cloud:

Step 1. Log in to Meraki Dashboard (https://dashboard.meraki.com).

Step 2. Navigate to **Secure Connect > Sites** (see Figure 10-52).

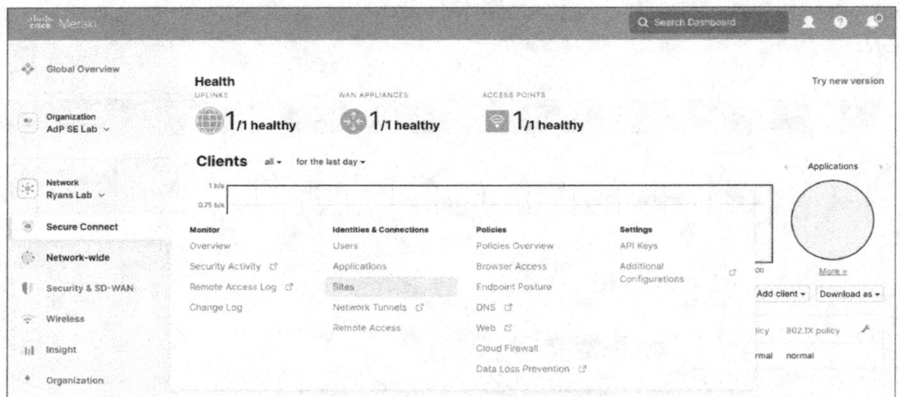

Figure 10-52 *Navigating to the Secure Connect Sites Page in Meraki Dashboard*

Step 3. In the Meraki Secure SD-WAN box, click the **Connect Meraki Networks** link, as shown in Figure 10-53.

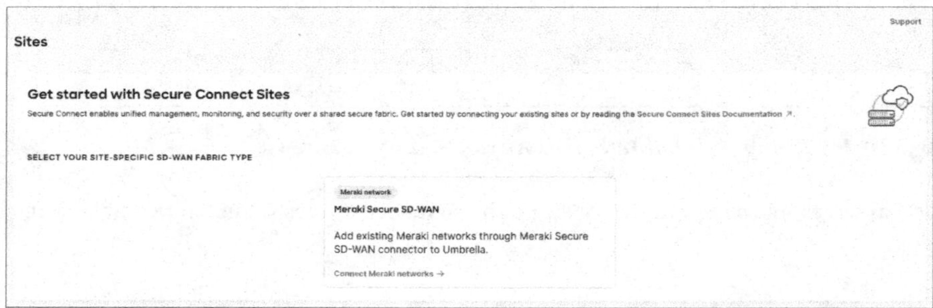

Figure 10-53 *The Get Started with Secure Connect Sites Page in Meraki Dashboard*

Step 4. Select the Meraki networks to attach to the Secure Connect cloud. Next, select the closest region from the **Assign to Region** drop-down menu. In this example (see Figure 10-54), we have selected **Australia-1.** Click **Next.**

Step 5. Click **Finish and Save** (see Figure 10-55).

Step 6. Back on the **Sites** page, you see the message "System is configuring routing." After this process has completed, you will see the newly added network in the **Sites** pane and the message "Site successfully configured," as shown in Figure 10-56.

Step 7. Click the site name to slide out a panel from the right, as shown in Figure 10-57. This panel confirms that a default route has been enabled for this spoke site. If this were a hub site, it would be disabled; however, it could be enabled on this same pane.

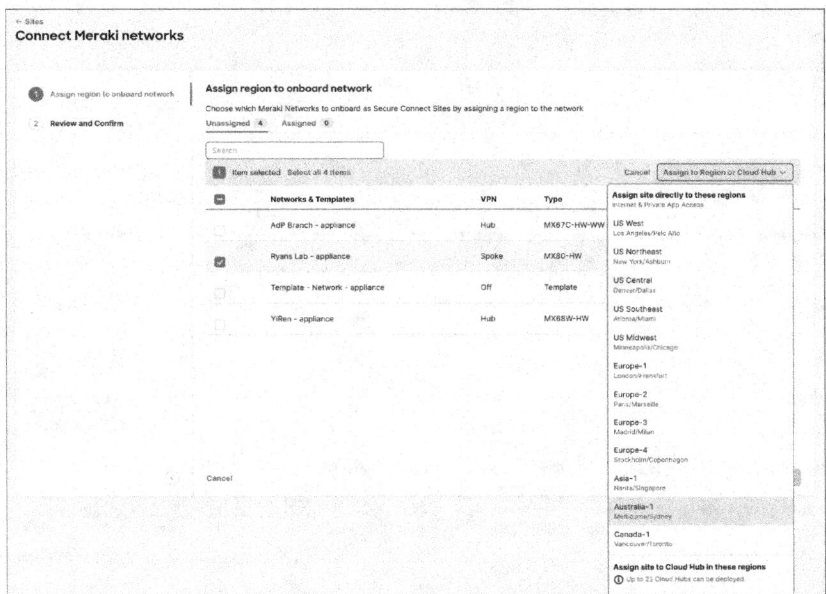

Figure 10-54 *The Assign Region to Onboard Network Page in Meraki Dashboard*

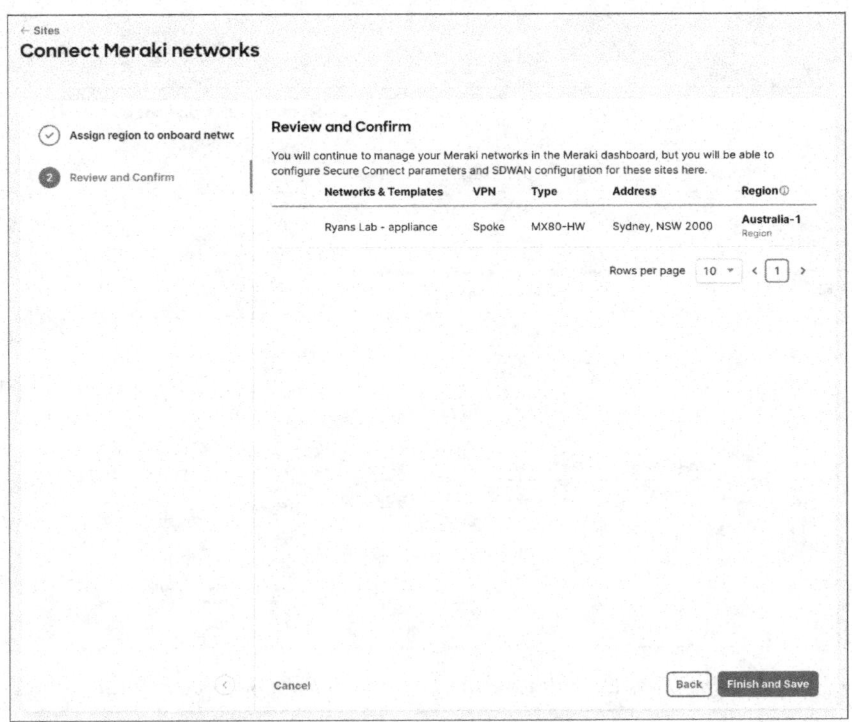

Figure 10-55 *Confirming the Meraki Network to Secure Connect Region Assignment in Meraki Dashboard*

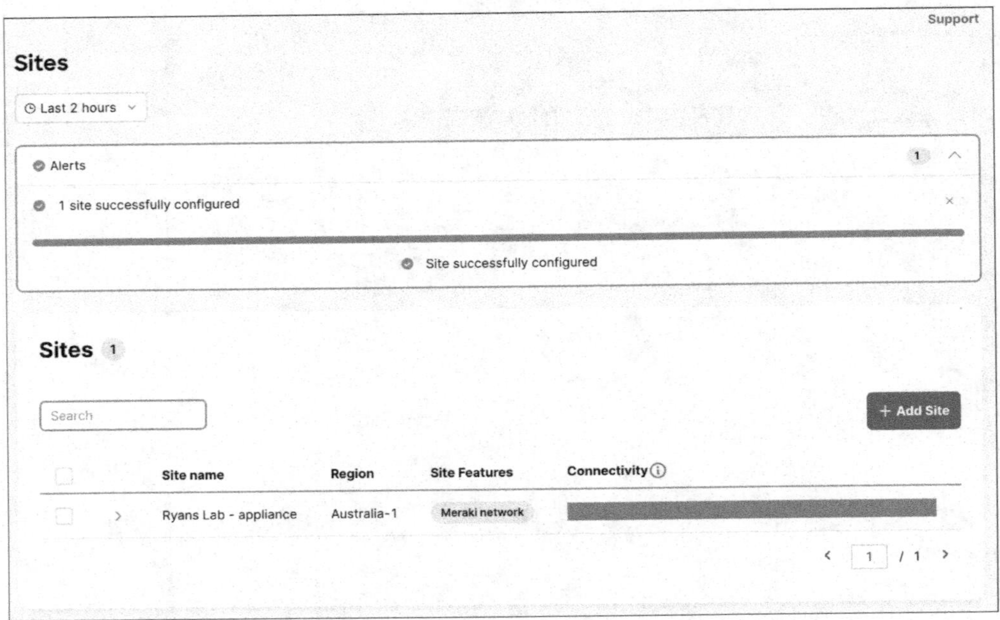

Figure 10-56 *The Sites Page After Successfully Adding a New Site to the Secure Connect Cloud*

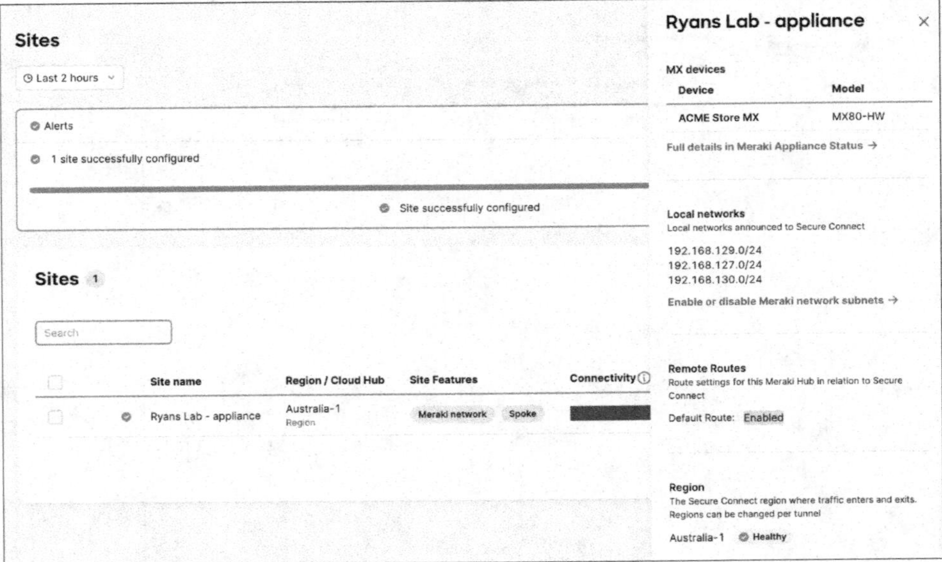

Figure 10-57 *Confirming That Default Routing Is Enabled for a Secure Connect Spoke Site*

You've now completed the steps required to attach spoke sites to the Secure Connect cloud. To learn more about Secure Connect sites, refer to https://documentation.meraki.com/CiscoPlusSecureConnect/Cisco__Secure_Connect_Now-_Sites.

Configuring DHCP to Assign Umbrella's DNS Servers

To ensure that Umbrella's security policies are applied, user DNS traffic must be forwarded to Umbrella's DNS servers. Typically, the local Meraki MX security appliance is also the DHCP server for each site. If another device is acting as the DHCP server, configure it to assign the following DNS server IP addresses: 208.67.222.222 and 208.67.220.220.

Follow these steps to configure a Meraki MX security appliance to assign Umbrella's DNS server IP addresses via DHCP:

Step 1. In Meraki Dashboard, navigate to **Security & SD-WAN > DHCP** (under Configure).

Step 2. For those subnets that are being advertised to Secure Connect, from the **DNS Nameservers** drop-down menu, select **Use Umbrella** (see Figure 10-58).

Click **Save Changes**.

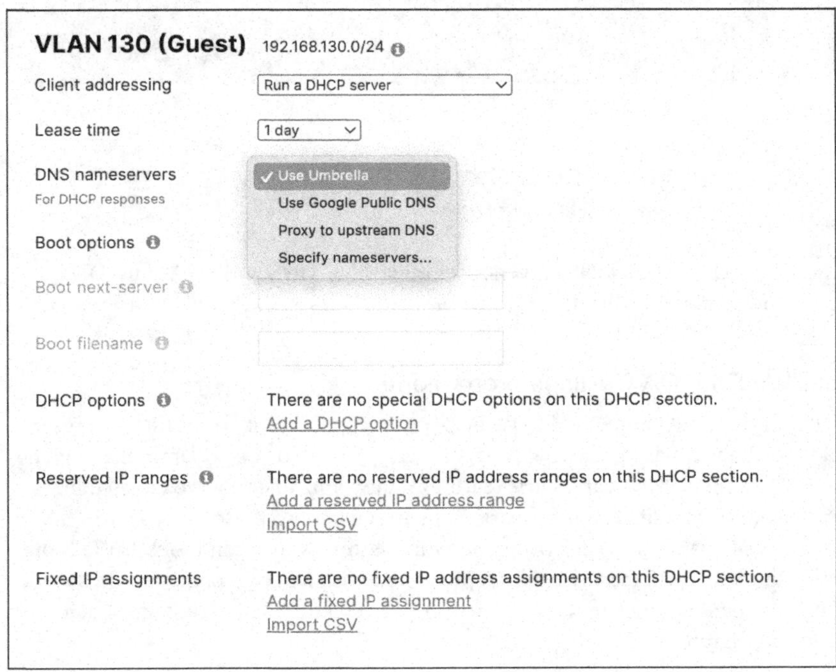

Figure 10-58 *A DHCP Subnet in Meraki Dashboard Configured to Use Umbrella's DNS Servers*

The DHCP server on Meraki MX then assigns the Umbrella DNS servers to clients. You can verify this by navigating to http://welcome.umbrella.com, where you will be presented with Cisco Umbrella's bright green welcome page (see Figure 10-59).

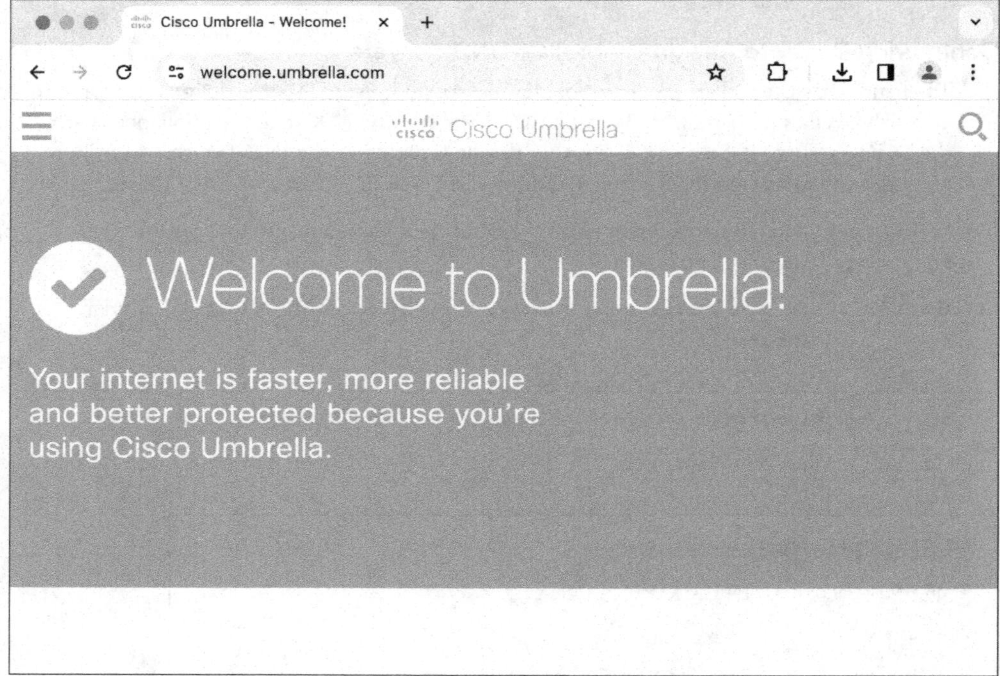

Figure 10-59 *The Cisco Umbrella Welcome Page*

To learn more about Umbrella's DNS servers, including IPv6 DNS and USA-only DNS, refer to https://docs.umbrella.com/deployment-umbrella/docs/point-your-dns-to-cisco.

Installing Umbrella's Root CA Certificate on Clients

A major upside of Secure Connect's HTTPS inspection capability is the ability to present users with a block page advising them why access was prevented. Cisco Umbrella, which provides the HTTPS inspection capability, features a customizable block page enabling organizations to present additional information, such as where to go for help or to request access. This capability is very different from platforms that can block HTTPS but can't inspect it. In these instances, the user is presented with an error page, often causing them to think that there is an issue with the network. The Umbrella block page is demonstrated later in this chapter.

For Umbrella to be able to present an HTTPS block page to users, the Umbrella Root CA certificate must be pushed to clients. The easiest way to do this is with a mobile device management (MDM) solution, like Meraki Systems Manager. Refer to the "Certificate Settings Payload" section in Chapter 11, "Securing End-User Devices," for a guide on how to push certificates to end-user devices. Before heading there, follow these steps to download the Umbrella Root CA certificate:

Step 1. Log in to the Cisco Umbrella Dashboard (https://dashboard.umbrella.com).

Step 2. Navigate to **Deployments > Root Certificate** (under Configuration).

Step 3. Expand the **Cisco Root Certificate Authority** pane and click the download icon to download the certificate (see Figure 10-60).

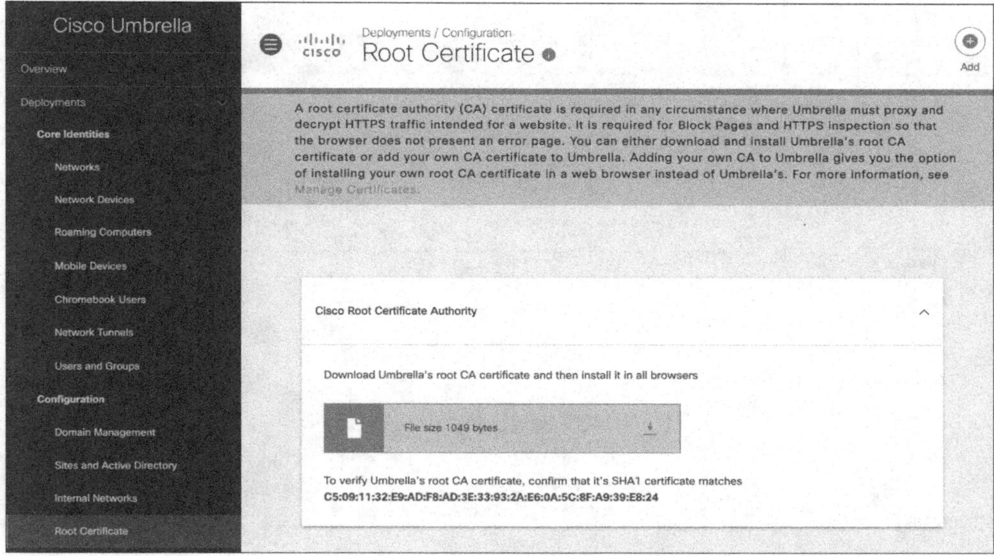

Figure 10-60 *Downloading the Umbrella Root CA Certificate*

For more ways to install the Umbrella Root CA certificate on client devices, including using Microsoft group policies, refer to https://docs.umbrella.com/umbrella-user-guide/docs/install-the-cisco-umbrella-root-certificate/.

Enabling Intelligent Proxy and SSL Decryption in Cisco Umbrella

Cisco Umbrella's intelligent proxy capability intercepts and proxies requests for URLs, potentially malicious files, and domain names associated with certain uncategorized or unknown domains. This allows Cisco to identify new threats and protect your network and users. Known domains—for example, content-carrying domains (CDNs) for Netflix or YouTube—are not proxied, and hence performance for users is not impacted.

By default, SSL decryption is not enabled. With the majority of sites using HTTPS today, it is vital that this capability be enabled because you can't control what you can't see. In addition to adding the Root CA certificate to clients, as shown in the preceding section, turning on SSL decryption is also required to present a block page to users for HTTPS sites.

Follow these steps to configure intelligent proxy and SSL decryption in Cisco Umbrella:

Step 1. Log in to Meraki Dashboard (https://dashboard.meraki.com).

Step 2. Navigate to **Secure Connect > DNS** (see Figure 10-61).

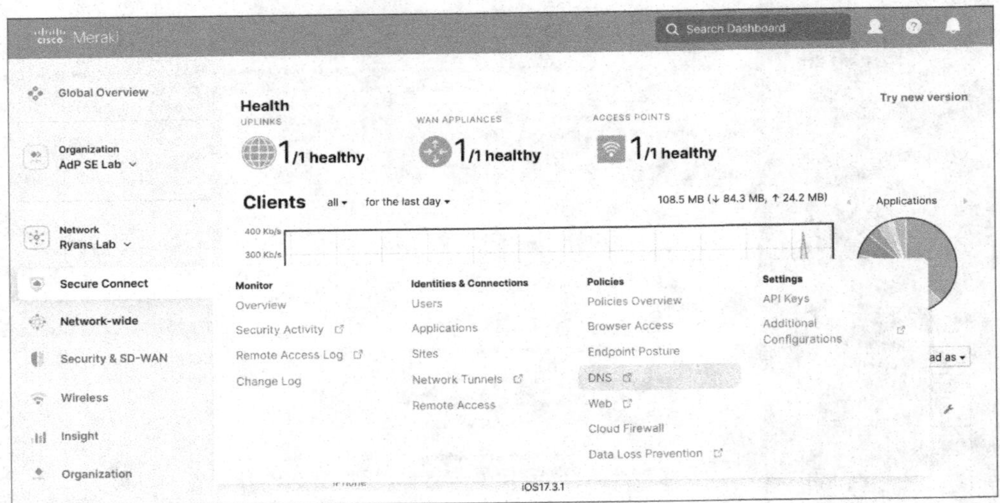

Figure 10-61 *Navigating to the Secure Connect DNS Page in Meraki Dashboard*

Step 3. In the Umbrella Dashboard, click **Default Policy** to expand it.

Under **Advanced Settings**, click the slider to enable **Intelligent Proxy** and check the box for **SSL Decryption**, as shown in Figure 10-62. Click **SAVE**.

You've completed the steps necessary to enable Intelligent Proxy and SSL decryption. To learn more about Intelligent Proxy, refer to https://docs.umbrella.com/umbrella-user-guide/docs/manage-the-intelligent-proxy.

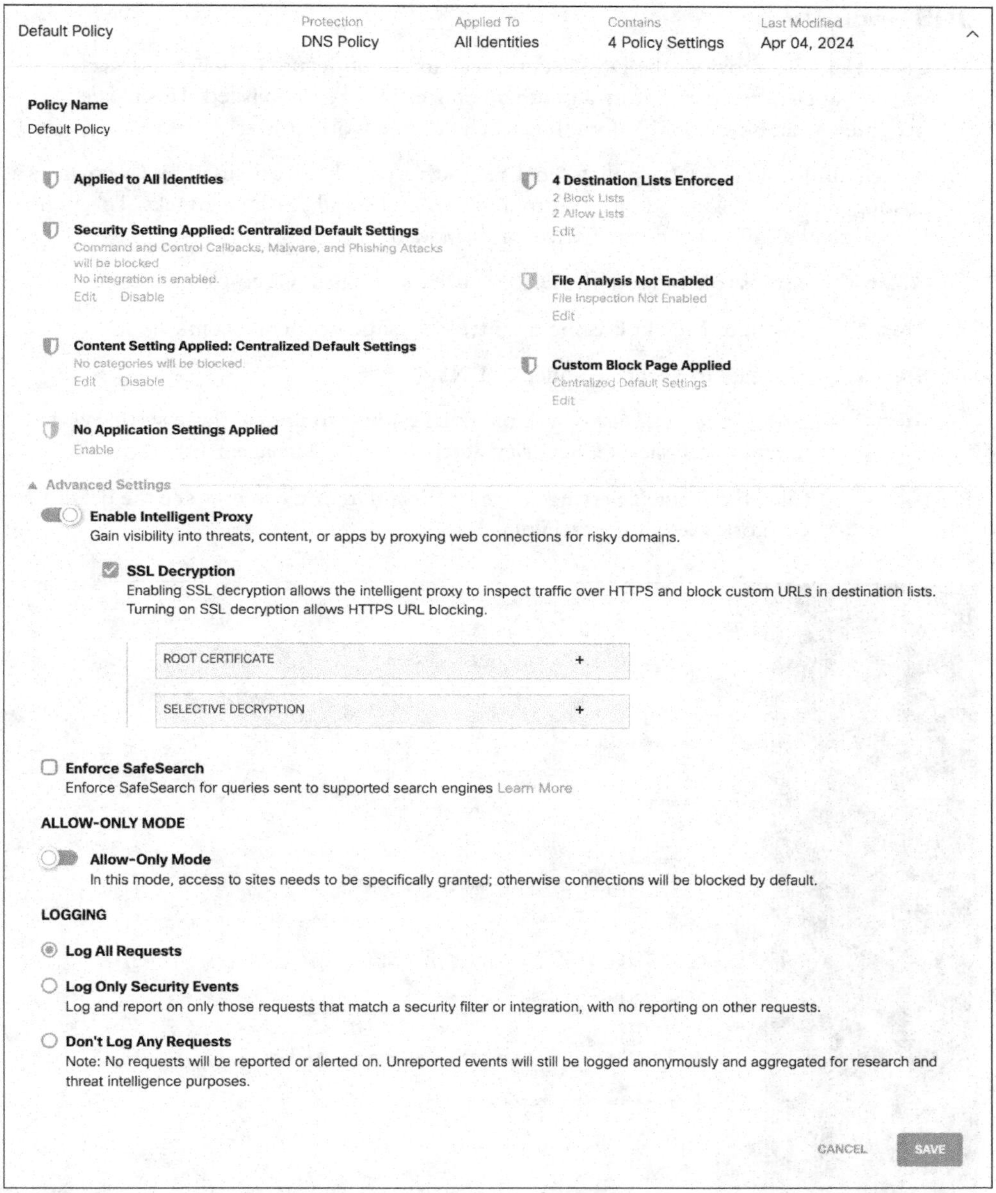

Default Policy

Protection	Applied To	Contains	Last Modified
DNS Policy	All Identities	4 Policy Settings	Apr 04, 2024

Policy Name
Default Policy

Applied to All Identities

Security Setting Applied: Centralized Default Settings
Command and Control Callbacks, Malware, and Phishing Attacks will be blocked
No integration is enabled.
Edit Disable

Content Setting Applied: Centralized Default Settings
No categories will be blocked.
Edit Disable

No Application Settings Applied
Enable

4 Destination Lists Enforced
2 Block Lists
2 Allow Lists
Edit

File Analysis Not Enabled
File Inspection Not Enabled
Edit

Custom Block Page Applied
Centralized Default Settings
Edit

Advanced Settings

Enable Intelligent Proxy
Gain visibility into threats, content, or apps by proxying web connections for risky domains.

SSL Decryption
Enabling SSL decryption allows the intelligent proxy to inspect traffic over HTTPS and block custom URLs in destination lists. Turning on SSL decryption allows HTTPS URL blocking.

ROOT CERTIFICATE +

SELECTIVE DECRYPTION +

Enforce SafeSearch
Enforce SafeSearch for queries sent to supported search engines Learn More

ALLOW-ONLY MODE

Allow-Only Mode
In this mode, access to sites needs to be specifically granted; otherwise connections will be blocked by default.

LOGGING

Log All Requests

Log Only Security Events
Log and report on only those requests that match a security filter or integration, with no reporting on other requests.

Don't Log Any Requests
Note: No requests will be reported or alerted on. Unreported events will still be logged anonymously and aggregated for research and threat intelligence purposes.

CANCEL SAVE

Figure 10-62 *Enabling Intelligent Proxy and SSL Decryption as Part of a DNS Policy*

DNS Security

Cisco Umbrella provides the DNS security capability of Secure Connect and works by inspecting DNS requests before any other connections are established. This means security threats can be stopped before they reach your network or users.

By default, Umbrella's DNS policy blocks sites that have been classified by Cisco Talos as hosting malware, command-and-control infrastructure, and phishing attacks. This policy is configurable, and further categories can be added.

Follow these steps to configure the DNS security settings in Cisco Umbrella:

Step 1. Log in to Meraki Dashboard (https://dashboard.meraki.com).

Step 2. Navigate to **Secure Connect > DNS**.

Step 3. In the Umbrella Dashboard, the quickest way to update these settings is to navigate to **Policies > Security Settings** (under Management).

Click the **Default Settings** pane to expand it. You can now see the default categories selected (see Figure 10-63).

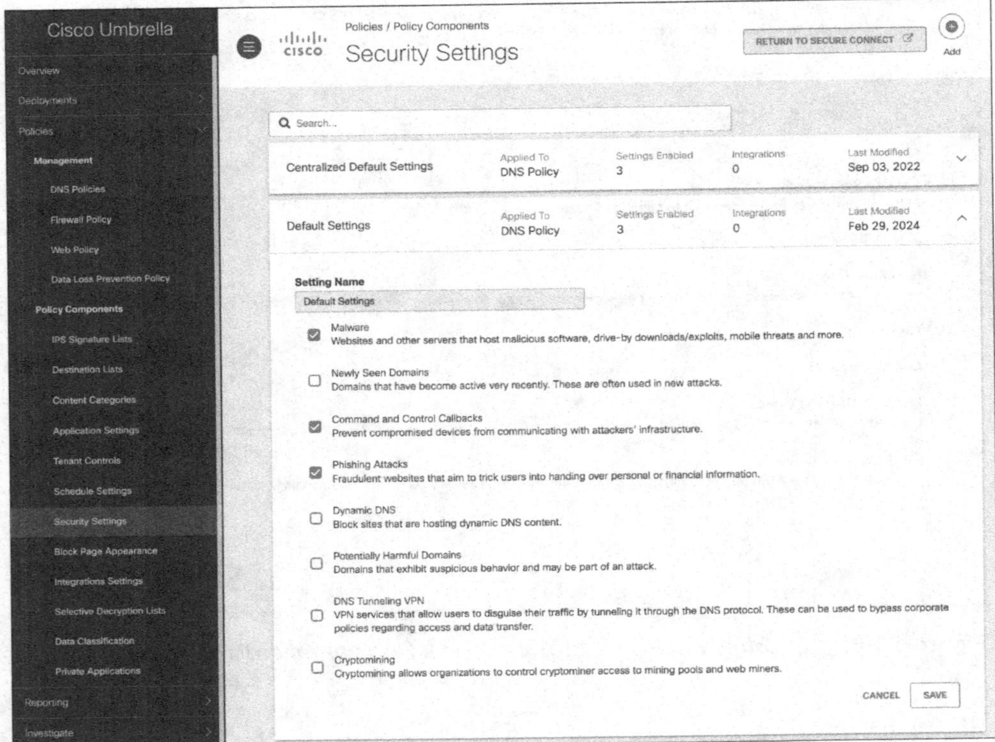

Figure 10-63 *The Default DNS Security Settings in Cisco Umbrella*

Step 4. In this example, add newly seen domains to the policy because they are commonly used in zero day exploits. On the screen shown in Figure 10-64, check **Newly Seen Domains** and click **SAVE**. Removing any of the default selections is not recommended.

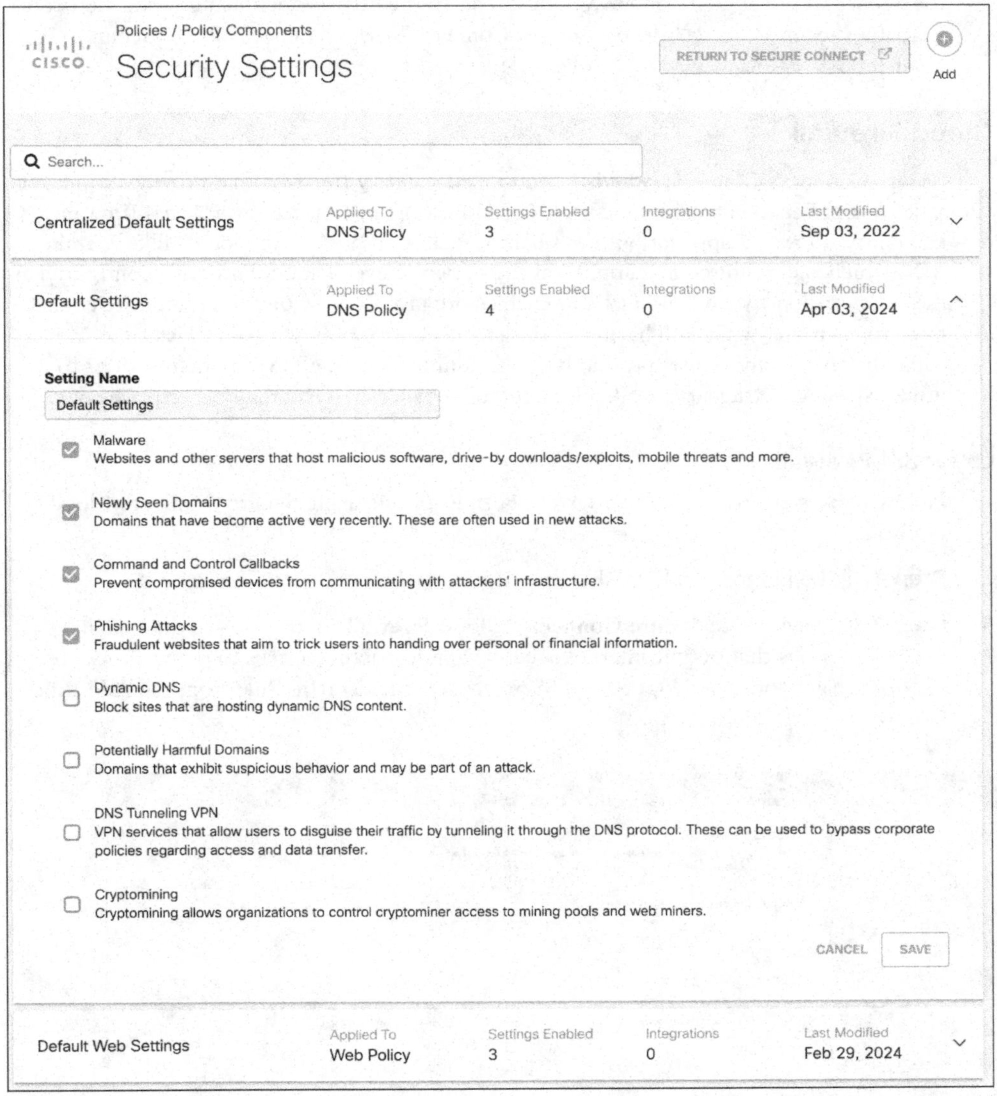

Policies / Policy Components

Security Settings

RETURN TO SECURE CONNECT

Add

Search...

	Applied To	Settings Enabled	Integrations	Last Modified
Centralized Default Settings	DNS Policy	3	0	Sep 03, 2022
Default Settings	DNS Policy	4	0	Apr 03, 2024

Setting Name

Default Settings

- [x] Malware
  Websites and other servers that host malicious software, drive-by downloads/exploits, mobile threats and more.
- [x] Newly Seen Domains
  Domains that have become active very recently. These are often used in new attacks.
- [x] Command and Control Callbacks
  Prevent compromised devices from communicating with attackers' infrastructure.
- [x] Phishing Attacks
  Fraudulent websites that aim to trick users into handing over personal or financial information.
- [ ] Dynamic DNS
  Block sites that are hosting dynamic DNS content.
- [ ] Potentially Harmful Domains
  Domains that exhibit suspicious behavior and may be part of an attack.
- [ ] DNS Tunneling VPN
  VPN services that allow users to disguise their traffic by tunneling it through the DNS protocol. These can be used to bypass corporate policies regarding access and data transfer.
- [ ] Cryptomining
  Cryptomining allows organizations to control cryptominer access to mining pools and web miners.

CANCEL SAVE

	Applied To	Settings Enabled	Integrations	Last Modified
Default Web Settings	Web Policy	3	0	Feb 29, 2024

Figure 10-64 *Adding the Newly Seen Domain Security Category to the Default Umbrella DNS Policy*

At this point, you've completed the simple steps to configure the blocking of sites in various security categories as part of a DNS policy in Cisco Umbrella. For a deeper explanation of these security categories, refer to https://docs.umbrella.com/umbrella-user-guide/docs/dns-security-cats. For information on DNS policy best practices, refer to https://docs.umbrella.com/umbrella-user-guide/docs/best-practices-for-dns-policies. Finally, for the Secure Connect guide on DNS policy, refer to the https://documentation.meraki.com/CiscoPlusSecureConnect/Cisco__Secure_Connect_Now_-_Policies/Cisco__Secure_Connect_Now_-_Manage_DNS_Policies.

Cloud Firewall

Secure Connect's Cloud Firewall is a centralized security function that provides an important control between trust boundaries. Cloud Firewall includes a Layer 3 to 4 firewall capability, a Layer 7 application firewall, as well as an IDS/IPS function. Unlike Meraki MX, which is configured and applied at the network level, Cloud Firewall is configured at the organization level. Cloud Firewall enables organizations to distribute Internet connections to each site, while still having a consistent security policy across those sites. This capability massively boosts productivity for administrators, allowing organizations to utilize SD-WAN efficiently, while providing direct access to cloud and enterprise apps.

Layer 3/4 Firewall

Follow these steps to configure a Layer 3/4 firewall rule using Secure Connect's Cloud Firewall:

Step 1. Log in to Meraki Dashboard (https://dashboard.meraki.com).

Step 2. Navigate to **Secure Connect > Cloud Firewall.** Here, you see the default rules that permit Internet access while restricting access to private apps and networks (see Figure 10-65). Select **Internet Traffic Rule** from the **Add Rule** drop-down menu.

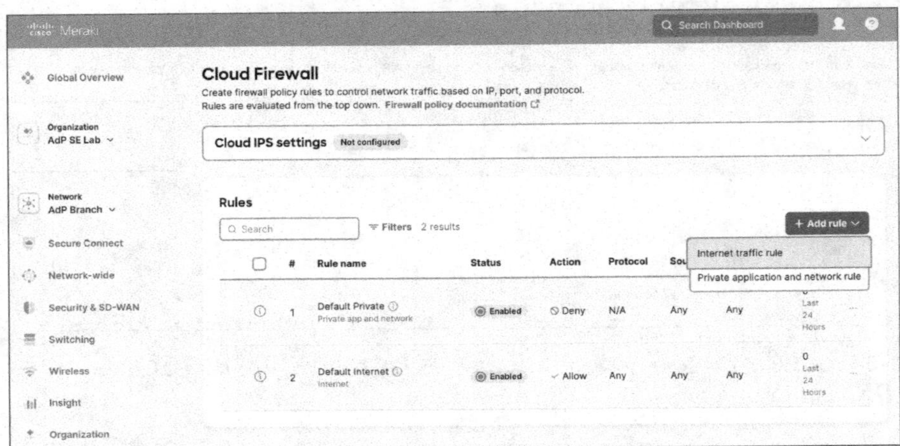

Figure 10-65 *The Cloud Firewall Page in Meraki Dashboard*

Step 3. Enter a meaningful name in the **Rule Name** field (see Figure 10-66). You cannot use special characters in the **Rule Name** or **Description** fields. In this example, we're seeking to block ping to an IP address on the Internet, hence the name **Block Ping.**

a. (Optional) Click **Add Description** to add a description. This description could be handy for referencing the business need for this rule or the change request number responsible for it.

b. Click **Next: Rule Intent** to continue.

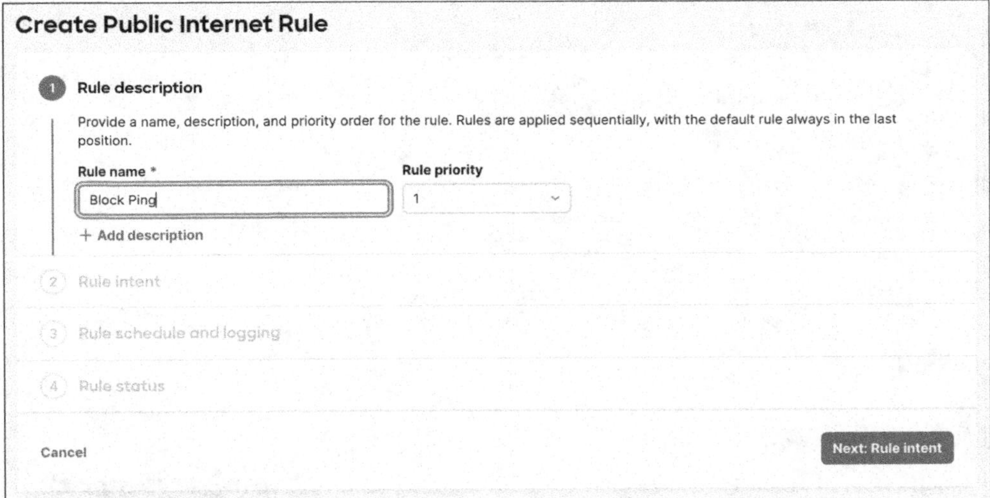

Figure 10-66 *Adding a Name to a New Cloud Firewall Rule in Meraki Dashboard*

Step 4. From the screen shown in Figure 10-67, do the following:

a. Under the **Action** heading, select the intent of the rule—in this case, **Deny.**

b. From the **Protocol** drop-down menu, select **ICMP**. Available options are **Any, TCP, UDP**, or **ICMP.**

c. In the **Sources** field, specify the subnet or an individual IP address (using CIDR notation), username, user group, or tunnel. If you don't specify a source, such as in this example, it will default to **Any.**

d. In the **Destinations** field, specify a subnet or an individual IP address (using CIDR notation), a public application category, or specific Apps from categories. In this example, we have entered a subnet. As you can see in Figure 10-67, when entering a subnet, you must also select it using the check box.

e. Click **Next: Rule Schedule and Logging.**

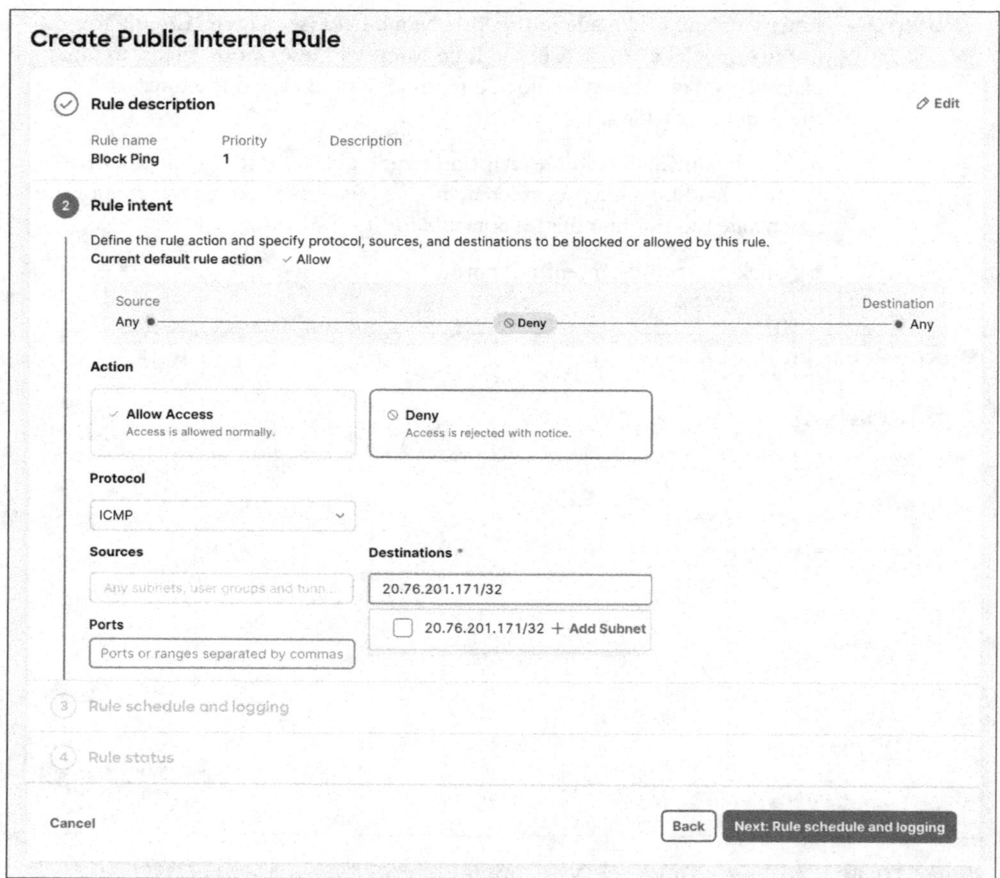

Figure 10-67 *Configuring the Rule Intent on a Cloud Firewall Rule in Meraki Dashboard*

Step 5. (Optional) Set a start date from the **Rule Starts** drop-down menu (see Figure 10-68), or an end date from the **Rule Ends** drop-down menu, if you wish.

Logging is enabled by default. Leave this setting as is.

Click **Next: Rule Status** to continue.

Step 6. New rules are enabled by default, so leave **Rule Status** as is (see Figure 10-69). Click **Save and Add Rule** to finish.

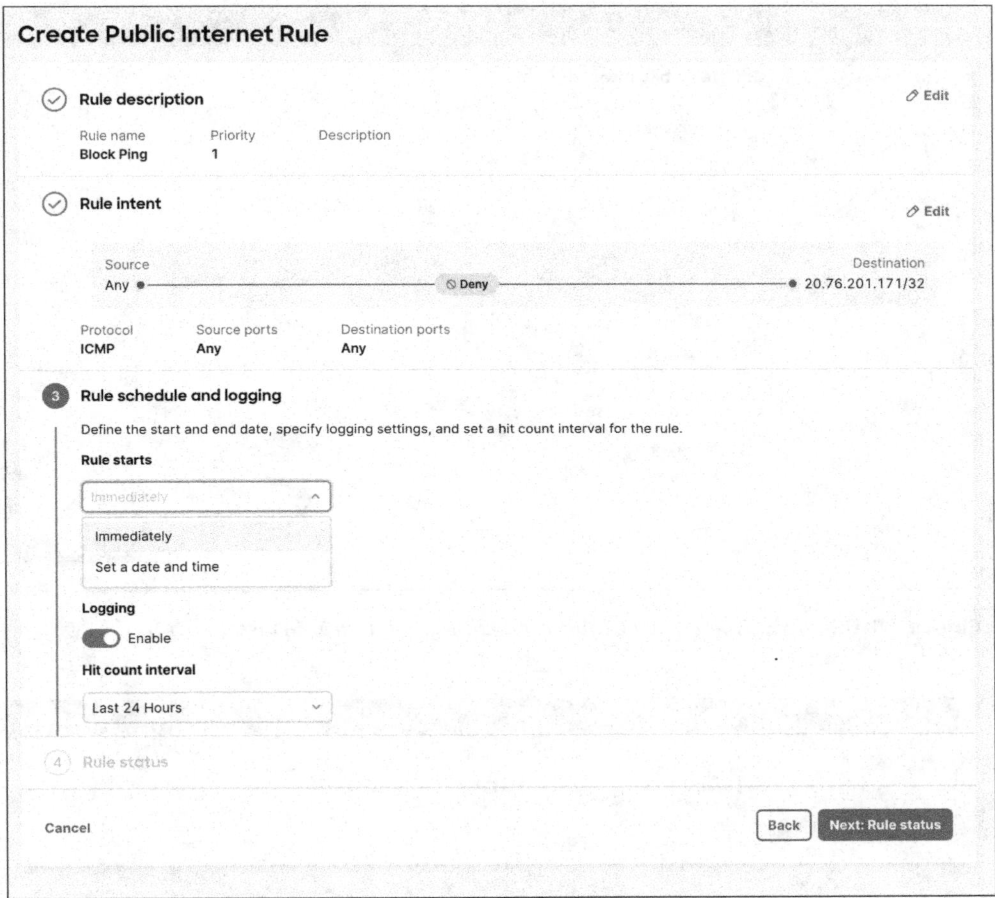

Figure 10-68 *Configuring the Rule Schedule and Logging for a Cloud Firewall Rule in Meraki Dashboard*

You then return to the **Cloud Firewall** page with the new rule displayed above the default rules, as shown in Figure 10-70.

At this point, you've completed the steps to successfully add a Layer 3 or 4 Cloud Firewall rule.

Follow these steps to verify that the rule is working as expected:

Step 1. Disable this new rule by selecting it. Then, from the **Change Status** drop-down menu, select **Disabled** (see Figure 10-71).

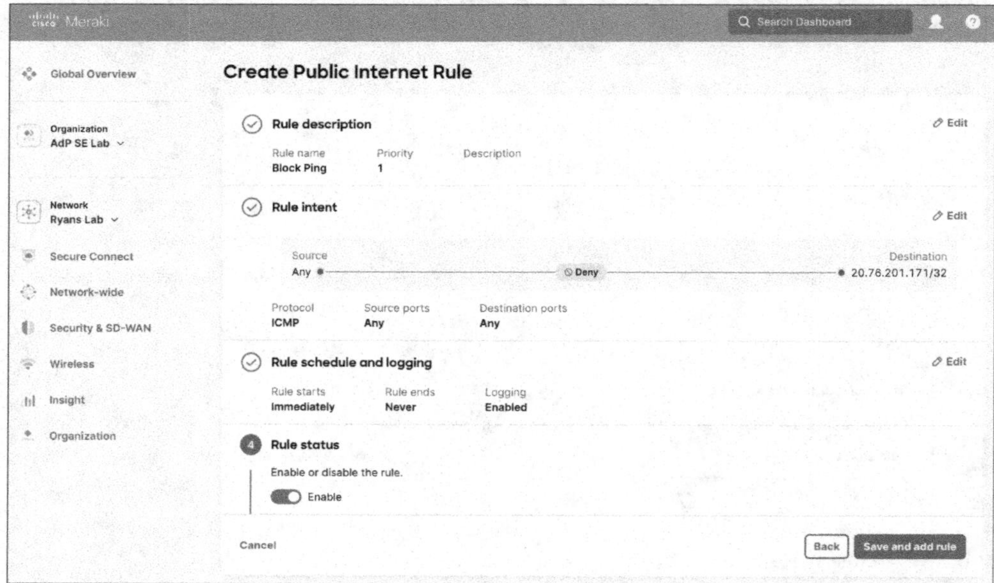

Figure 10-69 *Enabling a New Cloud Firewall Rule in Meraki Dashboard*

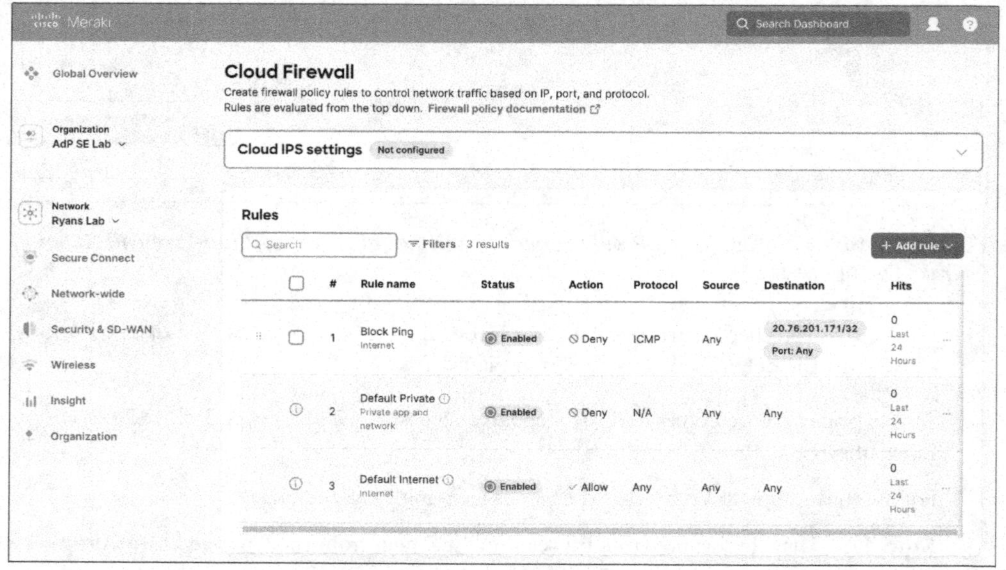

Figure 10-70 *The Cloud Firewall Page in Meraki Dashboard After Adding a New Rule*

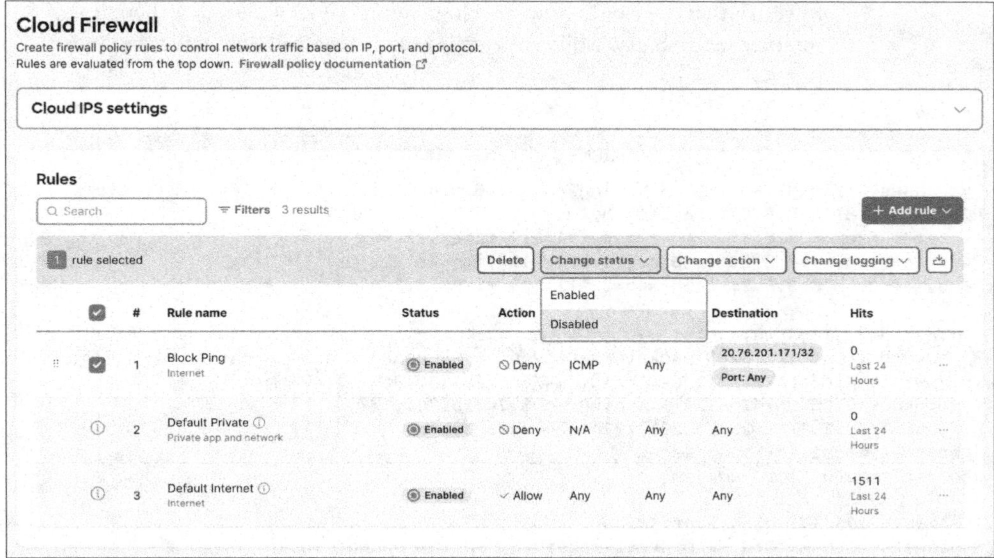

Figure 10-71 *Showing the Options Available After Selecting a Cloud Firewall Rule*

Step 2. Ping the destination IP address featured in the block rule. In this case, we sent a ping to 20.76.201.171 and verified that this address was reachable (see Figure 10-72).

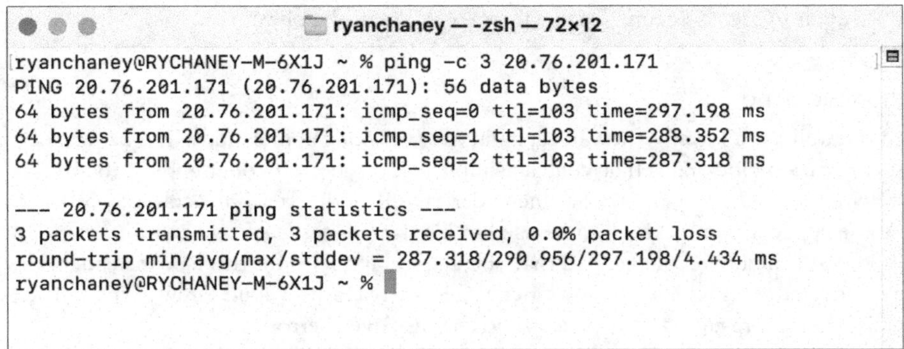

Figure 10-72 *Successful ping Before the New Cloud Firewall Rule Is Enabled*

Step 3. Reenable the firewall rule by selecting it again and selecting **Enabled** from the **Change Status** menu.

Step 4. Verify that Internet connectivity is working. In this example, this was done by sending ping packets to 8.8.8.8. Then ping the destination IP address again to verify that the rule is now working. Figure 10-73 shows that there is still Internet reachability, while the rule is now successfully blocking the desired traffic.

```
ryanchaney — -zsh — 74×18
ryanchaney@RYCHANEY-M-6X1J ~ % ping -c 3 8.8.8.8
PING 8.8.8.8 (8.8.8.8): 56 data bytes
64 bytes from 8.8.8.8: icmp_seq=0 ttl=119 time=137.068 ms
64 bytes from 8.8.8.8: icmp_seq=1 ttl=119 time=16.922 ms
64 bytes from 8.8.8.8: icmp_seq=2 ttl=119 time=13.344 ms

--- 8.8.8.8 ping statistics ---
3 packets transmitted, 3 packets received, 0.0% packet loss
round-trip min/avg/max/stddev = 13.344/55.778/137.068/57.499 ms
ryanchaney@RYCHANEY-M-6X1J ~ % ping -c 3 20.76.201.171
PING 20.76.201.171 (20.76.201.171): 56 data bytes
Request timeout for icmp_seq 0
Request timeout for icmp_seq 1

--- 20.76.201.171 ping statistics ---
3 packets transmitted, 0 packets received, 100.0% packet loss
ryanchaney@RYCHANEY-M-6X1J ~ %
```

Figure 10-73 *ping Showing the New Cloud Firewall Rule Working as Desired*

For more information on configuring a Cloud Firewall policy with Secure Connect, refer to https://documentation.meraki.com/CiscoPlusSecureConnect/Cisco__Secure_Connect_Now_-_Policies/Cisco__Secure_Connect_-_Cloud_Firewall_Policy.

Application Blocking

Cloud Firewall has a Layer 7 firewall capability for blocking applications. The benefit of using application blocking is that you can simply select the protocol or application by name, without needing to know what the underlying IP addresses, protocols, or ports are. While application blocking can be used to block websites (such as YouTube or Facebook), it is highly recommended that you use web policies for this task instead. Web policies present users with a friendly block page, whereas with Cloud Firewall the traffic is simply blocked, resulting in a "page cannot be displayed" error.

Follow these steps to configure an application-based firewall rule using Secure Connect:

Step 1. Log in to Meraki Dashboard (https://dashboard.meraki.com).

Step 2. Navigate to **Secure Connect > Cloud Firewall.** From the **Add Rule** drop-down menu, select **Internet Traffic Rule** (see Figure 10-74).

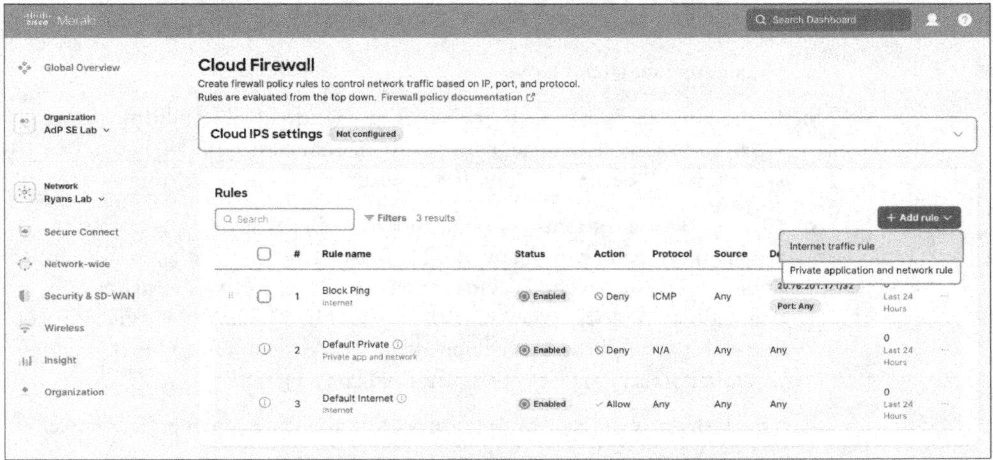

Figure 10-74 *Creating an Application-Based Cloud Firewall Rule in Meraki Dashboard*

Step 3. In this example, we create a simple firewall rule to block the Speedtest application.

a. In the **Rule Name** field, add a meaningful name. In this example, we have used the name **Block Speedtest**, as shown in Figure 10-75.

b. Click **Next: Rule Intent**.

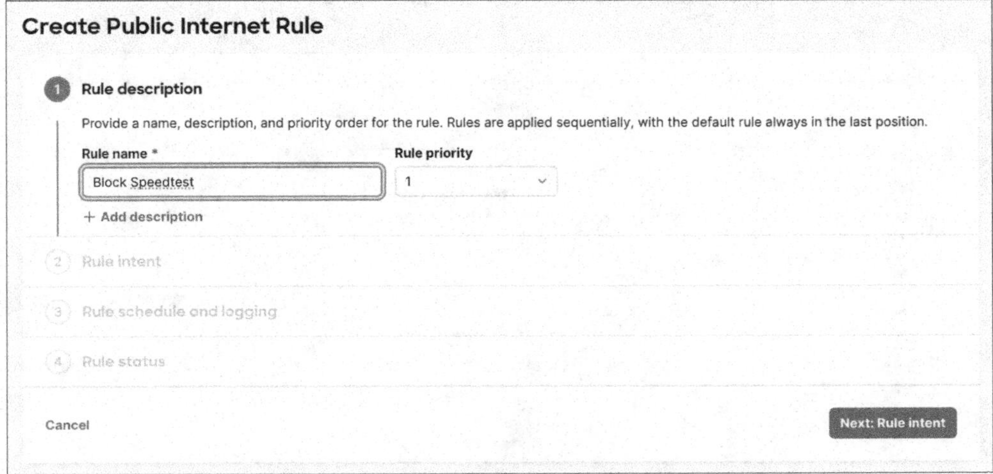

Figure 10-75 *Adding a Rule Name to a New Cloud Firewall Rule in Meraki Dashboard*

Step 4. Now it's time to define this rule's intent (see Figure 10-76).

a. Under **Action**, click **Deny**.

b. In the **Sources** field, specify a subnet or an individual IP address (using CIDR notation), username, user group, or tunnel. If you don't specify a source, it will default to **Any**. In this example, we have left this as **Any**.

c. Click into the **Destinations** field, and you will see groupings of public applications, each with many applications. Many of them are non-web applications, such as audio/video/messaging and software updates. You can choose to block either an entire group like IT Service Management or just select an application like Speedtest. The easiest way to block individual applications is to just type in the application name.

d. Check the box in front of the protocol or application name. In this example, we have selected **Speedtest**.

e. Click **Next: Rule Schedule and Logging**.

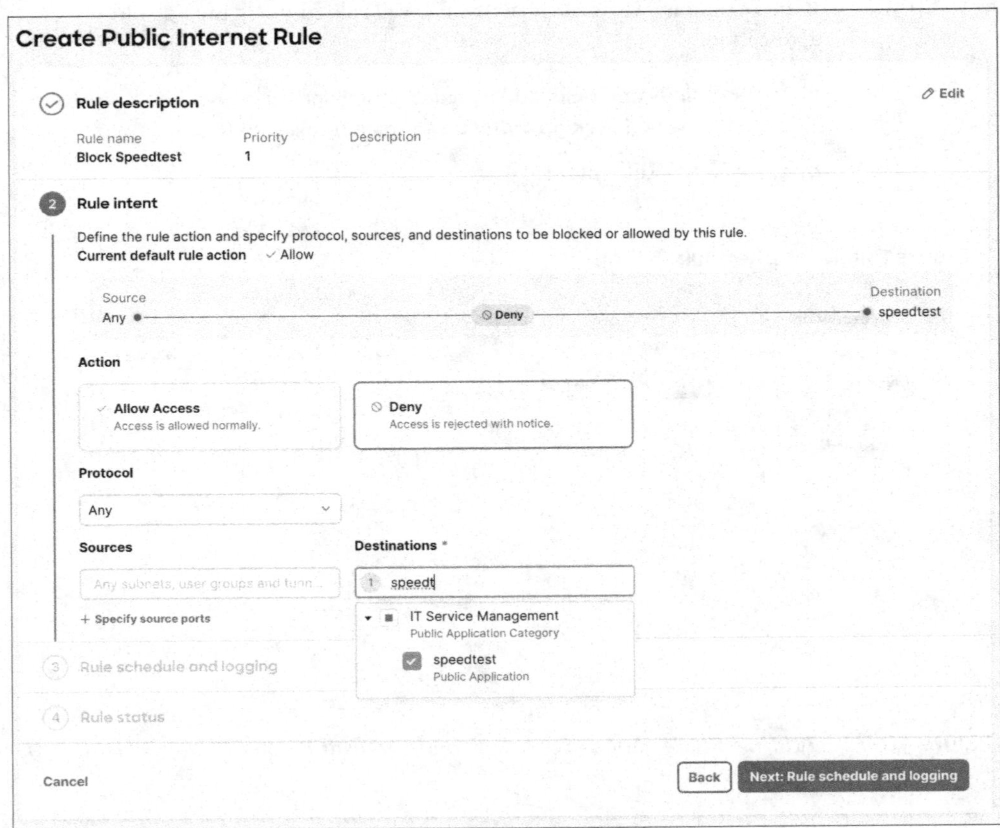

Figure 10-76 *Configuring the Intent on a New Cloud Firewall Rule in Meraki Dashboard*

Step 5. Under **Rule Starts**, you can schedule a start date, and under **Rule Ends**, an end date. In this example, we want this rule to start immediately and never end, which are the defaults (see Figure 10-77). Click **Next: Rule Status.**

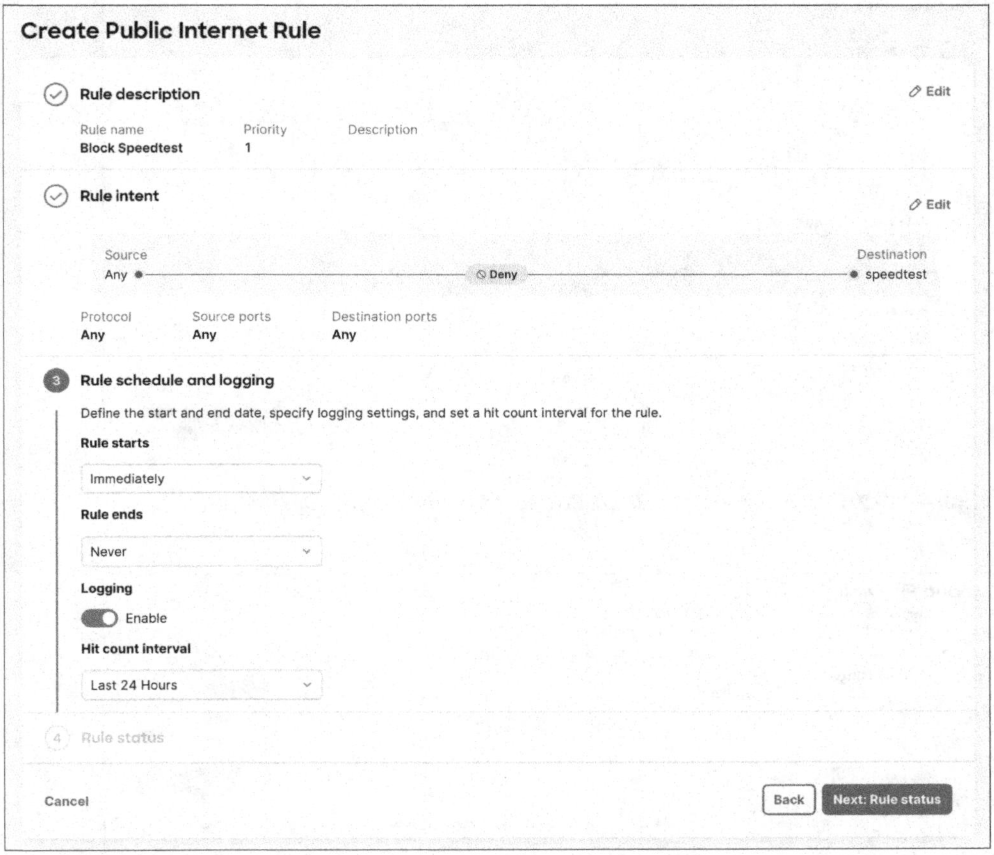

Figure 10-77 *Scheduling a New Cloud Firewall Rule Start and End Date in Meraki Dashboard*

Step 6. Click **Save and Add Rule** (see Figure 10-78). You then return to the **Cloud Firewall** page with the new firewall rule listed at the top, as shown in Figure 10-79.

At this point, you've completed the configuration of an application-based firewall rule in Meraki Dashboard. To verify that this rule is working, try running the Speedtest application. As demonstrated in Figure 10-80, the Speedtest application is not able to connect, proving that our rule is working.

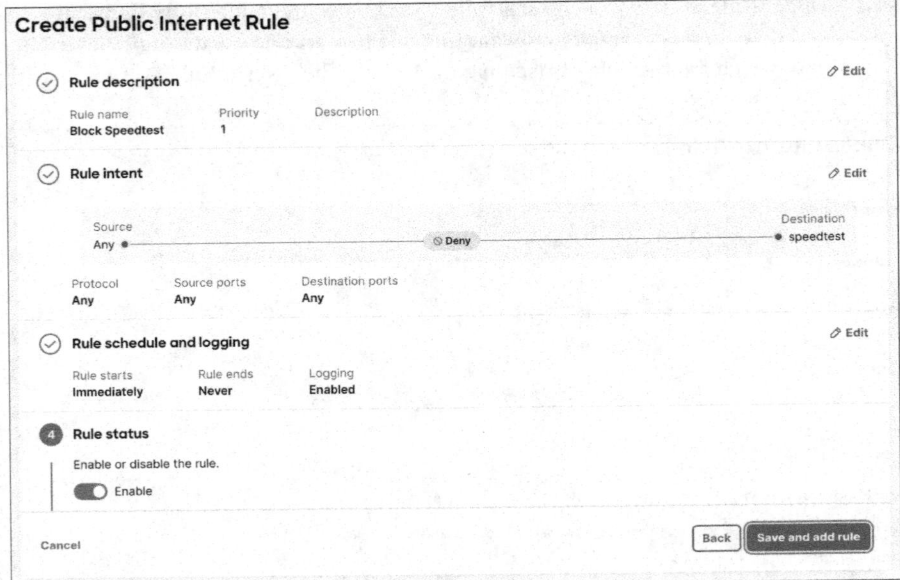

Figure 10-78 *Saving a New Cloud Firewall Rule in Meraki Dashboard*

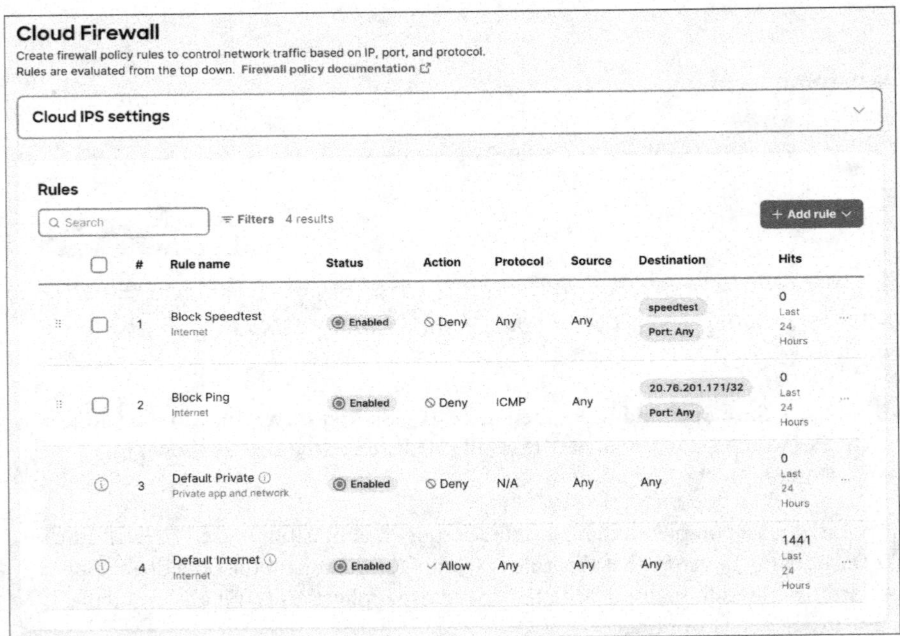

Figure 10-79 *The Cloud Firewall Page in Meraki Dashboard After Adding a New Rule*

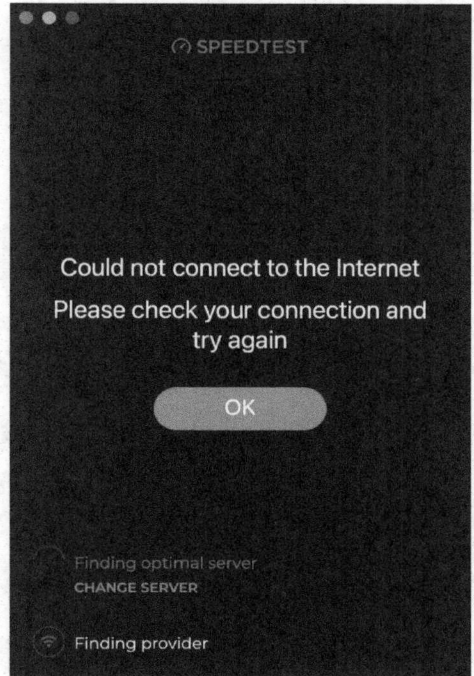

Figure 10-80 *The Speedtest Application Being Blocked by Cloud Firewall*

You also can verify this rule by using the Activity Search tool in the Umbrella Dashboard. Figure 10-81 shows that the Speedtest traffic is blocked by this firewall rule, with the rule name from Meraki Dashboard shown under the **Ruleset or Rule** column. You can find the Activity Search tool in Umbrella Dashboard by navigating to **Reporting > Activity Search** (under Core Reports).

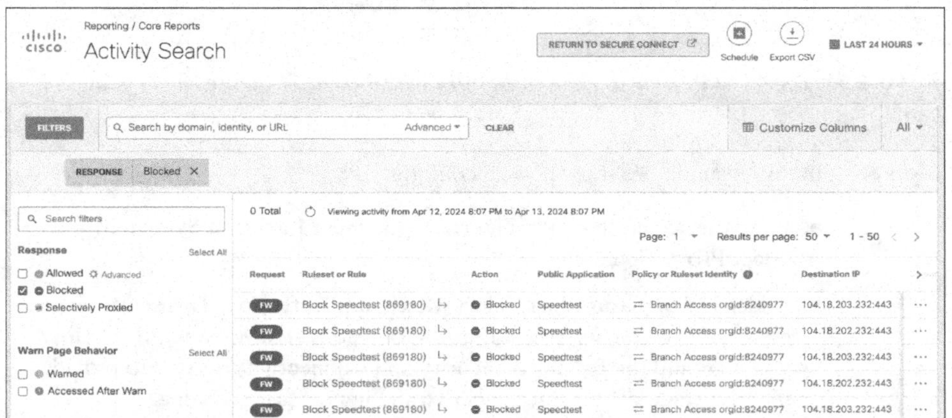

Figure 10-81 *The Umbrella Activity Search Tool Verifying That Cloud Firewall Is Blocking Speedtest*

You've now completed the configuration and verification of an application-based Cloud Firewall rule using Secure Connect. It's worth noting that you can also define private applications for your internal apps. To learn how to define private applications, refer to https://documentation.meraki.com/CiscoPlusSecureConnect/Cisco__Secure_Connect_-_Private_Applications_and_Networks_Access_Control/Cisco__Secure_Connect_-_Defining_Private_Applications.

Intrusion Detection and Prevention (IDS/IPS)

Cloud Firewall also includes a Snort3-based intrusion detection and prevention (IDS/IPS) function. IDS/IPS has been a requirement of security standards like PCI for many years. Secure Connect's IDS/IPS includes a database of over 40,000+ signatures developed and updated by the security researchers at Cisco Talos. Secure Connect's IDS/IPS function is not enabled by default.

Follow these steps to enable and configure the Cloud Firewall IDS/IPS function:

Step 1. Log in to Meraki Dashboard (https://dashboard.meraki.com).

Step 2. Navigate to **Secure Connect > Cloud Firewall** (see Figure 10-82). Click **Cloud IPS Settings** to expand it and then click **Configure IPS Settings.**

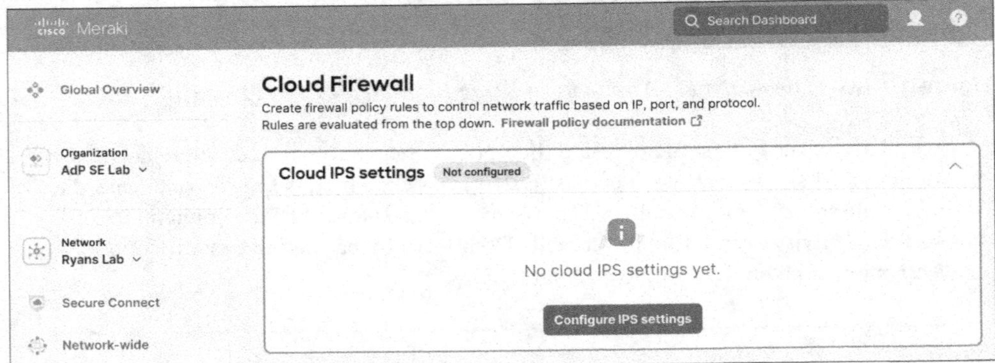

Figure 10-82 *The Cloud Firewall Page in Meraki Dashboard Showing the Default IPS Settings*

Step 3. In this example, we show how to configure IPS.

  a. From the screen shown in Figure 10-83, under **Intrusion System Mode**, select **Protection.**

  b. Under **IPS Signature List**, select **Maximum Detection.** This selection generates a lot of events, which is good for testing. However, in production, you may find the Balanced Security and Connectivity setting to provide the best trade-off between security and unnecessary alerting.

  c. Click **Save.**

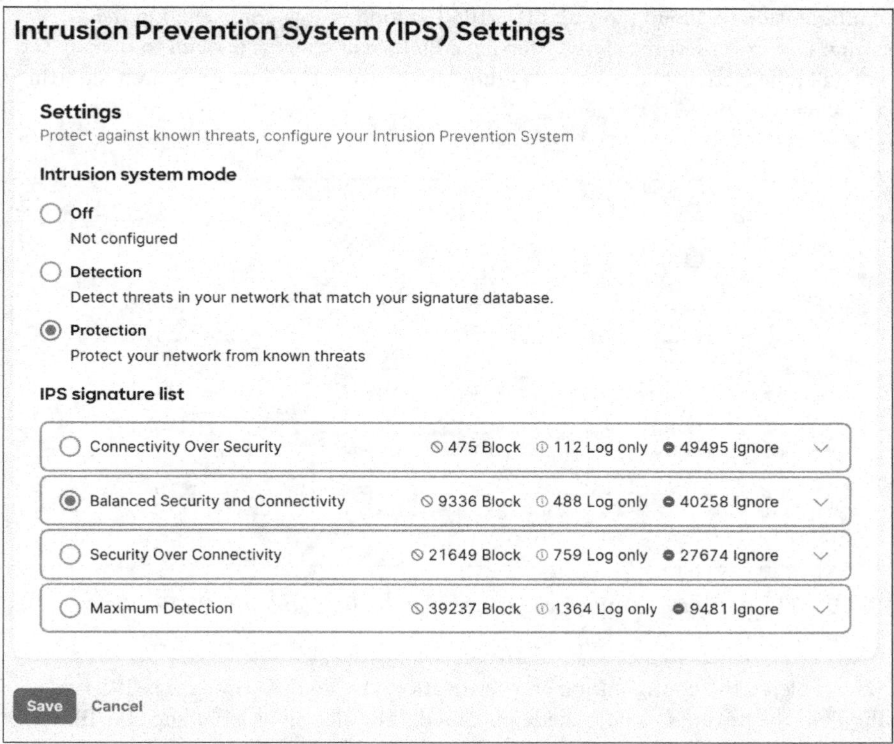

Figure 10-83 *Configuring Secure Connect's Intrusion Prevention System (IPS) Settings*

Step 4. You then return to the **Cloud Firewall** page. By expanding the **Cloud IPS Settings** pane again, you can now see that IPS is enabled (see Figure 10-84).

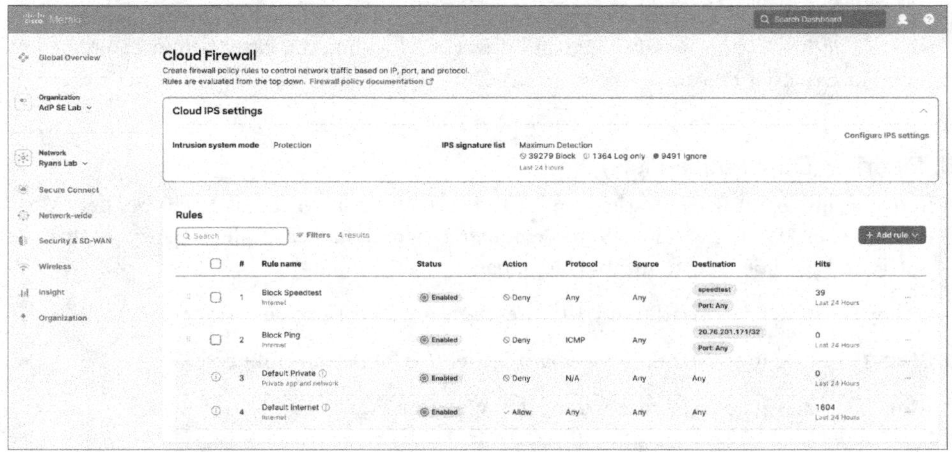

Figure 10-84 *The Cloud Firewall Page in Meraki Dashboard After Enabling IPS*

The configuration of Cloud Firewall's IDS/IPS function is now complete. On the Maximum Detection setting, simply starting a BitTorrent client is enough to quickly see IPS events in the Activity Search tool. Figure 10-85 shows the Activity Search reporting tool showing the IPS alerts triggered.

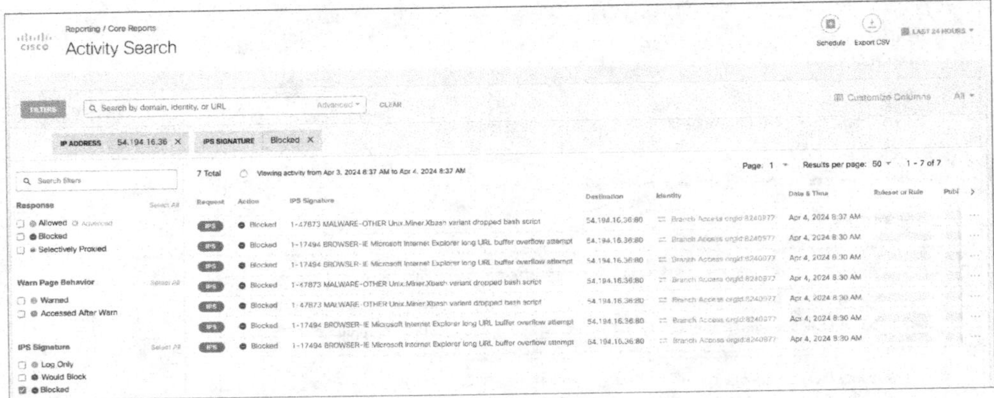

Figure 10-85 *The Activity Search Tool in Cisco Umbrella Showing IPS Events*

You've completed the configuration and verification of Cloud Firewall's IDS/IPS functionality. For the Secure Connect guide on Cloud Firewall policy, including IDS/IPS, refer to https://documentation.meraki.com/CiscoPlusSecureConnect/Cisco__Secure_Connect_Now_-_Policies/Cisco__Secure_Connect_-_Cloud_Firewall_Policy.

Secure Web Gateway (SWG)

Secure Web Gateway is where an administrator should configure policies for web traffic using ports 80 and 443. This section covers how to filter URLs and content categories, as well as File Inspection, sandboxing, and file type blocking, the latter being requirements found in Essential Eight.

URL Filtering (Destination Lists)

In this example, we use a destination list to block attempts to access YouTube. Because this site uses HTTPS, we are able to demonstrate Umbrella's capability to inspect this traffic and provide a customizable block page.

Follow these steps to configure URL filtering using a destination list:

Step 1. Log in to Meraki Dashboard (https://dashboard.meraki.com).

Step 2. Navigate to **Secure Connect > Web** (see Figure 10-86).

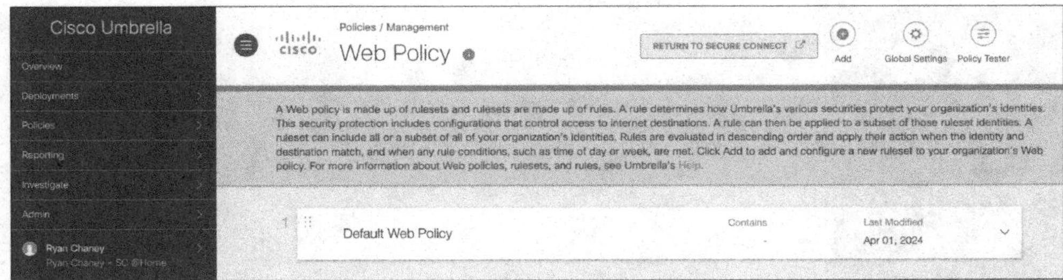

Figure 10-86 *The Default Web Policy Page in Cisco Umbrella*

Step 3. From the menu on the left, expand **Policies** and then click **Destination Lists** under **Policy Components** (see Figure 10-87).

Click **Add** in the top right.

Figure 10-87 *The Default Destinations List Page in Cisco Umbrella*

Step 4. On this page (see Figure 10-88), you can now configure the destination list.

a. In the **List Name** field, select the existing text and replace it with a meaningful name. Because the destination list will only block YouTube, in this example we have named our destination list **YouTube**.

b. Under **Destination List Type**, select **Web Policy**.

c. In the **Destinations** field, you can enter a domain name, URL, or subnet to match on. A single destination list can have up to 5,000 destinations, but it is recommended to keep entries to fewer than 100 for better performance. Enter **youtube.com** and then click the **ADD** button.

d. Click **SAVE**.

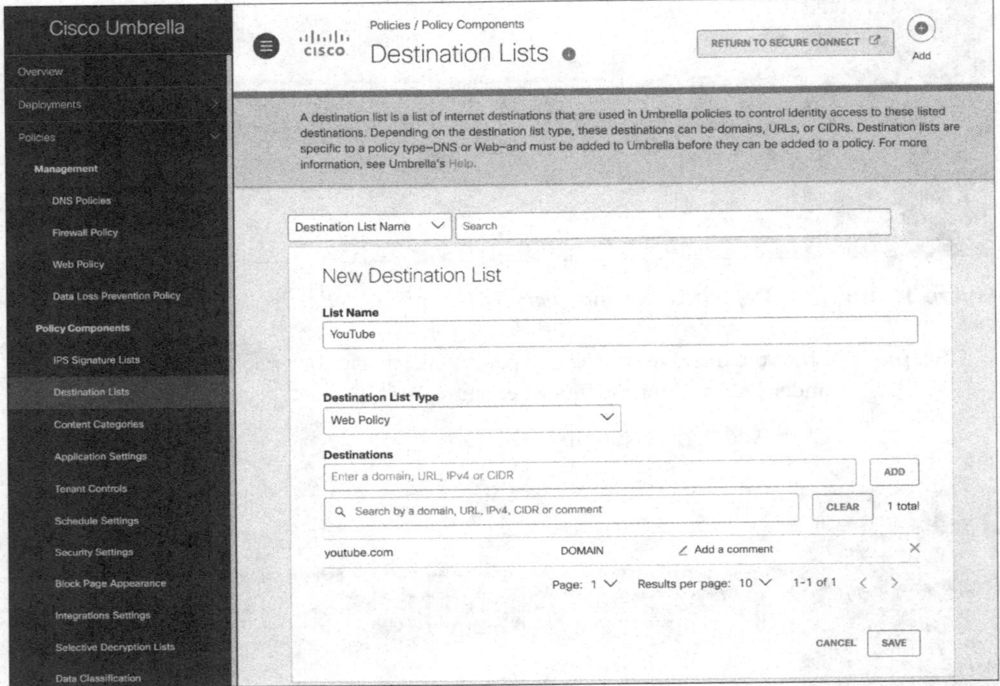

Figure 10-88 *Configuring a Destination List in Cisco Umbrella*

Step 5. With the destination list configured, the next step is to apply it using a policy.

a. Navigate to **Policies > Management > Web Policy.** You can have multiple rulesets here, which is recommended when the ruleset identities are different. For now, update the default Web policy because it will apply to all networks and users (that is, all identities).

b. Click **Default Web Policy** to expand it (see Figure 10-89).

Step 6. Click **Add Rule** (see Figure 10-90).

a. For the **Rule Name**, enter **Block YouTube.**

b. Leave the **Rule Action** as **Block**, which is the default.

c. Under **Identities**, click **Add Identity.** On the **IDENTITIES** pop-up window, click the slider for **Inherit Ruleset Identities** to enable it and then click **APPLY** to close the pop-up window.

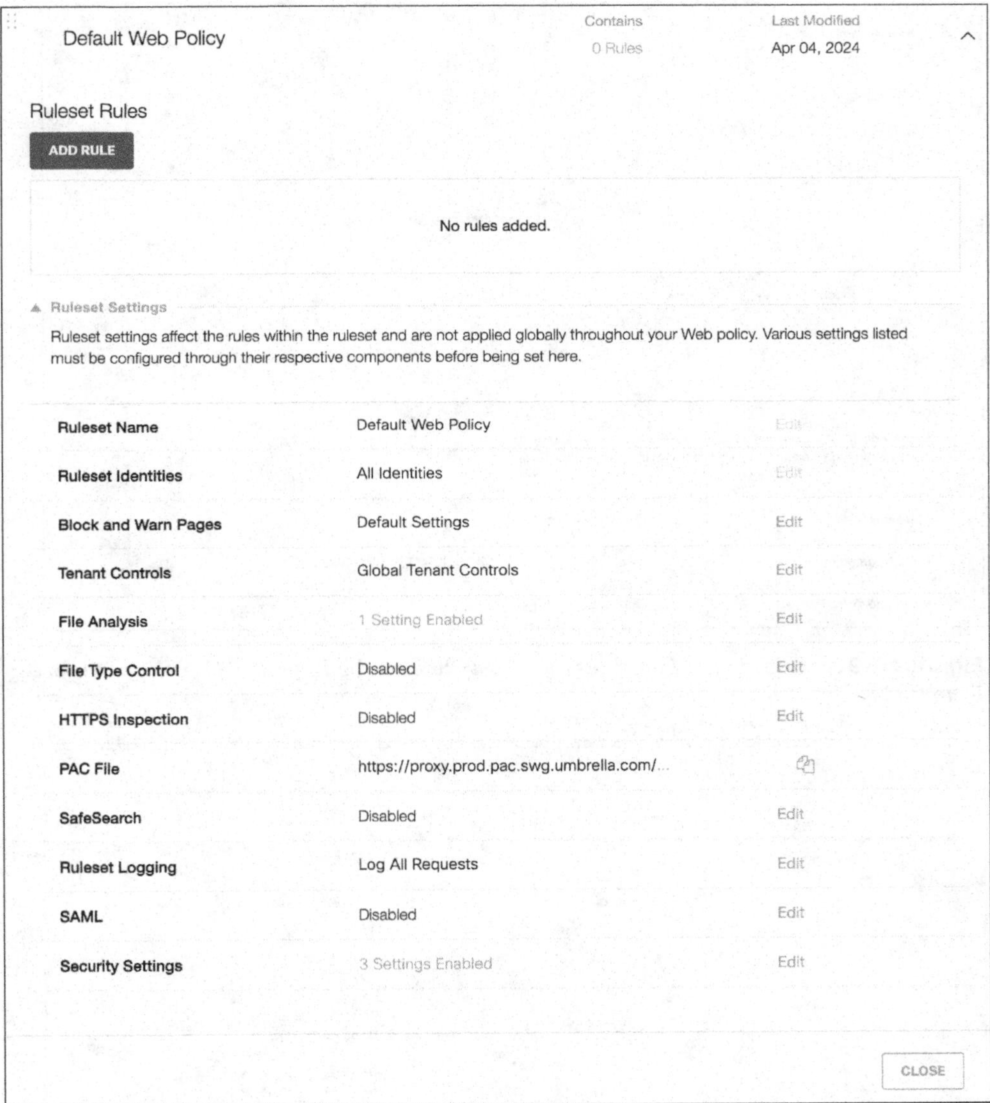

Figure 10-89 *The Default Web Policy Page in Cisco Umbrella*

Step 7. Back on the **ADD RULE** page again where you're configuring the Block YouTube rule, under **Destinations**, click **Add Destination** to bring up the **DESTINATIONS** pop-up window (see Figure 10-91).

a. Click **Destinations List** and then check the box to select the YouTube destination list created earlier.

b. Click **APPLY** to close this pop-up window.

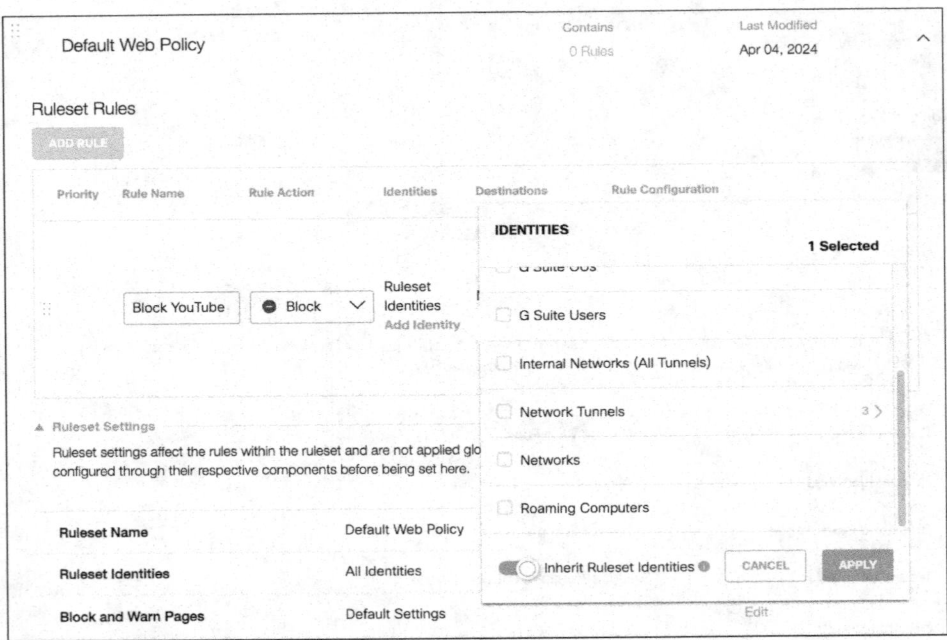

Figure 10-90 *Adding the Identities on a New Rule on the Default Web Policy in Cisco Umbrella*

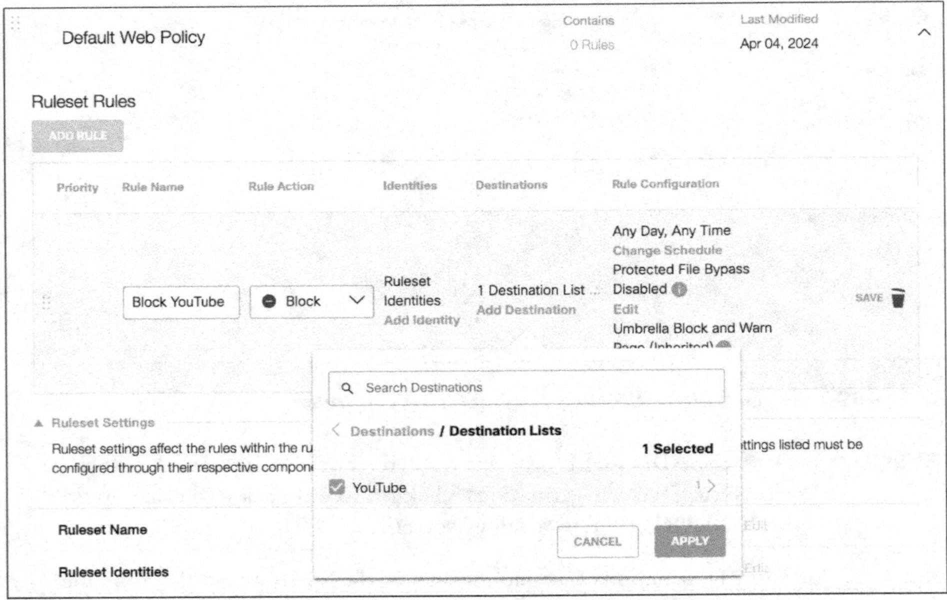

Figure 10-91 *Adding the Destination List on a New Rule on the Default Web Policy in Cisco Umbrella*

Step 8. Back on the **ADD RULE** page once again (see Figure 10-92), click **SAVE** to finish.

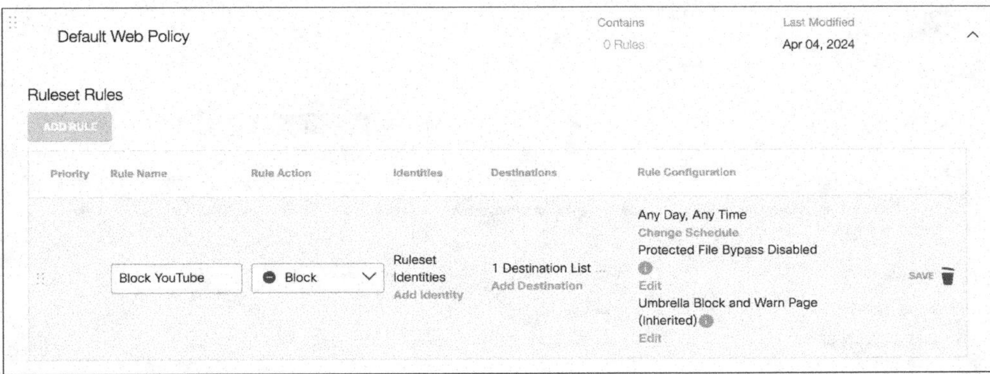

Figure 10-92 *Adding a New Rule to the Default Web Policy in Cisco Umbrella*

Step 9. Back on the **Default Web Policy** page shown in Figure 10-93, notice how the new rule is grayed out. To enable this rule, click the three dots (...) to the right of the rule and then click the **ENABLE RULE** slider so that it shifts across to the right.

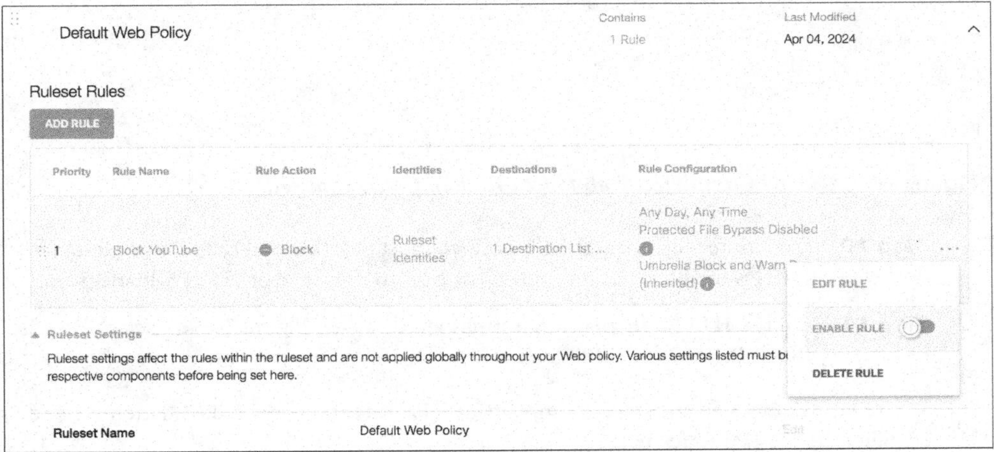

Figure 10-93 *Enabling a New Rule on the Default Web Policy in Cisco Umbrella*

The new rule blocking the youtube.com URL has now been successfully configured and enabled (see Figure 10-94).

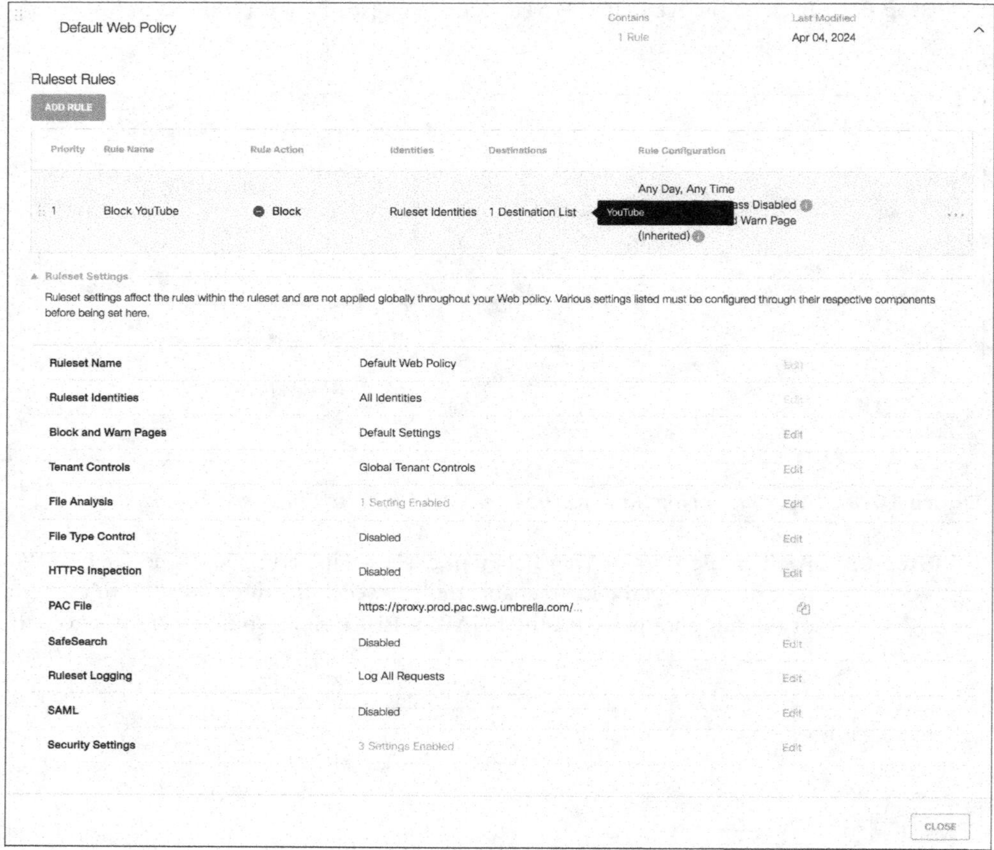

Figure 10-94 *The Completed Web Policy Rule in Cisco Umbrella*

Step 10. One more step is required before you test this rule and that is to enable the HTTPS block page function. Click **Edit** to the right of **HTTPS Inspection.**

Step 11. On the **HTTPS Inspection** pop-up window (see Figure 10-95), select **Display Block Page Over HTTPS** and then click **SAVE.**

You've now completed the steps to implement URL filtering using a destination list and enabling the HTTPS block page.

Follow these steps to verify that this site is now blocked:

Step 1. Open a web browser and navigate to https://www.youtube.com. The web browser is redirected to the default Umbrella block page (see Figure 10-96).

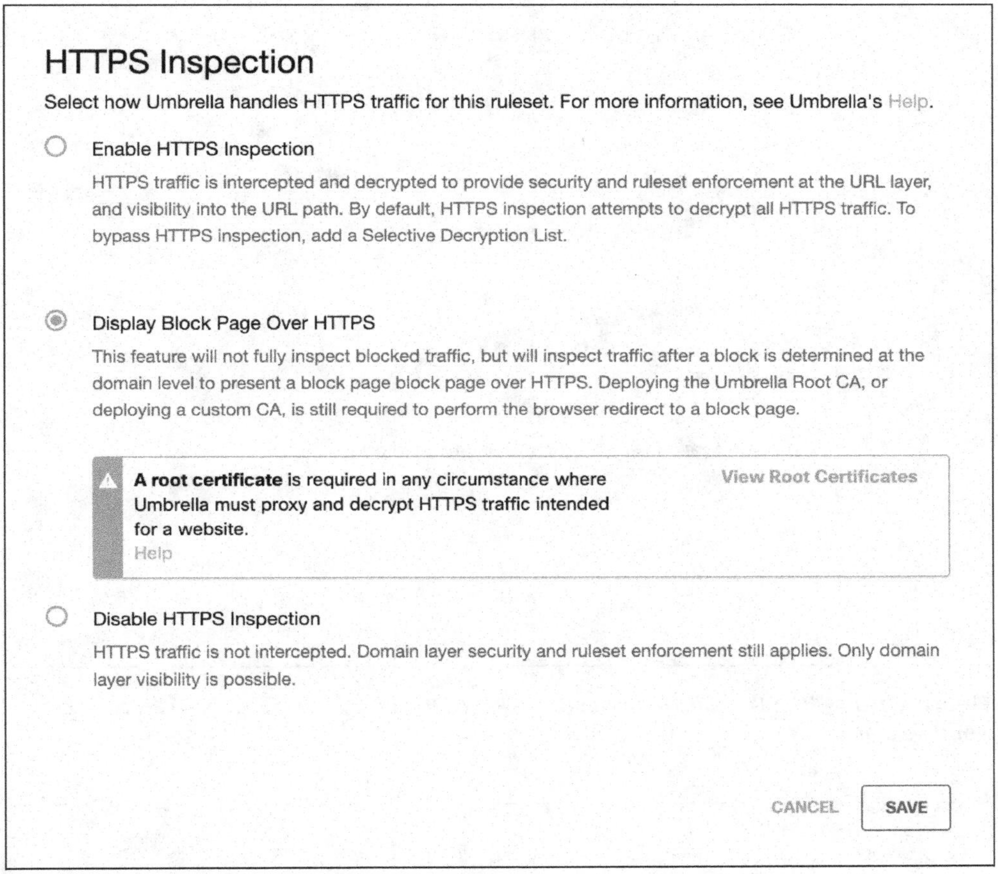

HTTPS Inspection

Select how Umbrella handles HTTPS traffic for this ruleset. For more information, see Umbrella's Help.

Enable HTTPS Inspection

HTTPS traffic is intercepted and decrypted to provide security and ruleset enforcement at the URL layer, and visibility into the URL path. By default, HTTPS inspection attempts to decrypt all HTTPS traffic. To bypass HTTPS inspection, add a Selective Decryption List.

Display Block Page Over HTTPS

This feature will not fully inspect blocked traffic, but will inspect traffic after a block is determined at the domain level to present a block page block page over HTTPS. Deploying the Umbrella Root CA, or deploying a custom CA, is still required to perform the browser redirect to a block page.

A root certificate is required in any circumstance where Umbrella must proxy and decrypt HTTPS traffic intended for a website.
Help

View Root Certificates

Disable HTTPS Inspection

HTTPS traffic is not intercepted. Domain layer security and ruleset enforcement still applies. Only domain layer visibility is possible.

CANCEL SAVE

Figure 10-95 *Enabling the Secure Web Gateway HTTPS Block Page in Cisco Umbrella*

Step 2. Using the Activity Search tool in Umbrella Dashboard (**Reporting** > **Activity Search**), you can verify that this traffic is indeed being blocked by Umbrella (see Figure 10-97).

At this point, you've completed the required steps to block individual websites using destination lists in Cisco Umbrella. For more information on configuring Secure Connect Web policies, refer to the guide available at https://documentation.meraki.com/CiscoPlusSecureConnect/Cisco__Secure_Connect_Now_-_Policies/Cisco__Secure_Connect_Now_-_Manage_the_Web_Policy.

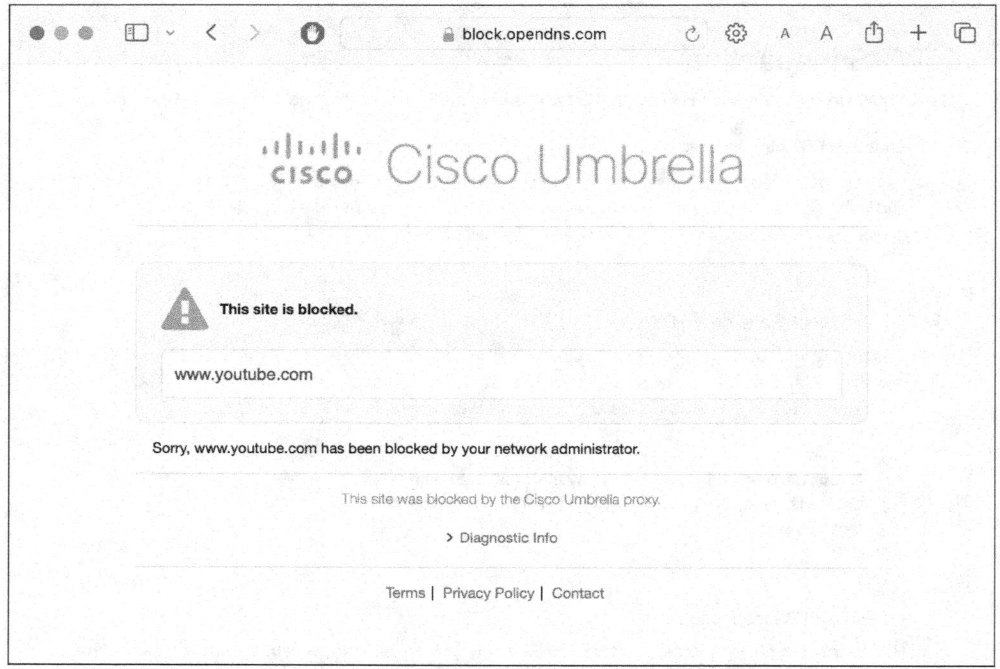

Figure 10-96 *The Default Umbrella Block Page Displayed when a User Tries to Access youtube.com*

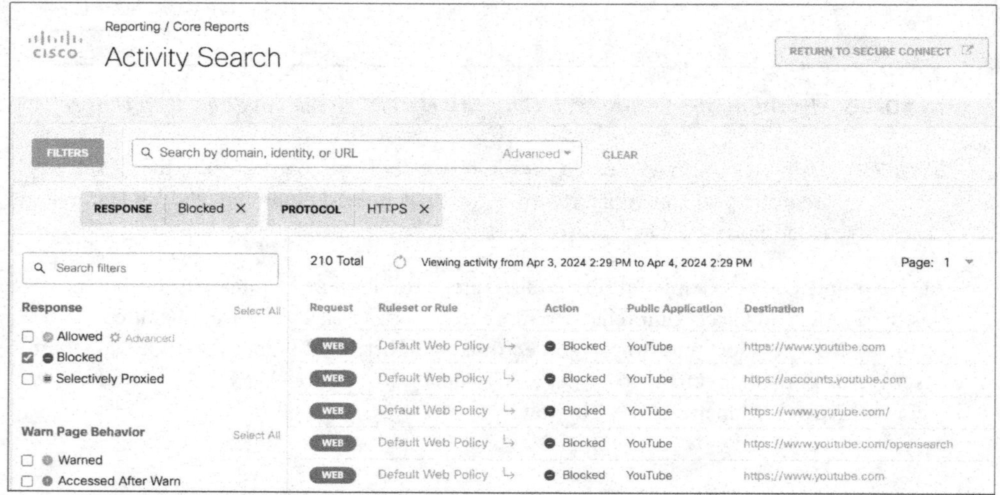

Figure 10-97 *The Activity Search Tool in Umbrella Dashboard Confirming youtube.com Is Being Blocked*

Content Filtering (Content Categories)

How many times have you heard stories of employees gambling away clients' money? Imagine for a moment that you're a network engineer at a major bank/accounting/law firm, and one day the board decides that it is good governance to ensure that employees are blocked from accessing gambling sites. How would you do this? Do you know all the gambling sites? How much time would you need to spend to ensure the list of gambling sites was always up to date? Thankfully, Cisco Talos does this work for you, and all you need to do is enable a Web policy in Cisco Umbrella.

It's important to know that content categories applied as part of web policies are URL-based, meaning that different parts of the same website can be classified differently. For example, consider www.reddit.com, which is classified in the Online Communities category. By applying content categories as part of a Web policy, you can still assign www.reddit.com/sports to Sports and www.reddit.com/nudepics to Adult. This is in contrast to content categories applied to DNS policies that are domain-based, meaning they only look at the domain name itself.

It's best practice to create your policies in a way that makes elements reusable. Although categories can be selected on a Web policy directly, using content categories makes it easy for the same grouping of categories to be applied elsewhere, as we demonstrate.

One of the requirements of Essential Eight is for organizations to have the capability to block Internet advertisements. We use this ability as our inspiration for the following configuration example. Follow these steps to block advertisements using Cisco Umbrella's content categories:

Step 1. Log in to Meraki Dashboard (https://dashboard.meraki.com).

Step 2. Navigate to **Secure Connect** > **Web**.

Step 3. In Umbrella, navigate to **Policies** > **Policy Components** > **Content Categories** (see Figure 10-98). Click the **Add** button in the top right.

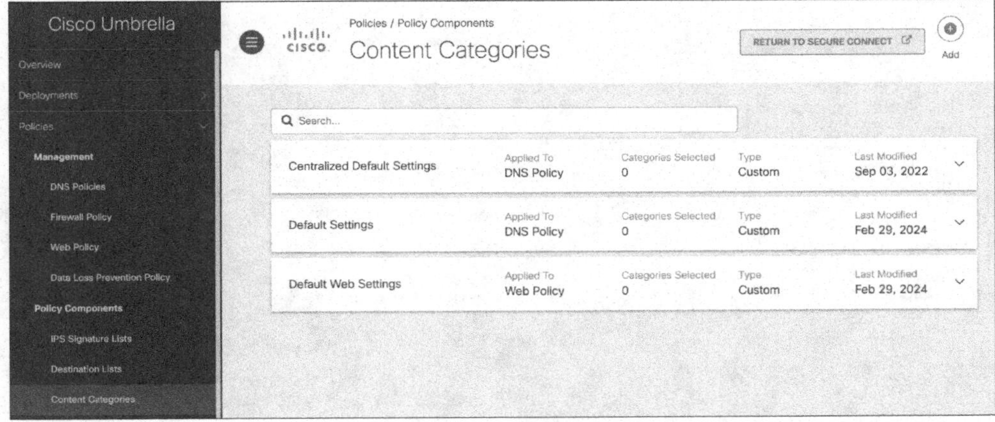

Figure 10-98 *The Default Content Categories Page in Cisco Umbrella*

Step 4. On the **Add New Content Setting** page (see Figure 10-99), under **Setting Name**, enter a meaningful name for this policy. Because ours is intended to block Internet advertising, we have simply named it **Advertising.**

a. From the **Policy Type** drop-down menu, select **Web Policies.**

b. In the **Categories** list, notice all the category options, which include gaming, gambling, social media, and many more. For reference, you can verify a website's content classification at https://www.talosintelligence.com/reputation_center. Each of the content categories is explained at https://docs.umbrella.com/umbrella-user-guide/docs/manage-content-categories-for-web-policies.

c. From the **Categories** listing, select **Advertisements** and then click **SAVE.** Note: Multiple categories can be selected if required.

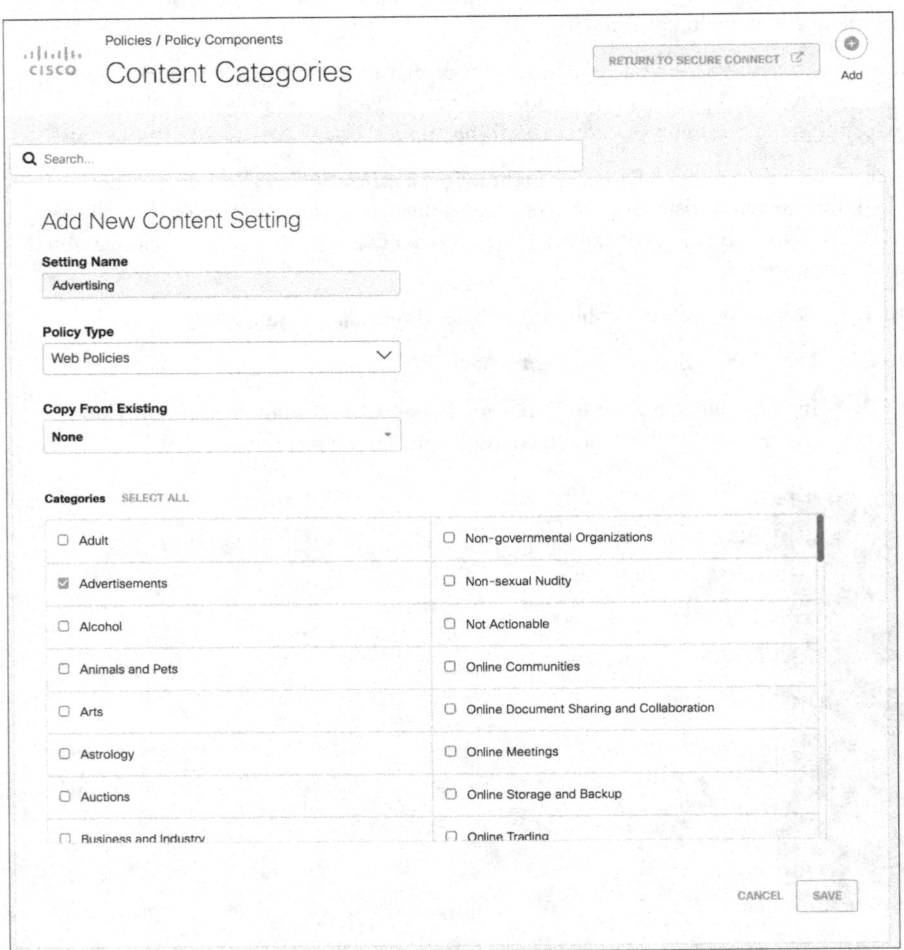

Figure 10-99 *Configuring a New Grouping of Content Categories in Cisco Umbrella*

Step 5. With the content categories defined, you now need to apply it through an update to the Web policy.

a. In Umbrella, navigate to **Policies > Management > Web Policy**.

b. Expand the **Default Web Policy** and click **ADD RULE**.

Step 6. On the new rule (see Figure 10-100), in the **Rule Name** field, enter **Block Advertising.** The name could refer to the categories contained or the identities to which this policy will be applied.

a. Leave **Rule Action** as **Block** (Default).

b. Under **Identities**, click **Add Identity.**

c. On the **IDENTITIES** pop-up window, click **Inherit Ruleset Identities** and then click **APPLY.**

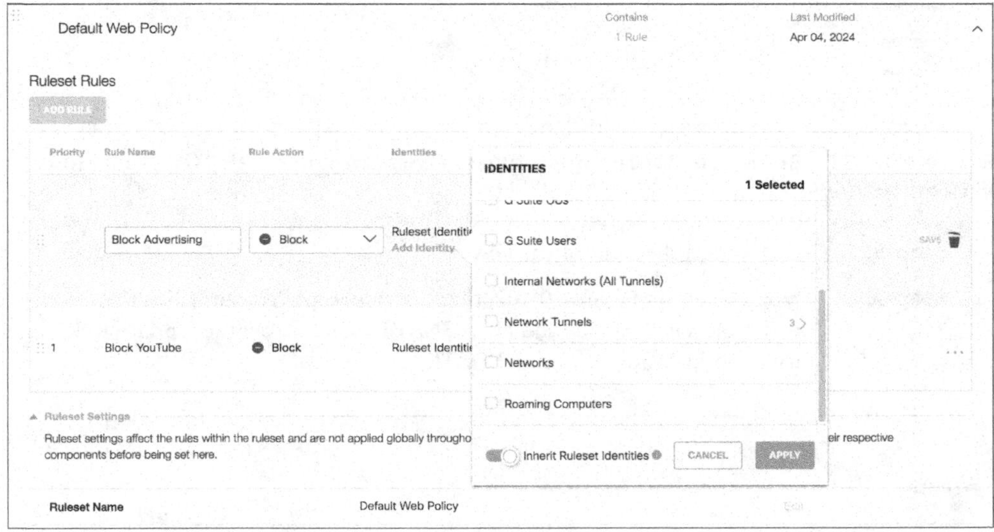

Figure 10-100 *Adding Identities to a New Rule on a Web Policy in Cisco Umbrella*

Step 7. Under **Destinations**, click **Add Destination.**

a. On the **DESTINATIONS** pop-up window, click **Content Categories.** From the **Select...** drop-down menu (see Figure 10-101), select the content category that was just created (in this case, **Advertising**), and then click **APPLY.**

b. The Destinations pop-up window closes, and you return to the configuration of the new rule.

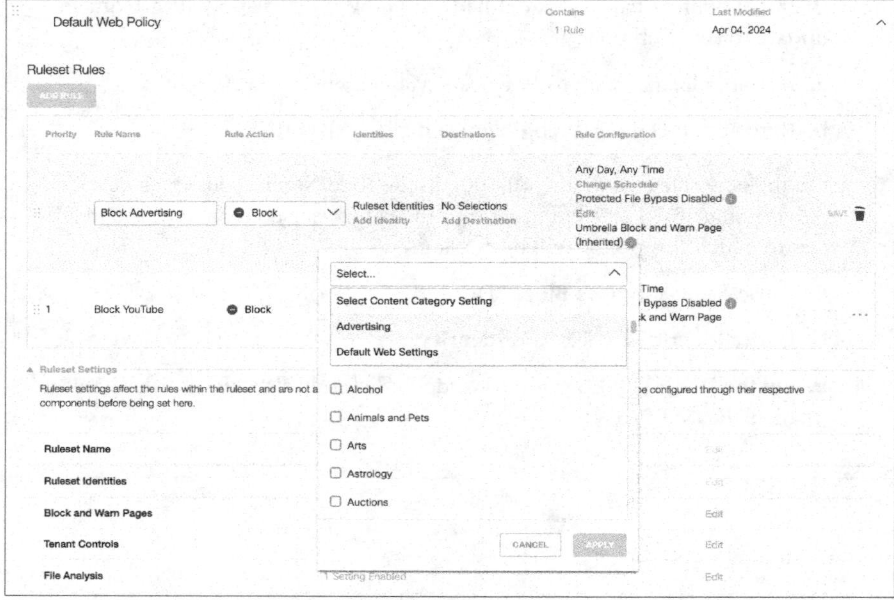

Figure 10-101 *Adding the Destination Content Categories on a New Web Policy Rule in Cisco Umbrella*

Step 8. Click **Save** on the right of the new rule.

Step 9. As you can see in Figure 10-102, the new rule is grayed out. Click the three dots (...) on the right side and click **ENABLE RULE.** On the **Update Rule Status** pop-up window, click **UPDATE.**

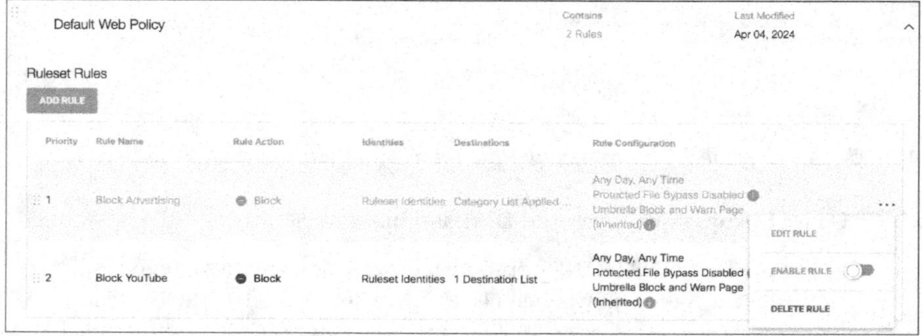

Figure 10-102 *Enabling a New Content Category Rule on the Default Web Policy in Cisco Umbrella*

This content category-based Web policy rule has now been configured successfully and is enabled (see Figure 10-103).

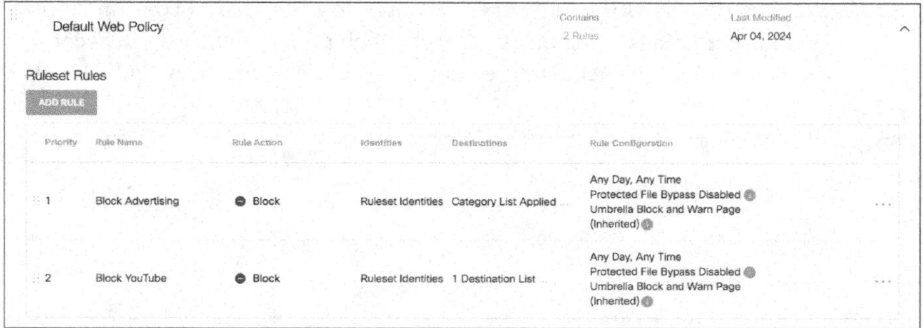

Figure 10-103 *The Default Web Policy in Cisco Umbrella After Successfully Adding a New Content Category Rule*

You've now completed the steps necessary to filter based on content category.

Follow these steps to verify that this configuration is working:

Step 1. Verify that the URL being tested is in a blocked content category by searching for it using Talos's IP and Domain Reputation Center at https://www.talosintelligence.com/reputation_center. The URL we're testing in this case is www.adforce.com.

Step 2. Open a web browser and navigate to www.adforce.com. The web browser is redirected to the default Umbrella block page. At the bottom of the page, users are informed that this site was blocked due to being classified in the category Advertisements (see Figure 10-104).

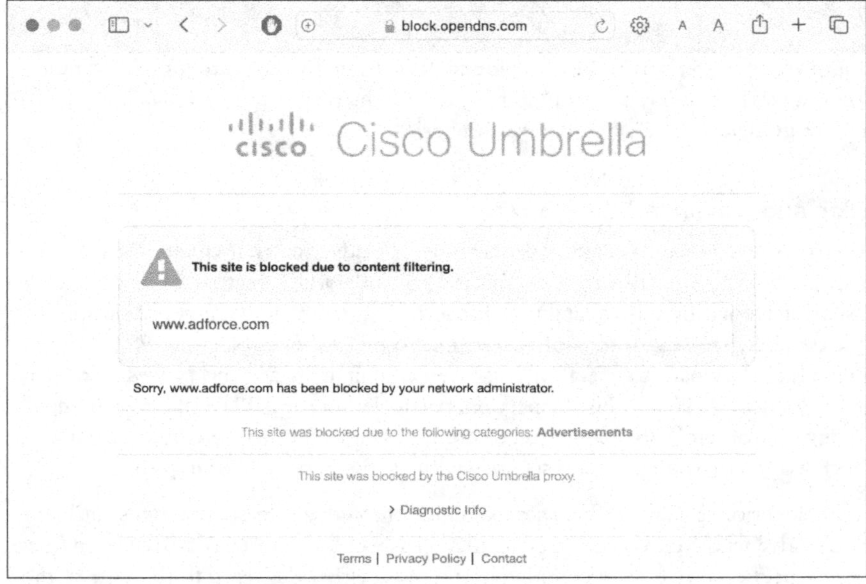

Figure 10-104 *The Umbrella Block Page for adforce.com*

Step 3. Figure 10-105 shows the log entry in the Activity Search tool confirming that www.adforce.com is being blocked by the Web policy. To reveal the Event Details pane shown, click the three dots (...) and then click **View Full Details.**

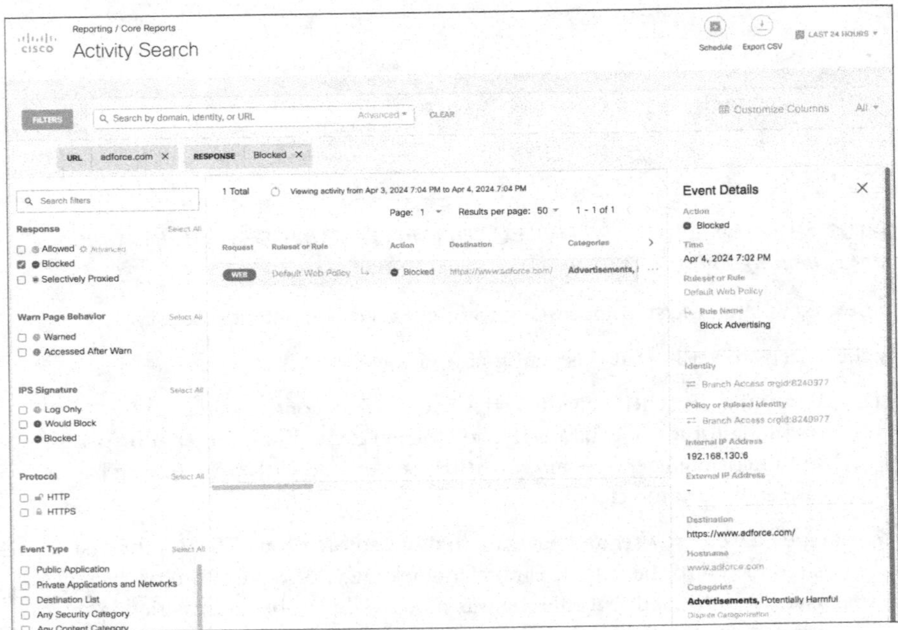

Figure 10-105 *The Activity Search Report Showing Traffic to adforce.com Blocked by a Web Policy*

You've completed the steps necessary to block URLs using content categories. For more on content categories including best practices, refer to https://docs.umbrella.com/umbrella-user-guide/docs/manage-content-categories.

File Inspection and Advanced Sandboxing

Anytime a user downloads a file, either deliberately or inadvertently, it creates the possibility for malware to enter the organization. This is a common attack vector. An example of a security standard requiring this capability is Essential Eight, which requires organizations to have the capability to scan Microsoft Office macro files for viruses. Using Web policies, you can scan file downloads to check whether they contain malware; this process is referred to as *File Inspection*. Typically, File Inspection, particularly over HTTPS, has a high impact on the throughput of hardware appliances. Shifting this capability to the cloud provides the best of both worlds, providing greater security without the performance impact.

When File Inspection is enabled, files are examined through a two-stage process utilizing both Cisco's Advanced Malware Protection (AMP) as well as Umbrella's antivirus engines. After both inspections have been completed, the file is either delivered to the user or the download is terminated, and the block page is displayed.

File Inspection is disabled by default. To enable File Inspection and advanced sandboxing, follow these steps.

Step 1. Log in to Meraki Dashboard (https://dashboard.meraki.com).

Step 2. Navigate to **Secure Connect > Web**.

Step 3. Expand the **Default Web Policy**. If you have created your own ruleset, the following steps are the same if you wish to update that.

Step 4. Under **Ruleset Settings** (see Figure 10-106), to the right of **File Analysis**, click **Edit**.

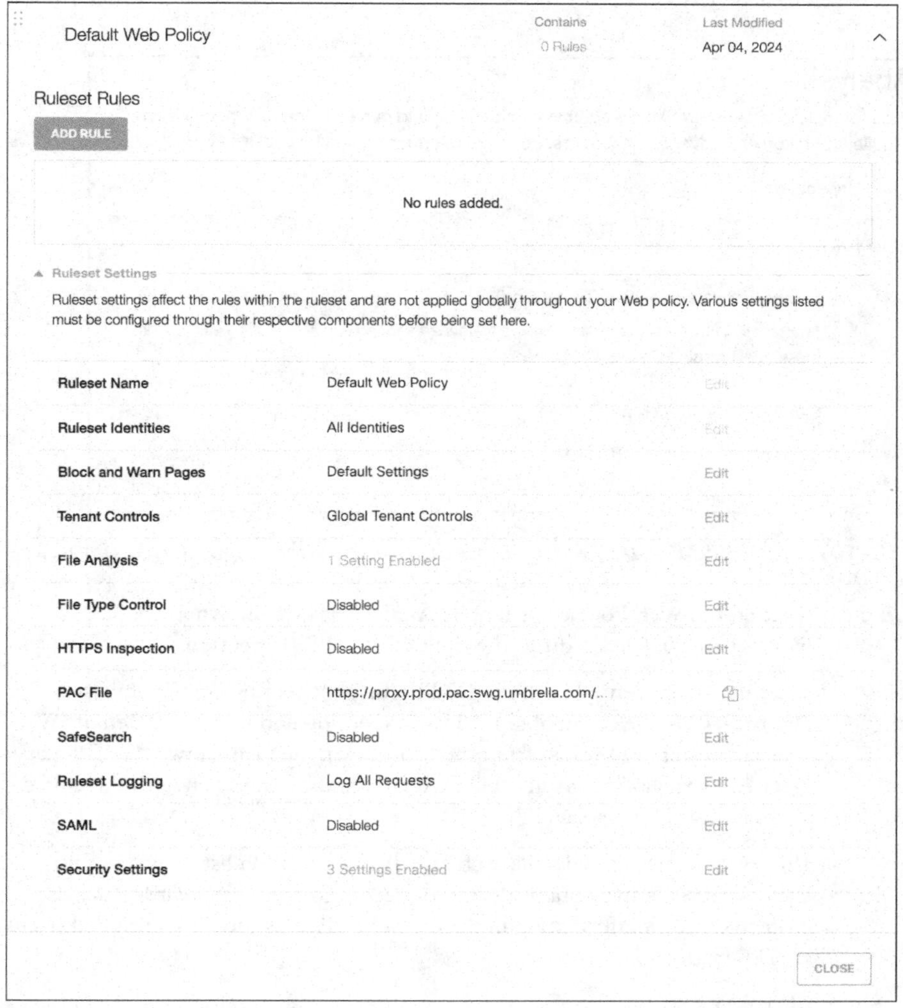

Figure 10-106 *The Default File-Related Settings on a Web Policy in Cisco Umbrella*

Step 5. Click the slider for **File Inspection** to enable the antivirus and malware scanning for attempted downloads (see Figure 10-107).

a. Click the slider to enable **Secure Malware Analytics (Threat Grid).** This option is not available as part of a DNS policy; hence, it is recommended that you enable File Inspection as part of a Web policy.

b. If this is the first time Secure Malware Analytics is being enabled, you will be asked to select a region—North America or Europe—in which you would like the sandboxing to occur. The region cannot be changed, so double-check before making this choice.

c. Click **SAVE.**

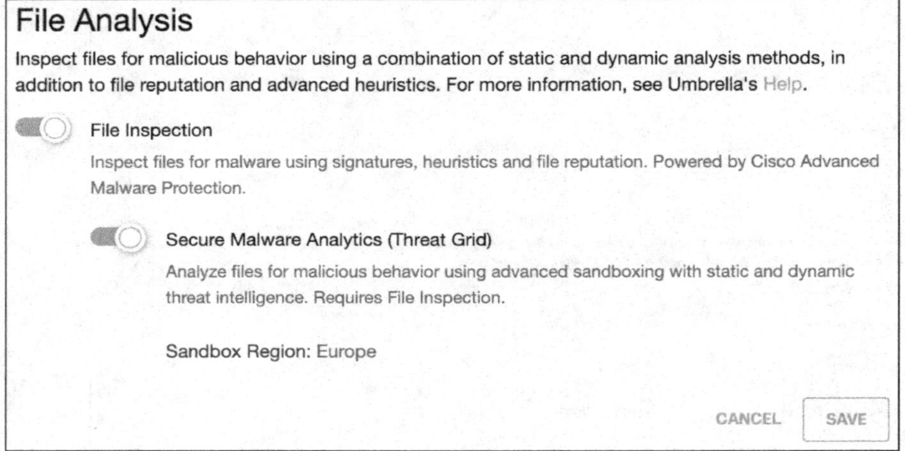

Figure 10-107 *Enabling File Inspection and Advanced Sandboxing in Cisco Umbrella*

Step 6. Back on the **Web Policies** page, **File Analysis** is now shown as enabled (see Figure 10-108). Click **Edit** to the right of **HTTPS Inspection.**

Step 7. You then are presented with the **HTTPS Inspection** pop-up window (see Figure 10-109). Select **Enable HTTPS Inspection** and select the **Default Web Selective Decryption List** from the drop-down menu as shown. HTTPS pages blocked by the existing rules will be unaffected by this change, and blocked pages will still be displayed.

This example uses the default web selective decryption list, which has no exclusions. Sensitive data protected by regulation or IT standards, such as protected health information in the case of HIPAA, should be excluded from HTTPS inspection.

Click **SAVE.**

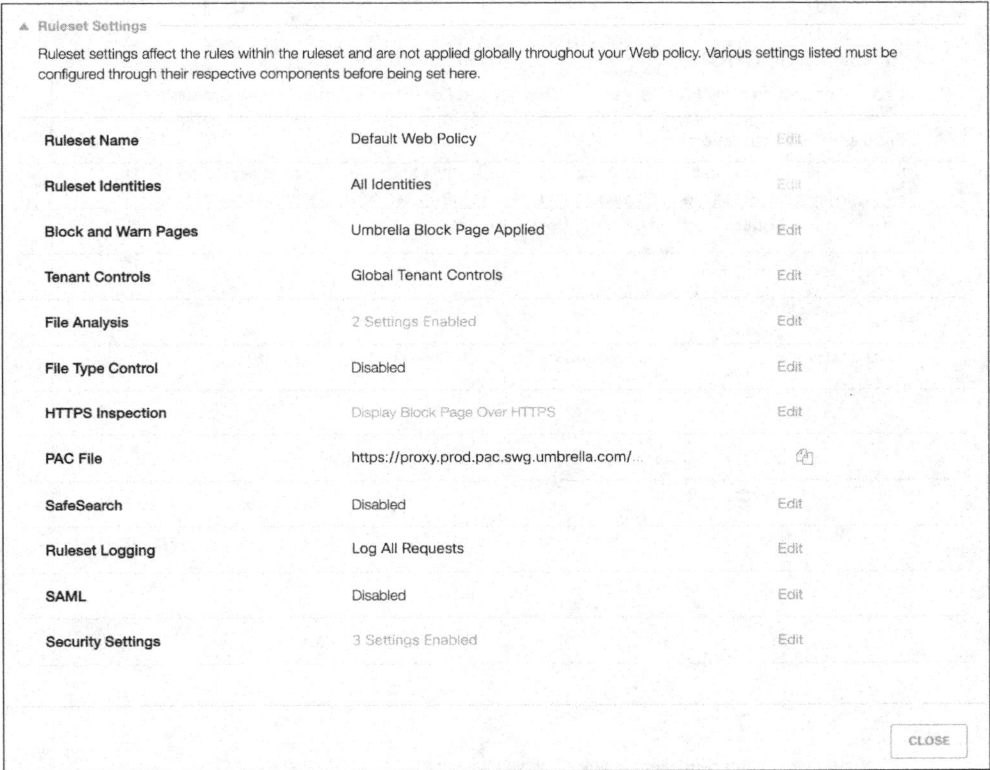

Figure 10-108 *A Cisco Umbrella Web Policy Ruleset After Enabling File Analysis*

You've completed the steps necessary to enable File Inspection and sandboxing.

As previously mentioned in the "Threat Protection" section, you can test this functionality without downloading files that contain real viruses and/or malware. EICAR test files trigger preventative measures, and as long as they are downloaded from a trustworthy source, they do not actually contain malware.

Follow these steps to verify that this configuration is working:

Step 1. Open https://eicar.eu in your web browser. The eicar.eu page should load, as shown in Figure 10-110.

Step 2. Click one of the HTTP links on the top row (for example, http://eicar.eu/eicar.com). The download is blocked, and the block page is then displayed, as shown in Figure 10-111.

HTTPS Inspection
Select how Umbrella handles HTTPS traffic for this ruleset. For more information, see Umbrella's Help.
Enable HTTPS Inspection
HTTPS traffic is intercepted and decrypted to provide security and ruleset enforcement at the URL layer, and visibility into the URL path. By default, HTTPS inspection attempts to decrypt all HTTPS traffic. To bypass HTTPS inspection, add a Selective Decryption List.
Default Web Selective Decryption List
0 Categories
0 Applications
0 Domains
No Categories
No Applications
No Domains
A root certificate is required in any circumstance where Umbrella must proxy and decrypt HTTPS traffic intended for a website.
Help
View Root Certificates
Display Block Page Over HTTPS
This feature will not fully inspect blocked traffic, but will inspect traffic after a block is determined at the domain level to present a block page block page over HTTPS. Deploying the Umbrella Root CA, or deploying a custom CA, is still required to perform the browser redirect to a block page.
Disable HTTPS Inspection
HTTPS traffic is not intercepted. Domain layer security and ruleset enforcement still applies. Only domain layer visibility is possible.
CANCEL
SAVE

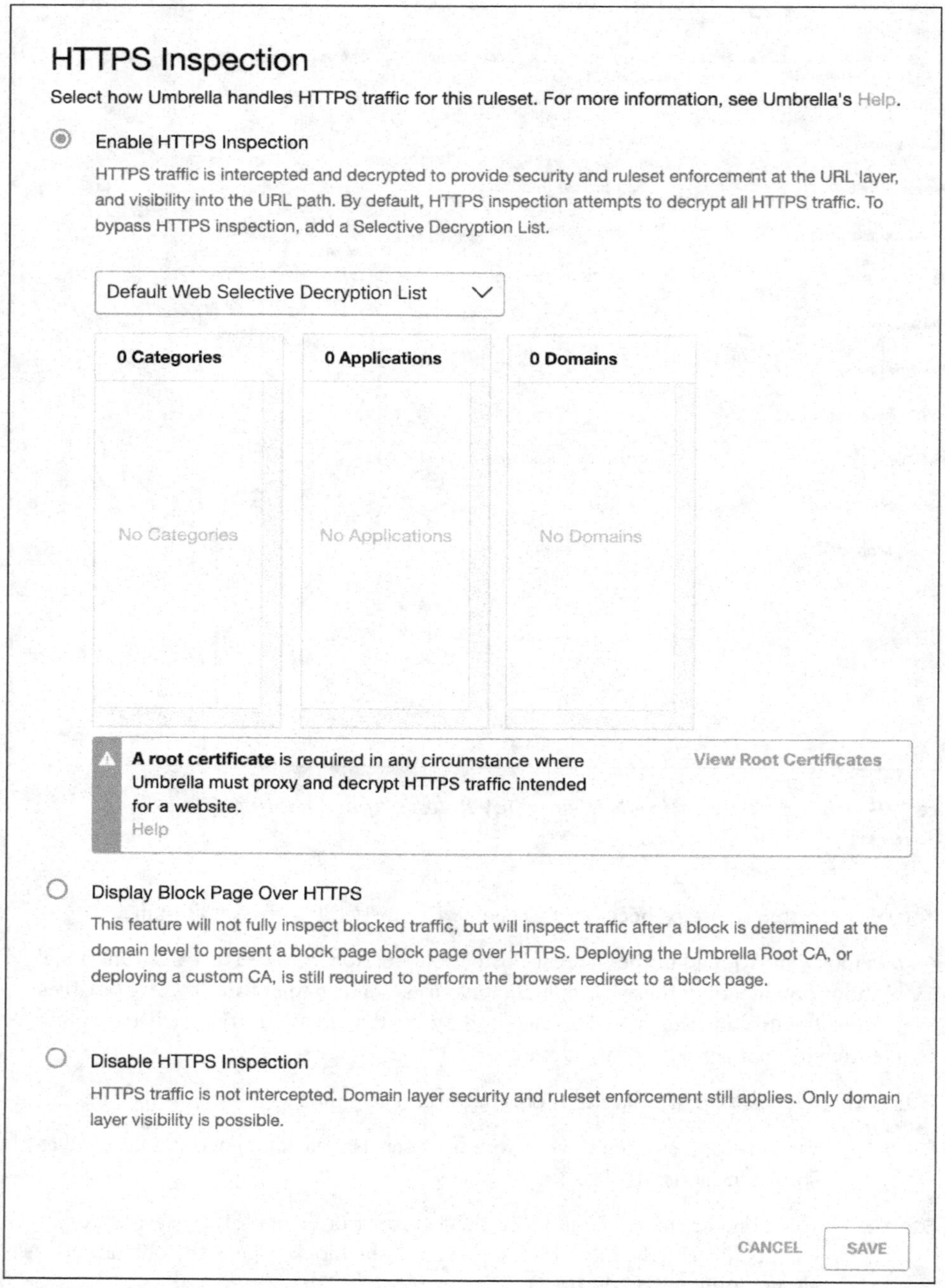

Figure 10-109 *The HTTPS Inspection Pop-Up Window on a Web Policy in Cisco Umbrella*

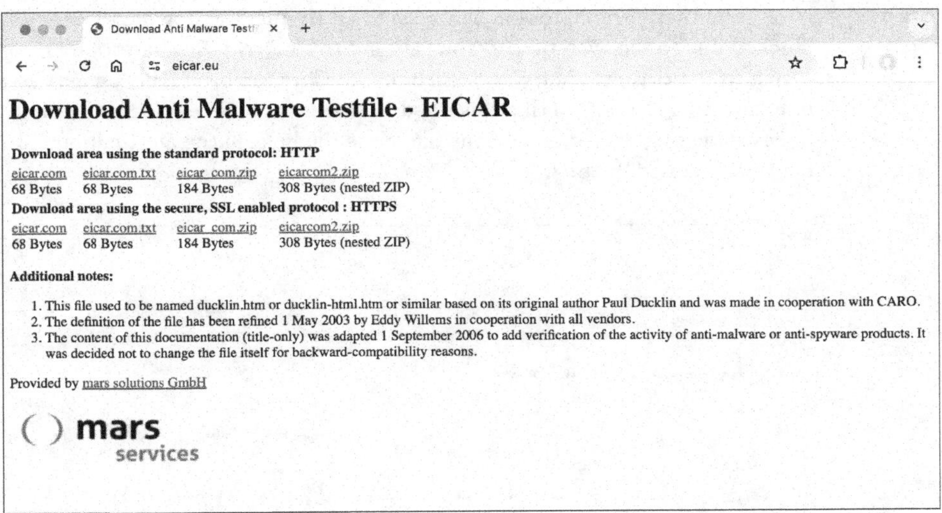

Figure 10-110 *The eicar.eu Home Page Showing the Test Files Available*

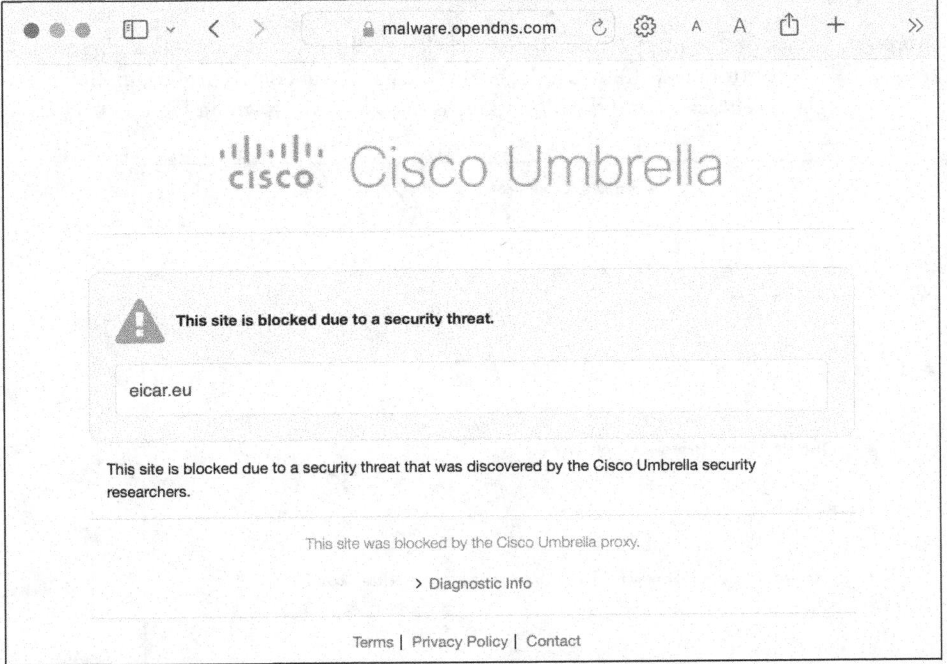

Figure 10-111 *The Umbrella Block Page Presented when Trying to Access an EICAR File over HTTP*

Step 3. Use the Activity Search tool in Umbrella to verify that the download was blocked due to the Web policy. You can find the Activity Search tool by navigating to **Reporting > Activity Search** (under Core Reports). The log entries in Figure 10-112 confirm that this file download was blocked due to the Web policy detecting this as a malicious file. Note the links in the Destination column starting with **http://**.

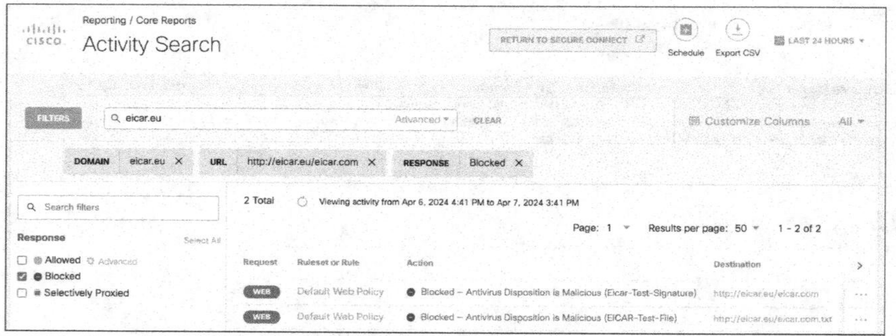

Figure 10-112 *Activity Search Entries Showing EICAR Downloads Being Blocked by the Web Policy*

Step 4. Back on the https://eicar.eu page, click any of the HTTPS download links on the bottom row (for example, https://eicar.eu/eicar.com). Once again, the download is blocked, and the block page is displayed, as shown in Figure 10-113.

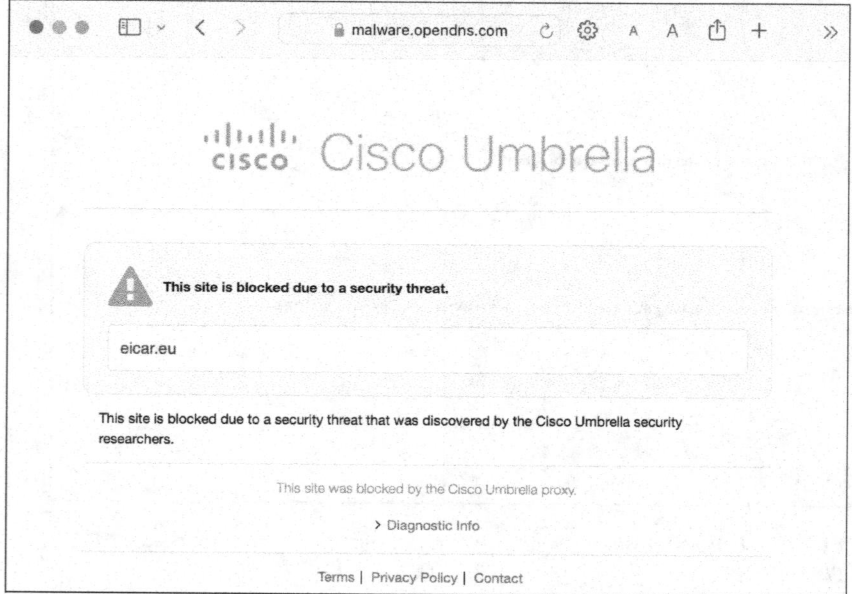

Figure 10-113 *The Umbrella Block Page Presented when Trying to Access an EICAR File over HTTPS*

Step 5. Use the Activity Search reporting tool to confirm that this file was blocked due to the Web policy. As you can see in Figure 10-114, once again, the web policy determined the file to be malicious. Note the links in the **Destination** column starting with **https://**.

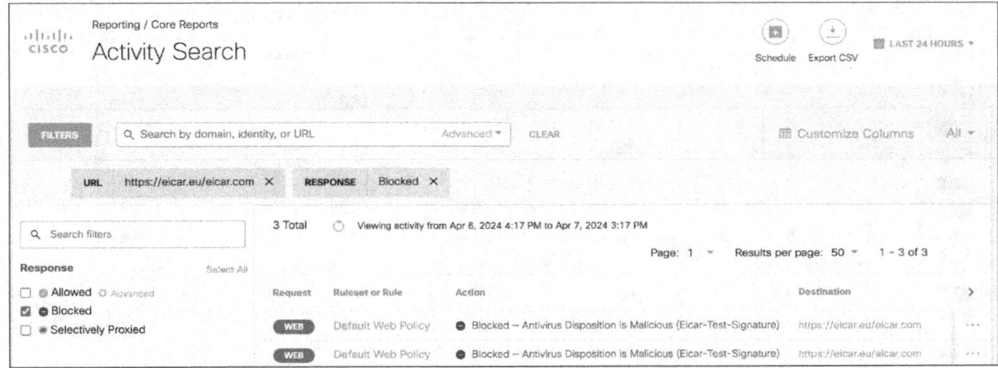

Figure 10-114 *Activity Search Entries Showing HTTPS EICAR Downloads Being Blocked by the Web Policy*

Step 6. This next test will validate that the AMP engine is working correctly over HTTP. Use this Umbrella HTTP test URL to attempt to download this text file: http://proxy.opendnstest.com/download/AMP_TEST_FILE.txt. Figure 10-115 shows that the file download was blocked.

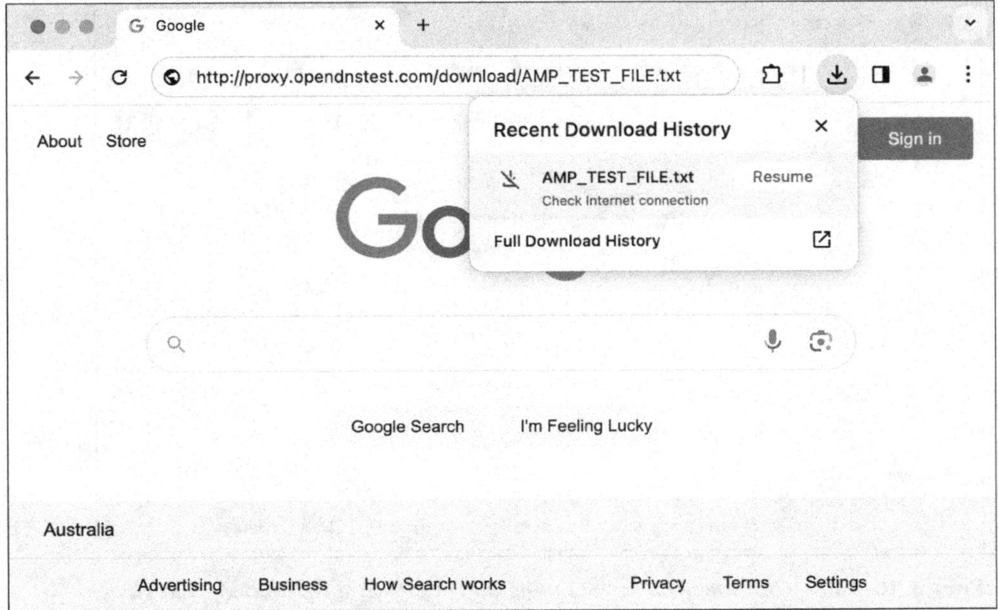

Figure 10-115 *Chrome Browser Showing an HTTP File Download That's Been Blocked*

Step 7. Use the Activity Search tool to confirm that this file was blocked due to the Web policy. As you can see in Figure 10-116, once again the web policy determined the file to be malicious. Notice the comment under the **Action** column stating that the Cisco AMP engine detected this malware. Also, check that the URL in the **Destination** column starts with **http://**.

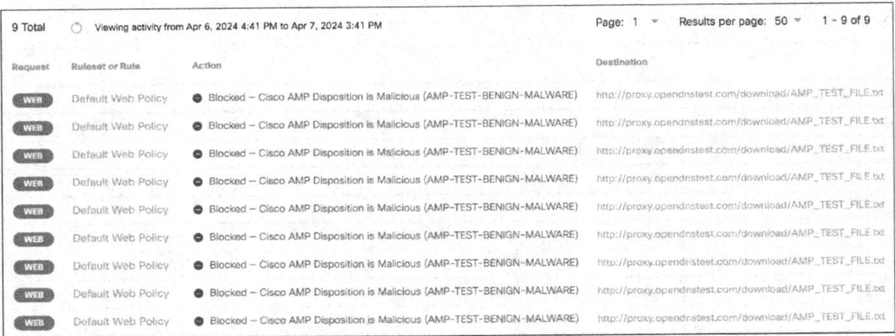

Figure 10-116 *Activity Search Entries Showing HTTP Downloads Containing Malware Blocked by the AMP Engine*

Step 8. This next test will validate that the AMP engine is working correctly over HTTPS. Use this Umbrella HTTPS test URL to attempt to download this text file: https://ssl-proxy.opendnstest.com/download/AMP_TEST_FILE.txt. Figure 10-117 shows that the file download was blocked.

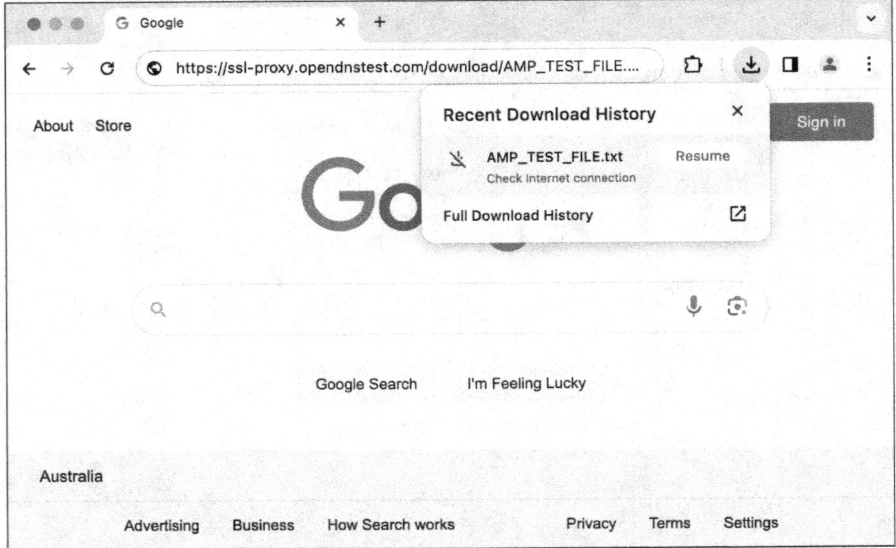

Figure 10-117 *Chrome Browser Showing an HTTPS File Download That's Been Blocked*

Step 9. Again, use the Activity Search reporting tool to confirm that this file was blocked due to the Web policy. As you can see in Figure 10-118, once again, the web policy determined the file to be malicious and blocked it. Notice the comment under the **Action** column stating that the Cisco AMP engine detected this malware. Also, check that the URL in the **Destination** column starts with **https://**.

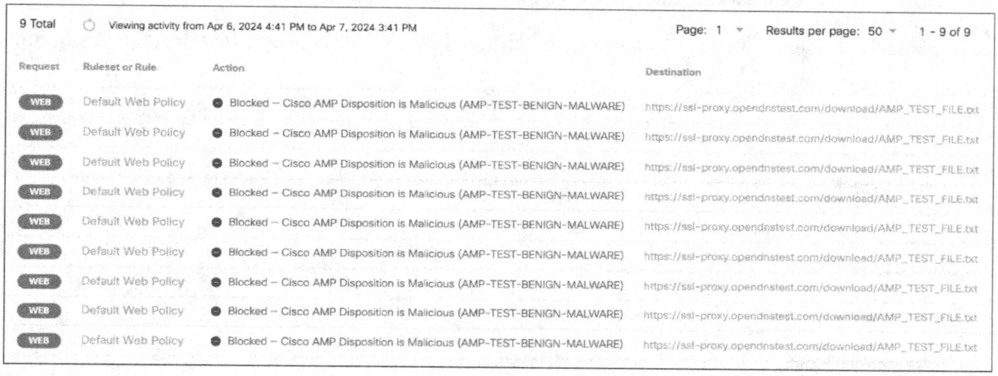

9 Total Viewing activity from Apr 6, 2024 4:41 PM to Apr 7, 2024 3:41 PM Page: 1 Results per page: 50 1 - 9 of 9

Request	Ruleset or Rule	Action	Destination
WEB	Default Web Policy	Blocked – Cisco AMP Disposition is Malicious (AMP-TEST-BENIGN-MALWARE)	https://ssl-proxy.opendnstest.com/download/AMP_TEST_FILE.txt
WEB	Default Web Policy	Blocked – Cisco AMP Disposition is Malicious (AMP-TEST-BENIGN-MALWARE)	https://ssl-proxy.opendnstest.com/download/AMP_TEST_FILE.txt
WEB	Default Web Policy	Blocked – Cisco AMP Disposition is Malicious (AMP-TEST-BENIGN-MALWARE)	https://ssl-proxy.opendnstest.com/download/AMP_TEST_FILE.txt
WEB	Default Web Policy	Blocked – Cisco AMP Disposition is Malicious (AMP-TEST-BENIGN-MALWARE)	https://ssl-proxy.opendnstest.com/download/AMP_TEST_FILE.txt
WEB	Default Web Policy	Blocked – Cisco AMP Disposition is Malicious (AMP-TEST-BENIGN-MALWARE)	https://ssl-proxy.opendnstest.com/download/AMP_TEST_FILE.txt
WEB	Default Web Policy	Blocked – Cisco AMP Disposition is Malicious (AMP-TEST-BENIGN-MALWARE)	https://ssl-proxy.opendnstest.com/download/AMP_TEST_FILE.txt
WEB	Default Web Policy	Blocked – Cisco AMP Disposition is Malicious (AMP-TEST-BENIGN-MALWARE)	https://ssl-proxy.opendnstest.com/download/AMP_TEST_FILE.txt
WEB	Default Web Policy	Blocked – Cisco AMP Disposition is Malicious (AMP-TEST-BENIGN-MALWARE)	https://ssl-proxy.opendnstest.com/download/AMP_TEST_FILE.txt
WEB	Default Web Policy	Blocked – Cisco AMP Disposition is Malicious (AMP-TEST-BENIGN-MALWARE)	https://ssl-proxy.opendnstest.com/download/AMP_TEST_FILE.txt

Figure 10-118 *Activity Search Entries Showing HTTPS Downloads Containing Malware Blocked by the AMP Engine*

At this point, you've completed the setup and verification of File Inspection using the antivirus and Cisco AMP engines. For more information on configuring File Inspection with Cisco Umbrella, refer to https://docs.umbrella.com/umbrella-user-guide/docs/enable-file-inspection-for-web-policies. More information on Cisco Secure Malware Analytics can be found at https://docs.umbrella.com/umbrella-user-guide/docs/enable-threat-grid-malware-analysis. Read on to learn more about Cisco Umbrella's file controls.

File Type Control

Secure Connect also has the capability to block file downloads based on a file's extension. Cisco Umbrella, which provides this functionality, uses an internal detection engine to determine the file type. This means file downloads can be prevented even if the file extension has been changed in an attempt to bypass this control. File Type Control can be enabled only as part of a Web policy and requires HTTPS inspection (this was enabled in the preceding section). An example of a security standard that requires this functionality is Essential Eight, which requires that organizations have the capability to block Microsoft Office macro files originating from the Internet. Microsoft Office macro files end in an *m*, such as *.docm*, *.xlsm*, and *.dotm*. We demonstrate how to block these file types in the following example.

Follow these steps to block the download of Microsoft Office macro files using Umbrella's file type controls:

Step 1. Log in to Meraki Dashboard (https://dashboard.meraki.com).

Step 2. Navigate to Secure **Connect** > **Web.**

Step 3. Expand the **Default Web Policy.** These steps are the same if you have previously created your own ruleset and wish to edit it.

Step 4. Under **Ruleset Settings** (see Figure 10-119), to the right of **File Type Control**, click **Edit.**

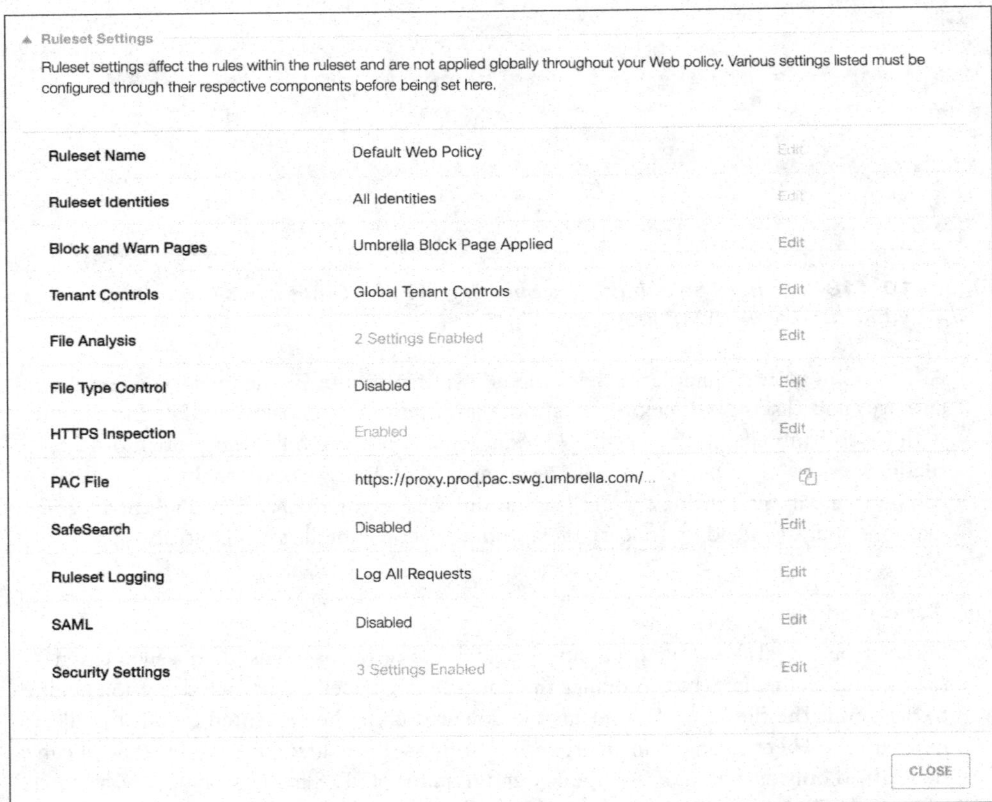

Figure 10-119 *A Web Policy in Cisco Umbrella Before Enabling File Type Control*

Step 5. On the **File Type Control** pop-up window, click **Documents** (see Figure 10-120).

Do not select the box to the left of **Documents** because this will block all file types categorized as documents.

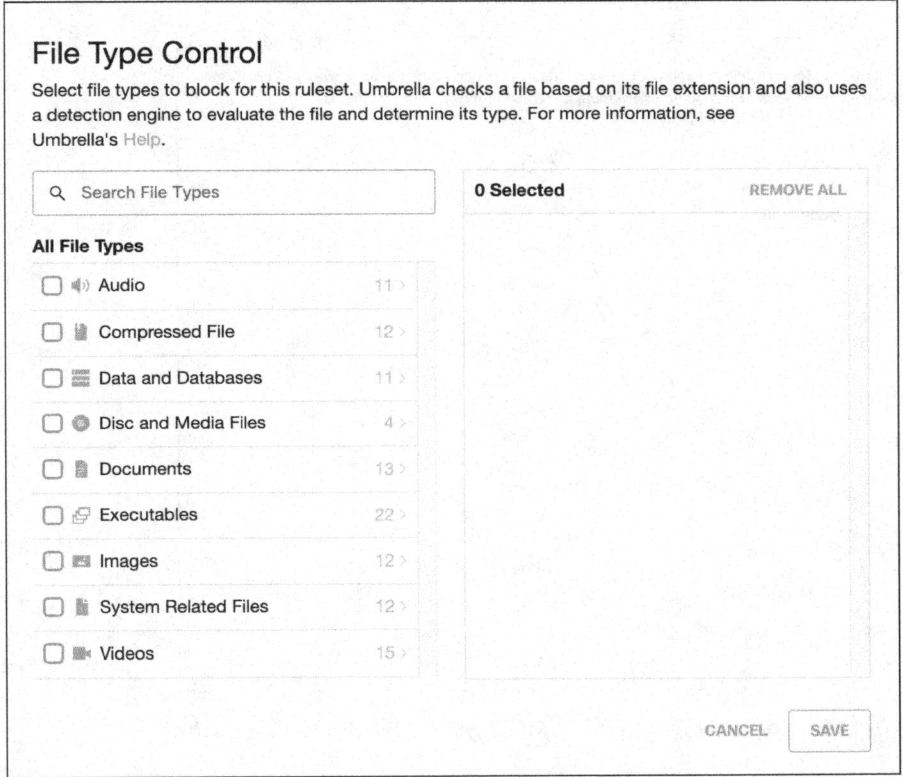

Figure 10-120 *The File Type Control Pop-Up Window Showing File Type Categories*

Step 6. In the window shown in Figure 10-121, select all the file types that end in *m*; these are Microsoft Office macro files. Click **SAVE**.

Step 7. Back on the **Web Policies** page, the **File Type Control** settings are now enabled.

Place your mouse pointer over **X File Types Blocked** to reveal the file extensions covered by this policy (see Figure 10-122).

You've now completed the steps required to block the downloading of Microsoft Office macro files using the File Type Control feature.

Follow these steps to verify that File Type Control is working as expected:

Step 1. Create a .dotm file using Word and an .xlsm file using Excel; then upload these files to an external website such as Office 365 or Google Drive. Next, try downloading the .dotm file using your web browser.

In this example, we attempted to download a .dotm file using Chrome from a site on the Internet. Cisco Umbrella prevented this download and displayed the block page shown in Figure 10-123.

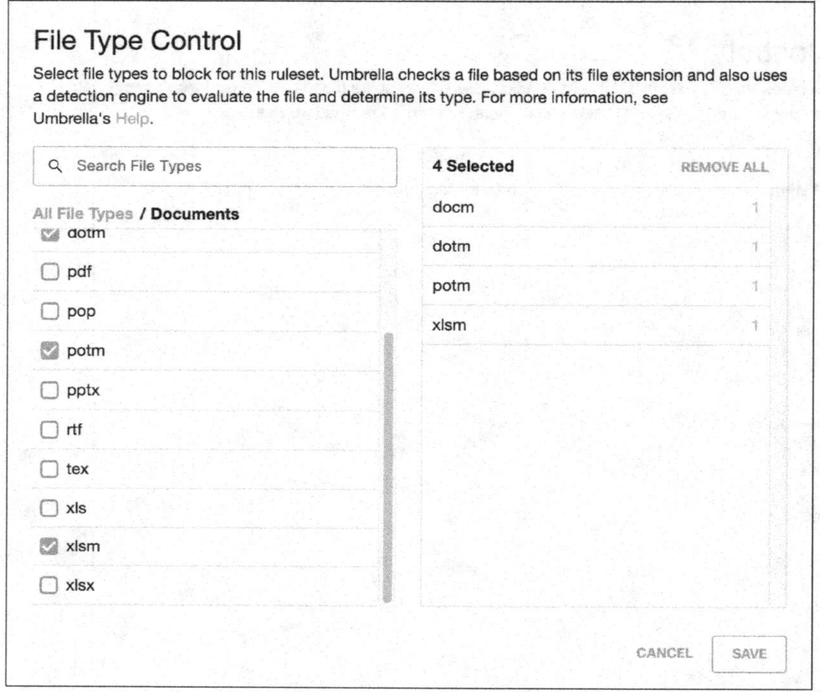

Figure 10-121 *Specifying Individual File Types to Block in Cisco Umbrella*

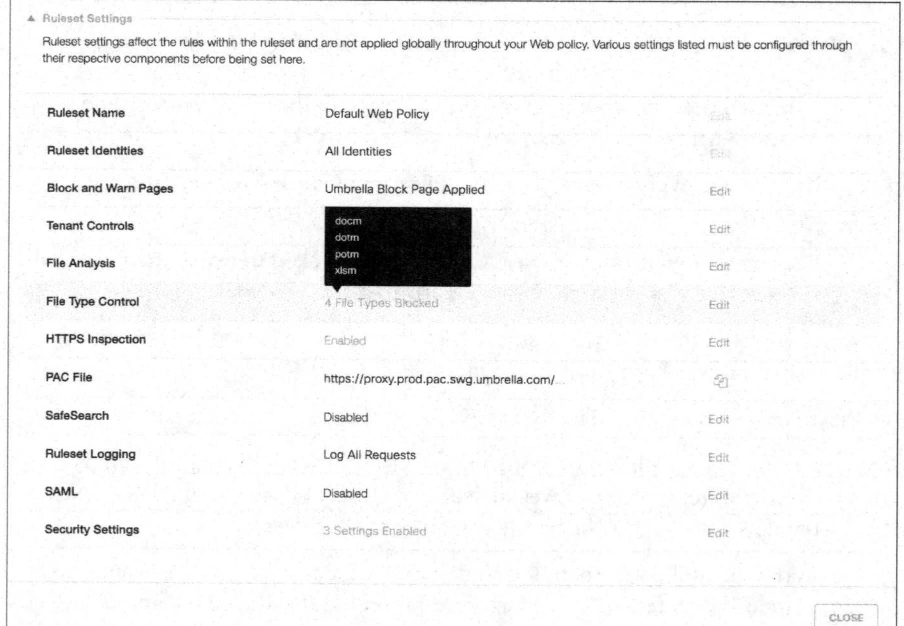

Figure 10-122 *A Web Policy in Cisco Umbrella with File Type Control Enabled*

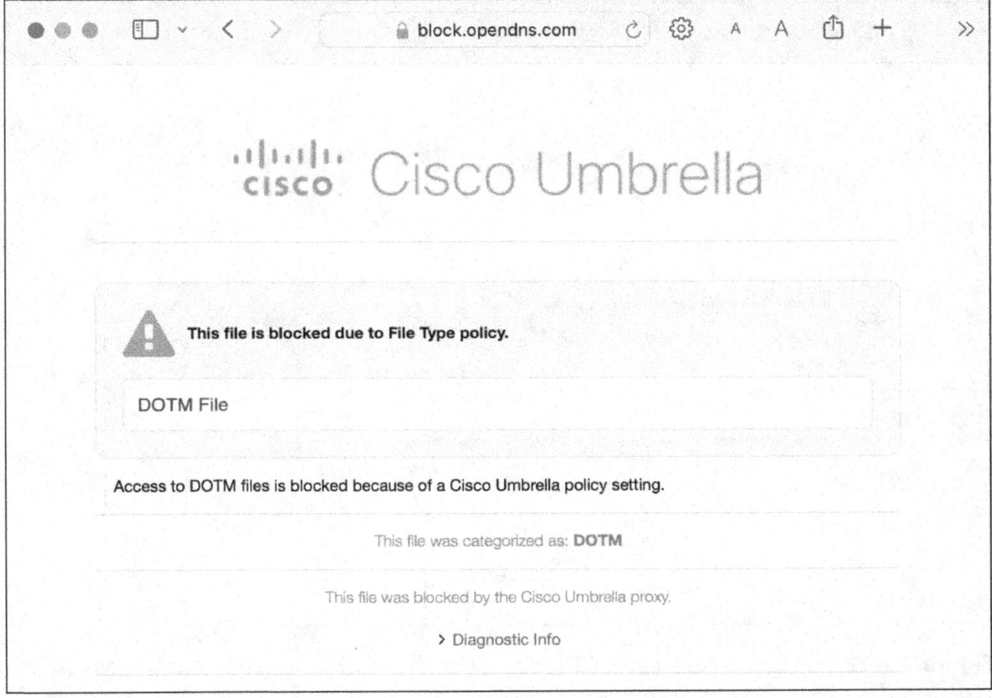

Figure 10-123 *The Umbrella Block Page Showing That a File with the Extension .dotm Has Been Blocked*

Step 2. Try downloading the .xlsm file using your web browser. Cisco Umbrella prevents this download and displays a block page, as shown in Figure 10-124.

You've now completed the setup and verification of the File Type Control feature in Cisco Umbrella. To learn more about File Type Control, refer to https://docs.umbrella.com/umbrella-user-guide/docs/manage-file-type-control.

Cloud Access Security Broker (CASB)

Cloud Access Security Broker might not be a category of security products that you have heard of before, but Cisco Umbrella's CASB functionality provides two really important capabilities. First, it provides the ability to see which cloud services are being used; these can be Software-as-a-Service (SaaS), Platform-as-a-Service (PaaS), or Infrastructure-as-a-Service (IaaS). Second, Umbrella can limit the functions that users can perform when using these cloud services, such as restricting file downloads or file uploads, posting, or sharing content.

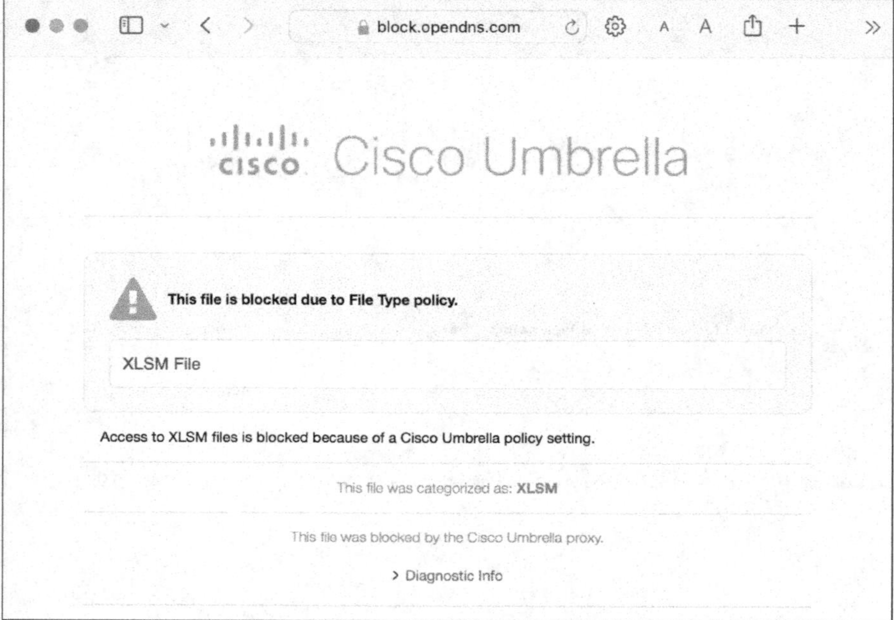

Figure 10-124 *The Umbrella Block Page Showing That a File with the Extension .xlsm Has Been Blocked*

Typically, network administrators have had tools to block access to websites but lacked the visibility into which cloud services users are actually using. The App Discovery report (**Secure Connect > Data Loss Prevention > Reporting > App Discovery**), available with Secure Connect, provides an insight into the cloud services being used, with a breakdown by category and risk profile (see Figure 10-125).

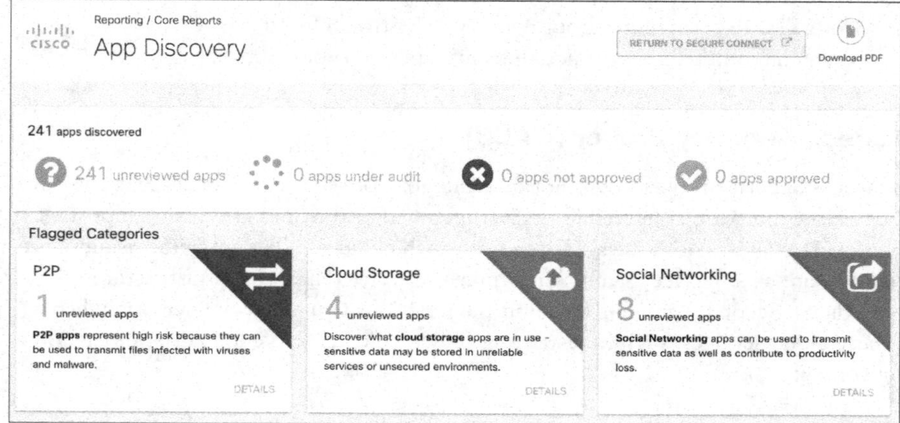

Figure 10-125 *A Portion of the App Discovery Report in Cisco Umbrella Showing Applications for Review*

The aim is to provide organizations with insight into what users are accessing and the confidence in knowing that adequate policies are in place. For example, the window in Figure 10-125 informs administrators that a number of cloud storage services are being used. Without sufficient controls in place, sensitive information could be stolen or leaked. Drilling into the details reveals the exact cloud services in use, and by whom, allowing administrators to implement a tailored security policy, as shown in Figure 10-126.

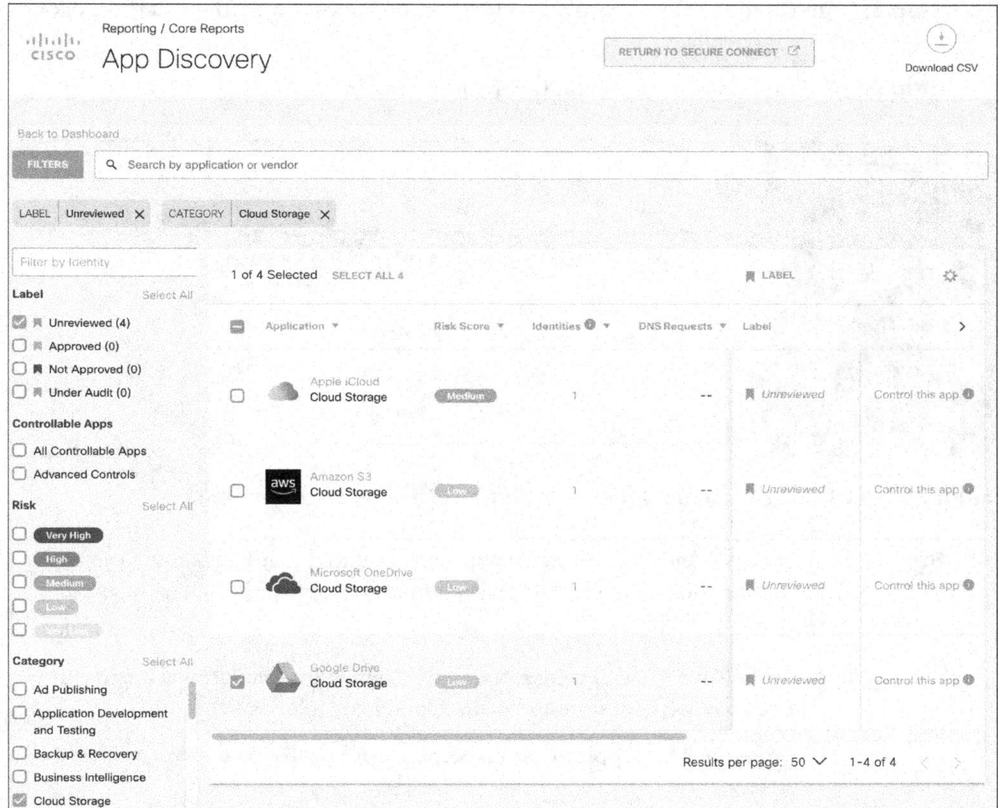

Figure 10-126 *Reviewing the Cloud Storage Apps That Are Being Used on the Network*

The real game-changer here, though, is the ability to control what users can do with cloud services. For example, rather than simply blocking sites like Google Drive, Box, and Dropbox, administrators can allow access but prevent users from uploading files. Likewise, perhaps it is permissible for users to access social media but not to post or share content. Both capabilities are important data loss prevention measures that can prevent sensitive data from leaving the organization's control. NIST 800-53 AC-4 requires the inspection of information flows to ensure they do not contravene a security or privacy policy. Additionally, PCI DSS 4.0 requirement 3.4.2 requires that organizations have technical controls to prevent the unauthorized transfer of credit card numbers. The following configuration examples demonstrate how requirements like these can be met using Secure Connect.

Follow these steps to configure a policy that prevents files from being uploaded to cloud storage services:

Step 1. In Cisco Umbrella, navigate to **Policies > Application Settings** (under Policy Components).

Step 2. Click **Add** in the top right (see Figure 10-127).

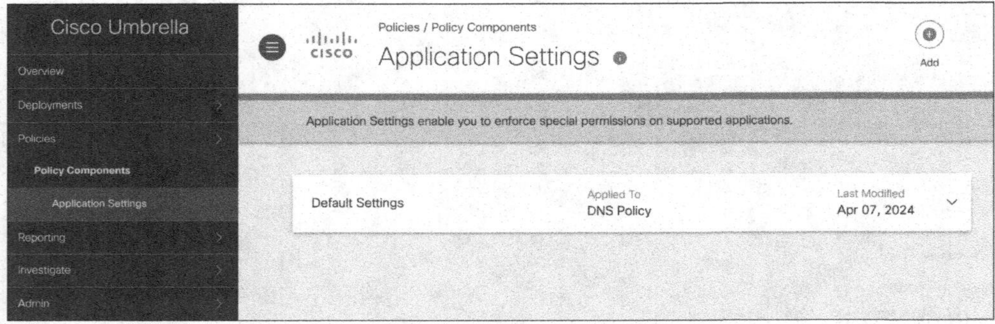

Figure 10-127 *The Default Application Settings Page in Cisco Umbrella*

Step 3. To start, you need to define an application setting that will contain the application functions you need to control. In this example, the aim is to restrict Google Drive uploads.

  a. In the **Give Your Setting a Name** field, enter a meaningful name. In this example, we have used the name **Block File Uploads.**

  b. From the **This Application List Applies To:** drop-down menu, select **Web Policy.**

  c. In the **Applications to Control** field, search for **Google** and then scroll down and select **Google Drive Uploads** (see Figure 10-128).

  d. Click **SAVE.**

Step 4. Remaining in Cisco Umbrella, navigate to **Policies > Web Policy.**

Expand the existing **Default Web Policy** (see Figure 10-129). Click **ADD RULE.**

Add New Application Setting

Give Your Setting a Name

Block File Uploads

This Application List applies to:

Web Policy

Applications To Control

Google

Google Code

Google Contacts

Google Docs

Google Drive

Google Drive Uploads

Google Drive Files to MS OneDrive

Google Duo

Google Earth

CANCEL SAVE

Figure 10-128 *Creating a New Application Setting in Cisco Umbrella*

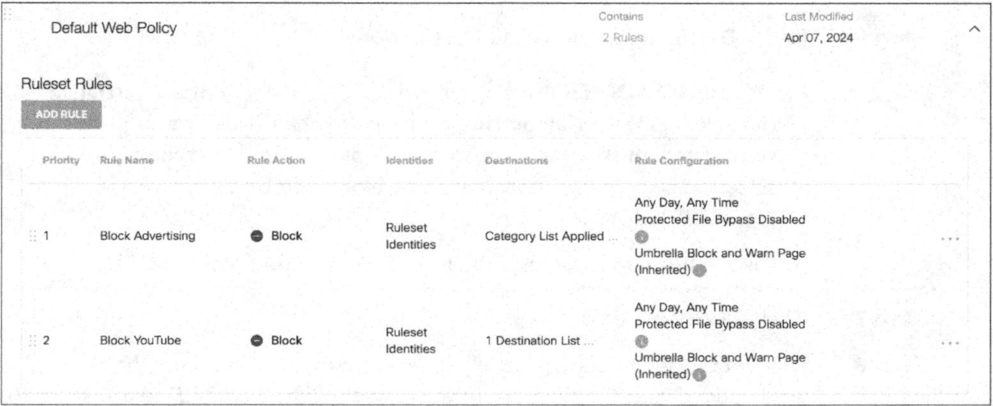

Figure 10-129 *The Existing Web Policy Before Adding an Application Settings–Based Rule*

Step 5. Now define the new rule using the application setting created earlier.

a. In the **Rule Name** field, enter a meaningful name. In this example, we have used **Block File Uploads.**

b. Leave the **Rule Action** as the default (**Block**).

c. Under **Identities**, click **Add Identity.** On the **IDENTITIES** pop-up window, click the slider to enable **Inherit Ruleset Identities** and then click **APPLY** to close the pop-up window shown in Figure 10-130.

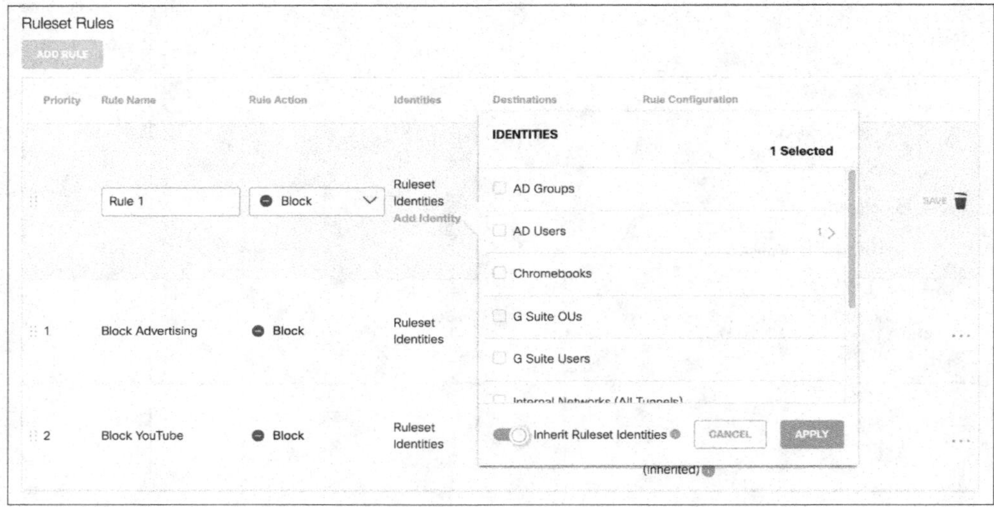

Figure 10-130 *Adding Identities to a New Application Settings–Based Rule in Cisco Umbrella*

Step 6. Under **Destinations**, click **Add Destination.**

a. On the **DESTINATIONS** pop-up window, click **Application Settings.** From the **Select Application Setting** drop-down menu, select the application setting previously created in Steps 1 through 3. In this example, we have selected the application setting titled **Block File Uploads** (see Figure 10-131).

b. Click **APPLY** to close the **DESTINATIONS** pop-up window.

Step 7. Click **SAVE** on the right.

Step 8. Back on the **Web Policy** page, click the three dots (...) on the right of the newly added rule. On the pop-up window, click the **ENABLE RULE** slider to enable the policy, as shown in Figure 10-132.

On the **Update Rule Status** pop-up window, click **UPDATE.**

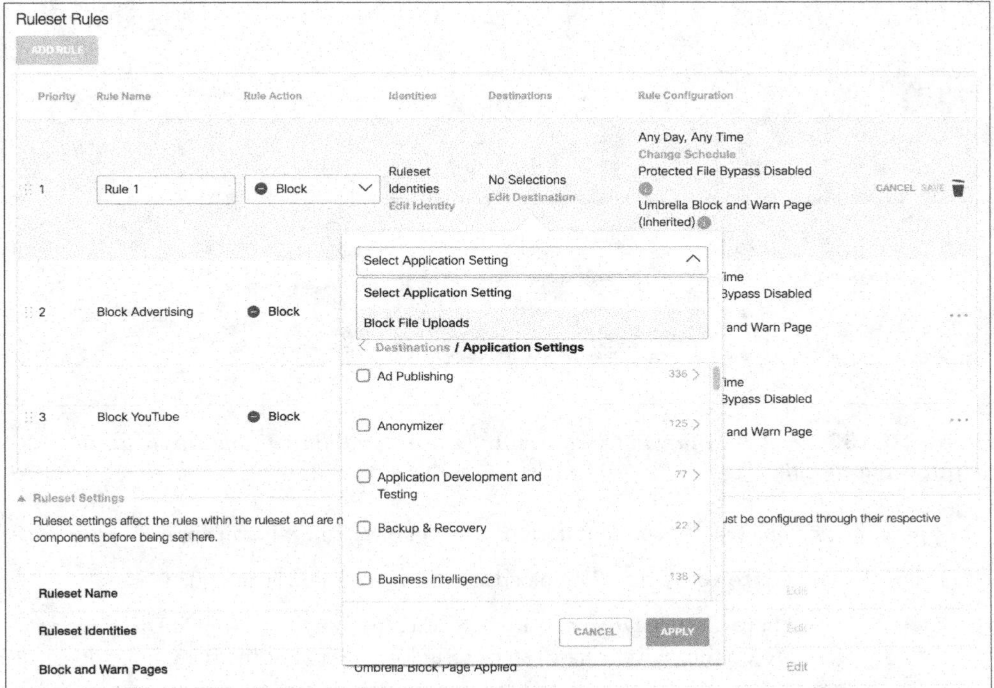

Figure 10-131 *Adding a Destination Application Setting to a New Web Policy Rule in Cisco Umbrella*

Ruleset Rules

ADD RULE

Priority	Rule Name	Rule Action	Identities	Destinations	Rule Configuration
1	Rule 1	Block	Ruleset Identities	Application List Applied ...	Any Day, Any Time Protected File Bypass Disabled Umbrella Block and Warn Page (Inherited)
2	Block Advertising	Block	Ruleset Identities	Category List Applied ...	Any Day, Any Time Protected File Bypass Disabled Umbrella Block and Warn Page (Inherited)
3	Block YouTube	Block	Ruleset Identities	1 Destination List ...	Any Day, Any Time Protected File Bypass Disabled Umbrella Block and Warn Page (Inherited)

EDIT RULE

ENABLE RULE

DELETE RULE

Figure 10-132 *Enabling the New Application Settings–Based Rule on a Web Policy in Cisco Umbrella*

The new rule is now configured, as shown in Figure 10-133. Notice that the rule is no longer grayed out, which confirms that it is enabled.

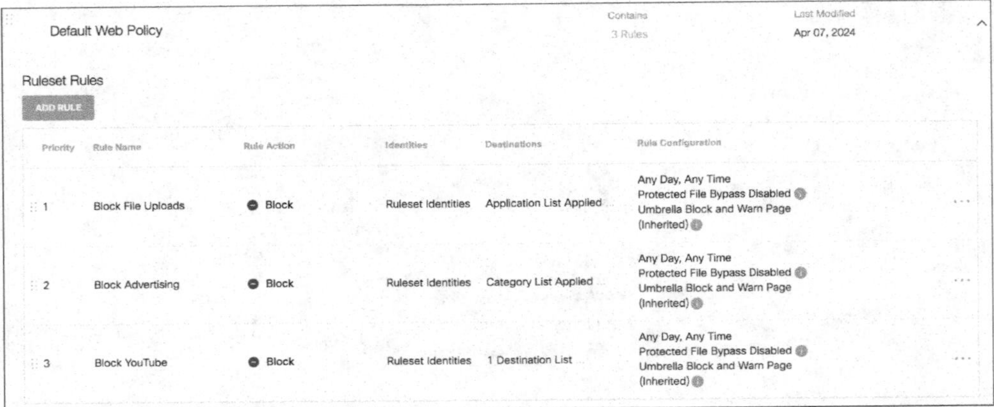

Figure 10-133 *A Web Policy in Cisco Umbrella After Enabling a New Application Settings–Based Rule*

You've now completed the configuration of a Web policy rule with an application list.

Follow these steps to verify that file uploads are now prevented as intended:

Step 1. Log in to Google Drive and attempt to upload any file. Google Drive allows you to go through the usual steps to upload a file, but the file upload doesn't start.

Step 2. Check the Activity Search report in Umbrella (**Reporting > Activity Search**). In Figure 10-134, you can see that the Web policy is successfully blocking these attempts to upload files to Google Drive.

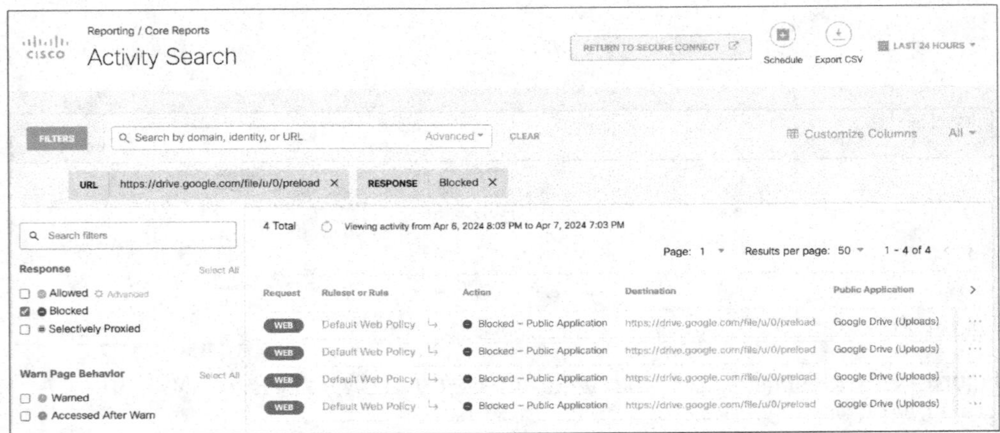

Figure 10-134 *Activity Search Logs Showing That the Web Policy Is Blocking File Uploads to Google Drive*

At this point, you've completed the steps necessary to implement and verify the types of advanced application controls possible with Secure Connect. For more information on advanced application controls, refer to https://docs.umbrella.com/umbrella-user-guide/docs/advanced-app-controls. To learn more about the Cloud Access Security Broker functionality available with Secure Connect, check out https://documentation.meraki.com/CiscoPlusSecureConnect/Cisco__Secure_Connect_Now_-_Policies/Cisco__Secure_Connect_-_Cloud_Access_Security_Broker_(CASB).

Data Loss Prevention (DLP)

Data Loss Prevention refers to a capability that allows administrators to prevent sensitive information from leaving the organization's control. For organizations that handle sensitive data, having a DLP capability is often recommended best practice. For example, NIST 800-53 AC-4 requires the capability to implement security or privacy filters to ensure only authorized information flows are occurring. Depending on the industry, sensitive information could include financial information such as credit card numbers, personally identifiable information (PII) like Social Security numbers, health information, documents classified as secret or confidential, and so on. Out of the box, Secure Connect can automatically detect whether an information flow contains GDPR, HIPAA, PII, or PCI data. Once Secure Connect's DLP function has determined what an information flow contains, DLP policies can then control where it can be transferred, where it can be stored, and who can access it.

Secure Connect's DLP function has three main capabilities:

- Real-Time Rules scan web traffic and prevent the exfiltration of sensitive data in real time. Use cases include
  - Preventing sensitive information from being input into generative AI engines like ChatGPT or being sent in the body of web-based email, like Gmail.
  - Preventing files containing sensitive information from being uploaded to cloud storage services, such as Google Drive, or being attached to web-based emails.
- SaaS API Rules extend DLP policies into cloud services like Microsoft Office 365. SaaS API Rules ensure files stored externally are being shared in accordance with their data classification and sensitivity.
- Discovery Scan scans services like Microsoft Office 365, Google Drive, and more to ensure files are being stored according to their data classification. For example, an organization might have a policy that says files containing PII must be stored on premises. The Discovery Scan feature scans these external locations and reports on compliance with this policy via the Data Loss Prevention report.

This section focuses on Real-Time Rules. For information on SaaS API rules and Discovery Scan, refer to https://documentation.meraki.com/CiscoPlusSecureConnect/Cisco__Secure_Connect_Now_-_Policies/Cisco___Secure_Connect_-_Manage_the_Data_Loss_Prevention_Policy. To apply similar controls on corporate email, check out Cisco's Secure Email product.

DLP policies apply to web requests, including web forms, such as the body of a web-based email, or a file upload, such as attaching a document to a web-based email. As of January 2024, DLP Real-Time Rules support thousands of applications including Box, ChatGPT, Dropbox, Gmail, Facebook Messenger, and Smartsheet. There is extensive file type support including PDF, common Microsoft Office file formats, RTF, ZIP files, CSV, and text files. For the full list of supported file types, refer to https://docs.umbrella.com/umbrella-user-guide/docs/supported-file-types.

DLP policies require HTTPS inspection to be enabled. This policy was enabled previously in the "File Inspection and Advanced Sandboxing" section.

In this example, we demonstrate how to configure Secure Connect DLP policies to stop the exfiltration of PCI data. Follow these steps to configure DLP policies, which prevent the exfiltration of PCI data using Real-Time Rules:

Step 1. Log in to Meraki Dashboard (https://dashboard.meraki.com).

Step 2. Navigate to **Secure Connect > Data Loss Prevention.** Doing so cross-launches into the Umbrella **Data Loss Prevention Policy** page, as shown in Figure 10-135.

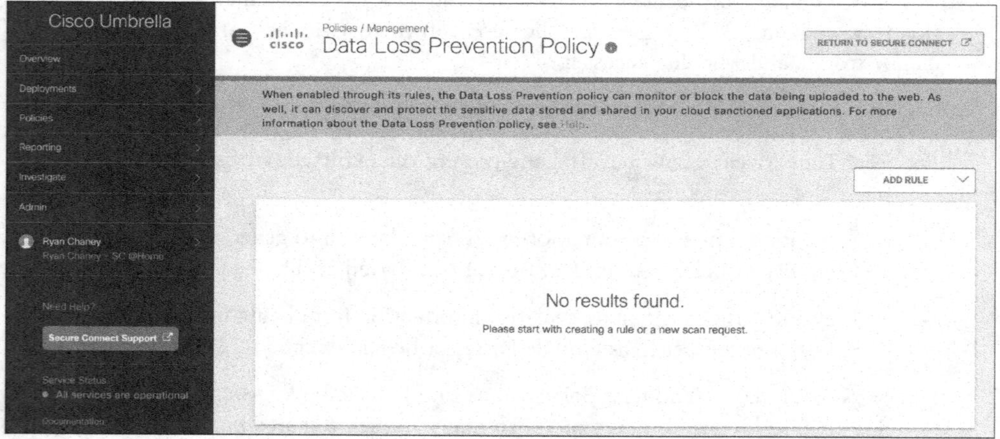

Figure 10-135 *The Default Data Loss Prevention Policy Page in Cisco Umbrella*

Step 3. On **the Data Loss Prevention Policy** page, click the **ADD RULE** drop-down menu, and select **Real Time Rule** from the drop-down menu, as shown in Figure 10-136.

Step 4. On the screen shown in Figure 10-137, in the **Rule Name** field, enter a meaningful name. In this example, we have used **Block Sensitive Data Exfiltration.**

a. From the **Severity** drop-down menu, choose a severity classification based on the perceived risk or importance. In this example, we have chosen **Critical**.

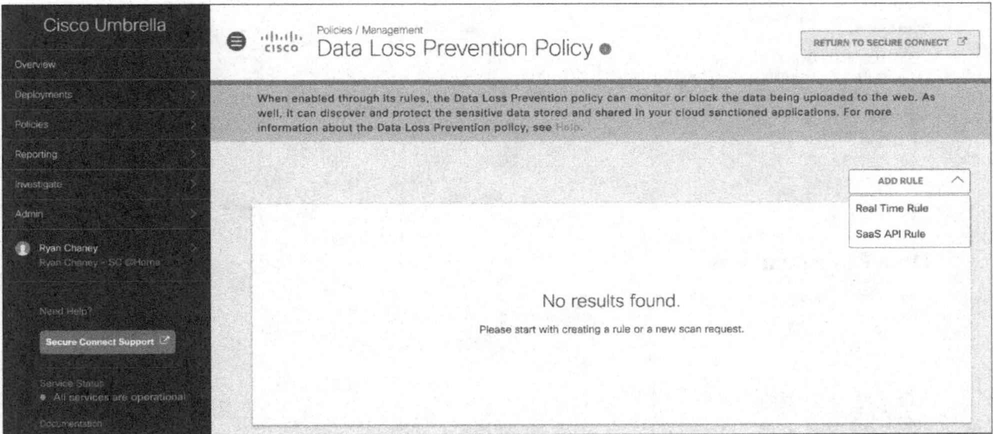

Figure 10-136 *Adding a New Data Loss Prevention Policy Real-Time Rule in Cisco Umbrella*

b. Under **Data Classifications**, under the heading **Select Where to Search for the Selected Data Classifications**, select **Content and File Name.**

c. In this example, we are using DLP policies to enforce compliance with PCI. Under the heading **Select Data Classifications to Add to This Rule**, select **Built-in PCI Classification.**

d. (Optional) If you place your mouse pointer over **Preview**, it will show what the data classification contains. To create your own custom data classifications, click **DATA CLASSIFICATION** or navigate to **Policies > Data Classification** (under Policy Components).

Step 5. Still on the **Data Loss Prevention Policy** page, scroll down to **File Labels.** Data labels look for values in the metadata attached to a document. This includes Microsoft Office document properties, Microsoft Office sensitivity labels, and Adobe PDF document properties. We do not use these in this example.

Under **Identities**, select the identities that this rule will apply to. In this example, we have selected all **Tunnels**, as shown in Figure 10-138.

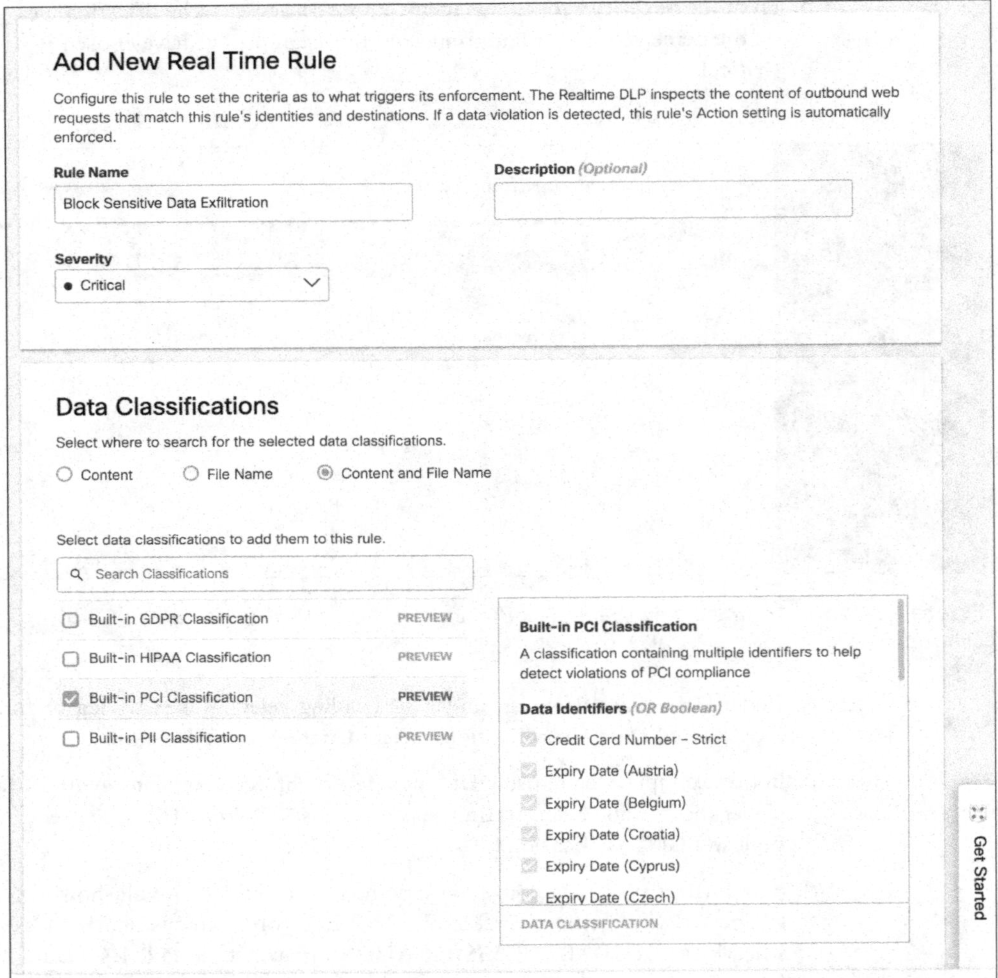

Figure 10-137 *Adding a New DLP Real-Time Rule in Cisco Umbrella (Part 1)*

Step 6. Scroll down to **Destinations** and select **All Destinations**, as shown in Figure 10-139.

a. Under **Action**, select **Block** from the drop-down menu.

b. Leave **User Notifications** disabled.

c. Click **SAVE**.

You've now completed the configuration of a Real-Time Rule on a Data Loss Prevention policy.

Follow these steps to verify that the Data Loss Prevention policy is now working as expected:

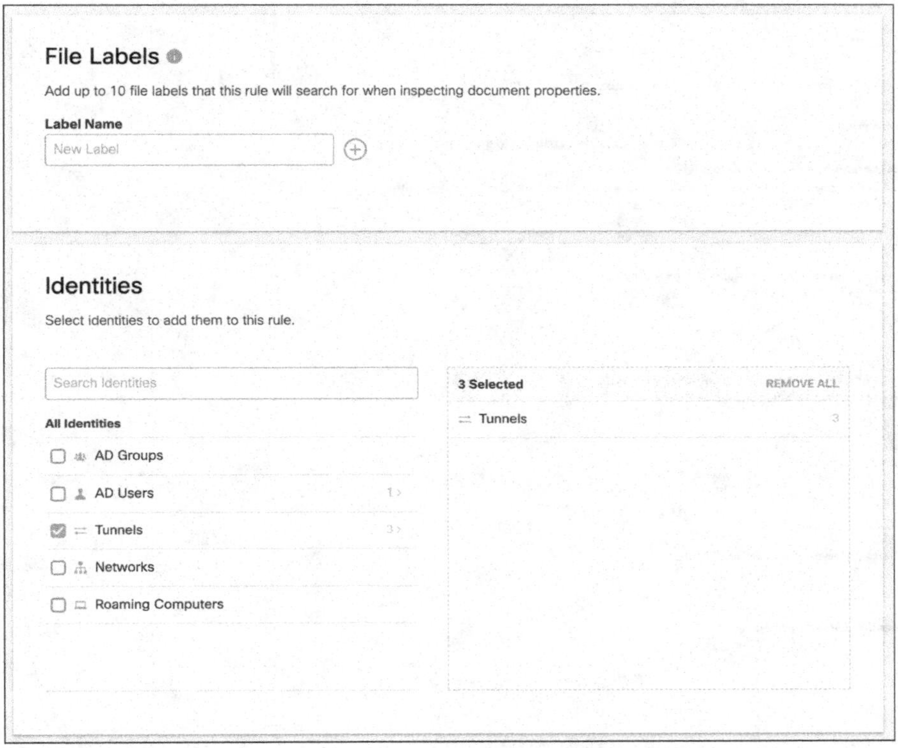

Figure 10-138 *Adding a New DLP Real-Time Rule in Cisco Umbrella (Part 2)*

Step 1. Log in to Gmail.

Note: Gmail appears to authenticate users using a YouTube URL. Because access to YouTube was blocked previously in the "Secure Web Gateway (SWG)" section, you might need to disable this rule to be able to log in successfully.

a. Once you're logged in, create a new email.

b. Attempt to upload a file containing dummy credit card information (examples can be found through a quick Google search). Note that when you're trying to attach a file containing credit card details, the upload is blocked, as shown in Figure 10-140.

Step 2. Verify that this was the result of the Real-Time Rule using the **Data Loss Prevention report** in Umbrella (**Reporting > Data Loss Prevention**). Notice that the event shown lists the file name of the attachment in the **File Name** column, and the details pane displays the last four digits of the credit card (see Figure 10-141).

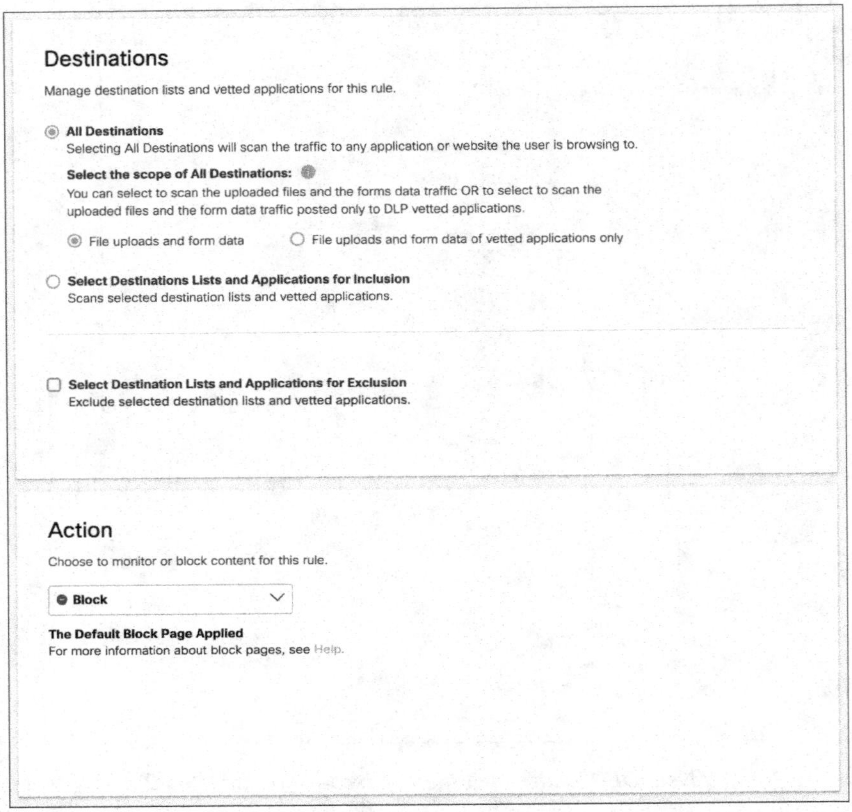

Destinations

Manage destination lists and vetted applications for this rule.

◉ **All Destinations**
Selecting All Destinations will scan the traffic to any application or website the user is browsing to.

Select the scope of All Destinations:
You can select to scan the uploaded files and the forms data traffic OR to select to scan the uploaded files and the form data traffic posted only to DLP vetted applications.

◉ File uploads and form data ○ File uploads and form data of vetted applications only

○ **Select Destinations Lists and Applications for Inclusion**
Scans selected destination lists and vetted applications.

☐ **Select Destination Lists and Applications for Exclusion**
Exclude selected destination lists and vetted applications.

Action

Choose to monitor or block content for this rule.

Block

The Default Block Page Applied
For more information about block pages, see Help.

Figure 10-139 *Adding a New DLP Real-Time Rule in Cisco Umbrella (Part 3)*

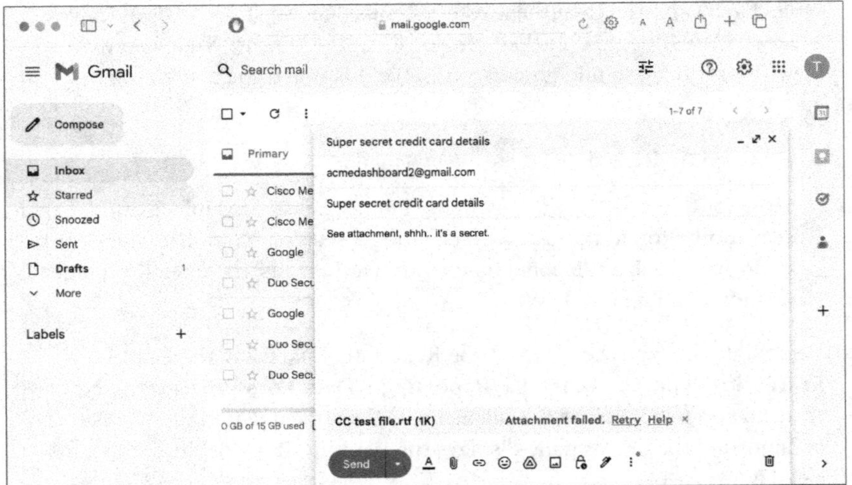

Figure 10-140 *Unsuccessfully Trying to Send an Email Attachment Containing Credit Card Information in Gmail*

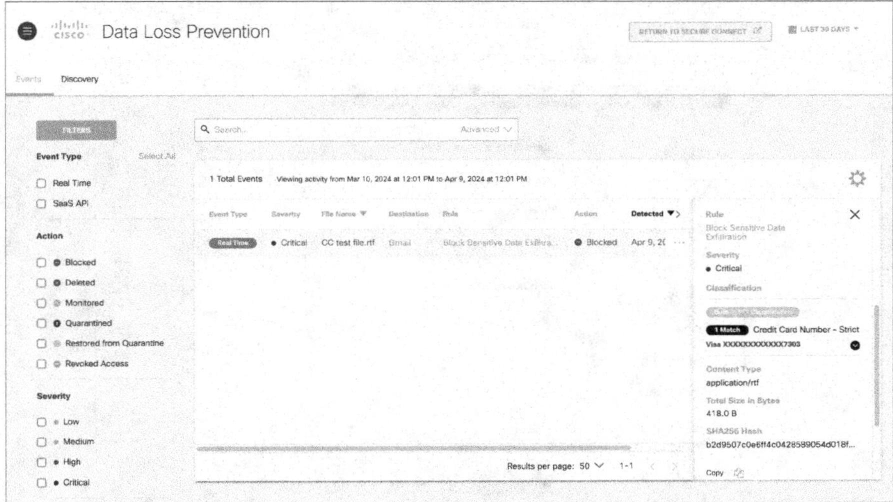

Figure 10-141 *Data Loss Prevention Report Showing Blocked Email Attachment Containing Credit Card Data*

Step 3. Create another new email (see Figure 10-142). Enter the dummy credit card details in the body of the email and click **Send**.

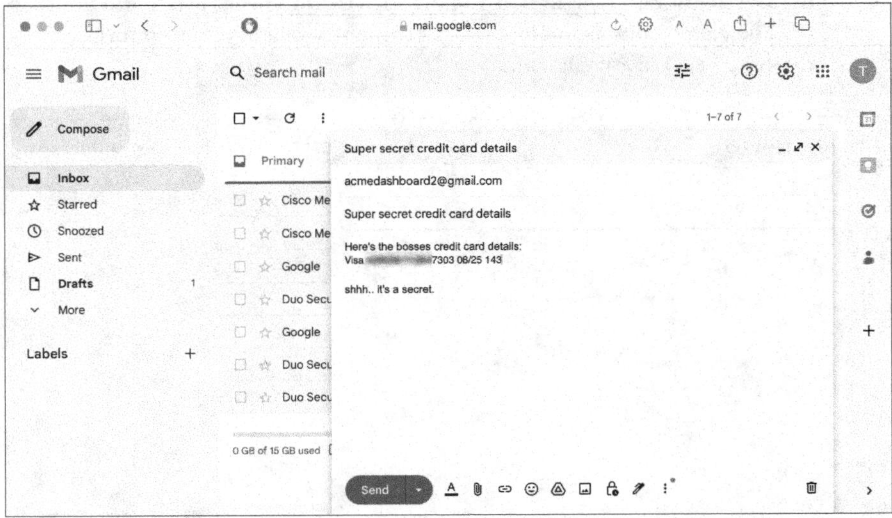

Figure 10-142 *Drafting an Email in Gmail with the Email Body Containing Credit Card Information*

Umbrella inspects the web form, finds the credit card information, and prevents the email from being sent (see Figure 10-143).

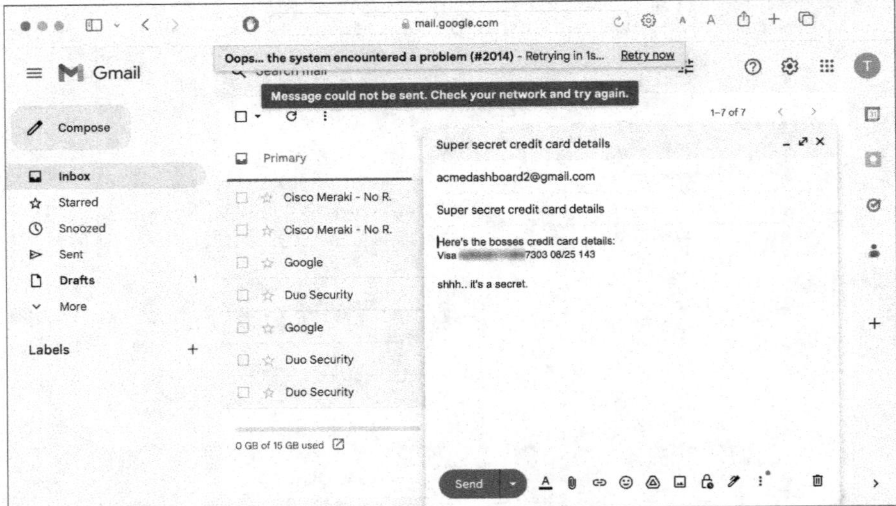

Figure 10-143 *Unsuccessfully Trying to Send an Email Body Containing Credit Card Information in Gmail*

Step 4. To confirm that it was the DLP policy that prevented this email from being sent, verify this using the **Data Loss Prevention report** in Umbrella (**Reporting > Data Loss Prevention**). Here, you can see **Gmail** listed as the **Destination** (see Figure 10-144). Notice the top result lists **Form** under the **File Name** column, indicating that this entry relates to a web form, as opposed to a file attachment.

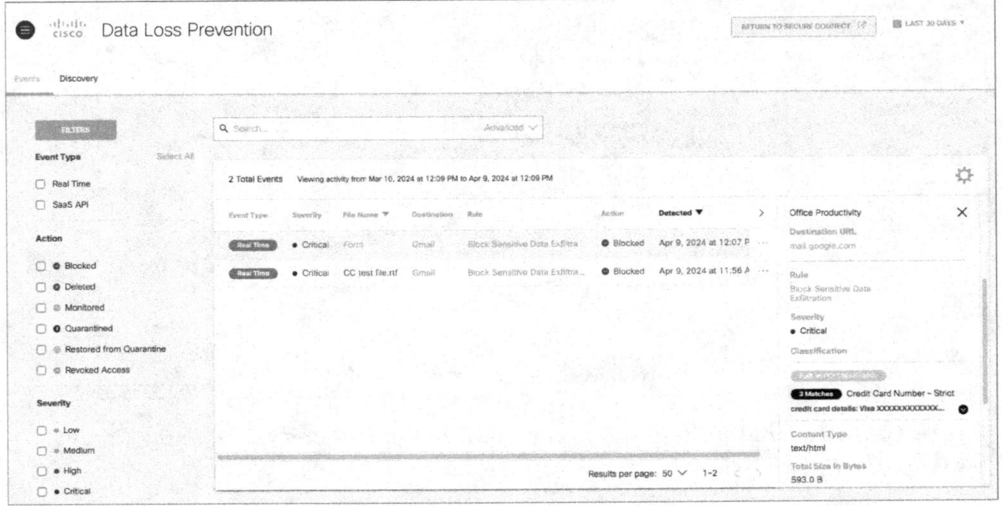

Figure 10-144 *Activity Search Report Showing That an Attempt to Email Credit Card Information Has Been Blocked*

Step 5. Verify that with this same policy you're able to prevent credit card data being used in queries using Generative AI tools—in this case, ChatGPT. In your web browser, navigate to https://chat.openai.com. Enter a query including your dummy credit card details and then click **Send Message** (see Figure 10-145).

Once again, the DLP policy detects the unauthorized use of PCI data and prevents the web form from being submitted. Note the error message in Figure 10-146.

Step 6. Using the **Data Loss Prevention report** in Umbrella (**Reporting > Data Loss Prevention**), you, as administrator, can verify that the blocked request was the result of the Real-Time Rule. Note the **Destination** of **OpenAI ChatGPT** and that **Form** is listed under **File Name** (see Figure 10-147).

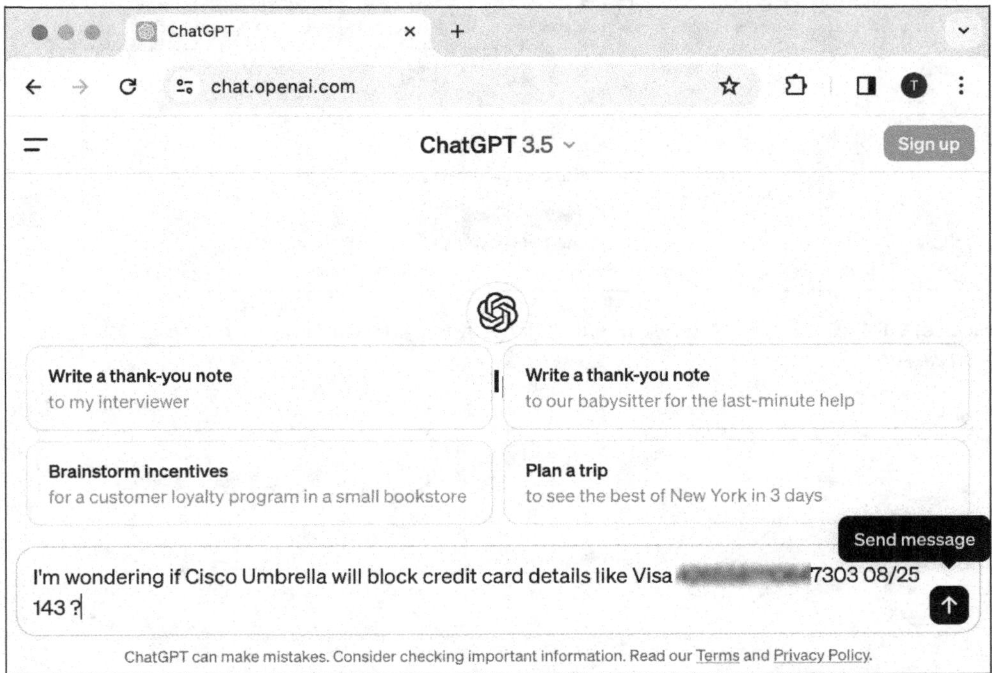

Figure 10-145 *Entering a Search Containing Credit Card Data into ChatGPT*

At this point, you've completed the configuration and verification of DLP policies using Real-Time Rules. You can do a lot more with Data Loss Prevention than we've been able to show here. To learn more about capabilities such as SaaS API Rules, Discovery Scan, and Remote Browser Isolation (RBI), refer to https://documentation.meraki.com/CiscoPlusSecureConnect/Cisco__Secure_Connect_Now_-_Policies/Cisco___Secure_Connect_-_Manage_the_Data_Loss_Prevention_Policy.

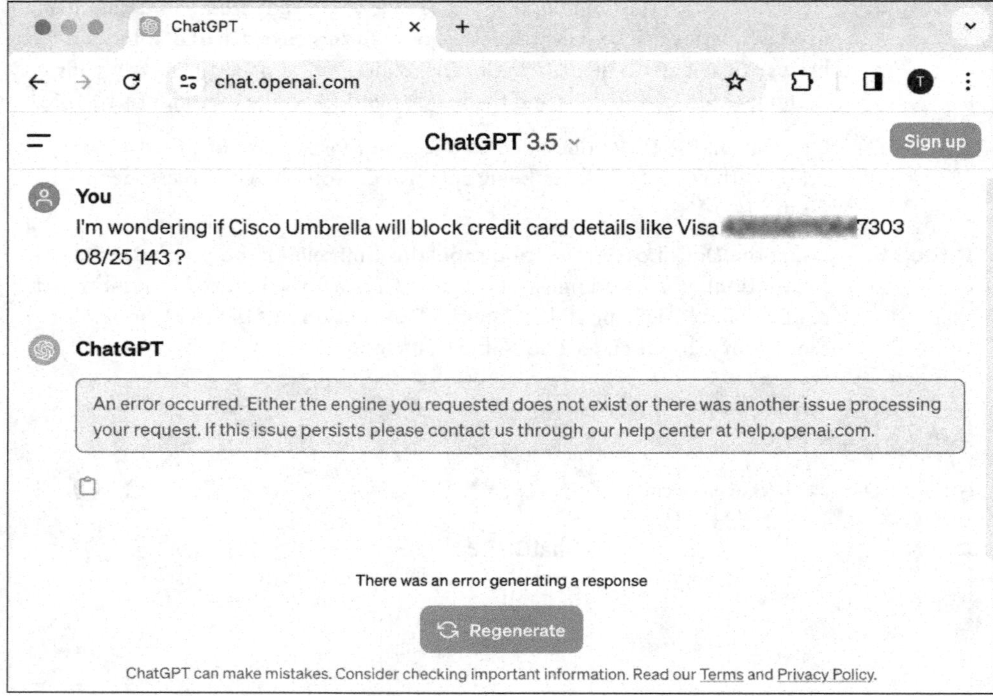

Figure 10-146 *Error Message in ChatGPT After Credit Card Information Is Blocked Successfully*

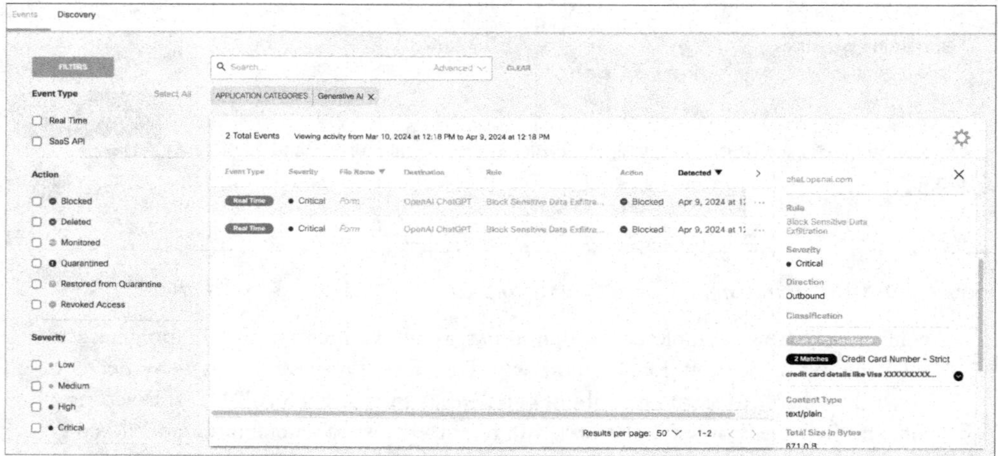

Figure 10-147 *Activity Search Report Showing That an Attempt to Enter Credit Card Details in ChatGPT Is Blocked*

Summary

This chapter covered those features and capabilities designed to secure user traffic and sensitive data. This included those features built into Meraki MX itself, such as firewalling, Geo-IP firewall and content filtering, as well as those available with Secure Connect, like Cloud Access Security Broker and Data Loss Prevention.

Cisco Secure Connect delivers required capabilities in a cost-effective way. With Secure Connect, organizations can offload existing security functions to the Secure Connect cloud, enabling them to deploy smaller and more power-efficient security appliances at each site. In addition, Secure Connect adds a ton of badly needed capabilities, which have been around for some time but have never been so accessible. This includes preventing malware through the capability to inspect file downloads before they enter the organization. Secure Connect also prevents sensitive data from leaving the organization's control, via webmail or webmail attachments, uploads to storage services like Google Drive, or through input into generative AI engines like ChatGPT. Secure Connect's wide range of functions replaces, or avoids the need for, multiple solutions and potentially multiple boxes onsite. In summary, Secure Connect delivers vital modern security capabilities while saving time and money, making it a must-have for all organizations, large and small.

Notes

[1] Cisco Meraki. (2023, January 30). MX Firewall Settings. https://documentation.meraki.com/MX/Firewall_and_Traffic_Shaping/MX_Firewall_Settings

[2] Cisco Meraki. (2024, February 15). Content Filtering Troubleshooting. https://documentation.meraki.com/MX/Content_Filtering_and_Threat_Protection/Content_Filtering/Content_Filtering_Troubleshooting

[3] Cisco Meraki. (2014, July 10). Off Limits: New MX Feature Allows Geography-Based Border Control. https://meraki.cisco.com/blog/2014/07/off-limits/

[4] Cisco Meraki. (2024, March 4). Advanced Malware Protection (AMP). https://documentation.meraki.com/MX/Content_Filtering_and_Threat_Protection/Advanced_Malware_Protection_(AMP)

[5] PCI Security Standards Council. (2022, December). *PCI DSS: v4.0*. https://www.pcisecuritystandards.org/document_library/

[6] Cisco Meraki. (2023, December 2). Cisco Secure Connect. https://documentation.meraki.com/CiscoPlusSecureConnect

Further Reading

Cisco Meraki. (2020, October 6). URL Filtering. https://documentation.meraki.com/MX/Content_Filtering_and_Threat_Protection/URL_Filtering

Cisco Meraki. (2023, August 23). Layer 3 and 7 Firewall Processing Order. https://documentation.meraki.com/General_Administration/Cross-Platform_Content/Layer_3_and_7_Firewall_Processing_Order

Cisco Meraki. (2023, November 9). Content Filtering. https://documentation.meraki.com/MX/Content_Filtering_and_Threat_Protection/Content_Filtering

Cisco Meraki. (2023, December 2). Cisco Secure Connect. https://documentation.meraki.com/CiscoPlusSecureConnect

Cisco Meraki. (2023, December 3). Cisco Secure Connect—Solution Overview. https://documentation.meraki.com/CiscoPlusSecureConnect/overview

Cisco Meraki. (2023, December 5). Setting Up Your Cisco Secure Connect Account. https://documentation.meraki.com/CiscoPlusSecureConnect/Cisco___Secure_Connect_Onboarding

Cisco Meraki. (2023, December 16). Cisco Secure Connect—Cloud Firewall Policy. https://documentation.meraki.com/CiscoPlusSecureConnect/Cisco__Secure_Connect_Now_-_Policies/Cisco__Secure_Connect_-_Cloud_Firewall_Policy

Cisco Meraki. (2024, January 10). Threat Protection. https://documentation.meraki.com/MX/Content_Filtering_and_Threat_Protection/Threat_Protection

Cisco Meraki. (2024a, January 12). Next-Gen Traffic Analytics—Network-Based Application Recognition (NBAR) *Integration*. https://documentation.meraki.com/General_Administration/Cross-Platform_Content/Next-gen_Traffic_Analytics_-_Network-Based_Application_Recognition_(NBAR)_Integration

Cisco Meraki. (2024b, January 12). Cisco Secure Connect Sites - Meraki SD-WAN Integration. https://documentation.meraki.com/CiscoPlusSecureConnect/Cisco__Secure_Connect_Now-_Sites/Cisco_Secure_Connect_Sites_-_Meraki_SD-WAN_Integration

Cisco Meraki. (2024a, January 27). Advanced Malware Protection (AMP). https://documentation.meraki.com/MX/Content_Filtering_and_Threat_Protection/Advanced_Malware_Protection_(AMP)

Cisco Meraki. (2024b, January 27). Site-to-Site VPN Settings. https://documentation.meraki.com/MX/Site-to-site_VPN/Site-to-Site_VPN_Settings

Cisco Meraki. (2024, January 30). MX Firewall Settings. https://documentation.meraki.com/MX/Firewall_and_Traffic_Shaping/MX_Firewall_Settings

Cisco Meraki. (2024, February 14). Meraki MX/Z Security and SD-WAN Licensing. https://documentation.meraki.com/General_Administration/Licensing/Meraki_MX_Security_and_SD-WAN_Licensing

Cisco Meraki. (2024, February 16). Customers with Both Meraki and Umbrella Organizations. https://documentation.meraki.com/CiscoPlusSecureConnect/Cisco___Secure_Connect_Onboarding/Customers_with_both_Meraki__and_Umbrella_Organizations

Cisco Meraki. (2024, April 5). Meraki SD-WAN Hub Integration with Secure Connect. https://documentation.meraki.com/CiscoPlusSecureConnect/Cisco__Secure_Connect_Now-_Sites/Meraki_SD-WAN_Hub_Integration_with_Secure_Connect

Cisco Meraki. (2024, May 15). Cisco Secure Connect—Account Setup Troubleshooting. https://documentation.meraki.com/CiscoPlusSecureConnect/Cisco___Secure_Connect_Troubleshooting_Guides/Cisco___Secure_Connect_-_Account_Setup_Troubleshooting

Cisco Systems. (2021, June). *Cisco Umbrella Design Guide*. https://www.cisco.com/c/dam/en/us/solutions/collateral/enterprise/design-zone-security/umbrella-design-guide.pdf

Cisco Systems. (2023, February 13). Configure MX Layer7 Geo-location Restriction and Troubleshoot in Meraki. https://www.cisco.com/c/en/us/support/docs/security/meraki-cloud-managed-security-appliances/220219-configure-mx-layer7-geo-location-restric.html

Cisco Umbrella. (2024a). DNS Security Categories. https://docs.umbrella.com/umbrella-user-guide/docs/dns-security-cats

Cisco Umbrella. (2024b). Enable Cisco Secure Malware Analytics (Threat Grid). https://docs.umbrella.com/umbrella-user-guide/docs/enable-threat-grid-malware-analysis

Cisco Umbrella. (2024c). Enable File Inspection for the Web Policy. https://docs.umbrella.com/umbrella-user-guide/docs/enable-file-inspection-for-web-policies

Cisco Umbrella. (2024d). Find Your Organization ID. https://docs.umbrella.com/deployment-umbrella/docs/find-your-organization-id

Cisco Umbrella. (2024e). Manage Content Categories. https://docs.umbrella.com/umbrella-user-guide/docs/manage-content-categories

Cisco Umbrella. (2024f). Point Your DNS to Cisco Umbrella. https://docs.umbrella.com/deployment-umbrella/docs/point-your-dns-to-cisco

CSF Tools. (n.d.). AC-4: Information Flow Enforcement. https://csf.tools/reference/nist-sp-800-53/r5/ac/ac-4/

National Institute of Standards and Technology (NIST). (2020, September). *NIST 800-53 Rev. 5: Security and Privacy Controls for Information Systems and Organizations*. https://nvlpubs.nist.gov/nistpubs/SpecialPublications/NIST.SP.800-53r5.pdf

PCI Security Standards Council. (2022, December). *PCI DSS: v4.0*. https://www.pcisecuritystandards.org/document_library/

Risto, J. (2023, May 22). What Is Common Vulnerability Scoring System (CVSS). *Sans.org*. https://www.sans.org/blog/what-is-cvss/

Sarband, M. (2023). Newly Seen Domains Security Category. https://support.umbrella.com/hc/en-us/articles/235911828-Newly-Seen-Domains-Security-Category

Chapter 11

Securing End-User Devices

In this chapter, you learn the following:

- What Meraki Systems Manager is and how it improves endpoint security and compliance with industry best practices
- How to greatly simplify the deployment of EAP-TLS using Sentry Wi-Fi
- How to enforce enterprise security policy through the use of Meraki Systems Manager profiles
- How to push out apps to provide increased security capabilities on user devices
- How Meraki Systems Manager and Cisco Duo complement each other in a coordinated approach toward security

In this era of hybrid work, where some staff may never connect to your organization's physical network, it could be argued that endpoint security has never been more important. Mobile device management (MDM) solutions, such as Cisco's own Meraki Systems Manager, are invaluable for securing end-user devices. Systems Manager provides secure, cloud-hosted policy management and auditing of endpoint devices. Meraki Systems Manager supports a wide range of endpoints and operating systems. This includes phones, tablets, and computers running Android, ChromeOS, IOS, tvOS, macOS, and Windows. Meraki Systems Manager is configured through Meraki Dashboard just like all other Meraki products, providing a single management interface for IT. A key reason to choose Systems Manager over competing products is the Sentry-based policies it enables. As demonstrated in Chapter 8, "Wired and Wireless LAN Security," and Chapter 9, "Meraki MX and WAN Security," Sentry-based Wi-Fi, LAN, and VPN are enabled with only a couple of clicks, saving huge amounts of time and expense.

Many of the key themes from the security standards apply equally to endpoint devices, as they do the rest of the IT infrastructure. Examples include

- Strong authentication, such as requirements relating to PINs for unlocking devices
- Encryption, in the form of disk encryption on devices

Additionally, specific requirements applicable to endpoints are also covered in this section, such as the ability to prevent the installation of "banned" applications. To understand the full capabilities of Meraki Systems Manager, refer to the data sheet at https://meraki.cisco.com/lib/pdf/meraki_datasheet_sm.pdf.

Systems Manager complements the functionality provided by Cisco Duo. As an example, one of the tasks of IT administrators is ensuring end-user devices are kept up to date and are receiving the latest security patches. Systems Manager can report on compliance with minimum software versions and push out software updates to enrolled devices. In contrast, Duo can warn users if they need to upgrade when connecting to the network and eventually block network access until a device is upgraded. This scenario also applies to other device characteristics such as screen lock, disk encryption, passcodes, and many more. The combination of Duo and Systems Manager allows for a defense-in-depth approach, where policy is reported on, managed, and enforced across the two platforms.

Before continuing with any of the configuration steps in the sections that follow, ensure that you do the following:

- Add Systems Manager device licenses to Meraki Dashboard. At least one is required, but you should have enough for all the devices you intend to enroll.
- Create a dedicated Systems Manager network if you don't already have one (**Organization > Create Network**). It is recommended that you keep all the devices managed by Systems Manager in the same network.

Integrating with Vender Mobile Device Enrollment Programs

For Meraki Systems Manager to communicate with an enrolled iOS or macOS device, Apple's Push Notification Service (APNS) first sends the device a silent notification. This notification prompts the device to check-in with the Meraki Dashboard and receive any pending commands.[1] For Apple's Push Notification server to trust commands from Systems Manager, a certificate must be installed in Meraki Dashboard. The equivalent steps for Android devices are detailed in the Android Enterprise Deployment Guide, which Meraki has published at https://documentation.meraki.com/SM/Deployment_Guides/Android_Enterprise_Deployment_Guide.

Follow these steps to install the Apple Push Notification certificate in Meraki Dashboard:

Step 1. Log in to Meraki Dashboard (https://dashboard.meraki.com).

Step 2. Navigate to **Organization > MDM** (under Configure).

Step 3. Under **Apple MDM Push Certificate**, click **+ Add Certificate**, as shown in Figure 11-1.

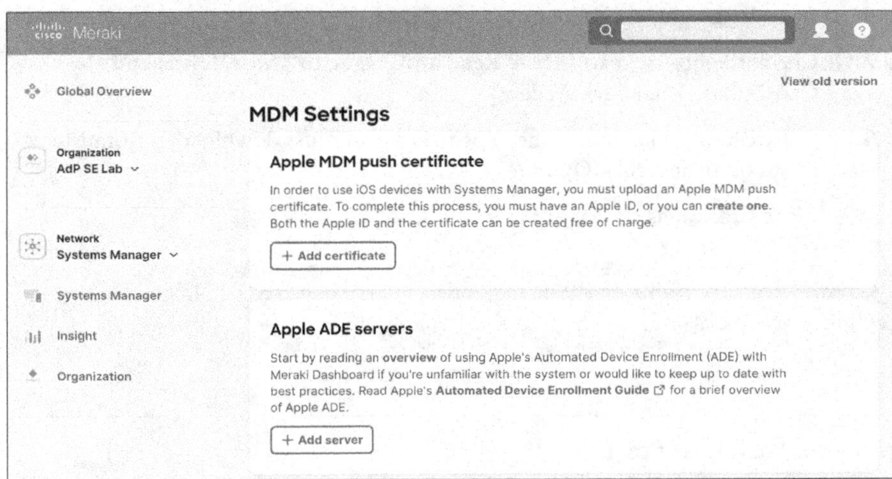

Figure 11-1 *The MDM Settings Page in Meraki Dashboard*

Step 4. On the **Add Certificate** pop-up window, click **Meraki_Apple_CSR.csr** to download the certificate signing request file, as shown in Figure 11-2.

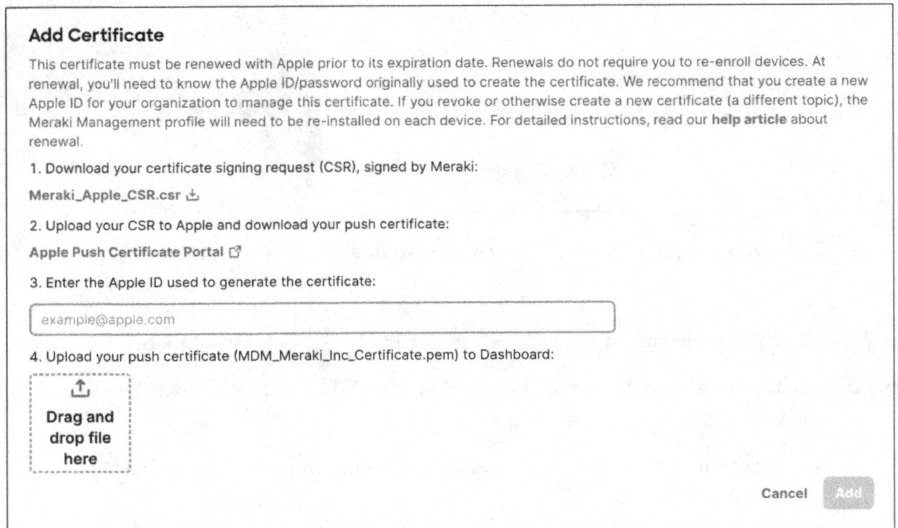

Figure 11-2 *The Add Certificate Pop-Up Window in Meraki Dashboard as Part of the Apple Integration*

Step 5. Click the link for **Apple Push Certificate Portal.** Clicking this link opens a new tab in your web browser and takes you to https://identity.apple.com/pushcert/. Log in with your Apple ID and complete the two-factor authentication.

Step 6. Once logged in, click **Create a Certificate.**

Step 7. Check the box next to **I Have Read and Agree to These Terms and Conditions.** Then click **Accept.**

Step 8. Click **Choose File**, locate the CSR file that was just downloaded from Meraki Dashboard, and click **Open.**

Click **Upload**, as shown in Figure 11-3.

> **Tip** If you receive an error with the CSR file, try switching back to the old version of the MDM Settings page and download the CSR file from there.

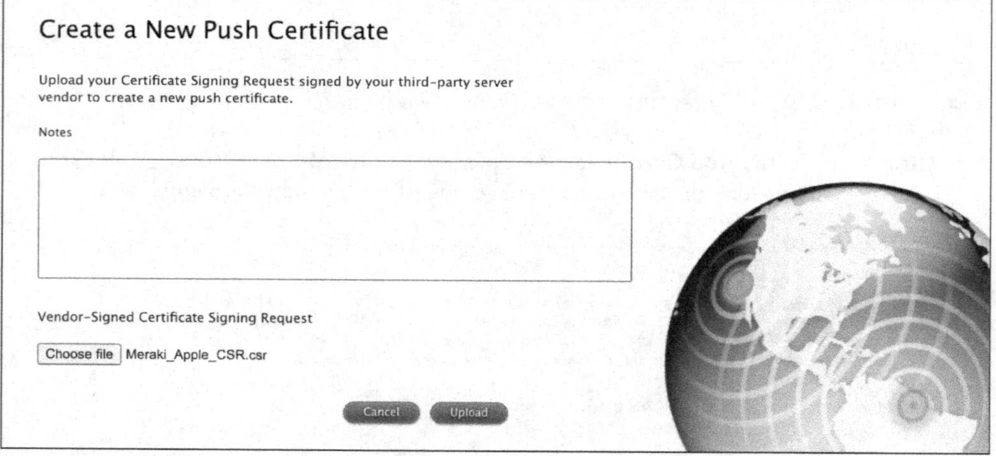

Figure 11-3 *The Create a New Push Certificate Page in the Apple Push Certificate Portal*

Step 9. On the confirmation page shown in Figure 11-4, click **Download.**

Step 10. Switch back to the browser tab open at the **Add Certificate** window in Meraki Dashboard (from Step 4).

a. Enter the Apple ID that you just used to log in to the Apple Push Certificate Portal.

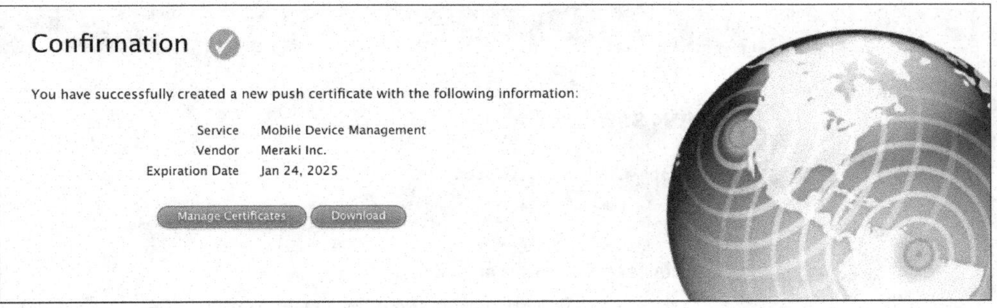

Figure 11-4 *Successful Creation of a New Push Certificate in the Apple Push Certificate Portal*

b. Click **Drag and Drop File Here**. In the window that opens, locate the certificate file (**MDM_Meraki Inc._Certificate.pem**) that was just downloaded from the Apple Push Certificate Portal, as shown in Figure 11-5, and click **Open**.

c. Click **Add** to finish.

Add Certificate

This certificate must be renewed with Apple prior to its expiration date. Renewals do not require you to re-enroll devices. At renewal, you'll need to know the Apple ID/password originally used to create the certificate. We recommend that you create a new Apple ID for your organization to manage this certificate. If you revoke or otherwise create a new certificate (a different topic), the Meraki Management profile will need to be re-installed on each device. For detailed instructions, read our **help article** about renewal.

1. Download your certificate signing request (CSR), signed by Meraki:

Meraki_Apple_CSR.csr

2. Upload your CSR to Apple and download your push certificate:

Apple Push Certificate Portal

3. Enter the Apple ID used to generate the certificate:

4. Upload your push certificate (MDM_Meraki_Inc_Certificate.pem) to Dashboard:

MDM_ Meraki Inc._Certificate.pem

Cancel Add

Figure 11-5 *Completing the Installation of the Apple Push Certificate on the Add Certificate Window in Dashboard*

You now go back to the **MDM Settings** page in Meraki Dashboard, as shown in Figure 11-6. The certificate details are displayed under the heading **CURRENT APPLE MDM PUSH CERTIFICATE**.

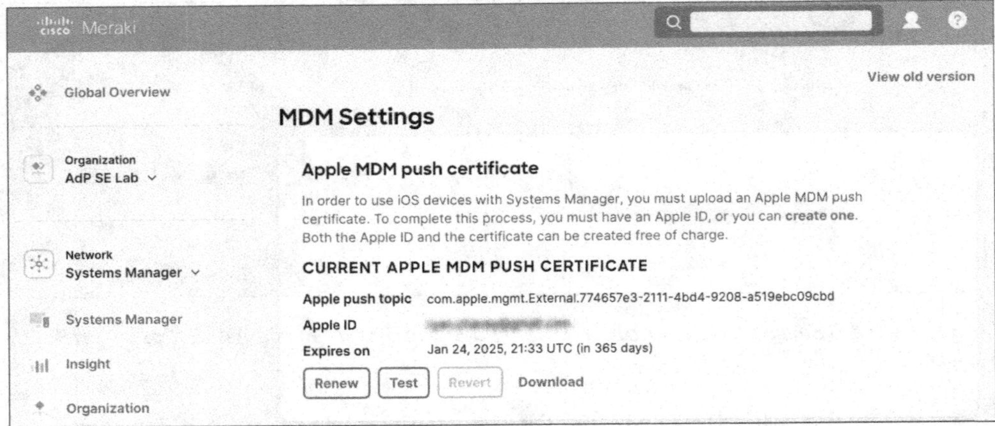

Figure 11-6 *The MDM Settings Page in Dashboard After the Successful Installation of the Apple Push Certificate*

You've completed the installation of the Apple push certificate, enabling Apple devices to now be enrolled. For further guidance on installing the Apple MDM push certificate, refer to https://documentation.meraki.com/SM/Device_Enrollment/Apple_MDM_Push_Certificate.

Enrolling Devices with Systems Manager

Devices need to be enrolled with Meraki Systems Manager to have profiles applied, provide data about the device, and enable the remote support functionality. The actual device enrollment process can be completed in a number of ways, which vary depending on the operating system. Where Apple devices are provided to employees, it is recommended to use Apple's enrollment program called Automated Device Enrollment (ADE). Doing so means that devices will arrive pre-enrolled, and administrators will have the widest range of policy capability. Administrators can manually enroll devices later in the ADE program, such as in the case of pre-owned devices.

Note Manually enrolling devices in the ADE program requires a factory reset, meaning it is not suitable for bring your own device (BYOD) deployments. The Android equivalent of ADE is called *device owner mode* and also requires a factory reset. For BYOD deployments, Android Enterprise devices support an alternative to device owner mode, where the organization data is containerized in a work profile and managed separately to the device itself. This is referred to as *managed profile mode*.

As part of the enrollment process, users are asked to authenticate. By default, Meraki Systems Manager defaults to using Meraki Cloud authentication. In an enterprise environment, it is highly likely that you will use a centralized identity management solution like Microsoft Entra or an authentication protocol such as SAML. If you wish to use one of these solutions for authenticating users during enrollment, configure this now. It is highly recommended that you use SAML with Cisco Duo or Cisco ISE, because you're likely already using these for securing admin access to Dashboard and/or Zero Trust. To configure authentication for Systems Manager enrollment in Meraki Dashboard, follow these steps:

Step 1. Navigate to **Systems Manager > General.**

Step 2. Scroll down to **End User Authentication Settings** and input the required parameters.

You can find guidance on configuring end-user authentication for Systems Manager enrollment at https://documentation.meraki.com/SM/Device_Enrollment/SM_Enrollment_Authentication.

Meraki publishes a wide range of enrollment guides, covering each of the supported device types. You can find these guides at https://documentation.meraki.com/SM/Device_Enrollment. Generally speaking, enrolling a device with Meraki Systems Manager starts with navigating to **Systems Manager > Devices**, clicking **Add Devices**, and following the prompts.

The configuration examples in this chapter were completed using an Apple device enrolled using the manual device enrollment process. To enroll an iOS device manually, follow the steps detailed at https://documentation.meraki.com/SM/Device_Enrollment/iOS_Enrollment.

Checking Compliance with Security Policy (Systems Manager Policies)

Systems Manager policies allow administrators to check the compliance of devices, including

- Checking whether devices have the required operating system version installed
- Checking for the presence of mandatory or banned apps
- Ensuring that mobile devices are not jailbroken
- Ensuring that mobile devices have a passcode lock configured and are "checking in" with Systems Manager regularly

Policies are for compliance reporting only. They do not push settings or software to devices; there are other tools for that purpose. It is recommended that you configure a Systems Manager policy before you configure profiles.

Follow these steps to configure a Systems Manager policy in Meraki Dashboard. This example focuses on iOS devices, but profiles are available for a range of operating systems and the steps are similar.

Step 1. Log in to Meraki Dashboard (https://dashboard.meraki.com).

Step 2. Navigate to **Systems Manager > Policies** (under Configure).

Step 3. Click **+ Add New**.

Step 4. This is where you configure all of the required compliance checks (see Figure 11-7).

a. Enter a name in the **Security Policy Name** field. This field does not allow spaces.

b. Select the settings you want to monitor. In this example, we have configured the following:

- A check to ensure that mobile devices have a passcode lock configured.
- A check to ensure that mobile devices are not jailbroken or rooted.
- Under **All Devices > Application Block List**, we have configured an application block list to block the TikTok application. The field directly underneath resolves the application name to the application's bundle ID; the bundle ID may or may not be intuitive.
- Under **All Devices > Mandatory Applications**, we have configured Cisco Secure Client.
- Under **All Devices > Minimum OS Version**, we have configured iOS devices to run at least version 17.1. The minimum OS can be specified for multiple different OS types.
- Last, a check to ensure that devices are checking in regularly—in our case, at least every 30 days. This helps to detect devices that may be lost or stolen or may have had Systems Manager removed.

c. Click **Save Changes**.

At this point, you've completed the configuration of policies in Systems Manager.

Follow these steps to see the compliance capabilities in action and enable alerting:

Step 1. Navigate to **Systems Manager > Devices**. By clicking the plus icon (on the right under General), you can change the columns displayed. Figure 11-8 shows two added columns indicating whether the devices are compliant with the corporate security policy and, if not, why.

> **Note** A beta version of this page is available; however, it does not have the Policy Reasons column available at the time of writing.

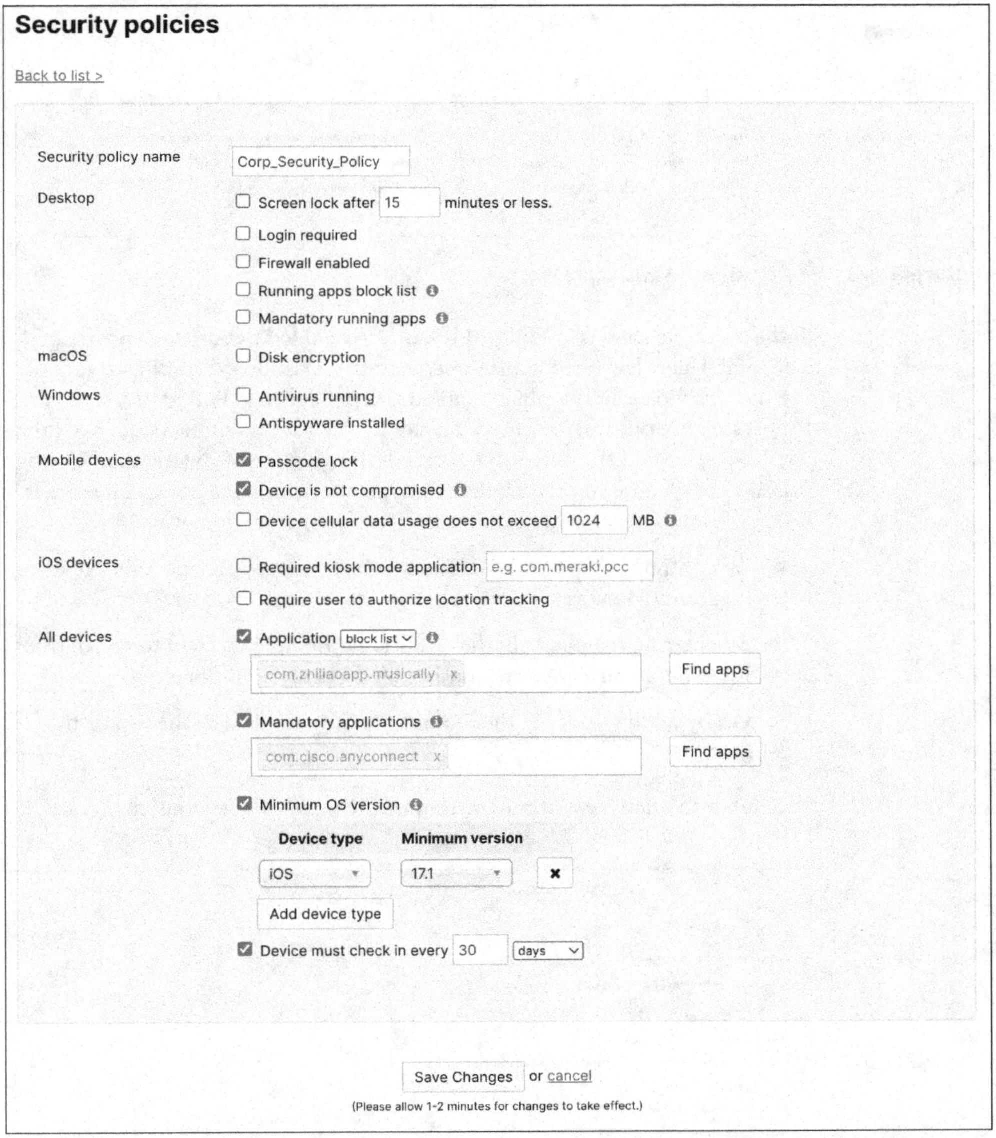

Figure 11-7 *The Systems Manager Security Policies Pane in Meraki Dashboard*

Step 2. It is possible to set up regular alerting and reporting, which will highlight any devices that are not compliant with the security policies and why. Navigate to **Systems Manager > Alerts** (under Configure).

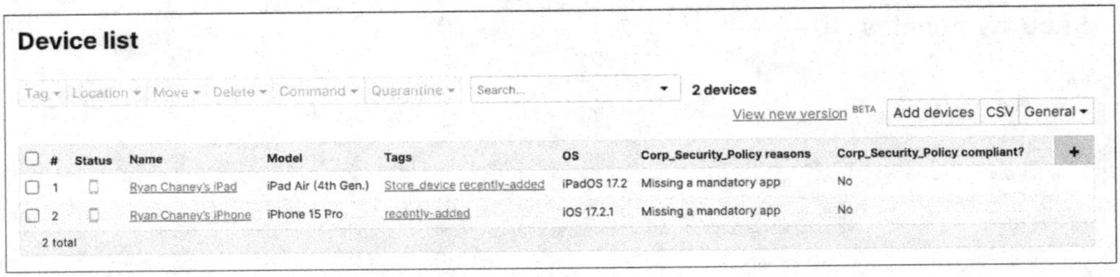

Device list

Tag ▾ | Location ▾ | Move ▾ | Delete ▾ | Command ▾ | Quarantine ▾ | Search... | **2 devices**

View new version BETA | Add devices | CSV | General ▾

#	Status	Name	Model	Tags	OS	Corp_Security_Policy reasons	Corp_Security_Policy compliant?
1		Ryan Chaney's iPad	iPad Air (4th Gen.)	Store_device recently-added	iPadOS 17.2	Missing a mandatory app	No
2		Ryan Chaney's iPhone	iPhone 15 Pro	recently-added	iOS 17.2.1	Missing a mandatory app	No

2 total

Figure 11-8 *The Systems Manager Devices List*

In this example shown in Figure 11-9, under **Enabled Security Reports**, a daily email alert has been configured to notify Dashboard administrators of any devices violating the policy named **Corp_Security_Policy**. If you created a separate network for Systems Manager devices as recommended, check that you have specified the recipients correctly for this new network. **All Network Admins**, as specified in the **Default Recipients** field, does not include organizational admins. Recipients can be specified in one of three ways:

- By configuring network admins for the Systems Manager Network (**Systems Manager > General**)
- By entering recipients in the **Additional Recipients** field to the right of **Enabled Security Alerts** and **Enabled Security Reports**
- Or, by adding users in the **Default Recipients** field at the top of the page

Remember to click **Save** at the bottom of the page to save your changes.

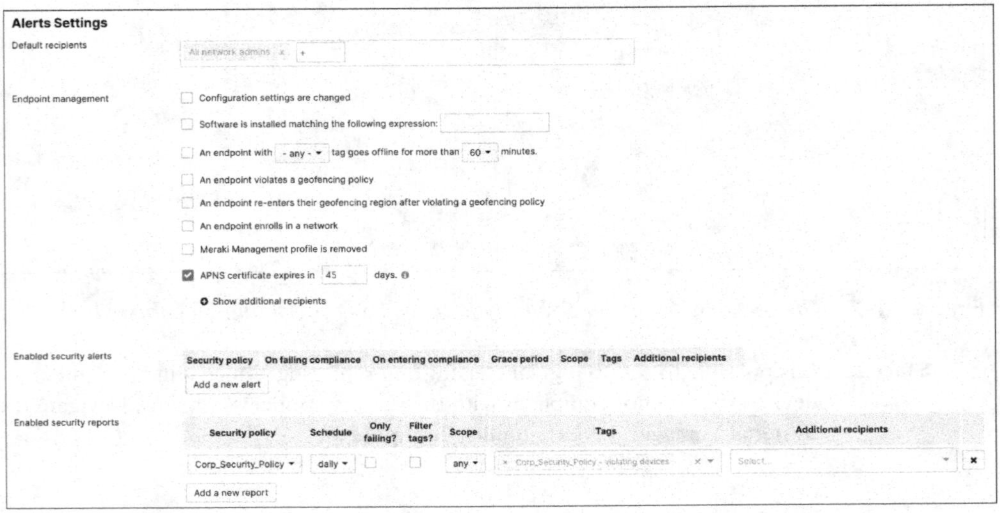

Alerts Settings

Default recipients: All network admins

Endpoint management:

- Configuration settings are changed
- Software is installed matching the following expression:
- An endpoint with - any - tag goes offline for more than 60 minutes.
- An endpoint violates a geofencing policy
- An endpoint re-enters their geofencing region after violating a geofencing policy
- An endpoint enrolls in a network
- Meraki Management profile is removed
- ☑ APNS certificate expires in 45 days.

Show additional recipients

Enabled security alerts: Security policy | On failing compliance | On entering compliance | Grace period | Scope | Tags | Additional recipients

Add a new alert

Enabled security reports:

Security policy	Schedule	Only failing?	Filter tags?	Scope	Tags	Additional recipients
Corp_Security_Policy	daily	☐	☐	any	Corp_Security_Policy - violating devices	Select...

Add a new report

Figure 11-9 *Configuring Systems Manager Alerts in Meraki Dashboard*

Note The difference between a *security alert* and a *security report* is that an alert is sent when compliance issues are detected, whereas a report is a summary that is sent out daily, weekly, or monthly.

Figure 11-10 shows a sample security report from Meraki Systems Manager. As an Easter egg, notice that the report features the original Meraki logo—very cool!

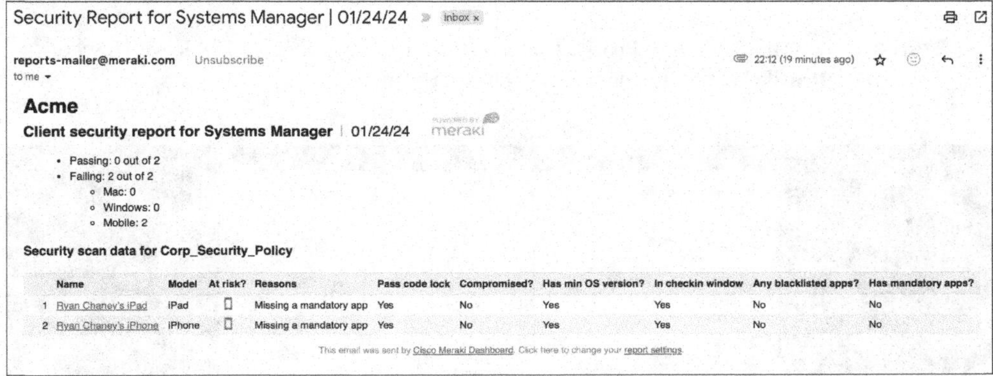

Figure 11-10 *A Security Report from Meraki Systems Manager*

You've now completed the setup of Systems Manager policies and alerting. With this setup in place, read on to learn how to manage client devices.

Creating a Systems Manager Profile

Profiles can contain one or more settings payloads and are used by Systems Manager to push out settings and certificates to devices. This section details how to configure a profile in Meraki Systems Manager, laying the foundation for the following sections, which detail the various payloads that can be added. In this example, we use the default device profile that can be used for all device types and operating systems.

Follow these steps to create a profile in Systems Manager:

Step 1. Log in to Meraki Dashboard (https://dashboard.meraki.com).

Step 2. Navigate to **Systems Manager > Settings** (under Manage).

Step 3. Click **+ Add Profile**, as shown in Figure 11-11.

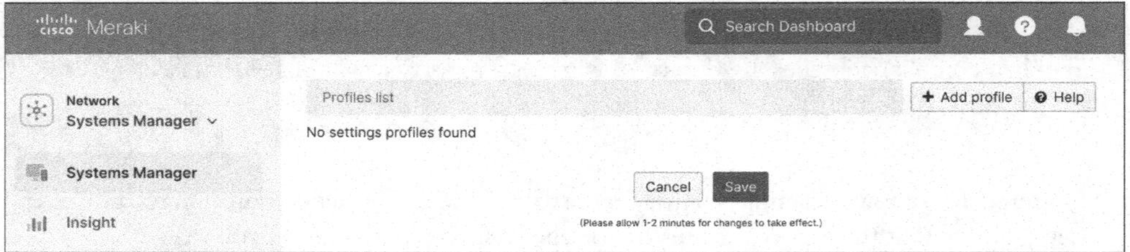

Figure 11-11 *Creating a Profile in Meraki Dashboard*

Step 4. On the **Add New Profile** pop-up window (see Figure 11-12), leave **Device Profile (Default)** selected and click **Continue.**

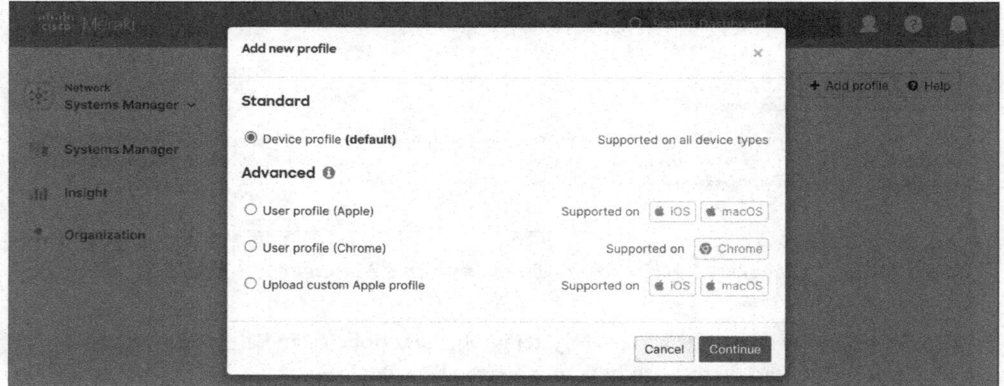

Figure 11-12 *Choosing a Device Profile from the Add New Profile Window in Meraki Dashboard*

Step 5. On the screen shown in Figure 11-13, enter a meaningful name for this profile in the **Name** field. You can either have multiple profiles, each with one payload, or one profile with lots of payloads. Take this into consideration when naming your profile.

It is recommended that each operating system has its own profile. This will make it clear as to how controls are to be implemented. For example, a passcode policy will be interpreted differently for iOS versus macOS. Think about version control and incorporate this into the **Name** or **Description.** For example, the **Description** field could be used to record the name, or initials, of the person who created or last made changes to this profile, as well as a brief description of that change.

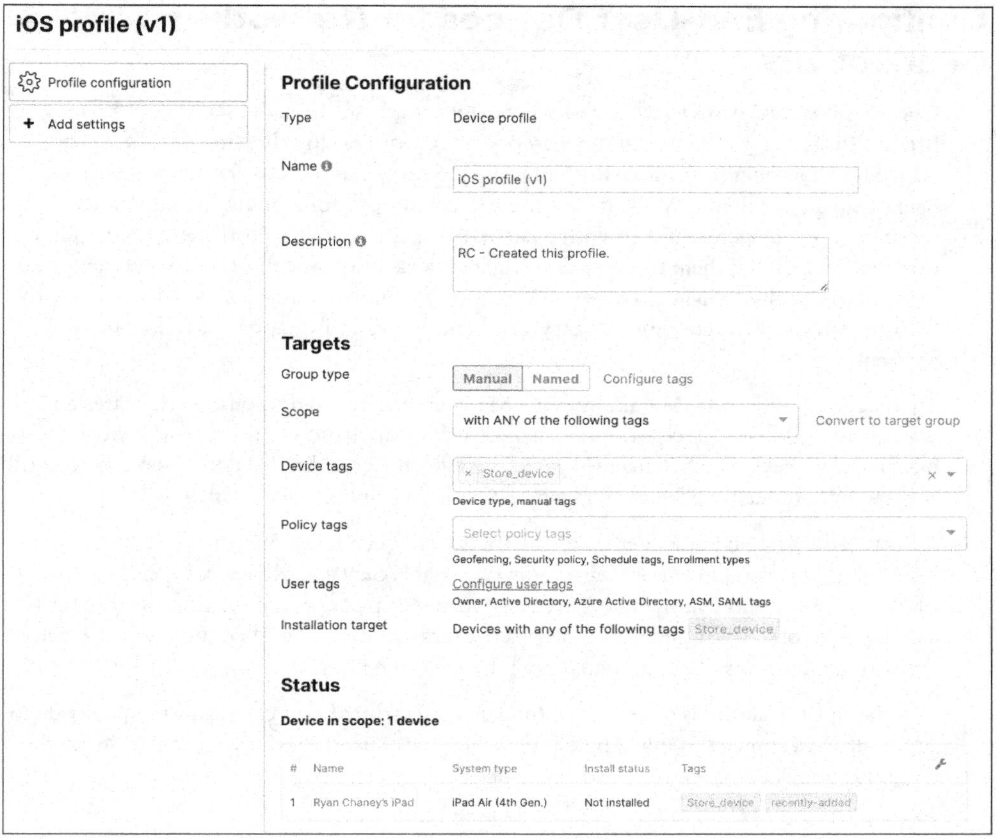

Figure 11-13 *Configuring a New Systems Manager Device Profile in Meraki Dashboard*

From the **Scope** drop-down menu, select how to determine which devices this policy will be applied to. There is plenty of flexibility here: all devices, devices with or without certain tags. In this example, we have chosen to apply this profile to all of Acme's store devices (devices with the tag **Store_device**). Policy tags are not required for this use case, but it's important to point out that profiles can be made conditional on such things as where a user is, whether their device is compliant with security policy, time of day, or who the owner of the device is.

Click **Save**.

The creation of a profile in Systems Manager is now complete. The following sections explain how to add the various payloads that apply your corporate security policy.

Configuring End-User Devices for Network Connectivity

One of the easiest ways to avoid risky behavior by users is to make security seamless. If users find it easy to get onto the network, they won't go looking for open SSIDs or introduce their own rogue access points. Using Sentry-based network access, such as Sentry Wi-Fi and Sentry VPN, makes life extremely easy for admins. When you use these features, devices enrolled with Systems Manager receive a profile and the required certificates enabling them to connect to the network automatically. Certificates are generated automatically by Meraki's own CA, relieving administrators of this burden. Refer to Chapter 8 for how to configure Sentry LAN and Wi-Fi and Chapter 9 for how to configure Sentry VPN.

This section covers how Meraki Systems Manager can be used to push certificates and settings to end-user devices. Even if the network setup is not compatible with Sentry-based access, such as when using WPA3 or AnyConnect today, Systems Manager can still substantially reduce the frustration when it comes to onboarding users.

Additionally, Systems Manager eases the transition when migrating to networks using Sentry-based access. In this scenario, you can enable Sentry-based access on the new Meraki network and use Meraki Systems Manager to push profiles to user devices for the existing network. With the profiles in place, users can continue to connect to the legacy network, and as sites are upgraded, they'll be able to migrate across seamlessly.

The aim in this section is to teach the fundamentals so that you can adapt the payloads to suit your environment. While Apple iOS devices were used for the verification steps, the configuration is the same for Android devices.

Certificate Settings Payload

The certificate settings payload is used to push X.509 certificates to devices. Systems Manager supports X.509 certificates with these filename extensions: .cer, .p12, .crt, and .pem.

In this example, we push two certificates as part of our Systems Manager profile. The first is a device certificate obtained using the Certificate Provisioning Portal in Cisco Identity Services Engine (ISE). The second is the ISE CA certificate. A certificate payload is required to specify which certificate to trust on a Wi-Fi payload. We require this in the following section. Rather than run you through the steps to add each certificate, we just show the steps once.

Follow these steps to configure a certificate settings payload on an existing Systems Manager profile:

Step 1. Open the existing profile that you wish to modify (**Systems Manager > Settings**).

Step 2. Click **+ Add Settings** and select **Certificate**, as shown in Figure 11-14.

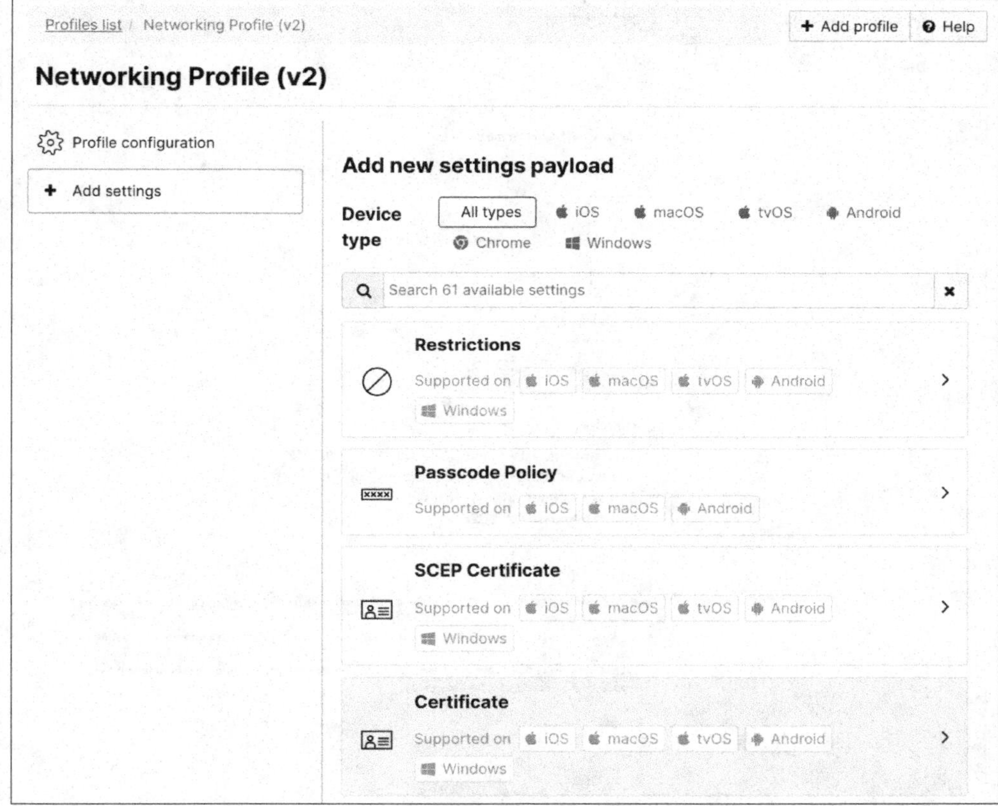

Figure 11-14 *Adding a Certificate Payload to a Profile in Meraki Systems Manager*

Step 3. On the screen shown in Figure 11-15, enter a **Name** to describe this certificate.

a. If your certificate has a password, enter it here; otherwise, leave this field blank.

b. The next step is to select the certificate that the client needs to trust and the one used by the authentication server (in this case, Cisco ISE). Under **Certificate**, click **Choose File**, select the certificate downloaded earlier from Cisco ISE, and click **Open**. The certificate details will populate after you click Save.

c. Click **Save**.

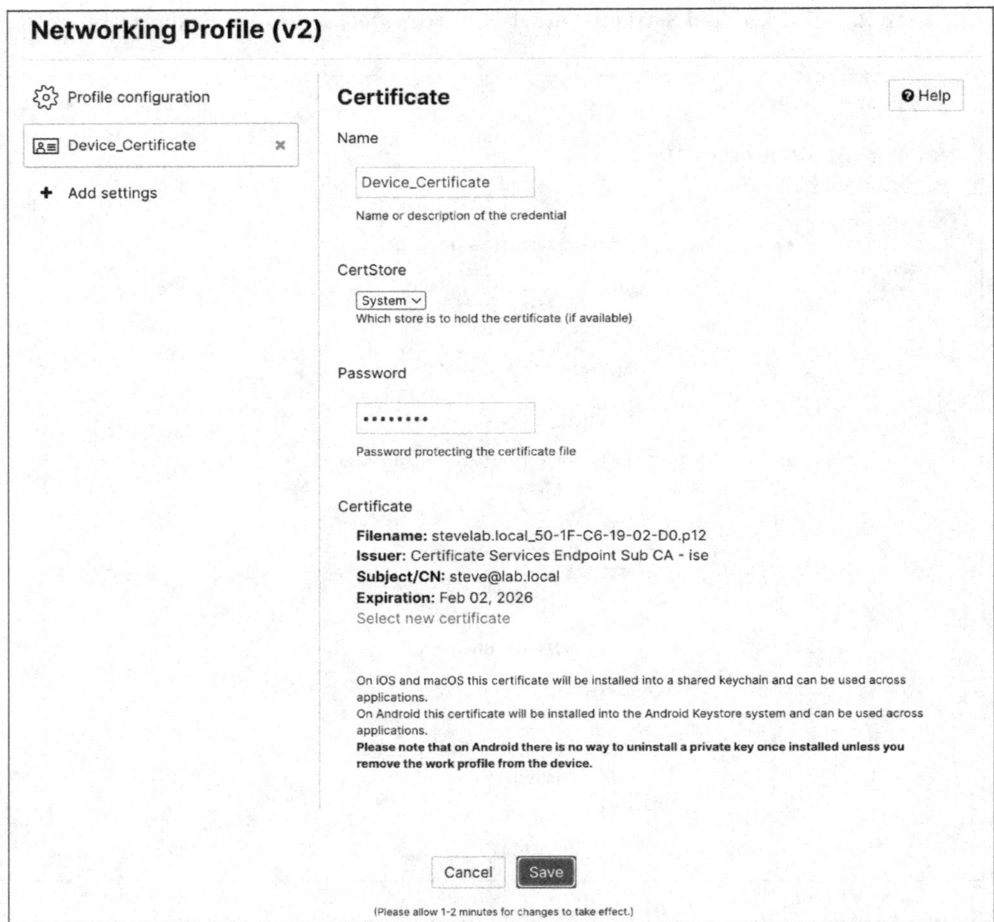

Figure 11-15 *Configuring a Certificate Payload in Meraki Systems Manager*

Now that you've completed the configuration of the Certificate settings payload in Systems Manager, you can refer to the following URL to learn more about creating certificate payloads: https://documentation.meraki.com/SM/Profiles_and_Settings/Certificates_Payload_(Pushing_Certificates).

Wi-Fi Settings Payload

Wi-Fi settings payloads push out wireless settings, effectively preconfiguring SSIDs on enrolled devices. Although Sentry Wi-Fi is certainly easier, Wi-Fi settings payloads are required for non-Meraki SSIDs, or where the configuration of the SSID is not compatible with Sentry Wi-Fi.

Follow these steps to configure a Wi-Fi settings payload on an existing Systems Manager profile:

Step 1. In Meraki Dashboard, navigate to **Systems Manager > Settings** (under Manage). Open an existing profile that you wish to modify.

> **Note** If you will be using an authentication type that requires certificates, such as EAP-TLS, ensure that you select a Systems Manager profile that includes a settings payload for both the device certificate and the Root CA certificate.

Step 2. Click **+ Add Settings** and then click **Wi-Fi Settings** on the **Add New Settings Payload** pane, as shown in Figure 11-16.

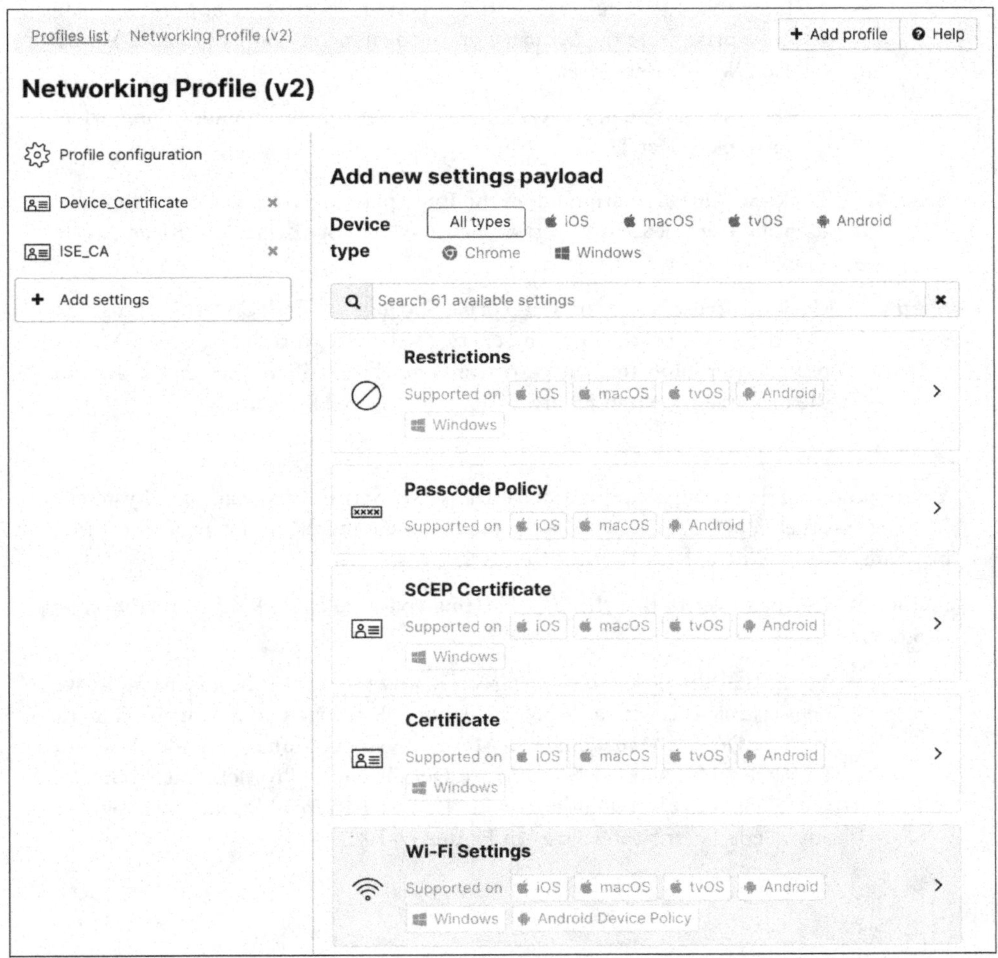

Figure 11-16 *Adding a Wi-Fi Settings Payload to a Systems Manager Profile*

Step 3. On the **Wi-Fi Settings** page (see Figure 11-17), ensure **Manual** is selected from the **Configuration** drop-down menu. This should be the default.

a. Enter the name of the SSID in the **SSID** field.

b. Select **Auto Join.**

c. The remaining settings on this pane must be tailored to match your wireless network setup. For guidance on configuring the Wi-Fi Settings payload to suit your network, refer to https://documentation.meraki.com/SM/Profiles_and_Settings/Systems_Manager_Wi-Fi_Settings_Payload.

d. In this example, disable MAC address randomization by checking **Disable MAC Address Randomization (iOS 14 or Later).**

e. To expose the Enterprise Settings section, choose any option that includes **Enterprise** from the **Security** drop-down menu. In this example, we have used **WPA2 Enterprise.**

f. Because you're using EAP-TLS, on the **Protocols** tab under **Enterprise Settings**, select **TLS.**

Step 4. Click the **Authentication** tab in the **Enterprise Settings** section. From the **Identity Certificate** drop-down menu, select your device certificate, as shown in Figure 11-18.

Step 5. Click the **Trust** tab in the **Enterprise Settings** section. Under the **Trusted Certificates** drop-down menu, check the box next to the Subject/CN displayed after importing the certificate into the certificate settings policy. In the example shown in Figure 11-19, this is **ise.selab.local.**

Click **Save.**

You've now completed the configuration of the Wi-Fi Settings payload for a Systems Manager profile. When devices receive the profile update with the Wi-Fi and certificate payloads, they will be able to connect to this SSID.

Follow these steps to verify that the Wi-Fi settings payload is working correctly on Apple iOS devices:

Step 1. Verify that the profile has been received by the device. In this example, we demonstrate this with an Apple iPad. On iOS, navigate to **Settings > General > VPN & Device Management > Meraki Systems Manager** (under MOBILE DEVICE MANAGEMENT) **> More Details** (under Profile). You should see the Wi-Fi SSID listed under **WI-FI NETWORK.** In addition, you should see any needed certificates listed in Figure 11-20.

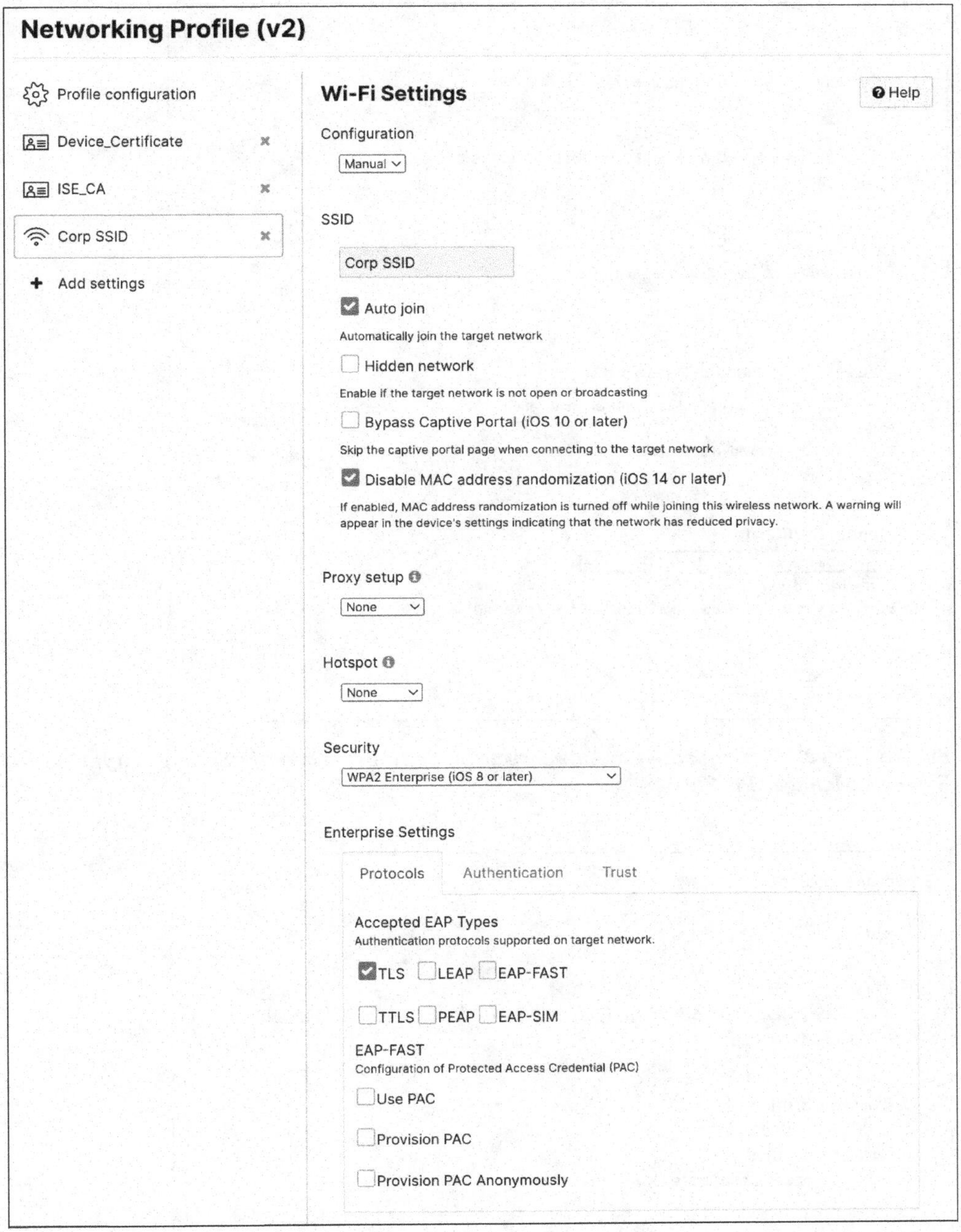

Figure 11-17 *Configuring a Wi-Fi Settings Payload on a Systems Manager Profile*

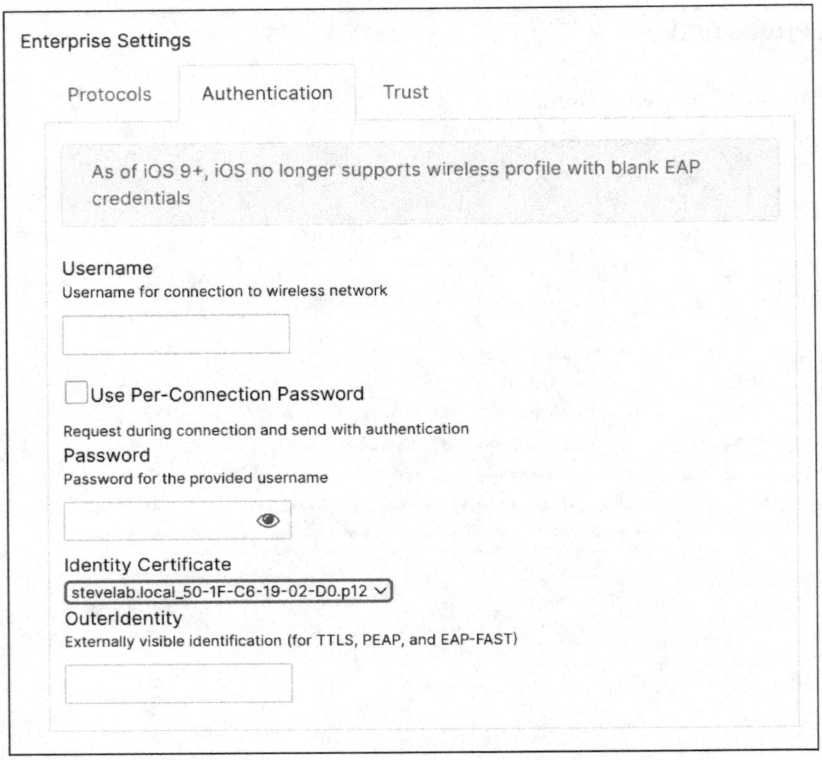

Figure 11-18 *Configuring the Authentication Settings on a Wi-Fi Settings Payload on a Systems Manager Profile*

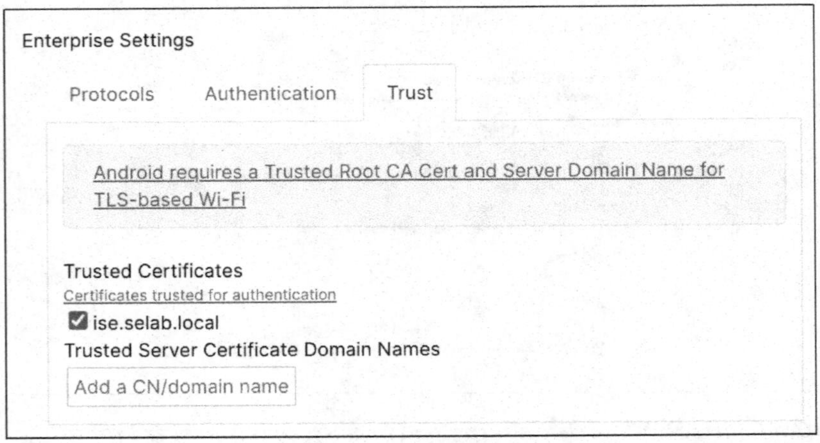

Figure 11-19 *Configuring the Trust Settings on a Wi-Fi Settings Payload on a Systems Manager Profile*

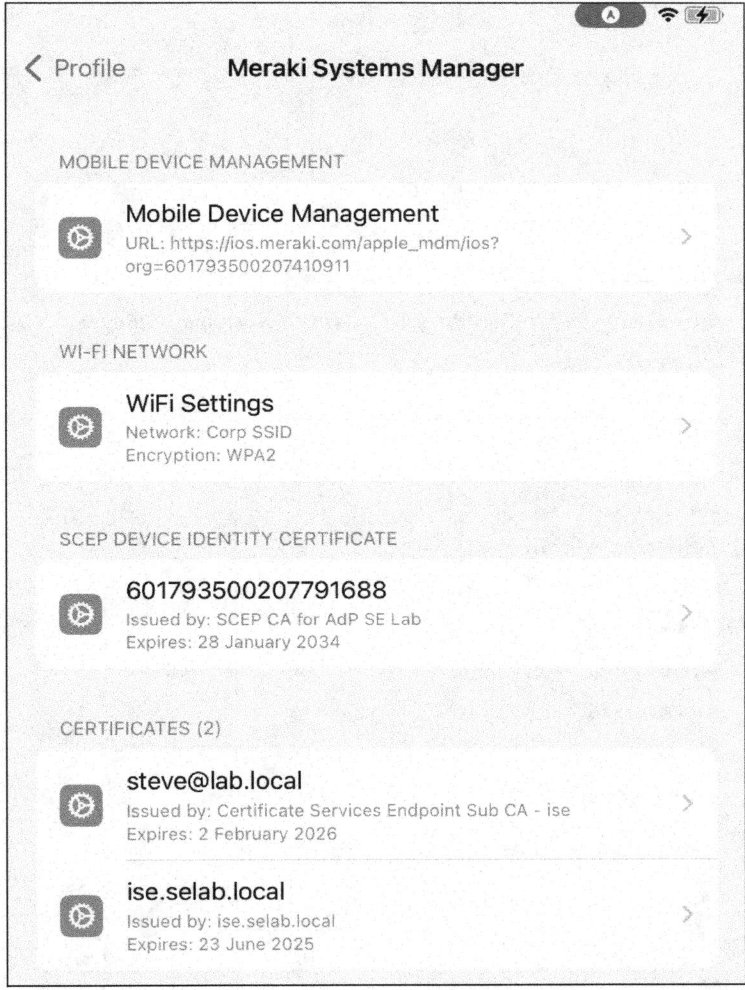

Figure 11-20 *A Systems Manager Profile on an iOS Device Showing the Wi-Fi Settings Payload and Certificates*

Step 2. Try connecting to the SSID and, if unsuccessful, check the appropriate logs either in Meraki Dashboard or, in this case, in Cisco ISE. In this example, with ISE already configured, this device was able to connect directly to the network without any user interaction, as shown in Figure 11-21.

Step 3. Because the intention was to use EAP-TLS in this example, you can also verify this by checking the live logs in Cisco ISE. In Figure 11-22, you can see this user was connecting using the authentication protocol EAP-TLS.

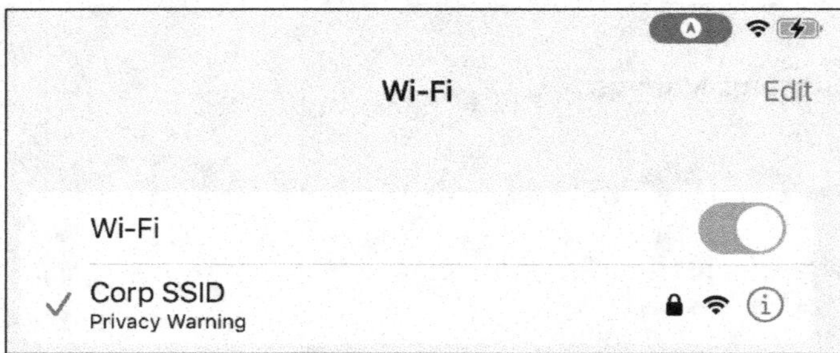

Figure 11-21 *Successfully Connected to Meraki Wi-Fi Using a Systems Manager Profile with Wi-Fi Settings*

Authentication Details

Source Timestamp	2024-02-03 12:56:39.431
Received Timestamp	2024-02-03 12:56:39.431
Policy Server	ise
Event	5200 Authentication succeeded
Username	steve@lab.local
Endpoint Id	50:1F:C6:19:02:D0
Calling Station Id	50-1F-C6-19-02-D0
Endpoint Profile	Apple-Device
Authentication Identity Store	Windows_2016_AD-10.200.155.100
Identity Group	Profiled
Authentication Method	dot1x
Authentication Protocol	EAP-TLS
Service Type	Framed
Network Device	ACME_Store_Wifi
Device Type	All Device Types
Location	All Locations
NAS IPv4 Address	192.168.129.2
NAS Port Type	Wireless - IEEE 802.11
Authorization Profile	PermitAccess
Response Time	97 milliseconds

Figure 11-22 *Confirming EAP-TLS Authentication as Per the Wi-Fi Settings Payload on a Systems Manager Profile*

At this point, you've completed the configuration and verification of a Wi-Fi settings payload in Meraki Systems Manager. For more information on Wi-Fi settings payloads, refer to https://documentation.meraki.com/SM/Profiles_and_Settings/Systems_Manager_Wi-Fi_Settings_Payload.

VPN Settings Payload

VPN settings payloads are used to push VPN settings to devices. Although using Sentry VPN is the far easier option where client VPN is being used, VPN settings payloads are required for non-Meraki VPN solutions.

In this example we show how to configure a client VPN using a VPN settings payload. Follow these steps to add a VPN settings payload to an existing Systems Manager profile:

Step 1. In Meraki Dashboard, navigate to **Systems Manager > Settings** (under Manage).

Step 2. Click the name of an existing profile where you wish to add a passcode policy or click **+ Add Profile** to create a new one.

> **Note** If you will be using a VPN that requires certificates, ensure that the profile also includes the necessary certificates.

Step 3. Click **+ Add Settings**, as shown in Figure 11-23.

Step 4. On the **VPN Settings** page, as shown in Figure 11-24, start by entering a **Connection Name.** In this example, we have used **Corp VPN.**

- **a.** Open the **IPsec Settings** page (**Security & SD-WAN > Client VPN**) in another browser tab. Copy the **Hostname** and paste it into the **Server** field on the **VPN Settings** page.
- **b.** Additionally, copy the **Shared Secret** from the **IPsec Settings** page and paste it into the **Shared Secret** field on the **VPN Settings** page.
- **c.** In this example, we've used a client VPN, so we need to select **L2TP** from the **Connection Type** drop-down menu. If you're not using a client VPN, select the connection type appropriate for your network setup from the available options.
- **d.** (Optional) Check **Send All Traffic** to disable split tunneling.
- **e.** Leave the remaining fields as their defaults and click **Save.**

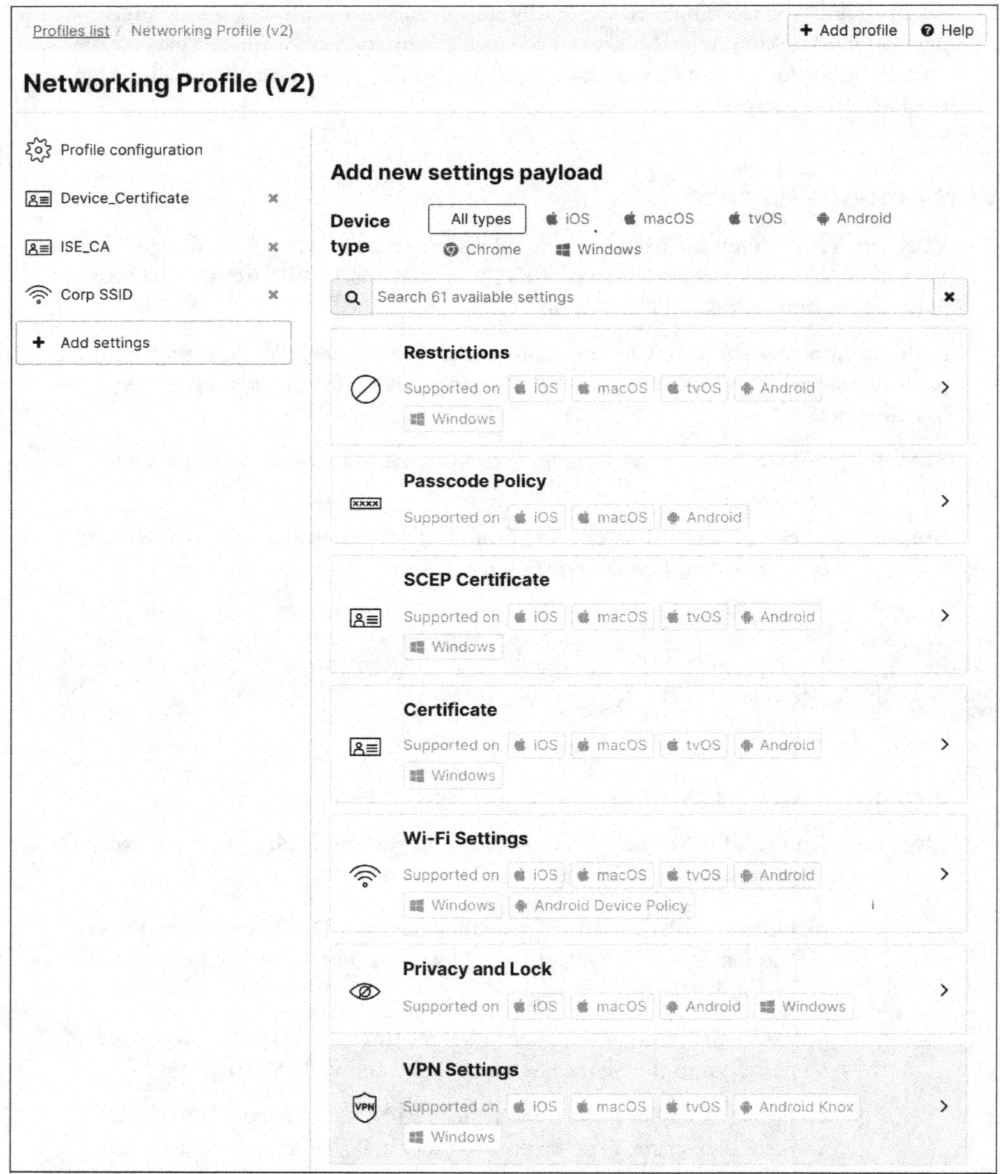

Figure 11-23 *Adding a VPN Settings Payload to an Existing Systems Manager Profile*

You've completed the configuration of the VPN Settings payload for a Systems Manager profile. When devices receive the profile update with the VPN settings, they will be able to connect.

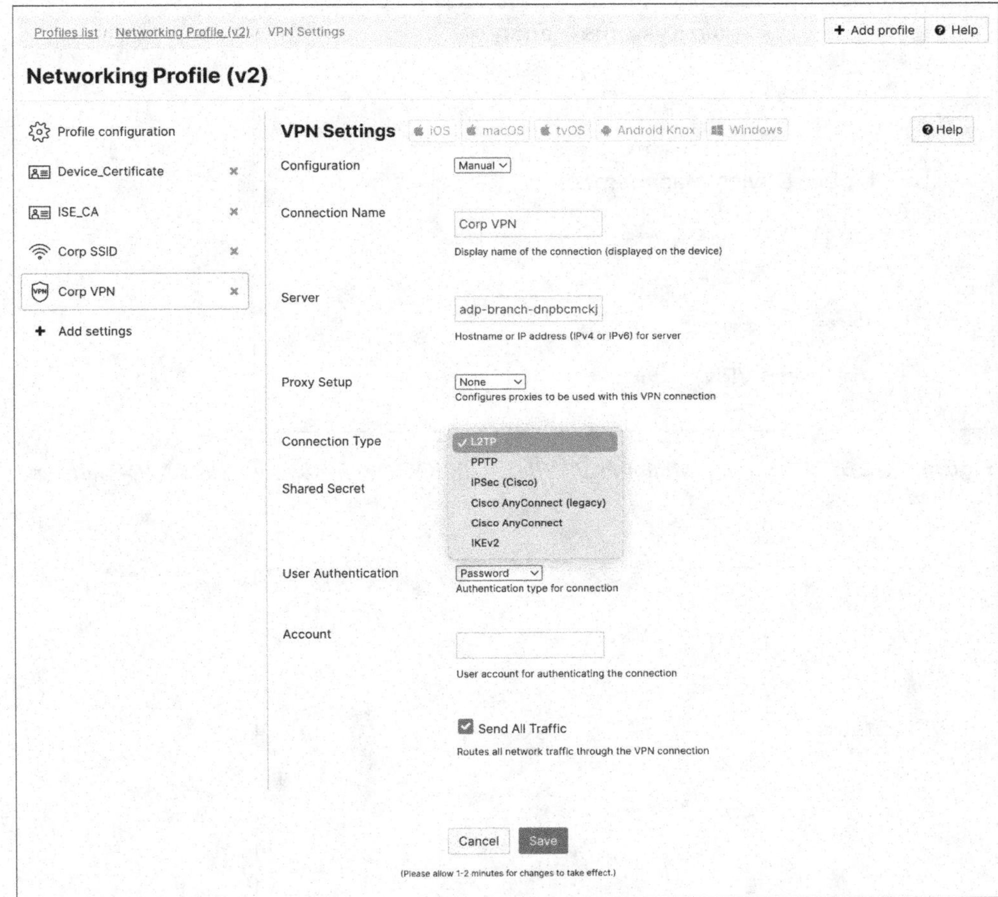

Figure 11-24 *Configuring a VPN Settings Payload on a Systems Manager Profile*

Follow these steps to verify that the VPN settings payload is working correctly on Apple iOS devices:

Step 1. Verify that the device has received the profile. In this example, we demonstrate this process with an Apple iPad. On iOS, navigate to **Settings > General > VPN & Device Management > Meraki Systems Manager** (under MOBILE DEVICE MANAGEMENT) > **More Details** (under Profile). You should see the VPN payload name listed under **VPN SETTINGS**, as shown in Figure 11-25.

Step 2. Try connecting to the VPN and, if unsuccessful, check the event log in Meraki Dashboard. In this example, this user was prompted for a username and password, then successfully connected to the VPN, as shown in Figure 11-26.

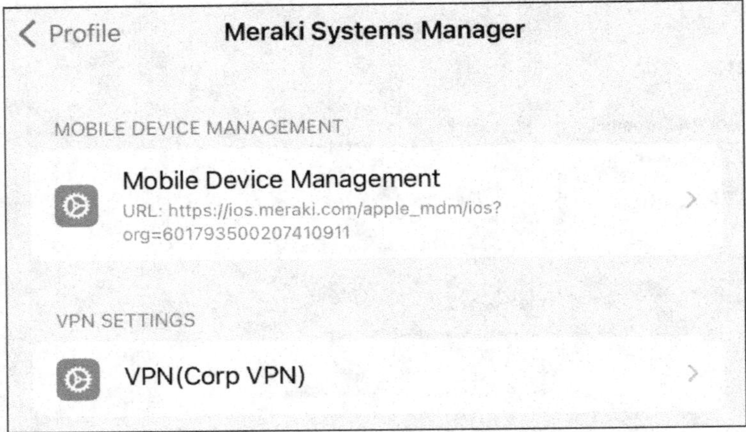

Figure 11-25 *A Systems Manager Profile on an iOS Device Showing the VPN Settings Payload*

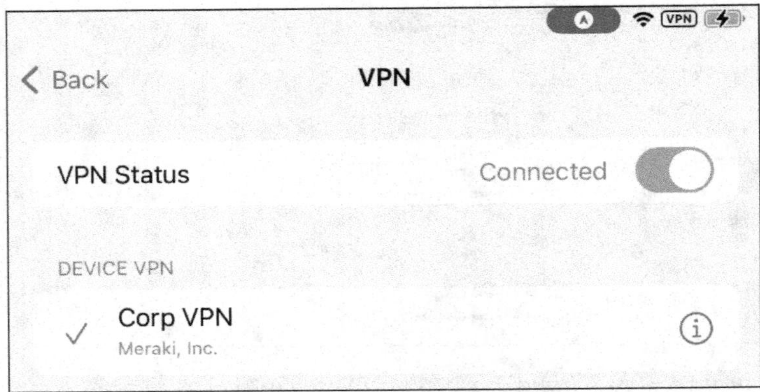

Figure 11-26 *Successfully Connecting to a Client VPN Using a Systems Manager Profile with VPN Settings*

> To avoid having to enter their username and password each time on iOS, users can save these details. To do this, navigate to **Settings > General > VPN & Device Management > VPN**. Then click the information symbol (the blue circle with the *I* in the center) and click **Edit**. Enter the username in the **Account** field and the **Password** in the password field; then click **Done**.

You've now completed the configuration and verification of VPN settings payloads in Meraki Systems Manager. For more information on VPN settings payloads, refer to https://documentation.meraki.com/SM/Profiles_and_Settings/Systems_Manager_VPN_Configurations_and_Sentry_VPN.

Applying Security Policy to Devices (Systems Manager Profiles)

This section details how to configure Systems Manager devices to meet the requirements of the security policy configured in the preceding section. Additionally, we address some extra requirements derived from industry best practices.

Passcode Policy (Includes Screen Lock)

Strong authentication is a key theme across IT security standards and should be a consideration for user devices also. NIST 800-53 has two requirements that can be met with a passcode policy. First, AC-11 requires that devices prevent access to systems (screen lock) after a period of inactivity and stay locked until a user reauthenticates. Second, NIST 800-53 AC-7(2) requires that mobile devices be configured to wipe themselves after a number of consecutive, unsuccessful device logon attempts. Note that setting a device PIN is typically required to enable encryption on the mobile device, making it even more important to enforce such a policy.

A passcode lock is required as part of the corporate security policy configured earlier in this chapter, so we can now configure a passcode payload to enforce this policy.

Follow these steps to configure a passcode policy as part of a Systems Manager profile:

Step 1. Navigate to **Systems Manager > Settings** (under Manage).

Step 2. Click the name of an existing profile where you wish to add a passcode policy or click **+ Add Profile** to create a new one.

Step 3. Click **+ Add Settings**.

Step 4. In this example, we create a simple passcode policy that requires PINs with a minimum length of six characters and sets devices to auto-lock after five minutes (see Figure 11-27).

- **a.** Set **Minimum Length** to **6**.
- **b.** Set **Auto-Lock** to **5** minutes.
- **c.** Set **Maximum Number of Failed Attempts** to **10**.
- **d.** Click **Save**.

Now that you've completed the configuration of the passcode settings payload, you can refer to the following URL for further explanation of the configuration options on this page: https://documentation.meraki.com/SM/Profiles_and_Settings/Systems_Manager_Passcode_Payload.

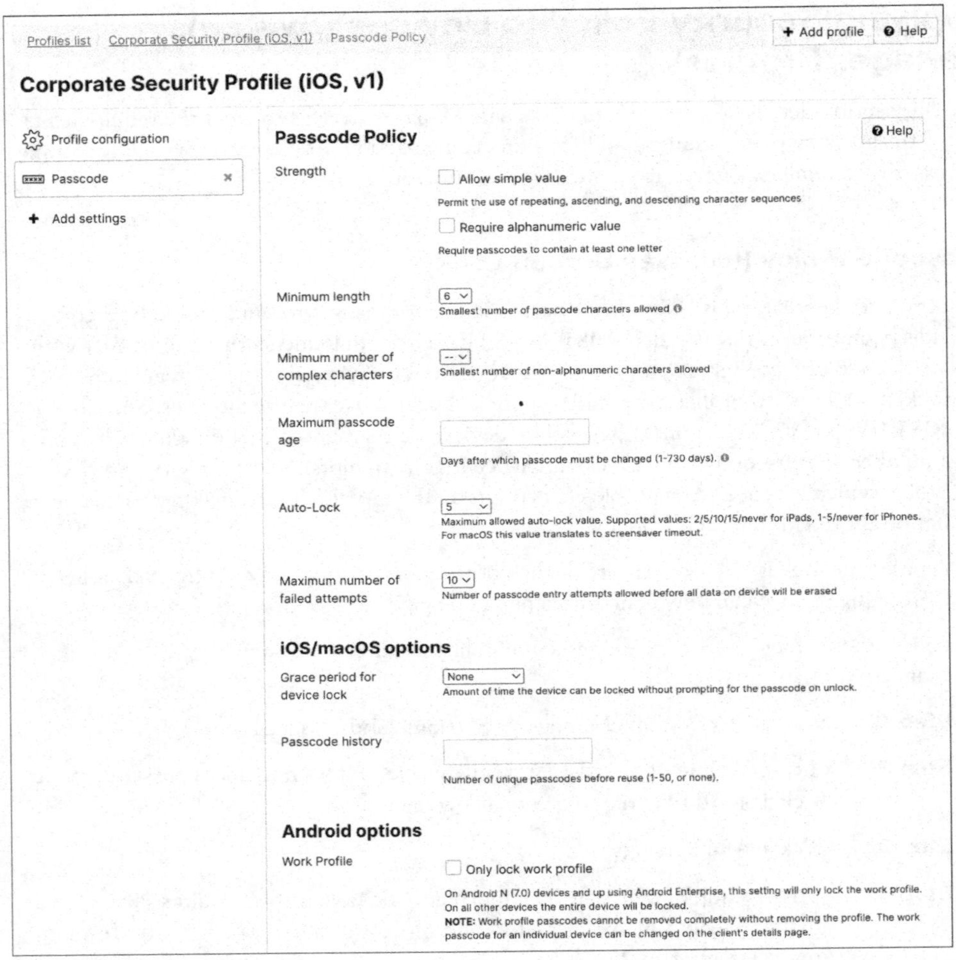

Figure 11-27 *Configuring a Passcode Settings Payload on a Systems Manager Profile*

Once this profile has been pushed to an enrolled device, you can check that the passcode policy is being enforced. Perform the following steps to verify that the passcode payload is working correctly on an Apple iOS device. On an Android 10+ device, you can test this policy by trying to change or remove the screen lock PIN by navigating to **Settings > Security > Screen Lock**.

Step 1. On an iOS device, navigate to **Settings > General > VPN & Device Management.** Under **MOBILE DEVICE MANAGEMENT**, click **Meraki Systems Manager.**

On the **Profile** page, next to **Contains**, you should see **Password Policy** listed, as shown in Figure 11-28.

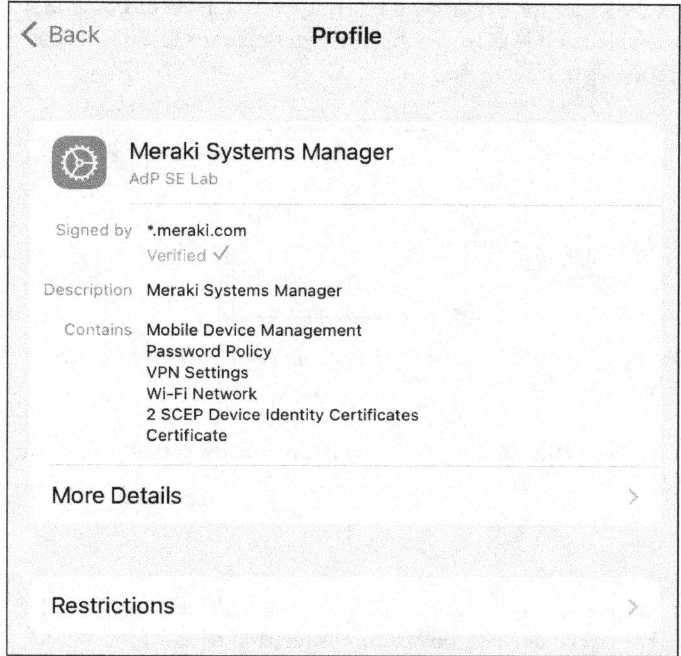

Figure 11-28 *A Profile with a Password Policy That Has Been Pushed to an iOS Device by Systems Manager*

Step 2. Click **Restrictions** and then **Passcode.** You can now see the details of the passcode policy matching what was configured in Systems Manager, as shown in Figure 11-29. This window confirms that the device has received the profile.

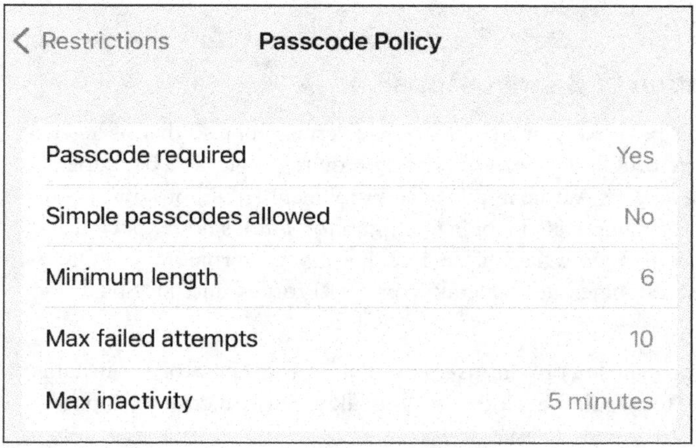

Restrictions

Passcode Policy

Passcode required	Yes
Simple passcodes allowed	No
Minimum length	6
Max failed attempts	10
Max inactivity	5 minutes

Figure 11-29 *The Details of the Passcode Policy Shown on an iOS Device*

Last, notice that the slider for **Erase Data** (**Settings > Touch ID & Passcode**) has changed to enabled and is grayed out, as shown in Figure 11-30. This confirms that the profile is in effect.

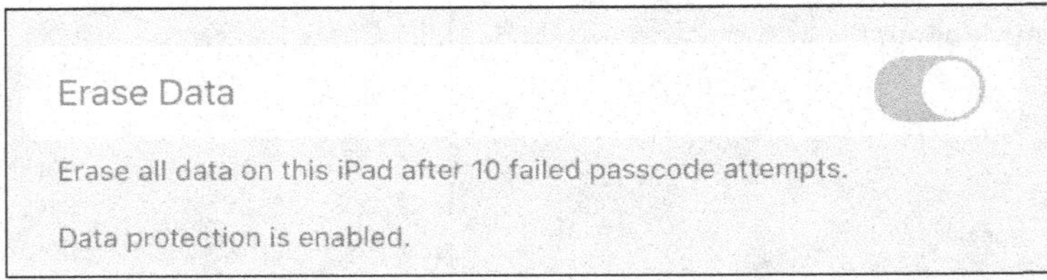

Figure 11-30 *The Erase Data Setting on iOS with the Passcode Policy Applied as Part of a Systems Manager Profile*

You've now completed the configuration and verification of a passcode policy payload in Meraki Systems Manager.

Disk Encryption

NIST 800-53 Access Control 19 requires disk encryption on mobile devices (either full device or container based). For Apple devices, this feature is referred to as *data protection* and is enabled by default. You can check this in iOS 17.2+ by navigating to **Settings > Face ID & Passcode.** Scroll down and the last line will read "Data protection is enabled." Likewise, with Android, as long as you set a PIN on the device, the storage is encrypted. So, in summary, you won't find a setting in Systems Manager to enforce disk encryption on mobile devices because it's not necessary. However, there is a settings payload for macOS FileVault to force Mac devices to use disk encryption, as shown in Figure 11-31. If disk encryption is required for Macs, you can also audit compliance as part of a Systems Manager policy.

Preventing the Installation of Banned Apps

Using a Restriction settings payload, you are able to hide certain apps so that users cannot access them. In the case of iOS devices, this setting requires devices to be "supervised," which means using Apple's Automated Device Enrollment (ADE) program. You can enable supervision with an app called Apple Configurator, but it's not expected that it would be workable with a large fleet of devices. For more information on iOS supervision, refer to https://documentation.meraki.com/SM/Profiles_and_Settings/iOS_Supervision.

For supervised devices, you can also prevent users from using the App Store or installing apps from the App Store. This would be another way to allow only sanctioned applications on devices.

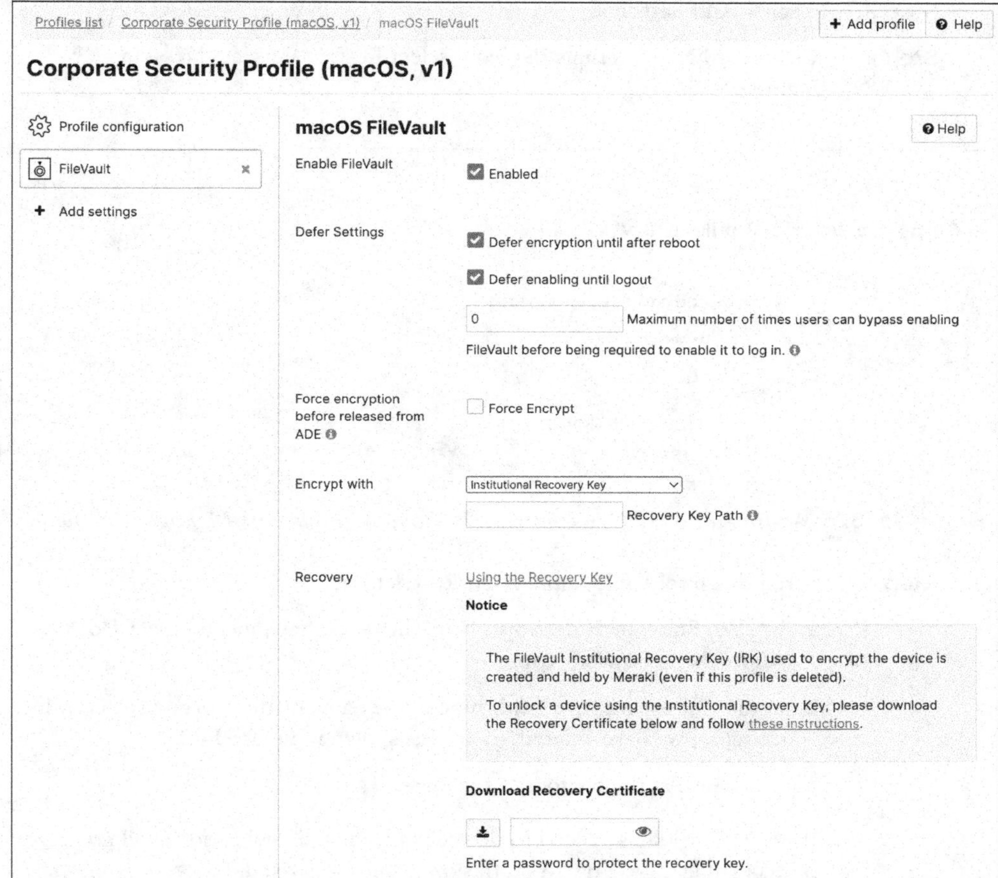

Figure 11-31 *Configuring macOS FileVault as Part of a Systems Manager Profile*

For non-supervised devices, it is possible to restrict apps based on their content (age) rating.

The TikTok application is on the application block list as part of the corporate security policy configured earlier in this chapter. We now configure a Restrictions payload to enforce this policy.

Follow these steps to configure a Restrictions policy as part of a Systems Manager profile:

Step 1. Navigate to **Systems Manager > Settings** (under Manage).

Step 2. Click the name of an existing profile where you wish to add a passcode policy or click **+ Add Profile** to create a new one.

Step 3. Click **+ Add Settings.**

Step 4. Under **Add New Settings Payload**, select **Restrictions**, as shown in Figure 11-32.

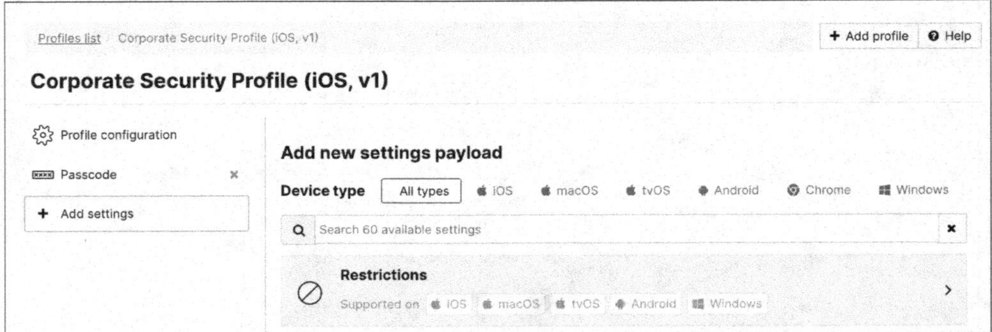

Figure 11-32 *Adding a Restrictions Settings Payload to a Systems Manager Profile*

Step 5. Scroll down to **Apple Supervised Restrictions.**

a. Next to **Show or Hide Apps**, from the drop-down menu, select **Do Not Allow the Following Apps.**

b. In the **Choose an App** field, type in the name of the app and select it. In this case, we have entered **TikTok**, as shown in Figure 11-33.

c. Click **Save** at the bottom of the page.

When the profile is synced to devices, the banned applications will no longer be accessible. If you try to do this on a non-supervised device, all non-system apps will be hidden.

You can verify the profile is working by searching for the banned app on an affected device. If the profile is pushed from Systems Manager, you will also see a Managed App restriction listed, as shown in Figure 11-34. (On iOS, navigate to **Settings > General > VPN & Device Management > Meraki Systems Manager**.)

At this point, you've completed the configuration of the various payloads necessary to support security requirements identified across industry best practices. There is a lot more that you can do with Systems Manager profiles. To find out more, visit https://documentation.meraki.com/SM/Profiles_and_Settings/Configuration_Settings_Payloads.

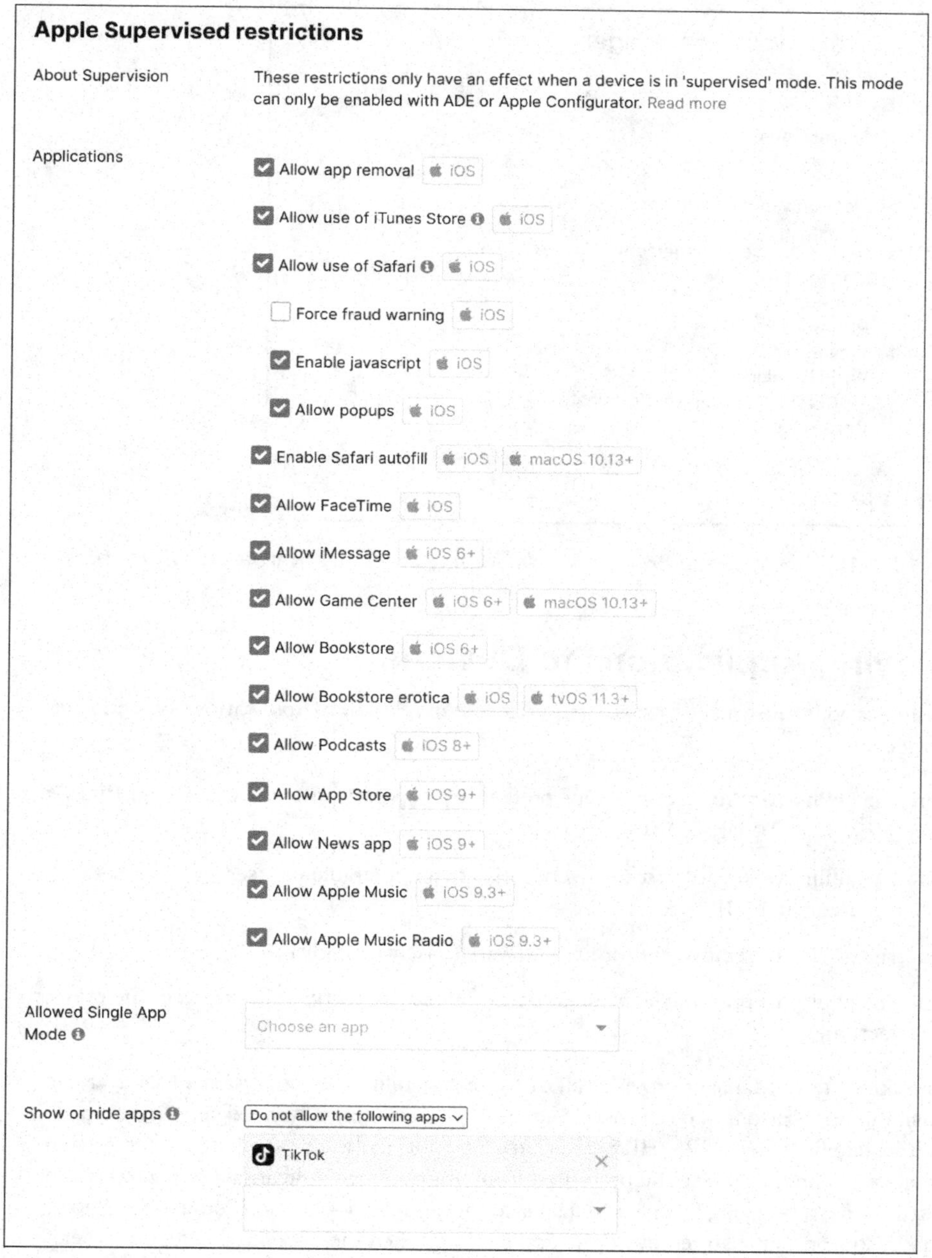

Apple Supervised restrictions

About Supervision — These restrictions only have an effect when a device is in 'supervised' mode. This mode can only be enabled with ADE or Apple Configurator. Read more

Applications

- [x] Allow app removal — iOS
- [x] Allow use of iTunes Store — iOS
- [x] Allow use of Safari — iOS
  - [ ] Force fraud warning — iOS
  - [x] Enable javascript — iOS
  - [x] Allow popups — iOS
- [x] Enable Safari autofill — iOS, macOS 10.13+
- [x] Allow FaceTime — iOS
- [x] Allow iMessage — iOS 6+
- [x] Allow Game Center — iOS 6+, macOS 10.13+
- [x] Allow Bookstore — iOS 6+
- [x] Allow Bookstore erotica — iOS, tvOS 11.3+
- [x] Allow Podcasts — iOS 8+
- [x] Allow App Store — iOS 9+
- [x] Allow News app — iOS 9+
- [x] Allow Apple Music — iOS 9.3+
- [x] Allow Apple Music Radio — iOS 9.3+

Allowed Single App Mode — Choose an app

Show or hide apps — Do not allow the following apps

TikTok

Figure 11-33 *Restricting the TikTok Application by Using a Restrictions Payload on a Systems Manager Profile*

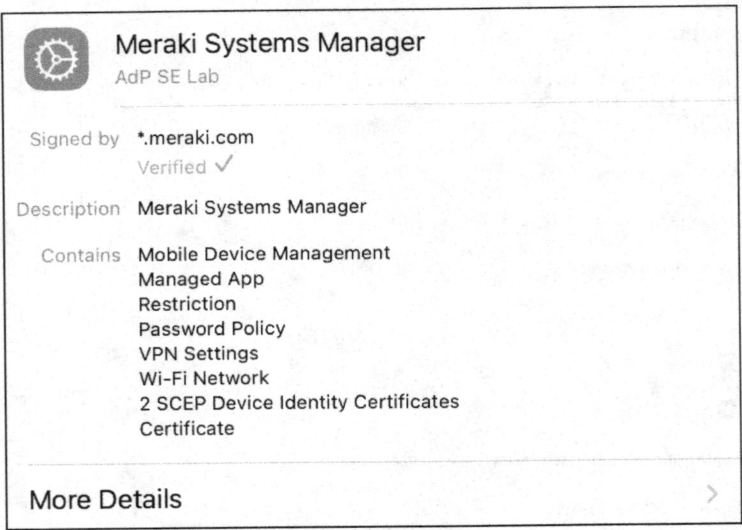

Figure 11-34 *Verifying the Presence of the Managed App Policy on an iOS Profile*

Deploying Applications to Devices

Organizations must meet four key requirements in relation to applications on end-user devices:

- The ability to install applications on devices to detect potential cybersecurity events (NIST CSF 2.0 DE.CM-03)
- The ability to ensure that these controls are not alterable by users (PCI DSS 4.0 requirement 1.5.1)
- The ability to remove end-of-life software (Essential Eight)
- The ability to prevent the installation of end-of-life software (covered in the previous section)

Meraki Systems Manager provides all of these capabilities. First, Systems Manager can push out applications such as Cisco Secure Client, bringing advanced security capabilities like host-based IPS (HIPS), NetFlow, and anti-malware capabilities to end-user devices. Second, users can be prevented from uninstalling applications or changing their settings. Last, by using Systems Manager to manage the applications on users' devices, administrators can also remove these applications when they go end of life, are superseded, or are no longer licensed, mitigating further compliance issues.

Follow these steps to push applications to devices enrolled with Meraki Systems Manager:

Step 1. Log in to Meraki Dashboard (https://dashboard.meraki.com).

Step 2. Navigate to **Systems Manager** > **Apps** (under Monitor).

Step 3. If the application you want to deploy is not listed, click the **+ Add App** button in the top right, as shown in Figure 11-35.

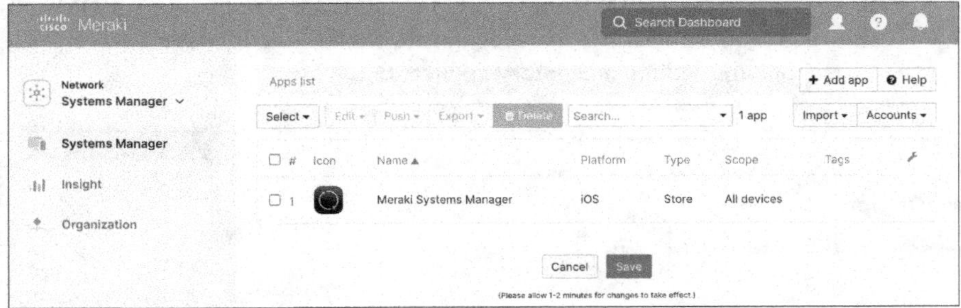

Figure 11-35 *The Apps Page in Meraki Systems Manager*

Step 4. Click the appropriate **App Platform**; as you can see, all the major vendors are represented. In this case, we're working with Apple devices, so **iOS** has been selected. For this example (see Figure 11-36), we're installing an app that can be found on the Apple App store, so **App Store App** has been selected. Using an app store is the typical option; however, you also have the option to install apps directly.

Click **Next.**

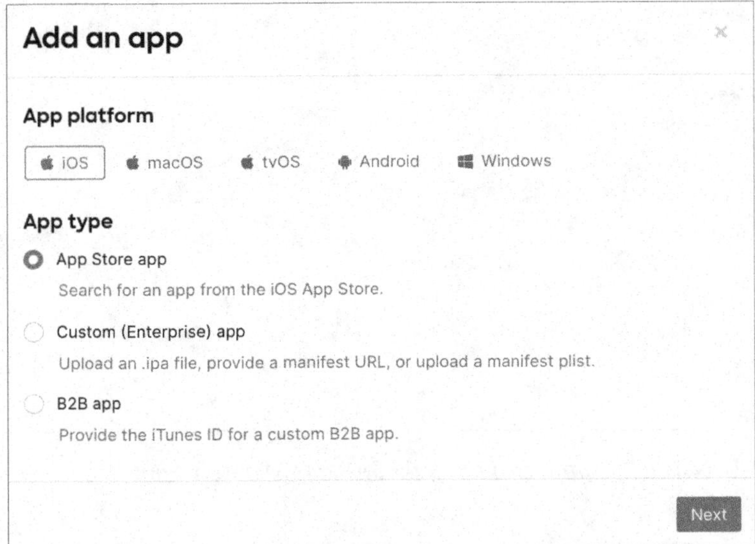

Figure 11-36 *Selecting the Source of an App on the Add an App Window in Systems Manager*

Step 5. Search for and select the name of the app that you want to publish. In this example, we're using Systems Manager to push out **Cisco Secure Client**. You can also choose the country for the app store you wish to download the app from. This will be relevant if the app is available only in certain locations.

We recommend selecting **Keep App Up to Date** and **Remove with MDM**, as shown in Figure 11-37. We also recommend unchecking **Removable** to prevent users from uninstalling mandatory applications.

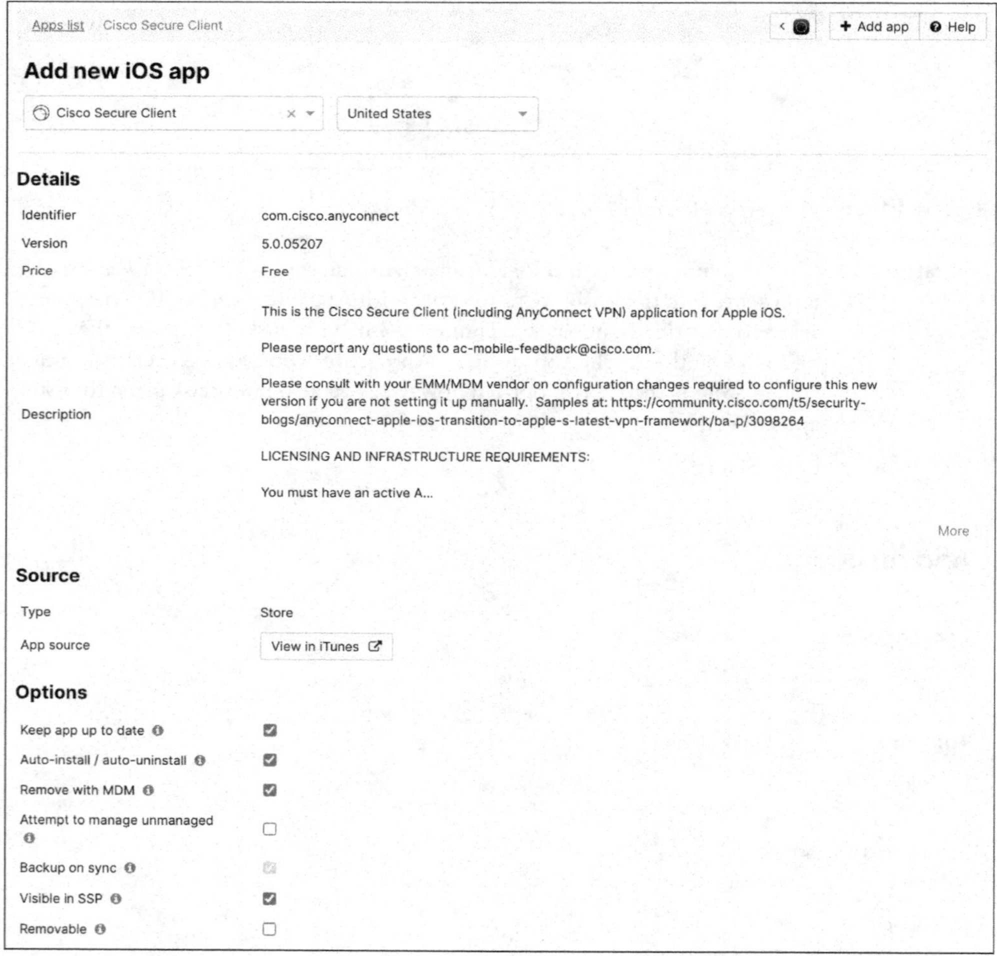

Figure 11-37 *The Add New iOS App Page in Meraki Systems Manager Showing Cisco Secure Client*

Step 6. Staying on the **Add New iOS App** page, scroll down to reveal the remaining settings.

a. To facilitate silent installs and avoid users being prompted to log in to the app store, choose a relevant **Purchase Method.** You can find more information on Apple's Volume Purchase Program (VPP) at https://documentation.meraki.com/SM/Apps_and_Software/Apple_Volume_Purchase_Program_(VPP) or contact your Apple specialist.

b. From the **Scope** drop-down menu, select the devices that need to receive this app. In this example, we have selected **All Devices**, as shown in Figure 11-38.

c. Click **Save** to apply these changes.

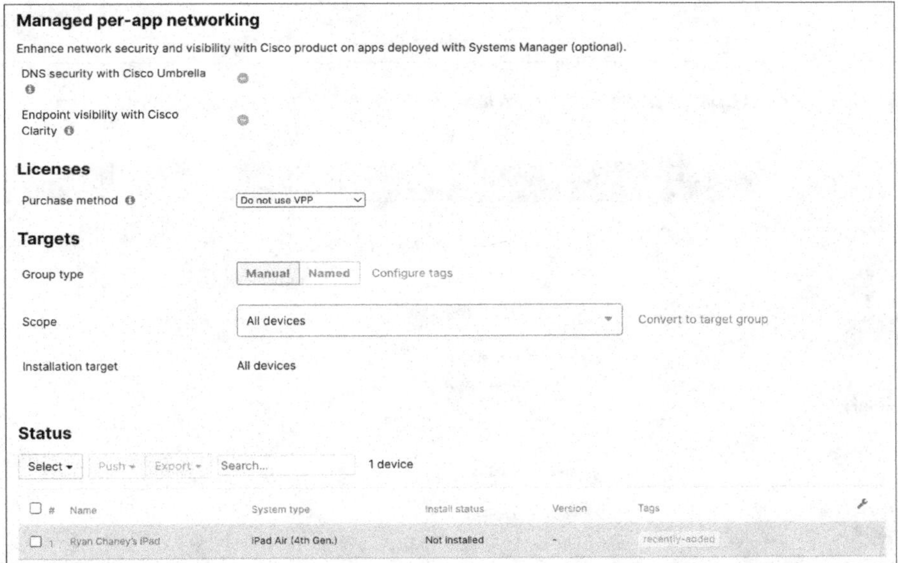

Figure 11-38 *Setting the Scope for a New App in Meraki Systems Manager*

Step 7. Click **Apps List** at the top of the page to take you back to the Apps page. On the **Apps** page, you can see that the Cisco Secure Client app has been added to the list with the correct scope, as shown in Figure 11-39.

Step 8. To push out the app, select it by checking the box next to its name. Then, from the **Push** drop-down menu, select **Push to All in Scope** and click **Confirm**, as shown in Figure 11-40.

If the Purchase method was not set, users will receive a notification on their devices (see Figure 11-41) to start the app installation. Users can cancel the app installation; however, Systems Manager will automatically retry later. Otherwise, the app will silently install, and its icon will show up on the device next to the existing ones.

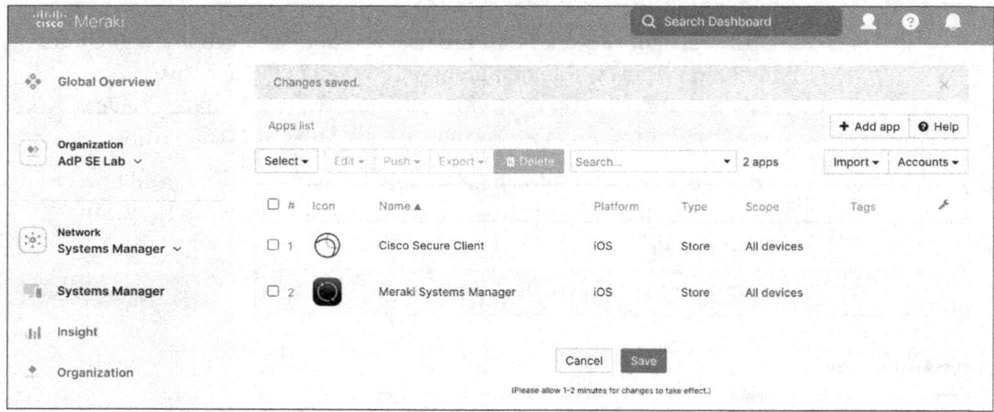

Figure 11-39 *The Apps Page in Systems Manager After Adding Cisco Secure Client*

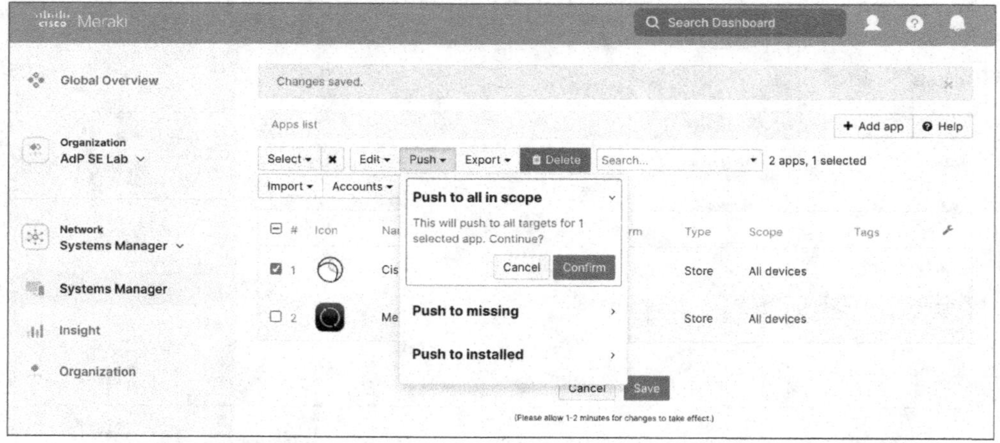

Figure 11-40 *Pushing an App to Devices from Meraki Systems Manager*

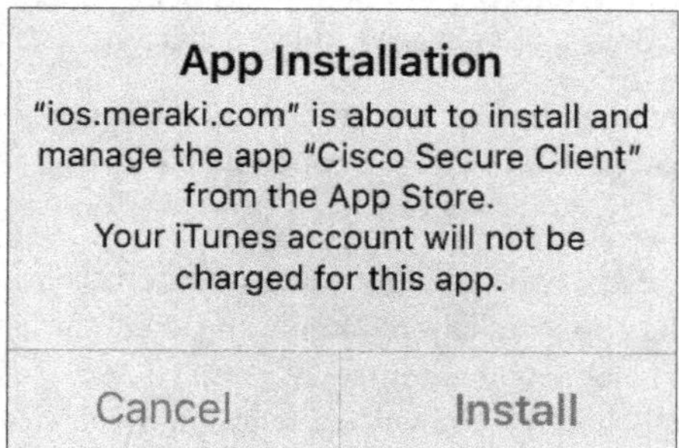

Figure 11-41 *The App Installation Notification for Cisco Secure Client on iOS*

You've now completed the steps to push out an application to a device using Meraki Systems Manager. To verify the app installation, in the case of iOS devices, navigate to **Settings > General > VPN & Device Management > Meraki Systems Manager** (see Figure 11-42) and click **Apps**. This screen lists the apps that have been pushed from Systems Manager, confirming that the app has been successfully installed (see Figure 11-43).

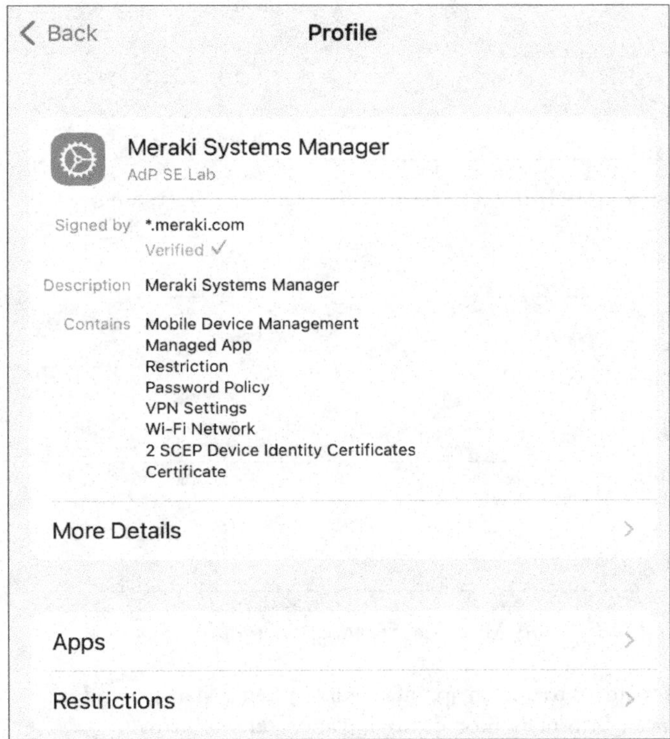

Figure 11-42 *An iOS Device Management Profile Where Apps Have Been Installed*

> **Note** Cisco AnyConnect is in the process of being rebranded; this is why the app name is shown as AnyConnect and not Cisco Secure Connect.

It's worth noting that the corporate security policy created earlier required devices to have Cisco Secure Client installed to be compliant. Previously, this device alerted because it was not compliant, but since pushing out the app, this device has come back into a compliant state, as shown in Figure 11-44.

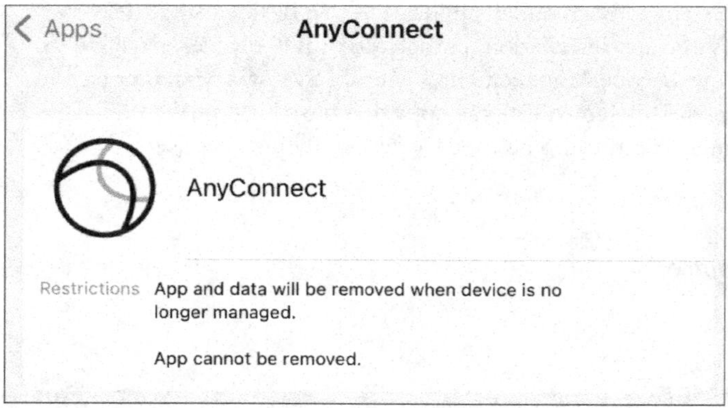

Figure 11-43 *Confirmation That the App Was Successfully Installed by Systems Manager on an iOS Device*

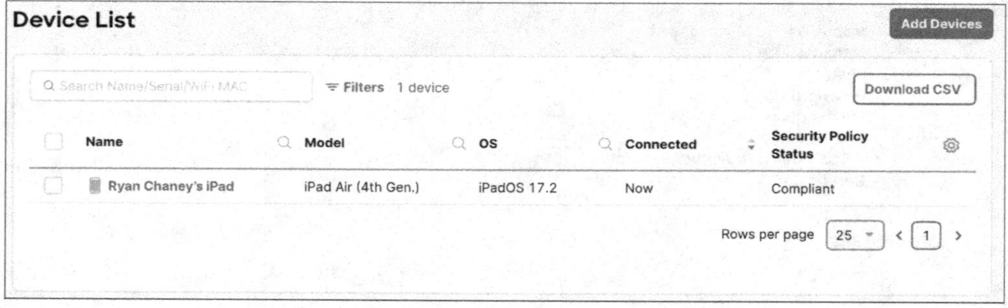

Figure 11-44 *The Devices List in Systems Manager Showing a Compliant Device*

You've completed the steps required to add an app in Meraki Systems Manager and push it out to devices. For more information on deploying apps, refer to https://documentation.meraki.com/SM/Apps_and_Software/Deploying_Store_Apps_for_iOS%2F%2FmacOS_and_Android.

We recommend that you also check out the Trusted Endpoints integration with Cisco Duo, which utilizes the Systems Manager capabilities discussed in this chapter. Cisco Duo's Trusted Endpoints feature offers an alternative to device certificates for determining the trustworthiness of user devices. The net effect of this is that Duo can verify which devices are trusted, allowing administrators to then permit or deny access based on whether devices are trusted or not. Systems Manager is utilized to

- Push out the Duo Mobile and Duo Desktop application to devices
- Configure the Duo app with the Trusted Endpoints configuration key and Trusted Endpoints identifier
- Provide its inventory data to Duo via an API integration

For instructions on how to configure Cisco Duo's Trusted Endpoints feature, refer to https://duo.com/docs/trusted-endpoints-meraki.

Pushing Operating System Updates to Devices

Ensuring that devices are running up-to-date operating systems reduces the risk of unpatched and end-of-life software. Security policies provide a way to track whether devices are running current releases. Where devices are not running a suitable operating system version, OS updates can be pushed to them via Systems Manager. As mentioned at the opening of this chapter, Cisco Duo can work hand in hand with Systems Manager to warn users of the need to upgrade and to block access where there is noncompliance.

To support OS updates, iOS devices must be enrolled with ADE (Automated Device Enrollment) and be "supervised."

Follow these steps to push out operating system updates to devices enrolled with Meraki Systems Manager:

Step 1. Log in to Meraki Dashboard (https://dashboard.meraki.com).

Step 2. Navigate to **Systems Manager** > **Devices** (under Monitor).

Step 3. Select the devices you want to update by checking the box next to their name. Select **Install Available OS Updates** from the **Command** drop-down menu, as shown in Figure 11-45.

Step 4. An **Install Available OS Updates** pane slides out from the right.

- **a.** Choose the **OS Version** to upgrade to.
- **b.** On iOS, updates are a two-step process where the software is downloaded to the device first and then the install is started later. Leave **Install Action** as the default, to first download the software and repeat this process to kick off the upgrade. Users will receive a message prompting them that their organization requires an upgrade. The update can be deferred up to three times before it must be completed to continue using the device.
- **c.** Click **Update** to start.

Step 5. Add the **OS Update Status** to the table of devices on the **Devices List** page. To do this, click the sprocket icon on the right and check **OS Update Status.** Refresh the page to see the progress of the updates for devices in the OS Update Status column.

At this point in the chapter, you've completed the steps necessary to push out OS updates using Meraki Systems Manager. For more information on installing OS updates with Systems Manager, refer to https://documentation.meraki.com/SM/Apps_and_Software/Deploying_OS_Updates_with_Systems_Manager. This support page from Apple also has additional helpful detail on the install actions and the software update process in general: https://support.apple.com/en-au/guide/deployment/depafd2fad80/web.

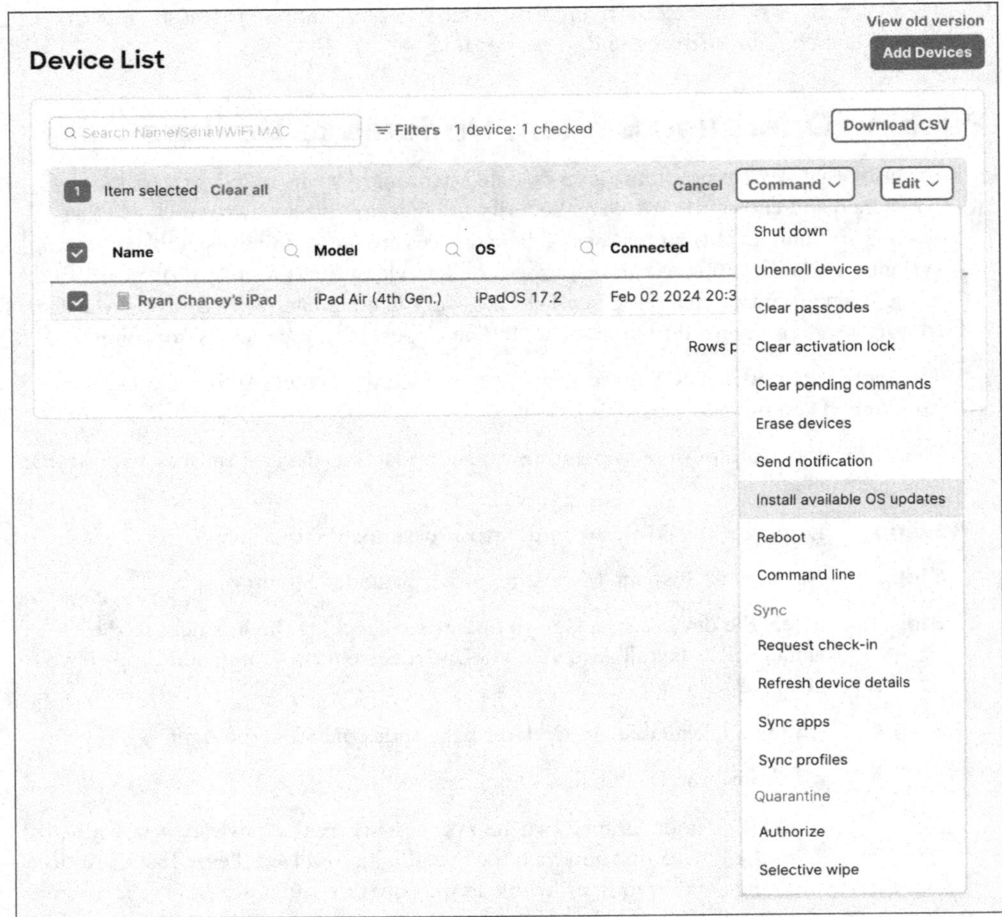

Figure 11-45 *Pushing Out OS Updates to Devices Using Meraki Systems Manager*

Summary

This chapter focused on Systems Manager, a fully featured cloud-hosted mobile device management solution that is part of the Meraki Cloud platform. In this chapter, we demonstrated how Systems Manager makes implementing secure networks seamless for users by utilizing profiles to preconfigure Wi-Fi and VPN settings and by pushing certificates to devices. Additionally, using profiles, Systems Manager ensures that devices meet the requirements of industry best practices, such as requiring PINs and screen lock. Systems Manager is highly complementary with Cisco Duo, with the combination working in tandem to meet the objectives of an organization's corporate security policy.

Notes

[1] Cisco Meraki. (2024, January 12). Apple MDM Push Certificate. https://documentation.meraki.com/SM/Device_Enrollment/Apple_MDM_Push_Certificate

Further Reading

Android. (2024, March 18). Device Management Overview. https://source.android.com/docs/devices/admin

Apple. (2021, February 18). Data Protection Overview. https://support.apple.com/en-au/guide/security/secf6276da8a/web

Apple. (2023, September 29). Use Automated Device Enrollment. https://support.apple.com/en-us/HT204142

Cisco. (2020, August 16). Integrate Cisco Meraki Systems Manager. https://www.cisco.com/c/en/us/td/docs/security/ise/UEM-MDM-Server-Integration/b_MDM_UEM_Servers_CiscoISE/m_integrate-meraki-systems-manager-with-ise.html

Cisco Meraki. (2020, October 6). Managed and Unmanaged Apps. https://documentation.meraki.com/SM/Apps_and_Software/Managed_and_Unmanaged_Apps#:~:text=A%20managed%20app%20is%20one,being%20deployed%20through%20Systems%20Manager

Cisco Meraki. (2022, June 8). Device Enrollment. https://documentation.meraki.com/SM/Device_Enrollment

Cisco Meraki. (2022, October 21). iOS Supervision. https://documentation.meraki.com/SM/Profiles_and_Settings/iOS_Supervision

Cisco Meraki. (2023, October 26). Android Enterprise Deployment Guide. https://documentation.meraki.com/SM/Deployment_Guides/Android_Enterprise_Deployment_Guide

Cisco Meraki. (2023, May 11). Apple Volume Purchase Program (VPP). https://documentation.meraki.com/SM/Apps_and_Software/Apple_Volume_Purchase_Program_(VPP)

Cisco Meraki. (2023, September 19). Certificate-based Wi-Fi authentication with Systems Manager and Meraki APs. https://documentation.meraki.com/General_Administration/Cross-Platform_Content/Certificate-based_Wi-Fi_authentication_with_Systems_Manager_and_Meraki_APs

Cisco Meraki. (2023, November 1). SM – Endpoint Management. https://documentation.meraki.com/SM

Cisco Meraki. (2023, December 19). Deploying OS Updates with Systems Manager. https://documentation.meraki.com/SM/Apps_and_Software/Deploying_OS_Updates_with_Systems_Manager

Cisco Meraki. (2024, January 11). Certificates Payload (Pushing Certificates). https://documentation.meraki.com/SM/Profiles_and_Settings/Certificates_Payload_(Pushing_Certificates)

Cisco Meraki. (2024, January 20). iOS Enrollment. https://documentation.meraki.com/SM/Device_Enrollment/iOS_Enrollment

CSF Tools. (n.d.a). AC-11: Device Lock. https://csf.tools/reference/nist-sp-800-53/r5/ac/ac-11/

CSF Tools. (n.d.b). AC-7(2): Purge or Wipe Mobile Device. https://csf.tools/reference/nist-sp-800-53/r5/ac/ac-7/ac-7-2/

CSF Tools (n.d.c). DE.CM-3: Personnel Activity Is Monitored to Detect Potential Cybersecurity Events. https://csf.tools/reference/nist-cybersecurity-framework/v1-1/de/de-cm/de-cm-3/

Kok, C. & Carter, K. (2023). *Protect Endpoints On the Zero-Trust Journey with Meraki Systems Manager*. Cisco Live. https://www.ciscolive.com/c/dam/r/ciscolive/global-event/docs/2023/pdf/BRKMER-1005.pdf

Chapter 12

Physical Security

In this chapter, you learn the following:

- Why physical security is an important part of IT security
- The steps Meraki takes to implement security in its MV product range
- How to monitor live video for events and how to find footage of events that have occurred in the past
- How to export video and snapshots to provide evidence in an investigation

In this chapter, we cover the capabilities of Meraki's smart camera product line that relate to an IT security use case, such as monitoring a data center. IT equipment can be expensive, making it a target for thieves looking to resell it. An example of just such an incident occurred in 2006, when UK ISP EasyNet had a break-in at a major central office (CO). Thieves literally pulled live networking equipment out of racks and took it away in a van. When operations staff investigated, they found the routers were simply ... missing. True story.

Industry best practice includes requirements related to the physical security of infrastructure and data. For example, NIST 800-53 PE-6 requires monitoring of physical access at sites where systems reside, thereby enabling organizations to detect and respond to incidents. Similarly, PCI DSS 4.0 requires that ingress and egress to sensitive areas are monitored with video cameras. Lastly, FIPS 200 also has requirements to limit physical access to information systems. Given a big enough incentive, if it's easier to just walk into a facility and physically take the data or the equipment it sits on, then criminals will try to do that.

Aside from just protecting assets and data, organizations must implement measures to improve physical security because doing so helps to deter crime and improve workplace safety. In the case of retail or logistics, improving security will help to mitigate product loss. If criminals think someone is watching them, or that they're more likely to get caught at your premises, they'll carry out their activities somewhere else. Certain industries, such as mining, infrastructure, and construction, report the frequency of and time lost to injuries in their annual reports, meaning safety has visibility at the board level. Video monitoring also increases workplace safety because staff are more likely to follow workplace safety rules if they know the "boss" is watching.

Meraki's MV smart camera product line utilizes the Meraki Cloud platform just like other Meraki devices. One of the key differentiators with Meraki's smart cameras compared to traditional CCTV systems is their extensibility. Meraki cameras can identify objects such as people or vehicles and make this data available through the Dashboard API. Additionally, the video itself is available to third-party applications via Real-Time Streaming Protocol (RTSP). This opens a wide range of use cases that are actively being developed. Today, you'll find Meraki cameras installed in countless locations, such as offices, schools, retail stores, and hospitals.

Meraki MV Security Cameras

Meraki has a range of both indoor and outdoor smart cameras. Because they do change over time, please refer to the Meraki website for the latest models: https://meraki.cisco.com/products/smart-cameras/models/. For all documentation, including installation and configuration on the MV product line, refer to https://documentation.meraki.com/MV.

Privacy

Meraki's smart cameras include a large number of features to maintain privacy in relation to video content. Meraki smart cameras inherit the same hardware and software trust model as other Meraki devices. This includes the following:

- Video is encrypted at rest as well as in transit. Video leaves the device only when being viewed or archived using the MV Cloud Archive feature.
- Access to view video is restricted using strong authentication controls, such as role-based access control (RBAC) and can be further restricted with multifactor authentication.

In addition, Meraki smart cameras feature video-specific privacy controls, as follows:

- The privacy windows feature allows administrators to block sensitive areas from a camera's feed while recording other areas. For details on how to configure privacy windows, see https://documentation.meraki.com/MV/Initial_Configuration/Privacy_Windows.
- Likewise, audio recording can be disabled if required by local regulation.

For more information on Meraki's hardware and software trust model, refer to Chapter 3, "Meraki Dashboard and Trust."

Monitoring Video

To monitor a large facility efficiently, organizations need an easy way to monitor multiple live cameras. Video walls support the streaming of up to 16 live camera feeds and are the primary way for a camera operator to monitor footage from multiple cameras. Once cameras are configured, a camera operator can access video walls in the following ways:

- **Via the Meraki Vision portal** (see Figure 12-1), which is specifically designed for the needs of camera operators. You can access the Meraki Vision portal at https://vision.meraki.com/ or by navigating to **Cameras > Meraki Vision Portal** in Meraki Dashboard. This is the recommended way for organizations to access, search, and export video footage.

Figure 12-1 *A Video Wall Showing a Retail Location in Meraki Vision*

- **Via Meraki Dashboard.** To locate video walls, simply navigate to **Cameras > Video Wall** (under Monitor), as shown in Figure 12-2.
- **On Apple TVs using the Meraki Display app.** Meraki Display is available from the App Store on Apple TV (which requires a Meraki Display license). The Meraki Display app is ideal for public spaces where you want to let visitors know they are being monitored. To force Apple TVs to be used only for Meraki Display, you can set them to single app mode using a Meraki Systems Manager profile.

Figure 12-2 *A Video Wall Showing a Retail Location in Meraki Dashboard*

- **Via the Meraki app on iPhone and iPad.** You can find the app by accessing https://apps.apple.com/us/app/meraki/id693056161 or by simply searching for "Meraki" in the Apple App Store.

Where an organization has multiple video walls configured, video wall rotation can be enabled to cycle through selected video walls based on a configured time interval. To start video wall rotation in Meraki Vision, navigate to **Video Walls**, and then at the bottom of the screen, click the blue **Start** button, as shown in Figure 12-3. The video wall rotation feature works with video walls within the same network and across multiple networks. Click the **Edit** button under **Video Wall Rotation** to set the time interval and the video walls that are of interest.

> **Note** For more information on multinetwork video walls, refer to https://documentation.meraki.com/MV/Viewing_Video/Multi_Network_Video_Walls_on_Vision_Portal_%5BBETA%5D.

For instructions on how to configure video walls, see https://documentation.meraki.com/MV/Advanced_Configuration/Video_Walls.

Figure 12-3 *The Video Wall Rotation Feature in Meraki Vision*

Motion Alerts

One way to bring important events to the attention of camera operators is using motion alerts. Motion alerts make it easy to add an extra level of monitoring for sensitive areas. For example, camera operators can be notified when a person or a vehicle has entered an area. Alerts can be tailored to a camera's entire field of view or just a defined area of interest. Being proactive plays a big part in keeping operations secure. You should think about how motion alerts could be operationalized as part of your security operations center (SOC).

Follow these steps to configure motion alerts in Meraki Dashboard:

Step 1. Log in to Meraki Dashboard (https://dashboard.meraki.com).

Step 2. Navigate to **Cameras > Cameras** (under Monitor).

Step 3. Click the camera name for which you want to enable motion alerts; then click the **Settings** tab. Next, click the **Motion Alerts** tab just above the video image, as shown in Figure 12-4.

Step 4. Next to **Alerting Schedule**, enable motion alerts by selecting **Always.** You can also set a schedule if you prefer.

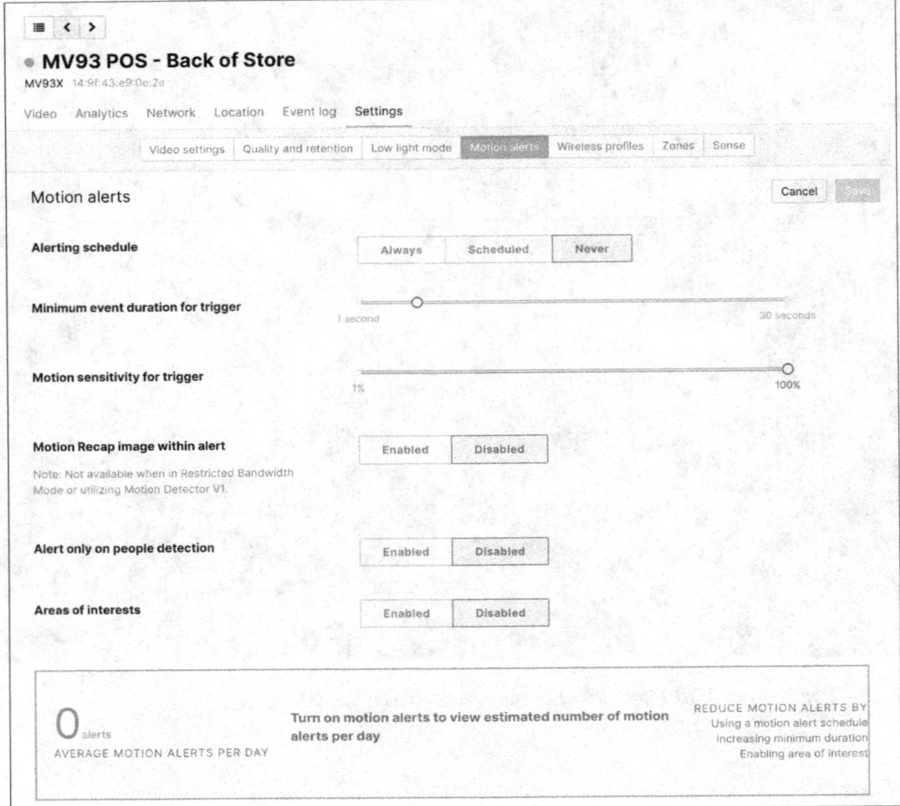

Figure 12-4 *The Motion Alerts Settings Page in Meraki Dashboard*

Step 5. (Optional) If you are interested only in detecting people, click **Enabled** next to **Alert Only on People Detection.** If you are interested in alerting on only a particular area of the frame, next to **Areas of Interests**, click **Enabled.** The video from this camera will appear below. You can draw a box to highlight an area of interest. You also can select multiple areas if required.

This step also enables Dashboard to determine the approximate number of motion alerts per day that the current settings will generate. Use **Minimum Event Duration for Trigger** and **Motion Sensitivity for Trigger** to reduce the number of alerts.

Step 6. Click **Save.** To quickly move to the next camera to configure, click one of the arrow buttons above the camera name.

Notifications can be sent for motion alerts just like any other alerts. Alerts appear in Meraki Dashboard in the network-wide event log and also under **Sensors > Event Log.** To configure alerting for motion alerts, navigate to **Network-wide > Alerts**, add your recipients to **Custom Recipients for Motion Alerts** (see Figure 12-5), and then click

Save. Alerts can be sent via SMS, email, and webhooks. To learn more about configuring alerts, refer to Chapter 6, "Security Operations."

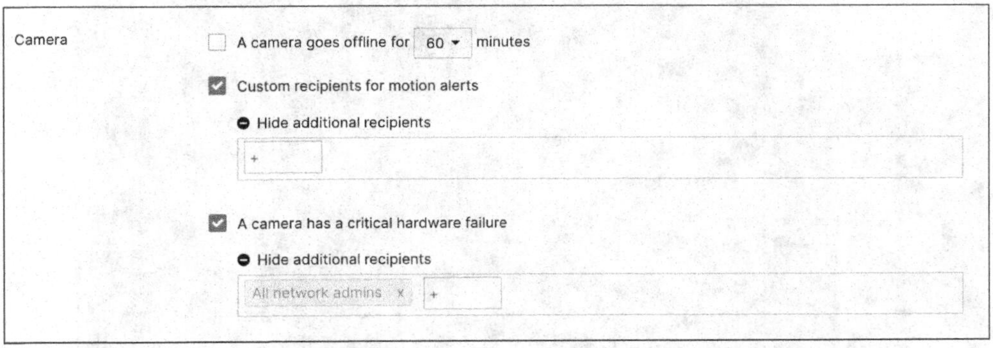

Figure 12-5 *Configuring Notifications for Motion Alerts in Meraki Dashboard*

For more details on configuring motion alerts, refer to https://documentation.meraki.com/MV/Advanced_Configuration/Motion_Alerts.

Motion Search

A common everyday task for camera operators is searching through videos to find footage of an incident or footage from a particular time period. Something might be missing from a secure area, for example, and the operator is trying to understand who accessed that room recently. Video footage might also be required as evidence in a police investigation or to support an insurance claim. Unlike they do in '80s cop shows, operators do not have to watch video on fast forward and pause when they notice motion. Meraki smart cameras can search video for motion in a particular area. An operator chooses a time period, frames an area of interest, and then Meraki Vision will return all the video of matching events.

Follow these steps to find footage of incidents using motion search in Meraki Vision:

Step 1. Log in to Meraki Vision (https://vision.meraki.com) and select the network you want to focus on.

Step 2. You should now be on the **Camera** tab. Select a camera of interest. Then click the **Motion** icon in the top-right corner, as shown in Figure 12-6.

Step 3. Select an area in the camera image by clicking and dragging a box covering the area of interest. Here, we highlighted the ladder in the right of the frame to try to find when one of the ladders was moved, as shown in Figure 12-7. Motion search instantly begins returning results on the right.

- **a.** On the Motion search pane, set the time range. Here, we set a time range covering the previous seven days.
- **b.** Click through the results until you find the one with what you're looking for.

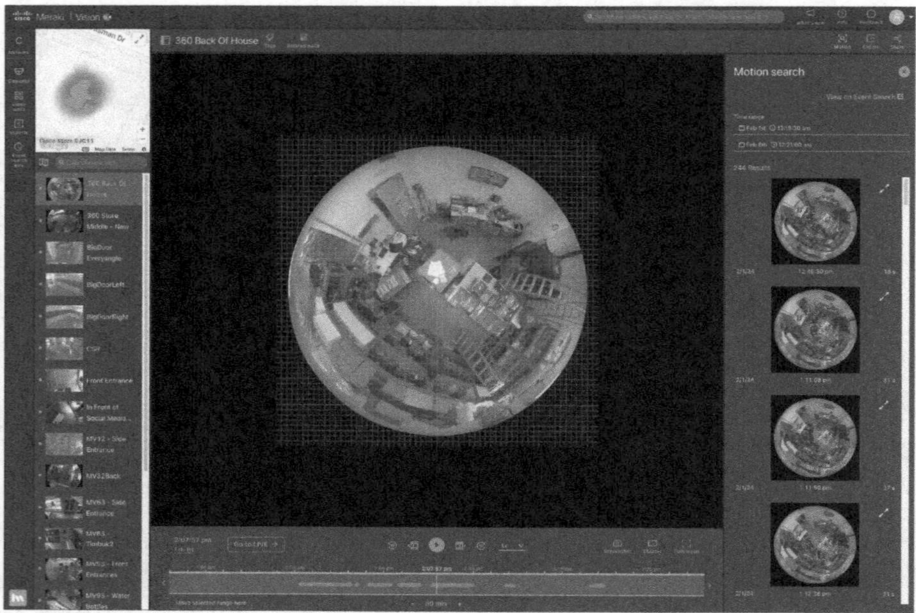

Figure 12-6 *The Cameras Page in Meraki Vision Showing a Live 360-Degree Image*

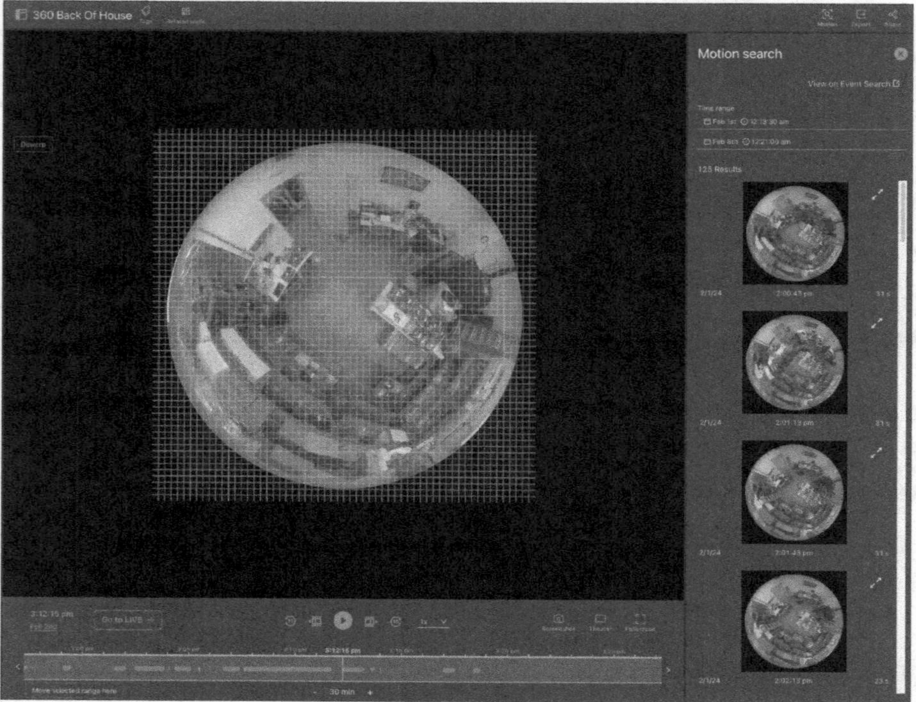

Figure 12-7 *The Cameras Page in Meraki Vision Showing a Search Area Highlighted*

Using the motion recap on the thumbnails, we were quickly able to locate video showing one of the ladders being moved on February 1 at 2:01 p.m., as shown in Figure 12-8.

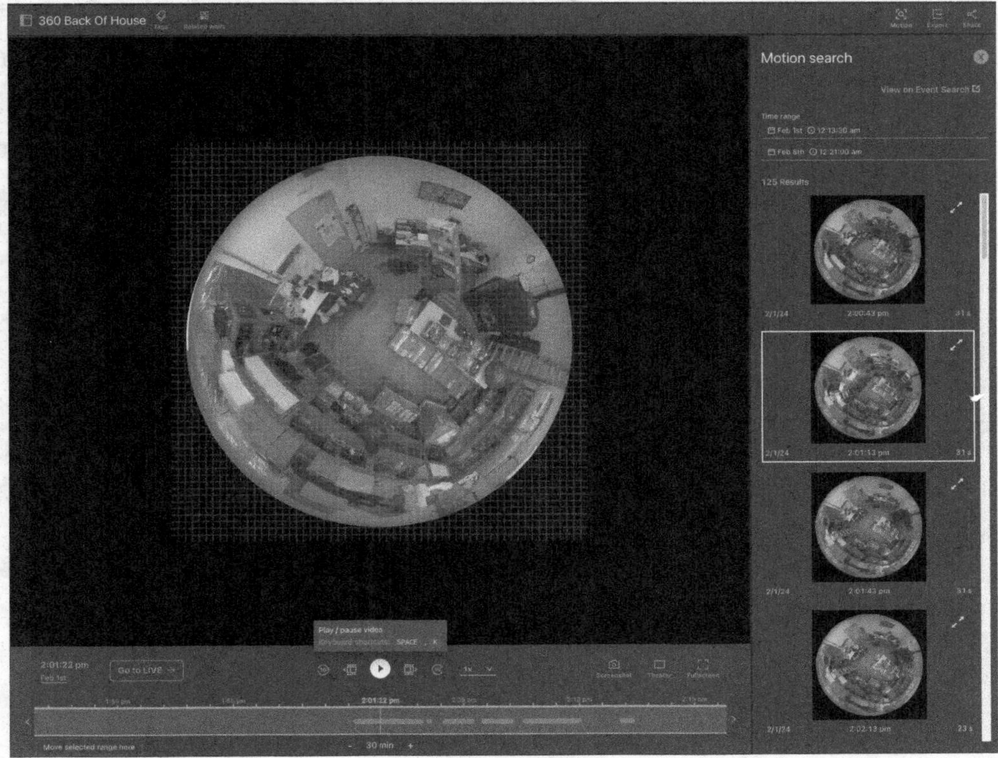

Figure 12-8 *The Motion Search Result Identifying When the Ladder Was Last Moved*

Step 4. From here, you can grab a screenshot using the **Screenshot** button in the lower right of the screen. This saves a .jpg file to your computer with the name of the camera, the date, and the time of the event in its filename.

a. If you want to share a URL of this video, click the **Share** button in the top right of the screen. This will copy a URL to your clipboard for pasting into an email or chat window.

b. You can export a video file using the **Export** button in the top-right corner. The video clip will then be available to download from the Exports page (from the menu on the left side). Figure 12-9 shows where to view the SHA256 checksum on the Exports page. This makes it possible to verify that an exported clip has not been modified since export, thereby providing a chain of custody.

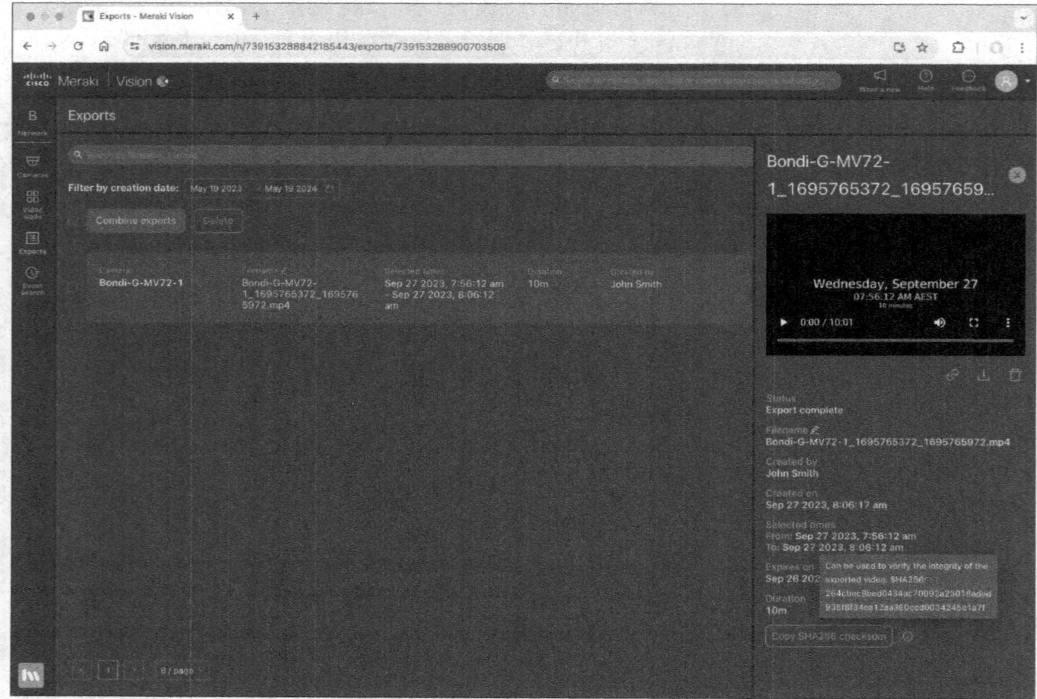

Figure 12-9 *Locating the SHA256 Checksum for an Exported Video in Meraki Vision*

Now you know how to search for footage of events in Meraki Vision and export snapshots, video, and URLs to share with others. It's worthwhile to note that you can also do motion searches on video walls. This capability is handy because it shows what was happening across an entire site at that point in time.

Sensor Sight (Meraki Smart Camera and Sensor Integration)

Any Meraki MT sensor can be linked to a Meraki MV smart camera. Once linked, sensor alerts will include an image from the smart camera and also flag the event in the camera's video timeline. Ideal use cases for this feature include monitoring sensitive areas such as cages or racks in data center locations, or a phone safe in a mobile phone retail store. To enable this capability, a door sensor would be deployed at the entrance-way and linked to an MV camera with a view of this entrance. With the events appearing in the MV video timeline, operators can save time by being able to jump straight to events. Figure 12-10 shows sensor alerts; note the last one for an open door sensor. Clicking the sensor name—in this case, **Small Rolling Door**—takes you to the sensor's device page.

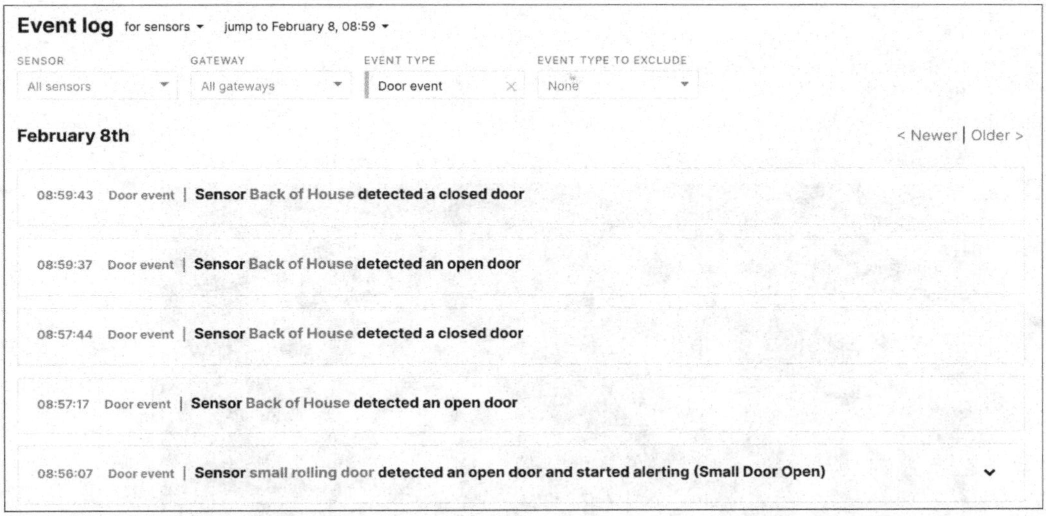

Event log for sensors ▾ jump to February 8, 08:59 ▾

SENSOR	GATEWAY	EVENT TYPE	EVENT TYPE TO EXCLUDE
All sensors	All gateways	Door event	None

February 8th < Newer | Older >

08:59:43 Door event | **Sensor** Back of House **detected a closed door**

08:59:37 Door event | **Sensor** Back of House **detected an open door**

08:57:44 Door event | **Sensor** Back of House **detected a closed door**

08:57:17 Door event | **Sensor** Back of House **detected an open door**

08:56:07 Door event | **Sensor** small rolling door **detected an open door and started alerting (Small Door Open)**

Figure 12-10 *The Event Log Showing Alerts from Meraki MT Sensors in Meraki Dashboard*

Under **Recent Snapshots**, you can see the same alert here, and by clicking **View Snapshot**, you can jump directly to the right camera and right point in time to review this footage (see Figure 12-11).

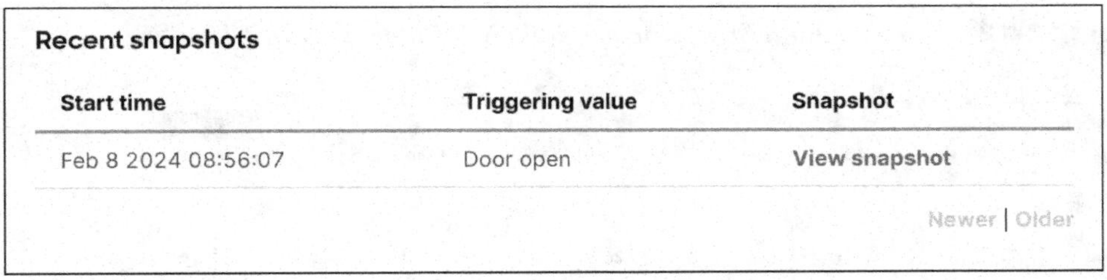

Recent snapshots

Start time	Triggering value	Snapshot
Feb 8 2024 08:56:07	Door open	View snapshot

Newer | Older

Figure 12-11 *The Recent Snapshots Pane from the Devices Page for a Meraki Sensor*

In this example, there is a door sensor on a roller door at the entrance to a retail location. The alert was triggered by a staff member opening the store for the day. In the MV video timeline, shown underneath the video image (see Figure 12-12), vertical bars indicate where there are sensor alerts.

> **Tip** In Meraki Dashboard you can see the linked MV cameras on the sensor list page by enabling the **Related MV** column using the sprocket icon (see Figure 12-13).

Figure 12-12 *A Sensor Alert Shown on a Meraki MV Camera's Video Timeline*

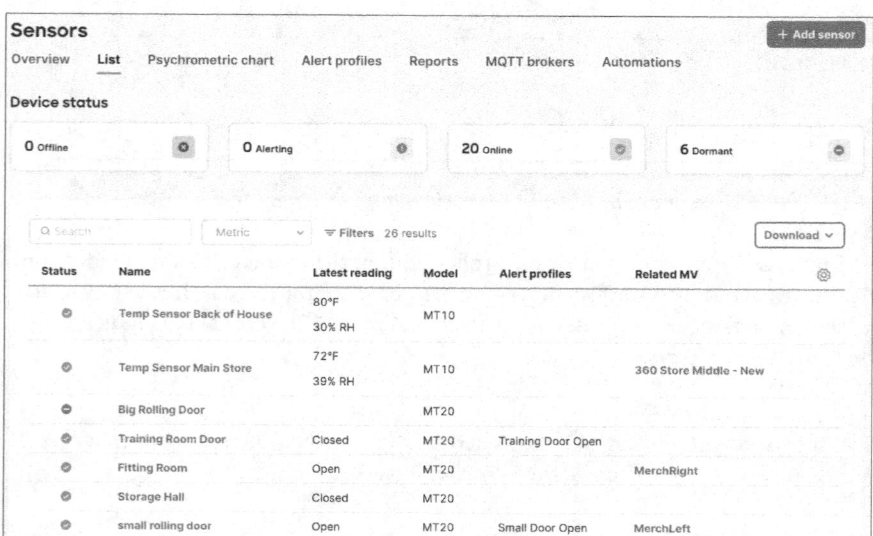

Status	Name	Latest reading	Model	Alert profiles	Related MV
	Temp Sensor Back of House	80°F 30% RH	MT10		
	Temp Sensor Main Store	72°F 39% RH	MT10		360 Store Middle - New
	Big Rolling Door		MT20		
	Training Room Door	Closed	MT20	Training Door Open	
	Fitting Room	Open	MT20		MerchRight
	Storage Hall	Closed	MT20		
	small rolling door	Open	MT20	Small Door Open	MerchLeft

Figure 12-13 *The Sensors Page in Dashboard Showing a List of Meraki Sensors and Their Related Meraki MV Camera*

For more details on configuring the Sensor Sight feature, refer to https://documentation.meraki.com/MT/MT_General_Articles/Sensor_Sight.

Summary

Often overlooked when thinking of cybersecurity, physical security is a key requirement of IT security standards. While video feeds are accessible in Meraki Dashboard, Meraki also provides Meraki Vision, a purpose-built graphical user interface for camera operators. Meraki Vision leverages the same Meraki Cloud to bring a distinctly Meraki experience to the monitoring of the physical environment. Focusing on the IT security use case, this chapter described how a camera operator would complete day-to-day tasks using the Meraki Vision portal. These tasks include monitoring video walls, using motion search to look for footage of incidents, and sharing snapshots and video footage. Finally, this chapter covered the integration of Meraki's MT sensor product line with Meraki MV smart cameras, known as Sensor Sight. Sensor Sight enables sensor alerts to be linked to cameras so that operators can jump straight to images of these events. Restricting access to live and historical video could be required for security and/or privacy reasons. For guidance on role-based access control, which can be used to restrict access to live and/or recorded video, refer to Chapter 4, "Role-Based Access Control," and the section on camera-only administrators.

Further Reading

Cisco Meraki. (2021, April 21). Video Walls. https://documentation.meraki.com/MV/Advanced_Configuration/Video_Walls

Cisco Meraki. (2023, June 27). Sensor Sight. https://documentation.meraki.com/MT/MT_General_Articles/Sensor_Sight

Cisco Meraki. (2024, January 11). Meraki Display. https://documentation.meraki.com/MV/Viewing_Video/Meraki_Display_Introduction

Cisco Meraki. (2024, January 30). Motion Alerts. https://documentation.meraki.com/MV/Advanced_Configuration/Motion_Alerts

Cisco Meraki. (2024, February 7). Alerts and Notifications. https://documentation.meraki.com/General_Administration/Cross-Platform_Content/Alerts_and_Notifications

Cisco Meraki. (n.d.). *Solution Guide: Meraki MV for Manufacturing*. https://meraki.cisco.com/product-collateral/meraki-mv-for-manufacturing-solution-guide

National Institute of Standards and Technology (NIST). (2006, March). *FIPS 200: Minimum Security Requirements for Federal Information and Information Systems*. https://csrc.nist.gov/pubs/fips/200/final

National Institute of Standards and Technology (NIST). (2020, September). *NIST 800-53 Rev. 5: Security and Privacy Controls for Information Systems and Organizations*. https://nvlpubs.nist.gov/nistpubs/SpecialPublications/NIST.SP.800-53r5.pdf

PCI Security Standards Council. (2022, December). *PCI DSS: v4.0*. https://www.pcisecuritystandards.org/document_library/

Appendix A

Comparison of Common Security Standards and Framework Requirements

Table A-1 shows the requirements addressed in this book and six of the most common IT security standards from which they are drawn. The subset of requirements identified here are those that would typically apply to the networking team or could be solved with a Cisco Meraki solution. Not all standards use the same language, time periods, and so on, so we've done our best to normalize them for easier comparison.

Table A-1 *Similarities Between Common Security Standards and Frameworks*

Requirement	Essential Eight (Australia)	NIST 800-53 (US, widely used globally)	PCI DSS v4.0 (Global)	HIPAA (US)	ISO 27001 (Global)	SOC2 (US)	Chapter	Topic
Security vulnerabilities are identified and managed.			X			X	3	Trust
Backups of platform software are conducted, protected, maintained, and tested.	X				X	X	3	Trust
All nonconsole (in-band) administrative access is encrypted using strong cryptography.			X				3	Trust
Strong cryptography is used to render all authentication factors unreadable during transmission and storage on all system components.			X				3	Trust
Software is patched, updated, replaced, and removed commensurate with risk.		X					3	Software and Hardware Trust Model
Privileged access to systems and applications is limited to only what is required for users and services to undertake their duties.	X	X	X	X	X	X	4	Role-Based Access Control (RBAC)
Unprivileged accounts cannot log on to privileged operating environments.	X	X	X	X	X	X	4–5	RBAC and Secure Admin Access to Dashboard

Requirement	Essential Eight (Australia)	NIST 800-53 (US, widely used globally)	PCI DSS v4.0 (Global)	HIPAA (US)	ISO 27001 (Global)	SOC2 (US)	Chapter	Topic
Administrative activities can be restricted to jump servers/hosts (IP whitelisting).	X						5	Secure Admin Access to Dashboard
Credentials for local administrator accounts and service accounts are long, unique, unpredictable, and managed.	X	X	X	X			5	Secure Admin Access to Dashboard
Multifactor authentication is used to authenticate privileged users of systems.	X	X	X	X	X	X	5	Secure Admin Access to Dashboard
If a user session has been idle for more than 15 minutes, the user is required to reauthenticate to reactivate the terminal or session.		X	X	X			5	Secure Admin Access to Dashboard
Invalid authentication attempts are limited by ■ Locking out the user ID after not more than 10 attempts. ■ Setting the lockout duration to a minimum of 30 minutes or until the user's identity is confirmed.		X	X				5	Secure Admin Access to Dashboard

Requirement	Essential Eight (Australia)	NIST 800-53 (US, widely used globally)	PCI DSS v4.0 (Global)	HIPAA (US)	ISO 27001 (Global)	SOC2 (US)	Chapter	Topic
If passwords/passphrases are used as authentication factors, they are set and reset for each user as follows: ■ Set to a unique value for first-time use and upon reset. ■ Forced to be changed immediately after the first use.			X	X			5	Secure Admin Access to Dashboard
If passwords/passphrases are used as an authentication factor, then they meet the following minimum level of complexity: ■ A minimum length of 12 characters (or *if* the system does not support 12 characters, a minimum length of 8 characters). ■ Contain both numeric and alphabetic characters.	X		X	X			5	Secure Admin Access to Dashboard
Individuals are not allowed to submit a new password/passphrase that is the same as any of the last four passwords/passphrases used.			X	X			5	Secure Admin Access to Dashboard

Requirement	Essential Eight (Australia)	NIST 800-53 (US, widely used globally)	PCI DSS v4.0 (Global)	HIPAA (US)	ISO 27001 (Global)	SOC2 (US)	Chapter	Topic
If passwords/passphrases are used as the only authentication factor for user access (that is, in any single-factor authentication implementation), then either ■ Passwords/passphrases are changed at least once every 90 days. or ■ The security posture of accounts is dynamically analyzed, and real-time access to resources is automatically determined accordingly		X	X	X			5	Secure Admin Access to Dashboard
Restrict the number of concurrent sessions on accounts.		X					5	Secure Admin Access to Dashboard
Provide a single sign-on capability for administrators.		X					5	Secure Admin Access to Dashboard
Privileged access is automatically disabled after 12 months unless revalidated.	X	X	X			X	5	Secure Admin Access to Dashboard

Requirement	Essential Eight (Australia)	NIST 800-53 (US, widely used globally)	PCI DSS v4.0 (Global)	HIPAA (US)	ISO 27001 (Global)	SOC2 (US)	Chapter	Topic
Privileged access is automatically disabled after 45 days of inactivity (90 days for PCI).	X	X	X			X	5	Secure Admin Access to Dashboard
The access control system(s) is set to *deny all* by default.			X				5	Secure Admin Access to Dashboard
All users are assigned a unique ID before access to system components or sensitive data is allowed.		X	X	X			5	Secure Admin Access to Dashboard
Automatically remove/disable temporary and emergency accounts after organization-defined time period.		X					5	Secure Admin Access to Dashboard
Enforce usage conditions for accounts such as by restricting usage to certain days of the week, time of day, or specific durations of time. Monitoring should generate alerts if the account is used in violation of specified parameters.	X	X	X	X			5	Secure Admin Access to Dashboard
Privileged access events are logged.	X	X	X	X	X		6	Centralized Logging and Audit Capabilities

Requirement	Essential Eight (Australia)	NIST 800-53 (US, widely used globally)	PCI DSS v4.0 (Global)	HIPAA (US)	ISO 27001 (Global)	SOC2 (US)	Chapter	Topic
Audit logs capture all changes to identification and authentication credentials including but not limited to ■ Creation of new accounts. ■ Elevation of privileges. ■ All changes, additions, or deletions to accounts with administrative access.	X	X	X	X	X		6	Centralized Logging and Audit Capabilities
Successful and unsuccessful multifactor authentication events are logged.	X			X	X		6	Centralized Logging and Audit Capabilities
Log records are generated for cybersecurity events and made available for continuous monitoring.	X				X		6	Centralized Logging and Audit Capabilities
Audit logs capture all invalid access attempts.			X	X	X		6	Centralized Logging and Audit Capabilities
Audit logs capture all creation and deletion of system-level objects.			X	X	X		6	Centralized Logging and Audit Capabilities

Requirement	Essential Eight (Australia)	NIST 800-53 (US, widely used globally)	PCI DSS v4.0 (Global)	HIPAA (US)	ISO 27001 (Global)	SOC2 (US)	Chapter	Topic
Audit logs record the following details for each auditable event: ■ User identification. ■ Type of event. ■ Date and time. ■ Success and failure indication. ■ Origination of event. ■ Identity or name of affected data, system component, resource, or service (for example, name and protocol.		X	X	X	X		6	Centralized Logging and Audit Capabilities
Audit log files are protected to prevent modifications by individuals.		X	X	X	X		6	Centralized Logging and Audit Capabilities
Retain audit log history for at least 12 months, with at least the most recent 3 months immediately available for analysis. (NIST800-53 uses the term *long-term retention*.)		X	X	X	X		6	Centralized Logging and Audit Capabilities

Requirement	Essential Eight (Australia)	NIST 800-53 (US, widely used globally)	PCI DSS v4.0 (Global)	HIPAA (US)	ISO 27001 (Global)	SOC2 (US)	Chapter	Topic
System clocks and time are synchronized using time-synchronization technology.		X	X		X		6	Centralized Logging and Audit Capabilities
Record timestamps for audit records.		X			X		6	Centralized Logging and Audit Capabilities
Audit logs for the anti-malware solution(s) are enabled and retained.			X	X			6	Centralized Logging and Audit Capabilities
Provide the capability to process, sort, and search audit records for events such as identities of individuals, event types, event locations, event dates and times, Internet Protocol addresses involved, or event success or failure.		X					6	Centralized Logging and Audit Capabilities
Audit logging for remote access.		X			X		6	Centralized Logging and Audit Capabilities

Requirement	Essential Eight (Australia)	NIST 800-53 (US, widely used globally)	PCI DSS v4.0 (Global)	HIPAA (US)	ISO 27001 (Global)	SOC2 (US)	Chapter	Topic
Implement cryptographic mechanisms to protect the integrity of audit information and audit tools.		X			X		6	Centralized Logging and Audit Capabilities
Authorize access to management of audit logging functionality to only those users whose role requires it.		X					4	RBAC
Authorize read-only access to audit information for only those users whose role requires it.		X					6	Centralized Logging and Audit Capabilities
Provide irrefutable evidence that an individual (or process acting on behalf of an individual) has performed an action.		X			X		6	Centralized Logging and Audit Capabilities
An organization must establish and maintain an inventory of organizational information systems including hardware, software, and firmware.	X				X	X	6	Inventory
An inventory of authorized wireless access points is maintained.			X				6	Inventory

Requirement	Essential Eight (Australia)	NIST 800-53 (US, widely used globally)	PCI DSS v4.0 (Global)	HIPAA (US)	ISO 27001 (Global)	SOC2 (US)	Chapter	Topic
Automated method of asset discovery is used.	X						6	Inventory
Organizations must establish and maintain baseline configurations (configuration templates).	X						6	Inventory
Configuration files for security controls are kept consistent with active network configurations.			X				6	Inventory
Hardware and software technologies in use are reviewed at least once every 12 months, including at least the following: ■ Analysis that the technologies continue to receive security fixes from vendors promptly and that this equipment is not end of life/support. ■ Analysis that the technologies continue to be an effective control.			X				6	Inventory

Requirement	Essential Eight (Australia)	NIST 800-53 (US, widely used globally)	PCI DSS v4.0 (Global)	HIPAA (US)	ISO 27001 (Global)	SOC2 (US)	Chapter	Topic
Representations of the organization's authorized network communication and network data flows are maintained. PCI asks that an accurate network diagram is maintained that shows all connections (and boundaries) between sensitive data environments and other networks, including any wireless networks.		X	X				6	Topology
Integration with third-party identity provider is supported.							6 and 7	SAML and RADIUS
Implement replay-resistant authentication mechanisms.		X	X				5	Multifactor Authentication (MFA)
Uniquely identify and authenticate devices and/or types of devices before establishing a network connection.	X	X				X	6	Zero Trust
Demonstrate the ability to prevent devices connecting to the network with end-of-life operating systems.	X						6	Zero Trust

Requirement	Essential Eight (Australia)	NIST 800-53 (US, widely used globally)	PCI DSS v4.0 (Global)	HIPAA (US)	ISO 27001 (Global)	SOC2 (US)	Chapter	Topic
Demonstrate the ability to separate and enforce policy between trusted and untrusted or dev/test/prod networks.	X	X	X	X	X	X	8	Security Group Tags (SGTs)
Anti-spoofing measures are implemented to detect and block forged source IP addresses from entering the trusted network.			X		X		8	DHCP and ARP Security
Vendor default accounts are managed as follows: ■ If the vendor default account will be used, the default password is changed. ■ If the vendor default account will not be used, the account is removed or disabled.			X	X			8	Device Hardening
Controls are implemented to restrict use of publicly accessible network jacks within the facility.			X			X	8	Port Security, Zero Trust

Requirement	Essential Eight (Australia)	NIST 800-53 (US, widely used globally)	PCI DSS v4.0 (Global)	HIPAA (US)	ISO 27001 (Global)	SOC2 (US)	Chapter	Topic
Wireless networks transmitting sensitive data use industry best practices for authentication and encryption.		X	X			X	8	Wireless Security
For wireless environments transmitting sensitive data, all wireless vendor defaults are changed at installation or are confirmed to be secure, including but not limited to ■ Default wireless encryption keys. ■ Passwords on wireless access points. ■ SNMP defaults. ■ Any other security-related wireless vendor defaults.			X				8	Wireless Security

Requirement	Essential Eight (Australia)	NIST 800-53 (US, widely used globally)	PCI DSS v4.0 (Global)	HIPAA (US)	ISO 27001 (Global)	SOC2 (US)	Chapter	Topic
Authorized and unauthorized wireless access points are managed as follows: ■ The presence of wireless (Wi-Fi) access points is tested for. ■ All authorized and unauthorized wireless access points are detected and identified. ■ Testing, detection, and identification occur at least once every three months. ■ If automated monitoring is used, personnel are notified via generated alerts.			X				8	Wireless Security
Select radio antennas and calibrate transmission power levels to reduce the probability that signals from wireless access points can be received outside of organization-controlled boundaries.		X				X	8	Wireless Security
The confidentiality, integrity, and availability of data-in-transit is protected.		X		X	X	X	9	VPN

Requirement	Essential Eight (Australia)	NIST 800-53 (US, widely used globally)	PCI DSS v4.0 (Global)	HIPAA (US)	ISO 27001 (Global)	SOC2 (US)	Chapter	Topic
Strong cryptography and security protocols are implemented as follows to safeguard sensitive data during transmission over open, public networks: ■ Only trusted keys and certificates are accepted. ■ Certificates used during transmission over open, public networks are confirmed as valid and are not expired or revoked. ■ The protocol in use supports only secure versions or configurations and does not support fallback to, or use of, insecure versions, algorithms, key sizes, or implementations. ■ The encryption strength is appropriate for the encryption methodology in use.		X	X	X		X	9	VPN

Requirement	Essential Eight (Australia)	NIST 800-53 (US, widely used globally)	PCI DSS v4.0 (Global)	HIPAA (US)	ISO 27001 (Global)	SOC2 (US)	Chapter	Topic
Accounts used by third parties to access, support, or maintain system components via remote access are managed as follows: ■ Enabled only during the time period needed and disabled when not in use. ■ Use is monitored for unexpected activity.		X	X			X	9	VPN
MFA is implemented for all remote network access originating from outside the entity's network that could access or impact sensitive data as follows: ■ All remote access by all personnel, both users and administrators, originating from outside the entity's network. ■ All remote access by third parties and vendors.		X	X			X	7	User Authentication

Requirement	Essential Eight (Australia)	NIST 800-53 (US, widely used globally)	PCI DSS v4.0 (Global)	HIPAA (US)	ISO 27001 (Global)	SOC2 (US)	Chapter	Topic
External service providers and the services they provide are monitored to find adverse cybersecurity events.		X					9	ThousandEyes
The deployed anti-malware solution ■ Detects all known types of malware. ■ Removes, blocks, or contains all known types of malware.			X	X	X		10	Anti-Malware Protection (AMP)
The anti-malware solution is kept current via automatic updates.			X	X	X		10	Anti-Malware Protection (AMP)
The anti-malware solution performs periodic scans and active or real-time scans.			X	X			10	Anti-Malware Protection (AMP)
Anti-malware mechanisms cannot be disabled or altered by users, unless specifically documented, and authorized by management on a case-by-case basis for a limited time period.			X	X			10	Anti-Malware Protection (AMP)

Requirement	Essential Eight (Australia)	NIST 800-53 (US, widely used globally)	PCI DSS v4.0 (Global)	HIPAA (US)	ISO 27001 (Global)	SOC2 (US)	Chapter	Topic
Access to external websites shall be managed to reduce exposure to malicious content.					X		10	Securing User Traffic
Demonstrate the ability to block Microsoft Office macros (or those containing malware) originating from the Internet.	X						10	Securing User Traffic
Demonstrate the ability to scan Microsoft Office macros for viruses.	X						10	Securing User Traffic
Demonstrate the ability to block Internet advertisements.	X						10	Securing User Traffic
Demonstrate the ability to prevent privileged accounts (excluding privileged service accounts) from accessing the Internet, email, and web services.	X	X					10	Securing User Traffic
Multifactor authentication is used by an organization's users if they authenticate to their organization's Internet-facing services.	X	X					10	Securing User Traffic

Requirement	Essential Eight (Australia)	NIST 800-53 (US, widely used globally)	PCI DSS v4.0 (Global)	HIPAA (US)	ISO 27001 (Global)	SOC2 (US)	Chapter	Topic
Multifactor authentication is used by an organization's users if they authenticate to third-party Internet-facing services that process, store, or communicate their organization's data.	X	X					10	Securing User Traffic
All services, protocols, and ports allowed are identified, approved, and have a defined business need.		X	X				10	Securing User Traffic
Inbound and outbound traffic to the trusted/sensitive environments (NIST 800-53 uses different level security domains) is restricted as follows: ■ To only traffic that is necessary. ■ All other traffic is specifically denied.		X	X	X			10	Securing User Traffic

Requirement	Essential Eight (Australia)	NIST 800-53 (US, widely used globally)	PCI DSS v4.0 (Global)	HIPAA (US)	ISO 27001 (Global)	SOC2 (US)	Chapter	Topic
Intrusion detection and/or intrusion prevention techniques are used to detect and/or prevent intrusions into the network as follows: ■ All traffic is monitored at the perimeter of the sensitive/trusted environments. ■ All traffic is monitored at critical points. ■ Personnel are alerted to suspected compromises. ■ All intrusion detection and prevention engines, baselines, and signatures are kept up to date.		X	X	X		X	10	Intrusion Detection and Prevention Systems (IDS/IPS)
Prevent encrypted information from bypassing controls by one of the following: decrypting the information; blocking the flow of the encrypted information; terminating communications sessions attempting to pass encrypted information.		X	X		X	X	10	Securing User Traffic

Requirement	Essential Eight (Australia)	NIST 800-53 (US, widely used globally)	PCI DSS v4.0 (Global)	HIPAA (US)	ISO 27001 (Global)	SOC2 (US)	Chapter	Topic
Demonstrate the ability to deploy agents that can perform host-based IPS functions such as (1) limiting the execution of executables, software libraries, scripts, installers, compiled HTML, HTML applications, and control panel applets by the operating system, web browsers, and email clients and (2) logging allowed and blocked execution events.	X					X	11	Securing End-User Devices
Demonstrate the ability to remove and prevent installation of software that has reached end of support.	X				X	X	11	Securing End-User Devices
Demonstrate the ability to prevent the installation of "banned" applications.	X				X	X	11	Securing End-User Devices
Ensure hosts are running the latest or previous OS release.	X				X		11	Securing End-User Devices
Inventories of physical devices managed by the organization are maintained.		X					11	Securing End-User Devices

Requirement	Essential Eight (Australia)	NIST 800-53 (US, widely used globally)	PCI DSS v4.0 (Global)	HIPAA (US)	ISO 27001 (Global)	SOC2 (US)	Chapter	Topic
Security controls are implemented on any computing devices, including company- and employee-owned devices, that connect to both untrusted networks (including the Internet) and trusted networks as follows: ■ Specific configuration settings are defined to prevent threats from being introduced into the entity's network. ■ Security controls are actively running. ■ Security controls are not alterable by users of the computing devices unless specifically documented and authorized by management on a case-by-case basis for a limited period.			X				11	Securing End-User Devices

Requirement	Essential Eight (Australia)	NIST 800-53 (US, widely used globally)	PCI DSS v4.0 (Global)	HIPAA (US)	ISO 27001 (Global)	SOC2 (US)	Chapter	Topic
Wipe information from mobile devices after consecutive unsuccessful device logon attempts.		X			X	X	11	Securing End-User Devices
Prevent access by enforcing a device lock after a period of inactivity and retain the device lock until the user reauthenticates.		X			X	X	11	Securing End-User Devices
Employ device encryption to protect the confidentiality and integrity of information on mobile devices.		X			X	X	11	Securing End-User Devices
Personnel activity and technology usage are monitored to find adverse cybersecurity events.		X					11	Securing End-User Devices
The physical environment is monitored to find adverse cybersecurity events (this includes environmental monitoring).				X	X	X	12	Physical Security

Requirement	Essential Eight (Australia)	NIST 800-53 (US, widely used globally)	PCI DSS v4.0 (Global)	HIPAA (US)	ISO 27001 (Global)	SOC2 (US)	Chapter	Topic
Individual physical access to sensitive areas is monitored with either video cameras or physical access control mechanisms (or both) as follows: ■ Entry and exit points to/from sensitive areas are monitored. ■ Monitoring devices or mechanisms are protected from tampering or disabling. ■ Collected data is reviewed and correlated with other entries. ■ Collected data is stored for at least three months, unless otherwise restricted by law.		X	X	X	X	X	12	Physical Security
Networks and network services are monitored to find adverse cybersecurity events.			X				6	Security Operations

Requirement	Essential Eight (Australia)	NIST 800-53 (US, widely used globally)	PCI DSS v4.0 (Global)	HIPAA (US)	ISO 27001 (Global)	SOC2 (US)	Chapter	Topic
Incidents and failures of critical security control systems are detected, alerted, and addressed promptly, including but not limited to failure of the following critical security control systems: ■ Network security controls. ■ IDS/IPS. ■ Change-detection mechanisms. ■ Anti-malware solutions. ■ Physical access controls. ■ Logical access controls. ■ Audit logging mechanisms. ■ Segmentation controls (if used). ■ Audit log review mechanisms. ■ Automated security testing tools (if used).		X	X		X	X	6	ServiceNow Integration

Requirement	Essential Eight (Australia)	NIST 800-53 (US, widely used globally)	PCI DSS v4.0 (Global)	HIPAA (US)	ISO 27001 (Global)	SOC2 (US)	Chapter	Topic
Audit log files are promptly backed up to a secure, central, internal log server(s) or other media that is difficult to modify (Syslog).	X	X	X		X	X	6	Security Operations
Provide and implement the capability to centrally review and analyze audit records from multiple components within the system.							6	Splunk Integration
Support the management of system accounts using automated mechanisms. This includes using automated mechanisms to create, enable, modify, disable, and remove accounts.		X					6	Meraki Dashboard API
Align account management processes with personnel termination and transfer processes		X					6	Meraki Dashboard API

Index

Numerics

A

B

C

D

E

F

G

H

I

J-K-L

M

N

O

P

Q-R

S

T

U

V

W

X-Y-Z